IET PROFESSIONAL APPLICATION OF COMPUTING SERIES 26

Handbook of Mathematical Models for Languages and Computation

Other volumes in this series:

Volume 1 **Knowledge Discovery and Data Mining** M.A. Bramer (Editor)
Volume 3 **Troubled IT Projects: Prevention and turnaround** J.M. Smith
Volume 4 **UML for Systems Engineering: Watching the wheels, 2nd Edition** J. Holt
Volume 5 **Intelligent Distributed Video Surveillance Systems** S.A. Velastin and P. Remagnino (Editors)
Volume 6 **Trusted Computing** C. Mitchell (Editor)
Volume 7 **SysML for Systems Engineering** J. Holt and S. Perry
Volume 8 **Modelling Enterprise Architectures** J. Holt and S. Perry
Volume 9 **Model-Based Requirements Engineering** J. Holt, S. Perry and M. Bownsword
Volume 13 **Trusted Platform Modules: Why, when and how to use them** Ariel Segall
Volume 14 **Foundations for Model-based Systems Engineering: From Patterns to Models** J. Holt, S. Perry and M. Bownsword
Volume 15 **Big Data and Software Defined Networks** J.Taheri (Editor)
Volume 18 **Modeling and Simulation of Complex Communication** M. A. Niazi (Editor)
Volume 20 **SysML for Systems Engineering: A Model-Based Approach, 3rd Edition** J.Holt and S. Perry
Volume 23 **Data as Infrastructure for Smart Cities** L. Suzuki and A. Finkelstein
Volume 24 **Ultrascale Computing Systems** J. Carretero, E. Jeannot and A. Zomaya
Volume 25 **Big Data-Enabled Internet of Things** M. Khan, S. Khan, A. Zomaya (Editors)
Volume 35 **Big Data Recommender Systems Vol 1 & 2** Osman Khalid, Samee U. Khan, Albert Y. Zomaya (Editors)

Handbook of Mathematical Models for Languages and Computation

Alexander Meduna, Petr Horáček and Martin Tomko

The Institution of Engineering and Technology

Published by The Institution of Engineering and Technology, London, United Kingdom

The Institution of Engineering and Technology is registered as a Charity in England & Wales (no. 211014) and Scotland (no. SC038698).

First published 2019

The Institution of Engineering and Technology
Michael Faraday House
Six Hills Way, Stevenage
Herts, SG1 2AY, United Kingdom

www.theiet.org

British Library Cataloguing in Publication Data
A catalogue record for this product is available from the British Library

ISBN 978-1-78561-659-4 (hardback)
ISBN 978-1-78561-660-0 (PDF)

Typeset in India by MPS Limited
Printed in the UK by CPI Group (UK) Ltd, Croydon

To my mother Jarmila, and my father Petr. PH

To Dagmara. AM

To my beloved grandmothers, Marta and Margita,
in memory of my grandfather Ján,
who passed away before I was born,
and in loving memory of my grandfather Emil,
who passed away during my work on this book. MT

Contents

Preface

From a theoretical viewpoint, the present handbook represents a theoretically oriented summary of the knowledge about crucially important mathematical models for languages and computation. It introduces all formalisms concerning these models with enough rigor to make all results quite clear and valid. Every complicated mathematical passage is preceded by its intuitive explanation so that even the most complex parts of the handbook are easy to grasp. Similarly, every new model is preceded by an explanation of its purpose and followed by some examples with comments to reinforce its understanding.

From a practical viewpoint, the handbook pays significant attention to the application and implementation of all the mathematical models. To make quite clear how to encode them, the text contains a large number of computer programs in C#, one of the most popular programming languages at present.

This book is intended for everybody who somehow makes use of mathematical models for languages and computation in their scientific fields. It can also be used as an accompanying text for a class involving these models. Used as a textbook, apart from the theory, it illustrates how to implement and apply the mathematical concepts in computational practice.

This handbook is self-contained in the sense that no other sources are needed to understand the material, so no previous knowledge concerning discrete mathematics is assumed. Nevertheless, a familiarity with the rudiments of high-school mathematics is helpful for a quicker comprehension of the present text. A basic familiarity with a high-level programming language, especially C#, is surely helpful in order to grasp the implementation portion of the text.

The text contains many algorithms. Strictly speaking, every algorithm requires a verification that it terminates and works correctly. However, the termination of the algorithms given in this book is always so obvious that its verification is omitted throughout. The correctness of complicated algorithms is verified. On the other hand, we most often give only the gist of the straightforward algorithms and leave their rigorous verification as an exercise. The text describes the algorithms in Pascal-like notation, which is so simple and intuitive that even the student unfamiliar with the Pascal programming language can immediately pick it up. In this description, a Pascal-like repeat loop is sometimes ended with **until no change**, meaning that the loop is repeated until no change can result from its further repetition. As the clear comprehensibility is of paramount importance in the book, the description of algorithms is often enriched by an explanation in words.

Regarding the technical organization of the text, all the algorithms, examples, conventions, definitions, lemmas, and theorems are sequentially numbered within chapters. Examples and figures are organized similarly.

For further backup materials concerning this handbook, we refer to

http://www.fit. vutbr.cz/~meduna/books/hmmlc.

Synopsis of this handbook

The entire text contains 20 chapters, which are divided into five parts, Parts I–V.

Part I, which consists of Chapters 1–3, reviews all mathematical concepts needed to follow the rest of this handbook. Chapter 1 recalls sets and sequences. It pays special attention to formal languages as sets of finite sequences of symbols because they underlie many central notions in the theory of computation. Chapter 2 examines several concepts concerning relations and functions. Chapter 3 examines a number of concepts from graph theory.

Part II defines classical models for languages and computation based on the mathematical concepts from Part I. Most of these models are underlain by rewriting systems, which are based upon binary relations whose members are called rules. By their rules, these systems repeatedly change sequences of symbols, called strings. They are classified into two categories—generative and accepting language models. Generative models or, briefly, grammars define strings of their languages by generating them from special start symbols. On the other hand, accepting models or, briefly, automata defines the strings of their languages by a rewriting process that starts from these strings and ends in a prescribed set of final strings. Part II consists of Chapters 4–10. Chapter 4 introduces the basic versions of rewriting systems while paying special attention to using them as language-defining devices. Chapter 5 presents finite automata as the simplest versions of automata covered in this book. Chapters 6 discusses generative models called context-free grammars, while Chapter 7 discusses their accepting counterparts—pushdown automata; indeed, both are equally powerful. In Part II, Chapters 8–10 form an inseparable unit, which is crucially important to Part II and, in fact, the book in its entirety. These chapters deal with Turing machines as basic language-defining models for computation. Indeed, based on them, Part II explores the very heart of the foundations of computation. More precisely, Chapter 8 introduces the mathematical notion of a Turing machine, which has become a universally accepted formalization of the intuitive notion of a procedure. Based upon this strictly mathematical notion, Chapters 9 and 10 study the general limits of computation in terms of computability and decidability. Regarding computability, Chapter 9 considers Turing machines as computers of functions over nonnegative integers and demonstrates the existence of functions whose computation cannot be specified by any procedure. As far as decidability is concerned, Chapter 10 formalizes problem-deciding algorithms by Turing machines that halt on every input. It formulates several important problems concerning the language models discussed in this book and constructs algorithms that decide them. On the other hand,

Chapter 10 describes several problems that are not decidable by any algorithm. Apart from giving several specific undecidable problems, this book builds up a general theory of undecidability. Finally, the text approaches decidability in a much finer and realistic way. Indeed, it reconsiders problem-deciding algorithms in terms of their computational complexity measured according to time and space requirements. Perhaps most importantly, it shows that although some problems are decidable in principle, they are intractable for absurdly high computational requirements of the algorithms that decide them.

Part III, which consists of Chapters 11–15, covers modern and alternative models for languages and computation. Chapter 11 discusses context-dependent versions of grammatical models. Chapter 12 covers automata and grammars that define languages under various kinds of mathematical regulation. Chapter 13 studies grammatical models that work in parallel. Chapter 14 investigates automata and grammars that work in a discontinuous way. Finally, Chapter 15 defines the automata based upon a generalized versions of pushdown lists.

Part IV, which consists of Chapters 16–19, demonstrates computational applications of mathematical models studied in Parts II and III. Chapter 16 makes many remarks on applications in general. Then, more specifically, Chapters 17 and 18 describe applications in syntax analysis of programming and natural languages, respectively. Chapter 19 shows applications in computational biology.

Part V, which consists of a single chapter—Chapter 20, closes the entire book by adding several important remarks concerning its coverage. It sums up all the coverage contained in the text. It also sketches important current investigation trends. Finally, Chapter 20 makes several bibliographical remarks.

Acknowledgements

This work was supported by The Ministry of Education, Youth and Sports of the Czech Republic from the National Programme of Sustainability (NPU II); project IT4Innovations excellence in science – LQ1602; the TAČR grant TE01020415; and the BUT grant FIT-S-17-3964.

List of implementations

List of symbols

Symbol	Description
$a \in A$	a is a member of A
$a \notin A$	a is not a member of A
$\emptyset$	empty set
$\{a_1, \ldots, a_n\}$	set containing $a_1, \ldots, a_n$
$\{a \mid \pi(a)\}$	set containing all elements that satisfy π
$\mathbb{N}$	set of all natural numbers (positive integers)
$_0\mathbb{N}$	set of all non-negative integers
$A \subseteq B$	A is a subset of B
$A \subset B$	A is a proper subset of B
$A \cup B$	union of A and B
$A \cap B$	intersection of A and B
$A - B$	difference of A and B
$\bar{A}$	complement of A
$\lvert x \rvert$	length of x
ε	empty sequence, empty string
Σ^*	set of all strings over Σ
Σ^+	set of all non-empty strings over Σ
x^i	ith power of a string x
L^i	ith power of a language L
L^*	closure of a language L (Kleene star)
L^+	positive closure of a language L (Kleene plus)
$\mathrm{lms}\, x$	leftmost symbol of a string x
$\mathrm{perm}(x)$	set of all permutations of a string x
$\mathrm{sym}(x, n)$	the nth symbol of a string x
(a, b)	ordered pair
$A \times B$	Cartesian product of A and B
$\rho \circ \chi$	composition of ρ with χ
$a\rho b$	synonym for $(a, b) \in \rho$
$a = \phi(b)$	synonym for $(a, b) \in \phi$ if ϕ is a function
ρ^k	k-fold product of ρ
ρ^+	transitive closure of ρ
ρ^*	reflexive and transitive closure of ρ
$x \rightarrow y$	rule with left-hand side x and right-hand side y
$\mathrm{lhs}\, p$	left-hand side of rule p
$\mathrm{rhs}\, p$	right-hand side of rule p

$u_M \Rightarrow v\ [x \rightarrow y]$	M rewrites u to v using rule $x \rightarrow y$
$_M\Rightarrow^k$	k-fold product of $_M\Rightarrow$
$_M\Rightarrow^+$	transitive closure of $_M\Rightarrow$
$_M\Rightarrow^*$	reflexive and transitive closure of $_M\Rightarrow$
$L(M)$	language of M
$F(G)$	set of all sentential forms of G
$\Rightarrow_{lm}$	leftmost derivation step
$\Rightarrow_{rm}$	rightmost derivation step
$_G\bot(A \rightarrow x)$	rule tree representing $A \rightarrow X$ in G
$_G\bot(u \Rightarrow^* v)$	derivation tree representing $u \Rightarrow^* v$ in G
$_\varepsilon L(M)$	language accepted by pushdown automaton M by empty pushdown
$_f L(M)$	language accepted by pushdown automaton M by final state
►	Turing machine start state
□	blank symbol
▷	left bounder
◁	right bounder
■	accepting state
♦	rejecting state
Ψ	set of all Turing machines
M-f	function computed by Turing machine M
$f^{\underline{m}}$	m-argument function
M-$f^{\underline{m}}$	m-argument function computed by M
$x \curvearrowright y$	jumping finite automaton makes a jump from x to y
$x\ _p\vdash y$	deep pushdown automaton pops its pushdown from x to y
$x\ _e\vdash y$	deep pushdown automaton expands its pushdown from x to y
$x \vdash y$	deep pushdown automaton makes a move from x to y
•	separator of rule items
↻	set of items

List of mathematical models

Abbreviation	**Description**
PSG	phrase-structure grammar
MONG	monotonous grammar
CSG	context-sensitive grammar
CFG	context-free grammar
LG	linear grammar
RLG	right-linear grammar
RG	regular grammar
gf-grammar	generalized forbidding grammar
sc-grammar	semi-conditional grammar
ssc-grammar	simple semi-conditional grammar
gcc-grammar	global context conditional grammar
MG	matrix grammar with appearance checking
${}_nEMG$	even matrix grammar of degree *n*
SFA	self-regulating finite automaton
n-first-SFA	*n*-turn first-move self-regulating finite automaton
n-all-SFA	*n*-turn all-move self-regulating finite automaton
n-PRLG	*n*-parallel right-linear grammar
n-PRLL	*n*-parallel right-linear language
n-RLSMG	*n*-right-linear simple matrix grammar
SPDA	self-regulating pushdown automaton
n-first-SPDA	*n*-turn first-move SPDA
n-all-SPDA	*n*-turn all-move SPDA
OA-RPDA	one-turn atomic regulated pushdown automaton
SCG	scattered context grammar
C-ET0L grammar	context-conditional ET0L grammar
C-EPT0L grammar	propagating context-conditional ET0L grammar
C-E0L grammar	context-conditional E0L grammar
C-EP0L grammar	propagating context-conditional E0L grammar
F-ET0L grammar	forbidding ET0L grammar
F-EPT0L grammar	propagating forbidding ET0L grammar
F-E0L grammar	forbidding E0L grammar
F-EP0L grammar	propagating forbidding E0L grammar
SSC-ET0L grammar	simple semi-conditional ET0L grammar
SSC-EPT0L grammar	propagating simple semi-conditional ET0L grammar

SSC-E0L grammar	simple semi-conditional E0L grammar
SSC-EP0L grammar	propagating simple semi-conditional E0L grammar
LRC-ET0L grammar	left random context ET0L grammar
LP-ET0L grammar	left permitting ET0L grammar
LF-ET0L grammar	left random context E0L grammar
LRC-EPT0L grammar	propagating left random context ET0L grammar
LP-EPT0L grammar	propagating left permitting ET0L grammar
LF-EPT0L grammar	propagating left forbidding ET0L grammar
LRC-E0L grammar	left random context E0L grammar
LP-E0L grammar	left permitting E0L grammar
LF-E0L grammar	left forbidding E0L grammar
RC-ET0L grammar	random context ET0L grammar
n-MGR	*n*-generative rule-synchronized grammar system
n-LMGR	leftmost *n*-generative rule-synchronized grammar system
n-LMGN	leftmost *n*-generative nonterminal-synchronized grammar system
GJFA	general jumping finite automaton
JFA	jumping finite automaton
DJFA	deterministic jumping finite automaton
CJFA	complete jumping finite automaton

List of language families

Abbreviation	**Name of family or defining model**
ET0L	ET0L grammars
EPT0L	EPT0L grammars
E0L	E0L grammars
EP0L	propagating E0L grammars
P	polynomially bounded (deterministic) Turing deciders
NP	polynomially bounded nondeterministic Turing deciders
PS	polynomially space-bounded (deterministic) Turing deciders
NPS	polynomially space-bounded nondeterministic Turing deciders
RE	recursively enumerable languages
CS	context-sensitive grammars
CF	context-free grammars
LIN	linear languages
REG	regular languages
FIN	finite languages
CG	context-conditional grammars
$\mathbf{CG}^{-\varepsilon}$	propagating context-conditional grammars
Per	permitting grammars
For	forbidding grammars
RC	random context grammars
$\mathbf{Per}^{-\varepsilon}$	propagating permitting grammars
$\mathbf{For}^{-\varepsilon}$	propagating forbidding grammars
$\mathbf{RC}^{-\varepsilon}$	propagating random context grammars
GF	generalized forbidding grammars
$\mathbf{GF}^{-\varepsilon}$	propagating gf-grammars
SCOND	semi-conditional grammars
PSCOND	propagating sc-grammars
SSCOND	simple semi-conditional grammars
PSSCOND	propagating ssc-grammars
GCC	global context conditional grammars
$\mathbf{GCC}^{-\varepsilon}$	propagating gcc-grammars
ST	state grammars
$\mathbf{ST}_n$	n-limited state grammars

$\mathbf{rC}_{ac}$	regular-controlled grammars with appearance checking
$\mathbf{rC}_{ac}^{-\varepsilon}$	propagating regular-controlled grammars with appearance checking
rC	regular-controlled grammars
$\mathbf{rC}^{-\varepsilon}$	propagating regular-controlled grammars
$\mathbf{M}_{ac}$	matrix grammars with appearance checking
$\mathbf{M}_{ac}^{-\varepsilon}$	propagating matrix grammars with appearance checking
M	matrix grammars
$\mathbf{M}^{-\varepsilon}$	propagating matrix grammars
$_n\mathbf{EM}(\varrho)$	$_nEMG$ by ϱ
$\mathbf{EM}(\varrho)$	all even matrix grammars by ϱ
$\mathbf{P}_{ac}$	programmed grammars of with appearance checking
$\mathbf{P}_{ac}^{-\varepsilon}$	propagating programmed grammars with appearance checking
P	programmed grammars
$\mathbf{P}^{-\varepsilon}$	propagating programmed grammars
$\mathbf{FSFA}_n$	*n*-first-SFA
$\mathbf{ASFA}_n$	*n*-all-SFA
$\mathbf{PRL}_n$	*n*-PRLG
$\mathbf{RLSM}_n$	*n*-RLSMG
$\mathbf{FSPDA}_n$	*n*-first-SPDA
$\mathbf{ASPDA}_n$	*n*-all-SPDA
$\mathbf{SCFA}(\mathscr{L})$	state-controlled finite automata controlled by languages from $\mathscr{L}$
$\mathbf{TCFA}(\mathscr{L})$	transition-controlled finite automata controlled by languages from $\mathscr{L}$
RPDA	regulated pushdown automata
OA - RPDA	one-turn atomic regulated pushdown automata
SC	scattered context grammars
PSC	propagating scattered context grammars
CET0L	C-ET0L grammars
CEPT0L	C-EPT0L grammars
CE0L	C-E0L grammars
CEP0L	C-EP0L grammars
FET0L	F-ET0L grammars
FEPT0L	F-EPT0L grammars
FE0L	F-E0L grammars
FEP0L	F-EP0L grammars
SSCET0L	SSC-ET0L grammars
SSCEPT0L	SSC-EPT0L grammars
SSCE0L	SSC-E0L grammars
SSCEP0L	SSC-EP0L grammars
LRCET0L	LRC-ET0L grammars

LPET0L	LP-ET0L grammars
LFET0L	LF-ET0L grammars
LRCEPT0L	LRC-PET0L grammars
LPEPT0L	LP-PET0L grammars
LFEPT0L	LF-PET0L grammars
LRCE0L	LRC-E0L grammars
LPE0L	LP-E0L grammars
LFE0L	LF-E0L grammars
RCET0L	RC-ET0L grammars
RCEPT0L	propagating RC-ET0L grammars
$\mathbf{MGR}_{n,X}$	n-MGRs in the X mode
$\mathbf{SC}(\varrho)$	scattered context grammars by ϱ
GJFA	general jumping finite automata
$\mathbf{GJFA}^{-\varepsilon}$	ε-free GJFA
JFA	jumping finite automata
$\mathbf{JFA}^{-\varepsilon}$	ε-free JFA
DJFA	deterministic jumping finite automata
$\mathbf{DPDA}_k$	deep pushdown automata of depth k
$\mathbf{DEPDA}_k$	deep pushdown automata of depth k by empty pushdown
${}_n\mathbf{DPDA}$	n-expandable deep pushdown automata
${}_n\mathbf{DPDA}_r$	n-expandable deep pushdown automata with # and no more than $(r-1)$ non-input pushdown symbols

Part I
Basic mathematical concepts

This opening three-chapter part reviews all mathematical concepts needed to follow Parts II–V. Chapter 1 recalls sets and sequences. It pays special attention to formal languages as sets of finite sequences of symbols because they underlie many central notions in the theory of computation. Chapter 2 examines basic concepts concerning relations and functions. Chapter 3 gives a number of concepts from graph theory.

Chapter 1

Sets, sequences, and languages

This chapter reviews the most basic concepts concerning sets and sequences. Special attention is paid to languages defined as sets whose elements are finite sequences of symbols because languages play an important role later in this book.

1.1 Sets

In what follows, we assume that there exist primitive objects, referred to as *elements*, taken from some prespecified *universe*, usually denoted by $\mathbb{U}$. We also assume that there are objects, referred to as *sets*, which represent collections of objects, each of which is an element or another set. If A contains an object a, we symbolically write $a \in A$ and refer to a as a *member of* A. On the other hand, to express that a is not a member of A, we write $a \notin A$.

If A has a finite number of members, A is a *finite set*; otherwise, it is an *infinite set*. The finite set that has no member is the *empty set*, denoted by $\emptyset$. The *cardinality of a finite set* A, card(A), is the number of members that belong to A; note that card($\emptyset$) $= 0$. A finite set A is customarily *specified by listing its members*, that is, $A = \{a_1, a_2, \ldots, a_n\}$, where a_1 through a_n are all members of A. As a special case, we have $\{\} = \emptyset$. An infinite set B is usually *defined by a property* π so that B contains all elements satisfying π; in symbols, this specification has the following general format: $B = \{a \mid \pi(a)\}$. Sometimes, an infinite set is *defined recursively* by explicitly naming the first few values (typically, just one first value) in the set and then defining later values in the set in terms of earlier values.

In this book, we denote the set of all natural numbers by $\mathbb{N}$. In other words, $\mathbb{N}$ denotes the set of all positive integers, so

$$\mathbb{N} = \{1, 2, \ldots\}.$$

Furthermore, ${}_0\mathbb{N}$ denotes the set of all nonnegative integers.

Example 1.1. Take $\mathbb{U} = \mathbb{N}$. Let X be the set of all even positive integers defined as

$$X = \{i \mid i \in \mathbb{N},\ i \text{ is even}\} \text{ or, alternatively, } X = \{j \mid j = 2i,\ i, j \in \mathbb{N}\}.$$

Let Y be the set of all even positive integers between 1 and 9. Define

$$Y = \{i \mid i \in X,\ 1 \leq i \leq 9\} \text{ or, simply, } Y = \{2, 4, 6, 8\}.$$

Observe that card(Y) $= 4$. Consider the next recursive definition of the set W

(i) 2 is in W;
(ii) if i is in W, then so is $2i$, for all $i \geq 2$.

By (i), W contains 2. Then, by (ii), it contains 4, too. By (ii) again, it includes 8 as well. Continuing in this way, we see that W contains $2, 4, 8, 16, \ldots$. In words, W consists of all positive integers that represent a power of two; mathematically,

$$W = \{j \mid j = 2i,\ i, j \in \mathbb{N}\} \text{ or, briefly, } \{2i \mid i \in \mathbb{N}\}.$$

Let A and B be two sets. A is a *subset of* B, symbolically written as $A \subseteq B$, if each member of A also belongs to B. A is a *proper subset of* B, written as $A \subset B$, if $A \subseteq B$ and B contains a member that is not in A. By $A \not\subseteq B$, we express that A is not a subset of B. If $A \subseteq B$ and $B \subseteq A$, A *equals* B, denoted by $A = B$; simply put, $A = B$ means that both sets are identical. By $A \neq B$, we express that A is not equal to B. The *power set of* A, denoted by power(A), is the set of all subsets of A; formally, power(A) $= \{B \mid A \subseteq B\}$.

For two sets, A and B, their *union*, *intersection*, and *difference* are denoted by $A \cup B$, $A \cap B$, and $A - B$, respectively, and defined as $A \cup B = \{a \mid a \in A \text{ or } a \in B\}$, $A \cap B = \{a \mid a \in A \text{ and } a \in B\}$, and $A - B = \{a \mid a \in A \text{ and } a \notin B\}$. If $A \cap B = \emptyset$, A and B are *disjoint*. More generally, n sets $C_1, C_2, \ldots, C_n$, where $n \geq 2$, are *pairwise disjoint* if $C_i \cap C_j = \emptyset$ for all $1 \leq i, j \leq n$ such that $i \neq j$. If A is a set over a universe $\mathbb{U}$, the *complement of* A is denoted by $\overline{A}$ and defined as $\overline{A} = \mathbb{U} - A$.

Sets whose members are other sets are usually called *classes* of sets rather than sets of sets.

Example 1.2. Consider the sets from Example 1.1. Observe that

$$\begin{aligned}
\text{power}(Y) = \{&\emptyset,\\
&\{2\}, \{4\}, \{6\}, \{8\},\\
&\{2,4\}, \{2,6\}, \{2,8\}, \{4,6\}, \{4,8\}, \{6,8\},\\
&\{2,4,6\}, \{2,4,8\}, \{2,6,8\}, \{4,6,8\},\\
&\{2,4,6,8\}\}.
\end{aligned}$$

Furthermore, $X \subset \mathbb{U}$ and $Y \subset X$. Set $W = \mathbb{U} - X$. In words, W is the set of all odd positive integers. As obvious, $X \cap W = \emptyset$, so X and W are disjoint. Notice that $Y \cup W = \{i \mid i \in \mathbb{U}, i \leq 8 \text{ or } i \text{ is even}\}$. Notice that

$$\bar{Y} = \{1, 3, 5, 7\} \cup \{i \mid i \in \mathbb{U},\ i \geq 9\}.$$

X, Y, and W are not pairwise disjoint because $X \cap W \neq \emptyset$. On the other hand, $\{2\}$, $\{8\}$, and $\{4, 6\}$ are pairwise disjoint. Observe that $\{j \mid j \in \mathbb{U}, j \neq j\}$ and $\emptyset$ are identical, symbolically written as

$$\{j \mid j \in \mathbb{U},\ j \neq j\} = \emptyset.$$

Sets $\mathbb{U}$ and $(X \cup W)$ are identical, too.

To illustrate a class of sets, consider Δ defined as

$$\Delta = \{U \mid U \subseteq \mathbb{U},\ 1 \in U\}.$$

In words, Δ consists of all subsets of $\mathbb{U}$ that contain 1; for instance, {1} and W are in Δ, but {2} and Y are not. Notice that $\mathbb{U} \in \Delta$, but $\mathbb{U} \not\subseteq \Delta$; indeed, Δ contains sets of positive integers while $\mathbb{U}$ contains positive integers, not sets.

Implementation 1.3. We now present a C# implementation of a finite set. The .NET Framework, which C# makes use of, provides interface `ISet<T>` (and its implementation `HashSet<T>`). Let us point out that this interface implements most notions concerning finite sets and operations over them. For instance, it contains property `Count` which corresponds to the cardinality of a finite set; furthermore, it includes method `IntersectWith`, which performs the intersection of the two sets.

Next, however, we implement these notions in a completely original way, which struggles to make the defined notions, so it follows their mathematical definitions above as literally as possible. The following generic class represents a finite set whose members are objects of type `T`.

```
public class FiniteSet<T> : IEnumerable<T>
{
    private List<T> elements;

    // constructor
    public FiniteSet()
    {
        this.elements = new List<T>();
    }

    // returns an enumerator that iterates through this set
    public IEnumerator<T> GetEnumerator()
    {
        return this.elements.GetEnumerator();
    }
    IEnumerator IEnumerable.GetEnumerator()
    {
        return this.GetEnumerator();
    }
}
```

First, we need to determine whether a set contains a given element. We simply expose `Contains` method of `List<T>` class which performs this test.

```
public bool Contains(T element)
{
    return this.elements.Contains(element);
}
```

Instances of `List<T>` class may contain the same element multiple times, which is not the case in terms of sets. Therefore, we first check whether a given element has already been included into the set, and only if the answer is no, we add it into the set.

```
public bool Add(T element)
{
    if (this.Contains(element)) return false;
    else
    {
        this.elements.Add(element);
        return true;
    }
}
```

For convenience, the return value states whether a new element has been added.

An element is removed by `Remove` method of `List<T>`. Again, the return value says whether any element has actually been removed.

```
public bool Remove(T element)
{
    return this.elements.Remove(element);
}
```

Recall that the cardinality of a finite set is simply the number of its members, so it is straightforwardly determined as follows:

```
public int Cardinality { get { return this.elements.Count; } }
```

Having determined the cardinality of a finite set, we can easily find out whether the set is empty.

```
public bool IsEmpty { get { return this.Cardinality == 0; } }
```

To print out finite sets, we make use of `ToString` as follows:

```
public override string ToString()
{
    if (this.IsEmpty) return "{ }";
    else
    {
        var result = new StringBuilder();
        result.Append("{ ");
        foreach (T element in this.elements)
        {
            result.Append(element);
            result.Append(", ");
        }
        result.Remove(result.Length - 2, 2); // remove last comma
        result.Append(" }");
        return result.ToString();
    }
}
```

For instance, with the set Y from Example 1.1, this method returns a `System.String`, which would be printed out as `{ 2, 4, 6, 8 }`. To give another example, the empty set is printed out as `{ }` in this way.

Next, we initialize a set with another set, so after performing this initialization, both sets are identical.

```
public FiniteSet(FiniteSet<T> source)
{
    this.elements = new List<T>(source);
}
```

Throughout the rest of this implementation, A and B represent two finite sets. Next, we implement the test whether $A = B$, so we find out whether card(A) = card(B), and if so, we verify that every member of A belongs to B.

```
public bool SetEquals(FiniteSet<T> other)
{
    if (ReferenceEquals(this, other)) return true;
    else if (ReferenceEquals(other, null)) return false;
    else if (this.Cardinality != other.Cardinality) return false;
    else
    {
        foreach (T element in this)
        {
            if (!other.Contains(element)) return false;
        }

        return true;
    }
}
```

Next, we implement $A \cup B$ so we extend A by all members of B.

```
public FiniteSet<T> Union(FiniteSet<T> other)
{
    if (other == null) return null;

    var result = new FiniteSet<T>(this);
    foreach (T element in other)
    {
        result.Add(element);
    }
    return result;
}
```

Recall that `Add` method first tests whether an element a is absent in A, and if so, it includes a into A; otherwise, it quits.

We perform $A \cap B$ by putting together all elements that simultaneously belong to A and B.

```
public FiniteSet<T> Intersection(FiniteSet<T> other)
{
    if (other == null) return null;

    var result = new FiniteSet<T>();
```

```
    foreach (T element in this)
    {
        if (other.Contains(element)) result.Add(element);
    }
    return result;
}
```

We implement $A - B$ so that all members of B are removed from A.

```
public FiniteSet<T> Difference(FiniteSet<T> other)
{
    if (other == null) return null;

    var result = new FiniteSet<T>();
    foreach (T element in this)
    {
        if (!other.Contains(element)) result.Add(element);
    }
    return result;
}
```

We can answer whether $A \cap B = \emptyset$ by using "`A.Intersection(B).IsEmpty`." In this implementation, however, we always compute the whole intersection. In a more efficient way, the next implementation answers no and stops upon the first occurrence of an element in $A \cap B$.

```
public bool IsDisjoint(FiniteSet<T> other)
{
    if (other == null) return false;

    foreach (T element in this)
    {
        if (other.Contains(element)) return false;
    }

    return true;
}
```

Next, we compute the power set of A.

Let A have n members, a_1 through a_n, where $n \in \mathbb{N}$. Order the n members as a_1, $a_2, \ldots, a_i, \ldots, a_n$. The following implementation represents each set X in the power set by a unique binary string of the form $b_1 b_2 \cdots b_i \cdots b_n$, so $b_i = 1$ if and only if $a_i \in X$, and $b_i = 0$ if and only if $a_i \notin X$, where each b_i is a binary digit, $1 \leq i \leq n$.

```
public FiniteSet<FiniteSet<T>> PowerSet()
{
    var result = new FiniteSet<FiniteSet<T>>();

    // there is a total of (2^Cardinality) possible subsets
    int subsetCount = 1;
    for (int i = 0; i < this.Cardinality; i++)
```

```
    {
        subsetCount *= 2;
    }

    for (int i = 0; i < subsetCount; i++)
    {
        var subset = new FiniteSet<T>();
        for (int j = 0; j < this.Cardinality; j++)
        {
            if ((i & (1 << j)) != 0) // j-th digit of i is 1
            {
                subset.Add(this.elements[j]);
            }
        }
        result.Add(subset);
    }

    return result;
}
```

We close this section by describing two important proof techniques—proofs by contradiction and proofs by induction, which are frequently applied throughout this handbook.

Considering a proposition, a *proof by contradiction* starts by assuming that the opposite proposition is true. Then, it demonstrates that this assumption leads to a contradiction. Thus, the assumption was wrong, so the proposition holds true.

A *proof by induction* demonstrates that a statement s_i is true for all integers $i \geq b$, where b is a nonnegative integer. In general, a proof of this kind is made in the following way:

Basis. Prove that s_b is true.

Induction Hypothesis. Suppose that there exists an integer n such that $n \geq b$ and s_m is true for all $b \leq m \leq n$.

Induction Step. Prove that s_{n+1} is true under the assumption that the inductive hypothesis holds.

We illustrate how to make proofs by contradiction and by induction.

Let P be the set of all primes (a natural number n is prime if and only if its only positive divisors are 1 and n).

A proof by contradiction. By contradiction, we next prove that P is infinite. That is, assume that P is finite. Set $k = \text{card}(P)$. Thus, P contains k numbers $p_1, p_2, \ldots, p_k$. Set $n = p_1p_2 \cdots p_k + 1$. Observe that n is not divisible by any p_i, $1 \leq i \leq k$. As a result, either n is a new prime or n equals a product of new primes. In either case, there exists a prime out of P, which contradicts that P contains all primes. Thus, P is infinite. Another proof by contradiction is given in Example 2.8.

A proof by induction. As already stated, *by induction* we prove that a statement s_i holds for all $i \geq b$, where $b \in \mathbb{N}$. To illustrate, consider the set $\{i^2 \mid i \in \mathbb{N}\}$ and let s_i state

$$1 + 3 + 5 + \cdots + 2i - 1 = i^2$$

for all $i \in \mathbb{N}$; in other words, s_i says that the sum of odd integers is a perfect square. An inductive proof of this statement is as follows:

Basis. As $1 = 1^2$, s_i is true.

Induction Hypothesis. Assume that s_m is true for all $1 \leq m \leq n$, where n is a natural number.

Induction Step. Consider $s_{n+1} = 1 + 3 + 5 + \cdots + (2n - 1) + (2(n + 1) - 1) = (n + 1)^2$. By the inductive hypothesis, $s_n = 1 + 3 + 5 + \cdots + (2n - 1) = n^2$. Hence, $1 + 3 + 5 + \cdots + (2n - 1) + (2(n + 1) - 1) = n^2 + 2n + 1 = (n + 1)^2$. Consequently, s_{n+1} holds, and the inductive proof is completed.

1.2 Sequences

A *sequence* is a list of elements from some universe. A sequence is *finite* if it consists of finitely many elements; otherwise, it is *infinite*. The *length of a finite sequence* x, denoted by $|x|$, is the number of elements in x. The *empty sequence*, denoted by ε, is the sequence consisting of no element, that is, $|\varepsilon| = 0$.

Let s be a sequence. If s is finite, it is defined by listing its elements. If s is infinite, it is specified by using ellipses provided that this specification is clear. Alternatively, s is defined recursively by explicitly naming the first few values in s and then deriving later values in s by a property applied to earlier values in s.

Example 1.4. For instance,

$$0, 1, 0, 0$$

represents a finite sequence whose length is four, symbolically written $|0, 1, 0, 0| = 4$.

The infinite sequence

$$1, 3, 5, 7, 9, 11, \ldots$$

is the sequence consisting of all odd positive integers. The famous infinite *Fibonacci sequence* of positive integers, F, is defined recursively by

(i) $F(1) = F(2) = 1$;
(ii) $F(n) = F(n - 2) + F(n - 1)$, for all $n \geq 3$.

Thus, F starts as

$$1, 1, 2, 3, 5, 8, 13, 21, 34, 55, 89, 144, \ldots$$

Implementation 1.5. Fibonacci Sequence The following C# implementation of F takes an integer n as its input argument and returns $F(n)$.

```
public static class Sequences
{
    public static int Fibonacci(int n)
    {
        if (n <= 0) throw new ArgumentOutOfRangeException(
            "n", "Element index must be greater than or equal to 1.");

        if (n == 1 || n == 2) return 1;
        else return Fibonacci(n - 2) + Fibonacci(n - 1);
    }
}
```

For instance, calling `Console.WriteLine(Sequences.Fibonacci(10))` prints out `55`.

This straightforward implementation follows the definition of F literally and, thereby, involves a double recursion, thus working somewhat inefficiently. Alternative versions of this implementation, which avoid double recursion, are left as exercises.

1.3 Formal languages

An *alphabet* Σ is a finite non-empty set, whose members are called *symbols*. Any non-empty subset of Σ is a *subalphabet of* Σ. A finite sequence of symbols from Σ is a *string over* Σ; specifically, the empty sequence ε is referred to as the *empty string*—that is, the string consisting of zero symbols. By Σ^*, we denote the set of all strings over Σ. Set $\Sigma^+ = \Sigma^* - \{\varepsilon\}$. Let $x \in \Sigma^*$. Like for any sequence, $|x|$ denotes the length of x—that is, the number of symbols in x. For any $a \in \Sigma$, $\text{occur}(x, a)$ denotes the number of occurrences of a in x. For any $n \in \{1, \ldots, |x|\}$, $\text{symbol}(x, n)$ denotes the nth symbol in x.

In strings, for brevity, we usually juxtapose the symbols and omit the parentheses and all separating commas. That is, we write $a_1a_2 \cdots a_n$ instead of $a_1, a_2, \ldots, a_n$ hereafter.

Any subset $L \subseteq \Sigma^*$ is a *formal language* or, briefly and preferably, a *language over* Σ. Any subset of L is a *sublanguage of* L. If L represents a finite set, L is a *finite language*; otherwise, L is an *infinite language*. When discussing strings over Σ, Σ^* fulfills the role of the universe $\mathbb{U}$ in terms of Section 1.1; accordingly, Σ^* is customarily called the *universal language over* Σ. By analogy with classes of sets (see Section 1.1), *classes of languages* refer to sets whose members are languages.

Example 1.6. Let Σ be the English alphabet, consisting of its 26 letters, together with a hyphen (-). Strings ε, *a-b-c*, *yes*, and *all-you-can-eat* are strings over Σ, while a/b and $u2$ are not because they contain symbols out of Σ. Languages $\emptyset$, $\{\varepsilon\}$, $\{a, an, the\}$, $\{aa, ab, ba, bb\}$ are finite languages over Σ. Notice that $\emptyset \neq \{\varepsilon\}$ because $\text{card}(\emptyset) = 0 \neq \text{card}(\{\varepsilon\}) = 1$. The set of all English words contained in this book represents a finite language over Σ. On the other hand, the language consisting of all compound words of the form

great-granduncle, great-great-granduncle, great-great-great-granduncle, . . .

is an infinite language over Σ. Of course, many languages over Σ contain strings out of the English vocabulary. Take, for instance, the infinite language consisting of all strings over Σ that start with *a*. This infinite language contains *about*, which belongs to the English vocabulary, but it also includes *axyz*, which does not belong to this vocabulary.

Any natural-language family is a language class according to the definition above. For instance, the English language belongs to the Indo-European family of languages. It is noteworthy that a finite language family may contain infinite languages. To illustrate, take the family of all programming languages that have ever been designed. This family is obviously finite. However, most of its members are infinite; for instance, the language consisting of all well-written C programs is obviously infinite.

Implementation 1.7. Many programming languages already contain built-in types which follow the formal definition of symbols and strings. In C#, standard type `System.Char` (or, simply, **`char`**) represents an Unicode character (e.g., letter or digit), and type `System.String` (or **`string`**) represents a finite sequence of these characters. However, here we define our own types so that we are not limited to the alphabet of Unicode characters.

The following class `Symbol` represents symbols denoted by labels which are sequences of Unicode characters.

```
public class Symbol : IEquatable<Symbol>
{
    private string label;

    // constructor
    public Symbol(string label)
    {
        if (string.IsNullOrEmpty(label)) this.label = string.Empty;
        else this.label = label;
    }
}
```

To illustrate valid representations of symbols by three trivial examples, observe that `a`, `a1`, and `<a>` are created by **`new`** `Symbol("a")`, **`new`** `Symbol("a1")`, and **`new`** `Symbol("<a>")`, respectively.

Next, we determine whether two instances of symbol class have the same label and, thereby, represent the same symbol. We implement equality checking in a way defined by the standard `IEquatable<T>` interface. First, we create a single static method which performs the actual check for two given instances.

```
public static bool Equals(Symbol a, Symbol b)
{
    if (ReferenceEquals(a, b)) return true;
    else if (ReferenceEquals(a, null) || ReferenceEquals(b, null))
```

```
    {
        return false;
    }
    else return string.Equals(a.label, b.label);
}
```

Notice that all the required methods can call the static method with appropriate parameters. We always make use of this pattern when implementing equality checking throughout this book.

```
public bool Equals(Symbol other) { return Symbol.Equals(this, other); }

public override bool Equals(object obj)
{
    return Symbol.Equals(this, obj as Symbol);
}

public static bool operator ==(Symbol a, Symbol b)
{
    return Symbol.Equals(a, b);
}

public static bool operator !=(Symbol a, Symbol b)
{
    return !Symbol.Equals(a, b);
}
```

Classes which override `Equals` method are also required to override `GetHashCode` method. We forward the work to the label in this case.

```
public override int GetHashCode() { return this.label.GetHashCode(); }
```

Next, symbols are represented directly by their labels.

```
public override string ToString() { return this.label.ToString(); }
```

Finally, we provide an implicit conversion from the standard `System.String` class.

```
public static implicit operator Symbol(string s)
{
    return s == null ? null : new Symbol(s);
}
```

In this way, we specify `Symbol` literals directly by using `System.String` literals. For example, `"a1"` specifies **new** `Symbol("a1")` provided that `System.String` is not applicable while `Symbol` is.

Having represented individual symbols, we further define class `HmmlcString` to represent a sequence of symbols. We use the prefix `Hmmlc` to disambiguate it from the standard `System.String` class.

```
public class HmmlcString : IEquatable<MFoC_String>, IEnumerable<Symbol>
{
    private List<Symbol> symbols;
```

```
    // constructor
    public HmmlcString(params Symbol[] symbols)
    {
        this.symbols = new List<Symbol>(symbols);
    }
}
```

The length of a string is simply the number of its symbols.

```
public int Length { get { return this.symbols.Count; } }
```

We also add a static, read-only field which represents the empty string.

```
public static readonly HmmlcString Empty = new HmmlcString();
```

Every string is a sequence, whose elements can be enumerated as implemented next.

```
public IEnumerator<Symbol> GetEnumerator()
{
    return this.symbols.GetEnumerator();
}
IEnumerator IEnumerable.GetEnumerator()
{
    return this.symbols.GetEnumerator();
}
```

The symbols which form a string can be indexed and accessed by the positions as follows:

```
public Symbol this[int i] { get { return this.symbols[i]; } }
```

Note that, as usual in C#, indexing starts from 0.

Next, we implement equality checking using the pattern introduced with `Symbol` class above.

```
public static bool Equals(HmmlcString x, HmmlcString y)
{
    if (ReferenceEquals(x, y)) return true;
    else if (ReferenceEquals(x, null) || ReferenceEquals(y, null))
    {
        return false;
    }
    else if (x.Length != y.Length) return false;
    else
    {
        for (int i = 0; i < x.Length; i++)
        {
            if (x[i] != y[i]) return false;
        }
        return true;
    }
}
```

```
public bool Equals(HmmlcString other)
{
    return HmmlcString.Equals(this, other);
}

public override bool Equals(object obj)
{
    return HmmlcString.Equals(this, obj as MFoC_String);
}

public static bool operator ==(MFoC_String x, MFoC_String y)
{
    return HmmlcString.Equals(x, y);
}

public static bool operator !=(MFoC_String x, MFoC_String y)
{
    return !HmmlcString.Equals(x, y);
}

public override int GetHashCode()
{
    return string.Concat(this.symbols).GetHashCode();
}
```

A `System.String` representation of a `HmmlcString` is obtained as the concatenation of all its symbols.

```
public override string ToString()
{
    return string.Concat(this.symbols);
}
```

The following method counts the number of occurrences of a given symbol *a* in a string.

```
public int Occur(Symbol a)
{
    int count = 0;
    foreach (Symbol b in this) { if (a == b) count++; }
    return count;
}
```

For example, create a string as follows:

```
var x = new HmmlcString("a1", "a2", "B", "a1");
```

Calling `Console.WriteLine(x)` results in printing out `a1a2aBa1`. Moreover, calling `Console.WriteLine(x.Occur("a1"))` outputs `2`.

To conclude with, recall that we have already implemented finite set (see Implementation 1.3). Since any alphabet is a special case of finite set, we can create a derived class as follows:

```
public class Alphabet : FiniteSet<Symbol>
{
    // constructor
    public Alphabet()
        : base()
    {
    }

    // copy constructor
    public Alphabet(Alphabet source)
        : base(source)
    {
    }
}
```

You may notice that this implementation allows an alphabet to be empty. Strictly according to definition, this should not be possible. However, imposing such restriction in our implementation would be nontrivial. Disregarding it, on the other hand, does not have any significant drawbacks for our purposes.

Language operations

Let $x, y \in \Sigma^*$ be two strings over an alphabet Σ, and let $L, K \subseteq \Sigma^*$ be two languages over Σ. As languages are defined as sets, all set operations apply to them. Specifically, $L \cup K$, $L \cap K$, and $L - K$ denote the union, intersection, and difference of languages L and K, respectively. Perhaps most importantly, the *concatenation of x with y*, denoted by xy, is the string obtained by appending y to x. Notice that for every $w \in \Sigma^*$, $w\varepsilon = \varepsilon w = w$. The *concatenation of L and K*, denoted by LK, is defined as $LK = \{xy \mid x \in L, y \in K\}$.

Apart from binary operations, we also make some unary operations with strings and languages. Let $x \in \Sigma^*$ and $L \subseteq \Sigma^*$. The *complement of L* is denoted by $\bar{L}$ and defined as $\bar{L} = \Sigma^* - L$. The *reversal of x*, denoted by reversal(x), is x written in the reverse order, and the *reversal of L*, reversal(L), is defined as reversal(L) $=$ $\{\text{reversal}(x) \mid x \in L\}$. Next, based on the recursive definitional method described in Section 1.1, we define for all $i \geq 0$, the *ith power of x*, denoted by x^i, as

(i) $x^0 = \varepsilon$;
(ii) $x^i = xx^{i-1}$, for $i \geq 1$.

To demonstrate the recursive aspect, consider, for instance, the ith power of x, x^i, with $i = 3$. By the second part of the definition, $x^3 = xx^2$. By applying the second part to x^2 again, $x^2 = xx^1$. By another application of this part to x^1, $x^1 = xx^0$. By the first part of this definition, $x^0 = \varepsilon$. Thus, $x^1 = xx^0 = x\varepsilon = x$. Hence, $x^2 = xx^1 = xx$. Finally, $x^3 = xx^2 = xxx$. By using this recursive method, we frequently introduce new notions, including the *ith power of L*, L^i, which is defined as

(i) $L^0 = \{\varepsilon\}$;
(ii) $L^i = LL^{i-1}$, for $i \geq 1$.

The *closure of L*, L^*, is defined as $L^* = L^0 \cup L^1 \cup L^2 \cup \cdots$, and the *positive closure of L*, L^+, is defined as $L^+ = L^1 \cup L^2 \cup \cdots$. Notice that $L^+ = LL^* = L^*L$, and $L^* = L^+ \cup \{\varepsilon\}$. Let $w, x, y, z \in \Sigma^*$. If $xz = y$, x is a *prefix of* y; if, in addition, $x \notin \{\varepsilon, y\}$, x is a *proper prefix of* y.

If $zx = y$, x is a *suffix of* y; if, in addition, $x \notin \{\varepsilon, y\}$, x is a *proper suffix of* y.

If $wxz = y$, x is a *substring of* y; if, in addition, $x \notin \{\varepsilon, y\}$, x is a *proper substring of* y. By substrings(y), we denote the set of all substrings of y.

Let $y \in \Sigma^*$. By symbols(y), prefixes(y), suffixes(y), substrings(y), and perm(y), we denote the sets of all symbols, prefixes, suffixes, substrings, and permutations of y, respectively, and by lms(y) we denote the leftmost symbol of y. Furthermore, for any $L \subseteq \Sigma^*$, set symbols(L) $= \bigcup_{y \in L}$ symbols(y), prefixes(L) $= \bigcup_{y \in L}$ prefixes(y), suffixes(L) $= \bigcup_{y \in L}$ suffixes(y), substrings(L) $= \bigcup_{y \in L}$ substrings(y), perm(L) $= \bigcup_{y \in L}$ perm(L), and let lmax(L) denote the length of the longest string in L. For any $n \in \{1, \ldots, |y|\}$, prefix (y, n) and suffix (y, n) denote the prefix of y of length n and the suffix of y of length n, respectively, substrings(y, n) $=$ substrings(y) $\cap \Sigma^n$, and let sym(y, n) denote the n-th symbol of y.

Example 1.8. Set $\Sigma = \{0, 1\}$. For instance, ε, 1, and 110 are strings over Σ. Notice that $|\varepsilon| = 0$, $|1| = 1$, $|110| = 3$. The concatenation of 1 and 110 is 1110. The third power of 1110 equals 111011101110. Observe that reversal(1110) $=$ 0111. We have prefixes(1110) $= \{\varepsilon, 1, 11, 111, 1110\}$, where 1, 11, and 111 are proper prefixes of 1110 while ε and 1110 are not. We have suffixes(1110) $= \{\varepsilon, 0, 10, 110, 1110\}$, substrings(1110) $= \{\varepsilon, 0, 1, 11, 10, 110, 1110\}$, and symbols(1110) $= \{0, 1\}$.

Set $K = \{1, 01\}$ and $L = \{0, 01\}$. Observe that $L \cup K$, $L \cap K$, and $L - K$ are equal to $\{0, 1, 01\}$, $\{01\}$, and $\{0\}$, respectively. The concatenation of K and L is $KL = \{10, 101, 010, 0101\}$. Notice that $\bar{L} = \Sigma^* - L$, so $\bar{L}$ contains all strings in $\{0, 1\}^*$ but 0 and 01. Furthermore, reversal(L) $= \{0, 10\}$ and $L^2 = \{00, 001, 010, 0101\}$. The strings in L^* that consist of three or fewer symbols are ε, 0, 00, 01, 000, 001, and 010. $L^+ = L^* \cup \{\varepsilon\}$. Notice that prefixes($L$) $= \{\varepsilon, 0, 01\}$, suffixes(L) $= \{\varepsilon, 1, 01\}$, substrings(L) $= \{\varepsilon, 0, 1, 01\}$, and symbols($L$) $= \{0, 1\}$.

Implementation 1.9. Next, a stack-based implementation of reversal is described. We add a new method `Reverse` to class `HmmlcSTring`. For a string $x \in \Sigma^*$, the implementation reads x and, simultaneously, stores it into a stack. When the whole string is processed in this way, the program first creates a new string, initialized to the empty string. Then it starts popping off symbols stored in the stack and appending them to the new string, thus producing reversal(x) as desired.

```
public HmmlcString Reverse()
{
    var stack = new Stack<Symbol>();
    foreach (Symbol a in this.symbols) { stack.Push(a); }

    var result = new HmmlcString();
    while (stack.Count > 0)
    {
        Symbol a = stack.Pop();
        result.symbols.Add(a);
    }

    return result;
}
```

Implementation 1.10. In class `HmmlcString`, we implement a method which concatenates a string with another string *s*.

```
public HmmlcString Concatenate(HmmlcString s)
{
    if (s == null) return this;
    else if (this == HmmlcString.Empty) return s;
    else if (s == HmmlcString.Empty) return this;
    else
    {
        var symbols = new List<Symbol>(this.symbols);

        foreach (Symbol a in s.symbols)
        {
            symbols.Add(a);
        }

        return new HmmlcString(symbols.ToArray());
    }
}
```

Next, we add a check whether a string is a prefix of another string *s*. We compare symbols of the two strings up to the length of the potential prefix.

```
public bool IsPrefixOf(HmmlcString s)
{
    if (s == null) return false;
    else if (this.Length > s.Length) return false;
    else
    {
        for (int i = 0; i < this.Length; i++)
        {
            if (this[i] != s[i])
            {
                return false;
            }
        }
        return true;
    }
}
```

The suffix relation can be implemented in a similar way—indeed, the two methods only differ in the position of the compared symbols in *s*.

```
public bool IsSuffixOf(HmmlcString s)
{
    if (s == null) return false;
    else if (this.Length > s.Length) return false;
    else
    {
        for (int i = 0; i < this.Length; i++)
```

```
        {
            if (this[i] != s[s.Length - this.Length + i])
            {
                return false;
            }
        }
        return true;
    }
}
```

We further add a method which returns the prefix of a given length.

```
public HmmlcString GetPrefix(int length)
{
    if (length == 0) return HmmlcString.Empty;
    else
    {
        var symbols = new List<Symbol>();

        for (int i = 0; i < length; i++)
        {
            symbols.Add(this[i]);
        }

        return new HmmlcString(symbols.ToArray());
    }
}
```

Making use of this method, obtaining the set of all prefixes is straightforward.

```
public FiniteSet<HmmlcString> GetAllPrefixes()
{
    var result = new FiniteSet<HmmlcString>();

    for (int i = 0; i <= this.Length; i++)
    {
        result.Add(this.GetPrefix(i));
    }

    return result;
}
```

To conclude with, we add analogous methods for suffixes.

```
public HmmlcString GetSuffix(int length)
{
    if (length == 0) return HmmlcString.Empty;
    else
    {
        var symbols = new List<Symbol>();

        for (int i = this.Length - length; i < this.Length; i++)
        {
```

```
            symbols.Add(this[i]);
        }

        return new HmmlcString(symbols.ToArray());
    }
}

public FiniteSet<HmmlcString> GetAllSuffixes()
{
    var result = new FiniteSet<HmmlcString>();

    for (int i = 0; i <= this.Length; i++)
    {
        result.Add(this.GetSuffix(i));
    }

    return result;
}
```

The next example defines a trivial function that represents all nonnegative integers by unary strings. Moreover, it shows how to perform some common mathematical operations, such as addition, in terms of this function.

Example 1.11. Let a be a symbol. We represent every $i \in {}_0\mathbb{N}$ (see Section 1.1) by a^i; to rephrase this mathematically, we define a function ν from ${}_0\mathbb{N}$ to $\{a\}^*$ as $\nu(i) = a^i$ for all $i \geq 0$, for instance, ν maps 0, 2, and 123 to ε, aa, and a^{123}, respectively.

Consider the operation of addition defined over ${}_0\mathbb{N}$. In terms of ν, by using concatenation, we define $i + j = |\nu(i)\nu(j)|$ for all $i, j \in {}_0\mathbb{N}$. For instance, take $2 + 3 = |\nu(2)\nu(3)| = |aaaaa|$. Similarly for multiplication, we define $ij = |\nu(i)^j|$ for all $i, j \in {}_0\mathbb{N}$. Finally, consider i^j for all $i, j \geq 0$. In terms of ν, we define $i^j = |\nu(i)|^j$ for all $i, j \in {}_0\mathbb{N}$.

Implementation 1.12. We present an implementation of ν from Example 1.11, which takes any number $i \in {}_0\mathbb{N}$ and produces a^i.

```
public static HmmlcString Nu(int i)
{
    var symbols = new List<string>();
    for (int j = 0; j < i; j++) { symbols.Add("a"); }
    return new HmmlcString(symbols.ToArray());
}
```

Chapter 2

Relations and functions

This chapter reviews rudimentary concepts concerning relations and their special cases called functions. These concepts underlie most formal models introduced in Part II of this book.

2.1 Relations

For two elements, a and b, (a, b) denotes the *ordered pair* consisting of a and b in this order. Let A and B be two sets. The *Cartesian product of A and B*, $A \times B$, is defined as $A \times B = \{(a, b) \mid a \in A \text{ and } b \in B\}$. A *binary relation* or, briefly, a *relation*, ρ, from A to B is any subset of $A \times B$, that is, $\rho \subseteq A \times B$. If ρ represents a finite set, it is a *finite relation*; otherwise, it is an *infinite relation*. The *domain of* ρ, denoted by domain (ρ), and the *range of* ρ, denoted by range (ρ), are defined as domain $(\rho) = \{a \mid (a, b) \in \rho \text{ for some } b \in B\}$ and range $(\rho) = \{b \mid (a, b) \in \rho \text{ for some } a \in A\}$. If $A = B$, ρ is a *relation on* A. A relation σ is a *subrelation of* ρ if $\sigma \subseteq \rho$. The *inverse of* ρ, denoted by inverse (ρ), is defined as inverse $(\rho) = \{(b, a) \mid (a, b) \in \rho\}$. Let $\chi \subseteq B \times C$ be a relation, where C is a set; the *composition of* ρ *with* χ is denoted by $\rho \circ \chi$ and defined as $\rho \circ \chi = \{(a, c) \mid (a, b) \in \rho, (b, c) \in \chi\}$.

As relations are defined as sets, the set operations apply to them, too. For instance, if ρ is a relation from A to B, its complement $\bar{\rho}$ is defined as $(A \times B) - \rho$.

Example 2.1. Set

$$\textit{articles} = \{a, an, the\} \text{ and } \textit{two-words} = \{author, reader\}.$$

The Cartesian product of *articles* and *two-words* is defined as

$$\begin{aligned} \textit{articles} \times \textit{two-words} = \{&(a, author), (a, reader), (an, author), \\ &(an, reader), (the, author), (the, reader)\}. \end{aligned}$$

Define the relation *proper-article* as

$$\textit{proper-article} = \{(a, reader), (an, author), (the, author), (the, reader)\}.$$

Observe that *proper-article* properly relates English articles to the members of the set *two-words*. Notice that

$$\text{inverse}\,(\textit{proper-article}) = \{(reader, a), (author, an), (author, the), (reader, the)\}.$$

Let $\rho \subseteq A \times B$ be a relation. To express that $(a, b) \in \rho$, we sometimes write $a\rho b$. That is, we use $(a, b) \in \rho$ and $a\rho b$ interchangeably in what follows.

Let A be a set and ρ be a relation on A. Then,

(i) if for all $a \in A$, $a\rho a$, then ρ is *reflexive*;
(ii) if for all $a, b \in A$, $a\rho b$ implies $b\rho a$, then ρ is *symmetric*;
(iii) if for all $a, b \in A$, ($a\rho b$ and $b\rho a$) implies $a = b$, then ρ is *antisymmetric*; and
(iv) if for all $a, b, c \in A$, ($a\rho b$ and $b\rho c$) implies $a\rho c$, then ρ is *transitive*.

Let A be a set, ρ be a relation on A, and $a, b \in A$. For $k \geq 1$, the *k-fold product of* ρ, ρ^k, is recursively defined as

(i) $a\rho^1 b$ iff $a\rho b$, and
(ii) $a\rho^k b$ iff there exists $c \in A$ such that $a\rho c$ and $c\rho^{k-1}b$, for $k \geq 2$.

Furthermore, $a\rho^0 b$ if and only if $a = b$. The *transitive closure of* ρ, ρ^+ is defined as $a\rho^+ b$ if and only if $a\rho^k b$, for some $k \geq 1$; consequently, ρ^+ is the smallest transitive relation that contains ρ. The *reflexive and transitive closure of* ρ, ρ^*, is defined as $a\rho^* b$ if and only if $a\rho^k b$, for some $k \geq 0$.

Example 2.2. Let A be the set of all people who have ever lived. Define the relation *parent* so

$(a, b) \in$ *parent* if and only if a is a parent of b, for all $a, b \in A$.

Observe that $parent^2$ represents the grandparenthood because $(a, b) \in parent^2$ if and only if a is a grandparent of b. Furthermore, $(a, b) \in parent^3$ if and only if a is a great-grandparent of b. Consequently, $parent^+$ corresponds to being an ancestor in the sense that $(a, b) \in parent^+$ iff a is an ancestor of b. Of course, $(a, a) \notin parent^+$ for any $a \in A$ because a cannot be an ancestor of a. On the other hand, notice that $(a, a) \in parent^*$ for all $a \in A$, so $(a, b) \in parent^*$ iff a is an ancestor of b or $a = b$.

Let A be a finite set, $A = \{a_1, \ldots, a_n\}$, for some $n \geq 1$. Let ρ be a relation on A. A useful way to represent ρ is by its *adjacency matrix* ${}_\rho M$. That is, ${}_\rho M$ is an $n \times n$ matrix whose entries are 0s and 1s. Its rows and columns are both denoted by a_1–a_n. For all $1 \leq i,j \leq n$, the entry ${}_\rho M_{ij}$ is 1 if and only if $(a_i, a_j) \in \rho$, so ${}_\rho M_{ij} = 0$ if and only if $(a_i, a_j) \notin \rho$.

From ${}_\rho M$, we can easily construct ${}_{\rho^+}M$, which represents the transitive closure of ρ, by using *Warshall's algorithm*, given next. In essence, this algorithm is based upon the idea that if ${}_{\rho^+}M_{ik} = 1$ and ${}_{\rho^+}M_{kj} = 1$, ${}_{\rho^+}M_{ij} = 1$. Starting from ${}_\rho M$, it repeatedly performs this implication until no new member can be added to the adjacency matrix.

Example 2.3. Let $A = \{1, 2, 3, 4\}$ and ρ be the relation on A defined as

$$\rho = \{(1, 2), (1, 4), (2, 1), (2, 3), (3, 4), (4, 3)\}.$$

Its adjacency matrix ${}_\rho M$ is as follows:

$$ {}_\rho M = \begin{bmatrix} 0 & 1 & 0 & 1 \\ 1 & 0 & 1 & 0 \\ 0 & 0 & 0 & 1 \\ 0 & 0 & 1 & 0 \end{bmatrix} $$

Algorithm 2.1: Warshall's algorithm

Input: An adjacency matrix ${}_\rho M$, where ρ is a relation on $A = \{a_1, \ldots, a_n\}$, for some $n \geq 1$.
Output: ${}_{\rho^+}M$.

begin
  set ${}_{\rho^+}M = {}_\rho M$
  repeat
    if ${}_{\rho^+}M_{ij} = 1$ *and* ${}_{\rho^+}M_{jk} = 1$, *where* $i, j, k = 1, \ldots, n$ **then**
      set ${}_{\rho^+}M_{ik} = 1$
    end
  until no change
end

We apply Warshall's algorithm to ${}_\rho M$ in order to obtain ${}_{\rho^+}M$, which represents the transitive closure of ρ. Strictly speaking, we give the first eight matrices produced by the innermost cycle in the implementation of this algorithm that follows the present example (see Implementation 2.1). Notice that some iterations result in a change of the current version of the matrix they work with, while others do not.

$$\begin{bmatrix} 0 & 1 & 0 & 1 \\ 1 & 0 & 1 & 0 \\ 0 & 0 & 0 & 1 \\ 0 & 0 & 1 & 0 \end{bmatrix} \begin{bmatrix} 0 & 1 & 0 & 1 \\ 1 & 0 & 1 & 0 \\ 0 & 0 & 0 & 1 \\ 0 & 0 & 1 & 0 \end{bmatrix} \begin{bmatrix} 0 & 1 & 0 & 1 \\ 1 & 0 & 1 & 0 \\ 0 & 0 & 0 & 1 \\ 0 & 0 & 1 & 0 \end{bmatrix} \begin{bmatrix} 0 & 1 & 0 & 1 \\ 1 & 0 & 1 & 0 \\ 0 & 0 & 0 & 1 \\ 0 & 0 & 1 & 0 \end{bmatrix}$$

$$\begin{bmatrix} 1 & 1 & 0 & 1 \\ 1 & 0 & 1 & 0 \\ 0 & 0 & 0 & 1 \\ 0 & 0 & 1 & 0 \end{bmatrix} \begin{bmatrix} 1 & 1 & 0 & 1 \\ 1 & 0 & 1 & 0 \\ 0 & 0 & 0 & 1 \\ 0 & 0 & 1 & 0 \end{bmatrix} \begin{bmatrix} 1 & 1 & 1 & 1 \\ 1 & 0 & 1 & 0 \\ 0 & 0 & 0 & 1 \\ 0 & 0 & 1 & 0 \end{bmatrix} \begin{bmatrix} 1 & 1 & 1 & 1 \\ 1 & 0 & 1 & 0 \\ 0 & 0 & 0 & 1 \\ 0 & 0 & 1 & 0 \end{bmatrix}$$

The resulting ${}_{\rho^+}M$, produced by this algorithm, is as follows:

$${}_{\rho^+}M = \begin{bmatrix} 1 & 1 & 1 & 1 \\ 1 & 1 & 1 & 1 \\ 0 & 0 & 1 & 1 \\ 0 & 0 & 1 & 1 \end{bmatrix}$$

Implementation 2.1. We can implement Algorithm 2.1 in C# as follows:

```
public static class Relations
{
    public static void Warshall(int[,] M)
    {
        int n = M.GetLength(0);
        if (n != M.GetLength(1)) throw new ArgumentException(
            "Adjacency matrix must be square (n times n).", "M");
```

```
        bool change;
        do
        {
            change = false;
            for (int i = 0; i < n; i++)
            {
                for (int j = 0; j < n; j++)
                {
                    for (int k = 0; k < n; k++)
                    {
                        if (M[i, k] == 0)
                        {
                            if (M[i, j] == 1 && M[j, k] == 1)
                            {
                                M[i, k] = 1;
                                change = true;
                            }
                        }
                    }
                }
            }
        }
        while (change);
    }
}
```

Note that array indexing in C# starts from 0, while our matrix indices start from 1. Consequently, M_{ij} corresponds to `M[i-1, j-1]` in the above implementation; for example, M_{11} and M_{24} translate to `M[0, 0]` and `M[1, 3]`, respectively.

To compute ${}_{\rho^+}M$ from ${}_{\rho}M$ defined in Example 2.3, we can use this implementation as follows:

```
int[,] rhoM = new int[,]
{
    { 0, 1, 0, 1 },
    { 1, 0, 1, 0 },
    { 0, 0, 0, 1 },
    { 0, 0, 1, 0 }
};

Relations.Warshall(rhoM);
```

Variable `rhoM` now contains the adjacency matrix of ρ^+ (see Example 2.3).

Let Σ be a set and ρ be a relation on Σ. If ρ is reflexive, symmetric, and transitive, then ρ is an *equivalence relation*. Let ρ be an equivalence relation on Σ. Then, ρ partitions Σ into disjoint subsets, called *equivalence classes*, so that for each $a \in \Sigma$, the equivalence class of a is denoted by $[a]$ and defined as $[a] = \{b \mid a\rho b\}$. As an exercise, explain why for all a and b in Σ, either $[a] = [b]$ or $[a] \cap [b] = \emptyset$.

Example 2.4. Let $\equiv_n$ denote the *relation of congruence modulo n* on ${}_0N$, defined as

$$\equiv_n = \{(x, y) \mid x, y \in {}_0N,\ x - y = kn,\ \text{for some integer } k\}.$$

Specifically, take $n = 3$. In other words,

$$\equiv_3 = \{(x, y) \mid x, y \in {}_0N,\ x - y \text{ is a multiple of } 3\}.$$

Notice that $\equiv_3$ is reflexive because $i - i = 0$, which is a multiple of 3. Furthermore, $\equiv_3$ is symmetric because $i - j$ is a multiple of 3 iff $j - i$ is a multiple of 3. Finally, it is transitive because whenever $i - j$ is a multiple of 3 and $j - k$ is a multiple of 3, $i - j = (i - j) + (j - k)$ is the sum of two multiples, so it is a multiple of 3, too. Thus, $\equiv_3$ represents an equivalence relation.

Observe that

$$\{0, 3, 6, \dots\}$$

forms an equivalence class because $3n \equiv_3 3m$ for all integers n and m. More generally, $\equiv_3$ partitions ${}_0N$ into these three equivalence classes

$$[0] = \{0, 3, 6, \dots\},$$
$$[1] = \{1, 4, 7, \dots\},$$
$$[2] = \{2, 5, 8, \dots\}.$$

Observe that [0], [1], [2] are pairwise disjoint and that ${}_0N = [0] \cup [1] \cup [2]$.

Let Σ be a set and ρ be a relation on Σ. If ρ is reflexive, antisymmetric, and transitive, then ρ is a *partial order*. If ρ is a partial order satisfying either $a\rho b$ or $b\rho a$, for all $a, b \in \Sigma$ such that $a \neq b$, then ρ is a *linear order*. As an exercise, illustrate these relations by specific examples.

2.2 Functions

A *function* ϕ from A to B is a relation ϕ from A to B such that if $a\phi b$ and $a\phi c$, then $b = c$; in other words, for every $a \in A$, there is no more than one $b \in B$ such that $a\phi b$. Let ϕ be a function from A to B. If domain $(\phi) = A$, ϕ is *total*. If we want to emphasize that ϕ may not satisfy domain $(\phi) = A$, we say that ϕ is *partial*.

Example 2.5. Reconsider the relation *parent* from Example 2.2, defined as

$(a, b) \in$ *parent* if and only if a is a parent of b, for all $a, b \in A$,

where A is the set of all people who have ever lived. Of course, *parent* is not a function because a parent may have two or more children. Neither is inverse (*parent*) a function because every child has two parents. Consider *one-child-parent* as the subrelation of *parent* defined as

$(a, b) \in$ *one-child-parent* if and only if a is a parent of a single child b, for all $a, b \in A$.

Clearly, *one-child-parent* is a partial function, but inverse (*one-child-parent*) is not a function.

Finally, take B as the set of all mothers who have a single child, so $B \subseteq A$. Consider *parent* defined over B. Observe that *parent* redefined over B coincides with the following definition of relation *one-daughter–mother* over B

$$(a, b) \in \textit{one-daughter–mother} \quad \text{if and only if both } a \text{ and } b \text{ are mothers of a single daughter, for all } a, b \in B.$$

As obvious, *one-daughter–mother* and its inverse are both total functions.

Let ϕ be a function from A to B. If for every $b \in B$, card $(\{a \mid a \in A \text{ and } \phi(a) = b\}) \leq 1$, ϕ is an *injection*. If for every $b \in B$, card $(\{a \mid a \in A \text{ and } \phi(a) = b\}) \geq 1$, ϕ is a *surjection*. If ϕ is a total function that is both a surjection and an injection, ϕ represents a *bijection*. Instead of $a\phi b$, where $a \in A$ and $b \in B$, we often write $\phi(a) = b$ and say that b is the *value* of ϕ for *argument* a.

Return to the set theory (see Section 1.1). Based upon bijections, we define the notion of a countable set, which fulfills an important role in the theory of computation (see above). That is, if there is a bijection from an infinite set Ψ to an infinite set Ξ, then Ψ and Ξ have the *same cardinality*. An infinite set, Ω, is *countable* or, synonymously, *enumerable*, if Ω and $\mathbb{N}$ have the same cardinality; otherwise, it is *uncountable* (as stated in Section 1.1, $\mathbb{N}$ denotes the set of natural numbers).

Example 2.6. Consider the set of all even natural numbers, E. Define the bijection $\phi(i) = 2i$, for all $i \in \mathbb{N}$. Observe that ϕ represents a bijection from $\mathbb{N}$ to E, so they have the same cardinality. Thus, E is countable. As an exercise, show that the set of all rational numbers is countable, too.

Example 2.7. Consider the set ς of all functions mapping $\mathbb{N}$ to $\{0, 1\}$. By contradiction, we prove that ς is uncountable. Suppose that ς is countable. Thus, there is a bijection from ς to $\mathbb{N}$. Let ${}_if$ be the function mapped to the ith positive integer, for all $i \geq 1$. Consider the total function g from $\mathbb{N}$ to $\{0, 1\}$ defined as $g(j) = 0$ if and only if ${}_jf(j) = 1$, for all $i \geq 1$, so $g(j) = 1$ if and only if ${}_jf(j) = 0$. As ς contains g, $g = {}_kf$ for some $k \geq 1$. Specifically, $g(k) = {}_kf(k)$. However, $g(k) = 0$ if and only if ${}_kf(k) = 1$, so $g(k) \neq {}_kf(k)$, thus contradicting $g(k) = {}_kf(k)$. Consequently, ς is uncountable.

The proof technique by which we have demonstrated that ς is uncountable is customarily called *diagonalization*. To see why, rephrase the above-described proof in terms of an infinite table with ${}_1f, {}_2f, \ldots$ listed down the rows and $1, 2, \ldots$ listed across the columns (see Table 2.1). Each entry contains either 0 or 1. Specifically, the entry in row ${}_if$ and column j contains 1 if and only if ${}_if(j) = 1$, so this entry contains 0 if and only if ${}_if(j) = 0$. A contradiction occurs at the diagonal entry in row ${}_kf$ and column k because $g(k) = 0$ if and only if ${}_kf(k) = 1$ and $g(k) = {}_kf(k)$; in other words, this diagonal entry contains 0 if and only if it contains 1, which is impossible. We make use of this proof technique later in this book.

Table 2.1 Diagonalization

	1	2	...	k	...
${}_1f$	0	1		0	
${}_2f$	1	1		1	
$\vdots$					
${}_kf = g$	0	0		$g(k)$	
$\vdots$					

Table 2.2 Morse code

Letter	μ	Letter	μ	Letter	μ
A	.–	J	.–––	S	...
B	–...	K	–.–	T	–
C	–.–.	L	.–..	U	..–
D	–..	M	––	V	...–
E	.	N	–.	W	.––
F	..–.	O	–––	X	–..–
G	––.	P	.––.	Y	–.––
H	....	Q	––.–	Z	––..
I	..	R	.–.		

We close this section by defining substitution and homomorphism, which represent two important types of functions that transform symbols in languages (see Section 1.3). Let T and U be two alphabets. A total function τ from T^* to power (U^*) such that $\tau(uv) = \tau(u)\tau(v)$ for every $u, v \in T^*$ is a *substitution* from T^* to U^*. By this definition, $\tau(\varepsilon) = \{\varepsilon\}$ and $\tau(a_1a_2 \cdots a_n) = \tau(a_1)\tau(a_2)\cdots\tau(a_n)$, where $a_i \in T$, $1 \leq i \leq n$, for some $n \geq 1$, so τ is completely specified by defining $\tau(a)$ for every $a \in T$. A total function ν from T^* to U^* such that $\nu(uv) = \nu(u)\nu(v)$ for every $u, v \in T^*$ is a *homomorphism* from T^* to U^*. For brevity, we write $\nu(u) = x$ instead of $\nu(u) = \{x\}$, where $x \in U^*$, hereafter. As any homomorphism is obviously a special case of a substitution, we simply specify ν by defining $\nu(a)$ for every $a \in T$; if $\nu(a) \neq \varepsilon$ for all $a \in T$, ν is said to be an *ε-free homomorphism*. It is worth noting that a homomorphism from T^* to U^* may not represent an injection from T^* to U^* as illustrated in the next example.

Example 2.8. Let ${}_{English}\Delta$ denote the English alphabet. The *Morse code*, denoted by μ, can be seen as a homomorphism from ${}_{English}\Delta^*$ to $\{\,.\,,\,-\}^*$ (see Table 2.2). For instance,

$$\mu(SOS) = \ldots --- \ldots$$

Notice that by no means, μ is an injection from ${}_{English}\Delta^*$ to $\{\,.\,,\,-\,\}^*$; for instance, $\mu(SOS) = \mu(IJS)$.

To give another example, suppose that we wish to change every digit in a binary string into its corresponding English name started with a capital letter. We can use the homomorphism o defined as $o(0) = Zero$ and $o(1) = One$. For instance, o changes 101 to *OneZeroOne*. Notice that o is an injection from $\{0, 1\}^*$ to $\{Zero, One\}^*$.

Chapter 3
Graphs

This chapter reviews the principal ideas and notions underlying graph theory. It restricts its attention to directed graphs, which are central to the theory of computation.

3.1 Directed graphs

Loosely speaking, a directed graph is a representation of a set with some pairs of its elements, called nodes, connected by directed links, called edges. Customarily, a graph is depicted as a set of dots for the vertices, joined by lines for the edges. A directed graph has its edges directed from one node to another.

More precisely, a *directed graph* or, briefly, a *graph* is a pair $G = (A, \rho)$, where A is a set and ρ is a relation on A. Members of A are called *nodes*, and ordered pairs in ρ are called *edges*. If $(a, b) \in \rho$, edge (a, b) *leaves* a and *enters* b. Let $a \in A$; the *in-degree of* a and the *out-degree of* a are card $(\{b \mid (b, a) \in \rho\})$ and card $(\{c \mid (a, c) \in \rho\})$. A sequence of nodes, $(a_0, a_1, \ldots, a_n)$, where $n \geq 1$, is a *path of length* n from a_0 to a_n if $(a_{i-1}, a_i) \in \rho$ for all $1 \leq i \leq n$; if, in addition, $a_0 = a_n$, then $(a_0, a_1, \ldots, a_n)$ is a *cycle of length* n. In this book, we frequently *label* the edges of G with some attached information. Pictorially, we represent $G = (A, \rho)$, so we draw each edge $(a, b) \in \rho$ as an arrow from a to b possibly with its label as illustrated in the next example.

Example 3.1. For a program p, its *call graph* $G = (P, \rho)$ is defined, so P represents the set of subprograms in p, and $(x, y) \in \rho$ iff subprogram x calls subprogram y. Suppose that $P = \{a, b, c, d\}$ and $\rho = \{(a, b), (a, c), (b, d), (c, c), (c, d), (d, a)\}$, which says that a calls b and c, b calls d, c calls itself and d, and d calls a (see Figure 3.1).

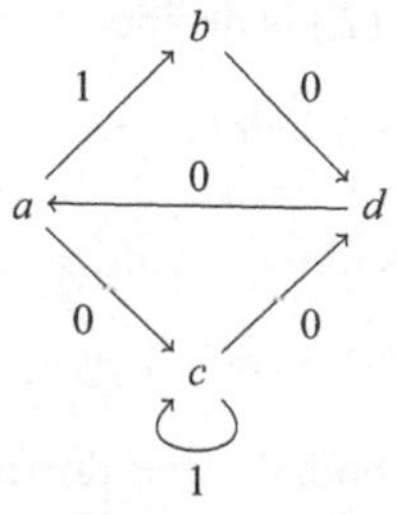

Figure 3.1 Graph

The in-degree of a is 1, and its out-degree is 2. Notice that (a, b, d) is a path of length 2 in G. G contains no cycle because none of its paths starts and ends in the same node. Suppose we want to express that the value of a global variable is zero when calls (a, b) and (c, c) occur; otherwise, it is one. To express this, we label the edges of G in the way given in the figure.

3.2 Trees

Let $G = (A, \rho)$ be a graph. The graph G is an *acyclic graph* if it contains no cycle. If $(a_0, a_1, \ldots, a_n)$ is a path in G, a_0 is an *ancestor of* a_n and a_n is a *descendant of* a_0; if in addition, $n = 1$, a_0 is a *direct ancestor of* a_n and a_n a *direct descendant of* a_0. A tree is an acyclic graph $T = (A, \rho)$ such that A contains a specified node, called the *root of* T and denoted by root (T), and every $a \in A - \{\text{root}(T)\}$ is a descendant of root (T) and its in-degree is one. If $a \in A$ is a node whose out-degree is 0, a is a *leaf*; otherwise, it is an *interior node*. In this book, a tree T is always considered as an *ordered tree* in which each interior node $a \in A$ has all its direct descendants, b_1 through b_n, where $n \geq 1$, ordered from the left to the right so that b_1 is the leftmost direct descendant of a and b_n is the rightmost direct descendant of a. At this point, a is the *parent* of its *children* b_1 through b_n, and all these nodes together with the edges connecting them, (a, b_1) through (a, b_n), are called a *parent–children portion of* T. The *frontier of* T, denoted by frontier (T), is the sequence of T's leaves ordered from the left to the right. The *depth of* T, depth (T), is the length of the longest path in T. A tree $S = (B, \nu)$ is a *subtree of* T if $\emptyset \subset B \subseteq A$, $\nu \subseteq \rho \cap (B \times B)$, and in T, no node in $A - B$ is a descendant of a node in B; S is an *elementary subtree of* T if depth $(S) = 1$.

Like any graph, a tree T can be described as a two-dimensional structure. To simplify this description, however, we draw a tree T with its root on the top and with all edges directed down. Each parent has its children drawn from the left to the right according to its ordering. Drawing T in this way, we always omit all arrowheads.

Apart from this two-dimensional representation, however, it is frequently convenient to specify T by a one-dimensional representation, denoted by odr (T), in which each subtree of T is represented by the expression appearing inside a balanced pair of $\langle$ and $\rangle$ with the node which is the root of that subtree appearing immediately to the left of $\langle$. More precisely, odr (T) is defined by the following recursive rules:

1. If T consists of a single node a, odr $(T) = a$.
2. Let (a, b_1) through (a, b_n), where $n \geq 1$, be the parent–children portion of T, root $(T) = a$, and T_k be the subtree rooted at b_k, $1 \leq k \leq n$, then

$$\text{odr}(T) = a\langle \text{odr}(T_1)\, \text{odr}(T_2) \cdots \text{odr}(T_n)\rangle.$$

The next example illustrates both the one-dimensional odr representation and the two-dimensional pictorial representation of a tree. For brevity, we prefer the former throughout the rest of this book.

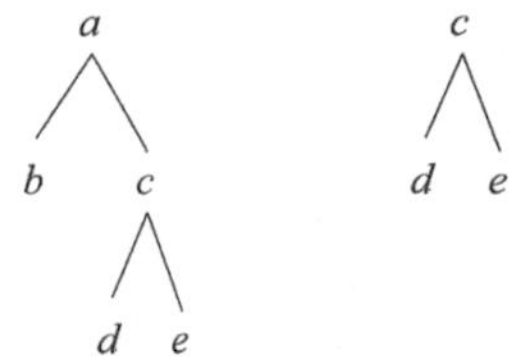

Figure 3.2 Tree and subtree

Example 3.2. Consider the tree $T = (P, \rho)$, where $P = \{a, b, c, d, e\}$ and ρ is defined as follows:

$$\rho = \{(a, b), (a, c), (c, d), (c, e)\}.$$

Nodes a and c are interior nodes while b, d, and e are leaves. The root of T is a. We define b and c as the first child of a and the second child of a, respectively. A parent–children portion of T is, for instance, (a, b) and (a, c). Notice that frontier $(T) = bd$, and depth $(T) = 2$. Following (1) and (2) above, we obtain the one-dimensional representation of T as

$$\text{odr}\,(T) = a\langle bc\langle de\rangle\rangle.$$

Its subtrees are $a\langle bc\langle de\rangle\rangle$, $c\langle de\rangle$, b, d, and e. In Figure 3.2, we pictorially describe $a\langle bc\langle de\rangle\rangle$ and $c\langle de\rangle$.

Implementation 3.1. A *binary tree* is a tree in which every interior node has exactly two children; for instance, T from Example 3.2 represents a binary tree. Next, we describe the implementation of a binary tree, in which every node is represented by a three-part structure. One part contains its data—for instance, the symbol which denotes the node. The others are blank if the node is a leaf; otherwise, they refer the two children of the node. As a whole, the tree implementation starts by a reference to its root node. Figure 3.3 illustrates this principle.

A C# implementation follows next. First, we create a generic class that represents a binary tree node. Each node can contain an object of type `T` as data.

```
public class BinaryTreeNode<T>
{
    public T Data { get; set; }
    public BinaryTreeNode<T> LeftChild { get; private set; }
    public BinaryTreeNode<T> RightChild { get; private set; }

    // constructor
    public BinaryTreeNode(T data)
    {
        this.Data = data;
        this.LeftChild = null;
        this.RightChild = null;
    }
}
```

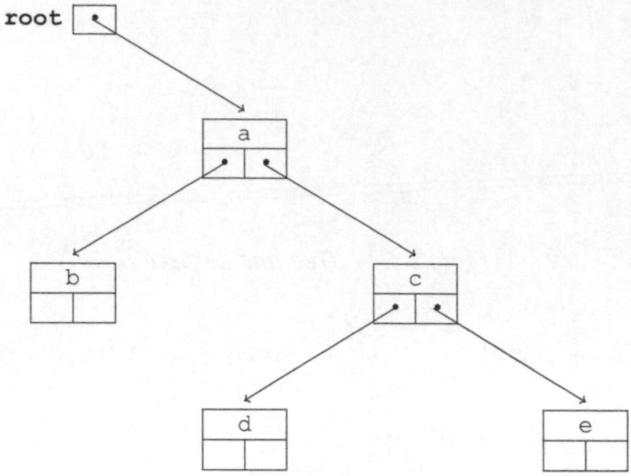

Figure 3.3 Diagram of binary tree implementation

We add a property which states whether a node is a leaf or an interior node.

```
public bool IsLeaf { get { return this.LeftChild == null; } }
```

To see why checking the existence of only one of the two potential child nodes is sufficient, recall the definition of binary tree above.

So far, we can only construct single, isolated nodes. The following method enables us to append new nodes to an existing node as its children. In order to maintain the invariants of binary tree, we add child nodes to leaf nodes only, and we always add both left and right child.

```
public void AddChildren(T leftChildData, T rightChildData)
{
    if (!this.IsLeaf) throw new InvalidOperationException(
        "Child nodes can only be added to leaf nodes.");

    this.LeftChild = new BinaryTreeNode<T>(leftChildData);
    this.RightChild = new BinaryTreeNode<T>(rightChildData);
}
```

The implementation of a binary tree as a whole is now straightforward.

```
public class BinaryTree<T>
{
   public BinaryTreeNode<T> Root { get; private set; }

    // constructor
    public BinaryTree(T rootData)
    {
        this.Root = new BinaryTreeNode<T>(rootData);
    }
}
```

Finally, we implement odr(T) directly following its recursive definition. We override ToString method in BinaryTreeNode<T> class.

```
public override string ToString()
{
    if (this.IsLeaf) return this.Data.ToString();
    else return this.Data.ToString() +
                "<" +
                this.LeftChild.ToString() +
                this.RightChild.ToString() +
                ">";
}
```

In BinaryTree<T> class, we only need to call ToString method of the root node.

```
public override string ToString()
{
    return this.Root.ToString();
}
```

In this implementation, binary tree T from Example 3.2 can be constructed as follows:

```
var T = new BinaryTree<Symbol>("a");
var a = T.Root;
a.AddChildren("b", "c");
var c = a.RightChild;
c.AddChildren("d", "e");
```

Calling Console.WriteLine(T) results in printing out a<bc<de>>.

Part II
Classical models for languages and computation

This book defines languages mathematically as sets of sequences consisting of symbols (see Section 1.3). This definition encompasses almost all languages as they are commonly understood. Indeed, natural languages, such as English, are included in this definition. All artificial languages introduced by various scientific disciplines can be viewed as formal languages. Most importantly, all computational processes are prescribed by programing languages, which obviously represent formal languages, too. It thus comes as no surprise that over its history, computer science has developed a mathematically systematized body of knowledge concerning formal languages, referred to as formal language theory, which is central to this book.

The strictly mathematical approach to languages also necessitates introducing mathematical models for them. Most models of this kind are underlain by *rewriting systems*, which are based upon binary relations whose members are called rules. By their rules, these systems repeatedly change sequences of symbols, called strings. Despite their broad variety, most of them can be classified into two categories—generative and accepting language models. Generative models or, more briefly, *grammars* define strings of their languages by generating them from special start symbols. On the other hand, accepting models or *automata* define strings of their languages by a rewriting process that starts from these strings and ends in a prescribed set of final strings.

Part II consists of Chapters 4–10. Chapter 4 introduces the basic versions of rewriting systems while paying special attention to using them as language-defining devices. Chapter 5 presents finite automata as the simplest versions of automata covered in this book. Chapter 6 discusses generative models called context-free grammars while Chapter 7 discusses their accepting counterparts—pushdown automata; indeed, both are equally powerful.

Chapters 8–10 form an inseparable unit, which is crucially important to Part II and, in fact, the book in its entirety. These chapters deal with Turing machines as basic language-defining models for computation. Indeed, based on them, Part II explores the very heart of the foundations of computation. More precisely, Chapter 8 introduces the mathematical notion of a Turing machine, which has become a universally accepted formalization of the intuitive notion of a procedure. Based upon this strictly mathematical notion, Chapters 9 and 10 study the general limits of computation in terms of computability and decidability. Regarding computability, Chapter 9 considers Turing machines as computers of functions over nonnegative integers and demonstrates the existence of functions whose computation cannot be specified by any procedure. As far as decidability is concerned, Chapter 10 formalizes problem-deciding algorithms by Turing machines that halt on every input. It formulates several important problems concerning the language models discussed in this book and constructs algorithms that decide them. On the other hand, Chapter 10 describes several problems that are not decidable by any algorithm. Apart from giving several specific undecidable problems, this book builds up a general theory of undecidability. Finally, the text approaches decidability in a much finer and realistic way. Indeed, it reconsiders problem-deciding algorithms in terms of their computational complexity measured according to time and space requirements. Perhaps most importantly, it shows that although some problems are decidable in principle, they are intractable for absurdly high computational requirements of the algorithms that decide them.

Chapter 4
Relations and language models

We all use a variety of languages, ranging from high-level programming languages up to machine codes, to express our ideas representing procedures, which prescribe computers how to execute computational processes we have in mind. Just like finite sets, finite languages might be specified by listing all the strings. Apart from listing some trivial few-word languages, however, most specifications of this kind would be unbearably extensive and clumsy. More importantly, infinite languages, including almost all programing and natural languages, obviously cannot be specified by an exhaustive enumeration of their strings at all. Consequently, mathematical finite-size models for languages are central to this book as a whole. We base these models, customarily referred to as rewriting systems, upon relations (see Section 2.1). As a matter of fact, these systems underlie almost all language models covered in this book.

Section 4.1 defines rewriting systems in general. Section 4.2 concentrates its attention on using these systems as language-defining devices.

4.1 Rewriting systems

Without further ado, we define rewriting systems in general.

Definition 4.1. *A* rewriting system *is a pair,* $M = (\Sigma, R)$*, where* Σ *is an alphabet, and* R *is a finite relation on* Σ^**.* Σ *is called the* total alphabet of M *or, simply, the* alphabet of M. *A member of* R *is called a* rule of M, *and accordingly,* R *is referred to as the* set of rules *in* M.

The rewriting relation *over* Σ^* *is denoted by* ${}_M\Rightarrow$ *and defined so that for every* $u, v \in \Sigma^*$, $u\ {}_M\Rightarrow v$ *in* M *iff there exist* $(x, y) \in R$ *and* $w, z \in \Sigma^*$ *such that* $u = wxz$ *and* $v = wyz$. *As usual,* ${}_M\Rightarrow^k$, ${}_M\Rightarrow^+$, *and* ${}_M\Rightarrow^*$ *denote the* k*-fold product, the transitive closure, and the transitive and reflexive closure of* ${}_M\Rightarrow$*, respectively.*

Let $M = (\Sigma, R)$ be a rewriting system. Each rule $(x, y) \in R$ is written as $x \to y$ throughout this book. For $x \to y \in R$, x and y represent the *left-hand side of* $x \to y$ and the *right-hand side of* $x \to y$, respectively. We drop M in ${}_M\Rightarrow$ and, thereby, simplify ${}_M\Rightarrow$ to $\Rightarrow$ whenever M is automatically understood. By $u \Rightarrow v\ [x \to y]$, where $u, v \in \Sigma^*$ and $x \to y \in R$, we express that M directly rewrites u as v according to $x \to y$. Of course, whenever the information regarding the applied rule is immaterial, we omit its specification; in other words, we simplify $u \Rightarrow v\ [x \to y]$ to $u \Rightarrow v$. By underlining, we specify the substring rewritten during a rewriting step if necessary. More formally, if $u = wxz$, $v = wyz$, $x \to y \in R$, where $u, v, x, y \in \Sigma^*$, then $w\underline{x}z \Rightarrow wyz\ [x \to y]$ means that the x occurring behind w is rewritten during this step by using $x \to y$ (we usually specify the rewritten occurrence of x in this way when other occurrences of x appear in w and z).

To give a straightforward insight into our approach, we now give a simple example that illustrates how we connect the mathematically oriented discussion of scattered context grammars in the previous chapters with the application-oriented discussion of the present chapter. As the principle subject of this section, we discuss languages and their representations. It is thus only natural to illustrate our discussion by linguistically oriented examples.

Example 4.1. *Let Δ denote the alphabet of English small letters (this alphabet is used in all examples of this section). In the present example, we introduce a rewriting system M that translates every digital string to the string in which every digit is converted to its corresponding English name followed by #; for instance,* 010 *is translated to zero#one#zero#.*

First, we define the finite function h from $\{0, 1, \ldots, 9\}$ to Δ^* as

$$
\begin{aligned}
h(0) &= zero,\\
h(1) &= one,\\
h(2) &= two,\\
h(3) &= three,\\
h(4) &= four,\\
h(5) &= five,\\
h(6) &= six,\\
h(7) &= seven,\\
h(8) &= eight,\\
h(9) &= nine.
\end{aligned}
$$

In words, h translates every member of $\{0, 1, \ldots, 9\}$ to its corresponding English name; for instance, $h(9) = nine$. Based upon h, we define $M = (\Sigma, R)$ with $\Sigma = \{0, 1, \ldots, 9\} \cup \Delta \cup \{\#\}$ and $R = \{i \to h(i)\# \mid i \in \{0, 1, \ldots, 9\}\}$. Finally, we define the function $T(M)$ from $\{0, 1, \ldots, 9\}^*$ to $(\Delta \cup \{\#\})^*$ as

$$T(M) = \{(s, t) \mid s \Rightarrow^* t,\ s \in \{0, 1, \ldots, 9\}^*,\ t \in (\Delta \cup \{\#\})^*\}.$$

For instance, $T(M)$ contains (911, nine#one#one#). Indeed, M translates 911 *to nine#one#one# as follows*

$$
\begin{array}{lll}
9\underline{1}1 & \Rightarrow\ 9one\#1 & [1 \to one\#],\\
9one\#\underline{1} & \Rightarrow\ 9one\#one\# & [1 \to one\#],\\
\underline{9}one\#one\# & \Rightarrow\ nine\#one\#one\# & [9 \to nine\#].
\end{array}
$$

Thus,

$$911 \Rightarrow^* nine\#one\#one\#\ [1 \to one\#, 1 \to one\#, 9 \to nine\#].$$

Therefore, $(911, nine\#one\#one\#) \in T(M)$. *Thus,* M *performs the desired translation.*

Example 4.2. *This example strongly resembles a simple morphological study—in linguistics,* morphology *studies the structure of words. Indeed, it discusses restructuring strings consisting of English letters, including strings that does not represent any English words, such as xxuy. More precisely, we introduce a rewriting system M that*

(i) *starts from non-empty strings consisting of small English letters delimited by angle brackets,*
(ii) *orders the letters lexicographically, and*
(iii) *eliminates the angle brackets.*

For instance, M changes $\langle xxuy \rangle$ *to* $uxxy$.

Let Δ *have the same meaning as in Example 4.1—that is,* Δ *denotes the alphabet of English lowercases. Let* $\angle$ *denote the standardly defined lexical order over* Δ*—that is,*

$$a \angle b \angle c \cdots \angle y \angle z.$$

We define $M = (\Sigma, R)$ *with* $\Sigma = \Delta \cup \{\langle, \rangle, 1, 2, 3\}$ *and R containing the following rules:*

(i) $\langle \to 12,\ 12 \to 3;$
(ii) $2\alpha \to \alpha 2$ *and* $\alpha 2 \to 2\alpha$ *for all* $\alpha \in \Delta;$
(iii) $\beta 2\alpha \to \alpha 2\beta$ *for all* $\alpha, \beta \in \Delta$ *such that* $\alpha \angle \beta;$
(iv) $3\alpha\beta \to \alpha 3\beta$ *for all* $\alpha, \beta \in \Delta$ *such that* $\alpha \angle \beta$ *or* $\alpha = \beta;$
(v) $3\alpha\rangle \to \alpha$ *for all* $\alpha \in \Delta.$

Define the function $T(M)$ *from* $(\{\langle, \rangle\} \cup \Delta)^+$ *to* Δ^+ *as*

$$T(M) = \{(\langle s \rangle, t) \mid \langle s \rangle \Rightarrow^* t, \text{ where } s, t \in \Delta^+\}.$$

Observe that $(\langle s \rangle, t) \in T(M)$ *if and only if t is a permutation of s such that t has its letters lexicographically ordered according to* $\angle$*. For instance,* $T(M)$ *contains* $(\langle order \rangle, deorr)$*. Indeed, M translates* $\langle order \rangle$ *to deorr as follows:*

$$\begin{array}{lcll}
\underline{\langle} order\rangle & \Rightarrow & 12order\rangle & [\langle \to 12], \\
1\underline{2o}rder\rangle & \Rightarrow & 1o2rder\rangle & [2o \to o2], \\
1o\underline{2r}der\rangle & \Rightarrow & 1or2der\rangle & [2r \to r2], \\
1o\underline{r2d}er\rangle & \Rightarrow & 1od2rer\rangle & [r2d \to d2r], \\
1od\underline{2r}er\rangle & \Rightarrow & 1odr2er\rangle & [2r \to r2], \\
1od\underline{r2e}r\rangle & \Rightarrow & 1ode2rr\rangle & [r2e \to e2r], \\
1od\underline{e2}rr\rangle & \Rightarrow & 1od2err\rangle & [e2 \to 2e], \\
1o\underline{d2}err\rangle & \Rightarrow & 1o2derr\rangle & [d2 \to 2d], \\
1\underline{o2d}err\rangle & \Rightarrow & 1d2oerr\rangle & [o2d \to d2o], \\
1d\underline{2o}err\rangle & \Rightarrow & 1do2err\rangle & [2o \to o2], \\
1d\underline{o2e}rr\rangle & \Rightarrow & 1de2orr\rangle & [o2e \to e2o],
\end{array}$$

$$
\begin{array}{llll}
1d\underline{e2}orr\rangle & \Rightarrow & 1d2eorr\rangle & [e2 \rightarrow 2e], \\
1\underline{d2}eorr\rangle & \Rightarrow & 12deorr\rangle & [d2 \rightarrow 2d], \\
\underline{12}deorr\rangle & \Rightarrow & 3deorr\rangle & [12 \rightarrow 3], \\
\underline{3de}orr\rangle & \Rightarrow & d3eorr\rangle & [3de \rightarrow d3e], \\
d\underline{3eo}rr\rangle & \Rightarrow & de3orr\rangle & [3eo \rightarrow e3o], \\
de\underline{3or}r\rangle & \Rightarrow & deo3rr\rangle & [3or \rightarrow o3r], \\
deo\underline{3rr}\rangle & \Rightarrow & deor3r\rangle & [3rr \rightarrow r3r], \\
deor\underline{3r\rangle} & \Rightarrow & deorr & [3r\rangle \rightarrow r].
\end{array}
$$

Observe that M can translate ⟨order⟩ to deorr by a number of different sequences of rewriting steps. In fact, it can translate infinitely many members of $T(M)$ in various ways. In general, this phenomenon is referred to as non-determinism; accordingly, rewriting systems working in this way are said to be non-deterministic. In mathematics, we usually design the basic versions of rewriting systems so they work non-deterministically. In terms of their implementation, however, we obviously prefer using their deterministic versions. Therefore, we usually place a restriction on the way the rules are applied so the rewriting systems restricted in this way necessarily work deterministically; simultaneously, we obviously want that the deterministic restricted versions perform the same job as their original unrestricted counterparts.

Implementation 4.1. *Returning to M discussed in Example 4.2, we next give its implementation based, in essence, upon applying the rules in a way that resembles the famous bubble sort. Indeed, the program works by repeatedly stepping through the string, comparing each pair of adjacent symbols and swapping them if they are in the wrong order; clearly, this swapping idea underlies (iii)—the key part of the construction above. The pass through the list is repeated until no swaps are needed, which indicates that the string is ordered.*

First, however, we need to add one more method to `HmmlcString` *class. This method will allow us to rewrite symbols in a given string. More precisely, it returns a new string that is identical to the original one with the exception of a single symbol at a given position (0-indexed) being replaced by a new symbol.*

```
public HmmlcString Rewrite(int i, Symbol a)
{
    var result = new HmmlcString(this.symbols);
    result.symbols[i] = a;
    return result;
}
```

We are now present a module that simulates the functionality of M. First, we implement a method that compares the lexical order of two given symbols, a and b. It returns 1 *if a is greater,* −1 *if b is greater, and* 0 *if a and b are equal.*

```
public static class RewritingSystemM
{
    private static int LexicalCompare(Symbol a, Symbol b)
    {
        if (object.ReferenceEquals(a, b)) return 0;
```

```
        else if (object.ReferenceEquals(a, null)) return -1;
        else if (object.ReferenceEquals(b, null)) return 1;
        else return string.Compare(a.ToString(), b.ToString());
    }
}
```

The next method added to class `RewritingSystemM` *compares two symbols at given positions in a given string and swaps them if the first symbol is greater than the second.*

```
private static HmmlcString CompareAndExchange(HmmlcString x,
                                              int i1, int i2)
{
    if (LexicalCompare(x[i1], x[i2]) <= 0) return x;
    else // wrong order
    {
        // swap the two symbols
        Symbol a1 = x[i1];
        Symbol a2 = x[i2];
        return x.Rewrite(i1, a2).Rewrite(i2, a1);
    }
}
```

The final helper method checks whether a given string is lexically sorted.

```
private static bool IsStringSorted(HmmlcString x)
{
    for (int i = 0; i < x.Length - 1; i++)
    {
        if (LexicalCompare(x[i], x[i + 1]) > 0) return false;
    }
    return true;
}
```

Using the above methods, we can sort a given string as follows.

```
public static HmmlcString SortString(HmmlcString x)
{
    HmmlcString y = x;
    while (!IsStringSorted(y))
    {
        for (int i = 0; i < y.Length - 1; i++)
        {
            y = CompareAndExchange(y, i, i + 1);
        }
    }
    return y;
}
```

Next, we explain how this implementation loosely reflects the application of some rules in M.

Concerning the rules introduced in (ii), the program simulates their application by circulating a right-direction traversal across the string. Concerning the rules constructed in (iii), function `CompareAndExchange()` *simulates their application in the swapping way sketched above. Finally, concerning the rules made in (iv), function* `IsStringSorted()` *implements their application by performing a left-to-right traversal across the string. It stops and returns* **`false`** *if it finds two adjacent letters improperly ordered; otherwise, it returns* **`true`**.

To illustrate the usage of this implementation, consider the following code, which prints `order =>* deorr` *to standard output.*

```
var x = new HmmlcString("o", "r", "d", "e", "r");
var y = RewritingSystemM.SortString(x);
Console.WriteLine("0 =>* 1", x, y);
```

It is noteworthy that during every iteration of the outer cycle (the **`while`** *loop), the program actually traverses the string twice. Indeed, during the first traversal, it checks whether or not the entire string is already ordered. If so, it stops. If not, it performs the second traversal, in which it orders adjacent letters, and repeats the loop.*

As obvious, the above-described C# implementation works strictly deterministically. As an exercise, show that it produces precisely $T(M)$, defined earlier in Example 4.2.

4.2 Language-defining models

In this section, we return to the key subject of this chapter, which consists in using rewriting systems as language-defining models.

Whenever we use a rewriting system, $M = (\Sigma, R)$, as a language-defining model, then for brevity, we denote the language that M defines by $L(M)$. In principal, M defines $L(M)$ so it either *generates* $L(M)$ or *accepts* $L(M)$. Next, we explain these two fundamental language-defining methods in a greater detail. Let $S \in \Sigma^*$ and $F \in \Sigma^*$ be a *start language* and a *final language*, respectively.

(i) The *language generated by M* is defined as the set of all strings $y \in F$ such that $x \Rightarrow^* y$ in M for some $x \in S$. M used in this way is generally referred to as a *language-generating model* or, more briefly, a *grammar*.
(ii) The *language accepted by M* is defined as the set of all strings $x \in S$ such that $x \Rightarrow^* y$ in M for some $y \in F$. M used in this way is referred to as a *language-accepting model* or, more briefly, an *automaton*.

Example 4.3. *Let Δ have the same meaning as in Examples 4.1 and 4.2—that is, Δ denotes the alphabet of English lowercases. Let L be the language consisting of all even-length palindromes over Δ—a* palindrome *is a string that is the same whether written forwards or backward. For instance, aa and noon belong to L, but b and oops do not. The present example introduces a grammar and an automaton that define L.*

Let $G = (\Sigma, P)$ be the rewriting system with $\Sigma = \Delta \cup \{\#\}$ and

$$P = \{\# \rightarrow a\#a \mid a \in \Delta\} \cup \{\# \rightarrow \varepsilon\}.$$

Set $S = \{\#\}$ *and* $F = \Delta^*$. *Define the language generated by G as*

$$L(G) = \{t \mid s \Rightarrow^* t,\ s \in S,\ t \in F\}.$$

In other words,

$$L(G) = \{t \mid \# \Rightarrow^* t \text{ with } t \in \Delta^*\}.$$

Observe that G acts as a grammar that generates L. For instance,

$$\# \Rightarrow n\#n \Rightarrow no\#on \Rightarrow noon$$

in G, so noon $\in L(G)$.

To give an automaton that accepts L, introduce the rewriting system $A = (\Sigma, R)$ *with* $\Sigma = \Delta \cup \{\#\}$ *and*

$$R = \{a\#a \rightarrow \# \mid a \in \Delta\}.$$

Set $S = \Delta^*\{\#\}\Delta^*$ *and* $F = \{\#\}$. *Define the language accepted by A as*

$$L(A) = \{st \mid s\#t \Rightarrow^* u, \text{ where } s, t \in \Delta^*,\ u \in F\}.$$

That is,

$$L(A) = \{st \mid s\#t \Rightarrow^* \#, \text{ where } s, t \in \Delta^*\}.$$

For instance, A accepts noon

$$n\underline{o\#o}n \Rightarrow \underline{n\#n} \Rightarrow \#$$

(as stated in the comments following Definition 4.1, the underlined substrings denote the substrings that are rewritten). On the other hand, consider this sequence of rewriting steps

$$n\underline{o\#o}nn \Rightarrow \underline{n\#n}n \Rightarrow \#n.$$

It starts from no#onn, and after performing two steps, it ends up with #n, which cannot be further rewritten. Since $\#n \notin F$, *which equals* $\{\#\}$, *M does not accept no#onn. As an exercise, based upon these observations, demonstrate that* $L = L(A)$, *so A acts as an automaton that accepts L.*

Before closing this section, we make use of Example 4.3 to explain and illustrate the concept of equivalence and that of determinism in terms of rewriting systems that define languages.

Equivalence

If some rewriting systems define the same language, they are said to be *equivalent*. For instance, take *G* and *A* in Example 4.3. Both define the same language, so they are equivalent.

Determinism

Recall that Example 4.2 has already touched the topic of determinism in terms of rewriting systems. Notice that the language-defining rewriting system *A* from Example 4.3 works deterministically in the sense that *A* rewrites any string from *K* by no more than one rule, where $K = S$, so $K = \Delta^*\{\#\}\Delta^*$. To express this concept of determinism more generally, let $M = (\Sigma, R)$ be a rewriting system and $K \subseteq \Sigma^*$. M is *deterministic over* K if for every $w \in K$, there is no more than one $r \in R$ such that $w \Rightarrow v$ $[r]$ with $v \in K$. Mathematically, if M is deterministic over K, then its rewriting relation $\Rightarrow$ represents a function over K—that is, for all $u, v, w \in K$, if $u \Rightarrow v$ and $u \Rightarrow w$, then $v = w$. When K is understood, we usually just say that M is *deterministic*; frequently, we take $K = \Sigma^*$.

As already noted in Example 4.2, the basic versions of language-defining rewriting systems are always introduced quite generally and, therefore, non-deterministically. That is also why we first define the basic versions of these models in a non-deterministic way throughout this book. In practice, however, we obviously prefer their deterministic versions because they are easy to implement. Therefore, we always study whether any non-deterministic version can be converted to an equivalent deterministic version, and if so, we want to perform this conversion algorithmically. More specifically, we reconsider this crucially important topic of determinism in terms of finite automata in Section 5.3.

Alternative notation. Language-defining rewriting systems represent pairs. Sometimes, however, we specify them as n-tuples, for some $n \geq 2$ because an alternative notation like this makes them easier to discuss. To illustrate, we next define queue grammars and their variants, which are frequently used in proofs of theorems in Part III.

Queue grammars

Queue grammars (see [1]) always rewrite the first and the last symbol in the strings in parallel; all the other symbols in between them remain unchanged. That is, as their name indicates, queue grammars rewrite strings in a way that resemble the standard way of working with an abstract data type referred to as a queue. Indeed, these grammars work on strings based upon the well-known first-in-first-out principle—that is, the first symbol added to the string will be the first one to be removed. More specifically, during every derivation step, these grammars attach a string as a suffix to the current sentential form while eliminating the leftmost symbol of this form; as a result, all symbols that were attached prior to this step have to be removed before the newly attached suffix is removed. Next, we define these grammars rigorously.

Definition 4.2. *A* queue grammar *is a sixtuple*

$$Q = (\Sigma, \Delta, W, F, R, g)$$

where Σ *and* W *are two alphabets satisfying* $\Sigma \cap W = \emptyset$, $\Delta \subset \Sigma$, $F \subset W$, $g \in (\Sigma - \Delta)(W - F)$, *and*

$$R \subseteq \Sigma \times (W - F) \times \Sigma^* \times W$$

is a finite relation such that for each $a \in \Sigma - \Delta$, *there exists an element* $(a, b, x, c) \in R$. *If* $u = arb$, $v = rxc$, *and* $(a, b, x, c) \in R$, $r, x \in \Sigma^*$, *where* $a \in \Sigma$ *and* $b, c \in W$, *then* Q *makes a* derivation step *from* u *to* v *according to* (a, b, x, c), *symbolically written as*

$$u \Rightarrow_Q v \; [(a, b, x, c)]$$

or, simply, $u \Rightarrow_Q v$. *We define* $\Rightarrow_Q^n$ $(n \geq 0)$, $\Rightarrow_Q^+$, *and* $\Rightarrow_Q^*$ *in the standard way. The* language *of Q, denoted by L(Q), is defined as*

$$L(Q) = \{x \in \Delta^* \mid g \Rightarrow_Q^* xf, f \in F\}.$$

As an example, consider a queue grammar $G = (\Sigma, \Delta, W, F, s, P)$, where $\Sigma = \{S, A, a, b\}$, $\Delta = \{a, b\}$, $W = \{Q, f\}$, $F = \{f\}$, $s = SQ$ and $P = \{p_1, p_2\}$, $p_1 = (S, Q, Aaa, Q)$ and $p_2 = (A, Q, bb, f)$. Then, there exists a derivation

$$s = SQ \Rightarrow AaaQ[p_1] \Rightarrow aabbf[p_2]$$

in this queue grammar, which generates *aabb*.

Theorem 4.1 (see [1]). *For every recursively enumerable language K, there is a queue grammar Q such that L(Q) = K.*

Next, we slightly modify the definition of a queue grammar.

Definition 4.3 (see [2,3,4]). *A* left-extended queue grammar *is a sixtuple*

$$Q = (\Sigma, \Delta, W, F, R, g),$$

where Σ, Δ, W, F, R, g *have the same meaning as in a queue grammar; in addition, assume that* $\# \notin \Sigma \cup W$. *If* $u, v \in \Sigma^*\{\#\}\Sigma^* W$ *so* $u = w\#arb$, $v = wa\#rzc$, $a \in \Sigma$, $r, z, w \in \Sigma^*$, $b, c \in W$, *and* $(u, b, z, c) \in R$, *then*

$$u \Rightarrow_Q v \; [(a, b, z, c)]$$

or, simply, $u \Rightarrow_Q v$. *In the standard manner, extend* $\Rightarrow_Q$ *to* $\Rightarrow_Q^n$, *where* $n \geq 0$. *Based on* $\Rightarrow_Q^n$, *define* $\Rightarrow_Q^+$ *and* $\Rightarrow_Q^*$. *The* language *of Q, denoted by L(Q), is defined as*

$$L(Q) = \{v \in \Delta^* \mid \#g \Rightarrow_Q^* w\#vf \text{ for some } w \in \Sigma^* \text{ and } f \in F\}.$$

Less formally, during every step of a derivation, a left-extended queue grammar shifts the rewritten symbol over #; in this way, it records the derivation history, which represents a property fulfilling a crucial role in several proofs later in this book.

For example, consider a left-extended queue grammar, which has the same components as the previously mentioned queue grammar *G*. Then, there exists a derivation

$$\#s = \#SQ \Rightarrow S\#AaaQ[p_1] \Rightarrow SA\#aabbf[p_2]$$

in this left-extended queue grammar, which generates *aabb*. Moreover, this type of queue grammar saves symbols from the first components of rules that were used in the derivation.

Theorem 4.2. *For every queue grammar Q, there is an equivalent left-extended queue grammar Q′ such that L(Q′) = L(Q).*

The proof is trivial and left to the reader.

Theorem 4.3. *For every recursively enumerable language K, there is a left-extended queue grammar Q such that L(Q) = K.*

Proof. Follows from Theorems 4.1 and 4.2. ■

Throughout Part II, we always define rewriting systems as pairs. In Parts III and IV, we use alternative notation with a single exception of Chapter 17, which uses pairs like in Part II.

Alternative rewriting. Notice that the queue grammars simultaneously rewrite the beginning and the end of strings. Consequently, they work in a semi-parallel way as opposed to the sequential way the standard language models work (see the beginning of this section). In fact, some language models, such as ET0L grammars defined next, work in a totally parallel way.

Definition 4.4. *An* ET0L grammar *is a $(t+3)$-tuple*

$$G = (\Sigma, \Delta, R_1, \dots, R_t, w),$$

where $t \geq 1$, and Σ, Δ, and w are the total alphabet, *the* terminal alphabet *($\Delta \subseteq \Sigma$), and the* start string *($w \in \Sigma^+$), respectively. Each R_i is a finite set of* rules *of the form*

$$a \rightarrow x,$$

where $a \in \Sigma$ and $x \in \Sigma^*$. If $a \rightarrow x \in R_i$ implies that $x \neq \varepsilon$ for all $i = 1, \dots, t$, then G is said to be propagating *(an EPT0L grammar for short).*

Let $u, v \in \Sigma^*$, $u = a_1a_2 \cdots a_q$, $v = v_1v_2 \cdots v_q$, $q = |u|$, $a_j \in \Sigma$, $v_j \in \Sigma^*$, and $p_1, p_2, \dots, p_q$ is a sequence of rules of the form $p_j = a_j \rightarrow v_j \in R_i$ for all $j = 1, \dots, q$, for some $i \in \{1, \dots, t\}$. Then, u directly derives *v according to the rules p_1 through p_q, denoted by*

$$u \Rightarrow_G v\ [p_1, p_2, \dots, p_q].$$

If p_1 through p_q are immaterial, we write just $u \Rightarrow_G v$. In the standard manner, we define the relations $\Rightarrow_G^n$ ($n \geq 0$), $\Rightarrow_G^*$, and $\Rightarrow_G^+$.

The language *of G, denoted by $L(G)$, is defined as*

$$L(G) = \{y \in \Delta^* \mid w \Rightarrow_G^* y\}.$$

The families of languages generated by ET0L and EPT0L grammars are denoted by **ET0L** and **EPT0L**, respectively.

Definition 4.5. *Let $G = (\Sigma, \Delta, R_1, \dots, R_t, w)$ be an ET0L grammar, for some $t \geq 1$. If $t = 1$, then G is called an* E0L grammar.

The families of languages generated by E0L and propagating E0L grammars (EP0L grammars for short) are denoted by **E0L** and **EP0L**, respectively.

As demonstrated in [5], the next theorem holds true.

Theorem 4.4. $\mathbf{E0L} = \mathbf{EP0L} \subset \mathbf{ET0L} = \mathbf{EPT0L} \subset \boldsymbol{CS}$.

Chapter 5
Finite automata

In this five-section chapter, we cover finite automata that represents perhaps the simplest language-accepting rewriting systems. In Section 5.1, we define their basic versions. Then, in Section 5.2, we introduce finite automata that read a symbol during every single computational step. In Section 5.3, we study deterministic finite automata. In Section 5.4, we cover several reduced and minimal versions of finite automata. Finally, in Section 5.5, we define regular expressions and demonstrate the equivalence between them and finite automata.

5.1 Mathematical elements of finite automata

In this section, we define finite automata as special cases of rewriting systems, introduced in Section 4.1. Therefore, we straightforwardly apply the mathematical terminology concerning rewriting systems to finite automata. Perhaps most significantly, we apply relations $\Rightarrow$, $\Rightarrow^n$, $\Rightarrow^+$, and $\Rightarrow^*$ to them.

Definition 5.1. *A* finite automaton *is a rewriting system* $M = (\Sigma, R)$, *where*

- Σ *contains subsets* Q, F, *and* Δ *such that* $\Sigma = Q \cup \Delta$, $F \subseteq Q$, *and* $Q \cap \Delta = \emptyset$ *and*
- R *is a finite* set of rules *of the form* $qa \rightarrow p$, *where* $q, p \in Q$ *and* $a \in \Delta \cup \{\varepsilon\}$.

Q, F, *and* Δ *are referred to as the* set of states, *the* set of final states, *and the* alphabet of input symbols, *respectively.* Q *contains a special state called the* start state, *usually denoted by* s. M accepts $w \in \Delta^*$ *if* $sw \Rightarrow^* f$ *in* M *with* $f \in F$. *The* language accepted by M *or, briefly, the* language of M *is denoted by* $L(M)$ *and defined as the set of all strings that* M *accepts; formally,*

$$L(M) = \{w \mid w \in \Delta^*,\ sw \Rightarrow^* f, f \in F\}.$$

Every string that M rewrites has the form qav, where $q \in Q$, $a \in \Delta \cup \{\varepsilon\}$, and $v \in \Delta^*$. By using a rule of the form $qa \rightarrow p$, where $q, p \in Q$ and $a \in \Delta \cup \{\varepsilon\}$, M reads a and changes q to p. By repeatedly performing rewriting steps like this, M reads the string of input symbols in a left-to-right way and, simultaneously, moves the current state closer toward its right end. M accepts $w \in \Delta^*$ if starting from sw, it reads all the input string and ends up in a final state.

As finite automata represent special cases of rewriting systems, all the notions concerning rewriting systems are applicable to finite automata as well (see Section 4.1). In addition, we next introduce some specific terminology concerning finite automata.

Let $M = (S, R)$ be a finite automaton. We automatically assume that S, D, Q, s, F, and R denote its total alphabet, the alphabet of input symbols, the set of states, the start state, the set of final states, and the set of rules of M, respectively. To explicitly express that S, D, Q, s, F, and R represent the components of M, we write ${}_MS$, ${}_MD$, ${}_MQ$, ${}_Ms$, ${}_MF$, and ${}_MR$ instead of plain S, D, Q, s, F, and R, respectively; we primarily make use of this M-related representation when several automata are discussed and, therefore, a confusion may arise. A *configuration of M* is a string of the form qv, where $v \in \Delta^*$ and $q \in Q$. ${}_M\Xi$ denotes the set of all configurations of M. If $b \Rightarrow c$ in M, where $b, c \in {}_M\Xi$, M makes a *move* or a *computational step* from b to c. M makes a *sequence of moves* or a *computation* from b to c if $b \Rightarrow^* c$ in M, where $b, c \in {}_M\Xi$. A computation of the form $sw \Rightarrow^* f$, where $w \in \Delta^*$ and $f \in F$, is called an *accepting computation*. Thus, $L(M)$ contains w if and only if M makes an accepting computation of the form $sw \Rightarrow^* f$.

5.1.1 How to specify finite automata

Let M be a finite automaton. Customarily, we represent M in one of the following four ways.

1. In an informal way, we describe M as a procedure while partially omitting some details concerning its components. Describing M in this way, we always make sure that the translation from this description to the corresponding formal description represents an utterly straightforward task.
2. In a tabular way, M is specified by its *state table* whose columns and rows are denoted with the members of $\Delta \cup \{\varepsilon\}$ and the states of Q, respectively. The start state denotes the first row. The final states are specified by underlining. For each $q \in Q$ and each $a \in \Delta \cup \{\varepsilon\}$, the entry in row q and column a contains $\{p \mid qa \rightarrow p \in R\}$. For brevity, we omit the braces in the sets of these entries; a blank entry means $\emptyset$.
3. In a graphical way, M is specified by its *state diagram* in a pictorial way. That is, this diagram is a labeled directed graph such that each node is labeled with a state $q \in Q$ and for two nodes $q, p \in Q$, there is an edge (q,p) labeled with $\{a \mid qa \rightarrow p \in R,\ a \in \Delta \cup \{\varepsilon\}\}$. For simplicity, we entirely omit every edge labeled with $\emptyset$ in the diagram. Furthermore, in the specification of edge-labeling non-empty sets, we omit the braces; for instance, instead of $\{a, b\}$ as an edge label, we just write a, b. To symbolically state that a state s is the start state, we point to it with a short arrow like in Figure 5.1. Final states are doubly circled.
4. In a formal way, we define M by spelling out all the states, symbols, and rules of M strictly according to Definition 5.1.

Table 5.1 State table

State	*a*	*b*	*ε*
1			2, 4
2	2, 3		
<u>3</u>		3	
4		4, 5	
<u>5</u>			

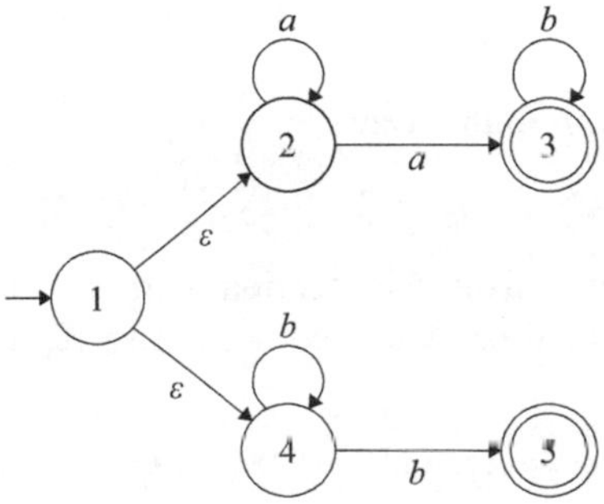

Figure 5.1 State diagram

Example 5.1. *In this example, we design a finite automaton M that accepts x iff x has either the form a^ib^j, where $i \geq 1$ and $j \geq 0$, or the form b^k, where $k \geq 1$. Briefly and mathematically,*

$$L(M) = \{a\}^+\{b\}^* \cup \{b\}^+.$$

We describe M in all four ways sketched above.

5.1.1.1 Informal description

M has five states—1 to 5, out of which 3 and 5 are final. From its start state 1, without reading any input symbol, *M* moves either to state 2 or 4. To accept a^ib^j, *M* loops in 2 while reading *a*s. Then, *M* makes a move from 2 to 3 with a single *a*. In 3, *M* reads any number of *b*s. As 3 is a final state, *M* completes the acceptance of a^ib^j in this way. To accept b^k, in 4, *M* reads any number of *b*s. Then, *M* makes a move from 4 to state 5 with *b*. Since 5 is a final state, *M* completes the acceptance of b^k.

5.1.1.2 State table

In Table 5.1, we describe *M* by its state table.

5.1.1.3 State diagram

In Figure 5.1, we describe *M* by its state diagram.

5.1.1.4 Formal description

Let $M = (\Sigma, R)$, where $\Sigma = Q \cup \Delta$ with $Q = \{1, 2, 3, 4, 5\}$, $\Delta = \{a, b\}$, $F = \{3, 5\}$, and 1 is the start state. Furthermore, R contains these seven rules

$$\begin{aligned} 1 &\to 2, \\ 1 &\to 4, \\ 2a &\to 2, \\ 2a &\to 3, \\ 3b &\to 3, \\ 4b &\to 4, \\ 4b &\to 5. \end{aligned}$$

For instance, M accepts aab in this way

$$1aab \Rightarrow 2aab \Rightarrow 2ab \Rightarrow 3b \Rightarrow 3.$$

Implementation 5.1. We close this section with an implementation of finite automaton using C# code. First, we need a class to represent a finite automaton state.

```
public class FiniteAutomatonState : IEquatable<FiniteAutomatonState>
{
    public Symbol Label { get; private set; }

    // constructor
    public FiniteAutomatonState(Symbol label)
    {
        this.Label = label;
    }

    // equality checking using pattern from Implementation 1.1
    public static bool Equals(FiniteAutomatonState q,
                              FiniteAutomatonState p)
    {
        if (ReferenceEquals(q, p)) return true;
        else if (ReferenceEquals(q, null) || ReferenceEquals(p, null))
        {
            return false;
        }
        else return q.Label == p.Label;
    }
    public bool Equals(FiniteAutomatonState other)
    {
        return FiniteAutomatonState.Equals(this, other);
    }
    public override bool Equals(object obj)
    {
        return FiniteAutomatonState.Equals(
            this, obj as FiniteAutomatonState);
    }
    public static bool operator ==(FiniteAutomatonState q,
                                   FiniteAutomatonState p)
```

```
    {
        return FiniteAutomatonState.Equals(q, p);
    }
    public static bool operator !=(FiniteAutomatonState q,
                                   FiniteAutomatonState p)
    {
        return !FiniteAutomatonState.Equals(q, p);
    }
    public override int GetHashCode()
    {
        return this.Label.GetHashCode();
    }

    // returns a System.String that represents this state
    public override string ToString()
    {
        return this.Label.ToString();
    }
}
```

We also add an implicit conversion so that we can use `System.String` literals to define states.

```
public static implicit operator FiniteAutomatonState(string s)
{
    return new FiniteAutomatonState(s);
}
```

The next class represents a finite automaton rule.

```
public class FiniteAutomatonRule : IEquatable<FiniteAutomatonRule>
{
    public FiniteAutomatonState CurrentState { get; private set; }
    public Symbol InputSymbol { get; private set; }
    public FiniteAutomatonState NextState { get; private set; }

    // constructor
    public FiniteAutomatonRule(FiniteAutomatonState currentState,
                               Symbol inputSymbol,
                               FiniteAutomatonState nextState)
    {
        this.CurrentState = currentState;
        this.InputSymbol = inputSymbol;
        this.NextState = nextState;
    }

    // equality checking using pattern from Implementation 1.1
    public static bool Equals(FiniteAutomatonRule r1,
                              FiniteAutomatonRule r2)
    {
        if (ReferenceEquals(r1, r2)) return true;
        else if (ReferenceEquals(r1, null) ||
                 ReferenceEquals(r2, null))
        {
            return false;
        }
        else
```

```
        {
            return r1.CurrentState == r2.CurrentState &&
                   r1.InputSymbol == r2.InputSymbol &&
                   r1.NextState == r2.NextState;
        }
    }
    public bool Equals(FiniteAutomatonRule other)
    {
        return FiniteAutomatonRule.Equals(this, other);
    }
    public override bool Equals(object obj)
    {
        return FiniteAutomatonRule.Equals(
            this, obj as FiniteAutomatonRule);
    }
    public static bool operator ==(FiniteAutomatonRule r1,
                                   FiniteAutomatonRule r2)
    {
       return FiniteAutomatonRule.Equals(r1, r2);
    }
    public static bool operator !=(FiniteAutomatonRule r1,
                                   FiniteAutomatonRule r2)
    {
        return !FiniteAutomatonRule.Equals(r1, r2);
    }
    public override int GetHashCode()
    {
        return this.ToString().GetHashCode();
    }

    // returns a System.String that represents this rule
    public override string ToString()
    {
        if (this.InputSymbol == null)
        {
            return string.Format("{0} -> {1}", this.CurrentState,
                                               this.NextState);
        }
        else
        {
            return string.Format("{0}{1} -> {2}", this.CurrentState,
                                                  this.InputSymbol,
                                                  this.NextState);
        }
    }
}
```

Using classes `FiniteAutomatonState` and `FiniteAutomatonRule` defined above, we now implement finite automaton as follows:

```
public class FiniteAutomaton
{
    public FiniteSet<FiniteAutomatonState> States { get; private set; }
    public FiniteAutomatonState StartState { get; set; }
    public FiniteSet<FiniteAutomatonState> FinalStates { get; private set; }
    public Alphabet InputAlphabet { get; private set; }
    public FiniteSet<FiniteAutomatonRule> Rules { get; private set; }
```

```
    // constructor
    public FiniteAutomaton()
    {
        this.States = new FiniteSet<FiniteAutomatonState>();
        this.StartState = null;
        this.FinalStates = new FiniteSet<FiniteAutomatonState>();
        this.InputAlphabet = new Alphabet();
        this.Rules = new FiniteSet<FiniteAutomatonRule>();
    }

    // returns a System.String that represents this finite automaton
    public override string ToString()
    {
        return "States = " + this.States +
               Environment.NewLine +
               "Start state = " + this.StartState +
               Environment.NewLine +
               "Final states = " + this.FinalStates +
               Environment.NewLine +
               "Input alphabet = " + this.InputAlphabet +
               Environment.NewLine +
               "Rules = " + this.Rules;
    }
}
```

5.2 Finite automata that always read

From a mathematical standpoint, the basic versions of finite automata introduced in the previous section are very convenient (see Definition 5.1). On the other hand, they are so general that they are difficult to use in practice. More specifically, they may loop endlessly on some input strings because they may perform moves during which they change states without reading any symbols. As obvious, we prefer using finite automata that read a symbol during every move, so they cannot end up in an endless loop. In this section, we explain how to transform any finite automaton to an equivalent finite automaton that always read. During this explanation, we demonstrate several results by the mathematical induction described in Section 1.1 in order to demonstrate the use of this proof method.

Let us point out that throughout this section, we often make use of the conventions introduced in Section 5.1. Specifically, recall that for a finite automaton M, sets Q, F, Σ, and R denote its set of states, the set of final states, the alphabet of input symbols, and the set of rules, respectively (see Definition 5.1).

Definition 5.2. *Let M be a finite automaton. An* ε-rule *is a rule of the form $q \to p \in R$, where $q, p \in Q$. M is an ε-free finite automaton if no rule in R is an ε-rule.*

By ε-rules, finite automata make *ε-moves* during which they change states without reading any symbols and, consequently, endlessly loop. To transform them to equivalent ε-free finite automata, we first explain how to determine the set of all states that they can reach by ε-moves. For this purpose, for any finite automaton M, we set

$$\varepsilon\text{-moves}(E) = \{q \mid o \Rightarrow^* q, \text{ where } o \in E,\ q \in Q\};$$

Algorithm 5.1: Determination of ε-moves

Input: A finite automaton M and $E \subseteq Q$.
Output: ε-moves $(E) = \{q \mid o \Rightarrow^* q, \text{ where } o \in E, q \in {}_MQ\}$.

begin
  set ε-moves (E) to E
  repeat
    ε-moves $(E) = \varepsilon$-moves $(E) \cup \{p \mid q \rightarrow p \in {}_MR$ and $q \in \varepsilon$-moves $(E)\}$
  until no change $\{\varepsilon$-moves (E) *cannot be further extended*$\}$
end

in words, by ε-moves (E), we denote the set of states that M can reach by sequences of ε-moves from states in E. We often omit the braces in E if E contains a single state; in other words, ε-moves $(\{p\})$ is shortened to ε-moves (p), where $p \in {}_MQ$.

Let M be a finite automaton and $E \subseteq Q$. To compute ε-moves (E), we initially set ε-moves $(E) = E$ because M can reach any state in E by zero ε-moves. If R contains $q \rightarrow p$ with $q \in \varepsilon$-moves (E), we add p to ε-moves (E). In this way, we repeat the extension of ε-moves (E) until no more states can be included into ε-moves (E). As obvious, the resulting set ε-moves (E) equals $\{q \mid o \Rightarrow^* q, \text{ where } o \in E, q \in {}_MQ\}$ as desired.

In Algorithm 5.1, the **repeat** loop is ended with **until no change**, meaning that the loop is repeated until no change can result from its further repetition. We end loops in this way throughout the rest of this book.

Next, we rigorously verify that this algorithm works correctly. We make this verification by using mathematical induction, explained in Section 1.1.

Lemma 5.1. *Algorithm 5.1 is correct.*

Proof. To establish this lemma, we prove Claims A and B, in which ε-moves (E_i) denotes the set of states that ε-moves (E) contains after the ith iteration of the `repeat` loop, where $i = 0, 1, \ldots, h$, for some $h \leq \text{card}({}_MQ)$.

Claim A. For every $j \geq 0$ and every $p \in {}_MQ$, if $p \in \varepsilon$-moves (E_j), there exists $q \in \varepsilon$-moves (E) such that $q \Rightarrow^* p$ in M.

Proof of Claim A (by induction on $j \geq 0$).

Basis. Let $j = 0$. Observe that $p \in \varepsilon$-moves (E_0) implies $p \in \varepsilon$-moves (E). As $p \Rightarrow^0 p$, the basis holds.

Induction Hypothesis. Assume that Claim A holds for all $j = 0, \ldots, i$, where i is a nonnegative integer.

Induction Step. Let $p \in \varepsilon$-moves (E_{i+1}). Next, we distinguish two cases—$p \in \varepsilon$-moves (E_j), for some $j \leq i$ and $p \in \varepsilon$-moves $(E_{i+1}) - \varepsilon$-moves (E_i).

(i) Let $p \in \varepsilon$-moves (E_j), for some $j \leq i$. By the induction hypothesis, there exists $q \in {}_MQ$ such that $q \Rightarrow^* p$ in M, so the inductive step holds in this case.

(ii) Let $p \in \varepsilon\text{-moves}(E_{i+1}) - \varepsilon\text{-moves}(E_i)$. Examine the `repeat` loop to see that there exists $o \to p \in {}_MR$ for some $o \in \varepsilon\text{-moves}(E_i)$. By the induction hypothesis, $q \Rightarrow^* o$ in M for some $q \in E$, so $q \Rightarrow^* o \Rightarrow p$ in M. Thus, $q \Rightarrow^* p$ in M, and the inductive step holds in this case as well.

Claim B. For all $j \geq 0$, if $q \Rightarrow^j p$ in M with $q \in E, p \in \varepsilon\text{-moves}(E)$.
Proof of Claim B (by induction on $j \geq 0$).

Basis. Let $j = 0$. That is, $q \Rightarrow^0 p$ in M with $q \in E$, so $q = p$. Then, the algorithm includes p into ε-moves (E) even before the first iteration of the `repeat` loop; formally, $p \in \varepsilon\text{-moves}(E_0)$. Thus, the basis holds.

Induction Hypothesis. Assume that Claim B holds for all $j = 0, \ldots, i$, where i is a nonnegative integer.

Induction Step. Let $q \Rightarrow^{i+1} p$ in M with $q \in E$. Next, we first consider $p \in \varepsilon\text{-moves}(E_j)$, for some $j \leq i$; then, we study the case when $p \notin \varepsilon\text{-moves}(E_j)$, for any $j \leq i$.

(i) Let $p \in \varepsilon\text{-moves}(E_j)$, for some $j \leq i$. Recall that no iteration of the `repeat` loop removes any states from ε-moves (E). Therefore, $p \in \varepsilon\text{-moves}(E)$.
(ii) Let $p \notin \varepsilon\text{-moves}(E_j)$, for any $j \leq i$. As $i + 1 > 1$, we can express $q \Rightarrow^{i+1} p$ in M as $q \Rightarrow^i o \Rightarrow p$, and the induction hypothesis implies $o \in \varepsilon\text{-moves}(E)$. ${}_MR$ contains $o \to p$ because $o \Rightarrow p$ in M. As $o \in \varepsilon\text{-moves}(E)$ and $o \to p \in {}_MR$, the `repeat` loop adds p to E during iteration $i + 1$, so $p \in \varepsilon\text{-moves}(E)$.

By Claims A and B, $q \Rightarrow^* p$ in M with $q \in E$ if and only if $p \in \varepsilon\text{-moves}(E)$. Hence, Algorithm 5.1 correctly determines $\varepsilon\text{-moves}(E) = \{q \mid o \Rightarrow^* q,\text{ where } o \in E,\ q \in Q\}$, so the lemma holds. ■

Example 5.2. *We apply Algorithm 5.1 to the finite automaton M given in Example 5.1 and a single-member state set* {1}.

First, we set $\varepsilon\text{-moves}(1) = \{1\}$. *Because* $1 \to 2$ *and* $1 \to 4$ *are* ε*-rules in* M, *we add* 2 *and* 4 *to* ε-moves (1), *thus producing* $\varepsilon\text{-moves}(1) = \{1, 2, 4\}$. *As there is no* ε*-rule* $2 \to p$ *or* $4 \to p$ *in* M *for any* p, *no more states can be added to* ε-moves (1) *at this point, and we are done.*

Implementation 5.2. *ε-rules* First, we extend the class `FiniteAutomatonRule` with the notion of ε-rules. We add a property that tells us whether a rule is an ε-rule, and also an alternate constructor for ε-rules.

```
public bool IsEpsilonRule { get { return this.InputSymbol == null; } }

public FiniteAutomatonRule(FiniteAutomatonState currentState,
                           FiniteAutomatonState nextState)
    : this(currentState, null, nextState)
{
}
```

Now we can add a property which indicates whether a finite automaton is ε-free to `FiniteAutomaton` class.

```
public bool IsEpsilonFree
{
    get
    {
        foreach (FiniteAutomatonRule r in this.Rules)
        {
            if (r.IsEpsilonRule) return false;
        }
        return true;
    }
}
```

Finally, the following method added to `FiniteAutomaton` class implements Algorithm 5.1.

```
public FiniteSet<FiniteAutomatonState> DetermineEpsilonMoves(
    FiniteSet<FiniteAutomatonState> E)
{
    var result = new FiniteSet<FiniteAutomatonState>();

    foreach (FiniteAutomatonState state in E)
    {
        result.Add(state);
    }

    bool changed = false;
    do
    {
        foreach (FiniteAutomatonRule r in this.Rules)
        {
            if (r.IsEpsilonRule && E.Contains(r.CurrentState))
            {
                result.Add(r.NextState);
            }
        }
    }
    while (changed);

    return result;
}
```

As in Example 5.1, we want to find ε-moves for the finite automaton M from Example 5.1 and state set {1}.

```
var M = new FiniteAutomaton()
{
    States = { "1", "2", "3", "4", "5" },
    StartState = "1",
    FinalStates = { "3", "5" },
    InputAlphabet = { "a", "b" },
    Rules =
    {
        new FiniteAutomatonRule("1", "2"),
        new FiniteAutomatonRule("1", "4"),
        new FiniteAutomatonRule("2", "a", "2"),
        new FiniteAutomatonRule("2", "a", "3"),
        new FiniteAutomatonRule("3", "b", "3"),
```

Algorithm 5.2: Removal of ε-rules

Input: A finite automaton $I = ({}_I\Sigma, {}_IR)$.
Output: An equivalent ε-free finite automaton $O = ({}_O\Sigma, {}_OR)$.

begin
set ${}_O\Sigma$ to ${}_I\Sigma$ with ${}_O\Delta = {}_I\Delta$, ${}_OQ = {}_IQ$, and ${}_Os = {}_Is$
set ${}_OF$ to $\{q \mid q \in {}_IQ,\ \varepsilon\text{-moves}(q) \cap {}_IF \neq \emptyset\}$
set ${}_OR$ to
$\{qa \to p \mid q \in {}_IQ,\ a \in {}_I\Delta,\ oa \to p \in {}_IR$ for some $o \in \varepsilon\text{-moves}(q)$ in $I\}$
end

```
        new FiniteAutomatonRule("4", "b", "4"),
        new FiniteAutomatonRule("4", "b", "5")
    }
};

var E = new FiniteSet<FiniteAutomatonState> { "1" };

FiniteSet<FiniteAutomatonState> epsilonMoves =
    M.DetermineEpsilonMoves(E);
```

We are now ready to convert any finite automaton I to an equivalent ε-free finite automaton O.

Basic Idea. By using Algorithm 5.1, we find out whether ${}_Is \Rightarrow^* f$ with $f \in {}_IF$, where ${}_Is$ denotes the start state of I. Thus, I accepts ε, and if this is the case, we include ${}_Is$ into ${}_OF$ so O accepts ε, too. Furthermore, set

$${}_OR = \{qa \to p \mid q \in {}_IQ,\ a \in {}_I\Delta,\ oa \to p \in {}_IR \text{ for some } o \in \varepsilon\text{-moves}(\{q\})\},$$

where ε-moves $(\{q\})$ is constructed by Algorithm 5.1; therefore, ${}_OR$ contains the set of all states I can reach by ε-moves from q. In this way, by $qa \to p \in {}_OR$, O simulates $qa \Rightarrow^* oa \Rightarrow p$ in I.

Theorem 5.1. *Algorithm 5.2 is correct. Consequently, for every finite automaton $I = ({}_I\Sigma, {}_IR)$, there is an equivalent ε-free finite automaton O.*

Proof. Notice that Algorithm 5.2 produces ${}_O\Delta = {}_I\Delta$, ${}_OQ = {}_IQ$, and ${}_Os = {}_Is$. Therefore, for simplicity, we just write Δ, Q, and s throughout this proof because there exists no danger of confusion. However, we carefully distinguish ${}_IF$ from ${}_OF$ because they may differ from each other.

As obvious, ${}_OR$ contains no ε-rules. To establish $L(O) = L(I)$, we first prove the following claim.

Claim 1. *For every $q, p \in Q$ and $w \in \Delta^+$, $qw \Rightarrow^+ p$ in O iff $qw \Rightarrow^+ p$ in I.*

Proof. Only If. By induction on $|w| \geq 1$, we next prove that for every $q, p \in Q$ and $w \in \Delta^+$, $qw \Rightarrow^+ p$ in O implies $qw \Rightarrow^+ p$ in I.

Basis. Let $|w| = 1$ and $qw \Rightarrow^+ p$ in O. Since $|w| = 1$, w is a symbol in Δ. As ${}_O R$ contains no ε-rules, $qw \Rightarrow^+ p$ is, in effect, a one-move computation of the form $qw \Rightarrow p$ in O. Thus, $qw \rightarrow p$ in ${}_O R$. By the definition of ${}_O R$, $ow \rightarrow p \in {}_I R$ for some $o \in \varepsilon$-moves$(\{q\})$ in I, so $q \Rightarrow^+ o$ and $ow \Rightarrow p$ in I. Consequently, $qw \Rightarrow^+ p$ in I.

Induction Hypothesis. Assume that the "only-if" part of this claim holds for all $w \in \Delta^+$ with $|w| \leq n$, where n is a nonnegative integer.

Induction Step. Let $qw \Rightarrow^+ p$ in O, where $q, p \in Q$ and $w \in \Delta^+$ with $|w| = n + 1$, so $|w| \geq 2$. Because $|w| \geq 1$ and ${}_O R$ contains no ε-rules, we can express $qw \Rightarrow^+ p$ as $qva \Rightarrow^+ ha \Rightarrow p$, where $h \in Q$, $a \in \Delta$, v is a prefix of w, and $|v| = n$. As $qv \Rightarrow^+ h$ in O and $|v| = n$, $qv \Rightarrow^+ h$ in I by the inductive hypothesis. Since $ha \Rightarrow p$ in O, $ha \rightarrow p \in {}_O R$. By the definition of ${}_O R$, $ha \Rightarrow^+ oa \Rightarrow p$ in I, where $o \in Q$. Putting $qv \Rightarrow^+ h$ and $ha \Rightarrow^+ oa \Rightarrow p$ in I together, $qva \Rightarrow^+ ha \Rightarrow^+ p$ in I. Because $va = w$, $qw \Rightarrow^+ p$ in I. Thus, the "only-if" part of the claim holds.

If. The "if" part of the claim is left as an exercise. □

To prove that $L(O) = L(I)$, consider the above claim for $q = s$. That is, $sw \Rightarrow^+ p$ in O iff $sw \Rightarrow^+ p$ in I for all $w \in \Delta^+$, so $L(O) - \{\varepsilon\} = L(I) - \{\varepsilon\}$. As ${}_O F = \{q \mid q \in {}_I Q,\ \varepsilon\text{-moves}(q) \cap {}_I F \neq \emptyset\}$, $s \Rightarrow^* p$ in O with $p \in {}_O F$ iff $s \Rightarrow^* p \Rightarrow^* f$ in I with $f \in {}_I F$. Therefore, $L(O) = L(I)$, and the theorem holds. ■

Example 5.3. *Return to the finite automaton M in Figure 5.1. By using Algorithm 5.1, we have determined ε-moves for each state of M as follows:*

$$\begin{aligned}
\varepsilon\text{-moves}(1) &= \{1, 2, 4\},\\
\varepsilon\text{-moves}(2) &= \{2\},\\
\varepsilon\text{-moves}(3) &= \{3\},\\
\varepsilon\text{-moves}(4) &= \{4\},\\
\varepsilon\text{-moves}(5) &= \{5\}.
\end{aligned}$$

Having constructed these sets, we apply Algorithm 5.2 to transform this automaton to an equivalent ε-free finite automaton. For instance, as ε-moves$(1) = \{1, 2, 4\}$ *and* $4b \rightarrow 5 \in R$, *this algorithm adds a rule of the form* $1b \rightarrow 5$ *into the output automaton. The complete list of the resulting automaton rules are as follows:*

$$\begin{aligned}
1a &\rightarrow 2,\\
1a &\rightarrow 3,\\
1b &\rightarrow 4,\\
1b &\rightarrow 5,\\
2a &\rightarrow 2,\\
2a &\rightarrow 3,\\
3b &\rightarrow 3,\\
4b &\rightarrow 4,\\
4b &\rightarrow 5.
\end{aligned}$$

Figure 5.2 shows the state diagram of the output automaton.

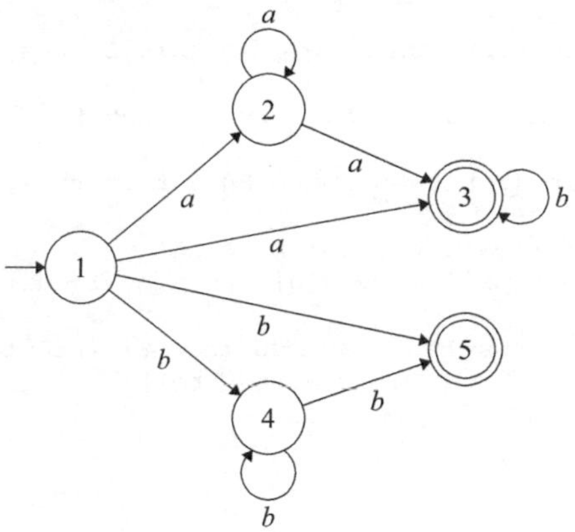

Figure 5.2 ε-Free finite automaton

Next, we give a C# implementation of Algorithm 5.2.

Implementation 5.3. *Removal of ε-rules* To implement Algorithm 5.2, we add the following method to the class `FiniteAutomaton`.

```
public FiniteAutomaton RemoveEpsilonRules()
{
    var result = new FiniteAutomaton()
    {
        // copy input alphabet, states, and start state
        InputAlphabet = new Alphabet(this.InputAlphabet),
        States = new FiniteSet<FiniteAutomatonState>(this.States),
        StartState = this.StartState,
    };

    // determine epsilon moves for each state
    var epsilonMoves =
        new Dictionary<FiniteAutomatonState,
                       FiniteSet<FiniteAutomatonState>>();
    foreach (FiniteAutomatonState q in this.States)
    {
        var E  = new FiniteSet<FiniteAutomatonState>();
        E.Add(q);
        epsilonMoves.Add(q, this.DetermineEpsilonMoves(E));
    }

    // compute final states
    foreach (FiniteAutomatonState q in this.States)
    {
        if (!epsilonMoves[q].IsDisjoint(this.FinalStates))
        {
            result.FinalStates.Add(q);
        }
    }
```

```
    // compute rules
    foreach (FiniteAutomatonState q in this.States)
    {
        foreach (Symbol a in this.InputAlphabet)
        {
            foreach (FiniteAutomatonRule r in this.Rules)
            {
                if (r.InputSymbol == a &&
                    epsilonMoves[q].Contains(r.CurrentState))
                {
                    result.Rules.Add (new FiniteAutomatonRule(
                        q, a, r.NextState));
                }
            }
        }
    }

    return result;
}
```

5.3 Determinism

Consider any finite automaton that always reads, $M = (\Sigma, R)$. In general, its set of rules R may contain several rules with the same left-hand side. To rephrase this feature mathematically, R represents a relation rather than a function, so it may relate a single member of $Q\Delta$ to several members of Q. As a consequence, M can make several different moves on the same symbol from the same state. For instance, take the automaton in Figure 5.2; from 1, it can enter state 2 or 3 on a. As obvious, this nondeterministic behavior complicates the use of M in practice. Therefore, in this section, we explain how to convert M to its equivalent deterministic version that makes precisely one move on every symbol from the same state. Mathematically speaking, we turn M to its equivalent version whose set of rules represents a total function.

Definition 5.3. *Let $M = (\Sigma, R)$ be any finite automaton that always reads (see Definition 5.2). M is a* deterministic finite automaton *if for every $q \in Q$ and every $a \in \Delta$, there exists precisely one $p \in Q$ such that $qa \to p \in {}_MR$.*

Basic Idea. Let $I = ({}_I\Sigma, {}_IR)$ be any finite automaton that always reads. To turn I to an equivalent deterministic finite automaton $O = ({}_O\Sigma, {}_OR)$, set ${}_OQ = \{\langle W \rangle \mid W \subseteq {}_IQ\}$—that is, any set $W \subseteq {}_IQ$ is represented by a unique symbol $\langle W \rangle$ (it is worth noting that ${}_OQ$ always contains $\langle \emptyset \rangle$). Furthermore, if $W \cap {}_IF \neq \emptyset$, include $\langle W \rangle$ into ${}_OF$. For every $\langle X \rangle \in {}_OQ$ and every $a \in \Delta$, add $\langle X \rangle a \to \langle Y \rangle$ to ${}_OR$ with $Y = \{q \mid xa \to q \in {}_IR,$ for some $x \in X$ and $a \in {}_I\Delta\}$. Consequently, $\langle\{{}_Is\}\rangle w \Rightarrow^* \langle Z \rangle$ in O iff ${}_Isw \Rightarrow *p$, for all $p \in Z$ and $w \in \Delta^*$. Specifically, for every $\langle E \rangle \in {}_OF$, $\langle\{{}_Is\}\rangle w \Rightarrow^* \langle E \rangle$ in O iff ${}_Isw \Rightarrow^* f$ in I, for some $f \in E \cap {}_IF$. In other words, O accepts w iff I accepts w, so $L(O) = L(I)$.

Algorithm 5.3: Determinization

Input: A finite automaton that always reads, $I = ({}_I\Sigma, {}_IR)$.
Output: A deterministic finite automaton $O = ({}_O\Sigma, {}_OR)$ such that $L(O) = L(I)$.

begin
  set ${}_O\Delta = {}_I\Delta$
  set ${}_OQ = \{\langle W\rangle \mid W \subseteq {}_IQ\}$
  set ${}_OF = \{\langle U\rangle \mid \langle U\rangle \in {}_OQ$ and $U \cap {}_IF \neq \emptyset\}$
  set ${}_Os = \langle\{{}_Is\}\rangle$
  for *every* $\langle X\rangle \in {}_OQ$ *and every* $a \in {}_O\Delta$ **do**
    add $\langle X\rangle a \to \langle Y\rangle$ to ${}_OR$ with $Y = \{q \mid pa \to q \in {}_IR, p \in X\}$
  end
end

Lemma 5.2. *Algorithm 5.3 is correct.*

Proof. Clearly, for any subset $O \subseteq {}_IQ$ and any input symbol $a \in {}_I\Delta$, there exists a single set, $P \subseteq {}_IQ$, satisfying this equivalence

$$p \in P \text{ iff } oa \to p \in {}_IR \text{ for some } o \in O.$$

Notice that ${}_I\Delta = {}_O\Delta$. Consequently, for any $\langle O\rangle \in {}_OQ$ and $a \in {}_O\Delta$, there exists a unique state $\langle P\rangle \in {}_OQ$, such that $\langle O\rangle a \to \langle P\rangle \in {}_OR$, so O is deterministic. A fully rigorous proof that $L(I) = L(O)$ is left as an exercise. ∎

Lemma 5.2 implies the following theorem.

Theorem 5.2. *For every finite automaton that always reads, I, there is an equivalent deterministic finite automaton O.*

For simplicity, we omit braces in the states of the form $\langle\{\dots\}\rangle$ and write $\langle\dots\rangle$ instead; for example, $\langle\{2, 3\}\rangle$ is simplified to $\langle 2, 3\rangle$.

Example 5.4. *Reconsider the automaton in Figure 5.2. Recall its rules*

$1a \to 2,$
$1a \to 3,$
$1b \to 4,$
$1b \to 5,$
$2a \to 2,$
$2a \to 3,$
$3b \to 3,$
$4b \to 4,$
$4b \to 5,$

Table 5.2 Deterministic finite automaton

State	*a*	*b*	State	*a*	*b*
$\langle 1\rangle$	$\langle 2,3\rangle$	$\langle 4,5\rangle$	$\langle 1,2,4\rangle$	$\langle 2,3\rangle$	$\langle 4,5\rangle$
$\langle 2\rangle$	$\langle 2,3\rangle$	$\langle\emptyset\rangle$	$\underline{\langle 1,2,5\rangle}$	$\langle 2,3\rangle$	$\langle 4,5\rangle$
$\underline{\langle 3\rangle}$	$\langle\emptyset\rangle$	$\langle 3\rangle$	$\underline{\langle 1,3,4\rangle}$	$\langle 2,3\rangle$	$\langle 3,4,5\rangle$
$\langle 4\rangle$	$\langle\emptyset\rangle$	$\langle 4,5\rangle$	$\underline{\langle 1,3,5\rangle}$	$\langle 2,3\rangle$	$\langle 3,4,5\rangle$
$\underline{\langle 5\rangle}$	$\langle\emptyset\rangle$	$\langle\emptyset\rangle$	$\underline{\langle 1,4,5\rangle}$	$\langle 2,3\rangle$	$\langle 4,5\rangle$
$\langle 1,2\rangle$	$\langle 2,3\rangle$	$\langle 4,5\rangle$	$\underline{\langle 2,3,4\rangle}$	$\langle 2,3\rangle$	$\langle 3,4,5\rangle$
$\underline{\langle 1,3\rangle}$	$\langle 2,3\rangle$	$\langle 3,4,5\rangle$	$\underline{\langle 2,3,5\rangle}$	$\langle 2,3\rangle$	$\langle 3\rangle$
$\langle 1,4\rangle$	$\langle 2,3\rangle$	$\langle 4,5\rangle$	$\underline{\langle 2,4,5\rangle}$	$\langle 2,3\rangle$	$\langle 4,5\rangle$
$\underline{\langle 1,5\rangle}$	$\langle 2,3\rangle$	$\langle 4,5\rangle$	$\underline{\langle 3,4,5\rangle}$	$\langle\emptyset\rangle$	$\langle 3,4,5\rangle$
$\underline{\langle 2,3\rangle}$	$\langle 2,3\rangle$	$\langle 3\rangle$	$\underline{\langle 1,2,3,4\rangle}$	$\langle 2,3\rangle$	$\langle 3,4,5\rangle$
$\langle 2,4\rangle$	$\langle 2,3\rangle$	$\langle 4,5\rangle$	$\underline{\langle 1,2,3,5\rangle}$	$\langle 2,3\rangle$	$\langle 3,4,5\rangle$
$\underline{\langle 2,5\rangle}$	$\langle 2,3\rangle$	$\langle\emptyset\rangle$	$\underline{\langle 1,2,4,5\rangle}$	$\langle 2,3\rangle$	$\langle 4,5\rangle$
$\underline{\langle 3,4\rangle}$	$\langle\emptyset\rangle$	$\langle 3,4,5\rangle$	$\underline{\langle 1,3,4,5\rangle}$	$\langle 2,3\rangle$	$\langle 3,4,5\rangle$
$\underline{\langle 3,5\rangle}$	$\langle\emptyset\rangle$	$\langle 3\rangle$	$\underline{\langle 2,3,4,5\rangle}$	$\langle 2,3\rangle$	$\langle 3,4,5\rangle$
$\underline{\langle 4,5\rangle}$	$\langle\emptyset\rangle$	$\langle 4,5\rangle$	$\underline{\langle 1,2,3,4,5\rangle}$	$\langle 2,3\rangle$	$\langle 3,4,5\rangle$
$\underline{\langle 1,2,3\rangle}$	$\langle 2,3\rangle$	$\langle 3,4,5\rangle$	$\langle\emptyset\rangle$	$\langle\emptyset\rangle$	$\langle\emptyset\rangle$

in which states 3 *and* 5 *are final. This automaton works nondeterministically. For instance, from* 1 *on b, it can make a move to* 4 *or* 5*. With this automaton as its input, Algorithm 5.3 produces the equivalent deterministic finite automaton in which every state that contains* 3 *or* 5 *is final. The state table of the resulting automaton is shown in Table 5.2.*

Implementation 5.4. *Determinization of Finite Automata, we can add a property which indicates whether a finite automaton is deterministic to the class* `FiniteAutomaton` *as follows:*

```
public bool IsDeterministic
{
    get
    {
        if (!this.IsEpsilonFree) return false;

        foreach (FiniteAutomatonState q in this.States)
        {
            foreach (Symbol a in this.InputAlphabet)
            {
                int ruleCount = 0;
                foreach (FiniteAutomatonRule r in this.Rules)
                {
                    if (r.CurrentState == q && r.InputSymbol == a)
                    {
                        ruleCount++;
                        if (ruleCount > 1) return false;
                    }
```

```
                }
            }
        }
        return true;
    }
}
```

In order to implement Algorithm 5.3, we first create a method which constructs a new state from a given set of states. For example, given a set of three states labeled `1`*,* `2`*, and* `3`*, it returns a state labeled* `<1,2,3>`*.*

```
private FiniteAutomatonState CreateCompositeState(
    FiniteSet<FiniteAutomatonState> originalStates)
{
    if (originalStates.IsEmpty) return new FiniteAutomatonState("<>");
    else
    {
        var stringBuilder = new StringBuilder();
        stringBuilder.Append("<");
        foreach (FiniteAutomatonState state in originalStates)
        {
            stringBuilder.Append(state);
            stringBuilder.Append(",");
        }
        stringBuilder.Remove(stringBuilder.Length - 1, 1);
        stringBuilder.Append(">");
        return new FiniteAutomatonState(stringBuilder.ToString());
    }
}
```

We are now ready to implement Algorithm 5.3.

```
public FiniteAutomaton Determinize()
{
    if (!this.IsEpsilonFree)
    {
        return this.RemoveEpsilonRules().Determinize();
    }

    var result = new FiniteAutomaton()
    {
        // copy input alphabet
        InputAlphabet = new Alphabet(this.InputAlphabet)
    };

    // compute states as power set of original states
    var stateSets = new Dictionary<FiniteAutomatonState,
                                    FiniteSet<FiniteAutomatonState>>();
    foreach (FiniteSet<FiniteAutomatonState> stateSet
        in this.States.PowerSet())
    {
        FiniteAutomatonState sW = CreateCompositeState(stateSet);
        result.States.Add(sW);
```

```
        stateSets.Add(sW, stateSet);
    }

    // set start state
    result.StartState = CreateCompositeState(
        new FiniteSet<FiniteAutomatonState> { this.StartState });

    // compute final states
    foreach (FiniteAutomatonState sU in result.States)
    {
        if (!stateSets[sU].IsDisjoint(this.FinalStates))
        {
            result.FinalStates.Add(sU);
        }
    }

    // compute rules
    foreach (FiniteAutomatonState sX in result.States)
    {
        foreach (Symbol a in result.InputAlphabet)
        {
            var Y = new FiniteSet<FiniteAutomatonState>();
            foreach (FiniteAutomatonRule r in this.Rules)
            {
                if (r.InputSymbol == a &&
                    stateSets[sX].Contains(r.CurrentState))
                {
                    Y.Add(r.NextState);
                }
            }
            foreach (var stateSet in stateSets)
            {
                if (stateSet.Value.SetEquals(Y))
                {
                    result.Rules.Add(new FiniteAutomatonRule(
                        sX, a, stateSet.Key));
                    break;
                }
            }
        }
    }

    return result;
}
```

Algorithm 5.3 produces $O = ({}_O\Sigma, {}_OR)$ with card $({}_OQ) =$ card (power $({}_IQ)$) and card $({}_OR) =$ card (power $({}_IQ) \times \Delta$).

For instance, in Example 5.4, the resulting automaton has 32 states because $2^5 = 32$.

Besides, Algorithm 5.3 may introduce some states completely uselessly. Specifically, it may introduce states that the output deterministic finite automaton can never reach from its start state. For instance, in Table 5.2, states $\langle 2\rangle$, $\langle 1, 3, 5\rangle$, or $\langle 1, 2, 3, 4, 5\rangle$ are obviously unreachable as follows from their absence in the table columns denoted

---

Algorithm 5.4: Determinization and reachability

Input: A finite automaton that always reads, $I = ({}_I\Sigma, {}_IR)$.
Output: A deterministic finite automaton $O = ({}_O\Sigma, {}_OR)$ such that $L(O) = L(I)$ and ${}_OQ$ contains only reachable states.

begin
  set ${}_O\Delta = {}_I\Delta$
  set ${}_OQ = \{\langle {}_Is \rangle\}$
  set ${}_Os = \langle {}_Is \rangle$
  repeat
    if $a \in {}_I\Delta$, $X \subseteq {}_IQ$, $\langle X \rangle \in {}_OQ$, $Y = \{p \mid qa \rightarrow p \in {}_IR \text{ with } q \in X\}$ **then**
      add $\langle Y \rangle$ to ${}_OQ$
      add $\langle X \rangle a \rightarrow \langle Y \rangle$ to ${}_OR$
    end
  until no change
  set ${}_OF = \{\langle Y \rangle \mid \langle Y \rangle \in {}_OQ, Y \cap {}_IF \neq \emptyset\}$
end

---

by either of the two input symbols. In fact, the same holds for most of the states in Table 5.2. As a result, we explain how to produce the resulting automaton in a more economical and sophisticated way.

Definition 5.4. *In a deterministic finite automaton M, a state $q \in Q$ is* reachable *if there exists $w \in \Delta^*$ such that $sw \Rightarrow^* q$ in M; otherwise, q is* unreachable *in M.*

The next algorithm converts any finite automaton that always reads to its deterministic version that contains only reachable states.

Basic Idea. Take any ε-free finite automaton, $I = ({}_I\Sigma, {}_IR)$. The following algorithm transforms I to an equivalent deterministic finite automaton, $O = ({}_OS, {}_OR)$, so it parallels the previous algorithm except that a new state is introduced into ${}_OQ$ only if it is reachable. Initially, ${}_OQ$ contains only the start state $\langle {}_Is \rangle$. Then, if ${}_OQ$ already contains $\langle W \rangle$, where $W \in {}_IQ$, and $P = \{p \mid oa \Rightarrow p \text{ for some } o \in W\}$ is non-empty, where $a \in \Delta$, then we add $\langle P \rangle$ to ${}_OQ$ and include $\langle W \rangle a \rightarrow \langle P \rangle$ into ${}_OR$.

Example 5.5. *In this example, we convert the automaton from Figure 5.2 to an equivalent deterministic finite automaton by using Algorithm 5.4, which initializes the start state of the deterministic finite automaton to $\langle 1 \rangle$. From* 1 *on a, the automaton enters* 2 *or* 3, *so introduce $\langle 2, 3 \rangle$ as a new state and $\langle 1 \rangle a \rightarrow \langle 2, 3 \rangle$ as a new rule in the output deterministic finite automaton. From* 2, *on $\langle a \rangle$, the automaton again enters* 2 *or* 3, *and from* 3, *on a, it does not enter any state; therefore, add $\langle 2, 3 \rangle a \rightarrow \langle 2, 3 \rangle$ to the set of rules in the deterministic finite automaton. Complete the construction of*

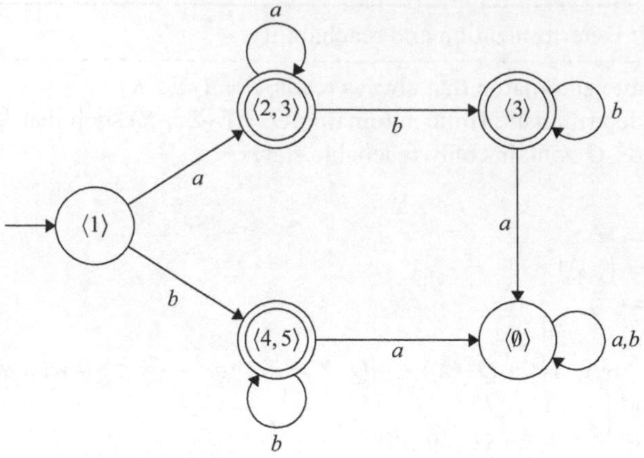

Figure 5.3 Deterministic finite automaton in which all states are reachable

the deterministic finite automaton as an exercise. The resulting deterministic finite automaton is defined by its rules

$$\begin{aligned}
\langle 1\rangle a &\rightarrow \langle 2,3\rangle,\\
\langle 1\rangle b &\rightarrow \langle 4,5\rangle,\\
\langle 2,3\rangle a &\rightarrow \langle 2,3\rangle,\\
\langle 2,3\rangle b &\rightarrow \langle 3\rangle,\\
\langle 4,5\rangle a &\rightarrow \langle \emptyset\rangle,\\
\langle 4,5\rangle b &\rightarrow \langle 4,5\rangle,\\
\langle 3\rangle a &\rightarrow \langle \emptyset\rangle,\\
\langle 3\rangle b &\rightarrow \langle 3\rangle,\\
\langle \emptyset\rangle a &\rightarrow \langle \emptyset\rangle,\\
\langle \emptyset\rangle b &\rightarrow \langle \emptyset\rangle,
\end{aligned}$$

where states $\langle 2,3\rangle$, $\langle 4,5\rangle$, and $\langle 3\rangle$ are final. Figure 5.3 gives the state diagram of the resulting output deterministic finite automaton. The corresponding state table is shown in Table 5.3.

Implementation 5.5. *To implement Algorithm 5.4, we add a new method to the class `FiniteAutomaton`. The method `CreateCompositeState` from Implementation 5.4 is used again.*

```
public FiniteAutomaton DeterminizeWithReachability()
{
    if (!this.IsEpsilonFree)
```

Table 5.3 Deterministic finite automaton in which all states are reachable

State	*a*	*b*
⟨1⟩	⟨2, 3⟩	⟨4, 5⟩
⟨3⟩	⟨∅⟩	⟨3⟩
⟨2, 3⟩	⟨2, 3⟩	⟨3⟩
⟨4, 5⟩	⟨∅⟩	⟨4, 5⟩
⟨∅⟩	⟨∅⟩	⟨∅⟩

```
{
    return this.RemoveEpsilonRules().DeterminizeWithReachability();
}

var result = new FiniteAutomaton()
{
    // copy input alphabet
    InputAlphabet = new Alphabet(this.InputAlphabet),
};

// create new start state
FiniteAutomatonState s = CreateCompositeState(
    new FiniteSet<FiniteAutomatonState> { this.StartState });
result.States.Add(s);
result.StartState = s;
var stateSets = new Dictionary<FiniteAutomatonState,
                               FiniteSet<FiniteAutomatonState>>();
stateSets.Add(
    s, new FiniteSet<FiniteAutomatonState> { this.StartState });

// compute states and rules
bool change;
do
{
    change = false;
    var states = new List<FiniteAutomatonState>(result.States);
    foreach (FiniteAutomatonState sX in states)
    {
        foreach (Symbol a in this.InputAlphabet)
        {
            var Y = new FiniteSet<FiniteAutomatonState>();
            foreach (FiniteAutomatonRule r in this.Rules)
            {
                if (r.InputSymbol == a &&
                    stateSets[sX].Contains(r.CurrentState))
                {
                    Y.Add(r.NextState);
                }
            }
            FiniteAutomatonState sY = null;
            foreach (var stateSet in stateSets)
```

```
                    {
                        if (stateSet.Value.SetEquals(Y))
                        {
                            sY = stateSet.Key;
                            break;
                        }
                    }
                    if (sY == null)
                    {
                        sY = CreateCompositeState(Y);
                        result.States.Add(sY);
                        stateSets.Add(sY, Y);
                    }
                    if (result.Rules.Add(new FiniteAutomatonRule(
                        sX, a, sY)))
                    {
                        change = true;
                    }
                }
            }
        }
        while (change);

        // compute final states
        foreach (FiniteAutomatonState sU in result.States)
        {
            if (!stateSets[sU].IsDisjoint(this.FinalStates))
            {
                result.FinalStates.Add(sU);
            }
        }

        return result;
    }
```

A deterministic finite automaton may also contain many useless states from which there is no computation that terminates in a final state.

Definition 5.5. *In a deterministic finite automaton, $M = (\Sigma, R)$, a state $q \in Q$ is* terminating *if there exists $w \in \Delta^*$ such that $qw \Rightarrow^* f$ in M with $f \in F$; otherwise, q is* nonterminating.

Consider a deterministic finite automaton, M. Of course, from its set of states Q, we want to remove as many nonterminating states as possible; however, we have to perform this removal carefully. Indeed, from a theoretical viewpoint, a total removal of these states might result into disturbing its determinism. That is, for a state $q \in Q$ and an input symbol $a \in \Delta$, the set of rules R may have no rule with qa on its left-hand side after the total removal, which violates Definition 5.3. Apart from this principal problem, from a more practical viewpoint, when occurring in q and reading a somewhere in the middle of an input string, M gets stuck, so it never completes reading the string. To illustrate, consider state $\langle\emptyset\rangle$ in the resulting automaton in Example 5.5. As obvious, this state is nonterminating, but its removal implies that the automaton cannot complete reading many input strings, such as *abab* or *baa*. Fortunately, as sketched in the rest of this section, we can always adapt any deterministic finite automaton so

1. it remains deterministic,
2. all its states are reachable, and
3. no more than one state is nonterminating.

As obvious, an automaton like this is suitable in terms of its implementation and use in practice; hence, its name is introduced next.

Definition 5.6. *A deterministic finite automaton is referred to as a* well-specified finite automaton *if all its states are reachable and no more than one state is nonterminating.*

In the rest of this section, we sketch a two-phase transformation of any deterministic finite automaton to an equivalent well-specified automaton. We only give a gist of this transformation while leaving its detailed description as an exercise.

Phase one

Consider any deterministic finite automaton, $I = ({}_I\Sigma, {}_IR)$. For I, we construct a well-specified finite automaton, $O = ({}_O\Sigma, {}_OR)$, such that $L(O) = L(I)$ by performing (1) and (2), given next.

1. Determine the set of all terminating states ${}_IQ_{term} \subseteq {}_IQ$. Observe that all final states are automatically terminating because ε takes I from any final state to the same state by making zero moves. Therefore, initialize ${}_IQ_{term}$ to F. If there exists $a \in \Delta$ and $p \in {}_IQ_{term}$ such that $oa \to p \in {}_IR$ with $o \in {}_IQ - {}_IQ_{term}$, then o is also terminating, so add o to ${}_IQ_{term}$. Repeat this extension of ${}_IQ_{term}$ until no more states can be added into ${}_IQ_{term}$. The resulting set ${}_IQ_{term}$ contains all terminating states in I.
2. Without any loss of generality, suppose that ${}_IQ$ only contains reachable states. Having determined all terminating states ${}_IQ_{term}$ in (1), we are now ready to construct O from I. If ${}_Is \notin {}_IQ_{term}$, $L(I) = \emptyset$, and the construction of O is trivial. If ${}_Is \in {}_IQ_{term}$, remove all nonterminating states from ${}_IQ$ and eliminate all rules containing nonterminating states in ${}_IR$. Denote the resulting automaton W.

Phase two

If W is already well-specified, we take O as W, and we are done. Suppose that W is not well-specified. To obtain an equivalent well-specified finite automaton O, set ${}_OQ$ to ${}_WQ \cup \{o\}$ and ${}_OR$ to ${}_WR \cup \{qa \to o \mid q \in {}_WQ,\ a \in {}_W\Delta$, and $qa \to p \in {}_WR$ for any $p \in {}_WQ\}$, where o is a new state.

As a result, we obtain the next theorem, whose rigorous proof is left as an exercise.

Theorem 5.3. *For every deterministic finite automaton, there exists an equivalent well-specified finite automaton.*

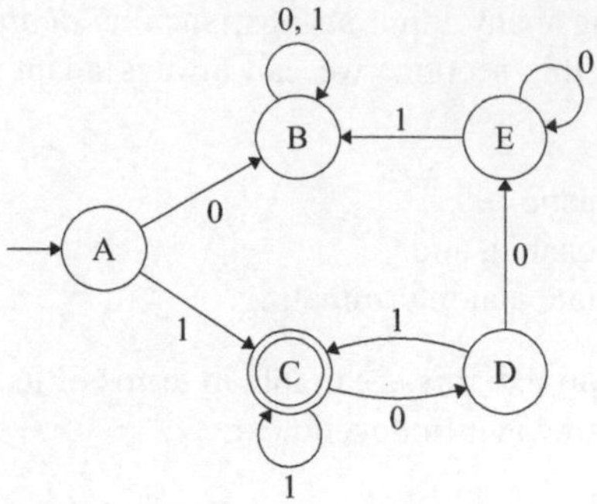

Figure 5.4 Deterministic finite automaton which is not well-specified

Example 5.6. *Observe that the deterministic finite automaton obtained in Example 5.5 represents a well-specified finite automaton. Therefore, to illustrate the two-phase transformation described above, we consider another deterministic finite automaton M, which is not well-specified. Specifically, let M be defined by rules*

$$A0 \to B,$$
$$A1 \to C,$$
$$B0 \to B,$$
$$B1 \to B,$$
$$C0 \to D,$$
$$C1 \to C,$$
$$D0 \to E,$$
$$D1 \to C,$$
$$E0 \to E,$$
$$E1 \to B.$$

The uppercases A to E denote states, where A is the start state and C is the only final state. 0 and 1 are input symbols. Its state diagram is shown in Figure 5.4. Observe that $L(M)$ consists of all binary strings starting with 1, in which every 0 is immediately followed by at least one 1; formally,

$$L(M) = \{1\}(\{0\}\{1\}^+)^*.$$

To convert this deterministic finite automaton to an equivalent well-specified deterministic finite automaton, follow the basic two-phase idea above. That is, by

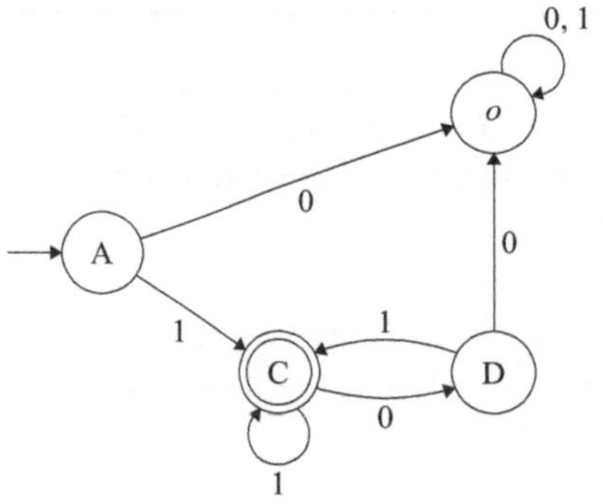

Figure 5.5 Well-specified finite automaton

using a new nonfinal state o, change this deterministic finite automaton to the completely specified deterministic finite automaton defined by its state diagram given in Figure 5.5

5.4 Reduction and minimization

Even a deterministic finite automaton M may contain some states that can be merged together without affecting $L(M)$. By merging these states, we can ultimately reduce the size of M with respect to the number of the states; as obvious, a reduction like this is frequently highly appreciated in practice. Before explaining how to achieve it, we need some terminology.

Definition 5.7. *Let* $M = (\Sigma, R)$ *be a well-specified finite automaton.*

(i) *A string* $w \in \Delta^*$ distinguishes *p from q, where* $p, q \in Q$, *if* $pw \Rightarrow^* u$ *and* $qw \Rightarrow^* v$ *in* M, *for some* $u, v \in Q$ *satisfying either* ($u \in F$ *and* $v \notin F$) *or* ($v \in F$ *and* $u \notin F$).

(ii) *State p is* distinguishable *from q if there exists an input string that distinguishes p from q; otherwise, p and q are* indistinguishable.

(iii) *M is a* reduced well-specified finite automaton *if each* $q \in Q$ *is distinguishable from all* $p \in Q - \{q\}$.

Next, we explain how to transform any well-specified finite automaton $I = ({}_I\Sigma, {}_IR)$ to a reduced well-specified automaton $O = ({}_O\Sigma, {}_OR)$ so both are equivalent. Since I represents a well-specified finite automaton, all its states are reachable and no more than one state is nonterminating (see Definition 5.6). Clearly, if ${}_IQ = {}_IF$, then $L(I) = {}_I\Delta^*$ because I is well-specified, and if ${}_IF = \emptyset$, $L(I) = \emptyset$. As obvious, in either case, the minimal finite automaton that accepts $L(I)$ has a single state. Therefore, we assume that ${}_IQ \neq {}_IF$ and ${}_IF \neq \emptyset$ in the rest of this section.

Algorithm 5.5: Reduction

Input: A well-specified finite automaton, $I = ({}_I\Sigma, {}_IR)$.
Output: A reduced well-specified finite automaton, $O = ({}_O\Sigma, {}_OR)$, such that $L(O) = L(I)$.

begin
set ${}_O\Delta = {}_I\Delta$ and ${}_OQ = \{\langle {}_IF\rangle, \langle {}_IQ - {}_IF\rangle\}$
while *there exist* $a \in {}_I\Delta$, $U, X \subset {}_IQ$ *such that*
$\emptyset \subset U \subset X$,
$\langle X\rangle \in O_Q$, *and*
$\{y \mid ua \Rightarrow y \text{ in } I,\ u \in U\}$ *and* $\{z \mid va \Rightarrow z \text{ in } I,\ v \in X - U\}$ *are two non-empty disjoint sets* **do**
set ${}_OQ = ({}_OQ - \{\langle X\rangle\}) \cup \{\langle U\rangle, \langle X - U\rangle\}$
end
set ${}_Os = \langle Y\rangle$, where $\langle Y\rangle \in {}_OQ$ with ${}_Is \in Y$
set ${}_OR = \{\langle X\rangle a \rightarrow \langle Y\rangle \mid qa \Rightarrow p,\ q \in X, p \in Y,\ a \in \Delta\}$
set ${}_OF = \{\langle Y\rangle \mid Y \subseteq {}_IF\}$
end

Basic Idea. First, the transformation of I to O constructs the set of states ${}_OQ$ so ${}_OQ \subseteq \{\langle W\rangle \mid W \subseteq {}_IQ\}$. Initially, set ${}_OQ$ to $\{\langle {}_IF\rangle, \langle {}_IQ\rangle - \langle {}_IF\rangle\}$ because ε obviously distinguishes $\langle {}_IF\rangle$ from $\langle {}_IQ\rangle - \langle {}_IF\rangle$, so $\langle {}_IF\rangle$ and $\langle {}_IQ\rangle - \langle {}_IF\rangle$ are necessarily distinguishable. Let $a \in {}_I\Delta$, $\emptyset \subset U \subset X \subset {}_IQ$, and $\langle X\rangle \in {}_OQ$. If $\{y \mid ua \Rightarrow y \text{ in } I, u \in U\}$ and $\{z \mid va \Rightarrow z \text{ in } I, v \in X - U\}$ are the two non-empty disjoint sets, then any state $u \in U$ is distinguishable from any state $v \in X - U$, so replace $\langle X\rangle$ with the two states, $\langle U\rangle$ and $\langle X - U\rangle$, and, thereby, increase card $({}_OQ)$ by one. Keep extending ${}_OQ$ in this way until no further extension is possible. To obtain O, set ${}_Os = \langle Y\rangle$, where $\langle Y\rangle \in {}_OQ$ with ${}_Is \in Y$, ${}_OF = \{\langle Y\rangle \mid Y \subseteq {}_IF\}$, and ${}_OR = \{\langle X\rangle a \rightarrow \langle Y\rangle \mid qa \Rightarrow p,\ q \in X,\ p \in Y,\ a \in {}_I\Delta\}$.

As an exercise, based upon the basic idea that precedes Algorithm 5.5, verify this algorithm.

Lemma 5.3. *Algorithm 5.5 is correct.*

From this lemma and Theorem 5.3, we obtain the next theorem.

Theorem 5.4. *For every deterministic finite automaton, there exists an equivalent reduced, well-specified finite automaton.*

Example 5.7. *Return to the well-specified finite automaton from Example 5.6. By Algorithm 5.5, convert this automaton to an equivalent minimum-state finite automaton O. This transformation first starts with two states* $\langle\langle 3\rangle, \langle 2, 3\rangle, \langle 4, 5\rangle\rangle$ *and* $\langle\langle 1\rangle, \langle\emptyset\rangle\rangle$.

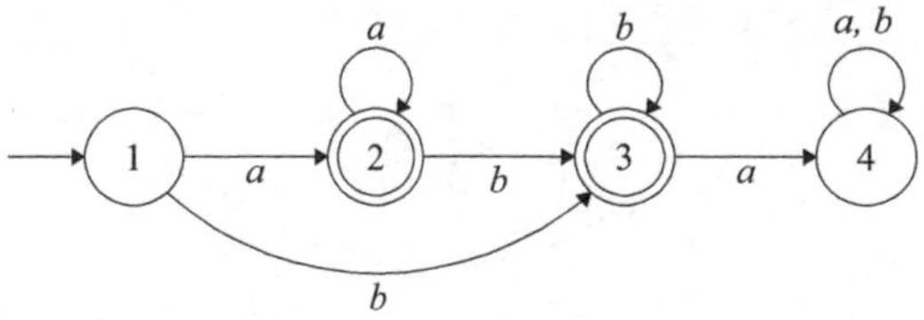

Figure 5.6 Reduced well-specified finite automaton

After this start, we replace $\langle\langle 3\rangle, \langle 2,3\rangle, \langle 4,5\rangle\rangle$ *with* $\langle\langle 2,3\rangle\rangle$ *and* $\langle\langle 3\rangle, \langle 4,5\rangle\rangle$ *as follows from these rules*

$$\langle 2,3\rangle a \rightarrow \langle 2,3\rangle,$$
$$\langle 2,3\rangle b \rightarrow \langle 3\rangle,$$
$$\langle 3\rangle a \rightarrow \langle \emptyset\rangle,$$
$$\langle 3\rangle b \rightarrow \langle 3\rangle,$$
$$\langle 4,5\rangle a \rightarrow \langle \emptyset\rangle,$$
$$\langle 4,5\rangle b \rightarrow \langle 4,5\rangle.$$

Then, we replace $\langle\langle 1\rangle, \langle\emptyset\rangle\rangle$ *with* $\langle\langle 1\rangle\rangle$ *and* $\langle\langle\emptyset\rangle\rangle$*. After this replacement, the set of states can no longer be extended by the algorithm. For simplicity, rename states* $\langle\langle 1\rangle\rangle$, $\langle\langle 2,3\rangle\rangle$, $\langle\langle 3\rangle, \langle 4,5\rangle\rangle$, *and* $\langle\langle\emptyset\rangle\rangle$ *to* 1, 2, 3, *and* 4, *respectively. States* 2 *and* 3 *are final. Construct the set of rules*

$$1a \rightarrow 2,$$
$$1b \rightarrow 3,$$
$$2a \rightarrow 2,$$
$$2b \rightarrow 3,$$
$$3a \rightarrow 4,$$
$$3b \rightarrow 3,$$
$$4a \rightarrow 4,$$
$$4b \rightarrow 4.$$

The resulting reduced well-specified finite automaton O is given in Figure 5.6.

Consider a reduced well-specified finite automaton with a nonterminating state. A removal of this state does not affect the accepted language. In fact, by this removal, we can even further minimize the number of states by one in the automaton. This minimization gives rise to the notion of a minimal finite automaton, defined next. Notice, however, that in a minimal finite automaton, there may exist a state q and an

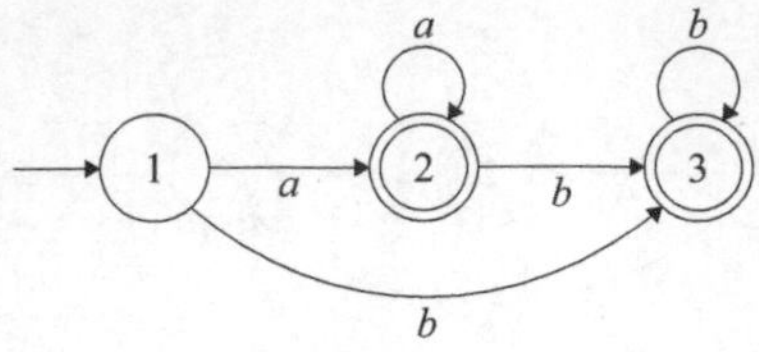

Figure 5.7 Minimal finite automaton

input symbol a such that no rule has qa on its left-hand side, which may represent an undesirable feature in terms of applications in practice.

Definition 5.8. *Let $M = (\Sigma, R)$ be a reduced well-specified finite automaton. We define the* minimal finite automaton, ${}_{\min}M$, underlying M *as follows:*

(i) If ${}_MQ$ has only terminating states, ${}_{\min}M$ coincides with M.
(ii) Let ${}_MQ$ have a nonterminating state q. ${}_{\min}M$ is constructed from M by removing q as well as all rules containing q.

A finite automaton O is a minimal finite automaton *if there exists a reduced well-specified finite automaton M such that O is the minimal finite automaton underlying M.*

From this definition, we obtain the next theorem.

Theorem 5.5. *For every reduced well-specified finite automaton, there exists an equivalent minimal finite automaton.*

Example 5.8. *Consider the reduced well-specified automaton constructed in Example 5.7. To obtain its underlying minimal finite automaton, we remove its single nonterminating state 4 as well as all rules containing it—that is, $3a \rightarrow 4$, $4a \rightarrow 4$, and $4b \rightarrow 4$. The state diagram of the minimal finite automaton is shown in Figure 5.7.*

Theorems 5.1, 5.2, 5.3, 5.4, and 5.5 imply the following summarizing theorem.

Theorem 5.6. *Finite automata, finite automata that always read, deterministic finite automata, well-specified finite automata, reduced well-specified finite automate, and minimal finite automata are all equally powerful.*

We close this section by noting that for any finite automaton I, there exists an essentially unique minimal finite automaton O equivalent with I—that is, any other minimal finite automaton equivalent to I completely coincides with O except that its names of states may differ. Specifically, consider the finite automaton from Example 5.1. This automaton accepts language

$$L = \{a\}^+\{b\}^* \cup \{b\}^+.$$

However, there exist infinitely many other finite automata that accept L as well. On the other hand, the only minimal finite automaton that accepts this language is the automaton in Figure 5.6.

5.5 Regular expressions

In this section, we introduce regular expressions and define regular languages by them. Then, we demonstrate that these expressions and finite automata are equivalent—more precisely, they both characterize the family of regular languages.

Regular expressions represent simple language-denoting formulas, based on the operations of concatenation, union, and closure.

Definition 5.9. *Let* Δ *be an alphabet. The* regular expressions *over* Δ *and the* languages that these expressions denote *are defined recursively as follows:*

(i) $\emptyset$ *is a regular expression denoting the empty set;*
(ii) ε *is a regular expression denoting* $\{\varepsilon\}$*;*
(iii) a*, where* $a \in \Delta$*, is a regular expression denoting* $\{a\}$*;*
(iv) if r *and* s *are regular expressions denoting the languages* R *and* S*, respectively, then*
  (a) $(r|s)$ *is a regular expression denoting* $R \cup S$*;*
  (b) (rs) *is a regular expression denoting* RS*;*
  (c) $(r)^*$ *is a regular expression denoting* R^*.

The language denoted by a regular expression r *is symbolically written as* $L(r)$*. A language* $L \subseteq \Delta^*$ *is* regular *iff there exists a regular expression* r *satisfying* $L = L(r)$*. The family of all regular languages is denoted by* ${}_{reg}\Phi$.

In practice as well as in theory, regular expressions sometimes use $+$ instead of $|$. This book uses the latter throughout.

Regular expressions are said to be *equivalent* if they define the same language. For instance, as a simple exercise, prove that $(a)^*$ and $((a)^*\varepsilon)$ are equivalent, but $(a)^*$ and $((a)^*\emptyset)$ are not.

In practice, we frequently simplify the *fully parenthesized regular expressions* created strictly by this definition by reducing the number of parentheses in them. To do so, we introduce the next convention concerning the priority of the three operators.

Convention 5.1. We automatically assume that * has higher precedence than operation concatenation, which has higher precedence than $|$. In addition, the expression rr^* and r^*r is usually written as r^+.

Based upon Convention 5.1, we can make regular expressions more succinct and readable. For instance, instead of $((a^*)(b(b^*)))$, we can write $(a^*)(b^+)$ or even a^*b^+. From a broader point of view, Convention 5.1 allows us to establish general equivalences between regular expressions. To illustrate, all the following regular expressions are equivalent

$$(r)^*,\ (r^*),\ ((r|\emptyset)^*),\ (r|\emptyset)^*,\ r^*|\emptyset^*,\ \text{and}\ r^*.$$

Specifically, instead of (r^*), we can thus equivalently write $(r)^*$ or r^*, and we frequently make use of these equivalent expressions later in this section (see, for instance, the proof of Lemma 5.4). Left as an exercise, there exist a number of other equivalences as well as algebraic laws obeyed by regular expressions, and many of them allow us to further simplify regular expressions.

An example concerning regular expressions applied to the English vocabulary is as follows.

Example 5.9. *We open this example in terms of formal English. Let* Δ *be the English alphabet together with a hyphen (-). Let* $W \subseteq \Delta^*$ *be the set of all possible well-formed English words, including compound words, such as made-up. Notice that* W *is infinite. For instance, consider the subset* $V \subseteq W$ *containing infinitely many words of the form*

(great-)^{i}grandparents

for all $i \geq 0$. *Purely theoretically speaking, they all represent well-formed English words although most of them such as*

great-great-great-great-great-great-great-great-great-great-great-grandparents

are rather uncommon words, which most people never utter during their lifetime. Although V *represents an infinite set of rather bizarre English words, it is easily and rigorously defined by a short regular expression of the form*

(great-)*grandparents.

To illustrate the use of regular expressions in terms of informal English, blah is a word that is repeatedly used to describe words or feelings where the specifics are considered unimportant or boring to the speaker or writer. It is usually seen in writing transcribing speech. An example of this use might be a sentence like this

He keeps making stupid excuses that he is tired and sleepy blah-blah-blah.

As the repetition of blah is unlimited, the set of all these compound words contains

blah, blah-blah, blah-blah-blah, blah-blah-blah-blah, . . .

Simply put, this set represents the infinite language $\{blah\text{-}\}^*\{blah\}$. *Observe that this language is denoted by a regular expressions of the form*

(blah-)*blah.

Equivalence with finite automata

First, we explain how to transform any deterministic finite automaton to an equivalent regular expression. Then, we describe the transformation of any regular expression to an equivalent finite automaton and, thereby, establish the equivalence between regular expressions and finite automata.

From finite automata to regular expressions

Next, we explain how to convert any deterministic finite automaton to an equivalent regular expression.

Basic Idea. Let $M = ({}_M\Sigma, {}_MR)$ be a deterministic finite automaton and card $(Q) = n$, for some $n \geq 1$. Rename states in M so $Q = \{q_1, \ldots, q_n\}$ with $q_1 = s$.

For all $i,j = 1, \ldots, n$ and all $k = 0, \ldots, n$, let $[i, k, j]$ denote the language consisting of all input strings on which M makes a computation from q_i to q_j during which every state q_l that M enters and leaves satisfies $l \leq k$. That is, for all $x \in \Delta^*$, $x \in [i, k, j]$ iff $q_i x \Rightarrow^+ q_j$ and for every $y \in$ prefixes $(x) - \{\varepsilon, x\}$, $q_i y \Rightarrow^+ q_l$ with $l \leq k$.

Definition 5.10. *For all $k = 0, \ldots, n$, we recursively define $[i, k, j]$ as*

(i) $[i, 0, j] = \{a \mid a \in \Delta \cup \{\varepsilon\},\ q_i a \Rightarrow^m q_j \text{ with } m \leq 1\}$;
(ii) *for* $k \geq 1$, $[i, k, j] = [i, k - l, j] \cup [i, k - 1, k][k, k - 1, k]^*[k, k - 1, j]$.

According to (i), $a \in [i, 0, j]$ iff $q_i a \rightarrow q_j \in R$, and $\varepsilon \in [i, 0, j]$ iff $i = j$. According to (ii), $[i, k - 1, j] \subseteq [i, k, j]$, so $[i, k, j]$ contains all input strings that take M from q_i to q_j during which it never passes through q_l with $l \geq k - 1$. Furthermore, $[i, k, j]$ includes $[i, k - 1, k][k, k - 1, k]^*[k, k - 1, j]$, which contain all input strings $x = uvw$ such that (a) u takes M from q_i to q_k, (b) v takes M from q_k back to q_k zero or more times, and (c) w takes M from q_k to q_j. Observe that during (a) through (c), M never enters and leaves q_l with $l \geq k - 1$. Furthermore, notice that M performs (b) zero times iff $v = \varepsilon$. Based upon these properties, the following lemma demonstrates that for every $[i, k, j]$, there is a regular expression ${}_{i,k,j}E$ such that $L({}_{i,k,j}E) = [i, k, j]$. From this lemma, Theorem 5.7 derives that $L(M)$ is denoted by the regular expression ${}_{1,n,j_1}E|{}_{1,n,j_2}E| \cdots |{}_{1,n,j_h}E$ with $F = \{q_{j_1}, q_{j_2}, \ldots, q_{j_h}\}$.

Lemma 5.4. *For all $i,j = 1, \ldots, n$ and all $k = 0, \ldots, n$, there exists a regular expression ${}_{i,k,j}E$ such that $L({}_{i,k,j}E) = [i, k, j]$, where $[i, k, j]$ has the meaning given in Definition 5.10.*

Proof. By induction on $k \geq 0$.

Basis. Let $i,j \in \{1, \ldots, n\}$ and $k = 0$. By (i) in Definition 5.10, $[i, 0, j] \subseteq \Delta \cup \{\varepsilon\}$, so there surely exists a regular expression ${}_{i,0,j}E$ such that $L({}_{i,0,j}E) = [i, 0, j]$.

Induction Hypothesis. Suppose that there exist $l \in \{1, \ldots, n\}$ such that for each $i,j \in \{1, \ldots, n\}$ and $k \leq l - 1$, there exists a regular expression ${}_{i,k,j}E$ such that $L({}_{i,k,j}E) = [i, k, j]$.

Induction Step. Consider any $[i, k, j]$, where $i,j \in \{1, \ldots, n\}$ and $k = l$. By the recursive formula (ii) above, $[i, k, j] = [i, k - 1, j] \cup [i, k - 1, k][k, k - 1, k]^*[k, k - 1, j]$. By the induction hypothesis, there exist regular expressions ${}_{i,k-1,j}E$, ${}_{i,k-1,k}E$, ${}_{k,k-1,k}E$, and ${}_{k,k-1,j}E$ such that $L({}_{i,k-1,j}E) = [i, k - 1, j]$, $L({}_{i,k-1,k}E) = [i, k - 1, k]$, $L({}_{k,k-1,k}E) = [k, k - 1, k]$, and $L({}_{k,k-1,j}E) = [k, k - 1, j]$. Thus, $[i, k, j]$ is denoted by the regular expression ${}_{i,k-1,j}E|{}_{i,k-1,k}E(k, k - 1, kE)^*k, k - 1, jE$. ■

Theorem 5.7. *For every deterministic finite automaton M, there exists an equivalent regular expression E.*

Proof. By the definition of $[i, k, j]$ for $k = n$ (see Definition 5.10), where $i,j \in \{1, \ldots, n\}$, $[i, n, j] = \{x \mid x \in \Delta^*,\ q_i x \Rightarrow^* q_j\}$. Thus, $L(M) = \{x \mid x \in \Delta^*,\ x \in [1, n, j],\ q_j \in F\}$. Thus,

$$L(M) = {}_{1,n,j_1}E|{}_{1,n,j_2}E| \cdots |{}_{1,n,j_h}E,$$

where $F = \{q_{j_1}, q_{j_2}, \ldots, q_{j_h}\}$. Consequently, the theorem holds true. ■

Example 5.10. *Consider the deterministic finite automaton M defined by its rules*

$$\begin{aligned} q_1a &\to q_1, \\ q_1b &\to q_2, \\ q_2b &\to q_2, \end{aligned}$$

where q_1 *is the start state and also the* q_2 *final state. Notice that* $L(M) = \{a\}^*\{b\}^+$. *Following the idea described above, construct*

$${}_{1,0,1}E = a|\varepsilon,\ {}_{1,0,2}E = b,\ {}_{2,0,2}E = b|\varepsilon,\ {}_{2,0,1}E = \emptyset.$$

Furthermore, we obtain

$$\begin{aligned}
{}_{1,1,1}E &= {}_{1,0,1}E|{}_{1,0,1}E({}_{1,0,1}E)^*{}_{1,0,1}E = (a|\varepsilon)|(a|\varepsilon)(a|\varepsilon)^*(a|\varepsilon) = a^*, \\
{}_{1,1,2}E &= {}_{1,0,2}E|{}_{1,0,1}E({}_{1,0,1}E)^*{}_{1,0,2}E = b|(a|\varepsilon)(a|\varepsilon)^*(b) = a^*b, \\
{}_{2,1,1}E &= {}_{2,0,1}E|{}_{2,0,1}E({}_{1,0,1}E)^*{}_{1,0,1}E = \emptyset|\emptyset(a|\varepsilon)^*(a|\varepsilon) = \emptyset, \\
{}_{2,1,2}E &= {}_{2,0,2}E|{}_{2,0,1}E({}_{1,0,1}E)^*{}_{1,0,2}E = (b|\varepsilon)|\emptyset(a|\varepsilon)^*b = b|\varepsilon, \\
{}_{1,2,1}E &= {}_{1,1,1}E|{}_{1,1,2}E({}_{2,1,2}E)^*{}_{2,1,1}E = a^*|a^*b(b|\varepsilon)^*\emptyset = a^*, \\
{}_{1,2,2}E &= {}_{1,1,2}E|{}_{1,1,2}E({}_{2,1,2}E)^*{}_{2,1,2}E = a^*b|a^*b(b|\varepsilon)^*(b|\varepsilon) = a^*b^+, \\
{}_{2,2,1}E &= {}_{2,1,1}E|{}_{2,1,2}E({}_{2,1,2}E)^*{}_{2,1,1}E = \emptyset|(b|\varepsilon)(b|\varepsilon)^*\emptyset = \emptyset, \\
{}_{2,2,2}E &= {}_{2,1,2}E|{}_{2,1,2}E({}_{2,1,2}E)^*{}_{2,1,2}E = (b|\varepsilon)|(b|\varepsilon)(b|\varepsilon)^*(b|\varepsilon) = b^*.
\end{aligned}$$

M has two states—q_1 *and* q_2*, where* q_1 *is the start state and* q_2 *is the only final state. Therefore,* ${}_{1,2,2}E$ *denotes* $L(M)$. *Indeed,* $L(M) = \{a\}^*\{b\}^+ = L({}_{1,2,2}E) = L(a^*b^+)$.

From regular expressions to finite automata

Consider fully parenthesized regular expressions over an alphabet—that is, regular expressions constructed strictly according to Definition 5.9 without involving any simplification introduced in Convention 5.1. Next, we transform these expressions to equivalent finite automata. To achieve this transformation, we first prove the following three statements:

1. There exist finite automata equivalent to the trivial regular expressions $\emptyset$, ε, and $a \in \Delta$.
2. For any pair of finite automata, I and J, there exist finite automata that accept $L(I) \cup L(J)$ and $L(I)L(J)$.
3. For any finite automaton, I, there exists a finite automaton that accepts $L(I)^*$.

By induction on the number of operators occurring in regular expressions, we then make use of these statements to obtain the desired transformation that turns any regular expression to an equivalent finite automaton.

Lemma 5.5. *There exist finite automata that accept the empty set,* $\{\varepsilon\}$, *and* $\{a\}$ *with* $a \in \Delta$.

Proof. First, any finite automaton with no final state accepts the empty set. Second, $\{\varepsilon\}$ is accepted by any one-state finite automaton that contains no rule. Its only state is the start state; simultaneously, this state is final. As obvious, this automaton accepts $\{\varepsilon\}$. Third, let $a \in \Delta$. Consider a one-rule finite automaton defined by one

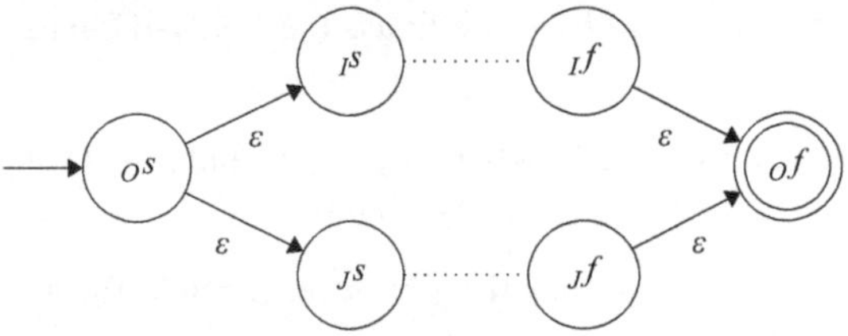

Figure 5.8 Finite automaton for union

Algorithm 5.6: Finite automaton for union

Input: Two finite automata, $I = ({}_I\Sigma, {}_IR)$ and $J = ({}_J\Sigma, {}_JR)$, such that ${}_IQ \cap {}_JQ = \emptyset$.
Output: A finite automaton, $O = ({}_O\Sigma, {}_OR)$, such that $L(O) = L(I) \cup L(J)$.

begin
set ${}_O\Sigma = {}_I\Sigma \cup {}_J\Sigma$
set ${}_OQ = {}_IQ \cup {}_JQ$
introduce two new states, ${}_Os$ and ${}_Of$, into ${}_OQ$, and define ${}_Os$ as the start state in O
set ${}_OF = \{{}_Of\}$
set ${}_OR = {}_IR \cup {}_JR \cup \{{}_Os \rightarrow {}_Is, {}_Os \rightarrow {}_Js\} \cup \{p \rightarrow {}_Of \mid p \in {}_IF \cup {}_JF\}$
end

---

rule $sa \rightarrow f$, where s is the start nonfinal state and f is the only final state. Clearly, $L(M) = \{a\}$. ∎

Next, we convert any two finite automata, I and J, to a finite automaton O satisfying $L(O) = L(I) \cup L(J)$.

Basic Idea (see Figure 5.8). Let us consider any two finite automata, I and J. Without any loss of generality, we assume that I and J have disjoint sets of states (if I and J contain some states in common, we rename states in either I or J so that they have no state in common). Construct O so that from its start state ${}_Os$, it enters ${}_Is$ or ${}_Js$ by an ε-move. From ${}_Is$, O simulates I, and from ${}_Js$, it simulates J. Whenever occurring in a final state of I or J, O can enter its only final state ${}_Of$ by an ε-move and stop. Thus, $L(O) = L(I) \cup L(J)$.

Lemma 5.6. *Algorithm 5.6 is correct.*

Proof. To establish $L(O) = L(I) \cup L(J)$, we first prove the following claim.

Claim 1. *For every $w \in {}_O\Delta^*$, $qw \Rightarrow^* p$ in O iff $qw \Rightarrow^* p$ in K with $K \in \{I, J\}$, $q, p \in {}_KQ$.*

Proof. Only If. By induction on $i \geq 0$, we prove for every $w \in {}_O\Delta^*$ and every $i \geq 0$,

$$qw \Rightarrow^i p \text{ in } O \text{ implies } qw \Rightarrow^i p \text{ in } K,$$

where $K \in \{I,J\}$ and $q,p \in {}_KQ$. As obvious, the "only-if" part follows from this implication.

Basis. Let $i = 0$, so $qw \Rightarrow^0 p$ in O, where $q,p \in {}_KQ$ and $K \in \{I,J\}$. Then, $q = p$ and $w = \varepsilon$. Clearly, $q \Rightarrow^0 q$ in K, and the basis holds.

Induction Hypothesis. Assume that the implication holds for all $0 \leq i \leq n$, where $n \in {}_0\mathbb{N}$.

Induction Step. Let $qw \Rightarrow^{n+1} p$ in O, where $q,p \in {}_KQ$ for some $K \in \{I,J\}$ and $w \in {}_O\Delta^*$. Because $n+1 \geq 1$, express $qw \Rightarrow^{n+1} p$ as $qva \Rightarrow^n oa \Rightarrow p$ in O, where $o \in {}_KQ$, $w = va$ with $a \in {}_O\Delta \cup \{\varepsilon\}$ and $v \in {}_O\Delta^*$. Since $oa \Rightarrow p$ in O, $oa \rightarrow p \in {}_OR$. Recall that $o,p \in {}_KQ$. Thus, by the definition of ${}_OR$ (see Algorithm 5.6), ${}_KR$ contains $oa \rightarrow p$, so $oa \rightarrow p$ in K. By the inductive hypothesis, $qv \Rightarrow^n o$ in K. Putting $qv \Rightarrow^n o$ and $oa \rightarrow p$ in K together, $qva \Rightarrow^n oa \Rightarrow p$ in K. Because $va = w$, $qw \Rightarrow^{n+1} p$ in K, which completes the induction step.

If. By analogy with the "only-if" part of the claim, prove its "if" part as an exercise. Consequently, the claim holds true. □

Observe that O makes every accepting computation so it starts by applying a rule from $\{{}_Os \rightarrow {}_Is, {}_Os \rightarrow {}_Js\}$ and ends by applying a rule from $\{p \rightarrow {}_Of \mid p \in {}_IF \cup {}_JF\}$. More formally, O accepts every $w \in L(O)$ by a computation of the form

$${}_Osw \Rightarrow {}_Ksw \Rightarrow^* {}_Kf \Rightarrow {}_Of,$$

where $K \in \{I,J\}$ and ${}_Kf \in {}_KF$. Consider the previous claim for $q = {}_Ks$ and $p = {}_Kf$ to obtain

$${}_Ksw \Rightarrow^* {}_Kf \text{ in } O \text{ iff } {}_Ksw \Rightarrow^* {}_Kf \text{ in } K.$$

Thus,

$${}_Osw \Rightarrow {}_Ksw \Rightarrow^* {}_Kf \Rightarrow {}_Of \text{ iff } {}_Ksw \Rightarrow^* {}_Kf \text{ in } K.$$

Hence, $w \in L(O)$ iff $w \in L(K)$. In other words, $L(O) = \{w \in L(K) \mid K \in \{I,J\}\}$. That is, $L(O) = L(I) \cup L(J)$, and the lemma holds. ■

Before going any further, we need the notion of a stop state, used in Algorithm 5.7.

Definition 5.11. *Let M be a finite automaton. In ${}_MQ$, a* stop state *is a state that does not occur on the left-hand side of any rule in ${}_MR$.*

By this definition, any finite automaton can never leave any of its stop states. By the next lemma, without any loss of generality, we can always assume that a finite automaton has precisely one final state, which is also a stop state.

Lemma 5.7. *For every finite automaton I, there exists an equivalent finite automaton O such that ${}_OF = \{{}_Of\}$ and ${}_Of$ is a stop state.*

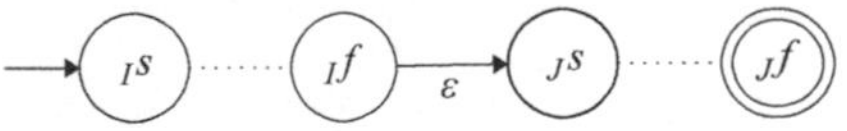

Figure 5.9 Finite automaton for concatenation

Algorithm 5.7: Finite automaton for concatenation

Input: Two finite automata, $I = ({}_I\Sigma, {}_IR)$ and $J = ({}_J\Sigma, {}_JR)$, such that ${}_IQ \cap {}_JQ = \emptyset$, ${}_IF = \{{}_If\}$, ${}_JF = \{{}_Jf\}$, ${}_If$ and ${}_JF$ are both stop states (see Lemma 5.7).

Output: A finite automaton, $O = ({}_O\Sigma, {}_OR)$, such that $L(O) = L(I)L(J)$.

begin
  set ${}_O\Sigma = {}_I\Sigma \cup {}_J\Sigma$
  set ${}_OQ = {}_IQ \cup {}_JQ$
  set ${}_Os = {}_Is$
  set ${}_OF = {}_Jf$
  set ${}_OR = {}_IR \cup {}_JR \cup \{{}_If \rightarrow {}_Js\}$
end

Proof. Let I be a finite automaton. Take any finite automaton J such that $L(J) = \emptyset$ (see Lemma 5.5). By using Algorithm 5.6, convert I and J to a finite automaton O satisfying $L(O) = L(I) \cup L(J) = L(I) \cup \emptyset = L(I)$. Observe that O constructed in this way has a single final state ${}_Of$, which is also a stop state. ■

We are now ready to convert any pair of finite automata, I and J, to a finite automaton O that accepts $L(O) = L(I)L(J)$.

Basic Idea (see Figure 5.9). Consider any two finite automata, I and J, such that ${}_IQ \cap {}_JQ = \emptyset$. Without any loss of generality, suppose that I has a single final state, ${}_If$, such that ${}_If$ is also a stop state, and J has also only one final state, ${}_Jf$, and this state is a stop state (see Lemma 5.7). Construct O as follows: starting from ${}_Is$, O simulates I until it enters ${}_If$, from which O makes an ε-move to ${}_Js$. From ${}_Js$, O simulates J until O enters ${}_Jf$, which is also the only final state in O. Thus, $L(O) = L(I)L(J)$.

Lemma 5.8. *Algorithm 5.7 is correct.*

Proof. Notice that O accepts every $w \in L(O)$ by a computation of the form

$${}_Isuv \Rightarrow^* {}_Ifv \Rightarrow {}_Jsv \Rightarrow^* {}_Jf,$$

where $w = uv$. Thus, ${}_Isu \Rightarrow^* {}_If$ in I, and ${}_Jsv \Rightarrow^* {}_Jf$ in J. Therefore, $u \in L(I)$ and $v \in L(J)$, so $L(O) \subseteq L(I)L(J)$. In a similar way, demonstrate $L(I)L(J) \subseteq L(O)$. Hence, $L(O) = L(I)L(J)$. A rigorous version of this proof is left as an exercise. ■

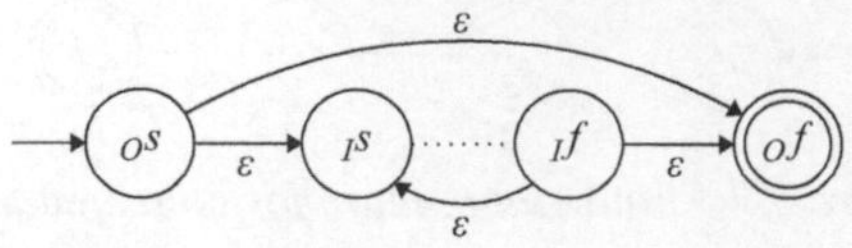

Figure 5.10 Finite automaton for iteration

Algorithm 5.8: Finite automaton for iteration.

Input: A finite automaton, $I = ({}_I\Sigma, {}_IR)$, such that ${}_IF = \{{}_If\}$ and ${}_If$ is a stop state (see Lemma 5.7).

Output: A finite automaton, $O = ({}_O\Sigma, {}_OR)$, such that $L(O) = L(I)^*$.

begin

set ${}_O\Sigma = {}_I\Sigma$

set ${}_OQ = {}_IQ$

introduce two new states, ${}_Os$ and ${}_Of$, into ${}_OQ$; define ${}_Os$ as the start state in O

set ${}_OF = \{{}_Of\}$

set ${}_OR = {}_IR \cup \{{}_Os \to {}_Of, {}_Os \to {}_Is, {}_If \to {}_Is, {}_If \to {}_Of\}$

end

We now convert any finite automaton I to a finite automaton O satisfying $L(I) = L(O)^*$.

Basic Idea (see Figure 5.10). Consider a finite automaton, I. Without any loss of generality, suppose that I has a single final state ${}_If$ such that ${}_If$ is also a stop state (see Lemma 5.7). Apart from all states from I, O has two new states, ${}_Os$ and ${}_Of$, where ${}_Os$ is its start state and ${}_Of$ is its only final state. From ${}_Os$, O can enter ${}_Of$ without reading any symbol, thus accepting $\emptyset$. In addition, it can make an ε-move to ${}_Is$ to simulate I. Occurring in ${}_If$, O can enter ${}_Is$ or ${}_Of$ by making an ε-move. If O enters ${}_Is$, it starts simulating another sequence of moves in I. If O enters ${}_Of$, it successfully completes its computation. Therefore, $L(O) = L(I)^*$.

Lemma 5.9. *Algorithm 5.8 is correct.*

Proof. To see the reason why $L(O) = L(I)^*$, observe that O accepts every $w \in L(O) - \{\varepsilon\}$ in this way

$$\begin{aligned} {}_Osv_1v_2\cdots v_n &\Rightarrow^* {}_Isv_1v_2\cdots v_n \\ &\Rightarrow^* {}_Ifv_2\cdots v_n \\ &\Rightarrow {}_Isv_2\cdots v_n \\ &\Rightarrow^* {}_Ifv_3\cdots v_n \\ &\vdots \\ &\Rightarrow {}_Isv_n \\ &\Rightarrow^* {}_If \\ &\Rightarrow {}_Of, \end{aligned}$$

where $n \in \mathbb{N}$, $w = v_1 v_2 \cdots v_n$ with $v_i \in L(I)$ for all $i = 1, \ldots, n$. Furthermore, O accepts ε as ${}_O s\varepsilon \Rightarrow {}_O f$. Therefore, $L(I)^* \subseteq L(O)$. Similarly, prove $L(O) \subseteq L(I)^*$. As $L(I)^* \subseteq L(O)$ and $L(O) \subseteq L(I)^*$, $L(O) = L(I)^*$. A rigorous version of this proof is left as an exercise. ■

We are now ready to prove that for any regular expression, there is an equivalent finite automaton. In the proof, we will consider fully parenthesized regular expressions defined strictly according to Definition 5.9 (that is, we do not consider their simplified versions introduced in Convention 5.1).

Theorem 5.8. *Let r be a regular expression, then there exists a finite automaton M such that $L(r) = L(M)$.*

Proof. By induction on the number of operators in r. Let r be a fully parenthesized regular expressions over an alphabet Δ (see Definition 5.9).

Basis. Let r be a fully parenthesized regular expression that contains no operator. By Definition 5.9, r is of the form $\emptyset$, ε, or a with $a \in \Delta$. Then, this basis follows from Lemma 5.5.

Induction Hypothesis. Suppose that Theorem 5.8 holds for every regular expression containing n or fewer operators, for some $n \in {}_0\mathbb{N}$.

Induction Step. Let e be any fully parenthesized regular expression containing $n + 1$ operators. Thus, e is of the form $(r|s)$, (rs), or $(r)^*$, where r and s are regular expressions with no more than n operators, so for r and s, Theorem 5.8 holds by the induction hypothesis. These three forms of e are considered next.

(i) Let $e = (r|s)$, so $L(e) = L(r) \cup L(s)$. As Theorem 5.8 holds for r and s, there are finite automata I and J such that $L(r) = L(I)$ and $L(s) = L(J)$. By using Algorithm 5.6, verified by Lemma 5.6, convert I and J to a finite automaton O satisfying $L(O) = L(I) \cup L(J)$, so $L(O) = L(e)$.

(ii) Let $e = (rs)$, so $L(e) = L(r)L(s)$. Let I and J be finite automata such that $L(r) = L(I)$ and $L(s) = L(J)$. By using Algorithm 5.7, turn I and J to a finite automaton O satisfying $L(O) = L(I)L(J)$, so $L(O) = L(e)$.

(iii) Let $e = (r)^*$, so $L(e) = L((r)^*)$. Let I be a finite automaton such that $L(r) = L(I)$. By using Algorithm 5.8, convert I to a finite automaton O satisfying $L(O) = L(I)^* = L(r)^* = L(e)$.

■

Taking a closer look at the previous proof, we see that it actually presents a method of converting any fully parenthesized regular expression to an equivalent finite automaton as sketched next.

Basic Idea. Consider any regular expression. Processing from the innermost parentheses out, determine how the expression is constructed by Definition 5.9. Follow the conversion described in the previous proof and simultaneously create

Table 5.4 Regular expressions and finite automata

	Regular expression	Finite automaton
1	a	M_1
2	b	M_2
3	c	M_3
4	$(b\|c)$	M_4
5	$((b\|c))^*$	M_5
6	$(a((b\|c))^*)$	M_6

the equivalent finite automata by the algorithms referenced in this proof. More specifically, let r and s be two regular expressions obtained during the construction.

(i) Let r be a regular expression of the form $\emptyset$, ε, or a, where $a \in \Delta$. Turn r to an equivalent finite automaton by the method given in the proof of Lemma 5.5.

(ii) Let r and s be two regular expressions, and let I and J be finite automata equivalent with r and s, respectively. Then,
- (a) $(r|s)$ is equivalent to the finite automaton constructed from I and J by Algorithm 5.6;
- (b) (rs) is equivalent to the finite automaton constructed from I and J by Algorithm 5.7;
- (c) $(r)^*$ is equivalent to the finite automaton constructed from I by Algorithm 5.8.

Leaving an algorithm that rigorously reformulates this method as an exercise, we next illustrate it by an example.

Example 5.11. *Consider $(a((b|c))^*)$ as a fully parenthesized regular expression. By Definition 5.9, we see that this expression is step-by-step constructed by making expressions a, b, c, $(b|c)$, $((b|c))^*$, and $(a((b|c))^*)$, numbered by* 1, 2, 3, 4, 5, *and* 6, *respectively, for brevity; in this example, we construct the six finite automata, M_1 through M_6, so M_i is equivalent to regular expression i, where $i = 1, \ldots, 6$ (see Table 5.4). During the construction of M_i, $1 \leq i \leq 5$, we always introduce two new states, denoted by ${}_is$ and ${}_if$ (during the construction of M_6, we need no new state).*

Consider the first three elementary subexpressions a, b, and c that denote languages $\{a\}$, $\{b\}$, and $\{c\}$, respectively. Based on the construction given in the proof of Lemma 5.5, we construct M_1, M_2, and M_3 that accept $\{a\}$, $\{b\}$, and $\{c\}$, respectively. From expressions b and c, we make expression $(b|c)$ that denotes $\{b\} \cup \{c\}$. Recall that M_2 and M_3 are equivalent to expressions b and c, respectively; that is, $L(M_2) = \{b\}$ and $L(M_3) = \{c\}$. Thus, with M_2 and M_3 as the input of Algorithm 5.6, we construct M_4 that accepts $L(M_2) \cup L(M_3) = \{b\} \cup \{c\} = \{b, c\}$. From $(b|c)$, we can make $((b|c))^*$ that denotes $(\{b\} \cup \{c\})^* = \{b, c\}^*$. Recall that M_4 is equivalent to regular expression 4. *Therefore, with M_4 as the input of Algorithm 5.8, we construct M_5 equivalent to regular expression* 5. *From regular expressions* 1 *and* 5, *we*

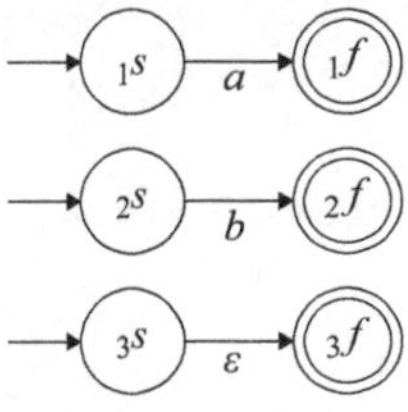

Figure 5.11 M_1, M_2, and M_3

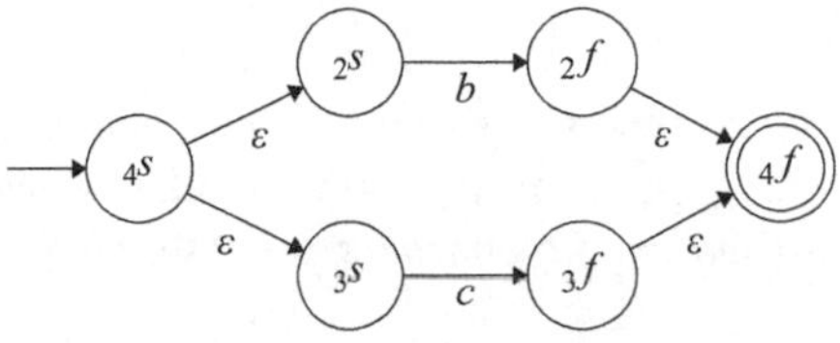

Figure 5.12 M_4

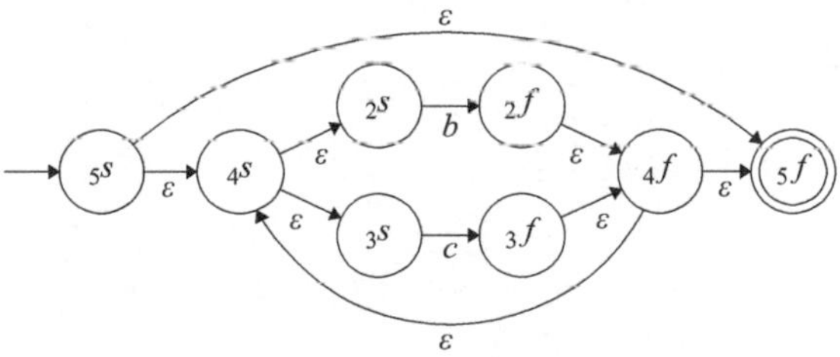

Figure 5.13 M_5

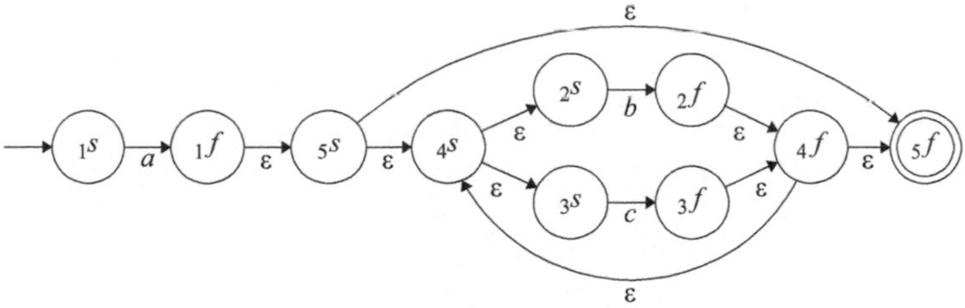

Figure 5.14 M_6

make regular expression 6 *that denotes* $\{a\}(\{b\} \cup \{c\})^* = \{a\}\{b, c\}^*$. *$M_1$ and M_5 are equivalent to regular expressions* 1 *and* 5, *respectively. Therefore, with M_1 and M_5 as the input of Algorithm 5.7, we construct a finite automaton M_6 equivalent to regular expression* 6 *as desired. Figures 5.11–5.14 summarize this construction.*

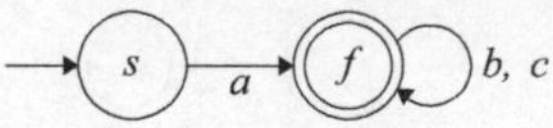

Figure 5.15 M_{min}

By algorithms given in Section 5.4, we can now turn M_6 *to an equivalent minimal finite automaton* M_{min} *depicted in Figure 5.15.*

We close this chapter by the next crucially important theorem, which summarizes Theorems 5.6, 5.7, and 5.8.

Theorem 5.9. *The regular expressions and the finite automata are equivalent—that is, they both characterize* $_{reg}\Phi$. *Consequently, all the restricted versions of finite automata mentioned in Theorem 5.6 characterize* $_{reg}\Phi$, *too.*

Chapter 6
Context-free grammars

Context-free grammars represent language-generating rewriting systems. Each of their rewriting rules has a single symbol on its left-hand sides. By repeatedly applying these rules, these grammars generate sentences of their languages.

This chapter gives a mathematical introduction into context-free grammars. First, Section 6.1 defines their basic versions. Then, Section 6.2 presents several mathematical methods that transform the basic versions so that the transformed versions are as powerful as the original versions but are much easier to handle in theory as well as in practice.

6.1 Mathematical elements of context-free grammars

As already stated, the mathematical notion of a context-free grammar represents a language-generating rewriting system based upon finitely many terminal symbols, nonterminal symbols, and grammatical rules. Terminal symbols occur in the language generated by the grammar, while nonterminal symbols do not. Each rule has a single nonterminal symbol on its left-hand side, while its right-hand side is a string, which may contain both terminal and nonterminal symbols. Starting from a special start symbol, the grammar repeatedly rewrites nonterminal symbols according to its rules until it obtains a sentence—that is, a string that solely consists of terminal symbols. The set of all sentences represents the language generated by the grammar.

Since context-free grammars represent special cases of rewriting systems (see Chapter 4), we often use the mathematical terminology concerning these systems throughout the present section. Specifically, we apply the relations $\Rightarrow$, $\Rightarrow^n$, $\Rightarrow^+$, and $\Rightarrow^*$ to these grammars.

Definition 6.1. *A* context-free grammar *is a rewriting system* $G = (\Sigma, R)$, *where*

- Σ *is divided into two disjoint subalphabets, denoted by* N *and* Δ *and*
- R *is a finite set of rules of the form* $A \to x$, *where* $A \in N$ *and* $x \in \Sigma^*$.

N *and* Δ *are referred to as the* alphabet of nonterminal symbols *and the* alphabet of terminal symbols, *respectively.* N *contains a special* start symbol, *denoted by* S. *Let* $p = x \to y \in R$ *be a rule. The strings* x *and* y *are called the* left-hand side *and* right-hand side *of* p, *denoted by* lhs p *and* rhs p, *respectively.*

If $S \Rightarrow^* w$, *where* $w \in \Sigma^*$, G derives w, *and* w *is a* sentential form. $F(G)$ *denotes the set of all sentential forms derived by* G. *The* language generated by G, *symbolically* *denoted by* $L(G)$, *is defined as* $L(G) = F(G) \cap \Delta^*$. *Members of* $L(G)$ *are called* sentences. *If* $S \Rightarrow^* w$ *and* w *is a sentence,* $S \Rightarrow^* w$ *is a* successful derivation *in* G.

Let L *be a language. If there exists a context-free grammar satisfying* $L = L(G)$, L *is called a* context-free language.

To give an intuitive insight into this strictly mathematical definition, take a string xAy and a rule $A \to u \in R$, where $A \in N$ and $x, y, u \in \Sigma^*$. By using $A \to u$, G makes a derivation step from xAy to xuy, so it changes A to u in xAy, symbolically written as $xAy \Rightarrow xuy$. If G makes a sequence of derivation steps from S to a string $w \in \Sigma^*$, then w is a sentential form. Every sentential form over Δ is a sentence, and the set of all sentences is the language of G, denoted by $L(G)$. As a result, every sentence w satisfies $S \Rightarrow^* w$ with $w \in \Delta^*$, so $L(G) = \{w \in \Delta^* \mid S \Rightarrow^* w\}$.

As already pointed out, all the notions introduced for rewriting systems are applicable to G. Specifically, by $u \Rightarrow v$ $[r]$, where $u, v \in \Sigma^*$ and $r \in R$, we say that G directly rewrites u to v by r or, as we customarily say in terms of context-free grammars, *G makes a derivation step from u to v by r*. Furthermore, to express that G makes $u \Rightarrow^* w$ according to a sequence of rules, $r_1 r_2 \cdots r_n$, we write $u \Rightarrow^* v$ $[r_1 r_2 \cdots r_n]$, which is read as a *derivation from u to v by using $r_1 r_2 \cdots r_n$*. On the other hand, whenever the information regarding the applied rules is immaterial, we omit these rules. In other words, we often simplify $u \Rightarrow v$ $[r]$ and $u \Rightarrow^* v$ $[r_1 r_2 \cdots r_n]$ to $u \Rightarrow v$ and $u \Rightarrow^* v$, respectively.

For any context-free grammar G, we automatically assume that Σ, N, Δ, S, and R denote the total alphabet, the alphabet of nonterminal symbols, the alphabet of terminal symbols, the start symbol, and the set of rules, respectively. If there exists a danger of confusion, we mark Σ, N, Δ, S, and R with G as ${}_G\Sigma$, ${}_GN$, ${}_G\Delta$, ${}_GS$, ${}_GR$, respectively, in order to clearly relate these components to G (in particular, we make these marks when several context-free grammars are simultaneously discussed). For brevity, we often abbreviate nonterminal symbols and terminal symbols to *nonterminals* and *terminals*, respectively. If we want to express that a nonterminal A forms the left-hand side of a rule, we refer to this rule as an *A-rule*. If we want to specify that A is rewritten during a derivation step, $xAy \Rightarrow xuy$, we underline this A as $x\underline{A}y \Rightarrow xuy$.

For brevity, G is often defined by simply listing its rules together with specifying its nonterminals and terminals, usually denoted by uppercases and lowercases, respectively.

Suppose we have designed a context-free grammar G for a language L. Having completed this design, we obviously want to verify that G generates precisely L. In other words, in a strictly mathematical way, we demonstrate that $L(G) = L$. As a rule, we prove this equation by using mathematical induction as illustrated in the rest of section.

Example 6.1. *Consider* $L = \{a^k b^k \mid k \geq 1\}$. *In principle, we generate the strings from* L *by a context-free grammar,* G, *so* G *derives sentential forms*

$$S, aSb, aaSbb, aaaSbbb, \ldots$$

in which G *rewrites* S *with* ab *during the very last derivation step. Formally,* $G = (\Sigma, R)$, *where* $\Sigma = \{a, b, S\}$ *and* $R = \{S \to aSb, S \to ab\}$. *In* Σ, $\Delta = \{a, b\}$ *is the alphabet of terminals and* $N = \{S\}$ *is the alphabet of nonterminals, where* S *is the start symbol of* G. *Let us label the two rules of* G *as*

$$\begin{aligned} 1 &: S \rightarrow aSb, \\ 2 &: S \rightarrow ab. \end{aligned}$$

Consider $aaSbb$. *By using rule* 1, G *rewrites* S *with* aSb *in this string, so* $aaSbb \Rightarrow aaaSbbb$ [1]. *By using rule* 2, G *rewrites* S *with* ab, *so* $aaSbb \Rightarrow aaabbb$ [2]. *By using the sequence of rules* 112, G *makes*

$$\begin{aligned} aaSbb &\Rightarrow aaaSbbb \quad [1] \\ &\Rightarrow aaaaSbbbb \quad [1] \\ &\Rightarrow aaaaabbbbb \quad [2]. \end{aligned}$$

Briefly, we write $aaSbb \Rightarrow^* aaaaabbbbb$ [112] *or, even more simply,* $aaSbb \Rightarrow^* aaaaabbbbb$.

To verify that G *generates* $\{a^k b^k \mid k \geq 1\}$, *recall that by using rule* 1, G *replaces* S *with* aSb, *and by rule* 2, G *replaces* S *with* ab. *Consequently, every successful derivation has the form*

$$S \Rightarrow aSb \Rightarrow aaSbb \Rightarrow \cdots \Rightarrow a^k Sb^k \Rightarrow a^{k+1} b^{k+1},$$

which G *makes according to a sequence of rules of the form* $1^k 2$, *for some* $k \geq 0$. *In symbols,* $S \Rightarrow^* a^{k+1} b^{k+1}$ $[1^k 2]$. *From these observations, we see* $L(G) = \{a^k b^k \mid k \geq 1\}$; *a detailed verification of this identity is left as an exercise.*

The two-rule context-free grammar considered in the previous example generates every sentence by a unique derivation, so the analysis of its derivation process is easy. As a result, the determination of its generated language represents a trivial task as well. In a general case, however, a context-free grammar G may contain several occurrences of nonterminals on the right-hand sides of their rules and generate their sentences by a variety of different derivations. Under these circumstances, a mathematical verification that G properly generates the language under consideration may be more complicated as shown in the next example.

From a more broader viewpoint, this example also illustrates a typical two-phase approach to achieving complicated results. During the first phase, a more general result is established. Then, as a consequence resulting from the general case, the desired result is derived during the second phase.

Example 6.2. *Let* K *be the language containing all non-empty strings consisting of an equal number of as and bs. To rephrase this mathematically,*

$$K = \{w \mid w \in \{a, b\}^+ \text{ and } \mathrm{occur}(w, a) = \mathrm{occur}(w, b)\}.$$

In this example, we prove that K is generated by the context-free grammar G defined as

$$1 : S \rightarrow aB,$$
$$2 : S \rightarrow bA,$$
$$3 : A \rightarrow a,$$
$$4 : A \rightarrow aS,$$
$$5 : A \rightarrow bAA,$$
$$6 : B \rightarrow b,$$
$$7 : B \rightarrow bS,$$
$$8 : B \rightarrow aBB.$$

We first prove the following claim, which says something more than we actually need to establish $K = L(G)$. From this claim, we subsequently obtain $K = L(G)$ as a straightforward consequence of this claim.

Claim 1. *For all $w \in \{a, b\}^*$, these three equivalences hold*

(i) $S \Rightarrow^* w$ *iff* occur $(a, w) =$ occur (b, w);
(ii) $A \Rightarrow^* w$ *iff* occur $(a, w) =$ occur $(b, w) + 1$;
(iii) $B \Rightarrow^* w$ *iff* occur $(b, w) =$ occur $(a, w) + 1$.

Proof. This claim is proved by induction on $|w| \geq 1$.

Basis. Let $|w| = 1$.

(i) From S, G generates no sentence of length one. On the other hand, no sentence of length one satisfies occur $(a, w) =$ occur (b, w). Thus, in this case, the basis holds vacuously.
(ii) Examine G to see that if $A \Rightarrow^* w$ with $|w| = 1$, then $w = a$. For $w = a$, $A \Rightarrow^* w$ [3]. Therefore, (ii) holds in this case.
(iii) Prove (iii) by analogy with the proof of (ii).

Consequently, the basis holds.

Induction Hypothesis. Assume that there exists a positive integer $n \geq 1$ such that the claim holds for every $w \in \{a, b\}^*$ satisfying $1 \leq |w| \leq n$.

Induction Step. Let $w \in \{a, b\}^*$ with $|w| = n + 1$.

Consider (i) in the claim. To prove its *only-if* part, consider any derivation of the form $S \Rightarrow^* w$ $[\rho]$, where ρ is a sequence of rules. This derivation starts from S. As only rules 1 and 2 have S on the left-hand side, express $S \Rightarrow^* w$ $[\rho]$ as $S \Rightarrow^* w[r\pi]$, where $\rho = r\pi$ and $r \in \{1, 2\}$.

(i) If $r = 1$, $S \Rightarrow^* w$ $[1\pi]$, where $1\colon S \rightarrow aB$. At this point, $w = av$, and $B \Rightarrow^* v$ $[\pi]$, where $|v| = n$. By the induction hypothesis, (iii) holds for v, so occur $(b, v) =$ occur $(a, v) + 1$. Therefore, occur $(a, w) =$ occur (b, w).
(ii) If $r = 2$, $S \Rightarrow^* w$ $[2\pi]$, where $2\colon S \rightarrow bA$. Thus, $w = bv$, and $A \Rightarrow^* v$ $[\pi]$, where $|v| = n$. By the induction hypothesis, (ii) holds for v, so occur $(a, v) =$ occur $(b, v) + 1$. As $w = bv$, occur $(a, w) =$ occur (b, w).

To prove the *if* part of (i), suppose that $\text{occur}(a, w) = \text{occur}(b, w)$. Clearly, $w = av$ or $w = bv$, for some $v \in \{a, b\}^*$ with $|v| = n$.

(i) Let $w = av$. Then, $|v| = n$ and $\text{occur}(a, v) + 1 = \text{occur}(b, v)$. As $|v| = n$, by the induction hypothesis, we have $B \Rightarrow^* v$ iff $\text{occur}(b, v) = \text{occur}(a, v) + 1$ from (iii). By using $1\colon S \to aB$, we obtain $S \Rightarrow aB$ [1]. Putting $S \Rightarrow aB$ and $B \Rightarrow^* v$ together, we have $S \Rightarrow aB \Rightarrow^* av$, so $S \Rightarrow^* w$ because $w = av$.

(ii) Let $w = bv$. Then, $|v| = n$ and $\text{occur}(a, v) = \text{occur}(b, v) + 1$. By the induction hypothesis, we have $A \Rightarrow^* v$ iff $\text{occur}(a, v) = \text{occur}(b, v) + 1$ (see (ii)). By $2\colon S \to bA$, G makes $S \Rightarrow bA$. Thus, $S \Rightarrow bA$ and $A \Rightarrow^* v$, so $S \Rightarrow^* w$.

Take (ii) in the claim. To prove its *only-if* part, consider any derivation of the form $A \Rightarrow^* w\ [\rho]$, where ρ is a sequence of rules in G. Express $A \Rightarrow^* w\ [\rho]$ as $A \Rightarrow^* w\ [r\pi]$, where $\rho = r\pi$ and $r \in \{3, 4, 5\}$ because rules $3\colon A \to a$, $4\colon A \to aS$, and $5\colon A \to bAA$ are all the A-rules in G.

(i) If $r = 3$, $A \Rightarrow^* w\ [r\pi]$ is a one-step derivation $A \Rightarrow a$ [3], so $w = a$, which satisfies $\text{occur}(a, w) = \text{occur}(b, w) + 1$.

(ii) If $r = 4$, $A \Rightarrow^* w\ [4\pi]$, where $4\colon A \Rightarrow aS$. Thus, $w = av$, and $S \Rightarrow^* v\ [\pi]$, where $|v| = n$. By the induction hypothesis, from (i), $\text{occur}(a, v) = \text{occur}(b, v)$, so $\text{occur}(a, w) = \text{occur}(b, w) + 1$.

(iii) If $r = 5$, $A \Rightarrow^* w\ [5\pi]$, where $5\colon A \Rightarrow bAA$. Thus, $w = buv$, $A \Rightarrow^* u$, $A \Rightarrow^* v$, where $|u| \le n$, $|v| \le n$. By the induction hypothesis, from (ii),

$$\text{occur}(a, u) = \text{occur}(b, u) + 1$$

and

$$\text{occur}(a, v) = \text{occur}(b, v) + 1,$$

so $\text{occur}(a, uv) = \text{occur}(b, uv) + 2$. Notice that

$$\text{occur}(b, uv) = \text{occur}(b, w) - 1$$

implies

$$\text{occur}(a, uv) - 2 = \text{occur}(b, w) - 1.$$

Furthermore, from

$$\text{occur}(a, uv) - 2 = \text{occur}(b, w) - 1$$

it follows that

$$\text{occur}(a, uv) = \text{occur}(a, w),$$

so

$$\text{occur}(a, w) = \text{occur}(b, w) + 1.$$

To prove the *if* part of (ii), suppose that $\text{occur}(a, w) = \text{occur}(b, w) + 1$. Obviously, $w = av$ or $w = bv$, for some $v \in \{a, b\}^*$ with $|v| = n$.

(i) Let $w = av$. At this point, $|v| = n$ and $\text{occur}(a, v) = \text{occur}(b, v)$. As $|v| = n$, by the induction hypothesis, we have $S \Rightarrow^* v$. By using $4\colon A \to aS$, $A \Rightarrow aS$ [4].

Putting $A \Rightarrow aS$ and $S \Rightarrow^* v$ together, we obtain $A \Rightarrow aS \Rightarrow^* av$, so $A \Rightarrow^* w$ because $w = av$.

(ii) Let $w = bv$. At this point, $|v| = n$ and $\text{occur}(a, v) = \text{occur}(b, v) + 2$. Express v as $v = uz$ so that $\text{occur}(a, u) = \text{occur}(b, u) + 1$ and $\text{occur}(a, z) = \text{occur}(b, z) + 1$; as an exercise, we leave a proof that $\text{occur}(a, v) = \text{occur}(b, v) + 2$ implies that v can always be expressed in this way. Since $|v| = n$, $|u| \leq n \geq |z|$. Thus, by the induction hypothesis (see (ii)), we have $A \Rightarrow^* u$ and $A \Rightarrow^* z$. By using $5: A \to bAA$, $A \Rightarrow bAA$ [5]. Putting $A \Rightarrow bAA$, $A \Rightarrow^* u$, and $A \Rightarrow^* z$ together, we obtain $A \Rightarrow bAA \Rightarrow^* buz$, so $A \Rightarrow^* w$ because $w = bv = buz$.

Prove (iii) by analogy with the proof of the inductive step of (ii), given above.

Having established this claim, we easily obtain the desired equation $L(G) = \{w \mid w \in \{a, b\}^+ \text{ and } \text{occur}(w, a) = \text{occur}(w, b)\}$ as a consequence of equivalence (i). Indeed, this equivalence says that for all $w \in \{a, b\}^*$, $S \Rightarrow^* w$ iff $\text{occur}(a, w) = \text{occur}(b, w)$. Consequently, $w \in L(G)$ iff $\text{occur}(a, w) = \text{occur}(b, w)$. As G has no ε-rules, $\varepsilon \notin L(G)$, so $L(G) = \{w \mid w \in \{a, b\}^+ \text{ and } \text{occur}(w, a) = \text{occur}(w, b)\}$. ■

Implementation 6.1. The following C# code provides an implementation of a context-free grammar rule.

```
public class ContextFreeRule : IEquatable<ContextFreeRule>
{
    public Symbol LeftHandSide { get; private set; }
    public HmmlcString RightHandSide { get; private set; }

    // constructor
    public ContextFreeRule(Symbol leftHandSide,
                           HmmlcString rightHandSide)
    {
        this.LeftHandSide = leftHandSide;
        this.RightHandSide = rightHandSide;
    }

    // equality checking using pattern from Implementation 1.1
    public static bool Equals(ContextFreeRule r1, ContextFreeRule r2)
    {
        if (ReferenceEquals(r1, r2)) return true;
        else if (ReferenceEquals(r1, null) ||
                 ReferenceEquals(r2, null))
        {
            return false;
        }
        else
        {
            return r1.LeftHandSide == r2.LeftHandSide &&
                   r1.RightHandSide == r2.RightHandSide;
        }
    }
```

```
    public bool Equals(ContextFreeRule other)
    {
        return ContextFreeRule.Equals(this, other);
    }
    public override bool Equals(object obj)
    {
        return ContextFreeRule.Equals(this, obj as ContextFreeRule);
    }
    public static bool operator ==(ContextFreeRule r1,
                                   ContextFreeRule r2)
    {
        return ContextFreeRule.Equals(r1, r2);
    }
    public static bool operator !=(ContextFreeRule r1,
                                   ContextFreeRule r2)
    {
        return !ContextFreeRule.Equals(r1, r2);
    }
    public override int GetHashCode()
    {
        return this.ToString().GetHashCode();
    }

    // returns a System.String that represents this rule
    public override string ToString()
    {
        return string.Format("{0} -> {1}", this.LeftHandSide,
                                           this.RightHandSide);
    }
}
```

Now we can implement context-free grammar as follows:

```
public class ContextFreeGrammar
{
    public Alphabet Nonterminals { get; private set; }
    public Alphabet Terminals { get; private set; }
    public FiniteSet<ContextFreeRule> Rules { get; private set; }
    public Symbol StartSymbol { get; set; }

    // constructor
    public ContextFreeGrammar()
    {
        this.Nonterminals = new Alphabet();
        this.Terminals = new Alphabet();
        this.Rules = new FiniteSet<ContextFreeRule>();
        this.StartSymbol = null;
    }

    // returns a System.String that represents this grammar
    public override string ToString()
```

```
    {
        return "Nonterminals = " + this.Nonterminals +
               Environment.NewLine +
               "Terminals = " + this.Terminals +
               Environment.NewLine +
               "Rules = " + this.Rules +
               Environment.NewLine +
               "Start symbol = " + this.StartSymbol;
    }
}
```

6.2 Canonical derivations and derivation trees

In a general case, context-free grammars may generate the same sentence by many different derivations, and this derivation multiplicity obviously complicates their investigation as well as application. To reduce this derivation multiplicity, we introduce two special types of *canonical derivations—leftmost derivations* and *rightmost derivations*. In addition, in terms of graph theory, we simplify the discussion concerning grammatical derivations by *derivation trees*, which represents derivations by graphically displaying rules but suppressing the order of their applications. We demonstrate that we can always restrict our attention only to canonical derivations and derivation trees in any context-free grammar G without affecting $L(G)$.

6.2.1 Leftmost derivations

A derivation is *leftmost* if during its every single derivation step, the leftmost occurrence of a nonterminal is rewritten in the sentential form.

Definition 6.2. *Let $G = (\Sigma, R)$ be a context-free grammar.*

(i) *Let $r: A \to z \in R$, $t \in \Delta^*$, $o \in \Sigma^*$. Then, G makes the* leftmost derivation step from tAo to tzo according to r, *symbolically written as* $tAo \Rightarrow_{lm} tzo\ [r]$.

(ii) Leftmost derivations in G *are defined recursively as follows:*

(a) *for all $u \in \Sigma^*$, G makes the* leftmost derivation from u to u according to ε, *symbolically written* $u \Rightarrow_{lm}^* u\ [\varepsilon]$;

(b) *if $u, w, v \in \Sigma^*$, $\rho = \sigma r$, $\sigma \in R^*$, $r \in R$, $u \Rightarrow_{lm}^* w\ [\sigma]$, and $w \Rightarrow_{lm} v\ [r]$ in G, then G makes the* leftmost derivation from u to v according to ρ, *symbolically written as* $u \Rightarrow_{lm}^* v\ [\rho]$ *in G.*

Next, we demonstrate that every context-free grammar can generate each sentence by a leftmost derivation.

Theorem 6.1. *Let G be a context-free grammar. Then, $w \in L(G)$ if and only if $S \Rightarrow_{lm}^* w$ in G.*

Proof. The *if* part of the proof says that $S \Rightarrow_{lm}^* w$ implies $w \in L(G)$, for every $w \in \Delta^*$. Since $S \Rightarrow_{lm}^* w$ can be seen a special case of $S \Rightarrow^* w$, this implication holds true.

Therefore, we only need to prove the *only-if* part that says that $w \in L(G)$ implies $S \Rightarrow^*_{lm} w$ in G. In other words, we need to show that for every $w \in L(G)$, $S \Rightarrow^*_{lm} w$. This statement follows from the next claim, which we prove by mathematical induction.

Claim 1. *For every* $w \in L(G)$, $S \Rightarrow^n w$ *implies* $S \Rightarrow^n_{lm} w$, *for all* $n \geq 0$.

Proof. We will prove this claim by induction on $n \geq 0$.

Basis. For $n = 0$, this implication is trivial.

Induction Hypothesis. Assume that there exists an integer $n \geq 0$ such that the claim holds for all derivations of length n or less.

Induction Step. Let $S \Rightarrow^{n+1} w\ [\rho]$, where $w \in L(G)$, $\rho \in R^+$, and $|\rho| = n + 1$. If $S \Rightarrow^{n+1} w\ [\rho]$ is leftmost, the induction step is completed. Assume that this derivation is not leftmost. Express $S \Rightarrow^{n+1} w\ [\rho]$ as

$$
\begin{aligned}
S &\Rightarrow^*_{lm} uAv\underline{B}x && [\sigma] \\
&\Rightarrow uAvyx && [r\colon B \to y] \\
&\Rightarrow^* w && [\theta],
\end{aligned}
$$

where $\rho, \theta \in R^*$, $\rho = \sigma r \theta$, $r\colon B \to y \in R$, $u \subset \text{prefixes}(w)$, $A \in N$, and $v, x, y \in \Sigma^*$. In other words, $S \Rightarrow^*_{lm} uAvBx$ is the longest leftmost derivation that begins $S \Rightarrow^{n+1} w$. As $w \in L(G)$ and $L(G) \subseteq \Delta^*$ (see Definition 6.1), $w \in \Delta^*$. Thus, $A \notin \text{symbols}(w)$ because $A \in N$. Hence, A is surely rewritten during $uAvyx \Rightarrow^* w$. Express $S \Rightarrow^{n+1} w$ as

$$
\begin{aligned}
S &\Rightarrow^*_{lm} uAv\underline{B}x && [\sigma] \\
&\Rightarrow uAvyx && [r\colon B \to y] \\
&\Rightarrow^* u\underline{A}z && [\pi] \\
&\Rightarrow_{lm} utz && [p\colon A \to t] \\
&\Rightarrow^* w && [o],
\end{aligned}
$$

where $\pi, o \in R^*$, $\theta = \pi p o$, $p\colon A \to t \in R$, $vyx \Rightarrow^* z$, $z \in \Sigma^*$. Rearrange this derivation so that the derivation step according to p is made right after the initial part $S \Rightarrow^*_{lm} uAvBx\ [\sigma]$; more formally written,

$$
\begin{aligned}
S &\Rightarrow^*_{lm} u\underline{A}vBx && [\sigma] \\
&\Rightarrow_{lm} utv\underline{B}x && [p\colon A \to t] \\
&\Rightarrow utvyx && [r\colon B \to y] \\
&\Rightarrow^* utz && [\pi] \\
&\Rightarrow^* w && [o].
\end{aligned}
$$

The resulting derivation $S \Rightarrow^* w\ [\sigma p r \pi o]$ begins with at least $|\sigma p|$ leftmost steps, so its leftmost beginning is definitely longer than the leftmost beginning of the original derivation $S \Rightarrow^{n+1} w\ [\rho]$. If $S \Rightarrow^* w\ [\sigma p r \pi o]$ is leftmost, the induction step is completed. If not, apply the derivation rearrangement described above to $S \Rightarrow^* w\ [\sigma p r \pi o]$. After no more than $n - 2$ repetitions of this rearrangement, we necessarily obtain $S \Rightarrow_{lm}^{*} w$, which completes the induction step, so the proof of the claim is completed. □

By this claim, we see that $w \in L(G)$ implies $S \Rightarrow_{lm}^{*} w$ in G, so the theorem holds. ■

It is worth noting that Theorem 6.1 does not hold in terms of all sentential forms. More formally speaking, if we replace $L(G)$ with $F(G)$ in the theorem, the resulting statement is untrue. Indeed, consider, for instance, a trivial context-free grammar having only these two rules—$S \to AA$ and $A \to a$. Observe that this grammar makes $S \Rightarrow AA \Rightarrow Aa$; however, there is no leftmost derivation of Aa in the grammar.

6.2.2 Rightmost derivations

In *rightmost derivations*, the rightmost occurrence of a nonterminal is rewritten during its every derivation step.

Definition 6.3. *Let $G = (\Sigma, R)$ be a context-free grammar.*

(i) *Let $r: A \to z \in R$, $t \in \Delta^*$, $o \in \Sigma^*$. Then, G makes the* rightmost derivation step from tAo to tzo according to r, *symbolically written as* $tAo \Rightarrow_{rm} tzo\ [r]$.

(ii) Rightmost derivations in G *are defined recursively as follows:*

  (a) *For all $u \in \Sigma^*$, G makes the* rightmost derivation from u to u according to ε, *symbolically written* $u \Rightarrow_{rm}^{*} u\ [\varepsilon]$.

  (b) *If $u, w, v \in \Sigma^*$, $\rho = \sigma r$, $\sigma \in R^*$, $r \in R$, $u \Rightarrow_{rm}^{*} w\ [\sigma]$ and $w \Rightarrow_{rm} v\ [r]$ in G, then G makes the* rightmost derivation from u to v according to ρ, *symbolically written as* $u \Rightarrow_{rm}^{*} v\ [\rho]$ *in G.*

Let $u, v \in \Sigma^*$, $\rho \in R^*$, and $u \Rightarrow_{rm}^{*} v\ [\rho]$ in G. If ρ represents an immaterial piece of information, we usually simplify $u \Rightarrow_{rm}^{*} v\ [\rho]$ to $u \Rightarrow_{rm}^{*} v$. Of course, in a general case, G can make $u \Rightarrow_{rm}^{*} v$ according to several different sequences of rules from R^*.

As an exercise, by analogy with Theorem 6.1, prove the next theorem.

Theorem 6.2. *Let G be a context-free grammar. Then, $w \in L(G)$ if and only if $S \Rightarrow_{rm}^{*} w$ in G.*

6.2.3 Derivation trees

In what follows, we frequently make use of the graph theory and its terminology introduced in Chapter 3.

Apart from the canonical derivations, we often simplify the discussion concerning grammatical derivations graphically by *derivation trees*, which represent compositions of *rule trees*. As their names indicate, rule trees describe grammatical rules, while derivation trees represent derivations by specifying the applied rules, expressed as rule trees, together with the nonterminals to which the rules are applied. However, they suppress the order of the applications of the rules, so we make use of these trees when this order is immaterial.

To give a more mathematical insight into these notions, take a context-free grammar, $G = (\Sigma, R)$, and a rule $A \to x \in R$. Let T be the elementary tree satisfying root $(T) = A$ and frontier $(T) = x$, then, T is the rule tree that represents $A \to x$. A derivation tree is any tree such that its root is from Σ, and each of its elementary subtrees is a rule tree that represents a rule from R.

Definition 6.4. *Let $G = (\Sigma, R)$ be a context-free grammar.*

(i) *For $l\colon A \to x \in R$, $A\langle x\rangle$ is the* rule tree that represents l.
(ii) *The* derivation trees representing derivations *in G are defined recursively as follows:*
   (a) *One-node tree X is the derivation tree corresponding to $X \Rightarrow^0 X$ in G, where $X \in \Sigma$.*
   (b) *Let d be the derivation tree representing $A \Rightarrow^* uBv$ $[\rho]$ with* frontier $(d) = uBv$, *and let $l\colon B \to z \in R$. The derivation tree that represents*

$$\begin{aligned} A &\Rightarrow^* u\underline{B}v\ [\sigma] \\ &\Rightarrow uzv\ [l] \end{aligned}$$

   is obtained by replacing the $(|u| + 1)$st leaf in d, B, with the rule tree corresponding to l, $B\langle z\rangle$.
(iii) *A* derivation tree *in G is any tree t for which there is a derivation represented by t (see (ii)).*

Let $G = (\Sigma, R)$ be a context-free grammar. For any $A \to x \in R$, ${}_G\bot(A \to x)$ denotes the rule tree representing $A \to x$. For any $A \Rightarrow^* x\ [\rho]$ in G, where $A \in N, x \in \Sigma^*$, and $\rho \in R^*$, ${}_G\Delta(A \Rightarrow^* x\ [\rho])$ denotes the derivation tree corresponding to $A \Rightarrow^* x\ [\rho]$. Just like we often write $A \Rightarrow^* x$ instead of $A \Rightarrow^* x\ [\rho]$, we sometimes simplify ${}_G\bot(A \Rightarrow^* x\ [\rho])$ to ${}_G\bot(A \Rightarrow^* x)$ in what follows if there is no danger of confusion. Finally, ${}_G\bot_{all}$ denotes the set of all derivation trees for G. If G is automatically understood, we often drop the subscript G in this terminology; for instance, instead of ${}_G\bot_{all}$, we just write $\bot_{all}$.

Theorem 6.3. *Let $G = (\Sigma, R)$ be a context-free grammar, $A \in N$, and $x \in \Sigma^*$. Then, $A \Rightarrow^* x$ in G if and only if there is $t \in \bot_{all}$ satisfying* root $(t) = A$ *and* frontier $(t) = x$.

Proof. Consider any context-free grammar, $G = (\Sigma, R)$. The *only-if* part of the equivalence says that for every derivation $A \Rightarrow^* x$, where $A \in N$ and $x \in \Sigma^*$, there exists $t \in \bot_{all}$ such that root $(t) = A$ and frontier $(t) = x$. From Definition 6.4, we know how to construct $\bot(A \Rightarrow^x\ )$, which satisfies these properties.

The *if* part says that for every $t \in \bot_{all}$ with root $(t) = A$ and frontier $(t) = x$, where $A \in N$ and $x \in \Sigma^*$, there exists $A \Rightarrow^* x$ in G. We prove the *if* part by induction on depth $(t) \geq 0$.

Basis. Consider any $t \in \bot_{all}$ such that depth $(t) = 0$. As depth $(t) = 0$, t is a tree consisting of one node, so root $(t) =$ frontier $(t) = A$, where $A \in N$. Observe that $A \Rightarrow^0 A$ in G; therefore, the basis holds.

Induction Hypothesis. Suppose that the *if* part holds for all trees of depth n or less, where $n \in {}_0\mathbb{N}$.

Induction Step. Consider any $t \in \perp_{all}$ with depth $(t) = n+1$, where root $(t) = A$, and frontier $(t) = x$, $A \in N$, $x \in \Sigma^*$. Consider the topmost rule tree, $\perp(p)$, occurring in t. That is, $\perp(p)$ is the rule tree whose root coincides with root (t). Let $p: A \to u \in R$. Distinguish these two cases—(i) $u = \varepsilon$ and (ii) $u \neq \varepsilon$.

(i) If $u = \varepsilon$, t has actually the form $A\langle\rangle$, which means $u = \varepsilon$ and depth $(t) = 1$, and at this point, $A \Rightarrow \varepsilon$ [p], so the induction step is completed.

(ii) Assume $u \neq \varepsilon$. Let $u = X_1X_2 \cdots X_m$, where $m \geq 1$. Thus, t is of the form $A\langle t_1t_2 \cdots t_m\rangle$, where each t_i is in $\perp_{all}$ and satisfies root $(t_i) = X_i$, $1 \leq i \leq m$, with depth $(t_i) \leq n$. Let frontier $(t_i) = y_i$, where $y_i \in \Sigma^*$, so $x = y_1y_2 \cdots y_m$. As depth $(t_i) \leq n$, by the induction hypothesis, $X_i \Rightarrow^* y_i$ in G, $1 \leq i \leq m$. Since $A \to u \in R$ with $u = X_1X_2 \cdots X_m$, we have $A \Rightarrow X_1X_2 \cdots X_m$. Putting together $A \to X_1X_2 \cdots X_m$ and $X_i \Rightarrow^* y_i$ for all $1 \leq i \leq m$, we obtain

$$\begin{aligned} A &\Rightarrow X_1X_2 \cdots X_m \\ &\Rightarrow^* y_1X_2 \cdots X_m \\ &\Rightarrow^* y_1y_2 \cdots X_m \\ &\vdots \\ &\Rightarrow^* y_1X_2 \cdots y_m. \end{aligned}$$

Thus, $A \Rightarrow^* x$ in G, the induction step is completed, and the *if* part of the equivalence holds true.

■

Corollary 6.1. *Let G be a context-free grammar. Then, $w \in L(G)$ iff $\perp_{all}$ contains t satisfying* root $(t) = S$ *and* frontier $(t) = w$.

Proof. Let $w \in \Delta^*$. Consider Theorem 6.3 with $A = S$ and $x = w$ to see that Corollary 6.1 holds true. ■

Theorems 6.3 and Corollary 6.1 imply the following important corollary, which says that without any loss of generality, we can always restrict our attention to the canonical derivations or derivation trees when discussing context-free languages.

Corollary 6.2. *Let G be a context-free grammar. The following languages are identical:*

- $L(G)$,
- $\{w \in \Delta^* \mid S \Rightarrow_{lm}^* w\}$,
- $\{w \in \Delta^* \mid S \Rightarrow_{rm}^* w\}$,
- $\{w \in \Delta^* \mid w =$ frontier (t), *where* $t \in \perp_{all}$ *with* root $(t) = S\}$.

6.2.4 Ambiguity

Before closing this section, we make use of the terminology introduced above to describe an undesirable phenomenon referred to as *ambiguity*, which occurs in some context-free grammars. Unfortunately, even if we reduce our attention only to canonical derivations or derivation trees, we may still face a derivation multiplicity of some sentences. Indeed, some context-free grammars make several different canonical derivations of the same sentences. In fact, some context-free languages are generated only by context-free grammars of this kind.

Definition 6.5. *Let* $G = (\Sigma, R)$ *be a context-free grammar.*

(i) G *is* ambiguous *if* $L(G)$ *contains a sentence* w *such that* $S \Rightarrow^{*}_{lm} w\ [\rho]$ *and* $S \Rightarrow^{*}_{lm} w\ [\sigma]$ *with* $\rho \neq \sigma$*, where* $\rho, \sigma \in R^*$*; otherwise,* G *is* unambiguous.
(ii) *A context-free language* L *is* inherently ambiguous *if every context-free grammar* H *satisfying* $L(H) = L$ *is ambiguous.*

Less formally, a context-free grammar G is ambiguous if it generates a sentence by two different leftmost derivations. We can rephrase this definition in terms of rightmost derivations as follows: G is ambiguous if it generates a sentence by two different rightmost derivations. Finally, in terms of derivation trees, G is ambiguous if ${}_G\bot_{all}$ contains t and u such that $t \neq u$ while frontier (t) = frontier (u).

We close this section by illustrating its key notions—canonical derivations, rule trees, derivation trees, and ambiguity.

Example 6.3. *Consider*

$$Z = \{a_i b_j c_k \mid i, j, k \geq 0,\ i = j \text{ or } j = k\}.$$

Observe that $Z = L(G)$*, where* G *is the context-free grammar defined by the following ten rules:*

$$\begin{aligned}
0 &: S \rightarrow AB,\\
1 &: A \rightarrow aAb,\\
2 &: A \rightarrow ab,\\
3 &: B \rightarrow cB,\\
4 &: B \rightarrow c,\\
5 &: S \rightarrow CD,\\
6 &: C \rightarrow aC,\\
7 &: C \rightarrow a,\\
8 &: D \rightarrow bDc,\\
9 &: D \rightarrow bc.
\end{aligned}$$

Indeed, G *uses rules 0–4 to generate* $\{a_i b_j c_k \mid i, j, k \geq 0,\ i = j\}$*. By using rules 5–9, it generates* $\{a_i b_j c_k \mid i, j, k \geq 0,\ j = k\}$*. As the union of these two languages coincides with* Z*,* $L(G) = Z$*.*

Notice that G *can generate every sentence by a variety of different derivations. For instance, consider* $aabbcc \in L(G)$*. Observe that* G *generates this sentence by the 12 different derivations, I–XII, listed in Table 6.1 (we specify the rewritten symbols by underlining).*

Table 6.2 describes the rule trees $\bot(0)$–$\bot(9)$ *corresponding to the ten rules in* G*. In addition,* $\bot(0)$ *is pictorially shown in Figure 6.1.*

Consider, for instance, the first derivation in Table 6.1. Table 6.3 presents this derivation together with its corresponding derivation tree constructed in a

Table 6.1 Twelve derivations of aabbcc

I		**II**		**III**	
$\underline{S}$		$\underline{S}$		$\underline{S}$	
$\Rightarrow \underline{A}B$	[0]	$\Rightarrow \underline{A}B$	[0]	$\Rightarrow \underline{A}B$	[0]
$\Rightarrow a\underline{A}bB$	[1]	$\Rightarrow aAb\underline{B}$	[1]	$\Rightarrow aAb\underline{B}$	[1]
$\Rightarrow aabb\underline{B}$	[2]	$\Rightarrow a\underline{A}bcB$	[3]	$\Rightarrow aAbc\underline{B}$	[3]
$\Rightarrow aabbc\underline{B}$	[3]	$\Rightarrow aabbc\underline{B}$	[2]	$\Rightarrow a\underline{A}bcc$	[4]
$\Rightarrow aabbcc$	[4]	$\Rightarrow aabbcc$	[4]	$\Rightarrow aabbcc$	[2]
IV		**V**		**VI**	
$\underline{S}$		$\underline{S}$		$\underline{S}$	
$\Rightarrow A\underline{B}$	[0]	$\Rightarrow A\underline{B}$	[0]	$\Rightarrow A\underline{B}$	[0]
$\Rightarrow \underline{A}cB$	[3]	$\Rightarrow Ac\underline{B}$	[3]	$\Rightarrow \underline{A}cB$	[3]
$\Rightarrow a\underline{A}bcB$	[1]	$\Rightarrow \underline{A}cc$	[4]	$\Rightarrow aAbc\underline{B}$	[1]
$\Rightarrow aabbc\underline{B}$	[2]	$\Rightarrow a\underline{A}bcc$	[1]	$\Rightarrow a\underline{A}bcc$	[4]
$\Rightarrow aabbcc$	[4]	$\Rightarrow aabbcc$	[2]	$\Rightarrow aabbcc$	[2]
VII		**VIII**		**IX**	
$\underline{S}$		$\underline{S}$		$\underline{S}$	
$\Rightarrow \underline{C}D$	[5]	$\Rightarrow \underline{C}D$	[5]	$\Rightarrow \underline{C}D$	[5]
$\Rightarrow a\underline{C}D$	[6]	$\Rightarrow aC\underline{D}$	[6]	$\Rightarrow aC\underline{D}$	[6]
$\Rightarrow aa\underline{D}$	[7]	$\Rightarrow a\underline{C}bDc$	[8]	$\Rightarrow aCb\underline{D}c$	[8]
$\Rightarrow aabb\underline{D}c$	[8]	$\Rightarrow aab\underline{D}c$	[7]	$\Rightarrow a\underline{C}bbcc$	[9]
$\Rightarrow aabbcc$	[9]	$\Rightarrow aabbcc$	[9]	$\Rightarrow aabbcc$	[7]
X		**XI**		**XII**	
$\underline{S}$		$\underline{S}$		$\underline{S}$	
$\Rightarrow C\underline{D}$	[5]	$\Rightarrow C\underline{D}$	[5]	$\Rightarrow C\underline{D}$	[5]
$\Rightarrow \underline{C}bDc$	[8]	$\Rightarrow Cb\underline{D}c$	[8]	$\Rightarrow \underline{C}bDc$	[8]
$\Rightarrow a\underline{C}bDcD$	[6]	$\Rightarrow \underline{C}bbcc$	[9]	$\Rightarrow aCb\underline{D}c$	[6]
$\Rightarrow aab\underline{D}c$	[7]	$\Rightarrow a\underline{C}bbcc$	[6]	$\Rightarrow a\underline{C}bbcc$	[9]
$\Rightarrow aabbcc$	[9]	$\Rightarrow aabbcc$	[7]	$\Rightarrow aabbcc$	[7]

Table 6.2 $\perp(0)$–$\perp(9)$

Rule	**Rule tree**
$0: S \rightarrow AB$	$S\langle AB\rangle$
$1: A \rightarrow aAb$	$A\langle aAb\rangle$
$2: A \rightarrow ab$	$A\langle ab\rangle$
$3: B \rightarrow cB$	$B\langle cB\rangle$
$4: B \rightarrow c$	$B\langle c\rangle$
$5: S \rightarrow CD$	$S\langle CD\rangle$
$6: C \rightarrow aC$	$C\langle aC\rangle$
$7: C \rightarrow a$	$C\langle a\rangle$
$8: D \rightarrow bDc$	$D\langle bDc\rangle$
$9: D \rightarrow bc$	$D\langle bc\rangle$

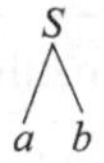

Figure 6.1 Rule tree ⊥(0) of the form $S\langle AB\rangle$

Table 6.3 Derivation I and its corresponding derivation tree

Derivation		**Derivation tree**
$\underline{S}$		S
$\Rightarrow \underline{A}B$	[0]	S $\langle AB\rangle$
$\Rightarrow a\underline{A}bB$	[1]	S $\langle A\langle aAb\rangle B\rangle$
$\Rightarrow aabb\underline{B}$	[2]	S $\langle A\langle aA\langle ab\rangle b\rangle B\rangle$
$\Rightarrow aabbc\underline{B}$	[3]	$\langle A\langle aA\langle ab\rangle b\rangle B\langle cB\rangle\rangle$
$\Rightarrow aabbcc$	[4]	$S\langle A\langle aA\langle ab\rangle b\rangle B\langle cB\rangle c\rangle\rangle\rangle$

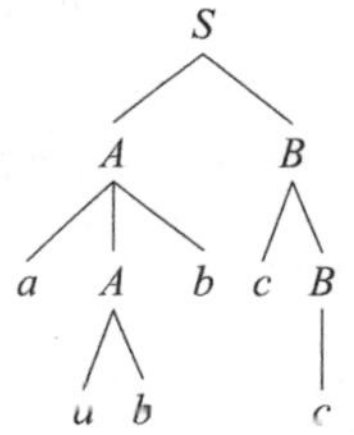

Figure 6.2 Derivation tree $S\langle A\langle aA\langle ab\rangle b\rangle B\langle cB\rangle c\rangle\rangle\rangle$

step-by-step way. In addition, the resulting derivation tree, $S\langle A\langle aA\langle ab\rangle b\rangle B\langle cB\rangle c\rangle\rangle\rangle$, is shown in Figure 6.2.

In Table 6.1, derivations I and VII represent two different leftmost derivations that generate aabbcc. Thus, G is ambiguous. In fact, as an exercise, prove that Z is inherently ambiguous because every context-free grammar that generates Z is ambiguous.

Example 6.3 demonstrates the existence of inherently ambiguous context-free languages. As obvious, these languages are difficult to use in practice because their generation always represents an ambiguous process.

Algorithm 6.1: Determination of terminating symbols

Input: A context-free grammar, $G = (\Sigma, R)$.
Output: The set T that contains all terminating symbols in G.

```
begin
    set T = Δ
    repeat
        if A → x ∈ _GR and x ∈ T* then
            add A to T
        end
    until no change
end
```

6.3 Useless symbols and their elimination

Context-free grammars sometimes contain symbols that fulfill no role regarding the generated languages. As obvious, these useless symbols needlessly obscure and increase the grammatical specification, so we next explain how to eliminate them.

To start with, consider symbols from which no strings of terminals are derivable. Clearly, they are utterly useless with respect to the generated languages, so we next describe how to remove them.

Definition 6.6. *Let $G = (\Sigma, R)$ be a context-free grammar and $X \in \Sigma$. Then, X is* terminating *if and only if $X \Rightarrow^* w$ in G for some $w \in \Delta^*$; otherwise, X is* nonterminating.

Basic Idea. Consider a context-free grammar G. Construct the set T containing all terminating symbols in G in the following way. First, set T to ${}_G\Delta$ because every terminal $a \in {}_G\Delta$ satisfies $a \Rightarrow^0 a$, so a is surely terminating by Definition 6.6. If $A \rightarrow x \in R$ satisfies $x \in T^*$, then $A \Rightarrow x \Rightarrow^* w$ in G, for some $w \in \Delta^*$; therefore, add A to T because $A \Rightarrow x \Rightarrow^* w$ and, consequently, A is terminating. In this way, keep extending T until no further terminating symbol can be added to T. The resulting set T contains only terminating symbols in G.

The following algorithm works based on this idea. A rigorous verification of this simple algorithm is left as an exercise.

Example 6.4. *Consider this context-free grammar*

$$
\begin{aligned}
S &\rightarrow SoS,\\
S &\rightarrow SoA,\\
S &\rightarrow A,\\
A &\rightarrow AoA,\\
S &\rightarrow (S),\\
S &\rightarrow i,\\
B &\rightarrow i,
\end{aligned}
$$

where o, i, (*and*) *are terminals, and the other symbols are nonterminals. Intuitively,* o *and* i *stand for an operator and an identifier, respectively. Notice, that the context-free grammar generates the set of expressions that can be built up using the terminal symbols; for instance,* $S \Rightarrow^* io(ioi)$.

Applying Algorithm 6.1, we first set $T = \{o, i, (,)\}$. *As* $S \to i$ *with* $i \in T$, *we add* S *to* T. *For the same reason,* $B \to i$ *leads to the inclusion of* B *to* T, *so* $T = \{o, i, (,), B, S\}$. *At this point,* T *cannot be increased any further, and we are done. As a result,* A *is nonterminating because* $A \notin T$.

Implementation 6.2. *We implement Algorithm 6.1 in C# by adding the following method to* `ContextFreeGrammar` *class.*

```
public Alphabet DetermineTerminatingSymbols()
{
    var result = new Alphabet(this.Terminals);

    bool change;
    do
    {
        change = false;
        foreach (ContextFreeRule r in this.Rules)
        {
            if (r.RightHandSide.Symbols.Difference(result).IsEmpty)
            {
                if (result.Add(r.LeftHandSide)) change = true;
            }
        }
    }
    while (change);

    return result;
}
```

We can apply this implementation to the context-free grammar from Example 6.4 as follows:

```
var G = new ContextFreeGrammar()
{
    Nonterminals =  "S", "A", "B" ,
    Terminals =  "o", "(", ")", "i" ,
    Rules =
    {
        new ContextFreeRule("S", new HmmlcString("S", "o", "S")),
        new ContextFreeRule("S", new HmmlcString("S", "o", "A")),
        new ContextFreeRule("S", new HmmlcString("A")),
        new ContextFreeRule("A", new HmmlcString("A", "o", "A")),
        new ContextFreeRule("S", new HmmlcString("(", "S", ")")),
        new ContextFreeRule("S", new HmmlcString("i")),
        new ContextFreeRule("B", new HmmlcString("i"))
    },
```

Algorithm 6.2: Determination of accessible symbols

Input: A context-free grammar, $G = (\Sigma, R)$.
Output: The set W that contains all accessible symbols in G.

begin
  set $W = \{S\}$
  repeat
    if $A \in W$ *for some* $A \to x \in R$ **then**
      add symbols (x) to W
    end
  until no change
end

```
    StartSymbol  =  "S"
};

Alphabet terminatingSymbols = G.DetermineTerminatingSymbols();
```

Consider a context-free grammar G and a symbol X in G. Suppose that there exists no derivation from the start symbol to a string that contains X. Of course, at this point, X is utterly useless in G, and its removal does not affect $L(G)$ at all. Formally, X is called an inaccessible symbol, and its definition follows next. Recall that $F(G)$, used in the next definition, denotes the set of all sentential forms derived by G (see Definition 6.1), and for the definition of symbols, see Section 1.3.

Definition 6.7. *Let* $G = (\Sigma, R)$ *be a context-free grammar* G *and* $X \in \Sigma$. *Then,* X *is* accessible *if and only if* $X \in$ symbols $(F(G))$; *otherwise,* X *is* inaccessible.

Basic Idea. Let $G = (\Sigma, R)$ be a context-free grammar. To construct the subalphabet $W \subseteq \Sigma$ that contains all accessible symbols, initialize W with the start symbol S, which is always accessible because $S \Rightarrow^0 S$. If $A \to x \in R$ with $A \in W$, we include symbols (x) into W because we can always change A to x by $A \to x$ in any sentential form, so symbols $(x) \subseteq$ symbols $(F(G))$. Keep extending W in this way until no further symbols can be added to W to obtain the set of all accessible symbols. The next algorithm, whose rigorous verification is left as an exercise, constructs W in this way.

Example 6.5. *Take the same context-free grammar as in Example 6.4—that is,*

$$\begin{aligned}
S &\to SoS,\\
S &\to SoA,\\
S &\to A,\\
A &\to AoA,\\
S &\to (S),\\
S &\to i,\\
B &\to i.
\end{aligned}$$

With this context-free grammar as its input, Algorithm 6.2 sets $W = \{S\}$. As $S \rightarrow SoS$, it adds o to W. Furthermore, since $S \rightarrow A$, the algorithm adds A there, too. Continuing in this way, the algorithm finishes with W containing all symbols but B, so B is the only inaccessible symbol in this context-free grammar.

Implementation 6.3. We give a C# implementation of Algorithm 6.2 as another method of `ContextFreeGrammar` class.

```
public Alphabet DetermineAccessibleSymbols()
{
    var result = new Alphabet { this.StartSymbol };

    bool change;
    do
    {
        change = false;
        foreach (ContextFreeRule r in this.Rules)
        {
            if (result.Contains(r.LeftHandSide))
            {
                foreach (Symbol a in r.RightHandSide.Symbols)
                {
                    if (result.Add(a)) change = true;
                }
            }
        }
    }
    while (change);

    return result;
}
```

Definition 6.8. *Let $G = (\Sigma, R)$ be a context-free grammar. A symbol $X \in \Sigma$ is* useful *in G if and only if X is both accessible and terminating in G; otherwise, X is* useless.

Making use of the previous two algorithms, we next explain how to turn any context-free grammar to an equivalent context-free grammar that contains only useful symbols.

Lemma 6.1. *Algorithm 6.3 is correct.*

Proof. By contradiction, prove that every nonterminal in O is useful. Assume that $X \in \Sigma$ is a useless symbol. Consequently,

(i) for every $y \in \Sigma^*$ such that $S \Rightarrow^* y$, $X \notin$ symbols(y), or
(ii) for every $x \in \Sigma^*$ such that $X \Rightarrow^* x$, $x \notin {}_O\Delta^*$.

Case (i) is ruled out because Algorithm 6.2 would eliminate A. Case (ii) is ruled out, too. Indeed, if for every $x \in \Sigma^*$ such that $X \Rightarrow^* x$, $x \notin {}_O\Delta^*$, then X would be eliminated by Algorithm 6.1. Therefore, $X \notin {}_O\Sigma$, which contradicts $X \in {}_O\Sigma$. As a result, all symbols in O are useful.

As an exercise, prove that $L(I) = L(O)$. ■

Algorithm 6.3: Removal of useless symbols

Input: A context-free grammar $I = ({}_I\Sigma, {}_IR)$.
Output: A context-free grammar $O = ({}_O\Sigma, {}_OR)$ such that $L(I) = L(O)$ and all symbols in O are useful.

begin
First, by using Algorithm 6.1, determine all terminating symbols in ${}_I\Sigma$. Then, eliminate all nonterminating symbols and the rules that contain them from I.
Consider the context-free grammar resulting from (1). By using Algorithm 6.2, determine all its accessible symbols. Then, eliminate all inaccessible symbols and the rules that contain them from the context-free grammar. Take the resulting context-free grammar as O.
end

Observe that the order of the two transformations in Algorithm 6.3 is important. Indeed, if we reverse them, this algorithm does not work properly. To demonstrate this, consider the following four-rule context-free grammar I:

$$
\begin{aligned}
S &\to a, \\
S &\to A, \\
A &\to AB, \\
B &\to a.
\end{aligned}
$$

Notice that $L(I) = \{a\}$. If we apply the transformations in Algorithm 6.3 properly, we obtain an equivalent one-rule grammar O defined as $S \to a$. That is, in this way, Algorithm 6.3 rightly detects and eliminates A and B as useless symbols. However, if we improperly apply Algorithm 6.2 before Algorithm 6.1, we obtain the two-rule context-free grammar $S \to a$ and $B \to a$, in which B is useless.

Example 6.6. *Once again, return to the context-free grammar*

$$
\begin{aligned}
S &\to SoS, \\
S &\to SoA, \\
S &\to A, \\
A &\to AoA, \\
S &\to (S), \\
S &\to i, \\
B &\to i,
\end{aligned}
$$

discussed in the previous two examples. Eliminate the nonterminating symbols from this context-free grammar by Algorithm 6.1. From Example 6.4, we already know that A is the only nonterminating symbol, so the elimination of all rules containing A produces the grammar defined as

$$S \rightarrow SoS,$$
$$S \rightarrow (S),$$
$$S \rightarrow i,$$
$$B \rightarrow i.$$

Use Algorithm 6.2 to detect B as the only inaccessible symbol in this grammar. Remove it together with $B \rightarrow i$ to obtain

$$S \rightarrow SoS,$$
$$S \rightarrow (S),$$
$$S \rightarrow i$$

as the resulting equivalent context-free grammar in which all symbols are useful.

Implementation 6.4. Making use of the methods introduced in Implementations 6.2 and 6.3, we close this section with an implementation of Algorithm 6.3.

```
public bool HasUselessSymbols
{
    get
    {
        int symbolCount = this.Nonterminals.Cardinality +
                          this.Terminals.Cardinality;

        Alphabet terminatingSymbols =
            this.DetermineTerminatingSymbols();
        if (terminatingSymbols.Cardinality < symbolCount)
        {
            return true; // some symbols are not terminating
        }

        Alphabet accessibleSymbols =
            this.DetermineAccessibleSymbols();
        if (accessibleSymbols.Cardinality < symbolCount)
        {
            return true; // some symbols are not accessible
        }

        return false; // all symbols are terminating and accessible
    }
}

public ContextFreeGrammar RemoveUselessSymbols()
{
    // first, remove all nonterminating symbols
    Alphabet terminatingSymbols =
        this.DetermineTerminatingSymbols();
```

```
var G = new ContextFreeGrammar()
{
    Terminals = new Alphabet(this.Terminals),
    StartSymbol = this.StartSymbol
};
foreach (Symbol a in this.Nonterminals)
{
    if (terminatingSymbols.Contains(a)) G.Nonterminals.Add(a);
}
foreach (ContextFreeRule r in this.Rules)
{
    if (terminatingSymbols.Contains(r.LeftHandSide))
    {
        bool canAddRule = true;
        foreach (Symbol a in r.RightHandSide.Symbols)
        {
            if (!terminatingSymbols.Contains(a))
            {
                canAddRule = false;
                break;
            }
        }
        if (canAddRule) G.Rules.Add(r);
    }
}

// G now contains only terminating symbols
// next, remove all inaccessible symbols from G
Alphabet accessibleSymbols = G.DetermineAccessibleSymbols();

var result = new ContextFreeGrammar()
{
    StartSymbol = G.StartSymbol
};
foreach (Symbol a in G.Nonterminals)
{
    if (accessibleSymbols.Contains(a))
    {
        result.Nonterminals.Add(a);
    }
}
foreach (Symbol a in G.Terminals)
{
    if (accessibleSymbols.Contains(a))
    {
        result.Terminals.Add(a);
    }
}
```

```
    foreach (ContextFreeRule r in G.Rules)
    {
        if (result.Nonterminals.Contains(r.LeftHandSide))
        {
            result.Rules.Add(r);
        }
    }

    return result;
}
```

6.4 Erasing rules and their elimination

Erasing rules or, synonymously, ε-rules represent the rules that have ε on their right-hand sides. If a context-free grammar does not have them, it can never make any sentential form shorter during a derivation step, and this property obviously simplifies its exploration as well as application. Therefore, we explain how to eliminate them in this section.

Definition 6.9. *Let $G = (\Sigma, R)$ be a context-free grammar. A rule of the form $A \rightarrow \varepsilon \in R$ is called an* erasing rule *or, briefly, an* ε-rule.

To eliminate all ε-rules from a context-free grammar, we need to detect all erasable nonterminals—that is, the nonterminals from which the grammar can derive ε.

Definition 6.10. *Let $G = (\Sigma, R)$ be a context-free grammar. A nonterminal $A \in N$ is an* erasable nonterminal *or, briefly, an* ε-nonterminal *in G if $A \Rightarrow^* \varepsilon$ in G.*

Basic Idea. Let I be a context-free grammar. To determine the set E that contains all ε-nonterminals in I, we initialize E with the left-hand sides of all these ε-rules; indeed, by using $A \rightarrow \varepsilon$, $A \Rightarrow \varepsilon$ in I. Then, we extend E by every nonterminal B for which there is $B \rightarrow x$ with $x \in E^*$, which obviously implies $B \Rightarrow^* \varepsilon$. To complete the construction of E, we keep repeating this extension until no further ε-nonterminals can be added to E.

A fully rigorous verification of this algorithm is left as an exercise.

Example 6.7. *Take*

$$S \rightarrow AB,$$
$$A \rightarrow aAb,$$
$$B \rightarrow cBd,$$
$$A \rightarrow \varepsilon,$$
$$B \rightarrow \varepsilon$$

as the input context-free grammar I. Observe that

$$L(I) = \{a^n b^n \mid n \geq 0\}\{c^m d^m \mid m \geq 0\}.$$

Algorithm 6.4: Detection of erasable nonterminals

Input: A context-free grammar, $I = (\Sigma, R)$.
Output: The set E that contains all erasable nonterminals in I.

begin
  set $E = \{A \mid A \rightarrow \varepsilon \in R\}$
  repeat
    if $B \rightarrow x \in R$ *with* $x \in E^*$ **then**
      add B to E
    end
  until no change
end

Algorithm 6.4 first initializes E with A and B because both nonterminals occur as the left-hand sides of the two ε-rules in I—that is, $A \rightarrow \varepsilon$ and $B \rightarrow \varepsilon$. Then, since $S \rightarrow AB$ with $AB \in E^*$, it includes S into E. After this inclusion, the algorithm cannot further increase E, so it ends.

Implementation 6.5. We give a C# implementation of Algorithm 6.4. Add the following method to `ContextFreeGrammar` class.

```
public FiniteSet<Symbol> DetermineErasableNonterminals()
{
    var result = new FiniteSet<Symbol>();
    foreach (ContextFreeRule r in this.Rules)
    {
        if (r.RightHandSide == HmmlcString.Empty)
        {
            result.Add(r.LeftHandSide);
        }
    }

    bool change;
    do
    {
        change = false;
        foreach (ContextFreeRule r in this.Rules)
        {
            if (r.RightHandSide.Symbols.Difference(result).IsEmpty)
            {
                if (result.Add(r.LeftHandSide)) change = true;
            }
        }
    }
```

Algorithm 6.5: Elimination of erasing rules

Input: A context-free grammar, $I = (\Sigma, R)$.
Output: A context-free grammar, $O = (\Sigma, R)$, that satisfies $L(O) = L(I) - \{\varepsilon\}$ and ${}_OR$ has no ε-rules.

begin
  set ${}_OR = \{A \rightarrow y \mid A \rightarrow y \in {}_IR, y \neq \varepsilon\}$
  use Algorithm 6.4 to determine ${}_IE$ that contains all ε-nonterminals in I
  repeat
    if $B \rightarrow x_0A_1x_1 \cdots A_nx_n$ *in* ${}_IR$ *where* $A_i \in {}_IE$, $x_i \in ({}_I\Sigma - {}_IE)^*$, *for all* $1 \leq i \leq n$, $0 \leq j \leq n$, *where n is a positive integer* **then**
      extend ${}_OR$ by
        $\{B \rightarrow x_0X_1x_1 \cdots X_nx_n \mid X_i \in \{\varepsilon, A_i\}, 1 \leq i \leq n, |X_1X_2 \cdots X_n| \geq 1\}$
    end
  until no change
end

```
    while (change);

    return result;
}
```

Note that this method returns a `FiniteSet<Symbol>` instead of an `Alphabet`. This is because there may be no erasable symbols, in which case the result will be the empty set. By definition, an alphabet cannot be empty.

We are now ready to eliminate all ε-rules from context-free grammars without decreasing their power. To be precise, without ε-rules, context-free grammars cannot generate ε. Therefore, we explain how to turn any context-free grammar I to a context-free grammar O so

(i) O generates $L(I) - \{\varepsilon\}$ and
(ii) no ε-rule occurs in O.

Basic Idea. Let I be a context-free grammar. Next, we explain how to transform I to a context-free grammar O that generates $L(I) - \{\varepsilon\}$ and, simultaneously, O contains no ε-rule. First, in I, detect all ε-nonterminals by Algorithm 6.4. Take any rule $B \rightarrow y$ with $y = x_0A_1x_1 \cdots A_nx_n$ in I, where A_1–A_n are ε-nonterminals. Add all possible rules of the form $B \rightarrow x_0X_1x_1 \cdots X_nx_n$ to O where $X_i \in \{\varepsilon, A_i\}$ and $X_1X_2 \cdots X_n \neq \varepsilon$ because each A_i can be erased by $A_i \Rightarrow^* \varepsilon$ in I. Repeat this extension of O until no further rule can be added therein.

As an exercise, prove that Algorithm 6.5 is correct.

Example 6.8. *Reconsider the context-free grammar defined as*

$$S \to AB,$$
$$A \to aAb,$$
$$B \to cBd,$$
$$A \to \varepsilon,$$
$$B \to \varepsilon$$

(see Example 6.7). Take this grammar as I. Initially, according to Algorithm 6.5, we set $_OR = \{S \to AB, A \to aAb, B \to cBd\}$. *Consider* $S \to AB$. *Both A and B are* ε*-nonterminals, so we add* $S \to AB$, $S \to B$, *and* $S \to A$ *to* $_OR$. *Analogically, from* $A \to aAb$ *and* $B \to cBd$, *we construct* $A \to aAb$, $B \to cBd$, $A \to ab$, *and* $B \to cd$, *respectively. In this way, as the resulting context-free grammar O without* ε*-rules, we obtain*

$$S \to AB,$$
$$S \to A,$$
$$S \to B,$$
$$A \to aAb,$$
$$B \to cBd,$$
$$A \to ab,$$
$$B \to cd.$$

Observe that O generates $\{a^n b^n \mid n \geq 0\}\{c^n d^n \mid n \geq 0\} - \{\varepsilon\}$, *so* $L(O) = L(I) - \{\varepsilon\}$.

Implementation 6.6. To implement Algorithm 6.5, we add the following new method to the class `ContextFreeGrammar`.

```
public ContextFreeGrammar RemoveErasingRules()
{
    var result = new ContextFreeGrammar
    {
        // copy nonterminals, terminals, and start symbol
        Nonterminals = new Alphabet(this.Nonterminals),
        Terminals = new Alphabet(this.Terminals),
        StartSymbol = this.StartSymbol
    };

    // determine erasable symbols
    FiniteSet<Symbol> erasableNonterminals =
        this.DetermineErasableNonterminals();

    // compute rules
    foreach (ContextFreeRule r in this.Rules)
    {
        // skip epsilon rules
        if (r.RightHandSide == HmmlcString.Empty) continue;

        int erasableCount =
            r.RightHandSide.Symbols
                               .Intersection(erasableNonterminals)
                               .Cardinality;
```

```
        if (erasableCount == 0)
        {
            // no erasable nonterminals, add rule as is
            result.Rules.Add(r);
        }
        else
        {
            // add rules to cover all possibilities
            // number of possibilities is 2^erasableCount
            int possibilityCount = 1 << erasableCount;
            for (int i = 0; i < possibilityCount; i++)
            {
                int erasableIndex = 0;
                var rhs = HmmlcString.Empty;
                foreach (Symbol a in r.RightHandSide)
                {
                    if (erasableNonterminals.Contains(a)) // erasable
                    {
                        // check if symbol should be included
                        // in this possibility
                        if ((i & (1 << erasableIndex)) != 0)
                        {
                            rhs = rhs.Concatenate(new HmmlcString(a));
                        }
                        erasableIndex++;
                    }
                    else // not erasable, must always be included
                    {
                        rhs = rhs.Concatenate(new HmmlcString(a));
                    }
                }
                if (rhs == HmmlcString.Empty)
                {
                    result.Rules.Add(
                        new ContextFreeRule(r.LeftHandSide, rhs));
                }
            }
        }
    }

    return result;
}
```

We also add a property which tells us whether a grammar contains any erasing rules.

```
public bool HasErasingRules
{
    get
    {
        foreach (ContextFreeRule r in this.Rules)
```

```
            {
                if (r.RightHandSide == HmmlcString.Empty) return true;
            }
            return false;
        }
}
```

Before closing this section, we make a final remark concerning the generation of ε. As already pointed out, if a context-free grammar contains no ε-rules, it cannot generate ε. Indeed, Algorithm 6.5 turns a context-free grammar I to a context-free grammar O so $L(O) = L(I) - \{\varepsilon\}$. If ε is not in $L(I)$, we actually have $L(O) = L(I)$. Suppose that ε belongs to $L(I)$. To generate $L(I)$ including ε, we can easily change O to $G = ({}_G\Sigma, {}_GR)$ so ${}_G\Sigma = {}_O\Sigma \cup \{{}_GS\}$ and ${}_GR = {}_OR \cup \{{}_GS \to {}_OS,\ {}_GS \to \varepsilon\}$, where ${}_GS$ is a newly introduced symbol, which is not in ${}_O\Sigma$. As obvious, $L(G) = L(I)$. As a result, we obtain the next theorem.

Theorem 6.4. *For every context-free language L such that $\varepsilon \in L$, there is a context-free grammar G simultaneously satisfying (i)–(iii), given as follows:*

(i) $L(G) = L$.
(ii) $S \to \varepsilon$ *is the only ε-rule in G, where S is the start symbol of G.*
(iii) *No rule contains S on its right-hand side in G.*

6.5 Single rules and their elimination

Single rules have a single nonterminal on the right-hand side, so they only rename their nonterminals; otherwise, they fulfill no role at all. As obvious, it is frequently desirable to remove them. The present section explains how to perform this removal.

Definition 6.11. *Let $G = (\Sigma, R)$ be a context-free grammar. A rule of the form $A \to B \in R$, where A and B are nonterminals, is called a* single rule.

Basic Idea. To transform a context-free grammar I to an equivalent context-free grammar O without single rules, observe that according to a sequence of single rules, every derivation is of the form $A \Rightarrow^* B$ in I, where A and B are nonterminals. Furthermore, notice that for any derivation of the form $A \Rightarrow^* B$, there exists a derivation from A to B during which no two identical rules are applied. Consider the set of all derivations that have the form $A \Rightarrow^* B \Rightarrow x$, where x differs from any nonterminal and $A \Rightarrow^* B$ is made according to a sequence of single rules so that this sequence contains no two identical rules. Notice that this set is finite because every derivation of the above form consists of no more than n steps with n being the number of rules in I. For any derivation $A \Rightarrow^* B \Rightarrow x$ in the set, which satisfies the above requirements, introduce $A \to x$ to obtain the resulting equivalent output context-free grammar O without single rules.

Algorithm 6.6: Elimination of single rules

Input: A context-free grammar I.
Output: A context-free grammar O such that $L(O) = L(I) - \{\varepsilon\}$ and no single rule occurs in O.

begin
set ${}_O\Sigma = {}_I\Sigma$
set ${}_OR = \emptyset$
repeat
if $A \Rightarrow^n B \Rightarrow x$ *in* I, *where* $A, B \in {}_IN$, $x \in {}_I\Sigma^* - {}_IN$, $0 \le n \le \text{card}\,({}_IR)$, *and* $A \Rightarrow^n B$ *is made by* n *single rules* **then**
add $A \to x$ to ${}_OR$
end
until no change
end

Example 6.9. *Reconsider the context-free grammar obtained in Example 6.8. This grammar has the following rules:*

$$\begin{aligned} S &\to AB, \\ S &\to A, \\ S &\to B, \\ A &\to aAb, \\ B &\to cBd, \\ A &\to ab, \\ B &\to cd. \end{aligned}$$

As obvious, $S \to A$ *and* $S \to B$ *are single rules. The program above transforms this context-free grammar to an equivalent context-free grammar without single rules as follows. From* $S \Rightarrow A \Rightarrow aAb$*, the program constructs* $S \to aAb$*. Similarly, from* $S \Rightarrow A \Rightarrow ab$*, it makes* $S \to ab$*. As the resulting context-free grammar, the program produces*

$$\begin{aligned} S &\to AB, \\ S &\to aAb, \\ S &\to ab, \\ S &\to cBd, \\ S &\to cd, \\ A &\to aAb, \\ B &\to cBd, \\ A &\to ab, \\ B &\to cd. \end{aligned}$$

Implementation 6.7. We first add a property to `ContextFreeGrammar` class which says whether any single rules are present.

```
public bool HasSingleRules
{
    get
    {
        foreach (ContextFreeRule r in this.Rules)
        {
            if (r.RightHandSide.Length == 1 &&
                this.Nonterminals.Contains(r.RightHandSide[0]))
            {
                return true;
            }
        }
        return false;
    }
}
```

Next, we give a C# implementation of Algorithm 6.6.

```
public ContextFreeGrammar RemoveSingleRules()
{
    var result = new ContextFreeGrammar
    {
        // copy nonterminals, terminals, and start symbol
        Nonterminals = new Alphabet(this.Nonterminals),
        Terminals = new Alphabet(this.Terminals),
        StartSymbol = this.StartSymbol
    };

    // compute rules
    foreach (Symbol a in this.Nonterminals)
    {
        // determine all nonterminals that can be derived from a
        // using single rules
        // a is always derivable (a =>^0 a)
        var derivableNonterminals = new FiniteSet<Symbol> { a };
        for (int n = 1; n < this.Rules.Cardinality; n++)
        {
            var nextDerivableNonterminals =
                new FiniteSet<Symbol>(derivableNonterminals);

            foreach (Symbol b in derivableNonterminals)
            {
                foreach (ContextFreeRule r in this.Rules)
                {
                    if (r.LeftHandSide == b &&
                        r.RightHandSide.Length == 1 &&
                        this.Nonterminals.Contains(r.RightHandSide[0]))
                    {
                        nextDerivableNonterminals.Add(
                            r.RightHandSide[0]);
```

```
                }
            }
        }

        derivableNonterminals = nextDerivableNonterminals;
    }

    // add rules rewriting a to all possible strings
    foreach (Symbol b in derivableNonterminals)
    {
        foreach (ContextFreeRule r in this.Rules)
        {
            if (r.LeftHandSide == b &&
                !(r.RightHandSide.Length == 1 &&
                this.Nonterminals.Contains(r.RightHandSide[0])))
            {
                result.Rules.Add(
                    new ContextFreeRule(a, r.RightHandSide));
            }
        }
    }
}

return result;
}
```

As an exercise, prove the next lemma.

Lemma 6.2. *Algorithm 6.6 is correct.*

We close this section by summarizing all the useful grammatical transformations given earlier in this chapter to demonstrate how to obtain a properly defined context-free grammar from any context-free grammar. Of course, first, we state what we actually mean by this notion.

Definition 6.12. *A context-free grammar G is* proper *if it contains neither useless symbols nor ε-rules nor single rules.*

Theorem 6.5. *For every context-free grammar I, there exists a proper context-free grammar O such that* $L(O) = L(I) - \{\varepsilon\}$.

Proof. As an exercise, prove this theorem by transformations given earlier in this chapter. ■

Implementation 6.8. Making use of Implementations 6.4, 6.6, and 6.7, we obtain a method that converts any context-free grammar to a proper one.

```
public bool IsProper
{
    get
    {
        return (!this.HasUselessSymbols &&
                !this.HasErasingRules &&
                !this.HasSingleRules);
    }
}

public ContextFreeGrammar ToProper()
{
    return this.RemoveUselessSymbols()
               .RemoveErasingRules()
               .RemoveSingleRules();
}
```

6.6 Chomsky normal form

In context-free grammars satisfying Chomsky normal form, every rule has on its right-hand side either one terminal or two nonterminals. In theory, formal language theory often makes use of this grammatical form to simplify proofs. In practice, this form is used in some methods of syntax analysis. The present section explains how to transform any context-free grammar to an equivalent proper grammar satisfying this form.

Definition 6.13. *A context-free grammar G is in* Chomsky normal form *if it is proper, and in addition, every rule $A \to x \in R$ has x consisting of a single terminal or two nonterminals.*

Basic Idea. Let $I = ({}_I\Sigma, {}_IR)$ be a proper context-free grammar. Start the transformation of I to an equivalent context-free grammar $O = ({}_O\Sigma, {}_OR)$ in Chomsky normal form by introducing nonterminal subalphabet $W = \{a' \mid a \in {}_I\Delta\}$ together with the bijection β from ${}_I\Sigma$ to $W \cup {}_IN$ that maps every $a \in {}_I\Delta$ to the nonterminal a' and every $A \in {}_IN$ to itself. Set ${}_O\Sigma = W \cup {}_I\Sigma$. For every $a \in {}_I\Delta$, include $a' \to a$ into ${}_OR$, and for every $A \to a \in {}_IR$, move $A \to a$ from ${}_IR$ to ${}_OR$. Furthermore, for each $A \to XY \in {}_IR$, where X and Y are in ${}_I\Sigma$, add $A \to \beta(X_1)\beta(X_2)$ to ${}_OR$ and, simultaneously, eliminate $A \to X_1X_2$ in ${}_IR$. Finally, for every $A \to X_1X_2X_3 \cdots X_{n-1}X_n \in {}_IR$ with $n \geq 3$, include new nonterminals $\langle X_2 \cdots X_n\rangle, \langle X_3 \cdots X_n\rangle, \ldots, \langle X_{n-2}X_{n-1}X_n\rangle, \langle X_{n-1}X_n\rangle$ into ${}_ON$ and add the rules $A \to \beta(X_1)\langle X_2 \cdots X_n\rangle$, $\langle X_2 \cdots X_n\rangle \to \beta(X_2)\langle X_3 \cdots X_n\rangle, \ldots,$ $\langle X_{n-2}X_{n-1}X_n\rangle \to \beta(X_{n-2})\langle X_{n-1}X_n\rangle$, $\langle X_{n-1}X_n\rangle \to \beta(X_{n-1})\beta(X_n)$ to ${}_OR$; notice that the added rules satisfy the Chomsky normal form. In this way,

$$A \Rightarrow X_1X_2X_3 \cdots X_{n-1}X_n \; [A \to X_1X_2X_3 \cdots X_{n-1}X_n]$$

in I is simulated in O as

$$\begin{aligned} A &\Rightarrow \beta(X_1)\langle X_2 \cdots X_n\rangle \\ &\Rightarrow \beta(X_1)\beta(X_2)\langle X_3 \cdots X_n\rangle \\ &\vdots \\ &\Rightarrow \beta(X_1)\beta(X_2)\cdots\beta(X_{n-2})\langle X_{n-1}\cdots X_n\rangle \\ &\Rightarrow \beta(X_1)\beta(X_2)\cdots\beta(X_{n-2})\beta(X_{n-1})\beta(X_n) \end{aligned}$$

and $\beta(X_j) \Rightarrow X_j$ $[\beta(X_j) \rightarrow X_j]$ in O, for every $X_j \in {}_I\Delta$, where $1 \leq j \leq n$.

O, constructed in this way, may contain some useless nonterminals; if it does, remove these useless symbols and all rules that contain them by using Algorithm 6.3.

Example 6.10. *Return to the context-free grammar obtained in Example 6.6—that is,*

$$\begin{aligned} S &\rightarrow SoS, \\ S &\rightarrow (S), \\ S &\rightarrow i, \end{aligned}$$

which obviously represents a proper context-free grammar. By using Algorithm 6.7 above, we convert this context-free grammar to an equivalent context-free grammar O in the Chomsky normal form. Initially, the algorithm introduces four new nonterminals; o', $('$, $)'$, and i'; and the bijection β from $\{S, o, (,), i\}$ to $\{S, o', (',)', i'\}$ that maps S, o, $($, $)$, and i to S, o', $('$, $)'$, and i', respectively. Then, it includes $o' \rightarrow o$, $(' \rightarrow ($, $)' \rightarrow)$, and $i' \rightarrow i$ into ${}_OR$. After this, it places $S \rightarrow i$ into ${}_OR$. From $S \rightarrow SoS$, this algorithm subsequently constructs $S \rightarrow S\langle oS\rangle$, $\langle oS\rangle \rightarrow o'S$. Analogously, from $S \rightarrow (S)$, it constructs $S \rightarrow ('\langle S)\rangle$, $\langle S)\rangle \rightarrow S)'$. The algorithm produces O defined as

$$\begin{aligned} o' &\rightarrow o, \\ (' &\rightarrow (, \\ )' &\rightarrow), \\ i' &\rightarrow i, \\ S &\rightarrow i, \\ S &\rightarrow S\langle oS\rangle, \\ \langle oS\rangle &\rightarrow o'S, \\ S &\rightarrow ('\langle S)\rangle, \\ \langle S)\rangle &\rightarrow S)'. \end{aligned}$$

This context-free grammar contains an inaccessible symbol i'. The algorithm detects this symbol as useless and removes it together with the rule $i' \rightarrow i$, which contains

---

Algorithm 6.7: Chomsky normal form

Input: A proper context-free grammar I.
Output: A context-free grammar O in Chomsky normal form such that $L(I) = L(O)$.

begin
  introduce $W = \{a' \mid a \in {}_I\Delta\}$ and the bijection β from ${}_I\Delta$ to $W \cup {}_IN$ defined as $\beta(a) = a'$ for all $a \in {}_I\Delta$, and $\beta(A) = A$ for all $A \in {}_IN$
  set ${}_O\Sigma = W \cup {}_I\Sigma$ and ${}_OR = \emptyset$
  for *all* $a \in {}_I\Delta$ **do**
    add $a' \to a$ to ${}_OR$
  end
  for *all* $A \to a \in {}_IR, A \in {}_IN, a \in {}_I\Delta$ **do**
    move $A \to a$ from ${}_IR$ to ${}_OR$
  end
  for *all* $A \to X_1X_2 \in {}_IR, A \in {}_IN, X_i \in {}_I\Sigma, i = 1, 2$ **do**
    add $A \to \beta(X_1)\beta(X_2)$ to ${}_OR$
    remove $A \to X_1X_2$ from ${}_IR$
  end
  repeat
    if *for some* $n \geq 3$, $A \to X_1X_2X_3 \cdots X_{n-1}X_n \in {}_IR, A \in {}_IN, X_i \in {}_I\Sigma, i = 1, \ldots, n$ **then**
      introduce new nonterminals $\langle X_2 \cdots X_n\rangle, \langle X_3 \cdots X_n\rangle, \ldots, \langle X_{n-2}X_{n-1}X_n\rangle, \langle X_{n-1}X_n\rangle$ into ${}_ON$
      add $A \to \beta(X_1)\langle X_2 \cdots X_n\rangle$, $\langle X_2 \cdots X_n\rangle \to \beta(X_2)\langle X_3 \cdots X_n\rangle, \ldots,$ $\langle X_{n-2}X_{n-1}X_n\rangle \to \beta(X_{n-2})\langle X_{n-1}X_n\rangle$, $\langle X_{n-1}X_n\rangle \to \beta(X_{n-1})\beta(X_n)$ to ${}_OR$
      remove $A \to X_1X_2X_3 \cdots X_{n-1}X_n$ from ${}_IR$
    end
  until no change
  remove all useless symbols and rules that contain them from O by Algorithm 6.3.
end

---

it. Rename S, $\langle oS\rangle$, o', $('$, $\langle S)\rangle$, *and* $)'$ *to* A_1, A_2, A_3, A_4, A_5, *and* A_6, *respectively, and order the rules according to their left-hand sides as follows:*

$$
\begin{aligned}
A_1 &\to A_1A_2,\\
A_1 &\to A_4A_5,\\
A_1 &\to i,\\
A_2 &\to A_3A_1,\\
A_3 &\to o,\\
A_4 &\to (,\\
A_5 &\to A_1A_6,\\
A_6 &\to),
\end{aligned}
$$

where A_1 is the start symbol. This context-free grammar represents the resulting version of the context-free grammar in the Chomsky normal form.

Implementation 6.9. First, we extend class `ContextFreeGrammar` with a property which tells us whether a context-free grammar is in Chomsky normal form.

```
public bool IsCNF
{
    get
    {
        if (!this.IsProper) return false;

        foreach (ContextFreeRule r in this.Rules)
        {
            if ((r.RightHandSide.Length == 1 &&
                 this.Terminals.Contains(r.RightHandSide[0])) ||
                (r.RightHandSide.Length == 2 &&
                 this.Nonterminals.Contains(r.RightHandSide[0]) &&
                 this.Nonterminals.Contains(r.RightHandSide[1])))
            {
                continue;
            }

            return false;
        }
        return true;
    }
}
```

We further add the following C# implementation of Algorithm 6.7. First, we create a helper method which implements bijection β.

```
private Symbol CnfBeta(Symbol a)
{
    if (this.Terminals.Contains(a)) return a + "'";
    else return a;
}
```

Now we can implement the conversion itself. Recall that `ToProper()` method was added in Implementation 6.8 and `RemoveUselessSymbols()` method in Implementation 6.4.

```
public ContextFreeGrammar ToChomskyNormalForm()
{
    // if grammar is not proper we convert it first
    if (!this.IsProper) return this.ToProper().ToChomskyNormalForm();

    var result = new ContextFreeGrammar()
    {
        // copy alphabet and start symbol
```

```
        Nonterminals = new Alphabet(this.Nonterminals),
        Terminals = new Alphabet(this.Terminals),
        StartSymbol = this.StartSymbol
    };

    // introduce new nonterminal and rule for each terminal
    foreach (Symbol a in this.Terminals)
    {
        result.Nonterminals.Add(a + "'");
        result.Rules.Add(new ContextFreeRule(
            a + "'",
            new HmmlcString(a)));
    }

    // make rules, introducing new nonterminals as needed
    foreach (ContextFreeRule r in this.Rules)
    {
        switch (r.RightHandSide.Length)
        {
            case 1:
                result.Rules.Add(r);
                break;
            case 2:
                result.Rules.Add(new ContextFreeRule(
                    r.LeftHandSide,
                    new HmmlcString(CnfBeta(r.RightHandSide[0]),
                                    CnfBeta(r.RightHandSide[1]))));
                break;
            default: // 3 or more symbols
                Symbol leftHandSide = r.LeftHandSide;
                for (int i = 0; i < r.RightHandSide.Length - 2; i++)
                {
                    // introduce new nonterminal <Xi+1...Xn>
                    var labelBuilder = new StringBuilder();
                    labelBuilder.Append("<");
                    for (int j = i + 1;
                         j < r.RightHandSide.Length;
                         j++)
                    {
                        labelBuilder.Append(r.RightHandSide[j]);
                    }
                    labelBuilder.Append(">");
                    var newNonterminal =
                        new Symbol(labelBuilder.ToString());
                    result.Nonterminals.Add(newNonterminal);

                    // add rule <Xi..Xn> -> Beta(Xi)<Xi+1...Xn>
                    // (or A -> Beta(X1)<X2...Xn> if first iteration)
```

```
                    result.Rules.Add(new ContextFreeRule(
                        leftHandSide,
                        new HmmlcString(CnfBeta(r.RightHandSide[i]),
                                    newNonterminal)));

                    leftHandSide = newNonterminal;
                }
                // add rule <Xn-1Xn> -> Beta(Xn-1)Beta(Xn)
                result.Rules.Add(new ContextFreeRule(
                    leftHandSide,
                    new HmmlcString(
                        CnfBeta(r.RightHandSide[
                            r.RightHandSide.Length - 2]),
                        CnfBeta(r.RightHandSide[
                            r.RightHandSide.Length - 1]))));
                break;
        }
    }

    // remove all useless symbols and rules
    result = result.RemoveUselessSymbols();

    return result;
}
```

Note that, for the sake of efficiency, this implementation processes all three types of rules in a single loop. Consequently, it produces the resulting rules in a different order than one might expect when strictly following Algorithm 6.7.

Prove the next theorem as an exercise.

Theorem 6.6. *Algorithm 6.7 is correct. Therefore, for every context-free language L, there exists a context-free grammar G such that* $L(G) = L - \{\varepsilon\}$ *and G satisfies the Chomsky normal form.*

6.7 Left recursion and its removal

In a context-free grammar, a *left recursive derivation* is a derivation of the form $A \Rightarrow^+ Ax$, where A is a nonterminal and x is a string. A derivation like this often represents an undesirable phenomenon because it causes the context-free grammar to enter an infinite loop during leftmost derivations. In fact, several grammatical transformations, such as achieving the Greibach normal form described in the next section, work only with non-left-recursive context-free grammars. Therefore, this section explains how to remove left recursion from any context-free grammar.

Definition 6.14. *Let $G = (\Sigma, R)$ be a context-free grammar and $A \in N$.*

(i) *A rule of the form $A \to Ay \in R$, where $y \in \Sigma^*$, is a* directly left-recursive rule, *and A is a* directly left-recursive nonterminal. *G is* directly left-recursive *if $_GN$ contains a directly left-recursive nonterminal.*
(ii) *A derivation of the form $A \Rightarrow^+ Ax$, where $x \in \Sigma^*$, is a* left-recursive derivation, *and A is a* left-recursive nonterminal *in G. G is* left-recursive *if $_GN$ contains a left-recursive nonterminal.*

Observe that directly left-recursive nonterminals are special cases of left-recursive nonterminals. Next, we explain how to remove them from any context-free grammar without affecting the generated language.

6.7.1 Direct left recursion and its elimination

Basic Idea. Let $G = ({}_G\Sigma, {}_GR)$ be a directly left-recursive context-free grammar. Without any loss of generality, suppose that G is proper (see Definition 6.12 and Theorem 6.5). Observe that for every nonterminal $A \in N$, there surely exists an A-rule that is not directly left-recursive; otherwise, A would be a useless symbol, which contradicts that G is proper. For every directly left-recursive, symbol A introduces a new nonterminal B into N, and for any pair of rules,

$$\begin{aligned} A &\to Aw, \\ A &\to u, \end{aligned}$$

where $u \in {}_G\Sigma^*$ and $A \to u$ is not a left-recursive rule, introduce

$$\begin{aligned} A &\to u, \\ A &\to uB, \\ B &\to wB, \\ B &\to w \end{aligned}$$

into $_GR$. Repeat this extension of G until nothing can be added to $_GN$ or $_GR$ in this way. Then, eliminate all the directly left-recursive A-rules in $_GR$, so the resulting context-free grammar is not a directly left-recursive. Consider, for instance,

$$A \Rightarrow Aw \Rightarrow Aww \Rightarrow uww,$$

made by two applications of $A \to Aw$ followed by one application of $A \to u$ in the original version of G. The modified version of G simulates the above derivation as

$$A \Rightarrow uB \Rightarrow uwB \Rightarrow uww$$

by applying $A \to u$, $B \to wB$, and $B \to w$. To illustrate this elimination by an example, take

$$\begin{aligned} S &\to SoS, \\ S &\to (S), \\ S &\to i \end{aligned}$$

as G (see Example 6.6). From this context-free grammar, the transformation sketched above produces

$$S \to (S),$$
$$S \to i,$$
$$S \to (S)B,$$
$$S \to iB,$$
$$B \to oSB,$$
$$B \to oS.$$

For instance, $S \Rightarrow SoS \Rightarrow Soi \Rightarrow ioi$ in the original context-free grammar is simulated by the transformed non-directly left-recursive context-free grammar as $S \Rightarrow iB \Rightarrow ioS \Rightarrow ioi$.

6.7.2 Left recursion and its elimination

Basic Idea. In essence, we eliminate general left recursion by the elimination of direct left recursion combined with a modification of rules so their right-hand sides start with nonterminals ordered in a way that rules out left recursion. More precisely, without any loss of generality (see Theorem 6.6), we consider a context-free grammar, $I = ({}_I\Sigma, {}_IR)$, in Chomsky normal form with ${}_IN = \{A_1, \ldots, A_n\}$, where card $({}_IN) = n$ (of course, we can always rename the nonterminals in I in this way). We next sketch how to turn I to an equivalent context-free grammar, $O = ({}_O\Sigma, {}_OR)$, with ${}_ON = \{A_1, \ldots, A_n\} \cup \{B_1, \ldots, B_m\}$, where B_1–B_m are new nonterminals ($m = 0$ actually means that ${}_ON = {}_IN$), and ${}_IR$ contains rules of these three forms:

(i) $A_i \to au$ with $a \in {}_O\Delta$ and $u \in {}_ON^*$;
(ii) $A_i \to A_jv$, for some $A_i, A_j \in \{A_k \mid 1 \leq k \leq n\}$ such that $i < j$, and $v \in {}_ON^+$; and
(iii) $B_i \to Cw$ with $C \in \{A_k \mid 1 \leq k \leq n\} \cup \{B_l \mid 1 \leq l \leq i-1\}$ and $w \in {}_ON^*$.

As demonstrated shortly (see the proof of Lemma 6.3), (i)–(iii) imply that O cannot make a derivation of the form $A_k \Rightarrow^+ A_kx$ or $B_l \Rightarrow^+ B_lx$, where $1 \leq k \leq n$ and $1 \leq l \leq i-1$; in other words, O is a non-left-recursive context-free grammar (of course, as opposed to I, O may not be in Chomsky normal form though).

The construction of O is based upon repeatedly changing I by (i) and (ii), given next, until I cannot be further modified. Then, O is defined as the final version of I, resulting from this repeated modification. To start with, set $k = 0$ and $i = 1$.

(i) In ${}_IR$, for every rule of the form $A_i \to A_jy$, where $j < i$, $y \in {}_IN^*$, extend ${}_IR$ by all A_i-rules of the form $A_i \to zy$, where $A_j \to z \in {}_IR$, $z \in {}_IN^+$ (recall that A_i-rule is a rule with A_i on its left-hand side according to conventions given in Section 4.1). After this extension, remove $A_i \to A_jy$ from ${}_IR$.
(ii) Rephrase and perform the elimination of direct recursion described above in terms of I instead of G. That is, let $A_i \in {}_IN$ be a directly left-recursive

nonterminal in I. Rephrase the above-described elimination of direct left recursion in terms of A_i as follows. Increase k by one and introduce a new nonterminal B_k into ${}_IN$. First, for every pair of rules,

$$A_i \rightarrow A_i w,$$
$$A_i \rightarrow u,$$

where $A_i \rightarrow u$ is not a left-recursive rule, add

$$A_i \rightarrow u,$$
$$A_i \rightarrow uB_k,$$
$$B_k \rightarrow wB_k,$$
$$B_k \rightarrow w$$

to ${}_IR$. Repeat this extension of ${}_IR$ until no more rules can be inserted into ${}_IR$ in this way. After this extension is completed, remove all directly left-recursive A_i-rules from ${}_IR$.

When ${}_IR$ cannot be modified by further repetition of (i) or (ii), increase i by 1. If $i \leq n$, repeat (i) and (ii) again in the same way; otherwise, set ${}_O\Sigma$ and ${}_OR$ to ${}_I\Sigma$ and ${}_IR$, respectively, in order to obtain $O = ({}_O\Sigma, {}_OR)$ as the resulting non-left-recursive context-free grammar equivalent with the original version of I (of course, as opposed to I, O may not satisfy the Chomsky normal form).

Based upon this basic idea, we next give an algorithm that turns I to O, satisfying the above properties.

Lemma 6.3. *Algorithm 6.8 is correct.*

Proof. By a straightforward examination of Algorithm 6.8, we see that each rule in ${}_OR$ has one of the forms (i)–(iii). Next, by contradiction, we prove that O is non-left-recursive. Suppose that O is left-recursive. We distinguish two cases—(a) $\{A_k \mid 1 \leq k \leq n\}$ contains a left-recursive nonterminal and (b) $\{B_l \mid 1 \leq l \leq m\}$ contains a left-recursive nonterminal.

(a) Let A_i be left-recursive, for some $A_i \in \{A_1, \ldots, A_n\}$. That is, there exists $x \in {}_ON^+$ such that $A_i \Rightarrow^+ A_i x$ in O. Recall that the right-hand side of every A_i-rule starts with a terminal or a nonterminal from $\{A_k \mid i \leq k \leq n\}$ (see (i) and (ii) in Algorithm 6.8), which rules out $A_i \Rightarrow^+ A_i x$ in O—a contradiction.

(b) Let B_i be left-recursive, for some $B_i \in \{B_1, \ldots, B_m\}$. That is, there exists $x \in {}_ON^+$ such that $B_i \Rightarrow^+ B_i x$ in O. Recall that the right-hand side of every B_i-rule starts with a nonterminal from $\{A_k \mid 1 \leq k \leq n\} \cup \{B_l \mid 1 \leq l \leq i\}$ (see (iii) in Algorithm 6.8). Furthermore, no right-hand side of any A_i-rule starts with a nonterminal from $\{B_l \mid 1 \leq l \leq m\}$, for all $1 \leq i \leq n$ (see (ii)). Thus, O cannot make $B_i \Rightarrow^+ B_i x$—a contradiction.

Thus, O is a non-left-recursive context-free grammar. As an exercise, complete this proof by demonstrating that $L(I) = L(O)$. ∎

Algorithm 6.8: Elimination of left recursion

Input: A context-free grammar I in Chomsky normal form with $_IN = \{A_1, \ldots, A_n\}$, for some $n \geq 1$.

Output: A non-left-recursive context-free grammar O such that $L(I) = L(O)$, $_ON = \{A_k \mid 1 \leq k \leq n\} \cup \{B_l \mid 1 \leq l \leq m\}$, for some $m \geq 0$, and each rule in $_OR$ has one of these three forms (i) $A_i \to au$ with $a \in {_O\Delta}$, and $u \in {_ON^*}$; (ii) $A_i \to A_jv$, for some $A_i, A_j \in \{A_k \mid 1 \leq k \leq n\}$ such that $i < j$, and $v \in {_ON^+}$; (iii) $B_i \to Cw$ with $C \in \{A_k \mid 1 \leq k \leq n\} \cup \{B_l \mid 1 \leq l \leq i-1\}$ and $w \in {_ON^*}$.

begin
  set $k = 0$
  for $i = 1, \ldots, n$ **do**
    repeat
      if $A_i \to A_jy \in {_IR}$, *where* $j < i$ *and* $y \in {_IN^*}$ **then**
        repeat
          if $A_j \to z \in {_IR}$, *where* $z \in {_IN^+}$ **then**
            add $A_i \to zy$ to $_IR$
          end
        until no change
        remove $A_i \to A_jy$ from $_IR$
      end
      if $A_i \in {_IN}$ *is a directly left-recursive nonterminal in* I **then**
        $k = k + 1$
        introduce a new nonterminal B_k into $_IN$
        repeat
          if $A_i \to A_iw$ *and* $A_i \to u$ *are in* $_IR$, *where* $w, u \in {_IN^+}$ *and* $A_i \to u$ *is not a directly left-recursive rule* **then**
            add $A_i \to uB_k$, $B_k \to wB_k$, and $B_k \to w$ to $_IR$
          end
        until no change
        remove all directly left-recursive A_i-rules from $_IR$ { notice that $A_i \to u$ remains in $_IR$ }
      end
    until no change
  end
  define $O = ({_O\Sigma}, {_OR})$ with $_O\Sigma = {_I\Sigma}$ and $_OR = {_IR}$
end

Example 6.11. *Reconsider the context-free grammar in the Chomsky normal form*

$A_1 \to A_1A_2,$
$A_1 \to A_4A_5,$

$A_1 \to i,$
$A_2 \to A_3A_1,$
$A_3 \to o,$
$A_4 \to ($,
$A_5 \to A_1A_6,$
$A_6 \to)$

from Example 6.10. Observe that this context-free grammar is left-recursive because A_1 is a directly left-recursive nonterminal. Consider the context-free grammar as the input grammar I in Algorithm 6.8. Observe that I satisfies all the properties required by Algorithm 6.8. Apply this algorithm to convert I to an equivalent non-left-recursive grammar O, satisfying the output properties described in Algorithm 6.8. In this application, $n = 6$ because I has six nonterminals: A_1–A_6. For $i = 1$, the `for` *loop replaces $A_1 \to A_1A_2$ with*

$A_1 \to A_4A_5,$
$A_1 \to A_4A_5B_1,$
$A_1 \to i,$
$A_1 \to iB_1,$
$B_1 \to A_2B_1,$
$B_1 \to A_2.$

After this replacement, for $i = 2, \ldots, 4$, the `for` *loop does not change any rule. For $i = 5$, this loop replaces $A_5 \to A_1A_6$ with*

$A_5 \to A_4A_5A_6,$
$A_5 \to A_4A_5B_1A_6,$
$A_5 \to iA_6,$
$A_5 \to iB_1A_6.$

After this replacement, it replaces $A_5 \to A_4A_5A_6$ with $A_5 \to (A_5A_6$. Finally, it replaces $A_5 \to A_4A_5B_1A_6$ with $A_5 \to (A_5B_1A_6$. For $k = 6$, the `for` *loop does not change any rule. Consequently, the resulting output grammar O produced by Algorithm 6.8 is defined as*

(i)	(ii)	(iii)
$A_1 \to i,$	$A_1 \to A_4A_5,$	$B_1 \to A_2B_1,$
$A_1 \to iB_1,$	$A_1 \to A_4A_5B_1,$	$B_1 \to A_2.$
$A_3 \to o,$	$A_2 \to A_3A_1,$	
$A_4 \to ($,		
$A_5 \to (A_5A_6,$		
$A_5 \to (A_5B_1A_6,$		
$A_5 \to iA_6,$		
$A_5 \to iB_1A_6,$		
$A_6 \to)$,		

Implementation 6.10. *Before we implement Algorithm 6.8, we first add the following helper method to* `ContextFreeGrammar` *class.*

```
private ContextFreeGrammar RenameNonteminals()
{
    var result = new ContextFreeGrammar()
    {
        Terminals = new Alphabet(this.Terminals)
    };

    var mapping = new Dictionary<Symbol, Symbol>();

    int i = 0;
    foreach (Symbol X in this.Nonterminals)
    {
        i++;
        Symbol Ai = "A" + i;
        mapping.Add(X, Ai);
        result.Nonterminals.Add(Ai);
    }

    foreach (ContextFreeRule r in this.Rules)
    {
        Symbol lhs = mapping[r.LeftHandSide];

        var rhsSymbols = new List<Symbol>();
        foreach (Symbol a in r.RightHandSide)
        {
            if (this.Nonterminals.Contains(a))
            {
                rhsSymbols.Add(mapping[a]);
            }
            else
            {
                rhsSymbols.Add(a);
            }
        }
        var rhs = new HmmlcString(rhsSymbols.ToArray());

        result.Rules.Add(new ContextFreeRule(lhs, rhs));
    }

    result.StartSymbol = mapping[this.StartSymbol];

    return result;
}
```

Now that we can convert any context-free grammar to Chomsky normal form (see Implementation 6.9) and rename the resulting nonterminals to $A_1, \ldots, A_n$, *we implement Algorithm 6.8 as follows:*

```
public ContextFreeGrammar RemoveLeftRecursion()
{
```

```
ContextFreeGrammar result = this.ToChomskyNormalForm()
                            .RenameNonteminals();

var ANonterminals = new Alphabet(result.Nonterminals);

int n = result.Nonterminals.Cardinality;

int k = 0;

for (int i = 1; i <= n; i++)
{
    Symbol Ai = "A" + i;

    bool change;
    do
    {
        change = false;

        foreach (ContextFreeRule r in result.Rules)
        {
            if (r.LeftHandSide == Ai &&
                r.RightHandSide.Length > 0 &&
                ANonterminals.Contains(r.RightHandSide[0]))
            {
                Symbol Aj = r.RightHandSide[0];
                int j = int.Parse(Aj.ToString().Substring(1));
                if (j < i)
                {
                    var currentRules =
                        new FiniteSet<ContextFreeRule>(
                            result.Rules);
                    foreach (ContextFreeRule r2 in currentRules)
                    {
                        if (r2.LeftHandSide == Aj &&
                            r2.RightHandSide.Length > 0)
                        {
                            HmmlcString z = r2.RightHandSide;
                            HmmlcString y =
                                r.RightHandSide.GetSuffix(
                                    r.RightHandSide.Length - 1);
                            result.Rules.Add(new ContextFreeRule(
                                Ai, z.Concatenate(y)));
                        }
                    }

                    result.Rules.Remove(r);

                    change = true;

                    break;
                }
            }
        }
```

```
bool AiDirectlyRecursive = false;
foreach (ContextFreeRule r2 in result.Rules)
{
    if (r2.LeftHandSide == Ai &&
        r2.RightHandSide.Length > 0 &&
        r2.RightHandSide[0] == Ai)
    {
        AiDirectlyRecursive = true;
        break;
    }
}
if (AiDirectlyRecursive)
{
    k++;
    Symbol Bk = "B" + k;
    result.Nonterminals.Add(Bk);
    var currentRules =
        new FiniteSet<ContextFreeRule>(result.Rules);
    foreach (ContextFreeRule r2 in currentRules)
    {
        if (r2.LeftHandSide == Ai &&
            r2.RightHandSide.Length > 0 &&
            r2.RightHandSide[0] == Ai)
        {
            foreach (ContextFreeRule r3 in currentRules)
            {
                if (r3.LeftHandSide == Ai &&
                    r3.RightHandSide.Length > 0 &&
                    r3.RightHandSide[0] != Ai)
                {
                    HmmlcString u = r3.RightHandSide;
                    HmmlcString w =
                        r2.RightHandSide.GetSuffix(
                            r2.RightHandSide.Length - 1);
                    HmmlcString BkString =
                        new HmmlcString(Bk);
                    result.Rules.Add(new ContextFreeRule(
                        Ai, u.Concatenate(BkString)));
                    result.Rules.Add(new ContextFreeRule(
                        Bk, w.Concatenate(BkString)));
                    result.Rules.Add(new ContextFreeRule(
                        Bk, w));
                }
            }
        }
    }
    foreach (ContextFreeRule r2 in currentRules)
    {
        if (r2.LeftHandSide == Ai &&
            r2.RightHandSide.Length > 0 &&
            r2.RightHandSide[0] == Ai)
```

```
                    {
                        result.Rules.Remove(r2);
                    }
                }

                change = true;
            }
        }
        while (change);
    }

    return result;
}
```

Algorithm 6.8 and Lemma 6.3 imply the next theorem.

Lemma 6.4. *For every context-free grammar I in Chomsky normal form, there exists an equivalent non-left-recursive context-free grammar O.*

Theorem 6.7. *For every context-free grammar I, there exists a non-left-recursive context-free grammar O satisfying L(I) = L(O).*

Proof. Consider any context-free grammar I. If $\varepsilon \notin L(I)$, this theorem follows from Theorem 6.6 and Lemma 6.4. Suppose that $\varepsilon \in L(I)$. Introduce the context-free grammar $O = ({}_O\Sigma, {}_OR)$ with ${}_O\Sigma = {}_O\Sigma \cup \{{}_OS\}$ and ${}_OR = {}_IR \cup \{{}_OS \rightarrow {}_IS, {}_OS \rightarrow \varepsilon\}$, where the start symbol ${}_OS$ is a newly introduced symbol, ${}_OS \notin {}_I\Sigma$. Observe that O is non-left-recursive and $L(I) = L(O)$. ■

6.7.3 Right recursion

By analogy with left recursion, we define its right counterpart.

Definition 6.15. *A context-free grammar G is* right-recursive *if $A \Rightarrow^+ xA$ in G, for some $A \in N$ and $x \in \Sigma^*$.*

As an exercise, prove the following theorem:

Theorem 6.8. *For every context-free grammar I, there exists a non-right-recursive context-free grammar O satisfying L(I) = L(O).*

6.8 Greibach normal form

In Greibach normal form, context-free grammars have the right-hand side of every rule started with a terminal followed by zero or more nonterminals. Just like Chomsky normal form, Greibach normal form simplifies proofs of results about context-free grammars. Therefore, we explain how to turn any context-free grammar into an equivalent context-free grammar that satisfies this form.

Definition 6.16. *Let $G = (\Sigma, R)$ be a context-free grammar. G is in* Greibach normal form *if in R, every rule is of the form $A \rightarrow ax$, where $A \in N$, $a \in \Delta$ and $x \in N^*$.*

Basic Idea. Without any loss of generality, suppose that a context-free grammar $I = ({}_I\Sigma, {}_IR)$ satisfies the properties of the context-free grammar produced by Algorithm 6.8 (see Lemma 6.3). That is, ${}_IN = \{A_k \mid 1 \leq k \leq n\} \cup \{B_l \mid 1 \leq l \leq m\}$, for some $n, m \geq 0$, and each rule in ${}_IR$ has one of these three forms:

(i) $A_i \to au$ with $a \in {}_I\Delta$, and $u \in {}_IN^*$;
(ii) $A_i \to A_jv$, for some $A_i, A_j \in \{A_k \mid 1 \leq k \leq n\}$ such that $i < j$ and $v \in {}_IN^+$; and
(iii) $B_i \to Cw$ with $C \in \{A_k \mid 1 \leq k \leq n\} \cup \{B_l \mid 1 \leq l \leq i-1\}$ and $w \in {}_IN^*$.

Consider all rules of the form $A_i \to au$ with $a \in {}_I\Delta$ and $u \in {}_IN^*$ (see (i)). As obvious, they are in Greibach normal form.

Consider any rule of the form $A_n \to u$ (see (i) and (ii)). As n is the greatest number in $\{1, \ldots, n\}$, $A_n \to u$ is not of the form (ii), so it is of the form (i). That is, u starts with a terminal and, therefore, $A_n \to u$ is in Greibach normal form. For every pair of rules $A_{n-1} \to A_nv$ and $A_n \to u$, introduce a rule $A_{n-1} \to uv$ into ${}_OR$, which is in Greibach normal form because so is $A_n \to u$. As a result, all the newly introduced A_{n-1}-rules are in Greibach normal form. Then, for every pair of rules $A_{n-2} \to A_jv$ and $A_j \to u$ in (ii) with $n-2 < j$—that is, $j = n-1$ or $j = n$, make an analogical introduction of new rules. Proceeding down toward $n = 1$ in this way, we eventually obtain all A_k-rules in Greibach normal form.

Consider any rule $B_1 \to u$ from (iii). For B_1, u starts with A_j for some $j = 1, \ldots, n$, and all the A_j-rules in ${}_OR$ are in Greibach normal form. Therefore, for every pair of rules $B_1 \to A_jy$ in ${}_IR$ and $A_j \to v$ in ${}_OR$, add $B_1 \to vy$ to ${}_OR$. As a result, all the newly introduced B_1-rules in ${}_OR$ are in Greibach normal form. Then, for every pair of rules $B_2 \to Cw$ in ${}_IR$ with $C \in \{A_k \mid 1 \leq k \leq n\} \cup \{B_1\}$ and a C-rule $C \to z$ in ${}_OR$, which is already in Greibach normal form, add $B_2 \to zw$ to ${}_OR$. Proceeding from 1 to m in this way, we eventually obtain all the B_l-rules in Greibach normal form, $1 \leq l \leq m$. The resulting context-free grammar is Greibach normal form and generates $L(I)$.

Consider the basic idea preceding Algorithm 6.9. Based on this idea, give a rigorous proof of the next lemma.

Lemma 6.5. *Algorithm 6.9 is correct.*

Example 6.12. *Consider the non-left-recursive context-free grammar*

(i)	*(ii)*	*(iii)*
$A_1 \to i,$	$A_1 \to A_4A_5,$	$B_1 \to A_2B_1,$
$A_1 \to iB_1,$	$A_1 \to A_4A_5B_1,$	$B_1 \to A_2,$
$A_3 \to o,$	$A_2 \to A_3A_1,$	
$A_4 \to ($,		
$A_5 \to (A_5A_6,$		
$A_5 \to (A_5B_1A_6,$		
$A_5 \to iA_6,$		
$A_5 \to iB_1A_6,$		
$A_6 \to)$		

obtained in Example 6.11. Let this context-free grammar be I in Algorithm 6.9. Notice that it satisfies all the input requirements stated in this algorithm.

Algorithm 6.9: Greibach normal form

Input: A non-left-recursive context-free grammar $I = ({}_I\Sigma, {}_IR)$ such that ${}_IN = \{A_k \mid 1 \leq k \leq n\} \cup \{B_l \mid 1 \leq l \leq m\}$, for some $n, m \geq 0$, and each rule in ${}_IR$ has one of these three forms (i) $A_i \rightarrow au$ with $a \in {}_I\Delta$, and $u \in {}_IN^*$; (ii) $A_i \rightarrow A_jv$, for some $A_i, A_j \in \{A_k \mid 1 \leq k \leq n\}$ such that $i < j$, and $v \in {}_IN^+$; (iii) $B_i \rightarrow Cw$ with $C \in \{A_k \mid 1 \leq k \leq n\} \cup \{B_l \mid 1 \leq l \leq i-1\}$ and $w \in {}_IN^*$.

Output: A context-free grammar O in Greibach normal form such that $L(O) = L(I)$.

begin
  set ${}_ON = {}_IN$, ${}_O\Delta = {}_I\Delta$, and ${}_OS = {}_IS$
  set ${}_OR = \{A_i \rightarrow au \mid A_i \rightarrow au$ with $a \in {}_I\Delta$ and $u \in {}_IN^*\}$
  for $i = n, n-1, \ldots, 1$ **do**
    for *each* $A_i \rightarrow A_jy \in {}_IR$, *where* $A_i, A_j \in \{A_k \mid 1 \leq k \leq n\}$ *such that* $i < j$, *and* $y \in {}_IN^+$ **do**
      ${}_OR = {}_OR \cup \{A_i \rightarrow zy \mid A_j \rightarrow z \in {}_OR, z \in {}_I\Delta_IN^*\}$
    end
  end
  for $i = 1, 2, \ldots, m$ **do**
    for *each* $B_i \rightarrow Cw \in {}_IR$ *with* $C \in \{A_k \mid 1 \leq k \leq n\} \cup \{B_l \mid 1 \leq l \leq i-1\}$ *and* $w \in {}_IN^*$ **do**
      ${}_OR = {}_OR \cup \{B_i \rightarrow zw \mid C \rightarrow z \in {}_OR, z \in {}_I\Delta_IN^*\}$
    end
  end
end

Consider (i). All these rules are in Greibach normal form. Thus, initialize ${}_OR$ *with them.*

Consider (ii). Notice that the first `for` *loop works with these rules. For* $i = 2$, *as* $A_2 \rightarrow A_3A_1$ *is in (ii) and* ${}_OR$ *contains* $A_3 \rightarrow o$; *this loop adds* $A_2 \rightarrow oA_1$ *to* ${}_OR$. *For* $i = 1$, *since* $A_1 \rightarrow A_4A_5$ *and* $A_1 \rightarrow A_4A_5B_1$ *are in (ii) and* $A_4 \rightarrow ($ *is in* ${}_OR$, *this loop also adds* $A1 \rightarrow (A_5$ *and* $A_1 \rightarrow (A_5B_1$ *to* ${}_OR$.

Consider (iii). The second for loop works with the two B_1*-rules listed in (iii). As* $B_1 \rightarrow A_2B_1$ *and* $B_1 \rightarrow A_2$ *are in (iii) and* $A_2 \rightarrow oA_1$ *is in* ${}_OR$, *the second* `for` *loop includes* $B_1 \rightarrow oA_1B_1$ *and* $B_1 \rightarrow oA_1$ *into* ${}_OR$.

Consequently, as O, Algorithm 6.9 produces this context-free grammar in Greibach normal form:

$A_1 \rightarrow i,$
$A_1 \rightarrow iB_1,$
$A_5 \rightarrow (A_5A_6,$
$A_5 \rightarrow (A_5B_1A_6,$

$$A_5 \to iA_6,$$
$$A_5 \to iB_1A_6,$$
$$A_3 \to o,$$
$$A_4 \to (,$$
$$A_6 \to),$$
$$A_2 \to oA_1,$$
$$A_1 \to (A_5,$$
$$A_1 \to (A_5B_1,$$
$$B_1 \to oA_1B_1,$$
$$B_1 \to oA_1.$$

As an exercise, verify that $L(I) = L(O)$.

Implementation 6.11. *Next, we present a C# implementation of Algorithm 6.9 by way of a method added to `ContextFreeGrammar` class. Recall that method `RemoveLeftRecursion` from Implementation 6.10 also converts the grammar to Chomsky normal form and renames nonterminals as required for the algorithm.*

```
public ContextFreeGrammar ToGreibachNormalForm()
{
    ContextFreeGrammar I = this.RemoveLeftRecursion();

    var result = new ContextFreeGrammar()
    {
        Nonterminals = new Alphabet(I.Nonterminals),
        Terminals = new Alphabet(I.Terminals),
        StartSymbol = I.StartSymbol
    };

    var ANonterminals = new FiniteSet<Symbol>();
    var BNonterminals = new FiniteSet<Symbol>();

    foreach (Symbol A in I.Nonterminals)
    {
        if (A.ToString().StartsWith("A"))
        {
            ANonterminals.Add(A);
        }
        else
        {
            BNonterminals.Add(A);
        }
    }

    int n = ANonterminals.Cardinality;
    int m = BNonterminals.Cardinality;
```

```
foreach (ContextFreeRule r in I.Rules)
{
    if (r.RightHandSide.Length > 0 &&
        I.Terminals.Contains(r.RightHandSide[0]))
    {
        result.Rules.Add(r);
    }
}

for (int i = n; i >= 1; i--)
{
    Symbol Ai = "A" + i;

    foreach (ContextFreeRule r in I.Rules)
    {
        if (r.LeftHandSide == Ai &&
            r.RightHandSide.Length >= 2 &&
            ANonterminals.Contains(r.RightHandSide[0]))
        {
            Symbol Aj = r.RightHandSide[0];
            int j = int.Parse(Aj.ToString().Substring(1));
            if (i < j)
            {
                HmmlcString y = r.RightHandSide.GetSuffix(
                    r.RightHandSide.Length - 1);

                var currentRules =
                    new FiniteSet<ContextFreeRule>(
                        result.Rules);
                foreach (ContextFreeRule r2 in currentRules)
                {
                    if (r2.LeftHandSide == Aj &&
                        r2.RightHandSide.Length > 0 &&
                        I.Terminals.Contains(r2.RightHandSide[0]))
                    {
                        HmmlcString z = r2.RightHandSide;
                        result.Rules.Add(new ContextFreeRule(
                            Ai, z.Concatenate(y)));
                    }
                }
            }
        }
    }
}

for (int i = 1; i <= m; i++)
{
    Symbol Bi = "B" + i;
```

```
        foreach (ContextFreeRule r in I.Rules)
        {
            if (r.LeftHandSide == Bi &&
                r.RightHandSide.Length > 0)
            {
                Symbol C = r.RightHandSide[0];
                HmmlcString w = r.RightHandSide.GetSuffix(
                    r.RightHandSide.Length - 1);

                var currentRules =
                    new FiniteSet<ContextFreeRule>(result.Rules);
                foreach (ContextFreeRule r2 in currentRules)
                {
                    if (r2.LeftHandSide == C &&
                        r2.RightHandSide.Length > 0 &&
                        I.Terminals.Contains(r2.RightHandSide[0]))
                    {
                        HmmlcString z = r2.RightHandSide;
                        result.Rules.Add(new ContextFreeRule(
                            Bi, z.Concatenate(w)));
                    }
                }
            }
        }
    }

    return result;
}
```

Algorithm 6.9, Lemma 6.5 and Theorem 6.7 imply the next theorem.

Theorem 6.9. *For every context-free grammar I, there exists a context-free grammar O in Greibach normal form such that $L(I) - \{\varepsilon\} = L(O)$.*

We close this section by taking a finer look at context-free grammars in Greibach normal form. Specifically, we discuss the number of nonterminals on the right-hand side of their rules. To do so, we introduce the notion of an *n*-standard Greibach normal form, where *n* is a nonnegative integer. That is, if a context-free grammar *G* in Greibach normal form has *n* or fewer nonterminals on the right-hand side of each rule, then *G* is in an *n*-standard Greibach normal form.

Definition 6.17. *Let n be a nonnegative integer and $G = (\Sigma, R)$ be a context-free grammar in Greibach normal form. G is in an n-*standard Greibach normal form *if every rule $A \to ax \in R$ satisfies $a \in \Delta$, $x \in N^*$, and $|x| \leq n$.*

Clearly, any zero-standard Greibach normal form context-free grammar generates ∅ or a language that represents an alphabet—that is, a finite language in which every string is of length one.

Theorem 6.10. *A language L is generated by a context-free grammar in a zero-standard Greibach normal form iff L represents a finite set of symbols.*

In a one-standard Greibach normal form context-free grammars, every rule is of the form $A \rightarrow aB$ or $A \rightarrow a$. These context-free grammars are as powerful as finite automata.

Theorem 6.11. *A language L is accepted by a finite automaton iff* $L - \{\varepsilon\}$ *is generated by a context-free grammar in a one-standard Greibach normal form.*

Proof. Leaving a fully detailed version of this proof as an exercise, we only give its sketch. First, convert any context-free grammar in a one-standard Greibach normal form to an equivalent finite automaton (see Definition 5.1). Then, turn any deterministic finite automaton M (see Definition 5.3) to a one-standard Greibach normal form context-free grammar that generates $L(M) - \{\varepsilon\}$. As finite automata and deterministic finite automata have the same power (see Theorem 5.4), Theorem 6.11 holds true. ■

Consider two-standard Greibach normal form context-free grammars. For instance, return to the context-free grammar discussed in Example 6.2—that is,

$$
\begin{aligned}
S &\rightarrow aB,\\
S &\rightarrow bA,\\
A &\rightarrow a,\\
A &\rightarrow aS,\\
A &\rightarrow bAA,\\
B &\rightarrow b,\\
B &\rightarrow bS,\\
B &\rightarrow aBB.
\end{aligned}
$$

This context-free grammar represents a context-free grammar in a two-standard Greibach normal form. According to the next theorem, every context-free grammar G can be turned to a context-free grammar in a two-standard Greibach normal form so that it generates $L(G) - \{\varepsilon\}$.

Theorem 6.12. *A language L is generated by a context-free grammar iff* $L - \{\varepsilon\}$ *is generated by a context-free grammar in a two-standard Greibach normal form.*

Proof. By Theorem 6.12, a language L is generated by a context-free grammar iff $L(G) - \{\varepsilon\}$ is generated by a context-free grammar in a two-standard Greibach normal form. Consider the basic idea underlying the transformation to the Chomsky normal form (see Algorithm 6.7). As an exercise, modify this idea to convert G to an equivalent context-free grammar G in a two-standard Greibach normal form. ■

Chapter 7
Pushdown automata

Pushdown automata represent, in essence, finite automata extended by potentially infinite stacks, commonly referred to as pushdown lists or, more briefly, pushdowns. In this chapter, we demonstrate that these automata are as powerful as context-free grammars, discussed in the previous chapter.

This chapter is divided into four sections. First, Section 7.1 defines pushdown automata. Then, Section 7.2 establishes the equivalence between them and context-free grammars. Section 7.3 introduces three ways of accepting languages by these automata. Finally, Section 7.4 narrows its attention to the deterministic versions of pushdown automata and demonstrates that they are less powerful than their nondeterministic versions.

7.1 Pushdown automata

We begin by defining pushdown automata as special cases of rewriting systems, introduced in Chapter 4. Therefore, in this definition as well as in the discussion that follows, we take advantage of all the mathematical terminology concerning these systems, such as relations $\Rightarrow$ and $\Rightarrow^*$.

Definition 7.1. *A* pushdown automaton *is a rewriting system,* $M = (\Sigma, R)$, *where*

- Σ *is divided into subalphabets* Q, Γ, Δ *such that* $Q \cap (\Gamma \cup \Delta) = \emptyset$.
- R *is a finite* set of rules *of the form* $x \to y$, *where* $x \in \Gamma^* Q(\Delta \cup \{\varepsilon\})$ *and* $y \in \Gamma^* Q$.

Q, Γ, *and* Δ *are referred to as the* set of states, *the* alphabet of pushdown symbols, *and the* alphabet of input symbols, *respectively.* Q *contains the* start state, *denoted by* s, *and a* set of final states, *denoted by* F. Γ *contains the* start symbol, S. *If* $Ssw \Rightarrow^* f$ *in* M *with* $f \in F$, M accepts w. *The set of all strings that* M *accepts is the* language accepted by M, *denoted by* $L(M)$, *so*

$$L(M) = \{w \mid w \in \Delta^*, Ssw \Rightarrow^* f, f \in F\}.$$

Let M be a pushdown automaton. A *configuration* of M is a string of the form wqv, where $w \in \Gamma^*$, $q \in Q$, and $v \in \Delta^*$. Unless $w = \varepsilon$, the rightmost symbol of w represents the *pushdown top* symbol. ${}_MX$ denotes the set of all configurations of M. If $\beta \Rightarrow \chi$ in M, where $\beta, \chi \in {}_MX$, M makes a *move* from b to c. M makes a *sequence of moves* or, more briefly, a *computation* from β to χ if $\beta \Rightarrow^* \chi$ in M, where $\beta, \chi \in {}_MX$.

Furthermore, we automatically assume that S, Γ, Δ, Q, s, S, F, and R denote the total alphabet, the alphabet of pushdown symbols, the alphabet of input symbols, the set of states, the start state, the start pushdown symbol, the set of final states, and the set of rules of M, respectively.

For brevity, M is often defined by simply listing its rules together with specifying the members of S, Γ, Δ, Q, and F.

Next, we illustrate the definition by two examples.

Example 7.1. *Take* $L = \{a^k b^k \mid k \geq 1\}$. *In this example, we construct a pushdown automaton* M *that accepts this language.*

To give an insight into the way M *works, it always performs two computational phases. First, it pushes down as. Then, when the first occurrence of b appears,* M *pops up as and pairs them off with bs. If the number of as and bs coincides,* M *accepts the input string; otherwise, it rejects.*

Formally, $M = (\Sigma, R)$ *with* $\Sigma = \Gamma \cup \Delta \cup Q$, $\Gamma = \{S, a\}$, $\Delta = \{a, b\}$, $Q = \{s, f\}$, $F = \{f\}$, *and*

$$R = \{Ssa \rightarrow as, asa \rightarrow aas, asb \rightarrow f, afb \rightarrow f\}.$$

Less formally, but more succinctly, we can specify M *by listing its four rules, labeled by* 1–4, *as*

$$\begin{aligned} 1 &: Ssa \rightarrow as, \\ 2 &: asa \rightarrow aas, \\ 3 &: asb \rightarrow f, \\ 4 &: afb \rightarrow f. \end{aligned}$$

For instance, on aaabbb, M *performs this sequence of moves*

$$\begin{aligned} Ssaaabbb &\Rightarrow asaabbb \ [1] \\ &\Rightarrow aasabbb \ [2] \\ &\Rightarrow aaasbbb \ [2] \\ &\Rightarrow aafbb \ [3] \\ &\Rightarrow afb \ [4] \\ &\Rightarrow f \ [4]. \end{aligned}$$

As f *is final,* M *accepts aaabbb.*

In general, observe that M *makes every acceptance so it applies once rule* 1, n *times rule* 2, *once rule* 3, *and* n *times rule* 4 *in this order, for some* $n \geq 0$; *in this way,* M *accepts* $a^{n+1}b^{n+1}$. *Consequently,* $L(M) = \{a^k b^k \mid k \geq 1\}$; *a rigorous proof of this identity is left as an exercise.*

Implementation 7.1. A C# implementation of pushdown automaton follows next. Notice the similarities with the code implementing finite automata (see Implementation 5.2). First, we implement a pushdown automaton state.

```
public class PushdownAutomatonState
    : IEquatable<PushdownAutomatonState>
{
    public Symbol Label { get; private set; }
```

```
// constructor
public PushdownAutomatonState(Symbol label)
{
    this.Label = label;
}

// equality checking using pattern from Implementation 1.3
public static bool Equals(PushdownAutomatonState q,
                          PushdownAutomatonState p)
{
    if (ReferenceEquals(q, p)) return true;
    else if (ReferenceEquals(q, null) ||
             ReferenceEquals(p, null))
    {
        return false;
    }
    else return q.Label == p.Label;
}
public bool Equals(PushdownAutomatonState other)
{
    return PushdownAutomatonState.Equals(this, other);
}
public override bool Equals(object obj)
{
    return PushdownAutomatonState.Equals(
        this, obj as PushdownAutomatonState);
}
public static bool operator ==(PushdownAutomatonState q,
                               PushdownAutomatonState p)
{
    return PushdownAutomatonState.Equals(q, p);
}
public static bool operator !=(PushdownAutomatonState q,
                               PushdownAutomatonState p)
{
    return !PushdownAutomatonState.Equals(q, p);
}
public override int GetHashCode()
{
    return this.Label.GetHashCode();
}

// returns a System.String that represents this state
public override string ToString()
{
    return this.Label.ToString();
}
```

```
    public static implicit operator PushdownAutomatonState(string s)
    {
        return new PushdownAutomatonState(s);
    }
}
```

Next, we create a class to represent a pushdown automaton rule.

```
public class PushdownAutomatonRule : IEquatable<PushdownAutomatonRule>
{
    public HmmlcString PushdownTop { get; private set; }
    public PushdownAutomatonState CurrentState { get; private set; }
    public Symbol InputSymbol { get; private set; }
    public HmmlcString StringToPush { get; private set; }
    public PushdownAutomatonState NextState { get; private set; }
    public bool IsEpsilonRule
    {
        get { return this.InputSymbol == null; }
    }

    // constructor
    public PushdownAutomatonRule(HmmlcString pushdownTop,
                                 PushdownAutomatonState currentState,
                                 Symbol inputSymbol,
                                 HmmlcString stringToPush,
                                 PushdownAutomatonState nextState)
    {
        this.PushdownTop = pushdownTop;
        this.CurrentState = currentState;
        this.InputSymbol = inputSymbol;
        this.StringToPush = stringToPush;
        this.NextState = nextState;
    }

    // constructor for epsilon rules
    public PushdownAutomatonRule(HmmlcString pushdownTop,
                                 PushdownAutomatonState currentState,
                                 HmmlcString stringToPush,
                                 PushdownAutomatonState nextState)
        : this(pushdownTop,
               currentState,
               null,
               stringToPush,
               nextState)
    {
    }

    // equality checking using pattern from Implementation 1.3
    public static bool Equals(PushdownAutomatonRule r1,
                              PushdownAutomatonRule r2)
```

```
{
    if (ReferenceEquals(r1, r2)) return true;
    else if (ReferenceEquals(r1, null) ||
            ReferenceEquals(r2, null))
    {
        return false;
    }
    else
    {
        return r1.PushdownTop == r2.PushdownTop &&
               r1.CurrentState == r2.CurrentState &&
               r1.InputSymbol == r2.InputSymbol &&
               r1.StringToPush == r2.StringToPush &&
               r1.NextState == r2.NextState;
    }
}
public bool Equals(PushdownAutomatonRule other)
{
    return PushdownAutomatonRule.Equals(this, other);
}
public override bool Equals(object obj)
{
    return PushdownAutomatonRule.Equals(
        this, obj as PushdownAutomatonRule);
}
public static bool operator ==(PushdownAutomatonRule r1,
                               PushdownAutomatonRule r2)
{
    return PushdownAutomatonRule.Equals(r1, r2);
}
public static bool operator !=(PushdownAutomatonRule r1,
                               PushdownAutomatonRule r2)
{
    return !PushdownAutomatonRule.Equals(r1, r2);
}
public override int GetHashCode()
{
    return this.ToString().GetHashCode();
}

// returns a System.String that represents this rule
public override string ToString()
{
    return string.Format("{0}{1}{2} -> {3}{4}",
                         this.PushdownTop != HmmlcString.Empty ?
                            this.PushdownTop.ToString() :
                            string.Empty,
                         this.CurrentState,
                         this.InputSymbol != null ?
```

```
                                this.InputSymbol.ToString() :
                                string.Empty,
                            this.StringToPush != HmmlcString.Empty ?
                                this.StringToPush.ToString() :
                                string.Empty,
                            this.NextState);
    }
}
```

Using classes `PushdownAutomatonState` and `PushdownAutomatonRule`, we now implement pushdown automaton itself.

```
public class PushdownAutomaton
{
    public FiniteSet<PushdownAutomatonState> States
    {
        get; private set;
    }
    public PushdownAutomatonState StartState { get; set; }
    public FiniteSet<PushdownAutomatonState> FinalStates
    {
        get; private set;
    }
    public Alphabet PushdownAlphabet { get; private set; }
    public Alphabet InputAlphabet { get; private set; }
    public FiniteSet<PushdownAutomatonRule> Rules
    {
        get; private set;
    }
    public Symbol StartSymbol { get; set; }

    // constructor
    public PushdownAutomaton()
    {
        this.States = new FiniteSet<PushdownAutomatonState>();
        this.StartState = null;
        this.FinalStates = new FiniteSet<PushdownAutomatonState>();
        this.PushdownAlphabet = new Alphabet();
        this.InputAlphabet = new Alphabet();
        this.Rules = new FiniteSet<PushdownAutomatonRule>();
        this.StartSymbol = null;
    }

    // returns a System.String that represents this automaton
    public override string ToString()
    {
        return "States = " + this.States +
               Environment.NewLine +
               "Start state = " + this.StartState +
```

```
                Environment.NewLine +
                "Final states = " + this.FinalStates +
                Environment.NewLine +
                "Pushdown alphabet = " + this.PushdownAlphabet +
                Environment.NewLine +
                "Input alphabet = " + this.InputAlphabet +
                Environment.NewLine +
                "Rules = " + this.Rules +
                Environment.NewLine +
                "Start symbol = " + this.StartSymbol;
    }
}
```

In this implementation, pushdown automaton M from Example 7.1 may be defined as follows.

```
var M = new PushdownAutomaton()
{
    States = { "s", "f" },
    StartState = "s",
    FinalStates = { "f" },
    PushdownAlphabet = { "S", "a" },
    InputAlphabet = { "a", "b" },
    Rules =
    {
        new PushdownAutomatonRule(new HmmlcString("S"), "s", "a",
                                  new HmmlcString("a"), "s"),
        new PushdownAutomatonRule(new HmmlcString("a"), "s", "a",
                                  new HmmlcString("a", "a"), "s"),
        new PushdownAutomatonRule(new HmmlcString("a"), "s", "b",
                                  HmmlcString.Empty, "f"),
        new PushdownAutomatonRule(new HmmlcString("a"), "⊥", "b",
                                  HmmlcString.Empty, "f"),
    },
    StartSymbol = "S"
};
```

Example 7.2. *Take*

$$L = \{vw \mid v, w \in \{a, b\}^*, v = \text{reversal}\,(w)\}.$$

Next, we construct a pushdown automaton M such that $L(M) = L$. In many respects, M works similarly to the pushdown automaton designed in the previous example. Indeed, let $z \in \{a, b\}^*$ be an input string. M first pushes down a prefix of z. Anytime, however, in an utterly nondeterministic way, it can decide that it has pushed down precisely $|z|/2$ initial symbols of z, so it starts to pop up the symbols from the pushdown and pair them off with the remaining symbols of w. When and if M simultaneously empties the pushdown and completes reading z, it accepts; otherwise, it rejects.

Algorithm 7.1: Conversion of context-free grammars to pushdown automata

Input: A context-free grammar $I = ({}_I\Sigma, {}_IR)$.
Output: A pushdown automaton $O = ({}_O\Sigma, {}_OR)$ such that $L(O) = L(I)$.

begin
 set ${}_O\Sigma = {}_I\Sigma \cup \{s\}$, where s is a new state
 set ${}_OQ = {}_OF = \{s\}$
 set ${}_O\Gamma = {}_I\Sigma$, ${}_O\Delta = {}_I\Delta$, and ${}_OS = {}_IS$
 set ${}_OR = \{As \to \text{reversal}(x)s \mid A \to x \in {}_IR\} \cup \{asa \to s \mid a \in {}_I\Delta\}$
end

Formally, $M = (\Sigma, R)$, where $\Sigma = \Gamma \cup \Delta \cup Q$, $\Gamma = \{S, a, b\}$, $\Delta = \{a, b\}$, $Q = \{s, q, f\}$, $F = \{f\}$, and

$$\begin{aligned} R = & \{Ssc \to Scs \mid c \in \{a, b\}\} \\ & \cup \{dsc \to dcs \mid c, d \in \{a, b\}\} \\ & \cup \{s \to q\} \\ & \cup \{cqc \to q \mid c \in \{a, b\}\} \\ & \cup \{Sq \to f\}. \end{aligned}$$

A proof that $L(M) = L$ is left as an exercise.

As already pointed out, M works in a nondeterministic way. In fact, L cannot be accepted by any pushdown automaton that works in a deterministic way. We return to this issue in Section 7.4.

7.2 Pushdown automata and context-free grammars are equivalent

In this section, we demonstrate the equivalence of context-free grammars and pushdown automata.

First, we explain how to turn any context-free grammar $I = ({}_I\Sigma, {}_IR)$ to an equivalent pushdown automaton $O = ({}_O\Sigma, {}_OR)$.

Basic Idea. In essence, from I, O is converted so that it uses its pushdown to simulate every leftmost derivation in I. In a greater detail, this simulation is performed in the following way. If a terminal a occurs as the pushdown top symbol, O removes a from the pushdown, and, simultaneously, reads a as the input symbol; in this way, it verifies their coincidence with each other. If a nonterminal A occurs as the pushdown top symbol, O simulates a leftmost derivation step made by a rule $A \to X_1X_2 \cdots X_n \in {}_IR$, where each $X_i \in {}_I\Sigma$, $1 \leq i \leq n$, for some $n \geq 0$ ($n = 0$ means $X_1X_2 \cdots X_n = \varepsilon$), so that it replaces the pushdown top A with $X_n \cdots X_1$.

Next, we give Algorithm 7.1, which describes the construction of O from I in a rigorous way.

As an exercise, prove the next theorem.

Theorem 7.1. *Algorithm 7.1 is correct. Therefore, for every context-free grammar, there is an equivalent pushdown automaton.*

Example 7.3. *Consider the following grammar, G*

$$S \to SS,$$
$$S \to aSb,$$
$$S \to \varepsilon.$$

Algorithm 7.1 turns G into this pushdown automaton M

$$\begin{aligned} Ss &\to SSs, \\ Ss &\to bSas, \\ Ss &\to s, \\ asa &\to s, \\ bsb &\to s. \end{aligned}$$

For instance, M accepts abaabb as

$$\begin{aligned} Ssabaabb &\Rightarrow SSsabaabb \\ &\Rightarrow SbSasabaabb \\ &\Rightarrow SbSsbaabb \\ &\Rightarrow Sbsbaabb \\ &\Rightarrow Ssaabb \\ &\Rightarrow bSasaabb \\ &\Rightarrow bSsabb \\ &\Rightarrow bbSasabb \\ &\Rightarrow bbSsbb \\ &\Rightarrow bbsbb \\ &\Rightarrow bsb \\ &\Rightarrow s. \end{aligned}$$

Implementation 7.2. Next, we implement Algorithm 7.1 by the following method to class `ContextFreeGrammar`.

```
public PushdownAutomaton ToPushdownAutomaton()
{
    var result = new PushdownAutomaton()
    {
        // we assume "s" is not in terminals or nonterminals
        States = { "s" },
        StartState = "s",
        FinalStates = { "s" },
        StartSymbol = this.StartSymbol
    };

    // copy symbols
    foreach (Symbol A in this.Nonterminals)
    {
        result.PushdownAlphabet.Add(A);
    }
```

```
    foreach (Symbol a in this.Terminals)
    {
        result.PushdownAlphabet.Add(a);
        result.InputAlphabet.Add(a);
    }

    // compute rules
    foreach (ContextFreeRule r in this.Rules)
    {
        result.Rules.Add(new PushdownAutomatonRule(
            new HmmlcString(r.LeftHandSide), "s",
            r.RightHandSide.Reverse(), "s"));
    }
    foreach (Symbol a in this.Terminals)
    {
        result.Rules.Add(new PushdownAutomatonRule(
            new HmmlcString(a), "s", a,
            HmmlcString.Empty, "s"));
    }

    return result;
}
```

Take a closer look at the output pushdown automaton O produced by Algorithm 7.1. Observe that the pushdown automaton O changes precisely one symbol on the pushdown top by using each of its rules. This observation leads to the next corollary, which fulfills an important role later in this section (see Theorem 7.3).

Corollary 7.1. *For every context-free grammar, there is an equivalent pushdown automaton* $M = (\Sigma, R)$*, in which every rule* $x \rightarrow y \in R$ *satisfies* $x \in \Gamma Q(\Delta \cup \{\varepsilon\})$ *and* $y \in \Gamma^* Q$.

Before we sketch how to turn any pushdown automaton to an equivalent context-free grammar, we explain how to transform any pushdown automaton to an equivalent pushdown automaton that satisfies the properties stated in Corollary 7.1.

Theorem 7.2. *For every pushdown automaton* $N = ({}_N\Sigma, {}_NR)$*, there exists an equivalent pushdown automaton* $M = ({}_M\Sigma, {}_MR)$ *with every rule* $x \rightarrow y \in {}_MR$ *satisfying* $x \in \Gamma Q(\Delta \cup \{\varepsilon\})$ *and* $y \in \Gamma^* Q$.

Proof. Let $N = ({}_N\Sigma, {}_NR)$ be any pushdown automaton such that $L(N) = L$. From N, we construct an equivalent pushdown automaton $M = ({}_M\Sigma, {}_MR)$ whose rules have the prescribed form so M simulates every move in N by several moves during which it records top pushdown symbols of N in its states. More precisely, suppose that N makes a move according to a rule of the form $xqa \rightarrow yp \in {}_NR$, where $q, p \in {}_NQ$,

---

Algorithm 7.2: Conversion of pushdown automata to context-free grammars

---

Input: A pushdown automaton $I = ({}_I\Sigma, {}_IR)$ in which every rule is of the form $Aqa \rightarrow yp \in {}_IR$ where $q, p \in {}_IQ$, $a \in {}_I\Delta \cup \{\varepsilon\}$, $y \in {}_I\Sigma^*$, and $A \in {}_I\Gamma$.
Output: A context-free grammar $O = ({}_O\Sigma, {}_OR)$ such that $L(O) = L(I)$.

begin
  set ${}_O\Sigma = {}_I\Delta \cup {}_ON \cup \{{}_OS\}$, where ${}_ON = \{\langle pAq \rangle \mid p, q \in {}_IQ, A \in {}_I\Gamma\}$ and ${}_OS$ is a newly introduced symbol, used as the start symbol of O
  set ${}_O\Delta = {}_I\Delta$
  set ${}_OR = \{{}_OS \rightarrow \mid f \in {}_IF$ (${}_Is$ and ${}_IS$ are the start state and the start pushdown symbol of I, respectively)$\}$
  add $\langle q_0Aq_{n+1} \rangle \rightarrow a\langle q_1X_1q_2 \rangle \langle q_2X_2q_3 \rangle \cdots \langle q_nX_nq_{n+1} \rangle$ to ${}_OR$ for all $Aq_0a \rightarrow X_n \cdots X_1q_1 \in {}_IR$, where $q_0, q_{n+1} \in {}_IQ$, $a \in {}_I\Delta$, $A \in {}_I\Gamma$, and $q_j \in {}_IQ$, $X_j \in {}_I\Gamma$, $\langle q_1X_jq_{j+1} \in {}_ON \rangle$, $1 \leq j \leq n$, for some $n \in {}_0\mathbb{N}$ ($n = 0$ means $X_n \cdots X_1 = \langle q_1X_1q_2 \rangle \cdots \langle q_nX_nq_{n+1} \rangle = \varepsilon$)
end

$a \in {}_N\Delta \cup \{\varepsilon\}$, $x, y \in {}_N\Gamma^*$. Assume that $|x| \geq 1$ so $x = Xz$, for some $X \in {}_N\Gamma$ and $z \in {}_N\Gamma^*$. M simulates this move in the following two-phase way:

(i) Starting from q, M makes $|z|$ moves during which in a symbol-by-symbol way, it stores the string u consisting of the top $|z|$ pushdown symbols into its state of the form $\langle uq \rangle$.
(ii) From $\langle uq \rangle$, by applying a rule of the form $X\langle zq \rangle a \rightarrow yp \in {}_MR$, M verifies that $z = u$, reads a, pushes y onto its pushdown, and moves to state p. In other words, M completes the simulation of this move in N, and it is ready to simulate another move of N.

As an exercise, explain how to make this simulation under the assumption that $|x| = 0$. Then, rephrase all this proof in a fully rigorous way. ■

We are now ready to sketch how to turn any pushdown automaton M whose rules have the form described in Theorem 7.2 to an equivalent context-free grammar.

Basic Idea. Suppose that $I = ({}_I\Sigma, {}_IR)$ is a pushdown automaton in which every rule has the form $Aqa \rightarrow yp \in {}_IR$, where $q, p \in {}_IQ$, $a \in {}_I\Delta \cup \{\varepsilon\}$, $y \in {}_I\Sigma^*$, and $A \in {}_I\Gamma$. To transform I to an equivalent context-free grammar O, the following algorithm constructs O so a leftmost derivation of $w \in {}_O\Delta^*$ in O simulates a sequence of moves made by I on w. O performs this simulation by using nonterminals of the form $\langle qAp \rangle$, where $q, p \in {}_IQ$, and $A \in {}_I\Gamma$. More precisely, $\langle qAp \rangle \Rightarrow^*_{lm} w$ in O iff $Aqw \Rightarrow^* p$ in I. In addition, we introduce a new symbol, ${}_OS$, as the start symbol of O and define all ${}_OS$-rules as $\{{}_OS \rightarrow \langle {}_Is_I Sf \rangle \mid f \in {}_IF\}$. Thus, ${}_OS \Rightarrow \langle {}_Is_ISf \rangle \Rightarrow^*_{lm} w$ in O iff ${}_IS_Isw \Rightarrow^* f$ in I with $f \in {}_IF$. As a result, $L(O) = L(I)$.

Based upon the basic idea preceding Algorithm 7.2, prove the next lemma.

Lemma 7.1. *Algorithm 7.2 is correct.*

From Theorem 7.2, Algorithm 7.2, and Lemma 7.1, we obtain the next theorem.

Theorem 7.3. *For every pushdown automaton, there exists an equivalent context-free grammar.*

Theorems 7.1 and 7.3 imply the next crucial theorem, which states the equal power of pushdown automata and context-free grammars.

Theorem 7.4. *Pushdown automata and context-free grammars are equivalent.*

7.3 Three types of acceptance by pushdown automata

Consider a pushdown automaton M. Its language is standardly defined as

$$L(M) = \{w \mid w \in \Delta^*,\ Ssw \Rightarrow^* f, f \in F\}.$$

In other words, *M accepts w by empty pushdown and final state* because after reading w, M has to (i) empty its pushdown and (ii) end up in a final state to accept $w \in \Delta^*$ (see Definition 7.1). Next, we modify this way of acceptance so that we only require either (i) or (ii).

Definition 7.2. *Let M be a pushdown automaton.*

(i) *If $Ssw \Rightarrow^* q$ in M with $q \in Q$, M* accepts w by empty pushdown. *The set of all strings that M accepts in this way is the* language accepted by M by empty pushdown, *denoted by ${}_{\varepsilon}L(M)$.*
(ii) *If $Ssw \Rightarrow^* vf$ in M with $v \in \Gamma^*$ and $f \in F$, M* accepts w by final state. *The set of all strings that M accepts in this way is the* language accepted by M by final state, *denoted by ${}_{f}L(M)$.*

Example 7.4. *Consider a pushdown automaton M defined by its five rules*

$$\begin{aligned} 1 &: Ssa \rightarrow Sas,\\ 2 &: asa \rightarrow aas,\\ 3 &: asb \rightarrow q,\\ 4 &: aqb \rightarrow q,\\ 5 &: Sq \rightarrow f, \end{aligned}$$

where $\Gamma = \{S, a\}$, $\Delta = \{a, b\}$, $Q = \{s, q, f\}$, and $F = \{s, f\}$. To describe how M works, observe that M reads a and pushes down Sa by using rule 1. *Then, M pushes down as by using rule* 2 *while remaining in the final state s. When and if the first occurrence of b appears, M begins to pop up as and pair them off with bs while remaining in the only nonfinal state q.*

For instance, on aa, M works as

$$\begin{aligned} Saa &\Rightarrow Sasa\ [1]\\ &\Rightarrow Saas\ [2]. \end{aligned}$$

On aabb, M works in the following way

$$\begin{aligned} Ssaabb &\Rightarrow Sasabb \; [1] \\ &\Rightarrow Saasbb \; [2] \\ &\Rightarrow Saqb \; [3] \\ &\Rightarrow Sq \; [4] \\ &\Rightarrow f \; [5]. \end{aligned}$$

As s and f are final, M accepts aa and aabb by final state.

Consider the three types of acceptance and corresponding three languages that M accepts—$_fL(M)$, $_\varepsilon L(M)$, and $L(M)$—in terms of Definitions 7.2 and 7.1. Observe that

$$_fL(M) = \{a^k b^k \mid k \geq 1\} \cup \{a\}^+ \text{ and } {_\varepsilon L(M)} = L(M) = \{a^k b^k \mid k \geq 1\}.$$

In the proofs of Lemmas 7.2–7.5, given next, we describe how to convert the three types of acceptance to each other.

Lemma 7.2. *For any pushdown automaton I, there is a pushdown automaton O such that $_fL(I) = {_\varepsilon L(O)}$.*

Proof. Let *I* be a pushdown automaton. *O* keeps its start symbol $_OS$ on the pushdown bottom; otherwise, it simulates *I* move by move. If *I* enters a final state and accepts, *O* completely empties its pushdown list, including $_OS$, and accepts too. If *I* empties its pushdown while occurring in a nonfinal state and, therefore, does not accept its input by final state, the pushdown of *O* contains $_OS$, so *O* does not accept its input either. A fully rigorous proof is left as an exercise. ■

Lemma 7.3. *For any pushdown automaton I, there is a pushdown automaton O such that $L(I) = {_fL(O)}$.*

Proof. Let *I* be a pushdown automaton. Construct *O* with $_OF = \{f\}$, where *f* is a new final state, by analogy with the proof of Lemma 7.2. That is, *O* keeps $_OS$ on the pushdown bottom while simulating *I*. If *I* empties its pushdown, enters a final state, and accepts, then after simulating this computation in *I*, *O* occurs in the same state with the pushdown containing $_OS$; from this configuration, *O* enters *f* in order to accept the input by final state. ■

Lemma 7.4. *For any pushdown automaton I, there is a pushdown automaton O such that $_\varepsilon L(I) = {_fL(O)} = L(O)$.*

Proof. Let *I* be a pushdown automaton. Construct *O* so it has the same final states as *I*. *O* keeps its start symbol $_OS$ on the pushdown bottom while simulating *I*. If *I* empties its pushdown and accepts its input, *O* has its pushdown containing only $_OS$, and from this configuration, it enters a final state while removing $_OS$ from the pushdown. Observe that *O* constructed in this way satisfies $_\varepsilon L(I) = {_fL(O)} = L(O)$. ■

Lemma 7.5. *For any pushdown automaton I, there is a pushdown automaton O such that $L(I) = {_\varepsilon L(O)}$.*

Proof. Let I be a pushdown automaton. Construct O so it keeps its start symbol ${}_OS$ on the pushdown bottom; otherwise, it simulates I move by move. If I empties its pushdown and enters a final state, then O has its pushdown containing only ${}_OS$, so it removes ${}_OS$ from the pushdown to accept the input by empty pushdown. ∎

The previous four lemmas and Theorem 7.4 imply the following main and concluding theorem of this section.

Theorem 7.5. *Let L be a language. The following statements are equivalent:*

(i) *there is a context-free grammar G such that* $L = L(G)$;
(ii) *there is a pushdown automaton M such that* $L = L(M)$;
(iii) *there is a pushdown automaton O such that* $L = {}_fL(O)$;
(iv) *there is a pushdown automaton K such that* $L = {}_\varepsilon L(K)$.

7.4 Determinism

In general, pushdown automatons work in a nondeterministic way—that is, they can make many different sequences of moves on the same input. Since this nondeterminism obviously complicates their implementation and application in practice, we study their deterministic versions in the present section. We show that the deterministic versions of pushdown automata are less powerful than pushdown automata although they are stronger than finite automata.

Definition 7.3. *Let M be a pushdown automaton. M is a* deterministic pushdown automaton *if for every rule* $xqa \to yp \in R$, *where* $x, y \in \Gamma^*$, $q, p \in Q$, *and* $a \in \Delta \cup \{\varepsilon\}$, *it holds that* $zxqb \to uo \notin R - \{xqa \to yp\}$, *for any* $z, u \in \Gamma^*$, $b \in \{a, \varepsilon\}$, $o \in Q$.

Implementation 7.3. To implement a check whether a pushdown automaton is deterministic, we add property `IsDeterministic` to class `PushdownAutomaton`.

```
public bool IsDeterministic
{
    get
    {
        foreach (PushdownAutomatonRule r in this.Rules)
        {
            foreach (PushdownAutomatonRule r2 in this.Rules)
            {
                if (r == r2) continue; // same rule, skip

                if ((r.CurrentState == r2.CurrentState)
                    &&
                    (r.InputSymbol == r2.InputSymbol ||
                    r2.IsEpsilonRule)
                    &&
                    (r.PushdownTop.IsSuffixOf(r2.PushdownTop)))
```

```
                {
                    return false;
                }
            }
        }

        return true;
    }
}
```

According to Definition 7.3, *M* makes no more than one moves from any configuration, so it makes a unique sequence of moves on any input—a property highly appreciated in practice. For instance, observe that *M* discussed in Example 7.1 is a deterministic pushdown automaton, and its implementation is relatively simple as shown next.

Implementation 7.4. Next, we implement *M* from Example 7.1 in C# as a function in a static class `PushdownAutomatonM` which takes a string and communicates whether the string is in *L*(*M*) or not by its return value. The first implementation presented here is quite pragmatic—that is, rather than strictly following the rules of the pushdown automaton, it is based on the understanding of its expected behavior. Instead of a pushdown, we use a counter to keep track of how many *a*s we have read so far, and once we start reading *b*s, we start to decrement it.

```
public static bool CheckString1(HmmlcString inputString)
{
    int state = 0; // 0 is start state, 1 is final state
    int count = 0;

    for (int i = 0; i < inputString.Length; i++)
    {
        Symbol currentInputSymbol = inputString[i];

        switch (state)
        {
            case 0: // start state, reading "a"s
                if (currentInputSymbol == "a")
                {
                    state = 0;
                    count++;
                }
                else if (currentInputSymbol == "b")
                {
                    if (count > 0)
                    {
                        state = 1; // start reading "b"s
                        count--;
                    }
                    else
```

```
                    {
                        // no "a"s read yet, reject
                        return false;
                    }
                }
                else
                {
                    // unexpected symbol, reject
                    return false;
                }
                break;
            case 1: // final state, reading "b"s
                if (currentInputSymbol == "b")
                {
                    if (count > 0)
                    {
                        state = 1;
                        count--;
                    }
                    else
                    {
                        // more "b"s than "a"s
                        return false;
                    }
                }
                else
                {
                    // mixed "a"s and "b"s or unexpected symbol
                    return false;
                }
                break;
            default: // unexpected state
                return false;
        }
    }

    // whole input read
    // accept if in final state and no "a"s are left over
    return state == 1 && count == 0;
}
```

The next function gives the same results but follows the definition of M more closely. We use standard .NET generic `Stack` class to implement the pushdown.

```
public static bool CheckString2(HmmlcString inputString)
{
    var pushdown = new Stack<Symbol>();
    pushdown.Push("S");
    PushdownAutomatonState currentState = "s";
```

```
int inputPosition = 0;

while (true)
{
    if (pushdown.Count == 0 &&
        currentState == "f" &&
        inputPosition == inputString.Length)
    {
        return true;
    }

    if (inputPosition == inputString.Length)
    {
        // whole input read but not in final state
        // or pushdown not empty, reject
        return false;
    }

    Symbol pushdownTop = pushdown.Count > 0 ?
        pushdown.Pop() : null;
    Symbol currentInputSymbol = inputString[inputPosition];

    if (pushdownTop == "S" &&
        currentState == "s" &&
        currentInputSymbol == "a")
    {
        pushdown.Push("a");
        currentState = "s";
    }
    else if (pushdownTop == "a" &&
             currentState == "s" &&
             currentInputSymbol == "a")
    {
        pushdown.Push("a");
        pushdown.Push("a");
        currentState = "s";
    }
    else if (pushdownTop == "a" &&
             currentState == "s" &&
             currentInputSymbol == "b")
    {
        currentState = "f";
    }
    else if (pushdownTop == "a" &&
             currentState == "f" &&
             currentInputSymbol == "b")
    {
        currentState = "f";
    }
```

```
        else // cannot apply any rule
        {
            return false;
        }

        inputPosition++;
    }
}
```

Notice that in `CheckString2()`, the rules of *M* are encoded directly in the C# program by way of several **`if–else`** statements. We can generalize the implementation as follows:

```
public static bool CheckString3(HmmlcString inputString)
{
    var M = new PushdownAutomaton()
    {
        States = { "s", "f" },
        StartState = "s",
        FinalStates = { "f" },
        PushdownAlphabet = { "S", "a" },
        InputAlphabet = { "a", "b" },
        Rules =
        {
            new PushdownAutomatonRule(new HmmlcString("S"), "s", "a",
                                      new HmmlcString("a"), "s"),
            new PushdownAutomatonRule(new HmmlcString("a"), "s", "a",
                                      new HmmlcString("a", "a"), "s"),
            new PushdownAutomatonRule(new HmmlcString("a"), "s", "b",
                                      HmmlcString.Empty, "f"),
            new PushdownAutomatonRule(new HmmlcString("a"), "f", "b",
                                      HmmlcString.Empty, "f"),
        },
        StartSymbol = "S"
    };

    var pushdown = new Stack<Symbol>();
    pushdown.Push(M.StartSymbol);
    PushdownAutomatonState currentState = M.StartState;
    int inputPosition = 0;

    while (true)
    {
        if (pushdown.Count == 0 &&
            M.FinalStates.Contains(currentState) &&
            inputPosition == inputString.Length)
        {
            return true;
        }
```

```
        if (inputPosition == inputString.Length)
        {
            // whole input read but not in final state
            // or pushdown not empty, reject
            return false;
        }

        Symbol pushdownTop = pushdown.Count > 0 ?
            pushdown.Pop() : null;
        Symbol currentInputSymbol = inputString[inputPosition];

        bool ruleApplied = false;

        foreach (PushdownAutomatonRule r in M.Rules)
        {
            if ((r.PushdownTop == HmmlcString.Empty ||
                pushdownTop == r.PushdownTop[0])
                &&
                (currentState == r.CurrentState)
                &&
                (r.IsEpsilonRule ||
                currentInputSymbol == r.InputSymbol))
            {
                foreach (Symbol symbol in r.StringToPush)
                {
                    pushdown.Push(symbol);
                }
                currentState = r.NextState;
                inputPosition++;
                ruleApplied = true;
                break;
            }
        }

        if (!ruleApplied)
        {
            // no rule could be applied, reject
            return false;
        }
    }
}
```

Function `CheckString3()` can be used to simulate any pushdown automaton M simply by changing the initialization of `M` to match the definition of M. Note however that M must still be deterministic; if it is not, the function may reject even some strings from $L(M)$ because it always uses the first applicable rule it finds and does not backtrack.

Unfortunately, deterministic pushdown automata have also their disadvantages. Most significantly, they are less powerful than their nondeterministic counterparts. Specifically, the next lemma gives a language that can be accepted by no deterministic pushdown automaton, but it can be accepted by a pushdown automaton that work nondeterministically.

Lemma 7.6. *Let* $L = \{vw \mid v, w \in \{a, b\}^*,\ v = \text{reversal}(w)\}$. *Any pushdown automaton M that accepts L is nondeterministic.*

Proof. We only give a gist underlying this proof. Any pushdown automaton M that accepts L necessarily works on its input $u \in \{a, b\}^*$ by performing these four computational phases:

(i) M pushes down a prefix of u.
(ii) M takes a guess that it is right in the middle of u, which means that the length of its current pushdown equals the length of the suffix that remains to be read.
(iii) M pops up the symbols from the pushdown and pairs them off with the same input symbols.
(iv) When and if M completes reading u, it accepts.

Notice, however, that M ends (i) and begins (ii) based on its guess, so M makes necessarily more than one moves from the same configuration at this point. As a result, M cannot work deterministically. ∎

Theorem 7.6. *Deterministic pushdown automata are less powerful than pushdown automata.*

Proof. Deterministic pushdown automata are special cases of pushdown automata. Lemma 7.6 gives a language that cannot be accepted by any deterministic pushdown automaton although it can be accepted by a pushdown automaton. Thus, Theorem 7.6 holds true. ∎

On the other hand, deterministic pushdown automata are stronger than finite automata.

Theorem 7.7. *Deterministic pushdown automata are more powerful than finite automata.*

Proof. Deterministic finite automata can be seen as deterministic pushdown automata that keeps its pushdown completely empty during any computation. Recall that deterministic finite automata are as powerful as their nondeterministic counterparts. Furthermore, return to the deterministic pushdown automaton M satisfying $L(M) = \{a^k b^k \mid k \geq 1\}$ (see Example 7.1). As obvious, no finite automaton accepts $\{a^k b^k \mid k \geq 1\}$ because by using a finite set of states, no finite automaton can keep track of k, which runs to infinity. Therefore, this theorem holds. ∎

Chapter 8
Turing machines

Simply put, Turing machines represent finite automata generalized in three ways. First, they can both read and write on their tapes. Second, their read–write heads can move both to the right and to the left on the tapes. Finally, the tapes can be limitlessly extended to the right.

As explained in the next chapter, in computer science, there exists a crucially important hypothesis, *referred to as the Church–Turing thesis*, saying that every effective computation is mechanically performable by a procedure if and only if it is carried out by a Turing machine. Consequently, any computation beyond the power of Turing machines is also beyond the power of any computer. Therefore, these machines are central to the study of computation from a practical, mathematical, logical, as well as philosophical standpoint.

8.1 Turing machines and their languages

Without further ado, we define the notion of a Turing machine.

Definition 8.1. *A* Turing machine *is a rewriting system* $M = (\Sigma, R)$, *where*

- Σ *contains subalphabets* Q, F, Γ, Δ, $\{\rhd, \lhd\}$ *such that* $\Sigma = Q \cup \Gamma \cup \{\rhd, \lhd\}$, $F \subseteq Q$, $\Delta \subseteq \Gamma$, $\Gamma - \Delta$ *always contains* $\Box$*—the* blank *symbol, and* $\{\rhd, \lhd\}$, Q, Γ *are pairwise disjoint.*
- R *is a finite* set of rules *of the form* $x \to y$ *satisfying*
  - *(i)* $\{x, y\} \in \{\rhd\}Q$, *or*
  - *(ii)* $\{x, y\} \in \Gamma Q \cup Q\Gamma$, *or*
  - *(iii)* $x \in Q\{\lhd\}$ *and* $y \in Q\{\Box\lhd, \lhd\}$.

Q, F, Γ, *and* Δ *are referred to as the* set of states, *the* set of final states, *the* alphabet of tape symbols, *and the* alphabet of input symbols, *respectively.* Q *contains the* start state, *denoted by* $\blacktriangleright$. *Relations* $\Rightarrow$ *and* $\Rightarrow^*$ *are defined like in any rewriting system (see Definition 4.1).* M accepts $w \in \Delta^*$ *if* $\rhd \blacktriangleright w\lhd \Rightarrow^* \rhd ufv\lhd$ *in* M, *where* $u, v \in \Gamma^*$, $f \in F$. *The* language accepted by M *or, briefly, the* language of M *is denoted by* $L(M)$ *and is defined as the set of all strings that* M *accepts; formally,*

$$L(M) = \{w \mid w \in \Delta^*,\ \rhd \blacktriangleright w\lhd \Rightarrow^* \rhd ufv\lhd,\ u, v \in \Gamma^*,\ f \in F\}.$$

A *configuration* of M is a string of the form $\triangleright uqv \triangleleft$, $u, v \in \Gamma^*$, $q \in Q$. Let ${}_M X$ denote the set of all configurations of M. We say that uv is on the *tape* of M, which is always delimited by $\triangleright$ and $\triangleleft$, referred to as the *left* and *right bounders*, respectively. In essence, $\triangleright uqv \triangleleft$ captures the current situation M occurs in. That is, in $\triangleright uqv \triangleleft$, q is the current state of M, whose read–write *head* occurs over the current *input symbol* defined as the leftmost symbol of $v\triangleleft$. If $\beta \Rightarrow \chi$ in M, where $\beta, \chi \in {}_M X$, we say that M makes a *move* or a *computational step* from β to χ. A move made by an *extending rule* of the form $q\triangleleft \rightarrow p\Box\triangleleft \in R$, where $q, p \in Q$, deserves our special attention because it actually extends the current tape by inserting a new occurrence of $\Box$ in front of $\triangleleft$; more formally and briefly, $\triangleright uq \triangleleft \Rightarrow \triangleright up\Box\triangleleft$, where $u \in \Gamma^*$. As follows from Definition 8.1, $\triangleright \blacktriangleright w\triangleleft \Rightarrow^* \chi$ implies $\chi \in {}_M X$. We say that M makes a *sequence of moves* or a *computation* from β to χ if $\beta \Rightarrow^* \chi$ in M, where $\beta, \chi \in {}_M X$.

For brevity, considering any Turing machine M, we automatically assume that Q, F, Γ, Δ, and R have exactly the same meaning as in Definition 8.1. If there exists any danger of confusion, we mark Q, F, Γ, Δ, and R with M as ${}_M Q$, ${}_M F$, ${}_M \Gamma$, ${}_M \Delta$, and ${}_M R$, respectively, in order to emphasize that they represent the components of M (in particular, we use these marks when several Turing machines are simultaneously discussed).

Example 8.1. *Consider* $L = \{x \mid x \in \{a, b, c\}^*, occur(x, a) = occur(x, b) = occur(x, c)$. *Less formally, x is in L iff x has an equal number of as, bs, and cs; for instance, babcca* $\in L$, *but babcc* $\notin L$. *In this example, we construct a Turing machine M such that L(M) = L.*

Gist. *M records symbols it has read by using its states from* power $(\{a, b, c\})$ *(see Section 1.1). That is, M moves on the tape in any direction. Whenever it reads an input symbol that is not already recorded in the current state, M can add this symbol into its current state while simultaneously changing it to* $\Box$ *on the tape. M can anytime change the state that records all three symbols to the state that records no symbol at all. By using a special state,* $\checkmark$, *M can scan the entire tape, so it starts from* $\triangleleft$ *and moves left toward* $\triangleright$ *in order to find out whether the tape is completely blank, and if this is the case, M accepts.*

Definition. *Define* $M = (\Sigma, R)$, *where* $\Sigma = Q \cup \Gamma \cup \{\triangleright, \triangleleft\}$, $\Gamma = \Delta \cup \{\Box\}$, $\Delta = \{a, b, c\}$, $Q = \{\blacktriangleright, \checkmark, \blacksquare\} \cup W$ *with* $W = \{\langle O \rangle \mid \langle O \rangle \subseteq \{a, b, c\}\}$ *and* $F = \{\blacksquare\}$. *Construct the rules of R by performing (i)–(v), given next. (As stated in Section 1.1,* $\{\}$ *denotes the empty set just like* $\emptyset$ *does. In this example, we use* $\{\}$ *for this purpose.)*

- *(i)* *Add* $\triangleright \blacktriangleright \rightarrow \triangleright\langle\{\}\rangle$ *to R.*
- *(ii)* *For every* $\langle O \rangle \in W$ *and every* $d \in \Delta \cup \{\Box\}$, *add* $\langle O \rangle d \rightarrow d\langle O \rangle$ *and* $d\langle O \rangle \rightarrow \langle O \rangle d$ *to R.*
- *(iii)* *For every* $\langle O \rangle \in W$ *such that* $O \in \{a, b, c\}$ *and every* $d \in \Delta - O$, *add* $\langle O \rangle d \rightarrow \langle O \cup \{d\}\rangle\Box$ *to R.*
- *(iv)* *Add* $\langle\{a, b, c\}\rangle d \rightarrow \langle\{\}\rangle d$ *to R, where* $d \in \Delta \cup \{\Box, \triangleleft\}$.
- *(v)* *Add* $\langle\{\}\rangle\triangleleft \rightarrow \checkmark\triangleleft$, $\Box\checkmark \rightarrow \checkmark\Box$, *and* $\triangleright\checkmark \rightarrow \triangleright\blacksquare$ *to R.*

Computation. *Consider both the informal and formal description of M. Observe that by (i), M starts every computation. By (ii), M moves on its tape. By (iii), M adds the input symbol into its current state from* power (Δ) *and, simultaneously, changes the input symbol to* $\Box$ *on the tape. By (iv), M empties $\{a, b, c\}$, so it changes this state to the state equal to the empty set. By (v), M makes a final scan of the tape, starting from* $\triangleleft$ *and moving left toward* $\triangleright$*, in order to make sure that the tape is completely blank, and if it is, M accepts.*

For instance, in this way, M accepts babcca as follows:

$$
\begin{aligned}
\triangleright \blacktriangleright babcca\triangleleft &\Rightarrow \triangleright\langle\{\}\rangle babcca\triangleleft \\
&\Rightarrow^* \triangleright babc\langle\{\}\rangle ca\triangleleft \\
&\Rightarrow \triangleright babc\langle\{c\}\rangle\Box a\triangleleft \\
&\Rightarrow^* \triangleright ba\langle\{c\}\rangle bc\Box a\triangleleft \\
&\Rightarrow \triangleright ba\langle\{b, c\}\rangle\Box c\Box a\triangleleft \\
&\Rightarrow^* \triangleright ba\Box c\Box\langle\{b, c\}\rangle a\triangleleft \\
&\Rightarrow \triangleright ba\Box c\Box\langle\{a, b, c\}\rangle\Box\triangleleft \\
&\Rightarrow^* \triangleright b\langle\{a, b, c\}\rangle a\Box c\Box\Box\triangleleft \\
&\Rightarrow \triangleright b\langle\{\}\rangle a\Box c\Box\Box\triangleleft \\
&\Rightarrow^* \triangleright\Box\Box\Box\Box\Box\Box\langle\{\}\rangle\triangleleft \\
&\Rightarrow^* \triangleright\Box\Box\Box\Box\Box\Box\checkmark\triangleleft \\
&\Rightarrow \triangleright\Box\Box\Box\Box\Box\checkmark\Box\triangleleft \\
&\Rightarrow^* \triangleright\checkmark\Box\Box\Box\Box\Box\Box\triangleleft \\
&\Rightarrow \triangleright\blacksquare\Box\Box\Box\Box\Box\Box\triangleleft .
\end{aligned}
$$

Notice, however, M accepts the same string in many other ways, including

$$
\begin{aligned}
\triangleright \blacktriangleright babcca\triangleleft &\Rightarrow \triangleright\langle\{\}\rangle babcca\triangleleft \\
&\Rightarrow \triangleright\Box\langle\{b\}\rangle abcca\triangleleft \\
&\Rightarrow \triangleright\Box\langle\{a, b\}\rangle\Box bcca\triangleleft \\
&\Rightarrow^* \triangleright\Box\Box b\langle\{a, b\}\rangle cca\triangleleft \\
&\Rightarrow \triangleright\Box\Box b\langle\{a, b, c\}\rangle\Box ca\triangleleft \\
&\Rightarrow \triangleright\Box\Box b\langle\{\}\rangle\Box ca\triangleleft \\
&\Rightarrow \triangleright\Box\Box\langle\{\}b\rangle\Box ca\triangleleft \\
&\Rightarrow \triangleright\Box\Box\langle\{b\}\rangle\Box\Box ca\triangleleft \\
&\Rightarrow^* \triangleright\Box\Box\Box\Box\Box\Box\checkmark\triangleleft \\
&\Rightarrow^* \triangleright\checkmark\Box\Box\Box\Box\Box\Box\triangleleft \\
&\Rightarrow \triangleright\blacksquare\Box\Box\Box\Box\Box\Box\triangleleft .
\end{aligned}
$$

Working on the same string in several different ways, M represents a nondeterministic rewriting system (see Chapter 4). In the next chapter, we explain how to turn any Turing machine to an equivalent Turing machine that works deterministically (see Theorem 8.1).

Implementation 8.1. Next, we present a C# implementation of Turing machine. Recall and compare Implementations 5.2 and 7.2 for finite and pushdown automata, respectively.

First we implement Turing machine state as follows:

```
public class TuringMachineState : IEquatable<TuringMachineState>
{
    public Symbol Label { get; private set; }

    // constructor
    public TuringMachineState(Symbol label)
    {
        this.Label = label;
    }

    // equality checking using pattern from Implementation 1.1
    public static bool Equals(TuringMachineState q,
                              TuringMachineState p)
    {
        if (ReferenceEquals(q, p)) return true;
        else if (ReferenceEquals(q, null) ||
                 ReferenceEquals(p, null))
        {
            return false;
        }
        else return q.Label == p.Label;
    }
    public bool Equals(TuringMachineState other)
    {
        return TuringMachineState.Equals(this, other);
    }
    public override bool Equals(object obj)
    {
        return TuringMachineState.Equals(
            this, obj as TuringMachineState);
    }
    public static bool operator ==(TuringMachineState q,
                                   TuringMachineState p)
    {
        return TuringMachineState.Equals(q, p);
    }
    public static bool operator !=(TuringMachineState q,
                                   TuringMachineState p)
    {
        return !TuringMachineState.Equals(q, p);
    }
    public override int GetHashCode()
    {
        return this.Label.GetHashCode();
    }

    // returns a System.String that represents this state
    public override string ToString()
```

```
    {
        return this.Label.ToString();
    }

    public static implicit operator TuringMachineState(string s)
    {
        return new TuringMachineState(s);
    }
}
```

We also need to represent the rules.

```
public class TuringMachineRule : IEquatable<TuringMachineRule>
{
    public HmmlcString LeftHandSide { get; private set; }
    public HmmlcString RightHandSide { get; private set; }

    // constructor
    public TuringMachineRule(HmmlcString leftHandSide,
                             HmmlcString rightHandSide)
    {
        this.LeftHandSide = leftHandSide;
        this.RightHandSide = rightHandSide;
    }

    // equality checking using pattern from Implementation 1.1
    public static bool Equals(TuringMachineRule r1,
                              TuringMachineRule r2)
    {
        if (ReferenceEquals(r1, r2)) return true;
        else if (ReferenceEquals(r1, null) ||
                 ReferenceEquals(r2, null))
        {
            return false;
        }
        else
        {
            return r1.LeftHandSide == r2.LeftHandSide &&
                   r1.RightHandSide == r2.RightHandSide;
        }
    }
    public bool Equals(TuringMachineRule other)
    {
        return TuringMachineRule.Equals(this, other);
    }
    public override bool Equals(object obj)
    {
        return TuringMachineRule.Equals(
            this, obj as TuringMachineRule);
    }
```

```
    public static bool operator ==(TuringMachineRule r1,
                                   TuringMachineRule r2)
    {
        return TuringMachineRule.Equals(r1, r2);
    }
    public static bool operator !=(TuringMachineRule r1,
                                   TuringMachineRule r2)
    {
        return !TuringMachineRule.Equals(r1, r2);
    }
    public override int GetHashCode()
    {
        return this.ToString().GetHashCode();
    }

    // returns a System.String that represents this rule
    public override string ToString()
    {
        return string.Format("{0} -> {1}", this.LeftHandSide,
                                           this.RightHandSide);
    }
}
```

As opposed to Definition 8.1, the code given earlier places no restriction on the form of rules. However, writing a program that checks whether Turing-machine rules satisfy the forms given in Definition 8.1 represents a trivial task left as an exercise.

At this point, we can implement Turing machine as follows:

```
public class TuringMachine
{
    public FiniteSet<TuringMachineState> States
    {
        get; private set;
    }
    public TuringMachineState StartState { get; set; }
    public FiniteSet<TuringMachineState> FinalStates
    {
        get; private set;
    }
    public Alphabet TapeAlphabet { get; private set; }
    public Alphabet InputAlphabet { get; private set; }
    public FiniteSet<TuringMachineRule> Rules { get; private set; }

    // constructor
    public TuringMachine()
    {
        this.States = new FiniteSet<TuringMachineState>();
        this.StartState = null;
        this.FinalStates = new FiniteSet<TuringMachineState>();
```

```
        this.TapeAlphabet = new Alphabet();
        this.InputAlphabet = new Alphabet();
        this.Rules = new FiniteSet<TuringMachineRule>();
    }

    // returns a System.String that represents this Turing machine
    public override string ToString()
    {
        return "TuringMachineStates = " + this.States +
               Environment.NewLine +
               "Start state = " + this.StartState +
               Environment.NewLine +
               "Final states = " + this.FinalStates +
               Environment.NewLine +
               "Tape alphabet = " + this.TapeAlphabet +
               Environment.NewLine +
               "Input alphabet = " + this.InputAlphabet +
               Environment.NewLine +
               "Rules = " + this.Rules;
    }
}
```

Last, we add some predefined special symbols and states to `TuringMachine` class.

```
public static readonly Symbol LeftBounder = new Symbol("|>|");
public static readonly Symbol RightBounder = new Symbol("|<|");
public static readonly Symbol Blank = new Symbol("_");

public static readonly TuringMachineState
    DefaultStartTuringMachineState = new TuringMachineState("S");
public static readonly TuringMachineState
    AcceptTuringMachineState = new TuringMachineState("#");
public static readonly TuringMachineState
    RejectTuringMachineState = new TuringMachineState("@");
```

As illustrated in Example 8.1, the strictly *formal description* of a Turing machine spells out the states, symbols, and rules of the Turing machine under discussion. It is the most detailed and, thereby, rigorous description. At the same time, this level of description tends to be tremendously lengthy and tedious. Thus, paradoxically, this fully detailed description frequently obscures what the Turing machine actually is designed for. For instance, without any intuitive comments included in Example 8.1, we would find somewhat difficult to figure out the way the Turing machine accepts its language. Therefore, in the sequel, we prefer an *informal description* of Turing machines. That is, we describe them as procedures, omitting various details concerning their components. Crucially, the Church–Turing thesis makes both ways of description perfectly legitimate because it assures us that every procedure is identifiable with a Turing machine defined in a rigorously mathematical way. As a matter of fact, whenever describing Turing machines in an informal way, we always make sure that the translation from this informal description to the corresponding formal description represents a straightforward task; unfortunately, this task is usually unbearably time-consuming too. To illustrate an informal description of Turing machines, we give the following example that informally describes a Turing machine as a Pascal-like procedure, which explains the changes of the tape but omits the specification of states or rules.

When informally describing a Turing machine as a Pascal-like procedure, we express that the machine accepts or rejects its input by ACCEPT or REJECT, respectively.

Example 8.2. *Consider $L = \{a^i \mid i \text{ is a prime number}\}$. This example constructs a Turing machine M satisfying $L(M) = L$. Therefore, from a more general viewpoint, Turing machines are able to recognize the primes. M is defined as a Pascal-like procedure in the following way.*

Let a^i be the input string on the tape, where $i \geq 1$;
if $i \leq 1$ **then**
    REJECT
end
change a^i to AAa^{i-2} on the tape
while $A^k a^h$ occurs on the tape with $k \leq h$ and $i = k + h$ **do**
    on the tape, change $A^k a^h$ to the unique string y satisfying
        $i = |y|$ and $y \in A^k\{a^k A^k\}^* z$ with $z \in \text{prefixes}\,(a^k A^{k-1})$;
    if $|z| = 0$ or $|z| = k$ **then**
        REJECT
    else
        change y to $A^{k+1}a^{h-1}$ on the tape
    end
end { of the while loop }
ACCEPT

*Observe that i is no prime iff an iteration of the **while** loop obtains $y = A^k a^k A^k \cdots a^k A^k$. Indeed, at this point, i is divisible by k, so M rejects a^i. On the other hand, if during every iteration, $y = A^k a^k A^k \cdots a^k A^k z$ such that $z \in \text{prefixes}\,(a^k A^{k-1}) - \{\varepsilon, a^k\}$, then after exiting from this loop, M accepts the input string because i is a prime.*

*In the **while** loop, consider the entrance test whether $A^k a^h$ occurs on the tape with $k \leq h$ and $i = k + h$. By using several states, tape symbols, and rules, we can easily reformulate this test to its strictly formal description in a straightforward way. However, a warning is in order: this reformulation also represents a painfully tedious task. As obvious, a strictly mathematical definition of the other parts of M is lengthy as well.*

Even more frequently and informally, we just use English prose to describe procedures representing Turing machines under consideration. As a matter of fact, this *highly informal description* of Turing machines is used in most proofs of theorems given in the sequel.

8.2 Determinism

In this section, we demonstrate how to turn any Turing machine to an equivalent deterministic Turing machine.

Definition 8.2. *A Turing machine is* deterministic *if it represents a rewriting system that can make no more than one move from any configuration.*

Theorem 8.1. *From every Turing machine I, we can construct an equivalent deterministic Turing machine O.*

Proof. Let I be any Turing machine. From I, we obtain an equivalent deterministic Turing machine O, so on every input string $x \in {}_I\Delta^*$, O works as follows: first, O saves x somewhere on the tape, so this string is available whenever needed. Then, O systematically produces the sequences of the rules from ${}_IR$ on its tape, for instance, in the lexicographical order. Always after producing a sequence of the rules from ${}_IR$ in this way, O simulates the moves that I performs on x according to this sequence. If the sequence causes I to accept, O accepts as well; otherwise, it proceeds to the simulation according to the next sequence of rules. If there exists a sequence of moves according to which I accepts x, O eventually produces this sequence and accepts x too. ■

Next, without affecting the power of Turing machines, we place further reasonable restrictions upon the way deterministic Turing machines work.

Definition 8.3. *Let M be a Turing machine. If from a configuration χ, M can make no move, then χ is a* halting configuration *of M.*

Theorem 8.2. *From every deterministic Turing machine I, we can construct an equivalent deterministic Turing machine $O = ({}_O\Sigma, {}_OR)$ such that ${}_OQ$ contains two new states, ■ and ♦, which do not occur on the left-hand side of any rule in ${}_OR$, ${}_OF = \{■\}$, and*

(i) every halting configuration $\chi \in {}_OX$ has the form $\chi = \rhd qu \lhd$ with $q \in \{■, ♦\}$ and $u \in {}_O\Gamma^*$, and every non-halting configuration $v \in {}_OX$ satisfies $\{■, ♦\} \cap$ symbols $(v) = \emptyset$;

(ii) on every input string $x \in {}_O\Delta^*$, O performs one of the following three kinds of computation:

(a) $\rhd$ ► $x \lhd \Rightarrow^* \rhd$■$u \lhd$ where $u \in {}_O\Gamma^*$,

(b) $\rhd$ ► $x \lhd \Rightarrow^* \rhd$♦$v \lhd$ where $v \in {}_O\Gamma^*$, and

(c) never enters any halting configuration.

Proof. Let I be a deterministic Turing machine. From I, construct O satisfying the properties of Theorem 8.2 as follows: in both I and O, ► is the start state. Introduce ■ and ♦ as two new states into ${}_OQ$. Define ■ as the only final state in O; formally, set ${}_OF = \{■\}$. On every input string x, O works as follows:

(i) O runs I on x.

(ii) If I halts in $\rhd yqv \lhd$, where $y, v \in {}_I\Gamma^*$ and $q \in {}_IQ$, O continues from $\rhd yqv \lhd$ and computes $\rhd yqv \lhd \Rightarrow^* \rhd qyv \lhd$.

(iii) If $q \in {}_IF$, O computes $\rhd qyv\lhd \Rightarrow \rhd\blacksquare yv\lhd$ and halts, and if $q \in {}_IQ - {}_IF$, O computes $\rhd qyv\lhd \Rightarrow \rhd\blacklozenge yv\lhd$ and halts.

As obvious, O satisfies the properties stated in Theorem 8.2. ∎

Convention 8.1. *In what follows, we automatically assume that every Turing machine has the properties satisfied by O stated in Theorems 8.1 and 8.2.*

Consider the three ways of computation described in Part II of Theorem 8.2—(a), (b), and (c). Let M be a Turing machine and $x \in {}_M\Delta^*$. We say that M *accepts* x iff on x, M makes a computation of the form (a). M *rejects* x iff on x, M makes a computation of the form (b). M *halts* on x iff it accepts or rejects x; otherwise, M *loops* on x—in other words, M loops on x iff it performs a computation of the form (c). States $\blacksquare$ and $\blacklozenge$ are referred to as the *accepting* and *rejecting states*, respectively; accordingly, configurations of the form $\rhd\blacksquare u\lhd$ and $\rhd\blacklozenge u\lhd$, where $u \in {}_M\Gamma^*$, are referred to as *accepting* and *rejecting configurations*, respectively.

We assume that Δ denotes the input alphabet of all Turing machines in what follows. Under this assumption, for brevity, we usually simply state that a Turing machine M works on an input string x instead of stating that M works on an input string x, where $x \in \Delta^*$. Furthermore, any language that is accepted by a Turing machine is called a *Turing language*.

Next, we prove that every Turing language is accepted by a Turing machine that never rejects any input x—that is, either O accepts x or O loops on x. It is worth noting that we cannot reformulate this result, so O never loops on any input. In other words, some Turing languages are accepted only by Turing machines that loop on some inputs as demonstrated later (see Theorem 10.14).

Theorem 8.3. *From any Turing machine I, we can construct a Turing machine O such that L(I) = L(O) and O never rejects any input.*

Proof. Consider any Turing machine I. In I, replace every rule with $\blacklozenge$ on its right-hand side with a set of rules that cause the machine to keep looping in the same configuration. Let O be the Turing machine resulting from this simple modification. Clearly, $L(I) = L(O)$ and O never rejects any input. A fully rigorous proof of this theorem is left to the reader. ∎

Next, we reduce the number of tape symbols in Turing machines without affecting their power.

Theorem 8.4. *From any Turing machine I with* $\mathrm{card}({}_I\Delta) \geq 2$, *we can construct a Turing machine O with* ${}_O\Gamma = {}_I\Delta \cup \{\square\}$.

Proof. Let $I = ({}_I\Sigma, {}_IR)$ be a Turing machine such that $a, b \in {}_I\Delta$. Let $2^{k-1} \leq \mathrm{card}({}_I\Gamma) \leq 2^k$, for some $k \in \mathbb{N}$. We encode every symbol in ${}_I\Gamma - \{\square\}$ as a unique string of length k over $\{a, b\}$ by a function f from ${}_I\Gamma - \{\square\}$ to $\{a, b\}^k$. Based upon f, define the homomorphism g from ${}_I\Sigma^*$ to $({}_IQ \cup \{\rhd, \lhd, \square, a, b\})^*$ so that for all $Z \in {}_I\Gamma - \{\square\}$, $g(Z) = f(Z)$, and for all $Z \in ({}_IQ \cup \{\rhd, \lhd, \square\})$, $g(Z) = Z$ (see Section 2.2 for the definition of homomorphism). Next, we construct a Turing machine O that simulates I over the configurations encoded by f in the following way:

(i) *Initialization.* Let $w = c_1c_2 \cdots c_n$ be an input string, where $c_1, \ldots, c_n$ are input symbols from ${}_I\Delta$. O starts its computation on w by changing w to $g(w)$; in greater detail, it changes $\rhd \blacktriangleright c_1c_2 \cdots c_n\lhd$ to $g(\rhd \blacktriangleright c_1c_2 \cdots c_n \lhd)$, which equals $\rhd \blacktriangleright f(c_1)f(c_2) \cdots f(c_n)\lhd$.

(ii) *Simulation of a Move.* If $\rhd d_1d_2 \cdots d_{i-1}qd_i \cdots d_m\lhd$ is the current configuration of I, where $q \in {}_IQ$ and $d_i \in {}_I\Gamma$, $1 \leq i \leq m$, then the corresponding configuration in ${}_OX$ encoded by g is

$$g(\rhd d_1d_2 \cdots d_{i-1}qd_i \cdots d_m\lhd) = \rhd f(d_1d_2 \cdots d_{i-1})qf(d_i \cdots d_m) \lhd .$$

Let $\chi, \kappa \in {}_IX$, and let I compute $\chi \Rightarrow \kappa$ by using $r \in {}_IR$. Then, O simulates $\chi \Rightarrow \kappa$ so it computes $g(\chi) \Rightarrow g(\kappa)$.

(iii) *Simulation of a Computation.* O continues the simulation of moves in I one by one. If I makes a move by which it accepts, O also accepts; otherwise, O continues the simulation.

■

Notice that we can apply the encoding technique employed in the proof of Theorem 8.4 even if a or b are not in ${}_I\Delta$, which gives rise to the next corollary.

Corollary 8.1. *Let I be a Turing machine. Then, there exists a Turing machine O such that $L(I) = L(O)$ and ${}_O\Gamma = \{a, b, \Box\} \cup {}_I\Delta$.*

The next theorem, whose proof is left as an exercise, says we can also place a limit on the number of states in Turing machines without affecting their power.

Theorem 8.5. *Let I be a Turing machine. Then, there exists a Turing machine O such that $L(I) = L(O)$ and* $\text{card}({}_OQ) \leq 3$.

The bottom line of all the restricted versions of Turing machines discussed in the present section is that they are as powerful as the general versions of Turing machines according to Definition 8.1. Of course, there also exist restrictions placed upon Turing machines that decrease their power. As a matter of fact, whenever we simultaneously place a limit on both the number of non-input tape symbols and the number of states, we decrease the power of Turing machines (a proof of this result is omitted because it is beyond the scope of this introductory text).

We close this section by an implementation of a deterministic Turing machine.

Implementation 8.2. The following C# code implements the behavior of Turing machine M from Example 8.1. Method `CheckString()` takes the input string as its argument and checks if this string contains an even number of as, bs, and cs (and there are no other symbols).

```
public class TuringMachineM
{
    public static bool CheckString(HmmlcString inputString)
    {
        HmmlcString tape = inputString;
```

```
bool aFound;
bool bFound;
bool cFound;
int aIndex = 0;
int bIndex = 0;
int cIndex = 0;

do
{
    aFound = false;
    bFound = false;
    cFound = false;

    for (int i = 0; i < tape.Length; i++)
    {
        if (!aFound && tape[i] == "a")
        {
            aFound = true;
            aIndex = i;
        }

        if (!bFound && tape[i] == "b")
        {
            bFound = true;
            bIndex = i;
        }

        if (!cFound && tape[i] == "c")
        {
            cFound = true;
            cIndex = i;
        }

        if (aFound && bFound && cFound)
        {
            tape = tape.Rewrite(aIndex, TuringMachine.Blank);
            tape = tape.Rewrite(bIndex, TuringMachine.Blank);
            tape = tape.Rewrite(cIndex, TuringMachine.Blank);
            break;
        }
    }
}
while (aFound && bFound && cFound);

foreach (Symbol a in tape)
{
    if (a != TuringMachine.Blank) return false;
}
```

```
            return true;
        }
    }
```

Notice that this implementation works strictly deterministically and the program always terminates. If there is at least one a, at least one b, and at least one c, we replace the first occurrence of each with the blank symbol and continue with the next iteration. As soon as any of the three symbols is not found, the loop ends, and we check if all symbols have been replaced by the blank symbol.

8.3 Universalness

Notice that a formally described Turing machine resembles the machine code of a program executed by a computer, which thus acts as a universal device that executes all possible programs of this kind. Considering the subject of this chapter, we obviously want to know whether there also exists a Turing machine acting as such a universal device, which simulates all Turing machines. The answer is yes, and in this section, we construct a *universal Turing machine* U that does the job—that is, U simulates every Turing machine M working on any input w. However, since the input of any Turing machine, including U, is always a string, we first show how to encode every Turing machine M as a string, symbolically denoted by $\langle M \rangle$, from which U interprets M before it simulates its computation. To be quite precise, as its input, U has the code of M followed by the code of w, denoted by $\langle M, w \rangle$, from which U decodes M and w to simulate M working on w so U accepts $\langle M, w \rangle$ iff M accepts w. As a result, before the construction of U, we explain how to obtain $\langle M \rangle$ and $\langle M, w \rangle$ for every Turing machine M and every input w.

8.3.1 Turing machine codes

Any reasonable encoding for Turing machines over a fixed alphabet $\vartheta \subseteq \Delta$ is acceptable provided that for every Turing machine M, U can mechanically and uniquely interpret $\langle M \rangle$ as M. Mathematically speaking, this encoding should represent a total function code from the set of all Turing machines to ϑ^* such that code $(M) = \langle M \rangle$ for every Turing machine M. In addition, we select an arbitrary but fixed Turing machine Z and define the decoding of Turing machines, decode, so for every $x \in$ range (code), decode $(x) =$ inverse (code(M)), and for every $y \in \vartheta^* -$ range (code), decode $(y) = Z$, so range (decode) equals the set of all Turing machines. As a result, decode is a total surjection because it maps every string in ϑ^*, including the strings that code maps to no Turing machine, to a Turing machine. Notice, on the other hand, that several binary strings in ϑ^* may be decoded to the same machine; mathematically, decode may not be an injection. From a more practical viewpoint, we just require that the mechanical interpretation of both code and decode is relatively easily performable. Apart from encoding and decoding all Turing machines, we also use code and decode to encode and decode the pairs consisting of Turing machines and input strings. Next, we illustrate code and decode in binary.

Consider any Turing machine M. Recall that we automatically apply the convention introduced in Definition 8.1 to M, including the meaning of Q, F, Γ, Δ, and R. Consider Q as the set of states of M. Rename these states to $q_1, q_2, q_3, q_4, \ldots, q_m$ so $q_1 = \blacktriangleright$, $q_2 = \blacksquare$, $q_3 = \blacklozenge$, where $m = \text{card}\,(Q)$. Rename the symbols of $\{\rhd, \lhd\} \cup \Gamma$ to $a_1, a_2, \ldots, a_n$ so $a_1 = \rhd$, $a_2 = \lhd$, where $n = \text{card}\,(\Gamma) + 2$. Introduce the homomorphism h from $Q \cup \Gamma$ to $\{0,1\}^*$ as $h(q_i) = 10^i$, $1 \leq i \leq m$, and $h(a_j) = 110^j$, $1 \leq j \leq n$ (homomorphism is defined in Section 2.2). Extend h so it is defined from $(\Gamma \cup Q)^*$ to $\{0,1\}^*$ in the standard way—that is, $h(\varepsilon) = \varepsilon$, and $h(X_1 \cdots X_k) = h(X_1)h(X_2) \cdots h(Xk)$, where $k \geq 1$, and $X_l \in \Gamma \cup Q$, $1 \leq l \leq k$ (see Section 2.2). Based on h, we now define the function code from R to $\{0,1\}^*$ so that for each rule $x \rightarrow y \in R$, code $(x \rightarrow y) = h(xy)$. Then, write the rules of R one after the other in an order as $x_1 \rightarrow y_1, x_2 \rightarrow y_2, \ldots, x_o \rightarrow y_o$ with $o = \text{card}\,(R)$; for instance, order them lexicographically. Set code $(R) =$ code $(x_1 \rightarrow y_1)111$ code $(x_2 \rightarrow y_2)111 \cdots$ code $(x_o \rightarrow y_o)111$. Finally, from code (R), we obtain the desired code (M) by setting code $(M) = 0^m10^n1$ code $(R)1$. Taking a closer look at code $(M) = 0^m10^n1$ code $(R)1$, 0^m1 and 0^n1 state that $m = \text{card}\,(Q)$ and $n = \text{card}\,(\Gamma) + 2$, respectively, and code (R) encodes the rules of R. Seen as a function from the set of all Turing machines to $\{0,1\}^*$, code obviously represents a total function the set of all Turing machines to ϑ^*. On the other hand, there are binary strings that represent no legal code of any Turing machine; mathematically, inverse (code) is a partial function, not a total function. For example, ε, any string in $\{0\}^* \cup 1^*$, or any string that starts with 1 are illegal codes, so their inverses are undefined. Select an arbitrary but fixed Turing machine Z; for instance, take Z as a Turing machine without any rules. Extend inverse (code) to the total function decode from $\{0,1\}^*$ to the set of all Turing machines so that decode maps all binary strings that represent no code of any Turing machine to Z. More precisely, for every $x \in \{0,1\}^*$, if x is a legal code of a Turing machine K, decode maps x to K, but if it is not, decode maps x to Z; equivalently and briefly, if x encodes K and, therefore, $x \in$ range (code), decode $(x) = K$, and if $x \in \{0,1\}^* -$ range (code), decode $(x) = Z$ (notice that decode represents a surjection).

To encode every $w \in \Delta^*$, we simply set code $(w) = h(w)$, where h is the homomorphism defined previously. Select an arbitrary but fixed $y \in \Delta^*$; for instance, take $y = \varepsilon$. Define the total surjection decode from $\{0,1\}^*$ to Δ^* so for every $x \in \{0,1\}^*$, if $x \in$ range (code), decode $(x) =$ inverse (code(w)); otherwise, decode $(x) = y$.

Let Ψ denote the set of all Turing machines. For every $(M, w) \in \Psi \times \Delta^*$, define code $(M, w) =$ code (M) code (w). Viewed as a function from $\Psi \times \Delta^*$ to $\{0,1\}^*$, code obviously represents a total function from $\Psi \times \Delta^*$ to ϑ^*. Define the total surjection decode from $\{0,1\}^*$ to $\Psi \times \Delta^*$ so decode $(xy) =$ decode (x) decode (y), where decode $(x) \in \Psi$ and decode $(y) \in \Delta^*$.

Example 8.3. *Consider this trivial Turing machine $M \in \Psi$, where $M = (\Sigma, R)$, $\Sigma = Q \cup \Gamma \cup \{\rhd, \lhd\}$, $Q = \{\blacktriangleright, \blacksquare, \blacklozenge, A, B, C, D\}$, $\Gamma = \Delta \cup \{\square\}$, $\Delta = \{b\}$, and R contains these rules*

$$\blacktriangleright \lhd \rightarrow \blacksquare \lhd,$$
$$\blacktriangleright b \rightarrow bA,$$

$$
\begin{aligned}
Ab &\rightarrow bB,\\
Bb &\rightarrow bA,\\
A\lhd &\rightarrow C\lhd,\\
B\lhd &\rightarrow D\lhd,\\
bD &\rightarrow D\square,\\
bC &\rightarrow C\square,\\
\rhd C &\rightarrow \rhd\blacklozenge,\\
\rhd D &\rightarrow \rhd\blacksquare.
\end{aligned}
$$

Leaving a simple proof that $L(M) = \{b^i \mid i \leq 0,\ i \text{ is even}\}$ *as an exercise, we next obtain the binary code of M by applying the encoding method described previously. Introduce the homomorphism h from* $Q \cup \{\rhd, \lhd\} \cup \Gamma$ *to* $\{0,1\}^*$ *as* $h(q_i) = 10^i$, $1 \leq i \leq 7$, *where* q_1, q_2, q_3, q_4, q_5, q_6, *and* q_7 *coincide with* $\blacktriangleright$, $\blacksquare$, $\blacklozenge$, *A, B, C, and D, respectively, and* $h(a_i) = 110^j$, $1 \leq j \leq 4$, *where* a_1, a_2, a_3, *and* a_4 *coincide with* $\rhd$, $\lhd$, $\square$, *and b, respectively. Extend h so it is defined from* $(Q \cup \{\rhd, tmr\} \cup \Gamma)^*$ *to* $\{0,1\}^*$ *in the standard way. Based on h, define the function* code *from R to* $\{0,1\}^*$, *so for each rule* $x \rightarrow y \in R$, code $(x \rightarrow y) = h(xy)$. *For example,* code $(\blacktriangleright b \rightarrow bA) =$ 1011000011000010000. *Take, for instance, the previous order of the rules from R, and set*

$$
\begin{aligned}
\mathrm{code}\,(R) &= \mathrm{code}\,(\blacktriangleright \lhd \rightarrow \blacksquare\lhd)111\,\mathrm{code}\,(\blacktriangleright b \rightarrow bA)1111\\
&\quad \mathrm{code}\,(Ab \rightarrow bB)111\,\mathrm{code}\,(Bb \rightarrow bA)111\\
&\quad \mathrm{code}\,(A\lhd \rightarrow C\lhd)111\,\mathrm{code}\,(B\lhd \rightarrow D\lhd)111\\
&\quad \mathrm{code}\,(bD \rightarrow D\square)111\,\mathrm{code}\,(bC \rightarrow C\square)111\\
&\quad \mathrm{code}\,(\rhd C \rightarrow \rhd\blacklozenge)111\,\mathrm{code}\,(\rhd D \rightarrow \rhd\blacksquare)111\\
&= 10110010011001111011000011000010000111\\
&\quad 1000011000011000010000011110000011000011000010000\\
&\quad 111\\
&\quad 1000011001000000110011110000011001000000001100111\\
&\quad 1100001000000010000000110001111100001000000100000\\
&\quad 011000111\\
&\quad 1101000000110100011111010000000110100111.
\end{aligned}
$$

To encode M as a whole, set

$$
\begin{aligned}
\mathrm{code}\,(M) &= 0^7 10^4 1\,\mathrm{code}\,(R)1\\
&= 000000010000 1\\
&\quad 10110010011001111011000011000010000111\\
&\quad 1000011000011000010000011110000011000011000010000\\
&\quad 111
\end{aligned}
$$

10000110010000000110011110000011001000000001100111

11000010000000100000000110001111100001000000100000

011000111

11010000000110100011111010000000110100111

1.

Take $w = bb$*, whose* $\text{code}(bb) = 110000110000$*. As a result, the binary string denoted by* $\text{code}(M, bb)$ *is*

$$\begin{array}{c}000000010000110110010011001111011000011000010000011110\\ 0001100001100001000000111100000110000110000100000111100\\ 00110010000000110011110000011001000000001100111100001\\ 000000010000000110001111100001000000010000000110001111\\ 1010000001101000111110100000001101001111110000110000.\end{array}$$

Implementation 8.3. Here, we present an implementation of code in C#. In order to convert a Turing machine (represented by an instance of `TuringMachine` class) to the corresponding binary string, we first need to encode its states and tape symbols. Because the set of states and the sets of states are, by definition, disjoint, and states are also identified by symbols, we can use a single mapping for both sets. The following helper method, `CodeSymbols()`, creates such mapping.

```
public static class UniversalTuringMachine
{
    private static readonly HmmlcString string0 =
        new HmmlcString("0");
    private static readonly HmmlcString string1 =
        new HmmlcString("1");

    private static IDictionary<Symbol, HmmlcString>
        CodeSymbols(TuringMachine M)
    {
        var result = new Dictionary<Symbol, HmmlcString>();

        // states
        var stateCode = new HmmlcString("1");

        foreach (TuringMachineState q in M.States)
        {
            stateCode = stateCode.Concatenate(string0);
            result.Add(q.Label, stateCode);
        }

        // tape symbols
        var tapeSymbolCode = new HmmlcString("11");
```

```
        tapeSymbolCode = tapeSymbolCode.Concatenate(string0);
        result.Add(TuringMachine.LeftBounder, tapeSymbolCode);

        tapeSymbolCode = tapeSymbolCode.Concatenate(string0);
        result.Add(TuringMachine.RightBounder, tapeSymbolCode);

        foreach (Symbol a in M.TapeAlphabet)
        {
            tapeSymbolCode = tapeSymbolCode.Concatenate(string0);
            result.Add(a, tapeSymbolCode);
        }

        return result;
    }
}
```

Now that we have mapped all states and tape symbols to their respective binary codes, encoding rules is straightforward. We add another helper method as follows:

```
private static HmmlcString CodeRule(TuringMachineRule r,
    IDictionary<Symbol, HmmlcString> symbolCodes)
{
    var result = HmmlcString.Empty;

    foreach (Symbol a in r.LeftHandSide)
    {
        result = result.Concatenate(symbolCodes[a]);
    }
    foreach (Symbol a in r.RightHandSide)
    {
        result = result.Concatenate(symbolCodes[a]);
    }

    return result;
}
```

We are now ready to implement code (*M*).

```
public static HmmlcString Code(TuringMachine M)
{
    var result = HmmlcString.Empty;

    IDictionary<Symbol, HmmlcString> symbolCodes = CodeSymbols(M);

    for (int i = 0; i < M.States.Cardinality; i++)
    {
        result = result.Concatenate(string0);
    }
    result = result.Concatenate(string1);
```

```
    for (int i = 0; i < M.TapeAlphabet.Cardinality + 2; i++)
    {
        result = result.Concatenate(string0);
    }
    result = result.Concatenate(string1);

    var string111 = new HmmlcString("111");
    foreach (TuringMachineRule r in M.Rules)
    {
        result = result.Concatenate(CodeRule(r, symbolCodes));
        result = result.Concatenate(string111);
    }
    result = result.Concatenate(string1);

    return result;
}
```

By analogy with `Code()`, we can easily implement code (M, w) for a Turing machine M and an input string w, as demonstrated in the exercises.

In what follows, we suppose there exists a fixed encoding and a fixed decoding of all Turing machines in Ψ. We just require that both are uniquely and mechanically interpretable; otherwise, they may differ from code and decode (in fact, they may not even be in binary). As already stated in the beginning of this section, we denote the code of $M \in \Psi$ by $\langle M \rangle$. Similarly, we suppose there exist an analogical encoding and decoding of the members of Δ^*, $\Psi \times \Delta^*$, $\Psi \times \Psi$, and $\Psi \times {}_0\mathbb{N}^*$. Again, for brevity, we denote the codes of $w \in \Delta^*$, $(M, w) \in \Psi \times \Delta^*$, $(M, N) \in \Psi \times \Psi$, and $(M, i) \in \Psi \times {}_0\mathbb{N}^*$ by $\langle w \rangle$, $\langle M, w \rangle$, $\langle M, N \rangle$, and $\langle M, i \rangle$, respectively (as an exercise, encode and decode the members of ${}_0\mathbb{N}^*$ similarly to encoding the machine in Ψ). Even more generally, for any automaton or grammar, X, discussed earlier in this book, $\langle X \rangle$ represents its code analogical to $\langle M \rangle$.

Out of all the terminology introduced in the previous convention, we need only $\langle M \rangle$ and $\langle M, w \rangle$ in rest of the present section. In the following sections of this chapter, however, we also make use of the other abbreviations as always explicitly pointed out therein.

8.3.2 Construction of universal Turing machines

We are now ready to construct U—that is, a universal Turing machine (see the beginning of this section). As a matter of fact, we construct two versions of U. The first version, denoted by ${}_{Acceptance}U$, simulates every $M \in \Psi$ on $w \in \Delta^*$ so ${}_{Acceptance}U$ accepts $\langle M, w \rangle$ iff M accepts w. In other words, $L({}_{Acceptance}U) = {}_{Acceptance}L$ with

$${}_{Acceptance}L = \{\langle M, w \rangle \mid M \in \Psi,\ w \in \Delta^*,\ M \text{ accepts } w\}.$$

The other version, denoted by ${}_{Halting}U$, simulates every $M \in \Psi$ on $w \in \Delta^*$ in such a way that ${}_{Halting}U$ accepts $\langle M, w\rangle$ iff M halts on w. To rephrase this in terms of formal languages, $L({}_{Halting}U) = {}_{Halting}L$ with

$$ {}_{Halting}L = \{\langle M, w\rangle \mid M \in \Psi,\ w \in \Delta^*,\ M \text{ halts on } w\}. $$

Strictly speaking, in the following proof, we should state that ${}_{Acceptance}U$ works on $\langle M, w\rangle$ so it first interprets $\langle M, w\rangle$ as M and w; then it simulates the moves of M on w. However, instead of a long and obvious statement like this, we just state that ${}_{Acceptance}U$ runs M on w. In a similar manner, we shorten the other proofs of results concerning Turing machines in the sequel whenever no confusion exists.

Theorem 8.6. *There exists* ${}_{Acceptance}U \in \Psi$ *such that* $L({}_{Acceptance}U) = {}_{Acceptance}L$.

Proof. On every input $\langle M, w\rangle$, ${}_{Acceptance}U$ works, so it runs M on w. ${}_{Acceptance}U$ accepts $\langle M, w\rangle$ if and when it finds out that M accepts w; otherwise, ${}_{Acceptance}U$ keeps simulating the moves of M in this way. ■

Observe that ${}_{Acceptance}U$ represents a procedure, not an algorithm because if M loops on w, so does ${}_{Acceptance}U$ on $\langle M, w\rangle$. As a matter of fact, later on (see Section 10.3), we demonstrate that no Turing machine can halt on every input and, simultaneously, act as a universal Turing machine (see Theorem 10.14). To reformulate this in terms of formal languages, no Turing machine accepts ${}_{Acceptance}L$ in such a way that it halts on all strings. Indeed, for all $X \in \Psi$ satisfying ${}_{Acceptance}L = L(X)$, $\Delta^* - {}_{Acceptance}L$ necessarily contains a string on which X loops. By analogy with the proof of Theorem 8.6, we next obtain ${}_{Halting}U$ that accepts ${}_{Halting}L$, defined previously.

Theorem 8.7. *There exists* ${}_{Halting}U \in \Psi$ *such that* $L({}_{Halting}U) = {}_{Halting}L$.

Proof. On every $\langle M, w\rangle$, ${}_{Halting}U$ works, so it runs M on w. ${}_{Halting}U$ accepts $\langle M, w\rangle$ iff M halts on w, which means that M either accepts or rejects w. Thus, ${}_{Halting}U$ loops on $\langle M, w\rangle$ iff M loops on w. $L({}_{Halting}U) = {}_{Halting}L$. ■

Chapter 9
Computability

In essence, computers are programmable electronic devices that perform their procedures, which accept input data, execute operations in accordance with their instructions and display the results. Consequently, from an utterly intuitive viewpoint, the notion of a procedure is understood as a finite set of instructions, each of which can be executed in a fixed amount of time; when performed, it reads input data, computes its instructions, and produces output data. As obvious, the notion of a procedure are more than significant in computer science in its entirety, which necessities its formalization in order to study them mathematically. According to the Church–Turing thesis, this formalization is provided by the strictly mathematical notion of a Turing machine, introduced in Chapter 8.

In other words, the Church–Turing thesis assures us that any computation performed by a procedure can be also carried out by a Turing machine. It thus comes as no surprise that these machines are central to computation as a whole. Perhaps most importantly, this theory makes use of Turing machines to demonstrate the mathematical limits of computation. Indeed, any computation beyond the power of Turing machines is also beyond the computer power in general as the Church–Turing thesis proclaims.

Algorithms represent important special cases of procedures that halt on all inputs. For instance, all C programs obviously represent procedures, but only those of them that never enter any endless loops are algorithms. As algorithms obviously fulfill a crucially important role in computer science, the present chapter and, perhaps even more significantly, the following chapter pay a special attention to them.

In Section 9.1, we view Turing machines as computers of nonnegative integer functions. Apart from functions computable in this way, we demonstrate the existence of functions that cannot be computed by any procedure, so they are not computable at all according to the Church–Turing thesis. Then, in Section 9.2, we give an introduction to the theory of computability from a more general point of view.

9.1 Functions computed by Turing machines

Considering the Turing machine model as the formalization of an effective procedure, we demonstrate the existence of functions whose computation cannot be specified by any procedure, so they can never be computed by any computer. As a matter of fact, the existence of these uncomputable functions immediately follows from the following counting argument. Consider the set of all functions that map $\mathbb{N}$ onto $\{0, 1\}$ and the set of all procedures. While the former is uncountable, the latter is countable under our assumption that every procedure has a finite description (see Section 8.1). Thus, there necessarily exist functions with no procedures to compute them. In this section, based upon the following Turing machine-based formalization, we take a more specific look at functions whose computation can or, in contrast, cannot be specified by any procedure.

Definition 9.1. *Let* $M \in \Psi$. *The* function computed by M, *symbolically denoted by* M-f, *is defined over* Δ^* *as* $M\text{-}f = \{(x, y) \mid x, y \in \Delta^*,\ \rhd \blacktriangleright x \lhd \Rightarrow^* \rhd \blacksquare yu \lhd$ *in* M, $u \in \{\square\}^*\}$.

Consider M-f, where $M \in \Psi$, and an argument $x \in \Delta^*$. In a general case, M-f is partial, so $M\text{-}f(x)$ may or may not be defined. Clearly, if $M\text{-}f(x) = y$ is defined, M computes $\rhd \blacktriangleright x \lhd \Rightarrow^* \rhd \blacksquare yu \lhd$, where $u \in \{\square\}^*$. However, if $M\text{-}f(x)$ is undefined, M, starting from $\rhd \blacktriangleright x \lhd$, never reaches a configuration of the form $\rhd \blacksquare vu \lhd$, where $v \in \Delta^*$ and $u \in \{\square\}^*$, so it either rejects x or loops on x (see Section 8.1).

Definition 9.2. *A function* f *is a* computable function *if there exists* $M \in \Psi$ *such that* $f = M$-f; *otherwise,* f *is an* uncomputable function.

Integer functions computed by Turing machines

By Definition 9.1, for every $M \in \Psi$, M-f is defined over Δ^*, where Δ is an alphabet. However, in mathematics, we usually study numeric functions defined over sets of infinitely many numbers. To use Turing machines to compute functions like these, we first need to represent these numbers by strings over Δ. In this introductory book, we restrict our attention only to integer functions over ${}_0\mathbb{N}$, so we need to represent every nonnegative integer $i \in {}_0\mathbb{N}$ as a string over Δ. Traditionally, we represent i in unary as unary (i) for all $i \in {}_0\mathbb{N}$, where unary is defined in Example 1.11. That is, unary $(j) = a^j$ for all $j \geq 0$; for instance, unary (0), unary (2), and unary (999) are equal to ε, aa, and a^{999}, respectively. Under this representation, used in the sequel, we obviously automatically assume that $\Delta = \{a\}$ simply because a is the only input symbol needed. Next, we formalize the computation of integer functions by Turing machines based upon unary.

Definition 9.3.

(i) *Let* g *be a function over* ${}_0\mathbb{N}$ *and* $M \in \Psi$. M computes g in unary *or, more briefly,* M computes g *iff* unary $(g) = M$-f.

(ii) *A function* h *over* ${}_0\mathbb{N}$ *is a* computable function *if there exists a Turing machine* M *such that* M *computes* h; *otherwise,* h *is an* uncomputable function.

In greater detail, part (i) of Definition 9.3 says that M computes an integer function g over ${}_0\mathbb{N}$ if this equivalence holds:

$$g(x) = y \text{ iff } (\text{unary}(x), \text{unary}(y)) \in M\text{-}f, \text{ for all } x, y \in {}_0\mathbb{N}.$$

Convention 9.1. *Whenever $M \in \Psi$ works on an integer $x \in {}_0\mathbb{N}$, x is expressed as* unary (x). *For brevity, whenever no confusion exists, instead of stating that M* works on x represented as unary (x), *we just state that M* works on x *in what follows.*

Implementations 9.1 and 9.2 simulate Turing machines given in Examples 9.1 and 9.2, respectively. Both implementations are described as simple high-level-language algorithms. Observe that this way of describing Turing machines is quite legitimate because the Church–Turing thesis (see the beginning of Chapter 8) assures us that for every Turing machine defined in a strictly mathematical way, there exists a procedure that performs exactly the same job as the machine does.

Example 9.1. *Let g be the* successor function *defined as $g(i) = i + 1$, for all $i \geq 0$. Construct a Turing machine M that computes $\rhd \blacktriangleright a^i \lhd \Rightarrow^* \rhd \blacksquare a^{i+1} \lhd$ so it moves across a^i to the right bounder $\lhd$, replaces it with $a\lhd$, and returns to the left to finish its accepting computation in $\rhd \blacksquare a^{i+1} \lhd$. As a result, M increases the number of as by one on the tape. Thus, by Definition 9.3, M computes g.*

Implementation 9.1. We implement M from Example 9.1 as another method in `TuringMachineM` module (see Implementation 8.4).

```
public static int Successor(int i)
{
    return i + 1;
}
```

Example 9.2. *Let g be the total function defined as $g(i) = j$, for all $i \geq 0$, where j is the smallest prime satisfying $i \leq j$. Construct a Turing machine M that tests whether i, represented by a^i, is a prime in the way described in Example 8.3. If i is prime, M accepts in the configuration $\rhd \blacksquare a^i \lhd$. If not, M continues its computation from $\rhd \blacktriangleright a^{i+1} \lhd$ and tests whether $i + 1$ is prime; if it is, it accepts in $\rhd \blacksquare a^{i+1} \lhd$. In this way, it continues increasing the number of as by one and testing whether the number is prime until it reaches a^j such that j is prime. As this prime j is obviously the smallest prime satisfying $i \leq j$, M accepts in $\rhd \blacksquare a^j \lhd$. Thus, M computes g.*

Implementation 9.2. To implement M from Example 9.2, we first add a helper method to `TuringMachineM` class, which follows the procedure from Example 8.3 to determine if a given number is prime.

```
private static bool IsPrime(int i)
{
    if (i <= 1) return false;

    int k = 2;
    int h = i - k;

    while (k <= h)
    {
        if (i % k == 0) return false;
        else
```

```
        {
            k++;
            h--;
        }
    }

    return true;
}
```

Using the previous method and the successor method from Implementation 9.1, the implementation of g is straightforward.

```
public static int NextPrime(int i)
{
    int j = i;

    while (!IsPrime(j))
    {
        j = Successor(j);
    }

    return j;
}
```

Both functions discussed in the previous two examples are total. However, there also exist partial integer functions, which may be undefined for some arguments. Suppose that g is a function over ${}_0\mathbb{N}$, which is undefined for some arguments. Let M be a Turing machine, and let M compute g. According to Definition 9.3, for any $x \in {}_0\mathbb{N}$, $g(x)$ is undefined iff $(\text{unary}(x), \text{unary}(y)) \notin M\text{-}f$ for all $y \in {}_0\mathbb{N}$. The next example illustrates a partial integer function computed in this way.

Convention 9.2. *As opposed to the previous two examples, the next function as well as all other functions discussed throughout the rest of this section are defined over the set of positive integers, $\mathbb{N}$, which excludes 0.*

Example 9.3. *In this example, we consider a partial function g over $\mathbb{N}$ that is defined for 1, 2, 4, 8, 16, ..., but it is undefined for the other positive integers. More precisely, $g(x) = 2x$ if $x = 2^n$, for some $n \in \mathbb{N}$; otherwise, $g(x)$ is undefined (see Table 9.1).*

We construct $M \in \Psi$ that computes g as follows. Starting from $\rhd \blacktriangleright a^i \lhd$, M computes $\rhd \blacktriangleright a^i \lhd \Rightarrow^* \rhd \blacktriangleright a^i A^j \lhd$ with j being the smallest natural number simultaneously satisfying $i \leq j$ and $j = 2^n$ with $n \in \mathbb{N}$. If $i = j$, then $i = 2^n$ and $g(i) = 2i = 2^{n+1}$, so M computes $\rhd \blacktriangleright a^i A^j \lhd \Rightarrow^* \rhd \blacksquare a^i a^j \lhd$ and, thereby, defines $g(i) = 2^{n+1}$. If $i < j$, then $2^{n-1} < i < 2^n$ and $g(i)$ is undefined, so M rejects a^i by $\rhd \blacktriangleright a^i A^j \lhd \Rightarrow^* \rhd \blacklozenge a^i \square^j \lhd$.

In somewhat greater detail, we describe M by the following Pascal-like algorithm that explains how M changes its configurations.

Let $\rhd \blacktriangleright a^i \lhd$ be the input, for some $i \in \mathbb{N}$;
change $\rhd \blacktriangleright a^i \lhd$ to $\rhd \blacktriangleright a^i A \lhd$
while the current configuration $\rhd \blacktriangleright a^i A^j \lhd$ satisfies $j \leq i$ **do**

Table 9.1 Partial function g discussed in Example 9.3

x	$g(x)$
1	2
2	4
3	Undefined
4	8
5	Undefined
6	Undefined
7	Undefined
8	16
⋮	⋮

if $i = j$ **then**
  ACCEPT by computing $\triangleright \blacktriangleright a^i A^j \triangleleft \Rightarrow^{\triangleright} \blacksquare a^i A^i \triangleleft$
   { because $i = j = 2^m$ for some $m \in \mathbb{N}$ }
else
  compute $\triangleright \blacktriangleright a^i A^j \triangleleft \Rightarrow^* \triangleright \blacktriangleright a^i A^{2j} \triangleleft$ by changing each A to AA
end
end { of the while loop }
REJECT by computing $\triangleright \blacktriangleright a^i A^j \Rightarrow^* \triangleright \blacklozenge \square^j \triangleleft$
 { because $j > i$, so $i \neq 2^m$ for any $m \in \mathbb{N}$ }

The set of all rewriting systems is countable because every definition of a rewriting system is finite, so this set can be put into a bijection with $\mathbb{N}$. For the same reason, the set of all Turing machines, which are defined as rewriting systems, is countable. However, the set of all functions is uncountable (see Example 9.3). From this observation, it straightforwardly follows the existence of uncomputable functions: there are just more functions than Turing machines. More surprisingly, however, even some simple total well-defined functions over $\mathbb{N}$ are uncomputable as the next example illustrates.

Example 9.4. *For every $k \in \mathbb{N}$, set*

$$_kX = \{M \in \Psi \mid \text{card}\,(_MQ) = k + 1,\ _M\Delta = \{a\}\}.$$

Informally, $_kX$ denotes the set of all Turing machines in Ψ with $k + 1$ states such that their languages are over $\{a\}$. Without any loss of generality, suppose that $_MQ = \{q_0, q_1, \ldots, q_k\}$ with $\blacktriangleright = q_0$ and $\blacksquare = q_k$. Let g be the total function over $\mathbb{N}$ defined for every $i \in \mathbb{N}$ so $g(i)$ equals the greatest integer $j \in \mathbb{N}$ satisfying $\triangleright q_0 a \triangleleft \Rightarrow^* \triangleright q_i a^j u \triangleleft$ in M with $M \in {_iX}$, where $u \in \{\square\}^*$. In other words, $g(i) = j$ iff j is the greatest positive integer satisfying $M\text{-}f(1) = j$, where $M \in {_iX}$. Consequently, for every Turing machine $K \in {_iX}$, either $K\text{-}f(1) \leq g(i)$ or $K\text{-}f(1)$ is undefined.

Observe that for every $i \in \mathbb{N}$, ${}_iX$ is finite. Furthermore, ${}_iX$ always contains $M \in \Psi$ such that $\triangleright q_0 a \triangleleft \Rightarrow^* \triangleright q_i a^j u \triangleleft$ in M with $j \in \mathbb{N}$, so g is total. Finally, $g(i)$ is defined quite rigorously because each Turing machine in ${}_iX$ is deterministic (see Convention 8.4). At first glance, these favorable mathematical properties might suggest that g is computable, yet we next demonstrate that g is uncomputable by a proof based upon diagonalization (see Example 2.8).

Gist. *To demonstrate that g is uncomputable, we proceed, in essence, as follows: we assume that g is computable. Under this assumption, Ψ contains a Turing machine M that computes g. We convert M to a Turing machine N, which we subsequently transform to a Turing machine O and demonstrate that O performs a computation that contradicts the definition of g, so our assumption that g is computable is incorrect. Thus, g is uncomputable.*

In greater detail, let $M \in \Psi$ be a Turing machine that computes g. We can easily modify M to another Turing machine $N \in \Psi$ such that N computes $h(x) = g(2x) + 1$ for every $x \in \mathbb{N}$. Let $N \in {}_mX$, where $m \in \mathbb{N}$, so ${}_NQ = \{q_0, q_1, \ldots, q_m\}$ with $\blacktriangleright = q_0$ and $\blacksquare = q_m$. Modify N to the Turing machine $O = ({}_O\Sigma, {}_OR)$, $O \in \Psi$, in the following way. Define q_m as a nonfinal state. Set ${}_OQ = \{q_0, q_1, \ldots, q_m, q_{m+1}, \ldots, q_{2m}\}$ with $\blacktriangleright = q_0$ and $\blacksquare = q_{2m}$, so $O \in {}_{2m}X$. Initialize ${}_OR$ with the rules of ${}_NR$. Then, extend ${}_OR$ by the following new rules:

- $q_m a \to a q_m$ *and* $q_m \square \to a q_m$;
- $q_h \triangleleft \to q_{h+1} \square \triangleleft$ *and* $q_{h+1} \square \to a q_{h+1}$, *for all* $m \leq h \leq 2m - 1$; *and*
- $a q_{2m} \to q_{2m} a$.

Starting from $\triangleright q_0 a \triangleleft$, O first computes $\triangleright q_0 a \triangleleft \Rightarrow^* \triangleright q_m a^{h(m)} u \triangleleft$ with $u \in \{\square\}^*$ just like N does. Then, by the newly introduced rules, O computes $\triangleright q_m a^{h(m)} u \triangleleft \Rightarrow^* \triangleright q_{2m} a^{h(m)} a^{|u|} a^m \triangleleft$ with $q_{2m} = \blacksquare$. In brief, $\triangleright q_0 a \triangleleft \Rightarrow^* \triangleright q_{2m} a^{h(m)} a^{|u|} a^m \triangleleft$ in O, which is impossible, however. Indeed, $|a^{h(m)} a^{|u|} a^m| = |a^{g(2m)+1} a^{|u|} a^m| > g(2m)$, so O-$f(1) > g(2m)$, which contradicts K-$f(1) \leq g(2m)$ for all $K \in {}_{2m}X$ because $O \in {}_{2m}X$. From this contradiction, we conclude that g is uncomputable.

9.2 Mathematical theory of computability: an introduction

Recall the Church–Turing thesis, which assures us that he intuitive notion of a procedure is functionally identical with the formal notion of a Turing machine (see the beginning of Chapter 8). This crucially important declaration, originated by Alonzo Church in 1936, brings us to the very heart of the theoretical foundations of computation and, thereby, makes the Turing machine exceptionally significant. Indeed, as the intuitive notion of an effective procedure is central to computation as a whole, we really do need to formalize it by an adequate formal model in order to explore these foundations quite clearly and validly, and the Church–Turing thesis assures us that the Turing machine fulfills this role properly.

Named after its inventor Alan Turing, the Turing machine represents a relatively simple language-defining model, and as follows from its description given shortly, it obviously constitutes a procedure. Much more surprisingly, the Church–Turing thesis also asserts that every procedure in the intuitive sense can be completely formalized by this strictly mathematical notion of a Turing machine. Observe that it is really a thesis, not a theorem because it cannot be proved. Indeed, any proof of this kind would necessitate a formalization of our intuitive notion of a procedure, so it can be rigorously compared with the notion of a Turing machine. At this point, however, there would be a problem whether this newly formalized notion is equivalent to the intuitive notion of a procedure, which would give rise to another thesis similar to the Church–Turing thesis. Therefore, any attempt to prove this thesis inescapably ends up with an infinite regression. However, the evidence supporting the Church–Turing thesis is hardly disputable because throughout its history, computer science has formalized the notion of a procedure in the intuitive sense by other mathematical models; including Post systems, μ-recursive functions, and λ-calculus; and all of them have eventually turned out to be equivalent with Turing machines. Even more importantly, nobody has ever come with a procedure in the intuitive sense and demonstrated that no Turing machine can formalize it. Thus, the strictly mathematical notion of a Turing machine has become the universally accepted formalization of the intuitive notion of a procedure. In other words, it is a general-enough mathematical model for the notion of a procedure in the intuitive sense, so any possible procedure can be realized as a Turing machine. Playing such a significant role, the Turing machine model underlies most fundamental ideas behind computation as demonstrated in the present section.

First, this section sketches the fundamental theory of computability. That is, it considers Turing machines as computers of functions over nonnegative integers and demonstrates the existence of functions whose computation cannot be specified by any procedure. In what follows, we often consider an enumeration of Ψ. In essence, to enumerate Ψ means to list all Turing machines in Ψ. We can easily obtain a list like this, for instance, by enumerating their codes according to length and alphabetic order. If the code of $M \in \Psi$ is the ith string in this lexicographic enumeration, we let M be the ith Turing machine in the list.

Convention 9.3. *In the sequel, ζ denotes some fixed enumeration of all possible Turing machines,*

$$\zeta = {}_1M, {}_2M, \ldots$$

Regarding ζ, we just require the existence of two algorithms—(1) an algorithm that translates every $i \in \mathbb{N}$ to ${}_iM$ and (2) an algorithm that translates every $M \in \Psi$ to i so $M = {}_iM$, where $i \in \mathbb{N}$. Let

$$\xi = {}_1M\text{-}f, {}_2M\text{-}f, \ldots$$

That is, ξ corresponds to ζ, so ξ denotes the enumeration of the functions computed by the Turing machines listed in ζ. The positive integer i of ${}_iM\text{-}f$ is referred to as the index of ${}_iM\text{-}f$; *in terms of ζ, i is referred to as the* index of ${}_iM$.

Throughout the rest of this chapter, we frequently discuss Turing machines that construct other Turing machines, represented by their codes, and the Turing machines constructed in this way may subsequently create some other machines, and so on. Let us note that a construction like this commonly occurs in real-world computer-science practice; for instance, a compiler produces a program that itself transforms the codes of some other programs, and so forth. Crucially, by means of universal Turing machines described in Section 8.3, we always know how to run any Turing machine on any string, including a string that encodes another Turing machine.

Recursion theorem

Consider any total computable function γ over $\mathbb{N}$ and apply γ to the indices of Turing machines in ζ (see Convention 9.3). The next theorem says that there necessarily exists $n \in \mathbb{N}$, customarily referred to as a *fixed point of* γ, such that ${}_nM$ and ${}_{\gamma(n)}M$ compute the same function—that is, in terms of ξ, ${}_nM\text{-}f = {}_{\gamma(n)}M\text{-}f$.

Theorem 9.1. *For every total computable function g over* $\mathbb{N}$*, there is* $n \in \mathbb{N}$ *such that* ${}_nM\text{-}f = {}_{\gamma(n)}M\text{-}f$ *in* ξ.

Proof. Let γ be any total computable function over $\mathbb{N}$, and let $X \in \Psi$ compute γ—that is, $X\text{-}f = \gamma$. First, for each $i \in \mathbb{N}$, introduce a Turing machine $N_i \in \Psi$ that works on every input $x \in \mathbb{N}$ as follows:

(i) N_i saves x.
(ii) N_i runs ${}_iM$ on i (according to Convention 9.3, ${}_iM$ denotes the Turing machine of index i in ζ).
(iii) If ${}_iM\text{-}f(i)$ is defined and, therefore, ${}_iM$ actually computes ${}_iM\text{-}f(i)$, then N_i runs X on ${}_iM\text{-}f(i)$ to compute $X\text{-}f({}_iM\text{-}f(i))$.
(iv) N_i runs ${}_{X\text{-}f({}_iM\text{-}f(i))}M$ on x to compute ${}_{X\text{-}f({}_iM\text{-}f(i))}M\text{-}f(x)$.

Let O be a Turing machine in ζ that computes the function $O\text{-}f$ over $\mathbb{N}$ such that for each $\in \mathbb{N}$, $O\text{-}f(i)$ is equal to the index of N_i in ζ, constructed previous. Note that although ${}_iM\text{-}f(i)$ may be undefined in (iii), $O\text{-}f$ is total because N_i is defined for all $i \in \mathbb{N}$. Furthermore, ${}_{O\text{-}f(i)}M\text{-}f = {}_{X\text{-}f({}_iM\text{-}f(i))}M\text{-}f$ because $O\text{-}f(i)$ is the index of N_i in ζ, and N_i computes $X\text{-}f({}_iM\text{-}f(i))M\text{-}f$. As $X\text{-}f = \gamma$, we have ${}_{X\text{-}f({}_iM\text{-}f(i))}M\text{-}f = {}_{\gamma({}_iM\text{-}f(i))}M\text{-}f$. Let $O = {}_kM$ in ζ, where $k \in \mathbb{N}$; in other words, k is the index of O. Set $n = O\text{-}f(k)$ to obtain ${}_nM\text{-}f = {}_{O\text{-}f(k)}M\text{-}f = {}_{X\text{-}f({}_kM\text{-}f(k))}M\text{-}f = {}_{\gamma({}_kM\text{-}f(k))}M\text{-}f = {}_{\gamma(O\text{-}f(k))}M\text{-}f = {}_{\gamma(n)}M\text{-}f$. Thus, n is a fixed point of γ, and Theorem 9.1 holds true. ■

The recursion theorem is a powerful tool frequently applied in the theory of computation as illustrated next.

Example 9.5. *Consider the enumeration* $\zeta = {}_1M, {}_2M, \ldots$ *(see Convention 9.3). Observe that Theorem 9.1 implies the existence of* $n \in \mathbb{N}$ *such that* ${}_nM\text{-}f = {}_{n+1}M\text{-}f$*, meaning that* ${}_nM$ *and* ${}_{n+1}M$ *compute the same function. Indeed, define the total computable function* γ *for each* $i \in \mathbb{N}$ *as* $\gamma(i) = i + 1$*. By Theorem 9.1, there is* $n \in \mathbb{N}$ *such that* ${}_nM\text{-}f = {}_{\gamma(n)}M\text{-}f$ *in* ξ*, and by the definition of* γ*,* $\gamma(n) = n + 1$*. Thus,* ${}_nM\text{-}f = {}_{n+1}M\text{-}f$.

From a broader perspective, this result holds in terms of any enumeration of Ψ*, which may differ from* ζ*, provided that it satisfies the simple requirements stated in*

Convention 9.3. That is, the enumeration can be based on any representation whatsoever provided that there exists an algorithm that translates each representation to the corresponding machine in Ψ and vice versa. As an exercise, consider an alternative enumeration of this kind and prove that it necessarily contains two consecutive Turing machines that compute the same function. To rephrase this generalized result in terms of the Turing–Church thesis, any enumeration of procedures contains two consecutive procedures that compute the same function.

Before closing this section, we generalize functions so they map multiple arguments to a set, and we briefly discuss their computation by Turing machines. For k elements, $a_1, \ldots, a_k$, where $k \in \mathbb{N}$, $(a_1, \ldots, a_k)$ denotes the *ordered k-tuple* consisting of a_1 through a_k in this order. Let $A_1, \ldots, A_k$ be k sets. The *Cartesian product of* $A_1, \ldots, A_k$ is denoted by $A_1 \times \cdots \times A_k$ and defined as

$$A_1 \times \cdots \times A_k = \{(a_1, \ldots, a_k) \mid a_i \in A_i,\ 1 \le i \le k\}.$$

Let $m \in \mathbb{N}$ and B be a set. Loosely speaking, an *m-argument function* from $A_1 \times \cdots \times A_m$ to B maps each $(a_1, \ldots, a_m) \in A_1 \times \cdots \times A_m$ to no more than one $b \in B$. To express that a function f represents an m-argument function, we write $f^{\underline{m}}$ (carefully distinguish $f^{\underline{m}}$ from f^m, which denotes the m-fold product of f, defined in the conclusion of Section 2.2). If $f^{\underline{m}}$ maps $(a_1, \ldots, a_m) \in A_1 \times \cdots \times A_m$ to $b \in B$, then $f^{\underline{m}}(a_1, \ldots, a_m)$ is defined as b, written as $f^{\underline{m}}(a_1, \ldots, a_m) = b$, where b is the *value* of $f^{\underline{m}}$ for arguments $a_1, \ldots, a_m$. If $f^{\underline{m}}$ maps $(a_1, \ldots, a_m)$ to no member of B, $f_m(a_1, \ldots, a_m)$ is *undefined*. If $f^{\underline{m}}(a_1, \ldots, a_m)$ is defined for all $(a_1, \ldots, a_m) \in A_1 \times \cdots \times A_m$, $f^{\underline{m}}$ is *total*. If we want to emphasize that $f^{\underline{m}}$ may not be total, we say that $f^{\underline{m}}$ is *partial*.

Next, we generalize Definition 9.3 to the m-argument function $M\text{-}f^{\underline{m}}$ computed by $M \in \Psi$. For the sake of this generalization, we assume that Δ contains #, used in the following definition to separate the m arguments of $M\text{-}f^{\underline{m}}$.

Definition 9.4. *Let $M \in \Psi$. The m-*argument function computed by *M is denoted by $M\text{-}f^{\underline{m}}$ and defined as*

$$M\text{-}f^{\underline{m}} = \{(x, y) \mid x \in \Delta^*,\ \text{occur}(x, \#) = m - 1,\ y \in (\Delta - \{\#\})^*,$$
$$\rhd \blacktriangleright x \lhd \Rightarrow^* \rhd \blacksquare yu \lhd \text{ in } M,\ u \in \{\square\}^*\}.$$

That is, $f^{\underline{m}}(x_1, x_2, \ldots, x_m) = y$ iff $\rhd \blacktriangleright x_1\#x_2\# \cdots \#x_m \lhd \Rightarrow^* \rhd \blacksquare yu \lhd$ in M with $u \in \{\square\}^*$, and $f^{\underline{m}}(x_1, x_2, \ldots, x_m)$ is undefined iff M loops on $x_1\#x_2\# \cdots x_m$ or rejects $x_1\#x_2\# \cdots x_m$. Notice that $M\text{-}f^{\underline{1}}$ coincides with $M\text{-}f$ (see Definition 9.3). According to Definition 9.4, for every Turing machine M and every $m \in \mathbb{N}$, there exists $M\text{-}f^{\underline{m}}$. At a glance, it is hardly credible that every Turing machine M defines $M\text{-}f^{\underline{m}}$ because Ψ obviously contains Turing machines that never perform a computation that defines any member of $M\text{-}f^{\underline{m}}$. However, if we realize that we might have $M\text{-}f^{\underline{m}}$ completely undefined—that is, $M\text{-}f^{\underline{m}} = \emptyset$, which is perfectly legal from a mathematical point of view, then the existence of $M\text{-}f^{\underline{m}}$ corresponding to every Turing machine M comes as no surprise.

Definition 9.5. *Let $m \in \mathbb{N}$. A function $f^{\underline{m}}$ is a* computable function *if there exists $M \in \Psi$ such that $f^{\underline{m}} = M\text{-}f^{\underline{m}}$; otherwise, $f^{\underline{m}}$ is* uncomputable.

To use Turing machines as computers of m-argument integer functions, we automatically assume that Turing machines work with the unary-based representation of integers by analogy with one-argument integer functions computed by Turing machines (see Definition 9.3 and Convention 9.1).

Definition 9.6. *Let $M \in \Psi$, $m \in \mathbb{N}$, and $f^{\underline{m}}$ be an m-argument function from $A_1 \times \ldots \times A_m$ to $\mathbb{N}$, where $A_i = \mathbb{N}$, for all $1 \leq i \leq m$. M computes $f^{\underline{m}}$ iff this equivalence holds*

$$f^{\underline{m}}(x_1, \ldots, x_m) = y \text{ iff } (\text{unary}(x_1)\# \cdots \# \text{unary}(x_m), \text{unary}(y)) \in M\text{-}f^{\underline{m}}.$$

Kleene's s-m-n theorem

The next theorem says that for all $m, n \in \mathbb{N}$, there is a total computable function s of $m + 1$ arguments such that

$$_iM\text{-}f^{\underline{m+n}}(x_1, \ldots, x_m, y_1, \ldots, y_n) = {}_{s^{\underline{m+1}}(i, x_1, \ldots, x_m)}M\text{-}f^{\underline{n}}(y_1, \ldots, y_n)$$

for all $i, x_1, \ldots, x_m, y_1, \ldots, y_n$. In other words, considering the Turing–Church thesis, there is an algorithm such that from $_iM$ and $x_1, \ldots, x_m$ it determines another Turing machine that computes $_iM\text{-}f^{\underline{m+n}}(x_1, \ldots, x_m, y_1, \ldots, y_n)$ with only n arguments $y_1, \ldots, y_n$. In this way, the number of arguments is lowered, yet the same function is computed.

Convention 9.4. *In this chapter, we often construct $M \in \Psi$ from a finite sequence of strings, $z_1, \ldots, z_n$ (see, for instance, Theorem 9.2 and Example 9.6), and in order to express this clearly and explicitly, we denote M constructed in this way by $M_{[z_1,\ldots,z_n]}$. Specifically, in the proof of the next theorem, $M_{[i,x_1,\ldots,x_m]}$ is constructed from $i, x_1, \ldots, x_m$, which are unary strings representing integers (see Convention 9.1).*

Theorem 9.2 (Kleene's *s-m-n* **Theorem).** *For all $i, m, n \in \mathbb{N}$, there is a total computable $(m + 1)$-argument function $s^{\underline{m+1}}$ such that $_iM\text{-}f^{\underline{m+n}}(x_1, \ldots, x_m, y_1, \ldots, y_n) = {}_{s^{\underline{m+1}}(i,x_1,\ldots,x_m)}M\text{-}f^{\underline{n}}(y_1, \ldots, y_n)$.*

Proof. We first construct a Turing machine $S \in \Psi$. Then, we demonstrate that $S\text{-}f^{\underline{m+1}}$ satisfies the properties of $s^{\underline{m+1}}$ stated in Theorem 9.2, so we just take $s^{\underline{m+1}} = S\text{-}f^{\underline{m+1}}$ to complete the proof.

Construction of S. Let $m, n \in \mathbb{N}$. We construct a Turing machine $S \in \Psi$ so S itself constructs another machine in Ψ and produces its index in ζ as the resulting output value. More precisely, given input $i\#x_1\# \cdots \#x_m$, S constructs a Turing machine, denoted by $M_{[i,x_1,\ldots,x_m]}$, for $i = 1, 2, \ldots$, and produces the index of $M_{[i,x_1,\ldots,x_m]}$—that is, j satisfying $M_{[i,x_1,\ldots,x_m]} = {}_jM$ in ζ—as the resulting output value. $M_{[i,x_1,\ldots,x_m]}$ constructed by S works as follows:

(i) When given input $y_1\# \cdots \#y_n$, $M_{[i,x_1,\ldots,x_m]}$ shifts $y_1\# \cdots \#y_n$ to the right, writes $x_1\# \cdots \#x_m\#$ to its left, so it actually changes $y_1\# \cdots \#y_n$ to $x_1\# \cdots \#x_m\#y_1\# \cdots \#y_n$.

(ii) $M_{[i,x_1,\ldots,x_m]}$ runs $_iM$ on $x_1\# \cdots \#x_m\#y_1\# \cdots \#y_n$.

Properties of $S\text{-}f^{\underline{m+1}}$. Consider the $(m+1)$-argument function $S\text{-}f^{\underline{m+1}}$ computed by S constructed above. Recall that $S\text{-}f^{\underline{m+1}}$ maps $(i, x_1, \ldots, x_m)$ to the resulting output value equal to the index of $M_{[i,x_1,\ldots,x_m]}$ in ζ. More briefly,

$$S\text{-}f^{\underline{m+1}}(i, x_1, \ldots, x_m) = j$$

with j satisfying $M_{[i,x_1,\ldots,x_m]} = {}_jM$ in ζ. Observe that $M_{[i,x_1,\ldots,x_m]}$ computes

$${}_iM\text{-}f^{\underline{m+n}}(x_1, \ldots, x_m, y_1, \ldots, y_n)$$

on every input $(y_1, \ldots, y_n)$, where ${}_iM\text{-}f^{\underline{m+n}}$ denotes the $(m+n)$-argument computable function. By these properties,

$$\begin{aligned}{}_iM\text{-}f^{\underline{m+n}}(x_1, \ldots, x_m, y_1, \ldots, y_n) &= {}_jM\text{-}f^{\underline{n}}(y_1, \ldots, y_n)\\ &= {}_{S\text{-}f^{\underline{m+1}}(i,x_1,\ldots,x_m)}M\text{-}f^{\underline{n}}(y_1, \ldots, y_n).\end{aligned}$$

Therefore, to obtain the total computable $(m+1)$-argument function $s^{\underline{m+1}}$ satisfying Theorem 9.2, set $s^{\underline{m+1}} = S\text{-}f^{\underline{m+1}}$. ■

Theorem 9.2 represents a powerful tool for demonstrating closure properties concerning computable functions. To illustrate, by using this theorem, we prove that the set of computable one-argument functions is closed with respect to composition in the next example.

Example 9.6. *There is a total computable* 2*-argument function* $g^{\underline{2}}$ *such that*

$${}_iM\text{-}f({}_jM\text{-}f(x)) = {}_{g^{\underline{2}}(i,j)}M\text{-}f(x)$$

for all $i, j, x \in \mathbb{N}$. *We define the* 3*-argument function* $h^{\underline{3}}$ *as* $h^{\underline{3}}(i,j,x) = {}_iM\text{-}f({}_jM\text{-}f(x))$ *for all* $i, j, x \in \mathbb{N}$. *First, we demonstrate that* $h^{\underline{3}}$ *is computable. Given* $i, j, x \in \mathbb{N}$, *we introduce a Turing machine H that computes* $h^{\underline{3}}$, *so it works on every input x as follows:*

(i) *H runs* ${}_jM$ *on x.*
(ii) *If* ${}_jM\text{-}f(x)$ *is defined and, therefore, produced by H in (i), H runs* ${}_iM$ *on* ${}_jM\text{-}f(x)$.
(iii) *If* ${}_iM\text{-}f({}_jM\text{-}f(x))$ *is defined, H produces* ${}_iM\text{-}f({}_jM\text{-}f(x))$, *so H computes*

$${}_iM\text{-}f({}_jM\text{-}f(x)).$$

Thus, $h^{\underline{3}}$ *is computable. Let* $h^{\underline{3}}$ *be computed by* ${}_kM$ *in* ζ. *That is,* ${}_kM\text{-}f^{\underline{3}} = h^{\underline{3}}$. *By Theorem 9.2, there is a total computable function s such that* ${}_{s^{\underline{3}}(k,i,j)}M\text{-}f^{\underline{1}}(x) = {}_kM\text{-}f^{\underline{3}}(i,j,x)$ *for all* $i, j, x \in \mathbb{N}$. *Set* $g^{\underline{2}}(i,j) = s^{\underline{3}}(k,i,j)$ *for all* $i, j \in \mathbb{N}$ *(of course, k has the same meaning as previous). Thus,* ${}_iM\text{-}f({}_jM\text{-}f(x)) = {}_{s^{\underline{3}}(k,i,j)}M\text{-}f(x) = {}_{g^{\underline{2}}(i,j)}M\text{-}f(x)$, *for all* $i, j, x \in \mathbb{N}$. *As already noted, from a broader perspective, we have actually proved that the composition of two computable functions is again computable, so the set of computable one-argument functions is closed with respect to composition. Establishing more closure properties concerning other common operations, such as addition and product, is left as an exercise.*

Most topics concerning the computability of multi-argument functions are far beyond this introductory text. Therefore, we narrow our attention to one-argument functions. In fact, we just consider total functions from Δ^* to $\{\varepsilon\}$, upon which we base the next section, which discusses *decidability* as a crucially important topic of the computation theory.

Chapter 10
Decidability

Recall that algorithms represent procedures that stop on all inputs, so they are formalized by Turing machines (TMs) that also halt on any input strings. In terms of these machines, we investigate the power of problem-deciding algorithms in this chapter. In fact, we restrict our attention only to the algorithmic decidability concerning problems related to the mathematical models discussed earlier in this book.

10.1 Turing deciders

Every problem P considered in this chapter is specified by (1) the set of all its instances and (2) a property π such that each instance either satisfies π or does not satisfy π. Given a particular instance $i \in \Pi$, P asks whether or not i satisfies π. To decide P by means of Turing deciders (TDs), which work on strings like any TMs, we represent P by an encoding language as

$$_P L = \{\langle i \rangle \mid i \in \Pi,\ i \text{ satisfies } \pi\},$$

where $\langle i \rangle$ is a string representing instance i. A TD M, which halts on all inputs, decides P if

1. M rejects every input that represents no instance from Π.
2. For every $\langle i \rangle$ with $i \in \Pi$, M accepts $\langle i \rangle$ iff i satisfies π, so M rejects $\langle i \rangle$ iff i does not satisfy π.

More formally, $L(M) = {}_P L$, and

$$\Delta^* - L(M) = (\Delta^* - \{\langle i \rangle \mid i \in \Pi\}) \cup \{\langle i \rangle \mid i \in \Pi,\ i \text{ does not satisfy } \pi\}.$$

In brief, we state P as

Problem. P.
Question: *A formulation of P.*
Language: $_P L$.

To illustrate our approach to decidability, we consider the problem referred to as *FA-Emptiness*. For any finite automaton (FA) M, *FA-Emptiness* asks whether the language accepted by M is empty. In what follows, *FA-Instances* denotes the set of all instances of FAs. The language encoding *FA-Emptiness* is defined as

$$_{FA\text{-}Emptiness}L = \{\langle M\rangle \mid M \in \textit{FA-Instances},\ L(M) = \emptyset\}.$$

Formally, *FA-Emptiness* is specified as

Problem. *FA-Emptiness.*
Question: *Let $M \in$ FA-Instances. Is $L(M)$ empty?*
Language: $_{FA\text{-}Emptiness}L = \{\langle M\rangle \mid M \in \textit{FA-Instances},\ L(M) = \emptyset\}$.

We can construct a TD for $_{FA\text{-}Emptiness}L$ in a trivial way as demonstrated shortly (see Theorem 10.2).

In general, a problem that can be decided by a TD is referred to as a *decidable problem*, while an *undecidable problem* cannot be decided by any TD. For instance, the above problem of emptiness reformulated in terms of TMs, symbolically referred to as *TM-Emptiness*, is undecidable as we demonstrate later in this chapter. That is, we denote the set of all instances of TMs by *TM-Instances*, and we encode this important undecidable problem by its encoding language

$$_{TM\text{-}Emptiness}L = \{\langle M\rangle \mid M \in \textit{TM-Instances},\ L(M) = \emptyset\}$$

and prove that no TD accepts $_{TM\text{-}Emptiness}L$ (see Theorem 10.17).

Next, we define TDs rigorously. As already pointed out, any TD M halts on every input string. In addition, we require that M always halts with its tape completely blank. The following definition makes use of M-f (see Definition 9.1) and the domain of a function (see Section 2.2), so recall both notions before reading it.

Definition 10.1.

(i) *Let $M \in$ TM-Instances. If M always halts and M-f is a function from Δ^* to $\{\varepsilon\}$, then M is a* TD.
(ii) *Let L be a language and M be a TD. M is a* TD for L *if* domain $(M\text{-}f) = L$.
(iii) *A language is* decidable *if there is a TD for it; otherwise, the language is* undecidable.

By (i) in Definition 10.1, $M \in$ *TM-Instances* is a TD if it never loops, and for every $x \in \Delta^*$, $\triangleright \blacktriangleright x\triangleleft \Rightarrow^* \triangleright iu\triangleleft$ in M with $i \in \{\blacksquare, \blacklozenge\}$ and $u \in \{\square\}^*$. By (ii), a TD M for a language L satisfies $\triangleright \blacktriangleright x\triangleleft \Rightarrow^* \triangleright\blacksquare u\triangleleft$ in M for every $x \in L$ and $\triangleright \blacktriangleright y\triangleleft \Rightarrow^* \triangleright\blacklozenge v\triangleleft$ in M for every $y \in {}_M\Delta^* - L$, where $u, v \in \{\square\}^*$.

In what follows, *TD-Instances* denotes the set of all TDs.

We close this section strictly in terms of formal languages. First, we give a specific decidable formal language in Example 10.1. Then, we state a relation between the language families defined by FAs, context-free grammars (CFGs), and TDs.

Example 10.1. *Return to Example 8.3, in which we have designed a TM that accepts* $L = \{x \mid x \in \{a, b, c\}^*,\ \text{occur}\,(x, a) = \text{occur}\,(x, b) = \text{occur}\,(x, c)\}$. *Recall that from Theorem 8.2 onwards, we automatically assume that every TM has the properties*

Table 10.1 Acceptance of babcca

Scan	Tape
0	*babcca*
1	□□*b*□*ca*
2	□□□□□□
3	ACCEPT

satisfied by O stated in Theorems 8.1 and 8.2. However, the TM constructed in Example 8.3 does not satisfy them; in fact, it is not even deterministic. As a result, it is out of TM-Instances, so it is definitely out of TD-Instances as well.

In the present example, we design another TM D such that D ∈ TD-Instances and D accepts L. D repeatedly scans across the tape in a left-to-right way, erasing the leftmost occurrence of a, b, and c during every single scan. When it reaches ◁ after erasing all these three occurrences, it moves left to ▷ and makes another scan like this. However, when D reaches ◁ while some of the three symbols are missing on the tape, it can decide whether the input string is accepted. Indeed, if all three symbols are missing, D accepts; otherwise, it rejects. Therefore, D performs its final return to ▷ in either of the following two ways:

- *If the tape is completely blank and, therefore, all as, bs, and cs have been erased during the previous scans, D moves its head left to ▷ and accepts in a configuration of the form ▷■□ ⋯ □◁.*
- *If the tape is not blank and, therefore, contains some occurrences of symbols from X, where $\emptyset \subset X \subset \{a, b, c\}$, then during its return to ▷, D changes all these occurrences to □ and rejects in a configuration of the form ▷♦□ ⋯ □◁.*

Omitting the state specification, Table 10.1 schematically describes the acceptance of babcca by D.

Clearly, D is a TD for L, so L is a decidable language. Symbolically and briefly, D ∈ TD-Instances, so L is a decidable language. Observe that D is, in fact, implemented in Implementation 8.4.

We are now ready to establish a relation between the power of FAs, that of CFGs and of TDs.

Theorem 10.1. *TDs are more powerful than CFGs, which are more powerful than FAs.*

Proof. From Theorems 7.6 and 7.14, it follows that CFGs are more powerful than FAs. As an exercise, prove that every language generated by a CFG is decidable. Consider L in Example 10.1. Again as an exercise, prove that L is generated by no CFG. Thus, by Example 10.1, TDs are more powerful than CFGs. ■

10.2 Decidable problems

In this section, we present several decidable problems for FAs and CFGs. However, we also point out that there exist problems that are decidable for FAs but undecidable for CFGs.

10.2.1 Decidable problems for finite automata

Let $M \in$ *FA-Instances*. We give algorithms for deciding the following three problems:

- Is the language accepted by M empty?
- Is the language accepted by M finite?
- Is the language accepted by M infinite?

In addition, for any input string w, we decide the next problem.

- Is w a member of the language accepted by M?

We suppose there exists a fixed encoding and decoding for all of the automata in *FA-Instances* by analogy with the encoding and decoding of TMs (see Section 8.3). That is, $\langle M \rangle$ represents the code of M from *FA-Instances*. Similarly, we suppose there exists an analogical encoding and decoding of the members of *FA-Instances* $\times \Delta^*$ and *FA-Instances* $\times$ *FA-Instances*. For brevity, we denote the codes of $(M, w) \in$ *FA-Instances* $\times \Delta^*$ and $(M, N) \in$ *FA-Instances* $\times$ *FA-Instances* by $\langle M, w \rangle$ and $\langle M, N \rangle$, respectively.

To slightly simplify our task, we automatically assume that all FAs we deal with in this section are completely specified deterministic finite automata (DFAs) because deciding the four problems for them turns out somewhat simpler than deciding these problems for the general versions of FAs. However, since any FA can be algorithmically converted to an equivalent completely specified DFA (see Section 5.3), all four problems are decidable for all FAs, too.

As already stated in Section 10.1, the *FA-Emptiness* problem asks whether the language accepted by an FA is empty. Next, we recall the formulation of this problem and prove that it is decidable by demonstrating that its encoding language ${}_{\textit{FA-Emptiness}}L$ is decidable.

Problem 10.1. *FA-Emptiness.*
Question: *Let $M \in$ FA-Instances. Is $L(M)$ empty?*
Language: ${}_{\textit{FA-Emptiness}}L = \{\langle M \rangle \mid M \in \textit{FA-Instances},\ L(M) = \emptyset\}$.

Theorem 10.2. *${}_{\textit{FA-Emptiness}}L$ is decidable.*

Proof. As M is completely specified, each of its states is reachable (see Definition 5.6). Thus, $L(M) = \emptyset$ iff M has no final state. Design a TD D that works on every $\langle M \rangle$ so D accepts $\langle M \rangle$ iff M has no final state, and D rejects $\langle M \rangle$ iff M has some final states. ■

The *FA-Membership* problem asks whether a string $w \in {}_M\Delta^*$ is a member of the language accepted by a completely specified DFA M. Like *FA-Emptiness*, *FA-Membership* is decidable.

Problem 10.2. *FA-Membership.*
Question: Let $M \in$ *FA-Instances* and $w \in {}_M\Delta^*$. Is w a member of $L(M)$?
Language: ${}_{FA\text{-}Membership}L = \{\langle M, w\rangle \mid M \in \textit{FA-Instances},\ w \in L(M)\}$.

Theorem 10.3. ${}_{FA\text{-}Membership}L$ *is decidable.*

Proof. Let $M \in$ *FA-Instances*. Recall that M reads exactly one input symbol during every move. Thus, after making precisely $|w|$ moves on $w \in \Delta^*$, M either accepts or rejects w. Therefore, construct a TD D that works on every $\langle M, w\rangle$ as follows:

(i) D runs M on w until M accepts or rejects w (after $|w|$ moves).
(ii) D accepts $\langle M, w\rangle$ iff M accepts w, and D rejects $\langle M, w\rangle$ iff M rejects w. ■

FA-Infiniteness is a problem that asks whether the language accepted by a completely specified DFA M is infinite. To demonstrate that the decidability of the same problem can be often proved in several different ways, we next give two alternative proofs that *FA-Infiniteness* is decidable. We only sketch the first proof while describing the other in detail.

Problem 10.3. *FA-Infiniteness.*
Question: Let $M \in$ *FA-Instances*. Is $L(M)$ infinite?
Language: ${}_{FA\text{-}Infiniteness}L = \{\langle M\rangle \mid M \in \textit{FA-Instances},\ L(M) \text{ is infinite}\}$.

Theorem 10.4. ${}_{FA\text{-}Infiniteness}L$ *is decidable.*

Proof. Let $M \in$ *FA-Instances*. Recall that M is automatically supposed to be a completely specified DFA. Under this assumption, we obviously see that $L(M)$ is infinite if and only if its state diagram contains a cycle. Thus, we can easily reformulate and decide this problem in terms of the graph theory in this way. Indeed, finding out whether a directed graph contains a cycle represents a simple task, left as an exercise. ■

Consequently, the next problem is decidable as well.

Problem 10.4. *FA-Finiteness.*
Question: Let $M \in$ *FA-Instances*. Is $L(M)$ finite?
Language: ${}_{FA\text{-}Finiteness}L = \{\langle M\rangle \mid M \in \textit{FA-Instances},\ L(M) \text{ is finite}\}$.

Corollary 10.1. ${}_{FA\text{-}Finiteness}L$ *is decidable.*

The *FA-Equivalance* problem asks whether two members of *FA-Instances* are equivalent; in other words, it asks whether both automata accept the same language. We decide this problem by using some elementary results of the set theory.

Problem 10.5. *FA-Equivalance.*
Question: Let $M, N \in$ *FA-Instances*. Are M and N equivalent?
Language: ${}_{FA\text{-}Equivalance}L = \{\langle M, N\rangle \mid M, N \in \textit{FA-Instances},\ L(M) = L(N)\}$.

Theorem 10.5. ${}_{FA\text{-}Equivalance}L$ *is decidable.*

Proof. Let $M, N \in$ *FA-Instances*. As an exercise, prove that $L(M) = L(N)$ iff $\emptyset = (L(M) \cap \overline{L(N)}) \cup (L(N) \cap \overline{L(M)})$. Construct a TD D that works on every $\langle M, N\rangle \in {}_{FA\text{-}Equivalance}L$ as follows:

(i) From M and N, D constructs a FA O such that $L(O) = (L(M) \cap \overline{L(N)}) \cup (L(N) \cap \overline{L(M)})$.
(ii) From O, D constructs an equivalent $P \in$ *FA-Instances*.
(iii) D decides whether $L(P) = \emptyset$ (see Theorem 10.2 and its proof).
(iv) If $L(P) = \emptyset$, $L(M) = L(N)$ and D accepts $\langle M, N\rangle$, and if $L(P) \neq \emptyset$, D rejects $\langle M, N\rangle$.

Consider (i) and (ii) above; as an exercise, describe them in detail. ■

10.2.2 Decidable problems for context-free grammars

Let G be any CFG. We give algorithms for deciding the following three problems:

- Is the language generated by G empty?
- Is the language generated by G finite?
- Is the language generated by G infinite?

In addition, for any input string w, we decide the next problem.

- Is w a member of the language generated by G?

Rather than discussing these problems for any CFGs, we decide them for CFGs in the Chomsky normal form, in which every rule has either a single terminal or two nonterminals on its right-hand side (see Definition 6.13). Making use of this form, we find easier to decide two of them—*CFG-Membership* and *CFG-Infiniteness*. As any CFG can be turned to an equivalent grammar in the Chomsky normal form by algorithms given in Section 6.6, deciding these problems for grammars satisfying the Chomsky normal form obviously implies their decidability for any CFGs as well.

Let *CFG-Instances* denote the set of all CFGs in Chomsky normal form. We suppose there exists a fixed encoding and decoding of the members in *CFG-Instances*. Let $\langle G\rangle$ represents the code of G from *CFG-Instances*. Similarly, we suppose there exists an analogical encoding and decoding of the members of *CFG-Instances* $\times\ \Delta^*$ and *CFG-Instances* $\times$ *CFG-Instances*. Again, for brevity, we denote the codes of $(G, w) \in$ *CFG-Instances* $\times\ \Delta^*$ and $(G, H) \in$ *CFG-Instances* $\times$ *CFG-Instances* by $\langle G, w\rangle$ and $\langle G, H\rangle$, respectively.

Problem 10.6. *CFG-Emptiness.*
Question: Let $G \in$ *CFG-Instances*. Is $L(G)$ empty?
Language: ${}_{CFG\text{-}Emptiness}L = \{\langle G\rangle \mid G \in CFG\text{-}Instances,\ L(G) = \emptyset\}$.

Theorem 10.6. ${}_{CFG\text{-}Emptiness}L$ *is decidable.*

Proof. Let $G \in$ *CFG-Instances*. Recall that a symbol in G is terminating if it derives a string of terminals (see Definition 6.6). As a result, $L(G)$ is non-empty iff S is terminating, where S denotes the start symbol of G. Therefore, construct a TD D that works on $\langle G\rangle$ as follows:

(i) D decides whether S is terminating by Algorithm 6.1;
(ii) D rejects $\langle G\rangle$ if S is terminating; otherwise, D accepts $\langle G\rangle$. ■

It is worth noting that the way we perform the decision of *CFG-Emptiness* described in the proof of Theorem 10.6 works for CFGs that are not in Chomsky normal form as well. During the decision of the next two problems, however, this form fulfills a significant role.

Given a string $w \in \Delta^*$ and a grammar $G \in$ *CFG-Instances*, the *CFG-Membership* problem asks whether w is a member of $L(G)$. Next, we show how to decide this problem by an algorithm based upon the Chomsky normal form.

Problem 10.7. *CFG-Membership.*
Question: Let $G \in$ *CFG-Instances* and $w \in \Delta^*$. Is w a member of $L(G)$?
Language: ${}_{\text{CFG-Membership}}L = \{\langle G, w\rangle \mid G \in \textit{CFG-Instances},\ w \in L(G)\}$.

The proof of the next lemma is simple and left as an exercise.

Lemma 10.1. *Let G be a CFG in the Chomsky normal form. Then, G generates every $w \in L(G)$ by making no more than $2|w| - 1$ derivation steps.*

Theorem 10.7. ${}_{\text{CFG-Membership}}L$ *is decidable.*

Proof. As all members of *CFG-Instances* are in the Chomsky normal form, none of them generates ε. Therefore, we construct the following TD D that works on every $\langle G, w\rangle$ in either of the following two ways (i) and (ii), depending on whether $w = \varepsilon$ or not.

(i) Let $w = \varepsilon$. Clearly, $\varepsilon \in L(G)$ iff the start symbol S is an ε-nonterminal—that is, S derives ε (see Definition 6.10). Thus, D decides whether S is an ε-nonterminal by Algorithm 6.4, and if so, D accepts $\langle G, w\rangle$; otherwise, D rejects $\langle G, w\rangle$.
(ii) Let $w \neq \varepsilon$. Then, D works on $\langle G, w\rangle$ as follows:
    (a) D constructs the set of all sentences that G generates by making no more than $2|w| - 1$ derivation steps.
    (b) If this set contains w, D accepts $\langle G, w\rangle$; otherwise, it rejects $\langle G, w\rangle$. ■

The *CFG-Infiniteness* problem asks whether the language generated by a CFG is infinite.

Problem 10.8. *CFG-Infiniteness.*
Question: Let $G \in$ *CFG-Instances*. Is $L(G)$ infinite?
Language: ${}_{\text{CFG-Infiniteness}}L = \{\langle G\rangle \mid G \in \textit{CFG-Instances},\ L(G) \text{ is infinite}\}$.

As an exercise, prove the next lemma.

Lemma 10.2. *Let G be a CFG in the Chomsky normal form. Then, $L(G)$ is infinite if and only if $L(G)$ contains a sentence x such that $k \leq |x| < 2k$ with $k = 2^n$, where n is the number of nonterminals in G.*

Theorem 10.8. ${}_{\textit{CFG-Infiniteness}}L$ *is decidable.*

Proof. Construct a TD D that works on every $G \in$ *CFG-Instances* as follows:

(i) D constructs the set of all sentences x in $L(G)$ satisfying $k \leq |x| < 2k$ with $k = 2^n$, where n is the number of nonterminals in G.
(ii) If this set is empty, D rejects $\langle G \rangle$; otherwise, D accepts $\langle G \rangle$. ■

Theorem 10.8 implies that we can also decide the following problem:

Problem 10.9. *CFG-Finiteness.*
Question: Let $G \in$ *CFG-Instances*. Is $L(G)$ finite?
Language: ${}_{\textit{CFG-Finiteness}}L = \{\langle G \rangle \mid G \in \textit{CFG-Instances}, \ L(G) \text{ is finite}\}$.

Corollary 10.2. ${}_{\textit{CFG-Finiteness}}L$ *is decidable.*

Recall that for FAs, we have formulated the problem *FA-Equivalance* and proved that it is decidable for them (see Theorem 10.5). However, we have not reformulated this problem for *CFG-Instances* in this section. The reason for this is that this problem is undecidable for *CFG-Instances*, which brings us to the topic of the next section—undecidable problems.

10.3 Undecidability: diagonalization

As the central topic of the present section, we consider several problems concerning TMs and demonstrate that they are undecidable. In addition, in a briefer way, we also mention some undecidable problems not concerning TMs in the conclusion of this section.

Let P be a problem concerning TMs, and let P be encoded by a language ${}_PL$. Demonstrating that P is undecidable consists in proving that ${}_PL$ is an undecidable language. Like every rigorous proof in mathematics, a proof like this requires some ingenuity. Nevertheless, it is usually achieved by contradiction based upon either of these two proof techniques—*diagonalization*, discussed in the present section, and *reduction*, explained in Sections 10.4 and 10.5.

As a rule, a diagonalization-based proof is schematically performed in the following way:

1. Assume that ${}_PL$ is decidable, and consider a TD D such that $L(D) = {}_PL$.
2. From D, construct another TD O; then, by using the diagonalization technique (see Example 2.8), apply O on its own description $\langle O \rangle$, so this application results into a contradiction.
3. The contradiction obtained in (2) implies that the assumption in (1) is incorrect, so ${}_PL$ is undecidable.

Following this proof scheme almost literally, we next demonstrate the undecidability of the famous *halting problem* that asks whether $M \in$ *TM-Instances* halts on input x. Observe that the following formulation of the *TM-Halting* problem makes use of the encoding language ${}_{Halting}L$, introduced in Section 8.3.

Problem 10.10. *TM-Halting.*
Question: Let $M \in$ *TM-Instances* and $w \in \Delta^*$. Does M halt on w?
Language: ${}_{TM\text{-}Halting}L = \{\langle M, w\rangle \mid M \in \textit{TM-Instances},\ w \in \Delta^*,\ M \text{ halts on } w\}$.

Theorem 10.9. ${}_{TM\text{-}Halting}L$ *is undecidable.*

Proof. Assume that ${}_{TM\text{-}Halting}L$ is decidable. Then, there exists a TD D such that $L(D) = {}_{TM\text{-}Halting}L$. That is, for any $\langle M,x\rangle \in {}_{Halting}L$, D accepts $\langle M,x\rangle$ if and only if M halts on x, and D rejects $\langle M,x\rangle$ if and only if M loops on x. From D, construct another TD O that works on every input w, where $w = \langle M\rangle$ with $M \in$ *TM-Instances* (recall that every input string encodes a TM in *TM-Instances*, so the case when w encodes, no TM is ruled out), as follows:

(i) O replaces w with $\langle M, M\rangle$, where $w = \langle M\rangle$.
(ii) O runs D on $\langle M, M\rangle$.
(iii) O accepts if and only if D rejects, and O rejects if and only if D accepts.

That is, for every $w = \langle M\rangle$, O accepts $\langle M\rangle$ if and only if D rejects $\langle M, M\rangle$, and since $L(D) = {}_{TM\text{-}Halting}L$, D rejects $\langle M, M\rangle$ if and only if M loops on $\langle M\rangle$. Thus, O accepts $\langle M\rangle$ if and only if M loops on $\langle M\rangle$. As O works on every input w, it also works on $w = \langle O\rangle$. Take this case. Since O accepts $\langle M\rangle$ if and only if M loops on $\langle M\rangle$ for every $w = \langle M\rangle$, this equivalence holds for $w = \langle O\rangle$ as well, so O accepts $\langle O\rangle$ if and only if O loops on $\langle O\rangle$. Thus, $\langle O\rangle \in L(O)$ if and only if $\langle O\rangle \notin L(O)$—a contradiction. Therefore, ${}_{TM\text{-}Halting}L$ is undecidable. ∎

Observe that Theorem 10.9 has its crucial consequences in practice as well as in theory. Indeed, considering the Turing–Church thesis, it rules out the existence of a universal algorithm that would decide, for any procedure, whether the procedure is, in fact, an algorithm—that is, a procedure that halts on all inputs (see the beginning of Chapter 9). As a result, although we would obviously appreciate an algorithm like this in practice very much, we have to give up its existence once and for all. Furthermore, this theorem straightforwardly implies that some TMs cannot be turned to equivalent TDs as the next theorem says.

Theorem 10.10. *TMs are more powerful than TDs.*

Proof. Of course, TDs are special cases of TMs. By Theorem 10.9, ${}_{TM\text{-}Halting}L$ is undecidable. However, by Theorem 8.8, a TM accepts ${}_{TM\text{-}Halting}L$. Thus, this theorem holds true. ∎

As *TM-Halting* is undecidable, it comes as no surprise that the problem that asks whether $M \in$ *TM-Instances* loops on input x is not decidable either.

Problem 10.11. *TM-Looping.*
Question: Let $M \in$ *TM-Instances* and $w \in \Delta^*$. Does M loop on w?
Language: ${}_{TM\text{-}Looping}L = \{\langle M, w\rangle \mid M \in \textit{TM-Instances},\ w \in \Delta^*,\ M \text{ loops on } w\}$.

To prove the undecidability of this problem, we establish the following two theorems. The first of them is obvious.

Theorem 10.11. *${}_{TM\text{-}Looping}L$ is the complement of ${}_{TM\text{-}Halting}L$.*

Next, we prove that a language L is decidable if and only if both L and $\bar{L}$ are Turing languages (see Section 8.2); in other words, there are $M, N \in$ *TM-Instances* such that $L = L(M)$ and $L(N) = \bar{L}$.

Theorem 10.12. *Let $L \subseteq \Delta^*$. L is decidable if and only if both L and $\bar{L}$ are Turing languages.*

Proof. To prove the *only if* part of the equivalence, take any decidable language L. By Theorem 10.10, L is a Turing language. In fact, by Definition 10.1, there is TD M such that $L = L(M)$. Change M to $N \in$ *TM-Instances* so that N enters a nonfinal state in which it keeps looping exactly when M enters the final state $\blacksquare$. As a result, $L(N) = \overline{L(M)} = \bar{L}$, so $\bar{L}$ is a Turing language. Thus, both L and $\bar{L}$ are Turing languages.

To prove the *if* part of the equivalence, let $N, O \in$ *TM-Instances* such that $L = L(N)$ and $L(O) = \bar{L}$. Observe that N and O cannot accept the same string because $L \cap \bar{L} = \emptyset$. On the other hand, every input w is accepted by either N or O because $L \cup \bar{L} = \Delta^*$. Based on these observations, we next construct a TD M from N and O so M decides L. That is, M works on every input w in the following way:

(i) M simultaneously runs N and O on w, so M executes by turns one move in N and O—that is, step-by-step, M computes the first move in N, the first move in O, the second move in N, the second move in O, and so forth.
(ii) M continues the simulation described in (i) until a move that would take N or O to an accepting configuration, and in this way, M finds out whether $w \in L(N)$ or $w \in L(O)$.
(iii) Instead of entering the accepting configuration in N or O, M halts and either accepts if $w \in L(N)$ or rejects if $w \in L(O)$. To express this in a more mathematical way, M changes the current configuration to a halting configuration of the form $\triangleright iu \triangleleft$, where $u \in \{\square\}^*$, $i \in \{\blacksquare, \blacklozenge\}$, $i = \blacksquare$ if and only if $w \in L(N)$, and $i = \blacklozenge$ if and only if $w \in L(O)$.

Observe that $L(M) = L$. Furthermore, M always halts, so L is decidable. ∎

Making use of Theorems 10.11 and 10.12, we easily demonstrate ${}_{TM\text{-}Looping}L$ as an undecidable problem. In fact, we prove a stronger result that says that ${}_{TM\text{-}Looping}L$ is not a Turing language.

Theorem 10.13. *${}_{TM\text{-}Looping}L$ is not a Turing language.*

Proof. For the sake of a contradiction, assume that ${}_{TM\text{-}Looping}L$ is a Turing language. Recall that ${}_{TM\text{-}Looping}L$ is the complement of ${}_{TM\text{-}Halting}L$ (see Theorem 10.11). Furthermore, ${}_{TM\text{-}Halting}L$ is a Turing language. Thus, Theorem 10.12 would imply that ${}_{TM\text{-}Halting}L$ is decidable, which contradicts Theorem 10.9. Thus, ${}_{TM\text{-}Looping}L$ is not a Turing language. ∎

Corollary 10.3. ${}_{TM\text{-}Looping}L$ *is not decidable.*

Proof. Theorems 10.12 and 10.13 imply this corollary. ■

10.4 Undecidability: reduction

Apart from diagonalization, discussed in the previous section, we often establish the undecidability of a problem P, so the decidability of P would imply the decidability of a well-known undecidable problem U, and from this contradiction, we conclude that P is undecidable. We usually say that we *reduce* U to P when demonstrating the undecidability of P in this way because we derive the undecidability of P from the previously known undecidability of U. In terms of the problem-encoding languages, to prove that a language ${}_PL$, which encodes P, is undecidable, we usually follow the following proof scheme:

1. For a contradiction, assume that ${}_PL$ is decidable, and consider a TD D such that $L(D) = {}_PL$.
2. Modify D to another TD that would decide a well-known undecidable language ${}_UL$—a contradiction.
3. The contradiction obtained in (2) implies that the assumption in (1) is incorrect, so ${}_PL$ is undecidable.

Based on this reduction-proof scheme, we next demonstrate the undecidability of the *TM-Membership* problem that asks whether input w is a member of $L(M)$, where $M \in$ *TM-Instances* and $w \in \Delta^*$. It is worth noting that the following formulation of this problem makes use of the encoding language ${}_{TM\text{-}Membership}L$ that coincides with ${}_{Acceptance}L$ defined in Section 8.3.

Problem 10.12. *TM-Membership.*
Question: Let $M \in$ *TM-Instances* and $w \in \Delta^*$. Is w a member of $L(M)$?
Language: ${}_{TM\text{-}Membership}L = \{\langle M, w\rangle \mid M \in \textit{TM-Instances},\ w \in L(M)\}$.

We prove the undecidability of this problem by reducing *TM-Halting* to it. That is, we show that if there were a way of deciding the *TM-Membership* problem, we could decide Problem 10.10 *TM-Halting*, which contradicts Theorem 10.9.

Theorem 10.14. ${}_{TM\text{-}Membership}L$ *is not decidable.*

Proof. Given $\langle M, x\rangle$, construct a TM N that coincides with M except that N accepts x if and only if M halts on x (recall that M halts on x if and only if M either accepts or rejects x). In other words, $x \in L(N)$ if and only if M halts on x. If there were a TD D for ${}_{TM\text{-}Membership}L$, we could use D and this equivalence to decide ${}_{TM\text{-}Halting}L$. Indeed, we could decide ${}_{TM\text{-}Halting}L$ by transforming M to N as described above and asking whether $x \in L(N)$; from $x \in L(N)$, we would conclude that M halts on x, while from $x \notin L(N)$, we would conclude that M loops on x. However, Problem 10.10 *TM-Halting* is undecidable (see Theorem 10.9), which rules out the existence of D. Thus, ${}_{TM\text{-}Membership}L$ is not decidable. ■

Next, we formulate the *TM-NonMembership* problem, and based upon Theorems 10.12 and 10.14, we prove that it is not decidable either.

Problem 10.13. *TM-NonMembership.*
Question: Let $M \in$ *TM-Instances* and $w \in \Delta^*$. Is w out of $L(M)$?
Language: ${}_{\textit{TM-NonMembership}}L = \{\langle M, w\rangle \mid M \in \textit{TM-Instances},\ w \in \Delta^*,\ w \notin L(M)\}$.

By analogy with the proof of Theorem 10.13, we prove that ${}_{\textit{TM-NonMembership}}L$ is not even a Turing language.

Theorem 10.15. ${}_{\textit{TM-NonMembership}}L$ *is not a Turing language.*

Proof. For the sake of obtaining a contradiction, suppose that ${}_{\textit{TM-NonMembership}}L$ is a Turing language. As already pointed out, ${}_{\textit{TM-Membership}}L = {}_{\textit{Acceptance}}L$, so the language ${}_{\textit{TM-Membership}}L$ is a Turing language (see Theorem 8.7). Clearly, the language ${}_{\textit{TM-NonMembership}}L$ is the complement of ${}_{\textit{TM-Membership}}L$. Thus, by Theorem 10.12, ${}_{\textit{TM-Membership}}L$ would be decidable, which contradicts Theorem 10.14. Thus, the language ${}_{\textit{TM-NonMembership}}L$ is not a Turing language. ■

From Theorems 10.12 and 10.15, we obtain the next corollary, saying that Problem 10.13 *TM-NonMembership* is an undecidable problem.

Corollary 10.4. ${}_{\textit{TM-NonMembership}}L$ *is undecidable.*

The next problem asks whether $L(M)$ is regular, where $M \in$ *TM-Instances*. By reducing *TM-Halting* to it, we prove its undecidability.

Problem 10.14. *TM-Regularness.*
Question: Let $M \in$ *TM-Instances*. Is $L(M)$ regular?
Language: ${}_{\textit{TM-Regularness}}L = \{\langle M\rangle \mid M \in \textit{TM-Instances},\ L(M) \text{ is regular}\}$.

Theorem 10.16. ${}_{\textit{TM-Regularness}}L$ *is undecidable.*

Proof. Consider ${}_{\textit{TM-Halting}}L = \{\langle M, w\rangle \mid M \in \textit{TM-Instances},\ w \in \Delta^*,\ M \text{ halts on } w\}$. Recall that ${}_{\textit{TM-Halting}}L$ is a Turing language, which is undecidable (see Theorems 8.8 and 10.9). Let O be any TM such that $L(O) = {}_{\textit{TM-Halting}}L$. Next, we construct a TM W so that W converts every input $\langle M, w\rangle$, where $M \in$ *TM-Instances* and $w \in \Delta^*$, to a new TM, denoted by $N_{[M,w]}$. Given $\langle M, w\rangle$, W constructs a TM $N_{[M,w]}$ that works on every input $y \in \Delta^*$ as follows:

(i) $N_{[M,w]}$ places w somewhere behind y on its tape.
(ii) $N_{[M,w]}$ runs M on w.
(iii) If M halts on w, $N_{[M,w]}$ runs O on y and accepts if and when O accepts.

If M loops on w, $N_{[M,w]}$ never gets behind (ii), so the language accepted by $N_{[M,w]}$ equals $\emptyset$ in this case. If M halts on w, $N_{[M,w]}$ accepts y in (iii) if and when O accepts y, so the language accepted by $N_{[M,w]}$ coincides with $L(O)$ in this case. Thus, the language accepted by $N_{[M,w]}$ equals $L(O)$ if and only if M halts on w, and the language accepted by $N_{[M,w]}$ equals $\emptyset$ if and only if M loops on w. Since $L(O)$ is a Turing language, which is undecidable, $L(O)$ is not regular (see Theorems 10.1 and 10.10). By Definition 5.9,

$\emptyset$ is regular. Thus, the language accepted by $N_{[M,w]}$ is regular if and only if M loops on w, and the language accepted by $N_{[M,w]}$ is non-regular if and only if M halts on w. For the sake of obtaining a contradiction, assume that ${}_{TM\text{-}Regularness}L$ is decidable by a TD V. Under this assumption, W could make use of V and the two equivalences to decide ${}_{TM\text{-}Halting}L$, which contradicts Theorem 10.9. Thus, ${}_{TM\text{-}Regularness}L$ is undecidable. ∎

As an exercise, demonstrate the undecidability of the following four problems by analogy with the proof of Theorem 10.13.

Problem 10.15. *TM-Emptiness.*
Question: Let $M \in$ *TM-Instances*. Is $L(M)$ empty?
Language: ${}_{TM\text{-}Emptiness}L = \{\langle M \rangle \mid M \in TM\text{-}Instances,\ L(M) = \emptyset\}$.

Theorem 10.17. *${}_{TM\text{-}Emptiness}L$ is undecidable.*

Problem 10.16. *TM-Finiteness.*
Question: Let $M \in$ *TM-Instances*. Is $L(M)$ finite?
Language: ${}_{TM\text{-}Finiteness}L = \{\langle M \rangle \mid M \in TM\text{-}Instances,\ L(M) \text{ is finite}\}$.

Theorem 10.18. *${}_{TM\text{-}Finiteness}L$ is undecidable.*

Problem 10.17. *TM-Contextfreeness.*
Question: Let $M \in$ *TM-Instances*. Is $L(M)$ context-free?
Language: ${}_{TM\text{-}Contextfreeness}L = \{\langle M \rangle \mid M \in TM\text{-}Instances,\ L(M) \text{ is context-free}\}$.

Theorem 10.19. *${}_{TM\text{-}Contextfreeness}L$ is undecidable.*

Problem 10.18. *TM-Universality.*
Question: Let $M \in$ *TM-Instances*. Is $L(M)$ equal to Δ^*?
Language: ${}_{TM\text{-}Universality}L = \{\langle M \rangle \mid M \in TM\text{-}Instances,\ L(M) = \Delta^*\}$.

Theorem 10.20. *${}_{TM\text{-}Universality}L$ is undecidable.*

More undecidable problems

We have concentrated our attention on the undecidability concerning TMs and their languages so far. However, undecidable problems arise in a large variety of areas in the formal language theory as well as out of this theory. Therefore, before concluding this section, we informally mention some of them while completely omitting proofs that demonstrate their undecidability.

Let G and H be any two CFGs (see Chapter 6). The following problems are undecidable:

- Are G and H equivalent?
- Does $L(G)$ contain $L(H)$?
- Is the intersection of $L(G)$ and $L(H)$ empty?
- Is $L(G)$ equal to ${}_G\Delta^*$?
- Is G ambiguous?

There also exist many undecidable problems concerning languages without involving their models, and some of them were introduced long time ago. To illustrate, in 1946, Post introduced a famous problem, which we here formulate in terms of ε-free homomorphisms, defined in Section 2.2. Let X, Y be two alphabets and g, h be two ε-free homomorphisms from X^* to Y^*; *Post's Correspondence Problem* is to determine whether there is $w \in X^+$ such that $g(w) = h(w)$. For example, consider $X = \{1, 2, 3\}$, $Y = \{a, b, c\}$, $g(1) = abbb$, $g(2) = a$, $g(3) = ba$, $h(1) = b$, $h(2) = aab$, and $h(3) = b$ and observe that $2231 \in X^+$ satisfies $g(2231) = h(2231)$. Consider a procedure that systematically produces all possible $w \in X^+$, makes $g(w)$ and $h(w)$, and tests whether $g(w) = h(w)$. If and when the procedure finds out that $g(w) = h(w)$, it halts and answers yes; otherwise, it continues to operate endlessly. Although there is a procedure like this, there is no algorithm, which halts on every input, to decide this problem. Simply put, Post's Correspondence Problem is undecidable.

Of course, there exist many undecidable problems that are out of the scope of this book. For instance, mathematics will never have a general algorithm that decides whether statements in number theory with the plus and times are true or false. Although these results are significant from a purely mathematical point of view, they are not really closely related to the subject of this book, so we leave out their discussion.

10.5 Undecidability: a general approach to reduction

As demonstrated in the previous section, many reduction-based proofs of undecidability are very similar (cf. the proofs of Theorems 10.13 and 10.15). This similarity has inspired mathematics to undertake a more general approach to reduction, based upon the next definition, which makes use of the notion of a computable function (see Definition 9.2).

Definition 10.2. *Let $K, L \subseteq \Delta^*$ be two languages. A total computable function f over Δ^* is a* reduction of K to L, *symbolically written as $K_f \angle L$, if for all $w \in \Delta^*$, $w \in K$ if and only if $f(w) \in L$.*

Let $K, L \in \Delta^*$. We write $K \angle L$ to express that there exists a reduction of K to L (instead of $\angle$, $\leq$ is also used in the literature sometimes).

First, we establish a general theorem concerning $\angle$ in terms of Turing languages.

Theorem 10.21. *Let $K, L \subseteq \Delta^*$. If $K \angle L$ and L is a Turing language, then K is a Turing language too.*

Proof. Let $K, L \subseteq \Delta^*$, $K \angle L$, and let L be a Turing language. Recall that $K \angle L$ means that there exists a reduction f of K to L, written as $K_f \angle L$ (see Definition 10.2). As L is a Turing language, there is a TM M satisfying $L = L(M)$. Construct a new TM N that works on every input $w \in \Delta^*$ as follows:

(i) N computes $f(w)$ (according to Definition 10.2, f is computable).
(ii) N runs M on $f(w)$.
(iii) If M accepts, then N accepts, and if M rejects, then N rejects.

Notice that N accepts w if and only if M accepts $f(w)$. As $L = L(M)$, M accepts $f(w)$ if and only if $f(w) \in L$. As $K \angle L$ (see Definition 10.2), $w \in K$ if and only if $f(w) \in L$. Thus, $K = L(N)$, so K is a Turing language. ∎

Corollary 10.5. *Let $K, L \subseteq \Delta^*$. If $K \angle L$ and K is not a Turing language, L is not a Turing language either.*

By Theorem 10.21, we can easily prove that a language K is a Turing language. Indeed, we take a Turing language L and construct a TM M that computes a reduction of K to L, so $K \angle L$. Then, by Theorem 10.21, K is a Turing language. For instance, from Theorem 8.7 (recall that ${}_{\textit{TM-Membership}}L = {}_{\textit{Acceptance}}L$), it follows that ${}_{\textit{TM-Membership}}L$ is a Turing language. Take this language. Demonstrate that ${}_{\textit{TM-Halting}}L \angle {}_{\textit{TM-Membership}}L$ to prove that ${}_{\textit{TM-Halting}}L$ is a Turing language. As a result, we have obtained an alternative proof that ${}_{\textit{TM-Halting}}L$ is a Turing language, which also follows from Theorem 8.7.

Consider Corollary 10.5. As a rule, this result saves us much work to prove that a language L is not a Turing language. Typically, a proof like this is performed based on methods (i) or (ii), sketched next.

(i) Take a well-known language K that is not a Turing language. Construct a TM M that computes a reduction of K to L, $K \angle L$. As a result, Corollary 10.5 implies that L is not a Turing language.
(ii) By Definition 10.2, if f is a reduction of K to L, then f is a reduction of $\bar{K}$ to $\bar{L}$ too. Therefore, to prove that a language L is not a Turing language, take a language K whose complement $\bar{K}$ is not a Turing language. Construct a TM that computes a reduction of K to $\bar{L}$. As $K \angle \bar{L}$, we have $\bar{K} \angle \bar{\bar{L}}$, so $\bar{K} \angle L$. By Corollary 10.5, L is not a Turing language.

As a matter of fact, we sometimes make use of Corollary 10.5 to demonstrate that neither a language nor its complement is a Turing language. To illustrate, set

$$ {}_{\textit{TM-Equivalence}}L = \{\langle M, N\rangle \mid M, N \in \textit{TM-Instances},\ L(M) = L(N)\}, \text{ and} $$
$$ {}_{\textit{TM-NonEquivalence}}L = \{\langle M, N\rangle \mid M, N \in \textit{TM-Instances},\ L(M) \neq L(N)\}. $$

Notice that the latter is the complement of the former. Next, we show that neither of them is a Turing language.

Theorem 10.22. *${}_{\textit{TM-Equivalence}}L$ is not a Turing language.*

Proof. We follow method (ii) above in this proof. More specifically, we prove that ${}_{\textit{TM-Membership}}L \angle {}_{\textit{TM-NonEquivalence}}L$ (see Problem 10.12); therefore, ${}_{\textit{TM-Equivalence}}L$ is not a Turing language because neither is ${}_{\textit{TM-Membership}}\bar{L}$. To establish the relation ${}_{\textit{TM-Membership}}L \angle {}_{\textit{TM-NonEquivalence}}L$, we construct a TM X that computes a reduction of ${}_{\textit{TM-Membership}}L$ to ${}_{\textit{TM-NonEquivalence}}L$. Specifically, X transforms any $\langle O, w\rangle$, where $O \in \textit{TM-Instances}$ and $w \in \Delta^*$, to the following two TMs, M and $N[O, w]$, and produces $\langle M, N[O, w]\rangle$ as output (we denote M without any information concerning

$\langle O, w \rangle$ because its construction is completely independent of it—that is, X produces the same M for every $\langle O, w \rangle$). M and $N[O, w]$ work as follows:

(i) M rejects every input.
(ii) On every input $x \in \Delta^*$, $N[O, w]$ works so it runs O on w and accepts x if and when O accepts w.

As obvious, $L(M) = \emptyset$. From the way $N[O, w]$ works on every input $x \in \Delta^*$, it follows:

- If $w \in L(O)$, then $L(N[O, w]) = \Delta^*$, which implies $L(M) \neq L(N[O, w])$.
- If $w \notin L(O)$, then $L(N[O, w]) = \emptyset$, which means $L(M) = L(N[O, w])$.

Thus, X computes ${}_{TM\text{-}Membership}L \angle {}_{TM\text{-}NonEquivalence}L$, so ${}_{TM\text{-}Equivalence}L$ is not a Turing language. ■

Observe that the proof of the following theorem, which says that the language ${}_{TM\text{-}NonEquivalence}L$ is not a Turing language, parallels the previous proof significantly. As a matter of fact, while in the previous proof, M always rejects, in the following proof, M always accepts; otherwise, both proofs coincide with each other.

Theorem 10.23. *${}_{TM\text{-}NonEquivalence}L$ is not a Turing language.*

Proof. To show that ${}_{TM\text{-}NonEquivalence}L$ is not a Turing language, we construct a TM X that computes ${}_{TM\text{-}Membership}L \angle {}_{TM\text{-}NonEquivalence}L$. X works so it transforms every $\langle O, w \rangle$, where $O \in$ *TM-Instances* and $w \in \Delta^*$, to the following two TMs M, $N[O, w]$ and produces $\langle M, N[O, w] \rangle$ as output. M and $N[O, w]$ are defined as follows:

(i) M accepts every input string.
(ii) On every input string x, $N[O, w]$ runs O on w and accepts x if and when O accepts w.

As obvious, $L(M) = \Delta^*$. If $w \in L(O)$, $L(N[O, w]) = \Delta^*$ and $L(M) = L(N[O, w])$; otherwise, $L(M) \neq L(N[O, w])$. Hence, ${}_{TM\text{-}Membership}L \angle {}_{TM\text{-}Equivalence}L$. Therefore, based on (ii) above, we conclude that ${}_{TM\text{-}NonEquivalence}L$ is not a Turing language. ■

Returning to the key topic of this section, we see that such results as Theorem 10.21 and Corollary 10.5 have often significant consequences in terms of undecidability. Indeed, unless L is a Turing language, a problem encoded by L is undecidable because every decidable language is a Turing language (see Theorem 10.10). Specifically, in this way, Theorem 10.21 and Corollary 10.5 imply the undecidability of the next two problems encoded by languages ${}_{TM\text{-}Equivalence}L$ and ${}_{TM\text{-}NonEquivalence}L$, introduced above.

Problem 10.19. *TM-Equivalence.*
Question: Let $M, N \in$ *TM-Instances*. Are M and N equivalent?
Language: ${}_{TM\text{-}Equivalence}L$

Problem 10.20. *TM-NonEquivalence.*
Question: Let $M, N \in$ *TM-Instances*. Are M and N nonequivalent?
Language: ${}_{TM\text{-}NonEquivalence}L$

Corollary 10.6. *Neither* ${}_{TM\text{-}Equivalence}L$ *nor* ${}_{TM\text{-}NonEquivalence}L$ *is decidable.*

Next, we establish results analogical to Theorem 10.21 and Corollary 10.5 in terms of decidable languages.

Theorem 10.24. *Let* $K, L \subseteq \Delta^*$. *If* $K \angle L$ *and* L *is decidable,* K *is decidable, too.*

Proof. Let $K, L \subseteq \Delta^*$, $K \angle L$, and L is decidable. Let f be a reduction of K to L. As already pointed out, by Definition 10.2, f is a reduction of $\bar{K}$ to $\bar{L}$, too. By Theorem 10.12, L is decidable if and only if L and $\bar{L}$ are Turing languages. By Theorem 10.21, K and $\bar{K}$ are Turing languages. Thus, K is decidable by Theorem 10.12. ■

Corollary 10.7. *Let* $K, L \subseteq \Delta^*$. *If* $K \angle L$ *and* K *is not decidable,* L *is not decidable either.*

Theorem 10.24 and Corollary 10.7 often save us much work when we demonstrate undecidability. In the following examples, we revisit some of an earlier result concerning undecidability to demonstrate how to establish it by using Corollary 10.7.

Example 10.2. *Reconsider Problem 10.15 TM-Emptiness and Theorem 10.17, stating that this problem is undecidable. In essence, this undecidability is established so that from any TM* M *and any string* x, *we algorithmically construct a TM* N *such that* $L(N) = \emptyset$ *if and only if* M *halts on* x. *To rephrase this in terms of languages, we define a reduction of* ${}_{TM\text{-}Halting}L$ *to* ${}_{TM\text{-}Emptiness}L$, *so* ${}_{TM\text{-}Halting}L \angle {}_{TM\text{-}Emptiness}L$. *As* ${}_{TM\text{-}Halting}L$ *is undecidable (see Theorem 10.9),* ${}_{TM\text{-}Emptiness}L$ *is undecidable by Corollary 10.7, so Problem 10.15 TM-Emptiness is undecidable.*

Rice's theorem

Next, we discuss the undecidability concerning properties of Turing languages. More specifically, we identify a property of Turing languages, π, with the subfamily of the Turing language family that contains precisely the Turing languages that satisfy π. For instance, the property of being finite equals

$$\{L \mid L \text{ is a Turing language and } L \text{ is finite}\}.$$

In this way, we consider π as a decidable property if there exists a TD D such that $L(D)$ consists of all descriptions of TMs whose languages are in the subfamily defined by π.

Definition 10.3. *Let* π *be a subfamily of the Turing language family. Then,* π *is said to be a* property of Turing languages.

(i) *A Turing language* L satisfies π *if* $L \in \pi$.
(ii) *Set* $L = \{\langle M \rangle \mid M \in \text{TM-Instances},\ L(M) \in \pi\}$. *We say that* π *is* decidable *if there is a TD* D *such that* $L(D) = {}_{\pi}L$; *otherwise,* π *is* undecidable.
(iii) *We say that* π *is* trivial *if either* π *is all the family of Turing languages or* $\pi = \emptyset$; *otherwise,* π *is* nontrivial.

For instance, the property of being finite is nontrivial because

$$\{L \mid L \text{ is a Turing language, } L \text{ is finite}\}$$

is a non-empty proper subfamily of the Turing language family. As a matter of fact, there are only two trivial properties—all the family of Turing languages and $\emptyset$, and both of them are trivially decidable because they are true either for all Turing languages or for no Turing language. As a result, we concentrate our attention on the nontrivial properties in what follows. Surprisingly, Rice's theorem, given next, says that all nontrivial properties are undecidable.

Theorem 10.25 (Rice's theorem). *Every nontrivial property is undecidable.*

Proof. Let π be a nontrivial property. Without any loss of generality, suppose that $\emptyset \notin \pi$ (if $\emptyset \in \pi$ reformulate this proof in terms of $\bar{pi}$ as an exercise). As π is nontrivial, π is non-empty, so there exists a Turing language K in π. Let N be a TM such that $K = L(N)$.

For the sake of obtaining a contradiction, assume that π is decidable. In other words, there exists a TD D that decides ${}_{\pi}L$. Next, we demonstrate that under this assumption, ${}_{\textit{TM-Halting}}L$ would be decidable, which contradicts Theorem 10.9. Indeed, we construct an algorithm that takes any $\langle M, x\rangle$, where M is a TM and $x \in \Delta^*$, and produces $\langle O\rangle$ as output, where O is a TM, so $\langle M, x\rangle \in {}_{\textit{TM-Halting}}L$ if and only if $\langle O\rangle \in {}_{\pi}L$, and by using this equivalence and D, we would decide ${}_{\textit{TM-Halting}}L$. O is designed so it works on every input string y as follows:

(i) Saves y and runs M on x.
(ii) If M halts on x, O runs N on y and accepts if and only if N accepts y.

If M loops on x, so does O. As O works on every y in this way, $L(O) = \emptyset$ if and only if M loops on x. If M halts on x, O runs N on y, and O accepts y if and only if N accepts y, so $L(O) = L(N) = K$ in this case (recall that the case when $K = \emptyset$ is ruled out because $\emptyset \notin \pi$). Thus, $\langle M, x\rangle \in {}_{\textit{TM-Halting}}L$ if and only if $\langle O\rangle \in {}_{\pi}L$. Apply D to decide whether $\langle O\rangle \in {}_{\pi}L$. If so, $\langle M, x\rangle \in {}_{\textit{TM-Halting}}L$, and if not, $\langle M, x\rangle \notin {}_{\textit{TM-Halting}}L$, so ${}_{\textit{TM-Halting}}L$ would be decidable, which contradicts Theorem 10.9. Therefore, ${}_{\pi}L$ is undecidable. ∎

Rice's theorem is a powerful result that has a great variety of consequences. For instance, consider the properties of being finite, regular, and context-free as properties of Turing languages. Rice's theorem straightforwardly implies that all these properties are undecidable.

10.6 Computational complexity

This section takes a finer look at TDs by discussing their *computational complexity*. This complexity is measured according to their time and space computational requirements. The *time complexity* equals the number of moves they need to make a decision while the *space complexity* is defined as the number of visited tape squares. Perhaps most importantly, this section points out that some problems are *tractable* for their reasonable computational requirements while others are *intractable* for their unmanageably high computational requirements to decide them. Simply put, there exist problems that are decidable in theory, but their decision is intractable in practice.

As most topics concerning complexity are too complicated to discuss them in this introductory text, the present section differs from the previous sections of this chapter, which have discussed their material in the form of mathematical formulas and proofs. Rather than giving a fully rigorous presentation of computational complexity, this section only explains the basic ideas underlying it. Indeed, it restricts its attention to the very fundamental concepts and results, which are usually described informally. The section omits mathematically precise proofs. On the other hand, it points out some important open problems concerning the computational complexity.

We begin with the explanation of time complexity, after which we briefly conceptualize space complexity.

10.6.1 Time complexity

Observe that the following definition that formalizes the time complexity of a TD considers the worst case scenario concerning this complexity.

Definition 10.4. *Let* $M = ({}_M\Sigma, {}_MR)$ *be a TD. The* time-complexity function of M, *denoted by* ${}_Mtime$, *is defined over* ${}_0\mathbb{N}$ *so for all* $n \in {}_0\mathbb{N}$, ${}_Mtime(n)$ *is the maximal number of moves M makes on an input string of length n before halting.*

Example 10.3. *Return to the TD D in Example 10.1 such that* $L(D) = \{x \mid x \in \{a, b, c\}^*, \text{occur}\,(x, a) = \text{occur}\,(x, b) = \text{occur}\,(x, c)\}$. *Recall that D scans across the tape in a left-to-right way while erasing the leftmost occurrence of a, b, and c. When it reaches* $\lhd$ *after erasing all three occurrences, it moves left to* $\rhd$ *and makes another scan of this kind. However, when D reaches* $\lhd$ *while some of the three symbols are missing on the tape, D makes its final return to* $\rhd$ *and halts by making one more move during which it accepts or rejects as described in Example 10.1. Let g be the integer function over* ${}_0\mathbb{N}$ *defined for all* ${}_0\mathbb{N}$, *so that if* $n \in {}_0\mathbb{N}$ *is divisible by* 3, $g(n) = n(2(n/3)) + 1$, *and if* $n \in {}_0\mathbb{N}$ *is indivisible by* 3, $g(n) = g(m) + 2n$, *where m is the smallest* $m \in {}_0\mathbb{N}$ *such that* $m \leq n$ *and m is divisible by* 3. *Observe that* ${}_Dtime(n) = g(n)$. *As an exercise, design another TD E such that* $L(D) = L(E)$ *and* ${}_Etime(n) < {}_Dtime(n)$, *for all* $n \in \mathbb{N}$.

As a general rule, for a TD M, ${}_Mtime$ is a complicated polynomial, whose determination represents a tedious and difficult task. Besides this difficulty, we are usually interested in the time complexity of M only when it is run on large inputs. As a result, rather than determine ${}_Mtime$ rigorously, we often consider the highest order term of ${}_Mtime$; on the other hand, we disregard the coefficient of this term as well as any lower terms. The elegant *big-O notation*, defined next, is customarily used for this purpose.

Definition 10.5.

(i) *Let f and g be two functions over* ${}_0\mathbb{N}$*. If there exist* $c, d \in \mathbb{N}$ *such that for every* $n \geq d$*,* $f(n)$ *and* $g(n)$ *are defined and* $f(n) \leq cg(n)$*, then g is an* upper bound *for f, written as* $f = \mathrm{O}(g)$*.*
(ii) *If* $f = \mathrm{O}(g)$ *and g is of the form* n^m*, where* $m \in \mathbb{N}$*, then g is a* polynomial bound *for f.*
(iii) *Let M be a TD. M is* polynomially bounded *if there is a polynomial bound for* ${}_M time$*.*

Let f and g be two polynomials. In essence, according to (i) and (ii) in Definition 10.5, $f = \mathrm{O}(g)$ says that f is less than or equal to g if we disregard differences regarding multiplicative constants and lower order terms. Indeed, $f = \mathrm{O}(g)$ implies $kf = \mathrm{O}(g)$ for any $k \in \mathbb{N}$, so the multiplication constants are ignored. As $f(n) = cg(n)$ holds for all $n \geq d$, the values of any $n \leq d$ are also completely ignored as well. In practice, to obtain $g = n^m$ as described in (ii), we simply take n^m as the highest order term of f without its coefficient; for instance, if $f(n) = 918,273,645n^5 + 999n^4 + 1,111n^3 + 71,178n^2 + 98,765,431n + 1,298,726$, then $f = \mathrm{O}(n^5)$. On the other hand, if $f \neq \mathrm{O}(g)$, there exist infinitely many values of n satisfying $f(n) > cg(n)$.

Based upon (iii) of Definition 10.5, from a more practical point of view, we next distinguish the decidable problems that are possible to compute from the decidable problems that are not.

Definition 10.6. *Let P be a decidable problem. If P is decided by a polynomially bounded TD, P is* tractable*; otherwise, P is* intractable.

Informally, this definition says that although intractable problems are decidable in principle, they can hardly be decided in reality as no decision maker can decide them in polynomial time. On the other hand, tractable problems can be decided in polynomial time, so they are central to practically oriented computer science. Besides, their practical significance, however, tractable problems lead to some crucial topics of theoretical computer science as demonstrated next.

According to Convention 8.4, up until now, we have automatically assumed that the TMs work deterministically. We also know that deterministic TMs are as powerful as their nondeterministic versions (see Definition 8.2 and Theorem 8.1). In terms of their time complexity, however, their relationship remains open as pointed out shortly. Before this, we reformulate some of the previous notions in terms of nondeterministic TMs.

Definition 10.7. *Let us define the following notions:*

(i) *Let M be a TM according to Definition 8.1 (thus, M may not be deterministic). M is a* nondeterministic TD *if M halts on every input string.*
(ii) *Let M be a nondeterministic TD. The* time complexity *of M,* ${}_M time$*, is defined by analogy with Definition 10.4—that is, for all* $n \in {}_0\mathbb{N}$*,* ${}_M time(n)$ *is the maximal number of moves M makes on an input string of length n before halting.*
(iii) *Like in Definition 10.5, M is* polynomially bounded *if there is a polynomial bound for* ${}_M time$*.*

Convention 10.1. *Consider polynomially bounded deterministic TDs and polynomially bounded non-deterministic TDs. In what follows, P and NP denote the language families accepted by the former and the latter, respectively.*

Notice that any TD represents a special case of a nondeterministic TD, so $P \subseteq NP$. However, it is a longstanding open problem whether $P = NP$, referred to as the *$P = NP$ problem*. By using various methods, theoretical computer science has intensively attempted to decide this problem. One of the most important approaches to this problem is based upon ordering the languages in NP. The equivalence classes defined by this ordering consist of languages coding equally difficult problems. Considering the class corresponding to the most difficult problems, any problem coded by a language from this family is as difficult as any other problem coded by a language from NP. Consequently, if we prove that this class contains a language that also belongs to P, then $P = NP$; on the other hand, if we demonstrate that this class contains a language that does not belong to P, then $P \subset NP$. Next, we describe this approach to the $P = NP$ problem in somewhat greater detail.

Definition 10.8. *Let Δ and ς be two alphabets, $J \subseteq \Delta^*$ and $K \subseteq \varsigma^*$. Then, J is* polynomially transformable *into K, symbolically written as $J \propto K$, if there is a polynomially bounded TD M such that M-f (see Definition 9.1) is a total function from Δ^* to ς^* satisfying $x \in J$ if and only if M-$f(x) \in K$.*

In other words, $J \propto K$ means that the difficulty of deciding J is no greater than the difficulty of deciding K, so the problem encoded by J is no more difficult than the problem encoded by K.

Definition 10.9. *Let $L \in NP$. If $J \propto L$ for every $J \in NP$, then L is NP*-complete.

A decision problem coded by an NP-complete language is an *NP-complete problem*. There exist a number of well-known NP-complete problems, such as the next problem.

Problem 10.21. *Time-Bounded Acceptance.*
Question: Let M be a nondeterministic TM, $w \in {}_M\Delta^*$, and $i \in \mathbb{N}$. Does M accept w by computing no more than i moves?
Language:

$$ {}_{\textit{Time-Bounded Acceptance}}L = \{\langle M, w, i\rangle \mid M \text{ is a nondeterministic TM},$$
$$w \in {}_M\Delta^*,\ i \in \mathbb{N},\ M \text{ accepts } w \text{ by computing } i \text{ or fewer moves}\}$$

Once again, by finding an NP-complete language L and proving either $L \in P$ or $L \notin P$, we would decide the $P = NP$ problem. Indeed, if $L \in P$, then $P = NP$, and if $L \notin P$, then $P \subset NP$. So far, however, a proof like this has not been achieved yet, and the $P = NP$ problem remains open.

10.6.2 Space complexity

We close this section by a remark about the space complexity of TDs.

Definition 10.10. *Let* $M = ({}_M\Sigma, {}_MR)$ *be a TD. A function g over* ${}_0\mathbb{N}$ *represents the* space complexity *of* M*, denoted by* ${}_Mspace$*, if* ${}_Mspace(i)$ *equals the minimal number* $j \in {}_0\mathbb{N}$ *such that for all* $x \in {}_M\Delta^i$, $y, v \in \Gamma^*$, $\rhd_M sx\lhd \Rightarrow^* \rhd yqv\lhd$ *in* M *implies* $|yv| \leq j$.

Thus, starting with an input string of length i, M always occurs in a configuration with no more than ${}_Mspace(i)$ symbols on the tape. As an exercise, define polynomially space (PS)-bounded (deterministic) TDs and PS-bounded nondeterministic TDs by analogy with the corresponding deciders in terms of time complexity (see Definitions 10.5 and 10.7).

PS denotes the family of languages accepted by PS-bounded (deterministic) TDs, and *NPS* denotes the family of languages accepted by PS-bounded nondeterministic TDs.

As opposed to the unknown relationship between *P* and *NP*, we know more about *PS* and *NPS*. Indeed, it holds that $PS = NPS$, and *NPS* is properly contained in the family of decidable languages. It is also well known that $NP \subseteq PS$, but it is not known whether this inclusion is proper—another important long-standing open problem in the theory of computation.

Part III
Alternative models for languages and computation

Working within a virtually endless and limitless computer environment such as the Internet, many modern information technologies cope with information of an enormous or even unlimited size largely fragmented and spread across all over this huge environment. Typically, in a parallel and discontinuous way, they perform a single computational step in the following three-phase way. First, they select several information elements, frequently occurring far away from each other within the entire body of information. Second, they simultaneously change them to new pieces of information, and as a result, they obtain entirely new information as a whole. Finally, based upon this new information, they prescribe and regulate the subsequent computational step. To illustrate this kind of modern computation performed in a discontinuous, parallel and regulated way, take a huge collection of sets, each of which contains many information elements concerning one person. The objective of an information technology working with these sets may consist in determining all the sets that contain scattered information satisfying some prescribed properties, which may imply some activities of the person. To give another example, consider many financial pieces of information spread across the business world. The objective of information technologies working with this huge information may consist of avoiding any financial crisis based upon a sophisticated computational method that can predict an undesirable situation like this and suggest how to prevent its occurrence under given circumstances. As these examples clearly illustrate, discontinuity, parallelism, and regulation are crucially important aspects of modern computation.

Some studies of modern computation simplify their investigation, so they consider only very few specific areas in which they work with some special case studies without any attempt to formalize the computation in general. Consequently, they produce fragmented knowledge that has hardly any relation to modern computation as a whole. Thus, rather than shedding some light on fundamental ideas of this computation, they produce little or no relevant results about it. Unless theoretically oriented computer science pays general attention to its research on principles and models that reflect and underlie modern computation, it fails in acting as a systematized theory concerning general ideas behind today's real-world computational methods. Simply and briefly stated, it fatefully loses its purpose.

Considering this urgent need for an in-depth theory of modern computation executed primarily in a discontinuous, parallel and regulated way, computer science obviously needs to create a systematic and compact body of rigorous knowledge that clearly and thoroughly explains the fundamentals underlying the computation. Naturally, a theory like this needs to be based upon formal models that adequately reflect the regulated and discontinuous computation in parallel. The traditional models, covered in Part II, fail to serve as adequate mathematical models for this purpose although we are fully aware of their significance in terms of the classical theory of computation. Indeed, an overwhelming majority of classical models work with strings continuously and sequentially, so these models necessarily fail to formalize modern computation. Fortunately, to put this sad situation into more positive perspectives, formal language theory has recently introduced some grammars and automata that work in a parallel, discontinuous, or regulated way. Out of them, the present part of this book covers the crucially important models that formalize computation performed in this way (see Chapters 12–14). Apart from them, it covers some other kinds of newly introduced models, such as deep pushdown automata (see Chapter 15).

Note on notation. Up until now, we have specified all rewriting systems as pairs in accordance with their definition in Section 4.1. From now on, however, we specify them as n-tuples, for some $n \geq 2$ (most often, they are specified as quadruples) because this extended notation makes the upcomming material much easier to explain and discuss.

Chapter 11
Context-dependent grammars

The present chapter gives an extensive and thorough coverage of grammars that generate languages under various context-related restrictions. First, it covers classical grammars based upon tight context restrictions (Section 11.1). Then, it studies context conditional grammars and their variants, including random context grammars, generalized forbidding grammars, semi-conditional grammars, and simple semi-conditional grammars (Section 11.2). They all are based upon loose context restrictions. More precisely, they have their rules enriched by permitting and forbidding strings, referred to as permitting and forbidding conditions, respectively. These grammars perform their language-generation process in such a way that they require the presence of permitting conditions and, simultaneously, the absence of forbidding conditions in the rewritten sentential forms.

11.1 Tightly context-dependent grammars

In this chapter, *tightly context-dependent grammars* are represented by traditional grammars, such as context-sensitive grammars (CSGs) and phrase-structure grammars (PSGs), defined next. As opposed to context-free grammars (CFGs), on the left-hand sides of their rules, they may have strings—that is, whole sequences of symbols and not necessarily single symbols. In effect, they thus restrict their derivations by prescribing sequences of neighboring symbols that can be rewritten during a derivation step. This kind of restriction is generally referred to as tight-context dependency to distinguish it from loose-context dependency, in which the symbol-neighborhood requirement is dropped (see Section 11.2).

Definition 11.1. *A* PSG *is a rewriting system* $G = (\Sigma, R)$*, where*

- Σ *is divided into two disjoint subalphabets, denoted by* N *and* Δ *and*
- R *is a finite set of rules of the form* $x \rightarrow y$*, where* $x \in \Sigma^+ - \Delta^*$ *and* $y \in \Sigma^*$.

N *and* Δ *are referred to as the* alphabet of nonterminal symbols *and the* alphabet of terminal symbols, *respectively.* N *contains a special* start symbol, *denoted by* S. *Let* $p = x \rightarrow y \in R$ *be a rule. The strings* x *and* y *are called the* left-hand side *and* right-hand side *of* p, *denoted by* lhs p *and* rhs p, *respectively.*

If $S \Rightarrow^* w$, *where* $w \in \Sigma^*$, G derives w, *and* w *is a* sentential form. $F(G)$ *denotes the set of all sentential forms derived by* G. *The* language generated by G, *symbolically* *denoted by L(G), is defined as* $L(G) = F(G) \cap \Delta^*$. *Members of L(G) are called* sentences. *If* $S \Rightarrow^* w$ *and w is a sentence,* $S \Rightarrow^* w$ *is a* successful derivation *in G.*

By analogy with any CFG, for any PSG G, we automatically assume that Σ, N, Δ, S, and R denote the total alphabet, the alphabet of nonterminal symbols, the alphabet of terminal symbols, the start symbol, and the set of rules, respectively. If we want to specify that x is rewritten during a derivation step, $uxv \Rightarrow uyv$, we underline this x as $u\underline{x}v \Rightarrow uyv$. For brevity, G is often defined by simply listing its rules together with specifying its nonterminals and terminals, usually denoted by uppercases and lowercases, respectively.

Considering PSGs, we next define some of their special cases, including their abbreviations. Let $G = (\Sigma; R)$ be a phrase-structure grammar, a PSG for short. G is *monotonous grammar*, a MONG for short, if every rule $x \to y$ in R satisfies $|x| \leq |y|$. G is *context sensitive grammar*, a CSG for short, if every rule r in R is of the form $xAy \to xuy$, where $x, y \in \Sigma^*, A \in N, u \in \Sigma^+$. Of course, G is a *context free grammar*, a CFG for short, if every rule $u \to v \in R$ satisfies $u \in N$. G is a *linear grammar*, an LG for short, if G is a CFG and every rule contains no more than one nonterminal on its right-hand side. G is a *right-linear grammar*, an RLG for short, if G is an LG and the right-hand side of every rule is in $T^*(N \cup \{\varepsilon\})$. G is a *regular grammar*, an RG for short, if G is an LG and the right-hand side of every rule is in $T(N \cup \{\varepsilon\})$.

Crucially, in what follows, instead of $G = (\Sigma; R)$, we write G as a quadruple of the form

$$G = (\Sigma, \Delta, R, S)$$

where all the symbols have the previous meaning.

PSGs are equivalent with Turing machines (see Chapter 8), and the language family they both define is called the family of *recursively enumerable languages*, **RE** for short. This family properly contains the family of *context-sensitive languages*, generated by CSGs and MONGs. The family of *context-free languages*, generated by CFGs, is properly contained in that of context-sensitive languages; however, it is a proper superfamily of the family of *linear languages*, **LIN** for short, generated by LGs. The family of linear languages properly contains the family of *regular languages*, **REG** for short, generated by RLGs and RGs. Finally, the family of *finite languages*, **FIN** for short, is a proper subfamily of the family of regular languages. As a whole, these results represent the Chomsky hierarchy of language families.

In general, CSGs and PSGs may have rules of various forms, and they may generate a very broad variety of completely different sentential forms during the generation of their languages. As is obvious, this inconsistency concerning the form of rules as well as rewritten strings represents an undesirable phenomenon in theory as well as in practice. From a theoretical viewpoint, the demonstration of properties concerning languages generated in this inconsistent way usually lead to unbearably tedious proofs. From a practical viewpoint, this kind of language generation is obviously difficult to apply and implement. Therefore, we pay special attention to arranging these grammars in such a way that they generate their languages in a more uniform way.

The present section consists of two subsections. First, it studies grammars with modified grammatical rules so they all satisfy some simple prescribed forms, generally referred to as normal forms. Second, it explains how to perform tight-context rewriting over strings that have a uniform form.

Normal forms

In this section, we convert CSGs and PSGs into several normal forms, including the Kuroda, Penttonen, and Geffert normal forms. We also reduce the number of context-free rules in these grammars. In addition, we describe the Greibach and Chomsky normal forms for CFGs.

Recall that for a grammar $G = (\Sigma, \Delta, R, S)$, N denotes the set of all nonterminal symbols, so $N = \Sigma - \Delta$.

Definition 11.2. *Let* $G = (\Sigma, \Delta, R, S)$ *be a PSG. G is in the* Kuroda normal form *(see [6]) if every rule in R is of one of the following four forms:*

$$\text{(i) } AB \rightarrow CD \qquad \text{(ii) } A \rightarrow BC \qquad \text{(iii) } A \rightarrow a \qquad \text{(iv) } A \rightarrow \varepsilon$$

where $A, B, C, D \in N$*, and* $a \in \Delta$.

Theorem 11.1 (see [6]). *For every PSG G, there is a PSG G′ in the Kuroda normal form such that* $L(G') = L(G) - \{\varepsilon\}$.

Definition 11.3. *Let* $G = (\Sigma, \Delta, R, S)$ *be a PSG. G is in the* Penttonen normal form *(see [7]) if every rule in R is of one of the following four forms:*

$$\text{(i) } AB \rightarrow AC \qquad \text{(ii) } A \rightarrow BC \qquad \text{(iii) } A \rightarrow a \qquad \text{(iv) } A \rightarrow \varepsilon$$

where $A, B, C \in N$*, and* $a \in \Delta$.

In other words, G is in the Penttonen normal form if G is in the Kuroda normal form and every $AB \rightarrow CD \in R$ satisfies that $A = C$

Theorem 11.2 (see [7]). *For every PSG G, there is a PSG G′ in the Penttonen normal form such that* $L(G') = L(G) - \{\varepsilon\}$.

Theorem 11.3 (see [7]). *For every CSG G, there is a CSG G′ in the Penttonen normal form such that* $L(G') = L(G)$.

Observe that if G is a CSG in the Penttonen normal form, then none of its rules are of the form (iv), which is not context-sensitive.

Theorems 11.2 and 11.3 can be further modified so that for every context-sensitive rule of the form $AB \rightarrow AC \in R$, where $A, B, C \in N$, there exist no $B \rightarrow x$ or $BD \rightarrow BE$ in R for any $x \in \Sigma^*$, $D, E \in N$:

Theorem 11.4. *Every context-sensitive language can be generated by a CSG* $G = (N_{CF} \cup N_{CS} \cup \Delta, \Delta, R, S)$*, where* N_{CF}*,* N_{CS}*, and* Δ *are pairwise disjoint alphabets, and every rule in R is either of the form* $AB \rightarrow AC$*, where* $B \in N_{CS}$*,* $A, C \in N_{CF}$*, or of the form* $A \rightarrow x$*, where* $A \in N_{CF}$ *and* $x \in N_{CS} \cup \Delta \cup N_{CF}^2$.

Proof. Let $G' = (\Sigma, \Delta, R', S)$ be a CSG in the Penttonen normal form (see Theorem 11.3). Then, let

$$G = (N_{CF} \cup N_{CS} \cup \Delta, \Delta, R, S)$$

be the CSG defined as follows:

$$\begin{aligned} N_{CF} &= N, \\ N_{CS} &= \{\widetilde{B} \mid AB \to AC \in R',\ A, B, C \in N\}, \\ R &= \{A \to x \mid A \to x \in R',\ A \in N,\ x \in \Delta \cup N^2\} \cup \\ &\quad \{B \to \widetilde{B},\ A\widetilde{B} \to AC \mid AB \to AC \in R',\ A, B, C \in N\}. \end{aligned}$$

Obviously, $L(G') = L(G)$ and G is of the required form, so the theorem holds. ■

Theorem 11.5. *Every recursively enumerable language can be generated by a PSG $G = (N_{CF} \cup N_{CS} \cup \Delta, \Delta, R, S)$, where N_{CF}, N_{CS}, and Δ are pairwise disjoint alphabets, and every rule in R is either of the form $AB \to AC$, where $B \in N_{CS}$, $A, C \in N_{CF}$, or of the form $A \to x$, where $A \in N_{CF}$ and $x \in N_{CS} \cup \Delta \cup N_{CF}^2 \cup \{\varepsilon\}$.*

Proof. The reader can prove this theorem by analogy with the proof of Theorem 11.4. ■

The next two normal forms limit the number of nonterminals and context-sensitive rules in PSGs.

Definition 11.4. *Let G be a PSG. G is in the* first Geffert normal form *(see [8]) if it is of the form*

$$G = (\{S, A, B, C\} \cup \Delta, \Delta, R \cup \{ABC \to \varepsilon\}, S)$$

where R contains context-free rules of the following three forms:

(i) $S \to uSa$ (ii) $S \to uSv$ (iii) $S \to uv$

where $u \in \{A, AB\}^*$, $v \in \{BC, C\}^*$, and $a \in \Delta$.

Theorem 11.6 (see [8]). *For every recursively enumerable language K, there exists a PSG G in the first Geffert normal form such that $L(G) = K$. In addition, every successful derivation in G is of the form $S \Rightarrow_G^* w_1 w_2 w$ by rules from R, where $w_1 \in \{A, AB\}^*$, $w_2 \in \{BC, C\}^*$, $w \in \Delta^*$, and $w_1 w_2 w \Rightarrow_G^* w$ is derived by $ABC \to \varepsilon$.*

Definition 11.5. *Let G be a PSG. G is in the* second Geffert normal form *(see [8]) if it is of the form*

$$G = (\{S, A, B, C, D\} \cup \Delta, \Delta, R \cup \{AB \to \varepsilon, CD \to \varepsilon\}, S)$$

where R contains context-free rules of the following three forms:

(i) $S \to uSa$ (ii) $S \to uSv$ (iii) $S \to uv$

where $u \in \{A, C\}^*$, $v \in \{B, D\}^*$, and $a \in \Delta$.

Theorem 11.7 (see [8]). *For every recursively enumerable language K, there exists a PSG G in the Geffert normal form such that* $L(G) = K$. *In addition, every successful derivation in G is of the form* $S \Rightarrow_G^* w_1 w_2 w$ *by rules from R, where* $w_1 \in \{A, C\}^*$, $w_2 \in \{B, D\}^*$, $w \in \Delta^*$, *and* $w_1 w_2 w \Rightarrow_G^* w$ *is derived by* $AB \rightarrow \varepsilon$ *and* $CD \rightarrow \varepsilon$.

Next, we establish two new normal forms for PSGs with a limited number of context-free rules in a prescribed form and, simultaneously, with non-context-free rules in a prescribed form. Specifically, we establish the following two normal forms of this kind:

1. First, we explain how to turn any PSG to an equivalent PSG that has $2 + n$ context-free rules, where n is the number of terminals, and every context-free rule is of the form $A \rightarrow x$, where x is a terminal, a two-nonterminal string, or the empty string. In addition, every non-context-free rule is of the form $AB \rightarrow CD$, where A, B, C, D arc nonterminals;
2. In the second normal form, PSGs have always only two context-free rules—that is, the number of context-free rules is reduced independently of the number of terminals as opposed to the first normal form. Specifically, we describe how to turn any PSG to an equivalent PSG that has two context-free rules of the forms $A \rightarrow \varepsilon$ and $A \rightarrow BC$, where A, B, C are nonterminals and ε denotes the empty string, and in addition, every non-context-free rule is of the form $AB \rightarrow CD$, where A, B, D are nonterminals and C is nonterminal or a terminal.

Theorem 11.8. *Let G be a PSG. Then, there is an equivalent PSG*

$$H = (\Sigma, \Delta, R_1 \cup R_2 \cup R_3, S)$$

with

$$\begin{aligned} R_1 &= \{AB \rightarrow CD \mid A, B, C, D \in N\}, \\ R_2 &= \{S \rightarrow S\#, \# \rightarrow \varepsilon\}, \\ R_3 &= \{A \rightarrow a \mid A \in N, a \in \Delta\} \end{aligned}$$

where $\# \in N$.

Proof. Let $G = (\Sigma, \Delta, R, S)$ be a PSG. By Theorem 11.1, we assume that G is in the Kuroda normal form. Set $\bar{\Delta} = \{\bar{a} \mid a \in \Delta\}$. Without any loss of generality, we assume that N, Δ, $\bar{\Delta}$, and $\{\#\}$ are pairwise disjoint. Construct the PSG

$$H = (\Sigma', \Delta, R'_1 \cup R'_2 \cup R'_3, S)$$

as follows: initially, set $\Sigma' = \Sigma \cup \bar{\Delta} \cup \{\#\}$, $R'_1 = \emptyset$, $R'_2 = \{S \rightarrow S\#, \# \rightarrow \varepsilon\}$, and $R'_3 = \{\bar{a} \rightarrow a \mid a \in \Delta\}$. Perform (1)–(5), given as follows:

(1) For each $AB \rightarrow CD \in R$, where $A, B, C, D \in N$, add $AB \rightarrow CD$ to R'_1;
(2) For each $A \rightarrow BC \in R$, where $A, B, C \in N$, add $A\# \rightarrow BC$ to R'_1;
(3) For each $A \rightarrow a \in R$, where $A \in N$ and $a \in \Delta$, add $A\# \rightarrow \bar{a}\#$ to R'_1;
(4) For each $A \rightarrow \varepsilon \in R$, where $A \in N$, add $A\# \rightarrow \#\#$ to R'_1;
(5) For each $A \in N$, add $A\# \rightarrow \#A$ and $\#A \rightarrow A\#$ to R'_1.

Before proving that $L(H) = L(G)$, let us give an insight into the construction. We simulate G by H using the following sequences of derivation steps.

First, by repeatedly using $S \rightarrow S\#$, we generate a proper number of #s. Observe that if the number of #s is too low, the derivation can be blocked since rules from (2) consume # during their application. Furthermore, notice that only rules from (4) and the initial rule $S \rightarrow S\#$ increase the number of #s in sentential forms of H.

Next, we simulate each application of a rule in G by several derivation steps in H. By using rules from (5), we can move # in the current sentential form as needed. If we have # or B in a proper position next to A, we can apply a rule from (1)–(4). We can also apply $\# \rightarrow \varepsilon$ to remove any occurrence of # from a sentential form of H.

To conclude the simulation, we rewrite the current sentential form by rules of the form $\bar{a} \rightarrow a$ to generate a string of terminals. Observe that a premature application of a rule of this kind may block the derivation in H. Indeed, #s then cannot move freely through such a sentential form.

To establish $L(H) = L(G)$, we prove four claims. Claim 1 demonstrates that every $w \in L(H)$ can be generated in two stages; first, only nonterminals are generated, and then, all nonterminals are rewritten to terminals. Claim 2 shows that we can arbitrarily generate and move #s within sentential forms of H during the first stage. Claim 3 shows how derivations of G are simulated by H. Finally, Claim 4 shows how derivations of every $w \in L(H)$ in H are simulated by G.

Set $N' = \Sigma' - \Delta$. Define the homomorphism τ from Σ'^* to Σ^* as $\tau(X) = X$ for all $X \in \Sigma$, $\tau(\bar{a}) = a$ for all $a \in \Delta$, and $\tau(\#) = \varepsilon$.

Claim 1. *Let $w \in L(H)$. Then, there exists a derivation $S \Rightarrow_H^* x \Rightarrow_H^* w$, where $x \in N'^+$, and during $x \Rightarrow_H^* w$, only rules of the form $\bar{a} \rightarrow a$, where $a \in \Delta$, are applied.*

Proof. Let $w \in L(H)$. Since there are no rules in $R'_1 \cup R'_2 \cup R'_3$ with symbols from Δ on their left-hand sides, we can always rearrange all the applications of the rules occurring in $S \Rightarrow_H^* w$ so the claim holds. □

Claim 2. *If $S \Rightarrow_H^* uv$, where $u, v \in \Sigma'^*$, then $S \Rightarrow_H^* u\#v$.*

Proof. By an additional application of $S \rightarrow S\#$, we get $S \Rightarrow_H^* S\#^{n+1}$ instead of $S \Rightarrow_H^* S\#^n$ for some $n \geq 0$, so we derive one more # in the sentential form. From Claim 1, by applying rules from (5), # can freely migrate through the sentential form as needed, until a rule of the form $\bar{a} \rightarrow a$ is used. □

Claim 3. *If $S \Rightarrow_G^k x$, where $x \in \Delta^*$, for some $k \geq 0$, then $S \Rightarrow_H^* x'$, where $\tau(x') = x$.*

Proof. This claim is established by induction on $k \geq 0$.

Basis. For $S \Rightarrow_G^0 S$, there is $S \Rightarrow_H^0 S$.

Induction Hypothesis. For some $k \geq 0$, $S \Rightarrow_G^k x$ implies that $S \Rightarrow_H^* x'$ such that $x = \tau(x')$.

Induction Step. Let $u, v \in N'^*$, $A, B, C, D \in N$, and $m \geq 0$. Assume that $S \Rightarrow_G^k y \Rightarrow_G x$. By the induction hypothesis, $S \Rightarrow_H^* y'$ with $y = \tau(y')$. Let us show the simulation of $y \Rightarrow_G x$ by an application of several derivation steps in H to get $y' \Rightarrow_H^+ x'$ with $\tau(x') = x$. This simulation is divided into the following four cases:

(i) *Simulation of* $AB \to CD$: $y' = uA\#^m Bv \Rightarrow_H^m u\#^m ABv \Rightarrow_H u\#^m CDv = x'$ using m derivation steps according to rules $A\# \to \#A$ from (5), and concluding the derivation by rule $AB \to CD$ from (1);

By the induction hypothesis and Claim 2, $y = \tau(u)A\tau(v)$ allows $y' = uA\#v$.

(ii) *Simulation of* $A \to BC$: $y' = uA\#v \Rightarrow_H uBCv = x'$ using rule $A\# \to BC$ from (2);
(iii) *Simulation of* $A \to a$: $y' = uA\#v \Rightarrow_H u\bar{a}\#v = x'$ using rule $A\# \to \bar{a}\#$ from (3);
(iv) *Simulation of* $A \to \varepsilon$: $y' = uA\#v \Rightarrow_H u\#\#v = x'$ using rule $A\# \to \#\#$ from (4).

□

Claim 4. *If* $S \Rightarrow_H^k x'$, *where* $x' \in N'^*$, *for some* $k \geq 0$, *then* $S \Rightarrow_G^* x$ *with* $x = \tau(x')$.

Proof. This claim is established by induction on $k \geq 0$.

Basis. For $S \Rightarrow_H^0 S$, there is $S \Rightarrow_G^0 S$.

Induction Hypothesis. For some $k \geq 0$, $S \Rightarrow_H^k x'$ implies that $S \Rightarrow_G^* x$ such that $x = \tau(x')$.

Induction Step. Let $u, v, w \in N'^*$ and $A, B, C, D \in N$. Assume that $S \Rightarrow_H^k y' \Rightarrow_H x'$. By the induction hypothesis, $S \Rightarrow_G^* y$ such that $y = \tau(y')$. Let us examine the following seven possibilities of $y' \Rightarrow_H x'$:

(i) $y' = uSv \Rightarrow_H uS\#v = x'$: Then,

$$\tau(y') = y = \tau(uSv) \Rightarrow_G^0 \tau(uS\#v) = \tau(uSv) = x = \tau(x');$$

(ii) $y' = uABv \Rightarrow_H uCDv = x'$: According to (1),

$$y = \tau(u)AB\tau(v) \Rightarrow_G \tau(u)CD\tau(v) = x;$$

(iii) $y' = uA\#v \Rightarrow_H uBCv = x'$: According to the source rule in (2),

$$y = \tau(u)A\tau(\#v) \Rightarrow_G \tau(u)BC\tau(\#v) = \tau(u)BC\tau(v) = x;$$

(iv) $y' = uA\#v \Rightarrow_H u\#\#v = x'$: By the corresponding rule $A \to \varepsilon$,

$$y = \tau(u)A\tau(v) \Rightarrow_G \tau(u\#\#v) = \tau(uv) = x;$$

(v) $y' = uA\#v \Rightarrow_H u\#Av = x'$ or $y' = u\#Av \Rightarrow_H uA\#v = x'$: In G,

$$y = \tau(uA\#v) = \tau(u)A\tau(\#v) \Rightarrow_G^0 \tau(u\#)A\tau(v) = x$$

or

$$y = \tau(u\#Av) = \tau(u\#)A\tau(v) \Rightarrow_G^0 \tau(u)A\tau(\#v) = x;$$

(vi) $y' = u\#v \Rightarrow_H uv = x'$: In G,

$$y = \tau(u\#v) \Rightarrow_G^0 \tau(uv) = x;$$

(vii) $y' = u\bar{a}v \Rightarrow_H uav = x'$: In G,

$$y = \tau(u\bar{a}v) = \tau(u)a\tau(v) \Rightarrow_G^0 \tau(u)a\tau(v) = x.$$ □

Next, we establish $L(H) = L(G)$. Consider Claim 3 with $x \in \Delta^*$. Then, $S \Rightarrow_G^* x$ implies that $S \Rightarrow_H^* x$, so $L(G) \subseteq L(H)$. Let $w \in L(H)$. By Claim 1, $S \Rightarrow_H^* x \Rightarrow_H^* w$, where $x \in N'^+$, and during $x \Rightarrow_H^* w$, only the rules of the form $\bar{a} \rightarrow a$, where $a \in \Delta$, are applied. By Claim 4, $S \Rightarrow_G^* \tau(x) = w$, so $L(H) \subseteq L(G)$. Hence, $L(H) = L(G)$.

Since H is of the required form, the theorem holds. ■

From the construction in the proof of Theorem 11.8, we obtain the following corollary concerning the number of nonterminals and rules in the resulting grammar.

Corollary 11.1. *Let $G = (\Sigma, \Delta, R, S)$ be a PSG in the Kuroda normal form. Then, there is an equivalent PSG in the normal form from Theorem 11.8*

$$H = (\Sigma', \Delta, R', S)$$

where

$$\text{card}(\Sigma') = \text{card}(\Sigma) + \text{card}(\Delta) + 1$$

and

$$\text{card}(R') = \text{card}(R) + \text{card}(\Delta) + 2(\text{card}(N) + 1).$$

If we drop the requirement on each symbol in the non-context-free rules to be a nonterminal, we can reduce the number of context-free rules even more.

Theorem 11.9. *Let G be a PSG. Then, there is an equivalent PSG*

$$H = (\Sigma, \Delta, R_1 \cup R_2, S)$$

with

$$R_1 = \{AB \rightarrow XD \mid A, B, D \in N, X \in N \cup \Delta\},$$
$$R_2 = \{S \rightarrow S\#, \# \rightarrow \varepsilon\}$$

where $\# \in N$.

Proof. Reconsider the proof of Theorem 11.8. Observe that we can obtain the new normal form by omitting the construction of R_3' and modifying step (3) in the following way

(3) For each $A \rightarrow a \in R$, where $A \in N$ and $a \in \Delta$, add $A\# \rightarrow a\#$ to R_1'.

The rest of the proof is analogical to the proof of Theorem 11.8, and it is left to the reader. ■

Next, we define two normal forms for CFGs—the Chomsky and Greibach normal forms (see [9] and [10]).

Definition 11.6. *Let G be a CFG. G is in the* Chomsky normal form *if every* $A \rightarrow x \in R$ *satisfies that* $x \in NN \cup \Delta$.

Theorem 11.10 (see [9]). *For every CFG G, there is a CFG G′ in the Chomsky normal form such that* $L(G') = L(G) - \{\varepsilon\}$.

Definition 11.7. *Let G be a CFG. G is in the* Greibach normal form *if every* $A \rightarrow x \in R$ *satisfies that* $x \in \Delta N^*$.

Theorem 11.11 (see [10]). *For every CFG G, there is a CFG G′ in the Greibach normal form such that* $L(G') = L(G) - \{\varepsilon\}$.

Finally, we define the following two normal forms for queue grammars and left-extended queue grammars.

Definition 11.8. *Let* $Q = (\Sigma, \Delta, W, F, R, g)$ *be a queue grammar (see Definition 4.2). Q satisfies the normal form, if* $\{!, f\} \subseteq W$, $F = \{f\}$, *and each* $(a, b, x, c) \in R$ *satisfies* $a \in \Sigma - \Delta$ *and either*

$$W' = W - \{!, f\}, b \in W', x \in (\Sigma - \Delta)^*, c \in W \quad or \quad b = !, x \in \Delta, c \in \{!, f\}.$$

Theorem 11.12. *For every queue grammar Q′, there is a queue grammar Q in the normal form of Definition 11.8 such that* $L(Q') = L(Q)$.

Note. Q generates every $y \in L(Q) - \{\varepsilon\}$ in this way:

$$\begin{array}{ll}
a_0q_0 \Rightarrow_Q x_0q_1 & [(a_0, q_0, z_0, q_1)] \\
\vdots & \\
\Rightarrow_Q x_{k-1}q_k & [(a_{k-1}, q_{k-1}, z_{k-1}, q_k)] \\
\Rightarrow_Q x_k! & [(a_k, q_k, z_k, !)] \\
\Rightarrow_Q x_{k+1}b_1! & [(a_{k+1}, !, b_1, !)] \\
\vdots & \\
\Rightarrow_Q x_{k+m-1}b_1 \cdots b_{m-1}! & [(a_{k+m-1}, !, b_{m-1}, !)] \\
\Rightarrow_Q b_1 \cdots b_m f & [(a_{k+m}, !, b_m, f)]
\end{array}$$

where $k, m \geq 1$, $g = a_0q_0$, $a_1, \ldots, a_{k+m} \in \Sigma - \Delta$, $b_1, \ldots, b_m \in \Delta$, $z_0, \ldots, z_k \in (\Sigma - \Delta)^*$, $q_0, \ldots, q_k, ! \in W - F$, $f \in F$, $x_0, \ldots, x_{k+m-1} \in (\Sigma - \Delta)^+$, and $y = b_1 \cdots b_m$.

Proof. Let $Q' = (\Sigma', \Delta, W', F', R', g')$ be any queue grammar. Set $\Phi = \{\bar{a} \mid a \in \Delta\}$. Define the homomorphism α from Σ'^* to $((\Sigma' - \Delta) \cup \Phi)^*$ as $\alpha(a) = \bar{a}$, for each $a \in \Delta$ and $\alpha(A) = A$, for each $A \in \Sigma' - \Delta$. Set $\Sigma = \Sigma' \cup \Phi$, $W = W' \cup \{!, f\}$, $F = \{f\}$, and $g = \alpha(a_0)q_0$ for $g' = a_0q_0$. Define the queue grammar $Q = (\Sigma, \Delta, W, F, R, g)$, with R constructed in the following way.

(1) For each $(a, b, x, c) \in R'$, where $c \in W' - F'$, add $(\alpha(a), b, \alpha(x), c)$ to R;
(2) For each $(a, b, x, c) \in R'$
  (2.1) where $x \neq \varepsilon$, $c \in F'$, add $(\alpha(a), b, \alpha(x), !)$ to R,
  (2.2) where $x = \varepsilon$, $c \in F'$, add $(\alpha(a), b, \varepsilon, f)$ to R;

(3) For each $a \in \Delta$,
    (3.1) add $(\bar{a}, !, a, !)$ to R;
    (3.2) add $(\bar{a}, !, a, f)$ to R.

Clearly, each $(a, b, x, c) \in R$ satisfies $a \in \Sigma - \Delta$ and either $b \in W'$, $x \in (\Sigma - \Delta)^*$, $c \in W' \cup \{!, f\}$ or $b = !$, $x \in \Delta$, $c \in \{!, f\}$.

To see that $L(Q') \subseteq L(Q)$, consider any $v \in L(Q')$. As $v \in L(Q')$, $g' \Rightarrow_{Q'}^* vt$, where $v \in \Delta^*$ and $t \in F'$. Express $g' \Rightarrow_{Q'}^* vt$ as

$$g' \Rightarrow_{Q'}^* axc \Rightarrow_{Q'} vt \ [(a, c, y, t)]$$

where $a \in \Sigma'$, $x, y \in \Delta^*$, $xy = v$, and $c \in W' - F'$. This derivation is simulated by Q as follows. First, Q uses rules from (1) to simulate $g' \Rightarrow_{Q'}^* axc$. Then, it uses a rule from (2) to simulate $axc \Rightarrow_{Q'} vt$. For $x = \varepsilon$, a rule from (2.2) can be used to generate $\varepsilon \in L(Q)$ in the case of $\varepsilon \in L(Q')$; otherwise, a rule from (2.1) is used. This part of simulation can be expressed as

$$g \Rightarrow_Q^* \alpha(ax)c \Rightarrow_Q \alpha(v)!.$$

At this point, $\alpha(v)$ satisfies $\alpha(v) = \bar{a}_1 \cdots \bar{a}_n$, where $a_i \in \Delta$ for all i, $1 \le i \le n$, for some $n \ge 1$. The rules from (3) of the form $(\bar{a}, !, a, !)$, where $a \in \Delta$, replace every $\bar{a}_j$ with a_j, where $1 \le j \le n - 1$, and, finally, $(\bar{a}, !, a, f)$, where $a \in \Delta$, replaces $\alpha(a_n)$ with a_n. As a result, we obtain the sentence vf, so $L(Q') \subseteq L(Q)$.

To establish $L(Q) \subseteq L(Q')$, observe that the use of a rule from (2.2) in Q before the sentential form is of the form $\alpha(ax)c$, where $a \in \Sigma'$, $x \in \Delta^*$, $c \in W' - F'$, leads to an unsuccessful derivation. Similarly, the use of (2.2) if $x \neq \varepsilon$ leads to an unsuccessful derivation as well. The details are left to the reader. As a result, $L(Q) \subseteq L(Q')$.

As $L(Q') \subseteq L(Q)$ and $L(Q) \subseteq L(Q')$, we obtain $L(Q) = L(Q')$. ■

Briefly, a queue grammar $Q = (\Sigma, \Delta, W, F, R, g)$ in normal form of Definition 11.8 generates every string in $L(Q) - \{\varepsilon\}$ in such a way that it passes through !. Before it enters !, it generates only strings from $(\Sigma - \Delta)^*$; after entering !, it generates only strings from Δ^*.

Definition 11.9. *Let $Q = (\Sigma, \Delta, W, F, R, g)$ be a left-extended queue grammar. Q satisfies the normal form, if $\Sigma = U \cup Z \cup \Delta$ and $W = X \cup Y \cup \{!\}$ such that U, Z, Δ, X, Y, {!} are pairwise disjoint, $F \subseteq Y$, $g \in UW$, and Q derives every $w \in L(Q)$ in this way:*

$$\begin{aligned}
\#g &\Rightarrow_Q^m a_0a_1 \cdots a_m\#b_1b_2 \cdots b_n! && [t_1t_2 \cdots t_m]\\
&\Rightarrow_Q a_0a_1 \cdots a_mb_1\#b_2 \cdots b_ny_1p_1 && [r_1]\\
&\Rightarrow_Q a_0a_1 \cdots a_mb_1b_2\#b_3 \cdots b_ny_1y_2p_2 && [r_2]\\
&\ \ \vdots\\
&\Rightarrow_Q a_0a_1 \cdots a_mb_1b_2 \cdots b_{n-1}\#b_ny_1y_2 \cdots y_{n-1}p_{n-1} && [r_{n-1}]\\
&\Rightarrow_Q a_0a_1 \cdots a_mb_1b_2 \cdots b_{n-1}b_n\#y_1y_2 \cdots y_np_n && [r_n]
\end{aligned}$$

where $m, n \in \mathbb{N}$, $a_j \in U$, $b_i \in Z$, $y_i \in \Delta^*$, $w = y_1y_2 \cdots y_n$, $p_i \in Y$, $p_n \in F$, $t_j, r_i \in R$, where $t_j = (a_j, b_j, x_j, c_j)$ satisfies $a_j \in U$, $b_j \in X$, $x_j \in (\Sigma - \Delta)^*$, $c_j \in X \cup \{!\}$, and $r_i = (a_i, b_i, x_i, c_i)$ satisfies $a_i \in Z$, $b_i \in (Y - F) \cup \{!\}$, $x_i \in \Delta^*$, $c_i \in Y$, for $j = 1, \cdots, m$ and $i = 1, \cdots, n$.

Theorem 11.13. *For every left-extended queue grammar K, there is a left-extended queue grammar Q in the normal form from Definition 11.9 such that* $L(K) = L(Q)$.

Proof. See Lemma 1 in [4]. ■

Uniform rewriting

The present section demonstrates that for every PSG G, there exists an equivalent PSG

$$G' = (\{S, 0, 1\} \cup \Delta, \Delta, R, S)$$

so that every $x \in F(G')$ satisfies

$$x \in \Delta^* \operatorname{perm}(w)^*$$

where $w \in \{0, 1\}^*$ (recall that $F(G')$ is defined in Definition 11.1). Then, it makes this conversion so that for every $x \in F(G)$,

$$x \in \operatorname{perm}(w)^* \Delta^*.$$

Let $G = (\Sigma, \Delta, R, S)$ be a PSG. Notice that $\operatorname{symbols}(L(G)) \subseteq \Delta$. If $a \in \Delta - \operatorname{symbols}(L(G))$, then a actually acts as a pseudoterminal because it appears in no string of $L(G)$. Every transformation described in this section assumes that its input grammar contains no pseudoterminals of this kind and does not contain any useless nonterminals either.

Let j be a natural number. Set

$$\mathbf{PS}[.j] = \{L \mid L = L(G), \text{ where } G = (\Sigma, \Delta, R, S) \text{ is a PSG such that } \operatorname{card}(\operatorname{symbols}(F(G)) - \Delta) = j \text{ and } F(G) \subseteq \Delta^* \operatorname{perm}(w)^*, \text{ where } w \in (\Sigma - \Delta)^*\}$$

Analogously, set

$$\mathbf{PS}[j.] = \{L \mid L = L(G), \text{ where } G = (\Sigma, \Delta, R, S) \text{ is a PSG such that } \operatorname{card}(\operatorname{symbols}(F(G)) - \Delta) = j \text{ and } F(G) \subseteq \operatorname{perm}(w)^* \Delta^*, \text{ where } w \in (\Sigma - \Delta)^*\}$$

Lemma 11.1. *Let G be a PSG. Then, there exists a PSG,* $G' = (\{S, 0, 1\} \cup \Delta, \Delta, R, S)$, *satisfying* $L(G') = L(G)$ *and* $F(G') \subseteq \Delta^* \operatorname{perm}(1^{n-2}00)^*$, *for some natural number* n.

Proof. Let $G = (\Sigma, \Delta, Q, \$)$ be a PSG, where Σ is the total alphabet of G, Δ is the terminal alphabet of G, Q is the set of rules of G, and $\$$ is the start symbol of G. Without any loss of generality, assume that $\Sigma \cap \{0, 1\} = \emptyset$. The following construction produces an equivalent PSG

$$G' = (\{S, 0, 1\} \cup \Delta, \Delta, R, S)$$

such that $F(G') \subseteq \Delta^* \operatorname{perm}(1^{n-2}00)^*$, for some natural number n.

For some integers m, n such that $m \geq 3$ and $2m = n$, introduce an injective homomorphism β from Σ to

$$(\{1\}^m\{1\}^*\{0\}\{1\}^*\{0\} \cap \{0,1\}^n) - \{1^{n-2}00\}.$$

Extend the domain of β to Σ^*. Define the PSG

$$G' = (\{S, 0, 1\} \cup \Delta, \Delta, R, S)$$

with

$$\begin{aligned} R = \{&S \rightarrow 1^{n-2}00\beta(\$)1^{n-2}00\} \cup \\ &\{\beta(x) \rightarrow \beta(y) \mid x \rightarrow y \in Q\} \cup \\ &\{1^{n-2}00\beta(a) \rightarrow a1^{n-2}00 \mid a \in \Delta\} \cup \\ &\{1^{n-2}001^{n-2}00 \rightarrow \varepsilon\}. \end{aligned}$$

Claim 1. *Let $S \Rightarrow^h_{G'} w$, where $w \in V^*$ and $h \geq 1$. Then,*
$w \in T^*(\{\varepsilon\} \cup \{1^{n-2}00\}(\beta(\Sigma))^*\{1^{n-2}00\})$.

Proof. The claim is proved by induction on $h \geq 1$.

Basis. Let $h = 1$. That is,

$$S \Rightarrow_{G'} 1^{n-2}00\beta(\$)1^{n-2}00 \ [\$ \rightarrow 1^{n-2}00\beta(\$)1^{n-2}00].$$

As

$$1^{n-2}00\beta(S)1^{n-2}00 \in \Delta^*(\{1^{n-2}00\}(\beta(\Sigma))^*\{1^{n-2}00\} \cup \{\varepsilon\}),$$

the basis holds.

Induction Hypothesis. Suppose that for some $k \geq 0$, if $S \Rightarrow^i_{G'} w$, where $i = 1, \ldots, k$ and $w \in \Sigma^*$, then $w \in \Delta^*(\{1^{n-2}00\}(\beta(\Sigma))^*\{1^{n-2}00\} \cup \{\varepsilon\})$.

Induction Step. Consider any derivation of the form

$$S \Rightarrow^{k+1}_{G'} w$$

where $w \in \Sigma^* - \Delta^*$. Express $S \Rightarrow^{k+1}_{G'} w$ as

$$\begin{aligned} S &\Rightarrow^k_{G'} u(\operatorname{lhs} p)v \\ &\Rightarrow_{G'} u(\operatorname{rhs} p)v \ [p] \end{aligned}$$

where $p \in R$ and $w = u(\operatorname{rhs} p)v$. Less formally, after k steps, G' derives $u(\operatorname{lhs} p)v$. Then, by using p, G' replaces $\operatorname{lhs} p$ with $\operatorname{rhs} p$ in $u(\operatorname{lhs} p)v$, so it obtains $u(\operatorname{rhs} p)v$. By the induction hypothesis,

$$u(\operatorname{lhs} p)v \in \Delta^*(\{1^{n-2}00\}(\beta(\Sigma))^*\{1^{n-2}00\} \cup \{\varepsilon\}).$$

As $\operatorname{lhs} p \notin \Delta^*$, $u(\operatorname{lhs} p)v \notin \Delta^*$. Therefore,

$$u(\operatorname{lhs} p)v \in \Delta^*\{1^{n-2}00\}(\beta(\Sigma))^*\{1^{n-2}00\}.$$

Let

$$u(\operatorname{lhs} p)v \in \Delta^*\{1^{n-2}00\}(\beta(\Sigma))^j\{1^{n-2}00\}$$

in G', for some $j \geq 1$. By the definition of R, p satisfies one of the following three properties:

(i) Let $\text{lhs}\, p = \beta(x)$ and $\text{rhs}\, p = \beta(y)$, where $x \to y \in Q$. At this point,

$$u \in \Delta^*\{1^{n-2}00\}\{\beta(\Sigma)\}^r$$

for some $r \geq 0$, and

$$v \in \{\beta(\Sigma)\}^{(j-|\text{lhs}\, p|-r)}\{1^{n-2}00\}.$$

Distinguish between these two cases: $|x| \leq |y|$ and $|x| > |y|$:

(i.a) Let $|x| \leq |y|$. Set $s = |y| - |x|$. Observe that
$u(\text{rhs}\, p)v \in \Delta^*\{1^{n-2}00\}(\beta(\Sigma))^{(j+s)}\{1^{n-2}00\}$
As $w = u(\text{rhs}\, p)v$,
$w \in \Delta^*(\{1^{n-2}00\}(\beta(\Sigma))^*\{1^{n-2}00\} \cup \{\varepsilon\})$;

(i.b) Let $|x| > |y|$. By analogy with 11.1, prove that
$w \in \Delta^*(\{1^{n-2}00\}(\beta(\Sigma))^*\{1^{n-2}00\} \cup \{\varepsilon\})$;

(ii) Assume that $\text{lhs}\, p = 1^{n-2}00\beta(a)$ and $\text{rhs}\, p = a1^{n-2}00$, for some $a \in \Delta$. Notice that

$$u(\text{lhs}\, p)v \in \Delta^*\{1^{n-2}00\}(\beta(\Sigma))^j\{1^{n-2}00\}$$

implies that $u \in \Delta^*$ and

$$v \in (\beta(\Sigma))^{(j-1)}\{1^{n-2}00\}.$$

Then,

$$u(\text{rhs}\, p)v \in \Delta^*\{a\}\{1^{n-2}00\}(\beta(\Sigma))^{(j-1)}\{1^{n-2}00\}.$$

As $w = u(\text{rhs}\, p)v$,

$$w \in \Delta^*(\{1^{n-2}00\}(\beta(\Sigma))^*\{1^{n-2}00\} \cup \{\varepsilon\});$$

(iii) Assume that $\text{lhs}\, p = 1^{n-2}001^{n-2}00$ and $\text{rhs}\, p = \varepsilon$. Then, $j = 0$ in

$$\Delta^*\{1^{n-2}00\}(\beta(\Sigma))^j\{1^{n-2}00\},$$

so

$$u(\text{lhs}\, p)v \in \Delta^*\{1^{n-2}00\}\{1^{n-2}00\}$$

and $u(\text{rhs}\, p)v \in \Delta^*$. As $w = u(\text{rhs}\, p)v$,

$$w \in \Delta^*(\{1^{n-2}00\}(\beta(\Sigma))^*\{1^{n-2}00\} \cup \{\varepsilon\}).$$

□

Claim 2. *Let* $S \Rightarrow^+_{G'} u \Rightarrow^*_{G'} z$, *where* $z \in \Delta^*$. *Then,* $u \in \Delta^*\Pi(1^{n-2}00)^*$.

Proof. Let $S \Rightarrow^+_{G'} u \Rightarrow^*_{G'} z$, where $z \in \Delta^*$. By Claim 1,

$$u \in \Delta^*(\{1^{n-2}00\}(\beta(\Sigma))^*\{1^{n-2}00\} \cup \{\varepsilon\})$$

and by the definition of β, $u \in \Delta^*\Pi(1^{n-2}00)^*$. □

Claim 3. *Let* $\$ \Rightarrow^m_G w$, *for some* $m \geq 0$. *Then,* $S \Rightarrow^+_{G'} 1^{n-2}00\beta(w)1^{n-2}00$.

Proof. The claim is proved by induction on $m \geq 0$.

Basis. Let $m = 0$. That is, $\$ \Rightarrow_G^0 \$$. As

$$S \Rightarrow_{G'} 1^{n-2}00\beta(\$)1^{n-2}00 \; [S \rightarrow 1^{n-2}00\beta(\$)1^{n-2}00],$$

the basis holds.

Induction Hypothesis. Suppose that for some $j \geq 1$, if $\$ \Rightarrow_G^i w$, where $i = 1, \ldots, j$ and $w \in \Sigma^*$, then $S \Rightarrow_{G'}^* \beta(w)$.

Induction Step. Let $\$ \Rightarrow_G^{j+1} w$. Express $\$ \Rightarrow_G^{j+1} w$ as

$$\$ \Rightarrow_G^j uxv \Rightarrow_G uyv \; [x \rightarrow y]$$

where $x \rightarrow y \in Q$ and $w = uyv$. By the induction hypothesis,

$$S \Rightarrow_{G'}^+ 1^{n-2}00\beta(uxv)1^{n-2}00.$$

Express $\beta(uxv)$ as $\beta(uxv) = \beta(u)\beta(x)\beta(v)$. As $x \rightarrow y \in R$, $\beta(x) \rightarrow \beta(y) \in R$. Therefore,

$$\begin{aligned} S &\Rightarrow_{G'}^+ 1^{n-2}00\beta(u)\beta(x)\beta(v)1^{n-2}00 \\ &\Rightarrow_{G'} 1^{n-2}00\beta(u)\beta(y)\beta(v)1^{n-2}00 \; [\beta(x) \rightarrow \beta(y)]. \end{aligned}$$

Because $w = uyv$, $\beta(w) = \beta(u)\beta(y)\beta(v)$, so

$$S \Rightarrow_{G'}^+ 1^{n-2}00\beta(w)1^{n-2}00.$$

□

Claim 4. $L(G) \subseteq L(G')$.

Proof. Let $w \in L(G)$. Thus, $\$ \Rightarrow_G^* w$ with $w \in T^*$. By Claim 3,

$$S \Rightarrow_{G'}^+ 1^{n-2}00\beta(w)1^{n-2}00.$$

Distinguish between these two cases: $w = \varepsilon$ and $w \neq \varepsilon$:

(i) If $w = \varepsilon$, $1^{n-2}00\beta(w)1^{n-2}00 = 1^{n-2}001^{n-2}00$. As $1^{n-2}001^{n-2}00 \rightarrow \varepsilon \in R$,

$$\begin{aligned} S &\Rightarrow_{G'}^* 1^{n-2}001^{n-2}00 \\ &\Rightarrow_{G'} \varepsilon \; [1^{n-2}001^{n-2}00 \rightarrow \varepsilon]. \end{aligned}$$

Thus, $w \in L(G')$.

(ii) Assume that $w \neq \varepsilon$. Express w as $w = a_1a_2 \cdots a_{n-1}a_n$ with $a_i \in \Delta$ for $i = 1, \ldots, n$, $n \geq 0$. Because

$$(\{1^{n-2}00\beta(a) \rightarrow a1^{n-2}00 \mid a \in \Delta\} \cup \{1^{n-2}001^{n-2}00 \rightarrow \varepsilon\}) \subseteq R,$$

there exists

$$\begin{aligned}
S &\Rightarrow_{G'}^{*} 1^{n-2}00\beta(a_1)\beta(a_2)\cdots\beta(a_{n-1})\beta(a_n)1^{n-2}00\\
&\Rightarrow_{G'} a_1 1^{n-2}00\beta(a_2)\cdots\beta(a_{n-1})\beta(a_n)1^{n-2}00\\
&\qquad [1^{n-2}00\beta(a_1) \rightarrow a_1 1^{n-2}00]\\
&\Rightarrow_{G'} a_1a_2 1^{n-2}00\beta(a_3)\cdots\beta(a_{n-1})\beta(a_n)1^{n-2}00\\
&\qquad [1^{n-2}00\beta(a_2) \rightarrow a_2 1^{n-2}00]\\
&\vdots\\
&\Rightarrow_{G'} a_1a_2\cdots a_{n-2}1^{n-2}00\beta(a_{n-1})\beta(a_n)1^{n-2}00\\
&\qquad [1^{n-2}00\beta(a_{n-2}) \rightarrow a_{n-2}1^{n-2}00]\\
&\Rightarrow_{G'} a_1a_2\cdots a_{n-2}a_{n-1}1^{n-2}00\beta(a_n)1^{n-2}00\\
&\qquad [1^{n-2}00\beta(a_{n-1}) \rightarrow a_{n-1}1^{n-2}00]\\
&\Rightarrow_{G'} a_1a_2\cdots a_{n-2}a_{n-1}a_n 1^{n-2}001^{n-2}00\\
&\qquad [1^{n-2}00\beta(a_n) \rightarrow a_n 1^{n-2}00]\\
&\Rightarrow_{G'} a_1a_2\cdots a_{n-2}a_{n-1}a_n\\
&\qquad [1^{n-2}001^{n-2}00 \rightarrow \varepsilon].
\end{aligned}$$

Therefore, $w \in L(G')$. □

Claim 5. *Let* $S \Rightarrow_{G'}^{m} 1^{n-2}00w1^{n-2}00$, *where* $w \in \{0, 1\}^*$, $m \geq 1$. *Also let inverse* β *denote the inverse of* β. *Then,* $\$ \Rightarrow_G^{*}$ inverse $\beta(w)$.

Proof. This claim is proved by induction on $m \geq 1$.

Basis. Let $m = 1$. That is,

$$S \Rightarrow_{G'} 1^{n-2}00w1^{n-2}00$$

where $w \in \{0, 1\}^*$. Then, $w = \beta(\$)$. As $\$ \Rightarrow_G^{0} \$$, the basis holds.

Induction Hypothesis. Suppose that for some $j \geq 1$, if $S \Rightarrow_{G'}^{i} 1^{n-2}00w1^{n-2}00$, where $i = 1, \ldots, j$ and $w \in \{0, 1\}^*$, then $\$ \Rightarrow_G^{+}$ inverse $\beta(w)$.

Induction Step. Let

$$S \Rightarrow_{G'}^{j+1} 1^{n-2}00w1^{n-2}00$$

where $w \in \{0, 1\}^*$. As $w \in \{0, 1\}^*$,

$$S \Rightarrow_{G'}^{j+1} 1^{n-2}00w1^{n-2}00$$

can be expressed as

$$\begin{aligned}
S &\Rightarrow_{G'}^{j} 1^{n-2}00u\beta(x)v1^{n-2}00\\
&\Rightarrow_{G'} 1^{n-2}00u\beta(y)v1^{n02}00 \;\; [\beta(x) \rightarrow \beta(y)]
\end{aligned}$$

where $x, y \in \Sigma^*$, $x \rightarrow y \in Q$, and $w = u\beta(y)v$. By the induction hypothesis,

$$S \Rightarrow_{G'}^{+} 1^{n-2}00 \,\text{inverse}\, \beta(u\beta(x)v)1^{n-2}00.$$

Express inverse $\beta(u\beta(x)v)$ as

$$\text{inverse}\, \beta(u\beta(x)v) = \text{inverse}\, \beta(u)x \,\text{inverse}\, \beta(v).$$

Since $x \to y \in Q$,

$$\begin{aligned} \$ &\Rightarrow_G^+ \text{inverse } \beta(u)x \text{ inverse } \beta(v) \\ &\Rightarrow_G \text{inverse } \beta(u)y \text{ inverse } \beta(v)\ [x \to y]. \end{aligned}$$

Because $w = u\beta(y)v$, inverse $\beta(w)$ = inverse $\beta(u)y$ inverse $\beta(v)$, so

$$\$ \Rightarrow_G^+ \text{inverse } \beta(w).$$ □

Claim 6. $L(G') \subseteq L(G)$.

Proof. Let $w \in L(G')$. Distinguish between $w = \varepsilon$ and $w \neq \varepsilon$.

(i) Let $w = \varepsilon$. Observe that G' derives ε as

$$\begin{aligned} S &\Rightarrow_{G'}^* 1^{n-2}001^{n-2}00 \\ &\Rightarrow_{G'} \varepsilon\ [1^{n-2}001^{n-2}00 \to \varepsilon]. \end{aligned}$$

Because

$$S \Rightarrow_{G'}^* 1^{n-2}001^{n-2}00.$$

Claim 5 implies that $\$ \Rightarrow_G^* \varepsilon$. Therefore, $w \in L(G)$.

(ii) Assume that $w \neq \varepsilon$. Let $w = a_1a_2 \cdots a_{n-1}a_n$ with $a_i \in \Delta$ for $i = 1, \ldots, n$, where $n \geq 1$. Examine R to see that in G', there exists this derivation:

$$\begin{aligned} S &\Rightarrow_{G'}^* 1^{n-2}00\beta(a_1)\beta(a_2) \cdots \beta(a_{n-1})\beta(a_n)1^{n-2}00 \\ &\Rightarrow_{G'} a_1 1^{n-2}00\beta(a_2) \cdots \beta(a_{n-1})\beta(a_n)1^{n-2}00 \\ &\qquad [1^{n-2}00\beta(a_1) \to a_1 1^{n-2}00] \\ &\Rightarrow_{G'} a_1a_2 1^{n-2}00\beta(a_3) \cdots \beta(a_{n-1})\beta(a_n)1^{n-2}00 \\ &\qquad [1^{n-2}00\beta(a_2) \to a_2 1^{n-2}00] \\ &\ \ \vdots \\ &\Rightarrow_{G'} a_1a_2 \cdots a_{n-2}1^{n-2}00\beta(a_{n-1})\beta(a_n)1^{n-2}00 \\ &\qquad [1^{n-2}00\beta(a_{n-2}) \to a_{n-2}1^{n-2}00] \\ &\Rightarrow_{G'} a_1a_2 \cdots a_{n-2}a_{n-1}1^{n-2}00\beta(a_n)1^{n-2}00 \\ &\qquad [1^{n-2}00\beta(a_{n-1}) \to a_{n-1}1^{n-2}00] \\ &\Rightarrow_{G'} a_1a_2 \cdots a_{n-2}a_{n-1}a_n 1^{n-2}001^{n-2}00 \\ &\qquad [1^{n-2}00\beta(a_n) \to a_n 1^{n-2}00] \\ &\Rightarrow_{G'} a_1a_2 \cdots a_{n-2}a_{n-1}a_n \\ &\qquad [1^{n-2}001^{n-2}00 \to \varepsilon]. \end{aligned}$$

Because

$$S \Rightarrow_{G'}^* 1^{n-2}00\beta(a_1)\beta(a_2) \cdots \beta(a_{n-1})\beta(a_n)1^{n-2}00.$$

Claim 5 implies that

$$\$ \Rightarrow_G^* a_1a_2 \cdots a_{n-1}a_n.$$

Hence, $w \in L(G)$. □

By Claims 4 and 6, $L(G) = L(G')$. By Claim 2, $F(G') \subseteq \Delta^*\Pi(1^{n-2}00)^*$. Thus, Lemma 11.1 holds. ■

Theorem 11.14. PS[.2] = RE

Proof. The inclusion **PS**[.2] $\subseteq$ **RE** follows from Turing–Church thesis. The inclusion **RE** $\subseteq$ **PS**[.2] follows from Lemma 11.1. Therefore, the theorem holds. ■

Lemma 11.2. *Let G be a PSG. Then, there exists a PSG* $G' = (\{S, 0, 1\} \cup \Delta, \Delta, R, S)$ *satisfying* $L(G) = L(G')$ *and* $F(G') \subseteq \Pi(1^{n-2}00)^*\Delta^*$*, for some* $n \geq 1$.

Proof. Let $G = (\Sigma, \Delta, Q, \$)$ be a PSG, where Σ is the total alphabet of G, Δ is the terminal alphabet of G, Q is the set of rules of G, and \$ is the start symbol of G. Without any loss of generality, assume that $\Sigma \cap \{0, 1\} = \emptyset$. The following construction produces an equivalent PSG

$$G' = (\{S, 0, 1\} \cup \Delta, \Delta, R, S)$$

such that $F(G') \subseteq \Pi(1^{n-2}00)^*\Delta^*$, for some $n \geq 1$.

For some $m \geq 3$ and n such that $2m = n$, introduce an injective homomorphism β from Σ to

$$(\{1\}^m\{1\}^*\{0\}\{1\}^*\{0\} \cap \{0, 1\}^n) - \{1^{n-2}00\}.$$

Extend the domain of β to Σ^*. Define the PSG

$$G' = (\Delta \cup \{S, 0, 1\}, \Delta, R, S)$$

with

$$\begin{aligned} R = {} & \{S \to 1^{n-2}00\beta(\$)1^{n-2}00\} \cup \\ & \{\beta(x) \to \beta(y) \mid x \to y \in Q\} \cup \\ & \{\beta(a)1^{n-2}00 \to 1^{n-2}00a \mid a \in \Delta\} \cup \\ & \{1^{n-2}001^{n-2}00 \to \varepsilon\}. \end{aligned}$$

Complete this proof by analogy with the proof of Lemma 11.1. ■

Theorem 11.15. PS[2.] = RE.

Proof. Clearly, **PS**[2.] $\subseteq$ **RE**. By Lemma 11.2, **RE** $\subseteq$ **PS**[2.]. Therefore, this theorem holds. ■

Corollary 11.2. PS[.2] = PS[2.] = RE.

There is an open problem area related to the results shown previously.

Open Problem 11.1. *Recall that in this section, we converted any PSG G to an equivalent PSG,* $G' = (\Sigma, \Delta, R, S)$*, so that for every* $x \in F(G')$, $x \in \Delta^*\Pi(w)^*$*, where w is a string over* $\Sigma - \Delta$*. Then, we made this conversion so that for every* $x \in F(G')$, $x \in \Pi(w)^*\Delta^*$*. Take into account the length of w. More precisely, for* $j, k \geq 1$ *set*

$$\mathbf{PS}[j, k] = \{L \mid L = L(G), \text{ where } G = (\Sigma, \Delta, R, S) \text{ is a PSG such that card } (\text{symbols}(F(G)) - \Delta) = j \text{ and } F(G) \subseteq \Delta^*\Pi(w)^*, \text{ where } w \in (\Sigma - \Delta)^* \text{ and } |w| = k\}.$$

Analogously, set

$$\mathbf{PS}[j,k.] = \{L \mid L = L(G), \text{ where } G = (\Sigma, \Delta, R, S) \text{ is a PSG such that card (symbols}(F(G)) - \Delta) = j \text{ and } F(G) \subseteq \Pi(w)^*\Delta^*, \text{ where } w \in (\Sigma - \Delta)^* \text{ and } |w| = k\}.$$

Reconsider this section in terms of these families of languages.

11.2 Loosely context-dependent grammars

Context-conditional grammars are based on context-free rules, each of which may be extended by finitely many *permitting* and *forbidding strings*. A rule like this can rewrite a sentential form on the condition that all its permitting strings occur in the current sentential form while none of its forbidding strings occur there.

This section first defines context-conditional grammars and, after that, it establishes their generative power.

Definitions

Without further ado, we define the basic versions of context-regulated grammars.

Definition 11.10. *A* context-conditional grammar *is a quadruple*

$$G = (\Sigma, \Delta, R, S)$$

where Σ, Δ, *and* S *are the* total alphabet, *the* terminal alphabet *(*$\Delta \subset \Sigma$*), and the* start symbol *(*$S \in \Sigma - \Delta$*), respectively.* P *is a finite set of* rules *of the form*

$$(A \to x, Per, For)$$

where $A \in \Sigma - \Delta$, $x \in \Sigma^*$, *and* $Per, For \subseteq \Sigma^+$ *are two finite sets. If* $Per \neq \emptyset$ *or* $For \neq \emptyset$, *the rule is said to be* conditional; *otherwise, it is called* context-free. G *has* degree (r, s), *where* r *and* s *are natural numbers, if for every* $(A \to x, Per, For) \in R$, max-len$(Per) \leq r$ *and* max-len$(For) \leq s$. *If* $(A \to x, Per, For) \in R$ *implies that* $x \neq \varepsilon$, G *is said to be* propagating. *Let* $u, v \in \Sigma^*$ *and* $(A \to x, Per, For) \in R$. *Then,* u directly derives v *according to* $(A \to x, Per, For)$ *in* G, *denoted by*

$$u \Rightarrow_G v\ [(A \to x, Per, For)],$$

provided that for some $u_1, u_2 \in \Sigma^*$, *the following conditions hold:*

(a) $u = u_1Au_2$,
(b) $v = u_1xu_2$,
(c) $Per \subseteq$ substrings(u), *and*
(d) $For \cap$ substrings$(u) = \emptyset$.

When no confusion exists, we simply write

$$u \Rightarrow_G v$$

instead of

$$u \Rightarrow_G v \, [(A \rightarrow x, Per, For)].$$

By analogy with CFGs, we extend $\Rightarrow_G$ *to* $\Rightarrow_G^k$ *(where* $k \geq 0$*),* $\Rightarrow_G^+$*, and* $\Rightarrow_G^*$*. The* language *of G, denoted by L(G), is defined as*

$$L(G) = \{w \in \Delta^* \mid S \Rightarrow_G^* w\}.$$

The families of languages generated by context-conditional grammars and propagating context-conditional grammars of degree (r, s) are denoted by $\mathbf{CG}(r, s)$ and $\mathbf{CG}^{-\varepsilon}(r, s)$, respectively. Furthermore, set

$$\mathbf{CG} = \bigcup_{r=0}^{\infty} \bigcup_{s=0}^{\infty} \mathbf{CG}(r, s)$$

and

$$\mathbf{CG}^{-\varepsilon} = \bigcup_{r=0}^{\infty} \bigcup_{s=0}^{\infty} \mathbf{CG}^{-\varepsilon}(r, s).$$

Generative power

Next, we prove several theorems concerning the generative power of the general versions of context-conditional grammars. Let us point out, however, that Sections 11.2–11.2 establish many more results about special cases of these grammars.

Theorem 11.16. $\mathbf{CG}^{-\varepsilon}(0, 0) = \mathbf{CG}(0, 0) = \mathbf{CF}$.

Proof. This theorem follows immediately from the definition. Clearly, context-conditional grammars of degree $(0, 0)$ are ordinary CFGs. ■

Lemma 11.3. $\mathbf{CG}^{-\varepsilon} \subseteq \mathbf{CS}$.

Proof. Let $r = s = 0$. Then, $\mathbf{CG}^{-\varepsilon}(0, 0) = \mathbf{CF} \subset \mathbf{CS}$. The rest of the proof establishes the inclusion for degrees (r, s) such that $r + s > 0$.

Consider a propagating context-conditional grammar

$$G = (\Sigma, \Delta, R, S)$$

of degree (r, s), where $r + s > 0$, for some $r, s \geq 0$. Let k be the greater number of r and s. Set

$$M = \{x \in \Sigma^+ \mid |x| \leq k\}.$$

Next, define

$$\text{cf-rules}\,(P) = \{A \rightarrow x \mid (A \rightarrow x, Per, For) \in R, \ A \in (\Sigma - \Delta), \ x \in \Sigma^+\}.$$

Then, set

$$\begin{aligned} N_F &= \{\lfloor X, x \rfloor \mid X \subseteq M,\ x \in M \cup \{\varepsilon\}\}, \\ N_T &= \{\langle X \rangle \mid X \subseteq M\}, \\ N_B &= \{\lceil p \rceil \mid p \in \text{cf-rules}\,(P)\} \cup \{\lceil \emptyset \rceil\}, \\ \Sigma' &= \Sigma \cup N_F \cup N_T \cup N_B \cup \{\rhd, \lhd, \$, S', \#\}, \\ \Delta' &= \Delta \cup \{\#\}. \end{aligned}$$

Construct the CSG

$$G' = (\Sigma', \Delta', R', S')$$

with the finite set of rules R' defined as follows:

(1) add $S' \to \rhd\lfloor \emptyset, \varepsilon \rfloor S \lhd$ to R';

(2) for all $X \subseteq M, x \in (\Sigma^k \cup \{\varepsilon\})$ and $y \in \Sigma^k$, extend R' by adding

$\lfloor X, x \rfloor y \to y \lfloor X \cup \text{substrings}(xy, k), y \rfloor$;

(3) for all $X \subseteq M, x \in (\Sigma^k \cup \{\varepsilon\})$ and $y \in \Sigma^+$, $|y| \leq k$, extend R' by adding

$\lfloor X, x \rfloor y \lhd \to y \langle X \cup \text{substrings}(xy, k) \rangle \lhd$;

(4) for all $X \subseteq M$ and every $p = A \to x \in \text{cf-rules}\,(R)$ such that there exists $(A \to x, Per, For) \in R$ satisfying $Per \subseteq X$ and $For \cap X = \emptyset$, extend R' by adding

$\langle X \rangle \lhd \to \lceil p \rceil \lhd$;

(5) for every $p \in \text{cf-rules}\,(R)$ and $a \in \Sigma$, extend R' by adding
$a \lceil p \rceil \to \lceil p \rceil a$;

(6) for every $p = A \to x \in \text{cf-rules}\,(R)$, $A \in (\Sigma - \Delta)$, $x \in \Sigma^+$, extend R' by adding

$A \lceil p \rceil \to \lceil \emptyset \rceil x$;

(7) for every $a \in \Sigma$, extend R' by adding

$a \lceil \emptyset \rceil \to \lceil \emptyset \rceil a$;

(8) add $\rhd \lceil \emptyset \rceil \to \rhd \lfloor \emptyset, \varepsilon \rfloor$ to R';

(9) add $\rhd \lfloor \emptyset, \varepsilon \rfloor \to \#\$$, $\$\lhd \to \#\#$, and $\$a \to a\$$, for all $a \in \Delta$, to R'.

Claim 1. *Every successful derivation in G' has the form*

$$\begin{aligned} S' &\Rightarrow_{G'} \rhd\lfloor \emptyset, \varepsilon \rfloor S \lhd \\ &\Rightarrow_{G'}^{+} \rhd\lfloor \emptyset, \varepsilon \rfloor x \lhd \\ &\Rightarrow_{G'} \#\$x\lhd \\ &\Rightarrow_{G'}^{|x|} \#x\$\lhd \\ &\Rightarrow_{G'} \#x\#\# \end{aligned}$$

such that $x \in \Delta^+$, and during

$$\rhd\lfloor \emptyset, \varepsilon \rfloor S \lhd \Rightarrow_{G'}^{+} \rhd\lfloor \emptyset, \varepsilon \rfloor x \lhd,$$

every sentential form w satisfies $w \in \{\rhd\}H^+\{\lhd\}$, where $H \subseteq \Sigma' - \{\rhd, \lhd, \#, \$, S'\}$.

Proof. Observe that the only rule that rewrites S' is $S' \to \rhd\lfloor\emptyset, \varepsilon\rfloor S\lhd$; thus,

$$S' \Rightarrow_{G'} \rhd\lfloor\emptyset, \varepsilon\rfloor S\lhd.$$

After that, every sentential form that occurs in

$$\rhd\lfloor\emptyset, \varepsilon\rfloor S\lhd \Rightarrow_{G'}^{+} \rhd\lfloor\emptyset, \varepsilon\rfloor x\lhd$$

can be rewritten by using any of the rules (2)–(8) from the construction of R'. By the inspection of these rules, it is obvious that the delimiting symbols $\rhd$ and $\lhd$ remain unchanged and no other occurrences of them appear inside the sentential form. Moreover, there is no rule generating a symbol from $\{\#, \$, S'\}$. Therefore, all these sentential forms belong to $\{\rhd\}H^{+}\{\lhd\}$.

Next, let us explain how G' generates a string from $L(G')$. Only $\rhd\lfloor\emptyset, \varepsilon\rfloor \to \#\$$ can rewrite $\rhd$ to a symbol from Δ (see (9) in the definition of R'). According to the left-hand side of this rule, we obtain

$$S' \Rightarrow_{G'} \rhd\lfloor\emptyset, \varepsilon\rfloor S\lhd \Rightarrow_{G'}^{*} \rhd\lfloor\emptyset, \varepsilon\rfloor x\lhd \Rightarrow_{G'} \#\$x\lhd$$

where $x \in H^{+}$. To rewrite $\lhd$, G' uses $\$\lhd \to \#\#$. Thus, G' needs $\$$ as the left neighbor of $\lhd$. Suppose that $x = a_1 a_2 \cdots a_q$, where $q = |x|$ and $a_i \in \Delta$, for all $i \in \{1, \ldots, q\}$. Since for every $a \in \Delta$ there is $\$a \to a\$ \in R'$ (see (9)), we can construct

$$\begin{aligned} \#\$a_1 a_2 \cdots a_n\lhd &\Rightarrow_{G'} \#a_1\$a_2 \cdots a_n\lhd \\ &\Rightarrow_{G'} \#a_1 a_2\$ \cdots a_n\lhd \\ &\Rightarrow_{G'}^{|x|-2} \#a_1 a_2 \cdots a_n\$\lhd. \end{aligned}$$

Notice that this derivation can be constructed only for x that belong to Δ^{+}. Then, $\$\lhd$ is rewritten to $\#\#$. As a result,

$$S' \Rightarrow_{G'} \rhd\lfloor\emptyset, \varepsilon\rfloor S\lhd \Rightarrow_{G'}^{+} \rhd\lfloor\emptyset, \varepsilon\rfloor x\lhd \Rightarrow_{G'} \#\$x\lhd \to_{G'}^{|x|} \#x\$\lhd \to_{G'} \#x\#\#$$

with the required properties. Thus, the claim holds. □

The following claim demonstrates how G' simulates a direct derivation from G—the heart of the construction.

Let $x \Rightarrow_{G'}^{\oplus} y$ denote the derivation $x \Rightarrow_{G'}^{+} y$ such that

$$x = \rhd\lfloor\emptyset, \varepsilon\rfloor u\lhd,\ y = \rhd\lfloor\emptyset, \varepsilon\rfloor v\lhd$$

for some $u, v \in \Sigma^{+}$, and during $x \Rightarrow_{G'}^{+} y$, there is no other occurrence of a string of the form $\rhd\lfloor\emptyset, \varepsilon\rfloor z\lhd$, $z \in \Sigma^{*}$.

Claim 2. *For every $u, v \in \Sigma^{*}$, it holds that*

$$\rhd\lfloor\emptyset, \varepsilon\rfloor u\lhd \Rightarrow_{G'}^{\oplus} \rhd\lfloor\emptyset, \varepsilon\rfloor v\lhd \quad \textit{if and only if} \quad u \Rightarrow_G v.$$

Proof. The proof is divided into the only-if part and the if part.

Only If. Let us show how G' rewrites $\triangleright\lfloor\emptyset,\varepsilon\rfloor u\triangleleft$ to $\triangleright\lfloor\emptyset,\varepsilon\rfloor v\triangleleft$. The simulation consists of two phases.

During the first, forward phase, G' scans u to get all nonempty substrings of length k or less. By repeatedly using rules $\lfloor X,x\rfloor y\rightarrow y\lfloor X\cup \text{substrings}\,(xy,k),y\rfloor$, $X\subseteq M$, $x\in(\Sigma^k\cup\{\varepsilon\})$, $y\in\Sigma^k$ (see (2) in the definition of R'), the occurrence of a symbol of the form $\lfloor X,x\rfloor$ is moved toward the end of the sentential form. Simultaneously, the substrings of u are recorded in X. The forward phase is finished by applying $\lfloor X,x\rfloor y\triangleleft\rightarrow y\langle X\cup\text{substrings}\,(xy,k)\rangle\triangleleft$, $x\in(\Sigma^k\cup\{\varepsilon\})$, $y\in\Sigma^+$, $|y|\leq k$ (see (3)); this rule reaches the end of u and completes $X=\text{substrings}\,(u,k)$. Formally,

$$\triangleright\lfloor\emptyset,\varepsilon\rfloor u\triangleleft\ \Rightarrow^+_{G'}\ \triangleright u\langle X\rangle\triangleleft$$

with $X=\text{substrings}\,(u,k)$.

The second, backward phase simulates the application of a conditional rule. Assume that $u=u_1Au_2$, $u_1,u_2\in\Sigma^*$, $A\in(\Sigma-\Delta)$, and there exists a rule $A\rightarrow x\in$ cf-rules(R) such that $(A\rightarrow x, Per, For)\in R$ for some $Per, For\subseteq M$, where $Per\subseteq X$, $For\cap X=\emptyset$. Let $u_1xu_2=v$. Then, G' derives

$$\triangleright u\langle X\rangle\triangleleft\Rightarrow^+_{G'}\triangleright\lfloor\emptyset,\varepsilon\rfloor v\triangleleft$$

by performing the following five steps:

(i) $\langle X\rangle$ is changed to $\lceil p\rceil$, where $p=A\rightarrow x$ satisfies the conditions previous (see (4) in the definition of R');
(ii) $\triangleright u_1Au_2\lceil p\rceil\triangleleft$ is rewritten to $\triangleright u_1A\lceil p\rceil u_2\triangleleft$ by using the rules of the form $a\lceil p\rceil\rightarrow\lceil p\rceil a$, $a\in V$ (see (5));
(iii) $\triangleright u_1A\lceil p\rceil u_2\triangleleft$ is rewritten to $\triangleright u_1\lceil\emptyset\rceil xu_2\triangleleft$ by using $A\lceil p\rceil\rightarrow\lceil\emptyset\rceil x$ (see (6));
(iv) $\triangleright u_1\lceil\emptyset\rceil xu_2\triangleleft$ is rewritten to $\triangleright\lceil\emptyset\rceil u_1xu_2\triangleleft$ by using the rules of the form $a\lceil\emptyset\rceil\rightarrow\lceil\emptyset\rceil a$, $a\in V$ (see (7));
(v) Finally, $\triangleright\lceil\emptyset\rceil$ is rewritten to $\triangleright\lfloor\emptyset,\varepsilon\rfloor$ by $\triangleright\lceil\emptyset\rceil\rightarrow\triangleright\lfloor\emptyset,\varepsilon\rfloor$.

As a result, we obtain

$$\begin{aligned}\triangleright\lfloor\emptyset,\varepsilon\rfloor u\triangleleft &\Rightarrow^+_{G'}\triangleright u\langle X\rangle\triangleleft\Rightarrow_{G'}\triangleright u\lceil p\rceil\triangleleft\\ &\Rightarrow^{|u|}_{G'}\triangleright\lceil\emptyset\rceil v\triangleleft\Rightarrow_{G'}\triangleright\lfloor\emptyset,\varepsilon\rfloor v\triangleleft.\end{aligned}$$

Observe that this is the only way of deriving

$$\triangleright\lfloor\emptyset,\varepsilon\rfloor u\triangleleft\Rightarrow^\oplus_{G'}\triangleright\lfloor\emptyset,\varepsilon\rfloor v\triangleleft.$$

Let us show that $u\Rightarrow_G v$. Indeed, the application of $A\lceil p\rceil\rightarrow\lceil\emptyset\rceil x$ implies that there exists $(A\rightarrow x, Per, For)\in R$, where $Per\subseteq\text{substrings}\,(u,k)$ and $For\cap\text{substrings}\,(u,k)=\emptyset$. Hence, there exists a derivation of the form

$$u\Rightarrow_G v\ [p]$$

where $u=u_1Au_2$, $v=u_1xu_2$ and $p=(A\rightarrow x, Per, For)\in R$.

If. The converse implication is similar to the only-if part, so we leave it to the reader.

□

Claim 3. $S' \Rightarrow_{G'}^{+} \triangleright\lfloor\emptyset, \varepsilon\rfloor x\triangleleft$ *if and only if* $S \Rightarrow_G^{*} x$, *for all* $x \in \Sigma^+$.

Proof. The proof is divided into the only-if part and the if part.

Only If. The only-if part is proved by induction on the ith occurrence of the sentential form w satisfying $w = \triangleright\lfloor\emptyset, \varepsilon\rfloor u\triangleleft$, $u \in \Sigma^+$ during the derivation in G'.

Basis. Let $i = 1$. Then, $S' \Rightarrow_{G'} \triangleright\lfloor\emptyset, \varepsilon\rfloor S\triangleleft$ and $S \Rightarrow_G^{0} S$.

Induction Hypothesis. Suppose that the claim holds for all $i \leq h$, for some $h \geq 1$.

Induction Step. Let $i = h + 1$. Since $h + 1 \geq 2$, we can express

$$S' \Rightarrow_{G'}^{+} \triangleright\lfloor\emptyset, \varepsilon\rfloor x_i\triangleleft$$

as

$$S' \Rightarrow_{G'}^{+} \triangleright\lfloor\emptyset, \varepsilon\rfloor x_{i-1}\triangleleft \Rightarrow_{G'}^{\oplus} \triangleright\lfloor\emptyset, \varepsilon\rfloor x_i\triangleleft$$

where $x_{i-1}, x_i \in \Sigma^+$. By the induction hypothesis,

$$S \Rightarrow_G^{*} x_{i-1}.$$

Claim 2 says that

$$\triangleright\lfloor\emptyset, \varepsilon\rfloor x_{i-1}\triangleleft \Rightarrow_{G'}^{\oplus} \triangleright\lfloor\emptyset, \varepsilon\rfloor x_i\triangleleft \quad \text{if and only if} \quad x_{i-1} \Rightarrow_G x_i.$$

Hence,

$$S \Rightarrow_G^{*} x_{i-1} \Rightarrow_G x_i$$

and the only-if part holds.

If. By induction on m, we prove that

$$S \Rightarrow_G^{m} x \text{ implies that } S' \Rightarrow_{G'}^{+} \triangleright\lfloor\emptyset, \varepsilon\rfloor x\triangleleft$$

for all $m \geq 0$, $x \in \Sigma^+$.

Basis. For $m = 0$, $S \Rightarrow_G^{0} S$ and $S' \Rightarrow_{G'} \triangleright\lfloor\emptyset, \varepsilon\rfloor S\triangleleft$.

Induction Hypothesis. Assume that the claim holds for all $m \leq n$, for some $n \geq 0$.

Induction Step. Let

$$S \Rightarrow_G^{n+1} x$$

with $x \in \Sigma^+$. Because $n + 1 \geq 1$, there exists $y \in \Sigma^+$ such that

$$S \Rightarrow_G^{n} y \Rightarrow_G x.$$

By the induction hypothesis, there is also a derivation

$$S' \Rightarrow_{G'}^{+} \triangleright\lfloor\emptyset, \varepsilon\rfloor y\triangleleft.$$

From Claim 2, it follows that

$$\triangleright\lfloor\emptyset, \varepsilon\rfloor y\triangleleft \Rightarrow_{G'}^{\oplus} \triangleright\lfloor\emptyset, \varepsilon\rfloor x\triangleleft.$$

Therefore,

$$S' \Rightarrow_{G'}^{+} \rhd\lfloor\emptyset, \varepsilon\rfloor x\lhd$$

and the converse implication holds as well. □

From Claims 1 and 3, we see that any successful derivation in G' is of the form

$$S' \Rightarrow_{G'}^{+} \rhd\lfloor\emptyset, \varepsilon\rfloor x\lhd \Rightarrow_{G'}^{+} \#x\#\#$$

such that

$$S \Rightarrow_{G}^{*} x, \; x \in \Delta^{+}.$$

Therefore, for each $x \in \Delta^{+}$,

$$S' \Rightarrow_{G'}^{+} \#x\#\# \quad \text{if and only if} \quad S \Rightarrow_{G}^{*} x.$$

Define the homomorphism h over $(\Delta \cup \{\#\})^{*}$ as $h(\#) = \varepsilon$ and $h(a) = a$ for all $a \in \Delta$. Observe that h is 4-linear erasing with respect to $L(G')$. Furthermore, notice that $h(L(G')) = L(G)$. Because **CS** is closed under linear erasing (see Theorem 10.4 on page 98 in [11]), $L \in$ **CS**. Thus, Lemma 11.3 holds. ■

Theorem 11.17. $\mathbf{CG}^{-\varepsilon} = \mathbf{CS}$.

Proof. By Lemma 11.3, we have $\mathbf{CG}^{-\varepsilon} \subseteq \mathbf{CS}$. $\mathbf{CS} \subseteq \mathbf{CG}^{-\varepsilon}$ holds as well. In fact, later in this book, we introduce several special cases of propagating context-conditional grammars and prove that even these grammars generate **CS** (see Theorems 11.32 and 11.34). As a result, $\mathbf{CG}^{-\varepsilon} = \mathbf{CS}$. ■

Lemma 11.4. $\mathbf{CG} \subseteq \mathbf{RE}$.

Proof. This lemma follows from Turing–Church thesis. To obtain an algorithm converting any context-conditional grammar to an equivalent PSG, use the technique presented in Lemma 11.3. ■

Theorem 11.18. $\mathbf{CG} = \mathbf{RE}$.

Proof. By Lemma 11.4, $\mathbf{CG} \subseteq \mathbf{RE}$. Later on, we define some special cases of context-conditional grammars and demonstrate that they characterize **RE** (see Theorems 11.24, 11.33, and 11.35). Thus, $\mathbf{RE} \subseteq \mathbf{CG}$. ■

Random-context grammars

This section discusses three special cases of context-conditional grammars whose conditions are nonterminal symbols, so their degree is not greater than $(1, 1)$. Specifically, *permitting grammars* are of degree $(1, 0)$. *Forbidding grammars* are of degree $(0, 1)$. Finally, *random context grammars* are of degree $(1, 1)$.

The present section, first, provides definitions and illustrates all the grammars under discussion and, then, it establishes their generative power.

Definitions and examples

We open this section by defining random context grammars and their two important special cases—permitting and forbidding grammars. Later in this section, we illustrate them.

Definition 11.11. *Let $G = (\Sigma, \Delta, R, S)$ be a context-conditional grammar. G is called a* random context grammar *provided that every $(A \rightarrow x, Per, For) \in R$ satisfies $Per \subseteq N$ and $For \subseteq N$.*

Definition 11.12. *Let $G = (\Sigma, \Delta, R, S)$ be a random context grammar. G is called a* permitting grammar *provided that every $(A \rightarrow x, Per, For) \in R$ satisfies $For = \emptyset$.*

Definition 11.13. *Let $G = (\Sigma, \Delta, R, S)$ be a random context grammar. G is called a* forbidding grammar *provided that every $(A \rightarrow x, Per, For) \in R$ satisfies $Per = \emptyset$.*

The following conventions simplify rules in permitting and forbidding grammars.

Let $G = (\Sigma, \Delta, R, S)$ be a permitting grammar, and let $p = (A \rightarrow x, Per, For) \in R$. Since $For = \emptyset$, we usually omit the empty set of forbidding conditions. That is, we write $(A \rightarrow x, Per)$ when no confusion arises.

Let $G = (V, T, P, S)$ be a forbidding grammar, and let $p = (A \rightarrow x, Per, For) \in R$. We write $(A \rightarrow x, For)$ instead of $(A \rightarrow x, Per, For)$ because $Per = \emptyset$ for all $p \in R$.

The families of languages defined by permitting grammars, forbidding grammars, and random context grammars are denoted by **Per**, **For**, and **RC**, respectively. To indicate that only propagating grammars are considered, we use the upper index $-\varepsilon$. That is, $\mathbf{Per}^{-\varepsilon}$, $\mathbf{For}^{-\varepsilon}$, and $\mathbf{RC}^{-\varepsilon}$ denote the families of languages defined by propagating permitting grammars, propagating forbidding grammars, and propagating random context grammars, respectively.

Example 11.1 (see [12]). *Let*

$$G = (\{S, A, B, C, D, A', B', C', a, b, c\}, \{a, b, c\}, R, S)$$

be a permitting grammar, where R is defined as follows:

$$\begin{aligned} R = \{&(S \rightarrow ABC, \emptyset), \\ &(A \rightarrow aA', \{B\}), \\ &(B \rightarrow bB', \{C\}), \\ &(C \rightarrow cC', \{A'\}), \\ &(A' \rightarrow A, \{B'\}), \\ &(B' \rightarrow B, \{C'\}), \\ &(C' \rightarrow C, \{A\}), \\ &(A \rightarrow a, \{B\}), \\ &(B \rightarrow b, \{C\}), \\ &(C \rightarrow c, \emptyset)\}. \end{aligned}$$

Consider the string aabbcc. G generates this string in the following way:

$$\begin{aligned} S &\Rightarrow ABC \Rightarrow aA'BC \Rightarrow aA'bB'C \Rightarrow aA'bB'cC' \Rightarrow \\ &aAbB'cC' \Rightarrow aAbBcC' \Rightarrow aAbBcC \Rightarrow \\ &aabBcC \Rightarrow aabbcC \Rightarrow aabbcc. \end{aligned}$$

Observe that G is propagating and

$$L(G) = \{a^n b^n c^n \mid n \geq 1\}$$

which is a non-context-free language.

Example 11.2 (see [12]). *Let*

$$G = (\{S, A, B, D, a\}, \{a\}, R, S)$$

be a random-context grammar. The set of rules R is defined as follows:

$$\begin{aligned} P = \{&(S \rightarrow AA, \emptyset, \{B, D\}),\\ &(A \rightarrow B, \emptyset, \{S, D\}),\\ &(B \rightarrow S, \emptyset, \{A, D\}),\\ &(A \rightarrow D, \emptyset, \{S, B\}),\\ &(D \rightarrow a, \emptyset, \{S, A, B\})\}. \end{aligned}$$

Notice that G is a propagating forbidding grammar. For aaaaaaaa, G makes the following derivation:

$$\begin{aligned} S &\Rightarrow AA \Rightarrow AB \Rightarrow BB \Rightarrow BS \Rightarrow SS \Rightarrow AAS \Rightarrow AAAA \Rightarrow BAAA \Rightarrow \\ &BABA \Rightarrow BBBA \Rightarrow BBBB \Rightarrow SBBB \Rightarrow SSBB \Rightarrow SSSB \Rightarrow \\ &SSSS \Rightarrow AASSS \Rightarrow^3 AAAAAAAA \Rightarrow^8 DDDDDDDD \Rightarrow^8 aaaaaaaa. \end{aligned}$$

Clearly, G generates this non-context-free language

$$L(G) = \left\{a^{2^n} \mid n \geq 1\right\}.$$

Generative power

We next establish several theorems concerning the generative power of the grammars defined in the previous section.

Theorem 11.19. $\mathbf{CF} \subset \mathbf{Per}^{-\varepsilon} \subset \mathbf{RC}^{-\varepsilon} \subset \mathbf{CS}$.

Proof. $\mathbf{CF} \subset \mathbf{Per}^{-\varepsilon}$ follows from Example 11.1. $\mathbf{Per}^{-\varepsilon} \subset \mathbf{RC}^{-\varepsilon}$ follows from Theorem 2.7 in Chapter 3 in [13]. Finally, $\mathbf{RC}^{-\varepsilon} \subset \mathbf{CS}$ follows from Theorems 1.2.4 and 1.4.5 in [12]. ■

Theorem 11.20. $\mathbf{Per}^{-\varepsilon} = \mathbf{Per} \subset \mathbf{RC} = \mathbf{RE}$.

Proof. $\mathbf{Per}^{-\varepsilon} = \mathbf{Per}$ follows from Theorem 1 in [14]. By Theorem 1.2.5 in [12], $\mathbf{RC} = \mathbf{RE}$. Furthermore, from Theorem 3.7 in Chapter 3 in [13], it follows that $\mathbf{Per} \subset \mathbf{RC}$; thus, the theorem holds. ■

Lemma 11.5. $\mathbf{ET0L} \subset \mathbf{For}^{-\varepsilon}$.

Proof. (See [15].) Let $L \in \mathbf{ET0L}$, $L = L(G)$ for some ET0L grammar,

$$G = (\Sigma, \Delta, R_1, \ldots, R_t, S).$$

Without loss of generality, we assume that G is propagating (see Theorem 4.2). We introduce the alphabets

$$\begin{aligned}
\Sigma^{(i)} &= \{a^{(i)} \mid a \in \Sigma\},\ 1 \le i \le t,\\
\Sigma' &= \{a' \mid a \in \Sigma\},\\
\Sigma'' &= \{a'' \mid a \in \Sigma\},\\
\bar{\Sigma} &= \{\bar{a} \mid a \in \Delta\}.
\end{aligned}$$

For $w \in \Sigma^*$, by $w^{(i)}$, w', w'', and $\bar{w}$, we denote the strings obtained from w by replacing each occurrence of a symbol $a \in \Sigma$ by $a^{(i)}$, a', a'', and $\bar{a}$, respectively. Let R' be the set of all random context rules defined as follows:

(1) For every $a \in \Sigma$, add $(a' \to a'', \emptyset, \bar{\Sigma} \cup \Sigma^{(1)} \cup \Sigma^{(2)} \cup \cdots \cup \Sigma^{(t)})$ to R';
(2) For every $a \in \Sigma$ for all $1 \le i \le t$, add

$$(a'' \to a^{(i)}, \emptyset, \bar{\Sigma} \cup \Sigma' \cup \Sigma^{(1)} \cup \Sigma^{(2)} \cup \cdots \cup \Sigma^{(i-1)} \cup \Sigma^{(i+1)} \cup \cdots \cup \Sigma^{(t)})$$

to R';
(3) For all $i \in \{1, \dots, t\}$ for every $a \to u \in R_i$, add $(a^{(i)} \to u', \emptyset, \Sigma'' \cup \bar{\Sigma})$ to R';
(4) For all $a \in \Delta$, add $(a' \to \bar{a}, \emptyset, \Sigma'' \cup \Sigma^{(1)} \cup \Sigma^{(2)} \cup \cdots \cup \Sigma^{(t)})$ to R';
(5) For all $a \in \Delta$, add $(\bar{a} \to a, \emptyset, \Sigma' \cup \Sigma'' \cup \Sigma^{(1)} \cup \Sigma^{(2)} \cup \cdots \cup \Sigma^{(t)})$ to R'.

Then, define the random context grammar

$$G' = (\Sigma' \cup \Sigma'' \cup \bar{\Sigma} \cup \Sigma^{(1)} \cup \Sigma^{(2)} \cup \cdots \cup \Sigma^{(t)}, \Delta, R', S)$$

that has only forbidding context conditions.

Let x' be a string over Σ'. To x', we can apply only rules whose left-hand side is in Σ'.

(a) We use $a' \to a''$ for some $a' \in \Sigma'$. The obtained sentential form contains symbols of Σ' and Σ''. Hence, we can use only rules of type (1). Continuing in this way, we get $x' \Rightarrow^*_{G'} x''$. By analogous arguments, we now have to rewrite all symbols of x'' by rules of (2) with the same index (i). Thus, we obtain $x^{(i)}$. To each symbol $a^{(i)}$ in $x^{(i)}$, we apply a rule $a^{(i)} \to u'$, where $a \to u \in R_i$. Since again all symbols in $x^{(i)}$ have to be replaced before starting with rules of another type, we simulate a derivation step in G and get z', where $x \Rightarrow_G z$ in G. Therefore, starting with a rule of (1), we simulate a derivation step in G, and conversely, each derivation step in G can be simulated in this way;
(b) We apply a rule $a' \to \bar{a}$ to x'. Next, each a' of Δ' occurring in x' has to be substituted by $\bar{a}$ and then by a by using the rules constructed in (5). Therefore, we obtain a terminal string only if $x' \in \Delta'^*$.

By these considerations, any successful derivation in G' is of the form

$$\begin{aligned}
S' &\Rightarrow_{G'} S'' \Rightarrow_{G'} S^{(i_0)}\\
&\Rightarrow_{G'} z'_1 \Rightarrow^*_{G'} z''_1 \Rightarrow^*_{G'} z_1^{(i_1)}\\
&\ \ \vdots\\
&\Rightarrow^*_{G'} z'_n \Rightarrow^*_{G'} z''_n \Rightarrow^*_{G'} z_n^{(i_n)}\\
&\Rightarrow^*_{G'} z_{n+1} \Rightarrow^*_{G'} \bar{z}_{n+1} \Rightarrow^*_{G'} z_{n+1},
\end{aligned}$$

and such a derivation exists if and only if

$$S \Rightarrow_G z_1 \Rightarrow_G z_2 \Rightarrow_G \cdots \Rightarrow_G z_n \Rightarrow_G z_{n+1}$$

is a successful derivation in G. Thus, $L(G) = L(G')$.

In order to finish the proof, it is sufficient to find a language that is not in **ET0L** and can be generated by a forbidding grammar. A language of this kind is

$$L = \{b(ba^m)^n \mid m \geq n \geq 0\},$$

which can be generated by the grammar

$$G = (\{S, A, A', B, B', B'', C, D, E\}, \{a, b\}, R, s)$$

with R consisting of the following rules:

$$(S \to SA, \emptyset, \emptyset),$$
$$(S \to C, \emptyset, \emptyset),$$
$$(C \to D, \emptyset, \{S, A', B', B'', D, E\}),$$
$$(B \to B'a, \emptyset, \{S, C, E\}),$$
$$(A \to B''a, \emptyset, \{S, C, E, B''\}),$$
$$(A \to A'a, \emptyset, \{S, C, E\}),$$
$$(D \to C, \emptyset, \{A, B\}),$$
$$(B' \to B, \emptyset, \{D\}),$$
$$(B'' \to B, \emptyset, \{D\}),$$
$$(A' \to A, \emptyset, \{D\}),$$
$$(D \to E, \emptyset, \{S, A, A', B', B'', C, E\}),$$
$$(B \to b, \emptyset, \{S, A, A', B', B'', C, D\}),$$
$$(E \to b, \emptyset, \{S, A, A', B, B', B'', C, D\}).$$

First, we have the derivation

$$S \Rightarrow_G^* SA^n \Rightarrow_G CA^n \Rightarrow_G DA^n.$$

Then, we have to replace all occurrences of A. If we want to replace an occurrence of A by a terminal string in some steps, it is necessary to use $A \to B''a$. However, this can be done at most once in a phase that replaces all As. Therefore, $m \geq n$. ■

Theorem 11.21. **CF** $\subset$ **ET0L** $\subset$ **For**$^{-\varepsilon}$ $\subseteq$ **For** $\subset$ **CS**.

Proof. According to Example 11.2, we already have **CF** $\subset$ **For**$^{-\varepsilon}$. By [5] and Lemma 11.5, **CF** $\subset$ **ET0L** $\subset$ **For**$^{-\varepsilon}$. Moreover, in [15], it has been proved that **For**$^{-\varepsilon}$ $\subseteq$ **For** $\subset$ **CS**. Therefore, the theorem holds. ■

The following corollary summarizes the relations of language families generated by random context grammars.

Corollary 11.3.

$$\mathbf{CF} \subset \mathbf{Per}^{-\varepsilon} \subset \mathbf{RC}^{-\varepsilon} \subset \mathbf{CS},$$

$$\mathbf{Per}^{-\varepsilon} = \mathbf{Per} \subset \mathbf{RC} = \mathbf{RE},$$

$$\mathbf{CF} \subset \mathbf{ET0L} \subset \mathbf{For}^{-\varepsilon} \subseteq \mathbf{For} \subset \mathbf{CS}.$$

Proof. This corollary follows from Theorems 11.19, 11.20, and 11.21. ■

Open Problem 11.2. *Are* $\mathbf{For}^{-\varepsilon}$ *and* $\mathbf{For}$ *identical?*

Forbidding context grammars

Generalized forbidding grammars represent a generalized variant of forbidding grammars (see Section 11.2) in which forbidding context conditions are formed by finite languages.

This section consists of two subsections: definitions and generative power and reduction. The former defines generalized forbidding grammars, and the latter establishes their power.

Definitions

Next, we define generalized forbidding grammars.

Definition 11.14. *Let* $G = (\Sigma, \Delta, R, S)$ *be a context-conditional grammar. If every* $(A \to x, Per, For)$ *satisfies* $Per = \emptyset$, *then* G *is said to be a* generalized forbidding grammar *(a* gf-grammar *for short).*

The following convention simplifies the notation of gf-grammars. Let $G = (\Sigma, \Delta, R, S)$ be a gf-grammar of degree (r, s). Since every $(A \to x, Per, For) \in R$ implies that $Per = \emptyset$, we omit the empty set of permitting conditions. That is, we write $(A \to x, For)$ instead of $(A \to x, Per, For)$. For simplicity, we also say that the degree of G is s instead of (r, s).

The families generated by gf-grammars and propagating gf-grammars of degree s are denoted by $\mathbf{GF}(s)$ and $\mathbf{GF}^{-\varepsilon}(s)$, respectively. Furthermore, set

$$\mathbf{GF} = \bigcup_{s=0}^{\infty} \mathbf{GF}(s)$$

and

$$\mathbf{GF}^{-\varepsilon} = \bigcup_{s=0}^{\infty} \mathbf{GF}^{-\varepsilon}(s).$$

Generative power and reduction

In the present section, we establish the generative power of generalized forbidding grammars, defined in the previous section. In fact, apart from establishing this power, we also give several related results concerning the reduction of these grammars. Indeed, we reduce these grammars with respect to the number of nonterminals, the number of forbidding rules, and the length of forbidding strings.

By analogy with Theorem 11.16, it is easy to see that gf-grammars of degree 0 are ordinary CFGs.

Theorem 11.22. $\mathbf{GF}^{-\varepsilon}(0) = \mathbf{GF}(0) = \mathbf{CF}$.

Furthermore, gf-grammars of degree 1 are as powerful as forbidding grammars.

Theorem 11.23. $\mathbf{GF}(1) = \mathbf{For}$.

Proof. This simple proof is left to the reader. ■

Theorem 11.24. $\mathbf{GF}(2) = \mathbf{RE}$.

Proof. It is straightforward to prove that $\mathbf{GF}(2) \subseteq \mathbf{RE}$; hence it is sufficient to prove the converse inclusion.

Let L be a recursively enumerable language. Without any loss of generality, we assume that L is generated by a PSG

$$G = (\Sigma, \Delta, R, S)$$

in the Penttonen normal form (see Theorem 11.2). Set $N = \Sigma - \Delta$.

Let @, \$, S' be new symbols and m be the cardinality of $\Sigma \cup \{@\}$. Clearly, $m \geq 1$. Furthermore, let f be an arbitrary bijection from $\Sigma \cup \{@\}$ onto $\{1, \ldots, m\}$ and f^{-1} be the inverse of f.

The gf-grammar

$$G' = (\Sigma' \cup \{@, \$, S'\}, \Delta, R', S')$$

of degree 2 is defined as follows:

$$\begin{aligned} \Sigma' &= W \cup \Sigma, \text{ where} \\ W &= \{[AB \rightarrow AC, j] \mid AB \rightarrow AC \in R,\ A, B, C \in N, 1 \leq j \leq m + 1\}. \end{aligned}$$

We assume that W, $\{@, \$, S'\}$, and Σ are pairwise disjoint alphabets. The set of rules R' is defined in the following way:

(1) add $(S' \rightarrow @S, \emptyset)$ to R';
(2) if $A \rightarrow x \in R$, $A \in N$, $x \in \{\varepsilon\} \cup \Delta \cup N^2$, then add $(A \rightarrow x, \{\$\})$ to R';
(3) if $AB \rightarrow AC \in R$, $A, B, C \in N$, then
  (3.a) add $(B \rightarrow \$[AB \rightarrow AC, 1], \{\$\})$ to R';
  (3.b) for all $j = 1, \ldots, m, f(A) \neq j$, extend R' by adding $([AB \rightarrow AC, j] \rightarrow [AB \rightarrow AC, j + 1], \{f^{-1}(j)\$\})$
  (3.c) add $([AB \rightarrow AC, f(A)] \rightarrow [AB \rightarrow AC, f(A) + 1], \emptyset)$ and $([AB \rightarrow AC, m + 1] \rightarrow C, \emptyset)$ to R'; and
(4) add$(@ \rightarrow \varepsilon, N \cup W \cup \{\$\})$ and $(\$ \rightarrow \varepsilon, W)$ to R'.

Basically, the application of $AB \to AC$ in G is simulated in G' in the following way. An occurrence of B is rewritten with $\$[AB \to AC, 1]$. Then, the left adjoining symbol of \$ is checked not to be any symbol from $(\Sigma \cup \{@\})$ except A. After this, the right adjoining symbol of \$ is $[AB \to AC, m+1]$. This symbol is rewritten with C. A formal proof is given later.

Immediately from the definition of R' it follows that

$$S' \Rightarrow_{G'}^{+} x$$

where $x \in (\Sigma' \cup \{@, S'\})^*$, implies that

(i) $S' \notin \text{symbols}(x)$;
(ii) if $\text{symbols}(x) \cap W \neq \emptyset$, then $\text{occur}(W, x) = 1$ and $\text{occur}(\{\$\}W, x) = 1$; and
(iii) if $x \notin \Delta^*$, then the leftmost symbol of x is @.

Next, we define a finite substitution g from Σ^* into Σ'^* such that for all $B \in \Sigma$,

$$g(B) = \{B\} \cup \{[AB \to AC, j] \in W \mid AB \to AC \in R,\ A, C \in N,\ j = 1, \ldots, m+1\}.$$

Let g^{-1} be the inverse of g.

To show that $L(G) = L(G')$, we first prove that

$$S \Rightarrow_{G}^{n} x \quad \text{if and only if} \quad S \Rightarrow_{G'}^{n'} x'$$

where $x' = @v'Xw'$, $X \in \{\$, \varepsilon\}$, $v'w' \in g(x)$, $x \in \Sigma^*$, for some $n \geq 0$, $n' \geq 1$.

Only If. This is established by induction on $n \geq 0$. That is, we have to demonstrate that $S \Rightarrow_{G}^{n} x$, $x \in \Sigma^*$, $n \geq 0$, implies that $S \Rightarrow_{G'}^{+} x'$ for some x' such that $x' = @v'Xw'$, $X \in \{\$, \varepsilon\}$, $v'w' \in g(x)$.

Basis. Let $n = 0$. The only x is S because $S \Rightarrow_{G}^{0} S$. Clearly, $S' \Rightarrow_{G'} @S$ and $S \in g(S)$.

Induction Hypothesis. Suppose that the claim holds for all derivations of length n or less, for some $n \geq 0$.

Induction Step. Let us consider any derivation of the form

$$S \Rightarrow_{G}^{n+1} x$$

with $x \in \Sigma^*$. Since $n + 1 \geq 1$, there is some $y \in V^+$ and $p \in R$ such that

$$S \Rightarrow_{G}^{n} y \Rightarrow_{G} x\ [p]$$

and by the induction hypothesis, there is also a derivation of the form

$$S \Rightarrow_{G'}^{n'} y'$$

for some $n' \geq 1$, such that $y' = @r'Ys'$, $Y \in \{\$, \varepsilon\}$, and $r's' \in g(y)$.

(i) Let us assume that $p = D \to y_2 \in R$, $D \in N$, $y_2 \in \{\varepsilon\} \cup \Delta \cup N^2$, $y = y_1Dy_3$, $y_1, y_3 \in \Sigma^*$, and $x = y_1y_2y_3$. From (2), it is clear that $(D \to y_2, \{\$\}) \in R'$;

(i.a) Let $\$ \notin \text{symbols}(y')$. Then, we have $y' = @r's' = @y_1Dy_3$,

$$S' \Rightarrow_{G'}^{n'} @y_1Dy_3 \Rightarrow_{G'} @y_1y_2y_3 \; [(D \rightarrow y_2, \{\$\})]$$

and $y_1y_2y_3 \in g(y_1y_2y_3) = g(x)$;

(i.b) Let $Y = \$ \in \text{substrings}(y')$ and $W \cap \text{substrings}(y') = \emptyset$. Then, there is the following
derivation in G':

$$S' \Rightarrow_{G'}^{n'} @r'\$s' \Rightarrow_{G'} @r's' \; [(\$ \rightarrow \varepsilon, W)]$$

By analogy with (i.a), we have $@r's' = @y_1Dy_2$, so

$$S' \Rightarrow_{G'}^{n'+1} @y_1Dy_3 \Rightarrow_{G'} @y_1y_2y_3 \; [(D \rightarrow y_2, \{\$\})]$$

where $y_1y_2y_3 \in g(x)$;

(i.c) Let $\$[AB \rightarrow AC, i] \in \text{substrings}(y')$ for some $i \in \{1, \ldots, m+1\}$, $AB \rightarrow AC \in R$, $A, B, C \in N$. Thus, $y' = @r'\$[AB \rightarrow AC, i]t'$, where $s' = [AB \rightarrow AC, i]t'$. By the inspection of the rules (see (3)) it can be seen (and the reader should be able to produce a formal proof) that we can express the derivation

$$S' \Rightarrow_{G'}^{*} y'$$

in the following form:

$$\begin{aligned} S' &\Rightarrow_{G'}^{*} @r'Bt' \\ &\Rightarrow_{G'} @r'\$[AB \rightarrow AC, 1]t' \; [(B \rightarrow \$[AB \rightarrow AC, 1], \{\$\})] \\ &\Rightarrow_{G'}^{i-1} @r'\$[AB \rightarrow AC, i]t' \end{aligned}$$

Clearly, $r'Bt' \in g(y)$ and $\$ \notin \text{symbols}(r'Bt')$. Thus, $r'Bt' = y_1Dy_3$, and there is a derivation

$$S' \Rightarrow_{G'}^{*} @y_1Dy_3 \Rightarrow_{G'} @y_1y_2y_3 \; [(D \rightarrow y_2, \{\$\})]$$

and $y_1y_2y_3 \in g(x)$;

(ii) Let $p = AB \rightarrow AC \in R$, $A, B, C \in N$, $y = y_1ABy_2$, $y_1, y_2 \in \Sigma^*$, and $x = y_1ACy_2$.

(a) Let $\$ \notin \text{symbols}(y')$. Thus, $r's' = y_1ABy_2$. By the inspection of the rules introduced in (3) (technical details are left to the reader), there is the following derivation in G':

$$\begin{aligned} S' &\Rightarrow_{G'}^{n'} @y_1ABy_2 \\ &\Rightarrow_{G'} @y_1A\$[AB \rightarrow AC, 1]y_2 \\ &\qquad [(B \rightarrow \$[AB \rightarrow AC, 1], \{\$\})] \\ &\Rightarrow_{G'} @y_1A\$[AB \rightarrow AC, 2]y_2 \\ &\qquad [([AB \rightarrow AC, 1] \rightarrow [AB \rightarrow AC, 2], \{f^{-1}(1)\$\})] \\ &\;\;\vdots \end{aligned}$$

$$\Rightarrow_{G'} @y_1A\$[AB \rightarrow AC, f(A)]y_2$$
$$[([AB \rightarrow AC, f(A) - 1] \rightarrow [AB \rightarrow AC, f(A)], \{f^{-1}(f(A) - 1)\$\})]$$
$$\Rightarrow_{G'} @y_1A\$[AB \rightarrow AC, f(A) + 1]y_2$$
$$[([AB \rightarrow AC, f(A)] \rightarrow [AB \rightarrow AC, f(A) + 1], \emptyset)]$$
$$\vdots$$
$$\Rightarrow_{G'} @y_1A\$[AB \rightarrow AC, m + 1]y_2$$
$$[([AB \rightarrow AC, m] \rightarrow [AB \rightarrow AC, m + 1], \{f^{-1}(m)\$\})]$$
$$\Rightarrow_{G'} @y_1A\$Cy_2$$
$$[([AB \rightarrow AC, m + 1] \rightarrow C, \emptyset)]$$

such that $y_1ACy_2 \in g(y_1ACy_2) = g(x)$;

(b) Let $\$ \in$ symbols (y'), symbols $(y') \cap W = \emptyset$. By analogy with (i.b), the derivation

$$S' \Rightarrow^*_{G'} @r's'$$

with $@r's' = @y_1ABy_2$, can be constructed in G'. Then, by analogy with (a), one can construct the derivation

$$S' \Rightarrow^*_{G'} @y_1ABy_2 \Rightarrow^*_{G'} @y_1A\$Cy_2$$

such that $y_1ACy_2 \in g(x)$;

(c) Let occur $(\{\$\}W, y') = 1$. By analogy with (i.c), one can construct the derivation

$$S' \Rightarrow^*_{G'} @y_1ABy_2$$

Next, by using an analogue from (a), the derivation

$$S' \Rightarrow^*_{G'} @y_1ABy_2 \Rightarrow^*_{G'} @y_1A\$Cy_2$$

can be constructed in G' so $y_1ACy_2 \in g(x)$.

In (i) and (ii), we have considered all possible forms of p. In cases (i.a), (i.b), and (i.c), we have considered all possible forms of y'. In any of these cases, we have constructed the desired derivation of the form

$$S' \Rightarrow^+_{G'} x'$$

such that $x' = @r'Xs', X \in \{\$, \varepsilon\}, r's' \in g(x)$. Hence, we have established the only-if part of our claim by the principle of induction.

If. This is also demonstrated by induction on $n' \geq 1$. We have to demonstrate that if $S' \Rightarrow^{n'}_{G'} x'$, $x' = @r'Xs'$, $X \in \{\$, \varepsilon\}$, $r's' \in g(x)$, $x \in \Sigma^*$, for some $n' \geq 1$, then $S \Rightarrow^*_G x$.

Basis. For $n' = 1$, the only x' is $@S$ since $S' \Rightarrow_{G'} @S$. Because $S \in g(S)$, we have $x = S$. Clearly, $S \Rightarrow_G^0 S$.

Induction Hypothesis. Assume that the claim holds for all derivations of length at most n' for some $n' \geq 1$. Let us show that it also holds for $n' + 1$.

Induction Step. Consider any derivation of the form

$$S' \Rightarrow_{G'}^{n'+1} x'$$

with $x' = @r'Xs'$, $X \in \{\$, \varepsilon\}$, $r's' \in g(x)$, $x \in V^*$. Since $n' + 1 \geq 2$, we have

$$S' \Rightarrow_{G'}^{n'} y' \Rightarrow_{G'} x' \ [p']$$

for some $p' = (Z' \to w', For) \in R'$, $y' = @q'Yt'$, $Y \in \{\$, \varepsilon\}$, $q't' \in g(y)$, $y \in \Sigma^*$, and by the induction hypothesis,

$$S \Rightarrow_G^* y.$$

Suppose:

(i) $Z' \in N$, $w' \in \{\varepsilon\} \cup \Delta \cup N^2$. By inspecting R' (see (2)), we have $For = \{\$\}$ and $Z' \to w' \in R$. Thus, $\$ \notin \text{symbols}(y')$ and so $q't' = y$. Hence, there is the following derivation:

$$S \Rightarrow_G^* y \Rightarrow_G x \ [Z' \to w'];$$

(ii) $g^{-1}(Z') = g^{-1}(w')$. But then $y = x$, and by the induction hypothesis, we have the derivation

$$S \Rightarrow_G^* y;$$

(iii) $p' = (B \to \$[AB \to AC, 1], \{\$\})$, that is, $Z' = B$, $w' = \$[AB \to AC, 1]$, $For = \{\$\}$ and so $w' \in \{\$\}g(Z')$, $Y = \varepsilon$, $X = \$$. By analogy with (ii), we have

$$S \Rightarrow_G^* y$$

and $y = x$;

(iv) $Z' = Y = \$$, that is, $p' = (\$ \to \varepsilon, W)$. Then, $X = \varepsilon$, $r's' = q't' \in g(y)$, and

$$S \Rightarrow_G^* y;$$

(v) $p' = ([AB \to AC, m+1] \to C, \emptyset)$, that is, $Z' = [AB \to AC, m+1]$, $w' = C$, $For = \emptyset$. From (3), it follows that there is a rule of the form $AB \to AC \in R$. Moreover, by inspecting (3), it is not too difficult to see (the technical details are left to the reader) that $Y = \$$, $r' = q'$, $t' = [AB \to AC, m+1]o'$, $s' = Co'$, and the derivation

$$S' \Rightarrow_{G'}^{n'} y' \Rightarrow_{G'} x' \ [p']$$

can be expressed as

$$\begin{array}{lll} S' & \Rightarrow_{G'}^{*} & @q'Bo' \\ & \Rightarrow_{G'} & @q'\$[AB \to AC, 1]o' \quad [(B \to \$[AB \to AC, 1], \{\$\})] \\ & \Rightarrow_{G'}^{m+1} & @q'\$[AB \to AC, m+1]o' \quad [h] \\ & \Rightarrow_{G'} & @q'\$Co' \quad [([AB \to AC, m+1] \to C, \emptyset)] \end{array}$$

where

$$h = h_1([AB \to AC, f(A)] \to [AB \to AC, f(A)+1], \emptyset)h_2,$$
$$h_1 = ([AB \to AC, 1] \to [AB \to AC, 2], \{f^{-1}(1)\$\})$$
$$([AB \to AC, 2] \to [AB \to AC, 3], \{f^{-1}(2)\$\})$$
$$\vdots$$
$$([AB \to AC, f(A)-1] \to [AB \to AC, f(A)], \{f^{-1}(f(A)-1)\$\})$$

in which $f(A) = 1$ implies that $h_1 = \varepsilon$,

$$h_2 = ([AB \to AC, f(A)+1] \to [AB \to AC, f(A)+2], \{f^{-1}(f(A)+1)\$\})$$
$$\vdots$$
$$([AB \to AC, m] \to [AB \to AC, m+1], \{f^{-1}(m)\$\})$$

in which $f(A) = m$ implies that $h_2 = \varepsilon$, that is, the rightmost symbol of $q' = r'$ must be A.

Since $q't' \in g(y)$, we have $y = q'Bo'$. Because the rightmost symbol of q' is A and $AB \to AC \in R$, we have

$$S \Rightarrow_G^* q'Bo' \Rightarrow_G q'Co' \; [AB \to AC]$$

where $q'Co' = x$.

By inspecting R', we see that (i) through (v) through cover all possible derivations of the form

$$S' \Rightarrow_{G'}^{n'} y' \Rightarrow_{G'} x',$$

and thus we have established that

$$S \Rightarrow_G^* x \quad \text{if and only if} \quad S' \Rightarrow_{G'}^+ x'$$

where $x' = @r'Xs'$, $r's' \in g(x)$, $X \in \{\$, \varepsilon\}$, $x \in \Sigma^*$, by the principle of induction.

A proof of the equivalence of G and G' can easily be derived from proofs given previously. By the definition of g, we have $g(a) = \{a\}$ for all $a \in T$. Thus, we have for any $x \in T^*$,

$$S \Rightarrow_G^* x \quad \text{if and only if} \quad S' \Rightarrow_{G'}^* @rXs,$$

where $X \in \{\$, \varepsilon\}$, $rs = x$. If $X = \varepsilon$, then

$$@x \Rightarrow_{G'} x \; [(@ \to \varepsilon, N \cup W \cup \{\$\})].$$

If $X = \$$, then

$$@r\$s \Rightarrow_{G'} @x \; [(\$ \to \varepsilon, W)] \Rightarrow_{G'} x \; [(@ \to \varepsilon, N \cup W \cup \{\$\})].$$

Hence,

$$S \Rightarrow_G^+ x \quad \text{if and only if} \quad S' \Rightarrow_{G'}^+ x$$

for all $x \in \Delta^*$, and so $L(G) = L(G')$. Thus, **RE** = **GF**(2). ■

Theorem 11.25. **GF**(2) = **GF** = **RE**.

Proof. This theorem follows immediately from the definitions and Theorem 11.24. ■

Examine the rules in G' in the proof of Theorem 11.24 to establish the following normal form.

Corollary 11.4. *Every recursively enumerable language L over some alphabet* Δ *can be generated by a gf-grammar* $G = (\Sigma, \Delta, R \cup \{p_1, p_2\}, S)$ *of degree 2 such that*

(i) $(A \to x, For) \in R$ *implies that* $|x| = 2$ *and the cardinality of For is at most 1;*
(ii) $p_i = (A_i \to \varepsilon, For_i)$, $i = 1, 2$, *where* $For_i \subseteq \Sigma$, *that is,* max-len $(For_i) \leq 1$.

In fact, the last corollary represents one of the reduced forms of gf-grammars of degree 2. Perhaps most importantly, it reduces the cardinality of the sets of forbidding conditions so that if a rule contains a condition of length two, this condition is the only context condition attached to the rule. Next, we study another reduced form of gf-grammars of degree 2. We show that we can simultaneously reduce the number of conditional rules and the number of nonterminals in gf-grammars of degree 2 without any decrease of their generative power.

Theorem 11.26. *Every recursively enumerable language can be defined by a gf-grammar of degree 2 with no more than 13 forbidding rules and 15 nonterminals.*

Proof. Let $L \in$ **RE**. By Theorem 11.7, without any loss of generality, we assume that L is generated by a PSG G of the form

$$G = (\Sigma, \Delta, R \cup \{AB \to \varepsilon, CD \to \varepsilon\}, S)$$

such that R contains only context-free rules and

$$\Sigma - \Delta = \{S, A, B, C, D\}.$$

We construct a gf-grammar of degree 2

$$G' = (\Sigma', \Delta, R', S'),$$

where

$$\Sigma' = \Sigma \cup W,$$
$$W = \{S', @, \widetilde{A}, \widetilde{B}, \langle \varepsilon_A \rangle, \$, \widetilde{C}, \widetilde{D}, \langle \varepsilon_C \rangle, \#\}, \ \Sigma \cap W = \emptyset,$$

in the following way. Let

$$N' = (\Sigma' - \Delta) - \{S', @\}.$$

Informally, N' denotes the set of all nonterminals in G' except S' and @. Then, the set of rules R' is constructed by performing (1)–(4), given next.

(1) If $H \to y \in R$, $H \in \Sigma - \Delta$, $y \in \Sigma^*$, then add $(H \to y, \emptyset)$ to R';
(2) Add $(S' \to @S@, \emptyset)$ and $(@ \to \varepsilon, N')$ to R';

(3) Extend R' by adding

$$
\begin{aligned}
&(A \to \widetilde{A}, \{\widetilde{A}\}),\\
&(B \to \widetilde{B}, \{\widetilde{B}\}),\\
&(\widetilde{A} \to \langle \varepsilon_A \rangle, \{\widetilde{A}a \mid a \in \Sigma' - \{\widetilde{B}\}\}),\\
&(\widetilde{B} \to \$, \{a\widetilde{B} \mid a \in \Sigma' - \{\langle \varepsilon_A \rangle\}\}),\\
&(\langle \varepsilon_A \rangle \to \varepsilon, \{\widetilde{B}\}),\\
&(\$ \to \varepsilon, \{\langle \varepsilon_A \rangle\});
\end{aligned}
$$

(4) Extend R' by adding

$$
\begin{aligned}
&(C \to \widetilde{C}, \{\widetilde{C}\}),\\
&(D \to \widetilde{D}, \{\widetilde{D}\}),\\
&(\widetilde{C} \to \langle \varepsilon_C \rangle, \{\widetilde{C}a \mid a \in \Sigma' - \{\widetilde{D}\}\}),\\
&(\widetilde{D} \to \#, \{a\widetilde{D} \mid a \in \Sigma' - \{\langle \varepsilon_C \rangle\}\}),\\
&(\langle \varepsilon_C \rangle \to \varepsilon, \{\widetilde{D}\}),\\
&(\# \to \varepsilon, \{\langle \varepsilon_C \rangle\}).
\end{aligned}
$$

Next, we prove that $L(G') = L(G)$.

Notice that G' has degree 2 and contains only 13 forbidding rules and 15 nonterminals. The rules of (3) simulate the application of $AB \to \varepsilon$ in G', and the rules of (4) simulate the application of $CD \to \varepsilon$ in G'.

Let us describe the simulation of $AB \to \varepsilon$. First, one occurrence of A and one occurrence of B are rewritten with $\widetilde{A}$ and $\widetilde{B}$, respectively (no sentential form contains more than one occurrence of $\widetilde{A}$ or $\widetilde{B}$). The right neighbor of $\widetilde{A}$ is checked to be $\widetilde{B}$ and $\widetilde{A}$ is rewritten with $\langle \varepsilon_A \rangle$. Then, analogously, the left neighbor of $\widetilde{B}$ is checked to be $\langle \varepsilon_A \rangle$ and $\widetilde{B}$ is rewritten with \$. Finally, $\langle \varepsilon_A \rangle$ and \$ are erased. The simulation of $CD \to \varepsilon$ is analogical.

To establish $L(G) = L(G')$, we first prove several claims.

Claim 1. *$S' \Rightarrow^{+}_{G'} w'$ implies that w' has one of the following forms:*

(I) $w' = @x'@$, $x' \in (N' \cup \Delta)^*$, symbols$(x') \cap N' \neq \emptyset$, *and*
(II) $w' = Xx'Y$, $x' \in \Delta^*$, $X, Y \in \{@, \varepsilon\}$.

Proof. The start symbol S' is always rewritten with $@S@$. After this initial step, @ can be erased in a sentential form provided that any nonterminal occurring in the sentential form belongs to $\{@, S'\}$ (see N' and (2) in the definition of R'). In addition, notice that only rules of (2) contain @ and S'. Thus, any sentential form containing some nonterminals from N' is of the form (I).

Case (II) covers sentential forms containing no nonterminal from N'. At this point, @ can be erased, and we obtain a string from $L(G')$. □

Claim 2. *$S' \Rightarrow^{*}_{G'} w'$ implies that* occur$(\widetilde{X}, w') \leq 1$ *for all $\widetilde{X} \in \{\widetilde{A}, \widetilde{B}, \widetilde{C}, \widetilde{D}\}$ and some $w' \in \Sigma'^*$.*

Proof. By the inspection of rules in R', the only rule that can generate $\widetilde{X}$ is of the form $(X \to \widetilde{X}, \{\widetilde{X}\})$. This rule can be applied only when no $\widetilde{X}$ occurs in the rewritten sentential form. Thus, it is impossible to derive w' from S' such that $\text{occur}(\widetilde{X}, w') \geq 2$. □

Informally, next claim says that every occurrence of $\langle \varepsilon_A \rangle$ in derivations from S' is always followed either by $\widetilde{B}$ or \$, and every occurrence of $\langle \varepsilon_C \rangle$ is always followed either by $\widetilde{D}$ or #.

Claim 3. *The following two statements hold true.*

(I) $S' \Rightarrow^*_{G'} y'_1 \langle \varepsilon_A \rangle y'_2$ *implies that* $y'_2 \in \Sigma'^+$ *and* $\text{lms}(y'_2) \in \{\widetilde{B}, \$\}$ *for any* $y'_1 \in \Sigma'^*$.
(II) $S' \Rightarrow^*_{G'} y'_1 \langle \varepsilon_C \rangle y'_2$ *implies that* $y'_2 \in \Sigma'^+$ *and* $\text{lms}(y'_2) \in \{\widetilde{D}, \#\}$ *for any* $y'_1 \in \Sigma'^*$.

Proof. We establish this claim by examination of all possible forms of derivations that may occur when deriving a sentential form containing $\langle \varepsilon_A \rangle$ or $\langle \varepsilon_C \rangle$.

(I) By the definition of R', the only rule that can generate $\langle \varepsilon_A \rangle$ is $p = (\widetilde{A} \to \langle \varepsilon_A \rangle, \{\widetilde{A}a \mid a \in \Sigma' - \{\widetilde{B}\}\})$. The rule can be applied provided that $\widetilde{A}$ occurs in a sentential form. It also holds that $\widetilde{A}$ has always a right neighbor (as follows from Claim 1), and according to the set of forbidding conditions in p, $\widetilde{B}$ is the only allowed right neighbor of $\widetilde{A}$. Furthermore, by Claim 2, no other occurrence of $\widetilde{A}$ or $\widetilde{B}$ can appear in the given sentential form. Consequently, we obtain a derivation

$$S' \Rightarrow^*_{G'} u'_1 \widetilde{A}\widetilde{B}u'_2 \Rightarrow_{G'} u'_1 \langle \varepsilon_A \rangle \widetilde{B}u'_2 \; [p]$$

for some $u'_1, u'_2 \in \Sigma'^*, \widetilde{A}, \widetilde{B} \notin \text{symbols}(u'_1 u'_2)$. Obviously, $\langle \varepsilon_A \rangle$ is always followed by $\widetilde{B}$ in $u'_1 \langle \varepsilon_A \rangle \widetilde{B}u'_2$.

Next, we discuss how G' can rewrite the substring $\langle \varepsilon_A \rangle \widetilde{B}$ in $u'_1 \langle \varepsilon_A \rangle \widetilde{B}u'_2$. There are only two rules having the nonterminals $\langle \varepsilon_A \rangle$ or $\widetilde{B}$ on their left-hand side, $p_1 = (\widetilde{B} \to \$, \{a\widetilde{B} \mid a \in \Sigma' - \{\langle \varepsilon_A \rangle\}\})$ and $p_2 = (\langle \varepsilon_A \rangle \to \varepsilon, \{\widetilde{B}\})$. G' cannot use p_2 to erase $\langle \varepsilon_A \rangle$ in $u'_1 \langle \varepsilon_A \rangle \widetilde{B}u'_2$ because p_2 forbids an occurrence of $\widetilde{B}$ in the rewritten string. However, we can rewrite $\widetilde{B}$ to \$ by using p_1 because its set of forbidding conditions defines that the left neighbor of $\widetilde{B}$ must be just $\langle \varepsilon_A \rangle$. Hence, we obtain a derivation of the form

$$\begin{aligned} S' &\Rightarrow^*_{G'} u'_1 \widetilde{A}\widetilde{B}u'_2 &&\Rightarrow_{G'} u'_1 \langle \varepsilon_A \rangle \widetilde{B}u'_2 \; [p] \\ &\Rightarrow^*_{G'} v'_1 \langle \varepsilon_A \rangle \widetilde{B}v'_2 &&\Rightarrow_{G'} v'_1 \langle \varepsilon_A \rangle \$ v'_2 \; [p_1]. \end{aligned}$$

Notice that during this derivation, G' may rewrite u'_1 and u'_2 with some v'_1 and v'_2, respectively ($v'_1, v'_2 \in \Sigma'^*$); however, $\langle \varepsilon_A \rangle \widetilde{B}$ remains unchanged after this rewriting.

In this derivation, we obtained the second symbol \$, which can appear as the right neighbor of $\langle \varepsilon_A \rangle$. It is sufficient to show that there is no other symbol that can appear immediately after $\langle \varepsilon_A \rangle$. By the inspection of R', only $(\$ \to \varepsilon, \{\langle \varepsilon_A \rangle\})$ can rewrite \$. However, this rule cannot be applied when $\langle \varepsilon_A \rangle$ occurs in the given sentential form. In other words, the occurrence of \$ in the substring $\langle \varepsilon_A \rangle \$$ cannot be rewritten before $\langle \varepsilon_A \rangle$ is erased by p_2. Hence, $\langle \varepsilon_A \rangle$ is always followed either by $\widetilde{B}$ or \$, so the first part of Claim 3 holds;

(II) By the inspection of rules simulating $AB \rightarrow \varepsilon$ and $CD \rightarrow \varepsilon$ in G' (see (3) and (4) in the definition of R'), these two sets of rules work analogously. Thus, part (II) of Claim 3 can be proved by analogy with part (I). □

Let us return to the main part of the proof. Let g be a finite substitution from $(N' \cup \Delta)^*$ to Σ^* defined as follows:

(a) for all $X \in \Sigma$, $g(X) = \{X\}$;
(b) $g(\widetilde{A}) = \{A\}$, $g(\widetilde{B}) = \{B\}$, $g(\langle\varepsilon_A\rangle) = \{A\}$, $g(\$) = \{B, AB\}$; and
(c) $g(\widetilde{C}) = \{C\}$, $g(\widetilde{D}) = \{D\}$, $g(\langle\varepsilon_C\rangle) = \{C\}$, $g(\#) = \{C, CD\}$.

Having this substitution, we can now prove the following claim.

Claim 4. *$S \Rightarrow_G^* x$ if and only if $S' \Rightarrow_{G'}^+ @x'@$ for some $x \in g(x')$, $x \in \Sigma^*$, $x' \in (N' \cup \Delta)^*$.*

Proof. The claim is proved by induction on the length of derivations.

Only If. We show that

$$S \Rightarrow_G^m x \quad \text{implies} \quad S' \Rightarrow_{G'}^+ @x@$$

where $m \geq 0, x \in \Sigma^*$; clearly $x \in g(x)$. This is established by induction on $m \geq 0$.

Basis. Let $m = 0$. That is, $S \Rightarrow_G^0 S$. Clearly, $S' \Rightarrow_{G'} @S@$.

Induction Hypothesis. Suppose that the claim holds for all derivations of length m or less, for some $m \geq 0$.

Induction Step. Let us consider any derivation of the form

$$S \Rightarrow_G^{m+1} x,\ x \in \Sigma^*.$$

Since $m + 1 \geq 1$, there is some $y \in \Sigma^+$ and $p \in R \cup \{AB \rightarrow \varepsilon, CD \rightarrow \varepsilon\}$ such that

$$S \Rightarrow_G^m y \Rightarrow_G x\ [p].$$

By the induction hypothesis, there is a derivation

$$S' \Rightarrow_{G'}^+ @y@.$$

There are the following three cases that cover all possible forms of p.

(i) Let $p = H \rightarrow y_2 \in R$, $H \in \Sigma - \Delta$, $y_2 \in \Sigma^*$. Then, $y = y_1Hy_3$ and $x = y_1y_2y_3$, $y_1, y_3 \in \Sigma^*$. Because we have $(H \rightarrow y_2, \emptyset) \in R'$,

$$S' \Rightarrow_{G'}^+ @y_1Hy_3@ \Rightarrow_{G'} @y_1y_2y_3@\ [(H \rightarrow y_2, \emptyset)]$$

and $y_1y_2y_3 = x$;

(ii) Let $p = AB \to \varepsilon$. Then, $y = y_1ABy_3$ and $x = y_1y_3$, $y_1, y_3 \in \Sigma^*$. In this case, there is the following derivation:

$$\begin{aligned}
S' &\Rightarrow^+_{G'} @y_1ABy_3@ \\
&\Rightarrow_{G'} @y_1\widetilde{A}By_3@ \quad [(A \to \widetilde{A}, \{\widetilde{A}\})] \\
&\Rightarrow_{G'} @y_1\widetilde{A}\widetilde{B}y_3@ \quad [(B \to \widetilde{B}, \{\widetilde{B}\})] \\
&\Rightarrow_{G'} @y_1\langle\varepsilon_A\rangle\widetilde{B}y_3@ \quad [(\widetilde{A} \to \langle\varepsilon_A\rangle, \{\widetilde{A}a \mid a \in \Sigma' - \{\widetilde{B}\}\})] \\
&\Rightarrow_{G'} @y_1\langle\varepsilon_A\rangle\$y_3@ \quad [(\widetilde{B} \to \$, \{a\widetilde{B} \mid a \in \Sigma' - \{\langle\varepsilon_A\rangle\}\})] \\
&\Rightarrow_{G'} @y_1\$y_3@ \quad [(\langle\varepsilon_A\rangle \to \varepsilon, \{\widetilde{B}\})] \\
&\Rightarrow_{G'} @y_1y_3@ \quad [(\$ \to \varepsilon, \{\langle\varepsilon_A\rangle\})];
\end{aligned}$$

(iii) Let $p = CD \to \varepsilon$. Then, $y = y_1CDy_3$ and $x = y_1y_3$, $y_1, y_3 \in \Sigma^*$. In this case, there exists the following derivation:

$$\begin{aligned}
S' &\Rightarrow^+_{G'} @y_1CDy_3@ \\
&\Rightarrow_{G'} @y_1\widetilde{C}Dy_3@ \quad [(C \to \widetilde{C}, \{\widetilde{C}\})] \\
&\Rightarrow_{G'} @y_1\widetilde{C}\widetilde{D}y_3@ \quad [(D \to \widetilde{D}, \{\widetilde{D}\})] \\
&\Rightarrow_{G'} @y_1\langle\varepsilon_C\rangle\widetilde{D}y_3@ \quad [(\widetilde{C} \to \langle\varepsilon_C\rangle, \{\widetilde{C}a \mid a \in V' - \{\widetilde{D}\}\})] \\
&\Rightarrow_{G'} @y_1\langle\varepsilon_C\rangle\#y_3@ \quad [(\widetilde{D} \to \#, \{a\widetilde{D} \mid a \in V' - \{\langle\varepsilon_C\rangle\}\})] \\
&\Rightarrow_{G'} @y_1\#y_3@ \quad [(\langle\varepsilon_C\rangle \to \varepsilon, \{\widetilde{D}\})] \\
&\Rightarrow_{G'} @y_1y_3@ \quad [(\# \to \varepsilon, \{\langle\varepsilon_C\rangle\})].
\end{aligned}$$

If. By induction on the length n of derivations in G', we prove that

$$S' \Rightarrow^n_{G'} @x'@ \quad \text{implies} \quad S \Rightarrow^*_G x$$

for some $x \in g(x')$, $x \in \Sigma^*$, $x' \in (N' \cup \Delta)^*$, $n \geq 1$.

Basis. Let $n = 1$. According to the definition of R', the only rule rewriting S' is $(S' \to @S@, \emptyset)$, so $S' \Rightarrow_{G'} @S@$. It is obvious that $S \Rightarrow^0_G S$ and $S \in g(S)$.

Induction Hypothesis. Assume that the claim holds for all derivations of length n or less, for some $n \geq 1$.

Induction Step. Consider any derivation of the form

$$S' \Rightarrow^{n+1}_{G'} @x'@, \; x' \in (N' \cup \Delta)^*.$$

Since $n + 1 \geq 2$, there is some $y' \in (N' \cup \Delta)^+$ and $p' \in R'$ such that

$$S' \Rightarrow^n_{G'} @y'@ \Rightarrow_{G'} @x'@ \; [p'],$$

and by the induction hypothesis, there is also a derivation

$$S \Rightarrow^*_G y$$

such that $y \in g(y')$.

By the inspection of R', the following cases cover all possible forms of p':

(i) Let $p' = (H \to y_2, \emptyset) \in R'$, $H \in \Sigma - \Delta$, $y_2 \in \Delta^*$. Then, $y' = y'_1Hy'_3$, $x' = y'_1y_2y'_3$, $y'_1, y'_3 \in (N' \cup \Delta)^*$, and y has the form $y = y_1Zy_3$, where $y_1 \in g(y'_1)$, $y_3 \in g(y'_3)$, and $Z \in g(H)$. Because for all $X \in \Sigma - \Delta$: $g(X) = \{X\}$, the only possible Z is H; thus, $y = y_1Hy_3$. By the definition of R' (see (1)), there exists a rule $p = H \rightarrow y_2$ in R, and we can construct the derivation

$$S \Rightarrow_G^* y_1Hy_3 \Rightarrow_G y_1y_2y_3 \ [p]$$

such that $y_1y_2y_3 = x$, $x \in g(x')$;

(ii) Let $p' = (A \rightarrow \widetilde{A}, \{\widetilde{A}\})$. Then, $y' = y_1'Ay_3'$, $x' = y_1'\widetilde{A}y_3'$, $y_1', y_3' \in (N' \cup \Delta)^*$ and $y = y_1Zy_3$, where $y_1 \in g(y_1')$, $y_3 \in g(y_3')$ and $Z \in g(A)$. Because $g(A) = \{A\}$, the only Z is A, so we can express $y = y_1Ay_3$. Having the derivation $S \Rightarrow_G^* y$ such that $y \in g(y')$, it is easy to see that also $y \in g(x')$ because $A \in g(\widetilde{A})$;

(iii) Let $p' = (B \rightarrow \widetilde{B}, \{\widetilde{B}\})$. By analogy with (ii), $y' = y_1'By_3'$, $x' = y_1'\widetilde{B}y_3'$, $y = y_1By_3$, where $y_1', y_3' \in (N' \cup \Delta)^*$, $y_1 \in g(y_1')$, $y_3 \in g(y_3')$; thus, $y \in g(x')$ because $B \in g(\widetilde{B})$;

(iv) Let $p' = (\widetilde{A} \rightarrow \langle \varepsilon_A \rangle, \{\widetilde{A}a \mid a \in \Sigma' - \{\widetilde{B}\}\})$. In this case, it holds that
- (iv.i) the application of p' implies that $\widetilde{A} \in$ symbols (y'), and moreover, by Claim 2, we have occur $(\widetilde{A}, y') \leq 1$;
- (iv.ii) $\widetilde{A}$ always has a right neighbor in $@y'@$;
- (iv.iii) according to the set of forbidding conditions in p', the only allowed right neighbor of $\widetilde{A}$ is $\widetilde{B}$.

Hence, y' must be of the form $y' = y_1'\widetilde{A}\widetilde{B}y_3'$, where $y_1', y_3' \in (N' \cup \Delta)^*$ and $\widetilde{A} \notin$ symbols $(y_1'y_3')$. Then, $x' = y_1'\langle \varepsilon_A \rangle \widetilde{B}y_3'$ and y is of the form $y = y_1Zy_3$, where $y_1 \in g(y_1')$, $y_3 \in g(y_3')$, and $Z \in g(\widetilde{A}\widetilde{B})$. Because $g(\widetilde{A}\widetilde{B}) = \{AB\}$, the only Z is AB; thus, we obtain $y = y_1ABy_3$. By the induction hypothesis, we have a derivation $S \Rightarrow_G^* y$ such that $y \in g(y')$. According to the definition of g, $y \in g(x')$ as well because $A \in g(\langle \varepsilon_A \rangle)$ and $B \in g(\widetilde{B})$;

(v) Let $p' = (\widetilde{B} \rightarrow \$, \{a\widetilde{B} \mid a \in \Sigma' - \{\langle \varepsilon_A \rangle\}\})$. Then, it holds the following:
- (v.i) $\widetilde{B} \in$ symbols (y') and, by Claim 2, occur $(\widetilde{B}, y') \leq 1$;
- (v.ii) $\widetilde{B}$ has always a left neighbor in $@y'@$;
- (v.iii) By the set of forbidding conditions in p', the only allowed left neighbor of $\widetilde{B}$ is $\langle \varepsilon_A \rangle$.

Therefore, we can express $y' = y_1'\langle \varepsilon_A \rangle \widetilde{B}y_3'$, where $y_1', y_3' \in (N' \cup \Delta)^*$ and $\widetilde{B} \notin$ symbols $(y_1'y_3')$. Then, $x' = y_1'\langle \varepsilon_A \rangle \$ y_3'$ and $y = y_1Zy_3$, where $y_1 \in g(y_1')$, $y_3 \in g(y_3')$, and $Z \in g(\langle \varepsilon_A \rangle \widetilde{B})$. By the definition of g, $g(\langle \varepsilon_A \rangle \widetilde{B}) = \{AB\}$, so $Z = AB$ and $y = y_1ABy_3$. By the induction hypothesis, we have a derivation $S \Rightarrow_G^* y$ such that $y \in g(y')$. Because $A \in g(\langle \varepsilon_A \rangle)$ and $B \in g(\$)$, $y \in g(x')$ as well;

(vi) Let $p' = (\langle \varepsilon_A \rangle \rightarrow \varepsilon, \{\widetilde{B}\})$. An application of $(\langle \varepsilon_A \rangle \rightarrow \varepsilon, \{\widetilde{B}\})$ implies that $\langle \varepsilon_A \rangle$ occurs in y'. Claim 3 says that $\langle \varepsilon_A \rangle$ has either $\widetilde{B}$ or \$ as its right neighbor. Since the forbidding condition of p' forbids an occurrence of $\widetilde{B}$ in y', the right neighbor of $\langle \varepsilon_A \rangle$ must be \$. As a result, we obtain $y' = y_1'\langle \varepsilon_A \rangle \$ y_3'$, where $y_1', y_3' \in (N' \cup \Delta)^*$. Then, $x' = y_1'\$ y_3'$, and y is of the form $y = y_1Zy_3$, where $y_1 \in g(y_1')$, $y_3 \in g(y_3')$, and $Z \in g(\langle \varepsilon_A \rangle \$)$. By the definition of g, $g(\langle \varepsilon_A \rangle \$) = \{AB, AAB\}$. If $Z = AB$, $y = y_1ABy_3$. Having the derivation $S \Rightarrow_G^* y$, it holds that $y \in g(x')$ because $AB \in g(\$)$;

(vii) Let $p' = (\$ \rightarrow \varepsilon, \{\langle \varepsilon_A \rangle\})$. Then, $y' = y_1'\$y_3'$ and $x' = y_1'y_3'$, where $y_1', y_3' \in (N' \cup \Delta)^*$. Express $y = y_1 Z y_3$ so that $y_1 \in g(y_1')$, $y_3 \in g(y_3')$, and $Z \in g(\$)$, where $g(\$) = \{B, AB\}$. Let $Z = AB$. Then, $y = y_1 AB y_3$, and there exists the derivation

$$S \Rightarrow_G^* y_1 AB y_3 \Rightarrow_G y_1 y_3 \ [AB \rightarrow \varepsilon]$$

where $y_1 y_3 = x$, $x \in g(x')$.

In cases (ii)–(vii), we discussed all six rules simulating the application of $AB \rightarrow \varepsilon$ in G' (see (3) in the definition of R'). Cases (viii)–(xiii) should cover the rules simulating the application of $CD \rightarrow \varepsilon$ in G' (see (4)). However, by the inspection of these two sets of rules, it is easy to see that they work analogously. Therefore, we leave this part of the proof to the reader.

We have completed the proof and established Claim 4 by the principle of induction. □

Observe that $L(G) = L(G')$ can be easily derived from the above claim. According to the definition of g, we have $g(a) = \{a\}$ for all $a \in \Delta$. Thus, from Claim 4, we have for any $x \in \Delta^*$

$$S \Rightarrow_G^* x \quad \text{if and only if} \quad S' \Rightarrow_{G'}^+ @x@.$$

Since

$$@x@ \Rightarrow_{G'}^2 x \ [(@ \rightarrow \varepsilon, N')(@ \rightarrow \varepsilon, N')],$$

we obtain for any $x \in \Delta^*$:

$$S \Rightarrow_G^* x \quad \text{if and only if} \quad S' \Rightarrow_{G'}^+ x.$$

Consequently, $L(G) = L(G')$, and the theorem holds. ■

Semi-conditional context grammars

The notion of a semi-conditional grammar, discussed in this section, is defined as a context-conditional grammar in which the cardinality of any context-conditional set is no more than one.

The present section consists of two subsections: definitions and examples, and generative power. The former defines and illustrates semi-conditional grammars, while the latter studies their generative power.

Definitions and examples

The definition of a semi-conditional grammar opens this section.

Definition 11.15. *Let $G = (\Sigma, \Delta, R, S)$ be a context-conditional grammar. G is called a* semi-conditional grammar *(an* sc-grammar *for short) provided that every $(A \rightarrow x, Per, For) \in R$ satisfies* card $(Per) \leq 1$ *and* card $(For) \leq 1$.

Let $G = (\Sigma, \Delta, R, S)$ be an sc-grammar, and let $(A \to x, Per, For) \in R$. For brevity, we omit braces in each $(A \to x, Per, For) \in R$, and instead of $\emptyset$, we write 0. For instance, we write $(A \to x, BC, 0)$ instead of $(A \to x, \{BC\}, \emptyset)$.

The families of languages generated by sc-grammars and propagating sc-grammars of degree (r, s) are denoted by **SCOND**(r, s) and **PSCOND**(r, s), respectively. The families of languages generated by sc-grammars and propagating sc-grammars of any degree are defined as

$$\mathbf{SCOND} = \bigcup_{r=0}^{\infty}\bigcup_{s=0}^{\infty}\mathbf{SCOND}(r, s)$$

and

$$\mathbf{PSCOND} = \bigcup_{r=0}^{\infty}\bigcup_{s=0}^{\infty}\mathbf{PSCOND}(r, s).$$

First, we give examples of sc-grammars with degrees $(1, 0)$, $(0, 1)$, and $(1, 1)$.

Example 11.3 (see [16]). *Let us consider an sc-grammar*

$$G = (\{S, A, B, A', B', a, b\}, \{a, b\}, R, S)$$

where

$$\begin{aligned} R = \{&(S \to AB, 0, 0), (A \to A'A', B, 0),\\ &(B \to bB', 0, 0), (A' \to A, B', 0),\\ &(B' \to B, 0, 0), (B \to b, 0, 0),\\ &(A' \to a, 0, 0), (A \to a, 0, 0)\}. \end{aligned}$$

Observe that A can be replaced by $A'A'$ only if B occurs in the rewritten string, and A' can be replaced by A only if B' occurs in the rewritten string. If there is an occurrence of B, the number of occurrences of A and A' can be doubled. However, the application of $(B \to bB', 0, 0)$ implies an introduction of one occurrence of b. As a result,

$$L(G) = \{a^n b^m \mid m \geq 1,\ 1 \leq n \leq 2^m\},$$

which is a non-context-free language.

Example 11.4 (see [16]). *Let*

$$G = (\{S, A, B, A', A'', B', a, b, c\}, \{a, b, c\}, R, S)$$

be an sc-grammar, where

$$\begin{aligned} P = \{&(S \to AB, 0, 0), (A \to A', 0, B'),\\ &(A' \to A''A'', 0, c), (A'' \to A, 0, B),\\ &(B \to bB', 0, 0), (B' \to B, 0, 0),\\ &(B \to c, 0, 0), (A \to a, 0, 0),\\ &(A'' \to a, 0, 0)\}. \end{aligned}$$

In this case, we get the non-context-free language

$$L(G) = \{a^n b^m c \mid m \geq 0,\ 1 \leq n \leq 2^{m+1}\}.$$

Example 11.5. *Let*

$$G = (\{S, P, Q, U, X, Y, Z, a, b, c, d, e, f\}, \{a, b, c, d, e, f\}, R, S)$$

be an sc-grammar, where

$$\begin{aligned} R = \{ & (S \to PQU, 0, 0), \\ & (P \to aXb, Q, Z), \\ & (Q \to cYd, X, Z), \\ & (U \to eZf, X, Q), \\ & (X \to P, Z, Q), \\ & (Y \to Q, P, U), \\ & (Z \to U, P, Y), \\ & (P \to \varepsilon, Q, Z), \\ & (Q \to \varepsilon, U, P), \\ & (U \to \varepsilon, 0, Y)\}. \end{aligned}$$

Note that this grammar is an sc-grammar of degree $(1, 1)$. *Consider* $aabbccddeeff$. *For this string,* G *makes the following derivation:*

$$\begin{aligned} S \Rightarrow\ & PQU \Rightarrow aXbQU \Rightarrow aXbcYdU \Rightarrow aXbcYdeZf \Rightarrow \\ & aPbcYdeZf \Rightarrow aPbcQdeZf \Rightarrow aPbcQdeUf \Rightarrow \\ & aaXbbcQdeUf \Rightarrow aaXbbccYddeUf \Rightarrow aaXbbccYddeeZff \Rightarrow \\ & aaPbbccYddeeZff \Rightarrow aaPbbccQddeeZff \Rightarrow aaPbbccQddeeUff \Rightarrow \\ & aabbccQddeeUff \Rightarrow aabbccddeeUff \Rightarrow aabbccddeeff. \end{aligned}$$

Clearly, G *generates the following language:*

$$L(G) = \{a^n b^n c^n d^n e^n f^n \mid n \geq 0\}.$$

As is obvious, this language is non-context-free.

Generative power

The present section establishes the generative power of sc-grammars.

Theorem 11.27. $\mathbf{PSCOND}(0,0) = \mathbf{SCOND}(0,0) = \mathbf{CF}$.

Proof. Follows directly from the definitions. ∎

Theorem 11.28. $\mathbf{CF} \subset \mathbf{PSCOND}(1,0)$, $\mathbf{CF} \subset \mathbf{PSCOND}(0,1)$.

Proof. In Examples 11.3 and 11.4, we show propagating sc-grammars of degrees $(1, 0)$ and $(0, 1)$ that generate non-context-free languages. Therefore, the theorem holds. ∎

Theorem 11.29. $\mathbf{PSCOND}(1,1) \subset \mathbf{CS}$.

Proof. Consider a propagating sc-grammar of degree $(1, 1)$

$$G = (\Sigma, \Delta, R, S).$$

If $(A \to x, A, \beta) \in R$, the permitting condition A does not impose any restriction. Hence, we can replace this rule by $(A \to x, 0, \beta)$. If $(A \to x, \alpha, A) \in R$, this rule cannot ever by applied; thus, we can remove it from R. Let $\Delta' = \{a' \mid a \in \Delta\}$ and $\Sigma' = \Sigma \cup \Delta' \cup \{S', X, Y\}$. Define a homomorphism τ from Σ^* to $((\Sigma - \Delta) \cup (\Delta'))^*$ as $\tau(a) = a'$ for all $a \in \Delta$ and $\tau(A) = A$ for every $A \in \Sigma - \Delta$. Furthermore, introduce a function g from $\Sigma \cup \{0\}$ to $2^{((\Sigma-\Delta)\cup\Delta')}$ as $g(0) = \emptyset$, $g(a) = \{a'\}$ for all $a \in \Delta$, and $g(A) = \{A\}$ for all $A \in \Sigma - \Delta$. Next, construct the propagating random context grammar

$$G' = (\Sigma', \Delta \cup \{c\}, R', S')$$

where

$$\begin{aligned} R' = \{&(S' \to SX, \emptyset, \emptyset), (X \to Y, \emptyset, \emptyset), (Y \to c, \emptyset, \emptyset)\} \cup \\ \{&(A \to \tau(x), g(\alpha) \cup \{X\}, g(\beta)) \mid (A \to x, \alpha, \beta) \in R\} \cup \\ \{&(a' \to a, \{Y\}, \emptyset) \mid a \in \Delta\}. \end{aligned}$$

It is obvious that $L(G') = L(G)\{c\}$. Therefore, $L(G)\{c\} \in \mathbf{RC}^{-\varepsilon}$. Recall that $\mathbf{RC}^{-\varepsilon}$ is closed under restricted homomorphisms (see page 48 in [12]), and by Theorem 11.19, it holds that $\mathbf{RC}^{-\varepsilon} \subset \mathbf{CS}$. Thus, we obtain $\mathbf{PSCOND}(1, 1) \subset \mathbf{CS}$. ■

The following corollary summarizes the generative power of propagating sc-grammars of degrees (1, 0), (0, 1), and (1, 1)—that is, the propagating sc-grammars containing only symbols as their context conditions.

Corollary 11.5.

$$\begin{aligned} &\mathbf{CF} \subset \mathbf{PSCOND}(0, 1) \subseteq \mathbf{PSCOND}(1, 1), \\ &\mathbf{CF} \subset \mathbf{PSCOND}(1, 0) \subseteq \mathbf{PSCOND}(1, 1), \\ &\quad \mathbf{PSCOND}(1, 1) \subseteq \mathbf{RC}^{-\varepsilon} \subset \mathbf{CS}. \end{aligned}$$

Proof. This corollary follows from Theorems 11.27, 11.28, and 11.29. ■

The next theorem says that propagating sc-grammars of degrees (1, 2), (2, 1) and propagating sc-grammars of any degree generate exactly the family of context-sensitive languages. Furthermore, if we allow erasing rules, these grammars generate the family of recursively enumerable languages.

Theorem 11.30.

$$\begin{array}{c} \mathbf{CF} \\ \subset \\ \mathbf{PSCOND}(2, 1) = \mathbf{PSCOND}(1, 2) = \mathbf{PSCOND} = \mathbf{CS} \\ \subset \\ \mathbf{SCOND}(2, 1) = \mathbf{SCOND}(1, 2) = \mathbf{SCOND} = \mathbf{RE}. \end{array}$$

Proof. In the next section, we prove a stronger result in terms of a special variant of sc-grammars—simple semi-conditional grammars (see Theorems 11.34 and 11.35). Therefore, we omit the proof here. ■

In [17], the following theorem is proved. It shows that **RE** can be characterized even by sc-grammars of degree (2, 1) with a reduced number of nonterminals and conditional rules.

Theorem 11.31 (see Theorem 1 in [17]). *Every recursively enumerable language can be generated by an sc-grammar of degree* (2, 1) *having no more than nine conditional rules and ten nonterminals.*

Simple semi-conditional context grammars

The notion of a simple semi-conditional grammar—that is, the subject of this section—is defined as an sc-grammar in which every rule has no more than one condition.

The present section consists of two subsections. First, it defines simple semi-conditional grammars, later, it discusses their generative power and reduction.

Definitions and examples

First, we define simple semi-conditional grammars. Then, we illustrate them.

Definition 11.16. *Let* $G = (\Sigma, \Delta, R, S)$ *be a semi-conditional grammar. G is a* simple semi-conditional grammar *(an* ssc-grammar *for short) if* $(A \to x, \alpha, \beta) \in R$ *implies that* $0 \in \{\alpha, \beta\}$.

In other words, G is an ssc-grammar if and only if every $(A \to x, Per, For) \in R$ satisfies $\text{card}\,(Per) + \text{card}\,(For) \leq 1$.

The families of languages generated by ssc-grammars and propagating ssc-grammars of degree (r, s) are denoted by $\mathbf{SSCOND}(r, s)$ and $\mathbf{PSSCOND}(r, s)$, respectively. Furthermore, set

$$\mathbf{SSCOND} = \bigcup_{r=0}^{\infty} \bigcup_{s=0}^{\infty} \mathbf{SSCOND}(r, s)$$

and

$$\mathbf{PSSCOND} = \bigcup_{r=0}^{\infty} \bigcup_{s=0}^{\infty} \mathbf{PSSCOND}(r, s).$$

Example 11.6. *Let*

$$G = (\{S, A, X, C, Y, a, b\}, \{a, b\}, R, S)$$

be an ssc-grammar, where

$$\begin{aligned} R = \{&(S \to AC, 0, 0),\\ &(A \to aXb, Y, 0),\\ &(C \to Y, A, 0),\\ &(Y \to Cc, 0, A),\\ &(A \to ab, Y, 0),\\ &(Y \to c, 0, A),\\ &(X \to A, C, 0)\}. \end{aligned}$$

Notice that G is propagating, and it has degree $(1,1)$. *Consider aabbcc. G derives this string as follows:*

$$S \Rightarrow AC \Rightarrow AY \Rightarrow aXbY \Rightarrow aXbCc \Rightarrow$$
$$aAbCc \Rightarrow aAbYc \Rightarrow aabbYc \Rightarrow aabbcc.$$

Obviously,

$$L(G) = \{a^n b^n c^n \mid n \geq 1\}.$$

Example 11.7. *Let*

$$G = (\{S, A, B, X, Y, a\}, \{a\}, R, S)$$

be an ssc-grammar, where

$$\begin{aligned} R = \{&(S \rightarrow a, 0, 0),\\ &(S \rightarrow X, 0, 0),\\ &(X \rightarrow YB, 0, A),\\ &(X \rightarrow aB, 0, A),\\ &(Y \rightarrow XA, 0, B),\\ &(Y \rightarrow aA, 0, B),\\ &(A \rightarrow BB, XA, 0),\\ &(B \rightarrow AA, YB, 0),\\ &(B \rightarrow a, a, 0)\}. \end{aligned}$$

G is a propagating ssc-grammar of degree $(2,1)$. *Consider the string aaaaaaaa. G derives this string as follows:*

$$S \Rightarrow X \Rightarrow YB \Rightarrow YAA \Rightarrow XAAA \Rightarrow XBBAA \Rightarrow XBBABB \Rightarrow$$
$$XBBBBBB \Rightarrow aBBBBBBB \Rightarrow aBBaBBBB \Rightarrow^6 aaaaaaaa.$$

Observe that G generates the following non-context-free language

$$L(G) = \left\{a^{2^n} \mid n \geq 0\right\}.$$

Generative power and reduction

The power and reduction of ssc-grammars represent the central topic discussed in this section.

Theorem 11.32. $\mathbf{PSSCOND}(2,1) = \mathbf{CS}$.

Proof. Because $\mathbf{PSSCOND}(2,1) \subseteq \mathbf{CG}^{-\varepsilon}$ and Lemma 11.3 implies that $\mathbf{CG}^{-\varepsilon} \subseteq \mathbf{CS}$, it is sufficient to prove the converse inclusion.

Let $G = (\Sigma, \Delta, R, S)$ be a CSG in the Penttonen normal form (see Theorem 11.3). We construct an ssc-grammar

$$G' = (\Sigma \cup W, \Delta, R', S)$$

that generates $L(G)$. Let

$$W = \{\widetilde{B} \mid AB \rightarrow AC \in P,\ A, B, C \in \Sigma - \Delta\}.$$

Define R' in the following way:

(1) If $A \rightarrow x \in R, A \in \Sigma - \Delta, x \in \Delta \cup (\Sigma - \Delta)^2$, then add $(A \rightarrow x, 0, 0)$ to R';
(2) If $AB \rightarrow AC \in P$, $A, B, C \in \Sigma - \Delta$, then add $(B \rightarrow \widetilde{B}, 0, \widetilde{B})$, $(\widetilde{B} \rightarrow C, A\widetilde{B}, 0)$, $(\widetilde{B} \rightarrow B, 0, 0)$ to R'.

Notice that G' is a propagating ssc-grammar of degree (2, 1). Moreover, from (2), we have for any $\widetilde{B} \in W$,

$$S \Rightarrow_{G'}^{*} w \quad \text{implies} \quad \text{occur}\,(\widetilde{B}, w) \leq 1$$

for all $w \in \Sigma'^*$ because the only rule that can generate $\widetilde{B}$ is of the form $(B \rightarrow \widetilde{B}, 0, \widetilde{B})$.

Let g be a finite substitution from Σ^* into $(\Sigma \cup W)^*$ defined as follows. For all $D \in \Sigma$,

(1) If $\widetilde{D} \in W$, then $g(D) = \{D, \widetilde{D}\}$;
(2) If $\widetilde{D} \notin W$, then $g(D) = \{D\}$.

Claim 1. *For any $x \in \Sigma^+$, $m, n \geq 0$, $S \Rightarrow_G^m x$ if and only if $S \Rightarrow_{G'}^n x'$ with $x' \in g(x)$.*

Proof. The proof is divided into the only-if part and the if part.

Only If. This is proved by induction on $m \geq 0$.

Basis. Let $m = 0$. The only x is S as $S \Rightarrow_G^0 S$. Clearly, $S \Rightarrow_{G'}^n S$ for $n = 0$ and $S \in g(S)$.

Induction Hypothesis. Assume that the claim holds for all derivations of length m or less, for some $m \geq 0$.

Induction Step. Consider any derivation of the form

$$S \Rightarrow_G^{m+1} x$$

where $x \in \Sigma^+$. Because $m + 1 \geq 1$, there is some $y \in \Sigma^*$ and $p \in R$ such that

$$S \Rightarrow_G^m y \Rightarrow_{G'} x\ [p].$$

By the induction hypothesis,

$$S \Rightarrow_{G'}^n y'$$

for some $y' \in g(y)$ and $n \geq 0$. Next, we distinguish between two cases: case (i) considers p with one nonterminal on its left-hand side, and case (ii) considers p with two nonterminals on its left-hand side.

(i) Let $p = D \rightarrow y_2 \in R$, $D \in \Sigma - \Delta$, $y_2 \in \Delta \cup (\Sigma - \Delta)^2$, $y = y_1 D y_3$, $y_1, y_3 \in \Sigma^*$, $x = y_1 y_2 y_3$, $y' = y_1' X y_3'$, $y_1' \in g(y_1)$, $y_3' \in g(y_3)$, and $X \in g(D)$. By (1) in the definition of R', $(D \rightarrow y_2, 0, 0) \in R$. If $X = D$, then

$$S \Rightarrow_{G'}^n y_1' D y_3' \Rightarrow_{G'} y_1' y_2 y_3'\ [(D \rightarrow y_2, 0, 0)].$$

Because $y_1' \in g(y_1)$, $y_3' \in g(y_3)$, and $y_2 \in g(y_2)$, we obtain $y_1' y_2 y_3' \in g(y_1 y_2 y_3) = g(x)$. If $X = \widetilde{D}$, we have $(X \rightarrow D, 0, 0)$ in R', so

$$S \Rightarrow_{G'}^n y_1' X y_3' \Rightarrow_{G'} y_1' D y_3' \Rightarrow_{G'} y_1' y_2 y_3'\ [(X \rightarrow D, 0, 0)(D \rightarrow y_2, 0, 0)]$$

and $y_1' y_2 y_3' \in g(x)$;

(ii) Let $p = AB \to AC \in R$, $A, B, C \in \Sigma - \Delta$, $y = y_1ABy_2$, $y_1, y_2 \in \Sigma^*$, $x = y_1ACy_2$, $y' = y'_1XYy'_2$, $y'_1 \in g(y_1)$, $y'_2 \in g(y_2)$, $X \in g(A)$, and $Y \in g(B)$. Recall that for any $\widetilde{B}$, occur $(\widetilde{B}, y') \leq 1$ and $(\widetilde{B} \to B, 0, 0) \in R'$. Then,

$$y' \Rightarrow^i_{G'} y'_1ABy'_2$$

for some $i \in \{0, 1, 2\}$. At this point, we have

$$\begin{aligned} S &\Rightarrow^*_{G'} y'_1ABy'_2 \\ &\Rightarrow_{G'} y'_1A\widetilde{B}y'_2 \ [(B \to \widetilde{B}, 0, \widetilde{B})] \\ &\Rightarrow_{G'} y'_1ACy'_2 \ [(\widetilde{B} \to C, A\widetilde{B}, 0)] \end{aligned}$$

where $y'_1ACy'_2 \in g(x)$.

If. This is established by induction on $n \geq 0$; in other words, we demonstrate that if $S \Rightarrow^n_{G'} x'$ with $x' \in g(x)$ for some $x \in \Sigma^+$, then $S \Rightarrow^*_G x$.

Basis. For $n = 0$, x' surely equals S as $S \Rightarrow^0_{G'} S$. Because $S \in g(S)$, we have $x = S$. Clearly, $S \Rightarrow^0_G S$.

Induction Hypothesis. Assume that the claim holds for all derivations of length n or less, for some $n \geq 0$.

Induction Step. Consider any derivation of the form

$$S \Rightarrow^{n+1}_{G'} x'$$

with $x' \in g(x)$, $x \in \Sigma^+$. As $n + 1 \geq 1$, there exists some $y \in \Sigma^+$ such that

$$S \Rightarrow^n_{G'} y' \Rightarrow_{G'} x' \ [p]$$

where $y' \in g(y)$. By the induction hypothesis,

$$S \Rightarrow^*_G y.$$

Let $y' = y'_1B'y'_2$, $y = y_1By_2$, $y'_1 \in g(y_1)$, $y'_2 \in g(y_2)$, $y_1, y_2 \in \Sigma^*$, $B' \in g(B)$, $B \in \Sigma - \Delta$, $x' = y'_1z'y'_2$, and $p = (B' \to z', \alpha, \beta) \in R'$. The following three cases cover all possible forms of the derivation step $y' \Rightarrow_{G'} x'$ $[p]$.

(i) Let $z' \in g(B)$. Then,

$$S \Rightarrow^*_G y_1By_2$$

where $y'_1z'y'_2 \in g(y_1By_2)$, that is, $x' \in g(y_1By_2)$;

(ii) Let $B' = B \in \Sigma - \Delta$, $z' \in \Delta \cup (\Sigma - \Delta)^2$, $\alpha = \beta = 0$. Then, there exists a rule, $B \to z' \in R$, so

$$S \Rightarrow^*_G y_1By_2 \Rightarrow_G y_1z'y_2 \ [B \to z'].$$

Since $z' \in g(z')$, we have $x = y_1z'y_2$ such that $x' \in g(x)$;

(iii) Let $B' = \widetilde{B}$, $z' = C$, $\alpha = A\widetilde{B}$, $\beta = 0$, $A, B, C \in \Sigma - \Delta$. Then, there exists a rule of the form $AB \to AC \in R$. Since occur $(Z, y') \leq 1$, $Z = \widetilde{B}$, and $A\widetilde{B} \in$ substrings (y'), we have $y'_1 = u'A$, $y_1 = uA$, $u' \in g(u)$ for some $u \in \Sigma^*$. Thus,

$$S \Rightarrow^*_G uABy_2 \Rightarrow_G uACy_2 \ [AB \to AC]$$

where $uACy_2 = y_1Cy_2$. Because $C \in g(C)$, we get $x = y_1Cy_2$ such that $x' \in g(x)$.

As cases (i)–(iii) cover all possible forms of a derivation step in G', we have completed the induction step and established Claim 1 by the principle of induction. □

The statement of Theorem 11.32 follows immediately from Claim 1. Because for all $a \in \Delta$, $g(a) = \{a\}$, we have for every $w \in \Delta^+$,

$$S \Rightarrow_G^* w \quad \text{if and only if} \quad S \Rightarrow_{G'}^* w.$$

Therefore, $L(G) = L(G')$, so the theorem holds. ■

Corollary 11.6.

$$\mathbf{PSSCOND}(2,1) = \mathbf{PSSCOND} = \mathbf{PSCOND}(2,1) = \mathbf{PSCOND} = \mathbf{CS}.$$

Proof. This corollary follows from Theorem 11.32 and the definitions of propagating ssc-grammars. ■

Next, we turn our investigation to ssc-grammars of degree (2, 1) with erasing rules. We prove that these grammars generate precisely the family of recursively enumerable languages.

Theorem 11.33. $\mathbf{SSCOND}(2,1) = \mathbf{RE}$.

Proof. Clearly, $\mathbf{SSCOND}(2,1) \subseteq \mathbf{RE}$; hence, it is sufficient to show that $\mathbf{RE} \subseteq \mathbf{SSCOND}(2,1)$. Every recursively enumerable language $L \in \mathbf{RE}$ can be generated by a PSG G in the Penttonen normal form (see Theorem 11.2). That is, the rules of G are of the form $AB \rightarrow AC$ or $A \rightarrow x$, where $A, B, C \in \Sigma - \Delta$, $x \in \{\varepsilon\} \cup \Delta \cup (\Sigma - \Delta)^2$. Thus, the inclusion $\mathbf{RE} \subseteq \mathbf{SSCOND}(2,1)$ can be proved by analogy with the proof of Theorem 11.32. The details are left to the reader. ■

Corollary 11.7.

$$\mathbf{SSCOND}(2,1) = \mathbf{SSCOND} = \mathbf{SCOND}(2,1) = \mathbf{SCOND} = \mathbf{RE}.$$

To demonstrate that propagating ssc-grammars of degree (1, 2) characterize **CS**, we first establish a normal form for CSGs.

Lemma 11.6. *Let $L' \in$ **CS** and $L = L' - \{\varepsilon\}$. Then, L can be generated by a CSG*

$$G = (\{S\} \cup N_{CF} \cup N_{CS} \cup \Delta, \Delta, R, S)$$

where $\{S\}$, N_{CF}, N_{CS}, and Δ are pairwise disjoint alphabets, and every rule in R is either of the form $S \rightarrow aD$ or $AB \rightarrow AC$ or $A \rightarrow x$, where $a \in \Delta$, $D \in N_{CF} \cup \{\varepsilon\}$, $B \in N_{CS}$, $A, C \in N_{CF}$, $x \in N_{CS} \cup \Delta \cup (\bigcup_{i=1}^{2} N_{CF}^i)$.

Proof. Let L be a context-sensitive language over an alphabet, Δ. Without any loss of generality, we can express L as $L = L_1 \cup L_2$, where $L_1 \subseteq \Delta$ and $L_2 \subseteq \Delta\Delta^+$. Thus, by analogy with the proofs of Theorems 1 and 2 in [16], L_2 can be represented as

$L_2 = \bigcup_{a\in\Delta} aL_a$, where each L_a is a context-sensitive language. Let L_a be generated by a CSG

$$G_a = (N_{CF_a} \cup N_{CS_a} \cup \Delta, \Delta, R_a, S_a)$$

of the form of Theorem 11.4. Clearly, we assume that for all as, the nonterminal alphabets N_{CF_a} and N_{CS_a} are pairwise disjoint. Let S be a new start symbol. Consider the CSG

$$G = (\{S\} \cup N_{CF} \cup N_{CS} \cup \Delta, \Delta, R, S)$$

where

$$\begin{aligned} N_{CF} &= \textstyle\bigcup_{a\in\Delta} N_{CF_a}, \\ N_{CS} &= \textstyle\bigcup_{a\in\Delta} N_{CS_a}, \\ R &= \textstyle\bigcup_{a\in\Delta} R_a \cup \{S \to aS_a \mid a \in \Delta\} \cup \{S \to a \mid a \in L_1\}. \end{aligned}$$

Obviously, G satisfies the required form, and we have

$$L(G) = L_1 \cup (\textstyle\bigcup_{a\in\Delta} aL(G_a)) = L_1 \cup (\textstyle\bigcup_{a\in\Delta} aL_a) = L_1 \cup L_2 = L.$$

Consequently, the lemma holds. ■

We are now ready to characterize **CS** by propagating ssc-grammars of degree $(1, 2)$.

Theorem 11.34. $\mathbf{CS} = \mathbf{PSSCOND}(1, 2)$

Proof. By Lemma 11.3, $\mathbf{PSSCOND}(1, 2) \subseteq \mathbf{CG}^{-\varepsilon} \subseteq \mathbf{CS}$; thus, it is sufficient to prove the converse inclusion.

Let L be a context-sensitive language. Without any loss of generality, we assume that L is generated by a CSG

$$G = (\{S\} \cup N_{CF} \cup N_{CS} \cup \Delta, \Delta, R, S)$$

of the form of Lemma 11.6. Set

$$\Sigma = \{S\} \cup N_{CF} \cup N_{CS} \cup \Delta.$$

Let q be the cardinality of Σ; $q \geq 1$. Furthermore, let f be an arbitrary bijection from Σ onto $\{1, \ldots, q\}$, and let f^{-1} be the inverse of f. Let

$$\widetilde{G} = (\widetilde{\Sigma}, \Delta, \widetilde{R}, S)$$

be a propagating ssc-grammar of degree $(1, 2)$, in which

$$\widetilde{\Sigma} = \left(\bigcup_{i=1}^{4} W_i \right) \cup \Sigma$$

where

$$\begin{aligned} W_1 &= \{\langle a, AB \to AC, j\rangle \mid a \in \Delta,\ AB \to AC \in R,\ 1 \leq j \leq 5\}, \\ W_2 &= \{[a, AB \to AC, j] \mid a \in \Delta,\ AB \to AC \in R,\ 1 \leq j \leq q + 3\}, \\ W_3 &= \{\widehat{B}, B', B'' \mid B \in N_{CS}\}, \\ W_4 &= \{\bar{a} \mid a \in \Delta\}. \end{aligned}$$

$\widetilde{R}$ is defined as follows:

(1) If $S \to aA \in R$, $a \in \Delta$, $A \in (N_{CF} \cup \{\varepsilon\})$, then add $(S \to \bar{a}A, 0, 0)$ to $\widetilde{R}$;
(2) If $a \in \Delta$, $A \to x \in R$, $A \in N_{CF}$, $x \in (\Sigma - \{S\}) \cup (N_{CF})^2$, then add $(A \to x, \bar{a}, 0)$ to $\widetilde{R}$;
(3) If $a \in \Delta$, $AB \to AC \in R$, $A, C \in N_{CF}$, $B \in N_{CS}$, then add the following rules to R' (an informal explanation of these rules can be found next):
 (3.a) $(\bar{a} \to \langle a, AB \to AC, 1\rangle, 0, 0)$,
 (3.b) $(B \to B', \langle a, AB \to AC, 1\rangle, 0)$,
 (3.c) $(B \to \widehat{B}, \langle a, AB \to AC, 1\rangle, 0)$,
 (3.d) $(\langle a, AB \to AC, 1\rangle \to \langle a, AB \to AC, 2\rangle, 0, B)$,
 (3.e) $(\widehat{B} \to B'', 0, B'')$,
 (3.f) $(\langle a, AB \to AC, 2\rangle \to \langle a, AB \to AC, 3\rangle, 0, \widehat{B})$,
 (3.g) $(B'' \to [a, AB \to AC, 1], \langle a, AB \to AC, 3\rangle, 0)$,
 (3.h) $([a, AB \to AC, j] \to [a, AB \to AC, j+1], 0, f^{-1}(j)[a, AB \to AC, j])$, for all $j = 1, \ldots, q, f(A) \neq j$,
 (3.i) $([a, AB \to AC, f(A)] \to [a, AB \to AC, f(A)+1], 0, 0)$,
 (3.j) $([a, AB \to AC, q+1] \to [a, AB \to AC, q+2], 0, B'[a, AB \to AC, q+1])$,
 (3.k) $([a, AB \to AC, q+2] \to [a, AB \to AC, q+3], 0, \langle a, AB \to AC, 3\rangle [a, AB \to AC, q+2])$,
 (3.l) $(\langle a, AB \to AC, 3\rangle \to \langle a, AB \to AC, 4\rangle, [a, AB \to AC, q+3], 0)$,
 (3.m) $(B' \to B, \langle a, AB \to AC, 4\rangle, 0)$,
 (3.n) $(\langle a, AB \to AC, 4\rangle \to \langle a, AB \to AC, 5\rangle, 0, B')$,
 (3.o) $([a, AB \to AC, q+3] \to C, \langle a, AB \to AC, 5\rangle, 0)$,
 (3.p) $(\langle a, AB \to AC, 5\rangle \to \bar{a}, 0, [a, AB \to AC, q+3])$.
(4) if $a \in \Delta$, then add $(\bar{a} \to a, 0, 0)$ to $\widetilde{R}$.

Let us informally explain the basic idea behind (3)—the heart of the construction. The rules introduced in (3) simulate the application of rules of the form $AB \to AC$ in G as follows: an occurrence of B is chosen, and its left neighbor is checked not to belong to $\widetilde{\Sigma} - \{A\}$. At this point, the left neighbor necessarily equals A, so B is rewritten with C.

Formally, we define a finite substitution g from Σ^* into $\widetilde{\Sigma}^*$ as follows:

(a) If $D \in \Sigma$, then add D to $g(D)$;
(b) If $\langle a, AB \to AC, j\rangle \in W_1$, $a \in \Delta$, $AB \to AC \in R$, $B \in N_{CS}$, $A, C \in N_{CF}$, $j \in \{1, \ldots, 5\}$, then add $\langle a, AB \to AC, j\rangle$ to $g(a)$;
(c) If $[a, AB \to AC, j] \in W_2$, $a \in \Delta$, $AB \to AC \in R$, $B \in N_{CS}$, $A, C \in N_{CF}$, $j \in \{1, \ldots, q+3\}$, then add $[a, AB \to AC, j]$ to $g(B)$;
(d) If $\{\widehat{B}, B', B''\} \subseteq W_3$, $B \in N_{CS}$, then include $\{\widehat{B}, B', B''\}$ into $g(B)$;
(e) If $\bar{a} \in W_4$, $a \in \Delta$, then add $\bar{a}$ to $g(a)$.

Let g^{-1} be the inverse of g. To show that $L(G) = L(\widetilde{G})$, we first prove three claims.

Claim 1. *$S \Rightarrow_G^+ x$, $x \in \Sigma^*$, implies that $x \in \Delta(\Sigma - \{S\})^*$.*

Proof. Observe that the start symbol S does not appear on the right side of any rule and that $S \to x \in R$ implies that $x \in \Delta \cup \Delta(\Sigma - \{S\})$. Hence, the claim holds. □

Claim 2. *If $S \Rightarrow^{+}_{\tilde{G}} x$, $x \in \tilde{\Sigma}^*$, then x has one of the following seven forms:*

(I) $x = ay$, *where* $a \in \Delta$, $y \in (\Sigma - \{S\})^*$;

(II) $x = \bar{a}y$, *where* $\bar{a} \in W_4$, $y \in (\Sigma - \{S\})^*$;

(III) $x = \langle a, AB \to AC, 1\rangle y$, *where* $\langle a, AB \to AC, 1\rangle \in W_1$, $y \in ((\Sigma - \{S\}) \cup \{B', \widehat{B}, B''\})^*$, occur $(B'', y) \leq 1$;

(IV) $x = \langle a, AB \to AC, 2\rangle y$, *where* $\langle a, AB \to AC, 2\rangle \in W_1$, $y \in ((\Sigma - \{S, B\}) \cup \{B', \widehat{B}, B''\})^*$, occur $(B', y) \leq 1$;

(V) $x = \langle a, AB \to AC, 3\rangle y$, *where* $\langle a, AB \to AC, 3\rangle \in W_1$, $y \in ((\Sigma - \{S, B\}) \cup \{B'\})^*(\{[a, AB \to AC, j] \mid 1 \leq j \leq q+3\} \cup \{\varepsilon, B''\})((\Sigma - \{S, B\}) \cup \{B'\})^*$;

(VI) $x = \langle a, AB \to AC, 4\rangle y$, *where* $\langle a, AB \to AC, 4\rangle \in W_1$, $y \in ((\Sigma - \{S\}) \cup \{B'\})^*[a, AB \to AC, q+3]((\Sigma - \{S\}) \cup \{B'\})^*$; *and*

(VII) $x = \langle a, AB \to AC, 5\rangle y$, *where* $\langle a, AB \to AC, 5\rangle \in W_1$, $y \in (\Sigma - \{S\})^*\{[a, AB \to AC, q+3], \varepsilon\}(\Sigma - \{S\})^*$.

Proof. The claim is proved by induction on the length of derivations.

Basis. Consider $S \Rightarrow_{\tilde{G}} x$, $x \in \tilde{\Sigma}^*$. By the inspection of the rules, we have

$$S \Rightarrow_{\tilde{G}} \bar{a}A \; [(S \to \bar{a}A, 0, 0)]$$

for some $\bar{a} \in W_4$, $A \in (\{\varepsilon\} \cup N_{CF})$. Therefore, $x = \bar{a}$ or $x = \bar{a}A$; in either case, x is a string of the required form.

Induction Hypothesis. Assume that the claim holds for all derivations of length n or less, for some $n \geq 1$.

Induction Step. Consider any derivation of the form

$$S \Rightarrow^{n+1}_{\tilde{G}} x$$

where $x \in \tilde{\Sigma}^*$. Since $n \geq 1$, we have $n + 1 \geq 2$. Thus, there is some z of the required form, $z \in \tilde{\Sigma}^*$, such that

$$S \Rightarrow^{n}_{\tilde{G}} z \Rightarrow_{\tilde{G}} x \; [p]$$

for some $p \in \tilde{R}$.

Let us first prove by contradiction that the first symbol of z does not belong to Δ. Assume that the first symbol of z belongs to Δ. As z is of the required form, we have $z = ay$ for some $a \in (\Sigma - \{S\})^*$. By the inspection of $\tilde{R}$, there is no $p \in \tilde{R}$ such that $ay \Rightarrow_{\tilde{G}} x \; [p]$, where $x \in \tilde{\Sigma}^*$. We have thus obtained a contradiction, so the first symbol of z is not in Δ.

Because the first symbol of z does not belong to Δ, z cannot have form (I); as a result, z has one of forms (II)–(VII). The following cases demonstrate that if z has one of these six forms, then x has one of the required forms, too.

(i) Assume that z is of form (II), that is, $z = \bar{a}y$, $\bar{a} \in W_4$, and $y \in (\Sigma - \{S\})^*$. By the inspection of the rules in $\tilde{R}$, we see that p has one of the following forms:
   - (i.a) $p = (A \to u, \bar{a}, 0)$, where $A \in N_{CF}$ and $u \in (\Sigma - \{S\}) \cup N^2_{CF}$;
   - (i.b) $p = (\bar{a} \to \langle a, AB \to AC, 1\rangle, 0, 0)$, where $\langle a, AB \to AC, 1\rangle \in W_1$;
   - (i.c) $p = (\bar{a} \to a, 0, 0)$, where $a \in \Delta$.

Note that rules of forms (i.a), (i.b), and (i.c) are introduced in construction steps (2), (3), and (4), respectively. If p has form (i.a), x has form (III), and if p has form (i.b), x has form (III). Finally, if p has form (i.c), then x has form (I). In any of these three cases, we obtain x that has one of the required forms;

(ii) Assume that z has form (III), that is, $z = \langle a, AB \rightarrow AC, 1\rangle y$ for some $\langle a, AB \rightarrow AC, 1\rangle \in W_1$, $\underset{\sim}{y} \in ((\Sigma - \{S\}) \cup \{B', \widehat{B}, B''\})^*$ and $\text{occur}(B'', y) \leq 1$. By the inspection of $\tilde{R}$, we see that z can be rewritten by rules of the following four forms:
   (ii.a) $(B \rightarrow B', \langle a, AB \rightarrow AC, 1\rangle, 0)$,
   (ii.b) $(B \rightarrow \widehat{B}, \langle a, AB \rightarrow AC, 1\rangle, 0)$,
   (ii.c) $(\widehat{B} \rightarrow B'', 0, B'')$ if $B'' \notin \text{symbols}(y)$, that is, $\text{occur}(B'', y) = 0$,
   (ii.d) $(\langle a, AB \rightarrow AC, 1\rangle \rightarrow \langle a, AB \rightarrow AC, 2\rangle, 0, B)$ if $B \notin \text{symbols}(y)$, that is, $\text{occur}(B, y) = 0$.

Clearly, in cases (ii.a) and (ii.b), we obtain x of form (III). If $z \Rightarrow_{\tilde{G}} x\ [p]$, where p is of form (ii.c), then $\text{occur}(B'', x) = 1$, so we get x of form (III). Finally, if we use the rule of form (ii.d), we obtain x of form (IV) because $\text{occur}(B, z) = 0$;

(iii) Assume that z is of form (IV), that is, $z = \langle a, AB \rightarrow AC, 2\rangle y$, where $\langle a, AB \rightarrow AC, 2\rangle \in W_1$, $\underset{\sim}{y} \in ((\Sigma - \{S, B\}) \cup \{B', \widehat{B}, B''\})^*$, and $\text{occur}(B'', y) \leq 1$. By the inspection of $\tilde{R}$, we see that the following two rules can be used to rewrite z
   (iii.a) $(\widehat{B} \rightarrow B'', 0, B'')$ if $B'' \notin \text{symbols}(y)$.
   (iii.b) $(\langle a, AB \rightarrow AC, 2\rangle \rightarrow \langle a, AB \rightarrow AC, 3\rangle, 0, \widehat{B})$ if $\widehat{B} \notin \text{symbols}(y)$.

In case (iii.a), we get x of form (IV). In case (iii.b), we have $\text{occur}(\widehat{B}, y) = 0$, so $\text{occur}(\widehat{B}, x) = 0$. Moreover, notice that $\text{occur}(B'', x) \leq 1$ in this case. Indeed, the symbol B'' can be generated only if there is no occurrence of B'' in a given rewritten string, so no more than one occurrence of B'' appears in any sentential form. As a result, we have $\text{occur}(B'', \langle a, AB \rightarrow AC, 3\rangle y) \leq 1$, that is, $\text{occur}(B'', x) \leq 1$. In other words, we get x of form (V);

(iv) Assume that z is of form (V), that is, $z = \langle a, AB \rightarrow AC, 3\rangle y$ for some $\langle a, AB \rightarrow AC, 3\rangle \in W_1$, $y \in ((\Sigma - \{S, B\}) \cup \{B'\})^*(\{[a, AB \rightarrow AC, j] \mid 1 \leq j \leq q+3\} \cup \{B'', \varepsilon\})((\Sigma - \{S, B\}) \cup \{B'\})^*$. Assume that $y = y_1 Y \underset{\sim}{y_2}$ with $y_1, y_2 \in ((\Sigma - \{S, B\}) \cup \{B'\})^*$. If $Y = \varepsilon$, then we can use no rule from $\tilde{R}$ to rewrite z. Because $z \Rightarrow_{\tilde{G}} x$, we have $Y \neq \varepsilon$. The following cases cover all possible forms of Y.
   (iv.a) Assume $Y = B''$. By the inspection of $\tilde{R}$, we see that the only rule that can rewrite z has the form
   $(B'' \rightarrow [a, AB \rightarrow AC, 1], \langle a, AB \rightarrow AC, 3\rangle, 0)$
   In this case, we get x of form (V);
   (iv.b) Assume $Y = [a, AB \rightarrow AC, j]$, $j \in \{1, \ldots, q\}$, and $f(A) \neq j$. Then, z can be rewritten only according to the rule

$$([a, AB \rightarrow AC, j] \rightarrow [a, AB \rightarrow AC, j+1], 0, f^{-1}(j)[a, AB \rightarrow AC, j])$$

   which can be used if the rightmost symbol of $\langle a, AB \rightarrow AC, 3\rangle y_1$ differs from $f^{-1}(j)$. Clearly, in this case, we again get x of form (V);

(iv.c) Assume $Y = [a, AB \to AC, j]$, $j \in \{1, \ldots, q\}$, $f(A) = j$. This case forms an analogy to case (iv.b) except that the rule of the form

$$([a, AB \to AC, f(A)] \to [a, AB \to AC, f(A) + 1], 0, 0)$$

is now used;

(iv.d) Assume $Y = [a, AB \to AC, q + 1]$. This case forms an analogy to case (iv.b); the only change is the application of the rule

$$([a, AB \to AC, q + 1] \to [a, AB \to AC, q + 2], \\ 0, B'[a, AB \to AC, q + 1]);$$

(iv.e) Assume $Y = [a, AB \to AC, q + 2]$. This case forms an analogy to case (iv.b) except that the rule

$$([a, AB \to AC, q + 2] \to [a, AB \to AC, q + 3], 0, \\ \langle a, AB \to AC, 3\rangle[a, AB \to AC, q + 2])$$

is used;

(iv.f) Assume $Y = [a, AB \to AC, q + 3]$. By the inspection of $\widetilde{R}$, we see that the only rule that can rewrite z is

$$(\langle a, AB \to AC, 3\rangle \to \langle a, AB \to AC, 4\rangle, [a, AB \to AC, q + 3], 0)$$

If this rule is used, we get x of form (VI);

(v) Assume that z is of form (VI), that is, $z = \langle a, AB \to AC, 4\rangle y$, where $\langle a, AB \to AC, 4\rangle \in W_1$ and $y \in ((\Sigma - \{S\}) \cup \{B'\})^*[a, AB \to AC, q + 3]((\Sigma - \{S\}) \cup \{B'\})^*$. By the inspection of $\widetilde{R}$, these two rules can rewrite z

(v.a) $(B' \to B, \langle a, AB \to AC, 4\rangle, 0)$,

(v.b) $(\langle a, AB \to AC, 4\rangle \to \langle a, AB \to AC, 5\rangle, 0, B')$ if $B' \notin \text{symbols}(y)$.

Clearly, in case (v.a), we get x of form (VI). In case (v.b), we get x of form (VII) because $\text{occur}(B', y) = 0$, so $y \in (\Sigma - \{S\})^*\{[a, AB \to AC, q + 3], \varepsilon\}(\Sigma - \{S\})^*$;

(vi) Assume that z is of form ((VII), that is, $z = \langle a, AB \to AC, 5\rangle y$, where $\langle a, AB \to AC, 5\rangle \in W_1$ and $y \in (\Sigma - \{S\})^*\{[a, AB \to AC, q + 3], \varepsilon\}(\Sigma - \{S\})^*$. By the inspection of $\widetilde{R}$, one of the following two rules can be used to rewrite z.

(vi.a) $([a, AB \to AC, q + 3] \to C, \langle a, AB \to AC, 5\rangle, 0)$,

(vi.b) $(\langle a, AB \to AC, 5\rangle \to \bar{a}, 0, [a, AB \to AC, q + 3])$ if $[a, AB \to AC, q + 3] \notin \text{symbols}(z)$.

In case (vi.a), we get x of form (VII). Case (vi.b) implies that $\text{occur}([a, AB \to AC, q + 3], y) = 0$; thus, x is of form (II).

This completes the induction step and establishes Claim 2. □

Claim 3. *It holds that*

$$S \Rightarrow^m_G w \quad \textit{if and only if} \quad S \Rightarrow^n_{\widetilde{G}} v$$

where $v \in g(w)$ *and* $w \in \Sigma^+$, *for some* $m, n \geq 0$.

Proof. The proof is divided into the only-if part and the if part.

Only If. The only-if part is established by induction on m, that is, we have to demonstrate that

$$S \Rightarrow^m_G w \quad \text{implies} \quad S \Rightarrow^*_{\widetilde{G}} v$$

for some $v \in g(w)$ and $w \in \Sigma^+$.

Basis. Let $m = 0$. The only w is S because $S \Rightarrow^0_G S$. Clearly, $S \Rightarrow^0_{\widetilde{G}} S$, and $S \in g(S)$.

Induction Hypothesis. Suppose that the claim holds for all derivations of length m or less, for some $m \geq 0$.

Induction Step. Let us consider any derivation of the form

$$S \Rightarrow^{m+1}_G x$$

where $x \in \Sigma^+$. Because $m + 1 \geq 1$, there are $y \in \Sigma^+$ and $p \in R$ such that

$$S \Rightarrow^m_G y \Rightarrow_G x \; [p]$$

and by the induction hypothesis, there is also a derivation

$$S \Rightarrow^n_{\widetilde{G}} \widetilde{y}$$

for some $\widetilde{y} \in g(y)$. The following cases cover all possible forms of p.

(i) Let $p = S \to aA \in R$ for some $a \in \Delta$, $A \in N_{CF} \cup \{\varepsilon\}$. Then, by Claim 1, $m = 0$, so $y = S$ and $x = aA$. By (1) in the construction of $\widetilde{G}$, $(S \to \bar{a}A, 0, 0) \in \widetilde{R}$. Hence,

$$S \Rightarrow_{\widetilde{G}} \widetilde{a}A$$

where $\widetilde{a}A \in g(aA)$;

(ii) Let us assume that $p = D \to y_2 \in R$, $D \in N_{CF}$, $y_2 \in (\Sigma - \{S\}) \cup N^2_{CF}$, $y = y_1Dy_3$, $y_1, y_3 \in \Sigma^*$, and $x = y_1y_2y_3$. From the definition of g, it is clear that $g(Z) = \{Z\}$ for all $Z \in N_{CF}$; therefore, we can express $\widetilde{y} = z_1Dz_3$, where $z_1 \in g(y_1)$ and $z_3 \in g(y_3)$. Without any loss of generality, we can also assume that $y_1 = au$, $a \in \Delta$, $u \in (\Sigma - \{S\})^*$ (see Claim 1), so $z_1 = a''u''$, $a'' \in g(a)$, and $u'' \in g(u)$. Moreover, by (2) in the construction, we have $(D \to y_2, \bar{a}, 0) \in \widetilde{R}$. The following cases cover all possible forms of a'':

(a) Let $a'' = \bar{a}$ (see (II) in Claim 2). Then, we have

$$S \Rightarrow^n_{\widetilde{G}} \bar{a}u''Dz_3 \Rightarrow_{\widetilde{G}} \bar{a}u''y_2z_3 \; [(D \to y_2, \bar{a}, 0)]$$

and $\bar{a}u''y_2z_3 = z_1y_2z_3 \in g(y_1y_2y_3) = g(x)$;

(b) Let $a'' = a$ (see (I) in Claim 2). By (4) in the construction of $\widetilde{G}$, we can express the derivation

$$S \Rightarrow^n_{\widetilde{G}} au''Dz_3$$

as

$$S \Rightarrow^{n-1}_{\widetilde{G}} \bar{a}u''Dz_3 \Rightarrow_{\widetilde{G}} au''Dz_3 \ [(\bar{a} \to a, 0, 0)].$$

Thus, there exists the derivation

$$S \Rightarrow^{n-1}_{\widetilde{G}} \bar{a}u''Dz_3 \Rightarrow_{\widetilde{G}} \bar{a}u''y_2z_3 \ [(D \to y_2, \bar{a}, 0)]$$

with $\bar{a}u''y_2z_3 \in g(x)$;

(c) Let $a'' = \langle a, AB \to AC, 5\rangle$ for some $AB \to AC \in R$ (see (VII) in Claim 2), and let $u''Dz_3 \in (\Sigma - \{S\})^*$, that is, $[a, AB \to AC, q+3] \notin \text{symbols}(u''Dz_3)$. Then, there exists the derivation

$$\begin{aligned} S &\Rightarrow^n_{\widetilde{G}} \langle a, AB \to AC, 5\rangle u''Dz_3 \\ &\Rightarrow_{\widetilde{G}} \bar{a}u''Dz_3 \ [(\langle a, AB \to AC, 5\rangle \to \bar{a}, 0, [a, AB \to AC, q+3])] \\ &\Rightarrow_{\widetilde{G}} \bar{a}u''y_2z_3 \ [(D \to y_2, \bar{a}, 0)] \end{aligned}$$

and $\bar{a}u''y_2z_3 \subset g(x)$;

(d) Let $a'' = \langle a, AB \to AC, 5\rangle$ (see (VII) in Claim 2). Let $[a, AB \to AC, q+3] \in \text{symbols}(u''Dz_3)$. Without any loss of generality, we can assume that $\widetilde{y} = \langle a, AB \to AC, 5\rangle u''Do''[a, AB \to AC, q+3]t''$, where $o''[a, AB \to AC, q+3]t'' = z_3$, $oBt = y_3$, $o'' \in g(t)$, $o, t \in (\Sigma - \{S\})^*$. By the inspection of $\widetilde{R}$ (see (3) in the construction of $\widetilde{G}$), we can express the derivation

$$S \Rightarrow^n_{\widetilde{G}} \widetilde{y}$$

as

$$\begin{aligned} S &\Rightarrow^*_{\widetilde{G}} \bar{a}u''Do''Bt'' \\ &\Rightarrow_{\widetilde{G}} \langle a, AB \to AC, 1\rangle u''Do''Bt'' \\ &\quad [(\bar{a} \to \langle a, AB \to AC, 1\rangle, 0, 0)] \\ &\Rightarrow^{1+|m_1m_2|}_{\widetilde{G}} \langle a, AB \to AC, 1\rangle u'Do'\widehat{B}t' \\ &\quad [m_1(B \to \widehat{B}, \langle a, AB \to AC, 1\rangle, 0)m_2] \\ &\Rightarrow_{\widetilde{G}} \langle a, AB \to AC, 2\rangle u'Do'\widehat{B}t' \\ &\quad [(\langle a, AB \to AC, 1\rangle \to \langle a, AB \to AC, 2\rangle, 0, B)] \\ &\Rightarrow_{\widetilde{G}} \langle a, AB \to AC, 2\rangle u'Do'B''t' \\ &\quad [\widehat{B} \to B'', 0, B''] \\ &\Rightarrow_{\widetilde{G}} \langle a, AB \to AC, 3\rangle u'Do'B''t' \\ &\quad [(\langle a, AB \to AC, 2\rangle \to \langle a, AB \to AC, 3\rangle, 0, \widehat{B})] \\ &\Rightarrow_{\widetilde{G}} \langle a, AB \to AC, 3\rangle u'Do'[a, AB \to AC, 1]t' \\ &\quad [(B'' \to [a, AB \to AC, 1], \langle a, AB \to AC, 3\rangle, 0)] \end{aligned}$$

$\Rightarrow_{\tilde{G}}^{q+2} \langle a, AB \rightarrow AC, 3\rangle u'Do'[a, AB \rightarrow AC, q+3]t'$
$[\omega]$
$\Rightarrow_{\tilde{G}} \langle a, AB \rightarrow AC, 4\rangle u'Do'[a, AB \rightarrow AC, q+3]t'$
$[(\langle a, AB \rightarrow AC, 3\rangle \rightarrow \langle a, AB \rightarrow AC, 4\rangle,$
$[a, AB \rightarrow AC, q+3], 0)]$
$\Rightarrow_{\tilde{G}}^{|m_3|} \langle a, AB \rightarrow AC, 4\rangle u''Do''[a, AB \rightarrow AC, q+3]t''$
$[m_3]$
$\Rightarrow_{\tilde{G}} \langle a, AB \rightarrow AC, 5\rangle u''Do''[a, AB \rightarrow AC, q+3]t''$
$[(\langle a, AB \rightarrow AC, 4\rangle \rightarrow \langle a, AB \rightarrow AC, 5\rangle, 0, B')]$

where $m_1, m_2 \in \{(B \rightarrow B', \langle a, AB \rightarrow AC, 1\rangle, 0)\}^*$, $m_3 \in \{(B' \rightarrow B, \langle a, AB \rightarrow AC, 4\rangle, 0)\}^*$, $|m_3| = |m_1 m_2|$,

$$\begin{aligned}\omega = {} & ([a, AB \rightarrow AC, 1] \rightarrow [a, AB \rightarrow AC, 2], 0,\\ & f^{-1}(1)[a, AB \rightarrow AC, 1]) \cdots\\ & ([a, AB \rightarrow AC, f(A) - 1] \rightarrow [a, AB \rightarrow AC, f(A)], 0,\\ & f^{-1}(f(A) - 1)[a, AB \rightarrow AC, f(A) - 1])\\ & ([a, AB \rightarrow AC, f(A)] \rightarrow [a, AB \rightarrow AC, f(A) + 1], 0, 0)\\ & ([a, AB \rightarrow AC, f(A) + 1] \rightarrow [a, AB \rightarrow AC, f(A) + 2], 0,\\ & f^{-1}(f(A) + 1)[a, AB \rightarrow AC, f(A) + 1]) \cdots\\ & ([a, AB \rightarrow AC, q] \rightarrow [a, AB \rightarrow AC, q + 1], 0,\\ & f^{-1}(q)[a, AB \rightarrow AC, q])\\ & ([a, AB \rightarrow AC, q + 1] \rightarrow [a, AB \rightarrow AC, q + 2], 0,\\ & B'[a, AB \rightarrow AC, q + 1])\\ & ([a, AB \rightarrow AC, q + 2] \rightarrow [a, AB \rightarrow AC, q + 3]), 0,\\ & \langle a, AB \rightarrow AC, 3\rangle[a, AB \rightarrow AC, q + 2]),\end{aligned}$$

$u' \in ((\text{symbols}(u'') - \{B\}) \cup \{B'\})^*$, $g^{-1}(u') = u$, $o' \in ((\text{symbols}(o'') - \{B\}) \cup \{B''\})^*$, $g^{-1}(o') = g^{-1}(o'') = o$, $t' \in ((\text{symbols}(t'') - \{B\}) \cup \{B'\})^*$, $g^{-1}(t') = g^{-1}(t'') = t$.
Clearly, $\bar{a}u''Do''Bt'' \in g(auDoBt) = g(auDy_3) = g(y)$. Thus, there exists the derivation
$S \Rightarrow_{\tilde{G}}^{*} \bar{a}u''Do''Bt'' \Rightarrow_{\tilde{G}} \bar{a}u''y_2o''Bt''$ $[(D \rightarrow y_2, \bar{a}, 0)]$
where $z_1y_2z_3 = \bar{a}u''y_2o''Bt'' \in g(auy_2oBt) = g(y_1y_2y_3) = g(x)$;

(e) Let $a'' = \langle a, AB \rightarrow AC, i\rangle$ for some $AB \rightarrow AC \in R$ and $i \in \{1, \ldots, 4\}$ (see (III)–(VI) in Claim 2). By analogy with (d), we can construct the derivation
$S \Rightarrow_{\tilde{G}}^{*} \bar{a}u''Do''Bt'' \Rightarrow_{\tilde{G}} \bar{a}u''y_2o''Bt''$ $[(D \rightarrow y_2, \bar{a}, 0)]$
such that $\bar{a}u''y_2o''Bt'' \in g(y_1y_2y_3) = g(x)$. The details are left to the reader;

(iii) Let $p = AB \rightarrow AC \in R$, $A, C \in N_{CF}$, $B \in N_{CS}$, $y = y_1ABy_3$, $y_1, y_3 \in \Sigma^*$, $x = y_1ACy_3$, $\widetilde{y} = z_1AYz_3$, $Y \in g(B)$, $z_i \in g(y_i)$ where $i \in \{1, 3\}$. Moreover, let $y_1 =$

au (see Claim 1), $z_1 = a''u''$, $a'' \in g(a)$, and $u'' \in g(u)$. The following cases cover all possible forms of a''.

(a) Let $a'' = \bar{a}$. Then, by Claim 2, $Y = B$. By (3) in the construction of $\widetilde{G}$, there exists the following derivation:

$$
\begin{aligned}
S &\Rightarrow^{n}_{\widetilde{G}} \bar{a}u''ABz_3 \\
&\Rightarrow_{\widetilde{G}} \langle a, AB \rightarrow AC, 1\rangle u''ABz_3 \\
&\quad [(\bar{a} \rightarrow \langle a, AB \rightarrow AC, 1\rangle, 0, 0)] \\
&\Rightarrow^{1+|m_1|}_{\widetilde{G}} \langle a, AB \rightarrow AC, 1\rangle u'A\widehat{B}u_3 \\
&\quad [m_1(B \rightarrow \widehat{B}, \langle a, AB \rightarrow AC, 1\rangle, 0)] \\
&\Rightarrow_{\widetilde{G}} \langle a, AB \rightarrow AC, 2\rangle u'A\widehat{B}u_3 \\
&\quad [(\langle a, AB \rightarrow AC, 1\rangle \rightarrow \langle a, AB \rightarrow AC, 2\rangle, 0, B)] \\
&\Rightarrow_{\widetilde{G}} \langle a, AB \rightarrow AC, 2\rangle u'AB''u_3 \\
&\quad [(\widehat{B} \rightarrow B'', 0, B'')] \\
&\Rightarrow_{\widetilde{G}} \langle a, AB \rightarrow AC, 3\rangle u'AB''u_3 \\
&\quad [(\langle a, AB \rightarrow AC, 2\rangle \rightarrow \langle a, AB \rightarrow AC, 3\rangle, 0, \widehat{B})] \\
&\Rightarrow_{\widetilde{G}} \langle a, AB \rightarrow AC, 3\rangle u'A[a, AB \rightarrow AC, 1]u_3 \\
&\quad [(B'' \rightarrow [a, AB \rightarrow AC, 1], \langle a, AB \rightarrow AC, 3\rangle, 0)] \\
&\Rightarrow^{q+2}_{\widetilde{G}} \langle a, AB \rightarrow AC, 3\rangle u'A[a, AB \rightarrow AC, q+3]u_3 \\
&\quad [\omega] \\
&\Rightarrow_{\widetilde{G}} \langle a, AB \rightarrow AC, 4\rangle u'A[a, AB \rightarrow AC, q+3]u_3 \\
&\quad [(\langle a, AB \rightarrow AC, 3\rangle \rightarrow \langle a, AB \rightarrow AC, 4\rangle, \\
&\qquad [a, AB \rightarrow AC, q+3], 0)] \\
&\Rightarrow^{|m_2|}_{\widetilde{G}} \langle a, AB \rightarrow AC, 4\rangle u''A[a, AB \rightarrow AC, q+3]z_3 \\
&\quad [m_2] \\
&\Rightarrow_{\widetilde{G}} \langle a, AB \rightarrow AC, 5\rangle u''A[a, AB \rightarrow AC, q+3]z_3 \\
&\quad [(\langle a, AB \rightarrow AC, 4\rangle \rightarrow \langle a, AB \rightarrow AC, 5\rangle, 0, B')] \\
&\Rightarrow_{\widetilde{G}} \langle a, AB \rightarrow AC, 5\rangle u''ACz_3 \\
&\quad [([a, AB \rightarrow AC, q+3] \rightarrow C, \langle a, AB \rightarrow AC, 5\rangle, 0)]
\end{aligned}
$$

where $m_1 \in \{(B \rightarrow B', \langle a, AB \rightarrow AC, 1\rangle, 0)\}^*$, $m_2 \in \{(B' \rightarrow B, \langle a, AB \rightarrow AC, 4\rangle, 0)\}^*$, $|m_1| = |m_2|$,

$$
\begin{aligned}
\omega = {} & ([a, AB \rightarrow AC, 1] \rightarrow [a, AB \rightarrow AC, 2], 0, \\
&\quad f^{-1}(1)[a, AB \rightarrow AC, 1]) \cdots \\
& ([a, AB \rightarrow AC, f(A) - 1] \rightarrow [a, AB \rightarrow AC, f(A)], 0, \\
&\quad f^{-1}(f(A) - 1)[a, AB \rightarrow AC, f(A) - 1]) \\
& ([a, AB \rightarrow AC, f(A)] \rightarrow [a, AB \rightarrow AC, f(A) + 1], 0, 0) \\
& ([a, AB \rightarrow AC, f(A) + 1] \rightarrow [a, AB \rightarrow AC, f(A) + 2], 0, \\
&\quad f^{-1}(f(A) + 1)[a, AB \rightarrow AC, f(A) + 1]) \cdots \\
& ([a, AB \rightarrow AC, q] \rightarrow [a, AB \rightarrow AC, q + 1], 0, \\
&\quad f^{-1}(q)[a, AB \rightarrow AC, q]) \\
& ([a, AB \rightarrow AC, q + 1] \rightarrow [a, AB \rightarrow AC, q + 2], 0, \\
&\quad B'[a, AB \rightarrow AC, q + 1])
\end{aligned}
$$

$$([a, AB \to AC, q+2] \to [a, AB \to AC, q+3]), 0,$$
$$\langle a, AB \to AC, 3\rangle [a, AB \to AC, q+2]),$$

$u_3 \in ((\text{symbols}(z_3) - \{B\}) \cup \{B'\})^*, g^{-1}(u_3) = g^{-1}(z_3) = y_3, u' \in ((\text{symbols}(u'') - \{B\}) \cup \{B'\})^*$, $g^{-1}(u') = g^{-1}(u'') = u$. It is clear that $\langle a, AB \to AC, 5\rangle \in g(a)$; thus, $\langle a, AB \to AC, 5\rangle u''ACz_3 \in g(auACy_3) = g(x)$;

(b) Let $a'' = a$. Then, by Claim 2, $Y = B$. By analogy with (ii.b) and (iii.a) in the proof of this claim (see above), we obtain

$$S \Rightarrow_{\tilde{G}}^{n-1} \bar{a}u''ABz_3 \Rightarrow_{\tilde{G}}^{*} \langle a, AB \to AC, 5\rangle u''ACz_3,$$

so $\langle a, AB \to AC, 5\rangle u''ACz_3 \in g(x)$;

(c) Let $a'' = \langle a, AB \to AC, 5\rangle$ for some $AB \to AC \in R$ (see (VII) in Claim 2), and let $u''AYz_3 \in (\Sigma - \{S\})^*$. At this point, $Y = B$. By analogy with (ii.c) and (iii.a) in the proof of this claim (see above), we can construct

$$S \Rightarrow_{\tilde{G}}^{n+1} \bar{a}u''ABz_3 \Rightarrow_{\tilde{G}}^{*} \langle a, AB \to AC, 5\rangle u''ACz_3,$$

so $\langle a, AB \to AC, 5\rangle u''ACz_3 \in g(x)$;

(d) Let $a'' = \langle a, AB \to AC, 5\rangle$ for some $AB \to AC \in R$ (see (VII) in Claim 2), and let $[a, AB \to AC, q+3] \in \text{symbols}(u''AYz_3)$. By analogy with (ii.d) and (iii.a) in the proof of this claim (see above), we can construct

$$S \Rightarrow_{\tilde{G}}^{*} \bar{a}u''ABz_3$$

and then

$$S \Rightarrow_{\tilde{G}}^{*} \bar{a}u''ABz_3 \Rightarrow_{\tilde{G}}^{*} \langle a, AB \to AC, 5\rangle u''ACz_3,$$

so that $\langle a, AB \to AC, 5\rangle u''ACz_3 \in g(auACy_3) = g(x)$;

(e) Let $a'' = \langle a, AB \to AC, i\rangle$ for some $AB \to AC \in R$, $i \in \{1, \ldots, 4\}$, see (III)–(VI) in Claim 2. By analogy with (c) and (d) in the proof of this claim, we can construct

$$S \Rightarrow_{\tilde{G}}^{*} \bar{a}u''ACz_3$$

where $\bar{a}u''ACz_3 \in g(x)$.

If. By induction on n, we next prove that if $S \Rightarrow_{\tilde{G}}^{n} v$ with $v \in g(w)$ and $w \in \Sigma^*$, for some $n \geq 0$, then $S \Rightarrow_{G}^{*} w$.

Basis. For $n = 0$, the only v is S as $S \Rightarrow_{\tilde{G}}^{0} S$. Because $\{S\} = g(S)$, we have $w = S$. Clearly, $S \Rightarrow_{G}^{0} S$.

Induction Hypothesis. Assume that the claim holds for all derivations of length n or less, for some $n \geq 0$. Let us show that it also holds true for $n + 1$.

Induction Step. For $n+1=1$, there only exists a direct derivation of the form

$$S \Rightarrow_{\tilde{G}} \bar{a}A \; [(S \rightarrow \bar{a}A, 0, 0)]$$

where $A \in N_{CF} \cup \{\varepsilon\}$, $a \in \Delta$, and $\bar{a}A \in g(aA)$. By (1), we have in R a rule of the form $S \rightarrow aA$ and, thus, a direct derivation $S \Rightarrow_G aA$.

Suppose that $n+1 \geq 2$ (i.e., $n \geq 1$). Consider any derivation of the form

$$S \Rightarrow_{\tilde{G}}^{n+1} x'$$

where $x' \in g(x)$, $x \in \Sigma^*$. Because $n+1 \geq 2$, there exist $\bar{a} \in W_4$, $A \in N_{CF}$, and $y \in \Sigma^+$ such that

$$S \Rightarrow_{\tilde{G}} \bar{a}A \Rightarrow_{\tilde{G}}^{n-1} y' \Rightarrow_{\tilde{G}} x' \; [p]$$

where $p \in \widetilde{R}$, $y' \in g(y)$, and by the induction hypothesis,

$$S \Rightarrow_G^* y.$$

Let us assume that $y' = z_1 Z z_2$, $y = y_1 D y_2$, $z_j \in g(y_j)$, $y_j \in (\Sigma - \{S\})^*$, $j = 1, 2$, $Z \in g(D)$, $D \in \Sigma - \{S\}$, $p = (Z \rightarrow u', \alpha, \beta) \in R'$, $\alpha = 0$ or $\beta = 0$, $x' = z_1 u' z_2$, $u' \in g(u)$ for some $u \in \Sigma^*$, that is, $x' \in g(y_1 u y_2)$. The following cases cover all possible forms of

$$y' \Rightarrow_{\tilde{G}} x' \; [p]:$$

(i) Let $Z \in N_{CF}$. By the inspection of $\widetilde{R}$, we see that $Z = D$, $p = (D \rightarrow u', \bar{u}, 0) \in \widetilde{R}$, $D \rightarrow u \in R$ and $u = u'$. Thus,

$$S \Rightarrow_G^* y_1 B y_2 \Rightarrow_G y_1 u y_2 \; [B \rightarrow u];$$

(ii) Let $u = D$. Then, by the induction hypothesis, we have the derivation

$$S \Rightarrow_G^* y_1 D y_2$$

and $y_1 D y_2 = y_1 u y_2$ in G;

(iii) Let $p = ([a, AB \rightarrow AC, q+3] \rightarrow C, \langle a, AB \rightarrow AC, 5\rangle, 0)$, $Z = [a, AB \rightarrow AC, q+3]$. Thus, $u' = C$ and $D = B \in N_{CS}$. By case (VI) in Claim 2 and the form of p, we have $z_1 = \langle a, AB \rightarrow AC, 5\rangle t$ and $y_1 = ao$, where $t \in g(o)$, $\langle a, AB \rightarrow AC, 5\rangle \in g(a)$, $o \in (\Sigma - \{S\})^*$, and $a \in \Delta$. From (3) in the construction of $\widetilde{G}$, it follows that there exists a rule of the form $AB \rightarrow AC \in R$. Moreover, (3) and Claim 2 imply that the derivation

$$S \Rightarrow_{\tilde{G}} \bar{a}A \Rightarrow_{\tilde{G}}^{n-1} y' \Rightarrow_{\tilde{G}} x' \; [p]$$

can be expressed in the form

$$
\begin{aligned}
S &\Rightarrow_{\tilde{G}} \bar{a}A \\
&\Rightarrow^{*}_{\tilde{G}} \bar{a}tBz_2 \\
&\Rightarrow_{\tilde{G}} \langle a, AB \to AC, 1\rangle tBz_2 \\
&\qquad [(\bar{a} \to \langle a, AB \to AC, 1\rangle, 0, 0)] \\
&\Rightarrow^{|\omega'|}_{\tilde{G}} \langle a, AB \to AC, 1\rangle v\widehat{B}w_2 \\
&\qquad [\omega'] \\
&\Rightarrow_{\tilde{G}} \langle a, AB \to AC, 1\rangle vB''w_2 \\
&\qquad [(\widehat{B} \to B'', 0, B'')] \\
&\Rightarrow_{\tilde{G}} \langle a, AB \to AC, 2\rangle vB''w_2 \\
&\qquad [(\langle a, AB \to AC, 1\rangle \to \langle a, AB \to AC, 2\rangle, 0, B)] \\
&\Rightarrow_{\tilde{G}} \langle a, AB \to AC, 3\rangle vB''w_2 \\
&\qquad [(\langle a, AB \to AC, 2\rangle \to \langle a, AB \to AC, 3\rangle, 0, \widehat{B})] \\
&\Rightarrow_{\tilde{G}} \langle a, AB \to AC, 3\rangle v[a, AB \to AC, 1]w_2 \\
&\qquad [(B'' \to [a, AB \to AC, 1], \langle a, AB \to AC, 3\rangle, 0)] \\
&\Rightarrow^{|\omega|}_{\tilde{G}} \langle a, AB \to AC, 3\rangle v[a, AB \to AC, q+3]w_2 \\
&\qquad [\omega] \\
&\Rightarrow_{\tilde{G}} \langle a, AB \to AC, 4\rangle v[a, AB \to AC, q+3]w_2 \\
&\qquad [(\langle a, AB \to AC, 3\rangle \to \langle a, AB \to AC, 4\rangle, \\
&\qquad\quad [a, AB \to AC, q+3], 0)] \\
&\Rightarrow^{|\omega'|-1}_{\tilde{G}} \langle a, AB \to AC, 4\rangle t[a, AB \to AC, q+3]z_2 \\
&\qquad [\omega''] \\
&\Rightarrow_{\tilde{G}} \langle a, AB \to AC, 5\rangle t[a, AB \to AC, q+3]z_2 \\
&\qquad [(\langle a, AB \to AC, 4\rangle \to \langle a, AB \to AC, 5\rangle, 0, B')] \\
&\Rightarrow_{\tilde{G}} \langle a, AB \to AC, 5\rangle tCz_2 \\
&\qquad [([a, AB \to AC, q+3] \to C, \langle a, AB \to AC, 5\rangle, 0)]
\end{aligned}
$$

where

$$
\begin{aligned}
\omega' \in\ & \{(B \to B', \langle a, AB \to AC, 1\rangle, 0)\}^* \\
& \{(B \to \widehat{B}, \langle a, AB \to AC, 1\rangle, 0)\} \\
& \{(B \to B', \langle a, AB \to AC, 1\rangle, 0)\}^*,
\end{aligned}
$$

$g(B) \cap \text{symbols}\,(vw_2) \subseteq \{B'\}, g^{-1}(v) = g^{-1}(t), g^{-1}(w_2) = g^{-1}(z_2),$

$$
\begin{aligned}
\omega = \omega_1 & \\
& ([a, AB \to AC, f(A)] \to [a, AB \to AC, f(A)+1], 0, 0)\omega_2 \\
& ([a, AB \to AC, q+1] \to [a, AB \to AC, q+2], 0 \\
& \quad B'[a, AB \to AC, q+1]) \\
& ([a, AB \to AC, q+2] \to [a, AB \to AC, q+3], 0, \\
& \quad \langle a, AB \to AC, 3\rangle[a, AB \to AC, q+2]),
\end{aligned}
$$

$$
\begin{aligned}
\omega_1 = & ([a, AB \to AC, 1] \to [a, AB \to AC, 2], 0, \\
& \quad f^{-1}(1)[a, AB \to AC, 1]) \cdots \\
& ([a, AB \to AC, f(A)-1] \to [a, AB \to AC, f(A)], 0, \\
& \quad f^{-1}(f(A)-1)[a, AB \to AC, f(A)-1]),
\end{aligned}
$$

where $f(A) = q$ implies that $q_1 = \varepsilon$,

$$\begin{aligned}\omega_2 = {} & ([a, AB \to AC, f(A)+1] \to [a, AB \to AC, f(A)+2], 0, \\ & f^{-1}(f(A)+1)[a, AB \to AC, f(A)+1]) \cdots \\ & ([a, AB \to AC, q] \to [a, AB \to AC, q+1], 0, \\ & \quad f^{-1}(q)[a, AB \to AC, q])\end{aligned}$$

where $f(A) = q$ implies that $q_2 = \varepsilon$, $\omega'' \in \{(B' \to B, \langle a, AB \to AC, 4\rangle, 0)\}^*$.

The derivation above implies that the rightmost symbol of t must be A. As $t \in g(o)$, the rightmost symbol of o must be A as well. That is, $t = s'A$, $o = sA$ and $s' \in g(s)$, for some $s \in (\Sigma - \{S\})^*$. By the induction hypothesis, there exists a derivation

$$S \Rightarrow_G^* asABy_2.$$

Because $AB \to AC \in R$, we get

$$S \Rightarrow_G^* asABy_2 \Rightarrow_G asACy_2 \; [AB \to AC]$$

where $asACy_2 = y_1uy_2$.

By (i)–(iii) and the inspection of $\tilde{R}$, we see that we have considered all possible derivations of the form

$$S \Rightarrow_{\tilde{G}}^{n+1} x',$$

so we have established Claim 3 by the principle of induction. □

The equivalence of G and $\tilde{G}$ can be easily derived from Claim 3. By the definition of g, we have $g(a) = \{a\}$ for all $a \in \Delta$. Thus, by Claim 3, we have for all $x \in \Delta^*$,

$$S \Rightarrow_G^* x \quad \text{if and only if} \quad S \Rightarrow_{\tilde{G}}^* x.$$

Consequently, $L(G) = L(\tilde{G})$, and the theorem holds. ■

Corollary 11.8.

$$\mathbf{PSSCOND}(1,2) = \mathbf{PSSCOND} = \mathbf{PSCOND}(1,2) = \mathbf{PSCOND} = \mathbf{CS}.$$

We now turn to the investigation of ssc-grammars of degree $(1, 2)$ with erasing rules.

Theorem 11.35. SSCOND(1, 2) = RE.

Proof. Clearly, we have $\mathbf{SSCOND}(1,2) \subseteq \mathbf{RE}$. Thus, we only need to show that $\mathbf{RE} \subseteq \mathbf{SSCOND}(1,2)$. Every language $L \in \mathbf{RE}$ can be generated by a PSG $G = (\Sigma, \Delta, R, S)$ in which each rule is of the form $AB \to AC$ or $A \to x$, where $A, B, C \in \Sigma - \Delta$, $x \in \{\varepsilon\} \cup \Delta \cup (\Sigma - \Delta)^2$ (see Theorem 11.5). Thus, the inclusion can be established by analogy with the proof of Theorem 11.34. The details are left to the reader. ■

Corollary 11.9.

$$\mathbf{SSCOND}(1,2) = \mathbf{SSCOND} = \mathbf{SCOND}(1,2) = \mathbf{SCOND} = \mathbf{RE}.$$

The following corollary summarizes the relations of language families generated by ssc-grammars.

Corollary 11.10.

$$\begin{array}{c} \mathbf{CF} \\ \subset \\ \mathbf{PSSCOND} = \mathbf{PSSCOND}(2,1) = \mathbf{PSSCOND}(1,2) = \\ = \mathbf{PSCOND} = \mathbf{PSCOND}(2,1) = \mathbf{PSCOND}(1,2) = \mathbf{CS} \\ \subset \\ \mathbf{SSCOND} = \mathbf{SSCOND}(2,1) = \mathbf{SSCOND}(1,2) = \\ = \mathbf{SCOND} = \mathbf{SCOND}(2,1) = \mathbf{SCOND}(1,2) = \mathbf{RE}. \end{array}$$

Proof. This corollary follows from Corollaries 11.6, 11.7, 11.8, and 11.9. ■

Next, we turn our attention to reduced versions of ssc-grammars. More specifically, we demonstrate that there exist several normal forms of ssc-grammars with a limited number of conditional rules and nonterminals.

Theorem 11.36. *Every recursively enumerable language can be defined by an ssc-grammar of degree* (2, 1) *with no more than 12 conditional rules and 13 nonterminals.*

Proof. Let L be a recursively enumerable language. By Theorem 11.7, we assume that L is generated by a grammar G of the form

$$G = (\Sigma, \Delta, R \cup \{AB \rightarrow \varepsilon, CD \rightarrow \varepsilon\}, S)$$

such that R contains only context-free rules and

$$\Sigma - \Delta = \{S, A, B, C, D\}.$$

Construct an ssc-grammar G' of degree (2, 1),

$$G' = (\Sigma', \Delta, R', S),$$

where

$$\Sigma' = \Sigma \cup W,$$
$$W = \{\widetilde{A}, \widetilde{B}, \langle\varepsilon_A\rangle, \$, \widetilde{C}, \widetilde{D}, \langle\varepsilon_C\rangle, \#\}, \ \Sigma \cap W = \emptyset.$$

The set of rules R' is defined in the following way:

(i) If $H \to y \in R$, $H \in \Sigma - \Delta$, $y \in \Sigma^*$, then add $(H \to y, 0, 0)$ to R';

(ii) Add the following six rules to R'

$$(A \to \widetilde{A}, 0, \widetilde{A}),$$
$$(B \to \widetilde{B}, 0, \widetilde{B}),$$
$$(\widetilde{A} \to \langle \varepsilon_A \rangle, \widetilde{A}\widetilde{B}, 0),$$
$$(\widetilde{B} \to \$, \langle \varepsilon_A \rangle \widetilde{B}, 0),$$
$$(\langle \varepsilon_A \rangle \to \varepsilon, 0, \widetilde{B}),$$
$$(\$ \to \varepsilon, 0, \langle \varepsilon_A \rangle);$$

(iii) Add the following six rules to R'

$$(C \to \widetilde{C}, 0, \widetilde{C}),$$
$$(D \to \widetilde{D}, 0, \widetilde{D}),$$
$$(\widetilde{C} \to \langle \varepsilon_C \rangle, \widetilde{C}\widetilde{D}, 0),$$
$$(\widetilde{D} \to \#, \langle \varepsilon_C \rangle \widetilde{D}, 0),$$
$$(\langle \varepsilon_C \rangle \to \varepsilon, 0, \widetilde{D}),$$
$$(\# \to \varepsilon, 0, \langle \varepsilon_C \rangle).$$

Notice that G' has degree (2, 1) and contains only 12 conditional rules and 13 nonterminals. The rules of (2) simulate the application of $AB \to \varepsilon$ in G', and the rules of (3) simulate the application of $CD \to \varepsilon$ in G'.

Let us describe the simulation of $AB \to \varepsilon$. First, one occurrence of A and one occurrence of B are rewritten to $\widetilde{A}$ and $\widetilde{B}$, respectively (no more than one $\widetilde{A}$ and one $\widetilde{B}$ appear in any sentential form). The right neighbor of $\widetilde{A}$ is checked to be $\widetilde{B}$ and $\widetilde{A}$ is rewritten to $\langle \varepsilon_A \rangle$. Then, analogously, the left neighbor of $\widetilde{B}$ is checked to be $\langle \varepsilon_A \rangle$ and $\widetilde{B}$ is rewritten to \$. Finally, $\langle \varepsilon_A \rangle$ and \$ are erased. The simulation of $CD \to \varepsilon$ is analogous.

To establish $L(G) = L(G')$, we first prove two claims.

Claim 1. $S \Rightarrow_{G'}^* x'$ *implies that* $\mathrm{occur}(\widetilde{X}, x') \leq 1$ *for all* $\widetilde{X} \in \{\widetilde{A}, \widetilde{B}, \widetilde{C}, \widetilde{D}\}$ *and* $x' \in \Sigma'^*$.

Proof. By the inspection of rules in R', the only rule that can generate $\widetilde{X}$ is of the form $(X \to \widetilde{X}, 0, \widetilde{X})$. This rule can be applied only when no $\widetilde{X}$ occurs in the rewritten sentential form. Thus, it is not possible to derive x' from S such that $\mathrm{occur}(\widetilde{X}, x') \geq 2$. □

Informally, the next claim says that every occurrence of $\langle \varepsilon_A \rangle$ in derivations from S is always followed by either $\widetilde{B}$ or \$, and every occurrence of $\langle \varepsilon_C \rangle$ is always followed by either $\widetilde{D}$ or #.

Claim 2. *The following holds:*

(I) $S \Rightarrow_{G'}^* y_1' \langle \varepsilon_A \rangle y_2'$ *implies* $y_2' \in \Sigma'^+$ *and* $\mathrm{lms}(y_2') \in \{\widetilde{B}, \$\}$ *for any* $y_1' \in \Sigma'^*$;

(II) $S \Rightarrow_{G'}^* y_1' \langle \varepsilon_C \rangle y_2'$ *implies* $y_2' \in \Sigma'^+$ *and* $\mathrm{lms}(y_2') \in \{\widetilde{D}, \#\}$ *for any* $y_1' \in \Sigma'^*$.

Proof. We base this proof on the examination of all possible forms of derivations that may occur during a derivation of a sentential form containing $\langle \varepsilon_A \rangle$ or $\langle \varepsilon_C \rangle$.

(I) By the definition of R', the only rule that can generate $\langle \varepsilon_A \rangle$ is $p = (\widetilde{A} \to \langle \varepsilon_A \rangle, \widetilde{A}\widetilde{B}, 0)$. This rule has the permitting condition $\widetilde{A}\widetilde{B}$, so it can be used provided that

$\widetilde{A}\widetilde{B}$ occurs in a sentential form. Furthermore, by Claim 1, no other occurrence of $\widetilde{A}$ or $\widetilde{B}$ can appear in the given sentential form. Consequently, we obtain a derivation

$$S \Rightarrow^*_{G'} u'_1\widetilde{A}\widetilde{B}u'_2 \Rightarrow_{G'} u'_1\langle\varepsilon_A\rangle\widetilde{B}u'_2 \ [p]$$

for some $u'_1, u'_2 \in \Sigma'^*, \widetilde{A}, \widetilde{B} \notin \text{symbols}(u'_1u'_2)$, which represents the only way of getting $\langle\varepsilon_A\rangle$. Obviously, $\langle\varepsilon_A\rangle$ is always followed by $\widetilde{B}$ in $u'_1\langle\varepsilon_A\rangle\widetilde{B}u'_2$.

Next, we discuss how G' can rewrite the substring $\langle\varepsilon_A\rangle\widetilde{B}$ in $u'_1\langle\varepsilon_A\rangle\widetilde{B}u'_2$. There are only two rules having the nonterminals $\langle\varepsilon_A\rangle$ or $\widetilde{B}$ on their left-hand side, $p_1 = (\widetilde{B} \to \$, \langle\varepsilon_A\rangle\widetilde{B}, 0)$ and $p_2 = (\langle\varepsilon_A\rangle \to \varepsilon, 0, \widetilde{B})$. G' cannot use p_2 to erase $\langle\varepsilon_A\rangle$ in $u'_1\langle\varepsilon_A\rangle\widetilde{B}u'_2$ because p_2 forbids an occurrence of $\widetilde{B}$ in the rewritten string. Rule p_1 has also a context condition, but $\langle\varepsilon_A\rangle\widetilde{B} \in \text{substrings}(u'_1\langle\varepsilon_A\rangle\widetilde{B}u'_2)$, and thus p_1 can be used to rewrite $\widetilde{B}$ with \$. Hence, we obtain a derivation of the form

$$\begin{aligned} S \Rightarrow^*_{G'} u'_1\widetilde{A}\widetilde{B}u'_2 \quad &\Rightarrow_{G'} u'_1\langle\varepsilon_A\rangle\widetilde{B}u'_2 \ [p] \\ \Rightarrow^*_{G'} v'_1\langle\varepsilon_A\rangle\widetilde{B}v'_2 &\Rightarrow_{G'} v'_1\langle\varepsilon_A\rangle\$v'_2 \ [p_1]. \end{aligned}$$

Notice that during this derivation, G' may rewrite u'_1 and u'_2 to some v'_1 and v'_2, respectively, where $v'_1, v'_2 \in \Sigma'^*$; however, $\langle\varepsilon_A\rangle\widetilde{B}$ remains unchanged after this rewriting.

In this derivation, we obtained the second symbol \$ that can appear as the right neighbor of $\langle\varepsilon_A\rangle$. It is sufficient to show that there is no other symbol that can appear immediately after $\langle\varepsilon_A\rangle$. By the inspection of R', only $(\$ \to \varepsilon, 0, \langle\varepsilon_A\rangle)$ can rewrite \$. However, this rule cannot be applied when $\langle\varepsilon_A\rangle$ occurs in the given sentential form. In other words, the occurrence of \$ in the substring $\langle\varepsilon_A\rangle\$$ cannot be rewritten before $\langle\varepsilon_A\rangle$ is erased by rule p_2. Hence, $\langle\varepsilon_A\rangle$ is always followed by either $\widetilde{B}$ or \$, and thus, the first part of Claim 2 holds;

(II) By the inspection of rules simulating $AB \to \varepsilon$ and $CD \to \varepsilon$ in G' (see (2) and (3) in the definition of R'), these two sets of rules work analogously. Thus, part (II) of Claim 2 can be proved by analogy with part (I). □

Let us return to the main part of the proof. Let g be a finite substitution from Σ'^* to Σ^* defined as follows:

(i) For all $X \in \Sigma, g(X) = \{X\}$;
(ii) $g(\widetilde{A}) = \{A\}, g(\widetilde{B}) = \{B\}, g(\langle\varepsilon_A\rangle) = \{A\}, g(\$) = \{B, AB\}$;
(iii) $g(\widetilde{C}) = \{C\}, g(\widetilde{D}) = \{D\}, g(\langle\varepsilon_C\rangle) = \{C\}, g(\#) = \{C, CD\}$.

Having this substitution, we can prove the following claim:

Claim 3. *$S \Rightarrow^*_G x$ if and only if $S \Rightarrow^*_{G'} x'$ for some $x \in g(x'), x \in \Sigma^*, x' \in \Sigma'^*$.*

Proof. The claim is proved by induction on the length of derivations.

Only If. We show that

$$S \Rightarrow^m_G x \quad \text{implies} \quad S \Rightarrow^*_{G'} x$$

where $m \geq 0, x \in \Sigma^*$; clearly $x \in g(x)$. This is established by induction on $m \geq 0$.

Basis. Let $m = 0$. That is, $S \Rightarrow_G^0 S$. Clearly, $S \Rightarrow_{G'}^0 S$.

Induction Hypothesis. Suppose that the claim holds for all derivations of length m or less, for some $m \geq 0$.

Induction Step. Consider any derivation of the form

$$S \Rightarrow_G^{m+1} x,\ x \in \Sigma^*.$$

Since $m + 1 \geq 1$, there is some $y \in \Sigma^+$ and $p \in R \cup \{AB \rightarrow \varepsilon, CD \rightarrow \varepsilon\}$ such that

$$S \Rightarrow_G^m y \Rightarrow_G x\ [p].$$

By the induction hypothesis, there is a derivation

$$S \Rightarrow_{G'}^* y.$$

The following three cases cover all possible forms of p.

(i) Let $p = H \rightarrow y_2 \in R$, $H \in \Sigma - \Delta$, $y_2 \in \Sigma^*$. Then, $y = y_1 H y_3$ and $x = y_1 y_2 y_3$, $y_1, y_3 \in \Sigma^*$. Because we have $(H \rightarrow y_2, 0, 0) \in R'$,

$$S \Rightarrow_{G'}^* y_1 H y_3 \Rightarrow_{G'} y_1 y_2 y_3\ [(H \rightarrow y_2, 0, 0)]$$

and $y_1 y_2 y_3 = x$;

(ii) Let $p = AB \rightarrow \varepsilon$. Then, $y = y_1 AB y_3$ and $x = y_1 y_3$, $y_1, y_3 \in \Sigma^*$. In this case, there is the derivation

$$\begin{aligned}
S &\Rightarrow_{G'}^* y_1 AB y_3 \\
&\Rightarrow_{G'} y_1 \tilde{A} B y_3 && [(A \rightarrow \tilde{A}, 0, \tilde{A})] \\
&\Rightarrow_{G'} y_1 \tilde{A}\tilde{B} y_3 && [(B \rightarrow \tilde{B}, 0, \tilde{B})] \\
&\Rightarrow_{G'} y_1 \langle\varepsilon_A\rangle \tilde{B} y_3 && [(\tilde{A} \rightarrow \langle\varepsilon_A\rangle, \tilde{A}\tilde{B}, 0)] \\
&\Rightarrow_{G'} y_1 \langle\varepsilon_A\rangle \$ y_3 && [(\tilde{B} \rightarrow \$, \langle\varepsilon_A\rangle\tilde{B}, 0)] \\
&\Rightarrow_{G'} y_1 \$ y_3 && [(\langle\varepsilon_A\rangle \rightarrow \varepsilon, 0, \tilde{B})] \\
&\Rightarrow_{G'} y_1 y_3 && [(\$ \rightarrow \varepsilon, 0, \langle\varepsilon_A\rangle)];
\end{aligned}$$

(iii) Let $p = CD \rightarrow \varepsilon$. Then, $y = y_1 CD y_3$ and $x = y_1 y_3$, $y_1, y_3 \in \Sigma^*$. By analogy with (ii), there exists the derivation

$$\begin{aligned}
S &\Rightarrow_{G'}^* y_1 CD y_3 \\
&\Rightarrow_{G'} y_1 \tilde{C} D y_3 && [(C \rightarrow \tilde{C}, 0, \tilde{C})] \\
&\Rightarrow_{G'} y_1 \tilde{C}\tilde{D} y_3 && [(D \rightarrow \tilde{D}, 0, \tilde{D})] \\
&\Rightarrow_{G'} y_1 \langle\varepsilon_C\rangle \tilde{D} y_3 && [(\tilde{C} \rightarrow \langle\varepsilon_C\rangle, \tilde{C}\tilde{D}, 0)] \\
&\Rightarrow_{G'} y_1 \langle\varepsilon_C\rangle \# y_3 && [(\tilde{D} \rightarrow \#, \langle\varepsilon_C\rangle\tilde{D}, 0)] \\
&\Rightarrow_{G'} y_1 \# y_3 && [(\langle\varepsilon_C\rangle \rightarrow \varepsilon, 0, \tilde{D})] \\
&\Rightarrow_{G'} y_1 y_3 && [(\# \rightarrow \varepsilon, 0, \langle\varepsilon_C\rangle)].
\end{aligned}$$

If. By induction on the length n of derivations in G', we prove that

$$S \Rightarrow_{G'}^n x' \quad \text{implies} \quad S \Rightarrow_G^* x$$

for some $x \in g(x')$, $x \in \Sigma^*$, $x' \in \Sigma'^*$.

Basis. Let $n = 0$. That is, $S \Rightarrow^0_{G'} S$. It is obvious that $S \Rightarrow^0_G S$ and $S \in g(S)$.

Induction Hypothesis. Assume that the claim holds for all derivations of length n or less, for some $n \geq 0$.

Induction Step. Consider any derivation of the form

$$S \Rightarrow^{n+1}_{G'} x',\ x' \in \Sigma'^*.$$

Since $n + 1 \geq 1$, there is some $y' \in \Sigma'^+$ and $p' \in R'$ such that

$$S \Rightarrow^n_{G'} y' \Rightarrow_{G'} x'\ [p']$$

and by the induction hypothesis, there is also a derivation

$$S \Rightarrow^*_G y$$

such that $y \in g(y')$.

By the inspection of R', the following cases cover all possible forms of p'.

(i) Let $p' = (H \rightarrow y_2, 0, 0) \in R'$, $H \in \Sigma - \Delta$, $y_2 \in \Sigma^*$. Then, $y' = y'_1 H y'_3$, $x' = y'_1 y_2 y'_3$, $y'_1, y'_3 \in \Sigma'^*$ and y has the form $y = y_1 Z y_3$, where $y_1 \in g(y'_1)$, $y_3 \in g(y'_3)$ and $Z \in g(H)$. Because $g(X) = \{X\}$ for all $X \in \Sigma - \Delta$, the only possible Z is H, and thus $y = y_1 H y_3$. By the definition of R', there exists a rule $p = H \rightarrow y_2$ in R, and we can construct the derivation

$$S \Rightarrow^*_G y_1 H y_3 \Rightarrow_G y_1 y_2 y_3\ [p]$$

such that $y_1 y_2 y_3 = x$, $x \in g(x')$;

(ii) Let $p' = (A \rightarrow \widetilde{A}, 0, \widetilde{A})$. Then, $y' = y'_1 A y'_3$, $x' = y'_1 \widetilde{A} y'_3$, $y'_1, y'_3 \in \Sigma'^*$, and $y = y_1 Z y_3$, where $y_1 \in g(y'_1)$, $y_3 \in g(y'_3)$ and $Z \in g(A)$. Because $g(A) = \{A\}$, the only Z is A, so we can express $y = y_1 A y_3$. Having the derivation $S \Rightarrow^*_G y$ such that $y \in g(y')$, it is easy to see that also $y \in g(x')$ because $A \in g(\widetilde{A})$;

(iii) Let $p' = (B \rightarrow \widetilde{B}, 0, \widetilde{B})$. By analogy with (ii), $y' = y'_1 B y'_3$, $x' = y'_1 \widetilde{B} y'_3$, $y = y_1 B y_3$, where $y'_1, y'_3 \in \Sigma'^*$, $y_1 \in g(y'_1)$, $y_3 \in g(y'_3)$, and thus $y \in g(x')$ because $B \in g(\widetilde{B})$;

(iv) Let $p' = (\widetilde{A} \rightarrow \langle \varepsilon_A \rangle, \widetilde{A}\widetilde{B}, 0)$. By the permitting condition of this rule, $\widetilde{A}\widetilde{B}$ surely occurs in y'. By Claim 1, no more than one $\widetilde{A}$ can occur in y'. Therefore, y' must be of the form $y' = y'_1 \widetilde{A}\widetilde{B} y'_3$, where $y'_1, y'_3 \in \Sigma'^*$ and $\widetilde{A} \notin \text{symbols}(y'_1 y'_3)$. Then, $x' = y'_1 \langle \varepsilon_A \rangle \widetilde{B} y'_3$ and y is of the form $y = y_1 Z y_3$, where $y_1 \in g(y'_1)$, $y_3 \in g(y'_3)$ and $Z \in g(\widetilde{A}\widetilde{B})$. Because $g(\widetilde{A}\widetilde{B}) = \{AB\}$, the only Z is AB; thus, we obtain $y = y_1 A B y_3$. By the induction hypothesis, we have a derivation $S \Rightarrow^*_G y$ such that $y \in g(y')$. According to the definition of g, $y \in g(x')$ as well because $A \in g(\langle \varepsilon_A \rangle)$ and $B \in g(\widetilde{B})$;

(v) Let $p' = (\widetilde{B} \rightarrow \$, \langle \varepsilon_A \rangle \widetilde{B}, 0)$. This rule can be applied provided that $\langle \varepsilon_A \rangle \widetilde{B} \in \text{substrings}(y')$. Moreover, by Claim 1, $\text{occur}(\widetilde{B}, y') \leq 1$. Hence, we can express $y' = y'_1 \langle \varepsilon_A \rangle \widetilde{B} y'_3$, where $y'_1, y'_3 \in \Sigma'^*$ and $\widetilde{B} \notin \text{symbols}(y'_1 y'_3)$. Then, $x' = y'_1 \langle \varepsilon_A \rangle \$ y'_3$ and $y = y_1 Z y_3$, where $y_1 \in g(y'_1)$, $y_3 \in g(y'_3)$ and $Z \in g(\langle \varepsilon_A \rangle \widetilde{B})$. By the definition of g, $g(\langle \varepsilon_A \rangle \widetilde{B}) = \{AB\}$, so $Z = AB$ and $y = y_1 A B y_3$. By the induction hypothesis, we have a derivation $S \Rightarrow^*_G y$ such that $y \in g(y')$. Because $A \in g(\langle \varepsilon_A \rangle)$ and $B \in g(\$)$, $y \in g(x')$ as well;

(vi) Let $p' = (\langle \varepsilon_A \rangle \to \varepsilon, 0, \widetilde{B})$. Application of $(\langle \varepsilon_A \rangle \to \varepsilon, 0, \widetilde{B})$ implies that $\langle \varepsilon_A \rangle$ occurs in y'. Claim 2 says that $\langle \varepsilon_A \rangle$ has either $\widetilde{B}$ or \$ as its right neighbor. Since the forbidding condition of p' forbids an occurrence of $\widetilde{B}$ in y', the right neighbor of $\langle \varepsilon_A \rangle$ must be \$. As a result, we obtain $y' = y'_1 \langle \varepsilon_A \rangle \$ y'_3$ where $y'_1, y'_3 \in \Sigma'^*$. Then, $x' = y'_1 \$ y'_3$ and y is of the form $y = y_1 Z y_3$, where $y_1 \in g(y'_1)$, $y_3 \in g(y'_3)$ and $Z \in g(\langle \varepsilon_A \rangle \$)$. By the definition of g, $g(\langle \varepsilon_A \rangle \$) = \{AB, AAB\}$. If $Z = AB$, $y = y_1 AB y_3$. Having the derivation $S \Rightarrow_G^* y$, it holds that $y \in g(x')$ because $AB \in g(\$)$;

(vii) Let $p' = (\$ \to \varepsilon, 0, \langle \varepsilon_A \rangle)$. Then, $y' = y'_1 \$ y'_3$ and $x' = y'_1 y'_3$, where $y'_1, y'_3 \in \Sigma'^*$. Express $y = y_1 Z y_3$ so that $y_1 \in g(y'_1)$, $y_3 \in g(y'_3)$ and $Z \in g(\$)$, where $g(\$) = \{B, AB\}$. Let $Z = AB$. Then, $y = y_1 AB y_3$, and there exists the derivation

$$S \Rightarrow_G^* y_1 AB y_3 \Rightarrow_G y_1 y_3 \; [AB \to \varepsilon]$$

where $y_1 y_3 = x$, $x \in g(x')$.

In cases (ii)–(vii), we discussed all six rules simulating the application of $AB \to \varepsilon$ in G' (see (2) in the definition of R'). Cases (viii)–(xiii) should cover rules simulating the application of $CD \to \varepsilon$ in G' (see (3)). However, by the inspection of these two sets of rules, it is easy to see that they work analogously. Therefore, we leave this part of the proof to the reader.

We have completed the proof and established Claim 3 by the principle of induction. □

Observe that $L(G) = L(G')$ follows from Claim 3. Indeed, according to the definition of g, we have $g(a) = \{a\}$ for all $a \in \Delta$. Thus, from Claim 3, we have for any $x \in \Delta^*$

$$S \Rightarrow_G^* x \quad \text{if and only if} \quad S \Rightarrow_{G'}^* x.$$

Consequently, $L(G) = L(G')$, and the theorem holds. ■

Let us note that in [18], Theorem 11.36 has been improved by demonstrating that even nine conditional rules and ten nonterminals are enough to generate every recursively enumerable language.

Theorem 11.37 (see [18]). *Every recursively enumerable language can be generated by an ssc-grammar of degree* (2, 1) *having no more than nine conditional rules and ten nonterminals.*

Continuing with the investigation of reduced ssc-grammars, we point out that Vaszil in [19] proved that if we allow permitting conditions of length three—that is, ssc-grammars of degree (3, 1), then the number of conditional rules and nonterminals can be further decreased.

Theorem 11.38. *Every recursively enumerable language can be generated by an ssc-grammar of degree* (3, 1) *with no more than 8 conditional rules and 11 nonterminals.*

Proof. (See [19].) Let L be a recursively enumerable language. Without any loss of generality, we assume that L is generated by a PSG

$$G = (\Sigma, \Delta, R \cup \{ABC \to \varepsilon\}, S)$$

where

$$\Sigma - \Delta = \{S, S', A, B, C\}$$

and R contains only context-free rules of the forms $S \rightarrow zSx$, $z \in \{A, B\}^*$, $x \in \Delta$, $S \rightarrow S'$, $S' \rightarrow uS'v$, $u \in \{A, B\}^*$, $v \in \{B, C\}^*$, $S' \rightarrow \varepsilon$ (see Theorem 11.6). Every successful derivation in G consists of the following two phases:

(i) $S \Rightarrow_G^* z_n \cdots z_1 S x_1 \cdots x_n$
$\Rightarrow_G z_n \cdots z_1 S' x_1 \cdots x_n \; ; z_i \in \{A, B\}^*, 1 \leq i \leq n;$

(ii) $z_n \cdots z_1 S' x_1 \cdots x_n \Rightarrow_G^* z_n \cdots z_1 u_m \cdots u_1 S' v_1 \cdots v_m x_1 \cdots x_n$
$\Rightarrow_G z_n \cdots z_1 u_m \cdots u_1 v_1 \cdots v_m x_1 \cdots x_n$
where $u_j \in \{A, B\}^*$, $v_j \in \{B, C\}^*$, $1 \leq j \leq m$, and the terminal string $x_1 \cdots x_n$ is generated by G if and only if by using the erasing rule $ABC \rightarrow \varepsilon$, the substring $z_n \cdots z_1 u_m \cdots u_1 v_1 \cdots v_m$ can be deleted.

Next, we introduce the ssc-grammar

$$G' = (\Sigma', \Delta, R', S)$$

of degree (3, 1), where

$$\Sigma' = \{S, S', A, A', A'', B, B', B'', C, C', C''\} \cup \Delta$$

and R' is constructed as follows:

(i) For every $H \rightarrow y \in R$, add $(H \rightarrow y, 0, 0)$ to R';
(ii) For every $X \in \{A, B, C\}$, add $(X \rightarrow X', 0, X')$ to R';
(iii) Add the following six rules to R':
$(C' \rightarrow C'', A'B'C', 0)$,
$(A' \rightarrow A'', A'B'C'', 0)$,
$(B' \rightarrow B'', A''B'C'', 0)$,
$(A'' \rightarrow \varepsilon, 0, C'')$,
$(C'' \rightarrow \varepsilon, 0, B')$,
$(B'' \rightarrow \varepsilon, 0, 0)$.

Observe that G' satisfies all the requirements of this theorem—that is, it contains only 8 conditional rules and 11 nonterminals. G' reproduces the first two phases of generating a terminal string in G by using the rules of the form $(H \rightarrow y, 0, 0) \in R'$. The third phase, during which $ABC \rightarrow \varepsilon$ is applied, is simulated by the additional rules. Examine these rules to see that all strings generated by G can also be generated by G'. Indeed, for every derivation step

$$y_1 ABC y_2 \Rightarrow_G y_1 y_2 \; [ABC \rightarrow \varepsilon]$$

in $G, y_1, y_2 \in \Sigma^*$, there exists the following derivation in G':

$$
\begin{aligned}
y_1ABCy_2 &\Rightarrow_{G'} y_1A'BCy_2 && [(A \to A', 0, A')] \\
&\Rightarrow_{G'} y_1A'B'Cy_2 && [(B \to B', 0, B')] \\
&\Rightarrow_{G'} y_1A'B'C'y_2 && [(C \to C', 0, C')] \\
&\Rightarrow_{G'} y_1A'B'C''y_2 && [(C' \to C'', A'B'C', 0)] \\
&\Rightarrow_{G'} y_1A''B'C''y_2 && [(A' \to A'', A'B'C'', 0)] \\
&\Rightarrow_{G'} y_1A''B''C''y_2 && [(B' \to B'', A''B'C'', 0)] \\
&\Rightarrow_{G'} y_1A''B''y_2 && [(C'' \to \varepsilon, 0, B')] \\
&\Rightarrow_{G'} y_1B''y_2 && [(A'' \to \varepsilon, 0, C'')] \\
&\Rightarrow_{G'} y_1y_2 && [(B'' \to \varepsilon, 0, 0)].
\end{aligned}
$$

As a result, $L(G) \subseteq L(G')$. In the following, we show that G' does not generate strings that cannot be generated by G; thus, $L(G') - L(G) = \emptyset$, so $L(G') = L(G)$.

Let us study how G' can generate a terminal string. All derivations start from S. While the sentential form contains S or S', its form is zSw or $zuS'vw$, $z, u, v \in \{A, B, C, A', B', C'\}^*$, $w \in \Delta^*$, where if $g(X') = X$ for $X \in \{A, B, C\}$ and $g(X) = X$ for all other symbols of Σ, then $g(zSw)$ or $g(zuS'vw)$ are valid sentential forms of G. Furthermore, zu contains at most one occurrence of A', v contains at most one occurrence of C', and zuv contains at most one occurrence of B' (see (ii) in the construction of R'). After $(S' \to \varepsilon, 0, 0)$ is used, we get a sentential form $zuvw$ with z, u, v, and w as above such that

$$S \Rightarrow_G^* g(zuvw).$$

Next, we demonstrate that

$$zuv \Rightarrow_{G'}^* \varepsilon \quad \text{implies} \quad g(zuv) \Rightarrow_G^* \varepsilon.$$

More specifically, we investigate all possible derivations rewriting a sentential form containing a single occurrence of each of the letters A', B', and C'.

Consider a sentential form of the form $zuvw$, where $z, u, v \in \{A, B, C, A', B', C'\}^*$, $w \in \Delta^*$, and occur $(A', zu) =$ occur $(B', zuv) =$ occur $(C', v) = 1$. By the definition of rules rewriting A', B', and C' (see (iii) in the construction of R'), we see that these three symbols must form a substring $A'B'C'$; otherwise, no next derivation step can be made. That is, $zuvw = z\bar{u}A'B'C'\bar{v}w$ for some $\bar{u}, \bar{v} \in \{A, B, C\}^*$. Next, observe that the only applicable rule is $(C' \to C'', A'B'C', 0)$. Thus, we get

$$z\bar{u}A'B'C'\bar{v}w \Rightarrow_{G'} z\bar{u}A'B'C''\bar{v}w.$$

This sentential form can be rewritten in two ways. First, we can rewrite A' to A'' by $(A' \to A'', A'B'C'', 0)$. Second, we can replace another occurrence of C with C'. Let us investigate the derivation

$$z\bar{u}A'B'C''\bar{v}w \Rightarrow_{G'} z\bar{u}A''B'C''\bar{v}w \; [(A' \to A'', A'B'C'', 0)].$$

As before, we can either rewrite another occurrence of A to A' or rewrite an occurrence of C to C' or rewrite B' to B'' by using $(B' \to B'', A''B'C'', 0)$. Taking into account all possible combinations of the previously described steps, we see that after the first application of $(B' \to B'', A''B'C'', 0)$, the whole derivation is of the form

$$z\bar{u}A'B'C'\bar{v}w \Rightarrow_{G'}^{+} zu_1Xu_2A''B''C''v_1Yv_2w$$

where $X \in \{A', \varepsilon\}$, $Y \in \{C', \varepsilon\}$, $u_1g(X)u_2 = \bar{u}$, and $v_1g(Y)v_2 = \bar{v}$. Let $zu_1Xu_2 = x$ and $v_1Yv_2 = y$. The next derivation step can be made in one of four ways. By an application of $(B \to B', 0, B')$, we can rewrite an occurrence of B in x or y. In both cases, this derivation is blocked in the next step. The remaining two derivations are

$$xA''B''C''yw \Rightarrow_{G'} xA''C''yw\ [(B'' \to \varepsilon, 0, 0)]$$

and

$$xA''B''C''yw \Rightarrow_{G'} xA''B''yw\ [(C'' \to \varepsilon, 0, B')].$$

Let us examine how G' can rewrite $xA''C''yw$. The following three cases cover all possible steps.

(i) If $xA''C''yw \Rightarrow_{G'} x_1B'x_2A''C''yw\ [(B \to B', 0, B')]$, where $x_1Bx_2 = x$, then the derivation is blocked;

(ii) If $xA''C''yw \Rightarrow_{G'} xA''C''y_1B'y_2w\ [(B \to B', 0, B')]$, where $y_1By_2 = y$, then no next derivation step can be made;

(iii) Let $xA''C''yw \Rightarrow_{G'} xA''yw\ [(C'' \to \varepsilon, 0, B')]$. Then, all the following derivations

$$xA''yw \Rightarrow_{G'} xyw$$

and

$$xA''yw \Rightarrow_{G'} x_1B'x_2A''yw \Rightarrow_{G'} x_1B'x_2yw$$

where $x_1Bx_2 = x$, and

$$xA''yw \Rightarrow_{G'} xA''y_1B'y_2w \Rightarrow_{G'} xy_1B'y_2w$$

where $y_1By_2 = y$, produce a sentential form in which the substring $A''B''C''$ is erased. This sentential form contains at most one occurrence of A', B', and C'.

Return to

$$xA''B''C''yw \Rightarrow_{G'} xA''B''yw.$$

Observe that by analogy with case (iii), any rewriting of $xA''B''yw$ removes the substring $A''B''$ and produces a sentential form containing at most one occurrence of A', B', and C'.

To summarize the considerations above, the reader can see that as long as there exists an occurrence of A'', B'', or C'' in the sentential form, only the erasing rules or $(B \to B', 0, B')$ can be applied. The derivation either enters a sentential form that blocks the derivation or the substring $A'B'C'$ is completely erased, after which new occurrences of A, B, and C can be changed to A', B', and C', respectively. That is,

$$z\bar{u}A'B'C'\bar{v}w \Rightarrow_{G'}^{+} xyw \quad \text{implies} \quad g(z\bar{u}A'B'C'\bar{v}w) \Rightarrow_{G} g(xyw)$$

where $z, \bar{u}, \bar{v} \in \{A, B, C\}^*$, $x, y \in \{A, B, C, A', B', C'\}^*$, $w \in \Delta^*$, and $z\bar{u} = g(x)$, $\bar{v}w = g(yw)$. In other words, the rules constructed in (ii) and (iii) correctly simulate the application of the only non-context-free rule $ABC \to \varepsilon$. Recall that $g(a) = a$, for all $a \in \Delta$. Hence, $g(xyw) = g(xy)w$. Thus, $L(G') - L(G) = \emptyset$.

Having $L(G) \subseteq L(G')$ and $L(G') - L(G) = \emptyset$, we get $L(G) = L(G')$, and the theorem holds. ■

Theorem 11.38 was further slightly improved in [17], where the following result was proved (the number of nonterminals was reduced from 11 to 9).

Theorem 11.39 (see [17]). *Every recursively enumerable language can be generated by an ssc-grammar of degree* $(3, 1)$ *with no more than eight conditional rules and nine nonterminals.*

Let us close this section by stating several open problems.

Open Problem 11.3. *In Theorems 11.32, 11.33, 11.34, and 11.35, we proved that ssc-grammars of degrees* $(1, 2)$ *and* $(2, 1)$ *generate the family of recursively enumerable languages, and propagating ssc-grammars of degrees* $(1, 2)$ *and* $(2, 1)$ *generate the family of context-sensitive languages. However, we did not discuss ssc-grammars of degree* $(1, 1)$*. According to Penttonen (see Theorem 11.29), propagating sc-grammars of degree* $(1, 1)$ *generate a proper subfamily of context-sensitive languages. That is,* $\mathbf{PSSCOND}(1, 1) \subseteq \mathbf{PSCOND}(1, 1) \subset \mathbf{CS}$*. Are propagating ssc-grammars of degree* $(1, 1)$ *as powerful as propagating sc-grammars of degree* $(1, 1)$*? Furthermore, consider ssc-grammars of degree* $(1, 1)$ *with erasing rules. Are they more powerful than propagating ssc-grammars of degree* $(1, 1)$*? Do they generate the family of all context-sensitive languages or, even more, the family of recursively enumerable languages?*

Open Problem 11.4. *In Theorems 11.36–11.39, several reduced normal forms of these grammars were presented. These normal forms give rise to the following questions. Can any of the results be further improved with respect to the number of conditional rules or nonterminals? Are there analogical reduced forms of ssc-grammars with degrees* $(1, 2)$ *and* $(1, 3)$*? Moreover, reconsider these results in terms of propagating ssc-grammars. Is it possible to achieve analogical results if we disallow erasing rules?*

Global context conditional grammars

In the present section, we go beyond the topic of this chapter. Indeed, rather than associating context conditions with grammatical rules, we associate them with a grammar as a whole.

Definition 11.17. *Let r be a natural number. A* global context conditional grammar *(a* gcc-grammar *for short)* of degree r *is a sixtuple,*

$$G = (\Sigma, \Delta, R, S, Per, For),$$

where (Σ, Δ, R, S) *is a CFG,* $For \subseteq \Sigma$, *and* $Per \subseteq \Sigma^+$ *such that* $y \in Per$ *implies* $|y| \leq r$. *G is said to be* propagating *if* $A \to x \in R$ *implies* $x \neq \varepsilon$.

Let $u, v \in \Sigma^*$, $p \in R$, $p = A \to x$, $u = u_1 A u_2$, $v = u_1 x u_2$, *for some* $A \in (\Sigma - \Delta)$, $x, u_1, u_2 \in \Sigma^*$, *then we write*

(a) $u\ {}^{p}\!\Rightarrow_G v\ [p]$ *if* $A \in$ symbols (substrings $(u) \cap Per$);
(b) $u\ {}^{f}\!\Rightarrow_G v\ [p]$ *if* symbols $(u) \cap For = \emptyset$; *and*
(c) $u \Rightarrow_G v\ [p]$ *if* $u\ {}^{p}\!\Rightarrow_G v\ [p]$ *or* $u\ {}^{f}\!\Rightarrow_G v\ [p]$.

Roughly speaking, such a production as $A \to x \in R$ *can be applied to a sentential form w provided that (a) A occurs in a permitting word from Per which is a subword of w or (b) no forbidding symbol from For occurs in w. Note that (a) requires any occurrence of A to appear in a permitting word that is a subword of u; but not necessarily the occurrence of A, which is rewritten in a given derivation step* $u\ {}^{p}\!\Rightarrow_G v$.

In the standard manner, we define $\Rightarrow_G^i$ *for* $i \geq 0$, $\Rightarrow_G^+$, *and* $\Rightarrow_G^*$. *The language of G, denoted by L(G), is defined as*

$$L(G) = \{w \in \Delta^* : S \Rightarrow_G^* w\}.$$

The family of languages generated by gcc*-grammars of degree r is denoted by*

$$\mathbf{GCC}(r).$$

Furthermore,

$$\mathbf{GCC} = \bigcup_{i=0}^{\infty} \mathbf{GCC}(i).$$

We use prefix ***prop-*** *if we consider only propagating* gcc*-grammars. That is,*

$$\mathbf{GCC}^{-\varepsilon}(r) \text{ and } \mathbf{GCC}^{-\varepsilon}$$

denote the family of languages generated by propagating gcc*-grammars of degree r and by propagating* gcc*-grammars of any degree, respectively.*

Next, we prove two fundamental results regarding the generative power of *gcc*-grammars:

(i) A language is context-sensitive if and only if it is generated by a propagating *gcc*-grammar of degree 2;
(ii) A language is recursively enumerable if and only if it is generated by a *gcc*-grammar of degree 2.

Theorem 11.40. $\mathbf{CS} = \mathbf{GCC}^{-\varepsilon}(2)$.

Proof. It is straightforward to prove that $\mathbf{GCC}^{-\varepsilon}(2) \subseteq \mathbf{CS}$, so it suffices to prove the converse inclusion.

Let L be a context-sensitive language. Without any loss of generality, we can assume that L is generated by a CSG

$$G = (N_{CF} \cup N_{CS} \cup \Delta, \Delta, R, S)$$

of the form described in Lemma 11.6. Let $\Sigma = N_{CF} \cup N_{CS} \cup \Delta$. Set

$$For = \{\langle A, B, C\rangle : AB \to AC \in R,\ A, C \in N_{CF},\ B \in N_{CS}\}.$$

The propagating *gcc*-grammar G' of degree 2 is defined as

$$G' = (\Sigma', \Delta, R', S, Per, For),$$

where $\Sigma' = \Sigma \cup For$ and

$$Per = \{A\langle A, B, C\rangle : A \in N_{CF},\ \langle A, B, C\rangle \in For\}.$$

The set of productions R' is defined in the following way:

(i) If $A \to x \in R, A \in N_{CF}, x \in N_{CS} \cup \Delta \cup N_{CF}^2$, then add $A \to x$ to R';
(ii) If $AB \to AC \in R, A, C \in N_{CF}, B \in N_{CS}$, then add the following two productions $B \to \langle A, B, C\rangle$, $\langle A, B, C\rangle \to C$ to R'.

Obviously, G' is a propagating *gcc*-grammar of degree 2. Moreover, observe that G is supposed to be of the form described by Lemma 11.6, so N_{CF} and N_{CS} are two disjoint alphabets. Thus, considering the construction of G', we should see that there is at most one occurrence of a symbol from *For* in any word derived from S, that is,

$$S \Rightarrow_{G'}^{*} x \quad \text{implies} \quad \#_{For} x \leq 1.$$

The formal proof is left to the reader.

Next, define a finite letter-to-letters substitution g from Σ^* into $(\Sigma \cup For)^*$ such that for all $Y \in \Sigma$,

$$g(Y) = \{Y\} \cup \{\langle X, Y, Z\rangle : \langle X, Y, Z\rangle \in For,\ X, Z \in N_{CF}\}.$$

Let inverse g be the inverse of g.

To show that $L(G) = L(G')$, we prove that

$$S \Rightarrow_{G}^{m} x \quad \text{if and only if} \quad S \Rightarrow_{G'}^{n} x',$$

where $x' \in g(x)$, $x \in \Sigma^+$, for some $m, n \geq 0$.

Only If. This is established by induction on the length m of derivations, that is, we have to demonstrate that

$$S \Rightarrow_{G}^{m} x \quad \text{implies} \quad S \Rightarrow_{G'}^{*} x'$$

for some $x' \in g(x)$, $x \in \Sigma^+$. This is our claim.

Basis. Let $m = 0$. The only x is S because $S \Rightarrow_{G}^{0} S$. Clearly, $S \Rightarrow_{G'}^{0} S$ in G' and $S \in g(S)$.

Induction Hypothesis. Suppose that our claim holds for all derivations of length at most m, for some $m \geq 0$.

Induction Step. Let us consider a derivation

$S \Rightarrow_G^{m+1} x,\ x \in \Sigma^+.$

Since $m + 1 \geq 1$, there is some $y \in \Sigma^+$ and $p \in R$ such that

$S \Rightarrow_G^{m} y \Rightarrow_G x\ [p],$

and by the induction hypothesis, there is also a derivation

$S \Rightarrow_{G'}^{n} y'$

for some $y' \in g(y)$.

(i) Let us assume that $p = D \rightarrow y_2 \in R$, $D \in N_{CF}$, $y_2 \in N_{CS} \cup \Delta \cup N_{CF}^2$, $y = y_1 D y_3$, $y_1, y_3 \in \Sigma^*$, and $x = y_1 y_2 y_3$. Since from the definition of g it is clear that $g(Z) = \{Z\}$ for all $Z \in N_{CF}$, we can express $y' = y'_1 D y'_3$, where $y'_1 \in g(y_1)$ and $y'_3 \in g(y_3)$. Clearly, $D \rightarrow y_2 \in R'$; see (i) in the definition of R'.

(a) If $For \cap \text{symbols}(y'_1 D y'_3) = \emptyset$, then

$S \Rightarrow_{G'}^{n} y'_1 D y'_3\ {}^{\mathrm{f}}\!\!\Rightarrow_{G'} y'_1 y_2 y'_3\ [D \rightarrow y_2]$

and $y'_1 y_2 y'_3 \in g(y_1 y_2 y_3) = g(x)$;

(b) If $For \cap \text{symbols}(y'_1 D y'_3) \neq \emptyset$, then $\#_{For} y'_1 D y'_3 = 1$. Next, suppose that $\langle X, Y, Z\rangle \in \text{symbols}(y'_1 D y'_3) \cap For$, $XY \rightarrow XZ \in R$, $X, Z \in N_{CF}$, $Y \in N_{CS}$; then, by (ii), we have $Y \rightarrow \langle X, Y, Z\rangle \in R'$. Clearly, we can express the derivation

$S \Rightarrow_{G'}^{n} y'_1 D y'_3$

in the following way:

$S \Rightarrow_{G'}^{n-1} \text{inverse}\, g(y'_1 D y'_3)\ {}^{\mathrm{f}}\!\!\Rightarrow_{G'} y'_1 D y'_3\ [Y \rightarrow \langle X, Y, Z\rangle],$

where

$\text{symbols}(\text{inverse}\, g(y'_1 D y'_3)) \cap For = \emptyset$ and $\text{inverse}\, g(y'_1 D y'_3) = y_1 D y_3$.

Thus,

$S \Rightarrow_{G'}^{n-1} y_1 D y_3 \Rightarrow_{G'} y_1 y_2 y_3\ [D \rightarrow y_2]$

and $y_1 y_2 y_3 \in g(x)$;

(ii) Let $p = AB \rightarrow AC \in R$, $A, C \in N_{CF}$, $B \in N_{CS}$, $y = y_1 A B y_2$, $y_1, y_2 \in \Sigma^*$, $x = y_1 A C y_2$, $y' = y'_1 X Y y'_2$, $y'_1 \in g(y_1)$, $y'_2 \in g(y_2)$, $X \in g(A)$, $Y \in g(B)$. Clearly,

$\{B \rightarrow \langle A, B, C\rangle, \langle A, B, C\rangle \rightarrow C\} \subseteq R'$

(see (ii) in the definition of R');

(a) If $For \cap \text{symbols}(y'_1 X Y y'_2) = \emptyset$, then $y'_1 X Y y'_2 = y_1 A B y_2$, and so

$$\begin{aligned} S &\Rightarrow_{G'}^{n} y_1 A B y_2 \\ &{}^{\mathrm{f}}\!\!\Rightarrow_{G'} y_1 A \langle A, B, C\rangle y_2\ [B \rightarrow \langle A, B, C\rangle] \\ &{}^{\mathrm{p}}\!\!\Rightarrow_{G'} y_1 A C y_2 \qquad [\langle A, B, C\rangle \rightarrow C] \end{aligned}$$

and $y_1 A C y_2 \in g(x)$;

(b) Let $For \cap \text{symbols}(y'_1 X Y y'_2) \neq \emptyset$. By analogy with (i), we can find the derivation

$S \Rightarrow_{G'}^{n-1} y_1 A B y_2$

in G', and so

$S \Rightarrow_{G'}^{n-1} y_1 A B y_2 \Rightarrow_{G'} y_1 A \langle A, B, C\rangle y_2 \Rightarrow_{G'} y_1 A C y_2,$

where $y_1 A C y_2 \in g(x)$.

Thus, the only-if part now follows by the principle of induction.

If. This is also established by induction, but in this case on n. We have to demonstrate that

$$S \Rightarrow_{G'}^{n} x' \quad \text{implies} \quad S \Rightarrow_{G}^{*} x,$$

where $x \in \Sigma^+$, $x = \text{inverse}\, g(x')$, and $n \geq 0$.

Basis. For $n = 0$ the only x' is S because $S \Rightarrow_{G'}^{0} S$. Since $S = \text{inverse}\, g(S)$, we have $x = S$. Clearly, $S \Rightarrow_{G}^{0} S$ in G.

Induction Hypothesis. Assume that the claim holds for all derivations of length at most n, for some $n \geq 0$.

Induction Step. Consider a derivation

$$S \Rightarrow_{G'}^{n+1} x',$$

where $x = \text{inverse}\, g(x')$ for some $x \in \Sigma^+$. Since $n + 1 \geq 1$, there is some $y \in \Sigma^+$, $y = \text{inverse}\, g(y')$, and $p \in R'$ such that

$$S \Rightarrow_{G'}^{n} y' \Rightarrow_{G'} x' \; [p]$$

in G'. By the induction hypothesis,

$$S \Rightarrow_{G}^{*} y.$$

Let $y' = r'Ds'$, $y = rBs$, $r = \text{inverse}\, g(r')$, $s = \text{inverse}\, g(s')$, $r, s \in \Sigma^*$, $B = \text{inverse}\, g(D)$, $x' = r'z's'$ and $p = D \rightarrow z' \in R'$. Moreover, let us consider the following three cases:

(i) Let $\text{inverse}\, g(z') = B$; see (ii). Then, $\text{inverse}\, g(x') = \text{inverse}\, g(r'z's') = rBs$. By the induction hypothesis, we have

$$S \Rightarrow_{G}^{*} rBs;$$

(ii) Let $z' \in \Delta \cup N_{CS} \cup N_{CF}^2$, $D = B \in N_{CF}$. Then, there is a production $B \rightarrow z' \in R$; see (i). Hence,

$$S \Rightarrow_{G}^{*} rBs \Rightarrow_{G} rz's \; [B \rightarrow z'].$$

Since $z' = \text{inverse}\, g(z')$, we have $x = rz's$ such that $\text{inverse}\, g(x') = x$;

(iii) Let $z' = C$, $D = \langle A, B, C \rangle \in For$; see (ii). Clearly,

$$y' \; {}^{\mathrm{p}}\!\Rightarrow_{G'} x' \; [p]$$

and $A\langle A, B, C \rangle \in \text{substrings}(y')$. By the definition of *For*, there is a production $AB \rightarrow AC \in R$. Since $\#_{For} y' \leq 1$, we have $r' = u'A$, $r = uA$, where $\text{inverse}\, g(u') = u$ and $u \in \Sigma^*$. Thus,

$$S \Rightarrow_{G}^{*} uABs \Rightarrow_{G} uACs \; [AB \rightarrow AC],$$

where $uACs = rCs$. Since $C = \text{inverse}\, g(C)$, we get $x = rCs$ such that

$$\text{inverse}\, g(x') = x.$$

By inspection of R', we have considered all possible derivations of the form

$$S \Rightarrow_{G'}^{n} y' \Rightarrow_{G'} x'$$

in G'. Thus, by the principle of induction, we have established that

$$S \Rightarrow_{G'}^{*} x' \quad \text{implies} \quad S \Rightarrow_{G}^{*} x,$$

where $x \in \Sigma^{+}$, inverse $g(x') = x$, and $n \geq 0$.

The equivalence of G and G' immediately follows from the statement above. Indeed, by the definition of g, we have $g(a) = \{a\}$ for all $a \in \Delta$. Therefore, we have for any $w \in \Delta^{*}$,

$$S \Rightarrow_{G}^{*} w \quad \text{if and only if} \quad S \Rightarrow_{G'}^{*} w,$$

that is, $L(G) = L(G')$. Hence, $\mathbf{GCC}^{-\varepsilon}(2) = \mathbf{CS}$. ■

Next, we turn to the investigation of *gcc*-grammars of degree 2 with erasing productions. We show that these grammars generate precisely the family of recursively enumerable languages.

Theorem 11.41. RE = GCC(2).

Proof. Clearly, $\mathbf{GCC}(2) \subseteq \mathbf{RE}$. Hence, it suffices to show that $\mathbf{RE} \subseteq \mathbf{GCC}(2)$. This inclusion can be proved by the technique used in Theorem 11.40, because every language $L \in \mathbf{RE}$ can be generated by a PSG whose productions are of the form $AB \rightarrow AC$ or $A \rightarrow x$, where $A, B, C \in \Sigma - \Delta$ and $x \in \{\varepsilon\} \cup \Delta \cup (\Sigma - \Delta)^2$ (see Theorems 11.2 and 11.5). The details are left to the reader. ■

The following corollary summarizes the results which were established in Theorems 11.40 and 11.41:

Corollary 11.11.

$$\begin{array}{c} \mathbf{GCC}^{-\varepsilon}(2) = \mathbf{GCC}^{-\varepsilon} = \mathbf{CS} \\ \subset \\ \mathbf{GCC}(2) = \mathbf{GCC} = \mathbf{RE}. \end{array}$$

Open problem

Consider an alternative definition of *gcc*-grammars. Specifically, define the notion of a forbidding *gcc*-grammar of degree r (for some natural number r) as a sixtuple $G = (\Sigma, \Delta, R, S, Per, For)$, where (Σ, Δ, R, S) is a CFG, $For \subseteq \Sigma^{+}$ such that $x \in For$ implies $|x| \leq r$, $Per \subseteq \Sigma$, and a production $A \rightarrow x$ can be applied to a word w when $Per \subseteq \text{symbols}(w)$ or $\emptyset = \Sigma^{*}\{A\}\Sigma^{*} \cap For \cap \text{substrings}(w)$. What is the language generating power of these grammars?

Chapter 12
Regulated models

This five-section chapter covers regulated language models, which are extended by additional mathematical mechanisms that prescribe the use of rules during the generation of their languages. An important advantage of these models lies in controlling their language-defining process and, therefore, operating in a more deterministic way than general models, which perform their derivations in a completely unregulated way. More significantly, the regulated versions of language models are stronger than their unregulated versions. The chapter covers grammars regulated by states (Section 12.1), grammars regulated by control languages (Section 12.2), matrix grammars (Section 12.3), programmed grammars (Section 12.4), and regulated automata (Section 12.5).

12.1 Grammars regulated by states

A *state grammar* G is a context-free grammar extended by an additional state mechanism that strongly resembles the finite-state control of finite automata. During every derivation step, G rewrites the leftmost occurrence of a nonterminal that can be rewritten in the current state; in addition, it moves from one state to another, which influences the choice of the rule to be applied in the next step. If the application of a rule always takes place within the first n occurrences of nonterminals, G is referred to as *n-limited*.

The present section consists of Sections 12.1.1 and 12.1.2. The former defines and illustrates state grammars. The latter describes their generative power.

12.1.1 Definitions and examples

In this section, we define state grammars and illustrate them by an example.

Definition 12.1. *A* state grammar *(see [20]) is a quintuple*

$$G = (\Sigma, W, \Delta, R, S)$$

where

- Σ *is a* total alphabet,
- W *is a finite set of* states,
- $\Delta \subset \Sigma$ *is an alphabet of* terminals,

- $S \in \Sigma - \Delta$ *is the* start symbol, *and*
- $R \subseteq (W \times (\Sigma - \Delta)) \times (W \times \Sigma^+)$ *is a finite relation.*

Instead of $(q, A, p, v) \in R$, *we write* $(q, A) \to (p, v) \in R$. *If* $(q, A) \to (p, v) \in R$, $x, y \in \Sigma^*$, *and for each* $B \in symbols(x)$, *R contains no rule with* (q, B) *on its left-hand side, then G makes a* derivation step *from* (q, xAy) *to* (p, xvy), *symbolically written as*

$$(q, xAy) \Rightarrow (p, xvy)\ [(q, A) \to (p, v)].$$

In addition, if n is a positive integer satisfying that $\mathrm{occur}(\Sigma - \Delta, xA) \leq n$, *we say that* $(q, xAy) \Rightarrow (p, xvy)\ [(q, A) \to (p, v)]$ *is n-*limited, *symbolically written as*

$$(q, xAy)\ {}_n\!\Rightarrow (p, xvy)\ [(q, A) \to (p, v)].$$

Whenever there is no danger of confusion, we simplify $(q, xAy) \Rightarrow (p, xvy)\ [(q, A) \to (p, v)]$ *and* $(q, xAy)\ {}_n\!\Rightarrow (p, xvy)\ [(q, A) \to (p, v)]$ *to*

$$(q, xAy) \Rightarrow (p, xvy)$$

and

$$(q, xAy)\ {}_n\!\Rightarrow (p, xvy),$$

respectively. In the standard manner, we extend $\Rightarrow$ *to* $\Rightarrow^m$, *where* $m \geq 0$; *then, based on* $\Rightarrow^m$, *we define* $\Rightarrow^+$ *and* $\Rightarrow^*$.

Let n be a positive integer, and let $\nu, \omega \in W \times \Sigma^+$. *To express that every derivation step in* $\nu \Rightarrow^m \omega$, $\nu \Rightarrow^+ \omega$, *and* $\nu \Rightarrow^* \omega$ *is n-limited, we write* $\nu\ {}_n\!\Rightarrow^m \omega$, $\nu\ {}_n\!\Rightarrow^+ \omega$, *and* $\nu\ {}_n\!\Rightarrow^* \omega$ *instead of* $\nu \Rightarrow^m \omega$, $\nu \Rightarrow^+ \omega$, *and* $\nu \Rightarrow^* \omega$, *respectively.*

By strings$(\nu\ {}_n\!\Rightarrow^* \omega)$, *we denote the set of all strings occurring in the derivation* $\nu\ {}_n\!\Rightarrow^* \omega$. *The* language *of G, denoted by L(G), is defined as*

$$L(G) = \{w \in \Delta^* \mid (q, S) \Rightarrow^* (p, w), q, p \in W\}.$$

Furthermore, for every $n \geq 1$, *define*

$$L(G, n) = \{w \in \Delta^* \mid (q, S)\ {}_n\!\Rightarrow^* (p, w), q, p \in W\}.$$

A derivation of the form $(q, S)\ {}_n\!\Rightarrow^* (p, w)$, *where* $q, p \in W$ *and* $w \in \Delta^*$, *represents a* successful *n*-limited generation *of w in G.*

Next, we illustrate the previous definition by an example.

Example 12.1. *Consider the state grammar*

$$G = (\{S, X, Y, a, b\}, \{p_0, p_1, p_2, p_3, p_4\}, \{a, b\}, R, S)$$

with the following nine rules in R:

$$\begin{array}{ll}
(p_0, S) \to (p_0, XY), & (p_0, X) \to (p_3, a), \\
(p_0, X) \to (p_1, aX), & (p_3, Y) \to (p_0, a), \\
(p_1, Y) \to (p_0, aY), & (p_0, X) \to (p_4, b), \\
(p_0, X) \to (p_2, bX), & (p_4, Y) \to (p_0, b), \\
(p_2, Y) \to (p_0, bY), &
\end{array}$$

Observe that G generates the non-context-free language

$$L(G) = \{ww \mid w \in \{a, b\}^+\}.$$

Indeed, first, S is rewritten to XY. Then, by using its states, G ensures that whenever X is rewritten to aX, the current state is changed to force the rewrite of Y to aY. Similarly, whenever X is rewritten to bX, the current state is changed to force the rewrite of Y to bY. Every successful derivation is finished by rewriting X to a or b and then Y to a or b, respectively.

For example, abab is produced by the following derivation:

$$\begin{aligned}(p_0, S) &\Rightarrow (p_0, XY) \quad [(p_0, S) \rightarrow (p_0, XY)]\\ &\Rightarrow (p_1, aXY) \quad [(p_0, X) \rightarrow (p_1, aX)]\\ &\Rightarrow (p_0, aXaY) \quad [(p_1, Y) \rightarrow (p_0, aY)]\\ &\Rightarrow (p_4, abaY) \quad [(p_0, X) \rightarrow (p_4, b)]\\ &\Rightarrow (p_0, abab) \quad [(p_4, Y) \rightarrow (p_0, b)].\end{aligned}$$

By **ST**, we denote the family of languages generated by state grammars. For every $n \geq 1$, $\mathbf{ST}_n$ denotes the family of languages generated by n-limited state grammars. Set

$$\mathbf{ST}_\infty = \bigcup_{n>1} \mathbf{ST}_n.$$

12.1.2 Generative power

In this section we give the key result concerning state grammars, originally established in [20].

Theorem 12.1. $\mathbf{CF} = \mathbf{ST}_1 \subset \mathbf{ST}_2 \subset \cdots \subset \mathbf{ST}_\infty \subset \mathbf{ST} = \mathbf{CS}$.

12.2 Grammars regulated by control languages

In essence, a *grammar with a control language* H is a context-free grammar G extended by a regular *control language* Ξ defined over the set of rules of G. Thus, each control string in Ξ represents, in effect, a sequence of rules in G. A terminal string w is in the language generated by H if and only if Ξ contains a control string according to which G generates w.

12.2.1 Definitions and examples

In this section, we define the notion of a regular-controlled grammar and illustrate it by examples.

Definition 12.2. *A* regular-controlled (context-free) grammar *(see [21]) is a pair*

$$H = (G, \Xi)$$

where

- $G = (\Sigma, \Delta, R, S)$ *is a context-free grammar, called the* core grammar;

- $\Xi \subseteq R^*$ *is a regular language, called the* control language.

The language *of* H*, denoted by* $L(H)$*, is defined as*

$$L(H) = \{w \in \Delta^* \mid S \Rightarrow_G^* w\ [\alpha] \text{ with } \alpha \in \Xi\}.$$

In other words, $L(H)$ in the above definition consists of all strings $w \in \Delta^*$ such that there is a derivation in G

$$S \Rightarrow_G w_1\ [r_1] \Rightarrow_G w_2\ [r_2] \Rightarrow_G \cdots \Rightarrow_G w_n\ [r_n]$$

where

$$w = w_n \text{ and } r_1 r_2 \cdots r_n \in \Xi \text{ for some } n \geq 1.$$

In what follows, instead of $x \Rightarrow_G y$, we sometimes write $x \Rightarrow_H y$—that is, we use $\Rightarrow_G$ and $\Rightarrow_H$ interchangeably.

Note that if $\Xi = R^*$, then there is no regulation, and thus $L(H) = L(G)$ in this case.

Example 12.2. *Let* $H = (G, \Xi)$ *be a regular-controlled grammar, where*

$$G = (\{S, A, B, C, a, b, c\}, \{a, b, c\}, R, S)$$

is a context-free grammar with R *consisting of the following seven rules:*

$$\begin{array}{lll} r_1 : S \rightarrow ABC, & r_4 : C \rightarrow cC, & r_7 : C \rightarrow \varepsilon, \\ & r_2 : A \rightarrow aA, & r_5 : A \rightarrow \varepsilon, \\ & r_3 : B \rightarrow bB, & r_6 : B \rightarrow \varepsilon, \end{array}$$

and $\Xi = \{r_1\}\{r_2 r_3 r_4\}^*\{r_5 r_6 r_7\}$.

First, r_1 *has to be applied. Then,* r_2*,* r_3*, and* r_4 *can be consecutively applied any number of times. The derivation is finished by applying* r_5*,* r_6*, and* r_7*. As a result, this grammar generates the non-context-free language*

$$L(H) = \{a^n b^n c^n \mid n \geq 0\}.$$

For example, the sentence aabbcc is obtained by the following derivation:

$$\begin{array}{lll} S & \Rightarrow_H ABC & [r_1] \\ & \Rightarrow_H aABC & [r_2] \\ & \Rightarrow_H aAbBC & [r_3] \\ & \Rightarrow_H aAbBcC & [r_4] \\ & \Rightarrow_H aaAbBcC & [r_2] \\ & \Rightarrow_H aaAbbBcC & [r_3] \\ & \Rightarrow_H aaAbbBccC & [r_4] \\ & \Rightarrow_H aabbBccC & [r_5] \\ & \Rightarrow_H aabbccC & [r_6] \\ & \Rightarrow_H aabbcc & [r_7]. \end{array}$$

As another example, the empty string is derived in this way:

$$S \Rightarrow_H ABC\ [r_1] \Rightarrow_H BC\ [r_5] \Rightarrow_H C\ [r_6] \Rightarrow_H \varepsilon\ [r_7].$$

Next, we introduce the concept of appearance checking. Informally, it allows us to skip the application of certain rules if they are not applicable to the current sentential form.

Definition 12.3. *A* regular-controlled grammar with appearance checking *(see [21]) is a triple*

$$H = (G, \Xi, W)$$

where

- *G and* Ξ *are defined as in a regular-controlled grammar,*
- $W \subseteq R$ *is the* appearance checking set.

We say that $x \in \Sigma^+$ *directly derives* $y \in \Sigma^*$ *in G in the* appearance checking mode *W by application of* $r\colon A \to w \in R$*, symbolically written as*

$$x \Rightarrow_{(G,W)} y\ [r]$$

if either

$$x = x_1 A x_2 \text{ and } y = x_1 w x_2$$

or

$$A \notin \text{symbols}(x), r \in W, \text{ and } x = y.$$

Define $\Rightarrow^k_{(G,W)}$ *for* $k \geq 0$, $\Rightarrow^+_{(G,W)}$, *and* $\Rightarrow^*_{(G,W)}$ *in the standard way. The* language *of H, denoted by L(H), is defined as*

$$L(H) = \{w \in \Delta^* \mid S \Rightarrow^*_{(G,W)} w\ [\alpha] \text{ with } \alpha \in \Xi\}.$$

According to Definition 12.2, in a regular-controlled grammar without appearance checking, once a control string has been started by G, all its rules have to be applied. G with an appearance checking set somewhat relaxes this necessity, however. Indeed, if the left-hand side of a rule is absent in the sentential form under scan and, simultaneously, this rule is in the appearance checking set, G skips its application and moves on to the next rule in the control string.

Observe that the only difference between a regular-controlled grammar with and without appearance checking is the derivation mode ($\Rightarrow_{(G,W)}$ instead of $\Rightarrow_G$). Furthermore, note that when $W = \emptyset$, these two modes coincide, so any regular-controlled grammar represents a special case of a regular-controlled grammar with appearance checking.

Example 12.3. *(from Chapter 3 of [13]). Let* $H = (G, \Xi, W)$ *be a regular-controlled grammar with appearance checking, where*

$$G = (\{S, A, X, a\}, \{a\}, R, S)$$

is a context-free grammar with R consisting of the following rules:

$$r_1\colon S \to AA, \qquad r_4\colon A \to X,$$
$$r_2\colon S \to X, \qquad r_5\colon S \to a,$$
$$r_3\colon A \to S,$$

and $\Xi = (\{r_1\}^*\{r_2\}\{r_3\}^*\{r_4\})^*\{r_5\}^*)$, $W = \{r_2, r_4\}$.

Assume that we have the sentential form

$$S^{2^m}$$

for some $m \geq 0$*, obtained by using a sequence of rules from* $(\{r_1\}^*\{r_2\}\{r_3\}^*\{r_4\})^*$. *This holds for the start symbol* ($m = 0$)*. We can either repeat this sequence or finish the derivation by using* r_5 *until we have*

$$a^{2^m}.$$

In the former case, we might apply r_1 *as many times as we wish. However, if we apply it only k many times, where* $k < m$*, then we have to use* r_2*, which blocks the derivation. Indeed, there is no rule with X on its left hand side. Thus, this rule guarantees that every S is eventually rewritten to AA. Notice that* $r_2 \in W$*. As a result, if no S occurs in the sentential form, we can skip it (it is not applicable), so we get*

$$S^{2^m} \Rightarrow^*_{(G,W)} (AA)^{2^m} = A^{2^{m+1}}.$$

Then, by analogy, we have to rewrite each A to S, so we get

$$A^{2^{m+1}} \Rightarrow^*_{(G,W)} S^{2^{m+1}}$$

which is of the same form as the sentential form from which we started the derivation. Therefore, this grammar generates the non-context-free language

$$L(H) = \left\{a^{2^n} \mid n \geq 0\right\}.$$

For example, the sentence aaaa is obtained by the following derivation:

$$\begin{aligned} S &\Rightarrow_{(G,W)} AA \quad [r_1] \\ &\Rightarrow_{(G,W)} AS \quad [r_3] \\ &\Rightarrow_{(G,W)} SS \quad [r_3] \\ &\Rightarrow_{(G,W)} AAS \quad [r_1] \\ &\Rightarrow_{(G,W)} AAAA \quad [r_1] \\ &\Rightarrow_{(G,W)} AASA \quad [r_3] \\ &\Rightarrow_{(G,W)} AASS \quad [r_3] \\ &\Rightarrow_{(G,W)} SASS \quad [r_3] \\ &\Rightarrow_{(G,W)} SSSS \quad [r_3] \\ &\Rightarrow_{(G,W)} SSSa \quad [r_5] \\ &\Rightarrow_{(G,W)} aSSa \quad [r_5] \\ &\Rightarrow_{(G,W)} aaSa \quad [r_5] \\ &\Rightarrow_{(G,W)} aaaa \quad [r_5]. \end{aligned}$$

As another example, a single a is generated by

$$S \Rightarrow_{(G,W)} a\ [r5].$$

We can disallow erasing rules in the underlying core grammar. This is formalized in the following definition.

Definition 12.4. *Let* $H = (G, \Xi)$ ($H = (G, \Xi, W)$) *be a regular-controlled grammar (with appearance checking). If G is propagating, H is said to be a* propagating regular-controlled grammar (with appearance checking).

By $\mathbf{rC}_{ac}$, $\mathbf{rC}_{ac}^{-\varepsilon}$, $\mathbf{rC}$, and $\mathbf{rC}^{-\varepsilon}$, we denote the families of languages generated by regular-controlled grammars with appearance checking, propagating regular-controlled grammars with appearance checking, regular-controlled grammars, and propagating regular-controlled grammars, respectively.

12.2.2 Generative power

The present section concerns the generative power of regular-controlled grammars. More specifically, the next theorem summarizes the relations between the language families defined in the conclusion of the previous section.

Theorem 12.2 (see Theorem 1 in [21]).

(i) All languages in $\mathbf{rC}$ over a unary alphabet are regular;
(ii) $\mathbf{CF} \subset \mathbf{rC}^{-\varepsilon} \subset \mathbf{rC}_{ac}^{-\varepsilon} \subset \mathbf{CS}$;
(iii) $\mathbf{CF} \subset \mathbf{rC}^{-\varepsilon} \subseteq \mathbf{rC} \subset \mathbf{rC}_{ac} = \mathbf{RE}$.

Open Problem 12.1. *Is* $\mathbf{rC} - \mathbf{rC}^{-\varepsilon}$ *empty? Put in other words, can any regular-controlled grammar be converted to an equivalent propagating regular-controlled grammar?*

12.3 Matrix grammars

As already pointed out in the beginning of this chapter, in essence, any matrix grammar can be viewed as a special regular-controlled grammar with a control language that has the form of the iteration of a finite language. More precisely, a *matrix grammar H* is a context-free grammar *G* extended by a finite set of sequences of its rules, referred to as *matrices*. In essence, *H* makes a derivation by selecting a matrix and afterwards applying all its rules one by one until it reaches the very last rule. Then, it either completes its derivation or it makes another selection of a matrix and continues the derivation in the same way.

This section is divided into three subsections. Section 12.3.1 defines and illustrates matrix grammars. Section 12.3.2 determines their power. Finally, Section 12.3.3 studies even matrix grammars as special cases of matrix grammars, which work in parallel. Consequently, in a very natural way, Section 12.3.3 actually introduces the central topic of the next chapter—grammatical parallelism (see Chapter 13).

12.3.1 Definitions and examples

We open this section by giving the rigorous definition of matrix grammars. Then, we illustrate this definition by an example.

Definition 12.5. *A* matrix grammar with appearance checking *(or MG for short; see [12]) is a triple*

$$H = (G, M, W)$$

where

- $G = (\Sigma, \Delta, R, S)$ *is a context-free grammar, called* core grammar*;*
- $M \subseteq R^+$ *is a finite language whose elements are called* matrices*; and*
- $W \subseteq R$ *is the* appearance checking set.

The direct derivation relation*, symbolically denoted by* $\Rightarrow_H$*, is defined over* Σ^* *as follows: for* $r_1 r_2 \cdots r_n \in M$*, for some* $n \geq 1$*, and* $x, y \in \Sigma^*$*,*

$$x \Rightarrow_H y$$

if and only if

$$x = x_0 \Rightarrow_{(G,W)} x_1\ [r_1] \Rightarrow_{(G,W)} x_2\ [r_2] \Rightarrow_{(G,W)} \cdots \Rightarrow_{(G,W)} x_n = y\ [r_n]$$

where $x_i \in \Sigma^*$*, for all i,* $1 \leq i \leq n-1$*, and the application of rules in the appearance checking mode is defined as in Definition 12.3.*

Define $\Rightarrow_H^k$ *for* $k \geq 0$*,* $\Rightarrow_H^+$*, and* $\Rightarrow_H^*$ *in the standard way. The* language *of H, denoted by L(H), is defined as*

$$L(H) = \{w \in \Delta^* \mid S \Rightarrow_H^* w\}.$$

Note that if $M = R$, then there is no regulation, and thus $L(H) = L(G)$ in this case.

Definition 12.6. *Let* $H = (G, M, W)$ *be a matrix grammar with appearance checking. If* $W = \emptyset$*, we say that H is a* matrix grammar without appearance checking *or, simply, a* matrix grammar *and we just write* $H = (G, M)$*.*

Without appearance checking, once a matrix has been started, H has to apply all its rules. However, with an appearance checking set of the rules in the matrices, H may sometimes skip the application of a rule within a matrix. More precisely, if the left-hand side of a rule is absent in the current sentential form while the corresponding rule of the applied matrix occurs in the appearance checking set, H moves on to the next rule in the matrix.

Example 12.4 (from [21]). *Let* $H = (G, M)$ *be a matrix grammar, where* $G = (\Sigma, \Delta, \Psi, R, S)$ *is a context-free grammar with* $\Sigma = \{S, A, B, a, b\}$*,* $\Delta = \{a, b\}$*, R consists of the following rules:*

$$\begin{array}{lll} r_1\colon S \rightarrow AB, & r_4\colon A \rightarrow bA, & r_7\colon B \rightarrow a, \\ r_2\colon A \rightarrow aA, & r_5\colon B \rightarrow bB, & r_8\colon A \rightarrow b, \\ r_3\colon B \rightarrow aB, & r_6\colon A \rightarrow a, & r_9\colon B \rightarrow b, \end{array}$$

and $M = \{r_1, r_2r_3, r_4r_5, r_6r_7, r_8r_9\}$*.*

We start with the only applicable matrix r_1 *and we get AB. Next, we can either*

- *terminate the derivation by using the matrix* r_6r_7 *and obtain aa,*
- *terminate the derivation by using the matrix* r_8r_9 *and obtain bb,*
- *rewrite AB to aAaB by using the matrix* r_2r_3*, or*
- *rewrite AB to bAbB by using the matrix* r_4r_5*.*

If the derivation is not terminated, we can continue analogously. For example, the sentence aabaab is obtained by the following derivation:

$$\begin{aligned} S &\Rightarrow_H AB \\ &\Rightarrow_H aAaB \\ &\Rightarrow_H aaAaaB \\ &\Rightarrow_H aabaab. \end{aligned}$$

Clearly, this grammar generates the non-context-free language

$$L(H) = \{ww \mid w \in \{a,b\}^+\}.$$

As with regular-controlled grammars, we can disallow erasing rules in the underlying core grammar.

Definition 12.7. *Let $H = (G, M, W)$ be a matrix grammar (with appearance checking). If G is propagating, H is a* propagating matrix grammar (with appearance checking).

The families of languages generated by matrix grammars with appearance checking, propagating matrix grammars with appearance checking, matrix grammars, and propagating matrix grammars are denoted by $\mathbf{M}_{ac}$, $\mathbf{M}_{ac}^{-\varepsilon}$, $\mathbf{M}$, and $\mathbf{M}^{-\varepsilon}$, respectively.

12.3.2 Generative power

This section states the relations between the language families defined in the conclusion of the previous section.

Theorem 12.3 (see Theorem 2 in [21]).

(i) $\mathbf{M}_{ac} = \mathbf{rC}_{ac}$;
(ii) $\mathbf{M}_{ac}^{-\varepsilon} = \mathbf{rC}_{ac}^{-\varepsilon}$;
(iii) $\mathbf{M} = \mathbf{rC}$;
(iv) $\mathbf{M}^{-\varepsilon} = \mathbf{rC}^{-\varepsilon}$.

Notice that the relations between the language families generated by matrix grammars are analogical to the relations between language families generated by regular-controlled grammars (see Theorem 12.2).

12.3.3 Even matrix grammars

In essence, even matrix grammars can be seen as sequences of context-free grammars, referred to as their components, which work in parallel. More precisely, for a positive integer n, an n-even matrix grammar is an ordered sequence of n context-free grammars with pairwise disjoint nonterminal alphabets and a shared terminal alphabet, whose rules are fixed n-tuples containing one rule of each component—that is, in every derivation step, each of these components rewrites a nonterminal occurring in its current sentential form. A sentential form of an n-even matrix grammar is a concatenation of sentential forms of all of its components from the first to the nth.

A derivation is successful if and only if all components generate a terminal string at once. Of course, one-component even matrix grammars are nothing but context-free grammars, so they characterize the family of context-free languages. Surprisingly, two-component even matrix grammars are significantly stronger as the present section demonstrates; indeed, they are as powerful as ordinary matrix grammars (see Section 12.3.1). This section also points out that even matrix grammars with more than two components are equivalent with two-component even matrix grammars. Then, it places and studies the following three leftmost derivation restrictions on even matrix grammars:

1. The first restriction requires that the leftmost possible occurences of nonterminals corresponding to the left-hand side of the selected rule be rewritten in each component. However, there is no restriction on rule selection;
2. The second restriction requires that a rule r be applied to a particular selection of nonterminals only if for any rule p with a different selection of nonterminals, when comparing the positions of selected nonterminals for each component from left to right, the nonterminal corresponding to r will be more to the left in the first component where the positions differ;
3. Finally, the third restriction simply requires the leftmost nonterminal in each component to be rewritten, paying no attention to whether any applicable rules exist.

As the section demonstrates, working under the second and third restriction, even matrix grammars are computational complete—that is, they are equivalent with Turing machines. The section has not precisely determined the generative power of even matrix grammars working under the first restriction, so this determination represents an open problem.

12.3.3.1 Definitions and examples

In this section, we define even matrix grammars. Furthermore, we introduce their leftmost variants and illustrate them by an example.

Definition 12.8. *Let $n \geq 1$. An* even matrix grammar of degree *n ($_n$EMG for short) is an $(n+3)$-tuple, $G_n = (N_1, N_2, \ldots, N_n, \Delta, R, S)$, where*

(1) $N_1, N_2, \ldots, N_n$ *are pairwise disjoint nonterminal alphabets;*
(2) Δ *is a terminal alphabet,* $\Delta \cap N_i = \emptyset$, *for* $1 \leq i \leq n$;
(3) S *is the* start symbol *such that* $S \notin N_1 \cup \cdots \cup N_n \cup \Delta$;
(4) R *is a finite set of rewriting rules of the form:*
  (4.a) $(S) \rightarrow (v)$, $v \in \Delta^*$.
  (4.b) $(S) \rightarrow (v_1 v_2 \cdots v_n)$, $v_i \in (N_i \cup \Delta)^*$, $symbols(v_i) \cap N_i \neq \emptyset$, *for* $1 \leq i \leq n$.
  (4.c) $(A_1, A_2, \ldots, A_n) \rightarrow (v_1, v_2, \ldots, v_n)$, $A_i \in N_i$, $v_i \in (N_i \cup \Delta)^*$, *for* $1 \leq i \leq n$.

Definition 12.9. *Let $G_n = (N_1, \ldots, N_n, \Delta, R, S)$ be an $_n$EMG, for some $n \geq 1$. Consider any string $u_1 A_1 w_1 \cdots u_n A_n w_n$, where $u_i w_i \in (N_i \cup \Delta)^*$, $A_i \in N_i$, and some rule $(A_1, \ldots, A_n) \rightarrow (v_1, \ldots, v_n)$, where $v_i \in (N_i \cup \Delta)^*$, for $1 \leq i \leq n$. Then, G_n makes a* derivation step

$$u_1 A_1 w_1 \cdots u_n A_n w_n \Rightarrow u_1 v_1 w_1 \cdots u_n v_n w_n.$$

Based on additional restrictions, we define the following three modes of leftmost derivations*:*

(1) *If* $A_i \notin \text{symbols}(u_i)$*, for* $1 \le i \le n$*, then write*

$$u_1 A_1 w_1 \cdots u_n A_n w_n \; {}_1\!\Rightarrow u_1 v_1 w_1 \cdots u_n v_n w_n;$$

(2) *If*

$$u_1 A_1 w_1 \cdots u_n A_n w_n = u'_1 B_1 w'_1 u'_2 B_2 w'_2 \cdots u'_n B_n w'_n$$

where $u'_i, w'_i \in (N_i \cup \Delta)^*$, $B_i \in N_i$*, there is an integer j satisfying* $1 \le j \le n$ *such that* $|u'_i| = |u_i|$ *for* $1 < i < j$ *and* $|u'_j| < |u_j|$*, and in R, there is no applicable rule*

$$(B_1, B_2, \ldots, B_n) \to (x_1, x_2, \ldots, x_n)$$

then write

$$u_1 A_1 w_1 \cdots u_n A_n w_n \; {}_2\!\Rightarrow u_1 v_1 w_1 \cdots u_n v_n w_n;$$

(3) *If* $N_i \cap \text{symbols}(u_i) = \emptyset$*, for* $1 \le i \le n$*, then write*

$$u_1 A_1 w_1 \cdots u_n A_n w_n \; {}_3\!\Rightarrow u_1 v_1 w_1 \cdots u_n v_n w_n.$$

In what follows, we write ${}_0\!\Rightarrow$ *instead of* $\Rightarrow$*. We say that* ${}_i\!\Rightarrow$ *represents the* direct derivation of mode *i, for* $i = 0, 1, 2, 3$.

For the clarity, let us informally describe the defined modes of leftmost derivations. In the first mode, any applicable rule is chosen and the leftmost possible nonterminals are rewritten. In the second mode, there is a specific rule chosen, which can rewrite nonterminals as to the left as possible—there exists no rule, which could be applied more leftmost, while the lower components are more prior. In the third mode, always the leftmost nonterminal of each component must be rewritten.

Definition 12.10. *Let* $G_n = (N_1, N_2, \ldots, N_n, \Delta, R, S)$ *be an* ${}_n$*EMG, and let* ρ *be any relation over* $(N_1 \cup \Delta)^*(N_2 \cup \Delta)^* \cdots (N_n \cup \Delta)^*$*. Set*

$$\mathscr{L}(G_n, \rho) = \{x \mid x \in \Delta^*, S\, \rho^*\, x\}.$$

$\mathscr{L}(G_n, \rho)$ *is said to be the* language that G_n generates by ρ.

$${}_n\mathbf{EM}(\rho) = \{\mathscr{L}(G_n, \rho) \mid G_n \text{ is a } {}_n\text{EMG}\}$$

is said to be the family of languages that ${}_n$*EMG*s generate by ρ. $\mathbf{EM}(\rho)$ *denotes the* family of languages generated by all even matrix grammars by ρ.

We illustrate the previous definitions by the next example.

Example 12.5. *Let* $G = (N_1, N_2, \Delta, R, S)$*, where* $N_1 = \{A, \overline{A}\}$, $N_2 = \{B, \overline{B}, C, \overline{C}\}$, $\Delta = \{a, b, c, d\}$*, be a* ${}_2$*EMG with R containing the following rules:*

(1)	$(S) \to (AABC)$,	*(6)*	$(A, \overline{B}) \to (aAb, c\overline{B}d)$,
(2)	$(A, B) \to (aAb, cBd)$,	*(7)*	$(A, \overline{C}) \to (aAb, c\overline{C}d)$,
(3)	$(A, C) \to (aAb, cCd)$,	*(8)*	$(A, \overline{B}) \to (\overline{A}, \varepsilon)$,
(4)	$(A, B) \to (\overline{A}, \overline{B})$,	*(9)*	$(\overline{A}, \overline{C}) \to (\varepsilon, \varepsilon)$.
(5)	$(\overline{A}, C) \to (\varepsilon, \overline{C})$,		

Next, we illustrate ${}_i\Rightarrow$, $0 \leq i \leq 3$, in terms of G.

0. *Using derivations of mode 0, after applying the starting rule (1), G uses (2) and/or (3). Then, rule (4) is applied; however, rule (3) is still applicable, until rule (5) is used. Next, the derivation proceeds by rules (6) and/or (7) and eventually finishes with rules (8) and (9). The derivation may proceed as follows:*

$$\begin{aligned} S \ {}_1&\Rightarrow AABC \\ {}_1&\Rightarrow^* a^k A b^k a^l A b^l c^m B d^m c^n C d^n \\ {}_1&\Rightarrow a^k A b^k a^l \overline{A} b^l c^m \overline{B} d^m c^n C d^n \\ {}_1&\Rightarrow^* a^{k+i+j} A b^{k+i+j} a^l \overline{A} b^l c^{m+i} \overline{B} d^{m+i} c^{n+j} C d^{n+j} \\ {}_1&\Rightarrow a^{k+i+j} A b^{k+i+j} a^l b^l c^{m+i} \overline{B} d^{m+i} c^{n+j} \overline{C} d^{n+j} \\ {}_1&\Rightarrow^* a^{k+i+j+o+p} A b^{k+i+j+o+p} a^l b^l c^{m+i+o} \overline{B} d^{m+i+o} c^{n+j+p} \overline{C} d^{n+j+p} \\ {}_1&\Rightarrow a^{k+i+j+o+p} \overline{A} b^{k+i+j+o+p} a^l b^l c^{m+i+o} d^{m+i+o} c^{n+j+p} \overline{C} d^{n+j+p} \\ {}_1&\Rightarrow a^{k+i+j+o+p} b^{k+i+j+o+p} a^l b^l c^{m+i+o} d^{m+i+o} c^{n+j+p} d^{n+j+p} \end{aligned}$$

for $i, j, k, l, m, n, o, p \geq 0$. Consequently,

$$\mathscr{L}(G, {}_1\Rightarrow) = \{a^k b^k a^l b^l c^m d^m c^n d^n \mid k + l = m + n, \text{ for } k, l, m, n \geq 0\},$$

which is a non-context-free language;

(i) *Using mode 1 leftmost derivations, after applying the starting rule (1), G continues using rules (2) and/or (3), until rule (4) is applied. Rule (3) is still applicable, until rule (5) is used. Next, the derivation proceeds by rules (6) and/or (7) and eventually finishes with rules (8) and (9):*

$$\begin{aligned} S \ {}_1&\Rightarrow AABC \\ {}_1&\Rightarrow^* a^{i+j} A b^{i+j} A c^i B d^i c^j C d^j \\ {}_1&\Rightarrow a^{i+j} \overline{A} b^{i+j} A c^i \overline{B} d^i c^j C d^j \\ {}_1&\Rightarrow^* a^{i+j} \overline{A} b^{i+j} a^k A b^k c^i \overline{B} d^i c^{j+k} C d^{j+k} \\ {}_1&\Rightarrow a^{i+j} b^{i+j} a^k A b^k c^i \overline{B} d^i c^{j+k} \overline{C} d^{j+k} \\ {}_1&\Rightarrow^* a^{i+j} b^{i+j} a^{k+o+p} A b^{k+o+p} c^{i+o} \overline{B} d^{i+o} c^{j+k+p} \overline{C} d^{j+k+p} \\ {}_1&\Rightarrow a^{i+j} b^{i+j} a^{k+o+p} \overline{A} b^{k+o+p} c^{i+o} d^{i+o} c^{j+k+p} \overline{C} d^{j+k+p} \\ {}_1&\Rightarrow a^{i+j} b^{i+j} a^{k+o+p} b^{k+o+p} c^{i+o} d^{i+o} c^{j+k+p} d^{j+k+p} \end{aligned}$$

for $i, j, k, o, p \geq 0$. Consequently,

$$\mathscr{L}(G, {}_1\Rightarrow) = \{a^k b^k a^l b^l c^m d^m c^n d^n \mid k + l = m + n, \text{ for } k, l, m, n \geq 0\};$$

(ii) *With derivations of leftmost mode 2, the situation is different. First, the starting rule (1) is applied, however, only rule (2) is applicable then, until rule (4) is used. Next, rule (5) must be applied. The derivation continues with applications of rule (6), since rule (7) is not applicable, until rules (8) and (9) are used:*

$$\begin{aligned} S \ {}_2&\Rightarrow AABC & {}_2&\Rightarrow^* a^i A b^i A c^i B d^i C \\ {}_2&\Rightarrow a^i \overline{A} b^i A c^i \overline{B} d^i C & {}_2&\Rightarrow a^i b^i A c^i \overline{B} d^i \overline{C} \\ {}_2&\Rightarrow^* a^i b^i a^j A b^j c^{i+j} \overline{B} d^{i+j} \overline{C} & {}_2&\Rightarrow a^i b^i a^j \overline{A} b^j c^{i+j} d^{i+j} \overline{C} \\ {}_2&\Rightarrow a^i b^i a^j b^j c^{i+j} d^{i+j} \end{aligned}$$

for $i, j \geq 0$. Consequently, $\mathscr{L}(G, {}_2\Rightarrow) = \{a^i b^i a^j b^j c^{i+j} d^{i+j} \mid \text{for } i, j \geq 0\}$;

(iii) *The derivation performed by the leftmost mode 3 derivations starts with rule (1), continues with applying rule (2) and eventually uses rule (4). However, then, the derivation is blocked, because there is no rule rewriting $\overline{A}$ and $\overline{B}$:*

$$S\ {}_3{\Rightarrow}\ AABC\ {}_3{\Rightarrow^*}\ a^iAb^iAc^iBd^iC\ {}_3{\Rightarrow}\ a^i\overline{A}b^iAc^i\overline{B}d^iC\ {}_3{\Rightarrow}\ \emptyset.$$

Consequently, $\mathscr{L}(G, {}_3{\Rightarrow}) = \emptyset$.

12.3.3.2 Generative power

In this section, we investigate the generative power of even matrix grammars working under the derivation modes introduced in the previous section. We pay a special attention to the number of their components.

Since any context-free grammar is ${}_1EMG$, we obtain the next theorem.

Theorem 12.4. $_1\mathbf{EM}({}_i{\Rightarrow}) = \mathbf{CF}$, for $i = 0, 1, 2, 3$.

Mode 0

From Theorem 12.4, every one-component even matrix grammar generates a context-free language. From Example 12.5, two-component even matrix grammars are more powerful than the one-component ones. Next we prove that additional components do not increase the power of even matrix grammars.

Theorem 12.5. $_n\mathbf{EM}({}_0{\Rightarrow}) = {}_2\mathbf{EM}({}_0{\Rightarrow})$, for $n \geq 2$.

Proof. Construction. Let $G = (N_1, N_2, \ldots, N_n, \Delta, R, S)$ be any ${}_nEMG$, for some $n \geq 2$. Suppose, the rules in R are of the form

$$r : (A_1, A_2, \ldots, A_n) \rightarrow (w_1, w_2, \ldots, w_n)$$

where $1 \leq r \leq \text{card}(R)$ is the unique numeric label. Set $N = N_1 \cup N_2 \cup \cdots \cup N_n$. Define ${}_2EMG$ $G' = (N, N', \Delta, R', S)$, where $N' = \{Q^i_j \mid 1 \leq i \leq \text{card}(R), 1 \leq j \leq n\}$. Construct R' as follows. Initially, set $R' = \emptyset$. Perform (1)–(3), given as follows:

(1) for each $r : (S) \rightarrow (w) \in R$, $w \in \Delta^*$, add $(S) \rightarrow (w)$ to R';
(2) for each $r : (S) \rightarrow (w) \in R$, $\text{symbols}(w) - \Delta \neq \emptyset$,
add $(S) \rightarrow (wQ^t_1)$, where $t \in \{1, 2, \ldots, \text{card}(R)\}$, to R';
(3) for each $r : (A_1, A_2, \ldots, A_n) \rightarrow (w_1, w_2, \ldots, w_n) \in R$, add
(3.a) $(A_i, Q^r_i) \rightarrow (w_i, Q^r_{i+1})$, for $1 \leq i < n$,
(3.b) $(A_n, Q^r_n) \rightarrow (w_n, Q^t_1)$, for $t \in \{1, 2, \ldots, \text{card}(R)\}$,
(3.c) $(A_n, Q^r_n) \rightarrow (w_n, \varepsilon)$, to R'.

Claim 1. $\mathscr{L}(G, {}_0{\Rightarrow}) = \mathscr{L}(G', {}_0{\Rightarrow})$.

Proof. We establish the proof by proving the following two claims.

Claim 2. $\mathscr{L}(G, {}_0{\Rightarrow}) \subseteq \mathscr{L}(G', {}_0{\Rightarrow})$.

Proof. To prove the claim, we show that for any sequence of derivation steps of G, generating the sentential form w, there is the corresponding sequence of derivation steps of G' generating the corresponding sentential form or the same terminal string, if it is successful, by induction on m—the number of the derivation steps of G.

Basis. Let $m = 0$. The correspondence of the sentential forms of G and G' is trivial. Let $m = 1$. Then, some starting rule from R of the form $(S) \rightarrow (v)$ is applied. However, in R', there is the corresponding rule $(S) \rightarrow (v)$, in case the derivation is finished, or $(S) \rightarrow (vQ_1^r)$ for $1 \leq r \leq \text{card}(R)$, otherwise. Without any loss of generality, suppose r is the label of the next rule applied by G. The basis holds.

Induction Hypothesis. Suppose that there exists $k \geq 1$ such that the assumption of correspondence holds for all sequences of the derivation steps of G of the length m, where $0 \leq m \leq k$.

Induction Step. Consider any sequence of moves

$$S\ {}_0{\Rightarrow}^{k+1}\ w.$$

Since $k + 1 \geq 1$, this sequence can be expressed as

$$S\ {}_0{\Rightarrow}^{k}\ v_1A_1u_1v_2A_2u_2 \cdots v_nA_nu_n\ {}_0{\Rightarrow}\ v_1x_1u_1v_2x_2u_2 \cdots v_nx_nu_n$$

where $A_i \in N_i$, $v_i, u_i \in (N_i \cup \Delta)^*$, and the last derivation step is performed by some rule

$$r : (A_1, A_2, \ldots, A_n) \rightarrow (x_1, x_2, \ldots, x_n) \in R.$$

Then, there exists a sequence of derivation steps of G'

$$S\ {}_0{\Rightarrow}^{*}\ v_1A_1u_1v_2A_2u_2 \cdots v_nA_nu_nQ_1^r.$$

From the construction of G', there exist rules

$$(A_1, Q_1^r) \rightarrow (x_1, Q_2^r), (A_2, Q_2^r) \rightarrow (x_2, Q_3^r), \ldots, (A_{n-1}, Q_{n-1}^r) \rightarrow (x_{n-1}, Q_n^r),$$
$$(A_n, Q_n^r) \rightarrow (x_n, Q_1^t), (A_n, Q_n^r) \rightarrow (x_n, \varepsilon)$$

for $1 \leq t \leq \text{card}(R)$. Therefore, in G', there is the sequence of derivation steps

$$\begin{aligned} S\ {}_0{\Rightarrow}^{*}\ & v_1A_1u_1v_2A_2u_2 \cdots v_nA_nu_nQ_1^r \\ {}_0{\Rightarrow}\ & v_1x_1u_1v_2A_2u_2 \cdots v_nA_nu_nQ_2^r \\ {}_0{\Rightarrow}\ & v_1x_1u_1v_2x_2u_2 \cdots v_nA_nu_nQ_3^r \\ {}_0{\Rightarrow}^{n-3}\ & v_1x_1u_1v_2x_2u_2 \cdots v_{n-1}x_{n-1}u_{n-1}v_nA_nu_nQ_n^r. \end{aligned}$$

Next, there are two possible situations. First, suppose the derivation of G is not finished and the rule labeled by some t is applied next. Then,

$$v_1x_1u_1v_2x_2u_2 \cdots v_nA_nu_nQ_n^r\ {}_0{\Rightarrow}\ v_1x_1u_1v_2x_2u_2 \cdots v_nx_nu_nQ_1^t$$

in G', generating the sentential form corresponding to the new sentential form of G, where $v_1x_1u_1v_2x_2u_2 \cdots v_nx_nu_nQ_1^t = wQ_1^t$. Second, suppose $w \in \Delta^*$. By the last of the highlighted rules of G'

$$v_1x_1u_1v_2x_2u_2 \cdots v_nA_nu_nQ_n^r\ {}_0{\Rightarrow}\ v_1x_1u_1v_2x_2u_2 \cdots v_nx_nu_n$$

where $v_1x_1u_1v_2x_2u_2 \cdots v_nx_nu_n = w$ and Claim 2 holds. □

Claim 3. $\mathscr{L}(G, {}_0{\Rightarrow}) \supseteq \mathscr{L}(G', {}_0{\Rightarrow})$.

Proof. To prove the claim, we show that for any sequence of derivation steps of G', generating the sentential form w, there is the corresponding sequence of derivation steps of G generating the corresponding sentential form or the same terminal string, if it is successful, by induction on m—the number of the derivation steps of G'. First, assume that in G', the symbols Q^x_y of the second component serve as states of computation. With the application of the starting rule, some symbol Q^r_1 is inserted. It means that G' is about to simulate the application of the rule r of G. The only applicable rule is then the rule rewriting Q^r_1 to Q^r_2. And it holds equally for any Q^x_y, where $y < n$. Therefore, except for the starting rules, these rules always have to be applied in sequence. We use this assumption in the next proof.

Basis. Let $m = 0$. The sentential forms of G and G' correspond. Let $m = 1$. Then, some starting rule from R' of the form $(S) \rightarrow (v)$ or $(S) \rightarrow (vQ^r_1)$, for some $r \in \{1, 2, \ldots, \text{card}(R)\}$ is applied. However, this rule is introduced by the rule $(S) \rightarrow (v)$ of R. Therefore, G can make the derivation step corresponding to the one made by G' and the basis holds.

Induction Hypothesis. Suppose that there exists $k \geq 1$ such that the assumption of correspondence holds for all sequences of derivation steps of G' of the length m, where $0 \leq m \leq k$.

Induction Step. Recall the previous assumption. Let us consider any sequence of moves

$$S \;{}_0\!\Rightarrow^{k+n} w.$$

This sequence can be written in the form

$$\begin{aligned} S \;{}_0\!\Rightarrow^{*} \;& v_1A_1u_1v_2A_2u_2 \cdots v_nA_nu_nQ^r_1 \\ {}_0\!\Rightarrow \;& v_1x_1u_1v_2A_2u_2 \cdots v_nA_nu_nQ^r_2 \\ {}_0\!\Rightarrow \;& v_1x_1u_1v_2x_2u_2 \cdots v_nA_nu_nQ^r_3 \\ {}_0\!\Rightarrow^{n-2} \;& v_1x_1u_1v_2x_2u_2 \cdots v_nx_nu_nX \end{aligned}$$

where $A_i \in N_i$, $v_i, u_i \in (N_i \cup \Delta)^*$ and $X = Q^t_1$, for $1 \leq t \leq \text{card}(R)$, or $X = \varepsilon$. There are n rules from R' used:

$$(A_1, Q^r_1) \rightarrow (x_1, Q^r_2), (A_2, Q^r_2) \rightarrow (x_2, Q^r_3), \ldots , (A_n, Q^r_n) \rightarrow (x_n, X).$$

These rules are introduced by the rule of G

$$r : (A_1, A_2, \ldots, A_n) \rightarrow (x_1, x_2, \ldots, x_n) \in R.$$

By the induction hypothesis, in the terms of G

$$S \;{}_0\!\Rightarrow^{*} v_1A_1u_1v_2A_2u_2 \cdots v_nA_nu_n.$$

Thus, using the rule r

$$v_1A_1u_1v_2A_2u_2 \cdots v_nA_nu_n \;{}_0\!\Rightarrow v_1x_1u_1v_2x_2u_2 \cdots v_nx_nu_n = w.$$

If $X = \varepsilon$, $w \in \Delta^*$ and G' generates the terminal string, G generates the same terminal string and Claim 3 holds. □

We have proved $\mathscr{L}(G, {}_0\Rightarrow) \subseteq \mathscr{L}(G', {}_0\Rightarrow)$ and $\mathscr{L}(G, {}_0\Rightarrow) \supseteq \mathscr{L}(G', {}_0\Rightarrow)$; therefore, $\mathscr{L}(G, {}_0\Rightarrow) = \mathscr{L}(G', {}_0\Rightarrow)$ and Claim 1 holds. □

Since G is any ${}_nEMG$, for some $n \geq 2$, and G' is ${}_2EMG$, Theorem 12.5 holds. ■

We have proved

$$\mathbf{CF} = {}_1\mathbf{EM}({}_0\Rightarrow) \subset {}_2\mathbf{EM}({}_0\Rightarrow) = \mathbf{EM}({}_0\Rightarrow).$$

However, this classification of even matrix languages is not very precise. Let us recall (see Theorems 12.2 and 12.3) that

$$\mathbf{CF} \subset \mathbf{M} \subset \mathbf{CS}.$$

By the following theorem, we prove that even matrix grammars characterize precisely the family of matrix languages.

Theorem 12.6. $\mathbf{EM}({}_0\Rightarrow) = \mathbf{M}$.

Proof. Without any loss of generality, we consider only ${}_2EMG$s.

Claim 1. ${}_2\mathbf{EM}({}_0\Rightarrow) \subseteq \mathbf{M}$.

Proof. Construction. Let $G = (N_1, N_2, \Delta, R, S)$ be any ${}_2EMG$. Suppose that the rules in R are of the form

$$r : (A_1, A_2) \rightarrow (w_1, w_2)$$

where $1 \leq r \leq \text{card}(R)$ is a unique numerical label. Define matrix grammar $H = (G', M)$, where $G' = (N_1 \cup N_2 \cup \{S\} \cup \Delta, \Delta, R', S)$. Construct R' and M as follows: Initially, set $R' = M = \emptyset$. Perform (1) and (2), given as follows:

(1) for each $r : (S) \rightarrow (w) \in R$,
 (1.a) add $r : S \rightarrow w$ to R',
 (1.b) add r to M;

(2) for each $r : (A_1, A_2) \rightarrow (w_1, w_2) \in R$,
 (2.a) add $r_1 : A_1 \rightarrow w_1$ and
 (2.b) add $r_2 : A_2 \rightarrow w_2$ to R',
 (2.c) add $r_1 r_2$ to M.

Claim 2. $\mathscr{L}(G, {}_0\Rightarrow) = \mathscr{L}(H)$.

Proof. Basic Idea. Every ${}_2EMG$ first applies some starting rule. Next, in every derivation step simultaneously in each component, there is a nonterminal rewritten to some string. This process can be simulated by MG as follows. For every starting rule of G, there is the same applicable rule of H. They both generate the equal terminal strings or a sentential forms $w_1 w_2$, where symbols$(w_1) \cap N_2 = \emptyset$ and symbols$(w_2) \cap N_1 = \emptyset$. Then, for every rule $(A_1, A_2) \rightarrow (x_1, x_2)$ in G, there are two rules $A_1 \rightarrow x_1$ and $A_2 \rightarrow x_2$ in H, which must be applied consecutively. Since $N_1 \cap N_2 = \emptyset$, every sentential form remains of the form $w_1 w_2$, where symbols$(w_1) \cap N_2 = \emptyset$ and symbols$(w_2) \cap N_1 = \emptyset$.

Thus, H simulates both separated components of G. A detailed version of the proof is left to the reader. □

Since for any ${}_2EMG$ we can construct an MG generating the same language, Claim 1 holds. □

Claim 3. ${}_2\mathbf{EM}({}_0\Rightarrow) \supseteq \mathbf{M}$.

Proof. Construction. Let $H = (G, M)$, where $G = (\Sigma, \Delta, R, S)$, $\Sigma - \Delta = N, S \in N$, be any MG. Without any loss of generality, suppose every $m \in M$ has its unique label. Define ${}_2EMG$ $G' = (N, N', \Delta, R', S')$, where $S' \notin N$,

$$N' = \{Q_i^r \mid r : p_1p_2 \cdots p_k \in M, i \in \{1, 2, \ldots, k\}, k \geq 1\}.$$

Construct R' as follows. Initially set $R' = \emptyset$. Perform (1) given as follows:

(1) for each $r : p_1p_2 \cdots p_k \in M$, $k \geq 1$, where $p_i : A_i \to w_i$, $i \in \{1, 2, \ldots, k\}$,
  (1.a) add $(S') \to (SQ_1^r)$,
  (1.b) $(A_i, Q_i^r) \to (w_i, Q_{i+1}^r)$, for $i < k$,
  (1.c) $(A_k, Q_k^r) \to (w_k, Q_1^t)$, for some $t : v \in M$, and
  (1.d) $(A_k, Q_k^r) \to (w_k, \varepsilon)$ to R'.

Claim 4. $\mathscr{L}(G', {}_0\Rightarrow) = \mathscr{L}(H)$.

Proof. We establish Claim 4 by proving the following two claims:

Claim 5. $\mathscr{L}(G', {}_0\Rightarrow) \supseteq \mathscr{L}(H)$.

Proof. We prove the claim by the induction on the number of derivation steps m.

Basis. Let $m = 0$. By the application of the rule $(S') \to (SQ_1^r)$, G' generates the sentential form corresponding to the starting symbol of H. Without any loss of generality, suppose r is the label of the next matrix applied by H. The basis holds.

Induction Hypothesis. Suppose that there exists $k \geq 0$ such that Claim 5 holds for all sequences of the derivation steps of the length m, where $0 \leq m \leq k$.

Induction Step. Consider any sequence of moves

$$S \Rightarrow^{k+1} w'$$

where $w' \in (N \cup \Delta)^*$. Since $k + 1 \geq 1$,

$$S \Rightarrow^k w \Rightarrow w'$$

for some $w \in (N \cup \Delta)^*$. Then, the last derivation step is performed by some matrix

$$r : p_1p_2 \cdots p_n$$

where $n \geq 1$. By the induction hypothesis

$$S' \,{}_0\Rightarrow SQ_1^s \,{}_0\Rightarrow^* wQ_1^r$$

in G', for some $s \in M$. By the construction of G', there exists the sequence of rules corresponding to the matrix r

$$(A_1, Q_1^r) \rightarrow (w_1, Q_2^r), (A_2, Q_2^r) \rightarrow (w_2, Q_3^r), \ldots, (A_n, Q_n^r) \rightarrow (w_n, X)$$

where $X = Q_1^t$ with $t \in M$ being the next matrix applied by H if symbols$(w') \cap N \neq \emptyset$, or $X = \varepsilon$ otherwise. By the application of this sequence of rules

$$wQ_1^r \ {}_0\!\Rightarrow^* w'X$$

which completes the proof. □

Claim 6. $\mathscr{L}(G', {}_0\!\Rightarrow) \subseteq \mathscr{L}(H)$.

Proof. We prove the claim by the induction on the number of derivation steps *m*.

Basis. Let $m = 1$. Then, G' applies some starting rule $(S') \rightarrow (SQ_1^r)$. The resulting sentential form corresponds to the starting sentential form of H. The basis holds.

Induction Hypothesis. Suppose that there exists $k \geq 1$ such that Claim 6 holds for all sequences of the derivation steps of the length m, where $1 \leq m \leq k$.

Induction Step. Notice that the rules of G', except the starting ones, form sequences

$$(A_1, Q_1^r) \rightarrow (w_1, Q_2^r), (A_2, Q_2^r) \rightarrow (w_2, Q_3^r), \ldots, (A_n, Q_n^r) \rightarrow (w_n, X)$$

where $X = Q_1^t, \varepsilon$, for some $t \in M$. These sequences must be always fully applied. Therefore, consider any sequence of moves

$$S' \ {}_0\!\Rightarrow S \ {}_0\!\Rightarrow^{k+l} w'$$

where $w' \in (N \cup \Delta)^*$ and $l \geq 1$ is the length of any such sequence of the rules, which is applied last. Then,

$$S' \ {}_0\!\Rightarrow S \ {}_0\!\Rightarrow^{k} w \ {}_0\!\Rightarrow^{l} w'.$$

The used sequence of the rules is introduced by some matrix $r : v \in M$. By the induction hypothesis

$$S \Rightarrow^* w$$

in H. However, by the matrix r

$$w \Rightarrow w'[r]$$

which completes the proof. □

Since $\mathscr{L}(G', {}_0\!\Rightarrow) \supseteq \mathscr{L}(H)$ and $\mathscr{L}(G', {}_0\!\Rightarrow) \subseteq \mathscr{L}(H)$, $\mathscr{L}(G', {}_0\!\Rightarrow) = \mathscr{L}(H)$. □

Since for any *MG* we can construct an ${}_2EMG$ generating the same language, Claim 3 holds. □

On the basis of Claims 1 and 3, Theorem 12.6 holds. ■

Mode 1

The following theorem can be proved by analogy with the proof of Theorem 12.5.

Theorem 12.7. $_n\mathbf{EM}(_1\Rightarrow) = {}_2\mathbf{EM}(_1\Rightarrow)$, for $n \geq 2$.

Proof. Left to the reader. ■

Open Problem 12.2. *Does* $_2\mathbf{EM}(_0\Rightarrow) = {}_2\mathbf{EM}(_1\Rightarrow)$ *hold?*

However, it is still an open problem whether mode 1 leftmost derivations increase the generative power of EMGs.

Mode 2

As we prove next, leftmost derivations of mode 2 significantly increase the generative power of even matrix grammars.

Theorem 12.8. $_2\mathbf{EM}(_2\Rightarrow) = \mathbf{RE}$.

By the Turing–Church thesis, $_2\mathbf{EM}(_2\Rightarrow) \subseteq \mathbf{RE}$. Thus, we only have to prove the opposite inclusion.

Proof. Construction. Let $L \in \mathbf{RE}$. Then, there exist context-free grammars $G_i = (N_i, \Delta, R_i, S_i)$, where $L(G_i) = L_i$, for $i = 1, 2$, and $L = h(L_1 \cap L_2)$, where h is a homomorphism from Δ^* to symbols$(L)^*$ (see Theorem 10.3.1 in [22]). Without any loss of generality, assume that $N_1 \cap N_2 = \emptyset$ and G_1, G_2 are in Greibach normal form (see Definition 11.7). Let $\Delta = \{a_1, \ldots, a_n\}$. Introduce four new symbols—$0, 1, \overline{0}, \overline{1} \notin (N_1 \cup N_2 \cup \Delta)$. Define the following homomorphisms:

(1) $c : a_i \mapsto 10^i$; $\overline{c} : a_i \mapsto \overline{1}\,\overline{0}^i$;

(2) $\pi_1 : N_1 \cup \Delta \mapsto N_1 \cup \Delta \cup \{0, 1\}$,
$$\begin{cases} A \mapsto A, & A \in N_1, \\ a \mapsto h(a)c(a), & a \in \Delta; \end{cases}$$

(3) $o : \overline{a} \mapsto a, a \in \{0, 1\}$;

(4) $\pi_2 : N_2 \cup \Delta \mapsto N_2 \cup \{\overline{0}, \overline{1}\}$,
$$\begin{cases} A \mapsto A, & A \in N_2, \\ a \mapsto \overline{c}(a), & a \in \Delta. \end{cases}$$

Then, let $G = (N_1', N_2', \Delta, R, S)$ be $_2EMG$, where $S \notin N_1' \cup N_2'$,

$$N_1' = N_1 \cup \{0, 1\}, N_2' = N_2 \cup \{\overline{0}, \overline{1}\}.$$

Construct R as follows. Initially, set $R = \emptyset$. Performs (1)–(3), given as follows:

(1) add $(S) \to (S_1 S_2)$ to R;
(2) for each $(A_1) \to (w_1) \in R_1$ and for each $(A_2) \to (w_2) \in R_2$, add $(A_1, A_2) \to (\pi_1(w_1), \pi_2(w_2))$ to R;
(3) add
    (a) $(0, \overline{0}) \to (\varepsilon, \varepsilon)$,
    (b) $(1, \overline{1}) \to (\varepsilon, \varepsilon)$,
    (c) $(0, \overline{1}) \to (0, \overline{1})$,
    (d) $(1, \overline{0}) \to (1, \overline{0})$ to R.

Claim 1. $\mathscr{L}(G, {}_2\Rightarrow) = L$.

Proof. Every derivation of G starts with the application of rule (1). Next, G simulates the leftmost derivations of G_1 and G_2, respectively, with rules (2). Without any loss of generality, suppose that for every $A \in N_1 \cup N_2$,

$$A \ {}_0{\Rightarrow}^* \ w, w \in \Delta^*.$$

Since G_1 and G_2 are in Greibach normal form, after every application of rule (2), the leftmost nonterminal symbol in both components of G is the beginning of the binary coding of some terminal symbol. Then,

$$S \ {}_2{\Rightarrow} \ S_1 S_2 \ {}_2{\Rightarrow} \ eaw\overline{a}w'$$

where $e \in \Delta$, $a, o(\overline{a}) \in \{0, 1\}^*$, $w \in N_1^*$, $w' \in N_2^*$. If and only if $a = o(\overline{a})$, by rules (3)a and (3)b,

$$eaw\overline{a}w' \ {}_2{\Rightarrow}^* \ eww'$$

and the derivation may possibly continue with an application of another rule (2). Suppose, $a \neq o(\overline{a})$. Then, $|a| \neq |\overline{a}|$ and a or $o(\overline{a})$ contains more 0s, which remain in the sentential form even after erasing the shorter coding. Next, two cases are possible. If the derivation already finished, the remaining 0s or $\overline{0}$s are permanent and the derivation is not terminating. Otherwise, another rule (2) is applied and other codings are inserted. However, then the leftmost nonterminal symbol in one component is 0 or 1 and in the second one is $\overline{1}$ or $\overline{0}$, respectively. Rule (3)c or (3)d must be applied and again infinitely many times, which blocks the derivation. Then, every application of rule (2) generates the binary codings $a, \overline{a}$, where $a = o(\overline{a})$, $a \in \{0, 1\}^*$, $\overline{a} \in \{\overline{0}, \overline{1}\}^*$, if and only if the derivation is terminating. Thus, if both components of G generate the corresponding encoded symbols in every derivation step of simulated G_1 and G_2, they generate the corresponding encoded strings. Therefore, obviously

$$S \ {}_2{\Rightarrow}^* \ x, x \in \Delta^*$$

where $x \in h(L_1 \cap L_2)$. Accordingly, $x \in L$, so $\mathscr{L}(G, {}_2{\Rightarrow}) = L$. □

Since L is an arbitrary recursively enumerable language, the proof of Theorem 12.8 is completed. ■

Mode 3

By the following theorem, we establish the generative power of even matrix grammars working under the leftmost mode 3 derivations.

Theorem 12.9. $_2\mathbf{EM}({}_3{\Rightarrow}) = \mathbf{RE}$.

We omit the proof, since the proof of Theorem 12.8 is fully applicable to prove Theorem 12.9. Only notice that rules (3)c and (3)d are not necessary, the more strict leftmost derivations would block the derivation anyway.

12.3.3.3 Summary

Let us state all the achieved results.

$$\mathbf{CF} = {}_1\mathbf{EM}({}_i\Rightarrow) \subset {}_2\mathbf{EM}({}_0\Rightarrow) = \mathbf{EM}({}_0\Rightarrow) = \mathbf{M} \subset \mathbf{CS}, i \in \{0, 1, 2, 3\},$$

$$\mathbf{CF} \subset {}_2\mathbf{EM}({}_1\Rightarrow) = \mathbf{EM}({}_1\Rightarrow) \subset \mathbf{CS},$$

$${}_2\mathbf{EM}({}_2\Rightarrow) = \mathbf{EM}({}_2\Rightarrow) = {}_2\mathbf{EM}({}_3\Rightarrow) = \mathbf{EM}({}_3\Rightarrow) = \mathbf{RE}.$$

We proved that even matrix grammars with two components are exactly as strong as matrix grammars. Additionally, we proved that the presence of more than two components has no influence on their generative power. Three leftmost modes of derivations were introduced and studied. The previous conclusion on the number of components still holds for leftmost derivations. The more strict leftmost derivations increase the generative power significantly—even matrix grammars become Turing complete. However, we are still not sure about the most liberal leftmost derivations; thus, we provide Open Problem 12.2, which we suggest for the future research.

Of course, even matrix grammars represent variants of ordinary matrix grammars, and as such, from a general viewpoint, they generate their languages in a regulated way. At the same time, however, they can be viewed as language generators working in parallel, which represents the central topic of the next chapter.

12.4 Programmed grammars

The regulation of a programmed grammar is based upon two binary relations, represented by two sets attached to the grammatical rules. More precisely, a *programmed grammar* G is a context-free grammar, in which two sets, σ_r and ϕ_r, are attached to each rule r, where σ_r and ϕ_r are subsets of the entire set of rules in G. G can apply r in the following two ways:

(1) If the left-hand side of r occurs in the sentential form under scan, G rewrites the left-hand side of r to its right-hand side, and during the next derivation step, it has to apply a rule from σ_r;
(2) If the left-hand side of r is absent in the sentential form under scan, G skips the application of r, and during the next derivation step, it has to apply a rule from ϕ_r.

This brief section consists of two subsections. Section 12.4.1 defines and illustrates programmed grammars, while Section 12.4.2 gives their generative power.

12.4.1 Definitions and examples

In this section, we define programmed grammars and illustrate them by an example. However, we must first introduce the following auxiliary concept to help us define programmed grammars.

Definition 12.11. *A* labeled context-free grammar *is a quintuple*

$$G = (\Sigma, \Delta, \Psi, R, S),$$

where (Σ, Δ, R, S) *is a context-free grammar, and* Ψ *is an alphabet of* labels, *such that* $\text{card}(\Psi) = \mathit{card}(R)$. *Furthermore, each rule* $A \to x \in R$ *is denoted by a unique label* $l \in \Psi$, *symbolically written as* $l : A \to x$, *referred to as the* rule labeled by l *or, briefly,* rule l.

Definition 12.12. *A* programmed grammar with appearance checking *(see [12])* G *is a labeled context-free grammar* $(\Sigma, \Delta, \Psi, R, S)$ *in which two sets* $\sigma_r, \varphi_r \subseteq \Psi$ *are attached to each rule* $r \in R$.

In other words, a programmed grammar is a quintuple

$$G = (\Sigma, \Delta, \Psi, R, S)$$

where

- Σ, Δ, Ψ, *and* S *are defined as in a labeled context-free grammar,* $\Sigma - \Delta = N$;
- $R \subseteq \Psi \times N \times \Sigma^* \times 2^\Psi \times 2^\Psi$ *is a finite relation, called the set of* rules, *such that* $\text{card}(\Psi) = \text{card}(R)$ *and if* $(r, A, x, \sigma_r, \phi_r), (s, A, x, \sigma_s, \phi_s) \in R$, *then* $(r, A, x, \sigma_r, \phi_r) = (s, A, x, \sigma_s, \phi_s)$.

Instead of $(r, A, x, \sigma_r, \phi_r) \in R$, *we write* $(r\colon A \to x, \sigma_r, \phi_r) \in R$. *For* $(r\colon A \to x, \sigma_r, \phi_r) \in R$, A *is referred to as the* left-hand side *of* r, *and* x *is referred to as the* right-hand side *of* r.

The direct derivation relation, *symbolically denoted by* $\Rightarrow_G$, *is defined over* $\Sigma^* \times \Psi$ *as follows: for* $(x_1, r), (x_2, s) \in \Sigma^* \times \Psi$,

$$(x_1, r) \Rightarrow_G (x_2, s)$$

if and only if either

$$x_1 = yAz, x_2 = ywz, (r\colon A \to w, \sigma_r, \phi_r) \in R, \text{ and } s \in \sigma_r, \text{ for some } y, z \in \Sigma^*,$$

or

$$x_1 = x_2, (r\colon A \to w, \sigma_r, \phi_r) \in R, A \notin \text{symbols}(x_1), \text{ and } s \in \phi_r.$$

Let $(r\colon A \to w, \sigma_r, \phi_r) \in R$. *Then,* σ_r *and* ϕ_r *are called the* success field *of* r *and the* failure field *of* r, *respectively. Observe that due to our definition of the relation of a direct derivation, if* $\sigma_r \cup \phi_r = \emptyset$, *then* r *is never applicable. Therefore, we assume that* $\sigma_r \cup \phi_r \neq \emptyset$, *for all* $(r\colon A \to w, \sigma_r, \phi_r) \in R$. *Define* $\Rightarrow_G^k$ *for* $k \geq 0$, $\Rightarrow_G^*$, *and* $\Rightarrow_G^+$ *in the standard way. Let* $(S, r) \Rightarrow_G^* (w, s)$, *where* $r, s \in \Psi$ *and* $w \in \Sigma^*$. *Then,* (w, s) *is called a* configuration. *The* language *of* G *is denoted by* $L(G)$ *and defined as*

$$L(G) = \{w \in \Delta^* \mid (S, r) \Rightarrow_G^* (w, s), \text{ for some } r, s \in \Psi\}.$$

Definition 12.13. *Let* $G = (\Sigma, \Delta, \Psi, R, S)$ *be a programmed grammar with appearance checking.* G *is* propagating *if every* $(r\colon A \to x, \sigma_r, \phi_r) \in R$ *satisfies that* $|x| \geq 1$. *Rules of the form* $(r\colon A \to \varepsilon, \sigma_r, \phi_r)$ *are called* erasing rules. *If every*

$(r\colon A \to x, \sigma_r, \phi_r) \in R$ *satisfies that* $\phi_r = \emptyset$, *then G is a* programmed grammar without appearance checking *or, simply, a* programmed grammar. *Then, for brevity, instead of* $(r\colon A \to x, \sigma_r, \emptyset)$, *we write* $(r\colon A \to x, \sigma_r)$.

If every sentential form derived by G contains k or fewer nonterminals, it is a programmed grammar of index k (with appearance checking).

Example 12.6 (from [12]). *Consider the programmed grammar with appearance checking*

$$G = (\{S, A, a\}, \{a\}, \{r_1, r_2, r_3\}, R, S)$$

where R consists of the three rules

$$(r_1\colon S \to AA, \{r_1\}, \{r_2, r_3\}),$$
$$(r_2\colon A \to S, \{r_2\}, \{r_1\}),$$
$$(r_3\colon A \to a, \{r_3\}, \emptyset).$$

Since the success field of r_i *is* $\{r_i\}$, *for each* $i \in \{1,2,3\}$, *the rules* r_1, r_2, *and* r_3 *have to be used as many times as possible. Therefore, starting from* S^n, *for some* $n \geq 1$, *the successful derivation has to pass to* A^{2n} *and then, by using* r_2, *to* S^{2n}, *or, by using* r_3, *to* a^{2n}. *A cycle like this, consisting of the repeated use of* r_1 *and* r_2, *doubles the number of symbols. In conclusion, we obtain the non-context-free language*

$$L(G) = \left\{a^{2^n} \mid n \geq 1\right\}.$$

For example, the sentence aaaa is obtained by the following derivation:

$$\begin{aligned}(S, r_1) &\Rightarrow_G (AA, r_2)\\ &\Rightarrow_G (AS, r_2)\\ &\Rightarrow_G (SS, r_1)\\ &\Rightarrow_G (AAS, r_1)\\ &\Rightarrow_G (AAAA, r_2)\\ &\Rightarrow_G (AASA, r_2)\\ &\Rightarrow_G (AASS, r_2)\\ &\Rightarrow_G (SASS, r_2)\\ &\Rightarrow_G (SSSS, r_3)\\ &\Rightarrow_G (SSSa, r_3)\\ &\Rightarrow_G (aSSa, r_3)\\ &\Rightarrow_G (aaSa, r_3)\\ &\Rightarrow_G (aaaa, r_3).\end{aligned}$$

Notice the similarity between G from this example and H from Example 12.3.

By $\mathbf{P}_{ac}$, $\mathbf{P}_{ac}^{-\varepsilon}$, $\mathbf{P}$, and $\mathbf{P}^{-\varepsilon}$, we denote the families of languages generated by programmed grammars with appearance checking, propagating programmed grammars with appearance checking, programmed grammars, and propagating programmed grammars, respectively.

For a positive integer k, by ${}_k\mathbf{P}_{ac}$, ${}_k\mathbf{P}_{ac}^{-\varepsilon}$, ${}_k\mathbf{P}$, and ${}_k\mathbf{P}^{-\varepsilon}$, we denote the families of languages generated by programmed grammars of index k with appearance checking, propagating programmed grammars of index k with appearance checking, programmed grammars of index k, and propagating programmed grammars of index k, respectively.

12.4.2 Generative power

The next theorem states the power of programmed grammars.

Theorem 12.10 (see Theorem 5.3.4 in [23]).

(i) $\mathbf{P}_{ac} = \mathbf{M}_{ac}$;
(ii) $\mathbf{P}_{ac}^{-\varepsilon} = \mathbf{M}_{ac}^{-\varepsilon}$;
(iii) $\mathbf{P} = \mathbf{M}$;
(iv) $\mathbf{P}^{-\varepsilon} = \mathbf{M}^{-\varepsilon}$.

Observe that programmed grammars, matrix grammars, and regular-controlled grammars are equally powerful (see Theorems 12.3 and 12.10).

Programmed grammars of finite index establish an infinite hierarchy of language families.

Theorem 12.11 (see Theorems 3.1.2i and 3.1.7 in [12]). ${}_k\mathbf{P} \subset {}_{k+1}\mathbf{P}$ for any $k \geq 1$.

12.5 Regulated automata and computation

Just like there exist regulated grammars, which formalize regulated computation, there also exist their automata-based counterparts for this purpose. Basically, in a very natural and simple way, these automata regulate the selection of rules according to which their sequences of moves are made. These regulated automata represent the principal subject of the present section, which covers their most essential types.

Consider Definition 5.1. In what follows, instead of specifying a finite automaton M as a pair, we specify M as a quintuple

$$M = (Q, \Delta, R, s, F)$$

whose components have the same meaning as in Definition 5.1. Similarly, consider Definition 7.1. In what follows, instead of specifying a pushdown automaton M as a pair, we specify M as a septuple

$$M = (Q, \Delta, \Gamma, R, s, S, F)$$

whose components have the same meaning as in Definition 7.1.

12.5.1 Self-regulating automata

This subsection focuses on finite and pushdown automata that regulate the selection of a rule according to which the current move is made by a rule according to which a previous move was made, hence their name—self-regulating automata. To give a more precise insight into self-regulating automata, consider a finite automaton M with a finite binary relation P over the set of rules in M. Furthermore, suppose that M makes a sequence of moves ρ that leads to the acceptance of a string, so ρ can be expressed as a concatenation of $n + 1$ consecutive subsequences, $\rho = \rho_0\rho_1 \cdots \rho_n$, where $|\rho_k| = |\rho_j|$, $0 \leq k, j \leq n$, in which r_i^j denotes the rule according to which the ith move in ρ_j is made, for all $0 \leq j \leq n$ and $1 \leq i \leq |\rho_j|$ (as usual, $|\rho_j|$ denotes the length of ρ_j). If for all $0 \leq j < n$, $(r_1^j, r_1^{j+1}) \in P$, then M represents an *n-turn first-move self-regulating finite automaton (SFA) (n-first-SFA) with respect to P*. If for all $0 \leq j < n$ and all $1 \leq i \leq |\rho_i|$, $(r_i^j, r_i^{j+1}) \in P$, then M represents an *n-turn all-move SFA (n-all-SFA) with respect to P*.

In this section, based on the number of turns, we establish two infinite hierarchies of language families that lie between the families of regular and context-sensitive languages. First, we demonstrate that n-first-SFAs give rise to an infinite hierarchy of language families coinciding with the hierarchy resulting from $(n + 1)$-parallel right-linear grammars (PRLGs) (see [24–27]). Recall that n-PRLGs generate a proper language subfamily of the language family generated by $(n + 1)$-PRLGs (see Theorem 5 in [25]). As a result, n-first-SFAs accept a proper language subfamily of the language family accepted by $(n + 1)$-turn first-move SFAs, for all $n \geq 0$. Similarly, we prove that n-all-SFAs give rise to an infinite hierarchy of language families coinciding with the hierarchy resulting from $(n + 1)$-right-linear simple matrix grammars (RLSMGs) (see [12,27,28]). As n-RLSMGs generate a proper subfamily of the language family generated by $(n + 1)$-RLSMGs (see Theorem 1.5.4 in [12]), n-all-SFAs accept a proper language subfamily of the language family accepted by $(n + 1)$-turn all-move SFAs. Furthermore, since the families of right-linear simple matrix languages (RLSMLs) coincide with the language families accepted by multi-tape non-writing automata (see [29]) and by finite-turn checking automata (see [30]), all-move SFAs characterize these families, too. Finally, we summarize the results about both infinite hierarchies.

Afterwards, by analogy with SFAs, we introduce and discuss *self-regulating pushdown automata (SPDAs)*. Regarding self-regulating all-move pushdown automata, we prove that they do not give rise to any infinite hierarchy analogical to the achieved hierarchies resulting from the SFAs. Indeed, zero-turn all-move SPDAs define the family of context-free languages while one-turn all-move SPDAs define the family of recursively enumerable languages. On the other hand, as far as self-regulating first-move pushdown automata are concerned, the question whether they define an infinite hierarchy is open.

12.5.2 Self-regulating finite automata

First, the present section defines n-first-SFAs and n-all-SFAs. Then, it determines the accepting power of these automata.

12.5.2.1 Definitions and examples

In this section, we define and illustrate n-first-SFAs and n-all-SFAs.

Definition 12.14. *An* SFA *is an octuple*

$$M = (Q, D, \Psi, R, q_0, q_t, F, P)$$

where

(i) (Q, D, R, q_0, F) *is a finite automaton;*
(ii) Ψ *is an alphabet of* labels *such that* card Ψ = card R, *and each rule* $qa \to p \in R$ *is denoted by a unique label* $l \in R$, *symbolically written as* $l : qa \to p$, *referred to as the* rule labeled by l *or, briefly,* rule l;
(iii) $q_t \in Q$ *is a* turn state; *and*
(iv) $P \subseteq \Psi \times \Psi$ *is a finite relation on the alphabet of rule labels.*

In this section, we consider two ways of self-regulation—first-move and all-move. According to these two types of self-regulation, two types of n-turn SFAs are defined.

Definition 12.15. *Let* $n \geq 0$ *and* $M = (Q, D, \Psi, R, q_0, q_t, F, P)$ *be an SFA. M is said to be an n-first-SFA if every* $w \in L(M)$ *is accepted by M in the following way:*

$$q_0 w \vdash_M^* f\,[\mu]$$

such that

$$\mu = r_1^0 \cdots r_k^0 r_1^1 \cdots r_k^1 \cdots r_1^n \cdots r_k^n$$

where $k \geq 1$, r_k^0 *is the first rule of the form* $qx \to q_t$, *for some* $q \in Q$, $x \in D^*$, *and*

$$(r_1^j, r_1^{j+1}) \in P$$

for all $j = 0, 1, \ldots, n$.

The family of languages accepted by n-first-SFAs is denoted by $\mathbf{FSFA}_n$.

Example 12.7. *Consider a* 1*-first-SFA*

$$M = (\{s, t, f\}, \{a, b\}, \{1, 2, 3, 4\}, R, s, t, \{f\}, \{(1, 3)\})$$

with R containing rules (see Figure 12.1)

$1: sa \to s,$
$2: sa \to t,$
$3: tb \to f,$
$4: fb \to f.$

With aabb, M makes

$$saabb \vdash_M sabb\,[1] \vdash_M tbb\,[2] \vdash_M fb\,[3] \vdash_M f\,[4].$$

In brief, $saabb \vdash_M^* f\,[1234]$. *Observe that* $L(M) = \{a^n b^n \mid n \geq 1\}$, *which belongs to* $\mathbf{CF} - \mathbf{REG}$.

Definition 12.16. *Let* $n \geq 0$ *and* $M = (Q, D, \Psi, R, q_0, q_t, F, P)$ *be an SFA. M is said to be an n-all-SFA if every* $w \in L(M)$ *is accepted by M in the following way:*

$$q_0 w \vdash_M^* f\,[\mu]$$

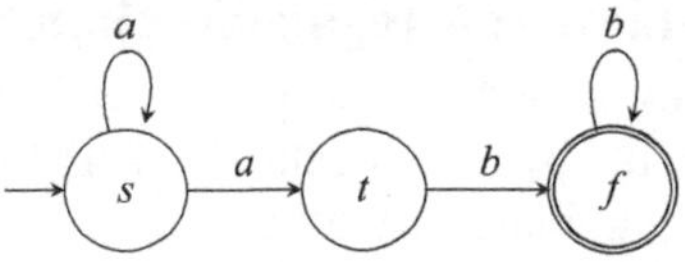

Figure 12.1 1-Turn first-move self-regulating finite automaton M

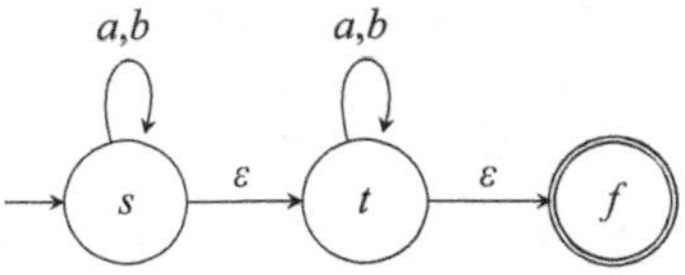

Figure 12.2 1-Turn all-move self-regulating finite automaton M

such that

$$\mu = r_1^0 \cdots r_k^0 r_1^1 \cdots r_k^1 \cdots r_1^n \cdots r_k^n$$

where $k \geq 1$, r_k^0 *is the first rule of the form* $qx \rightarrow q_t$, *for some* $q \in Q$, $x \in D^*$, *and*

$$(r_i^j, r_i^{j+1}) \in P$$

for all $i = 1, 2, \ldots, k$ *and* $j = 0, 1, \ldots, n-1$.

The family of languages accepted by n-all-SFAs is denoted by $\mathbf{ASFA}_n$.

Example 12.8. *Consider a* 1*-all-SFA*

$$M = (\{s, t, f\}, \{a, b\}, \{1, 2, 3, 4, 5, 6\}, R, s, t, \{f\}, \{(1, 4), (2, 5), (3, 6)\})$$

with R containing the following rules (see Figure 12.2):

$1: sa \rightarrow s,$
$2: sb \rightarrow s,$
$3: s \rightarrow t,$
$4: ta \rightarrow t,$
$5: tb \rightarrow t,$
$6: t \rightarrow f.$

With abab, M makes

$$sabab \vdash_M sbab\,[1] \vdash_M sab\,[2] \vdash_M tab\,[3] \vdash_M tb\,[4] \vdash_M t\,[5] \vdash_M f\,[6].$$

In brief, $sabab \vdash_M^* f\,[123456]$. *Observe that* $L(M) = \{ww \mid w \in \{a, b\}^*\}$, *which belongs to* **CS** − **CF**.

12.5.2.2 Accepting power

In this section, we discuss the accepting power of n-first-SFAs and n-all-SFAs.

12.5.2.3 *n*-Turn first-move self-regulating finite automata

We prove that the family of languages accepted by n-first-SFAs coincides with the family of languages generated by the so-called $(n+1)$-PRLGs (see [24–27]). First, however, we define these grammars formally.

Definition 12.17. *For $n \geq 1$, an n-*PRLG *(see [24–27]) is an $(n+3)$-tuple*

$$G = (N_1, \ldots, N_n, \Delta, S, R)$$

where N_i, $1 \leq i \leq n$, are pairwise disjoint nonterminal alphabets, *Δ is a* terminal alphabet, *$S \notin N$ is an* initial symbol, *where $N = N_1 \cup \cdots \cup N_n$, and R is a finite set of* rules *that contains these three kinds of rules*

1. $S \rightarrow X_1 \cdots X_n$, $\quad X_i \in N_i$, $1 \leq i \leq n$;
2. $X \rightarrow wY$, $\quad X, Y \in N_i$ *for some* i, $1 \leq i \leq n$, $w \in \Delta^*$;
3. $X \rightarrow w$, $\quad X \in N$, $w \in \Delta^*$.

For $x, y \in (N \cup \Delta \cup \{S\})^*$,

$$x \Rightarrow_G y$$

if and only if

(i) *either* $x = S$ *and* $S \rightarrow y \in R$,
(ii) *or* $x = y_1X_1 \cdots y_nX_n$, $y = y_1x_1 \cdots y_nx_n$, *where* $y_i \in \Delta^*$, $x_i \in \Delta^*N \cup \Delta^*$, $X_i \in N_i$, *and* $X_i \rightarrow x_i \in R$, $1 \leq i \leq n$.

Let $x, y \in (N \cup \Delta \cup \{S\})^*$ *and* $\ell > 0$. *Then,* $x \Rightarrow_G^{\ell} y$ *if and only if there exists a sequence*

$$x_0 \Rightarrow_G x_1 \Rightarrow_G \cdots \Rightarrow_G x_\ell$$

where $x_0 = x$, $x_\ell = y$. *As usual,* $x \Rightarrow_G^+ y$ *if and only if there exists* $\ell > 0$ *such that* $x \Rightarrow_G^{\ell} y$, *and* $x \Rightarrow_G^* y$ *if and only if* $x = y$ *or* $x \Rightarrow_G^+ y$.

The language *of G is defined as*

$$L(G) = \{w \in \Delta^* \mid S \Rightarrow_G^+ w\}.$$

*A language $K \subseteq \Delta^*$ is an n-*parallel right-linear language *(n-PRLL for short) if there is an n-PRLG G such that $K = L(G)$.*

The family of n-PRLLs is denoted by $\mathbf{PRL}_n$.

Definition 12.18. *Let $G = (N_1, \ldots, N_n, \Delta, S, R)$ be an n-PRLG, for some $n \geq 1$, and $1 \leq i \leq n$. By the* ith component *of G, we understand the* 1-*PRLG*

$$G = (N_i, \Delta, S', R')$$

where R' contains rules of the following forms:

1. $S' \rightarrow X_i$ $\quad$ *if* $S \rightarrow X_1 \cdots X_n \in R$, $X_i \in N_i$;
2. $X \rightarrow wY$ $\quad$ *if* $X \rightarrow wY \in R$ *and* $X, Y \in N_i$;
3. $X \rightarrow w$ $\quad$ *if* $X \rightarrow w \in R$ *and* $X \in N_i$.

To prove that the family of languages accepted by n-first-SFAs coincides with the family of languages generated by $(n+1)$-PRLGs, we need the following normal form of PRLGs.

Lemma 12.1. *For every n-PRLG $G = (N_1, \ldots, N_n, \Delta, S, R)$, there is an equivalent n-PRLG $G' = (N'_1, \ldots, N'_n, \Delta, S, R')$ that satisfies:*

(i) *if $S \to X_1 \cdots X_n \in R'$, then X_i does not occur on the right-hand side of any rule, for $i = 1, 2, \ldots, n$;*
(ii) *if $S \to \alpha$, $S \to \beta \in R'$ and $\alpha \neq \beta$, then* $\text{symbols}(\alpha) \cap \text{symbols}(\beta) = \emptyset$.

Proof. If G does not satisfy the conditions from the lemma, then we construct a new n-PRLG

$$G' = (N'_1, \ldots, N'_n, \Delta, S, R')$$

where R' contains all rules of the form $X \to \beta \in R, X \neq S$ and $N_j \subseteq N'_j$, $1 \leq j \leq n$. For each rule $S \to X_1 \cdots X_n \in R$, we add new nonterminals $Y_j \notin N'_j$ into N'_j, and rules include $S \to Y_1 \cdots Y_n$ and $Y_j \to X_j$ in R', $1 \leq j \leq n$. Clearly,

$$S \Rightarrow_G X_1 \cdots X_n \text{ if and only if } S \Rightarrow_{G'} Y_1 \cdots Y_n \Rightarrow_{G'} X_1 \cdots X_n.$$

Thus, $L(G) = L(G')$. ■

Lemma 12.2. *Let G be an n-PRLG. Then, there is an $(n-1)$-first-SFA M such that $L(G) = L(M)$.*

Proof. Informally, M is divided into n parts (see Figure 12.3). The ith part represents a finite automaton accepting the language of the ith component of G, and P also connects the ith part to the $(i+1)$st part as depicted in Figure 12.3.

Formally, without loss of generality, we assume $G = (N_1, \ldots, N_n, \Delta, S, R)$ to be in the form from Lemma 12.1. We construct an $(n-1)$-first-SFA

$$M = (Q, \Delta, \Psi, R, q_0, q_t, F, P)$$

where

$$\begin{aligned}
Q &= \{q_0, \ldots, q_n\} \cup N, N = N_1 \cup \cdots \cup N_n, \{q_0, q_1, \ldots, q_n\} \cap N = \emptyset, \\
F &= \{q_n\}, \\
R &= \{q_i \to X_{i+1} \mid S \to X_1 \cdots X_n \in R, 0 \leq i < n\} \cup \\
&\quad \{Xw \to Y \mid X \to wY \in R\} \cup \\
&\quad \{Xw \to q_i \mid X \to w \in R, w \in \Delta^*, X \in N_i, i \in \{1, \ldots, n\}\}, \\
q_t &= q_1, \\
\Psi &= R, \\
P &= \{(q_i \to X_{i+1}, q_{i+1} \to X_{i+2}) \mid S \to X_1 \cdots X_n \in R, 0 \leq i \leq n-2\}.
\end{aligned}$$

Next, we prove that $L(G) = L(M)$. To prove that $L(G) \subseteq L(M)$, consider any derivation of w in G and construct an acceptance of w in M depicted in Figure 12.3.

This figure clearly demonstrates the fundamental idea behind this part of the proof; its complete and rigorous version is left to the reader. Thus, M accepts every $w \in \Delta^*$ such that $S \Rightarrow_G^* w$.

$$
\begin{array}{ccccc}
& S & & & \\
& \Downarrow & & & \\
X_1^1 & X_1^2 & \cdots & X_1^n & \\
& \Downarrow & & & \\
x_1^1 X_2^1 & x_1^2 X_2^2 & \cdots & x_1^n X_2^n & \\
& \Downarrow & & & \\
& \vdots & & & \\
& \Downarrow & & & \\
x_1^1 \cdots x_{k-1}^1 X_k^1 & x_1^2 \cdots X_k^2 & \cdots & x_1^n \cdots X_k^n & \\
& \Downarrow & & & \\
w = x_1^1 \cdots x_k^1 & x_1^2 \cdots x_k^2 & \cdots & x_1^n \cdots x_k^n &
\end{array}
$$

in G

$$
\begin{array}{cccc}
q_0 & & & \\
\varepsilon \downarrow & \varepsilon \downarrow & & \varepsilon \downarrow \\
X_1^1 & X_1^2 & & X_1^n \\
x_1^1 \downarrow & x_1^2 \downarrow & & x_1^n \downarrow \\
X_2^1 & X_2^2 & & X_2^n \\
x_2^1 \downarrow & x_2^2 \downarrow & & x_2^n \downarrow \\
\vdots & \vdots & & \vdots \\
x_{k-1}^1 \downarrow & x_{k-1}^2 \downarrow & & x_{k-1}^n \downarrow \\
X_k^1 & X_k^2 & & X_k^n \\
x_k^1 \downarrow & x_k^2 \downarrow & & x_k^n \downarrow \\
q_1 & q_2 & & q_n
\end{array}
$$

in M

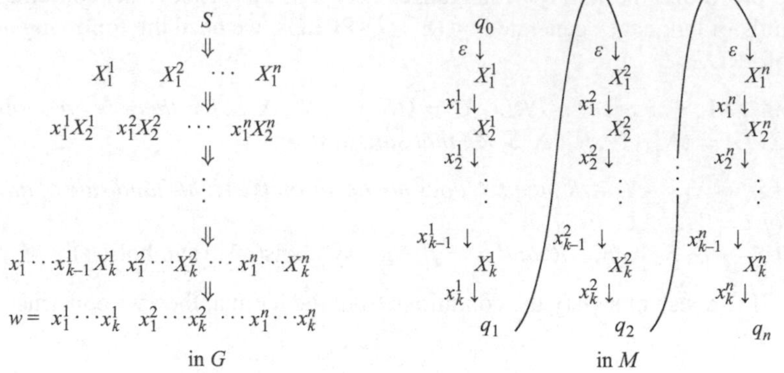

Figure 12.3　A derivation of w in G and the corresponding acceptance of w in M

To prove that $L(M) \subseteq L(G)$, consider any $w \in L(M)$ and any acceptance of w in M. Observe that the acceptance is of the form depicted on the right-hand side of Figure 12.3. It means that the number of steps M made from q_{i-1} to q_i is the same as from q_i to q_{i+1} since the only rule in the relation with $q_{i-1} \to X_1^i$ is the rule $q_i \to X_1^{i+1}$. Moreover, M can never come back to a state corresponding to a previous component. (By a component of M, we mean the finite automaton

$$
M_i = (Q, D, R, q_{i-1}, \{q_i\})
$$

for $1 \le i \le n$.) Next, construct a derivation of w in G. By Lemma 12.1, we have

$$
\mathrm{card}(\{X \mid (q_i \to X_1^{i+1}, q_{i+1} \to X) \in P\}) = 1
$$

for all $0 \le i < n - 1$. Thus, $S \to X_1^1 X_1^2 \cdots X_1^n \in R$. Moreover, if $X_j^i x_j^i \to X_{j+1}^i$, we apply $X_j^i \to x_j^i X_{j+1}^i \in R$, and if $X_k^i x_k^i \to q_i$, we apply $X_k^i \to x_k^i \in R$, $1 \le i \le n$, $1 \le j < k$.

Hence, Lemma 12.2 holds. ■

Lemma 12.3. *Let M be an n-first-SFA. Then, there is an $(n+1)$-PRLG G such that $L(G) = L(M)$.*

Proof. Let $M = (Q, D, \Psi, R, q_0, q_t, F, P)$. Consider

$$
G = (N_0, \ldots, N_n, D, S, R)
$$

where

$$\begin{aligned}
N_i &= (QD^l \times Q \times \{i\} \times Q) \cup (Q \times \{i\} \times Q),\\
l &= \max(\{|w| \mid qw \to p \in R\}), 0 \le i \le n,\\
R &= \{S \to [q_0x_0, q^0, 0, q_t][q_tx_1, q^1, 1, q_{i_1}][q_{i_1}x_2, q^2, 2, q_{i_2}] \cdots\\
&\qquad [q_{i_{n-1}}x_n, q^n, n, q_{i_n}] \mid\\
&\quad r_0\colon q_0x_0 \to q^0, r_1\colon q_tx_1 \to q^1, r_2\colon q_{i_1}x_2 \to q^2, \ldots,\\
&\qquad r_n\colon q_{i_{n-1}}x_n \to q^n \in R,\\
&\quad (r_0, r_1), (r_1, r_2), \ldots, (r_{n-1}, r_n) \in P,\ q_{i_n} \in F\} \cup\\
&\quad \{[px, q, i, r] \to x[q, i, r]\} \cup\\
&\quad \{[q, i, q] \to \varepsilon \mid q \in Q\} \cup\\
&\quad \{[q, i, p] \to w[q', i, p] \mid qw \to q' \in R\}.
\end{aligned}$$

Next, we prove that $L(G) = L(M)$. To prove that $L(G) \subseteq L(M)$, observe that we make $n+1$ copies of M and go through them similarly to Figure 12.3. Consider a derivation of w in G. Then, in a greater detail, this derivation is of the form

$$\begin{aligned}
S &\Rightarrow_G [q_0x_0^0, q_1^0, 0, q_t][q_tx_0^1, q_1^1, 1, q_{i_1}] \cdots [q_{i_{n-1}}x_0^n, q_1^n, n, q_{i_n}]\\
&\Rightarrow_G x_0^0[q_1^0, 0, q_t]x_0^1[q_1^1, 1, q_{i_1}] \cdots x_0^n[q_1^n, n, q_{i_n}]\\
&\Rightarrow_G x_0^0x_1^0[q_2^0, 0, q_t]x_0^1x_1^1[q_2^1, 1, q_{i_1}] \cdots x_0^nx_1^n[q_2^n, n, q_{i_n}] \qquad (12.1)\\
&\ \ \vdots\\
&\Rightarrow_G x_0^0x_1^0 \cdots x_k^0[q_t, 0, q_t]x_0^1x_1^1 \cdots x_k^1[q_{i_1}, 1, q_{i_1}] \cdots x_0^nx_1^n \cdots x_k^n[q_{i_n}, n, q_{i_n}]\\
&\Rightarrow_G x_0^0x_1^0 \cdots x_k^0x_0^1x_1^1 \cdots x_k^1 \cdots x_0^nx_1^n \cdots x_k^n
\end{aligned}$$

and

$$r_0\colon q_0x_0^0 \to q_1^0, r_1\colon q_tx_0^1 \to q_1^1, r_2\colon q_{i_1}x_0^2 \to q_1^2, \ldots, r_n\colon q_{i_{n-1}}x_0^n \to q_1^n \in R,$$

$$(r_0, r_1), (r_1, r_2), \ldots, (r_{n-1}, r_n) \in P$$

and $q_{i_n} \in F$.

Thus, the sequence of rules used in the acceptance of w in M is

$$\begin{aligned}
\mu = {} & (q_0x_0^0 \to q_1^0)(q_1^0x_1^0 \to q_2^0) \cdots (q_k^0x_k^0 \to q_t)\\
& (q_tx_0^1 \to q_1^1)(q_1^1x_1^1 \to q_2^1) \cdots (q_k^1x_k^1 \to q_{i_1})\\
& (q_{i_1}x_0^2 \to q_1^2)(q_1^2x_1^2 \to q_2^2) \cdots (q_k^2x_k^2 \to q_{i_2}) \qquad (12.2)\\
& \ \ \vdots\\
& (q_{i_{n-1}}x_0^n \to q_1^n)(q_1^nx_1^n \to q_2^n) \cdots (q_k^nx_k^n \to q_{i_n}).
\end{aligned}$$

Next, we prove that $L(M) \subseteq L(G)$. Informally, the acceptance is divided into $n+1$ parts of the same length. Grammar G generates the ith part by the ith component and records the state from which the next component starts.

Let μ be a sequence of rules used in an acceptance of

$$w = x_0^0x_1^0 \cdots x_k^0x_0^1x_1^1 \cdots x_k^1 \cdots x_0^nx_1^n \cdots x_k^n$$

in M of the form (12.2). Then, the derivation of the form (12.1) is the corresponding derivation of w in G since $[q^i_j, i, p] \rightarrow x^i_j[q^i_{j+1}, i, p] \in R$ and $[q, i, q] \rightarrow \varepsilon$, for all $0 \leq i \leq n$, $1 \leq j < k$.

Hence, Lemma 12.3 holds. ■

The first main result of this section follows next.

Theorem 12.12. For all $n \geq 0$, $\mathbf{FSFA}_n = \mathbf{PRL}_{n+1}$.

Proof. This proof follows from Lemmas 12.2 and 12.3. ■

Corollary 12.1. *The following statements hold true.*

(i) $\mathbf{REG} = \mathbf{FSFA}_0 \subset \mathbf{FSFA}_1 \subset \mathbf{FSFA}_2 \subset \cdots \subset \mathbf{CS}$*;*
(ii) $\mathbf{FSFA}_1 \subset \mathbf{CF}$*;*
(iii) $\mathbf{FSFA}_2 \not\subseteq \mathbf{CF}$*;*
(iv) $\mathbf{CF} \not\subseteq \mathbf{FSFA}_n$ *for any* $n \geq 0$*;*
(v) *For all* $n \geq 0$, $\mathbf{FSFA}_n$ *is closed under union, finite substitution, homomorphism, intersection with a regular language, and right quotient with a regular language;*
(vi) *For all* $n \geq 1$, $\mathbf{FSFA}_n$ *is not closed under intersection and complement.*

Proof. Recall the following statements that are proved in [25].

- $\mathbf{REG} = \mathbf{PRL}_1 \subset \mathbf{PRL}_2 \subset \mathbf{PRL}_3 \subset \cdots \subset \mathbf{CS}$;
- $\mathbf{PRL}_2 \subset \mathbf{CF}$;
- $\mathbf{CF} \not\subseteq \mathbf{PRL}_n$, $n \geq 1$;
- For all $n \geq 1$, $\mathbf{PRL}_n$ is closed under union, finite substitution, homomorphism, intersection with a regular language, and right quotient with a regular language;
- For all $n \geq 2$, $\mathbf{PRL}_n$ is not closed under intersection and complement.

These statements and Theorem 12.12 imply statements (i), (ii), (iv), (v), and (vi) in Corollary 12.1. Moreover, observe that

$$\{a^n b^n c^{2n} \mid n \geq 0\} \in \mathbf{FSFA}_2 - \mathbf{CF}$$

which proves (iii). ■

Theorem 12.13. For all $n \geq 1$, $\mathbf{FSFA}_n$ is not closed under inverse homomorphism.

Proof. For $n = 1$, let $L = \{a^k b^k \mid k \geq 1\}$, and let the homomorphism $h : \{a, b, c\}^* \rightarrow \{a, b\}^*$ be defined as $h(a) = a$, $h(b) = b$, and $h(c) = \varepsilon$. Then, $L \in \mathbf{FSFA}_1$, but

$$L' = h^{-1}(L) \cap c^* a^* b^* = \{c^* a^k b^k \mid k \geq 1\} \notin \mathbf{FSFA}_1.$$

Assume that L' is in $\mathbf{FSFA}_1$. Then, by Theorem 12.12, there is a 2-PRLG

$$G = (N_1, N_2, \Delta, S, R)$$

such that $L(G) = L'$. Let

$$k > \text{card}(R) \cdot \max(\{|w| \mid X \rightarrow wY \in R\}).$$

Consider a derivation of $c^k a^k b^k \in L'$. The second component can generate only finitely many as; otherwise, it derives $\{a^k b^n \mid k < n\}$, which is not regular. Analogously, the first component generates only finitely many bs. Therefore, the first component generates any number of as, and the second component generates any number of bs. Moreover, there is a derivation of the form $X \Rightarrow_G^m X$, for some $X \in N_2$, and $m \geq 1$, used in the derivation in the second component. In the first component, there is a derivation $A \Rightarrow_G^l a^s A$, for some $A \in N_1$, and $s, l \geq 1$. Then, we can modify the derivation of $c^k a^k b^k$ so that in the first component, we repeat the cycle $A \Rightarrow_G^l a^s A$ $(m+1)$-times, and in the second component, we repeat the cycle $X \Rightarrow_G^m X$ $(l+1)$-times. The derivations of both components have the same length—the added cycles are of length ml, and the rest is of the same length as in the derivation of $c^k a^k b^k$. Therefore, we have derived $c^k a^r b^k$, where $r > k$, which is not in L'—a contradiction.

For $n > 1$, the proof is analogous and left to the reader. ■

Corollary 12.2. *For all $n \geq 1$,* $\mathbf{FSFA}_n$ *is not closed under concatenation. Therefore, it is not closed under Kleene closure either.*

Proof. For $n = 1$, let $L_1 = \{c\}^*$ and $L_2 = \{a^k b^k \mid k \geq 1\}$. Then,

$$L_1 L_2 = \{c^j a^k b^k \mid k \geq 1, j \geq 0\}.$$

Analogously, prove this corollary for $n > 1$. ■

n-Turn all-move self-regulating finite automata

We next turn our attention to n-all-SFAs. We prove that the family of languages accepted by n-all-SFAs coincides with the family of languages generated by the so-called n-RLSMGs (see [12,27,28]). First, however, we define these grammars formally.

Definition 12.19. *For $n \geq 1$, an n-right-linear simple matrix grammar (n-RLSMG for short) (see [12,27,28]) is an $(n+3)$-tuple*

$$G = (N_1, \ldots, N_n, \Delta, S, R)$$

where N_i, $1 \leq i \leq n$, are pairwise disjoint nonterminal alphabets, Δ *is* a terminal alphabet, $S \notin N$ *is an* initial symbol, *where $N = N_1 \cup \cdots \cup N_n$, and R is a finite set of* matrix rules. *A matrix rule can be in one of the following three forms:*

1. $(S \to X_1 \cdots X_n)$, $\quad X_i \in N_i,\ 1 \leq i \leq n$;
2. $(X_1 \to w_1 Y_1, \ldots, X_n \to w_n Y_n)$, $\quad w_i \in \Delta^*,\ X_i, Y_i \in N_i,\ 1 \leq i \leq n$;
3. $(X_1 \to w_1, \ldots, X_n \to w_n)$, $\quad X_i \in N_i,\ w_i \in \Delta^*,\ 1 \leq i \leq n$.

Let m be a matrix. Then, $m[i]$ denotes the ith rule of m. For $x, y \in (N \cup \Delta \cup \{S\})^*$,

$$x \Rightarrow_G y$$

if and only if

(i) *either $x = S$ and $(S \to y) \in R$,*
(ii) *or $x = y_1 X_1 \cdots y_n X_n$, $y = y_1 x_1 \cdots y_n x_n$, where $y_i \in \Delta^*$, $x_i \in \Delta^* N \cup \Delta^*$, $X_i \in N_i$, $1 \leq i \leq n$, and $(X_1 \to x_1, \ldots, X_n \to x_n) \in R$.*

We define $x \Rightarrow_G^+ y$ *and* $x \Rightarrow_G^* y$ *as in Definition 12.17.*

The language *of G is defined as*

$$L(G) = \{w \in \Delta^* \mid S \Rightarrow_G^* w\}.$$

A language $K \subseteq \Delta^*$ *is an n-right-linear simple matrix language (n-RLSML for short) if there is an n-RLSMG G such that* $K = L(G)$.

The family of n-RLSMLs is denoted by $\mathbf{RLSM}_n$. Furthermore, the ith component of an n-RLSMG is defined analogously to the ith component of an n-PRLG (see Definition 12.18).

To prove that the family of languages accepted by n-all-SFAs coincides with the family of languages generated by n-RLSMGs, the following lemma is needed.

Lemma 12.4. *For every n-RLSMG,* $G = (N_1, \ldots, N_n, \Delta, S, R)$, *there is an equivalent n-RLSMG* G' *that satisfies (i)–(iii), given as follows:*

(i) *If* $(S \to X_1 \cdots X_n)$, *then* X_i *does not occur on the right-hand side of any rule,* $1 \le i \le n$;
(ii) *If* $(S \to \alpha), (S \to \beta) \in R$ *and* $\alpha \neq \beta$, *then* $\text{symbols}(\alpha) \cap \text{symbols}(\beta) = \emptyset$;
(iii) *For any two matrices* $m_1, m_2 \in R$, *if* $m_1[i] = m_2[i]$, *for some* $1 \le i \le n$, *then* $m_1 = m_2$.

Proof. The first two conditions can be proved analogously to Lemma 12.1. Suppose that there are matrices m and m' such that $m[i] = m'[i]$, for some $1 \le i \le n$. Let

$$\begin{aligned} m &= (X_1 \to x_1, \ldots, X_n \to x_n), \\ m' &= (Y_1 \to y_1, \ldots, Y_n \to y_n). \end{aligned}$$

Replace these matrices with matrices

$$\begin{aligned} m_1 &= (X_1 \to X_1', \ldots, X_n \to X_n'), \\ m_2 &= (X_1' \to x_1, \ldots, X_n' \to x_n), \\ m_1' &= (Y_1 \to Y_1'', \ldots, Y_n \to Y_n''), \\ m_2' &= (Y_1'' \to y_1, \ldots, Y_n'' \to y_n), \end{aligned}$$

where X_i', Y_i'' are new nonterminals for all i. These new matrices satisfy condition (iii). Repeat this replacement until the resulting grammar satisfies the properties of G' given in this lemma. ∎

Lemma 12.5. *Let G be an n-RLSMG. There is an* $(n-1)$*-all-SFA M such that* $L(G) = L(M)$.

Proof. Without the loss of generality, we assume that $G = (N_1, \ldots, N_n, \Delta, S, R)$ is in the form described in Lemma 12.4. We construct an $(n-1)$-all-SFA

$$M = (Q, \Delta, \Psi, R, q_0, q_t, F, P)$$

where

$$
\begin{aligned}
Q &= \{q_0, \ldots, q_n\} \cup N, N = N_1 \cup \cdots \cup N_n, \{q_0, q_1, \ldots, q_n\} \cap N = \emptyset,\\
F &= \{q_n\},\\
R &= \{q_i \to X_{i+1} \mid (S \to X_1 \cdots X_n) \in R,\ 0 \leq i < n\} \cup\\
&\quad \{X_i w_i \to Y_i \mid (X_1 \to w_1 Y_1, \ldots, X_n \to w_n Y_n) \in R,\ 1 \leq i \leq n\} \cup\\
&\quad \{X_i w_i \to q_i \mid (X_1 \to w_1, \ldots, X_n \to w_n) \in R,\ w_i \in \Delta^*,\ 1 \leq i \leq n\},\\
q_t &= q_1,\\
\Psi &= R,\\
P &= \{(q_i \to X_{i+1}, q_{i+1} \to X_{i+2}) \mid\\
&\qquad (S \to X_1 \cdots X_n) \in R,\ 0 \leq i \leq n-2\} \cup\\
&\quad \{(X_i w_i \to Y_i, X_{i+1} w_{i+1} \to Y_{i+1}) \mid\\
&\qquad (X_1 \to w_1 Y_1, \ldots, X_n \to w_n Y_n) \in R,\ 1 \leq i < n\} \cup\\
&\quad \{(X_i w_i \to q_i, X_{i+1} w_{i+1} \to q_{i+1}) \mid\\
&\qquad (X_1 \to w_1, \ldots, X_n \to w_n) \in R,\ w_i \in \Delta^*,\ 1 \leq i < n\}.
\end{aligned}
$$

Next, we prove that $L(G) = L(M)$. A proof of $L(G) \subseteq L(M)$ can be made by analogy with the proof of the same inclusion of Lemma 12.2, which is left to the reader.

To prove that $L(M) \subseteq L(G)$, consider $w \in L(M)$ and an acceptance of w in M. As in Lemma 12.2, the derivation looks like the one depicted on the right-hand side of Figure 12.3. Next, we describe how G generates w. By Lemma 12.4, there is a matrix

$$(S \to X_1^1 X_1^2 \cdots X_1^n) \in R.$$

Moreover, if $X_j^i x_j^i \to X_{j+1}^i$, $1 \leq i \leq n$, then

$$(X_j^i \to x_j^i X_{j+1}^i, X_j^{i+1} \to x_j^{i+1} X_{j+1}^{i+1}) \in P$$

for $1 \leq i < n$, $1 \leq j < k$. We apply

$$(X_j^1 \to x_j^1 X_{j+1}^1, \ldots, X_j^n \to x_j^n X_{j+1}^n) \in R.$$

If $X_k^i x_k^i \to q_i$, $1 \leq i \leq n$, then

$$(X_k^i \to x_k^i, X_k^{i+1} \to x_k^{i+1}) \in P$$

for $1 \leq i < n$, and we apply

$$(X_k^1 \to x_k^1, \ldots, X_k^n \to x_k^n) \in R.$$

Thus, $w \in L(G)$.

Hence, Lemma 12.5 holds. ■

Lemma 12.6. *Let M be an n-all-SFA. There is an $(n+1)$-RLSMG G such that $L(G) = L(M)$.*

Proof. Let $M = (Q, D, \Psi, R, q_0, q_t, F, P)$. Consider

$$G = (N_0, \ldots, N_n, D, S, R)$$

where

$$\begin{aligned}
N_i &= (QD^l \times Q \times \{i\} \times Q) \cup (Q \times \{i\} \times Q),\\
l &= \max(\{|w| \mid qw \to p \in R\}), 0 \leq i \leq n,\\
R &= \{(S \to [q_0x_0, q^0, 0, q_t][q_tx_1, q^1, 1, q_{i_1}] \cdots [q_{i_{n-1}}x_n, q^n, n, q_{i_n}]) \mid\\
&\qquad r_0\colon q_0x_0 \to q^0, r_1\colon q_tx_1 \to q^1, \ldots, r_n\colon q_{i_{n-1}}x_n \to q^n \in R\\
&\qquad (r_0, r_1), \ldots, (r_{n-1}, r_n) \in P, q_{i_n} \in F\} \cup\\
&\quad \{([p_0x_0, q_0, 0, r_0] \to x_0[q_0, 0, r_0], \ldots,\\
&\qquad [p_nx_n, q_n, n, r_n] \to x_n[q_n, n, r_n])\} \cup\\
&\quad \{([q_0, 0, q_0] \to \varepsilon, \ldots, [q_n, n, q_n] \to \varepsilon) : q_i \in Q, 0 \leq i \leq n\} \cup\\
&\quad \{([q_0, 0, p_0] \to w_0[q'_0, 0, p_0], \ldots, [q_n, n, p_n] \to w_n[q'_n, n, p_n]) \mid\\
&\qquad r_j\colon q_jw_j \to q'_j \in R, 0 \leq j \leq n, (r_i, r_{i+1}) \in P, 0 \leq i < n\}.
\end{aligned}$$

Next, we prove that $L(G) = L(M)$. To prove that $L(G) \subseteq L(M)$, consider a derivation of w in G. Then, the derivation is of the form (12.1) and there are rules

$$r_0\colon q_0x_0^0 \to q_1^0, r_1\colon q_tx_0^1 \to q_1^1, \ldots, r_n\colon q_{i_{n-1}}x_0^n \to q_1^n \in R$$

such that $(r_0, r_1), \ldots, (r_{n-1}, r_n) \in P$. Moreover, $(r_j^l, r_j^{l+1}) \in P$, where $r_j^l\colon q_j^lx_j^l \to q_{j+1}^l \in R$, and $(r_k^l, r_k^{l+1}) \in P$, where $r_k^l\colon q_k^lx_k^l \to q_{i_l} \in R$, $0 \leq l < n$, $1 \leq j < k$, q_{i_0} denotes q_t, and $q_{i_n} \in F$. Thus, M accepts w with the sequence of rules μ of the form (12.2).

To prove that $L(M) \subseteq L(G)$, consider $w \in L(M)$ and an acceptance of w in M. As in Lemma 12.2, the derivation looks like the one depicted on the right-hand side of Figure 12.3. Next, we describe how G generates w. By Lemma 12.4, there is a matrix

$$(S \to X_1^1X_1^2 \cdots X_1^n) \in R.$$

Moreover, if $X_j^ix_j^i \to X_{j+1}^i$, $1 \leq i \leq n$, then

$$(X_j^i \to x_j^iX_{j+1}^i, X_j^{i+1} \to x_j^{i+1}X_{j+1}^{i+1}) \in P$$

for $1 \leq i < n$, $1 \leq j < k$. We apply

$$(X_j^1 \to x_j^1X_{j+1}^1, \ldots, X_j^n \to x_j^nX_{j+1}^n) \in R.$$

If $X_k^ix_k^i \to q_i$, $1 \leq i \leq n$, then

$$(X_k^i \to x_k^i, X_k^{i+1} \to x_k^{i+1}) \in P$$

for $1 \leq i < n$, and we apply

$$(X_k^1 \to x_k^1, \ldots, X_k^n \to x_k^n) \in R.$$

Thus, $w \in L(G)$.

Hence, Lemma 12.6 holds. ■

Next, we establish another important result of this section.

Theorem 12.14. For all $n \geq 0$, $\mathbf{ASFA}_n = \mathbf{RLSM}_{n+1}$.

Proof. This proof follows from Lemmas 12.5 and 12.6. ■

Corollary 12.3. *The following statements hold true.*

(i) $\mathbf{REG} = \mathbf{ASFA}_0 \subset \mathbf{ASFA}_1 \subset \mathbf{ASFA}_2 \subset \cdots \subset \mathbf{CS}$;
(ii) $\mathbf{ASFA}_1 \not\subseteq \mathbf{CF}$;
(iii) $\mathbf{CF} \not\subseteq \mathbf{ASFA}_n$, *for every* $n \geq 0$;
(iv) *For all* $n \geq 0$, $\mathbf{ASFA}_n$ *is closed under union, concatenation, finite substitution, homomorphism, intersection with a regular language, and right quotient with a regular language;*
(v) *For all* $n \geq 1$, $\mathbf{ASFA}_n$ *is not closed under intersection, complement, and Kleene closure.*

Proof. Recall the following statements that are proved in [27].

- $\mathbf{REG} = \mathbf{RLSM}_1 \subset \mathbf{RLSM}_2 \subset \mathbf{RLSM}_3 \subset \cdots \subset \mathbf{CS}$;
- For all $n \geq 1$, $\mathbf{RLSM}_n$ is closed under union, finite substitution, homomorphism, intersection with a regular language, and right quotient with a regular language;
- For all $n \geq 2$, $\mathbf{RLSM}_n$ is not closed under intersection and complement.

Furthermore, recall these statements proved in [31] and [30].

- For all $n \geq 1$, $\mathbf{RLSM}_n$ is closed under concatenation;
- For all $n \geq 2$, $\mathbf{RLSM}_n$ is not closed under Kleene closure.

These statements and Theorem 12.14 imply statements (i), (iv), and (v) of Corollary 12.3. Moreover, observe that

$$\{ww \mid w \in \{a,b\}^*\} \in \mathbf{ASFA}_1 - \mathbf{CF}$$

(see Example 12.8), which proves (ii). Finally, let

$$L = \{wcw^R \mid w \in \{a,b\}^*\}.$$

By Theorem 1.5.2 in [12], $L \notin \mathbf{RLSM}_n$, for any $n \geq 1$. Thus, (iii) follows from Theorem 12.14. ■

The following theorem, Theorem 12.15, follows from Theorem 12.14 and from Corollary 3.3.3 in [30]. However, Corollary 3.3.3 in [30] is not proved effectively. We next prove Theorem 12.15 effectively.

Theorem 12.15. $\mathbf{ASFA}_n$ is closed under inverse homomorphism, for all $n \geq 0$.

Proof. For $n = 1$, let $M = (Q, D, \Psi, R, q_0, q_t, F, P)$ be a 1-all-SFA, and let $h : \Delta^* \to D^*$ be a homomorphism. Next, we construct a 1-all-SFA

$$M' = (Q', \Delta, \Psi, R', q_0', q_t', \{q_f'\}, P')$$

accepting $h^{-1}(L(M))$ as follows. Set

$$k = \max(\{|w| \mid qw \to p \in R\}) + \max(\{|h(a)| \mid a \in \Delta\})$$

and

$$Q' = \{q'_0\} \cup \{[x, q, y] \mid x, y \in D^*, |x|, |y| \leq k, q \in Q\}.$$

Initially, set R' and P' to $\emptyset$. Then, extend R' and P' by performing (1)–(5), given as follows:

(1) For $y \in D^*$, $|y| \leq k$, add
$(q'_0 \rightarrow [\varepsilon, q_0, y], q'_t \rightarrow [y, q_t, \varepsilon])$ to P';
(2) For $A \in Q'$, $q \neq q_t$, add
$([x, q, y]a \rightarrow [xh(a), q, y], A \rightarrow A)$ to P';
(3) For $A \in Q'$, add
$(A \rightarrow A, [x, q, \varepsilon]a \rightarrow [xh(a), q, \varepsilon])$ to P';
(4) For $(qx \rightarrow p, q'x' \rightarrow p') \in P$, $q \neq q_t$, add
$([xw, q, y] \rightarrow [w, p, y], [x'w', q', \varepsilon] \rightarrow [w', p', \varepsilon])$ to P';
(5) For $q_f \in F$, add
$([y, q_t, y] \rightarrow q'_t, [\varepsilon, q_f, \varepsilon] \rightarrow q'_f)$ to P'.

In essence, M' simulates M in the following way. In a state of the form $[x, q, y]$, the three components have the following meaning:

- $x = h(a_1 \cdots a_n)$, where $a_1 \cdots a_n$ is the input string that M' has already read,
- q is the current state of M,
- y is the suffix remaining as the first component of the state that M' enters during a turn; y is thus obtained when M' reads the last symbol right before the turn occurs in M; M reads y after the turn.

More precisely, $h(w) = w_1 y w_2$, where w is an input string, w_1 is accepted by M before making the turn—that is, from q_0 to q_t, and yw_2 is accepted by M after making the turn—that is, from q_t to $q_f \in F$. A rigorous version of this proof is left to the reader.

For $n > 1$, the proof is analogous and left to the reader. ■

12.5.2.4 Language families accepted by *n*-first-SFAs and *n*-all-SFAs

Next, we compare the family of languages accepted by *n*-first-SFAs with the family of languages accepted by *n*-all-SFAs.

Theorem 12.16. For all $n \geq 1$, $\mathbf{FSFA}_n \subset \mathbf{ASFA}_n$.

Proof. In [25] and [27], it is proved that for all $n > 1$, $\mathbf{PRL}_n \subset \mathbf{RLSM}_n$. The proof of Theorem 12.16 thus follows from Theorems 12.12 and 12.14. ■

Theorem 12.17. $\mathbf{FSFA}_n \not\subseteq \mathbf{ASFA}_{n-1}$, $n \geq 1$.

Proof. Recall that $\mathbf{FSFA}_n = \mathbf{PRL}_{n+1}$ (see Theorem 12.12) and $\mathbf{ASFA}_{n-1} = \mathbf{RLSM}_n$ (see Theorem 12.14). It is easy to see that

$$L = \{a_1^k a_2^k \cdots a_{n+1}^k \mid k \geq 1\} \in \mathbf{PRL}_{n+1}.$$

However, Lemma 1.5.6 in [12] implies that

$$L \notin \mathbf{RLSM}_n.$$

Hence, the theorem holds. ■

Lemma 12.7. *For each regular language L,* $\{w^n \mid w \in L\} \in \mathbf{ASFA}_{n-1}$.

Proof. Let $L = L(M)$, where M is a finite automaton. Make n copies of M. Rename their states so all the sets of states are pairwise disjoint. In this way, also rename the states in the rules of each of these n automata; however, keep the labels of the rules unchanged. For each rule label r, include (r, r) into P. As a result, we obtain an n-all-SFA that accepts $\{w^n \mid w \in L\}$. A rigorous version of this proof is left to the reader. ■

Theorem 12.18. $\mathbf{ASFA}_n - \mathbf{FSFA} \neq \emptyset$, for all $n \geq 1$, where $\mathbf{FSFA} = \bigcup_{m=1}^{\infty} \mathbf{FSFA}_m$.

Proof. By induction on $n \geq 1$, we prove that

$$L = \{(cw)^{n+1} \mid w \in \{a,b\}^*\} \notin \mathbf{FSFA}.$$

From Lemma 12.7, it follows that $L \in \mathbf{ASFA}_n$.

Basis. For $n = 1$, let G be an m-PRLG generating L, for some positive integer m. Consider a sufficiently large string $cw_1cw_2 \in L$ such that $w_1 = w_2 = a^{n_1}b^{n_2}$, $n_2 > n_1 > 1$. Then, there is a derivation of the form

$$\begin{aligned} S &\Rightarrow_G^p x_1A_1x_2A_2 \cdots x_mA_m \\ &\Rightarrow_G^k x_1y_1A_1x_2y_2A_2 \cdots x_my_mA_m \end{aligned} \tag{12.3}$$

in G, where cycle (12.3) generates more than one a in w_1. The derivation continues as

$$\begin{aligned} x_1y_1A_1 \cdots x_my_mA_m &\Rightarrow_G^r \\ x_1y_1z_1B_1 \cdots x_my_mz_mB_m &\Rightarrow_G^l x_1y_1z_1u_1B_1 \cdots x_my_mz_mu_mB_m \end{aligned} \tag{12.4}$$

$$\text{(cycle (12.4) generates no } a\text{s)} \Rightarrow_G^s cw_1cw_2.$$

Next, modify the left derivation, the derivation in components generating cw_1, so that the a-generating cycle (12.3) is repeated $(l + 1)$-times. Similarly, modify the right derivation, the derivation in the other components, so that the no-a-generating cycle (12.4) is repeated $(k + 1)$-times. Thus, the modified left derivation is of length

$$p + k(l+1) + r + l + s = p + k + r + l(k+1) + s$$

which is the length of the modified right derivation. Moreover, the modified left derivation generates more as in w_1 than the right derivation in w_2—a contradiction.

Induction Hypothesis. Suppose that the theorem holds for all $k \leq n$, for some $n \geq 1$.

Induction Step. Consider $n + 1$ and let

$$\{(cw)^{n+1} \mid w \in \{a,b\}^*\} \in \mathbf{FSFA}_l$$

for some $l \geq 1$. As $\mathbf{FSFA}_l$ is closed under the right quotient with a regular language, and language $\{cw \mid w \in \{a,b\}^*\}$ is regular, we obtain

$$\{(cw)^n \mid w \in \{a,b\}^*\} \in \mathbf{FSFA}_l \subseteq \mathbf{FSFA},$$

which is a contradiction. ■

12.5.3 Self-regulating pushdown automata

We will now define n-turn first-move SPDAs (n-first-SPDAs) and n-turn all-move SPDAs (n-all-SPDAs). Afterwards, we will determine the accepting power of n-all-SPDAs.

12.5.3.1 Definitions

Definition 12.20. *An* SPDA M *is a ten-tuple*

$$M = (Q, D, \Gamma, \Psi R, q_0, q_t, Z_0, F, P)$$

where

(i) $(Q, D, \Gamma, R, \ q_0, Z_0, F)$ *is a pushdown automaton entering a final state and emptying its pushdown,*
(ii) Ψ *is an alphabet of* labels *such that* card Ψ = card R, *and each rule* $x \to y \in R$ *is denoted by a unique label* $l \in R$, *symbolically written as* $l : x \to y$, *referred to as the* rule labeled by l *or, briefly,* rule l,
(iii) $q_t \in Q$ *is a* turn state, *and*
(iv) $P \subseteq \Psi \times \Psi$ *is a finite relation on the alphabet of rule labels.*

Definition 12.21. *Let* $n \geq 0$ *and*

$$M = (Q, D, \Gamma, \Psi, R, q_0, q_t, Z_0, F, P)$$

be an SPDA. M is said to be an n-first-SPDA if every $w \in L(M)$ *is accepted by M in the following way*

$$Z_0 q_0 w \vdash_M^* f\ [\mu]$$

such that

$$\mu = r_1^0 \cdots r_k^0 r_1^1 \cdots r_k^1 \cdots r_1^n \cdots r_k^n$$

where $k \geq 1$, r_k^0 *is the first rule of the form* $Zqx \to \gamma q_t$, *for some* $Z \in \Gamma$, $q \in Q$, $x \in D^*$, $\gamma \in \Gamma^*$, *and*

$$(r_1^j, r_1^{j+1}) \in P$$

for all $0 \leq j < n$.

The family of languages accepted by n-first-SPDAs is denoted by $\mathbf{FSPDA}_n$.

Definition 12.22. *Let* $n \geq 0$ *and*

$$M = (Q, D, \Gamma, \Psi, R, q_0, q_t, Z_0, F, P)$$

be an SPDA. M is said to be an n-all-SPDA if every $w \in L(M)$ *is accepted by M in the following way:*

$$Z_0 q_0 w \vdash_M^* f\ [\mu]$$

such that

$$\mu = r_1^0 \cdots r_k^0 r_1^1 \cdots r_k^1 \cdots r_1^n \cdots r_k^n$$

where $k \geq 1$, r_k^0 *is the first rule of the form* $Zqx \rightarrow \gamma q_t$, *for some* $Z \in \Gamma$, $q \in Q$, $x \in D^*$, $\gamma \in \Gamma^*$, *and*

$$(r_i^j, r_i^{j+1}) \in P$$

for all $1 \leq i \leq k$, $0 \leq j < n$.

The family of languages accepted by n-all-SPDAs is denoted by $\mathbf{ASPDA}_n$.

12.5.3.2 Accepting power

In this section, we investigate the accepting power of SPDAs.

As every n-first-SPDA and every n-all-SPDA without any turn state represents, in effect, an ordinary pushdown automaton, we obtain the following theorem:

Theorem 12.19. $\mathbf{FSPDA}_0 = \mathbf{ASPDA}_0 = \mathbf{CF}$.

However, if we consider 1-all-SPDAs, their power is that of phrase-structure grammars.

Theorem 12.20. $\mathbf{ASPDA}_1 = \mathbf{RE}$.

Proof. For any $L \in \mathbf{RE}$, $L \subseteq \Delta^*$, there are context-free grammars G and H and a homomorphism $h : D^* \rightarrow \Delta^*$ such that

$$L = h(L(G) \cap L(H))$$

(see Theorem 10.3.1 in [22]). Suppose that $G = (\Sigma_G, D, R_G, S_G)$ and $H = (\Sigma_H, D, R_H, S_H)$ are in the Greibach normal form (see Definition 11.7)—that is, all rules are of the form $A \rightarrow a\alpha$, where A is a nonterminal, a is a terminal, and α is a (possibly empty) string of nonterminals. Also let $N_G = \Sigma_G - D$ and $N_H = \Sigma_H - D$. Let us construct a 1-all-SPDA

$$M = (\{q_0, q, q_t, p, f\}, \Delta, D \cup N_G \cup N_H \cup \{Z\}, \Psi, R, q_0, Z, \{f\}, P)$$

where $Z \notin D \cup N_G \cup N_H$, with P constructed by performing (1)–(4), stated as follows:

(1) Add $(Zq_0 \rightarrow ZS_Gq, Zq_t \rightarrow ZS_Hp)$ to P;
(2) Add $(Aq \rightarrow B_n \cdots B_1aq, Cp \rightarrow D_m \cdots D_1ap)$ to P if
    $A \rightarrow aB_1 \cdots B_n \in R_G$ and
    $C \rightarrow aD_1 \cdots D_m \in R_H$;
(3) Add $(aqh(a) \rightarrow q, ap \rightarrow p)$ to P;
(4) Add $(Zq \rightarrow Zq_t, Zp \rightarrow f)$ to P.

Moreover, R contains only the rules from the definition of P.

Next, we prove that $w \in h(L(G) \cap L(H))$ if and only if $w \in L(M)$.

Only If. Let $w \in h(L(G) \cap L(H))$. There are $a_1, a_2, \ldots, a_n \in D$ such that

$$a_1a_2 \cdots a_n \in L(G) \cap L(H)$$

and $w = h(a_1a_2 \cdots a_n)$, for some $n \geq 0$. There are leftmost derivations

$$S_G \Rightarrow_G^n a_1a_2 \cdots a_n$$

and

$$S_H \Rightarrow_H^n a_1 a_2 \cdots a_n$$

of length n in G and H, respectively, because in every derivation step, exactly one terminal element is derived. Thus, M accepts $h(a_1)h(a_2)\cdots h(a_n)$ as

$$\begin{aligned}
&Zq_0 h(a_1)h(a_2)\cdots h(a_n)\\
\vdash_M\ & ZS_G q h(a_1)h(a_2)\cdots h(a_n)\\
&\vdots\\
\vdash_M\ & Za_n q h(a_n)\\
\vdash_M\ & Zq\\
\vdash_M\ & Zq_t\\
\vdash_M\ & ZS_H p\\
&\vdots\\
\vdash_M\ & Za_n p\\
\vdash_M\ & Zp\\
\vdash_M\ & f.
\end{aligned}$$

In state q, by using its pushdown, M simulates a derivation of $a_1 \cdots a_n$ in G but reads $h(a_1)\cdots h(a_n)$ as the input. In p, M simulates a derivation of $a_1 a_2 \cdots a_n$ in H but reads no input. As $a_1 a_2 \cdots a_n$ can be derived in both G and H by making the same number of steps, the automaton can successfully complete the acceptance of w.

If. Notice that in one step, M can read only $h(a) \in \Delta^*$, for some $a \in D$. Let $w \in L(M)$, then $w = h(a_1)h(a_2)\cdots h(a_n)$, for some $a_1, a_2, \ldots, a_n \in D$. Consider the following acceptance of w in M:

$$\begin{aligned}
&Zq_0 h(a_1)h(a_2)\cdots h(a_n)\\
\vdash_M\ & ZS_G q h(a_1)h(a_2)\cdots h(a_n)\\
&\vdots\\
\vdash_M\ & Za_n q h(a_n)\\
\vdash_M\ & Zq\\
\vdash_M\ & Zq_t\\
\vdash_M\ & ZS_H p\\
&\vdots\\
\vdash_M\ & Za_n p\\
\vdash_M\ & Zp\\
\vdash_M\ & f.
\end{aligned}$$

As stated above, in q, M simulates a derivation of $a_1 a_2 \cdots a_n$ in G, and then in p, M simulates a derivation of $a_1 a_2 \cdots a_n$ in H. It successfully completes the acceptance of w only if $a_1 a_2 \cdots a_n$ can be derived in both G and H. Hence, the if part holds, too. ∎

12.5.4 Open problems

Although the fundamental results about self-regulating automata have been achieved in this section, there still remain several open problems concerning them.

Open Problem 12.3. *What is the language family accepted by n-first-SPDAs, when $n \geq 1$ (see Definition 12.21)?*

Open Problem 12.4. *By analogy with the standard deterministic finite and pushdown automata (see Chapters 5 and 7, respectively), introduce the deterministic versions of self-regulating automata. What is their power?*

Open Problem 12.5. *Discuss the closure properties of other language operations, such as the reversal.*

12.5.5 Regulated acceptance with control languages

This section discusses automata in which the application of rules is regulated by control languages by analogy with context-free grammars regulated by control languages (see Section 12.2). The topic is first studied in terms of finite automata and afterwards in terms of pushdown automata. More precisely, this section discusses finite automata working under two kinds of regulation—*state-controlled regulation* and *transition-controlled regulation*. It establishes conditions under which any state-controlled finite automaton (SCFA) can be turned to an equivalent transition-controlled finite automaton (TCFA) and vice versa. Then, it proves that under either of the two regulations, finite automata controlled by regular languages characterize the family of regular languages, and an analogical result is then reformulated in terms of context-free languages. However, this section also demonstrates that finite automata controlled by languages generated by propagating programmed grammars with appearance checking increase their power significantly; in fact, they are computationally complete. Afterwards, this section shows that pushdown automata regulated by regular languages are as powerful as ordinary pushdown automata. Then, however, it proves that pushdown automata regulated by linear languages characterize the family of recursively enumerable languages; in fact, this characterization holds even in terms of one-turn pushdown automata.

12.5.6 Finite automata regulated by control languages

The present section studies finite automata regulated by control languages. In fact, it studies two kinds of this regulation—*state-controlled regulation* and *transition-controlled regulation*. To give an insight into these two types of regulation, consider a finite automaton M controlled by a language C, and a sequence $\tau \in C$ that resulted into the acceptance of an input word w. Working under the former regulation, M has C defined over the set of states, and it accepts w by going through all the states in τ and ending up in a final state. Working under the latter regulation, M has C defined over the set of transitions, and it accepts w by using all the transitions in τ and ending up in a final state.

First, we define these two types of controlled finite automata formally. After that, we establish conditions under which it is possible to convert any SCFA to an equivalent TCFA and vice versa (Theorem 12.21). Then, we prove that under both regulations, finite automata controlled by regular languages characterize the family of regular languages (Theorem 12.22 and Corollary 12.4). Finally, we show that finite automata controlled by context-free languages characterize the family of context-free languages (Theorem 12.23 and Corollary 12.5).

After that, we demonstrate a close relation of controlled finite automata to programmed grammars with appearance checking (see Section 12.4). Recall that programmed grammars with appearance checking are computationally complete—that is, they are as powerful as phrase-structure grammars; the language family generated by propagating programmed grammars with appearance checking is properly included in the family of context-sensitive languages (see Theorems 12.2, 12.3, and 12.10). This section proves that finite automata that are controlled by languages generated by propagating programmed grammars with appearance checking are computationally complete (Theorem 12.24 and Corollary 12.6). More precisely, SCFAs are computationally complete with $n + 1$ states, where n is the number of symbols in the accepted language (Corollary 12.7). TCFAs are computationally complete with a single state (Theorem 12.25).

12.5.6.1 Definitions

We begin by defining state-controlled and TCFAs formally.

Definition 12.23. *Let $M = (Q, D, R, s, F)$ be a finite automaton. Based on $\vdash_M$, we define a relation $\triangleright_M$ over $QD^* \times Q^*$ as follows: if $\alpha \in Q^*$ and $pax \vdash_M qx$, where $p, q \in Q$, $x \in D^*$, and $a \in D \cup \{\varepsilon\}$, then*

$$(pax, \alpha) \triangleright_M (qx, \alpha p).$$

Let $\triangleright_M^n$, $\triangleright_M^*$, and $\triangleright_M^+$ denote the nth power of $\triangleright_M$, for some $n \geq 0$, the reflexive-transitive closure of $\triangleright_M$, and the transitive closure of $\triangleright_M$, respectively.

Let $C \subseteq Q^*$ be a control language. *The* state-controlled language of M with respect to C *is denoted by ${}_\triangleright L(M, C)$ and defined as*

$${}_\triangleright L(M, C) = \{w \in D^* \mid (sw, \varepsilon) \triangleright_M^* (f, \alpha), f \in F, \alpha \in C\}.$$

The pair (M, C) is called an SCFA.

Definition 12.24. *Let $M = (Q, D, \Psi, R, s, F)$ be a finite automaton. Based on $\vdash_M$, we define a relation $\blacktriangleright_M$ over $QD^* \times \Psi^*$ as follows: if $\beta \in \Psi^*$ and $pax \vdash_M qx\ [r]$, where $r: pa \rightarrow q \in R$ and $x \in D^*$, then*

$$(pax, \beta) \blacktriangleright_M (qx, \beta r).$$

Let $\blacktriangleright_M^n$, $\blacktriangleright_M^*$, and $\blacktriangleright_M^+$ denote the nth power of $\blacktriangleright_M$, for some $n \geq 0$, the reflexive-transitive closure of $\blacktriangleright_M$, and the transitive closure of $\blacktriangleright_M$, respectively.

Let $C \subseteq \Psi^*$ be a control language. *The* transition-controlled language of M with respect to C *is denoted by ${}_\blacktriangleright L(M, C)$ and defined as*

$${}_\blacktriangleright L(M, C) = \{w \in D^* \mid (sw, \varepsilon) \blacktriangleright_M^* (f, \beta), f \in F, \beta \in C\}.$$

The pair (M, C) *is called an* TCFA.

For any family of languages $\mathscr{L}$, **SCFA(**$\mathscr{L}$**)** and **TCFA(**$\mathscr{L}$**)** denote the language families defined by state-controlled finite automata controlled by languages from $\mathscr{L}$ and transition-controlled finite automata controlled by languages from $\mathscr{L}$, respectively.

12.5.6.2 Conversions

First, we show that under certain circumstances, it is possible to convert any SCFA to an equivalent TCFA and vice versa. These conversions will be helpful to prove that

$$\mathbf{SCFA}(\mathscr{L}) = \mathbf{TCFA}(\mathscr{L}) = \mathscr{J},$$

where $\mathscr{L}$ satisfies the required conditions, we only have to prove that either

$$\mathbf{SCFA}(\mathscr{L}) = \mathscr{J}$$

or

$$\mathbf{TCFA}(\mathscr{L}) = \mathscr{J}.$$

Lemma 12.8. *Let* $\mathscr{L}$ *be a language family that is closed under finite* ε*-free substitution. Then,* **SCFA(**$\mathscr{L}$**)** $\subseteq$ **TCFA(**$\mathscr{L}$**)**.

Proof. Let $\mathscr{L}$ be a language family that is closed under finite ε-free substitution, $M = (Q, D, R, s, F)$ be a finite automaton, and $C \in \mathscr{L}$ be a control language. Without any loss of generality, assume that $C \subseteq Q^*$. We next construct a finite automaton M' and a language $C' \in \mathscr{L}$ such that ${}_{\triangleright}L(M, C) = {}_{\blacktriangleright}L(M', C')$. Define

$$M' = (Q, D, \Psi, R', s, F)$$

where

$$\begin{aligned} \Psi &= \{\langle p, a, q\rangle \mid pa \rightarrow q \in R\}, \\ R' &= \{\langle p, a, q\rangle : pa \rightarrow q \mid pa \rightarrow q \in R\}. \end{aligned}$$

Define the finite ε-free substitution π from Q^* to Ψ^* as

$$\pi(p) = \{\langle p, a, q\rangle \mid pa \rightarrow q \in R\}.$$

Let $C' = \pi(C)$. Since $\mathscr{L}$ is closed under finite ε-free substitution, $C' \in \mathscr{L}$. Observe that $(sw, \varepsilon) \triangleright^n_M (f, \alpha)$, where $w \in D^*$, $f \in F$, $\alpha \in C$, and $n \geq 0$, if and only if $(sw, \varepsilon) \blacktriangleright^n_{M'} (f, \beta)$, where $\beta \in \pi(\alpha)$. Hence, ${}_{\triangleright}L(M, C) = {}_{\blacktriangleright}L(M', C')$, so the lemma holds. ∎

Lemma 12.9. *Let* $\mathscr{L}$ *be a language family that contains all finite languages and is closed under concatenation. Then,* **TCFA(**$\mathscr{L}$**)** $\subseteq$ **SCFA(**$\mathscr{L}$**)**.

Proof. Let $\mathscr{L}$ be a language family that contains all finite languages and is closed under concatenation, $M = (Q, D, \Psi, R, s, F)$ be a finite automaton, and $C \in \mathscr{L}$ be a control language. Without any loss of generality, assume that $C \subseteq \Psi^*$. We next construct a finite automaton M' and a language $C' \in \mathscr{L}$ such that ${}_\blacktriangleright L(M, C) = {}_\triangleright L(M', C')$. Define

$$M' = (Q', D, R', s', F')$$

where

$$\begin{aligned} Q' &= \Psi \cup \{s', \ell\} \quad (s', \ell \notin \Psi), \\ R' &= \{s' \to r \mid r \colon sa \to q \in R\} \cup \\ &\quad\ \{ra \to t \mid r \colon pa \to q, t \colon qb \to m \in R\} \cup \\ &\quad\ \{ra \to \ell \mid r \colon pa \to q \in R, q \in F\}, \\ F' &= \{r \mid r \colon pa \to q \in R, p \in F\} \cup \{\ell\}. \end{aligned}$$

Finally, if $s \in F$, add s' to F'. Set $C' = \{s', \varepsilon\}C$. Since $\mathscr{L}$ is closed under concatenation and contains all finite languages, $C' \in \mathscr{L}$. Next, we prove that ${}_\blacktriangleright L(M, C) = {}_\triangleright L(M', C')$. First, notice that $s \in F$ if and only if $s' \in F$. Hence, by the definition of C', it is sufficient to consider nonempty sequences of moves of both M and M'. Indeed, $(s, \varepsilon) \blacktriangleright_M^0 (s, \varepsilon)$ with $s \in F$ and $\varepsilon \in C$ if and only if $(s', \varepsilon) \triangleright_{M'}^0 (s', \varepsilon)$ with $s' \in F$ and $\varepsilon \in C'$. Observe that

$$(sw, \varepsilon) \blacktriangleright_M (p_1w_1, r_1) \blacktriangleright_M (p_2w_2, r_1r_2) \blacktriangleright_M \cdots \blacktriangleright_M (p_nw_n, r_1r_2 \cdots r_n)$$

by

$$\begin{aligned} r_1 \colon \ & p_0a_1 \to p_1, \\ r_2 \colon \ & p_1a_2 \to p_2, \\ & \quad \vdots \\ r_n \colon \ & p_{n-1}a_n \to p_n, \end{aligned}$$

where $w \in D^*$, $p_i \in Q$ for $i = 1, 2, \ldots, n$, $p_n \in F$, $w_i \in D^*$ for $i = 1, 2, \ldots, n$, $a_i \in D \cup \{\varepsilon\}$ for $i = 1, 2, \ldots n$, and $n \geq 1$ if and only if

$$(s'w, \varepsilon) \triangleright_{M'} (r_1w, s') \triangleright_{M'} (r_2w_1, s'r_1) \triangleright_{M'} \cdots \triangleright_{M'} (r_{n+1}w_n, s'r_1r_2 \cdots r_n)$$

by

$$\begin{aligned} s' &\to r_1, \\ r_1a_1 &\to r_2, \\ r_2a_2 &\to r_3, \\ &\ \ \vdots \\ r_na_n &\to r_{n+1}, \end{aligned}$$

with $r_{n+1} \in F'$ (recall that $p_n \in F$). Hence, ${}_\blacktriangleright L(M, C) = {}_\triangleright L(M', C')$ and the lemma holds. ∎

Theorem 12.21. Let $\mathscr{L}$ be a language family that is closed under finite ε-free substitution, contains all finite languages, and is closed under concatenation. Then, $\mathbf{SCFA}(\mathscr{L}) = \mathbf{TCFA}(\mathscr{L})$.

Proof. This theorem follows directly from Lemmas 12.8 and 12.9. ■

12.5.6.3 Regular-controlled finite automata

Initially, we consider finite automata controlled by regular control languages.

Lemma 12.10. SCFA(REG) ⊆ REG.

Proof. Let $M = (Q, D, R, s, F)$ be a finite automaton and $C \subseteq Q^*$ be a regular control language. Since C is regular, there is a complete finite automaton $H = (\hat{Q}, Q, \hat{R}, \hat{s}, \hat{F})$ such that $L(H) = C$. We next construct a finite automaton M' such that $L(M') = {}_{\triangleright}L(M, L(H))$. Define

$$M' = (Q', D, R', s', F')$$

where

$$\begin{aligned} Q' &= \{\langle p, q\rangle \mid p \in Q, q \in \hat{Q}\},\\ R' &= \{\langle p, r\rangle a \rightarrow \langle q, t\rangle \mid pa \rightarrow q \in R, rp \rightarrow t \in \hat{R}\},\\ s' &= \langle s, \hat{s}\rangle,\\ F' &= \{\langle p, q\rangle \mid p \in F, q \in \hat{F}\}. \end{aligned}$$

Observe that a move in M' by $\langle p, r\rangle a \rightarrow \langle q, t\rangle \in R'$ simultaneously simulates a move in M by $pa \rightarrow q \in R$ and a move in H by $rp \rightarrow t \in \hat{R}$. Based on this observation, it is rather easy to see that M' accepts an input string $w \in D^*$ if and only if M reads w and enters a final state after going through a sequence of states from $L(H)$. Therefore, $L(M') = {}_{\triangleright}L(M, L(H))$. A rigorous proof of the identity $L(M') = {}_{\triangleright}L(M, L(H))$ is left to the reader. ■

The following theorem shows that finite automata controlled by regular languages are of little or no interest because they are as powerful as ordinary finite automata.

Theorem 12.22. SCFA(REG) = REG.

Proof. The inclusion **REG ⊆ SCFA(REG)** is obvious. The converse inclusion follows from Lemma 12.10. ■

Combining Theorems 12.21 and 12.22, we obtain the following corollary (recall that **REG** satisfies all the conditions from Theorem 12.21).

Corollary 12.4. TCFA(REG) = REG.

12.5.6.4 Context-free-controlled finite automata

Next, we consider finite automata controlled by context-free control languages.

Lemma 12.11. SCFA(CF) ⊆ CF.

Proof. Let $M = (Q, D, R, s, F)$ be a finite automaton and $C \subseteq Q^*$ be a context-free control language. Since C is context free, there is a pushdown automaton $H = (\hat{Q}, Q, \Gamma, \hat{R}, \hat{s}, \hat{Z}, \hat{F})$ such that $L(H) = C$. Without any loss of generality, we assume that $bpa \to wq \in \hat{R}$ implies that $a \neq \varepsilon$ (see Lemma 5.2.1 in [32]). We next construct a pushdown automaton M' such that $L(M') = {}_{\triangleright}L(M, L(H))$. Define

$$M' = (Q', D, \Gamma, R', s', Z, F')$$

where

$$\begin{aligned} Q' &= \{\langle p, q\rangle \mid p \in Q, q \in \hat{Q}\}, \\ R' &= \{b\langle p, r\rangle a \to w\langle q, t\rangle \mid pa \to q \in R, bpr \to wt \in \hat{R}\}, \\ s' &= \langle s, \hat{s}\rangle, \\ F' &= \{\langle p, q\rangle \mid p \in F, q \in \hat{F}\}. \end{aligned}$$

By a similar reasoning as in Lemma 12.10, we can prove that $L(M') = {}_{\triangleright}L(M, L(H))$. A rigorous proof of the identity $L(M') = {}_{\triangleright}L(M, L(H))$ is left to the reader. ■

The following theorem says that even though finite automata controlled by context-free languages are more powerful than finite automata, they cannot accept any non-context-free language.

Theorem 12.23. SCFA(CF) = CF.

Proof. The inclusion **CF** ⊆ **SCFA(CF)** is obvious. The converse inclusion follows from Lemma 12.11. ■

Combining Theorems 12.21 and 12.23, we obtain the following corollary (recall that **CF** satisfies all the conditions from Theorem 12.21).

Corollary 12.5. TCFA(CF) = CF.

12.5.6.5 Program-controlled finite automata

In this section, we show that there is a language family, strictly included in the family of context-sensitive languages, which significantly increases the power of finite automata. Indeed, finite automata controlled by languages generated by propagating programmed grammars with appearance checking have the same power as phrase-structure grammars. This result is of some interest because $\mathbf{P}_{ac}^{-\varepsilon} \subset \mathbf{CS}$ (see Theorem 12.10).

More specifically, we show how to algorithmically convert any programmed grammar with appearance checking G to a finite automaton M and a propagating programmed grammar with appearance checking G' such that ${}_{\triangleright}L(M, L(G')) = L(G)$. First, we give an insight into Algorithm 12.1, which performs this conversion.

Let $\Delta = \text{symbols}(L(G))$ and let $s \notin \Delta$ be a new symbol. From G, we construct the propagating programmed grammar with appearance checking G' such that $w \in L(G)$ if and only if $sws^k \in L(G')$, where $k \geq 1$. Then, the set of states of M will be $\Delta \cup \{s\}$, where s is the starting and also the only final state. For every $a, b \in \Delta$, we introduce

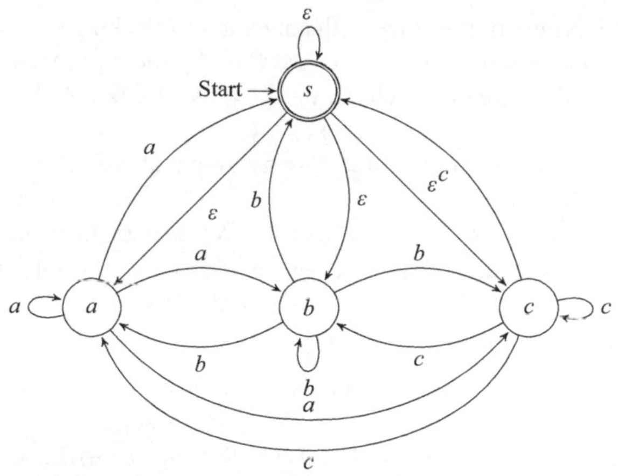

Figure 12.4 Example of a finite automaton constructed by Algorithm 12.1

$aa \to b$ to M. For every $a \in \Delta$, we introduce $s \to a$ and $aa \to s$. Finally, we add $s \to s$. An example of such a finite automaton when $\Delta = \{a, b, c\}$ can be seen in Figure 12.4. The key idea is that when M is in a state $a \in \Delta$, in the next move, it has to read a. Hence, with $sws^k \in L(G')$, M moves from s to a state in Δ, then reads every symbol in w, ends up in s, and uses k times the rule $s \to s$.

G' works in the following way. Every intermediate sentential form is of the form xvZ, where x is a string of symbols that are not erased in the rest of the derivation, v is a string of nonterminals that are erased in the rest of the derivation, and Z is a nonterminal. When simulating a rule of G, G' nondeterministically selects symbols that are erased, appends them using Z to the end of the currently generated string, and replaces an occurrence of the left-hand side of the original rule with the not-to-be-erased symbols from the right-hand side. To differentiate the symbols in x and v, v contains barred versions of the nonterminals. If G' makes an improper nondeterministic selection—that is, the selection does not correspond to a derivation in G—then G' is not able to generate a terminal string as explained in the notes following the algorithm.

Before proving that this algorithm is correct, we make some informal comments concerning the purpose of the rules of G'. The rules introduced in (1) are used to simulate an application of a rule where some of the symbols on its right-hand side are erased in the rest of the derivation, while some others are not erased. The rules introduced in (2) are used to simulate an application of a rule which erases a nonterminal by making one or more derivation steps. The rules introduced in (3) are used to simulate an application of a rule in the appearance checking mode. Observe that when simulating $(r\colon A \to y, \sigma_r, \rho_r) \in R$ in the appearance checking mode, we have to check the absence of both A and $\bar{A}$. If some of these two nonterminals appear in

Algorithm 12.1:

Input: A programmed grammar with appearance checking $G = (N, \Delta, \Psi, R, S)$.

Output: A finite automaton $M = (Q, \Delta, R, s, F)$ and a propagating programmed grammar with appearance checking $G' = (N', Q, \Psi', R', S')$ such that ${}_{\triangleright}L(M, L(G')) = L(G)$.

Note: Without any loss of generality, we assume that $s, S', Z, \# \notin (Q \cup N \cup \Delta)$ and $\ell_0, \bar{\ell}_0, \ell_s \notin \Psi$.

Method: Set $\Sigma = N \cup \Delta$ and $\bar{N} = \{\bar{A} \mid A \in N\}$. Define the function τ from N^* to $\bar{N}^* \cup \{\ell_s\}$ as $\tau(\varepsilon) = \ell_s$ and $\tau(A_1A_2 \cdots A_m) = \bar{A}_1\bar{A}_2 \cdots \bar{A}_m$, where $A_i \in N$ for $i = 1, 2, \dots, m$, for some $m \geq 1$. Initially, set

$$\begin{aligned}
Q &= \Delta \cup \{s\}, \qquad F = \{s\},\\
R &= \{s \rightarrow s\} \cup \{s \rightarrow a \mid a \in \Delta\} \cup \{aa \rightarrow b \mid a \in \Delta, b \in \Delta \cup \{s\}\},\\
N' &= N \cup \bar{N} \cup \{S', Z\}, \qquad \Psi' = \{\ell_0, \bar{\ell}_0, \ell_s\},\\
R' &= \{(\ell_0 \colon S' \rightarrow sSZ, \{r \mid (r \colon S \rightarrow x, \sigma_r, \rho_r) \in R, x \in \Sigma^*\}, \emptyset)\} \cup\\
&\quad\ \{(\bar{\ell}_0 \colon S' \rightarrow s\bar{S}Z, \{r \mid (r \colon S \rightarrow x, \sigma_r, \rho_r) \in R, x \in \Sigma^*\}, \emptyset)\} \cup\\
&\quad\ \{(\ell_s \colon Z \rightarrow s, \{\ell_s\}, \emptyset)\}.
\end{aligned}$$

Repeat (1)–(3), given next, until none of the sets Ψ' and R' can be extended in this way.

(1) **If** $(r \colon A \rightarrow y_0Y_1y_1Y_2y_2 \cdots Y_my_m, \sigma_r, \rho_r) \in R$, where $y_i \in \Sigma^*$, $Y_j \in N$, for $i = 0, 1, \dots, m$ and $j = 1, 2, \dots, m$, for some $m \geq 1$

then

(1.1) add $\ell = \langle r, y_0, Y_1y_1, Y_2y_2, \dots, Y_my_m \rangle$ to Ψ';

(1.2) add ℓ' to Ψ', where ℓ' is a new unique label;

(1.3) add $(\ell \colon A \rightarrow y_0y_1 \cdots y_m, \{\ell'\}, \emptyset)$ to R';

(1.4) add $(\ell' \colon Z \rightarrow \bar{y}Z, \sigma_r, \emptyset)$, where $\bar{y} = \tau(Y_1Y_2 \cdots Y_m)$ to R';

(2) **If** $(r \colon A \rightarrow y, \sigma_r, \rho_r) \in R$, where $y \in N^*$

then

(2.1) add $\bar{r}$ to Ψ', where $\bar{r}$ is a new unique label;

(2.2) add $(\bar{r} \colon \bar{A} \rightarrow \bar{y}, \sigma_r, \emptyset)$ to R', where $\bar{y} = \tau(y)$;

(3) **If** $(r \colon A \rightarrow y, \sigma_r, \rho_r) \in R$, where $y \in \Sigma^*$,

then

(3.1) add $\hat{r}$ to Ψ', where $\hat{r}$ is a new unique label;

(3.2) add $\hat{r}'$ to Ψ', where $\hat{r}'$ is a new unique label;

(3.3) add $(\hat{r} \colon A \rightarrow \#y, \emptyset, \{\hat{r}'\})$ to R';

(3.4) add $(\hat{r}' \colon \bar{A} \rightarrow \#y, \emptyset, \rho_r)$ to R'.

Finally, for every $t \in \Psi$, let Ψ'_t denote the set of rule labels introduced in steps (1.1), (2.2), and (3.3) from a rule labeled with t.

Replace every $(\ell' \colon Z \rightarrow \bar{y}Z, \sigma_r, \emptyset)$ from (1.1) satisfying $\sigma_r \neq \emptyset$ with

$$(\ell' \colon Z \rightarrow \bar{y}Z, \sigma'_r \cup \{\ell_s\}, \emptyset) \text{ where } \sigma'_r = \textstyle\bigcup_{t \in \sigma_r} \Psi'_t.$$

Replace every $(\bar{r} \colon \bar{A} \rightarrow \bar{y}, \sigma_r, \emptyset)$ from (2.2) satisfying $\sigma_r \neq \emptyset$ with

$$(\bar{r} \colon \bar{A} \rightarrow \bar{y}, \sigma'_r \cup \{\ell_s\}, \emptyset) \text{ where } \sigma'_r = \textstyle\bigcup_{t \in \sigma_r} \Psi'_t.$$

Replace every $(\hat{r}' \colon \bar{A} \rightarrow \#y, \emptyset, \rho_r)$ from (3.3) satisfying $\rho_r \neq \emptyset$ with

$$(\hat{r}' \colon \bar{A} \rightarrow \#y, \emptyset, \rho'_r \cup \{\ell_s\}) \text{ where } \rho'_r = \textstyle\bigcup_{t \in \rho_r} \Psi'_t.$$

the current configuration, the derivation is blocked because rules from (3) have empty success fields. Finally, notice that the final part of the algorithm ensures that after a rule $t \in R$ is applied, ℓ_s or any of the rules introduced in (1.1), (2.2), or (3.3) from rules in σ_t or ρ_t can be applied.

Reconsider (1). Notice that the algorithm works correctly although it makes no predetermination of nonterminals from which ε can be derived. Indeed, if the output grammar improperly selects a nonterminal that is not erased throughout the rest of the derivation, this occurrence of the nonterminal never disappears, so a terminal string cannot be generated under this improper selection.

We next prove that Algorithm 12.1 is correct.

Lemma 12.12. *Algorithm 12.1 converts any programmed grammar with appearance checking $G = (N, \Delta, \Psi, R, S)$ to a finite automaton $M = (Q, \Delta, R, s, F)$ and a propagating programmed grammar with appearance checking $G' = (N', Q, \Psi', R', S')$ such that ${}_{\triangleright}L(M, L(G')) = L(G)$.*

Proof. Clearly, the algorithm always halts. Consider the construction of G'. Observe that every string in $L(G')$ is of the form sws^k, where $k \geq 1$. From the construction of M, it is easy to see that $w \in {}_{\triangleright}L(M, L(G'))$ for $w \in \Delta^*$ if and only if $sws^k \in L(G')$ for some $k \geq 1$. Therefore, to prove that ${}_{\triangleright}L(M, L(G')) = L(G)$, it is sufficient to prove that $w \in L(G)$ for $w \in \Delta^*$ if and only if $sws^k \in L(G')$ for some $k \geq 1$.

We establish this equivalence by proving two claims. First, we prove that $w \in L(G)$ for $w \in \Delta^+$ if and only if $sws^k \in L(G')$ for some $k \geq 1$. Then, we show that $\varepsilon \in L(G)$ if and only if $\varepsilon \in L(G')$.

In what follows, we denote a string w which is to be erased as ${}^{\varepsilon}w$; otherwise, to denote that w is not to be erased, we write ${}^{\not\varepsilon}w$.

The next claim shows how G' simulates G.

Claim 1. *If $(S, t_1) \Rightarrow_G^m ({}^{\not\varepsilon}x_0 {}^{\varepsilon}X_1 {}^{\not\varepsilon}x_1 {}^{\varepsilon}X_2 {}^{\not\varepsilon}x_2 \cdots {}^{\varepsilon}X_h {}^{\not\varepsilon}x_h, t_2) \Rightarrow_G^* (z, t_3)$, where $z \in \Delta^+$, t_1, t_2, $t_3 \in \Psi$, $x_i \in \Sigma^*$ for $i = 0, 1, \ldots, h$, $X_j \in N$ for $j = 1, 2, \ldots, h$, for some $h \geq 0$ and $m \geq 0$, then $(S', \ell_0) \Rightarrow_{G'}^* (sx_0x_1x_2 \cdots x_h vZ, t_2')$, where $v \in \mathrm{perm}(\tau(X_1X_2 \cdots X_h)\xi)$, $\xi \in \{s\}^*$, and t_2' can be ℓ_s or any rule constructed from t_2 in (1.1), (2.2), or (3.3).*

Proof. This claim is established by induction on $m \geq 0$.

Basis. Let $m = 0$. Then, for $(S, t_1) \Rightarrow_G^0 (S, t_1) \Rightarrow_G^* (z, t_2)$, there is $(S', \ell_0) \Rightarrow_{G'} (sSZ, t_1')$, where t_1' can be ℓ_s or any rule constructed from t_1 in (1.1), (2.2), or (3.3). Hence, the basis holds.

Induction Hypothesis. Suppose that there exists $n \geq 0$ such that the claim holds for all derivations of length m, where $0 \leq m \leq n$.

Induction Step. Consider any derivation of the form

$$(S, t_1) \Rightarrow_G^{n+1} (w, t_3) \Rightarrow_G^* (z, t_4)$$

where $w \in \Sigma^+$ and $z \in \Delta^+$. Since $n + 1 \geq 1$, this derivation can be expressed as

$$(S, t_1) \Rightarrow_G^n ({}^{\not\varepsilon}x_0 {}^{\varepsilon}X_1 {}^{\not\varepsilon}x_1 {}^{\varepsilon}X_2 {}^{\not\varepsilon}x_2 \cdots {}^{\varepsilon}X_h {}^{\not\varepsilon}x_h, t_2) \Rightarrow_G (w, t_3) \Rightarrow_G^* (z, t_4)$$

where $x_i \in \Sigma^*$ for $i = 0, 1, \ldots, h$, $X_j \in \Sigma$ for $j = 1, 2, \ldots, h$, for some $h \geq 0$. By the induction hypothesis,

$$(S', \ell_0) \Rightarrow^*_{G'} (sx_0x_1x_2 \cdots x_h vZ, t'_2)$$

where $v \in \mathrm{perm}(\tau(X_1X_2 \cdots X_h)\xi)$, $\xi \in \{s\}^*$, and t'_2 can be ℓ_s or any rule constructed from t_2 in (1.1), (2.2), or (3.3).

Let $x = {}^{\not\varepsilon}x_0{}^{\varepsilon}X_1{}^{\not\varepsilon}x_1{}^{\varepsilon}X_2{}^{\not\varepsilon}x_2 \cdots {}^{\varepsilon}X_h{}^{\not\varepsilon}x_h$. Next, we consider all possible forms of the derivation $(x, t_2) \Rightarrow_G (w, t_3)$, covered by the following three cases—(i)–(iii).

(i) *Application of a rule that rewrites a symbol in some* x_j. Let $x_j = x'_jAx''_j$ and $(t_2 \colon A \to y_0Y_1y_1Y_2y_2 \cdots Y_my_m, \sigma_{t_2}, \rho_{t_2}) \in R$ for some $j \in \{0, 1, \ldots, h\}$ and $m \geq 0$, where $y_i \in \Sigma^*$ for $i = 0, 1, \ldots, m$, $Y_i \in N$ for $i = 1, \ldots, m$, and $t_3 \in \sigma_{t_2}$ so that

$$\begin{aligned}&({}^{\not\varepsilon}x_0{}^{\varepsilon}X_1{}^{\not\varepsilon}x_1{}^{\varepsilon}X_2{}^{\not\varepsilon}x_2 \cdots {}^{\varepsilon}X_j{}^{\not\varepsilon}x'_j{}^{\not\varepsilon}A{}^{\not\varepsilon}x''_j \cdots {}^{\varepsilon}X_h{}^{\not\varepsilon}x_h, t_2) \Rightarrow_G\\ &({}^{\not\varepsilon}x_0{}^{\varepsilon}X_1{}^{\not\varepsilon}x_1{}^{\varepsilon}X_2{}^{\not\varepsilon}x_2 \cdots {}^{\varepsilon}X_j{}^{\not\varepsilon}y_0{}^{\varepsilon}Y_1{}^{\not\varepsilon}y_1{}^{\varepsilon}Y_2{}^{\not\varepsilon}y_2 \cdots {}^{\varepsilon}Y_m{}^{\not\varepsilon}y_m \cdots {}^{\varepsilon}X_h{}^{\not\varepsilon}x_h, t_3).\end{aligned}$$

By (1) and by the final step of the algorithm, R' contains

$$\begin{aligned}&(\ell \colon A \to y_0y_1 \cdots y_m, \{\ell'\}, \emptyset),\\ &(\ell' \colon Z \to \bar{y}Z, \sigma_{\ell'}, \emptyset), \text{ where } \bar{y} = \tau(Y_1Y_2 \cdots Y_m).\end{aligned}$$

By the induction hypothesis, we assume that $t'_2 = \ell$. Then,

$$\begin{aligned}&(sx_0x_1x_2 \cdots x'_jAx''_j \cdots x_hvZ, \ell) && \Rightarrow_{G'}\\ &(sx_0x_1x_2 \cdots x'_jy_0y_1y_2 \cdots y_mx''_j \cdots x_hvZ, \ell') && \Rightarrow_{G'}\\ &(sx_0x_1x_2 \cdots x'_jy_0y_1y_2 \cdots y_mx''_j \cdots x_hv\bar{y}Z, t'_3)\end{aligned}$$

with $t'_3 \in \sigma_{\ell'}$. By the final step of the algorithm, t'_3 can be ℓ_s or any rule constructed from t_3 in (1.1), (2.2), or (3.3). As $x_0x_1x_2 \cdots x'_jy_0y_1y_2 \cdots y_mx''_j \cdots x_hv\bar{y}Z$ is of the required form, the induction step for (i) is completed;

(ii) *Application of a rule that rewrites some* X_j. Let $(t_2 \colon X_j \to y, \sigma_{t_2}, \rho_{t_2}) \in R$ for some $j \in \{1, 2, \ldots, h\}$, where $y \in N^*$ and $t_3 \in \sigma_{t_2}$ so that

$$\begin{aligned}&({}^{\not\varepsilon}x_0{}^{\varepsilon}X_1{}^{\not\varepsilon}x_1{}^{\varepsilon}X_2{}^{\not\varepsilon}x_2 \cdots {}^{\varepsilon}X_j{}^{\not\varepsilon}x_j \cdots {}^{\varepsilon}X_h{}^{\not\varepsilon}x_h, t_2) \Rightarrow_G\\ &({}^{\not\varepsilon}x_0{}^{\varepsilon}X_1{}^{\not\varepsilon}x_1{}^{\varepsilon}X_2{}^{\not\varepsilon}x_2 \cdots {}^{\varepsilon}y{}^{\not\varepsilon}x_j \cdots {}^{\varepsilon}X_h{}^{\not\varepsilon}x_h, t_3).\end{aligned}$$

By the induction hypothesis, $v = v_1\bar{X}_jv_2$ for some $v_1, v_2 \in \bar{N}^*$. By (2) and by the final step of the algorithm,

$$(\bar{t}_2 \colon \bar{X}_j \to \bar{y}, \sigma_{\bar{t}_2}, \emptyset) \in R' \text{ where } \bar{y} = \tau(y).$$

By the induction hypothesis, we assume that $t'_2 = \bar{t}_2$. Then,

$$(sx_0x_1x_2 \cdots x_hv_1\bar{X}_jv_2Z, \bar{t}_2) \Rightarrow_{G'} (sx_0x_1x_2 \cdots x_hv_1\bar{y}v_2Z, t'_3)$$

with $t'_3 \in \sigma_{\bar{t}_2}$. By the final step of the algorithm, t'_3 can be ℓ_s or any rule that was constructed from t_3 in (1.1), (2.2), or (3.3). Since $x_0x_1x_2 \cdots x_hv_1\bar{y}_jv_2Z$ is of the required form, the induction step for (ii) is completed.

(iii) *Application of a rule in the appearance checking mode.* Let $(t_2 \colon A \to y, \sigma_{t_2}, \rho_{t_2}) \in R$, where $A \notin \mathrm{symbols}(x)$, $y \in \Sigma^*$ and $t_3 \in \rho_{t_2}$ so that

$$(x, t_2) \Rightarrow_G (x, t_3).$$

By the induction hypothesis, we assume that t_2' was constructed from t_2 in (3.3). By (3) and by, the final step of the algorithm, R', contains

$$(\hat{r} : A \to \#y, \emptyset, \{\hat{r}'\}),$$
$$(\hat{r}' : \bar{A} \to \#y, \emptyset, \rho_{\hat{r}'}).$$

Since $A \notin \text{symbols}(x)$, $\bar{A} \notin \text{symbols}(x_0x_1x_2 \cdots x_h vZ)$. Then,

$$(sx_0x_1x_2 \cdots x_h vZ, \hat{r}) \Rightarrow_{G'}$$
$$(sx_0x_1x_2 \cdots x_h vZ, \hat{r}') \Rightarrow_{G'}$$
$$(sx_0x_1x_2 \cdots x_h vZ, t_3')$$

where t_3' can be ℓ_s or any rule that was constructed from t_3 in (1.1), (2.2), or (3.3). Since $x_0x_1x_2 \cdots x_h vZ$ is of the required form, the induction step for (iii) is completed.

Observe that cases (i)–(iii) cover all possible forms of $(x, t_2) \Rightarrow_G (w, t_3)$. Thus, the claim holds. □

To simplify the second claim and its proof, we define a generalization of $\Rrightarrow_{G'}$. In this generalization, we use the property that whenever a rule introduced in (1.1) or (3.3) is applied during a successful derivation, it has to be followed by its corresponding rule from (1.1) or (3.3), respectively. Let $\Sigma' = N' \cup \Delta$. Define the binary relation $\Rrightarrow_{G'}$ over $\Sigma'^* \times \Psi'$ as

$$(x, r) \Rrightarrow_{G'} (w, t)$$

if and only if either

$$(x, r) \Rightarrow_{G'} (w, t)$$

where $r, t \in \Psi'$ such that t is not introduced in (1.1) and (3.3), or

$$(x, r) \Rightarrow_{G'} (y, r') \Rightarrow_{G'} (w, t)$$

where r is a rule introduced in (1.1) or (3.3) and r' is its corresponding second rule introduced in (1.1) or (3.3), respectively. Define $\Rrightarrow_{G'}^n$ for $n \geq 0$ and $\Rrightarrow_{G'}^*$ in the usual way.

The next claim shows how G simulates G'. Define the homomorphism ι from Σ'^* to Σ^* as $\iota(X) = X$ for $X \in \Sigma$, $\iota(\bar{X}) = X$ for $X \in N$, and $\iota(s) = \iota(S') = \iota(Z) = \varepsilon$.

Claim 2. *If* $(S', \ell_0) \Rrightarrow_{G'}^m (sxu, t) \Rrightarrow_{G'}^* (z, g)$, *where* $x \in \Sigma^+$, $u \in (\bar{N} \cup \{s\})^*\{Z, \varepsilon\}$, $z \in Q^+$, $t, g \in \Psi'$, *and* $m \geq 1$, *then* $(S, t_1) \Rightarrow_G^* (x_0X_1x_1X_2x_2 \cdots X_hx_h, t')$, *where* $x = x_0x_1 \cdots x_h$, $X_1X_2 \cdots X_h \in \text{perm}(\iota(u))$, $h \geq 0$, *and* t' *is the rule from which* t *was constructed or any rule in* R *if* t *was not constructed from any rule in* R.

Proof. This claim is established by induction on $m \geq 1$.

Basis. Let $m = 1$. Then, for $(S', \ell_0) \Rrightarrow_{G'}^m (sSZ, t) \Rrightarrow_{G'}^* (z, g)$, where $t, g \in \Psi'$ and $z \in Q^+$, there is $(S, t') \Rightarrow_G^0 (S, t')$, where t' is the rule from which t was constructed. Hence, the basis holds.

Induction Hypothesis. Suppose that there exists $n \geq 1$ such that the claim holds for all derivations of length m, where $0 \leq m \leq n$.

Induction Step. Consider any derivation of the form

$$(S', \ell_0) \Rrightarrow_{G'}^{n+1} (swv, p) \Rrightarrow_{G'}^{*} (z, g)$$

where $n \geq 1$, $w \in \Sigma^+$, $v \in (\bar{N} \cup \{s\})^*\{Z, \varepsilon\}$, $z \in Q^+$, and $p, g \in \Psi'$. Since $n + 1 \geq 1$, this derivation can be expressed as

$$(S', \ell_0) \Rrightarrow_{G'}^{n} (sxu, t) \Rrightarrow_{G'} (swv, p) \Rrightarrow_{G'}^{*} (z, g)$$

where $x \in \Sigma^+$, $u \in (\bar{N} \cup \{s\})^*\{Z, \varepsilon\}$, and $t \in \Psi'$. By the induction hypothesis,

$$(S, t_1) \Rrightarrow_{G}^{*} (x_0X_1x_1X_2x_2 \cdots X_hx_h, t')$$

where $x = x_0x_1 \cdots x_h$, $X_1X_2 \cdots X_h \in \text{perm}(\iota(u))$, $h \geq 0$, and t' is the rule from which t was constructed or any rule in R if t was not constructed from any rule in R.

Next, we consider all possible forms of $(sxu, t) \Rrightarrow_{G'} (swv, p)$, covered by the following four cases—(i)–(iv).

(i) *Application of* $(\ell_s \colon Z \to s, \{\ell_s\}, \emptyset)$. Let $t = \ell_s$, so

$$(swu'Z, \ell_s) \Rrightarrow_{G'} (swu's, \ell_s)$$

where $u = u'Z$. Then, the induction step for (i) follows directly from the induction hypothesis (recall that $\iota(Z) = \iota(s) = \varepsilon$);

(ii) *Application of two rules introduced in (1).* Let $x = x'Ax''$ and $(\ell \colon A \to y_0y_1 \cdots y_m, \{\ell'\}, \emptyset)$, $(\ell' \colon Z \to \bar{y}Z, \sigma_{\ell'}, \emptyset) \in R'$ be two rules introduced in (1) from $(r \colon A \to y_0Y_1y_1Y_2y_2 \cdots Y_my_m, \sigma_r, \rho_r) \in R$, where $y_i \in \Sigma^*$, $Y_j \in N$, for $i = 0, 1, \ldots, m$ and $j = 1, 2, \ldots, m$, for some $m \geq 1$, and $\bar{y} = \tau(Y_1Y_2 \cdots Y_m)$. Then,

$$(sx'Ax''uZ, \ell) \Rrightarrow_{G'} (sx'y_0y_1 \cdots y_mx''u\bar{y}Z, p)$$

by applying ℓ and ℓ' ($p \in \sigma_{\ell'}$). By the induction hypothesis, $t' = r$ and $x_i = x_i'Ax_i''$ for some $i \in \{0, 1, \ldots, h\}$. Then,

$$(x_0X_1x_1X_2x_2 \cdots X_ix_i'Ax_i'' \cdots X_hx_h, r) \Rrightarrow_G$$
$$(x_0X_1x_1X_2x_2 \cdots X_ix_i'y_0Y_1y_1Y_2y_2 \cdots Y_my_mx_i'' \cdots X_hx_h, t'').$$

Clearly, both configurations are of the required forms, so the induction step is completed for (ii);

(iii) *Application of a rule introduced in (2).* Let $u = u'\bar{A}u''$ and $(\bar{r} \colon \bar{A} \to \bar{y}, \sigma_{\bar{r}}, \emptyset) \in R'$ be a rule introduced in (2) from $(r \colon A \to y, \sigma_r, \rho_r) \in R$, where $y \in N^*$ and $\bar{y} = \tau(y)$. Then,

$$(sxu'\bar{A}u''Z, \bar{r}) \Rrightarrow_{G'} (sxu'\bar{y}u''Z, p)$$

where $p \in \sigma_{\bar{r}}$. By the induction hypothesis, $t' = r$ and $X_i = A$ for some $i \in \{1, \ldots, h\}$. Then,

$$(x_0X_1x_1X_2x_2 \cdots X_ix_i \cdots X_hx_h, r) \Rrightarrow_G$$
$$(x_0X_1x_1X_2x_2 \cdots yx_i \cdots X_hx_h, t'').$$

Clearly, both configurations are of the required forms, so the induction step is completed for (iii);

(iv) *Application of two rules introduced in (3).* Let $(\hat{r}: A \to \#y, \emptyset, \{\hat{r}'\})$, $(\hat{r}': \bar{A} \to \#y, \emptyset, \rho_{\hat{r}'}) \in R'$ be two rules introduced in (3) from $(r: A \to y, \sigma_r, \rho_r) \in R$, where $y \in \Sigma^*$, such that $\{A, \bar{A}\} \cap \text{symbols}(sxuZ) = \emptyset$. Then,

$$(sxu, \hat{r}) \Rrightarrow_{G'} (sxu, p)$$

by applying $\hat{r}$ and $\hat{r}'$ in the appearance checking mode ($p \in \rho_{\hat{r}'}$). By the induction hypothesis, $t' = r$ and $A \notin \text{symbols}(x_0X_1x_1X_2x_2 \cdots X_hx_h)$, so

$$(x_0X_1x_1X_2x_2 \cdots X_hx_h, r) \Rightarrow_G (x_0X_1x_1X_2x_2 \cdots X_hx_h, t'').$$

Clearly, both configurations are of the required forms, so the induction step is completed for (iv).

Observe that cases (i)–(iv) cover all the possible forms of $(sxu, t) \Rrightarrow_{G'} (swv, p)$. Thus, the claim holds. □

Consider Claim 1 with $h = 0$. Then,

$$(S, t_1) \Rightarrow_G^* (z, r)$$

implies that

$$(S', \ell_0) \Rrightarrow_{G'} (szs^k, r').$$

where $k \geq 1$, $t_1, r \in \Psi$, and $r' \in \Psi'$. Consider Claim 2 with $x \in \Delta^+$ and $u \in \{s\}^+$. Then,

$$(S', \ell_0) \Rrightarrow_{G'}^* (sxu, t)$$

implies that

$$(S, t_1) \Rightarrow_G^* (x, t')$$

Hence, we have $w \in L(G)$ for $w \in \Delta^+$ if and only if $sws^k \in L(G')$ for some $k \geq 1$.

It remains to be shown that $\varepsilon \in L(G)$ if and only if $\varepsilon \in L(G')$. This can be proved by analogy with proving Claims 1 and 2, where G' uses $\bar{\ell}_0$ instead of ℓ_0 (see the initialization part of the algorithm). We leave this part of the proof to the reader. Hence, ${}_{\triangleright}L(M, L(G')) = L(G)$, and the lemma holds. ■

Lemma 12.13. $\mathbf{RE} \subseteq \mathbf{SCFA}(\mathbf{P}_{ac}^{-\varepsilon})$.

Proof. Let $I \in \mathbf{RE}$ and $\Delta = \text{symbols}(I)$. By Theorem 12.10, there is a programmed grammar with appearance checking $G = (\Sigma, \Lambda, \Psi, R, S)$ such that $L(G) = I$. Let $M = (Q, \Delta, R, s, F)$ and $G' = (\Sigma', Q, \Psi', R', S')$ be the finite automaton and the propagating programmed grammar with appearance checking, respectively, constructed by Algorithm 12.1 from G. By Lemma 12.12, ${}_{\triangleright}L(M, L(G')) = L(G) = I$, so the lemma holds. ■

Theorem 12.24. $\mathbf{SCFA}(\mathbf{P}_{ac}^{-\varepsilon}) = \mathbf{RE}$.

Proof. The inclusion **SCFA**($\mathbf{P}_{ac}^{-\varepsilon}$) $\subseteq$ **RE** follows from Turing–Church thesis. The converse inclusion **RE** $\subseteq$ **SCFA**($\mathbf{P}_{ac}^{-\varepsilon}$) follows from Lemma 12.13. ∎

Combining Theorems 12.21 and 12.24, we obtain the following corollary (recall that $\mathbf{P}_{ac}^{-\varepsilon}$ satisfies all the conditions from Theorem 12.21, see [12]).

Corollary 12.6. **TCFA**($\mathbf{P}_{ac}^{-\varepsilon}$) = **RE**.

Finally, we briefly investigate a reduction of the number of states in controlled finite automata. First, observe that the finite automaton $M = (Q, \Delta, R, s, F)$ from Algorithm 12.1 has $\text{card}(\Delta) + 1$ states. Therefore, we obtain the following corollary.

Corollary 12.7. *Let I be a recursively enumerable language, and let $\Delta = \text{symbols}(I)$. Then, there is a finite automaton $M = (Q, \Delta, R, s, F)$ such that $\text{card}(Q) = \text{card}(\Delta) + 1$, and a propagating programmed grammar with appearance checking G such that ${}_{\triangleright}L(M, L(G)) = I$.*

In a comparison to Corollary 12.7, a more powerful result holds in terms of TCFAs. In this case, the number of states can be decreased to a single state as stated in the following theorem.

Theorem 12.25. Let I be a recursively enumerable language. Then, there is a finite automaton $M = (Q, \Delta, R, s, F)$ such that $\text{card}(Q) = 1$, and a propagating programmed grammar with appearance checking G such that ${}_{\blacktriangleright}L(M, L(G)) = I$.

Proof. Reconsider Algorithm 12.1. We modify the construction of $M = (Q, \Delta, R, s, F)$ in the following way. Let $G = (\Sigma, \Delta, \Psi, R, S)$ be the input programmed grammar with appearance checking. Construct the finite automaton

$$M = (Q, \Phi, R, s, F)$$

where

$$\begin{aligned} Q &= \{s\}, \\ \Phi &= \{s\} \cup \Delta, \\ R &= \{s\colon s \to s\} \cup \{a\colon sa \to s \mid a \in \Delta\}, \\ F &= \{s\}. \end{aligned}$$

Observe that $\text{card}(Q) = 1$ and that this modified algorithm always halts. The correctness of the modified algorithm—that is, the identity ${}_{\blacktriangleright}L(M, L(G')) = L(G)$, where G' is the propagating programmed grammar constructed by Algorithm 12.1—can be established by analogy with the proof of Lemma 12.12, so we leave the proof to the reader. The rest of the proof of this theorem parallels the proof of Lemma 12.13, so we omit it. ∎

We close this section by presenting three open-problem areas that are related to the achieved results.

Open Problem 12.6. *In general, the state-controlled and TCFAs in Theorem 12.24 and Corollary 12.6 are nondeterministic. Do these results hold in terms of deterministic versions of these automata?*

Open Problem 12.7. *By using control languages from* **CF**, *we characterize* **CF**. *By using control languages from* $\mathbf{P}_{ac}^{-\varepsilon}$, *we characterize* **RE**. *Is there a language family* $\mathscr{L}$ *such that* $\mathbf{CF} \subset \mathscr{L} \subset \mathbf{P}_{ac}^{-\varepsilon}$ *by which we can characterize* **CS**?

Open Problem 12.8. *Theorem 12.21 requires* $\mathscr{L}$ *to contain all finite languages and to be closed under finite* ε*-free substitution and concatenation. Does the same result hold if there are fewer requirements placed on* $\mathscr{L}$?

12.5.7 Pushdown automata regulated by control languages

The section consists of four subsections. First, we define pushdown automata that regulate the application of their rules by control languages by analogy with context-free grammars regulated in this way (see Section 12.2). Then, we demonstrate that this regulation has no effect on the power of pushdown automata if the control languages are regular. Considering this result, we point out that pushdown automata regulated by regular languages are of little interest because their power coincides with the power of ordinary pushdown automata. Next, however, we prove that pushdown automata increase their power remarkably if they are regulated by linear languages; indeed, they characterize the family of recursively enumerable languages. Finally, we continue with the discussion of regulated pushdown automata, but we narrow our attention to their special cases, such as one-turn pushdown automata.

12.5.7.1 Definitions

Without further ado, we next define pushdown automata regulated by control languages.

Definition 12.25. *Let* $M = (Q, D, \Gamma, R, s, S, F)$ *be a pushdown automaton, and let* Ψ *be an alphabet of its rule labels. Let* Ξ *be a* control language *over* Ψ, *that is,* $\Xi \subseteq \Psi^*$. *With* Ξ, *M defines the following three types of accepted languages*

- $L(M, \Xi, 1)$—*the* language accepted by final state,
- $L(M, \Xi, 2)$—*the* language accepted by empty pushdown, and
- $L(M, \Xi, 3)$—*the* language accepted by final state and empty pushdown

defined as follows. Let $\chi \in \Gamma^* Q D^*$. *If* $\chi \in \Gamma^* F$, $\chi \in Q$, $\chi \in F$, *then* χ *is a* 1-final configuration, 2-final configuration, 3-final configuration, *respectively. For* $i = 1, 2, 3$, *we define* $L(M, \Xi, i)$ *as*

$$L(M, \Xi, i) = \{w \mid w \in D^* \text{ and } Ssw \vdash_M^* \chi\ [\sigma] \text{ for an } i\text{-final configuration } \chi \text{ and } \sigma \in \Xi\}.$$

The pair (M, Ξ) *is called a* controlled pushdown automaton.

For any family of languages $\mathscr{L}$ and $i \in \{1, 2, 3\}$, define

$$\mathbf{RPDA}(\mathscr{L}, i) = \{L \mid L = L(M, \Xi, i), \text{ where } M \text{ is a pushdown automaton and } \Xi \in \mathscr{L}\}.$$

We demonstrate that

$$\mathbf{CF} = \mathbf{RPDA(REG, 1)} = \mathbf{RPDA(REG, 2)} = \mathbf{RPDA(REG, 3)}$$

and

$$\mathbf{RE} = \mathbf{RPDA(LIN, 1)} = \mathbf{RPDA(LIN, 2)} = \mathbf{RPDA(LIN, 3)}.$$

12.5.7.2 Regular-controlled pushdown automata

This section proves that if the control languages are regular, the regulation of pushdown automata has no effect on their power. The proof of the following lemma presents a transformation that converts any regular grammar G and any pushdown automaton K to an ordinary pushdown automaton M such that $L(M) = L(K, L(G), 1)$.

Lemma 12.14. *For every regular grammar G and every pushdown automaton K, there exists a pushdown automaton M such that $L(M) = L(K, L(G), 1)$.*

Proof. Let $G = (\Sigma_G, \Delta_G, R_G, S_G)$ be any regular grammar, $N_G = \Sigma_G - \Delta_G$, and let $K = (Q_K, D_K, \Gamma_K, R_K, s_K, S_K, F_K)$ be any pushdown automaton. Next, we construct a pushdown automaton M that simultaneously simulates G and K so that $L(M) = L(K, L(G), 1)$.

Let f be a new symbol. Define M as

$$M = (Q_M, D_M, \Gamma_M, R_M, s_M, S_M, F_M)$$

where

$$\begin{aligned}
Q_M &= \{\langle qB\rangle \mid q \in Q_K, B \in N_G \cup \{f\}\},\\
D_M &= D_K,\\
\Gamma_M &= \Gamma_K,\\
s_M &= \langle s_K S_G\rangle,\\
S_M &= S_K,\\
F_M &= \{\langle qf\rangle \mid q \in F_K\},\\
R_M &= \{C\langle qA\rangle b \to x\langle pB\rangle \mid a\colon Cqb \to xp \in R_K, A \to aB \in R_G\} \cup\\
&\quad\ \{C\langle qA\rangle b \to x\langle pf\rangle \mid a\colon Cqb \to xp \in R_K, A \to a \in R_G\}.
\end{aligned}$$

Observe that a move in M according to $C\langle qA\rangle b \to x\langle pB\rangle \in R_M$ simulates a move in K according to $a\colon Cqb \to xp \in R_K$, where a is generated in G by using $A \to aB \in R_G$. Based on this observation, it is rather easy to see that M accepts an input string w if and only if K reads w and enters a final state after using a complete string of $L(G)$; therefore, $L(M) = L(K, L(G), 1)$. A rigorous proof that $L(M) = L(K, L(G), 1)$ is left to the reader. ■

Theorem 12.26. For $i \in \{1, 2, 3\}$, $\mathbf{CF} = \mathbf{RPDA(REG}, i\mathbf{)}$.

Proof. To prove that **CF** = **RPDA(REG,** 1), notice that **RPDA(REG,** 1) ⊆ **CF** follows from Lemma 12.14. Clearly, **CF** ⊆ **RPDA(REG,** 1), so **RPDA(REG,** 1) = **CF**. By analogy with the demonstration of **RPDA(REG,** 1) = **CF**, we can prove that **CF** = **RPDA(REG,** 2) and **CF** = **RPDA(REG,** 3). ■

Let us point out that most of the fundamental regulated grammars use control mechanisms that can be expressed in terms of regular control languages, as shown previously in this chapter. However, pushdown automata introduced by analogy with these grammars are of little or no interest because they are as powerful as ordinary pushdown automata (see Theorem 12.26).

12.5.7.3 Linear-controlled pushdown automata

This section demonstrates that pushdown automata regulated by linear control languages are more powerful than ordinary pushdown automata. In fact, it proves that

$$\mathbf{RE} = \mathbf{RPDA(LIN, 1)} = \mathbf{RPDA(LIN, 2)} = \mathbf{RPDA(LIN, 3)}.$$

Recall the normal form for left-extended queue grammars from Definition 11.9, which is needed to prove the following:

Lemma 12.15. *Let Q be a left-extended queue grammar that satisfies the normal form of Definition 11.9. Then, there exist a linear grammar G and a pushdown automaton M such that $L(Q) = L(M, L(G), 3)$.*

Proof. Let $Q = (\Sigma_Q, \Delta_Q, W_Q, F_Q, R_Q, g_Q)$ be a left-extended queue grammar satisfying the normal form of Definition 11.9. Without any loss of generality, assume that $\{@, \P, \S, \$, \lfloor, \rceil\} \cap (\Sigma_Q \cup W_Q) = \emptyset$. Define the coding ζ from Σ_Q^* to $\{\langle as \rangle_\Psi \mid a \in \Sigma_Q\}^*$ as $\zeta(a) = \langle as \rangle_\Psi$ (s is used as the start state of the pushdown automaton M defined later in this proof).

Construct the linear grammar $G = (N_G, \Delta_G, R_G, S_G)$ in the following way: initially, set

$$\begin{aligned}
N_G^{(0)} &= \{S_G, \langle ! \rangle, \langle !, 1 \rangle\} \cup \{\langle f \rangle \mid f \in F_Q\}, \\
\Delta_G^{(0)} &= \zeta(\Sigma_Q) \cup \{\langle \S s \rangle_\Psi, \langle @ \rangle_\Psi\} \cup \{\langle \S f \rangle_\Psi \mid f \in F_Q\}, \\
R_G^{(0)} &= \{S_G \to \langle \S s \rangle_\Psi \langle f \rangle \mid f \in F_Q\} \cup \{\langle ! \rangle \to \langle !, 1 \rangle \langle @ \rangle_\Psi\}.
\end{aligned}$$

Extend N_G, Δ_G, and R_G by performing (1)–(3), given as follows:

(1) For every $(a, p, x, q) \in R_Q$, where $p, q \in W_Q$, $a \in Z$, and $x \in \Delta^*$,

$$\begin{aligned}
N_G^{(1)} &= N_G^{(0)} \cup \{\langle apxqk \rangle \mid k = 0, \ldots, |x|\} \cup \{\langle p \rangle, \langle q \rangle\}, \\
\Delta_G^{(1)} &= \Delta_G^{(0)} \cup \{\langle \mathrm{sym}(x, k) \rangle_\Psi \mid k = 1, \ldots, |x|\} \cup \{\langle apxq \rangle_\Psi\}, \\
R_G^{(1)} &= R_G^{(0)} \cup \{\langle q \rangle \to \langle apxq|x| \rangle \langle apxq \rangle_\Psi, \langle apxq0 \rangle \to \langle p \rangle\} \\
&\quad \cup \{\langle apxqk \rangle \to \langle apxq(k-1) \rangle \langle \mathrm{sym}(x, k) \rangle_\Psi \mid k = 1, \ldots, |x|\};
\end{aligned}$$

(2) For every $(a, p, x, q) \in R_Q$ with $p, q \in W_Q$, $a \in U$, and $x \in \Sigma_Q^*$,

$$\begin{aligned} N_G^{(2)} &= N_G^{(1)} \cup \{\langle p, 1\rangle, \langle q, 1\rangle\}, \\ R_G^{(2)} &= R_G^{(1)} \cup \{\langle q, 1\rangle \to \text{reversal}(\zeta(x))\langle p, 1\rangle\zeta(a)\}; \end{aligned}$$

(3) For every $(a, p, x, q) \in R_Q$ with $ap = q_Q, p, q \in W_Q$, and $x \in \Sigma_Q^*$,

$$\begin{aligned} N_G &= N_G^{(2)} \cup \{\langle q, 1\rangle\}, \\ R_G &= R_G^{(2)} \cup \{\langle q, 1\rangle \to \text{reversal}(x)\langle \$s\rangle_\Psi\}. \end{aligned}$$

The construction of G is completed. Set $\Psi = \Delta_G$. Ψ represents the alphabet of rule labels corresponding to the rules of the pushdown automaton M, defined as

$$M = (Q_M, D_M, \Gamma_M, R_M, s_M, S_M, \{\urcorner\}).$$

Throughout the rest of this proof, s_M is abbreviated to s. Initially, set

$$\begin{aligned} Q_M &= \{s, \langle \P ! \rangle, \llcorner, \urcorner\}, \\ D_M &= \Delta_Q, \\ \Gamma_M &= \{S_M, \S\} \cup \Sigma_Q, \\ R_M &= \{\langle \S s\rangle_\Psi : S_M s \to \S s\} \cup \{\langle \S f\rangle_\Psi : \S\langle \P f\rangle \to \urcorner \mid f \in F_M\}. \end{aligned}$$

Extend Q_M and R_M by performing (A)–(D), given as follows:

(A) Set $R_M = R_M \cup \{\langle bs\rangle_\Psi : as \to abs \mid a \in \Gamma_M - \{S_M\}, b \in \Gamma_M\}$;
(B) Set $R_M = R_M \cup \{\langle \$s\rangle_\Psi : as \to a\llcorner \mid a \in \Sigma_Q\} \cup \{\langle a\rangle_\Psi : a\llcorner \to \llcorner \mid a \in \Sigma_Q\}$;
(C) Set $R_M = R_M \cup \{\langle @\rangle_\Psi : a\llcorner \to a\langle \P !\rangle \mid a \in Z\}$;
(D) For every $(a, p, x, q) \in R_Q$, where $p, q \in W_Q$, $a \in Z$, $x \in \Delta_Q^*$, set

$$\begin{aligned} Q_M &= Q_M \cup \{\langle \P p\rangle\} \cup \{\langle \P qu\rangle \mid u \in \text{prefix}(x)\}, \\ R_M &= R_M \cup \{\langle b\rangle_\Psi : a\langle \P qy\rangle b \to a\langle \P qyb\rangle \mid b \in \Delta_Q, y \in \Delta_Q^*, \\ &\qquad yb \in \text{prefix}(x)\} \\ &\qquad \cup \{\langle apxq\rangle_\Psi : a\langle \P qx\rangle \to \langle \P p\rangle\}. \end{aligned}$$

The construction of M is completed. Notice that several components of G and M have this form: $\langle x\rangle_y$. Intuitively, if $y = \Psi$, then $\langle x\rangle_y \in \Psi$, or Δ_G, respectively. If x begins with ¶, then $\langle x\rangle_y \in Q_M$. Otherwise, $\langle x\rangle_y \in N_G$.

First, we only sketch the reason why $L(Q)$ contains $L(M, L(G), 3)$. According to a string from $L(G)$, M accepts every string w as

$$\begin{aligned}
\S s w_1 \cdots w_{m-1} w_m &\vdash_M^+ \S b_m \cdots b_1 a_n \cdots a_1 s w_1 \cdots w_{m-1} w_m \\
&\vdash_M \S b_m \cdots b_1 a_n \cdots a_1 \lfloor w_1 \cdots w_{m-1} w_m \\
&\vdash_M^n \S b_m \cdots b_1 \lfloor w_1 \cdots w_{m-1} w_m \\
&\vdash_M \S b_m \cdots b_1 \langle \P q_1 \rangle w_1 \cdots w_{m-1} w_m \\
&\vdash_M^{|w_1|} \S b_m \cdots b_1 \langle \P q_1 w_1 \rangle w_2 \cdots w_{m-1} w_m \\
&\vdash_M \S b_m \cdots b_2 \langle \P q_2 \rangle w_2 \cdots w_{m-1} w_m \\
&\vdash_M^{|w_2|} \S b_m \cdots b_2 \langle \P q_2 w_2 \rangle w_3 \cdots w_{m-1} w_m \\
&\vdash_M \S b_m \cdots b_3 \langle \P q_3 \rangle w_3 \cdots w_{m-1} w_m \\
&\vdots \\
&\vdash_M \S b_m \langle \P q_m \rangle w_m \\
&\vdash_M^{|w_m|} \S b_m \langle \P q_m w_m \rangle \\
&\vdash_M \S \langle \P q_{m+1} \rangle \\
&\vdash_M \rceil
\end{aligned}$$

where $w = w_1 \cdots w_{m-1} w_m$, $a_1 \cdots a_n b_1 \cdots b_m = x_1 \cdots x_{n+1}$, and R_Q contains (a_0, p_0, x_1, p_1), (a_1, p_1, x_2, p_2), $\ldots$, (a_n, p_n, x_{n+1}, q_1), (b_1, q_1, w_1, q_2), (b_2, q_2, w_2, q_3), $\ldots$, (b_m, q_m, w_m, q_{m+1}). According to these members of R_Q, Q makes

$$\begin{aligned}
\#a_0 p_0 &\Rightarrow_Q a_0 \# y_0 x_1 p_1 && [(a_0, p_0, x_1, p_1)] \\
&\Rightarrow_Q a_0 a_1 \# y_1 x_2 p_2 && [(a_1, p_1, x_2, p_2)] \\
&\Rightarrow_Q a_0 a_1 a_2 \# y_2 x_3 p_3 && [(a_2, p_2, x_3, p_3)] \\
&\vdots \\
&\Rightarrow_Q a_0 a_1 a_2 \cdots a_{n-1} \# y_{n-1} x_n p_n && [(a_{n-1}, p_{n-1}, x_n, p_n)] \\
&\Rightarrow_Q a_0 a_1 a_2 \cdots a_n \# y_n x_{n+1} q_1 && [(a_n, p_n, x_{n+1}, q_1)] \\
&\Rightarrow_Q a_0 \cdots a_n b_1 \# b_2 \cdots b_m w_1 q_2 && [(b_1, q_1, w_1, q_2)] \\
&\Rightarrow_Q a_0 \cdots a_n b_1 b_2 \# b_3 \cdots b_m w_1 w_2 q_3 && [(b_2, q_2, w_2, q_3)] \\
&\vdots \\
&\Rightarrow_Q a_0 \cdots a_n b_1 \cdots b_{m-1} \# b_m w_1 w_2 \cdots w_{m-1} q_m && [(b_{m-1}, q_{m-1}, w_{m-1}, q_m)] \\
&\Rightarrow_Q a_0 \cdots a_n b_1 \cdots b_m \# w_1 w_2 \cdots w_m q_{m+1} && [(b_m, q_m, w_m, q_{m+1})].
\end{aligned}$$

Therefore, $L(M, L(G), 3) \subseteq L(Q)$.

More formally, to demonstrate that $L(Q)$ contains $L(M, L(G), 3)$, consider any $h \in L(G)$. G generates h as

$$\begin{aligned}
S_G &\Rightarrow_G \langle \S s \rangle_\Psi \langle q_{m+1} \rangle \\
&\Rightarrow_G^{|w_m|+1} \langle \S s \rangle_\Psi \langle q_m \rangle t_m \langle b_m q_m w_m q_{m+1} \rangle_\Psi \\
&\Rightarrow_G^{|w_{m-1}|+1} \langle \S s \rangle_\Psi \langle q_{m-1} \rangle t_{m-1} \langle b_{m-1} q_{m-1} w_{m-1} q_m \rangle_\Psi t_m \langle b_m q_m w_m q_{m+1} \rangle_\Psi \\
&\vdots \\
&\Rightarrow_G^{|w_1|+1} \langle \S s \rangle_\Psi \langle q_1 \rangle o \\
&\Rightarrow_G^{|w_1|+1} \langle \S s \rangle_\Psi \langle q_1, 1 \rangle \langle @ \rangle_\Psi o \\
&\qquad [\langle q_1 \rangle \rightarrow \langle q_1, 1 \rangle \langle @ \rangle_\Psi]
\end{aligned}$$

$$\begin{aligned}
\Rightarrow_G \quad & \langle \S s\rangle_\Psi \zeta(\text{reversal}(x_{n+1}))\langle p_n, 1\rangle\langle a_n\rangle_\Psi\langle @\rangle_\Psi o \\
& [\langle q_1, 1\rangle \to \text{reversal}(\zeta(x_{n+1}))\langle p_n, 1\rangle\langle a_n\rangle_\Psi\langle @\rangle_\Psi] \\
\Rightarrow_G \quad & \langle \S s\rangle_\Psi \zeta(\text{reversal}(x_n x_{n+1}))\langle p_{n-1}, 1\rangle\langle a_{n-1}\rangle_\Psi\langle a_n\rangle_\Psi\langle @\rangle_\Psi o \\
& [\langle p_n, 1\rangle \to \text{reversal}(\zeta(x_n))\langle p_{n-1}, 1\rangle\langle a_{n-1}\rangle_\Psi] \\
& \vdots \\
\Rightarrow_G \quad & \langle \S s\rangle_\Psi \zeta(\text{reversal}(x_2 \cdots x_n x_{n+1}))\langle p_1, 1\rangle\langle a_1\rangle_\Psi\langle a_2\rangle_\Psi \cdots \langle a_n\rangle_\Psi\langle @\rangle_\Psi o \\
& [\langle p_2, 1\rangle \to \text{reversal}(\zeta(x_2))\langle p_1, 1\rangle\langle a_1\rangle_\Psi] \\
\Rightarrow_G \quad & \langle \S s\rangle_\Psi \zeta(\text{reversal}(x_1 \cdots x_n x_{n+1}))\langle \$ s\rangle_\Psi\langle a_1\rangle_\Psi\langle a_2\rangle_\Psi \cdots \langle a_n\rangle_\Psi\langle @\rangle_\Psi o \\
& [\langle p_1, 1\rangle \to \text{reversal}(\zeta(x_1))\langle \$ s\rangle_\Psi]
\end{aligned}$$

where

$n, m \geq 1,$
$a_i \in U$ for $i = 1, \ldots, n,$
$b_k \in Z$ for $k = 1, \ldots, m,$
$x_l \in \Sigma^*$ for $l = 1, \ldots, n + 1,$
$p_i \in W$ for $i = 1, \ldots, n,$
$q_l \in W$ for $l = 1, \ldots, m + 1$ with $q_1 = !$ and $q_{m+1} \in F,$

and

$$\begin{aligned}
t_k &= \langle \text{sym}(w_k, 1)\rangle_\Psi \cdots \langle \text{sym}(w_k, |w_k| - 1)\rangle_\Psi\langle \text{sym}(w_k, |w_k|)\rangle_\Psi \\
&\quad \text{for } k = 1, \ldots, m, \\
o &= t_1\langle b_1 q_1 w_1 q_2\rangle_\Psi \cdots t_{m-1}\langle b_{m-1} q_{m-1} w_{m-1} q_m\rangle_\Psi t_m\langle b_m q_m w_m q_{m+1}\rangle_\Psi, \\
h &= \langle \S s\rangle_\Psi \zeta(\text{reversal}(x_1 \cdots x_n x_{n+1}))\langle \$\rangle_\Psi\langle a_1\rangle_\Psi\langle a_2\rangle_\Psi \cdots \langle a_n\rangle_\Psi\langle @\rangle_\Psi o.
\end{aligned}$$

We describe this derivation in a greater detail. Initially, G makes $S_G \Rightarrow_G \langle \S s\rangle_\Psi\langle q_{m+1}\rangle$ according to $S_G \to \langle \S s\rangle_\Psi\langle q_{m+1}\rangle$. Then, G makes

$$\begin{aligned}
& \langle \S s\rangle_\Psi\langle q_{m+1}\rangle \\
\Rightarrow_G^{|w_m|+1} \quad & \langle \S s\rangle_\Psi\langle q_m\rangle t_m\langle b_m q_m w_m q_{m+1}\rangle_\Psi \\
\Rightarrow_G^{|w_{m-1}|+1} \quad & \langle \S s\rangle_\Psi\langle q_{m-1}\rangle t_{m-1}\langle b_{m-1} q_{m-1} w_{m-1} q_m\rangle_\Psi t_m\langle b_m q_m w_m q_{m+1}\rangle_\Psi \\
& \vdots \\
\Rightarrow_G^{|w_1|+1} \quad & \langle \S s\rangle_\Psi\langle q_1\rangle o
\end{aligned}$$

according to rules introduced in (1). Then, G makes

$$\langle \S s\rangle_\Psi\langle q_1\rangle o \Rightarrow_G \langle \S s\rangle_\Psi\langle q_1, 1\rangle\langle @\rangle_\Psi o$$

according to $\langle ! \rangle \rightarrow \langle !, 1\rangle\langle @\rangle_\Psi$ (recall that $q_1 = !$). After this step, G makes

$$\begin{aligned}
&\langle \S s\rangle_\Psi \langle q_1, 1\rangle\langle @\rangle_\Psi o \\
\Rightarrow_G\ &\langle \S s\rangle_\Psi \zeta(\text{reversal}(x_{n+1}))\langle p_n, 1\rangle\langle a_n\rangle_\Psi\langle @\rangle_\Psi o \\
\Rightarrow_G\ &\langle \S s\rangle_\Psi \zeta(\text{reversal}(x_n x_{n+1}))\langle p_{n-1}, 1\rangle\langle a_{n-1}\rangle_\Psi\langle a_n\rangle_\Psi\langle @\rangle_\Psi o \\
&\vdots \\
\Rightarrow_G\ &\langle \S s\rangle_\Psi \zeta(\text{reversal}(x_2 \cdots x_n x_{n+1}))\langle p_1, 1\rangle\langle a_1\rangle_\Psi\langle a_2\rangle_\Psi \cdots \langle a_n\rangle_\Psi\langle @\rangle_\Psi o
\end{aligned}$$

according to rules introduced in (2). Finally, according to

$$\langle p_1, 1\rangle \rightarrow \text{reversal}(\zeta(x_1))\langle \$\rangle_\Psi,$$

which is introduced in (3), G makes

$$\begin{aligned}
&\langle \S s\rangle_\Psi \zeta(\text{reversal}(x_2 \cdots x_n x_{n+1}))\langle p_1, 1\rangle\langle a_1\rangle_\Psi\langle a_2\rangle_\Psi \cdots \langle a_n\rangle_\Psi\langle @\rangle_\Psi o \\
\Rightarrow_G\ &\langle \S s\rangle_\Psi \zeta(\text{reversal}(x_1 \cdots x_n x_{n+1}))\langle \$\rangle_\Psi\langle a_1\rangle_\Psi\langle a_2\rangle_\Psi \cdots \langle a_n\rangle_\Psi\langle @\rangle_\Psi o.
\end{aligned}$$

If $a_1 \cdots a_n b_1 \cdots b_m$ differs from $x_1 \cdots x_{n+1}$, then M does not accept according to h. Assume that $a_1 \cdots a_n b_1 \cdots b_m = x_1 \cdots x_{n+1}$. At this point, according to h, M makes this sequence of moves

$$\begin{aligned}
\S s w_1 \cdots w_{m-1} w_m \vdash_M^+\ &\S b_m \cdots b_1 a_n \cdots a_1 s w_1 \cdots w_{m-1} w_m \\
\vdash_M\ &\S b_m \cdots b_1 a_n \cdots a_1 \lfloor w_1 \cdots w_{m-1} w_m \\
\vdash_M^n\ &\S b_m \cdots b_1 \lfloor w_1 \cdots w_{m-1} w_m \\
\vdash_M\ &\S b_m \cdots b_1 \langle ¶ q_1\rangle w_1 \cdots w_{m-1} w_m \\
\vdash_M^{|w_1|}\ &\S b_m \cdots b_1 \langle ¶ q_1 w_1\rangle w_2 \cdots w_{m-1} w_m \\
\vdash_M\ &\S b_m \cdots b_2 \langle ¶ q_2\rangle w_2 \cdots w_{m-1} w_m \\
\vdash_M^{|w_2|}\ &\S b_m \cdots b_2 \langle ¶ q_2 w_2\rangle w_3 \cdots w_{m-1} w_m \\
\vdash_M\ &\S b_m \cdots b_3 \langle ¶ q_3\rangle w_3 \cdots w_{m-1} w_m \\
&\vdots \\
\vdash_M\ &\S b_m \langle ¶ q_m\rangle w_m \\
\vdash_M^{|w_m|}\ &\S b_m \langle ¶ q_m w_m\rangle \\
\vdash_M\ &\S \langle ¶ q_{m+1}\rangle \\
\vdash_M\ &\rceil.
\end{aligned}$$

In other words, according to h, M accepts $w_1 \cdots w_{m-1} w_m$. Return to the generation of h in G. By the construction of R_G, this generation implies that R_Q contains (a_0, p_0, x_1, p_1), (a_1, p_1, x_2, p_2), $\ldots$, $(a_{j-1}, p_{j-1}, x_j, p_j)$, $\ldots$, (a_n, p_n, x_{n+1}, q_1), (b_1, q_1, w_1, q_2), (b_2, q_2, w_2, q_3), $\ldots$, (b_m, q_m, w_m, q_{m+1}).

Thus, in Q,

$$
\begin{array}{lll}
\#a_0p_0 & \Rightarrow_Q a_0\#y_0x_1p_1 & [(a_0,p_0,x_1,p_1)] \\
& \Rightarrow_Q a_0a_1\#y_1x_2p_2 & [(a_1,p_1,x_2,p_2)] \\
& \Rightarrow_Q a_0a_1a_2\#y_2x_3p_3 & [(a_2,p_2,x_3,p_3)] \\
& \vdots & \\
& \Rightarrow_Q a_0a_1a_2\cdots a_{n-1}\#y_{n-1}x_np_n & [(a_{n-1},p_{n-1},x_n,p_n)] \\
& \Rightarrow_Q a_0a_1a_2\cdots a_n\#y_nx_{n+1}q_1 & [(a_n,p_n,x_{n+1},q_1)] \\
& \Rightarrow_Q a_0\cdots a_nb_1\#b_2\cdots b_mw_1q_2 & [(b_1,q_1,w_1,q_2)] \\
& \Rightarrow_Q a_0\cdots a_nb_1b_2\#b_3\cdots b_mw_1w_2q_3 & [(b_2,q_2,w_2,q_3)] \\
& \vdots & \\
& \Rightarrow_Q a_0\cdots a_nb_1\cdots b_{m-1}\#b_mw_1w_2\cdots w_{m-1}q_m & [(b_{m-1},q_{m-1},w_{m-1},q_m)] \\
& \Rightarrow_Q a_0\cdots a_nb_1\cdots b_m\#w_1w_2\cdots w_mq_{m+1} & [(b_m,q_m,w_m,q_{m+1})].
\end{array}
$$

Therefore, $w_1w_2\cdots w_m \in L(Q)$. Consequently, $L(M, L(G), 3) \subseteq L(Q)$. A proof that $L(Q) \subseteq L(M, L(G), 3)$ is left to the reader. As $L(Q) \subseteq L(M, L(G), 3)$ and $L(M, L(G), 3) \subseteq L(Q)$, $L(Q) = L(M, L(G), 3)$. Therefore, Lemma 12.15 holds. ∎

Theorem 12.27. For $i \in \{1, 2, 3\}$, $\mathbf{RE} = \mathbf{RPDA(LIN}, i\mathbf{)}$.

Proof. Obviously, $\mathbf{RPDA(LIN}, 3\mathbf{)} \subseteq \mathbf{RE}$. To prove that $\mathbf{RE} \subseteq \mathbf{RPDA(LIN}, 3\mathbf{)}$ also holds, consider any recursively enumerable language $L \in \mathbf{RE}$. By Theorem 4.3, $L(Q) = L$, for some left-extended queue grammar Q. Furthermore, by Theorem 11.14 and Lemma 12.15, $L(Q) = L(M, L(G), 3)$, for a linear grammar G and a pushdown automaton M. Thus, $L = L(M, L(G), 3)$. Hence, $\mathbf{RE} \subseteq \mathbf{RPDA(LIN}, 3\mathbf{)}$. As $\mathbf{RPDA(LIN}, 3\mathbf{)} \subseteq \mathbf{RE}$ and $\mathbf{RE} \subseteq \mathbf{RPDA(LIN}, 3\mathbf{)}$, $\mathbf{RE} = \mathbf{RPDA(LIN}, 3\mathbf{)}$.

By analogy with the demonstration of $\mathbf{RE} = \mathbf{RPDA(LIN}, 3\mathbf{)}$, we can prove that $\mathbf{RE} = \mathbf{RPDA(LIN}, i\mathbf{)}$ for $i = 1, 2$. ∎

12.5.7.4 One-turn linear-controlled pushdown automata

In the present section, we continue with the discussion of regulated pushdown automata, but we narrow our attention to their special cases—*one-turn regulated pushdown automata*. To give an insight into one-turn pushdown automata, consider two consecutive moves made by an ordinary pushdown automaton M. If during the first move, M does not shorten its pushdown and during the second move it does, then M makes a *turn* during the second move. A pushdown automaton is *one turn* if it makes no more than one turn with its pushdown during any computation starting from a start configuration. Recall that one-turn pushdown automata characterize the family of linear languages (see [22]), while their unrestricted versions characterize the family of context-free languages (see Theorem 7.6). As a result, one-turn pushdown automata are less powerful than the pushdown automata.

As the most surprising result, we demonstrate that linear-regulated versions of one-turn pushdown automata characterize the family of recursively enumerable languages. Thus, as opposed to the ordinary one-turn pushdown automata, one-turn linear-regulated pushdown automata are as powerful as linear-regulated pushdown automata that can make any number of turns.

In fact, this characterization holds even for some restricted versions of one-turn regulated pushdown automata, including their atomic and reduced versions, which are sketched next.

(I) During a move, an *atomic* one-turn regulated pushdown automaton changes a state and, in addition, performs exactly one of the following three actions:
- It pushes a symbol onto the pushdown;
- It pops a symbol from the pushdown;
- It reads an input symbol;

(II) A *reduced* one-turn regulated pushdown automaton has a limited number of some components, such as the number of states, pushdown symbols, or transition rules.

We establish the abovementioned characterization in a formal way.

Definition 12.26. *An* atomic pushdown automaton *is a pushdown automaton (see Definition 7.1)* $M = (Q, D, \Gamma, R, s, S, F)$, *where for every rule* $Apa \rightarrow wq \in R$, $|Aaw| = 1$. *That is, each of the rules from R has one of the following forms:*

(1) $Ap \rightarrow q$ *(*popping rule*),*
(2) $p \rightarrow wq$ *(*pushing rule*),*
(3) $pa \rightarrow q$ *(*reading rule*).*

Definition 12.27. *Let* $M = (Q, D, \Gamma, R, s, S, F)$ *be a pushdown automaton. Let* $x, x', x'' \in \Gamma^*$, $y, y', y'' \in D^*$, $q, q', q'' \in Q$, *and* $xqy \vdash_M x'q'y' \vdash_M x''q''y''$. *If* $|x| \leq |x'|$ *and* $|x'| > |x''|$, *then* $x'q'y' \vdash_M x''q''y''$ *is a* turn. *If M makes no more than one turn during any sequence of moves starting from a start configuration, then M is said to be* one turn.

One-turn pushdown automata represent an important restricted version of automata, and the formal language theory has studied their properties in detail (see Section 5.7 in [22] and Section 6.1 in [33]).

Definition 12.28. *Let M be a pushdown automaton. If M satisfies the conditions from Definitions 12.26 and 12.27, it is said to be* one-turn atomic pushdown automaton. *Additionally, if M is regulated (see Definition 12.5); it is a* one-turn atomic regulated pushdown automaton *(OA-RPDA for short).*

For any family of language $\mathscr{L}$ *and* $i \in \{1, 2, 3\}$, *define*

$$\textbf{OA-RPDA}(\mathscr{L}, i) = \{L \mid L = L(M, \Xi, i), \text{ where } M \text{ is a one-turn atomic pushdown automaton and } \Xi \in \mathscr{L}\}.$$

We next prove that one-turn atomic pushdown automata regulated by linear languages characterize the family of recursively enumerable languages. In fact, these automata need no more than one state and two pushdown symbols to achieve this characterization.

Lemma 12.16. *Let Q be a left-extended queue grammar satisfying the normal form of Definition 11.9. Then, there is a linear grammar G and a one-turn atomic pushdown* *automaton* $M = (\{\lfloor\}, \tau, \{0, 1\}, H, \lfloor, 0, \{\lfloor\})$ *such that* $\mathrm{card}(H) = \mathrm{card}(\tau) + 4$ *and* $L(Q) = L(M, L(G), 3)$.

Proof. Let $Q = (\Sigma, \tau, W, F, R, g)$ be a queue grammar satisfying the normal form of Definition 11.9. For some $n \geq 1$, introduce a homomorphism f from R to X, where

$$X = \{1\}^*\{0\}\{1\}^*\{1\}^n \cap \{0, 1\}^{2n}.$$

Extend f so it is defined from R^* to X^*. Define the substitution h from Σ^* to X^* as

$$h(a) = \{f(r) \mid r = (a, p, x, q) \in R \text{ for some } p, q \in W, x \in \Sigma^*\}.$$

Define the coding d from $\{0, 1\}^*$ to $\{2, 3\}^*$ as $d(0) = 2$, $d(1) = 3$. Construct the linear grammar

$$G = (N, \Delta, R, S)$$

as follows. Initially, set

$$\begin{aligned} \Delta &= \{0, 1, 2, 3\} \cup \tau, \\ N &= \{S\} \cup \{\tilde{q} \mid q \in W\} \cup \{\hat{q} \mid q \in W\}, \\ R &= \{S \rightarrow \tilde{f}2 \mid f \in F\} \cup \{\tilde{!} \rightarrow \hat{!}\}. \end{aligned}$$

Extend R by performing (1)–(3), given as follows:

(i) For every $r = (a, p, x, q) \in R, p, q \in w, x \in \Delta^*$

$R = R \cup \{\tilde{q} \rightarrow \tilde{p}d(f(r))x\}$;

(ii) For every $(a, p, x, q) \in R$,

$R = R \cup \{\hat{q} \rightarrow y\hat{p}b \mid y \in \mathrm{reversal}(h(x)), b \in h(a)\}$;

(iii) For every $(a, p, x, q) \in R$, $ap = S, p, q \in W, x \in \Sigma^*$,

$R = R \cup \{\hat{q} \rightarrow y \mid y \in \mathrm{reversal}(h(x))\}$.

Define the atomic pushdown automaton

$$M = (\{\lfloor\}, \tau, \{0, 1\}, H, \lfloor, 0, \{\lfloor\})$$

where H contains the following transition rules:

$$\begin{aligned} &0\colon \lfloor \rightarrow 0\lfloor, \\ &1\colon \lfloor \rightarrow 1\lfloor, \\ &2\colon 0\lfloor \rightarrow \lfloor, \\ &3\colon 1\lfloor \rightarrow \lfloor, \\ &a\colon \lfloor a \rightarrow \lfloor \text{ for every } a \in \tau. \end{aligned}$$

We next demonstrate that $L(M, L(G), 3) = L(Q)$. Observe that M accepts every string $w = w_1 \cdots w_{m-1}w_m$ as

$$
\begin{array}{lll}
0\lfloor w_1 \cdots w_{m-1}w_m & \vdash_M^+ & 0\bar{b}_m \cdots \bar{b}_1\bar{a}_n \cdots \bar{a}_1 \lfloor w_1 \cdots w_{m-1}w_m \\
& \vdash_M^{|\bar{a}_n \cdots \bar{a}_1|} & 0\bar{b}_m \cdots \bar{b}_1 \lfloor w_1 \cdots w_{m-1}w_m \\
& \vdash_M^{|w_1|} & 0\bar{b}_m \cdots \bar{b}_1 \lfloor w_2 \cdots w_{m-1}w_m \\
& \vdash_M^{|\bar{b}_1|} & 0\bar{b}_m \cdots \bar{b}_2 \lfloor w_2 \cdots w_{m-1}w_m \\
& \vdash_M^{|w_2|} & 0\bar{b}_m \cdots \bar{b}_2 \lfloor w_3 \cdots w_{m-1}w_m \\
& \vdash_M^{|\bar{b}_2|} & 0\bar{b}_m \cdots \bar{b}_3 \lfloor w_3 \cdots w_{m-1}w_m \\
& \vdots & \\
& \vdash_M & 0\bar{b}_m \lfloor w_m \\
& \vdash_M^{|w_m|} & 0\bar{b}_m \lfloor \\
& \vdash_M^{|\bar{b}_m|} & 0\lfloor \\
& \vdash_M & \lfloor
\end{array}
$$

according to a string of the form $\beta\alpha\alpha'\beta' \in L(G)$, where

$$
\begin{aligned}
\beta &= \text{reversal}(f(r_m))\,\text{reversal}(f(r_{m-1}))\cdots\text{reversal}(f(r_1)),\\
\alpha &= \text{reversal}(f(t_n))\,\text{reversal}(f(t_{n-1}))\cdots\text{reversal}(f(t_1)),\\
\alpha' &= f(t_0)f(t_1)\cdots f(t_n),\\
\beta' &= d(f(r_1))w_1d(f(r_2))w_2\cdots d(f(r_m))w_m
\end{aligned}
$$

for some $m, n \geq 1$ so that for $i = 1, \ldots, m$,

$$t_i = (b_i, q_i, w_i, q_{i+1}) \in R, b_i \in \Sigma - \tau, q_i, q_{i+1} \in Q, \bar{b}_i = f(t_i)$$

and for $j = 1, \ldots, n+1$, $r_j = (a_{j-1}, p_{j-1}, x_j, p_j)$, $a_{j-1} \in \Sigma - \tau, p_{j-1}, p_j \in Q - F, x_j \in (\Sigma - \tau)^*$, $\bar{a}_j = f(r_j)$, $q_{m+1} \in F$, $\bar{a}_0p_0 = g$. Thus, in Q,

$$
\begin{array}{lll}
\#a_0p_0 & \Rightarrow_Q a_0\#y_0x_1p_1 & [(a_0,p_0,x_1,p_1)]\\
& \Rightarrow_Q a_0a_1\#y_1x_2p_2 & [(a_1,p_1,x_2,p_2)]\\
& \Rightarrow_Q a_0a_1a_2\#y_2x_3p_3 & [(a_2,p_2,x_3,p_3)]\\
& \vdots & \\
& \Rightarrow_Q a_0a_1a_2\cdots a_{n-1}\#y_{n-1}x_np_n & [(a_{n-1},p_{n-1},x_n,p_n)]\\
& \Rightarrow_Q a_0a_1a_2\cdots a_n\#y_nx_{n+1}q_1 & [(a_n,p_n,x_{n+1},q_1)]\\
& \Rightarrow_Q a_0\cdots a_nb_1\#b_2\cdots b_mw_1q_2 & [(b_1,q_1,w_1,q_2)]\\
& \Rightarrow_Q a_0\cdots a_nb_1b_2\#b_3\cdots b_mw_1w_2q_3 & [(b_2,q_2,w_2,q_3)]\\
& \vdots & \\
& \Rightarrow_Q a_0\cdots a_nb_1\cdots b_{m-1}\#b_mw_1\cdots w_{m-1}q_m & [(b_{m-1},q_{m-1},w_{m-1},q_m)]\\
& \Rightarrow_Q a_0\cdots a_nb_1\cdots b_m\#w_1\cdots w_mq_{m+1} & [(b_m,q_m,w_m,q_{m+1})].
\end{array}
$$

Therefore, $w_1w_2\cdots w_m \in L(Q)$. Consequently, $L(M, L(G), 3) \subseteq L(Q)$. A proof of $L(Q) \subseteq L(M, L(G), 3)$ is left to the reader.

As $L(Q) \subseteq L(M, L(G), 3)$ and $L(M, L(G), 3) \subseteq L(Q)$, $L(Q) = L(M, L(G), 3)$. Observe that M is one-turn atomic. Furthermore, $\text{card}(H) = \text{card}(\tau) + 4$. Thus, Lemma 12.16 holds. ■

Theorem 12.28. For every $L \in$ **RE**, there is a linear language Ξ and a one-turn atomic pushdown automaton $M = (Q, D, \Gamma, R, s, \$, F)$ such that $\text{card}(Q) \leq 1$, $\text{card}(\Gamma) \leq 2$, $\text{card}(R) \leq \text{card}(D) + 4$, and $L(M, \Xi, 3) = L$.

Proof. By Theorem 4.3, for every $L \in$ **RE**, there is a left-extended queue grammar Q such that $L = L(Q)$. Thus, this theorem follows from Theorem 11.4 and Lemma 12.16. ■

Theorem 12.29. For every $L \in$ **RE**, there is a linear language Ξ and a one-turn atomic pushdown automaton $M = (Q, D, \Gamma, R, s, \$, F)$ such that $\text{card}(Q) \leq 1$, $\text{card}(\Gamma) \leq 2$, $\text{card}(R) \leq \text{card}(D) + 4$, and $L(M, \Xi, 1) = L$.

Proof. This theorem can be proved by analogy with the proof of Theorem 12.28. ■

Theorem 12.30. For every $L \in$ **RE**, there is a linear language Ξ and a one-turn atomic pushdown automaton $M = (Q, D, \Gamma, R, s, \$, F)$ such that $\text{card}(Q) \leq 1$, $\text{card}(\Gamma) \leq 2$, $\text{card}(R) \leq \text{card}(D) + 4$, and $L(M, \Xi, 2) = L$.

Proof. This theorem can be proved by analogy with the proof of Theorem 12.28. ■

From the previous three theorems, we obtain the following corollary:

Corollary 12.8. *For* $i \in \{1, 2, 3\}$, **RE** = **OA-RPDA**(**LIN**, i).

We close this section by suggesting some open-problem areas concerning regulated automata.

Open Problem 12.9. *For* $i = 1, \ldots, 3$, *consider* **RPDA**($\mathscr{L}, i$), *where* $\mathscr{L}$ *is a language family satisfying* **REG** $\subset \mathscr{L} \subset$ **LIN**. *For instance, consider* $\mathscr{L}$ *as the family of* minimal linear languages *(see page 76 in [11]). Compare* **RE** *with* **RPDA**($\mathscr{L}, i$).

Open Problem 12.10. *Investigate special cases of regulated pushdown automata, such as their deterministic versions.*

Open Problem 12.11. *By analogy with regulated pushdown automata, introduce and study some other types of regulated automata.*

12.5.8 Self-reproducing pushdown transducers

Throughout this entire book, we cover modern language-defining models. In the final section of this Chapter 12, however, we make a single exception. Indeed, we explain how to modify these models in a very natural way so that they define translations rather than languages. Consider the notion of a pushdown automaton (see Chapter 7). Based upon this notion, we next introduce and discuss the notion of a self-reproducing pushdown transducer, which defines a translation, not a language. In essence, the transducer makes its translation as follows. After a translation of an input string, x, to an output string, y, a self-reproducing pushdown transducer can make a self-reproducing step during which it moves y to its input tape and translates it again. In this self-reproducing way, it can repeat the translation n-times, for $n \geq 1$. This section demonstrates that every recursively enumerable language can be characterized by the domain of the translation obtained from a self-reproducing pushdown transducer that repeats its translation no more than three times. This characterization is of some interest because it does not hold in terms of ordinary pushdown transducers. Indeed, the domain obtained from any ordinary pushdown transducer is a context-free language (see [22]).

12.5.9 Definitions

Definition 12.29. *A* self-reproducing pushdown transducer *is an eight-tuple*

$$M = (Q, \Gamma, D, \Omega, R, s, S, O)$$

where Q *is a finite set of states,* Γ *is a total alphabet such that* $Q \cap \Gamma = \emptyset$, $D \subseteq \Gamma$ *is an input alphabet,* $\Omega \subseteq \Gamma$ *is an output alphabet,* R *is a finite set of* translation rules *of the form* $u_1qw \rightarrow u_2pv$ *with* $u_1, u_2, w, v \in \Gamma^*$ *and* $q, p \in Q$, $s \in Q$ *is the* start state, $S \in \Gamma$ *is the* start pushdown symbol, $O \subseteq Q$ *is the set of* self-reproducing states.

A configuration *of* M *is any string of the form* $\$zqy\$x$, *where* $x, y, z \in \Gamma^*$, $q \in Q$, *and* $\$$ *is a special* bounding symbol ($\$ \notin Q \cup \Gamma$). *If* $u_1qw \rightarrow u_2pv \in R$, $y = \$hu_1qwz\$t$, *and* $x = \$hu_2pz\$tv$, *where* $h, u_1, u_2, w, t, v, z \in \Gamma^*$, $q, p \in Q$, *then* M *makes a* translation step *from* y *to* x *in* M, *symbolically written as* $y\ {}_t\!\Rightarrow x\ [u_1qw \rightarrow u_2pv]$ *or, simply* $y\ {}_t\!\Rightarrow x$ *in* M. *If* $y = \$hq\$t$ *and* $x = \$hqt\$$, *where* $t, h \in \Gamma^*$, $q \in O$, *then* M *makes a* self-reproducing step *from* y *to* x *in* M, *symbolically written as* $y\ {}_r\!\Rightarrow x$. *Write* $y \Rightarrow x$ *if* $y\ {}_t\!\Rightarrow x$ *or* $y\ {}_r\!\Rightarrow x$. *In the standard manner, extend* $\Rightarrow$ *to* $\Rightarrow^n$, *where* $n \geq 0$; *then, based on* $\Rightarrow^n$, *define* $\Rightarrow^+$ *and* $\Rightarrow^*$.

Let $w, v \in \Gamma^*$; M translates w *to* v *if* $\$Ssw\$ \Rightarrow^* \$q\$v$ *in* M. The translation obtained from M, $T(M)$, *is defined as* $T(M) = \{(w, v) : \$Ssw\$ \Rightarrow^* \$q\$v$ *with* $w \in D^*$, $v \in \Omega^*$, $q \in Q\}$. *Set* $\text{domain}(T(M)) = \{w : (w, x) \in T(M)\}$ *and* $\text{range}(T(M)) = \{x : (w, x) \in T(M)\}$.

Let n *be a nonnegative integer; if during every translation,* M *makes no more than* n *self-reproducing steps, then* M *is an* n-self-reproducing pushdown transducer. *Two self-reproducing transducers are equivalent if they both define the same translation.*

In the literature, there often exists a requirement that a pushdown transducer, $M = (Q, \Gamma, D, \Omega, R, s, S, O)$, replaces no more than one symbol on its pushdown and reads no more than one symbol during every move. As stated next, we can always turn any self-reproducing pushdown transducer to an equivalent self-reproducing pushdown transducer that satisfies this requirement.

Theorem 12.31. Let M be a self-reproducing pushdown transducer. Then, there is an equivalent self-reproducing pushdown transducer

$$N = (Q, \Gamma, D, \Omega, R, s, S, O)$$

in which every translation rule, $u_1qw \rightarrow u_2pv \in R$, where $u_1, u_2, w, v \in \Gamma^*$ and $q, p \in Q$, satisfies $|u_1| \leq 1$ and $|w| \leq 1$.

Proof. Basic Idea. Consider every rule $u_1qw \rightarrow u_2pv$ in M with $|u_1| \geq 2$ or $|w| \geq 2$. N simulates a move made according to this rule as follows. First, N leaves q for a new state and makes $|w|$ consecutive moves during which it reads w symbol by symbol so that after these moves, it has w recorded in a new state, $\langle qw \rangle$. From this new state, it makes $|u_1|$ consecutive moves during which it pops u_1 symbol by symbol from the pushdown so that after these moves, it has both u_1 and w recorded in another new state, $\langle u_1qw \rangle$. To complete this simulation, it performs a move according to $\langle u_1qw \rangle \rightarrow u_2pv$. Otherwise, N works as M. A detailed version of this proof is left to the reader. ■

12.5.10 Results

Recall that every recursively enumerable language is generated by a left-extended queue grammar (see Theorem 4.3).

Lemma 12.17. *Let Q be a left-extended queue grammar satisfying the normal form introduced in Definition 11.9. Then, there exists a two-self-reproducing pushdown transducer, M, such that* $\text{domain}(T(M)) = L(Q)$ *and* $\text{range}(T(M)) = \{\varepsilon\}$.

Proof. Let $G = (\Sigma, \Delta, W, F, s, R)$ be a left-extended queue grammar satisfying the normal form introduced in Definition 11.9. Without any loss of generality, assume that $\{0,1\} \cap (\Sigma \cup W) = \emptyset$. For some positive integer, n, define an injection, ι, from R to $(\{0,1\}^n - \{1\}^n)$ so that ι is an injective homomorphism when its domain is extended to $(VW)^*$; after this extension, ι thus represents an injective homomorphism from $(VW)^*$ to $(\{0,1\}^n - \{1\}^n)^*$; a proof that such an injection necessarily exists is simple and left to the reader. Based on ι, define the substitution, ν, from Σ to $(\{0,1\}^n - \{1\}^n)$ so that for every $a \in \Sigma$, $\nu(a) = \{\iota(p) : p \in R,\ p = (a,b,x,c)$ for some $x \in \Sigma^*;\ b,c \in W\}$. Extend the domain of ν to Σ^*. Furthermore, define the substitution, μ, from W to $(\{0,1\}^n - \{1\}^n)$ so that for every $q \in W$, $\mu(q) = \{\iota(p) : p \in R,\ p = (a,b,x,c)$ for some $a \in \Sigma,\ x \in \Sigma^*;\ b,c \in W\}$. Extend the domain of μ to W^*.

Construction. Introduce the self-reproducing pushdown transducer

$$M = (Q, \Delta \cup \{0,1,S\}, \Delta, \emptyset, R, z, S, O)$$

where $Q = \{o,c,f,z\} \cup \{\langle p,i \rangle : p \in W \text{ and } i \in \{1,2\}\}$, $O = \{o,f\}$, and R is constructed by performing the following steps:

(1) If $a_0q_0 = s$, where $a \in \Sigma - \Delta$ and $q \in W - F$, then add $Sz \rightarrow uS\langle q_0,1\rangle w$ to R, for all $w \in \mu(q_0)$ and all $u \in \nu(a_0)$;
(2) If $(a,q,y,p) \in R$, where $a \in \Sigma - \Delta$, $p,q \in W - F$, and $y \in (\Sigma - \Delta)^*$, then add $S\langle q,1\rangle \rightarrow uS\langle p,1\rangle w$ to R, for all $w \in \mu(p)$ and $u \in \nu(y)$;
(3) For every $q \in W - F$, add $S\langle q,1\rangle \rightarrow S\langle q,2\rangle$ to R;
(4) If $(a,q,y,p) \in R$, where $a \in \Sigma - \Delta$, $p,q \in W - F$, and $y \in \Delta^*$, then add $S\langle q,2\rangle y \rightarrow S\langle p,2\rangle w$ to R, for all $w \in \mu(p)$;
(5) If $(a,q,y,p) \in R$, where $a \in \Sigma - \Delta$, $q \in W - F$, $y \in \Delta^*$, and $p \in F$, then add $S\langle q,2\rangle y \rightarrow SoS$ to R;

(6) Add $o0 \to 0o$, $o1 \to 1o$, $oS \to c$, $0c \to c0$, $1c \to c1$, $Sc \to f$, $0f0 \to f$, $1f1 \to f$ to R.

For brevity, the following proofs omit some obvious details, which the reader can easily fill in. The next claim describes how M accepts each string from $L(M)$.

Claim 1. *M accepts every $h \in L(M)$ in the following way*

$$
\begin{aligned}
&\$Szy_1y_2\cdots y_{m-1}y_m\$\\
&\Rightarrow\ \$g_0\langle q_0,1\rangle y_1y_2\cdots y_{m-1}y_m\$t_0\\
&\Rightarrow\ \$g_1\langle q_1,1\rangle y_1y_2\cdots y_{m-1}y_m\$t_1\\
&\quad\vdots\\
&\Rightarrow\ \$g_k\langle q_k,1\rangle y_1y_2\cdots y_{m-1}y_m\$t_k\\
&\Rightarrow\ \$g_k\langle q_k,2\rangle y_1y_2\cdots y_{m-1}y_m\$t_k\\
&\Rightarrow\ \$g_k\langle q_{k+1},2\rangle y_1y_2\cdots y_{m-1}y_m\$t_{k+1}\\
&\Rightarrow\ \$g_k\langle q_{k+2},2\rangle y_2\cdots y_{m-1}y_m\$t_{k+2}\\
&\quad\vdots\\
{}_t&\Rightarrow\ \$g_k\langle q_{k+m},2\rangle y_m\$t_{k+m}\\
{}_t&\Rightarrow\ \$g_kSo\$t_{k+m}S\\
{}_r&\Rightarrow\ \$g_kSot_{k+m}S\$\\
{}_t&\Rightarrow^{l}\ \$g_kSt_{k+m}oS\$\\
{}_t&\Rightarrow\ \$g_kSt_{k+m}c\$\\
{}_t&\Rightarrow^{l}\ \$u_1Sc\$v_1\\
{}_t&\Rightarrow\ \$u_1f\$v_1\\
{}_r&\Rightarrow\ \$u_1fv_1\$\\
&\Rightarrow\ \$u_2fv_2\$\\
&\quad\vdots\\
&\Rightarrow\ \$u_lfv_l\$\\
&\Rightarrow\ \$f\$
\end{aligned}
$$

in M, where $k, m \geq 1$; $q_0, q_1, \ldots, q_{k+m} \in W - F$; $y_1, \ldots, y_m \in \Delta^*$; $t_i \in \mu(q_0q_1\cdots q_i)$ for $i = 0, 1, \ldots, k+m$; $g_j \in \nu(d_0d_1\cdots d_j)$ with $d_1, \ldots, d_j \in (\Sigma - \Delta)^*$ for $j = 0, 1, \ldots, k$; $d_0d_1\cdots d_k = a_0a_1\cdots a_{k+m}$ where $a_1, \ldots, a_{k+m} \in \Sigma - \Delta$, $d_0 = a_0$, and $s = a_0q_0$; $g_k = t_{k+m}$ (notice that $\nu(a_0a_1\cdots a_{k+m}) = \mu(q_0q_1\cdots q_{k+m})$);

$$v_i \in \text{prefix}\,(\mu(q_0q_1\cdots q_{k+m}), |\mu(q_0q_1\cdots q_{k+m})| - i)$$

for $i = 1, \ldots, \upsilon$ with $\upsilon = |\mu(q_0q_1\cdots q_{k+m})|$;

$$u_j \in \text{suffix}\,(\nu(a_0a_1\cdots a_{k+m}), |\nu(a_0a_1\cdots a_{k+m})| - j)$$

for $j = 1, \ldots, l$ with $l = |\nu(a_0a_1\cdots a_{k+m})|$; $h = y_1y_2\cdots y_{m-1}y_m$.

Proof. Examine steps (1)–(6) of the construction of R. Notice that during every successful computation, M uses the rules introduced in step i before it uses the rules introduced in step $i+1$, for $i = 1, \ldots, 5$. Thus, in greater detail, every successful computation $\$Szh\$ \Rightarrow^* \$f\$$ can be expressed as

$$
\begin{aligned}
&\$Szy_1y_2\cdots y_{m-1}y_m\$ \\
&\Rightarrow \ \$g_0\langle q_0,1\rangle y_1y_2\cdots y_{m-1}y_m\$t_0 \\
&\Rightarrow \ \$g_1\langle q_1,1\rangle y_1y_2\cdots y_{m-1}y_m\$t_1 \\
&\quad \vdots \\
&\Rightarrow \ \$g_k\langle q_k,1\rangle y_1y_2\cdots y_{m-1}y_m\$t_k \\
&\Rightarrow \ \$g_k\langle q_k,2\rangle y_1y_2\cdots y_{m-1}y_m\$t_k \\
&\Rightarrow \ \$g_k\langle q_{k+1},2\rangle y_1y_2\cdots y_{m-1}y_m\$t_{k+1} \\
&\Rightarrow \ \$g_k\langle q_{k+2},2\rangle y_2y_3\cdots y_{m-1}y_m\$t_{k+2} \\
&\Rightarrow \ \$g_k\langle q_{k+3},2\rangle y_3y_4\cdots y_{m-1}y_m\$t_{k+3} \\
&\quad \vdots \\
&{}_t\!\Rightarrow \ \$g_k\langle q_{k+m},2\rangle y_m\$t_{k+m} \\
&{}_t\!\Rightarrow \ \$g_kSo\$t_{k+m}S \\
&\Rightarrow^* \ \$f\$
\end{aligned}
$$

where $k,m \geq 1$; $h = y_1y_2\cdots y_{m-1}y_m$; $q_0,q_1,\dots,q_{k+m} \in W - F$; $y_1,\dots,y_m \in \Delta^*$; $t_i \in \mu(q_0q_1\cdots q_i)$ for $i = 0,1,\dots,k+m$; $g_j \in \nu(d_0d_1\cdots d_j)$ with $d_1,\dots,d_j \in (\Sigma - \Delta)^*$ for $j = 0,1,\dots,k$; $d_0d_1\cdots d_k = a_0a_1\cdots a_{k+m}$ where $a_1,\dots,a_{k+m} \in \Sigma - \Delta$, $d_0 = a_0$, and $s = a_0q_0$.

During $\$g_kSo\$t_{k+m}S \Rightarrow^* \$f\$$ only the rules of (6) are used. Recall these rules: $o0 \rightarrow 0o$, $o1 \rightarrow 1o$, $oS \rightarrow c$, $0c \rightarrow c0$, $1c \rightarrow c1$, $Sc \rightarrow f$, $0f0 \rightarrow f$, $1f1 \rightarrow f$. Observe that to obtain $\$f\$$ from $\$g_kSo\$t_{k+m}S$ by using these rules, M performs $\$g_kSo\$t_{k+m}S \Rightarrow^* \$f\$$ as follows:

$$
\begin{aligned}
&\$g_kSo\$t_{k+m}S \\
&{}_r\!\Rightarrow \ \$g_kSot_{k+m}S\$ \\
&{}_t\!\Rightarrow^\iota \ \$g_kSt_{k+m}oS\$ \\
&{}_t\!\Rightarrow \ \$g_kSt_{k+m}c\$ \\
&{}_t\!\Rightarrow^\iota \ \$u_1Sc\$v_1 \\
&{}_t\!\Rightarrow \ \$u_1f\$v_1 \\
&{}_r\!\Rightarrow \ \$u_1fv_1\$ \\
&\Rightarrow \ \$u_2fv_2\$ \\
&\quad \vdots \\
&\Rightarrow \ \$u_lfv_l\$ \\
&\Rightarrow \ \$f\$
\end{aligned}
$$

in M, where $g_k = t_{k+m}$; $v_i \in \text{prefix}\,(\mu(q_0q_1\cdots q_{k+m}), |\mu(q_0q_1\cdots q_{k+m})| - i)$ for $i = 1,\dots,\upsilon$ with $\upsilon = |\mu(q_0q_1\cdots q_{k+m})|$; $u_j \in \text{suffix}\,(\nu(a_0a_1\cdots a_{k+m}), |\nu(a_0a_1\cdots a_{k+m}) - j)$ for $j = 1,\dots,l$ with $l = |\nu(a_0a_1\cdots a_{k+m})|$. This computation implies $g_k = t_{k+m}$. As a result, the claim holds.

□

Let M accepts $h \in L(M)$ in the way described in the above claim. Examine the construction of R to see that at this point R contains

$$(a_0, q_0, z_0, q_1), \ldots, (a_k, q_k, z_k, q_{k+1}), (a_{k+1}, q_{k+1}, y_1, q_{k+2}), \ldots,$$
$$(a_{k+m-1}, q_{k+m-1}, y_{m-1}, q_{k+m}), (a_{k+m}, q_{k+m}, y_m, q_{k+m+1})$$

where $z_1, \ldots, z_k \in (\Sigma - \Delta)^*$, so G makes the generation of h in the way described in Definition 11.9. Thus $h \in L(G)$. Consequently, $L(M) \subseteq L(G)$.

Let G generate $h \in L(G)$ in the way described in Definition 11.9. Then, M accepts h in the way described in the above claim, so $L(G) \subseteq L(M)$; a detailed proof of this inclusion is left to the reader.

As $L(M) \subseteq L(G)$ and $L(G) \subseteq L(M)$, $L(G) = L(M)$.

From the above Claim, it follows that M is a two-self-reproducing pushdown transducer. Thus, Lemma 12.17 holds. ■

Theorem 12.32. For every recursively enumerable language, L, there exists a two-self-reproducing pushdown transducer, M, such that

$$\text{domain}(T(M)) = L$$

and

$$\text{range}(T(M)) = \{\varepsilon\}.$$

Proof. This theorem follows from Theorems 4.3 and 11.4 and Lemma 12.17. ■

Chapter 13
Parallel grammatical models

Many modern information technologies work in parallel, so they make use of mutually cooperating multiprocessor computers. It thus comes as no surprise that the investigation of parallel computation fulfills a central role within computer science as a whole. In order to build up a systematized body of knowledge about computation in parallel, we need its proper formalization in the first place. The present chapter describes several types of parallel grammars, which can act as a grammatical formalization like this very well.

To give an insight into parallel grammars, recall that up until now, in all grammars under consideration, a single rule was applied during every derivation step. To obtain parallel grammars, this one-rule application is generalized to the application of several rules during a single step. Parallel grammars represent the subject of this chapter. First, it studies partially parallel generation of languages (see Section 13.1), after which it investigates the totally parallel generation of languages (see Section 13.2).

13.1 Partially parallel grammars

Partially parallel language generation is represented by the notion of a scattered context grammar (SCG), which is based on finite sequences of context-free rules. According to these sequences, the grammar simultaneously rewrites several nonterminals during a single derivation step while keeping the rest of the rewritten string unchanged.

13.1.1 Definitions and examples

In this section, we define SCGs and illustrate them by examples.

Definition 13.1. *An SCG is a quadruple*

$$G = (\Sigma, \Delta, R, S); \quad N = \Sigma - T$$

where

- Σ *is a* total alphabet*;*
- $\Delta \subset \Sigma$ *an alphabet of* terminals*;*

- $R \subseteq \bigcup_{m=1}^{\infty} (N^m \times (\Sigma^*)^m)$ *is a finite set of* rules *of the form*

  $$(A_1, A_2, \ldots, A_n) \to (x_1, x_2, \ldots, x_n)$$

  where $A_i \in N$, *and* $x_i \in \Sigma^*$, *for* $1 \leq i \leq n$, *for some* $n \geq 1$;
- $S \in \Sigma - \Delta$ *is the* start symbol;
- N *is an alphabet of* nonterminals.

If

$$u = u_1 A_1 \cdots u_n A_n u_{n+1},$$
$$v = u_1 x_1 \cdots u_n x_n u_{n+1},$$

and $p = (A_1, \ldots, A_n) \to (x_1, \ldots, x_n) \in R$, *where* $u_i \in \Sigma^*$, *for all* i, $1 \leq i \leq n+1$, *then* G *makes a* derivation step *from* u *to* v *according to* p, *symbolically written as*

$$u \Rightarrow_G v \; [p],$$

or, simply, $u \Rightarrow_G v$. *Set*

$$\text{lhs}\, p = A_1 \cdots A_n,$$
$$\text{rhs}\, p = x_1 \cdots x_n,$$

and

$$\text{len}\,(p) = n.$$

If $\text{len}\,(p) \geq 2$, p *is said to be a* context-sensitive rule *while for* $\text{len}\,(p) = 1$, p *is said to be* context free. *Define* $\Rightarrow_G^k$, $\Rightarrow_G^*$, *and* $\Rightarrow_G^+$ *in the standard way. The* language *of* G *is denoted by* $L(G)$ *and defined as*

$$L(G) = \{w \in \Delta^* \mid S \Rightarrow_G^* w\}.$$

A language L *is a* scattered context language *if there exists an SCG* G *such that* $L = L(G)$.

Definition 13.2. *A* propagating SCG *is an SCG*

$$G = (\Sigma, \Delta, R, S)$$

in which every $(A_1, \ldots, A_n) \to (x_1, \ldots, x_n) \in R$ *satisfies* $|x_i| \geq 1$, *for all* i, $1 \leq i \leq n$. *A* propagating scattered context language *is a language generated by a propagating SCG.*

Example 13.1. Consider the non-context-free language $L = \{a^n b^n c^n \mid n \geq 1\}$. This language can be generated by the SCG

$$G = (\{S, A, a, b, c\}, \{a, b, c\}, R, S)$$

where

$$R = \{(S) \to (aAbAcA),$$
$$(A, A, A) \to (aA, bA, cA),$$
$$(A, A, A) \to (\varepsilon, \varepsilon, \varepsilon)\}.$$

For example, the sentence *aabbcc* is generated by G as follows:

$$S \Rightarrow_G aAbAcA \Rightarrow_G aaAbbAccA \Rightarrow_G aabbcc.$$

Notice, however, that L can be also generated by the propagating SCG

$$G' = (\{S, A, a, b, c\}, \{a, b, c\}, R', S)$$

where

$$\begin{aligned} R' = \{&(S) \to (AAA), \\ &(A, A, A) \to (aA, bA, cA), \\ &(A, A, A) \to (a, b, c)\}. \end{aligned}$$

For brevity, we often label rules of SCGs with labels (just like we do in other grammars), as illustrated in the next example.

Example 13.2. Consider the non-context-free language

$$L = \{(ab^n)^m \mid m \geq n \geq 2\}.$$

This language is generated by the propagating SCG

$$G = (\{S, S_1, S_2, B, M, X, Y, Z, a, b\}, \{a, b\}, R, S)$$

with R containing the rules

$$\begin{aligned} &1 : (S) \to (MS), \\ &2 : (S) \to (S_1S_2), \\ &3 : (S_1, S_2) \to (MS_1, BS_2), \\ &4 : (S_1, S_2) \to (MX, BY), \\ &5 : (X, B, Y) \to (BX, Y, b), \\ &6 : (M, X, Y) \to (X, Y, ab), \\ &7 : (M, X, Y) \to (Z, Y, ab), \\ &8 : (Z, B, Y) \to (Z, b, Y), \\ &9 : (Z, Y) \to (a, b). \end{aligned}$$

Clearly, by applying rules 1–4, G generates a string from

$$\{M\}^+\{X\}\{B\}^+\{Y\}.$$

In what follows, we demonstrate that the string is of the form $M^{m-1}XB^{n-1}Y$, where m, $n \geq 2$. Rule 1 allows G to add Ms to the beginning of the sentential form, so $m \geq n$ holds true. Observe that each of the rules 5–8 either shifts the last nonterminal Y left or keeps its position unchanged. As a result, the rightmost nonterminal preceding Y has to be replaced with Y by rules 5–7; otherwise, the skipped nonterminals cannot be rewritten during the rest of the derivation. For the same reason, the rightmost nonterminal M preceding X has to be rewritten by the rule 6. Rules 5 and 6 are applied in a cycle consisting of $n-1$ applications of 5 and one application of 6:

$$\begin{aligned} M^{m-1}XB^{n-1}Y &\Rightarrow_G^{n-1} M^{m-1}B^{n-1}XYb^{n-1} \quad [5^{n-1}] \\ &\Rightarrow_G M^{m-2}XB^{n-1}Yab^n \quad [6]. \end{aligned}$$

At this point, the substring preceding Y differs from the original string only in the number of Ms decremented by 1, and the cycle can be repeated again. After repeating this cycle $m-2$ times, we obtain $MXB^{n-1}Y(ab^n)^{m-2}$. The derivation is completed as follows:

$$\begin{aligned} MXB^{n-1}Y(ab^n)^{m-2} &\Rightarrow_G^{n-1} MB^{n-1}XYb^{n-1}(ab^n)^{m-2} && [5^{n-1}] \\ &\Rightarrow_G ZB^{n-1}Y(ab^n)^{m-1} && [7] \\ &\Rightarrow_G^{n-1} Zb^{n-1}Y(ab^n)^{m-1} && [8^{n-1}] \\ &\Rightarrow_G (ab^n)^m && [9]. \end{aligned}$$

Example 13.3 (see [34], [35]). Consider the non-context-free language

$$L = \{a^{2^n} \mid n \geq 0\}.$$

This language is generated by the propagating SCG

$$G = (\{S, W, X, Y, Z, A, a\}, \{a\}, R, S)$$

with R containing the rules

$$\begin{aligned} &1: (S) \rightarrow (a), \\ &2: (S) \rightarrow (aa), \\ &3: (S) \rightarrow (WAXY), \\ &4: (W, A, X, Y) \rightarrow (a, W, X, AAY), \\ &5: (W, X, Y) \rightarrow (a, W, AXY), \\ &6: (W, X, Y) \rightarrow (Z, Z, a), \\ &7: (Z, A, Z) \rightarrow (Z, a, Z), \\ &8: (Z, Z) \rightarrow (a, a). \end{aligned}$$

In what follows, we demonstrate that $L(G) = L$. Rules 1 and 2 generate a and aa, respectively. Rule 3 starts off the derivation of longer strings in L. Consider the following derivation of $a^{16} \in L(G)$:

$$\begin{aligned} S &\Rightarrow_G WAXY && [3] \\ &\Rightarrow_G aWXA^2Y && [4] \\ &\Rightarrow_G a^2WA^3XY && [5] \\ &\Rightarrow_G a^3WA^2XA^2Y && [4] \\ &\Rightarrow_G a^4WAXA^4Y && [4] \\ &\Rightarrow_G a^5WXA^6Y && [4] \\ &\Rightarrow_G a^6WA^7XY && [5] \\ &\Rightarrow_G a^6ZA^7Za && [6] \\ &\Rightarrow_G^7 a^{13}ZZa && [7^7] \\ &\Rightarrow_G a^{16} && [8]. \end{aligned}$$

Observe that in any successful derivation, rules 4 and 5 are applied in a cycle, and after the required number of As is obtained, the derivation is finished by rules 6–8. In greater detail, observe that the rule $(W, A, X, Y) \rightarrow (a, W, X, AAY)$ removes one A between W and X and inserts two As between X and Y. In a successful derivation, this rule has to rewrite the leftmost nonterminal A. After all As are removed between W and X, the rule $(W, X, Y) \rightarrow (a, W, AXY)$ can be used to bring all As occurring between X and Y back between W and X, and the cycle can be repeated again. Alternatively, rule 6 can be used, which initializes the final phase of the derivation in which all As are replaced with as by rules 7 and 8.

By adding one more stage, the above grammar can be extended so that it generates the language

$$\left\{a^{2^{2^n}} \mid n \geq 0\right\}.$$

The first stage, similar to the above grammar, generates 2^n identical symbols that serve as a counter for the second stage. In the second stage, a string consisting of identical symbols, which are different from those generated during the first stage, is doubled 2^n times, thus obtaining 2^{2^n} identical symbols. This doubling starts from a string consisting of a single symbol. See [35] for the details.

The families of languages generated by SCGs and propagating SCGs are denoted by **SC** and **PSC**, respectively.

13.1.2 Generative power

This brief section establishes the power of SCGs. In addition, it points out a crucially important open problem, referred to as the *PSC = CS problem*, which asks whether **PSC** and **CS** coincide.

Theorem 13.1 (see [36]). $\mathbf{CF} \subset \mathbf{PSC} \subseteq \mathbf{CS} \subset \mathbf{SC} = \mathbf{RE}$.

Open Problem 13.1. Is the inclusion $\mathbf{PSC} \subseteq \mathbf{CS}$, in fact, an identity?

13.1.3 Normal forms

This section demonstrates how to transform any propagating SCG to an equivalent *2-limited propagating SCG*, which represents an important normal form of propagating SCGs. More specifically, in a 2-limited propagating SCG, each rule consists of no more than two context-free rules, either of which has, on their right-hand side, no more than two symbols.

Definition 13.3. *A* 2-limited propagating SCG *is a propagating SCG, $G = (\Sigma, \Delta, R, S)$, such that*

- $(A_1, \ldots, A_n) \rightarrow (w_1, \ldots, w_n) \in R$ *implies that* $n \leq 2$, *and for every* i, $1 \leq i \leq n$, $1 \leq |w_i| \leq 2$, *and* $w_i \in (\Sigma - \{S\})^*$ *and*
- $(A) \rightarrow (w) \in R$ *implies that* $A = S$.

The proof of the transformation is divided into two lemmas.

Lemma 13.1. *If $L \subseteq \Delta^*$ is a language generated by a propagating SCG, $G = (\Sigma, \Delta, R, S)$, and if c is a symbol such that $c \notin \Delta$, there is a 2-limited propagating SCG, $\bar{G}$, such that $L(\bar{G}) = L\{c\}$.*

Proof. Let $\bar{n}$ be the number of the rules in R. Number the rules of R from 1 to $\bar{n}$. Let $(A_{i1}, \ldots, A_{in_i}) \rightarrow (w_{i1}, \ldots, w_{in_i})$ be the ith rule. Let C and $\bar{S}$ be new symbols,

$$W = \{\langle i,j\rangle \mid 1 \leq i \leq \bar{n}, 1 \leq j \leq n_i\},$$
$$\bar{\Sigma} = \Sigma \cup \{C, \bar{S}\} \cup W \cup \{\langle C,i\rangle \mid 1 \leq i \leq \bar{n}\}.$$

Let $G' = (\bar{\Sigma}, \Delta \cup \{c\}, R', \bar{S})$ be a propagating SCG, where R' is defined as follows:

(i) for each $1 \le i \le \bar{n}$, add
$(\bar{S}) \to (S\langle C, i\rangle)$ to R';

(ii) for each i such that $n_i = 1$ and $1 \le k \le \bar{n}$, add
$(A_{i1}, \langle C, i\rangle) \to (w_{i1}, \langle C, k\rangle)$ to R';

(iii) for each i such that $n_i > 1$, $1 \le j \le n_i - 1$, $1 \le k \le \bar{n}$, add
  (a) $(A_{i1}, \langle C, i\rangle) \to (\langle i, 1\rangle, C)$,
  (b) $(\langle i,j\rangle, A_{i(j+1)}) \to (w_{ij}, \langle i,j+1\rangle)$, and
  (c) $(\langle i, n_i\rangle, C) \to (w_{in_i}, \langle C, k\rangle)$ to R';

(iv)
  (a) for each i such that $n_i = 1$, add
  $(A_{i1}, \langle C, i\rangle) \to (w_{i1}, c)$ to R';
  (b) for each i such that $n_i > 1$, add
  $(\langle i, n_i\rangle, C) \to (w_{in_i}, c)$ to R'.

Clearly, $L(G') = L\{c\}$. Since for some i and j, w_{ij} may satisfy $|w_{ij}| > 2$, G' may not be a 2-limited propagating SCG. However, by making use of standard techniques, one can obtain a 2-limited propagating SCG $\bar{G}$ from G' such that $L(\bar{G}) = L(G')$. □

Lemma 13.2. *If $L \subseteq \Delta^+$, c is a symbol such that $c \notin \Delta$, and $G = (\Sigma, \Delta \cup \{c\}, R, S)$ is a 2-limited propagating SCG satisfying $L(G) = L\{c\}$, then there is a 2-limited propagating SCG $\bar{G}$ such that $L(\bar{G}) = L$.*

Proof. For each $a \in \Delta \cup \{S\}$, let $\bar{a}$ be a new symbol. Let

$$L_1 = \{A_1A_2A_3 \mid S \Rightarrow_G^* A_1A_2A_3, A_i \in \Sigma, \text{ for all } i = 1, 2, 3\},$$
$$L_2 = \{A_1A_2A_3A_4 \mid S \Rightarrow_G^* A_1A_2A_3A_4, A_i \in \Sigma, \text{ for all } i = 1, 2, 3, 4\}.$$

Let h be the homomorphism from Σ^* to $(\{\bar{a} \mid a \in \Delta\} \cup (\Sigma - \Delta))^*$ defined as $h(a) = \bar{a}$, for each $a \in \Delta$, and $h(A) = A$, for each $A \in \Sigma - \Delta$. Let

$$\Sigma' = h(\Sigma) \cup \Delta \cup \{S'\} \cup \{\langle a, b\rangle \mid a, b \in \Sigma\}.$$

Let $G' = (\Sigma', \Delta, R', S')$, where for all $a, b \in \Delta$, $A_1, \ldots, A_6 \in \Sigma$, $A \in h(\Sigma)$, R' is defined as follows:

(i)
  (a) for each $a \in \Delta \cap L$, add
  $(S') \to (a)$ to R';
  (b) for each $A_1A_2A_3 \in L_1$, add
  $(S') \to (h(A_1)\langle A_2, A_3\rangle)$ to R';
  (c) for each $A_1A_2A_3A_4 \in L_2$, add
  $(S') \to (h(A_1A_2)\langle A_3, A_4\rangle)$ to R';

(ii)
  (a) for each $(A_1, A_2) \to (w_1, w_2) \in R$, add
  $(A_1, A_2) \to (h(w_1), h(w_2))$ to R';

(b) for each $(A_1, A_2) \rightarrow (w_1, w_2) \in R$,
  (i) where $|w_2| = 1$, add
    (A) $(A_1, \langle A_2, A_3 \rangle) \rightarrow (h(w_1), \langle w_2, A_3 \rangle)$, and
    (B) $(A_1, \langle A_3, A_2 \rangle) \rightarrow (h(w_1), \langle A_3, w_2 \rangle)$ to R';
  (ii) where $w_2 = A_4A_5$, add
    (A) $(A_1, \langle A_2, A_3 \rangle) \rightarrow (h(w_1), h(A_4)\langle A_5, A_3 \rangle)$, and
    (B) $(A_1, \langle A_3, A_2 \rangle) \rightarrow (h(w_1), h(A_3)\langle A_4, A_5 \rangle)$ to R'.
(c) for each $(A_1, A_2) \rightarrow (w_1, w_2) \in R$,
  (i) where $|w_1| = |w_2| = 1$, add
    $(A, \langle A_1, A_2 \rangle) \rightarrow (A, \langle w_1, w_2 \rangle)$ to R';
  (ii) where $w_1w_2 = A_3A_4A_5$, add
    $(A, \langle A_1, A_2 \rangle) \rightarrow (A, h(A_3)\langle A_4, A_5 \rangle)$ to R';
  (iii) where $w_1w_2 = A_3A_4A_5A_6$, add
    $(A, \langle A_1, A_2 \rangle) \rightarrow (A, h(A_3A_4)\langle A_5, A_6 \rangle)$ to R';

(iii) for each $a, b \in \Delta$, add
  (a) $(\bar{a}, \langle b, c \rangle) \rightarrow (a, \langle b, c \rangle)$, and
  (b) $(\bar{a}, \langle b, c \rangle) \rightarrow (a, b)$ to R'.

Note that the construction simply combines the symbol c with the symbol to its left. The reason for introducing a new symbol $\bar{a}$ for each $a \in \Delta$ is to guarantee that there always exists a nonterminal A whenever a rule from ((ii).(c)) is to be applied, and a nonterminal $\bar{a}$ that enables $\langle b, c \rangle$ to be converted to b by a rule from (iii). Clearly, $L(G') = L$. G' may not be a 2-limited propagating SCG since in ((ii).(c)), $|h(A_3A_4)\langle A_5, A_6 \rangle| = 3$. Once again, by standard techniques, we can obtain a 2-limited propagating SCG $\bar{G}$ from G' such that $L(\bar{G}) = L(G')$. □

By Lemmas 13.1 and 13.2, any propagating SCG can be converted to an equivalent 2-limited propagating SCG as stated in the following theorem:

Theorem 13.2. *If G is a propagating SCG, there exists a 2-limited propagating SCG $\bar{G}$ such that $L(\bar{G}) = L(G)$.*

13.1.4 Reduction

The present section discusses the reduction of SCGs. Perhaps most importantly, it studies how to reduce the size of their components, such as the number of nonterminals or the number of context-sensitive rules, without any decrease of their generative power. Indeed, any reduction like this is highly appreciated in both theory and practice because it makes scattered context rewriting more succinct and economical while preserving its power.

Definition 13.4. *Let $G = (\Sigma, \Delta, R, S)$ be an SCG. Then, its* degree of context sensitivity, *symbolically written as* dcs (G), *is defined as*

$$\text{dcs}(G) = \text{card}(\{p \mid p \in R, \text{len}(p) \geq 2\}).$$

The maximum context sensitivity *of G, denoted by* mcs (G), *is defined as*

$$\text{mcs}(G) = \max(\{\text{len}(p) - 1 \mid p \in R\}).$$

The overall context sensitivity *of G, denoted by* ocs (*G*), *is defined as*

$$\text{ocs}(G) = \text{len}(p_1) + \cdots + \text{len}(p_n) - n$$

where $R = \{p_1, \ldots, p_n\}$.

We present several results that reduce one of these measures while completely ignoring the other. Frequently, however, results of this kind are achieved at the cost of an enormous increase of the other measures. Therefore, we also undertake a finer approach to this descriptional complexity by simultaneously reducing several of these measures while keeping the generative power unchanged.

We start by pointing out a result regarding SCGs with a single nonterminal.

Theorem 13.3 (see Theorem 5 in [1]). *One-nonterminal SCGs cannot generate all recursively enumerable languages.*

For SCGs containing only one context-sensitive rule (see Definition 13.1), the following theorem holds:

Theorem 13.4. *There exists an SCG G such that G defines a non-context-free language, and*

$$\text{dcs}(G) = \text{mcs}(G) = \text{ocs}(G) = 1.$$

Proof. Consider the SCG

$$G = (\{S, A, C, a, b, c\}, \{a, b, c\}, R, S)$$

where the set of rules R is defined as

$$\begin{aligned} R = \{&(S) \rightarrow (AC),\\ &(A) \rightarrow (aAb),\\ &(C) \rightarrow (cC),\\ &(A, C) \rightarrow (\varepsilon, \varepsilon)\}. \end{aligned}$$

It is easy to verify that $L(G) = \{a^n b^n c^n \mid n \geq 0\}$ and $\text{dcs}(G) = \text{mcs}(G) = \text{ocs}(G) = 1$. □

Next, we concentrate our attention on reducing the number of nonterminals in SCGs. We first demonstrate how the number of nonterminals can be reduced to three.

Theorem 13.5. *For every recursively enumerable language L, there is an SCG* $G = (\Sigma, \Delta, R, S)$ *such that* $L(G) = L$, *and*

$$\text{card}(\Sigma - \Delta) = 3.$$

Proof. Let L be a recursively enumerable language. By Theorem 4.1, there exists a queue grammar $Q = (\bar{\Sigma}, \Delta, W, F, R, g)$ such that $L = L(Q)$. Without any loss of generality, assume that Q satisfies the normal form of Definition 11.8. Set $n = \text{card}(\bar{\Sigma} \cup W)$. Introduce a bijective homomorphism β from $\bar{\Sigma} \cup W$ to $\{B\}^*\{A\}\{B\}^* \cap$

$\{A, B\}^n$. Without any loss of generality, assume that $(\bar{\Sigma} \cup W) \cap \{A, B, S\} = \emptyset$. Define the SCG

$$G = (\Delta \cup \{A, B, S\}, \Delta, R, S)$$

where R is constructed in the following way:

(1) for $g = ab$, where $a \in \bar{\Sigma} - \Delta$ and $b \in W - F$, add $(S) \rightarrow (\beta(b)SS\beta(a)SA)$ to R;

(2) for each $a \in \{A, B\}$, add $(S, S, a, S) \rightarrow (S, \varepsilon, aS, S)$ to R;

(3) for each $(a, b, x, c) \in R$, where $a \in \bar{\Sigma} - \Delta$, $x \in (\bar{\Sigma} - \Delta)^*$, and $b, c \in W - F - \{1\}$, extend R by adding

$$\begin{aligned}&(b_1, \ldots, b_n, S, a_1, \ldots, a_n, S, S)\\ \rightarrow &(c_1, \ldots, c_n, \varepsilon, e_1, \ldots, e_n, SS, \beta(x)S)\end{aligned}$$

where $b_1 \cdots b_n = \beta(b)$, $a_1 \cdots a_n = \beta(a)$, $c_1 \cdots c_n = \beta(c)$, and $e_1 \cdots e_n = \varepsilon$;

(4) for each $(a, b, x, c) \in R$, where $a \in \bar{\Sigma} - \Delta$, $b \in W - F - \{1\}$, $x \in (\bar{\Sigma} - \Delta)^*$, and

(4.1) $c = 1$, extend R by adding
$$\begin{aligned}&(b_1, \ldots, b_n, S, a_1, \ldots, a_n, S, S)\\ \rightarrow &(c_1, \ldots, c_n, \varepsilon, e_1, \ldots, e_n, SS, \beta(x)S);\end{aligned}$$

(4.2) $c \in F$ and $x = \varepsilon$, extend R by adding
$$\begin{aligned}&(b_1, \ldots, b_n, S, a_1, \ldots, a_n, S, S, A)\\ \rightarrow &(e_1, \ldots, e_n, \varepsilon, e_{n+1}, \ldots, e_{2n}, \varepsilon, \varepsilon, \varepsilon)\end{aligned}$$

where $b_1 \cdots b_n = \beta(b)$, $a_1 \cdots a_n = \beta(a)$, $c_1 \cdots c_n = \beta(c)$, and $e_1 \cdots e_{2n} = \varepsilon$; and

(5) for each $(a, 1, x, c) \in R$, where $a \in \bar{\Sigma} - \Delta$, $x \in \Delta$, and

(5.1) $c = 1$, extend R by adding
$$\begin{aligned}&(b_1, \ldots, b_n, S, a_1, \ldots, a_n, S, S)\\ \rightarrow &(c_1, \ldots, c_n, \varepsilon, e_1, \ldots, e_n, SS, xS);\end{aligned}$$

(5.2) $c \in F$, extend R by adding
$$\begin{aligned}&(b_1, \ldots, b_n, S, a_1, \ldots, a_n, S, S, A)\\ \rightarrow &(e_1, \ldots, e_n, \varepsilon, e_{n+1}, \ldots, e_{2n}, \varepsilon, \varepsilon, x)\end{aligned}$$

where $b_1 \cdots b_n = \beta(1)$, $a_1 \cdots a_n = \beta(a)$, $c_1 \cdots c_n = \beta(c)$, and $e_1 \cdots e_{2n} = \varepsilon$.

The constructed SCG G simulates the queue grammar Q that satisfies the normal form of Definition 11.8. The rule from (1), applied only once, initializes the derivation. One of the rules from (4.2) and (5.2) terminates the derivation. In a greater detail, a rule from (4.2) is used in the derivation of $\varepsilon \in L(Q)$; in a derivation of every other string, a rule from (5.2) is used in the last step of the derivation.

Every sentential form of G can be divided into two parts. The first n nonterminals encode the state of Q. The second part represents the queue, where the first symbol S always occurs at the beginning of the queue and the third S always occurs at the end of the queue, followed by the ultimate nonterminal A.

During any successful derivation of G, a rule introduced in (2) is always applied after the application of a rule introduced in (1), (3), (4.1), and (5.1). More precisely, to go on performing the successful derivation, after applying rules from (1), (3), (4.1), and (5.1), G shifts the second occurrence of S right in the current sentential form. G makes this shift by using rules introduced in (2) to obtain a sentential form having precisely n occurrences of $d \in \{A, B\}$ between the first occurrence of S and the second occurrence of S.

The following claims demonstrate that the rule from (1) can be used only once during a successful derivation.

Claim 1. Let $S \Rightarrow_G^* x$ be a derivation during which G uses the rules introduced in (1) i times, for some $i \geq 1$. Then, occur $(S, x) = 1 + 2i - 3j$, occur $(B, x) = (n - 1)k$, and occur $(A, x) = k + i - j$, where k is a nonnegative integer and j is the number of applications of rules introduced in (4.2) and (5.2) such that $j \geq 1$ and $1 + 2i \geq 3j$.

Proof. Notice that the rules introduced in (2), (3), (4.1), and (5.1) preserve the number of As, Bs, and Ss present in the sentential form. Next, observe that every application of the rule from (1) adds 2 Ss to the sentential form and every application of a rule from (4.2) or (5.2) removes 3 Ss from the sentential form. Finally, notice the last A on the right-hand side of the rule from (1) and on the left-hand sides of the rules from (4.2) and (5.2). Based on these observations, it is easy to see that Claim 1 holds. □

Claim 2. Let $S \Rightarrow_G^* x$ be a derivation during which G applies the rule introduced in (1) two or more times. Then, $x \notin \Delta^*$.

Proof. Let $S \Rightarrow_G^* x$, where $x \in \Delta^*$. Because $x \in \Delta^*$, occur $(S, x) =$ occur $(B, x) =$ occur $(A, x) = 0$. As a result, we get $k = 0$, and $i = j = 1$ from the equations introduced in Claim 1. Thus, for $i \geq 2$, $x \notin \Delta^*$. □

Next, we demonstrate that rules from (4.2) and (5.2) can only be used during the last derivation step of a successful derivation.

Claim 3. G generates every $w \in L(G)$ as follows:

$$S \Rightarrow_G u\ [p] \Rightarrow_G^* v \Rightarrow_G w\ [q]$$

where p is the rule introduced in (1); q is a rule introduced in (4.2) or (5.2); and during $u \Rightarrow_G^* v$, G makes every derivation step by a rule introduced in (2), (3), (4.1), or (5.1).

Proof. Let $w \in L(G)$. By Claim 2, as $w \in \Delta^*$, G uses the rule introduced in (1) only once. Because $S \Rightarrow_G^* w$ begins from S, we can express $S \Rightarrow_G^* w$ as

$$S \Rightarrow_G u\ [p] \Rightarrow_G^* w$$

where p is the rule introduced in (1) and G never uses this rule during $u \Rightarrow_G^* w$. Observe that every rule r introduced in (2), (3), (4.1), and (5.1) satisfies occur $(S, \text{lhs}\, r) = 3$ and occur $(S, \text{rhs}\, r) = 3$. Furthermore, notice that every rule q introduced in (4.2) and (5.2) satisfies occur $(S, \text{lhs}\, q) = 3$ and occur $(S, \text{rhs}\, q) = 0$. These observations imply

$$S \Rightarrow_G u\ [p] \Rightarrow_G^* v \Rightarrow_G w\ [q]$$

where p is the rule introduced in (1), q is a rule introduced in (4.2) or (5.2), and during $u \Rightarrow_G^* v$, G makes every step by a rule introduced in (2), (3), (4.1), or (5.1). □

In what follows, we demonstrate that in order to apply a rule from (3) to (5), there have to be exactly n nonterminals between the first and the second occurrence of S. This can be accomplished by one or more applications of a rule from (2).

Claim 4. If $x \Rightarrow_G y\ [p]$ is a derivation step in a successful derivation of G, where p is a rule from (3) to (5), then $x = x_1Sx_2Sx_3SA$, where $x_1,\ x_2,\ x_3 \in (\Delta \cup \{A, B\})^+$, occur $(\{A, B\}, x_1) = k$, occur $(\{A, B\}, x_2) = m$, and $k = m = n$.

Proof. If $k < n$ or $m < n$, no rule introduced in (3)–(5) can be used. Therefore, $k \geq n$ and $m \geq n$.

Assume that $k > n$. The only rules that remove the symbols from $\{A, B\}$ in front of the first symbol S are those introduced in (4.2) and (5.2), and these rules remove precisely n nonterminals preceding the first symbol S. For $k > n$, $k - n$ nonterminals remain in the sentential form after the last derivation step so the derivation is unsuccessful. Therefore, $k = n$.

Assume that $m > n$. Then, after the application of a rule introduced in (3)–(5), m symbols from $\{A, B\}$ appear in front of the first S. Therefore, the number of nonterminals appearing in front of the first occurrence of S is greater than n, which contradicts the argument given in the previous paragraph. As a result, $m = n$. □

Based on Claims 1–4 and the properties of Q, we can express every successful derivation of G as

- either $S \Rightarrow_G \text{rhs}\, p_1\ [p_1] \Rightarrow_G^* u\ [\Xi] \Rightarrow_G v\ [p_{4a}] \Rightarrow_G^* w\ [\Psi] \Rightarrow_G z\ [p_{5b}]$ for $z \neq \varepsilon$;
- or $S \Rightarrow_G \text{rhs}\, p_1\ [p_1] \Rightarrow_G^* u\ [\Xi] \Rightarrow_G \varepsilon\ [p_{4b}]$
  where p_1, p_{4a}, p_{4b}, and p_{5b} are the rules introduced in (1), (4.1), (4.2), and (5.2), respectively, Ξ is a sequence of rules from (2) and (3), Ψ is a sequence of rules from (2) and (5.1), and the derivation satisfies the following properties:

- Every derivation step in $\text{rhs}\, p_1 \Rightarrow_G^* u\ [\Xi]$ has one of these forms:

  $$\beta(b_1)Sa_1'Sa_1''d_1y_1'SA \Rightarrow_G \beta(b_1)Sa_1'a_1''d_1Sy_1'SA\ [p_2], \text{ or}$$
  $$\beta(b_1)S\beta(a_1)S\beta(y_1)SA \Rightarrow_G \beta(c_1)SS\beta(y_1x_1)SA\ [p_3]$$

  where $a_1', a_1'', y_1' \in \{A, B\}^*$, $d_1 \in \{A, B\}$, $(a_1, b_1, x_1, c_1) \in R$, $b_1 \neq 1$, $c_1 \neq 1$, $y_1 \in (\bar{\Sigma} - \Delta)^*$, and p_2, p_3 are rules introduced in (2), (3), respectively;
- The derivation step $u \Rightarrow_G v\ [p_{4a}]$ has the form

  $$\beta(b_2)S\beta(a_2)S\beta(y_2)SA \Rightarrow_G \beta(1)SS\beta(y_2x_2)SA\ [p_{4a}]$$

  where $(a_2, b_2, x_2, 1) \in R$, $b_2 \neq 1$, and $y_2 \in (\bar{\Sigma} - \Delta)^+$. Observe that if $y_2x_2 = \varepsilon$, no rule is applicable after this step and the derivation is blocked;
- The derivation step $u \Rightarrow_G \varepsilon\ [p_{4b}]$ has the form

  $$\beta(b_3)S\beta(a_3)S\beta(y_3)SA \Rightarrow_G \varepsilon\ [p_{4b}]$$

  where $(a_3, b_3, \varepsilon, c_3) \in R$, $b_3 \neq 1$, $c_3 \in F$ and $y_3 = \varepsilon$. As no rule can be applied after a rule from (4.2) is used, if $y_3 \neq \varepsilon$, there remain some nonterminals in the sentential form, so the derivation is unsuccessful;

- Every derivation step in $v \Rightarrow_G^* w\ [\Psi]$ has one of these forms:

$$\beta(1)Sa'_4Sa''_4d_4y'_4t_4SA \Rightarrow_G \beta(1)Sa'_4a''_4d_4Sy_4t_4SA\ [p_2], \text{ or}$$
$$\beta(1)S\beta(a_4)S\beta(y_4)t_4SA \Rightarrow_G \beta(1)SS\beta(y_4)t_4x_4SA\ [p_{5a}]$$

  where $a'_4, a''_4, y'_4 \in \{A, B\}^*$, $d_4 \in \{A, B\}$, $(a_4, 1, x_4, 1) \in R$, $y_4 \in (\Sigma - \Delta)^*$, $t_4 \in \Delta^*$, and p_2, p_{5a} are the rules introduced in (2), (5.1), respectively;
- The derivation step $w \Rightarrow_G z\ [p_{5b}]$ has the form

$$\beta(1)S\beta(a_5)St_5SA \Rightarrow_G t_5x_5\ [p_{5b}]$$

  where $(a_5, 1, x_5, c_5) \in R$, $c_5 \in F$, and $t_5 \in \Delta^*$.

  Observe that

$$S \Rightarrow_G \text{rhs}\, p_1\ [p_1] \Rightarrow_G^* u\ [\Xi] \Rightarrow_G v\ [p_{4a}] \Rightarrow_G^* w\ [\Psi] \Rightarrow_G z\ [p_{5b}], \text{ for } z \neq \varepsilon$$

if and only if

$$g \Rightarrow_Q^* a_2y_2b_2 \Rightarrow_Q y_2x_21\ [(a_2, b_2, x_2, 1)]$$
$$\Rightarrow_Q^* a_5t_51 \ \Rightarrow_Q zc_5 \quad [(a_5, 1, x_5, c_5)],$$

or

$$S \Rightarrow_G \text{rhs}\, p_1\ [p_1] \Rightarrow_G^* u\ [\Xi] \Rightarrow_G \varepsilon\ [p_{4b}]$$

if and only if

$$g \Rightarrow_Q^* a_3y_3b_3 \Rightarrow_Q c_3\ [(a_3, b_3, \varepsilon, c_3)].$$

As a result, $L(Q) = L(G)$, so the theorem holds. □

Recall that one-nonterminal SCGs are incapable of generating all recursively enumerable languages (see Theorem 13.3). By Theorem 13.5, three-nonterminal SCGs characterize **RE**. As stated in the following theorem, the optimal bound for the needed number of nonterminals is, in fact, two. This very recent result is proved in [38].

Theorem 13.6 (see [38]). *For every recursively enumerable language L, there is an SCG $G = (\Sigma, \Delta, R, S)$ such that $L(G) = L$, and*

$$\text{card}(\Sigma - \Delta) = 2.$$

Up until now, we have reduced only one measure of descriptional complexity regardless of all the other measures. We next reconsider this topic in a finer way by simultaneously reducing several measures. It turns out that this simultaneous reduction results in an increase of all the measures involved. In addition, reducing the number of nonterminals necessarily leads to an increase of the number of context-sensitive rules and vice versa.

Theorem 13.7. *For every recursively enumerable language L, there is an SCG G = (Σ, Δ, R, S) such that L(G) = L, and*

$$\begin{aligned} \text{card}\,(\Sigma - \Delta) &= 5, \\ \text{dcs}\,(G) &= 2, \\ \text{mcs}\,(G) &= 3, \\ \text{ocs}\,(G) &= 6. \end{aligned}$$

Proof. (See [19].) Let

$$G' = (\{S', A, B, C, D\} \cup \Delta, \Delta, R' \cup \{AB \to \varepsilon, CD \to \varepsilon\}, S')$$

be a phrase-structure grammar in the Geffert normal form, where R' is a set of context-free rules, and $L(G') = L$ (see Theorem 11.7). Define the homomorphism h from $\{A, B, C, D\}^*$ to $\{0, 1\}^*$ so that $h(A) = h(B) = 00$, $h(C) = 10$, and $h(D) = 01$. Define the SCG

$$G = (\{S, \bar{S}, 0, 1, \$\} \cup \Delta, \Delta, R, S)$$

with R constructed as follows:

(1) for each $S' \to zS'a \in R'$, where $z \in \{A, C\}^*$, $a \in \Delta$, extend R by adding

$(S) \to (h(z)Sa)$;

(2) add $(S) \to (\bar{S})$ to R;

(3) for each $S' \to uS'v \in R'$, where $u \in \{A, C\}^*$, $v \in \{B, D\}^*$, extend R by adding

$(\bar{S}) \to (h(u)\bar{S}h(v))$;

(4) extend R by adding
(4.a) $(\bar{S}) \to (\$\$)$,
(4.b) $(0, \$, \$, 0) \to (\$, \varepsilon, \varepsilon, \$)$,
(4.c) $(1, \$, \$, 1) \to (\$, \varepsilon, \varepsilon, \$)$,
(4.d) $(\$) \to (\varepsilon)$.

Observe that G' generates every $a_1 \cdots a_k \in L(G')$ in the following way:

$$\begin{aligned} S' &\Rightarrow_{G'} z_{a_k} S' a_k \\ &\Rightarrow_{G'} z_{a_k} z_{a_{k-1}} S' a_{k-1} a_k \\ &\;\;\vdots \\ &\Rightarrow_{G'} z_{a_k} \cdots z_{a_2} S' a_2 \cdots a_k \\ &\Rightarrow_{G'} z_{a_k} \cdots z_{a_2} z_{a_1} S' a_1 a_2 \cdots a_k \\ &\Rightarrow_{G'} z_{a_k} \cdots z_{a_2} z_{a_1} u_l S' v_l a_1 a_2 \cdots a_k \\ &\;\;\vdots \end{aligned}$$

$$
\begin{aligned}
&\Rightarrow_{G'} z_{a_k} \cdots z_{a_1} u_l \cdots u_2 S' v_2 \cdots v_l a_1 \cdots a_k \\
&\Rightarrow_{G'} z_{a_k} \cdots z_{a_1} u_l \cdots u_2 u_1 v_1 v_2 \cdots v_l a_1 \cdots a_k \\
&= \quad d_m \cdots d_2 d_1 e_1 e_2 \cdots e_n a_1 \cdots a_k \\
&\Rightarrow_{G'} d_m \cdots d_2 e_2 \cdots e_n a_1 \cdots a_k \\
&\quad \vdots \\
&\Rightarrow_{G'} d_m e_n a_1 \cdots a_k \\
&\Rightarrow_{G'} a_1 \cdots a_k
\end{aligned}
$$

where $a_1, \ldots, a_k \in \Delta$, $z_{a_1}, \ldots, z_{a_k}$, $u_1, \ldots, u_l \in \{A, C\}^*$, $v_1, \ldots, v_l \in \{B, D\}^*$, $d_1, \ldots, d_m \in \{A, C\}$, and $e_1, \ldots, e_n \in \{B, D\}$. After erasing S' from the sentential form, G' verifies that the generated strings $z_{a_k} \cdots z_{a_1}$, $u_l \cdots u_1$, and $v_1 \cdots v_l$ are identical. If $m \neq n$, or $d_i e_i \notin \{AB, CD\}$, for some $i \geq 1$, the generated strings do not coincide, and the derivation is blocked, so $a_1 \cdots a_k$ does not belong to the generated language.

The above derivation can be straightforwardly simulated by G as follows:

$$
\begin{aligned}
S &\Rightarrow_G h(z_{a_k}) S a_k \\
&\Rightarrow_G h(z_{a_k}) h(z_{a_{k-1}}) S a_{k-1} a_k \\
&\quad \vdots \\
&\Rightarrow_G h(z_{a_k}) \cdots h(z_{a_2}) S a_2 \cdots a_k \\
&\Rightarrow_G h(z_{a_k}) \cdots h(z_{a_2}) h(z_{a_1}) S a_1 a_2 \cdots a_k \\
&\Rightarrow_G h(z_{a_k} \cdots z_{a_2} z_{a_1}) \bar{S} a_1 a_2 \cdots a_k && [p_2] \\
&\Rightarrow_G h(z_{a_k} \cdots z_{a_2} z_{a_1}) h(u_l) \bar{S} h(v_l) a_1 a_2 \cdots a_k \\
&\quad \vdots \\
&\Rightarrow_G h(z_{a_k} \cdots z_{a_1}) h(u_l) \cdots h(u_2) \bar{S} h(v_2) \cdots h(v_l) a_1 \cdots a_k \\
&\Rightarrow_G h(z_{a_k} \cdots z_{a_1}) h(u_l) \cdots h(u_2) h(u_1) \bar{S} h(v_1) h(v_2) \cdots h(v_l) a_1 \cdots a_k \\
&\Rightarrow_G h(z_{a_k} \cdots z_{a_1}) h(u_l \cdots u_2 u_1) \$\$ h(v_1 v_2 \cdots v_l) a_1 \cdots a_k && [p_{4a}] \\
&= \quad f_r \cdots f_2 f_1 \$\$ g_1 g_2 \cdots g_s a_1 \cdots a_k \\
&\Rightarrow_G f_r \cdots f_2 \$\$ g_2 \cdots g_s a_1 \cdots a_k \\
&\quad \vdots \\
&\Rightarrow_G f_r \$\$ g_s a_1 \cdots a_k \\
&\Rightarrow_G \$\$ a_1 \cdots a_k \\
&\Rightarrow_G \$ a_1 \cdots a_k && [p_{4d}] \\
&\Rightarrow_G a_1 \cdots a_k && [p_{4d}]
\end{aligned}
$$

where $f_1, \ldots, f_r, g_1, \ldots, g_s \in \{0, 1\}$, and p_2, p_{4a}, and p_{4d} are rules introduced in (2), (4.a), and (4.d), respectively. In this derivation, the context-free rules of G' are simulated by the rules introduced in (1)–(3), and the context-sensitive rules of G' are simulated by the rules introduced in (4.b) and (4.c). There are the following differences between the derivations in G' and G.

- Instead of verifying the identity of $z_{a_k} \cdots z_{a_1}$, $u_l \cdots u_1$, and $v_1 \cdots v_l$, G verifies that $h(z_{a_k} \cdots z_{a_1}, u_l \cdots u_1)$ and $h(v_1 \cdots v_l)$ coincide. This means that instead of comparing strings over $\{A, B, C, D\}$, G compares the strings $f_r \cdots f_1$ and $g_1 \cdots g_s$ over $\{0, 1\}$;

- The rule introduced in (2) guarantees that no rule from (1) can be used after its application. Similarly, the rule introduced in (4.a) prevents the rules of (1)–(3) from being applied;
- When applying the rules from (4.b) and (4.c), some symbols f_i and g_j, where i, $j \geq 1$, can be skipped. However, if some 0s and 1s that do not directly neighbor with the \$s are rewritten, the form of these rules guarantees that the skipped nonterminals can never be rewritten later in the derivation, so the derivation is necessarily unsuccessful in this case;
- The rule from (4.d) can be used anytime the symbol \$ appears in the sentential form. However, when this rule is used and some nonterminals from $\{0, 1\}$ occur in the sentential form, these nonterminals can never be removed from the sentential form, so the derivation is blocked. As a result, the rule from (4.d) has to be applied at the very end of the derivation.

These observations imply that $L = L(G) = L(G')$. As is obvious, $\text{card}\,(\Sigma - \Delta) = 5$, $\text{dcs}\,(G) = 2$, $\text{mcs}\,(G) = 3$, $\text{ocs}\,(G) = 6$. Thus, the theorem holds. □

Theorem 13.8. *For every recursively enumerable language L, there is an SCG* $\bar{G} = (\Sigma, \Delta, \bar{R}, S)$ *such that* $L(\bar{G}) = L$, *and*

$$\begin{aligned} \text{card}\,(\Sigma - \Delta) &= 8, \\ \text{dcs}\,(\bar{G}) &= 6, \\ \text{mcs}\,(\bar{G}) &= 1, \\ \text{ocs}\,(\bar{G}) &= 6. \end{aligned}$$

Proof. We slightly modify the construction given in the proof of Theorem 13.7. Define the SCG

$$\bar{G} = (\{S, \bar{S}, 0, 1, \$_L, \$_R, \$_0, \$_1\} \cup \Delta, \Delta, \bar{R}, S)$$

and initialize $\bar{R}$ with the set of all rules introduced in steps (1)–(3) of the construction given in the proof of Theorem 13.7. Then, add the following rules to $\bar{R}$:

(4)

(4.a) $(\bar{S}) \to (\$_L\$_R)$,
(4.b) $(0, \$_L) \to (\$_0, \varepsilon)$, $(\$_R, 0) \to (\varepsilon, \$_0)$, $(\$_0, \$_0) \to (\$_L, \$_R)$,
(4.c) $(1, \$_L) \to (\$_1, \varepsilon)$, $(\$_R, 1) \to (\varepsilon, \$_1)$, $(\$_1, \$_1) \to (\$_L, \$_R)$,
(4.d) $(\$_L) \to (\varepsilon)$, and $(\$_R) \to (\varepsilon)$.

Observe that a single derivation step made by a rule introduced in step (4.b) or (4.c) of the construction of G is simulated in $\bar{G}$ by the above rules from (4.b) or (4.c) in three derivation steps. In greater detail, a derivation of the form

$$x0\$\$0yz \Rightarrow_G x\$\$yz \; [(0, \$, \$, 0) \to (\$, \varepsilon, \varepsilon, \$)]$$

is simulated by $\bar{G}$ as follows:

$$\begin{aligned} x0\$_L\$_R0yz &\Rightarrow_{\bar{G}} x\$_0\$_R0yz \; [(0, \$_L) \rightarrow (\$_0, \varepsilon)] \\ &\Rightarrow_{\bar{G}} x\$_0\$_0yz \; [(\$_R, 0) \rightarrow (\varepsilon, \$_0)] \\ &\Rightarrow_{\bar{G}} x\$_L\$_Ryz \; [(\$_0, \$_0) \rightarrow (\$_L, \$_R)] \end{aligned}$$

where x, $y \in \{0, 1\}^*$, and $z \in \Delta^*$. The rest of the proof resembles the proof of Theorem 13.7 and is, therefore, left to the reader. □

Theorem 13.9. *For every recursively enumerable language L, there is an SCG $G = (\Sigma, \Delta, R, S)$ such that $L(G) = L$, and*

$$\begin{aligned} \text{card}\,(\Sigma - \Delta) &= 4, \\ \text{dcs}\,(G) &= 4, \\ \text{mcs}\,(G) &= 5, \\ \text{ocs}\,(G) &= 20. \end{aligned}$$

Proof. Let

$$G' = (\{S', A, B, C, D\} \cup \Delta, \Delta, R' \cup \{AB \rightarrow \varepsilon, CD \rightarrow \varepsilon\}, S')$$

be a phrase-structure grammar in the Geffert normal form, where R' is a set of context-free rules and $L(G') = L$ (see Theorem 11.7). Define the homomorphism h from $\{A, B, C, D\}^*$ to $\{0, 1\}^*$ so that $h(A) = h(B) = 00$, $h(C) = 10$, and $h(D) = 01$. Define the SCG

$$G = (\{S, 0, 1, \$\} \cup \Delta, \Delta, R, S)$$

with R constructed as follows:

(1) add $(S) \rightarrow (11S11)$ to R;
(2) for each $S' \rightarrow zS'a \in R'$, add $(S) \rightarrow (h(z)S1a1)$ to R;
(3) for each $S' \rightarrow uS'v \in R'$, add $(S) \rightarrow (h(u)Sh(v))$ to R;
(4) for each $S' \rightarrow uv \in R'$, add $(S) \rightarrow (h(u)\$\$h(v))$ to R; and
(5) add
  (5.a) $(0, 0, \$, \$, 0, 0) \rightarrow (\$, \varepsilon, \varepsilon, \varepsilon, \varepsilon, \$)$,
  (5.b) $(1, 0, \$, \$, 0, 1) \rightarrow (\$, \varepsilon, \varepsilon, \varepsilon, \varepsilon, \$)$,
  (5.c) $(1, 1, \$, \$, 1, 1) \rightarrow (11\$, \varepsilon, \varepsilon, \varepsilon, \varepsilon, \$)$, and
  (5.d) $(1, 1, \$, \$, 1, 1) \rightarrow (\varepsilon, \varepsilon, \varepsilon, \varepsilon, \varepsilon, \varepsilon)$ to R.

Every successful derivation starts by an application of the rule introduced in (1), and this rule is not used during the rest of the derivation. Rules from (2) to (4) simulate the context-free rules of G'. After the rule from (4) is used, only rules from (5) are applicable. The rules from (5.a) and (5.b) verify that the strings over $\{0, 1\}$, generated by the rules from (2) to (4), coincide. The rule from (5.c) removes the 1s between the terminal symbols and, in addition, makes sure that rules from (2) can never be used in a successful derivation after a rule from (3) is applied. Finally, the rule from (5.d) completes the derivation.

The proof of the theorem is based on five claims, established next.

Claim 1. Every successful derivation in G can be expressed as

$$\begin{aligned} S &\Rightarrow_G^* v\ [\Xi] \\ &\Rightarrow_G w\ [p_4] \\ &\Rightarrow_G^* y\ [\Psi] \\ &\Rightarrow_G z\ [p_{5d}] \end{aligned}$$

where

$$\begin{aligned} &v \in \{0,1\}^*\{S\}(\{0,1\} \cup \Delta)^*, \\ &w \in \{0,1\}^+\{\$\}\{\$\}(\{0,1\} \cup \Delta)^*, \\ &y \in \{1\}\{1\}\{\$\}\Delta^*\{\$\}\Delta^*\{1\}\Delta^*\{1\}\Delta^*, \end{aligned}$$

$z \in \Delta^*$, p_4 and p_{5d} are rules introduced in (4) and (5.d), respectively, and Ξ and Ψ are sequences of rules introduced in (1)–(3) and (5.a)–(5.c), respectively.

Proof. As S appears on the left-hand side of every rule introduced in (1)–(4), all of them are applicable, while S occurs in the sentential form. On the other hand, no rule from (5) can be used at this point. After p_4 is used, it replaces S with \$\$, so rules from (1) to (4) are not applicable, and only rules from (5) can be used. Therefore, the beginning of the derivation can be expressed as

$$\begin{aligned} S &\Rightarrow_G^* v\ [\Xi] \\ &\Rightarrow_G w\ [p_4]. \end{aligned}$$

Because all rules except for p_{5d} contain nonterminals on their right-hand sides, p_{5d} has to be applied in the last derivation step, and no other rule can be applied after its use. Applications of rules from (2) to (4) may introduce some nonterminals 0 and 1 to the sentential form, so in this case, the rules from (5.a) and (5.b) are applied to remove them. As a result,

$$\begin{aligned} w &\Rightarrow_G^* y\ [\Psi] \\ &\Rightarrow_G z\ [p_{5d}] \end{aligned}$$

and the sentential forms satisfy the conditions given in the claim. □

Claim 2. In $w \Rightarrow_G^+ z$ from Claim 1, every sentential form s satisfies

$$s \in \{0,1\}^*\{\$\}\Delta^*\{\$\}(\{0,1\} \cup \Delta)^*.$$

Proof. The form of the rules introduced in (5) implies that whenever a nonterminal appears between the two occurrences of \$, it can never be removed during the rest of the derivation. Therefore, the claim holds. □

Claim 3. In $w \Rightarrow_G^+ z$ from Claim 1, every sentential form s satisfies

$$s \in \{1\}\{1\}(\{1\}\{0\} \cup \{0\}\{0\})^*\{\$\}\Delta^*\{\$\}(\{0,1\} \cup \Delta)^*.$$

Proof. Claim 2 implies that whenever rules from (5) are used, each of these rules is applied to the nonterminals from $\{0, 1\}$ immediately preceding the first occurrence of \$ and immediately following the second occurrence of \$; otherwise, the derivation is unsuccessful. As a result, the only rule that removes the substring 11 preceding the first occurrence of \$ is (5.d). However, by Claim 1, (5.d) is used during the very last derivation step, so the substring 11 has to appear at the beginning of the sentential form in order to generate a string over Δ. □

Claim 4. The derivation

$$S \Rightarrow_G^* v\ [\Xi]$$

from Claim 1 can be expressed, in greater detail, as

$$\begin{aligned} S &\Rightarrow_G 11S11\ [p_1] \\ &\Rightarrow_G^* v \end{aligned}$$

where p_1 is the rule introduced in (1) and this rule is not used during the rest of the derivation.

Proof. The rule introduced in (1) is the only rule that introduces the substring 11 in front of the first occurrence of \$. By Claim 3, in front of the first \$, this substring appears only at the beginning of every sentential form in $w \Rightarrow_G^+ z$, so p_1 has to be applied at the beginning of the derivation and cannot be used later in the derivation. □

Claim 5. The derivation

$$\begin{aligned} w &\Rightarrow_G^* y\ [\Psi] \\ &\Rightarrow_G z\ [p_{5d}] \end{aligned}$$

from Claim 1 can be expressed, in greater detail, as

$$\begin{aligned} w &\Rightarrow_G^* x\ [\Psi_1] \\ &\Rightarrow_G^* y\ [\Psi_2] \\ &\Rightarrow_G z\ [p_{5d}] \end{aligned}$$

where

$$x \in \{1\}\{1\}(\{1\}\{0\} \cup \{0\}\{0\})^*\{\$\}\Delta^*\{\$\}(\{0, 1\} \cup \Delta)^*,$$

Ψ_1 is a sequence of rules introduced in (5.a) and (5.b), and Ψ_2 is a sequence of rules introduced in (5.c).

Proof. The proof of this claim follows immediately from Claims 2 and 3. □

Claim 6. The derivation

$$11S11 \Rightarrow_G^* v$$

from Claims 1 and 4 can be expressed in a greater detail as

$$\begin{aligned} 11S11 &\Rightarrow_G^* u \ [\Xi_1] \\ &\Rightarrow_G^* v \ [\Xi_2] \end{aligned}$$

where

$$u \in \{1\}\{1\}(\{1\}\{0\} \cup \{0\}\{0\})^* S(\{0\}\{1\} \cup \{0\}\{0\})^*(\{1\}\Delta\{1\})^*\{1\}\{1\}$$

and Ξ_1, Ξ_2 are sequences of rules introduced in (2), (3), respectively.

Proof. By Claim 4, every derivation starts by an application of the rule from (1). Therefore, u ends with 11. Next, notice that the two nonterminals 1 surrounding a, where $a \in \Delta$, introduced by every application of a rule from (2) can only be removed by the rule from (5.c). Indeed, by Claim 2, any other rule leaves a nonterminal between the two symbols \$, so the derivation is unsuccessful. By Claim 5, rules from (5.a) and (5.b) cannot be applied after the rule from (5.c) is used. As a result, the generation of the strings over {0, 1} by rules from (2) and (3) has to correspond to their removal by (5.a), (5.b), and (5.c). This implies that rules from (2) have to be applied before rules from (3). □

Based upon Claims 1–6, we see that every successful derivation is of the form

$$\begin{aligned} S &\Rightarrow_G 11S11 && [p_1] \\ &\Rightarrow_G^* u && [\Xi_1] \\ &\Rightarrow_G^* v && [\Xi_2] \\ &\Rightarrow_G w && [p_4] \\ &\Rightarrow_G^* x && [\Psi_1] \\ &\Rightarrow_G^* y && [\Psi_2] \\ &\Rightarrow_G z && [p_{5d}]. \end{aligned}$$

As the rest of this proof can be made by analogy with the proof of Theorem 13.7, we leave it to the reader. □

13.1.5 Economical transformations

The generation of languages is frequently performed in a specifically required way and based upon a prescribed set of grammatical components, such as a certain collection of nonterminals or rules. On the other hand, if these requirements are met, the generation can be based upon grammars of various types. For this purpose, we often make use of transformations that convert grammars of some type to equivalent grammars of another type, so the transformed grammars strongly resemble the original grammars regarding the way they work as well as the components they consist of. In other words, we want the output grammars resulting from these transformations to work similarly to the way the given original grammars work and, perhaps even more importantly, to contain the same set of grammatical components possibly extended by very few additional components. Transformations that produce SCGs in this economical way are discussed throughout the rest of this section. Because phrase-structure grammars represent one of the very basic grammatical models in formal language theory (see

Section 11.1), this section pays special attention to the economical transformations that convert these fundamental grammars to equivalent SCGs.

To compare the measures of scattered context and phrase-structure grammars, we first define the degree of context-sensitivity of phrase-structure grammars analogously to the degree of context sensitivity of SCGs (see Definition 13.4).

Definition 13.5. *Let* $G = (\Sigma, \Delta, R, S)$ *be a phrase-structure grammar. Its* degree of context sensitivity, *symbolically written as* $\mathrm{dcs}(G)$, *is defined as*

$$\mathrm{dcs}(G) = \mathrm{card}(\{x \to y \mid x \to y \in R, |x| \geq 2\}).$$

Theorem 13.10. *For every phrase-structure grammar* $G = (\Sigma, \Delta, R, S)$ *in the Kuroda normal form, there is an SCG* $\bar{G} = (\bar{\Sigma}, \Delta, \bar{R}, \bar{S})$ *such that* $L(\bar{G}) = L(G)$, *and*

$$\begin{aligned} \mathrm{card}(\bar{\Sigma}) &= \mathrm{card}(\Sigma) + 5, \\ \mathrm{card}(\bar{R}) &= \mathrm{card}(R) + 4, \\ \mathrm{dcs}(\bar{G}) &= \mathrm{dcs}(G) + 2. \end{aligned}$$

Proof. Let $G = (\Sigma, \Delta, R, S)$ be a phrase-structure grammar in the Kuroda normal form. Without any loss of generality, assume that $\Sigma \cap \{\bar{S}, F, 0, 1, \$\} = \emptyset$. Set $\bar{\Sigma} = \Sigma \cup \{\bar{S}, F, 0, 1, \$\}$. Define the SCG

$$\bar{G} = (\bar{\Sigma}, \Delta, \bar{R}, \bar{S})$$

where $\bar{R}$ is constructed as follows:

(1) add $(\bar{S}) \to (FFFS)$ to $\bar{R}$;
(2) for each $AB \to CD \in R$, add $(A, B) \to (C0, 1D)$ to $\bar{R}$;
(3) for each $A \to BC \in R$, add $(A) \to (BC)$ to $\bar{R}$;
(4) for each $A \to a \in R$, where $a \in \Delta \cup \{\varepsilon\}$, add $(A) \to (\$a)$ to $\bar{R}$; and
(5) add
  (5.a) $(F, 0, 1, F, F) \to (\varepsilon, F, F, \varepsilon, F)$,
  (5.b) $(F, F, F, \$) \to (\varepsilon, \varepsilon, F, FF)$,
  (5.c) $(F) \to (\varepsilon)$ to $\bar{R}$.

The rule from (1) starts a derivation and introduces three occurrences of the nonterminal F, which are present in every sentential form until three applications of the rule from (5.c) complete the derivation. Rules from (2), (3), and (4) simulate the corresponding rules of the Kuroda normal form behind the last occurrence of F. The rules from (5.a) and (5.b) guarantee that before (5.c) is applied for the first time, every sentential form in a successful derivation belongs to

$$\Delta^*\{F\}(\Delta \cup \{\varepsilon\})\{0^i 1^i \mid i \geq 0\}\{F\}\{F\}(\Sigma \cup \{0, 1, \$\})^*$$

and, thereby, the simulation of every derivation of G is performed properly. Notice that there are only terminals in front of the first nonterminal F. Moreover, the only nonterminals appearing between the first occurrence and the second occurrence of F are from $\{0, 1\}$, and there is no symbol between the second and the third occurrence of F in a successful derivation.

Next, we establish several claims to demonstrate that $L(G) = L(\bar{G})$ in a rigorous way.

Claim 1. Every successful derivation of $\bar{G}$ can be expressed as

$$\begin{aligned}\bar{S} &\Rightarrow_{\bar{G}} FFFS \quad [p_1]\\ &\Rightarrow_{\bar{G}}^{*} uFvFxFy \; [\Psi]\\ &\Rightarrow_{\bar{G}}^{*} w\\ &\Rightarrow_{\bar{G}}^{3} z \qquad [p_{5c}p_{5c}p_{5c}]\end{aligned}$$

where $u, z \in \Delta^*$, $v, x, y \in (\bar{\Sigma} - \{\bar{S}, F\})^*$, $w \in (\bar{\Sigma} - \{\bar{S}\})^*$, p_1 and p_{5c} are rules introduced in (1) and (5.c), respectively, and Ψ is a sequence of rules introduced in (2)–(5.b).

Proof. The only rule with $\bar{S}$ on its left-hand side is the rule introduced in (1), and because no rule contains $\bar{S}$ on its right-hand side, this rule is not used during the rest of the derivation process. As a result,

$$\bar{S} \Rightarrow_{\bar{G}} FFFS \; [p_1].$$

Observe that no rule from (2) to (4) contains the nonterminal F, and rules from (5.a) and (5.b) contain three nonterminals F on their left-hand sides as well as their right-hand sides. The rule from (5.c), which is the only rule with its right-hand side over Δ, removes F from the sentential form, so no rule from (5.a) and (5.b) can be used once it is applied. Notice that rules from (4) simulate $A \to a$, where $A \in \Sigma - \Delta$, $a \in \Delta \cup \{\varepsilon\}$, and these rules introduce \$ to the sentential form. In addition, observe that only the rule from (5.b) rewrites \$. Consequently, to generate a string over Δ, rules from (2) to (4) cannot be used after the rule from (5.c) is applied. Therefore,

$$w \Rightarrow_{\bar{G}}^{3} z \; [p_{5c}p_{5c}p_{5c}].$$

Notice that rules from (5.a) and (5.b) cannot rewrite any symbol in u. If symbols $u \cap (\bar{\Sigma} - \Delta) \neq \emptyset$, a nonterminal from $\{0, 1, \$\}$ remains in front of the first F because rules from (2) to (4) cannot rewrite u to a string over Δ, so the derivation would be unsuccessful in this case. Therefore, $u \in \Delta^*$, and the claim holds. □

Claim 2. Let

$$\bar{S} \Rightarrow_{\bar{G}}^{+} uFvFxFy \Rightarrow_{\bar{G}}^{*} w \Rightarrow_{\bar{G}}^{3} z$$

where $u, z \in \Delta^*$, $v, x, y \in (\bar{\Sigma} - \{\bar{S}, F\})^*$, and $w \in (\bar{\Sigma} - \{\bar{S}\})^*$. Then, $x \in \Delta^*$.

Proof. First, notice that if $(\bar{\Sigma} - \Delta) \cap$ symbols $x \neq \emptyset$, x cannot be rewritten to a string over Δ by using only rules from (2) to (4). Next, examine the rules from (5.a) and (5.b) to see that these rules cannot rewrite any symbol from x, and the rule from (5.b) moves x in front of the first occurrence of F. However, by Claim 1, no nonterminal can appear in front of the first F. As a result, $(\bar{\Sigma} - \Delta) \cap$ symbols $x = \emptyset$, so $x \in \Delta^*$. □

Claim 3. Let

$$\bar{S} \Rightarrow_{\bar{G}}^{+} uFvFxFy \Rightarrow_{\bar{G}}^{*} w \Rightarrow_{\bar{G}}^{3} z$$

where $u, z \in \Delta^*$, $v, x, y \in (\bar{\Sigma} - \{\bar{S}, F\})^*$, and $w \in (\bar{\Sigma} - \{\bar{S}\})^*$. Then, $v = v'v''$, where $v' \in (\{0\} \cup \Delta)^*$, $v'' \in (\{1\} \cup \Delta)^*$, and occur $(0, v') =$ occur $(1, v'')$.

Proof. First, notice that if $(\bar{\Sigma} - \Delta) \cap \text{symbols}(v) \neq \emptyset$, v cannot be rewritten to a string over Δ by using only rules from (2) to (4). Next, examine the rules from (5.a) and (5.b).

First, observe that the rule from (5.b) can only be applied if $v \in \Delta^*$. Indeed, (5.b) moves v in front of the first F, and if $(\bar{\Sigma} - \Delta) \cap \text{symbols}(v) \neq \emptyset$, Claim 1 implies that the derivation is unsuccessful. Therefore, $(\bar{\Sigma} - \Delta) \cap \text{symbols}(v) = \emptyset$ before the rule from (5.b) is applied. Second, observe that because the rule from (5.a) rewrites only nonterminals over $\{0, 1\}$ in v, $((\Sigma - \Delta) \cup \{\$\}) \cap \text{symbols}(v) = \emptyset$. Finally, observe that the rule from (5.a) has to be applied so that the first 0 following the first F and the first 1 preceding the second F is rewritten by (5.a). If this property is not satisfied, the form of (5.a) implies that 0 appears in front of the first F or 1 appears in between the second F and the third F. However, by Claims 1 and 2, this results in an unsuccessful derivation.

Based on these observations, we see that in order to generate $z \in \Delta^*$, v has to satisfy $v = v'v''$, where $v' \in (\{0\} \cup \Delta)^*$, $v'' \in (\{1\} \cup \Delta)^*$, and occur $(0, v') =$ occur $(1, v'')$. □

Claim 4. Let

$$\bar{S} \Rightarrow_{\bar{G}}^{+} uFvFxFy \Rightarrow_{\bar{G}}^{*} w \Rightarrow_{\bar{G}}^{3} z$$

where $u, z \in \Delta^*$, $v, x, y \in (\bar{\Sigma} - \{\bar{S}, F\})^*$, and $w \in (\bar{\Sigma} - \{\bar{S}\})^*$. Then,

$$y \in (\Delta \cup \{\varepsilon\})(\{0^i 1^i \mid i \geq 0\}K)^*$$

with $K = (\Sigma - \Delta) \cup \{\$\}(\Delta \cup \{\varepsilon\})$, $v \in (\Delta \cup \{\varepsilon\})\{0^i 1^i \mid i \geq 0\}$, and $x = \varepsilon$.

Proof. First, consider the rule introduced in (5.b). This rule rewrites \$ to FF in its last component. Because the nonterminal \$ is introduced by rules from (4), \$ may be followed by $a \in \Delta$. Therefore, after (5.b) is applied, the last nonterminal F may be followed by a. As a result, the prefix of y is always over $\Delta \cup \{\varepsilon\}$.

Second, notice that when the rule (5.b) is used, the first nonterminal \$ following the third nonterminal F has to be rewritten. In addition, the substring appearing between these symbols has to be in $\{0^i 1^i \mid i \geq 0\}$. The form of the rule introduced in (5.b) implies that after its application, this substring is moved in between the first occurrence of F and the second occurrence of F, so the conditions given by Claim 3 are satisfied. Therefore,

$$v \in (\Delta \cup \{\varepsilon\})\{0^i 1^i \mid i \geq 0\}$$

and because no terminal appears in the suffix of v, the proof of Claim 3 implies that $x = \varepsilon$. By induction, prove that

$$y \in (\Delta \cup \{\varepsilon\})(\{0^i 1^i \mid i \geq 0\}K)^*.$$

The induction part is left to the reader. □

Next, we define the homomorphism α from $\bar{\Sigma}^*$ to Σ^* as $\alpha(\bar{A}) = \varepsilon$, for all $\bar{A} \in \bar{\Sigma} - \Sigma$, and $\alpha(A) = A$, for all $A \in \Sigma$, and use this homomorphism in the following claims.

Claim 5. Let $\bar{S} \Rightarrow^m_{\bar{G}} w \Rightarrow^*_{\bar{G}} z$, where $m \geq 1$, $z \in \Delta^*$, and $w \in \bar{\Sigma}^*$. Then, $S \Rightarrow^*_G \alpha(w)$.

Proof. This claim is established by induction on $m \geq 1$.

Basis. Let $m = 1$. Then, $\bar{S} \Rightarrow_{\bar{G}} FFFS$. Because $\alpha(FFFS) = S$, $S \Rightarrow^0_G S$, so the basis holds.

Induction Hypothesis. Suppose that the claim holds for every $m \leq j$, for some $j \geq 1$.

Induction Step. Let $\bar{S} \Rightarrow^{j+1}_{\bar{G}} w \Rightarrow^*_{\bar{G}} z$, where $z \in \Delta^*$ and $w \in \bar{\Sigma}^*$. Based on Claims 1 and 4, express this derivation as

$$\begin{aligned} \bar{S} &\Rightarrow^j_{\bar{G}} uFvFxFy \\ &\Rightarrow_{\bar{G}} w\ [p] \\ &\Rightarrow^*_{\bar{G}} z \end{aligned}$$

where $u \in \Delta^*$, $x = \varepsilon$,

$$y \in (\Delta \cup \{\varepsilon\})(\{0^i 1^i \mid i \geq 0\}K)^*$$

with $K = (\Sigma - \Delta) \cup \{\$\}(\Delta \cup \{\varepsilon\})$, and

$$v \in (\Delta \cup \{\varepsilon\})\{0^i 1^i \mid i \geq 0\}.$$

By the induction hypothesis, $S \Rightarrow^*_G \alpha(uFvFxFy)$. Next, this proof considers all possible forms of p.

- Assume that $p = (A, B) \to (C0, 1D) \in \bar{R}$, where $A, B, C, D \in \Sigma - \Delta$. Claim 4 and its proof imply $y = y'Ay''By'''$, where $y'' \in \{0^i 1^i \mid i \geq 0\}$, and

  $$w = uFvFxFy'C0y''1Dy'''.$$

  As $(A, B) \to (C0, 1D) \in \bar{R}$, $AB \to CD \in R$ holds true. Because $\alpha(y'') = \varepsilon$,

  $$\alpha(uFvFxFy'Ay''By''') \Rightarrow_G \alpha(uFvFxFy'C0y''1Dy''').$$

  Therefore, $S \Rightarrow^*_G \alpha(w)$;
- Assume that $p = (A) \to (BC) \in \bar{R}$, where $A, B, C \in \Sigma - \Delta$. Claim 4 implies that $y = y'Ay''$, and

  $$w = uFvFxFy'BCy''.$$

As $(A) \to (BC) \in \bar{R}$, $A \to BC \in R$ holds true. Notice that

$$\alpha(uFvFxFy'Ay'') \Rightarrow_G \alpha(uFvFxFy'BCy'').$$

Therefore, $S \Rightarrow_G^* \alpha(w)$;

- Assume that $p = (A) \to (\$a) \in \bar{R}$, where $A \in \Sigma - \Delta$ and $a \in \Delta \cup \{\varepsilon\}$. Claim 4 implies that $y = y'Ay''$, and

  $$w = uFvFxFy'\$ay''.$$

  As $(A) \to (\$a) \in \bar{R}$, $A \to a \in R$ holds true. Notice that

  $$\alpha(uFvFxFy'Ay'') \Rightarrow_G \alpha(uFvFxFy'\$ay'').$$

  Therefore, $S \Rightarrow_G^* \alpha(w)$;
- Assume that p is a rule from (5). Notice that these rules rewrite only nonterminals over $\{0, 1, F, \$\}$. Therefore, $\alpha(w) = \alpha(uFvFxFy)$, so $S \Rightarrow_G^* \alpha(w)$.

Based on the arguments above, $\bar{S} \Rightarrow_{\bar{G}}^j uFvFxFy \Rightarrow_{\bar{G}} w\ [p]$, for any $p \in \bar{R}$, implies that $S \Rightarrow_G^* \alpha(w)$. Thus, the claim holds. □

Claim 6. $L(\bar{G}) \subseteq L(G)$.

Proof. By Claim 5, if $\bar{S} \Rightarrow_{\bar{G}}^+ z$ with $z \in \Delta^*$, then $S \Rightarrow_G^* z$. Therefore, the claim holds. □

Claim 7. Let $S \Rightarrow_G^m w \Rightarrow_G^* z$, where $m \geq 0$, $w \in \Sigma^*$, and $z \in \Delta^*$. Then, $\bar{S} \Rightarrow_{\bar{G}}^+ uFvFxFy$, where $u \in \Delta^*$,

$$y \in (\Delta \cup \{\varepsilon\})(\{0^i 1^i \mid i \geq 0\}K)^*$$

with $K = (\Sigma - \Delta) \cup \{\$\}(\Delta \cup \{\varepsilon\})$,

$$v \in (\Delta \cup \{\varepsilon\})\{0^i 1^i \mid i \geq 0\}$$

and $x = \varepsilon$, so that $w = \alpha(uFvFxFy)$.

Proof. This claim is established by induction on $m \geq 0$.

Basis. Let $m = 0$. Then, $S \Rightarrow_G^0 S \Rightarrow_G^* z$. Notice that $\bar{S} \Rightarrow_{\bar{G}} FFFS$ by using the rule introduced in (1), and $S = \alpha(FFFS)$. Thus, the basis holds.

Induction Hypothesis. Suppose that the claim holds for every $m \leq j$, where $j \geq 1$.

Induction Step. Let $S \Rightarrow_G^{j+1} w \Rightarrow_G^* z$, where $w \in \Sigma^*$ and $z \in \Delta^*$. Express this derivation as

$$\begin{aligned} S &\Rightarrow_G^j t \\ &\Rightarrow_G w\ [p] \\ &\Rightarrow_G^* z \end{aligned}$$

where $w \in \Sigma^*$ and $p \in R$. By the induction hypothesis, $\bar{S} \Rightarrow^+_{\bar{G}} uFvFxFy$, where $u \in \Delta^*$,

$$y \in (\Delta \cup \{\varepsilon\})(\{0^i 1^i \mid i \geq 0\}K)^*$$

with $K = (\Sigma - \Delta) \cup \{\$\}(\Delta \cup \{\varepsilon\})$,

$$v \in (\Delta \cup \{\varepsilon\})\{0^i 1^i \mid i \geq 0\}$$

and $x = \varepsilon$ so that $t = \alpha(uFvFxFy)$. Next, this proof considers all possible forms of p:

- Assume that $p = AB \rightarrow CD \in R$, where $A, B, C, D \in \Sigma - \Delta$. Express $t \Rightarrow_G w$ as $t'ABt'' \Rightarrow_G t'CDt''$, where $t'ABt'' = t$ and $t'CDt'' = w$. Claim 4 implies that $y = y'A0^k 1^k By''$, where $k \geq 0$, $\alpha(uFvFxFy') = t'$, and $\alpha(y'') = t''$. As $AB \rightarrow CD \in R$, $(A, B) \rightarrow (C0, 1D) \in \bar{R}$ holds true. Then,

  $$uFvFxFy'A0^k 1^k By'' \Rightarrow_{\bar{G}} uFvFxFy'C0^{k+1} 1^{k+1} Dy''.$$

  Therefore,

  $$\bar{S} \Rightarrow^+_{\bar{G}} uFvFxFy'C0^{k+1} 1^{k+1} Dy''$$

  and $w = \alpha(uFvFxFy'C0^{k+1} 1^{k+1} Dy'')$;
- Assume that $p = A \rightarrow BC \in R$, where A, B, $C \in \Sigma - \Delta$. Express $t \Rightarrow_G w$ as $t'At'' \Rightarrow_G t'BCt''$, where $t'At'' = t$ and $t'BCt'' = w$. Claim 4 implies that $y = y'Ay''$, where $\alpha(uFvFxFy') = t'$ and $\alpha(y'') = t''$. As $A \rightarrow BC \in R$, $(A) \rightarrow (BC) \in \bar{R}$ holds true. Then,

  $$uFvFxFy'Ay'' \Rightarrow_{\bar{G}} uFvFxFy'BCy''.$$

  Therefore,

  $$\bar{S} \Rightarrow^+_{\bar{G}} uFvFxFy'BCy''$$

  and $w = \alpha(uFvFxFy'BCy'')$;
- Assume that $p = A \rightarrow a \in R$, where $A \in \Sigma - \Delta$ and $a \in \Delta \cup \{\varepsilon\}$. Express $t \Rightarrow_G w$ as $t'At'' \Rightarrow_G t'at''$, where $t'At'' = t$ and $t'at'' = w$. Claim 4 implies that $y = y'Ay''$, where $\alpha(uFvFxFy') = t'$ and $\alpha(y'') = t''$. As $A \rightarrow a \in R$, $(A) \rightarrow (\$a) \in \bar{R}$ holds true. Then,

  $$uFvFxFy'Ay'' \Rightarrow_{\bar{G}} uFvFxFy'\$ay''.$$

  Therefore,

  $$\bar{S} \Rightarrow^+_{\bar{G}} uFvFxFy'\$ay''$$

  and $w = \alpha(uFvFxFy'\$ay'')$.

Consider the arguments above to see that $S \Rightarrow^j_G t \Rightarrow_G w$ [p], for any $p \in R$, implies that $\bar{S} \Rightarrow^+_{\bar{G}} s$, where $w = \alpha(s)$. Thus, the claim holds. □

Claim 8. $L(G) \subseteq L(\bar{G})$.

Proof. By Claims 1, 4, and 7, if $S \Rightarrow_G^* z$, where $z \in \Delta^*$, then $\bar{S} \Rightarrow_{\bar{G}}^+ z$. Therefore, Claim 8 holds. □

By Claims 6 and 8, $L(\bar{G}) = L(G)$. Observe that $\text{card}(\bar{\Sigma}) = \text{card}(\Sigma) + 5$, $\text{card}(\bar{R}) = \text{card}(R) + 4$, and $\text{dcs}(\bar{G}) = \text{dcs}(G) + 2$. Thus, the theorem holds. □

In the conclusion of this section, we point out several open problem areas.

Open Problem 13.2. By Theorem 13.7, SCGs with two context-sensitive rules characterize **RE**. What is the generative power of SCGs with one context-sensitive rule?

Open Problem 13.3. Revert the transformation under discussion and study economical transformations of SCGs to phrase-structure grammars.

Open Problem 13.4. From a much broader perspective, apart from the transformations between SCGs and phrase-structure grammars, study economical transformations between other types of grammars.

13.2 Totally parallel grammars

The totally parallel generation of languages works so that all symbols of the current sentential form are simultaneously rewritten during every single derivation step. The present section discusses this rewriting performed by *Extended tabled zero-sided Lindenmayer grammars* or, more briefly, ET0L grammars (see Section 4.2). Recall that these grammars can be understood as generalized parallel versions of context-free grammars. More precisely, there exist three main conceptual differences between them and context-free grammars. First, instead of a single set of rules, they have finitely many sets of rules. Second, the left-hand side of a rule may be formed by any grammatical symbol, including a terminal. Third, all symbols of a string are simultaneously rewritten during a single derivation step. The present section restricts its attention to ET0L grammars that work in a context-conditional way. Specifically, by analogy with context-conditional grammars that work in a sequential way (see Section 11.2), the section discusses *context-conditional ET0L grammars* that capture this dependency, so each of their rules may be associated with finitely many strings representing *permitting conditions* and, in addition, finitely many strings representing *forbidding conditions*. A rule like this can rewrite a symbol if all its permitting conditions occur in the current rewritten sentential form and, simultaneously, all its forbidding conditions do not. Otherwise, these grammars work just like ordinary ET0L grammars. The section consists of four subsections. Section 13.2.1 defines the basic version of context-conditional ET0L grammars. The other sections investigate three variants of the basic version—*forbidding ET0L (F-ET0L) grammars* (Section 13.2.2), *simple semi-conditional ET0L (SSC-ET0L) grammars* (Section 13.2.3), and *left random context ET0L (LRC-ET0L) grammars* (Section 13.2.4). All these sections concentrate their attention on establishing the generative power of the ET0L grammars under investigation.

13.2.1 Context-conditional ET0L grammars

In the present subsection, we demonstrate that context-conditional ET0L grammars characterize the family of recursively enumerable languages (see Theorem 13.13), and, without erasing rules, they characterize the family of context-sensitive languages (see Theorem 13.12).

13.2.1.1 Definitions

In this section, we define context-conditional ET0L grammars.

Definition 13.6. *A* context-conditional ET0L grammar *(a C-ET0L grammar for short) is a* $(t+3)$*-tuple*

$$G = (\Sigma, \Delta, R_1, \ldots, R_t, S)$$

where $t \geq 1$*, and* Σ*,* Δ*, and* S *are the* total alphabet*, the* terminal alphabet *(*$\Delta \subset \Sigma$*), and the* start symbol *(*$S \in \Sigma - \Delta$*), respectively. Every* R_i*, where* $1 \leq i \leq t$*, is a finite set of rules of the form*

$$(a \to x, Per, For)$$

with $a \in \Sigma$*,* $x \in \Sigma^*$*, and* $Per, For \subseteq \Sigma^+$ *are finite languages. If every* $(a \to x,\ Per,\ For) \in R_i$ *for* $i = 1, 2, \ldots, t$ *satisfies that* $|x| \geq 1$*, then* G *is said to be* propagating *(a C-EPT0L grammar for short).* G *has* degree (r, s)*, where* r *and* s *are natural numbers, if for every* $i = 1, \ldots, t$ *and* $(a \to x, Per, For) \in R_i$*,* max-len $(Per) \leq r$ *and* max-len $(For) \leq s$*.*

Let $u, v \in \Sigma^*$*,* $u = a_1 a_2 \cdots a_q$*,* $v = v_1 v_2 \cdots v_q$*,* $q = |u|$*,* $a_j \in \Sigma$*,* $v_j \in \Sigma^*$*, and* $p_1, p_2, \ldots, p_q$ *be a sequence of rules* p_j*:* $(a_j \to v_j, Per_j, For_j) \in R_i$ *for all* $j = 1, \ldots, q$ *and some* $i \in \{1, \ldots, t\}$*. If for every* p_j*,* $Per_j \subseteq$ substrings (u) *and* $For_j \cap$ substrings $(u) = \emptyset$*, then* u directly derives v *according to* $p_1, p_2, \ldots, p_q$ *in* G*, denoted by*

$$u \Rightarrow_G v\ [p_1, p_2, \ldots, p_q].$$

In the standard way, define $\Rightarrow_G^k$ *for* $k \geq 0$*,* $\Rightarrow_G^*$*, and* $\Rightarrow_G^+$*. The* language *of* G *is denoted by* $L(G)$ *and defined as*

$$L(G) = \{x \in \Delta^* \mid S \Rightarrow_G^* x\}.$$

Definition 13.7. *Let* $G = (\Sigma,\ \Delta,\ R_1,\ \ldots,\ R_t,\ S)$ *be a C-ET0L grammar, for some* $t \geq 1$*. If* $t = 1$*, then* G *is called a* context-conditional E0L *grammar (a C-E0L grammar for short). If* G *is a propagating C-E0L grammar,* G *is said to be a* C-EP0L grammar.

The language families defined by C-EPT0L, C-ET0L, C-EP0L, and C-E0L grammars of degree (r,s) are denoted by $\mathbf{CEPT0L}(r,s)$, $\mathbf{CET0L}(r,s)$, $\mathbf{CEP0L}(r,s)$, and $\mathbf{CE0L}(r,s)$, respectively. Set

$$\mathbf{CEPT0L} = \bigcup_{r=0}^{\infty}\bigcup_{s=0}^{\infty}\mathbf{CEPT0L}(r,s), \qquad \mathbf{CET0L} = \bigcup_{r=0}^{\infty}\bigcup_{s=0}^{\infty}\mathbf{CET0L}(r,s),$$

$$\mathbf{CEP0L} = \bigcup_{r=0}^{\infty}\bigcup_{s=0}^{\infty}\mathbf{CEP0L}(r,s), \qquad \mathbf{CE0L} = \bigcup_{r=0}^{\infty}\bigcup_{s=0}^{\infty}\mathbf{CE0L}(r,s).$$

13.2.1.2 Generative power

In this section, we discuss the generative power of context-conditional grammars.

Lemma 13.3.

$$\mathbf{CEP0L} \subseteq \mathbf{CEPT0L} \subseteq \mathbf{CET0L}$$

and

$$\mathbf{CEP0L} \subseteq \mathbf{CE0L} \subseteq \mathbf{CET0L}.$$

For any $r, s \geq 0$,

$$\mathbf{CEP0L}(r,s) \subseteq \mathbf{CEPT0L}(r,s) \subseteq \mathbf{CET0L}(r,s),$$

and

$$\mathbf{CEP0L}(r,s) \subseteq \mathbf{CE0L}(r,s) \subseteq \mathbf{CET0L}(r,s).$$

Proof. This lemma follows from Definitions 13.6 and 13.7. □

Theorem 13.11.

$$\begin{gathered}\mathbf{CF}\\ \subset\\ \mathbf{CE0L}(0,0) = \mathbf{CEP0L}(0,0) = \mathbf{E0L} = \mathbf{EP0L}\\ \subset\\ \mathbf{CET0L}(0,0) = \mathbf{CEPT0L}(0,0) = \mathbf{ET0L} = \mathbf{EPT0L}\\ \subset\\ \mathbf{CS}.\end{gathered}$$

Proof. Clearly, C-EP0L and C-E0L grammars of degree $(0,0)$ are ordinary EP0L and E0L grammars, respectively. Analogously, C-EPT0L and C-ET0L grammars of degree $(0,0)$ are EPT0L and ET0L grammars, respectively. Since $\mathbf{CF} \subset \mathbf{E0L} = \mathbf{EP0L} \subset \mathbf{ET0L} = \mathbf{EPT0L} \subset \mathbf{CS}$ (see Theorem 4.4), we get $\mathbf{CF} \subset \mathbf{CE0L}(0,0) = \mathbf{CEP0L}(0,0) = \mathbf{E0L} \subset \mathbf{CET0L}(0,0) = \mathbf{CEPT0L}(0,0) = \mathbf{ET0L} \subset \mathbf{CS}$; therefore, the theorem holds. □

Lemma 13.4. $\mathbf{CEPT0L}(r,s) \subseteq \mathbf{CS}$, *for any* $r \geq 0$, $s \geq 0$.

Proof. For $r = 0$ and $s = 0$, we have

$$\mathbf{CEPT0L}(0,0) = \mathbf{EPT0L} \subset \mathbf{CS}.$$

The following proof demonstrates that the inclusion holds for any r and s such that $r + s \geq 1$.

Let L be a language generated by a C-EPT0L grammar

$$G = (\Sigma, \Delta, P_1, \ldots, P_t, S)$$

of degree (r, s), for some $r, s \geq 0$, $r + s \geq 1$, $t \geq 1$. Let k be the greater number of r and s. Set

$$M = \{x \in \Sigma^+ \mid |x| \leq k\}.$$

For every P_i, where $1 \leq i \leq t$, define

$$\text{cf-rules}\,(P_i) = \{a \to z \mid (a \to z, Per, For) \in P_i,\ \ a \in \Sigma,\ \ z \in \Sigma^+\}.$$

Then, set

$$\begin{aligned} N_F &= \{\lfloor X, x \rfloor \mid X \subseteq M,\ x \in M \cup \{\varepsilon\}\},\\ N_\Delta &= \{\langle X \rangle \mid X \subseteq M\},\\ N_B &= \{\lceil Q \rceil \mid Q \subseteq \text{cf-rules}(P_i)\ 1 \leq i \leq t\},\\ \Sigma' &= \Sigma \cup N_F \cup N_\Delta \cup N_B \cup \{\rhd, \lhd, \$, S', \#\},\\ \Delta' &= \Delta \cup \{\#\}. \end{aligned}$$

Construct the context-sensitive grammar

$$G' = (\Sigma', \Delta', R', S')$$

with the finite set of rules R' constructed by performing (1)–(7), given next.

(1) Add $S' \to \rhd \lfloor \emptyset, \varepsilon \rfloor S \lhd$ to R';

(2) For all $X \subseteq M$, $x \in (\Sigma^k \cup \{\varepsilon\})$ and $y \in \Sigma^k$, extend R' by adding

$$\lfloor X, x \rfloor y \to y \lfloor X \cup \text{substrings}\,(xy, k), y \rfloor;$$

(3) For all $X \subseteq M$, $x \in (\Sigma^k \cup \{\varepsilon\})$ and $y \in \Sigma^+$, $|y| \leq k$, extend R' by adding

$$\lfloor X, x \rfloor y \lhd \to y \langle X \cup \text{substrings}\,(xy, k) \rangle \lhd;$$

(4) For all $X \subseteq M$ and $Q \subseteq \text{cf-rules}(P_i)$, where $i \in \{1, \ldots, t\}$, such that for every $a \to z \in Q$, there exists $(a \to z, Per, For) \in P_i$ satisfying $Per \subseteq X$ and $For \cap X = \emptyset$, extend R' by adding

$$\langle X \rangle \lhd \to \lceil Q \rceil \lhd;$$

(5) For every $Q \subseteq \text{cf-rules}(P_i)$ for some $i \in \{1, \ldots, t\}$, $a \in \Sigma$ and $z \in \Sigma^+$ such that $a \to z \in Q$, extend R' by adding

$$a \lceil Q \rceil \to \lceil Q \rceil z;$$

(6) For all $Q \subseteq \text{cf-rules}(P_i)$ for some $i = \{1, \ldots, t\}$, extend R' by adding

$$\rhd \lceil Q \rceil \to \rhd \lfloor \emptyset, \varepsilon \rfloor;$$

(7) Add $\triangleright\lfloor\emptyset,\varepsilon\rfloor \rightarrow \#\$$, $\$\triangleleft \rightarrow \#\#$, and $\$a \rightarrow a\$$, for all $a \in \Delta$, to R'.

To prove that $L(G) = L(G')$, we first establish Claims 1–3.

Claim 1. Every successful derivation in G' has the form

$$\begin{aligned} S' &\Rightarrow_{G'} \triangleright\lfloor\emptyset,\varepsilon\rfloor S\triangleleft \\ &\Rightarrow_{G'}^{+} \triangleright\lfloor\emptyset,\varepsilon\rfloor x\triangleleft \\ &\Rightarrow_{G'} \#\$x\triangleleft \\ &\Rightarrow_{G'}^{|x|} \#x\$\triangleleft \\ &\Rightarrow_{G'} \#x\#\# \end{aligned}$$

such that $x \in \Delta^+$ and during $\triangleright\lfloor\emptyset,\varepsilon\rfloor S\triangleleft \Rightarrow_{G'}^{+} \triangleright\lfloor\emptyset,\varepsilon\rfloor x\triangleleft$, every sentential form w satisfies $w \in \{\triangleright\}H^+\{\triangleleft\}$, where $H \subseteq \Sigma' - \{\triangleright, \triangleleft, \#, \$, S'\}$.

Proof. The only rule that can rewrite the start symbol is $S' \rightarrow \triangleright\lfloor\emptyset,\varepsilon\rfloor S\triangleleft$; thus,

$$S' \Rightarrow_{G'} \triangleright\lfloor\emptyset,\varepsilon\rfloor S\triangleleft.$$

After that, every sentential form that occurs in

$$\triangleright\lfloor\emptyset,\varepsilon\rfloor S\triangleleft \Rightarrow_{G'}^{+} \triangleright\lfloor\emptyset,\varepsilon\rfloor x\triangleleft$$

can be rewritten by using any of the rules introduced in (2)–(6) from the construction of R'. By the inspection of these rules, it is obvious that the edge symbols $\triangleright$ and $\triangleleft$ remain unchanged and no other occurrences of them appear inside the sentential form. Moreover, there is no rule generating a symbol from $\{\#, \$, S'\}$. Therefore, all these sentential forms belong to $\{\triangleright\}H^+\{\triangleleft\}$.

Next, let us explain how G' generates a string from $L(G')$. Only $\triangleright\lfloor\emptyset,\varepsilon\rfloor \rightarrow \#\$$ can rewrite $\triangleright$ to a symbol from Δ (see (7) in the definition of R'). According to the left-hand side of this rule, we obtain

$$S' \Rightarrow_{G'} \triangleright\lfloor\emptyset,\varepsilon\rfloor S\triangleleft \Rightarrow_{G'}^{*} \triangleright\lfloor\emptyset,\varepsilon\rfloor x\triangleleft \Rightarrow_{G'} \#\$x\triangleleft$$

where $x \in H^+$. To rewrite $\triangleleft$, G' uses $\$\triangleleft \rightarrow \#\#$. Thus, G' needs $\$$ as the left neighbor of $\triangleleft$. Suppose that $x = a_1a_2 \cdots a_q$, where $q = |x|$ and $a_i \in \Delta$, for all $i \in \{1, \dots, q\}$. Since for every $a \in \Delta$, there is $\$a \rightarrow a\$ \in R'$ (see (7)), we can construct

$$\begin{aligned} \#\$a_1a_2 \cdots a_n\triangleleft &\Rightarrow_{G'} \#a_1\$a_2 \cdots a_n\triangleleft \\ &\Rightarrow_{G'} \#a_1a_2\$ \cdots a_n\triangleleft \\ &\Rightarrow_{G'}^{|x|-2} \#a_1a_2 \cdots a_n\$\triangleleft. \end{aligned}$$

Notice that this derivation can be constructed only for x that belong to Δ^+. Then, $\$\triangleleft$ is rewritten to $\#\#$. As a result,

$$S' \Rightarrow_{G'} \triangleright\lfloor\emptyset,\varepsilon\rfloor S\triangleleft \Rightarrow_{G'}^{+} \triangleright\lfloor\emptyset,\varepsilon\rfloor x\triangleleft \Rightarrow_{G'} \#\$x\triangleleft \Rightarrow_{G'}^{|x|} \#x\$\triangleleft \Rightarrow_{G'} \#x\#\#$$

with the required properties. Thus, the claim holds. □

The following claim demonstrates how G' simulates a direct derivation from G—the heart of the construction.

Let $x \Rightarrow_{G'}^{\oplus} y$ denote the derivation $x \Rightarrow_{G'}^{+} y$ such that $x = \rhd\lfloor\emptyset, \varepsilon\rfloor u\lhd$, $y = \rhd\lfloor\emptyset, \varepsilon\rfloor v\lhd$, $u, v \in \Sigma^{+}$, and during $x \Rightarrow_{G'}^{+} y$, there is no other occurrence of a string of the form $\rhd\lfloor\emptyset, \varepsilon\rfloor z\lhd$, $z \in \Sigma^{*}$.

Claim 2. For every $u, v \in \Sigma^{*}$,

$$\rhd\lfloor\emptyset, \varepsilon\rfloor u\lhd \Rightarrow_{G'}^{\oplus} \rhd\lfloor\emptyset, \varepsilon\rfloor v\lhd \quad \text{if and only if} \quad u \Rightarrow_{G} v.$$

Proof. The proof is divided into the only-if part and the if part.

Only If. Let us show how G' rewrites $\rhd\lfloor\emptyset, \varepsilon\rfloor u\lhd$ to $\rhd\lfloor\emptyset, \varepsilon\rfloor v\lhd$ by performing a derivation consisting of a forward and a backward phase.

During the first, forward phase, G' scans u to obtain all nonempty substrings of length k or less. By repeatedly using rules

$$\lfloor X, x\rfloor y \rightarrow y\lfloor X \cup \text{substrings}\,(xy, k), y\rfloor$$

where $X \subseteq M$, $x \in (\Sigma^{k} \cup \{\varepsilon\})$, $y \in \Sigma^{k}$ (see (2) in the definition of R'), the occurrence of a symbol with form $\lfloor X, x\rfloor$ is moved toward the end of the sentential form. Simultaneously, the substrings of u are collected in X. The forward phase is finished by

$$\lfloor X, x\rfloor y\lhd \rightarrow y\langle X \cup \text{substrings}\,(xy, k)\rangle\lhd$$

where $x \in (\Sigma^{k} \cup \{\varepsilon\})$, $y \in \Sigma^{+}$, $|y| \leq k$ (see (3)); the rule reaches the end of u and completes $X = \text{substrings}\,(u, k)$. Formally,

$$\rhd\lfloor\emptyset, \varepsilon\rfloor u\lhd \Rightarrow_{G'}^{+} \rhd u\langle X\rangle\lhd$$

such that $X = \text{substrings}\,(u, k)$. Then, $\langle X\rangle$ is changed to $\lceil Q\rceil$, where

$$\begin{aligned} Q = \{a \rightarrow z \mid\ & (a \rightarrow z, Per, For) \in P_i,\ a \in \Sigma,\ z \in \Sigma^{+}, \\ & Per, For \subseteq M,\ Per \subseteq X,\ For \cap X = \emptyset\} \end{aligned}$$

for some $i \in \{1, \ldots, t\}$, by

$$\langle X\rangle\lhd \rightarrow \lceil Q\rceil\lhd$$

(see (4)). In other words, G' selects a subset of rules from P_i that could be used to rewrite u in G.

The second, backward phase simulates rewriting of all symbols in u in parallel. Since

$$a\lceil Q\rceil \rightarrow \lceil Q\rceil z \in R'$$

for all $a \rightarrow z \in Q$, $a \in \Sigma$, $z \in \Sigma^{+}$ (see (5)),

$$\rhd u\lceil Q\rceil\lhd \Rightarrow_{G'}^{|u|} \rhd\lceil Q\rceil v\lhd$$

such that $\lceil Q \rceil$ moves left and every symbol $a \in \Sigma$ in u is rewritten to some z provided that $a \to z \in Q$. Finally, $\lceil Q \rceil$ is rewritten to $\lfloor \emptyset, \varepsilon \rfloor$ by

$$\rhd \lceil Q \rceil \to \rhd \lfloor \emptyset, \varepsilon \rfloor.$$

As a result, we obtain

$$\begin{aligned} \rhd \lfloor \emptyset, \varepsilon \rfloor u \lhd &\Rightarrow^{+}_{G'} \rhd u \langle X \rangle \lhd \Rightarrow_{G'} \rhd u \lceil Q \rceil \lhd \\ &\Rightarrow^{|u|}_{G'} \rhd \lceil Q \rceil v \lhd \Rightarrow_{G'} \rhd \lfloor \emptyset, \varepsilon \rfloor v \lhd. \end{aligned}$$

Observe that this is the only way of deriving

$$\rhd \lfloor \emptyset, \varepsilon \rfloor u \lhd \Rightarrow^{\oplus}_{G'} \rhd \lfloor \emptyset, \varepsilon \rfloor v \lhd.$$

Let us show that $u \Rightarrow_G v$. Indeed, because we have $(a \to z, Per, For) \in P_i$ for every $a\lceil Q \rceil \to \lceil Q \rceil z \in R$ used in the backward phase, where $Per \subseteq \text{substrings}\,(u, k)$ and $For \cap \text{substrings}\,(u, k) = \emptyset$ (see the construction of Q), there exists a derivation

$$u \Rightarrow_G v\ [p_1 \cdots p_q]$$

where $|u| = q$, and p_j: $(a \to z, Per, For) \in P_i$ such that $a\lceil Q \rceil \to \lceil Q \rceil z$ has been applied in the $(q - j + 1)$th derivation step in

$$\rhd u \lceil Q \rceil \lhd \Rightarrow^{|u|}_{G'} \rhd \lceil Q \rceil v \lhd$$

where $a \in \Sigma$, $z \in \Sigma^{+}$, $1 \le j \le q$.

If. The converse implication can be proved similarly to the only-if part, so we leave it to the reader. □

Claim 3. $S' \Rightarrow^{+}_{G'} \rhd \lfloor \emptyset, \varepsilon \rfloor x \lhd$ if and only if $S \Rightarrow^{*}_{G} x$, for all $x \in \Sigma^{+}$.

Proof. The proof is divided into the only-if part and the if part.

Only If. The only-if part is proved by induction on the ith occurrence of the sentential form w satisfying $w = \rhd \lfloor \emptyset, \varepsilon \rfloor u \lhd$, $u \in \Sigma^{+}$, during the derivation in G'.

Basis. Let $i = 1$. Then, $S' \Rightarrow_{G'} \rhd \lfloor \emptyset, \varepsilon \rfloor S \lhd$ and $S \Rightarrow^{0}_{G} S$.

Induction Hypothesis. Suppose that the claim holds for all $1 \le i \le h$, for some $h \ge 1$.

Induction Step. Let $i = h + 1$. Since $h + 1 \ge 2$, we can express

$$S' \Rightarrow^{+}_{G'} \rhd \lfloor \emptyset, \varepsilon \rfloor x_i \lhd$$

as

$$S' \Rightarrow^{+}_{G'} \rhd \lfloor \emptyset, \varepsilon \rfloor x_{i-1} \lhd \Rightarrow^{\oplus}_{G'} \rhd \lfloor \emptyset, \varepsilon \rfloor x_i \lhd$$

where $x_{i-1}, x_i \in \Sigma^{+}$. By the induction hypothesis,

$$S \Rightarrow^{*}_{G} x_{i-1}.$$

Claim 2 says that

$$\rhd \lfloor \emptyset, \varepsilon \rfloor x_{i-1} \lhd \Rightarrow^{\oplus}_{G'} \rhd \lfloor \emptyset, \varepsilon \rfloor x_i \lhd \quad \text{if and only if} \quad x_{i-1} \Rightarrow_G x_i.$$

Hence,

$$S \Rightarrow_G^* x_{i-1} \Rightarrow_G x_i,$$

and the only-if part holds.

If. By induction on h, we prove that

$$S \Rightarrow_G^h x \quad \text{implies that} \quad S' \Rightarrow_{G'}^+ \rhd\lfloor\emptyset, \varepsilon\rfloor x\lhd$$

for all $h \geq 0, x \in \Sigma^+$.

Basis. For $h = 0$, $S \Rightarrow_G^0 S$ and $S' \Rightarrow_{G'} \rhd\lfloor\emptyset, \varepsilon\rfloor S\lhd$.

Induction Hypothesis. Assume that the claim holds for all $0 \leq h \leq n$, for some $n \geq 0$.

Induction Step. Consider any derivation of the form

$$S \Rightarrow_G^{n+1} x$$

where $x \in \Sigma^+$. Since $n + 1 \geq 1$, there exists $y \in \Sigma^+$ such that

$$S \Rightarrow_G^n y \Rightarrow_G x$$

and by the induction hypothesis, there is also a derivation

$$S' \Rightarrow_{G'}^+ \rhd\lfloor\emptyset, \varepsilon\rfloor y\lhd.$$

From Claim 2, we have

$$\rhd\lfloor\emptyset, \varepsilon\rfloor y\lhd \Rightarrow_{G'}^{\oplus} \rhd\lfloor\emptyset, \varepsilon\rfloor x\lhd.$$

Therefore,

$$S' \Rightarrow_{G'}^+ \rhd\lfloor\emptyset, \varepsilon\rfloor y\lhd \Rightarrow_{G'}^{\oplus} \rhd\lfloor\emptyset, \varepsilon\rfloor x\lhd$$

and the converse implication holds as well. □

From Claims 1 and 3, we see that any successful derivation in G' is of the form

$$S' \Rightarrow_{G'}^+ \rhd\lfloor\emptyset, \varepsilon\rfloor x\lhd \Rightarrow_{G'}^+ \#x\#\#$$

such that

$$S \Rightarrow_G^* x, \quad x \in \Delta^+.$$

Therefore, for each $x \in \Delta^+$, we have

$$S' \Rightarrow_{G'}^+ \#x\#\# \quad \text{if and only if} \quad S \Rightarrow_G^* x.$$

Define the homomorphism h over $(\Delta \cup \{\#\})^*$ as $h(\#) = \varepsilon$ and $h(a) = a$ for all $a \in \Delta$. Observe that h is 4-linear erasing with respect to $L(G')$. Furthermore, notice that $h(L(G')) = L(G)$. Since **CS** is closed under linear erasing (see Theorem 10.4 on page 98 in [11]), $L \in$ **CS**. Thus, Lemma 13.4 holds. □

Theorem 13.12. **CEPT0L** $=$ **CS**.

Proof. By Lemma 13.4, **CEPT0L** $\subseteq$ **CS**. Later in this section, we define two special cases of C-EPT0L grammars and prove that they generate all the family of context-sensitive languages (see Theorems 13.16 and 13.19). Therefore, **CS** $\subseteq$ **CEPT0L**, and hence **CEPT0L** $=$ **CS**. □

Lemma 13.5. **CET0L** $\subseteq$ **RE**.

Proof. This lemma follows from Turing–Church thesis. To obtain an algorithm converting any C-ET0L grammar to an equivalent phrase-structure grammar, use the technique presented in Lemma 13.4. □

Theorem 13.13. **CET0L** $=$ **RE**.

Proof. By Lemma 13.5, **CET0L** $\subseteq$ **RE**. In Sections 13.2.2 and 13.2.3, we introduce two special cases of C-ET0L grammars and demonstrate that even these grammars generate **RE** (see Theorems 13.17 and 13.18); therefore, **RE** $\subseteq$ **CET0L**. As a result, **CET0L** $=$ **RE**. □

13.2.2 Forbidding ET0L grammars

F-ET0L grammars, discussed in the present section, represent context-conditional ET0L grammars in which no rule has any permitting condition. First, this section defines and illustrates them. Then, it establishes their generative power and reduces their degree without affecting the power.

13.2.2.1 Definitions and examples

In this section, we define F-ET0L grammars.

Definition 13.8. *Let* $G = (\Sigma, \Delta, P_1, \ldots, P_t, S)$ *be a C-ET0L grammar. If every* $p\colon (a \to x, \mathrm{Per}, \mathrm{For}) \in P_i$*, where* $i = 1, \ldots, t$*, satisfies* $\mathrm{Per} = \emptyset$*, G is said to be an F-ET0L grammar. If G is a propagating F-ET0L grammar, then G is said to be an* F-EPT0L grammar. *If* $t = 1$*, G is called an* F-E0L grammar. *If G is a propagating F-E0L grammar, G is called an* F-EP0L grammar.

Let $G = (\Sigma, \Delta, P_1, \ldots, P_t, S)$ be an F-ET0L grammar of degree (r, s). From the above definition, $(a \to x, Per, For) \in P_i$ implies that $Per = \emptyset$ for all $i = 1, \ldots, t$. By analogy with sequential forbidding grammars, we thus omit the empty set in the rules. For simplicity, we also say that the degree of G is s instead of (r, s).

The families of languages generated by F-E0L grammars, F-EP0L grammars, F-ET0L grammars, and F-EPT0L grammars of degree s are denoted by **FE0L**(s), **FEP0L**(s), **FET0L**(s), and **FEPT0L**(s), respectively. Moreover, set

$$\mathbf{FEPT0L} = \bigcup_{s=0}^{\infty} \mathbf{FEPT0L}(s), \qquad \mathbf{FET0L} = \bigcup_{s=0}^{\infty} \mathbf{FET0L}(s),$$

$$\mathbf{FEP0L} = \bigcup_{s=0}^{\infty} \mathbf{FEP0L}(s), \qquad \mathbf{FE0L} = \bigcup_{s=0}^{\infty} \mathbf{FE0L}(s).$$

Example 13.4. Let

$$G = (\{S, A, B, C, a, \bar{a}, b\}, \{a, b\}, R, S)$$

be an F-EP0L grammar, where

$$\begin{aligned} R = \{&(S \to ABA, \emptyset),\\ &(A \to aA, \{\bar{a}\}),\\ &(B \to bB, \emptyset),\\ &(A \to \bar{a}, \{\bar{a}\}),\\ &(\bar{a} \to a, \emptyset),\\ &(B \to C, \emptyset),\\ &(C \to bC, \{A\}),\\ &(C \to b, \{A\}),\\ &(a \to a, \emptyset),\\ &(b \to b, \emptyset)\}. \end{aligned}$$

Obviously, G is an F-EP0L grammar of degree 1. Observe that for every string from $L(G)$, there exists a derivation of the form

$$\begin{aligned} S &\Rightarrow_G ABA\\ &\Rightarrow_G aAbBaA\\ &\Rightarrow_G^+ a^{m-1}Ab^{m-1}Ba^{m-1}A\\ &\Rightarrow_G a^{m-1}\bar{a}b^{m-1}Ca^{m-1}\bar{a}\\ &\Rightarrow_G a^m b^m C a^m\\ &\Rightarrow_G^+ a^m b^{n-1} C a^m\\ &\Rightarrow_G a^m b^n a^m \end{aligned}$$

with $1 \le m \le n$. Hence,

$$L(G) = \{a^m b^n a^m \mid 1 \le m \le n\}.$$

Note that $L(G) \notin$ **E0L** (see page 268 in [39]); however, $L(G) \in$ **FEP0L**(1). As a result, F-EP0L grammars of degree 1 are more powerful than ordinary E0L grammars.

13.2.2.2 Generative power and reduction

Next, we investigate the generative power of F-ET0L grammars of all degrees.

Theorem 13.14. FEPT0L(0) = EPT0L, **FET0L(0) = ET0L**, **FEP0L(0) = EP0L**, *and* **FE0L(0) = E0L**.

Proof. This theorem follows from Definition 13.8. □

Lemmas 13.6–13.9, given next, inspect the generative power of F-ET0L grammars of degree 1. As a conclusion, in Theorem 13.15, we demonstrate that both F-EPT0L(1) and F-ET0L(1) grammars generate precisely the family of ET0L languages.

Lemma 13.6. EPT0L ⊆ FEP0L(1).

Proof. Let

$$G = (\Sigma, \Delta, P_1, \ldots, P_t, S)$$

be an EPT0L grammar, where $t \geq 1$. Set

$$W = \{\langle a, i\rangle \mid a \in \Sigma,\ i = 1, \ldots, t\}$$

and

$$F_i = \{\langle a, j\rangle \in W \mid j \neq i\}.$$

Then, construct an F-EP0L grammar of degree 1

$$G' = (\Sigma', \Delta, R', S)$$

where $\Sigma' = \Sigma \cup W$, $(\Sigma \cap W = \emptyset)$ and the set of rules R' is defined as follows:

(1) for each $a \in \Sigma$ and $i = 1, \ldots, t$, add $(a \rightarrow \langle a, i\rangle, \emptyset)$ to R' and
(2) if $a \rightarrow z \in P_i$ for some $i \in \{1, \ldots, t\}$, $a \in \Sigma$, $z \in \Sigma^+$, add $(\langle a, i\rangle \rightarrow z, F_i)$ to R'.

Next, to demonstrate that $L(G) = L(G')$, we prove Claims 1 and 2.

Claim 1. For each derivation $S \Rightarrow^n_{G'} x,\ \ n \geq 0$,

(I) if $n = 2k + 1$ for some $k \geq 0$, $x \in W^+$ and
(II) if $n = 2k$ for some $k \geq 0$, $x \in \Sigma^+$.

Proof. The claim follows from the definition of R'. Indeed, every rule in R' is either of the form $(a \rightarrow \langle a, i\rangle, \emptyset)$ or $(\langle a, i\rangle \rightarrow z, F_i)$, where $a \in \Sigma$, $\langle a, i\rangle \in W$, $z \in \Sigma^+$, $i \in \{1, \ldots, t\}$. Since $S \in \Sigma$,

$$S \Rightarrow^{2k+1}_{G'} x \quad \text{implies} \quad x \in W^+$$

and

$$S \Rightarrow^{2k}_{G'} x \quad \text{implies} \quad x \in \Sigma^+.$$

Thus, the claim holds. □

Define the finite substitution γ from Σ^* to Σ'^* such that for every $a \in \Sigma$,

$$\gamma(a) = \{a\} \cup \{\langle a, i\rangle \in W \mid i = 1, \ldots, t\}.$$

Claim 2. $S \Rightarrow_G^* x$ if and only if $S \Rightarrow_{G'}^* x'$ for some $x' \in \gamma(x), x \in \Sigma^+, x' \in \Sigma'^+$.

Proof. The proof is divided into the only-if part and the if part.

Only If. By induction on $h \geq 0$, we show that for all $x \in \Sigma^+$,

$$S \Rightarrow_G^h x \quad \text{implies} \quad S \Rightarrow_{G'}^{2h} x.$$

Basis. Let $h = 0$. Then, the only x is S; therefore, $S \Rightarrow_G^0 S$ and also $S \Rightarrow_{G'}^0 S$.

Induction Hypothesis. Suppose that

$$S \Rightarrow_G^h x \quad \text{implies} \quad S \Rightarrow_{G'}^{2h} x$$

for all derivations of length $0 \leq h \leq n$, for some $n \geq 0$.

Induction Step. Consider any derivation of the form

$$S \Rightarrow_G^{n+1} x.$$

Since $n + 1 \geq 1$, this derivation can be expressed as

$$S \Rightarrow_G^n y \Rightarrow_G x \; [p_1, p_2, \ldots, p_q]$$

such that $y \in \Sigma^+$, $q = |y|$, and $p_j \in P_i$ for all $j = 1, \ldots, q$ and some $i \in \{1, \ldots, t\}$. By the induction hypothesis,

$$S \Rightarrow_{G'}^{2n} y.$$

Suppose that $y = a_1 a_2 \cdots a_q$, $a_j \in \Sigma$. Let

$$\begin{aligned} S &\Rightarrow_{G'}^{2n} a_1 a_2 \cdots a_q \\ &\Rightarrow_{G'} \langle a_1, i\rangle\langle a_2, i\rangle \cdots \langle a_q, i\rangle \quad [p'_1, p'_2, \ldots, p'_q] \\ &\Rightarrow_{G'} z_1 z_2 \cdots z_q \quad [p''_1, p''_2, \ldots, p''_q] \end{aligned}$$

where $p'_j\colon (a_j \rightarrow \langle a_j, i\rangle, \emptyset)$ and $p''_j\colon (\langle a_j, i\rangle \rightarrow z_j, F_i)$ such that $p_j\colon a_j \rightarrow z_j$, $z_j \in \Sigma^+$, for all $j = 1, \ldots, q$. Then, $z_1 z_2 \cdots z_q = x$; therefore,

$$S \Rightarrow_{G'}^{2(n+1)} x.$$

If. The converse implication is established by induction on $h \geq 0$. That is, we prove that

$$S \Rightarrow_{G'}^h x' \quad \text{implies} \quad S \Rightarrow_G^* x$$

for some $x' \in \gamma(x)$, $h \geq 0$.

Basis. For $h = 0$, $S \Rightarrow_{G'}^0 S$ and $S \Rightarrow_G^0 S$; clearly, $S \in \gamma(S)$.

Induction Hypothesis. Assume that there exists a natural number n such that the claim holds for every h, where $0 \leq h \leq n$.

Induction Step. Consider any derivation of the form

$$S \Rightarrow_{G'}^{n+1} x'.$$

Express this derivation as

$$S \Rightarrow^n_{G'} y' \Rightarrow_{G'} x' \; [p'_1, p'_2, \ldots, p'_q]$$

where $y' \in \Sigma'^+$, $q = |y'|$, and $p'_1, p'_2, \ldots, p'_q$ is a sequence of rules from R'. By the induction hypothesis,

$$S \Rightarrow^*_G y$$

where $y \in \Sigma^+$, $y' \in \gamma(y)$. Claim 1 says that there exist the following two cases—(i) and (ii).

(i) Let $n = 2k$ for some $k \geq 0$. Then, $y' \in \Sigma^+$, $x' \in W^+$, and every rule

$$p'_j\colon (a_j \rightarrow \langle a_j, i\rangle, \emptyset)$$

where $a_j \in \Sigma$, $\langle a_j, i\rangle \in W$, $i \in \{1, \ldots, t\}$, $1 \leq j \leq q$. In this case, $\langle a_j, i\rangle \in \gamma(a_j)$ for every a_j and any i (see the definition of g); hence, $x' \in \gamma(y)$ as well;

(ii) Let $n = 2k + 1$. Then, $y' \in W^+$, $x' \in \Sigma^+$, and each p'_j is of the form

$$p'_j\colon (\langle a_j, i\rangle \rightarrow z_j, F_i)$$

where $\langle a_j, i\rangle \in W$, $z_j \in \Sigma^+$, $i \in \{1, \ldots, t\}$, $1 \leq j \leq q$. Moreover, according to the forbidding conditions of p'_j, all $\langle a_j, i\rangle$ in y' have the same i. Thus, $y' = \langle a_1, i\rangle\langle a_2, i\rangle \cdots \langle a_q, i\rangle$, $y = \gamma^{-1}(y') = a_1 a_2 \cdots a_q$, and $x' = z_1 z_2 \cdots z_q$. By the definition of R',

$$(\langle a_j, i\rangle \rightarrow z_j, F_i) \in R' \quad \text{implies} \quad a_j \rightarrow z_j \in P_i.$$

Therefore,

$$S \Rightarrow^*_G a_1 a_2 \cdots a_q \Rightarrow_G z_1 z_2 \cdots z_q \; [p_1, p_2, \ldots, p_q]$$

where $p_j\colon a_j \rightarrow z_j \in P_i$ such that $p'_j\colon (\langle a_j, i\rangle \rightarrow z_j, F_i)$. Obviously, $x' = x = z_1 z_2 \cdots z_q$.

This completes the induction and establishes Claim 2. □

By Claim 2, for any $x \in \Delta^+$,

$$S \Rightarrow^*_G x \quad \text{if and only if} \quad S \Rightarrow^*_{G'} x.$$

Therefore, $L(G) = L(G')$, so the lemma holds. □

In order to simplify the notation in the proof of the following lemma, for every subset of rules

$$R \subseteq \{(a \rightarrow z, F) \mid a \in \Sigma,\ z \in \Sigma^*,\ F \subseteq \Sigma\}$$

define

$$\mathit{left}(R) = \{a \mid (a \rightarrow z, F) \in R\}.$$

Informally, *left*(R) denotes the set of the left-hand sides of all rules in R.

Lemma 13.7. FEPT0L(1) $\subseteq$ EPT0L.

Proof. Let

$$G = (\Sigma, \Delta, P_1, \ldots, P_t, S)$$

be an F-EPT0L grammar of degree 1, $t \geq 1$. Let Q be the set of all subsets $O \subseteq P_i$, $1 \leq i \leq t$, such that every $(a \to z, F) \in O$, $a \in \Sigma$, $z \in \Sigma^+$, $F \subseteq \Sigma$, satisfies $F \cap \text{left}(O) = \emptyset$. Introduce a new set Q' so that for each $O \in Q$, add

$$\{a \to z \mid (a \to z, F) \in O\}$$

to Q'. Express

$$Q' = \{Q'_1, \ldots, Q'_m\}$$

where m is the cardinality of Q'. Then, construct the EPT0L grammar

$$G' = (\Sigma, \Delta, Q'_1, \ldots, Q'_m, S).$$

To see the basic idea behind the construction of G', consider a pair of rules $p_1: (a_1 \to z_1, F_1)$ and $p_2: (a_2 \to z_2, F_2)$ from P_i, for some $i \in \{1, \ldots, t\}$. During a single derivation step, p_1 and p_2 can concurrently rewrite a_1 and a_2 provided that $a_2 \notin F_1$ and $a_1 \notin F_2$, respectively. Consider any $O \subseteq P_i$ containing no pair of rules $(a_1 \to z_1, F_1)$ and $(a_2 \to z_2, F_2)$ such that $a_1 \in F_2$ or $a_2 \in F_1$. Observe that for any derivation step based on O, no rule from O is blocked by its forbidding conditions; thus, the conditions can be omitted. A formal proof is given next.

Claim 1. $S \Rightarrow_G^h x$ if and only if $S \Rightarrow_{G'}^h x$, $x \in \Sigma^*$, $m \geq 0$.

Proof. The claim is proved by induction on $h \geq 0$.

Only If. By induction $h \geq 0$, we prove that

$$S \Rightarrow_G^h x \quad \text{implies} \quad S \Rightarrow_{G'}^h x$$

for all $x \in \Sigma^*$.

Basis. Let $h = 0$. As obvious, $S \Rightarrow_G^0 S$ and $S \Rightarrow_{G'}^0 S$.

Induction Hypothesis. Suppose that the claim holds for all derivations of length $0 \leq h \leq n$, for some $n \geq 0$.

Induction Step. Consider any derivation of the form

$$S \Rightarrow_G^{n+1} x.$$

Since $n + 1 \geq 1$, there exists $y \in \Sigma^+$, $q = |y|$, and a sequence $p_1, \ldots, p_q$, where $p_j \in P_i$ for all $j = 1, \ldots, q$ and some $i \in \{1, \ldots, t\}$, such that

$$S \Rightarrow_G^n y \Rightarrow_G x \; [p_1, \ldots, p_q].$$

By the induction hypothesis,

$$S \Rightarrow_{G'}^{n} y.$$

Set

$$O = \{p_j \mid 1 \leq j \leq q\}.$$

Observe that

$$y \Rightarrow_G x\ [p_1, \ldots, p_q]$$

implies that symbols $(y) =$ left (O). Moreover, every $p_j\colon (a \to z, F) \in O$, $a \in \Sigma$, $z \in \Sigma^+$, $F \subseteq \Sigma$, satisfies $F \cap$ symbols $(y) = \emptyset$. Hence, $(a \to z, F) \in O$ implies $F \cap$ left $(O) = \emptyset$. Inspect the definition of G' to see that there exists

$$Q'_r = \{a \to z \mid (a \to z, F) \in O\}$$

for some r, $1 \leq r \leq m$. Therefore,

$$S \Rightarrow_{G'}^{n} y \Rightarrow_{G'} x\ [p'_1, \ldots, p'_q]$$

where $p'_j\colon a \to z \in Q'_r$ such that $p_j\colon (a \to z, F) \in O$, for all $j = 1, \ldots, q$.

If. The if part demonstrates for every $h \geq 0$,

$$S \Rightarrow_{G'}^{h} x \text{ implies that } S \Rightarrow_{G}^{h} x$$

where $x \in \Sigma^*$.

Basis. Suppose that $h = 0$. As obvious, $S \Rightarrow_{G'}^{0} S$ and $S \Rightarrow_{G}^{0} S$.

Induction Hypothesis. Assume that the claim holds for all derivations of length $0 \leq h \leq n$, for some $n \geq 0$.

Induction Step. Consider any derivation of the form

$$S \Rightarrow_{G'}^{n+1} x.$$

As $n + 1 \geq 1$, there exists a derivation

$$S \Rightarrow_{G'}^{n} y \Rightarrow_{G'} x\ [p'_1, \ldots, p'_q]$$

such that $y \in \Sigma^+$, $q = |y|$, each $p'_i \in Q'_r$ for some $r \in \{1, \ldots, m\}$, and by the induction hypothesis,

$$S \Rightarrow_{G}^{n} y.$$

Then, by the definition of Q'_r, there exists P_i and $O \subseteq P_i$ such that every $(a \to z, F) \in O$, $a \in \Sigma$, $z \in \Sigma^+$, $F \subseteq \Sigma$, satisfies $a \to z \in Q'_r$ and $F \cap \mathit{left}(O) = \emptyset$. Since symbols $(y) \subseteq$ left(O), $(a \to z, F) \in O$ implies that $F \cap$ symbols $(y) = \emptyset$. Hence,

$$S \Rightarrow_{G}^{n} y \Rightarrow_G x\ [p_1, \ldots, p_q]$$

where $p_j\colon (a \to z, F) \in O$ for all $j = 1, \ldots, q$. □

From the claim above,

$$S \Rightarrow_G^* x \quad \text{if and only if} \quad S \Rightarrow_{G'}^* x$$

for all $x \in \Delta^*$. Consequently, $L(G) = L(G')$, and the lemma holds. □

The following two lemmas can be proved by analogy with the proofs of Lemmas 13.6 and 13.7. The details are left to the reader.

Lemma 13.8. $\mathbf{ET0L} \subseteq \mathbf{FE0L}(1)$.

Lemma 13.9. $\mathbf{FET0L}(1) \subseteq \mathbf{ET0L}$.

Theorem 13.15.

$$\mathbf{FEP0L}(1) = \mathbf{FEPT0L}(1) = \mathbf{FE0L}(1) = \mathbf{FET0L}(1) = \mathbf{ET0L} = \mathbf{EPT0L}.$$

Proof. By Lemmas 13.6 and 13.7, $\mathbf{EPT0L} \subseteq \mathbf{FEP0L}(1)$ and $\mathbf{FEPT0L}(1) \subseteq \mathbf{EPT0L}$, respectively. Since $\mathbf{FEP0L}(1) \subseteq \mathbf{FEPT0L}(1)$, we get

$$\mathbf{FEP0L}(1) = \mathbf{FEPT0L}(1) = \mathbf{EPT0L}.$$

Analogously, from Lemmas 13.8 and 13.9, we have

$$\mathbf{FE0L}(1) = \mathbf{FET0L}(1) = \mathbf{ET0L}.$$

Theorem 4.4 implies that $\mathbf{EPT0L} = \mathbf{ET0L}$. Therefore,

$$\mathbf{FEP0L}(1) = \mathbf{FEPT0L}(1) = \mathbf{FE0L}(1) = \mathbf{FET0L}(1) = \mathbf{EPT0L} = \mathbf{ET0L}.$$

Thus, the theorem holds. □

Next, we investigate the generative power of F-EPT0L grammars of degree 2. The following lemma establishes a normal form for context-sensitive grammars so that the grammars satisfying this form generate only sentential forms containing no nonterminal from N_{CS} as the leftmost symbol of the string. We make use of this normal form in Lemma 13.11.

Lemma 13.10. *Every context-sensitive language $L \in \mathbf{CS}$ can be generated by a context-sensitive grammar, $G = (N_1 \cup N_{CF} \cup N_{CS} \cup \Delta, \Delta, R, S_1)$, where N_1, N_{CF}, N_{CS}, and Δ are pairwise disjoint alphabets, $S_1 \in N_1$, and in R, every rule has one of the following forms*

- *(i)* $AB \rightarrow AC$, *where* $A \in (N_1 \cup N_{CF})$, $B \in N_{CS}$, $C \in N_{CF}$;
- *(ii)* $A \rightarrow B$, *where* $A \in N_{CF}$, $B \in N_{CS}$;
- *(iii)* $A \rightarrow a$, *where* $A \in (N_1 \cup N_{CF})$, $a \in \Delta$;
- *(iv)* $A \rightarrow C$, *where* $A, C \in N_{CF}$;
- *(v)* $A_1 \rightarrow C_1$, *where* $A_1, C_1 \in N_1$;

(vi) $A \to DE$, where $A, D, E \in N_{CF}$; or
(vii) $A_1 \to D_1E$, where $A_1, D_1 \in N_1$, $E \in N_{CF}$.

Proof. Let

$$G' = (N_{CF} \cup N_{CS} \cup \Delta, \Delta, R', S)$$

be a context-sensitive grammar of the form defined in Theorem 11.4. From this grammar, we construct a grammar

$$G = (N_1 \cup N_{CF} \cup N_{CS} \cup \Delta, \Delta, R, S_1)$$

where

$$\begin{aligned} N_1 &= \{X_1 \mid X \in N_{CF}\}, \\ R &= R' \cup \{A_1B \to A_1C \mid AB \to AC \in R', A, C \in N_{CF}, B \in N_{CS}, A_1 \in N_1\} \\ &\quad \cup \{A_1 \to a \mid A \to a \in R', A \in N_{CF}, A_1 \in N_1, a \in \Delta\} \\ &\quad \cup \{A_1 \to C_1 \mid A \to C \in R', A, C \in N_{CF}, A_1, C_1 \in N_1\} \\ &\quad \cup \{A_1 \to D_1E \mid A \to DE \in R', A, D, E \in N_{CF}, A_1, D_1 \in N_1\}. \end{aligned}$$

G works by analogy with G' except that in G, every sentential form starts with a symbol from $N_1 \cup \Delta$ followed by symbols that are not in N_1. Notice, however, that by $AB \to AC$, G' can never rewrite the leftmost symbol of any sentential form. Based on these observations, it is rather easy to see that $L(G) = L(G')$; a formal proof of this identity is left to the reader. As G is of the required form, Lemma 13.10 holds. □

Lemma 13.11. CS $\subseteq$ FEP0L(2).

Proof. Let L be a context-sensitive language generated by a grammar

$$G = (N_1 \cup N_{CF} \cup N_{CS} \cup \Delta, \Delta, R, S_1)$$

of the form of Lemma 13.10. Set

$$\begin{aligned} \Sigma &= N_1 \cup N_{CF} \cup N_{CS} \cup \Delta, \\ P_{CS} &= \{AB \to AC \mid AB \to AC \in R, A \in (N_1 \cup N_{CF}), B \in N_{CS}, C \in N_{CF}\}, \\ P_{CF} &= R - P_{CS}. \end{aligned}$$

Informally, P_{CS} and P_{CF} are the sets of context-sensitive and context-free rules in R, respectively, and Σ denotes the total alphabet of G.

Let f be an arbitrary bijection from Σ to $\{1, \ldots, m\}$, where m is the cardinality of Σ, and let f^{-1} be the inverse of f.

Construct an F-EP0L grammar of degree 2

$$G' = (\Sigma', \Delta, R', S_1)$$

with Σ' defined as

$$\begin{aligned} W_0 &= \{\langle A, B, C\rangle \mid AB \to AC \in P_{CS}\}, \\ W_S &= \{\langle A, B, C, j\rangle \mid AB \to AC \in P_{CS}, 1 \leq j \leq m + 1\}, \\ W &= W_0 \cup W_S, \\ \Sigma' &= \Sigma \cup W, \end{aligned}$$

where Σ, W_0, and W_S are pairwise disjoint alphabets. The set of rules R' is constructed by performing (1)–(3), given next.

(1) For every $X \in \Sigma$, add $(X \to X, \emptyset)$ to R';
(2) For every $A \to u \in P_{CF}$, add $(A \to u, W)$ to R';
(3) For every $AB \to AC \in P_{CS}$, extend R' by adding
  (3.a) $(B \to \langle A, B, C \rangle, W)$;
  (3.b) $(\langle A, B, C \rangle \to \langle A, B, C, 1 \rangle, W - \{\langle A, B, C \rangle\})$;
  (3.c) $(\langle A, B, C, j \rangle \to \langle A, B, C, j+1 \rangle, \{f^{-1}(j)\langle A, B, C, j \rangle\})$ for all $1 \le j \le m$ such that $f(A) \ne j$;
  (3.d) $(\langle A, B, C, f(A) \rangle \to \langle A, B, C, f(A)+1 \rangle, \emptyset)$; and
  (3.e) $(\langle A, B, C, m+1 \rangle \to C, \{\langle A, B, C, m+1 \rangle^2\})$.

Let us informally explain how G' simulates the non-context-free rules of the form $AB \to AC$ (see rules of (3) in the construction of R'). First, chosen occurrences of B are rewritten to $\langle A, B, C \rangle$ by $(B \to \langle A, B, C \rangle, W)$. The forbidding condition of this rule guarantees that there is no simulation already in process. After that, left neighbors of all occurrences of $\langle A, B, C \rangle$ are checked not to be any symbols from $\Sigma - \{A\}$. In greater detail, G' rewrites $\langle A, B, C \rangle$ with $\langle A, B, C, i \rangle$ for $i = 1$. Then, in every $\langle A, B, C, i \rangle$, G' increments i by one as long as i is less or equal to the cardinality of Σ; simultaneously, it verifies that the left neighbor of every $\langle A, B, C, i \rangle$ differs from the symbol that f maps to i except for the case when $f(A) = i$. Finally, G' checks that there are no two adjoining symbols $\langle A, B, C, m+1 \rangle$. At this point, the left neighbors of $\langle A, B, C, m+1 \rangle$ are necessarily equal to A, so every occurrence of $\langle A, B, C, m+1 \rangle$ is rewritten to C.

Observe that the other symbols remain unchanged during the simulation. Indeed, by the forbidding conditions, the only rules that can rewrite symbols $X \notin W$ are of the form $(X \to X, \emptyset)$. Moreover, the forbidding condition of $(\langle A, B, C \rangle \to \langle A, B, C, 1 \rangle, W - \{\langle A, B, C \rangle\})$ implies that it is not possible to simulate two different non-context-free rules at the same time.

To establish that $L(G) = L(G')$, we first prove Claims 1–5.

Claim 1. $S_1 \Rightarrow_{G'}^{h} x'$ implies that $\text{lms}(x') \in (N_1 \cup \Delta)$ for every $h \ge 0, x' \in \Sigma'^*$.

Proof. The claim is proved by induction on $h \ge 0$.

Basis. Let $h = 0$. Then, $S_1 \Rightarrow_{G'}^{0} S_1$ and $S_1 \in N_1$.

Induction Hypothesis. Assume that the claim holds for all derivations of length $h \le n$, for some $n \ge 0$.

Induction Step. Consider any derivation of the form

$$S_1 \Rightarrow_{G'}^{n+1} x'$$

where $x' \in \Sigma'^*$. Since $n + 1 \ge 1$, there is a derivation

$$S_1 \Rightarrow_{G'}^{n} y' \Rightarrow_{G'} x' \; [p_1, \ldots, p_q]$$

where $y' \in \Sigma'^*, q = |y'|$, and by the induction hypothesis, $\mathrm{lms}(y') \in (N_1 \cup \Delta)$. Inspect R' to see that the rule p_1 that rewrites the leftmost symbol of y' is one of the following forms $(A_1 \to A_1, \emptyset)$, $(a \to a, \emptyset)$, $(A_1 \to a, W)$, $(A_1 \to C_1, W)$, or $(A_1 \to D_1E, W)$, where $A_1, C_1, D_1 \in N_1$, $a \in \Delta$, $E \in N_{CF}$ (see (1) and (2) in the definition of R' and Lemma 13.10). It is obvious that the leftmost symbols of the right-hand sides of these rules belong to $(N_1 \cup \Delta)$. Hence, $\mathrm{lms}(x') \in (N_1 \cup \Delta)$, so the claim holds. □

Claim 2. $S_1 \Rightarrow^n_{G'} y'_1Xy'_3$, where $X \in W_S$, implies that $y'_1 \in \Sigma'^+$ and $y'_3 \in \Sigma'^*$, for any $n \geq 0$.

Proof. Informally, the claim says that every occurrence of a symbol from W_S always has a left neighbor. Clearly, this claim follows from the statement of Claim 1. Since $W_S \cap (N_1 \cup \Delta) = \emptyset$, X cannot be the leftmost symbol in a sentential form and the claim holds. □

Claim 3. $S_1 \Rightarrow^h_{G'} x'$, $h \geq 0$, implies that x' has one of the following three forms:

(I) $x' \in \Sigma^*$;
(II) $x' \in (\Sigma \cup W_0)^*$ and $\mathrm{occur}(W_0, x') > 0$;
(III) $x' \in (\Sigma \cup \{\langle A, B, C, j\rangle\})^*$, $\mathrm{occur}(\{\langle A, B, C, j\rangle\} x') > 0$, and

$$\{f^{-1}(k)\langle A, B, C, j\rangle \mid 1 \leq k < j, k \neq f(A)\} \cap \mathrm{substrings}(x') = \emptyset,$$

where $\langle A, B, C, j\rangle \in W_S$, $A \in (N_1 \cup N_{CF})$, $B \in N_{CS}$, $C \in N_{CF}$, $1 \leq j \leq m+1$.

Proof. We prove the claim by induction on $h \geq 0$.

Basis. Let $h = 0$. Clearly, $S_1 \Rightarrow^0_{G'} S_1$ and S_1 is of type (I).

Induction Hypothesis. Suppose that the claim holds for all derivations of length $h \leq n$, for some $n \geq 0$.

Induction Step. Consider any derivation of the form

$$S_1 \Rightarrow^{n+1}_{G'} x'.$$

Since $n+1 \geq 1$, there exists $y' \in \Sigma'^*$ and a sequence of rules $p_1, \ldots, p_q$, where $p_i \in R'$, $1 \leq i \leq q$, $q = |y'|$, such that

$$S_1 \Rightarrow^n_{G'} y' \Rightarrow_{G'} x' \; [p_1, \ldots, p_q].$$

Let $y' = a_1a_2 \cdots a_q$, $a_i \in \Sigma'$.

By the induction hypothesis, y' can only be of forms (I)–(III). Thus, the following three cases cover all possible forms of y'.

(i) Let $y' \in \Sigma^*$ (form (I)). In this case, every rule p_i can be either of the form $(a_i \to a_i, \emptyset)$, $a_i \in \Sigma$, or $(a_i \to u, W)$ such that $a_i \to u \in P_{CF}$, or $(a_i \to \langle A, a_i, C\rangle, W)$, $a_i \in N_{CS}$, $\langle A, a_i, C\rangle \in W_0$ (see the definition of R').

Suppose that for every $i \in \{1,\ldots,q\}$, p_i has one of the first two listed forms. According to the right-hand sides of these rules, we obtain $x' \in \Sigma^*$, that is, x' is of form (I).

If there exists i such that p_i: $(a_i \rightarrow \langle A, a_i, C\rangle, W)$ for some $A \in (N_1 \cup N_{CF})$, $a_i \in N_{CS}$, $C \in N_{CF}$, $\langle A, a_i, C\rangle \in W_0$, we get $x' \in (\Sigma \cup W_0)^*$ with occur $(W_0, x') > 0$. Thus, x' belongs to (II);

(ii) Let $y' \in (\Sigma \cup W_0)^*$ and occur $(W_0, y') > 0$ (form (II)). At this point, p_i is either $(a_i \rightarrow a_i, \emptyset)$ (rewriting $a_i \in \Sigma$ to itself) or $(\langle A,B,C\rangle \rightarrow \langle A,B,C,1\rangle, W - \{\langle A,B,C\rangle\})$ rewriting $a_i = \langle A,B,C\rangle \in W_0$ to $\langle A,B,C,1\rangle \in W_S$, where $A \in (N_1 \cup N_{CF})$, $B \in N_{CS}$, $C \in N_{CF}$. Since occur $(W_0, y') > 0$, there exists at least one i such that $a_i = \langle A,B,C\rangle \in W_0$. The corresponding rule p_i can be used provided that occur $(W - \{\langle A,B,C\rangle\}y') = 0$. Therefore, $y' \in (\Sigma \cup \{\langle A,B,C\rangle\})^*$, so $x' \in (\Sigma \cup \{\langle A,B,C,1\rangle\})^*$, occur $(\{\langle A,B,C,1\rangle\}x') > 0$. That is, x' is of type (III);

(iii) Assume that $y' \in (\Sigma \cup \{\langle A,B,C,j\rangle\})^*$, occur $(\{\langle A,B,C,j\rangle\}y') > 0$, and

$$\text{substrings}\,(y') \cap \{f^{-1}(k)\langle A,B,C,j\rangle \mid 1 \le k < j,\ k \ne f(A)\} = \emptyset$$

where $\langle A,B,C,j\rangle \in W_S$, $A \in (N_1 \cup N_{CF})$, $B \in N_{CS}$, $C \in N_{CF}$, $1 \le j \le m+1$ (form (III)). By the inspection of R', we see that the following four forms of rules can be used to rewrite y' to x'

(iii.a) $(a_i \rightarrow a_i, \emptyset)$, $a_i \in \Sigma$;
(iii.b) $(\langle A,B,C,j\rangle \rightarrow \langle A,B,C,j+1\rangle, \{f^{-1}(j)\langle A,B,C,j\rangle\})$, $1 \le j \le m$, $j \ne f(A)$;
(iii.c) $(\langle A,B,C,f(A)\rangle \rightarrow \langle A,B,C,f(A)+1\rangle, \emptyset)$;
(iii.d) $(\langle A,B,C,m+1\rangle \rightarrow C, \{\langle A,B,C,m+1\rangle^2\})$.

Let $1 \le j \le m, j \ne f(A)$. Then, symbols from Σ are rewritten to themselves (case (iii.a)) and every occurrence of $\langle A,B,C,j\rangle$ is rewritten to $\langle A,B,C,j+1\rangle$ by (iii.b). Clearly, we obtain $x' \in (\Sigma \cup \{\langle A,B,C,j+1\rangle\})^*$ such that

$$\text{occur}\left(\{\langle A,B,C,j+1\rangle\}x'\right) > 0.$$

Furthermore, (iii.b) can be used only when $f^{-1}(j)\langle A,B,C,j\rangle \notin$ substrings (y'). As

$$\text{substrings}\,(y') \cap \{f^{-1}(k)\langle A,B,C,j\rangle \mid 1 \le k < j,\ \ k \ne f(A)\} = \emptyset,$$

it holds that

$$\text{substrings}\,(y') \cap \{f^{-1}(k)\langle A,B,C,j\rangle \mid 1 \le k \le j,\ \ k \ne f(A)\} = \emptyset.$$

Since every occurrence of $\langle A,B,C,j\rangle$ is rewritten to $\langle A,B,C,j+1\rangle$ and other symbols are unchanged,

$$\text{substrings}\,(x') \cap \{f^{-1}(k)\langle A,B,C,j+1\rangle \mid 1 \le k < j+1,\ k \ne f(A)\} = \emptyset.$$

Therefore, x' is of form (III).

Next, assume that $j = f(A)$. Then, all occurrences of $\langle A, B, C, j\rangle$ are rewritten to $\langle A, B, C, j+1\rangle$ by (iii.c), and symbols from Σ are rewritten to themselves. As before, we obtain $x' \in (\Sigma \cup \{\langle A, B, C, j+1\rangle\})^*$ and $\text{occur}(\{\langle A, B, C, j+1\rangle\} x') > 0$. Moreover, because

$$\text{substrings}(y') \cap \{f^{-1}(k)\langle A, B, C, j\rangle \mid 1 \leq k < j,\ k \neq f(A)\} = \emptyset$$

and j is $f(A)$,

$$\text{substrings}(x') \cap \{f^{-1}(k)\langle A, B, C, j+1\rangle \mid 1 \leq k < j+1,\ k \neq f(A)\} = \emptyset$$

and x' belongs to (III) as well.

Finally, let $j = m + 1$. Then, every occurrence of $\langle A, B, C, j\rangle$ is rewritten to C (case (iii.d)). Therefore, $x' \in \Sigma^*$, so x' has form (I).

In (i), (ii), and (iii), we have considered all derivations that rewrite y' to x', and in each of these cases, we have shown that x' has one of the requested forms. Therefore, Claim 3 holds. □

To prove the following claims, we need a finite symbol-to-symbol substitution γ from Σ^* into Σ'^* defined as

$$\begin{aligned}\gamma(X) = {} & \{X\} \cup \{\langle A, X, C\rangle \mid \langle A, X, C\rangle \in W_0\} \\ & \cup \{\langle A, X, C, j\rangle \mid \langle A, X, C, j\rangle \in W_S,\ 1 \leq j \leq m+1\}\end{aligned}$$

for all $X \in \Sigma$, $A \in (N_1 \cup N_{CF})$, $C \in N_{CF}$. Let γ^{-1} be the inverse of γ.

Claim 4. Let $y' = a_1 a_2 \cdots a_q$, $a_i \in \Sigma'$, $q = |y'|$, and $\gamma^{-1}(a_i) \Rightarrow_G^{h_i} \gamma^{-1}(u_i)$ for all $i \in \{1, \ldots, q\}$ and some $h_i \in \{0, 1\}$, $u_i \in \Sigma'^+$. Then, $\gamma^{-1}(y') \Rightarrow_G^{r} \gamma^{-1}(x')$ such that $x' = u_1 u_2 \cdots u_q$, $r = \sum_{i=1}^{q} h_i$, $r \leq q$.

Proof. First, consider any derivation of the form

$$\gamma^{-1}(X) \Rightarrow_G^{h} \gamma^{-1}(u)$$

where $X \in \Sigma'$, $u \in \Sigma'^+$, $h \in \{0, 1\}$. If $h = 0$, $\gamma^{-1}(X) = \gamma^{-1}(u)$. Let $h = 1$. Then, there surely exists a rule $p\colon \gamma^{-1}(X) \rightarrow \gamma^{-1}(u) \in R$ such that

$$\gamma^{-1}(X) \Rightarrow_G \gamma^{-1}(u)\ [p].$$

Return to the statement of this claim. We can construct

$$\begin{aligned}\gamma^{-1}(a_1)\gamma^{-1}(a_2)\cdots\gamma^{-1}(a_q) & \Rightarrow_G^{h_1} \gamma^{-1}(u_1)\gamma^{-1}(a_2)\cdots\gamma^{-1}(a_q) \\ & \Rightarrow_G^{h_2} \gamma^{-1}(u_1)\gamma^{-1}(u_2)\cdots\gamma^{-1}(a_q) \\ & \ \ \vdots \\ & \Rightarrow_G^{h_q} \gamma^{-1}(u_1)\gamma^{-1}(u_2)\cdots\gamma^{-1}(u_q)\end{aligned}$$

where

$$\gamma^{-1}(y') = \gamma^{-1}(a_1)\cdots\gamma^{-1}(a_q)$$

and

$$\gamma^{-1}(u_1)\cdots\gamma^{-1}(u_q) = \gamma^{-1}(u_1\cdots u_q) = \gamma^{-1}(x').$$

In such a derivation, each $\gamma^{-1}(a_i)$ is either left unchanged (if $h_i = 0$) or rewritten to $\gamma^{-1}(u_i)$ by the corresponding rule $\gamma^{-1}(a_i) \rightarrow \gamma^{-1}(u_i)$. Obviously, the length of this derivation is $\sum_{i=1}^{q} h_i$. □

Claim 5. $S_1 \Rightarrow_G^* x$ if and only if $S_1 \Rightarrow_{G'}^* x'$, where $x \in \Sigma^*$, $x' \in \Sigma'^*$, $x' \in \gamma(x)$.

Proof. The proof is divided into the only-if part and the if part.

Only If. The only-if part is established by induction on $h \geq 0$. That is, we show that

$$S_1 \Rightarrow_G^h x \quad \text{implies} \quad S_1 \Rightarrow_{G'}^* x$$

where $x \in \Sigma^*$, for $h \geq 0$.

Basis. Let $h = 0$. Then, $S_1 \Rightarrow_G^0 S_1$ and $S_1 \Rightarrow_{G'}^0 S_1$ as well.

Induction Hypothesis. Assume that the claim holds for all derivations of length $0 \leq h \leq n$, for some $n \geq 0$.

Induction Step. Consider any derivation of the form

$$S_1 \Rightarrow_G^{n+1} x.$$

Since $n + 1 > 0$, there exists $y \in \Sigma^*$ and $p \in R$ such that

$$S_1 \Rightarrow_G^n y \Rightarrow_G x\ [p]$$

and by the induction hypothesis, there is also a derivation

$$S_1 \Rightarrow_{G'}^* y.$$

Let $y = a_1a_2\cdots a_q$, $a_i \in \Sigma$, $1 \leq i \leq q$, $q = |y|$. The following cases (i) and (ii) cover all possible forms of p.

(i) Let $p\colon A \rightarrow u \in P_{CF}$, $A \in (N_1 \cup N_{CF})$, $u \in \Sigma^*$. Then, $y = y_1Ay_3$ and $x = y_1uy_3$, $y_1, y_3 \in \Sigma^*$. Let $s = |y_1| + 1$. Since we have $(A \rightarrow u, W) \in R'$, we can construct a derivation

$$S_1 \Rightarrow_{G'}^* y \Rightarrow_{G'} x\ [p_1, \ldots, p_q]$$

such that $p_s\colon (A \rightarrow u, W)$ and $p_i\colon (a_i \rightarrow a_i, \emptyset)$ for all $i \in \{1, \ldots, q\}$, $i \neq s$;

(ii) Let $p\colon AB \to AC \in P_{CS}, A \in (N_1 \cup N_{CF}), B \in N_{CS}, C \in N_{CF}$. Then, $y = y_1ABy_3$ and $x = y_1ACy_3, y_1, y_3 \in \Sigma^*$. Let $s = |y_1| + 2$. In this case, there is the derivation

$$
\begin{aligned}
S_1 &\Rightarrow^*_{G'} y_1ABy_3 \\
&\Rightarrow_{G'} y_1A\langle A,B,C\rangle y_3 && [p_s\colon (B \to \langle A,B,C\rangle, W)] \\
&\Rightarrow_{G'} y_1A\langle A,B,C,1\rangle y_3 && [p_s\colon (\langle A,B,C\rangle \to \langle A,B,C,1\rangle, \\
&&& \quad W - \{\langle A,B,C\rangle\})] \\
&\Rightarrow_{G'} y_1A\langle A,B,C,2\rangle y_3 && [p_s\colon (\langle A,B,C,1\rangle \to \langle A,B,C,2\rangle, \\
&&& \quad \{f^{-1}(1)\langle A,B,C,j\rangle\})] \\
&\vdots \\
&\Rightarrow_{G'} y_1A\langle A,B,C,f(A)\rangle y_3 && [p_s\colon (\langle A,B,C,f(A)-1\rangle \to \\
&&& \quad \langle A,B,C,f(A)\rangle, \{f^{-1}(f(A)-1) \\
&&& \quad \langle A,B,C,f(A)-1\rangle\})] \\
&\Rightarrow_{G'} y_1A\langle A,B,C,f(A)+1\rangle y_3 && [p_s\colon (\langle A,B,C,f(A)\rangle \to \\
&&& \quad \langle A,B,C,f(A)+1\rangle, \emptyset)] \\
&\Rightarrow_{G'} y_1A\langle A,B,C,f(A)+2\rangle y_3 && [p_s\colon (\langle A,B,C,f(A)+1\rangle \to \\
&&& \quad \langle A,B,C,f(A)+2\rangle, \{f^{-1}(f(A)+1) \\
&&& \quad \langle A,B,C,f(A)+1\rangle\})] \\
&\vdots \\
&\Rightarrow_{G'} y_1A\langle A,B,C,m+1\rangle y_3 && [p_s\colon (\langle A,B,C,m\rangle \to \langle A,B,C,m+1\rangle, \\
&&& \quad \{f^{-1}(m)\langle A,B,C,m\rangle\})] \\
&\Rightarrow_{G'} y_1ACy_3 && [p_s\colon (\langle A,B,C,m+1\rangle \to C, \\
&&& \quad \{\langle A,B,C,m+1\rangle^2\})]
\end{aligned}
$$

such that $p_i\colon (a_i \to a_i, \emptyset)$ for all $i \in \{1, \ldots, q\}, i \neq s$.

If. By induction on $h \geq 0$, we prove that

$$S_1 \Rightarrow^h_{G'} x' \quad \text{implies} \quad S_1 \Rightarrow^*_G x$$

where $x' \in \Sigma'^*, x \in \Sigma^*$ and $x' \in \gamma(x)$.

Basis. Let $h = 0$. The only x' is S_1 because $S_1 \Rightarrow^0_{G'} S_1$. Obviously, $S_1 \Rightarrow^0_G S_1$ and $S_1 \in \gamma(S_1)$.

Induction Hypothesis. Suppose that the claim holds for any derivation of length $0 \leq h \leq n$, for some $n \geq 0$.

Induction Hypothesis. Consider any derivation of the form

$$S_1 \Rightarrow^{n+1}_{G'} x'.$$

Since $n + 1 \geq 1$, there exists $y' \in \Sigma'^*$ and a sequence of rules $p_1, \ldots, p_q$ from R', $q = |x'|$, such that

$$S_1 \Rightarrow^n_{G'} y' \Rightarrow_{G'} x' \; [p_1, \ldots, p_q].$$

Let $y' = a_1 a_2 \cdots a_q$, $a_i \in \Sigma'$, $1 \le i \le q$. By the induction hypothesis, we have

$$S_1 \Rightarrow_G^* y$$

where $y \in \Sigma^*$ such that $y' \in \gamma(y)$.

From Claim 3, y' has one of the following forms (i), (ii), or (iii), described next.

(i) Let $y' \in \Sigma'^*$ (see (I) in Claim 3). Inspect R' to see that there are three forms of rules rewriting symbols a_i in y':

(i.a) $p_i\colon (a_i \to a_i, \emptyset) \in R'$, $a_i \in \Sigma$. In this case,
$\gamma^{-1}(a_i) \Rightarrow_G^0 \gamma^{-1}(a_i)$,

(i.b) $p_i\colon (a_i \to u_i, W) \in R'$ such that $a_i \to u_i \in P_{CF}$. Since $a_i = \gamma^{-1}(a_i)$, $u_i = \gamma^{-1}(u_i)$ and $a_i \to u_i \in R$,
$\gamma^{-1}(a_i) \Rightarrow_G \gamma^{-1}(u_i)\ [a_i \to u_i]$,

(i.c) $p_i\colon (a_i \to \langle A, a_i, C\rangle, W) \in R'$, $a_i \in N_{CS}$, $A \in (N_1 \cup N_{CF})$, $C \in N_{CF}$. Since $\gamma^{-1}(a_i) = \gamma^{-1}(\langle A, a_i, C\rangle)$, we have
$\gamma^{-1}(a_i) \Rightarrow_G^0 \gamma^{-1}(\langle A, a_i, C\rangle)$.

We see that for all a_i, there exists a derivation

$$\gamma^{-1}(a_i) \Rightarrow_G^{h_i} \gamma^{-1}(z_i)$$

for some $h_i \in \{0, 1\}$, where $z_i \in \Sigma'^+$, $x' = z_1 z_2 \cdots z_q$. Therefore, by Claim 4, we can construct

$$S_1 \Rightarrow_G^* y \Rightarrow_G^r x$$

where $0 \le r \le q$, $x = \gamma^{-1}(x')$;

(ii) Let $y' \in (\Sigma \cup W_0)^*$ and occur $(W_0, y') > 0$ (see (II)). At this point, the following two forms of rules can be used to rewrite a_i in y'—(ii.a) or (ii.b).

(ii.a) $p_i\colon (a_i \to a_i, \emptyset) \in R'$, $a_i \in \Sigma$. As in case (i.a);
$\gamma^{-1}(a_i) \Rightarrow_G^0 \gamma^{-1}(a_i)$;

(ii.b) $p_i\colon (\langle A, B, C\rangle \to \langle A, B, C, 1\rangle, W - \{\langle A, B, C\rangle\})$, $a_i = \langle A, B, C\rangle \in W_0$, $A \in (N_1 \cup N_{CF})$, $B \in N_{CS}$, $C \in N_{CF}$. Since $\gamma^{-1}(\langle A, B, C\rangle) = \gamma^{-1}(\langle A, B, C, 1\rangle)$,
$\gamma^{-1}(\langle A, B, C\rangle) \Rightarrow_G^0 \gamma^{-1}(\langle A, B, C, 1\rangle)$.

Thus, there exists a derivation

$$S_1 \Rightarrow_G^* y \Rightarrow_G^0 x$$

where $x = \gamma^{-1}(x')$;

(iii) Let $y' \in (\Sigma \cup \{\langle A, B, C, j\rangle\})^*$, occur $(\{\langle A, B, C, j\rangle\} y') > 0$, and

$$\text{substrings}(y') \cap \{f^{-1}(k)\langle A, B, C, j\rangle \mid 1 \le k < j,\ k \ne f(A)\} = \emptyset$$

where $\langle A, B, C, j\rangle \in W_S$, $A \in (N_1 \cup N_{CF})$, $B \in N_{CS}$, $C \in N_{CF}$, $1 \le j \le m + 1$ (see (III)). By the inspection of R', the following four forms of rules can be used to rewrite y' to x':

(iii.a) $p_i\colon (a_i \to a_i, \emptyset)$, $a_i \in \Sigma$;

(iii.b) $p_i\colon (\langle A, B, C, j\rangle \to \langle A, B, C, j+1\rangle, \{f^{-1}(j)\langle A, B, C, j\rangle\})$, $1 \le j \le m$, $j \ne f(A)$;

(iii.c) p_i: $(\langle A, B, C, f(A)\rangle \to \langle A, B, C, f(A)+1\rangle, \emptyset)$;
(iii.d) p_i: $(\langle A, B, C, m+1\rangle \to C, \{\langle A, B, C, m+1\rangle^2\})$.

Let $1 \leq j \leq m$. G' can rewrite such y' using only rules (iii.a)–(iii.c). Since $\gamma^{-1}(\langle A, B, C, j\rangle) = \gamma^{-1}(\langle A, B, C, j+1\rangle)$ and $\gamma^{-1}(a_i) = \gamma^{-1}(a_i)$, by analogy with (ii), we obtain

$$S_1 \Rightarrow_G^* y \Rightarrow_G^0 x$$

such that $x = \gamma^{-1}(x')$.

Let $j = m+1$. In this case, only rules (iii.a) and (iii.d) can be used. Since occur $(\{\langle A, B, C, j\rangle\}y') > 0$, there is at least one occurrence of $\langle A, B, C, m+1\rangle$ in y', and by the forbidding condition of rule (iii.d), $\langle A, B, C, m+1\rangle^2 \notin$ substrings (y'). Observe that for $j = m+1$,

$$\begin{aligned}&\{f^{-1}(k)\langle A, B, C, m+1\rangle \mid 1 \leq k < j,\ k \neq f(A)\}\\ &\quad = \{X\langle A, B, C, m+1\rangle \mid X \in \Sigma,\ X \neq A\}\end{aligned}$$

and thus

$$\text{substrings}\,(y') \cap \{X\langle A, B, C, m+1\rangle \mid X \in \Sigma,\ X \neq A\} = \emptyset.$$

According to Claim 2, $\langle A, B, C, m+1\rangle$ always has a left neighbor in y'. As a result, the left neighbor of every occurrence of $\langle A, B, C, m+1\rangle$ is A. Therefore, we can express y', y, and x' as follows:

$$\begin{aligned}y' &= y_1A\langle A, B, C, m+1\rangle y_2A\langle A, B, C, m+1\rangle y_3 \cdots y_rA\langle A, B, C, m+1\rangle y_{r+1},\\ y &= \gamma^{-1}(y_1)AB\gamma^{-1}(y_2)AB\gamma^{-1}(y_3)\cdots\gamma^{-1}(y_r)AB\gamma^{-1}(y_{r+1}),\\ x' &= y_1ACy_2ACy_3\cdots y_rACy_{r+1},\end{aligned}$$

where $r \geq 1$, $y_s \in \Sigma^*$, $1 \leq s \leq r+1$. Since we have $p\colon AB \to AC \in R$, there is a derivation

$$\begin{aligned}S_1 &\Rightarrow_G^* \gamma^{-1}(y_1)AB\gamma^{-1}(y_2)AB\gamma^{-1}(y_3)\cdots\gamma^{-1}(y_r)AB\gamma^{-1}(y_{r+1})\\ &\Rightarrow_G \gamma^{-1}(y_1)AC\gamma^{-1}(y_2)AB\gamma^{-1}(y_3)\cdots\gamma^{-1}(y_r)AB\gamma^{-1}(y_{r+1})\ [p]\\ &\Rightarrow_G \gamma^{-1}(y_1)AC\gamma^{-1}(y_2)AC\gamma^{-1}(y_3)\cdots\gamma^{-1}(y_r)AB\gamma^{-1}(y_{r+1})\ [p]\\ &\ \ \vdots\\ &\Rightarrow_G \gamma^{-1}(y_1)AC\gamma^{-1}(y_2)AC\gamma^{-1}(y_3)\cdots\gamma^{-1}(y_r)AC\gamma^{-1}(y_{r+1})\ [p]\end{aligned}$$

where

$$\gamma^{-1}(y_1)AC\gamma^{-1}(y_2)AC\gamma^{-1}(y_3)\cdots\gamma^{-1}(y_r)AC\gamma^{-1}(y_{r+1}) = \gamma^{-1}(x') = x.$$

Since cases (i), (ii), and (iii) cover all possible forms of y', we have completed the induction and established Claim 5. □

The equivalence of G and G' follows from Claim 5. Indeed, observe that by the definition of γ, we have $\gamma(a) = \{a\}$ for all $a \in \Delta$. Therefore, by Claim 5, we have for any $x \in \Delta^*$,

$$S_1 \Rightarrow_G^* x \quad \text{if and only if} \quad S_1 \Rightarrow_{G'}^* x.$$

Thus, $L(G) = L(G')$, and the lemma holds. □

Theorem 13.16. CS = FEP0L(2) = FEPT0L(2) = FEP0L = FEPT0L.

Proof. By Lemma 13.11, **CS** $\subseteq$ **FEP0L**(2) $\subseteq$ **FEPT0L**(2) $\subseteq$ **FEPT0L**. From Lemma 13.4 and the definition of F-ET0L grammars, **FEPT0L**(s) $\subseteq$ **FEPT0L** $\subseteq$ **CEPT0L** $\subseteq$ **CS** for any $s \geq 0$. Moreover, **FEP0L**(s) $\subseteq$ **FEP0L** $\subseteq$ **FEPT0L**. Thus, **CS** = **FEP0L**(2) = **FEPT0L**(2) = **FEP0L** = **FEPT0L**, and the theorem holds. □

Return to the proof of Lemma 13.11. Observe the form of the rules in the F-EP0L grammar G'. This observation gives rise to the next corollary.

Corollary 1. *Every context-sensitive language can be generated by an F-EP0L grammar* $G = (\Sigma, \Delta, R, S)$ *of degree 2 such that every rule from R has one of the following forms:*

(i) $(a \rightarrow a, \emptyset)$, $a \in \Sigma$;
(ii) $(X \rightarrow x, F)$, $X \in \Sigma - \Delta$, $|x| \in \{1, 2\}$, max-len$(F) = 1$;
(iii) $(X \rightarrow Y, \{z\})$, $X, Y \in \Sigma - \Delta$, $z \in \Sigma^2$.

Next, we demonstrate that the family of recursively enumerable languages is generated by the forbidding E0L grammars of degree 2.

Lemma 13.12. RE $\subseteq$ **FE0L**(2).

Proof. Let L be a recursively enumerable language generated by a phrase-structure grammar

$$G = (\Sigma, \Delta, R, S)$$

having the form defined in Theorem 11.5, where

$$\begin{aligned} \Sigma &= N_{CF} \cup N_{CS} \cup \Delta, \\ P_{CS} &= \{AB \rightarrow AC \in R \mid A, C \in N_{CF}, B \in N_{CS}\}, \\ P_{CF} &= R - P_{CS}. \end{aligned}$$

Let \$ be a new symbol and m be the cardinality of $\Sigma \cup \{\$\}$. Furthermore, let f be an arbitrary bijection from $\Sigma \cup \{\$\}$ onto $\{1, \dots, m\}$, and let f^{-1} be the inverse of f.

Define the F-E0L grammar

$$G' = (\Sigma', \Delta, R', S')$$

of degree 2 as follows:

$$\begin{aligned} W_0 &= \{\langle A, B, C\rangle \mid AB \rightarrow AC \in R\}, \\ W_S &= \{\langle A, B, C, j\rangle \mid AB \rightarrow AC \in R, 1 \leq j \leq m\}, \\ W &= W_0 \cup W_S, \\ \Sigma' &= \Sigma \cup W \cup \{S', \$\}, \end{aligned}$$

where $A, C \in N_{CF}, B \in N_{CS}$, and Σ, W_0, W_S, and $\{S', \$\}$ are pairwise disjoint alphabets. The set of rules R' is constructed by performing (1)–(4), given as follows:

(1) Add $(S' \to \$S, \emptyset)$, $(\$ \to \$, \emptyset)$ and $(\$ \to \varepsilon, \Sigma' - \Delta - \{\$\})$ to R';
(2) For all $X \in \Sigma$, add $(X \to X, \emptyset)$ to R';
(3) For all $A \to u \in P_{CF}$, $A \in N_{CF}$, $u \in \{\varepsilon\} \cup N_{CS} \cup \Delta \cup (\bigcup_{i=1}^{2} N_{CF}^i)$, add $(A \to u, W)$ to R';
(4) If $AB \to AC \in P_{CS}, A, C \in N_{CF}, B \in N_{CS}$, then add the following rules into R'.
   (4.a) $(B \to \langle A, B, C\rangle, W)$;
   (4.b) $(\langle A, B, C\rangle \to \langle A, B, C, 1\rangle, W - \{\langle A, B, C\rangle\})$;
   (4.c) $(\langle A, B, C, j\rangle \to \langle A, B, C, j+1\rangle, \{f^{-1}(j)\langle A, B, C, j\rangle\})$ for all $1 \le j \le m$ such that $f(A) \ne j$;
   (4.d) $(\langle A, B, C, f(A)\rangle \to \langle A, B, C, f(A)+1\rangle, \emptyset)$;
   (4.e) $(\langle A, B, C, m+1\rangle \to C, \{\langle A, B, C, m+1\rangle^2\})$.

Let us only give a gist of the reason why $L(G) = L(G')$. The construction above resembles the construction in Lemma 13.11 very much. Indeed, to simulate the non-context-free rules $AB \to AC$ in F-E0L grammars, we use the same technique as in F-EP0L grammars from Lemma 13.11. We only need to guarantee that no sentential form begins with a symbol from N_{CS}. This is solved by an auxiliary nonterminal \$ in the definition of G'. The symbol is always generated in the first derivation step by $(S' \to \$S, \emptyset)$ (see (1) in the definition of R'). After that, it appears as the leftmost symbol of all sentential forms containing some nonterminals. The only rule that can erase it is $(\$ \to \varepsilon, \Sigma' - \Delta - \{\$\})$.

Therefore, by analogy with the technique used in Lemma 13.11, we can establish

$$S \Rightarrow_G^* x \quad \text{if and only if} \quad S' \Rightarrow_{G'}^+ \$x'$$

such that $x \in \Sigma^*$, $x' \in (\Sigma' - \{S', \$\})^*$, $x' \in \gamma(x)$, where γ is a finite substitution from Σ^* into $(\Sigma' - \{S', \$\})^*$ defined as

$$\begin{aligned}\gamma(X) = \{X\} &\cup \{\langle A, X, C\rangle \mid \langle A, X, C\rangle \in W_0\}\\ &\cup \{\langle A, X, C, j\rangle \mid \langle A, X, C, j\rangle \in W_S, 1 \le j \le m+1\}\end{aligned}$$

for all $X \in \Sigma, A, C \in N_{CF}$. The details are left to the reader.

As in Lemma 13.11, we have $\gamma(a) = \{a\}$ for all $a \in \Delta$; hence, for all $x \in \Delta^*$,

$$S \Rightarrow_G^* x \quad \text{if and only if} \quad S' \Rightarrow_{G'}^+ \$x.$$

Since

$$\$x \Rightarrow_{G'} x \; [(\$ \to \varepsilon, \Sigma' - \Delta - \{\$\})],$$

we obtain

$$S \Rightarrow_G^* x \quad \text{if and only if} \quad S' \Rightarrow_{G'}^+ x.$$

Consequently, $L(G) = L(G')$; thus, $\mathbf{RE} \subseteq \mathbf{FE0L}(2)$. ☐

Theorem 13.17. $\mathbf{RE} = \mathbf{FE0L}(2) = \mathbf{FET0L}(2) = \mathbf{FE0L} = \mathbf{FET0L}$.

Proof. By Lemma 13.12, we have **RE** $\subseteq$ **FE0L**(2) $\subseteq$ **FET0L**(2) $\subseteq$ **FET0L**. From Lemma 13.5, it follows that **FET0L**(s) $\subseteq$ **FET0L** $\subseteq$ **CET0L** $\subseteq$ **RE**, for any $s \geq 0$. Thus, **RE** = **FE0L**(2) = **FET0L**(2) = **FE0L** = **FET0L**, so the theorem holds. □

By analogy with Corollary 1, we obtain the following normal form.

Corollary 2. *Every recursively enumerable language can be generated by an F-E0L grammar* $G = (\Sigma, \Delta, R, S)$ *of degree 2 such that every rule from R has one of the following forms*

(i) $(a \rightarrow a, \emptyset)$, $a \in \Sigma$;
(ii) $(X \rightarrow x, F)$, $X \in \Sigma - \Delta$, $|x| \leq 2$, $F \neq \emptyset$, *and* max-len $(F) = 1$;
(iii) $(X \rightarrow Y, \{z\})$, $X, Y \in \Sigma - \Delta$, $z \in \Sigma^2$.

Moreover, we obtain the following relations between F-ET0L language families.

Corollary 3.

$$
\begin{gathered}
\mathbf{CF} \\
\subset \\
\mathbf{FEP0L}(0) = \mathbf{FE0L}(0) = \mathbf{EP0L} = \mathbf{E0L} \\
\subset \\
\mathbf{FEP0L}(1) = \mathbf{FEPT0L}(1) = \mathbf{FE0L}(1) = \mathbf{FET0L}(1) \\
= \mathbf{FEPT0L}(0) = \mathbf{FET0L}(0) = \mathbf{EPT0L} = \mathbf{ET0L} \\
\subset \\
\mathbf{FEP0L}(2) = \mathbf{FEPT0L}(2) = \mathbf{FEP0L} = \mathbf{FEPT0L} = \mathbf{CS} \\
\subset \\
\mathbf{FE0L}(2) = \mathbf{FET0L}(2) = \mathbf{FE0L} = \mathbf{FET0L} = \mathbf{RE}.
\end{gathered}
$$

Proof. This corollary follows from Theorems 13.14, 13.15, 13.16, and 13.17. □

13.2.3 Simple semi-conditional ET0L grammars

SSC-ET0L grammars represent another variant of context-conditional ET0L grammars with restricted sets of context conditions. By analogy with sequential simple semi-conditional grammars (see Section 11.2), these grammars are context-conditional ET0L grammars in which every rule contains no more than one context condition. This section defines them, establishes their power, and reduces their degree.

13.2.3.1 Definitions

In this section, we define SSC-ET0L grammars.

Definition 13.9. *Let* $G = (\Sigma, \Delta, P_1, \ldots, P_t, S)$ *be a context-conditional ET0L grammar, for some* $t \geq 1$. *If for all* p: $(a \rightarrow x, Per, For) \in P_i$ *for every* $i = 1, \ldots, t$ *holds that* card (Per) + card $(For) \leq 1$, *G is said to be an SSC-ET0L. If G is a propagating SSC-ET0L grammar, G is called an* SSC-EPT0L grammar. *If* $t = 1$, *then G is called an* SSC-E0L grammar; *if, in addition, G is a propagating SSC-E0L grammar, G is said to be an* SSC-EP0L grammar.

Let $G = (\Sigma, \Delta, P_1, \ldots, P_t, S)$ be an SSC-ET0L grammar of degree (r, s). By analogy with ssc-grammars (see Section 11.2), in each rule $(a \to x, Per, For) \in P_i$, $i = 1, \ldots, t$, we omit braces and instead of $\emptyset$, we write 0. For example, we write $(a \to x, EF, 0)$ instead of $(a \to x, \{EF\}, \emptyset)$.

Let **SSCEPT0L**(r, s), **SSCET0L**(r, s), **SSCEP0L**(r, s), and **SSCE0L**(r, s) denote the families of languages generated by SSC-EPT0L, SSC-ET0L, SSC-EP0L, and SSC-E0L grammars of degree (r, s), respectively. Furthermore, the families of languages generated by SSC-EPT0L, SSC-ET0L, SSC-EP0L, and SSC-E0L grammars of any degree are denoted by **SSCEPT0L**, **SSCET0L**, **SSCEP0L**, and **SSCE0L**, respectively. Moreover, set

$$\mathbf{SSCEPT0L} = \bigcup_{r=0}^{\infty} \bigcup_{s=0}^{\infty} \mathbf{SSCEPT0L}(r, s),$$

$$\mathbf{SSCET0L} = \bigcup_{r=0}^{\infty} \bigcup_{s=0}^{\infty} \mathbf{SSCET0L}(r, s),$$

$$\mathbf{SSCEP0L} = \bigcup_{r=0}^{\infty} \bigcup_{s=0}^{\infty} \mathbf{SSCEP0L}(r, s),$$

$$\mathbf{SSCE0L} = \bigcup_{r=0}^{\infty} \bigcup_{s=0}^{\infty} \mathbf{SSCE0L}(r, s).$$

13.2.3.2 Generative power and reduction

Next, let us investigate the generative power of SSC-ET0L grammars. The following lemma proves that every recursively enumerable language can be defined by an SSC-E0L grammar of degree $(1, 2)$.

Lemma 13.13. RE $\subseteq$ SSCE0L$(1, 2)$.

Proof. Let

$$G = (N_{CF} \cup N_{CS} \cup \Delta, \Delta, R, S)$$

be a phrase-structure grammar of the form of Theorem 11.5. Then, let $\Sigma = N_{CF} \cup N_{CS} \cup \Delta$ and m be the cardinality of Σ. Let f be an arbitrary bijection from Σ to $\{1, \ldots, m\}$, and inverse$f$ be the inverse of f. Set

$$\begin{aligned} M = \; & \{\#\} \\ & \cup \{\langle A, B, C \rangle \mid AB \to AC \in R, A, C \in N_{CF}, B \in N_{CS}\} \\ & \cup \{\langle A, B, C, i \rangle \mid AB \to AC \in R, A, C \in N_{CF}, B \in N_{CS}, 1 \leq i \leq m + 2\} \end{aligned}$$

and

$$W = \{[A, B, C] \mid AB \to AC \in R, A, C \in N_{CF}, B \in N_{CS}\}.$$

Next, construct an SSC-E0L grammar of degree $(1, 2)$

$$G' = (\Sigma', \Delta, R', S')$$

where

$$\Sigma' = \Sigma \cup M \cup W \cup \{S'\}.$$

Without any loss of generality, we assume that Σ, M, W, and $\{S'\}$ are pairwise disjoint. The set of rules R' is constructed by performing (1)–(5), given as follows:

(1) Add $(S' \rightarrow \#S, 0, 0)$ to R';
(2) For all $A \rightarrow x \in R, A \in N_{CF}, x \in \{\varepsilon\} \cup N_{CS} \cup \Delta \cup N_{CF}^2$, add $(A \rightarrow x, \#, 0)$ to R';
(3) For every $AB \rightarrow AC \in R,\ \ A, C \in N_{CF},\ B \in N_{CS}$, add the following rules to R':
  (3.a) $(\# \rightarrow \langle A, B, C \rangle, 0, 0)$;
  (3.b) $(B \rightarrow [A, B, C], \langle A, B, C \rangle, 0)$;
  (3.c) $(\langle A, B, C \rangle \rightarrow \langle A, B, C, 1 \rangle, 0, 0)$;
  (3.d) $([A, B, C] \rightarrow [A, B, C], 0, \langle A, B, C, m+2 \rangle)$;
  (3.e) $(\langle A, B, C, i \rangle \rightarrow \langle A, B, C, i+1 \rangle, 0, f^{-1}(i)[A, B, C])$ for all $1 \leq i \leq m, i \neq f(A)$;
  (3.f) $(\langle A, B, C, f(A) \rangle \rightarrow \langle A, B, C, f(A)+1 \rangle, 0, 0)$;
  (3.g) $(\langle A, B, C, m+1 \rangle \rightarrow \langle A, B, C, m+2 \rangle, 0, [A, B, C]^2)$;
  (3.h) $(\langle A, B, C, m+2 \rangle \rightarrow \#, 0, \langle A, B, C, m+2 \rangle [A, B, C])$;
  (3.i) $([A, B, C] \rightarrow C, \langle A, B, C, m+2 \rangle, 0)$;
(4) For all $X \in \Sigma$, add $(X \rightarrow X, 0, 0)$ to R';
(5) Add $(\# \rightarrow \#, 0, 0)$ and $(\# \rightarrow \varepsilon, 0, 0)$ to R'.

Let us explain how G' works. During the simulation of a derivation in G, every sentential form starts with an auxiliary symbol from M, called the master. This symbol determines the current simulation mode and controls the next derivation step. Initially, the master is set to # (see (1) in the definition of R'). In this mode, G' simulates context-free rules (see (2)); notice that symbols from Σ can always be rewritten to themselves by (4). To start the simulation of a non-context-free rule of the form $AB \rightarrow AC$, G' rewrites the master to $\langle A, B, C \rangle$. In the following step, chosen occurrences of B are rewritten to $[A, B, C]$; no other rules can be used except rules introduced in (4). At the same time, the master is rewritten to $\langle A, B, C, i \rangle$ with $i = 1$ (see (3.c)). Then, i is repeatedly incremented by one until i is greater than the cardinality of Σ (see rules (3.e) and (3.f)). Simultaneously, the master's conditions make sure that for every i such that inverse $f(i) \neq A$, no inverse $f(i)$ appears as the left neighbor of any occurrence of $[A, B, C]$. Finally, G' checks that there are no two adjoining $[A, B, C]$ (see (3.g)) and that $[A, B, C]$ does not appear as the right neighbor of the master (see (3.h)). At this point, the left neighbors of $[A, B, C]$ are necessarily equal to A and every occurrence of $[A, B, C]$ is rewritten to C. In the same derivation step, the master is rewritten to #.

Observe that in every derivation step, the master allows G' to use only a subset of rules according to the current mode. Indeed, it is not possible to combine context-free and non-context-free simulation modes. Furthermore, no two different non-context-free rules can be simulated at the same time. The simulation ends when # is erased by $(\# \rightarrow \varepsilon, 0, 0)$. After this erasure, no other rule can be used.

The following three claims demonstrate some important properties of derivations in G' to establish $L(G) = L(G')$.

Claim 1. $S' \Rightarrow_{G'}^{+} w'$ implies that $w' \in M(\Sigma \cup W)^*$ or $w' \in (\Sigma \cup W)^*$. Furthermore, if $w' \in M(\Sigma \cup W)^*$, every v' such that $S' \Rightarrow_{G'}^{+} v' \Rightarrow_{G'}^{*} w'$ belongs to $M(\Sigma \cup W)^*$ as well.

Proof. When deriving w', G' first rewrites S' to $\#S$ by using $(S' \rightarrow \#S, 0, 0)$, where $\# \in M$ and $S \in \Sigma$. Next, inspect R' to see that every symbol from M is always rewritten to a symbol belonging to M or, in the case of #, erased by $(\# \rightarrow \varepsilon, 0, 0)$. Moreover, there are no rules generating new occurrences of symbols from $(M \cup \{S'\})$. Thus, all sentential forms derived from S' belong either to $M(\Sigma \cup W)^*$ or to $(\Sigma \cup W)^*$. In addition, if a sentential form belongs to $M(\Sigma \cup W)^*$, all previous sentential forms (except for S') are also from $M(\Sigma \cup W)^*$. □

Claim 2. Every successful derivation in G' is of the form

$$S' \Rightarrow_{G'} \#S \Rightarrow_{G'}^{+} \#u' \Rightarrow_{G'} w' \Rightarrow_{G'}^{*} w'$$

where $u' \in \Sigma^*$, $w' \in \Delta^*$.

Proof. From Claim 1 and its proof, every successful derivation has the form

$$S' \Rightarrow_{G'} \#S \Rightarrow_{G'}^{+} \#u' \Rightarrow_{G'} v' \Rightarrow_{G'}^{*} w'$$

where $u', v' \in (\Sigma \cup W)^*$, $w' \in \Delta^*$. This claim shows that

$$\#u' \Rightarrow_{G'} v' \Rightarrow_{G'}^{*} w'$$

implies that $u' \in \Sigma^*$ and $v' = w'$. Consider

$$\#u' \Rightarrow_{G'} v' \Rightarrow_{G'}^{*} w'$$

where $u', v' \in (\Sigma \cup W)^*$, $w' \in \Delta^*$. Assume that u' contains a nonterminal $[A, B, C] \in W$. There are two rules rewriting $[A, B, C]$:

$$p_1 : ([A, B, C] \rightarrow [A, B, C], 0, \langle A, B, C, m + 2\rangle)$$

and

$$p_2 : ([A, B, C] \rightarrow C, \langle A, B, C, m + 2\rangle, 0).$$

Because of its permitting condition, p_2 cannot be applied during $\#u' \Rightarrow_{G'} v'$. If $[A, B, C]$ is rewritten by p_1—that is, $[A, B, C] \in \text{symbols}(v')$—$[A, B, C]$ necessarily occurs in all sentential forms derived from v'. Thus, no u' containing a nonterminal from W results in a terminal string; hence, $u' \in \Sigma^*$. By analogical considerations, establish that also $v' \in \Sigma^*$. Next, assume that v' contains some $A \in N_{CF}$ or $B \in N_{CS}$. The first one can be rewritten by $(A \rightarrow z, \#, 0)$, $z \in \Sigma^*$, and the second one by

$(B \to [A,B,C], \langle A,B,C\rangle, 0)$, $[A,B,C] \in W$, $\langle A,B,C\rangle \in M$. In both cases, the permitting condition forbids an application of the rule. Consequently, $v' \in \Delta^*$. It is sufficient to show that $v' = w'$. Indeed, every rule rewriting a terminal is of the form $(a \to a, 0, 0)$, $a \in \Delta$. □

Claim 3. Let $S' \Rightarrow_{G'}^{n} Zx'$, $Z \in M$, $x' \in (\Sigma \cup W)^*$, $n \geq 1$. Then, Zx' has one of the following forms:

(I) $Z = \#, x' \in \Sigma^*$;
(II) $Z = \langle A,B,C\rangle, x' \in \Sigma^*$, for some $A, C \in N_{CF}, B \in N_{CS}$;
(III) $Z = \langle A,B,C,i\rangle, x' \in (\Sigma \cup \{[A,B,C]\})^*, 1 \leq i \leq m+1$, and $\{f^{-1}(j)[A,B,C] \mid 1 \leq j < i, j \neq f(A)\} \cap \text{substrings}(x') = \emptyset$ for some $A, C \in N_{CF}, B \in N_{CS}$; and
(IV) $Z = \langle A,B,C,m+2\rangle$, $x' \in (\Sigma \cup \{[A,B,C]\})^*$, $\{X[A,B,C] \mid X \in \Sigma,\ X \neq A\} \cap \text{substrings}(x') = \emptyset$, and $[A,B,C]^2 \notin \text{substrings}(x')$ for some $A, C \in N_{CF}$, $B \in N_{CS}$.

Proof. This claim is proved by induction on $h \geq 1$.

Basis. Let $h = 1$. Then, $S' \Rightarrow_{G'} \#S$, where $\#S$ is of type (I).

Induction Hypothesis. Suppose that the claim holds for all derivations of length $1 \leq h \leq n$, for some $n \geq 1$.

Induction Step. Consider any derivation of the form

$$S' \Rightarrow_{G'}^{n+1} Qx'$$

where $Q \in M, x' \in (\Sigma \cup W)^*$. Since $n+1 \geq 2$, by Claim 1, there exists $Zy' \in M(\Sigma \cup W)^*$ and a sequence of rules $p_0, p_1, \ldots, p_q$, where $p_i \in R'$, $0 \leq i \leq q$, $q = |y'|$, such that

$$S' \Rightarrow_{G'}^{n} Zy' \Rightarrow_{G'} Qx' \ [p_0, p_1, \ldots, p_q].$$

Let $y' = a_1 a_2 \cdots a_q$, where $a_i \in (\Sigma \cup W)$ for all $i = 1, \ldots, q$. By the induction hypothesis, the following cases (i)–(iv) cover all the possible forms of Zy'.

(i) Let $Z = \#$ and $y' \in \Sigma^*$ (form (I)). According to the definition of R', p_0 is either $(\# \to \langle A,B,C\rangle, 0, 0)$, $A, C \in N_{CF}$, $B \in N_{CS}$, or $(\# \to \#, 0, 0)$, or $(\# \to \varepsilon, 0, 0)$, and every p_i is either of the form $(a_i \to z, \#, 0)$, $z \in \{\varepsilon\} \cup N_{CS} \cup \Delta \cup N_{CF}^2$, or $(a_i \to a_i, 0, 0)$. Obviously, y' is always rewritten to a string $x' \in \Sigma^*$. If $\#$ is rewritten to $\langle A,B,C\rangle$, we get $\langle A,B,C\rangle x'$ that is of form (II). If $\#$ remains unchanged, $\#x'$ is of type (I). In case that $\#$ is erased, the resulting sentential form does not belong to $M(\Sigma \cup W)^*$ as required by this claim (which also holds for all strings derived from x' (see Claim 1));
(ii) Let $Z = \langle A,B,C\rangle$, $y' \in \Sigma^*$, for some $A, C \in N_{CF}$, $B \in N_{CS}$ (form (II)). In this case, p_0: $(\langle A,B,C\rangle \to \langle A,B,C,1\rangle, 0, 0)$ and every p_i is either $(a_i \to [A,B,C], \langle A,B,C\rangle, 0)$ or $(a_i \to a_i, 0, 0)$ (see the definition of R'). It is easy to see that $\langle A,B,C,1\rangle x'$ belongs to (III);
(iii) Let $Z = \langle A,B,C,j\rangle$, $y' \in (\Sigma \cup \{[A,B,C]\})^*$, and y' satisfies

$$\{f^{-1}(k)[A,B,C] \mid 1 \leq k < j,\ k \neq f(A)\} \cap \text{substrings}(y') = \emptyset$$

where $1 \leq j \leq m+1$, for some $A, C \in N_{CF}, B \in N_{CS}$ (form III). The only rules rewriting symbols from y' are $(a_i \to a_i, 0, 0)$, $a_i \in \Sigma$, and

$$([A,B,C] \to [A,B,C], 0, \langle A,B,C,m+2\rangle);$$

thus, y' is rewritten to itself. By the inspection of R', p_0 can be of the following three forms.

(a) If $j \neq f(A)$ and $j < m+1$,
$p_0 = (\langle A,B,C,j\rangle \to \langle A,B,C,j+1\rangle, 0, f^{-1}(j)[A,B,C])$.
Clearly, p_0 can be used only when $f^{-1}(j)[A,B,C] \notin$ substrings (Zy'). As
$\{f^{-1}(k)[A,B,C] \mid 1 \leq k < j,\ k \neq f(A)\} \cap$ substrings $(y') = \emptyset$,
also
$\{f^{-1}(k)[A,B,C] \mid 1 \leq k \leq j,\ k \neq f(A)\} \cap$ substrings $(y') = \emptyset$.
Since $\langle A,B,C,j\rangle$ is rewritten to $\langle A,B,C,j+1\rangle$ and y' is unchanged, we get $\langle A,B,C,j+1\rangle y'$ with
$\{f^{-1}(k)[A,B,C] \mid 1 \leq k < j+1,\ k \neq f(A)\} \cap$ substrings $(y') = \emptyset$.
which is of form (III);

(b) If $j = f(A)$,
$p_0 = (\langle A,B,C,f(A)\rangle \to \langle A,B,C,f(A)+1\rangle, 0, 0)$.
As before, $Qx' = \langle A,B,C,j+1\rangle y'$. Moreover, because
$\{f^{-1}(k)[A,B,C] \mid 1 \leq k < j,\ k \neq f(A)\} \cap$ substrings $(y') = \emptyset$
and $j = f(A)$,
$\{f^{-1}(k)[A,B,C] \mid 1 \leq k < j+1,\ k \neq f(A)\} \cap$ substrings $(x') = \emptyset$.
Consequently, Qx' belongs to (III) as well;

(c) If $j = m+1$,
$p_0 = (\langle A,B,C,m+1\rangle \to \langle A,B,C,m+2\rangle, 0, [A,B,C]^2)$.
Then, $Qx' = \langle A,B,C,m+2\rangle y'$. The application of p_0 implies that $[A,B,C]^2 \notin$ substrings (x'). In addition, observe that for $j = m+1$,
$\{f^{-1}(k)[A,B,C] \mid 1 \leq k < j,\ \ k \neq f(A)\}$
$\quad = \{X[A,B,C] \mid X \in \Sigma,\ \ X \neq A\}$.
Hence,
$\{X[A,B,C] \mid X \in \Sigma,\ \ X \neq A\} \cap$ substrings $(x') = \emptyset$.
As a result, Qx' is of form (IV);

(iv) Let $Z = \langle A,B,C,m+2\rangle$, $y' \in (\Sigma \cup \{[A,B,C]\})^*$, $[A,B,C]^2 \notin$ substrings (y'), and

$$\{X[A,B,C] \mid X \in \Sigma,\ X \neq A\} \cap \text{substrings}\ (y') = \emptyset$$

for some $A, C \in N_{CF}$, $B \in N_{CS}$ (form (IV)). Inspect R' to see that

$$p_0 = (\langle A,B,C,m+2\rangle \to \#, 0, \langle A,B,C,m+2\rangle[A,B,C])$$

and p_i is either

$$(a_i \to a_i, 0, 0),\ a_i \in V$$

or

$$([A, B, C] \to C, \langle A, B, C, m+2\rangle, 0)$$

where $1 \le i \le q$. According to the right-hand sides of these rules, $Qx' \in \{\#\}\Sigma^*$, that is, Qx' belongs to (I).

In cases (i)–(iv), we have demonstrated that every sentential form obtained in $n+1$ derivation steps satisfies the statement of this claim. Therefore, we have finished the induction step and established Claim 3. □

To prove the following claims, define the finite substitution γ from Σ^* into $(\Sigma \cup W)^*$ as

$$\gamma(X) = \{X\} \cup \{[A, B, C] \in W \mid A, C \in N_{CF},\ B \in N_{CS}\}$$

for all $X \in \Sigma$. Let inverse γ be the inverse of γ.

Claim 4. Let $y' = a_1 a_2 \cdots a_q$, $a_i \in (\Sigma \cup W)^*$, $q = |y'|$, and $\gamma^{-1}(a_i) \Rightarrow_G^{h_i} \gamma^{-1}(x'_i)$ for all $i \in \{1, \ldots, q\}$ and some $h_i \in \{0, 1\}$, $x'_i \in (\Sigma \cup W)^*$. Then, $\gamma^{-1}(y') \Rightarrow_G^{h} \gamma^{-1}(x')$ such that $x' = x'_1 x'_2 \cdots x'_q$, $h = \sum_{i=1}^{q} h_i$, $h \le q$.

Proof. Consider any derivation of the form

$$\gamma^{-1}(X) \Rightarrow_G^{l} \gamma^{-1}(u)$$

where $X \in (\Sigma \cup W)$, $u \in (\Sigma \cup W)^*$, $l \in \{0, 1\}$. If $l = 0$, $\gamma^{-1}(X) = \gamma^{-1}(u)$. Let $l = 1$. Then, there surely exists a rule $p\colon \gamma^{-1}(X) \to \gamma^{-1}(u) \in R$ such that

$$\gamma^{-1}(X) \Rightarrow_G \gamma^{-1}(u)\ [p].$$

Return to the statement of this claim. We can construct the derivation

$$\begin{aligned}
\gamma^{-1}(a_1)\gamma^{-1}(a_2)\cdots\gamma^{-1}(a_q) &\Rightarrow_G^{h_1} \gamma^{-1}(x'_1)\gamma^{-1}(a_2)\cdots\gamma^{-1}(a_q) \\
&\Rightarrow_G^{h_2} \gamma^{-1}(x'_1)\gamma^{-1}(x'_2)\cdots\gamma^{-1}(a_q) \\
&\ \vdots \\
&\Rightarrow_G^{h_q} \gamma^{-1}(x'_1)\gamma^{-1}(x'_2)\cdots\gamma^{-1}(x'_q)
\end{aligned}$$

where

$$\gamma^{-1}(y') = \gamma^{-1}(a_1)\cdots\gamma^{-1}(a_q)$$

and

$$\gamma^{-1}(x'_1)\cdots\gamma^{-1}(x'_q) = \gamma^{-1}(x'_1\cdots x'_q) = \gamma^{-1}(x').$$

In such a derivation, each $\gamma^{-1}(a_i)$ is either left unchanged (if $h_i = 0$) or rewritten to $\gamma^{-1}(x_i')$ by the corresponding rule $\gamma^{-1}(a_i) \to \gamma^{-1}(x_i')$. Obviously, the length of this derivation is $\sum_{i=1}^{q} h_i$. □

Claim 5. $S \Rightarrow_G^* x$ if and only if $S' \Rightarrow_{G'}^+ Qx'$, where $\gamma^{-1}(x') = x$, $Q \in M$, $x \in \Sigma^*$, $x' \in (\Sigma \cup W)^*$.

Proof. The proof is divided into the only-if part and the if part.

Only If. By induction on $h \geq 0$, we show that

$$S \Rightarrow_G^h x \quad \text{implies} \quad S' \Rightarrow_{G'}^+ \#x$$

where $x \in \Sigma^*$, $h \geq 0$. Clearly, $\gamma^{-1}(x) = x$.

Basis. Let $h = 0$. Then, $S \Rightarrow_G^0 S$. In G', $S' \Rightarrow_{G'} \#S$ by using $(S' \to \#S, 0, 0)$.

Induction Hypothesis. Assume that the claim holds for all derivations of length $0 \leq h \leq n$, for some $n \geq 0$.

Induction Step. Consider any derivation of the form

$$S \Rightarrow_G^{n+1} x.$$

As $n + 1 \geq 1$, there exists $y \in \Sigma^*$ and $p \in R$ such that

$$S \Rightarrow_G^n y \Rightarrow_G x \ [p].$$

Let $y = a_1 a_2 \cdots a_q$, $a_i \in \Sigma$ for all $1 \leq i \leq q$, where $q = |y|$. By the induction hypothesis,

$$S' \Rightarrow_{G'}^+ \#y.$$

The following cases investigate all possible forms of p.

(i) Let $p\colon A \to z$, $A \in N_{CF}$, $z \in \{\varepsilon\} \cup N_{CS} \cup \Delta \cup N_{CF}^2$. Then, $y = y_1 A y_3$ and $x = y_1 z y_3$, $y_1, y_3 \in \Sigma^*$. Let $l = |y_1| + 1$. In this case, we can construct

$$S' \Rightarrow_{G'}^+ \#y \Rightarrow_{G'} \#x \ [p_0, p_1, \ldots, p_q]$$

such that $p_0\colon (\# \to \#, 0, 0)$, $p_l\colon (A \to z, \#, 0)$, and $p_i\colon (a_i \to a_i, 0, 0)$ for all $1 \leq i \leq q$, $i \neq l$;

(ii) Let p: $AB \rightarrow AC$, $A, C \in N_{CF}$, $B \in N_{CS}$. Then, $y = y_1ABy_3$ and $x = y_1ACy_3$, $y_1, y_3 \in \Sigma^*$. Let $l = |y_1| + 2$. At this point, there exists the derivation

$$\begin{aligned} S' &\Rightarrow^+_{G'} \#y_1ABy_3 \\ &\Rightarrow_{G'} \langle A, B, C\rangle y_1ABy_3 \\ &\Rightarrow_{G'} \langle A, B, C, 1\rangle y_1A[A, B, C]y_3 \\ &\Rightarrow_{G'} \langle A, B, C, 2\rangle y_1A[A, B, C]y_3 \\ &\vdots \\ &\Rightarrow_{G'} \langle A, B, C, f(A)\rangle y_1A[A, B, C]y_3 \\ &\Rightarrow_{G'} \langle A, B, C, f(A)+1\rangle y_1A[A, B, C]y_3 \\ &\vdots \\ &\Rightarrow_{G'} \langle A, B, C, m+1\rangle y_1A[A, B, C]y_3 \\ &\Rightarrow_{G'} \langle A, B, C, m+2\rangle y_1A[A, B, C]y_3 \\ &\Rightarrow_{G'} \#y_1ACy_3. \end{aligned}$$

If. The if part establishes that

$$S' \Rightarrow^h_{G'} Qx' \quad \text{implies} \quad S \Rightarrow^*_{G'} x$$

where $\gamma^{-1}(x') = x$, $Q \in M$, $x' \in (\Sigma \cup W)^*$, $x \in \Sigma^*$, $h \geq 1$. This claim is proved by induction on $h \geq 1$.

Basis. Assume that $h = 1$. Since the only rule that can rewrite S' is $(S' \rightarrow \#S, 0, 0)$, $S' \Rightarrow_{G'} \#S$. Clearly, $S \Rightarrow^0_G S$ and $\gamma^{-1}(S) = S$.

Induction Hypothesis. Suppose that the claim holds for any derivation of length $1 \leq h \leq n$, for some $n \geq 1$.

Induction Step. Consider any derivation of the form

$$S' \Rightarrow^{n+1}_{G'} Qx'$$

where $Qx' \in M(\Sigma \cup W)^*$. Since $n + 1 \geq 2$, by Claim 1, there exists a derivation

$$S' \Rightarrow^+_{G'} Zy' \Rightarrow_{G'} Qx' \; [p_0, p_1, \ldots, p_q]$$

where $Zy' \in M(\Sigma \cup W)^*$, and $p_i \in R'$ for all $i \in \{0, 1, \ldots, q\}$, $q = |y'|$. By the induction hypothesis, there is also a derivation

$$S \Rightarrow^*_{G'} y$$

where $y \in \Sigma^*$, $\gamma^{-1}(y') = y$. Let $y' = a_1a_2 \cdots a_q$. Claim 3 says that Zy' has one of the following forms:

(i) Let $Z = \#$ and $y' \in \Sigma^*$. Then, there are the following two forms of rules rewriting a_i in y'.

  (i.a) Let $(a_i \rightarrow a_i, 0, 0)$, $a_i \in \Sigma$. In this case,
  $\gamma^{-1}(a_i) \Rightarrow^0_G \gamma^{-1}(a_i)$;

(i.b) Let $(a_i \rightarrow x_i, \#, 0)$, $x_i \in \{\varepsilon\} \cup N_{CS} \cup \Delta \cup N_{CF}^2$. Since $a_i = \gamma^{-1}(a_i)$, $x_i = \gamma^{-1}(x_i)$ and $a_i \rightarrow x_i \in R$,
$\gamma^{-1}(a_i) \Rightarrow_G \gamma^{-1}(x_i)\ [a_i \rightarrow x_i]$.

We see that for all a_i, there exists a derivation

$$\gamma^{-1}(a_i) \Rightarrow_G^{h_i} \gamma^{-1}(x_i)$$

for some $h_i \in \{0, 1\}$, where $x_i \in \Sigma^*$, $x' = x_1x_2 \cdots x_q$. Therefore, by Claim 4, we can construct

$$S' \Rightarrow_G^* y \Rightarrow_G^{\overline{h}} x$$

where $0 \leq \overline{h} \leq q$, $x = \gamma^{-1}(x')$;

(ii) Let $Z = \langle A, B, C\rangle$, $y' \in \Sigma^*$, for some $A, C \in N_{CF}$, $B \in N_{CS}$. At this point, the following two forms of rules can be used to rewrite a_i in y'.

(ii.a) Let $(a_i \rightarrow a_i, 0, 0)$, $a_i \in \Sigma$. As in case (i.a),
$\gamma^{-1}(a_i) \Rightarrow_G^0 \gamma^{-1}(a_i)$;

(ii.b) Let $(a_i \rightarrow [A, B, C], \langle A, B, C\rangle, 0)$, $a_i = B$. Since $\gamma^{-1}([A, B, C]) = \gamma^{-1}(B)$, we have
$\gamma^{-1}(a_i) \Rightarrow_G^0 \gamma^{-1}([A, B, C])$.

Thus, there exists the derivation

$$S \Rightarrow_G^* y \Rightarrow_G^0 x,\ x = \gamma^{-1}(x').$$

(iii) Let $Z = \langle A, B, C, j\rangle$, $y' \in (\Sigma \cup \{[A, B, C]\})^*$, and

$$\{f^{-1}(k)[A, B, C] \mid 1 \leq k < j,\ k \neq f(A)\} \cap \text{substrings}\ (y') = \emptyset$$

where $1 \leq j \leq m + 1$, for some $A, C \in N_{CF}$, $B \in N_{CS}$. Then, the only rules rewriting symbols from y' are

$$(a_i \rightarrow a_i, 0, 0),\ a_i \in V$$

and

$$([A, B, C] \rightarrow [A, B, C], 0, \langle A, B, C, m + 2\rangle).$$

Hence, $x' = y'$. Since we have

$$S \Rightarrow_G^* y,\ \gamma^{-1}(y') = y,$$

it also holds that $\gamma^{-1}(x') = y$;

(iv) Let $Z = \langle A, B, C, m + 2\rangle$, $y' \in (\Sigma \cup \{[A, B, C]\})^*$, $[A, B, C]^2 \notin$ substrings y',

$$\{X[A, B, C] \mid X \in \Sigma,\ X \neq A\} \cap \text{substrings}\ (y') = \emptyset$$

for some $A, C \in N_{CF}$, $B \in N_{CS}$. G' rewrites $\langle A, B, C, m + 2\rangle$ by using

$$(\langle A, B, C, m + 2\rangle \rightarrow \#, 0, \langle A, B, C, m + 2\rangle[A, B, C]),$$

which forbids $\langle A, B, C, m + 2\rangle[A, B, C]$ as a substring of Zy'. As a result, the left neighbor of every occurrence of $[A, B, C]$ in $\langle A, B, C, m + 2\rangle y'$ is A. Inspect R' to see that a_i can be rewritten either by $(a_i \rightarrow a_i, 0, 0)$, $a_i \in \Sigma$, or by $([A, B, C] \rightarrow C, \langle A, B, C, m+2\rangle, 0)$. Therefore, we can express

$$\begin{aligned} y' &= y_1A[A,B,C]y_2A[A,B,C]y_3 \cdots y_lA[A,B,C]y_{l+1},\\ y &= y_1ABy_2ABy_3 \cdots y_lABy_{l+1},\\ x' &= y_1ACy_2ACy_3 \cdots y_lACy_{l+1}, \end{aligned}$$

where $l \geq 0$, $y_k \in \Sigma^*$, $1 \leq k \leq l+1$. Since we have $p\colon AB \rightarrow AC \in R$, there is a derivation

$$\begin{aligned} S &\Rightarrow_G^* y_1ABy_2ABy_3 \cdots y_lABy_{l+1}\\ &\Rightarrow_G y_1ACy_2ABy_3 \cdots y_lABy_{l+1} \quad [p]\\ &\Rightarrow_G y_1ACy_2ACy_3 \cdots y_lABy_{l+1} \quad [p]\\ &\;\;\vdots\\ &\Rightarrow_G y_1ACy_2ACy_3 \cdots y_lACy_{l+1} \quad [p]. \end{aligned}$$

Since cases (i)–(iv) cover all possible forms of y', we have completed the induction and established Claim 5. □

Let us finish the proof of Lemma 13.13. Consider any derivation of the form

$$S \Rightarrow_G^* w,\ w \in \Delta^*.$$

From Claim 5, it follows that

$$S' \Rightarrow_{G'}^+ \#w,$$

because $\gamma(a) = \{a\}$ for every $a \in \Delta$. Then, as shown in Claim 2,

$$S' \Rightarrow_{G'}^+ \#w \Rightarrow_{G'} w,$$

and hence,

$$S \Rightarrow_G^* w \quad \text{implies} \quad S' \Rightarrow_{G'}^+ w$$

for all $w \in \Delta^*$. To prove the converse implication, consider a successful derivation of the form

$$S' \Rightarrow_{G'}^+ \#u \Rightarrow_{G'} w \Rightarrow_{G'}^* w$$

for some $u \in \Sigma^*$, $w \in \Delta^*$ (see Claim 2). Observe that by the definition of R', for every

$$S' \Rightarrow_{G'}^+ \#u \Rightarrow_{G'} w,$$

there also exists a derivation

$$S' \Rightarrow_{G'}^+ \#u \Rightarrow_{G'}^* \#w \Rightarrow_{G'} w.$$

Then, according to Claim 5, $S \Rightarrow_G^* w$. Consequently, we get for every $w \in \Delta^*$,

$$S \Rightarrow_G^* w \quad \text{if and only if} \quad S' \Rightarrow_{G'}^* w.$$

Therefore, $L(G) = L(G')$. □

Lemma 13.14. **SSCET0L**$(r,s) \subseteq$ **RE** *for any* $r,s \geq 0$.

Proof. By Lemma 13.5, **CET0L** $\subseteq$ **RE**. Since **SSCET0L**$(r,s) \subseteq$ **CET0L** for all $r,s \geq 0$ (see Definition 13.9), **SSCET0L**$(r,s) \subseteq$ **RE** for all $r,s \geq 0$ as well. □

Inclusions established in Lemmas 13.13 and 13.14 imply the following theorem:

Theorem 13.18.

$$\mathbf{SSCE0L}(1,2) = \mathbf{SSCET0L}(1,2) = \mathbf{SSCE0L} = \mathbf{SSCET0L} = \mathbf{RE}.$$

Proof. From Lemmas 13.13 and 13.14, we have that

$$\mathbf{RE} \subseteq \mathbf{SSCE0L}(1,2)$$

and

$$\mathbf{SSCET0L}(r,s) \subseteq \mathbf{RE}$$

for any $r,s \geq 0$. By the definitions it holds that

$$\mathbf{SSCE0L}(1,2) \subseteq \mathbf{SSCET0L}(1,2) \subseteq \mathbf{SSCET0L}$$

and

$$\mathbf{SSCE0L}(1,2) \subseteq \mathbf{SSCE0L} \subseteq \mathbf{SSCET0L}.$$

Hence,

$$\mathbf{SSCE0L}(1,2) = \mathbf{SSCET0L}(1,2) = \mathbf{SSCE0L} = \mathbf{SSCET0L} = \mathbf{RE}.$$

□

Next, let us investigate the generative power of propagating SSC-ET0L grammars.

Lemma 13.15. **CS** $\subseteq$ **SSCEP0L**$(1,2)$.

Proof. We can base this proof on the same technique as in Lemma 13.13. However, we have to make sure that the construction produces no erasing rules. This requires some modifications of the original algorithm; in particular, we have to eliminate the rule $(\# \to \varepsilon, 0, 0)$.

Let L be a context-sensitive language generated by a context-sensitive grammar

$$G = (\Sigma, \Delta, R, S)$$

of the normal form of Theorem 11.4, where

$$\Sigma = N_{CF} \cup N_{CS} \cup T.$$

Let m be the cardinality of Σ. Define a bijection f from Σ to $\{1, \ldots, m\}$. Let inverse f be the inverse of f. Set

$$\begin{aligned} M &= \{\langle \# \mid X\rangle \mid X \in \Sigma\} \\ &\quad \cup\{\langle A,B,C \mid X\rangle \mid AB \rightarrow AC \in R,\ X \in \Sigma\} \\ &\quad \cup\{\langle A,B,C,i \mid X\rangle \mid AB \rightarrow AC \in R,\ 1 \le i \le m+2,\ X \in \Sigma\}, \\ W &= \{[A,B,C,X] \mid AB \rightarrow AC \in R,\ X \in \Sigma\}, \text{ and} \\ \Sigma' &= \Sigma \cup M \cup W, \end{aligned}$$

where Σ, M, and W are pairwise disjoint. Then, construct the SSC-EP0L grammar of degree $(1, 2)$

$$G' = (\Sigma', \Delta, R', \langle \# \mid S\rangle)$$

with the set of rules R' constructed by performing (1)–(4), given as follows:

(1) For all $A \rightarrow x \in R, A \in N_{CF}, x \in \Delta \cup N_{CS} \cup N_{CF}^2$,
   (1.a) for all $X \in \Sigma$, add $(A \rightarrow x, \langle \# \mid X\rangle, 0)$ to R';
   (1.b) if $x \in \Delta \cup N_{CS}$, add $(\langle \# \mid A\rangle \rightarrow \langle \# \mid x\rangle, 0, 0)$ to R';
   (1.c) if $x = YZ$, $YZ \in N_{CF}^2$, add $(\langle \# \mid A\rangle \rightarrow \langle \# \mid Y\rangle Z, 0, 0)$ to R';
(2) For all $X \in \Sigma$ and for every $AB \rightarrow AC \in R$, $A, C \in N_{CF}$, $B \in N_{CS}$, extend R' by adding
   (2.a) $(\langle \# \mid X\rangle \rightarrow \langle A,B,C \mid X\rangle, 0, 0)$;
   (2.b) $(B \rightarrow [A,B,C,X], \langle A,B,C \mid X\rangle, 0)$;
   (2.c) $(\langle A,B,C \mid X\rangle \rightarrow \langle A,B,C,1 \mid X\rangle, 0, 0)$;
   (2.d) $([A,B,C,X] \rightarrow [A,B,C,X], 0, \langle A,B,C,m+2\rangle X)$;
   (2.e) $(\langle A,B,C,i \mid X\rangle \rightarrow \langle A,B,C,i+1 \mid X\rangle, 0, f^{-1}(i)[A,B,C,X])$ for all $1 \le i \le m, i \ne f(A)$;
   (2.f) $(\langle A,B,C,f(A) \mid X\rangle \rightarrow \langle A,B,C,f(A)+1 \mid X\rangle, 0, 0)$;
   (2.g) $(\langle A,B,C,m+1 \mid X\rangle \rightarrow \langle A,B,C,m+2 \mid X\rangle, 0, [A,B,C,X]^2)$;
   (2.h) $(\langle A,B,C,m+2 \mid X\rangle \rightarrow \langle \# \mid X\rangle, 0, 0)$ for $X = A$,
   $(\langle A,B,C,m+2 \mid X\rangle \rightarrow \langle \# \mid X\rangle, 0, \langle A,B,C,m+2 \mid X\rangle[A,B,C,X])$ otherwise; and
   (2.i) $([A,B,C,X] \rightarrow C, \langle A,B,C,m+2 \mid X\rangle, 0)$;
(3) For all $X \in \Sigma$, add $(X \rightarrow X, 0, 0)$ to R';
(4) For all $X \in \Sigma$, add $(\langle \# \mid X\rangle \rightarrow \langle \# \mid X\rangle, 0, 0)$ and $(\langle \# \mid X\rangle \rightarrow X, 0, 0)$ to R'.

Consider the construction above and the construction used in the proof of Lemma 13.13. Observe that the present construction does not attach the master as an extra symbol before sentential forms. Instead, the master is incorporated with its right neighbor into one composite symbol. For example, if G generates $AabCadd$, the corresponding sentential form in G' is $\langle \# \mid A\rangle abCadd$, where $\langle \# \mid A\rangle$ is one symbol. At this point, we need no rule erasing #; the master is simply rewritten to the symbol with which it is incorporated (see rules of (4)). In addition, this modification involves some changes to the algorithm: first, G' can rewrite symbols incorporated with the master (see rules of (1.b) and (1.c)). Second, conditions of the rules depending on the master refer to the composite symbols. Finally, G' can make context-sensitive rewriting of the composite master's right neighbor (see rules of (2.h)). For instance, if

$$ABadC \Rightarrow_G ACadC\ [AB \rightarrow AC]$$

in G, G' derives

$$\langle \# \mid A \rangle BadC \Rightarrow_{G'}^{+} \langle \# \mid A \rangle CadC.$$

Based on the observations above, the reader can surely establish $L(G) = L(G')$ by analogy with the proof of Lemma 13.13. Thus, the fully rigorous version of this proof is omitted. □

Lemma 13.16. **SSCEPT0L**$(r, s) \subseteq$ **CS**, *for all* $r, s \geq 0$.

Proof. By Lemma 13.4, **CEPT0L**$(r, s) \subseteq$ **CS**, for any $r \geq 0, s \geq 0$. Since every SSC-EPT0L grammar is a special case of a C-EPT0L grammar (see Definition 13.9), we obtain **SSCEPT0L**$(r, s) \subseteq$ **CS**, for all $r, s \geq 0$. □

Theorem 13.19.

$$\mathbf{CS} = \mathbf{SSCEP0L}(1,2) = \mathbf{SSCEPT0L}(1,2) = \mathbf{SSCEP0L} = \mathbf{SSCEPT0L}.$$

Proof. By Lemma 13.15, we have

$$\mathbf{CS} \subseteq \mathbf{SSCEP0L}(1,2).$$

Lemma 13.16 says that

$$\mathbf{SSCEPT0L}(r,s) \subseteq \mathbf{CS}$$

for all $r, s \geq 0$. From the definitions, it follows that

$$\mathbf{SSCEP0L}(1,2) \subseteq \mathbf{SSCEPT0L}(1,2) \subseteq \mathbf{SSCEPT0L}$$

and

$$\mathbf{SSCEP0L}(1,2) \subseteq \mathbf{SSCEP0L} \subseteq \mathbf{SSCEPT0L}.$$

Hence, we have the identity

$$\mathbf{SSCEP0L}(1,2) = \mathbf{SSCEPT0L}(1,2) = \mathbf{SSCEP0L} = \mathbf{SSCEPT0L} = \mathbf{CS},$$

so the theorem holds. □

The following corollary summarizes the established relations between the language families generated by SSC-ET0L grammars.

Corollary 4.

$$\begin{array}{c}\mathbf{CF}\\ \subset\\ \mathbf{SSCEP0L}(0,0)=\mathbf{SSCE0L}(0,0)=\mathbf{EP0L}=\mathbf{E0L}\\ \subset\\ \mathbf{SSCEPT0L}(0,0)=\mathbf{SSCET0L}(0,0)=\mathbf{EPT0L}=\mathbf{ET0L}\\ \subset\\ \mathbf{SSCEP0L}(1,2)=\mathbf{SSCEPT0L}(1,2)=\mathbf{SSCEP0L}=\mathbf{SSCEPT0L}=\mathbf{CS}\\ \subset\\ \mathbf{SSCE0L}(1,2)=\mathbf{SSCET0L}(1,2)=\mathbf{SSCE0L}=\mathbf{SSCET0L}=\mathbf{RE}.\end{array}$$

Open Problem 13.5. Notice that Corollary 4 does not include some related language families. For instance, it contains no language families generated by SSC-ET0L grammars with degrees $(1, 1)$, $(1, 0)$, and $(0, 1)$. What is their generative power? What is the generative power of SSC-ET0L grammars of degree $(2, 1)$? Are they as powerful as SSC-ET0L grammars of degree $(1, 2)$?

13.2.4 Left random context ET0L grammars

As their name indicates, *LRC-ET0L grammars* represent another variant of context-conditional ET0L grammars. In this variant, a set of *permitting symbols* and a set of *forbidding symbols* are attached to each of their rules, just like in random context grammars (see Section 11.2). A rule like this can rewrite a symbol if each of its permitting symbols occurs to the left of the rewritten symbol in the current sentential form, while each of its forbidding symbols does not occur there. LRC-ET0L grammars represent the principal subject of this section.

In the present section, we demonstrate that LRC-ET0L grammars are computationally complete—that is, they characterize the family of recursively enumerable languages (see Theorem 13.21). In fact, we prove that the family of recursively enumerable languages is characterized even by LRC-ET0L grammars with a limited number of nonterminals (see Theorem 13.22). We also demonstrate how to characterize the family of context-sensitive languages by these grammars without erasing rules (see Theorem 13.20).

In addition, we study a variety of special cases of LRC-ET0L grammars. First, we introduce *left random context E0L grammars* (LRC-E0L grammars for short), which represent LRC-ET0L grammars with a single set of rules. We prove that the above characterizations hold in terms of LRC-E0L grammars as well. Second, we introduce *left permitting E0L grammars* (LP-E0L grammars for short), which represent LRC-E0L grammars where each rule has only a set of permitting symbols. Analogously, we define *left forbidding E0L grammars* (LF-E0L grammars for short) as LRC-E0L grammars where each rule has only a set of forbidding symbols. We demonstrate that LP-E0L grammars are more powerful than ordinary E0L grammars and that LF-E0L grammars are at least as powerful as ordinary ET0L grammars.

13.2.4.1 Definitions and examples

In this section, we define LRC-ET0L grammars and their variants. In addition, we illustrate them by examples.

Definition 13.10. *A LRC-ET0L grammar is an $(n+3)$-tuple*

$$G = (\Sigma, \Delta, P_1, P_2, \ldots, P_n, w)$$

where Σ, Δ, and w are defined as in an ET0L grammar, $N = \Sigma - \Delta$ is the alphabet of nonterminals, *and $P_i \subseteq \Sigma \times \Sigma^* \times$* power $(N) \times$ power (N) *is a finite relation, for all i, $1 \leq i \leq n$, for some $n \geq 1$. By analogy with phrase-structure grammars, elements of P_i are called* rules *and instead of $(X, y, U, W) \in P_i$, we write $(X \to y, U, W)$ throughout this section. The* direct derivation relation *over Σ^*, symbolically denoted by $\Rightarrow_G$, is defined as follows:*

$$u \Rightarrow_G v$$

if and only if

- $u = X_1X_2 \cdots X_k$,
- $v = y_1y_2 \cdots y_k$,
- $(X_i \to y_i, U_i, W_i) \in P_h$,
- $U_i \subseteq$ symbols $(X_1X_2 \cdots X_{i-1})$, *and*
- symbols $(X_1X_2 \cdots X_{i-1}) \cap W_i = \emptyset$,

for all i, $1 \leq i \leq k$, for some $k \geq 1$ and $h \leq n$. For $(X \to y, U, W) \in P_i$, U and W are called the left permitting context *and the* left forbidding context, *respectively. Let $\Rightarrow_G^m$, $\Rightarrow_G^*$, and $\Rightarrow_G^+$ denote the mth power of $\Rightarrow_G$, for $m \geq 0$, the reflexive-transitive closure of $\Rightarrow_G$, and the transitive closure of $\Rightarrow_G$, respectively. The* language *of G is denoted by $L(G)$ and defined as*

$$L(G) = \{x \in \Delta^* \mid w \Rightarrow_G^* x\}.$$

Definition 13.11. *Let $G = (\Sigma, \Delta, P_1, P_2, \ldots, P_n, w)$ be an LRC-ET0L grammar, for some $n \geq 1$. If every $(X \to y, U, W) \in P_i$ satisfies that $W = \emptyset$, for all i, $1 \leq i \leq n$, then G is a* left permitting ET0L grammar *(an LP-ET0L grammar for short). If every $(X \to y, U, W) \in P_i$ satisfies that $U = \emptyset$, for all i, $1 \leq i \leq n$, G is a* left-forbidding ET0L grammar *(an LF-ET0L grammar for short).*

By analogy with ET0L grammars (see their definition in Section 4.2), we define *LRC-EPT0L, LP-EPT0L, LF-EPT0L, LRC-E0L, LP-E0L, LF-E0L, LRC-EP0L, LP-EP0L*, and *LF-EP0L grammars.*

The language families that are generated by LRC-ET0L, LP-ET0L, LF-ET0L, LRC-EPT0L, LP-EPT0L and LF-EPT0L grammars are denoted by **LRCET0L**, **LPET0L**, **LFET0L**, **LRCEPT0L**, **LPEPT0L**, and **LFEPT0L**, respectively. The language families generated by LRC-E0L, LP-E0L, LF-E0L, LRC-EP0L, LP-EP0L, and LF-EP0L grammars are denoted by **LRCE0L**, **LPE0L**, **LFE0L**, **LRCEP0L**, **LPEP0L**, and **LFEP0L**, respectively.

Next, we illustrate the above-introduced notions by two examples.

Example 13.5. Consider $K = \{a^m b^n a^m \mid 1 \leq m \leq n\}$. This language is generated by the LF-EP0L grammar

$$G = (\{A, B, B', \bar{a}, a, b\}, \{a, b\}, R, ABA)$$

with R containing the following nine rules:

$$\begin{array}{lll} (A \to aA, \emptyset, \{\bar{a}\}), & (a \to a, \emptyset, \emptyset), & (B' \to bB', \emptyset, \{A\}), \\ (A \to \bar{a}, \emptyset, \{\bar{a}\}), & (B \to bB, \emptyset, \emptyset), & (B' \to b, \emptyset, \{A\}), \\ (\bar{a} \to a, \emptyset, \{A\}), & (B \to B', \emptyset, \emptyset), & (b \to b, \emptyset, \emptyset). \end{array}$$

To rewrite A to a string not containing A, $(A \to \bar{a}, \emptyset, \{\bar{a}\})$ has to be used. Since the only rule which can rewrite $\bar{a}$ is $(\bar{a} \to a, \emptyset, \{A\})$, and the rules that can rewrite A have $\bar{a}$ in their forbidding contexts, it is guaranteed that both As are rewritten to $\bar{a}$ simultaneously; otherwise, the derivation is blocked. The rules $(B' \to bB', \emptyset, \{A\})$ and $(B' \to b, \emptyset, \{A\})$ are applicable only if there is no A to the left of B'. Therefore, after these rules are applied, no more as can be generated. Consequently, we see that for every string from $L(G)$, there exists a derivation of the form

$$\begin{aligned} ABA &\Rightarrow_G^* a^{m-1}Ab^{m-1}Ba^{m-1}A \\ &\Rightarrow_G a^{m-1}\bar{a}b^{m-1}B'a^{m-1}\bar{a} \\ &\Rightarrow_G^+ a^m b^n a^m \end{aligned}$$

with $1 \leq m \leq n$. Hence, $L(G) = K$.

Recall that $K \notin$ **E0L** (see page 268 in [39]); however, $K \in$ **LFEP0L**. As a result, LF-EP0L grammars are more powerful than ordinary E0L grammars.

The next example shows how to generate K by an LP-EP0L grammar, which implies that LP-E0L grammars have greater expressive power than E0L grammars.

Example 13.6. Consider the LRC-EP0L grammar

$$H = (\{S, A, A', B, B', \bar{a}, a, b\}, \{a, b\}, R, S)$$

with R containing the following 14 rules:

$$\begin{array}{lll} (S \to ABA', \emptyset, \emptyset), & (A' \to aA', \{A\}, \emptyset), & (B \to bB, \emptyset, \emptyset), \\ (S \to \bar{a}B'\bar{a}, \emptyset, \emptyset), & (A' \to \bar{a}, \{\bar{a}\}, \emptyset), & (B \to bB', \emptyset, \emptyset), \\ (A \to aA, \emptyset, \emptyset), & (\bar{a} \to \bar{a}, \emptyset, \emptyset), & (B' \to bB', \{\bar{a}\}, \emptyset), \\ (A \to a\bar{a}, \emptyset, \emptyset), & (\bar{a} \to a, \emptyset, \emptyset), & (B' \to b, \emptyset, \{\bar{a}\}, \emptyset), \\ & (a \to a, \emptyset, \emptyset), & (b \to b, \emptyset, \emptyset). \end{array}$$

If the first applied rule is $(S \to \bar{a}B'\bar{a}, \emptyset, \emptyset)$, the generated string of terminals clearly belongs to K from Example 13.5. By using this rule, we can obtain a string with only two as, which is impossible if $(S \to ABA', \emptyset, \emptyset)$ is used instead. Therefore, we assume that $(S \to ABA', \emptyset, \emptyset)$ is applied as the first rule. Observe that $(A' \to aA', \{A\}, \emptyset)$ can be used only when there is A present to the left of A' in the current sentential form. Also, $(A' \to a, \{\bar{a}\}, \emptyset)$ can be applied only after $(A \to a\bar{a}, \emptyset, \emptyset)$ is used. Finally, note that $(B' \to bB', \{\bar{a}\}, \emptyset)$ and $(B' \to b, \emptyset, \{\bar{a}\}, \emptyset)$ can be applied only if there is $\bar{a}$ to the left of B'. Therefore, after these rules are used, no more as can be generated. Consequently, we see that for every string from $L(G)$ with more than two as, there exists a derivation of the form

$$\begin{aligned} S &\Rightarrow_H ABA' \\ &\Rightarrow_H^* a^{m-2}Ab^{m-2}Ba^{m-2}A' \\ &\Rightarrow_H a^{m-1}\bar{a}b^{m-1}B'a^{m-1}A' \\ &\Rightarrow_H^+ a^{m-1}\bar{a}b^{n-1}B'a^{m-1}\bar{a} \\ &\Rightarrow_H a^m b^n a^m \end{aligned}$$

with $2 \leq m \leq n$. Hence, $L(H) = K$.

13.2.4.2 Generative power and reduction

In this section, we establish the generative power of LRC-ET0L grammars and their special variants. More specifically, we prove that **LRCEPT0L** = **LRCEP0L** = **CS** (Theorem 13.20), **LRCET0L** = **LRCE0L** = **RE** (Theorem 13.21), **ET0L** $\subseteq$ **LFEP0L** (Theorem 13.23), and **E0L** $\subset$ **LPEP0L** (Theorem 13.24).

First, we consider LRC-EPT0L and LRC-EP0L grammars.

Lemma 13.17. CS $\subseteq$ **LRCEP0L.**

Proof. Let $G = (\Sigma, \Delta, R, S)$ be a context-sensitive grammar and let $N = \Sigma - \Delta$. Without any loss of generality, making use of Theorem 11.3, we assume that G is in the Penttonen normal form. Next, we construct an LRC-EP0L grammar H such that $L(H) = L(G)$. Set

$$\begin{aligned} \bar{N} &= \{\bar{A} \mid A \in N\}, \\ \hat{N} &= \{\hat{A} \mid A \in N\}, \\ N' &= N \cup \bar{N} \cup \hat{N}. \end{aligned}$$

Without any loss of generality, we assume that $\bar{N}$, $\hat{N}$, N, and Δ are pairwise disjoint. Construct

$$H = (\Sigma', \Delta, R', S)$$

as follows. Initially, set $\Sigma' = N' \cup \Delta$ and $R' = \emptyset$. Perform (1)–(5), given as follows:

(1) For each $A \to a \in R$, where $A \in N$ and $a \in \Delta$, add $(A \to a, \emptyset, N')$ to R';
(2) For each $A \to BC \in R$, where $A, B, C \in N$, add $(A \to BC, \emptyset, \bar{N} \cup \hat{N})$ to R';
(3) For each $AB \to AC \in R$, where $A, B, C \in N$,
    (3.1) add $(B \to C, \{\hat{A}\}, N \cup (\hat{N} - \{\hat{A}\}))$ to R' and
    (3.2) for each $D \in N$, add $(D \to D, \{\hat{A}, B\}, \hat{N} - \{\hat{A}\})$ to R';
(4) For each $D \in N$, add $(D \to \bar{D}, \emptyset, \bar{N} \cup \hat{N})$, $(D \to \hat{D}, \emptyset, \bar{N} \cup \hat{N})$, $(\bar{D} \to D, \emptyset, N \cup \hat{N})$, and $(\hat{D} \to D, \emptyset, N \cup \hat{N})$ to R';
(5) For each $a \in \Delta$ and each $D \in N$, add $(a \to a, \emptyset, N')$ and $(D \to D, \emptyset, \bar{N} \cup \hat{N})$ to R'.

Before proving that $L(H) = L(G)$, let us give an insight into the construction. The simulation of context-free rules of the form $A \rightarrow BC$, where $A, B, C \in N$, is done by rules introduced in (2). Rules from (5) are used to rewrite all the remaining symbols.

H simulates context-sensitive rules—that is, rules of the form $AB \rightarrow AC$, where $A, B, C \in N$—as follows. First, it rewrites all nonterminals to the left of A to their barred versions by rules from (4), A to $\hat{A}$ by $(A \rightarrow \hat{A}, \emptyset, \bar{N} \cup \hat{N})$ from (4), and all the remaining symbols by passive rules from (5). Then, it rewrites B to C by $(B \rightarrow C, \{\hat{A}\}, N \cup (\hat{N} - \{\hat{A}\}))$ from (3.1), barred nonterminals to non-barred nonterminals by rules from (4), $\hat{A}$ back to A by $(\hat{A} \rightarrow A, \emptyset, N \cup \hat{N})$ from (4), all other nonterminals by passive rules from (3.2), and all terminals by passive rules from (5). For example, for

$$abXYABZ \Rightarrow_G abXYACZ$$

there is

$$abXYABZ \Rightarrow_H ab\bar{X}\bar{Y}\hat{A}BZ \Rightarrow_H abXYACZ.$$

Observe that if H makes an improper selection of the symbols rewritten to their barred and hatted versions, like in $AXB \Rightarrow_H \hat{A}\bar{X}B$, then the derivation is blocked because every rule of the form $(\bar{D} \rightarrow D, \emptyset, N \cup \hat{N})$, where $D \in D$, requires that there are no hatted nonterminals to the left of $\bar{D}$.

To prevent $AAB \Rightarrow_H AaB \Rightarrow_H \hat{A}aB \Rightarrow_H AaC$, rules simulating $A \rightarrow a$, where $A \in N$ and $a \in \Delta$, introduced in (1), can be used only if there are no nonterminals to the left of A. Therefore, a terminal can never appear between two nonterminals, and so every sentential form generated by H is of the form x_1x_2, where $x_1 \in \Delta^*$ and $x_2 \in N'^*$.

To establish $L(H) = L(G)$, we prove three claims. Claim 1 demonstrates that every $y \in L(G)$ can be generated in two stages; first, only nonterminals are generated, and then, all nonterminals are rewritten to terminals. Claim 2 shows how such derivations of every $y \in L(G)$ in G are simulated by H. Finally, Claim 3 shows how derivations of H are simulated by G.

Claim 1. Let $y \in L(G)$. Then, in G, there exists a derivation $S \Rightarrow_G^* x \Rightarrow_G^* y$, where $x \in N^+$, and during $x \Rightarrow_G^* y$, only rules of the form $A \rightarrow a$, where $A \in N$ and $a \in \Delta$, are applied.

Proof. Let $y \in L(G)$. Since there are no rules in R with symbols from Δ on their left-hand sides, we can always rearrange all the applications of the rules occurring in $S \Rightarrow_G^* y$ so the claim holds. □

Claim 2. If $S \Rightarrow_G^h x$, where $x \in N^+$, for some $h \geq 0$, then $S \Rightarrow_H^* x$.

Proof. This claim is established by induction on $h \geq 0$.

Basis. For $h = 0$, this claim obviously holds.

Induction Hypothesis. Suppose that there exists $n \geq 0$ such that the claim holds for all derivations of length h, where $0 \leq h \leq n$.

Induction Step. Consider any derivation of the form

$$S \Rightarrow_G^{n+1} w$$

where $w \in N^+$. Since $n + 1 \geq 1$, this derivation can be expressed as

$$S \Rightarrow_G^n x \Rightarrow_G w$$

for some $x \in N^+$. By the induction hypothesis, $S \Rightarrow_H^* x$.

Next, we consider all possible forms of $x \Rightarrow_G w$, covered by the following two cases—(i) and (ii).

(i) Let $A \to BC \in R$ and $x = x_1Ax_2$, where $A, B, C \in N$ and $x_1, x_2 \in N^*$. Then, $x_1Ax_2 \Rightarrow_G x_1BCx_2$. By (2), $(A \to BC, \emptyset, \bar{N} \cup \hat{N}) \in R'$, and by (5), $(D \to D, \emptyset, \bar{N} \cup \hat{N}) \in R'$, for each $D \in N$. Since $\text{symbols}(x_1Ax_2) \cap (\bar{N} \cup \hat{N}) = \emptyset$,

$$x_1Ax_2 \Rightarrow_H x_1BCx_2,$$

which completes the induction step for (i);

(ii) Let $AB \to AC \in R$ and $x = x_1ABx_2$, where $A, B, C \in N$ and $x_1, x_2 \in N^*$. Then, $x_1ABx_2 \Rightarrow_G x_1BCx_2$. Let $x_1 = X_1X_2 \cdots X_k$, where $X_i \in N$, for all i, $1 \leq i \leq k$, for some $k \geq 1$. By (4), $(X_i \to \bar{X}_i, \emptyset, \bar{N} \cup \hat{N}) \in R'$, for all i, $1 \leq i \leq k$, and $(A \to \hat{A}, \emptyset, \bar{N} \cup \hat{N}) \in R'$. By (5), $(D \to D, \emptyset, \bar{N} \cup \hat{N}) \in R'$, for all $D \in \text{symbols}(Bx_2)$. Since $\text{symbols}(x_1ABx_2) \cap (\bar{N} \cup \hat{N}) = \emptyset$,

$$X_1X_2 \cdots X_kABx_2 \Rightarrow_H \bar{X}_1\bar{X}_2 \cdots \bar{X}_k\hat{A}Bx_2.$$

By (3.1), $(B \to C, \{\hat{A}\}, N \cup (\hat{N} - \{\hat{A}\})) \in R'$. By (4), $(\bar{X}_i \to X_i, \emptyset, N \cup \hat{N}) \in R'$, for all i, $1 \leq i \leq k$, and $(\hat{A} \to A, \emptyset, N \cup \hat{N}) \in R'$. By (3.2), $(D \to D, \{\hat{A}, B\}, \hat{N} - \{\hat{A}\}) \in R'$, for all $D \in \text{symbols}(x_2)$. Since $\text{symbols}(\bar{X}_1\bar{X}_2 \cdots \bar{X}_k) \cap (N \cup \hat{N}) = \emptyset$,

$$\bar{X}_1\bar{X}_2 \cdots \bar{X}_k\hat{A}Bx_2 \Rightarrow_H X_1X_2 \cdots X_kACx_2,$$

which completes the induction step for 13.2.4.2.

Observe that cases (i) and (ii) cover all possible forms of $x \Rightarrow_G w$. Thus, the claim holds. □

Define the homomorphism τ from Σ'^* to Σ^* as $\tau(\bar{A}) = \tau(\hat{A}) = \tau(A) = A$, for all $A \in N$, and $\tau(a) = a$, for all $a \in \Delta$.

Claim 3. If $S \Rightarrow_H^h x$, where $x \in \Sigma'^+$, for some $h \geq 0$, then $S \Rightarrow_G^* \tau(x)$, and x is of the form x_1x_2, where $x_1 \in \Delta^*$ and $x_2 \in N'^*$.

Proof. This claim is established by induction on $h \geq 0$.

Basis. For $h = 0$, this claim obviously holds.

Induction Hypothesis. Suppose that there exists $n \geq 0$ such that the claim holds for all derivations of length h, where $0 \leq h \leq n$.

Induction Step. Consider any derivation of the form

$$S \Rightarrow_H^{n+1} w.$$

Since $n+1 \geq 1$, this derivation can be expressed as

$$S \Rightarrow_H^n x \Rightarrow_H w$$

for some $x \in \Sigma'^+$. By the induction hypothesis, $S \Rightarrow_G^* \tau(x)$, and x is of the form x_1x_2, where $x_1 \in \Delta^*$ and $x_2 \in N'^*$.

Next, we make the following four observations regarding the possible forms of $x \Rightarrow_H w$:

(i) A rule from (1) can be applied only to the leftmost occurrence of a nonterminal in x_2. Therefore, w is always of the required form;

(ii) Rules from (1) and (2) can be applied only if symbols $(x) \cap (\bar{N} \cup \hat{N}) = \emptyset$. Furthermore, every rule from (1) and (2) is constructed from some $A \rightarrow a \in R$ and $A \rightarrow BC \in R$, respectively, where $A, B, C \in N$ and $a \in \Delta$. If two or more rules are applied at once, G can apply them sequentially;

(iii) When a rule from (3.1)—that is, $(B \rightarrow C, \{\hat{A}\}, N \cup (\hat{N} - \{\hat{A}\}))$—is applied, $\hat{A}$ has to be right before the occurrence of B that is rewritten to C. Otherwise, the symbols between $\hat{A}$ and that occurrence of B cannot be rewritten by any rule and, therefore, the derivation is blocked. Furthermore, H can apply only a single such rule. Since every rule in (3.1) is constructed from some $AB \rightarrow AC \in R$, where $A, B, C \in N$, G applies $AB \rightarrow AC$ to simulate this rewrite;

(iv) If rules introduced in (3.2), (4), or (5) are applied, the induction step follows directly from the induction hypothesis.

Based on these observations, we see that the claim holds. □

Next, we establish $L(H) = L(G)$. Let $y \in L(G)$. Then, by Claim 1, in G, there exists a derivation $S \Rightarrow_G^* x \Rightarrow_G^* y$ such that $x \in N^+$, and during $x \Rightarrow_G^* y$, G uses only rules of the form $A \rightarrow a$, where $A \in N$ and $a \in \Delta$. By Claim 2, $S \Rightarrow_H^* x$. Let $x = X_1X_2\cdots X_k$ and $y = a_1a_2\cdots a_k$, where $X_i \in N$, $a_i \in \Delta$, $X_i \rightarrow a_i \in R$, for all i, $1 \leq i \leq k$, for some $k \geq 1$. By (1), $(X_i \rightarrow a_i, \emptyset, N') \in R'$, for all i. By (5), $(a_i \rightarrow a_i, \emptyset, N') \in R'$ and $(X_i \rightarrow X_i, \emptyset, \bar{N} \cup \hat{N}) \in R'$, for all i. Therefore,

$$\begin{aligned} X_1X_2\cdots X_k &\Rightarrow_H a_1X_2\cdots X_k \\ &\Rightarrow_H a_1a_2\cdots X_k \\ &\vdots \\ &\Rightarrow_H a_1a_2\cdots a_k. \end{aligned}$$

Consequently, $y \in L(G)$ implies that $y \in L(H)$, so $L(G) \subseteq L(H)$.

Consider Claim 3 with $x \in \Delta^+$. Then, $x \in L(H)$ implies that $\tau(x) = x \in L(G)$, so $L(H) \subseteq L(G)$. As $L(G) \subseteq L(H)$ and $L(H) \subseteq L(G)$, $L(H) = L(G)$, so the lemma holds. □

Lemma 13.18. LRCEPT0L $\subseteq$ CS.

Proof. Let $G = (\Sigma, \Delta, P_1, P_2, \ldots, P_n, w)$ be an LRC-EPT0L grammar, for some $n \geq 1$. From G, we can construct a phrase-structure grammar, $H = (N', \Delta, R', S)$, such that $L(G) = L(H)$ and if $S \Rightarrow_H^* x \Rightarrow_H^* z$, where $x \in (N' \cup \Delta)^+$ and $z \in \Delta^+$, then $|x| \leq 4|z|$. Consequently, by the workspace theorem (see Section 7.2 and Theorem 3.3.15 in [23]), $L(H) \in$ **CS**. Since $L(G) = L(H)$, $L(G) \in$ **CS**, so the lemma holds. □

Theorem 13.20. LRCEPT0L = LRCEP0L = CS.

Proof. **LRCEP0L** $\subseteq$ **LRCEPT0L** follows from the definition of an LRC-EP0L grammar. By Lemma 13.17, we have **CS** $\subseteq$ **LRCEP0L**, which implies that **CS** $\subseteq$ **LRCEP0L** $\subseteq$ **LRCEPT0L**. Since **LRCEPT0L** $\subseteq$ **CS** by Lemma 13.18,

$$\mathbf{LRCEP0L} \subseteq \mathbf{LRCEPT0L} \subseteq \mathbf{CS}.$$

Hence, **LRCEPT0L** = **LRCEP0L** = **CS**, so the theorem holds. □

Hence, LRC-EP0L grammars characterize **CS**. Next, we focus on LRC-ET0L and LRC-E0L grammars.

Theorem 13.21. LRCET0L = LRCE0L = RE.

Proof. The inclusion **LRCE0L** $\subseteq$ **LRCET0L** follows from the definition of an LRC-E0L grammar. The inclusion **LRCET0L** $\subseteq$ **RE** follows from the Turing–Church thesis. The inclusion **RE** $\subseteq$ **LRCE0L** can be proved by analogy with the proof of Lemma 13.17. Observe that by Theorem 11.2, G can additionally contain rules of the form $A \rightarrow \varepsilon$, where $A \in N$. We can simulate these context-free rules in the same way we simulate $A \rightarrow BC$, where $A, B, C \in N$—that is, for each $A \rightarrow \varepsilon \in R$, we introduce $(A \rightarrow \varepsilon, \emptyset, \bar{N} \cup \hat{N})$ to R'. As **LRCE0L** $\subseteq$ **LRCET0L** $\subseteq$ **RE** and **RE** $\subseteq$ **LRCE0L** $\subseteq$ **LRCET0L**, **LRCET0L** = **LRCE0L** = **RE**, so the theorem holds. □

The following corollary compares the generative power of LRC-E0L and LRC-ET0L grammars to the power of E0L and ET0L grammars.

Corollary 5.

$$\begin{array}{c} \mathbf{CF} \subset \mathbf{E0L} = \mathbf{EP0L} \subset \mathbf{ET0L} = \mathbf{EPT0L} \\ \subset \\ \mathbf{LRCEPT0L} = \mathbf{LRCEP0L} = \mathbf{CS} \\ \subset \\ \mathbf{LRCET0L} = \mathbf{LRCE0L} = \mathbf{RE}. \end{array}$$

Proof. This corollary follows from Theorem 4.4 in Section 4.2 and from Theorems 13.20 and 13.21 above. □

Next, we show that the family of recursively enumerable languages is characterized even by LRC-E0L grammars with a limited number of nonterminals. Indeed, we prove that every recursively enumerable language can be generated by an LRC-E0L grammar with seven nonterminals.

Theorem 13.22. *Let K be a recursively enumerable language. Then, there is an LRC-E0L grammar, $H = (\Sigma, \Delta, R, w)$, such that $L(H) = K$ and* card $(\Sigma - \Delta) = 7$.

Proof. Let K be a recursively enumerable language. By Theorem 11.6, there is a phrase-structure grammar in the Geffert normal form

$$G = (\{S, A, B, C\}, \Delta, R \cup \{ABC \to \varepsilon\}, S)$$

satisfying $L(G) = K$. Next, we construct an LRC-E0L grammar H such that $L(H) = L(G)$. Set $N = \{S, A, B, C\}$, $\Sigma = N \cup \Delta$, and $N' = N \cup \{\bar{A}, \bar{B}, \#\}$ (without any loss of generality, we assume that $\Sigma \cap \{\bar{A}, \bar{B}, \#\} = \emptyset$). Construct

$$H = (\Sigma', \Delta, R', S\#)$$

as follows. Initially, set $\Sigma' = N' \cup \Delta$ and $R' = \emptyset$. Perform 1–8, given next.

(1) For each $a \in \Delta$,
add $(a \to a, \emptyset, \emptyset)$ to R';
(2) For each $X \in N$,
add $(X \to X, \emptyset, \{\bar{A}, \bar{B}, \#\})$ and $(X \to X, \{\bar{A}, \bar{B}, C\}, \{S, \#\})$ to R';
(3) Add $(\# \to \#, \emptyset, \{\bar{A}, \bar{B}\})$, $(\# \to \#, \{\bar{A}, \bar{B}, C\}, \{S\})$, and $(\# \to \varepsilon, \emptyset, N' - \{\#\})$ to R';
(4) For each $S \to uSa \in R$, where $u \in \{A, AB\}^*$ and $a \in \Delta$,
add $(S \to uS\#a, \emptyset, \{\bar{A}, \bar{B}, \#\})$ to R';
(5) For each $S \to uSv \in R$, where $u \in \{A, AB\}^*$ and $v \in \{BC, C\}^*$,
add $(S \to uSv, \emptyset, \{\bar{A}, \bar{B}, \#\})$ to R';
(6) For each $S \to uv \in R$, where $u \in \{A, AB\}^*$ and $v \in \{BC, C\}^*$,
add $(S \to uv, \emptyset, \{\bar{A}, \bar{B}, \#\})$ to R';
(7) Add $(A \to \bar{A}, \emptyset, \{S, \bar{A}, \bar{B}, \#\})$ and $(B \to \bar{B}, \emptyset, \{S, \bar{A}, \bar{B}, \#\})$ to R';
(8) Add $(\bar{A} \to \varepsilon, \emptyset, \{S, \bar{A}, \bar{B}, C, \#\})$, $(\bar{B} \to \varepsilon, \{\bar{A}\}, \{S, \bar{B}, C, \#\})$, and $(C \to \varepsilon, \{\bar{A}, \bar{B}\}, \{S, C, \#\})$ to R'.

Before proving that $L(H) = L(G)$, let us informally explain (1)–(8). H simulates the derivations of G that satisfy the form described in Theorem 11.6. Since H works in a parallel way, rules from (1) to (3) are used to rewrite symbols that are not actively rewritten. The context-free rules in R are simulated by rules from (4) to (6). The context-sensitive rule $ABC \to \varepsilon$ is simulated in a two-step way. First, rules introduced in (7) rewrite A and B to $\bar{A}$ and $\bar{B}$, respectively. Then, rules from (8) erase $\bar{A}$, $\bar{B}$, and C; for example,

$$AABCBC\#a\# \Rightarrow_H A\bar{A}\bar{B}CBC\#a\# \Rightarrow_H ABC\#a\#.$$

The role of # is 2-fold. First, it ensures that every sentential form of H is of the form $w_1 w_2$, where $w_1 \in (N' - \{\#\})^*$ and $w_2 \in (\Delta \cup \{\#\})^*$. Since left permitting and left forbidding contexts cannot contain terminals, a mixture of symbols from Δ and N in H could produce a terminal string out of $L(G)$. For example, observe that $AaBC \Rightarrow_H^* a$, but such a derivation does not exist in G. Second, if any of $\bar{A}$ and $\bar{B}$ are present, $ABC \to \varepsilon$ has to be simulated. Therefore, it prevents derivations of the form $Aa \Rightarrow_H \bar{A}a \Rightarrow_H a$ (notice that the start string of H is $S\#$). Since H works in a parallel way, if rules from (7) are used improperly, the derivation is blocked, so no partial erasures are possible.

Observe that every sentential form of G and H contains at most one occurrence of S. In every derivation step of H, only a single rule from $R \cup \{ABC \to \varepsilon\}$ can be simulated at once. $ABC \rightarrow \varepsilon$ can be simulated only if there is no S. #s can be eliminated by an application of rules from (7); however, only if no nonterminals occur to the left of # in the current sentential form. Consequently, all #s are erased at the end of every successful derivation. Based on these observations and on Theorem 11.6, we see that every successful derivation in H is of the form

$$\begin{aligned} S\# &\Rightarrow_H^* w_1 w_2 \# a_1 \# a_2 \cdots \# a_n \# \\ &\Rightarrow_H^* \# a_1 \# a_2 \cdots \# a_n \# \\ &\Rightarrow_H^* a_1 a_2 \cdots a_n \end{aligned}$$

where $w_1 \in \{A, AB\}^*$, $w_2 \in \{BC, C\}^*$, and $a_i \in \Delta$ for all $i = 1, \ldots, n$, for some $n \geq 0$.

To establish $L(H) = L(G)$, we prove two claims. First, Claim 1 shows how derivations of G are simulated by H. Then, Claim 2 demonstrates the converse—that is, it shows how derivations of H are simulated by G.

Define the homomorphism ϕ from Σ^* to Σ'^* as $\phi(X) = X$ for all $X \in N$, and $\phi(a) = \#a$ for all $a \in \Delta$.

Claim 1. If $S \Rightarrow_G^h x \Rightarrow_G^* z$, for some $h \geq 0$, where $x \in \Sigma^*$ and $z \in \Delta^*$, then $S\# \Rightarrow_H^* \phi(x)\#$.

Proof. This claim is established by induction on $h \geq 0$.

Basis. For $h = 0$, this claim obviously holds.

Induction Hypothesis. Suppose that there exists $n \geq 0$ such that the claim holds for all derivations of length h, where $0 \leq h \leq n$.

Induction Step. Consider any derivation of the form

$$S \Rightarrow_G^{n+1} w \Rightarrow_G^* z$$

where $w \in \Sigma^*$ and $z \in \Delta^*$. Since $n + 1 \geq 1$, this derivation can be expressed as

$$S \Rightarrow_G^n x \Rightarrow_G w \Rightarrow_G^* z$$

for some $x \in \Sigma^+$. Without any loss of generality, we assume that $x = x_1x_2x_3x_4$, where $x_1 \in \{A,\ AB\}^*$, $x_2 \in \{S,\ \varepsilon\}$, $x_3 \in \{BC,\ C\}^*$, and $x_4 \in \Delta^*$ (see Theorem 11.6 and the form of rules in R). Next, we consider all possible forms of $x \Rightarrow_G w$, covered by the following four cases—(i)–(iv).

(i) *Application of* $S \rightarrow uSa \in R$. Let $x = x_1Sx_4$, $w = x_1uSax_4$, and $S \rightarrow uSa \in R$, where $u \in \{A,\ AB\}^*$ and $a \in \Delta$. Then, by the induction hypothesis,

$$S\# \Rightarrow_H^* \phi(x_1Sx_4)\#.$$

By (4), $r\colon (S \rightarrow uS\#a, \emptyset, \{\bar{A}, \bar{B}, \#\}) \in R'$. Since $\phi(x_1Sx_4)\# = x_1S\phi(x_4)\#$ and symbols $(x_1S) \cap \{\bar{A},\ \bar{B},\ \#\} = \emptyset$, by (1), (2), (3), and by r,

$$x_1S\phi(x_4)\# \Rightarrow_H x_1uS\#a\phi(x_4)\#.$$

As $\phi(x_1uSax_4)\# = x_1uS\#a\phi(x_4)\#$, the induction step is completed for (i);

(ii) *Application of* $S \rightarrow uSv \in R$. Let $x = x_1Sx_3x_4$, $w = x_1uSvx_3x_4$, and $S \rightarrow uSv \in R$, where $u \in \{A, AB\}^*$ and $v \in \{BC, C\}^*$. To complete the induction step for (ii), proceed by analogy with (i) but use a rule from (5) instead of a rule from (4);

(iii) *Application of* $S \rightarrow uv \in R$. Let $x = x_1Sx_3x_4$, $w = x_1uvx_3x_4$, and $S \rightarrow uv \in R$, where $u \in \{A, AB\}^*$ and $v \in \{BC, C\}^*$. To complete the induction step for (iii), proceed by analogy with (i) but use a rule from (6) instead of a rule from (4);

(iv) *Application of* $ABC \rightarrow \varepsilon$. Let $x = x_1'ABCx_3'x_4$, $w = x_1'x_3'x_4$, where $x_1x_2x_3 = x_1'ABCx_3'$, so $x \Rightarrow_G w$ by $ABC \rightarrow \varepsilon$. Then, by the induction hypothesis,

$$S\# \Rightarrow_H^* \phi(x_1'ABCx_3'x_4)\#.$$

Since $\phi(x_1'ABCx_3'x_4)\# = x_1'ABCx_3'\phi(x_4)\#$ and $\text{symbols}(x_1'ABCx_3') \cap \{\bar{A}, \bar{B}, \#\} = \emptyset$,

$$x_1'ABCx_3'\phi(x_4)\# \Rightarrow_H x_1'\bar{A}\bar{B}Cx_3'\phi(x_4)\#$$

by rules from (1), (2), (3), and (7). Since $\text{symbols}(x_1') \cap \{S, \bar{A}, \bar{B}, C, \#\} = \emptyset$, $\{\bar{A}\} \subseteq \text{symbols}(x_1'\bar{A})$, $\text{symbols}(x_1'\bar{A}) \cap \{S, \bar{B}, C, \#\} = \emptyset$, $\{\bar{A}, \bar{B}\} \subseteq \text{symbols}(x_1'\bar{A}\bar{B})$, and $\{S, C, \#\} \cap \text{symbols}(x_1'\bar{A}\bar{B}) = \emptyset$,

$$x_1'\bar{A}\bar{B}Cx_3'\phi(x_4)\# \Rightarrow_H x_1'x_3'\phi(x_4)\#$$

by rules from (1), (2), (3), and (8). As $\phi(x_1'x_3'x_4)\# = x_1'x_3'\phi(x_4)\#$, the induction step is completed for (iv).

Observe that cases (i)–(iv) cover all possible forms of $x \Rightarrow_G w$, so the claim holds. □

Define the homomorphism τ from Σ'^* to Σ^* as $\tau(X) = X$ for all $X \in N$, $\tau(a) = a$ for all $a \in \Delta$, and $\tau(\bar{A}) = A$, $\tau(\bar{B}) = B$, $\tau(\#) = \varepsilon$.

Claim 2. If $S\# \Rightarrow_H^h x \Rightarrow_H^* z$, for some $h \geq 0$, where $x \in \Sigma'^*$ and $z \in \Delta^*$, then $S \Rightarrow_G^* \tau(x)$.

Proof. This claim is established by induction on $h \geq 0$.

Basis. For $h = 0$, this claim obviously holds.

Induction Hypothesis. Suppose that there exists $n \geq 0$ such that the claim holds for all derivations of length h, where $0 \leq h \leq n$.

Induction Step. Consider any derivation of the form

$$S\# \Rightarrow_H^{n+1} w \Rightarrow_H^* z$$

where $w \in \Sigma'^*$ and $z \in \Delta^*$. Since $n + 1 \geq 1$, this derivation can be expressed as

$$S\# \Rightarrow_H^n x \Rightarrow_H w \Rightarrow_H^* z$$

for some $x \in \Sigma'^+$. By the induction hypothesis, $S \Rightarrow_G^* \tau(x)$. Next, we consider all possible forms of $x \Rightarrow_H w$, covered by the following five cases—(i)–(v).

(i) Let $x = x_1Sx_2$ and $w = x_1uS\#ax_2$, where $x_1, x_2, \in \Sigma'^*$, such that

$$x_1Sx_2 \Rightarrow_H x_1uS\#ax_2$$

by $(S \rightarrow uS\#a,\ \emptyset,\ \{\bar{A},\ \bar{B},\ \#\})$—introduced in (4) from $S \rightarrow uSa \in R$, where $u \in \{A, AB\}^*$, $a \in \Delta$—and by the rules introduced in (1), (2), and (3). Since $\tau(x_1Sx_2) = \tau(x_1)S\tau(x_2)$,

$$\tau(x_1)S\tau(x_2) \Rightarrow_G \tau(x_1)uSa\tau(x_2).$$

As $\tau(x_1)uSa\tau(x_2) = \tau(x_1uS\#ax_2)$, the induction step is completed for (i);

(ii) Let $x = x_1Sx_2$ and $w = x_1uSvx_2$, where $x_1, x_2, \in \Sigma'^*$, such that $x_1Sx_2 \Rightarrow_H x_1uSvx_2$ by $(S \rightarrow uSv,\ \emptyset,\ \{\bar{A},\ \bar{B},\ \#\})$—introduced in (5) from $S \rightarrow uSv \in R$, where $u \in \{A, AB\}^*$, $v \in \{BC, C\}^*$—and by the rules introduced in (1), (2), and (3). Proceed by analogy with (i);

(iii) Let $x = x_1Sx_2$ and $w = x_1uvx_2$, where $x_1, x_2, \in \Sigma'^*$, such that $x_1Sx_2 \Rightarrow_H x_1uvx_2$ by $(S \rightarrow uv,\ \emptyset,\ \{\bar{A},\ \bar{B},\ \#\})$—introduced in (6) from $S \rightarrow uv \in R$, where $u \in \{A, AB\}^*$, $v \in \{BC, C\}^*$—and by the rules introduced in (1), (2), and (3). Proceed by analogy with (i);

(iv) Let $x = x_1\bar{A}\bar{B}Cx_2$ and $w = x_1'x_2$, where $x_1,\ x_2 \in \Sigma'^*$ and $\tau(x_1') = x_1$, such that $x_1\bar{A}\bar{B}Cx_2 \Rightarrow_H x_1'x_2$ by rules introduced in (1), (2), (3), (7), and (8). Since $\tau(x_1\bar{A}\bar{B}Cx_2) = \tau(x_1)ABC\tau(x_2)$,

$$\tau(x_1)ABC\tau(x_2) \Rightarrow_G \tau(x_1)\tau(x_2)$$

by $ABC \rightarrow \varepsilon$. As $\tau(x_1)\tau(x_2) = \tau(x_1'x_2)$, the induction step is completed for (iv);

(v) Let $x \Rightarrow_H w$ only by rules from (1), (2), (3), and from (7). As $\tau(x) = \tau(w)$, the induction step is completed for (v).

Observe that cases (i)–(v) cover all possible forms of $x \Rightarrow_H w$, so the claim holds. □

Next, we prove that $L(H) = L(G)$. Consider Claim 1 with $x \in \Delta^*$. Then, $S \Rightarrow_G^* x$ implies that $S\# \Rightarrow_H^* \phi(x)\#$. By (3), $(\# \rightarrow \varepsilon, \emptyset, N' - \{\#\}) \in R'$, and by (1), $(a \rightarrow a, \emptyset, \emptyset) \in R'$ for all $a \in \Delta$. Since symbols $(\phi(x)\#) \cap (N' - \{\#\}) = \emptyset$, $\phi(x)\# \Rightarrow_H x$. Hence, $L(G) \subseteq L(H)$. Consider Claim 2 with $x \in \Delta^*$. Then, $S\# \Rightarrow_H^* x$ implies that $S \Rightarrow_G^* x$. Hence, $L(H) \subseteq L(G)$. Since card $(N') = 7$, the theorem holds. □

We turn our attention to LRC-E0L grammars containing only forbidding conditions.

Lemma 13.19. EPT0L $\subseteq$ LFEP0L.

Proof. Let $G = (\Sigma,\ \Delta,\ P_1,\ P_2,\ \ldots,\ P_t,\ w)$ be an EPT0L grammar, for some $t \geq 1$. Set

$$R = \{\langle X, i\rangle \mid X \in \Sigma, 1 \leq i \leq t\}$$

and

$$F_i = \{\langle X, j\rangle \in R \mid j \neq i\} \text{ for } i = 1, 2, \ldots, t.$$

Without any loss of generality, we assume that $\Sigma \cap R = \emptyset$. Define the LF-EP0L grammar

$$H = (\Sigma', \Delta, R', w)$$

where $\Sigma' = \Sigma \cup R$, and R' is constructed by performing the following two steps:

(1) For each $X \in \Sigma$ and each $i \in \{1, 2, \ldots, t\}$, add $(X \rightarrow \langle X, i\rangle, \emptyset, \emptyset)$ to R';
(2) For each $X \rightarrow y \in P_i$, where $1 \leq i \leq t$, add $(\langle X, i\rangle \rightarrow y, \emptyset, F_i)$ to R'.

To establish $L(H) = L(G)$, we prove three claims. Claim 1 points out that every sentential form in H is formed either by symbols from R or from Σ, depending on whether the length of the derivation is even or odd. Claim 2 shows how derivations of G are simulated by H. Finally, Claim 3 demonstrates the converse—that is, it shows how derivations of H are simulated by G.

Claim 1. For every derivation $w \Rightarrow_H^n x$, where $n \geq 0$,

(i) if $n = 2k + 1$, for some $k \geq 0$, then $x \in R^+$ and
(ii) if $n = 2k$, for some $k \geq 0$, then $x \in \Sigma^+$.

Proof. The claim follows from the construction of R'. Indeed, every rule in R' is either of the form $(X \rightarrow \langle X, i\rangle, \emptyset, \emptyset)$ or $(\langle X, i\rangle \rightarrow y, \emptyset, F_i)$, where $X \in \Sigma$, $1 \leq i \leq t$, and $y \in \Sigma^+$. Since $w \in \Sigma^+$, $w \Rightarrow_H^{2k+1} x$ implies that $x \in R^+$, and $w \Rightarrow_H^{2k} x$ implies that $x \in \Sigma^+$. Thus, the claim holds. □

Claim 2. If $w \Rightarrow_G^h x$, where $x \in \Sigma^+$, for some $h \geq 0$, then $w \Rightarrow_H^* x$.

Proof. This claim is established by induction on $h \geq 0$.

Basis. For $h = 0$, this claim obviously holds.

Induction Hypothesis. Suppose that there exists $n \geq 0$ such that the claim holds for all derivations of length h, where $0 \leq h \leq n$.

Induction Step. Consider any derivation of the form

$$w \Rightarrow_G^{n+1} y$$

where $y \in \Sigma^+$. Since $n + 1 \geq 1$, this derivation can be expressed as

$$w \Rightarrow_G^n x \Rightarrow_G y$$

for some $x \in \Sigma^+$. Let $x = X_1X_2 \cdots X_h$ and $y = y_1y_2 \cdots y_h$, where $h = |x|$. As $x \Rightarrow_G y$, $X_i \rightarrow y_i \in P_m$, for all i, $1 \leq i \leq h$, for some $m \leq t$.

By the induction hypothesis, $w \Rightarrow_H^* x$. By (1), $(X_i \rightarrow \langle X_i, m\rangle, \emptyset, \emptyset) \in R'$, for all i, $1 \leq i \leq h$. Therefore,

$$X_1X_2 \cdots X_h \Rightarrow_H \langle X_1, m\rangle\langle X_2, m\rangle \cdots \langle X_h, m\rangle.$$

By (2), $(\langle X_i, m\rangle \rightarrow y_i, \emptyset, F_m) \in R'$, for all i, $1 \leq i \leq h$. Since

$$\text{symbols}\,(\langle X_1, m\rangle\langle X_2, m\rangle \cdots \langle X_h, m\rangle) \cap F_m = \emptyset,$$

it holds that

$$\langle X_1, m\rangle\langle X_2, m\rangle\cdots\langle X_h, m\rangle \Rightarrow_H y_1y_2\cdots y_h,$$

which proves the induction step. □

Define the homomorphism ψ from Σ'^* to Σ^* as $\psi(X) = \psi(\langle X, i\rangle) = X$, for all $X \in \Sigma$ and all i, $1 \leq i \leq t$.

Claim 3. If $w \Rightarrow_H^h x$, where $x \in \Sigma'^+$, for some $h \geq 0$, then $w \Rightarrow_G^* \psi(x)$.

Proof. This claim is established by induction on $h \geq 0$.

Basis. For $h = 0$, this claim obviously holds.

Induction Hypothesis. Suppose that there exists $n \geq 0$ such that the claim holds for all derivations of length h, where $0 \leq h \leq n$.

Induction Step. Consider any derivation of the form

$$w \Rightarrow_H^{n+1} y$$

where $y \in \Sigma'^+$. Since $n + 1 \geq 1$, this derivation can be expressed as

$$w \Rightarrow_H^n x \Rightarrow_H y$$

for some $x \in \Sigma'^+$. By the induction hypothesis, $w \Rightarrow_G^* \psi(x)$. By Claim 1, there exist the following two cases—(i) and (ii).

(i) Let $n = 2k + 1$, for some $k \geq 0$. Then, $x \in R^+$, so let $x = \langle X_1, m_1\rangle\langle X_2, m_2\rangle\cdots\langle X_h, m_h\rangle$, where $h = |x|$, $X_i \in \Sigma$, for all i, $1 \leq i \leq h$, and $m_j \in \{1, 2, \ldots, t\}$, for all j, $1 \leq j \leq h$. The only possible derivation in H is

$$\langle X_1, m_1\rangle\langle X_2, m_2\rangle\cdots\langle X_h, m_h\rangle \Rightarrow_H y_1y_2\cdots y_h$$

by rules introduced in (2), where $y_i \in \Sigma^*$, for all i, $1 \leq i \leq h$. Observe that $m_1 = m_2 = \cdots = m_h$; otherwise, $\langle X_h, m_h\rangle$ cannot be rewritten (see the form of left forbidding contexts of the rules introduced to R' in (2)). By (2), $X_j \to y_j \in P_{m_h}$, for all j, $1 \leq j \leq h$. Since $\psi(x) = X_1X_2\cdots X_h$,

$$X_1X_2\cdots X_h \Rightarrow_G y_1y_2\cdots y_h,$$

which proves the induction step for (i);

(ii) Let $n = 2k$, for some $k \geq 0$. Then, $x \in \Sigma^+$, so let $x = X_1X_2\cdots X_h$, where $h = |x|$. The only possible derivation in H is

$$X_1X_2\cdots X_h \Rightarrow_H \langle X_1, m_1\rangle\langle X_2, m_2\rangle\cdots\langle X_h, m_h\rangle$$

by rules introduced in (1), where $m_j \in \{1, 2, \ldots, t\}$, for all j, $1 \leq j \leq h$. Since $\psi(y) = \psi(x)$, where $y = \langle X_1, m_1\rangle\langle X_2, m_2\rangle\cdots\langle X_h, m_h\rangle$, the induction step for (ii) follows directly from the induction hypothesis.

Hence, the claim holds. □

Next, we establish $L(H) = L(G)$. Consider Claim 2 with $x \in \Delta^+$. Then, $w \Rightarrow_G^* x$ implies that $w \Rightarrow_H^* x$, so $L(G) \subseteq L(H)$. Consider Claim 3 with $x \in \Delta^+$. Then, $w \Rightarrow_H^* x$ implies that $w \Rightarrow_G^* \psi(x) = x$, so $L(H) \subseteq L(G)$. Hence, $L(H) = L(G)$, so the lemma holds. □

Theorem 13.23.

$$\mathbf{E0L} = \mathbf{EP0L} \subset \mathbf{ET0L} = \mathbf{EPT0L} \subseteq \mathbf{LFEP0L} \subseteq \mathbf{LFE0L}.$$

Proof. The inclusions $\mathbf{E0L} = \mathbf{EP0L}$, $\mathbf{ET0L} = \mathbf{EPT0L}$, and $\mathbf{E0L} \subset \mathbf{ET0L}$ follow from Theorem 4.4. From Lemma 13.19, we have $\mathbf{EPT0L} \subseteq \mathbf{LFEP0L}$. The inclusion $\mathbf{LFEP0L} \subseteq \mathbf{LFE0L}$ follows directly from the definition of an LF-E0L grammar. □

Next, we briefly discuss LRC-E0L grammars containing only permitting conditions.

Theorem 13.24.

$$\mathbf{E0L} = \mathbf{EP0L} \subset \mathbf{LPEP0L} \subseteq \mathbf{LPE0L}.$$

Proof. The identity

$$\mathbf{E0L} = \mathbf{EP0L}$$

follows from Theorem 4.4. The inclusions

$$\mathbf{EP0L} \subseteq \mathbf{LPEP0L} \subseteq \mathbf{LPE0L}$$

follow directly from the definition of an LP-E0L grammar. The properness of the inclusion

$$\mathbf{EP0L} \subset \mathbf{LPEP0L}$$

follows from Example 13.6. □

To conclude this section, we compare LRC-ET0L grammars and their special variants to a variety of conditional ET0L grammars with respect to their generative power. Then, we formulate some open problem areas.

Consider *random context ET0L grammars* (abbreviated *RC-ET0L grammars*), see [40,41] and Section 8 in [12]. These grammars have been recently discussed in connection to various grammar systems (see [42–49]) and membrane systems (P systems, see [50]). Recall that as a modification of LRC-ET0L grammars, they check the occurrence of symbols in the entire sequential form. Notice, however, that contrary to our definition of LRC-ET0L grammars, in [40,41] and in other works, RC-ET0L grammars are defined so that they have permitting and forbidding conditions attached to whole sets of rules rather than to each single rule. Since we also study LRC-E0L grammars, which contain just a single set of rules, attachment to rules is more appropriate in our case, just like in terms of other types of regulated ET0L grammars discussed in this section.

The language families generated by RC-ET0L grammars and propagating RC-ET0L grammars are denoted by **RCET0L** and **RCEPT0L**, respectively (for the definitions of these families, see [48]).

Theorem 13.25 (see 44).

$$\mathbf{RCEPT0L} \subset \mathbf{CS} \textit{ and } \mathbf{RCET0L} \subseteq \mathbf{RE}.$$

Let us point out that it is not known whether the inclusion **RCET0L** $\subseteq$ **RE** is, in fact, proper (see [42,48,50]).

Corollary 6.

$$\mathbf{RCEPT0L} \subset \mathbf{LRCEP0L} \textit{ and } \mathbf{RCET0L} \subseteq \mathbf{LRCE0L}.$$

Proof. This corollary follows from Theorems 13.20, 13.21, and 13.25. □

Corollary 6 is of some interest because LRC-E0L grammars (i) have only a single set of rules and (ii) they check only prefixes of sentential forms.

A modification of LF-ET0L grammars, called F-ET0L grammars, is introduced and discussed in Section 13.2.2. Recall that as opposed to LF-ET0L grammars, these grammars check for the absence of forbidding symbols in the entire sentential form. Furthermore, recall that **FET0L**(1) denotes the family of languages generated by F-ET0L grammars whose forbidding strings are of length one.

Corollary 7. **FET0L**(1) $\subseteq$ **LFEP0L**.

Proof. This corollary follows from Lemma 13.19 and from Theorem 13.15, which says that **FET0L**(1) = **ET0L**. □

This result is also of some interest because LF-EP0L grammars (i) have only a single set of rules, (ii) have no rules of the form $(A \to \varepsilon, \emptyset, W)$, and (iii) they check only prefixes of sentential forms.

Furthermore, consider context-conditional ET0L grammars (C-ET0L grammars for short) and SSC-ET0L grammars from Sections 13.2.1 and 13.2.3, respectively. Recall that these grammars differ from RC-ET0L grammars by the form of their permitting and forbidding sets. In C-ET0L grammars, these sets contain strings rather than single symbols. SSC-ET0L grammars are C-ET0L grammars in which every rule can either forbid or permit the occurrence of a single string.

Recall that **CET0L** and **CEPT0L** denote the language families generated by C-ET0L grammars and propagating C-ET0L grammars, respectively. The language families generated by SSC-ET0L grammars and propagating SSC-ET0L grammars are denoted by **SSCET0L** and **SSCEPT0L**, respectively.

Corollary 8.

$$\begin{array}{c}\mathbf{CEPT0L} = \mathbf{SSCEPT0L} = \mathbf{LRCEP0L} \\ \subset \\ \mathbf{CET0L} = \mathbf{SSCET0L} = \mathbf{LRCE0L}.\end{array}$$

Proof. This corollary follows from Theorems 13.20 and 13.21 and from Theorems 13.12, 13.13, 13.19, and 13.18, which say that **CEPT0L** = **SSCEPT0L** = **CS** and **CET0L** = **SSCET0L** = **RE**. □

We close this section by formulating several open problem areas suggested as topics of future investigation related to the present study.

Open Problem 13.6. By Theorem 13.23, **ET0L** $\subseteq$ **LFE0L**. Is this inclusion, in fact, an identity?

Open Problem 13.7. ET0L and EPT0L grammars have the same generative power (see Theorem 4.4). Are LF-E0L and LF-EP0L grammars equally powerful? Are LP-E0L and LP-EP0L grammars equally powerful?

Open Problem 13.8. What is the relation between the language families generated by ET0L grammars and by LP-E0L grammars?

Open Problem 13.9. Establish the generative power of LP-ET0L and LF-ET0L grammars.

Open Problem 13.10. Theorem 13.22 has proved that every recursively enumerable language can be generated by an LRC-E0L grammar with seven nonterminals. Can this result be improved?

Open Problem 13.11. Recall that LRC-E0L grammars without erasing the rules that characterize the family of context-sensitive languages (see Theorem 13.20). Can we establish this characterization based upon these grammars with a limited number of nonterminals?

13.3 Multigenerative grammar systems and parallel computation

Today's environment of cooperating multiprocessor computers allows us to base modern-information technologies on a large combination of simultaneously running processes, which make use of this powerful environment as much as possible. Consequently, parallel computation plays a crucially important role in computer science at present as already pointed out in the beginning of Chapter 13.

Recall that parallel computation is conceptually accomplished by breaking a large computational task into many independent subtasks, which are simultaneously executed. Once they are completed, their results are combined together. Of course, to obtain solid knowledge about this way of computation, we need formal models that adequately formalize computational parallelism, including the final combination of the achieved results. The present section describes multigenerative grammar systems, which can serve for this purpose very well. Indeed, they consist of several simultaneously working components represented by context-free grammars, so they reflect and formalize concurrent computation in a natural and proper way.

This section consists of two subsections. The first subsection introduces the basic versions of multigenerative grammar systems. During one generation step, each of their grammatical components rewrites a nonterminal in its sentential form. After this simultaneous generation is completed, all the generated strings are composed into a single string by some common operation, such as union or concatenation. More precisely, for a positive integer n, an n-generative grammar system works with n context-free grammatical components, each of which makes a derivation, and these n derivations are simultaneously controlled by a finite set of n-tuples consisting of rules. In this way, the grammar system generates n terminal strings, which are combined together by operation union, concatenation, or the selection of the first generated string. We show that these systems characterize the family of matrix languages. In addition, we demonstrate that multigenerative grammar systems with any number of grammatical components can be transformed to equivalent two-component versions of these systems.

The second subsection discusses leftmost versions of multigenerative grammar systems in which each generation step is performed in the leftmost manner. That is, all the grammatical components of these versions rewrite the leftmost nonterminal occurrence in their sentential forms; otherwise, they work as the basic versions. We prove that leftmost multigenerative grammar systems are more powerful than their basic versions. Indeed, they generate the family of recursively enumerable languages, which properly contains the family of matrix languages (see Theorems 12.2 and 12.3). We also consider regulation by n-tuples of nonterminals rather than rules and prove that leftmost multigenerative grammar systems regulated by rules or nonterminals have the same generative power. In addition, like for the basic versions, we demonstrate that leftmost multigenerative grammar systems with any number of grammatical components can be transformed to equivalent two-component versions of these systems.

13.3.1 Multigenerative grammar systems

In this section, we define multigenerative grammar systems and demonstrate that they are as powerful as matrix grammars. We also show that any multigenerative grammar system can be transformed to an equivalent two-component multigenerative grammar system.

Definition 13.12. *An* n-generative rule-synchronized grammar system *(an n-MGR for short) is an* $n+1$ *tuple*

$$\Gamma = (G_1, G_2, \ldots, G_n, Q)$$

where

- $G_i = (\Sigma_i, T_i, P_i, S_i)$ *is a context-free grammar, for each* $i = 1, \ldots, n$ *and*
- Q *is a finite set of n-tuples of the form* $(p_1, p_2, \ldots, p_n)$*, where* $p_i \in P_i$*, for all* $i = 1, \ldots, n$.

A sentential n-form *is an n-tuple of the form* $\chi = (x_1, x_2, \ldots, x_n)$*, where* $x_i \in \Sigma_i^*$*, for all* $i = 1, \ldots, n$*. Let* $\chi = (u_1A_1v_1, u_2A_2v_2, \ldots, u_nA_nv_n)$ *and* $\bar{\chi} = (u_1x_1v_1, u_2x_2v_2, \ldots, u_nx_nv_n)$ *be two sentential n-forms, where* $A_i \in N_i$ *and* $u_i, v_i, x_i \in \Sigma_i^*$*, for all* $i =$

$1, \ldots, n$. Let $(p_i\colon A_i \to x_i) \in P_i$ for all $i = 1, \ldots, n$ and $(p_1, p_2, \ldots, p_n) \in Q$. Then, χ directly derives $\bar{\chi}$ in Γ, denoted by

$$\chi \Rightarrow_\Gamma \bar{\chi}.$$

In the standard way, we generalize $\Rightarrow_\Gamma$ to $\Rightarrow_\Gamma^k$, for all $k \geq 0$, $\Rightarrow_\Gamma^*$, and $\Rightarrow_\Gamma^+$.

The n-language *of Γ, denoted by n-$L(\Gamma)$, is defined as*

$$n\text{-}L(\Gamma) = \{(w_1, w_2, \ldots, w_n) \mid (S_1, S_2, \ldots, S_n) \Rightarrow_\Gamma^* (w_1, w_2, \ldots, w_n), w_i \in T_i^*, \text{for all } i = 1, \ldots, n\}.$$

The language generated by Γ in the union mode, *$L_{union}(\Gamma)$, is defined as*

$$L_{union}(\Gamma) = \bigcup_{i=1}^{n} \{w_i \mid (w_1, w_2, \ldots, w_n) \in n\text{-}L(\Gamma)\}.$$

The language generated by Γ in the concatenation mode, *$L_{conc}(\Gamma)$, is defined as*

$$L_{conc}(\Gamma) = \{w_1 w_2 \ldots w_n \mid (w_1, w_2, \ldots, w_n) \in n\text{-}L(\Gamma)\}.$$

The language generated by Γ in the first mode, *$L_{first}(\Gamma)$, is defined as*

$$L_{first}(\Gamma) = \{w_1 \mid (w_1, w_2, \ldots, w_n) \in n\text{-}L(\Gamma)\}.$$

We illustrate the above definition by an example.

Example 13.7. Consider the 2-MGR $\Gamma = (G_1, G_2, Q)$, where

- $G_1 = (\{S_1, A_1, a, b, c\}, \{a, b, c\}, \{1\colon S_1 \to aS_1, 2\colon S_1 \to aA_1, 3\colon A_1 \to bA_1c, 4\colon A_1 \to bc\}, S_1)$,
- $G_2 = (\{S_2, A_2, d\}, \{d\}, \{1\colon S_2 \to S_2A_2, 2\colon S_2 \to A_2, 3\colon A_2 \to d\}, S_2)$,
- $Q = \{(1, 1), (2, 2), (3, 3), (4, 3)\}$.

Observe that

- $2\text{-}L(\Gamma) = \{(a^nb^nc^n, d^n) \mid n \geq 1\}$,
- $L_{union}(\Gamma) = \{a^nb^nc^n \mid n \geq 1\} \cup \{d^n \mid n \geq 1\}$,
- $L_{conc}(\Gamma) = \{a^nb^nc^nd^n \mid n \geq 1\}$, and
- $L_{first}(\Gamma) = \{a^nb^nc^n \mid n \geq 1\}$.

Next, we prove that multigenerative grammar systems under all of the defined modes are equivalent to matrix grammars.

Theorem 13.26. *Let $\Gamma = (G_1, G_2, \ldots, G_n, Q)$ be an n-MGR. With Γ as its input, Algorithm 1 halts and correctly constructs a matrix grammar, $H = (G, M)$, such that $L_{union}(\Gamma) = L(H)$.*

Proof. Let $(p\colon A \to x)$ be a rule. Then, for simplicity and brevity, $\bar{p}$ denotes the rule $h(A) \to h(x)$. To prove this theorem, we first establish Claims 1 and 2.

Claim 1. Let $(S_1, S_2, \ldots, S_n) \Rightarrow_\Gamma^m (y_1, y_2, \ldots, y_n)$, where $m \geq 0, y_i \in \Sigma_i^*$, for all $i = 1, \ldots, n$. Then, $S \Rightarrow_H^{m+1} h(y_1)h(y_2) \cdots h(y_{j-1})y_jh(y_{j+1}) \cdots h(y_n)$, for any $j = 1, \ldots, n$.

Conversion of an n-MGR in the union mode to an equivalent matrix grammar.

An n-MGR, $\Gamma = (G_1, G_2, \ldots, G_n, Q)$.

A matrix grammar, $H = (G, M)$, satisfying $L_{union}(\Gamma) = L(H)$.

Let $G_i = (\Sigma_i, T_i, P_i, S_i)$, for all $i = 1, \ldots, n$, and without any loss of generality, we assume that N_1 through N_n are pairwise disjoint. Let us choose arbitrary S satisfying $S \notin \bigcup_{j=1}^{n} N_j$. Then, construct

$$G = (\Sigma, \Delta, R, S)$$

where

- $N = \{S\} \cup (\bigcup_{i=1}^{n} N_i) \cup (\bigcup_{i=1}^{n} \{\bar{A} \mid A \in N_i\})$;
- $\Delta = \bigcup_{i=1}^{n} T_i$;
- $R = \{(s_1 : S \to S_1 h(S_2) \cdots h(S_n)),$
  $(s_2 : S \to h(S_1) S_2 \cdots h(S_n)),$
  $\vdots$
  $(s_n : S \to h(S_1) h(S_2) \cdots S_n)\}$
  $\cup (\bigcup_{i=1}^{n} P_i)$
  $\cup (\bigcup_{i=1}^{n} \{h(A) \to h(x) \mid A \to x \in P_i\})$,
  where h is a homomorphism from $((\bigcup_{i=1}^{n} \Sigma_i))^*$ to $(\bigcup_{i=1}^{n} \{\bar{A} \mid A \in N_i\})^*$, defined as $h(a) = \varepsilon$, for all $a \in \bigcup_{i=1}^{n} T_i$, and $h(A) = \bar{A}$, for all $A \in \bigcup_{i=1}^{n} N_i$;
- $M = \{s_1, s_2, \ldots, s_n\}$
  $\cup \{p_1 \bar{p_2} \cdots \bar{p_n} \mid (p_1, p_2, \ldots, p_n) \in Q\}$
  $\cup \{\bar{p_1} p_2 \cdots \bar{p_n} \mid (p_1, p_2, \ldots, p_n) \in Q\}$
  $\vdots$
  $\cup \{\bar{p_1} \bar{p_2} \cdots p_n \mid (p_1, p_2, \ldots, p_n) \in Q\}$.

Proof. This claim is proved by induction on $m \geq 0$.

Basis. Let $m = 0$. Then, $(S_1, S_2, \ldots, S_n) \Rightarrow_{\Gamma}^{0} (S_1, S_2, \ldots, S_n)$. Notice that

$$S \Rightarrow_H h(S_1) h(S_2) \cdots h(S_{j-1}) S_j h(S_{j+1}) \cdots h(S_n)$$

for any $j = 1, \ldots, n$, because

$$(s_j : S \to h(S_1) h(S_2) \cdots h(S_{j-1}) S_j h(S_{j+1}) \cdots h(S_n)) \in M.$$

Induction Hypothesis. Assume that the claim holds for all m-step derivations, where $m = 0, \ldots, k$, for some $k \geq 0$.

Induction Step. Consider any derivation of the form

$$(S_1, S_2, \ldots, S_n) \Rightarrow_{\Gamma}^{k+1} (y_1, y_2, \ldots, y_n).$$

Then, there exists a sentential n-form $(u_1A_1v_1, u_2A_2v_2, \ldots, u_nA_nv_n)$, where $u_i, v_i \in \Sigma_i^*, A_i \in N_i$ such that

$$\begin{aligned}(S_1, S_2, \ldots, S_n) &\Rightarrow_\Gamma^k (u_1A_1v_1, u_2A_2v_2, \ldots, u_nA_nv_n)\\ &\Rightarrow_\Gamma (u_1x_1v_1, u_2x_2v_2, \ldots, u_nx_nv_n)\end{aligned}$$

where $u_ix_iv_i = y_i$, for all $i = 1, \ldots, n$. First, observe that

$$(S_1, S_2, \ldots, S_n) \Rightarrow_\Gamma^k (u_1A_1v_1, u_2A_2v_2, \ldots, u_nA_nv_n)$$

implies that

$$\begin{aligned}S \Rightarrow_H^{k+1}\ & h(u_1A_1v_1)h(u_2A_2v_2)\cdots h(u_{j-1}A_{j-1}v_{j-1})\\ & u_jA_jv_jh(u_{j+1}A_{j+1}v_{j+1})\cdots h(u_nA_nv_n)\end{aligned}$$

for any $j = 1, \ldots, n$ by the induction hypothesis. Furthermore, let

$$(u_1A_1v_1, u_2A_2v_2, \ldots, u_nA_nv_n) \Rightarrow_\Gamma (u_1x_1v_1, u_2x_2v_2, \ldots, u_nx_nv_n).$$

Then, $((p_1 : A_1 \to x_1), (p_2 : A_2 \to x_2), \ldots, (p_n : A_n \to x_n)) \in Q$. Algorithm 1 implies that $\bar{p_1}\bar{p_2}\cdots\bar{p_{j-1}}p_j\bar{p_{j+1}}\cdots\bar{p_n} \in M$, for any $j = 1, \ldots, n$. Hence,

$$\begin{aligned}& h(u_1A_1v_1)h(u_2A_2v_2)\cdots h(u_{j-1}A_{j-1}v_{j-1})u_jA_jv_jh(u_{j+1}A_{j+1}v_{j+1})\cdots h(u_nA_nv_n) \Rightarrow_H\\ & \quad h(u_1x_1v_1)h(u_2x_2v_2)\cdots h(u_{j-1}x_{j-1}v_{j-1})u_jx_jv_jh(u_{j+1}x_{j+1}v_{j+1})\cdots h(u_nx_nv_n)\end{aligned}$$

by matrix $\bar{p_1}\bar{p_2}\cdots\bar{p_{j-1}}p_j\bar{p_{j+1}}\cdots\bar{p_n}$, for any $j = 1, \ldots, n$. As a result, we obtain

$$\begin{aligned}S \Rightarrow_H^{k+2}\ & h(u_1x_1v_1)h(u_2x_2v_2)\cdots h(u_{j-1}x_{j-1}v_{j-1})\\ & u_jx_jv_jh(u_{j+1}x_{j+1}v_{j+1})\cdots h(u_nx_nv_n)\end{aligned}$$

for any $j = 1, \ldots, n$. □

Claim 2. Let $S \Rightarrow_H^m y$, where $m \geq 1, y \in \Sigma^*$. Then, there exist $j \in \{1, \ldots, n\}$ and $y_i \in \Sigma_i^*$, for $i = 1, \ldots, n$, such that

$$(S_1, \ldots, S_n) \Rightarrow_\Gamma^{m-1} (y_1, \ldots, y_n)$$

and

$$y = h(y_1)\cdots h(y_{j-1})y_jh(y_{j+1})\cdots h(y_n).$$

Proof. This claim is proved by induction on $m \geq 1$.

Basis. Let $m = 1$. Then, there exists exactly one of the following one-step derivations in H:

$S \Rightarrow_H S_1h(S_2)\cdots h(S_n)$ by matrix s_1, or

$S \Rightarrow_H h(S_1)S_2\cdots h(S_n)$ by matrix s_2, or

$\ldots$, or

$S \Rightarrow_H h(S_1)h(S_2)\cdots S_n$ by matrix s_n.

Notice that trivially $(S_1, S_2, \ldots, S_n) \Rightarrow_\Gamma^0 (S_1, S_2, \ldots, S_n)$.

Induction Hypothesis. Assume that the claim holds for all m-step derivations, where $m = 1, \ldots, k$, for some $k \geq 1$.

Induction Step. Consider any derivation of the form

$$S \Rightarrow_H^{k+1} y.$$

Then, there exists a sentential form w such that

$$S \Rightarrow_H^k w \Rightarrow_H y$$

where $w, y \in (N \cup \Delta)^*$. As $w \Rightarrow_H y$, this derivation step can use only a matrix of the form $\bar{p}_1\bar{p}_2 \cdots \bar{p}_{j-1}p_j\bar{p}_{j+1} \cdots \bar{p}_n \in Q$, where p_j is a rule from P_j and $\bar{p}_i \in h(P_i)$, for $i = 1, \ldots, j-1, j+1, \ldots, n$. Hence, $w \Rightarrow_H y$ can be written as

$$h(w_i) \cdots h(w_{j-1})w_jh(w_{j+1}) \cdots h(w_n) \Rightarrow_H z_1 \cdots z_n$$

where $w_j \Rightarrow_H z_j$ by the rule p_j and $h(w_i) \Rightarrow_H z_i$ by $\bar{p}_i$, for $i = 1, \ldots, j-1, j+1, \ldots, n$. Each rule $\bar{p}_i$ rewrites a barred nonterminal $\bar{A}_i \in h(N_i)$. Of course, then each rule p_i can be used to rewrite the respective occurrence of a non-barred nonterminal A_i in w_i in such a way that $w_i \Rightarrow_H y_i$ and $h(y_i) = z_i$, for all $i = 1, \ldots, j-1, j+1, \ldots, n$. By setting $y_j = z_j$, we obtain

$$(w_1, \ldots, w_n) \Rightarrow_\Gamma (y_1, \ldots, y_n)$$

and $y = h(y_1) \cdots h(y_{j-1})y_jh(y_{j+1}) \cdots h(y_n)$. As a result, we obtain

$$(S_1, S_2, \ldots, S_{j-1}, S_j, S_{j+1}, \ldots, S_n) \Rightarrow_\Gamma^k$$
$$(u_1x_1v_1, u_2x_2v_2, \ldots, u_{j-1}x_{j-1}v_{j-1}, u_jx_jv_j, u_{j+1}x_{j+1}v_{j+1}, \ldots, u_nx_nv_n),$$

so $y = u_1x_1v_1u_2x_2v_2 \cdots u_{j-1}x_{j-1}v_{j-1}u_jx_jv_ju_{j+1}x_{j+1}v_{j+1} \cdots u_nx_nv_n$. □

Consider Claim 1 for $y_i \in T_i^*$, for all $i = 1, \ldots, n$. Notice that $h(a) = \varepsilon$, for all $a \in T_i$. We obtain an implication of the form

if $(S_1, S_2, \ldots, S_n) \Rightarrow_\Gamma^* (y_1, y_2, \ldots, y_n)$,
then $S \Rightarrow_H^* y_j$, for any $j = 1, \ldots, n$.

Hence, $L_{union}(\Gamma) \subseteq L(H)$. Consider Claim 1 for $y \in \Delta^*$. Notice that $h(a) = \varepsilon$, for all $a \in T_i$. We obtain an implication of the form

if $S \Rightarrow_H^* y$,
then $(S_1, S_2, \ldots, S_n) \Rightarrow_\Gamma^* (y_1, y_2, \ldots, y_n)$,

and there exist an index $j = 1, \ldots, n$ such that $y = y_j$. Hence, $L(H) \subseteq L_{union}(\Gamma)$. □

Theorem 13.27. *Let* $\Gamma = (G_1, G_2, \ldots, G_n, Q)$ *be an n-MGR. On input* Γ, *Algorithm 2 halts and correctly constructs a matrix grammar,* $H = (G, M)$, *such that* $L_{conc}(\Gamma) = L(H)$.

Proof. To prove this theorem, we first establish Claims 1 and 2.

Claim 1. Let $(S_1, S_2, \ldots, S_n) \Rightarrow_\Gamma^m (y_1, y_2, \ldots, y_n)$, where $m \geq 0, y_i \in \Sigma_i^*$, for all $i = 1, \ldots, n$. Then, $S \Rightarrow_H^{m+1} y_1y_2 \cdots y_n$.

Conversion of an n-MGR in the concatenation mode to an equivalent matrix grammar.
An n-MGR, $\Gamma = (G_1, G_2, \ldots, G_n, Q)$.
A matrix grammar, $H = (G, M)$, satisfying $L_{conc}(\Gamma) = L(H)$.
Let $G_i = (\Sigma_i, T_i, P_i, S_i)$, for all $i = 1, \ldots, n$, and without any loss of generality, we assume that N_1 through N_n are pairwise disjoint. Let us choose arbitrary S satisfying $S \notin \bigcup_{j=1}^{n} N_j$. Construct

$$G = (\Sigma, \Delta, R, S)$$

where

- $N = \{S\} \cup (\bigcup_{i=1}^{n} N_i)$;
- $\Delta = \bigcup_{i=1}^{n} T_i$;
- $R = \{(s\colon S \to S_1S_2 \cdots S_n)\} \cup (\bigcup_{i=1}^{n} P_i)$.

Finally, set $M = \{s\} \cup \{p_1p_2 \cdots p_n \mid (p_1, p_2, \ldots, p_n) \in Q\}$.

Proof. This claim is proved by induction on $m \geq 0$.

Basis. Let $m = 0$. Then, $(S_1, S_2, \ldots, S_n) \Rightarrow_{\Gamma}^{0} (S_1, S_2, \ldots, S_n)$. Notice that $S \Rightarrow_H S_1S_2 \cdots S_n$, because $(s\colon S \to S_1S_2 \cdots S_n) \in M$.

Induction Hypothesis. Assume that the claim holds for all m-step derivations, where $m = 0, \ldots, k$, for some $k \geq 0$.

Induction Step. Consider any derivation of the form

$$(S_1, S_2, \ldots, S_n) \Rightarrow_{\Gamma}^{k+1} (y_1, y_2, \ldots, y_n).$$

Then, there exists a sentential n-form $(u_1A_1v_1, u_2A_2v_2, \ldots, u_nA_nv_n)$, where $u_i, v_i \in \Sigma_i^*, A_i \in N_i$ such that

$$\begin{aligned}(S_1, S_2, \ldots, S_n) &\Rightarrow_{\Gamma}^{k} (u_1A_1v_1, u_2A_2v_2, \ldots, u_nA_nv_n)\\ &\Rightarrow_{\Gamma} (u_1x_1v_1, u_2x_2v_2, \ldots, u_nx_nv_n)\end{aligned}$$

where $u_ix_iv_i = y_i$, for all $i = 1, \ldots, n$. First, observe that

$$(S_1, S_2, \ldots, S_n) \Rightarrow_{\Gamma}^{k} (u_1A_1v_1, u_2A_2v_2, \ldots, u_nA_nv_n)$$

implies that

$$S \Rightarrow_{H}^{k+1} u_1A_1v_1u_2A_2v_2 \cdots u_nA_nv_n$$

by the induction hypothesis. Furthermore, let

$$(u_1A_1v_1, u_2A_2v_2, \ldots, u_nA_nv_n) \Rightarrow_{\Gamma} (u_1x_1v_1, u_2x_2v_2, \ldots, u_nx_nv_n).$$

Then, it holds that $((p_1: A_1 \to x_1), (p_2: A_2 \to x_2), \ldots, (p_n: A_n \to x_n)) \in Q$. Algorithm 2 implies that $p_1p_2 \cdots p_n \in M$. Hence,

$$u_1A_1v_1u_2A_2v_2 \cdots u_nA_nv_n \Rightarrow_H \\ u_1x_1v_1u_2x_2v_2 \cdots u_nx_nv_n$$

by matrix $p_1p_2 \cdots p_n$. As a result, we obtain

$$S \Rightarrow_H^{k+2} u_1x_1v_1u_2x_2v_2 \cdots u_nx_nv_n.$$ □

Claim 2. Let $S \Rightarrow_H^m y$, where $m \geq 1, y \in \Sigma^*$. Then, $(S_1, S_2, \ldots, S_n) \Rightarrow_\Gamma^{m-1} (y_1, y_2, \ldots, y_n)$ such that $y = y_1y_2 \cdots y_n$, where $y_i \in \Sigma_i^*$, for all $i = 1, \ldots, n$.

Proof. This claim is proved by induction on $m \geq 1$.

Basis. Let $m = 1$. Then, there exists exactly one one-step derivation in H: $S \Rightarrow_H S_1S_2 \cdots S_n$ by matrix s. Notice that $(S_1, S_2, \ldots, S_n) \Rightarrow_\Gamma^0 (S_1, S_2, \ldots, S_n)$ trivially.

Induction Hypothesis. Assume that the claim holds for all m-step derivations, where $m = 1, \ldots, k$, for some $k \geq 1$.

Induction Step. Consider any derivation of the form

$$S \Rightarrow_H^{k+1} y.$$

Then, there exists a sentential form w such that

$$S \Rightarrow_H^k w \Rightarrow_H y$$

where $w, y \in \Sigma^*$. First, observe that $S \Rightarrow_H^k w$ implies that

$$(S_1, S_2, \ldots, S_n) \Rightarrow_\Gamma^{k-1} (w_1, w_2, \ldots, w_n)$$

and $w = w_1w_2 \cdots w_n$, where $w_i \in \Sigma_i^*$, for all $i = 1, \ldots, n$, by the induction hypothesis. Furthermore, let $w \Rightarrow_H y$ by matrix $p_1p_2 \cdots p_n \in M$, where $w = w_1w_2 \cdots w_n$. Let p_i be a rule of the form $A_i \to x_i$. The rule p_i can be applied only inside substring w_i, for all $i = 1, \ldots, n$. Assume that $w_i = u_iA_iv_i$, where $u_i, v_i \in \Sigma^*, A_i \in N_i$, for all $i = 1, \ldots, n$. There exist a derivation step

$$u_1A_1v_1u_2A_2v_2 \cdots u_nA_nv_n \Rightarrow_H \\ u_1x_1v_1u_2x_2v_2 \cdots u_nx_nv_n$$

by matrix $p_1p_2 \cdots p_n \in M$. Algorithm 2 implies that

$$((p_1: A_1 \to x_1), (p_2: A_2 \to x_2), \ldots, (p_n: A_n \to x_n)) \in Q,$$

because $p_1p_2 \cdots p_n \in M$. Hence,

$$(u_1A_1v_1, u_2A_2v_2, \ldots, u_nA_nv_n \Rightarrow_\Gamma \\ (u_1x_1v_1, u_2x_2v_2, \ldots, u_nx_nv_n).$$

As a result, we obtain

$$(S_1, S_2, \ldots, S_n) \Rightarrow_\Gamma^k (u_1x_1v_1, u_2x_2v_2, \ldots, u_nx_nv_n)$$

and $y = u_1x_1v_1u_2x_2v_2 \cdots u_nx_nv_n$. □

Consider Claim 1 for $y_i \in T_i^*$, for all $i = 1, \ldots, n$. We obtain an implication of the form

$$\text{if } (S_1, S_2, \ldots, S_n) \Rightarrow_\Gamma^* (y_1, y_2, \ldots, y_n),$$
$$\text{then } S \Rightarrow_H^* y_1y_2 \cdots y_n.$$

Hence, $L_{conc}(\Gamma) \subseteq L(H)$. Consider Claim 2 for $y \in \Delta^*$. We obtain an implication of the form

$$\text{if } S \Rightarrow_H^* y, \text{then } (S_1, S_2, \ldots, S_n) \Rightarrow_\Gamma^* (y_1, y_2, \ldots, y_n), \text{ with } y = y_1y_2 \cdots y_n.$$

Hence, $L(H) \subseteq L_{conc}(\Gamma)$. □

Conversion of an n-MGR in the first mode to an equivalent matrix grammar.

An n-MGR, $\Gamma = (G_1, G_2, \ldots, G_n, Q)$.

A matrix grammar, $H = (G, M)$, satisfying $L_{first}(\Gamma) = L(H)$.

Let $G_i = (\Sigma_i, T_i, P_i, S_i)$, for all $i = 1, \ldots, n$, and without any loss of generality, we assume that N_1 through N_n are pairwise disjoint. Let us choose arbitrary S satisfying $S \notin \bigcup_{j=1}^{n} N_j$. Construct

$$G = (\Sigma, \Delta, R, S)$$

where

- $N = \{S\} \cup N_1 \cup (\bigcup_{i=2}^{n} \{\bar{A} : A \in N_i\})$;
- $\Delta = T_1$;
- $R = \{(s : S \rightarrow S_1h(S_2) \cdots h(S_n))\} \cup P_1$
  $\cup (\bigcup_{i=2}^{n} \{h(A) \rightarrow h(x) \mid A \rightarrow x \in P_i\})$,
  where h is a homomorphism from $((\bigcup_{i=2}^{n} \Sigma_i))^*$ to $(\bigcup_{i=2}^{n} \{\bar{A} \mid A \in N_i\})^*$ defined as $h(a) = \varepsilon$, for all $a \in \bigcup_{i=2}^{n} T_i$ and $h(A) = \bar{A}$, for all $A \in \bigcup_{i=2}^{n} N_i$.

Finally, set $M = \{s\} \cup \{p_1\bar{p_2} \cdots \bar{p_n} \mid (p_1, p_2, \ldots, p_n) \in Q\}$.

Theorem 13.28. *Let $\Gamma = (G_1, G_2, \ldots, G_n, Q)$ be an n-MGR. With Γ as its input, Algorithm 3 halts and correctly constructs a matrix grammar, $H = (G, M)$, such that $L_{first}(\Gamma) = L(H)$.*

Proof. Let $(p : A \rightarrow x)$ be a rule. Then, for simplicity and brevity, $\bar{p}$ denotes the rule $h(A) \rightarrow h(x)$. To prove this theorem, we first establish Claims 1 and 2.

Claim 1. Let $(S_1, S_2, \ldots, S_n) \Rightarrow_\Gamma^m (y_1, y_2, \ldots, y_n)$, where $m \geq 0$, $y_i \in \Sigma_i^*$, for all $i = 1, \ldots, n$. Then, $S \Rightarrow_H^{m+1} y_1h(y_2) \cdots h(y_n)$.

Proof. This claim is proved by induction on $m \geq 0$.

Basis. Let $m = 0$. Then, $(S_1, S_2, \ldots, S_n) \Rightarrow_\Gamma^0 (S_1, S_2, \ldots, S_n)$. Notice that $S \Rightarrow_H S_1h(S_2)\cdots h(S_n)$, because $(s\colon S \to S_1h(S_2)\cdots h(S_n)) \in M$.

Induction Hypothesis. Assume that the claim holds for all m-step derivations, where $m = 0, \ldots, k$, for some $k \geq 0$.

Induction Step. Consider any derivation of the form

$$(S_1, S_2, \ldots, S_n) \Rightarrow_\Gamma^{k+1} (y_1, y_2, \ldots, y_n).$$

Then, there exists a sentential n-form $(u_1A_1v_1, u_2A_2v_2, \ldots, u_nA_nv_n)$, where $u_i, v_i \in \Sigma_i^*, A_i \in N_i$ such that

$$\begin{aligned}(S_1, S_2, \ldots, S_n) &\Rightarrow_\Gamma^k (u_1A_1v_1, u_2A_2v_2, \ldots, u_nA_nv_n)\\ &\Rightarrow_\Gamma (u_1x_1v_1, u_2x_2v_2, \ldots, u_nx_nv_n)\end{aligned}$$

where $u_ix_iv_i = y_i$, for all $i = 1, \ldots, n$. First, observe that

$$(S_1, S_2, \ldots, S_n) \Rightarrow_\Gamma^k (u_1A_1v_1, u_2A_2v_2, \ldots, u_nA_nv_n)$$

implies that

$$S \Rightarrow_H^{k+1} u_1A_1v_1h(u_2A_2v_2)\cdots h(u_nA_nv_n)$$

by the induction hypothesis. Furthermore, let

$$\begin{aligned}&(u_1A_1v_1, u_2A_2v_2, \ldots, u_nA_nv_n) \Rightarrow_\Gamma\\ &\quad (u_1x_1v_1, u_2x_2v_2, \ldots, u_nx_nv_n).\end{aligned}$$

Then, it holds $((p_1\colon A_1 \to x_1), (p_2\colon A_2 \to x_2), \ldots, (p_n\colon A_n \to x_n)) \in Q$. Algorithm 3 implies that $p_1\bar{p_2}\cdots\bar{p_n} \in M$. Hence,

$$\begin{aligned}&u_1A_1v_1h(u_2A_2v_2)\cdots h(u_nA_nv_n) \Rightarrow_H\\ &\quad u_1x_1v_1h(u_2x_2v_2)\cdots h(u_nx_nv_n)\end{aligned}$$

by matrix $p_1\bar{p_2}\cdots\bar{p_n}$. As a result, we obtain

$$S \Rightarrow_H^{k+2} u_1x_1v_1h(u_2x_2v_2)\cdots h(u_nx_nv_n).$$ □

Claim 2. Let $S \Rightarrow_H^m y$, where $m \geq 1, y \in \Sigma^*$. Then, $(S_1, S_2, \ldots, S_n) \Rightarrow_\Gamma^{m-1} (y_1, y_2, \ldots, y_n)$, where $y_i \in \Sigma_i^*$, for all $i = 1, \ldots, n$ so that $y = y_1h(y_2)\cdots h(y_n)$.

Proof. This claim is proved by induction on $m \geq 1$.

Basis. Let $m = 1$. Then, there exists exactly one one-step derivation in H: $S \Rightarrow_H S_1h(S_2)\cdots h(S_n)$ by matrix s. Notice that $(S_1, S_2, \ldots, S_n) \Rightarrow_\Gamma^0 (S_1, S_2, \ldots, S_n)$ trivially.

Induction Hypothesis. Assume that the claim holds for all m-step derivations, where $m = 1, \ldots, k$, for some $k \geq 1$.

Induction Step. Consider any derivation of the form

$$S \Rightarrow_H^{k+1} y.$$

Then, there is w such that

$$S \Rightarrow_H^k w \Rightarrow_H y$$

where $w, y \in \Sigma^*$. First, observe that $S \Rightarrow_H^k w$ implies that

$$(S_1, S_2, \ldots, S_n) \Rightarrow_\Gamma^{k-1} (w_1, w_2, \ldots, w_n)$$

and $w = w_1 h(w_2) \cdots h(w_n)$, where $w_i \in \Sigma_i^*$, for all $i = 1, \ldots, n$, by the induction hypothesis. Furthermore, let $w \Rightarrow_H y$, where $w = w_1 h(w_2) \cdots h(w_n)$. Let p_1 be a rule of the form $A_1 \to x_1$. Let $\bar{p_i}$ be a rule of the form $h(A_i) \to h(x)$, for all $i = 2, \ldots, n$. The rule p_1 can be applied only inside substring w_1, the rule $\bar{p_i}$ can be applied only inside substring w_i, for all $i = 2, \ldots, n$. Assume that $w_i = u_i A_i v_i$, where $u_i, v_i \in \Sigma_i^*, A_i \in N_i$, for all $i = 1, \ldots, n$. There exists a derivation step

$$\begin{aligned}&u_1 A_1 v_1 h(u_2 A_2 v_2) \cdots h(u_n A_n v_n) \Rightarrow_H \\ &\quad u_1 x_1 v_1 h(u_2 x_2 v_2) \cdots h(u_n x_n v_n)\end{aligned}$$

by matrix $p_1 \bar{p_2} \cdots \bar{p_n} \in M$. Algorithm 3 implies that

$$((p_1 \colon A_1 \to x_1), (p_2 \colon A_2 \to x_2), \ldots, (p_n \colon A_n \to x_n)) \in Q$$

because $p_1 \bar{p_2} \cdots \bar{p_n} \in M$. Hence,

$$\begin{aligned}&(u_1 A_1 v_1, u_2 A_2 v_2, \ldots, u_n A_n v_n) \Rightarrow_\Gamma \\ &\quad (u_1 x_1 v_1, u_2 x_2 v_2, \ldots, u_n x_n v_n).\end{aligned}$$

As a result, we obtain

$$(S_1, S_2, \ldots, S_n) \Rightarrow_\Gamma^k (u_1 x_1 v_1, u_2 x_2 v_2, \ldots, u_n x_n v_n)$$

and $y = u_1 x_1 v_1 h(u_2 x_2 v_2) \cdots h(u_n x_n v_n)$. □

Consider Claim 1 for $y_i \in T_i^*$, for all $i = 1, \ldots, n$. Notice that $h(a) = \varepsilon$, for all $a \in T_i$. We obtain an implication of the form

if $(S_1, S_2, \ldots, S_n) \Rightarrow_\Gamma^* (y_1, y_2, \ldots, y_n)$,
then $S \Rightarrow_H^* y_1$.

Hence, $L_{first}(\Gamma) \subseteq L(H)$. Consider Claim 2 for $y \in \Delta^*$. Notice that $h(a) = \varepsilon$, for all $a \in T_i$. We obtain an implication of the form

if $S \Rightarrow_H^* y$,
then $(S_1, S_2, \ldots, S_n) \Rightarrow_\Gamma^* (y_1, y_2, \ldots, y_n)$, such that $y = y_1$.

Hence, $L(H) \subseteq L_{first}(\Gamma)$. Therefore, $L(H) = L_{first}(\Gamma)$. □

Theorem 13.29. *Let H be a matrix grammar and $\bar{w}$ be a string. With H and $\bar{w}$ as its input, Algorithm 4 halts and correctly constructs a 2-MGR, $\Gamma = (G_1, G_2, Q)$, such that $\{w_1 \mid (w_1, \bar{w}) \in 2\text{-}L(\Gamma)\} = L(H)$.*

Proof. To prove this theorem, we first establish Claims 1–4.

Conversion of a matrix grammar to an equivalent 2-MGR.

A matrix grammar, $H = (G, M)$, and a string, $\bar{w} \in \bar{\Delta}^*$, where $\bar{\Delta}$ is any alphabet.
A 2-MGR, $\Gamma = (G_1, G_2, Q)$, satisfying $\{w_1 \mid (w_1, \bar{w}) \in 2\text{-}L(\Gamma)\} = L(H)$.
Let $G = (\Sigma, \Delta, R, S)$. Then, set $G_1 = G$ and construct

$$G_2 = (\Sigma_2, T_2, P_2, S_2)$$

where

- $N_2 = \{\langle p_1p_2 \cdots p_k, j\rangle \mid p_1, \ldots, p_k \in R, p_1p_2 \cdots p_k \in M, 1 \leq j \leq k-1\} \cup \{S_2\}$;
- $T_2 = \bar{\Delta}$;
- $P_2 = \{S_2 \rightarrow \langle p_1p_2 \cdots p_k, 1\rangle \mid p_1, \ldots, p_k \in R, p_1p_2 \cdots p_k \in M, k \geq 2\}$
  $\cup \{\langle p_1p_2 \cdots p_k, j\rangle \rightarrow \langle p_1p_2 \cdots p_k, j+1\rangle \mid p_1p_2 \cdots p_k \in M, k \geq 2, 1 \leq j \leq k-2\}$
  $\cup \{\langle p_1p_2 \cdots p_k, k-1\rangle \rightarrow S_2 \mid p_1, \ldots, p_k \in R, p_1p_2 \cdots p_k \in M, k \geq 2\}$
  $\cup \{S_2 \rightarrow S_2 \mid p_1 \in M, |p_1| = 1\}$
  $\cup \{\langle p_1p_2 \cdots p_k, k-1\rangle \rightarrow \bar{w} \mid p_1, \ldots, p_k \in R, p_1p_2 \cdots p_k \in M, k \geq 2\}$
  $\cup \{S_2 \rightarrow \bar{w} \mid p_1 \in M, |p_1| = 1\}$;
- $Q = \{(p_1, S_2 \rightarrow \langle p_1p_2 \cdots p_k, 1\rangle) \mid p_1, \ldots, p_k \in R, p_1p_2 \cdots p_k \in M, k \geq 2\}$
  $\cup \{(p_{j+1}, \langle p_1p_2 \cdots p_k, j\rangle \rightarrow \langle p_1p_2 \cdots p_k, j+1\rangle) \mid p_1p_2 \cdots p_k \in M, k \geq 2, 1 \leq j \leq k-2\}$
  $\cup \{(p_k, \langle p_1p_2 \cdots p_k, k-1\rangle \rightarrow S_2) \mid p_1, \ldots, p_k \in R, p_1p_2 \cdots p_k \in M, k \geq 2\}$
  $\cup \{(p_1, S_2 \rightarrow S_2) \mid p_1 \in M, |p_1| = 1\}$
  $\cup \{(p_k, \langle p_1p_2 \cdots p_k, k-1\rangle \rightarrow \bar{w}) \mid p_1, \ldots, p_k \in R, p_1p_2 \cdots p_k \in M, k \geq 2\}$
  $\cup \{(p_1, S_2 \rightarrow \bar{w}) \mid p_1 \in M, |p_1| = 1\}$.

Claim 1. Let $x \Rightarrow_H y$, where $x, y \in \Sigma^*$. Then, $(x, S_2) \Rightarrow_\Gamma^* (y, S_2)$ and $(x, S_2) \Rightarrow_\Gamma^* (y, \bar{w})$.

Proof. In this proof, we distinguish two cases—(I) and (II). In (I), we consider any derivation step of the form $x \Rightarrow_H y$ by a matrix consisting of a single rule. In (II), we consider $x \Rightarrow_H y$ by a matrix consisting of several rules.

(I) Consider any derivation step of the form $x \Rightarrow_H y$ by a matrix which contains only one rule $(p_1\colon A_1 \rightarrow x_1)$. It implies that $uA_1v \Rightarrow_G ux_1v\ [p_1]$, where $uA_1v = x, ux_1v = y$. Algorithm 4 implies that $(A_1 \rightarrow x_1, S_2 \rightarrow S_2) \in Q$ and $(A_1 \rightarrow x_1, S_2 \rightarrow \bar{w}) \in Q$. Hence, $(uA_1v, S_2) \Rightarrow_\Gamma (ux_1v, S_2)$ and $(uA_1v, S_2) \Rightarrow_\Gamma (ux_1v, \bar{w})$;

(II) Let $x \Rightarrow_H y$ by a matrix of the form $p_1p_2 \cdots p_k$, where $p_i, \ldots, p_k \in R, k \geq 2$. It implies that

$$\begin{aligned} x &\Rightarrow_H y_1 && [p_1] \\ &\Rightarrow_H y_2 && [p_2] \\ &\vdots \\ &\Rightarrow_H y_{k-1} && [p_{k-1}] \\ &\Rightarrow_H y_k && [p_k] \end{aligned}$$

where $y_k = y$. Algorithm 4 implies that

- $(p_1, S_2 \rightarrow \langle p_1p_2 \cdots p_k, 1\rangle) \in Q$,
- $(p_{j+1}, \langle p_1p_2 \cdots p_k, j\rangle \rightarrow \langle p_1p_2 \cdots p_k, j+1\rangle) \in Q$, where $j = 1, \ldots, k-2$,
- $(p_k, \langle p_1p_2 \cdots p_k, k-1\rangle \rightarrow S_2) \in Q$,
- $(p_k, \langle p_1p_2 \cdots p_k, k-1\rangle \rightarrow \bar{w}) \in Q$.

Hence,

$$\begin{aligned} (x, S_2) &\Rightarrow_\Gamma (y_1, \langle p_1p_2 \cdots p_k, 1\rangle) \\ &\Rightarrow_\Gamma (y_2, \langle p_1p_2 \cdots p_k, 2\rangle) \\ &\vdots \\ &\Rightarrow_\Gamma (y_{k-1}, \langle p_1p_2 \cdots p_k, k-1\rangle) \\ &\Rightarrow_\Gamma (y_k, S_2) \end{aligned}$$

and

$$\begin{aligned} (x, S_2) &\Rightarrow_\Gamma (y_1, \langle p_1p_2 \cdots p_k, 1\rangle) \\ &\Rightarrow_\Gamma (y_2, \langle p_1p_2 \cdots p_k, 2\rangle) \\ &\vdots \\ &\Rightarrow_\Gamma (y_{k-1}, \langle p_1p_2 \cdots p_k, k-1\rangle) \\ &\Rightarrow_\Gamma (y_k, \bar{w}) \end{aligned}$$

where $y_k = y$. □

Claim 1. Let $x \Rightarrow_H^m y$, where $m \geq 1, y \in \Sigma^*$. Then, $(x, S_2) \Rightarrow_\Gamma^* (y, \bar{w})$.

Proof. This claim is proved by induction on $m \geq 1$.

Basis. Let $m = 1$ and let $x \Rightarrow_H y$. Claim 1 implies that $(x, S_2) \Rightarrow_\Gamma^* (y, \bar{w})$.

Induction Hypothesis. Assume that the claim holds for all m-step derivations, where $m = 1, \ldots, k$, for some $k \geq 1$.

Induction Step. Consider any derivation of the form

$$S \Rightarrow_H^{k+1} y.$$

Then, there exists w such that

$$S \Rightarrow_H w \Rightarrow_H^k y$$

where $w, y \in \Sigma^*$. First, observe that $w \Rightarrow_H^k y$ implies that

$$(w, S_2) \Rightarrow_\Gamma^* (y, \bar{w})$$

by the induction hypothesis. Furthermore, let $x \Rightarrow_H w$. Claim 1 implies that

$$(x, S_2) \Rightarrow_\Gamma^* (w, S_2).$$

As a result, we obtain

$$(x, S_2) \Rightarrow_\Gamma^* (y, \bar{w}).$$

□

Claim 3. Let

$$\begin{aligned} (y_0, S_2) &\Rightarrow_\Gamma (y_1, z_1) \\ &\Rightarrow_\Gamma (y_2, z_2) \\ &\vdots \\ &\Rightarrow_\Gamma (y_{k-1}, z_{k-1}) \\ &\Rightarrow_\Gamma (y_k, S_2) \end{aligned} \quad \text{or} \quad \begin{aligned} (y_0, S_2) &\Rightarrow_\Gamma (y_1, z_1) \\ &\Rightarrow_\Gamma (y_2, z_2) \\ &\vdots \\ &\Rightarrow_\Gamma (y_{k-1}, z_{k-1}) \\ &\Rightarrow_\Gamma (y_k, \bar{w}) \end{aligned}$$

where $z_i \neq S_2$, for all $i = 1, \ldots, k-1$. Then, there exists a direct derivation step $y_0 \Rightarrow_H y_k$.

Proof. In this proof, we distinguish two cases—(I) and (II) In (I), we consider any derivation step of the form $x \Rightarrow_H y$ by a matrix consisting of a single rule. In (II), we consider $x \Rightarrow_H y$ by a matrix consisting of several rules.

(I) Consider any derivation step of the form

$$(uA_1v, S_2) \Rightarrow_\Gamma (ux_1v, S_2)$$

or

$$(uA_1v, S_2) \Rightarrow_\Gamma (ux_1v, \bar{w})$$

where $uA_1v = y_0, ux_1v = y_1$. Then, $(A_1 \to x_1, S_2 \to S_2) \in Q$ or $(A_1 \to x_1, S_2 \to \bar{w}) \in Q$. Algorithm 4 implies that there exists a matrix of the form $(p_1 \colon A_1 \to x_1) \in M$. Hence,

$$uA_1v \Rightarrow_H ux_1v;$$

(II) Let

$$\begin{aligned} (y_0, S_2) &\Rightarrow_\Gamma (y_1, z_1) \\ &\Rightarrow_\Gamma (y_2, z_2) \\ &\vdots \\ &\Rightarrow_\Gamma (y_{k-1}, z_{k-1}) \\ &\Rightarrow_\Gamma (y_k, S_2) \end{aligned} \quad \text{or} \quad \begin{aligned} (y_0, S_2) &\Rightarrow_\Gamma (y_1, z_1) \\ &\Rightarrow_\Gamma (y_2, z_2) \\ &\vdots \\ &\Rightarrow_\Gamma (y_{k-1}, z_{k-1}) \\ &\Rightarrow_\Gamma (y_k, \bar{w}) \end{aligned}$$

where $z_i \neq S_2$, for all $i = 1, \ldots, k-1$ and $k \geq 2$. Algorithm 4 implies that there exists a matrix $p_1p_2 \cdots p_k \in M$ and that $z_i = \langle p_1p_2 \cdots p_k, i\rangle$, for all $i = 1, \ldots, k-1$. Hence,

$$y_0 \Rightarrow_H y_k.$$

□

Claim 4. Let

$$\begin{aligned}(y_0, S_2) &\Rightarrow_\Gamma (y_1, z_1)\\ &\Rightarrow_\Gamma (y_2, z_2)\\ &\vdots\\ &\Rightarrow_\Gamma (y_{r-1}, z_{r-1})\\ &\Rightarrow_\Gamma (y_r, \bar{w}).\end{aligned}$$

Set $m = \text{card}(\{i \mid 1 \leq i \leq r-1, z_i = S_2\})$. Then, $y_0 \Rightarrow_H^{m+1} y_r$.

Proof. This claim is proved by induction on $m \geq 0$.

Basis. Let $m = 0$. Then, $z_i \neq S_2$, for all $i = 1, \ldots, k-1$. Claim 3 implies that there exists a derivation step $y_0 \Rightarrow_H y_r$.

Induction Hypothesis. Assume that the claim holds for all m-step derivations, where $m = 0, \ldots, k$, for some $k \geq 0$.

Induction Step. Consider any derivation of the form

$$\begin{aligned}(y_0, S_2) &\Rightarrow_\Gamma (y_1, z_1)\\ &\Rightarrow_\Gamma (y_2, z_2)\\ &\vdots\\ &\Rightarrow_\Gamma (y_{r-1}, z_{r-1})\\ &\Rightarrow_\Gamma (y_r, \bar{w})\end{aligned}$$

where $\text{card}(\{i \mid 1 \leq i \leq r-1, z_i = S_2\}) = k+1$. Then, there exists $p \in \{1, \ldots, r-1\}$ such that $z_p = S_2$, $\text{card}(\{i \mid 1 \leq i \leq p-1, z_i = S_2\}) = 0$, $\text{card}(\{i \mid p+1 \leq i \leq r-1, z_i = S_2\}) = k$, and

$$\begin{aligned}(y_0, z_0) &\rightarrow_\Gamma (y_1, z_1)\\ &\vdots\\ &\Rightarrow_\Gamma (y_p, z_p)\\ &\vdots\\ &\Rightarrow_\Gamma (y_{r-1}, z_{r-1})\\ &\Rightarrow_\Gamma (y_r, \bar{w}).\end{aligned}$$

First, observe that from

$$\begin{aligned}(y_p, z_p) &\Rightarrow_\Gamma (y_{p+1}, z_{p+1})\\ &\vdots\\ &\Rightarrow_\Gamma (y_{r-1}, z_{r-1})\\ &\Rightarrow_\Gamma (y_r, \bar{w})\end{aligned}$$

where $z_p = S_2$ and $\text{card}(\{i \mid p+1 \leq i \leq r-1, z_i = S_2\}) = k$, it follows that

$$y_p \Rightarrow_H^{k+1} y_r$$

by the induction hypothesis. Furthermore, let

$$\begin{aligned}(y_0, z_0) &\Rightarrow_\Gamma (y_1, z_1)\\ &\vdots\\ &\Rightarrow_\Gamma (y_p, z_p)\end{aligned}$$

where $\text{card}(\{i \mid 1 \le i \le p-1, z_i = S_2\}) = 0$ implies that $z_i \neq S_2$, for all $i = 1, \ldots, p-1$. Claim 3 implies that there exists a derivation step $y_0 \Rightarrow_H y_p$. As a result, we obtain

$$y_0 \Rightarrow_H^{k+2} y_r. \qquad \square$$

We next prove the following two identities, (1) and (2).

(1) $\{w_1 \mid (w_1, \bar{w}) \in 2\text{-}L(\Gamma)\} = L(H)$. Consider Claim 1 for $x = S$ and $y \in \Delta^*$. We obtain an implication of the form

if $S \Rightarrow_H^* y$,
then $(S, S_2) \Rightarrow_\Gamma^* (y, \bar{w})$.

Hence, $L(H) \subseteq \{w_1 \mid (w_1, \bar{w}) \in 2\text{-}L(\Gamma)\}$. Consider Claim 4 for $y_0 = S$ and $y_r \in \Delta^*$. We see that

if $(S, S_2) \Rightarrow_\Gamma^* (y_r, \bar{w})$,
then $S \Rightarrow_H^* y_r$.

Hence, $\{w_1 \mid (w_1, \bar{w}) \in 2\text{-}L(\Gamma)\} \subseteq L(H)$;

(2) $\{(w_1, w_2) \mid (w_1, w_2) \in 2\text{-}L(\Gamma), w_2 \neq \bar{w}\} = \emptyset$. Notice that Algorithm 4 implies that $G_2 = (N_2, T_2, P_2, S_2)$ contains only rules of the form $A \to B$ and $A \to \bar{w}$, where $A, B \in N_2$. Hence, G_2 generates $\emptyset$ or $\{\bar{w}\}$. Γ contains G_2 as a second component; hence, $\{(w_1, w_2) \mid (w_1, w_2) \in 2\text{-}L(\Gamma), w_2 \neq \bar{w}\} = \emptyset$. $\square$

Theorem 13.30. *For every matrix grammar H, there is a 2-MGR Γ such that $L(H) = L_{union}(\Gamma)$.*

Proof. To prove this theorem, we make use of Algorithm 4 with matrix grammar H and $\bar{w}$ as input, where $\bar{w}$ is any string in $L(H)$, provided that $L(H)$ is nonempty. Otherwise, if $L(H)$ is empty, let $\bar{w}$ be any string. We prove that $L(H) = L_{union}(\Gamma)$.

(i) If $L(H) = \emptyset$, take any string $\bar{w}$ and use Algorithm 4 to construct Γ. Observe that $L_{union}(\Gamma) = \emptyset = L(H)$;
(ii) If $L(H) \neq \emptyset$, take any $\bar{w} \in L(H)$ and use Algorithm 4 to construct Γ. As is obvious, $L_{union}(\Gamma) = L(H) \cup \bar{w} = L(H)$. $\square$

Theorem 13.31. *For every matrix grammar H, there is a 2-MGR Γ such that $L(H) = L_{conc}(\Gamma)$.*

Proof. To prove this theorem, we make use of Algorithm 4 with matrix grammar H and $\bar{w} = \varepsilon$ as input. We prove that $L(H) = L_{conc}(\Gamma)$. Theorem 13.29 says that

$$\{w_1 \mid (w_1, \bar{w}) \in 2\text{-}L(\Gamma)\} = L(H)$$

and

$$\{(w_1, w_2) \mid (w_1, w_2) \in 2\text{-}L(\Gamma), w_2 \neq \bar{w}\} = \emptyset.$$

Then,

$$\begin{aligned} L_{conc}(\Gamma) &= \{w_1 w_2 \mid (w_1, w_2) \in 2\text{-}L(\Gamma)\} \\ &= \{w_1 w_2 \mid (w_1, w_2) \in 2\text{-}L(\Gamma), w_2 = \bar{w}\} \\ &\quad \cup \{w_1 w_2 \mid (w_1, w_2) \in 2\text{-}L(\Gamma), w_2 \neq \bar{w}\} \\ &= \{w_1 \bar{w} \mid (w_1, \bar{w}) \in 2\text{-}L(\Gamma)\} \cup \emptyset \\ &= \{w_1 \bar{w} \mid (w_1, \bar{w}) \in 2\text{-}L(\Gamma)\} \\ &= L(H) \end{aligned}$$

because $\bar{w} = \varepsilon$. □

Theorem 13.32. *For every matrix grammar H, there is a 2-MGR Γ such that $L(H) = L_{first}(\Gamma)$.*

Proof. To prove this theorem, we make use of Algorithm 4 with matrix grammar H and any $\bar{w}$ as input. We prove that $L(H) = L_{first}(\Gamma)$. Theorem 13.29 says that

$$\{w_1 \mid (w_1, \bar{w}) \in 2\text{-}L(\Gamma)\} = L(H)$$

and

$$\{(w_1, w_2) \mid (w_1, w_2) \in 2\text{-}L(\Gamma), w_2 \neq \bar{w}\} = \emptyset.$$

Then,

$$\begin{aligned} L_{first}(\Gamma) &= \{w_1 \mid (w_1, w_2) \in 2\text{-}L(\Gamma)\} \\ &= \{w_1 \mid (w_1, w_2) \in 2\text{-}L(\Gamma), w_2 = \bar{w}\} \\ &\quad \cup \{w_1 \mid (w_1, w_2) \in 2\text{-}L(\Gamma), w_2 \neq \bar{w}\} \\ &= \{w_1 \mid (w_1, \bar{w}) \in 2\text{-}L(\Gamma)\} \cup \emptyset \\ &= \{w_1 \mid (w_1, \bar{w}) \in 2\text{-}L(\Gamma)\} \\ &= L(H). \end{aligned}$$

Hence, the theorem holds. □

Let $\mathbf{MGR}_{n,X}$ denote the language families defined by n-MGRs in the X mode, where $X \in \{union, conc, first\}$. From the previous results, we obtain the following corollary.

Corollary 9. $\mathbf{M} = \mathbf{MGR}_{n,X}$*, where $n \geq 2$, $X \in \{union, conc, first\}$.*

To summarize all the results, multigenerative grammar systems with any number of grammatical components are equivalent with two-component versions of these systems. Perhaps even more importantly, these systems are equivalent with matrix grammars, which generate a proper subfamily of the family of recursively enumerable languages (see Theorem 12.3).

We close this section by suggesting two open problem areas.

Open Problem 13.12. Consider other operations, like intersection, and study languages generated in this way by multigenerative grammar systems.

Open Problem 13.13. Study multigenerative grammar systems that are based on other grammars than context-free grammars. Specifically, determine the generative power of multigenerative grammar systems with regular or right-linear grammars as components.

13.3.2 Leftmost multigenerative grammar systems

In this section, we study leftmost versions of multigenerative grammar systems, whose basic versions were defined and investigated in the previous subsection of this section. We prove that they characterize the family of recursively enumerable languages, which properly contains the family of matrix languages (see Theorems 12.2 and 12.3). We also consider regulation by n-tuples of nonterminals rather than rules, and we prove that leftmost multigenerative grammar systems regulated by rules or nonterminals have the same generative power. Just like for multigenerative grammar systems in the previous section, we explain how to reduce the number of grammatical components in leftmost multigenerative grammar systems to two.

Definition 13.13. *A* leftmost n-generative rule-synchronized grammar system *(an n-LMGR for short) is an n-MGR (see Definition 13.12), where for two sentential n-forms* $\chi = (u_1A_1v_1, u_2A_2v_2, \ldots, u_nA_nv_n)$ *and* $\bar{\chi} = (u_1x_1v_1, u_2x_2v_2, \ldots, u_nx_nv_n)$, *where* $A_i \in N_i, u_i, v_i, x_i \in \Sigma_i^*$, *and an n-tuple* $(p_1, p_2, \ldots, p_n) \in Q$, *where* $(p_i: A_i \to x_i) \in P_i$,

$$\chi \Rightarrow_\Gamma \bar{\chi}$$

if and only if $u_i \in T_i^*$, *for all* $i = 1, \ldots, n$.

Next, we introduce regulation by n-tuples of nonterminals rather than rules.

Definition 13.14. *A* leftmost n-generative nonterminal-synchronized grammar system *(an n-LMGN for short) is an* $n + 1$ *tuple*

$$\Gamma = (G_1, G_2, \ldots, G_n, Q)$$

where

- $G_i = (\Sigma_i, T_i, P_i, S_i)$ *is a context-free grammar, for each* $i = 1, \ldots, n$;
- Q *is a finite set of n-tuples of the form* $(A_1, A_2, \ldots, A_n)$, *where* $A_i \in N_i$, *for all* $i = 1, \ldots, n$.

A sentential n-form *is defined as a sentential n-form of an n-LMGR. Let* $\chi = (u_1A_1v_1, u_2A_2v_2, \ldots, u_nA_nv_n)$ *and* $\bar{\chi} = (u_1x_1v_1, u_2x_2v_2, \ldots, u_nx_nv_n)$ *be two sentential n-forms, where* $A_i \in N_i$, $u_i \in \Delta^*$, *and* $v_i, x_i \in \Sigma_i^*$, *for all* $i = 1, \ldots, n$. *Let* $(p_i: A_i \to x_i) \in P_i$, *for all* $i = 1, \ldots, n$ *and* $(A_1, A_2, \ldots, A_n) \in Q$. *Then,* χ *directly derives* $\bar{\chi}$ *in* Γ, *denoted by*

$$\chi \Rightarrow_\Gamma \bar{\chi}.$$

In the standard way, we generalize $\Rightarrow_\Gamma$ *to* $\Rightarrow_\Gamma^k$, *for all* $k \geq 0$, $\Rightarrow_\Gamma^*$, *and* $\Rightarrow_\Gamma^+$.

*An n-*language *for an n-LMGN is defined as the n-language for an n-LMGR, and a language generated by an n-LMGN in the X mode, for each X* $\in$ *{union, conc, first}, is defined as the language generated by an n-LMGR in the X mode.*

Example 13.8. Consider the 2-LMGN $\Gamma = (G_1, G_2, Q)$, where

- $G_1 = (\{S_1, A_1, a, b, c\}, \{a, b, c\}, \{S_1 \rightarrow aS_1, S_1 \rightarrow aA_1, A_1 \rightarrow bA_1c, A_1 \rightarrow bc\}, S_1)$,
- $G_2 = (\{S_2, A_2, d\}, \{d\}, \{S_2 \rightarrow S_2A_2, S_2 \rightarrow A_2, A_2 \rightarrow d\}, S_2)$,
- $Q = \{(S_1, S_2), (A_1, A_2)\}$.

Observe that

- $2\text{-}L(\Gamma) = \{(a^n b^n c^n, d^n) \mid n \geq 1\}$,
- $L_{union}(\Gamma) = \{a^n b^n c^n \mid n \geq 1\} \cup \{d^n \mid n \geq 1\}$,
- $L_{conc}(\Gamma) = \{a^n b^n c^n d^n \mid n \geq 1\}$, and
- $L_{first}(\Gamma) = \{a^n b^n c^n \mid n \geq 1\}$.

Lemma 13.20. *Let* Γ *be an n-LMGN and let* $\bar{\Gamma}$ *be an n-LMGR such that* $n\text{-}L(\Gamma) = n\text{-}L(\bar{\Gamma})$*. Then,* $L_X(\Gamma) = L_X(\bar{\Gamma})$*, for each X* $\in$ *{union, conc, first}.*

Proof.

(I) First, we prove that $L_{union}(\Gamma) = L_{union}(\bar{\Gamma})$ as follows:

$$\begin{aligned} L_{union}(\Gamma) &= \{w \mid (w_1, \ldots, w_n) \in n\text{-}L(\Gamma), w \in \{w_i \mid 1 \leq i \leq n\}\} \\ &= \{w \mid (w_1, \ldots, w_n) \in n\text{-}L(\bar{\Gamma}), w \in \{w_i \mid 1 \leq i \leq n\}\} \\ &= L_{union}(\bar{\Gamma}); \end{aligned}$$

(II) Second, we prove that $L_{conc}(\Gamma) = L_{conc}(\bar{\Gamma})$ as follows:

$$\begin{aligned} L_{conc}(\Gamma) &= \{w_1 \cdots w_n \mid (w_1, \ldots, w_n) \in n\text{-}L(\Gamma)\} \\ &= \{w_1 \cdots w_n \mid (w_1, \ldots, w_n) \in n\text{-}L(\bar{\Gamma})\} \\ &= L_{conc}(\bar{\Gamma}); \end{aligned}$$

(III) Finally, we prove that $L_{first}(\Gamma) = L_{first}(\bar{\Gamma})$ as follows:

$$\begin{aligned} L_{first}(\Gamma) &= \{w_1 \mid (w_1, \ldots, w_n) \in n\text{-}L(\Gamma)\} \\ &= \{w_1 \mid (w_1, \ldots, w_n) \in n\text{-}L(\bar{\Gamma})\} \\ &= L_{first}(\bar{\Gamma}). \end{aligned}$$

□

Theorem 13.33. *Let* $\Gamma = (G_1, G_2, \ldots, G_n, Q)$ *be an n-LMGN. With* Γ *as its input, Algorithm 5 halts and correctly constructs an n-LMGR,* $\bar{\Gamma} = (G_1, G_2, \ldots, G_n, \bar{Q})$*, such that* $n\text{-}L(\Gamma) = n\text{-}L(\bar{\Gamma})$*, and* $L_X(\Gamma) = L_X(\bar{\Gamma})$*, for each X* $\in$ *{union, conc, first}.*

Proof. To prove this theorem, we first establish Claims 1 and 2.

Claim 1. Let $(S_1, S_2, \ldots, S_n) \Rightarrow_{\Gamma}^{m} (y_1, y_2, \ldots, y_n)$, where $m \geq 0$, $y_i \in \Sigma_i^*$, for all $i = 1, \ldots, n$. Then, $(S_1, S_2, \ldots, S_n) \Rightarrow_{\bar{\Gamma}}^{m} (y_1, y_2, \ldots, y_n)$.

Conversion of an n-LMGN to an equivalent n-LMGR.
An n-LMGN, $\Gamma = (G_1, G_2, \ldots, G_n, Q)$.
An n-LMGR, $\bar{\Gamma} = (G_1, G_2, \ldots, G_n, \bar{Q})$, such that $n\text{-}L(\Gamma) = n\text{-}L(\bar{\Gamma})$.
Let $G_i = (\Sigma_i, T_i, P_i, S_i)$, for all $i = 1, \ldots, n$, and set

$$\bar{Q} = \{(A_1 \to x_1, A_2 \to x_2, \ldots, A_n \to x_n) \mid A_i \to x_i \in P_i, \text{ for all } i = 1, \ldots, n, \text{ and } (A_1, A_2, \ldots, A_n) \in Q\}.$$

Proof. This claim is proved by induction on $m \geq 0$.

Basis. The basis is clear.

Induction Hypothesis. Assume that Claim 1 holds for all m-step derivations, where $m = 0, \ldots, k$, for some $k \geq 0$.

Induction Step. Consider any derivation of the form

$$(S_1, S_2, \ldots, S_n) \Rightarrow_{\Gamma}^{k+1} (y_1, y_2, \ldots, y_n).$$

Then, there exists a sentential n-form $(u_1A_1v_1, u_2A_2v_2, \ldots, u_nA_nv_n)$, where $u_i \in T_i^*$, $A_i \in N_i$, and $v_i \in \Sigma_i^*$, such that

$$\begin{aligned}(S_1, S_2, \ldots, S_n) &\Rightarrow_{\Gamma}^{k} (u_1A_1v_1, u_2A_2v_2, \ldots, u_nA_nv_n)\\ &\Rightarrow_{\Gamma} (u_1x_1v_1, u_2x_2v_2, \ldots, u_nx_nv_n),\end{aligned}$$

where $u_ix_iv_i = y_i$, for all $i = 1, \ldots, n$. Then, by the induction hypothesis, we have

$$(S_1, S_2, \ldots, S_n) \Rightarrow_{\bar{\Gamma}}^{k} (u_1A_1v_1, u_2A_2v_2, \ldots, u_nA_nv_n).$$

Since

$$(u_1A_1v_1, u_2A_2v_2, \ldots, u_nA_nv_n) \Rightarrow_{\Gamma} (u_1x_1v_1, u_2x_2v_2, \ldots, u_nx_nv_n),$$

$(A_1, A_2, \ldots, A_n) \in Q$ and $A_i \to x_i \in P_i$, for all $i = 1, \ldots, n$. Algorithm 5 implies that $(A_1 \to x_1, A_2 \to x_2, \ldots, A_n \to x_n) \in \bar{Q}$, so

$$(u_1A_1v_1, u_2A_2v_2, \ldots, u_nA_nv_n) \Rightarrow_{\bar{\Gamma}} (u_1x_1v_1, u_2x_2v_2, \ldots, u_nx_nv_n),$$

which proves the induction step. Therefore, Claim 1 holds. □

Claim 2. Let $(S_1, S_2, \ldots, S_n) \Rightarrow_{\bar{\Gamma}}^{m} (y_1, y_2, \ldots, y_n)$, where $m \geq 0$, $y_i \in \Sigma_i^*$, for all $i = 1, \ldots, n$. Then, $(S_1, S_2, \ldots, S_n) \Rightarrow_{\Gamma}^{m} (y_1, y_2, \ldots, y_n)$.

Proof. This claim is proved by induction on $m \geq 0$.

Basis. The basis is clear.

Induction Hypothesis. Assume that Claim 2 holds for all m-step derivations, where $m = 0, \ldots, k$, for some $k \geq 0$.

Induction Step. Consider any derivation of the form

$$(S_1, S_2, \ldots, S_n) \Rightarrow_{\bar{\Gamma}}^{k+1} (y_1, y_2, \ldots, y_n).$$

Then, there exists a sentential n-form $(u_1A_1v_1,\ u_2A_2v_2,\ \ldots,\ u_nA_nv_n)$, where $u_i \in T_i^*$, $A_i \in N_i$, $v_i \in \Sigma_i^*$, such that

$$\begin{aligned}(S_1, S_2, \ldots, S_n) &\Rightarrow_{\bar{\Gamma}}^{k} (u_1A_1v_1, u_2A_2v_2, \ldots, u_nA_nv_n)\\ &\Rightarrow_{\bar{\Gamma}} (u_1x_1v_1, u_2x_2v_2, \ldots, u_nx_nv_n)\end{aligned}$$

where $u_ix_iv_i = y_i$, for all $i = 1, \ldots, n$. Then, by the induction hypothesis, we have

$$(S_1, S_2, \ldots, S_n) \Rightarrow_{\Gamma}^{k} (u_1A_1v_1, u_2A_2v_2, \ldots, u_nA_nv_n).$$

Since

$$\begin{aligned}&(u_1A_1v_1, u_2A_2v_2, \ldots, u_nA_nv_n) \Rightarrow_{\Gamma}\\ &\quad (u_1x_1v_1, u_2x_2v_2, \ldots, u_nx_nv_n),\end{aligned}$$

$(A_1 \rightarrow x_1, A_2 \rightarrow x_2, \ldots, A_n \rightarrow x_n) \in \bar{Q}$, for all $i = 1, \ldots, n$. Algorithm 5 implies that $(A_1, A_2, \ldots, A_n) \in Q$ and $A_i \rightarrow x_i \in P_i$, so

$$\begin{aligned}&(u_1A_1v_1, u_2A_2v_2, \ldots, u_nA_nv_n) \Rightarrow_{\Gamma}\\ &\quad (u_1x_1v_1, u_2x_2v_2, \ldots, u_nx_nv_n),\end{aligned}$$

which proves the induction step. Therefore, Claim 2 holds. □

Consider Claim 1 for $y_i \in T_i^*$, for all $i = 1, \ldots, n$. At this point, if

$$(S_1, S_2, \ldots, S_n) \Rightarrow_{\Gamma}^{*} (y_1, y_2, \ldots, y_n),$$

then

$$(S_1, S_2, \ldots, S_n) \Rightarrow_{\bar{\Gamma}}^{*} (y_1, y_2, \ldots, y_n).$$

Hence, n-$L(\Gamma) \subseteq n$-$L(\bar{\Gamma})$. Consider Claim 2 for $y_i \in T_i^*$, for all $i = 1, \ldots, n$. At this point, if

$$(S_1, S_2, \ldots, S_n) \Rightarrow_{\bar{\Gamma}}^{*} (y_1, y_2, \ldots, y_n),$$

then

$$(S_1, S_2, \ldots, S_n) \Rightarrow_{\Gamma}^{*} (y_1, y_2, \ldots, y_n).$$

Hence, n-$L(\bar{\Gamma}) \subseteq n$-$L(\Gamma)$. As n-$L(\Gamma) \subseteq n$-$L(\bar{\Gamma})$ and n-$L(\bar{\Gamma}) \subseteq n$-$L(\Gamma)$, n-$L(\Gamma) = n$-$L(\bar{\Gamma})$. By Lemma 13.20, this identity implies that $L_X(\Gamma) = L_X(\bar{\Gamma})$, for each $X \in \{$*union*, *conc*, *first*$\}$. Therefore, Theorem 13.33 holds. □

Theorem 13.34. *Let $\Gamma = (G_1, G_2, \ldots, G_n, Q)$ be an n-LMGR. With Γ as its input, Algorithm 6 halts and correctly constructs an n-LMGN, $\bar{\Gamma} = (\bar{G}_1, \bar{G}_2, \ldots, \bar{G}_n, \bar{Q})$, such that n-$L(\Gamma) =$ n-$L(\bar{\Gamma})$, and $L_X(\Gamma) = L_X(\bar{\Gamma})$, for each $X \in \{$union, conc, first$\}$.*

Proof. To prove this theorem, we first establish Claims 1 and 2.

Conversion of an n-LMGR to an equivalent n-LMGN.
An n-LMGR, $\Gamma = (G_1, G_2, \dots, G_n, Q)$.
An n-LMGN, $\bar{\Gamma} = (\bar{G}_1, \bar{G}_2, \dots, \bar{G}_n, \bar{Q})$, such that $n\text{-}L(\Gamma) = n\text{-}L(\bar{\Gamma})$.
Let $G_i = (\Sigma_i, T_i, P_i, S_i)$, for all $i = 1, \dots, n$, and set

- $\bar{G}_i = (\bar{\Sigma}_i, T_i, \bar{R}_i, S_i)$, for all $i = 1, \dots, n$, where
  $\bar{N}_i = \{\langle A, x\rangle \mid A \to x \in P_i\} \cup \{S_i\}$;
  $\bar{R}_i = \{\langle A, x\rangle \to y \mid A \to x \in P_i, y \in \tau_i(x)\} \cup \{S_i \to y \mid y \in \tau_i(S_i)\}$,
  where τ_i is a finite substitution from Σ_i^* to $\bar{\Sigma}_i^*$ defined as $\tau_i(a) = \{a\}$, for all $a \in \Delta$, and $\tau_i(A) = \{\langle A, x\rangle \mid A \to x \in P_i\}$, for all $A \in N_i$;
- $\bar{Q} = \{(\langle A_1, x_1\rangle, \langle A_2, x_2\rangle, \dots, \langle A_n, x_n\rangle) \mid (A_1 \to x_1, A_2 \to x_2, \dots, A_n \to x_n) \in Q\} \quad \cup \{(S_1, S_2, \dots, S_n)\}$.

Claim 1. Let $(S_1, S_2, \dots, S_n) \Rightarrow_\Gamma^m (z_1, z_2, \dots, z_n)$, where $m \geq 0$, $z_i \in \Sigma_i^*$, for all $i = 1, \dots, n$. Then, $(S_1, S_2, \dots, S_n) \Rightarrow_{\bar{\Gamma}}^{m+1} (\bar{z}_1, \bar{z}_2, \dots, \bar{z}_n)$, for any $\bar{z}_i \in \tau_i(z_i)$.

Proof. This claim is proved by induction on $m \geq 0$.

Basis. Let $m = 0$. Then,

$$(S_1, S_2, \dots, S_n) \Rightarrow_\Gamma^0 (S_1, S_2, \dots, S_n).$$

Observe that

$$(S_1, S_2, \dots, S_n) \Rightarrow_{\bar{\Gamma}}^1 (\bar{z}_1, \bar{z}_2, \dots, \bar{z}_n)$$

for any $\bar{z}_i \in \tau_i(z_i)$, because Algorithm 6 implies that $(S_1, S_2, \dots, S_n) \in \bar{Q}$ and $S_i \to \bar{z}_i \in \bar{R}_i$, for any $\bar{z}_i \in \tau_i(z_i)$, for all $i = 1, \dots, n$. Thus, the basis holds.

Induction Hypothesis. Assume that the claim holds for all m-step derivations, where $m = 0, \dots, k$, for some $k \geq 0$.

Induction Step. Consider any derivation of the form

$$(S_1, S_2, \dots, S_n) \Rightarrow_\Gamma^{k+1} (y_1, y_2, \dots, y_n).$$

Then, there exists a sentential n-form $(u_1A_1v_1, u_2A_2v_2, \dots, u_nA_nv_n)$, where $u_i \in T_i^*$, $A_i \in N_i$, $v_i \in \Sigma_i^*$, such that

$$\begin{aligned}(S_1, S_2, \dots, S_n) &\Rightarrow_\Gamma^k (u_1A_1v_1, u_2A_2v_2, \dots, u_nA_nv_n)\\ &\Rightarrow_\Gamma (u_1x_1v_1, u_2x_2v_2, \dots, u_nx_nv_n)\end{aligned}$$

where $u_ix_iv_i = y_i$, for all $i = 1, \dots, n$. Then, by the induction hypothesis, we have

$$(S_1, S_2, \dots, S_n) \Rightarrow_{\bar{\Gamma}}^{k+1} (\bar{w}_1, \bar{w}_2, \dots, \bar{w}_n)$$

for any $\bar{w}_i \in \tau_i(u_iA_iv_i)$, for all $i = 1, \dots, n$. Since

$$(u_1A_1v_1, u_2A_2v_2, \dots, u_nA_nv_n) \Rightarrow_\Gamma (u_1x_1v_1, u_2x_2v_2, \dots, u_nx_nv_n),$$

$(A_1 \to x_1, A_2 \to x_2, \ldots, A_n \to x_n) \in Q$. Algorithm 6 implies that $(\langle A_1,x_1\rangle, \langle A_2,x_2\rangle, \ldots, \langle A_n,x_n\rangle) \in \bar{Q}$ and $\langle A_i,x_i\rangle \to \bar{y}_i \in \bar{R}_i$, for any $\bar{y}_i \in \tau_i(x_i)$, for all $i = 1,\ldots,n$. Let $\bar{w}_i$ be any sentential form of the form $\bar{u}_i\langle A_i,x_i\rangle\bar{v}_i$, for all $i = 1,\ldots,n$, where $\bar{u}_i \in \tau_i(u_i)$ and $\bar{v}_i \in \tau_i(v_i)$. Then,

$$(\bar{u}_1\langle A_1,x_1\rangle\bar{v}_1, \bar{u}_2\langle A_2,x_2\rangle\bar{v}_2, \ldots, \bar{u}_n\langle A_n,x_n\rangle\bar{v}_n) \Rightarrow_{\bar{\Gamma}} (\bar{u}_1\bar{y}_1\bar{v}_1, \bar{u}_2\bar{y}_2\bar{v}_2, \ldots, \bar{u}_n\bar{y}_n\bar{v}_n)$$

where $\bar{u}_i\bar{y}_i\bar{v}_i$ is any sentential form, $\bar{u}_i\bar{y}_i\bar{v}_i \in \tau_i(u_iy_iv_i)$, for all $i = 1,\ldots,n$, which proves the induction step. Therefore, Claim 1 holds. □

Claim 2. Let $(S_1, S_2, \ldots, S_n) \Rightarrow_{\bar{\Gamma}}^m (\bar{z}_1, \bar{z}_2, \ldots, \bar{z}_n)$, where $m \geq 1$, $\bar{z}_i \in \bar{\Sigma}_i^*$, for all $i = 1,\ldots,n$. Then, $(S_1, S_2, \ldots, S_n) \Rightarrow_{\Gamma}^{m-1} (z_1, z_2, \ldots, z_n)$, where $\bar{z}_i \in \tau_i(z_i)$, for all $i = 1,\ldots,n$.

Proof. This claim is proved by induction on $m \geq 1$.

Basis. Let $m = 1$. Then,

$$(S_1, S_2, \ldots, S_n) \Rightarrow_{\bar{\Gamma}} (\bar{z}_1, \bar{z}_2, \ldots, \bar{z}_n)$$

implies that $S_i \to \bar{z}_i \in \bar{R}_i$, for all $i = 1,\ldots,n$. Algorithm 6 implies that $\bar{z}_i \in \tau_i(S_i)$, for all $i = 1,\ldots,n$, so

$$(S_1, S_2, \ldots, S_n) \Rightarrow_{\bar{\Gamma}}^0 (S_1, S_2, \ldots, S_n).$$

Since $\bar{z}_i \in \tau_i(S_i)$, for all $i = 1,\ldots,n$, the basis holds.

Induction Hypothesis. Assume that the claim holds for all m-step derivations, where $m = 1,\ldots,k$, for some $k \geq 1$.

Induction Step. Consider any derivation of the form

$$(S_1, S_2, \ldots, S_n) \Rightarrow_{\bar{\Gamma}}^{k+1} (\bar{y}_1, \bar{y}_2, \ldots, \bar{y}_n).$$

Then, there exists a sentential n-form

$$(\bar{u}_1\langle A_1,x_1\rangle\bar{v}_1, \bar{u}_2\langle A_2,x_2\rangle\bar{v}_2, \ldots, \bar{u}_n\langle A_n,x_n\rangle\bar{v}_n)$$

where $\bar{u}_i \in T_i^*$, $\langle A_i,x_i\rangle \in \bar{N}_i$, $\bar{v}_i \in \bar{\Sigma}_i^*$, such that

$$\begin{aligned}(S_1, S_2, \ldots, S_n) &\Rightarrow_{\bar{\Gamma}}^k (\bar{u}_1\langle A_1,x_1\rangle\bar{v}_1, \bar{u}_2\langle A_2,x_2\rangle\bar{v}_2, \ldots, \bar{u}_n\langle A_n,x_n\rangle\bar{v}_n)\\ &\Rightarrow_{\bar{\Gamma}} (\bar{u}_1\bar{x}_1\bar{v}_1, \bar{u}_2\bar{x}_2\bar{v}_2, \ldots, \bar{u}_n\bar{x}_n\bar{v}_n)\end{aligned}$$

where $\bar{u}_i\bar{x}_i\bar{v}_i = \bar{y}_i$ for all $i = 1,\ldots,n$. Then, by the induction hypothesis, we have

$$(S_1, S_2, \ldots, S_n) \Rightarrow_{\Gamma}^{k-1} \Rightarrow_{\Gamma} (w_1, w_2, \ldots, w_n)$$

where $\bar{u}_i\langle A_i,x_i\rangle\bar{v}_i \in \tau_i(w_i)$, for all $i = 1,\ldots,n$. Since

$$(\bar{u}_1\langle A_1,x_1\rangle\bar{v}_1, \bar{u}_2\langle A_2,x_2\rangle\bar{v}_2, \ldots, \bar{u}_n\langle A_n,x_n\rangle\bar{v}_n) \Rightarrow_{\bar{\Gamma}} (\bar{u}_1\bar{x}_1\bar{v}_1, \bar{u}_2\bar{x}_2\bar{v}_2, \ldots, \bar{u}_n\bar{x}_n\bar{v}_n),$$

there are $(\langle A_1, x_1\rangle, \langle A_2, x_2\rangle, \ldots, \langle A_n, x_n\rangle) \in \bar{Q}$ and $\langle A_i, x_i\rangle \to \bar{x}_i \in \bar{R}_i$ for all $i = 1, \ldots, n$. Algorithm 6 implies that $(A_1 \to x_1, A_2 \to x_2, \ldots, A_n \to x_n) \in Q$ and $A_i \to x_i \in P_i$ where $\bar{x}_i \in \tau_i(x_i)$ for all $i = 1, \ldots, n$. We can express w_i as $w_i = u_i A_i v_i$, where $\bar{u}_i \in \tau_i(u_i)$, $\bar{v}_i \in \tau_i(v_i)$, and observe that $\langle A_i, x_i\rangle \in \tau_i(A_i)$ holds by the definition of τ_i, for all $i = 1, \ldots, n$. Then,

$$(u_1A_1v_1, u_2A_2v_2, \ldots, u_nA_nv_n) \Rightarrow_{\Gamma} (u_1x_1v_1, u_2x_2v_2, \ldots, u_nx_nv_n)$$

where $\bar{u}_i \in \tau_i(u_i)$, $\bar{v}_i \in \tau_i(v_i)$, and $\bar{x}_i \in \tau_i(x_i)$ for all $i = 1, \ldots, n$, which means that $\bar{u}_i\bar{x}_i\bar{v}_i \in \tau_i(u_ix_iv_i)$ for all $i = 1, \ldots, n$. Therefore,

$$\begin{aligned}(S_1, S_2, \ldots, S_n) &\Rightarrow_{\Gamma}^{k+1} (u_1A_1v_1, u_2A_2v_2, \ldots, u_nA_nv_n)\\ &\Rightarrow_{\Gamma} (u_1x_1v_1, u_2x_2v_2, \ldots, u_nx_nv_n)\end{aligned}$$

where $\bar{u}_i\bar{x}_i\bar{v}_i \in \tau_i(u_ix_iv_i)$ for all $i = 1, \ldots, n$. Let $\bar{z}_i = \bar{u}_i\bar{x}_i\bar{v}_i$ and $z_i = u_ix_iv_i$ for all $i = 1, \ldots, n$. Then,

$$(S_1, S_2, \ldots, S_n) \Rightarrow_{\Gamma}^{k+2} (z_1, z_2, \ldots, z_n)$$

for all $\bar{z}_i \in \tau_i(z_i)$, which proves the induction step. Therefore, Claim 2 holds. □

Consider Claim 1 when $z_i \in T_i^*$, for all $i = 1, \ldots, n$. At this point, if

$$(S_1, S_2, \ldots, S_n) \Rightarrow_{\Gamma}^{*} (z_1, z_2, \ldots, z_n),$$

then

$$(S_1, S_2, \ldots, S_n) \Rightarrow_{\bar{\Gamma}}^{*} (\bar{z}_1, \bar{z}_2, \ldots, \bar{z}_n)$$

where $\bar{z}_i \in \tau_i(z_i)$ for all $i = 1, \ldots, n$. Since $\tau_i(a_i) = a_i$ for all $a_i \in T_i$, $\bar{z}_i = z_i$. Hence, $n\text{-}L(\Gamma) \subseteq n\text{-}L(\bar{\Gamma})$. Consider Claim 2 when $\bar{z}_i \in T_i^*$ for all $i = 1, \ldots, n$. At this point, if

$$(S_1, S_2, \ldots, S_n) \Rightarrow_{\bar{\Gamma}}^{m} (\bar{z}_1, \bar{z}_2, \ldots, \bar{z}_n),$$

then

$$(S_1, S_2, \ldots, S_n) \Rightarrow_{\Gamma}^{m-1} (z_1, z_2, \ldots, z_n)$$

where $\bar{z}_i \in \tau_i(z_i)$ for all $i = 1, \ldots, n$. Since $\tau_i(a_i) = a_i$ for all $a_i \in T_i$, $z_i = \bar{z}_i$. Hence, $n\text{-}L(\bar{\Gamma}) \subseteq n\text{-}L(\Gamma)$. As $n\text{-}L(\Gamma) \subseteq n\text{-}L(\bar{\Gamma})$ and $n\text{-}L(\bar{\Gamma}) \subseteq n\text{-}L(\Gamma)$, $n\text{-}L(\Gamma) = n\text{-}L(\bar{\Gamma})$. By Lemma 13.20, this identity implies that $L_X(\Gamma) = L_X(\bar{\Gamma})$, for each $X \in \{$*union*, *conc*, *first*$\}$. Therefore, Theorem 13.34 holds. □

From the achieved results, we immediately obtain the following corollary.

Corollary 10. *The family of languages generated by n-LMGN in the X mode coincides with the family of languages generated by n-LMGR in the X mode, where X* $\in \{$*union, conc, first*$\}$.

Theorem 13.35. *For every recursively enumerable language L over some alphabet* Δ, *there exits a 2-LMGR,* $\Gamma = ((\bar{\Sigma}_1, \Delta, \bar{R}_1, S_1), (\bar{\Sigma}_2, \Delta, \bar{R}_2, S_2), Q)$, *such that*

(i) $\{w \in \Delta^* \mid (S_1, S_2) \Rightarrow_\Gamma^* (w, w)\} = L$,
(ii) $\{w_1 w_2 \in \Delta^* \mid (S_1, S_2) \Rightarrow_\Gamma^* (w_1, w_2), w_1 \neq w_2\} = \emptyset$.

Proof. Recall that for every recursive enumerable language L over some alphabet Δ, there exist two context-free grammars, $G_1 = (\Sigma_1, \bar{\Delta}, P_1, S_1)$, $G_2 = (\Sigma_2, \bar{\Delta}, P_2, S_2)$, and a homomorphism h from $\bar{\Delta}^*$ to Δ^* such that $L = \{h(x) \mid x \in L(G_1) \cap L(G_2)\}$ (see Theorem 10.3.1 in [22]). Furthermore, by Theorem 11.12, for every context-free grammar, there exists an equivalent context-free grammar in the Greibach normal form (see Definition 11.7). Hence, without any loss of generality, we assume that G_1 and G_2 are in the Greibach normal form. Consider the 2-LMGR

$$\Gamma = (G_1, G_2, Q)$$

where

- $G_i = (\bar{\Sigma}_i, \Delta, \bar{R}_i, S_i)$, where
  $\bar{N}_i = N_i \cup \{\bar{a} \mid a \in \bar{\Delta}\}$,
  $\bar{R}_i = \{A \rightarrow \bar{a}x \mid A \rightarrow ax \in P_i, a \in \bar{\Delta}, x \in N_i^*\} \cup \{\bar{a} \rightarrow h(a) \mid a \in \bar{\Delta}\}$,
  for $i = 1, 2$;
- $Q = \{(A_1 \rightarrow \bar{a}x_1, A_2 \rightarrow \bar{a}x_2) \mid A_1 \rightarrow \bar{a}x_1 \in P_1, A_2 \rightarrow \bar{a}x_2 \in P_2, a \in \bar{\Delta}\}$
  $\cup \{(\bar{a} \rightarrow h(a), \bar{a} \rightarrow h(a)) \mid a \in \bar{\Delta}\}$.

Consider properties (i) and (ii) in Theorem 13.35. Next, Claims 1 and 2 establish (i) and (ii), respectively.

Claim 1. $\{w \in \Delta^* \mid (S_1, S_2) \Rightarrow_\Gamma^* (w, w)\} = L$.

Proof. (I) We prove that $L \subseteq \{w \in \Delta^* \mid (S_1, S_2) \Rightarrow_\Gamma^* (w, w)\}$. Let $w \in L$. Then, there exists a string, $a_1 a_2 \cdots a_n \in \bar{\Delta}^*$, such that

- $a_1 a_2 \cdots a_n \in L(G_1)$,
- $a_1 a_2 \cdots a_n \in L(G_2)$, and
- $h(a_1 a_2 \cdots a_n) = w$.

This means that there exist the following derivations in G_1 and G_2:

$$\begin{array}{lll} S_1 & \Rightarrow_{G_1} a_1 x_1 & [p_1] \\ & \Rightarrow_{G_1} a_1 a_2 x_2 & [p_2] \\ & \vdots & \\ & \Rightarrow_{G_1} a_1 a_2 \cdots a_n & [p_n], \end{array}$$

$$\begin{array}{lll} S_2 & \Rightarrow_{G_2} a_1 y_1 & [r_1] \\ & \Rightarrow_{G_2} a_1 a_2 y_2 & [r_2] \\ & \vdots & \\ & \Rightarrow_{G_2} a_1 a_2 \cdots a_n & [r_n], \end{array}$$

where $a_i \in \bar{\Delta}, x_i \in N_i^*, y_i \in N_2^*, p_i \in P_1, r_i \in P_2$, for all $i = 1, \ldots, n$. Observe that $\text{sym}(\text{rhs}\, p_i, 1) = \text{sym}(\text{rhs}\, r_i, 1) = a_i$, for all $i = 1, \ldots, n$ (see Definition 6.1 for rhs). The construction of Q implies the following two statements.

- Let $p_i\colon A_i \to a_i u_i \in \bar{R}_1, r_i\colon B_i \to a_i v_i \in \bar{R}_2$. Then, $(A_i \to \bar{a}_i u_i, B_i \to \bar{a}_i v_i) \in Q$, for all $i = 1, \ldots, n$;
- Q contains $(\bar{a}_i \to h(a_i), \bar{a}_i \to h(a_i))$, for all $i = 1, \ldots, n$.

Therefore, there exists

$$\begin{aligned}
(S_1, S_2) &\Rightarrow_\Gamma (\bar{a}_1 x_1, \bar{a}_1 y_1)\\
&\Rightarrow_\Gamma (h(a_1)x_1, h(a_1)y_1)\\
&\Rightarrow_\Gamma (h(a_1)\bar{a}_2 x_2, h(a_1)\bar{a}_2 y_2)\\
&\Rightarrow_\Gamma (h(a_1)h(a_2)x_2, h(a_1)h(a_2)y_2)\\
&\vdots\\
&\Rightarrow_\Gamma (h(a_1)h(a_2)\cdots h(a_n), h(a_1)h(a_2)\cdots h(a_n))\\
& = (h(a_1 a_2 \cdots a_n), h(a_1 a_2 \cdots a_n))\\
& = (w, w).
\end{aligned}$$

In brief, $(S_1, S_2) \Rightarrow_\Gamma^* (w, w)$. Hence, $L \subseteq \{w \in \Delta^* \mid (S_1, S_2) \Rightarrow_\Gamma^* (w, w)\}$.

(II) We prove that $\{w \in \Delta^* \mid (S_1, S_2) \Rightarrow_\Gamma^* (w, w)\} \subseteq L$. Let $(S_1, S_2) \Rightarrow_\Gamma^* (w, w)$. Then, there exists

$$\begin{aligned}
(S_1, S_2) &\Rightarrow_\Gamma (\bar{a}_1 x_1, \bar{a}_1 y_1)\\
&\Rightarrow_\Gamma (h(a_1)x_1, h(a_1)y_1)\\
&\Rightarrow_\Gamma (h(a_1)\bar{a}_2 x_2, h(a_1)\bar{a}_2 y_2)\\
&\Rightarrow_\Gamma (h(a_1)h(a_2)x_2, h(a_1)h(a_2)y_2)\\
&\vdots\\
&\Rightarrow_\Gamma (h(a_1)h(a_2)\cdots h(a_n), h(a_1)h(a_2)\cdots h(a_n))\\
& = (h(a_1 a_2 \cdots a_n), h(a_1 a_2 \cdots a_n))\\
& = (w, w).
\end{aligned}$$

By analogy with part 13.3.2, we can prove that there exist derivations in G_1 and G_2 of the forms

$$\begin{aligned}
S_1 &\Rightarrow_{G_1} a_1 x_1 && [p_1]\\
&\Rightarrow_{G_1} a_1 a_2 x_2 && [p_2]\\
&\vdots\\
&\Rightarrow_{G_1} a_1 a_2 \cdots a_n && [p_n],
\end{aligned}$$

$$\begin{aligned}
S_2 &\Rightarrow_{G_2} a_1 y_1 && [r_1]\\
&\Rightarrow_{G_2} a_1 a_2 y_2 && [r_2]\\
&\vdots\\
&\Rightarrow_{G_2} a_1 a_2 \cdots a_n && [r_n].
\end{aligned}$$

This implies that $a_1 a_2 \cdots a_n \in L(G_1)$, $a_1 a_2 \cdots a_n \in L(G_2)$, and $h(a_1 a_2 \cdots a_n) = w$, so $w \in L$. Hence, $\{w \in \Delta^* \mid (S_1, S_2) \Rightarrow_\Gamma^* (w, w)\} \subseteq L$. Therefore, Claim 1 holds.

□

Claim 2. $\{w_1 w_2 \in \Delta^* \mid (S_1, S_2) \Rightarrow_\Gamma^* (w_1, w_2), w_1 \neq w_2\} = \emptyset$.

Proof. By contradiction. Let $\{w_1w_2 \in \Delta^* \mid (S_1, S_2) \Rightarrow_\Gamma^* (w_1, w_2), w_1 \neq w_2\} \neq \emptyset$. Then, there have to exist two different strings, $w_1 = h(a_1)h(a_2)\cdots h(a_n)$ and $w_2 = h(b_1)h(b_2)\cdots h(b_n)$, such that $(S_1, S_2) \Rightarrow_\Gamma^* (w_1, w_2)$.

(I) Assume that $a_i = b_i$, for all $i = 1, \ldots, n$. Then, $w_1 = h(a_1)h(a_2)\cdots h(a_n) = h(b_1)h(b_2)\cdots h(b_n) = w_2$, which contradicts $w_1 \neq w_2$.

(II) Assume that there exists some $k \leq n$ such that $a_k \neq b_k$. Then, there exists a derivation of the form

$$\begin{aligned}(S_1, S_2) &\Rightarrow_\Gamma (\bar{a}_1x_1, \bar{a}_1y_1)\\ &\Rightarrow_\Gamma (h(a_1)x_1, h(a_1)y_1)\\ &\Rightarrow_\Gamma (h(a_1)\bar{a}_2x_2, h(a_1)\bar{a}_2y_2)\\ &\Rightarrow_\Gamma (h(a_1)h(a_2)x_2, h(a_1)h(a_2)y_2)\\ &\vdots\\ &\Rightarrow_\Gamma (h(a_1)h(a_2)\cdots h(a_{k-1})x_{k-1}, h(a_1)h(a_2)\cdots h(a_{k-1})y_{k-1}).\end{aligned}$$

Then, there has to exist a derivation.

$(x_{k-1}, y_{k-1}) \Rightarrow_\Gamma (\bar{a}_kx_k, \bar{b}_ky_k)$

where $\bar{a}_k \neq \bar{b}_k$. By the definition of Q, there has to be $(p, r) \in Q$ such that

$\mathrm{sym}(\mathrm{rhs}\, p, 1) = \mathrm{sym}(\mathrm{rhs}\, r, 1)$.

Therefore, the next derivation has to be of the form

$(x_{k-1}, y_{k-1}) \Rightarrow_\Gamma (\bar{a}_kx_k, \bar{b}_ky_k)$

where $\bar{a}_k = \bar{b}_k$, which is a contradiction. Therefore, Claim 2 holds. □

Claims 1 and 2 imply that Theorem 13.35 holds. □

Theorem 13.36. *For any recursively enumerable language L over an alphabet Δ, there exists a 2-LMGR, $\Gamma = (G_1, G_2, Q)$, such that $L_{union}(\Gamma) = L$.*

Proof. By Theorem 13.35, for every recursively enumerable language L over an alphabet Δ, there exits a 2-LMGR

$$\bar{\Gamma} = ((\Sigma_1, \Delta, P_1, S_1), (\Sigma_2, \Delta, P_2, S_2), Q)$$

such that

$$\{w \in \Delta^* \mid (S_1, S_2) \Rightarrow_\Gamma^* (w, w)\} = L$$

and

$$\{w_1w_2 \in \Delta^* \mid (S_1, S_2) \Rightarrow_\Gamma^* (w_1, w_2), w_1 \neq w_2\} = \emptyset.$$

Let $\Gamma = \bar{\Gamma}$. Then,

$$\begin{aligned}
L_{union}(\Gamma) &= \{w \mid (S_1, S_2) \Rightarrow^*_\Gamma (w_1, w_2), w_i \in \Delta^*, \text{ for } i = 1, 2, \\
&\qquad w \in \{w_1, w_2\}\} \\
&= \{w \mid (S_1, S_2) \Rightarrow^*_\Gamma (w, w)\} \cup \{w \mid (S_1, S_2) \Rightarrow^*_\Gamma (w_1, w_2), \\
&\qquad w_i \in \Delta^*, \text{ for } i = 1, 2, w \in \{w_1, w_2\}, w_1 \neq w_2\} \\
&= \{w \mid (S_1, S_2) \Rightarrow^*_\Gamma (w, w)\} \cup \emptyset \\
&= \{w \mid (S_1, S_2) \Rightarrow^*_\Gamma (w, w)\} \\
&= L.
\end{aligned}$$

Therefore, Theorem 13.36 holds. □

Theorem 13.37. *For any recursively enumerable language L over an alphabet Δ, there exists a 2-LMGR, $\Gamma = (G_1, G_2, Q)$, such that $L_{first}(\Gamma) = L$.*

Proof. By Theorem 13.35, for every recursively enumerable language L over an alphabet Δ, there exits a 2-LMGR

$$\bar{\Gamma} = ((\Sigma_1, \Delta, P_1, S_1), (\Sigma_2, \Delta, P_2, S_2), Q)$$

such that

$$\{w \in \Delta^* \mid (S_1, S_2) \Rightarrow^*_\Gamma (w, w)\} = L$$

and

$$\{w_1 w_2 \in \Delta^* \mid (S_1, S_2) \Rightarrow^*_\Gamma (w_1, w_2), w_1 \neq w_2\} = \emptyset.$$

Let $\Gamma = \bar{\Gamma}$. Then,

$$\begin{aligned}
L_{first}(\Gamma) &= \{w_1 \mid (S_1, S_2) \Rightarrow^*_\Gamma (w_1, w_2), w_i \in \Delta^*, \text{ for } i = 1, 2\} \\
&= \{w \mid (S_1, S_2) \Rightarrow^*_\Gamma (w, w)\} \cup \{w_1 \mid (S_1, S_2) \Rightarrow^*_\Gamma (w_1, w_2), \\
&\qquad w_i \in \Delta^*, \text{ for } i = 1, 2, w_1 \neq w_2\} \\
&= \{w \mid (S_1, S_2) \Rightarrow^*_\Gamma (w, w)\} \cup \emptyset \\
&= \{w \mid (S_1, S_2) \Rightarrow^*_\Gamma (w, w)\} \\
&= L.
\end{aligned}$$

Therefore, Theorem 13.37 holds. □

Theorem 13.38. *For any recursively enumerable language L over an alphabet Δ, there exists a 2-LMGR, $\Gamma = (G_1, G_2, Q)$, such that $L_{conc}(\Gamma) = L$.*

Proof. By Theorem 13.35, we have that for every recursively enumerable language L over an alphabet Δ, there exits a 2-LMGR

$$\bar{\Gamma} = ((\Sigma_1, \Delta, P_1, S_1), (\Sigma_2, \Delta, P_2, S_2), Q)$$

such that

$$\{w \in \Delta^* \mid (S_1, S_2) \Rightarrow^*_\Gamma (w, w)\} = L$$

and

$$\{w_1w_2 \in \Delta^* \mid (S_1, S_2) \Rightarrow_\Gamma^* (w_1, w_2), w_1 \neq w_2\} = \emptyset.$$

Let $G_1 = (\Sigma_1, \Delta, P_1, S_1)$ and $G_2 = (\Sigma_2, \emptyset, \bar{R}_2, S_2)$, where $\bar{R}_2 = \{A \rightarrow g(x) \mid A \rightarrow x \in P_2\}$, where g is a homomorphism from Σ_2^* to N_2^* defined as $g(X) = X$, for all $X \in N_2$, and $g(a) = \varepsilon$, for all $a \in \Delta$. We prove that $L_{conc}(\Gamma) = L$.

(I) We prove that $L \subseteq L_{conc}(\Gamma)$. Let $w \in L$. Then, there exists a derivation of the form

$(S_1, S_2) \Rightarrow_\Gamma^* (w, w)$.

Thus, there exist a derivation of the form

$(S_1, S_2) \Rightarrow_\Gamma^* (w, g(w))$.

Since $g(a) = \varepsilon$, for all $a \in \Delta$, $g(w) = \varepsilon$, for all $w \in \Delta^*$. Thus,

$(S_1, S_2) \Rightarrow_\Gamma^* (w, \varepsilon)$.

Hence, $w\varepsilon = w$ and $w \in L_{conc}(\Gamma)$;

(II) We prove that $L_{conc}(\Gamma) \subseteq L$. Let $w \in L$. Then, there exists a derivation of the form

$(S_1, S_2) \Rightarrow_\Gamma^* (w, \varepsilon)$,

because $L(G_2) = \{\varepsilon\}$. Since $g(x) = \varepsilon$ in Γ, for all $x \in \Delta^*$, there is a derivation of the form

$(S_1, S_2) \Rightarrow_\Gamma^* (w, x)$

where x is any string. Theorem 13.35 implies that $x = w$. Thus,

$(S_1, S_2) \Rightarrow_\Gamma^* (w, w)$.

Hence, $w \in L$.

By (I) and (II), Theorem 13.38 holds. □

We close this section by suggesting the next open-problem area.

Open Problem 13.14. By analogy with leftmost n-generative rule synchronized grammar systems, discussed in this section, introduce leftmost n-generative nonterminal-synchronized grammar systems and study their generative power.

Chapter 14
Jumping models

Take a typical program p that processes information i within the framework of today's information technologies. During a computational step, p usually reads a piece of information x in i, erases it, generates a new piece of information y, and inserts y into somewhere into i, whereas the position of this insertion may occur far away from the original position of x, which was erased. Therefore, to put it simply, during its computation, p keeps jumping across i as a whole. To investigate this kind of modern computation mathematically, the language theory should provide computer science with appropriate mathematical models.

The classical versions of automata and grammars work on words strictly continuously, however. Consequently, they can hardly serve as appropriate models for this purpose. A proper formalization of processors that work in the way sketched above necessitates an adaptation of classical grammars, so they work on words discontinuously. At the same time, any adaptation of this kind should conceptually maintain the original structure of these models as much as possible, so computer science can quite naturally base its investigation upon these newly adapted grammatical models by analogy with the standard approach based upon their classical versions. That is, these new models should work on words in a discontinuous way while keeping their structural conceptualization unchanged. This chapter discusses models that work in this discontinuous way. Indeed, automata and grammars discussed in this section are conceptualized just like their classical versions except that during the applications of their rules, they can jump over symbols in either direction within the rewritten strings, and in this jumping way, they define their languages.

The chapter consists of three sections. Section 14.1 studies jumping grammars, which work in a sequential way. Section 14.2 discusses their parallel versions. Finally, Section 14.3 covers jumping automata.

14.1 Sequential jumping grammars

Recall that a classical phrase-structure grammar (PSG) G (see Section 11.1) represents a language-generating rewriting system based upon an alphabet of symbols and a finite set of rules. The alphabet of symbols is divided into two disjoint subalphabets—the alphabet of terminal symbols and the alphabet of nonterminal symbols. Each rule is of the form $x \rightarrow y$, where x and y are strings over the alphabet of G, where x and y are referred to as the left-hand side and the right-hand side of $x \rightarrow y$. G applies $x \rightarrow y$ strictly sequentially, so it rewrites a string z according to $x \rightarrow y$ so it (1) selects an occurrence of x in z, (2) erases it, and (3) inserts y precisely at the position of this erasure. More mathematically speaking, let $z = uxv$, where u and v are strings. By using $x \rightarrow y$, G rewrites uxv as uyv. Starting from a special start nonterminal symbol, G repeatedly rewrites strings according to its rules in this sequential way until it obtains a sentence—that is, a string that solely consists of terminal symbols; the set of all sentences represents the language generated by the grammar.

In essence, the notion of a jumping grammar, discussed in this chapter, is conceptualized just like that of a classical grammar; however, it rewrites strings in a jumping way. Consider G, described above, as a grammar that works in a jumping way. Let z and $x \rightarrow y$ have the same meaning as above. G rewrites a string z according to a rule $x \rightarrow y$ in such a way that it selects an occurrence of x in z, erases it, and inserts y anywhere in the rewritten string, so this insertion may occur at a different position than the erasure of x. In other words, G rewrites a string z according to $x \rightarrow y$, so it performs (1) and (2) as described above, but during (3), G can jump over a portion of the rewritten string in either direction and insert y there. Formally, by using $x \rightarrow y$, G rewrites ucv as udv, where $u; v; w; c; d$ are strings such that either (1) $c = xw$ and $d = wy$ or (2) $c = wx$ and $d = yw$.

The present section primarily investigates the generative power of jumping grammars. First, it compares the generative power of jumping grammars with the accepting power of jumping finite automata (JFAs). More specifically, it demonstrates that regular jumping grammars are as powerful as JFAs. Regarding grammars, the general versions of jumping grammars are as powerful as classical PSGs. As there exist many important special versions of these classical grammars, we discuss their jumping counterparts in the present section as well. We study the jumping versions of context-free grammars (CFGs) and their special cases, including regular grammars (RGs), right-linear grammars (RLGs), and linear grammars (LGs). Surprisingly, all of them have a different power than their classical counterparts. In the conclusion of this section, the section formulates several open problems and suggests future investigation areas.

Next, we introduce four modes of derivation relations, three of which represent jumping derivation steps. We also briefly recall some terminology, such as the notion of a PSG, introduced earlier in this book (see Section 11.1).

Definition 14.1. *Let $G = (\Sigma, \Delta, R, S)$ be a PSG. We introduce four* modes of derivation steps *as derivation relations over Σ^*—namely, ${}_s\Rightarrow$, ${}_{lj}\Rightarrow$, ${}_{rj}\Rightarrow$, and ${}_j\Rightarrow$.*

Let $u, v \in \Sigma^*$. We define the four derivation relations as follows:

(i) $u \; {}_s\Rightarrow v$ *in G iff there exist $x \rightarrow y \in R$ and $w, z \in \Sigma^*$ such that $u = wxz$ and $v = wyz$.*

(ii) $u \; {}_{lj}\Rightarrow v$ *in G iff there exist $x \rightarrow y \in R$ and $w, t, z \in \Sigma^*$ such that $u = wtxz$ and $v = wytz$.*

(iii) $u \; {}_{rj}\Rightarrow v$ *in G iff there exist $x \rightarrow y \in R$ and $w, t, z \in \Sigma^*$ such that $u = wxtz$ and $v = wtyz$.*

(iv) $u \; {}_j\Rightarrow v$ *in G iff $u \; {}_{lj}\Rightarrow v$ or $u \; {}_{rj}\Rightarrow v$ in G.*

Let ${}_h\Rightarrow$ be one of the four derivation relations (i)–(iv) over Σ^*; in other words, h equals s, lj, rj, or j. As usual, for every $n \geq 0$, the nth power of ${}_h\Rightarrow$ is denoted by ${}_h\Rightarrow^n$. The transitive-reflexive closure and the transitive closure of ${}_h\Rightarrow$ are denoted by ${}_h\Rightarrow^*$ and ${}_h\Rightarrow^+$, respectively.

Example 14.1. *Consider the following RG:*

$$G = (\{A, B, C, a, b, c\}, \Delta = \{a, b, c\}, R, A),$$

where $R = \{A \to aB,\ B \to bC,\ C \to cA,\ C \to c\}$. *Observe that*

$$L(G,\ {}_s\Rightarrow) = \{abc\}\{abc\}^*, \text{ but}$$

$$L(G,\ {}_j\Rightarrow) = \{w \in \Delta^* \mid \text{occur}(\{a\}, w) = \text{occur}(\{b\}, w) = \text{occur}(\{c\}, w)\}.$$

Notice that although $L(G,\ {}_s\Rightarrow)$ *is regular,* $L(G,\ {}_j\Rightarrow) \in \mathbf{CS}$ *is a well-known non-context-free language.*

Example 14.2. *Consider the following context-sensitive grammar (CSG)* $G = (\{S, A, B, a, b\}, \{a, b\}, R, S)$ *containing the following rules:*

$$\begin{aligned} S &\to aABb, \\ S &\to ab, \\ AB &\to AABB, \\ aA &\to aa, \\ Bb &\to bb. \end{aligned}$$

Trivially, $L(G,\ {}_s\Rightarrow) = \{a^n b^n \mid n \geq 1\}$. *Using* ${}_j\Rightarrow$, *we can make the following derivation sequence (the rewritten substring is underlined):*

$$\underline{S}\ {}_j\Rightarrow a\underline{AB}b\ {}_j\Rightarrow aAAB\underline{Bb}\ {}_j\Rightarrow \underline{aA}ABbb\ {}_j\Rightarrow a\underline{aA}Bbb\ {}_j\Rightarrow a\underline{Bb}baa\ {}_j\Rightarrow abbbaa.$$

Notice that $L(G,\ {}_s\Rightarrow)$ *is context-free, but we cannot generate this language by any CFG, CSG or even MONG in jumping derivation mode.*

Lemma 14.1. $\{a\}^*\{b\}^* \notin \mathscr{L}(\Gamma_{MONG},\ {}_j\Rightarrow)$.

Proof. Assume that there exists a MONG $G = (\Sigma, \Delta, R, S)$ such that $L(G,\ {}_j\Rightarrow) = \{a\}^*\{b\}^*$. Let $p\colon x \to y \in R$ be the last applied rule during a derivation $S\ {}_j\Rightarrow^+ w$, where $w \in L(G,\ {}_j\Rightarrow)$, that is, $S\ {}_j\Rightarrow^* uxv\ {}_j\Rightarrow w\ [p]$, where $u, v, w \in \Delta^*$ and $y \in \{a\}^+ \cup \{b\}^+ \cup \{a\}^+\{b\}^+$. In addition, assume that the sentential form uxv is longer than x such that $uv \in \{a\}^+\{b\}^+$.

(i) If y contains at least one symbol b, the last jumping derivation step can place y at the beginning of the sentence and create a string from

$$\{a, b\}^*\{b\}\{a, b\}^*\{a\}\{a, b\}^*$$

that does not belong to $\{a\}^*\{b\}^*$.

(ii) By analogy, if y contains at least one symbol a, the last jumping derivation step can place y at the end of the sentence and, therefore, place at least one a behind some bs.

This is a contradiction, so there is no MONG that generates the regular language $\{a\}^*\{b\}^*$ using ${}_j\Rightarrow$. ■

We reopen a discussion related to Lemma 14.1 at the end of this section.

Corollary 14.1. *The following pairs of language families are incomparable, but not disjoint:*

(i) **REG** *and* $\mathscr{L}(\Gamma_{MONG}, {}_j\Rightarrow)$,
(ii) **CF** *and* $\mathscr{L}(\Gamma_{MONG}, {}_j\Rightarrow)$,
(iii) **REG** *and* $\mathscr{L}(\Gamma_{RG}, {}_j\Rightarrow)$,
(iv) **CF** *and* $\mathscr{L}(\Gamma_{RG}, {}_j\Rightarrow)$.

Proof. Since **REG** $\subset$ **CF**, it is sufficient to prove that **REG** $-$ $\mathscr{L}(\Gamma_{MONG}, {}_j\Rightarrow)$, $\mathscr{L}(\Gamma_{RG}, {}_j\Rightarrow)$ $-$ **CF**, and **REG** $\cap$ $\mathscr{L}(\Gamma_{RG}, {}_j\Rightarrow)$ are non-empty. By Lemma 14.1,

$$\{a\}^*\{b\}^* \in \mathbf{REG} - \mathscr{L}(\Gamma_{MONG}, {}_j\Rightarrow).$$

In Example 14.1, we define a jumping RG that generates a non-context-free language that belongs to $\mathscr{L}(\Gamma_{RG}, {}_j\Rightarrow)$ $-$ **CF**. Observe that regular language $\{a\}^*$ belongs to $\mathscr{L}(\Gamma_{RG}, {}_j\Rightarrow)$, so **REG** $\cap$ $\mathscr{L}(\Gamma_{RG}, {}_j\Rightarrow)$ is non-empty. ■

As even some very simple regular language such as $\{a\}^+\{b\}^+$ cannot be generated by jumping derivation in CSGs or even MONGs, we pinpoint the following open problem and state a theorem comparing these families with context-sensitive languages.

Open Problem 14.1. *Is* $\mathscr{L}(\Gamma_{CSG}, {}_j\Rightarrow) \subseteq \mathscr{L}(\Gamma_{MONG}, {}_j\Rightarrow)$ *proper?*

Theorem 14.1. $\mathscr{L}(\Gamma_{MONG}, {}_j\Rightarrow) \subset$ **CS**.

Proof. To see that $\mathscr{L}(\Gamma_{MONG}, {}_j\Rightarrow) \subseteq$ **CS**, we demonstrate how to transform any jumping MONG, $G = (\Sigma_G, \Delta, R_G, S)$, to a MONG, $H = (\Sigma_H, \Delta, R_H, S)$, such that $L(G, {}_j\Rightarrow) = L(H, {}_s\Rightarrow)$. Set $\Sigma_H = N_H \cup \Delta$ and $N_H = N_G \cup \{\bar{X} \mid X \in \Sigma_G\}$. Let π be the homomorphism from Σ_G^* to Σ_H^* defined by $\pi(X) = \bar{X}$ for all $X \in \Sigma_G$. Set $R_H = R_1 \cup R_2$, where

$$R_1 = \bigcup_{\alpha \to \beta \in R_G} \{\alpha \to \pi(\beta), \pi(\beta) \to \beta\}$$

and

$$R_2 = \bigcup_{\alpha \to \beta \in R_G} \{X\pi(\beta) \to \pi(\beta)X, \pi(\beta)X \to X\pi(\beta) \mid X \in \Sigma_G\}.$$

As obvious, $L(G, {}_j\Rightarrow) = L(H, {}_s\Rightarrow)$. Clearly, $\{a\}^*\{b\}^* \in$ **CS**. Thus, by Lemma 14.1, **CS** $-$ $\mathscr{L}(\Gamma_{MONG}, {}_j\Rightarrow) \neq \emptyset$, so this theorem holds. ■

Example 14.3. *Consider the language of all well-written arithmetic expressions with parentheses* (,) *and* [,]. *Eliminate everything but the parentheses in this language to obtain the language* $L(G, {}_s\Rightarrow)$ *defined by the CFG* $G = (\Sigma = \{E, (,), [,]\}, \Delta = \{(,), [,]\}, \{E \to (E)E, E \to [E]E, E \to \varepsilon\}, E)$. *G is not of a finite index (see Example 10.1 on page 210 in [11]). Consider the jumping RLG* $H = (\Sigma, \Delta, R_H, E)$, *where* R_H *contains*

$$E \to ()E,$$
$$E \to []E,$$
$$E \to \varepsilon.$$

Since H is a RLG, there is at most one occurrence of E in any sentential form derived from E in H, so H is of index 1. *Next, we sketch a proof that* $L(G, {}_s\Rightarrow) = L(H, {}_j\Rightarrow)$. *As obvious,* $\{\varepsilon, (), []\} \subseteq L(G, {}_s\Rightarrow) \cap L(H, {}_j\Rightarrow)$. *Consider*

$$\alpha E\beta \; {}_s\Rightarrow \alpha(E)E\beta \; [E \to (E)E] \; {}_s\Rightarrow^* \alpha(\gamma)\delta\beta$$

in G with $\gamma \neq \varepsilon$. *H can simulate this derivation as follows:*

$$\alpha E\beta \; {}_j\Rightarrow \alpha()E\beta \; {}_j\Rightarrow^* \alpha()\delta' E\delta''\beta \; {}_j\Rightarrow \alpha(xE)\delta\beta \; {}_j\Rightarrow^* \alpha(\gamma)\delta\beta,$$

where $\delta = \delta'\delta''$, $x \in \{(), []\}$, *and* $\alpha, \beta, \gamma, \delta \in \Sigma^*$. *For* $\gamma = \varepsilon$, *we modify the previous jumping derivation so that we make a jumping derivation step from* $\alpha()\delta' E\delta''\beta$ *to* $\alpha()\delta\beta$ *by* $E \to \varepsilon$ *in H. We deal with* $E \to [E]E$ *analogically, so* $L(G, {}_s\Rightarrow) \subseteq L(H, {}_j\Rightarrow)$. *Since* $L(G, {}_s\Rightarrow)$ *contains all proper strings with the three types of parentheses, to prove* $L(H, {}_j\Rightarrow) \subseteq L(G, {}_s\Rightarrow)$, *we have to show that H cannot generate an improper string of parentheses. As each non-erasing rule of H inserts both left and right parenthesis in the sentential form at once, the numbers of parentheses are always well-balanced. In addition, in H, we cannot generate an improper mixture of the two kinds of parentheses, such as* ([)], *or an improper parenthesis order, such as*)(, *so* $L(G, {}_s\Rightarrow) = L(H, {}_j\Rightarrow)$.

Results

Relations between the language families resulting from various jumping grammars

We establish several relations between the language families generated by jumping versions of grammars defined earlier in this section.

Theorem 14.2. $\mathscr{L}(\Gamma_{RLG}, {}_j\Rightarrow) = \mathscr{L}(\Gamma_{LG}, {}_j\Rightarrow) = \bigcup_{k\geq 1} \mathscr{L}(\Gamma_{CFG}, {}_j\Rightarrow_k)$.

Proof. Since $\mathscr{L}(\Gamma_{RLG}, {}_j\Rightarrow) \subseteq \mathscr{L}(\Gamma_{LG}, {}_j\Rightarrow) \subseteq \bigcup_{k\geq 1} \mathscr{L}(\Gamma_{CFG}, {}_j\Rightarrow_k)$ follows from the definitions, it suffices to proof that $\bigcup_{k\geq 1} \mathscr{L}(\Gamma_{CFG}, {}_j\Rightarrow_k) \subseteq \mathscr{L}(\Gamma_{RLG}, {}_j\Rightarrow)$.

Construction. Let Σ and Δ be an alphabet and an alphabet of terminals, respectively. Set $N = \Sigma - \Delta$. Let $\eta\colon \Sigma \to N \cup \{\varepsilon\}$ be the homomorphism such that $\eta(X) = X$ if $X \in N$; otherwise, $\eta(X) = \varepsilon$. Let $\tau\colon \Sigma \to \Delta \cup \{\varepsilon\}$ be the homomorphism such that $\tau(X) = X$ if $X \in \Delta$; otherwise, $\eta(X) = \varepsilon$. As usual, extend η and τ to strings of symbols.

For every CFG $G = (\Sigma_G, \Delta, R_G, S)$ and index $k \geq 1$, we construct an RLG $H = (\Sigma_H, \Delta, R_H, \langle S \rangle)$ such that $L(G, {}_j\Rightarrow_k) = L(H, {}_j\Rightarrow)$. Set

$$\Sigma_H = \left\{ \langle x \rangle \mid x \in \bigcup_{i=1}^{k} (\Sigma_G - \Delta)^i \right\} \cup \Delta$$

and set

$$R_H = \{\langle \alpha A \beta \rangle \to \tau(x)\langle \gamma \rangle \mid A \to x \in R_G, \alpha, \beta \in N^*, \gamma = \alpha\beta\eta(x), 1 \leq |\gamma| \leq k\}$$
$$\cup \{\langle A \rangle \to x \mid A \to x \in R_G, x \in \Delta^*\}.$$

Basic Idea. CFG G working with index k means that every sentential form contains at most k nonterminal symbols. In jumping derivation mode, the position of nonterminal symbol does not matter for context-free rewriting. Together with the finiteness of N, we can store the list of nonterminals using just one nonterminal from constructed $\Sigma_H - \Delta$ in the simulating RLG.

For every jumping derivation step $\gamma A \delta \ {}_j\Rightarrow_k \gamma' x \delta'$ by $A \to x$ in G, there is a simulating jumping derivation step $\tau(\bar{\gamma})\langle \eta(\gamma A \delta) \rangle \tau(\bar{\delta}) \ {}_j\Rightarrow \tau(\bar{\gamma}')\tau(x)\langle \eta(\gamma \delta x) \rangle \tau(\bar{\delta}')$ in H, where $\gamma\delta = \gamma'\delta' = \bar{\gamma}\bar{\delta} = \bar{\gamma}'\bar{\delta}'$. The last simulating step of jumping application of $A \to w$ with $w \in \Delta^*$ replaces the only nonterminal of the form $\langle A \rangle$ by w that can be placed anywhere in the string. ■

Consider the finite index restriction in the family $\bigcup_{k \geq 1} \mathscr{L}(\Gamma_{CFG}, {}_j\Rightarrow_k)$ in Theorem 14.2. Dropping this restriction gives rise to the question whether the inclusion $\bigcup_{k \geq 1} \mathscr{L}(\Gamma_{CFG}, {}_j\Rightarrow_k) \subseteq \mathscr{L}(\Gamma_{CFG}, {}_j\Rightarrow)$ is proper or not. The next theorem was recently proved.

Theorem 14.3 (see Theorem 3.10 in [51]).

$$\bigcup_{k \geq 1} \mathscr{L}(\Gamma_{CFG}, {}_j\Rightarrow_k) \subset \mathscr{L}(\Gamma_{CFG}, {}_j\Rightarrow).$$

Indeed, from a broader perspective, an investigation of finite-index-based restrictions placed upon various jumping grammars and their effect on the resulting generative power represents a challenging open-problem area as illustrated by Example 14.3.

Theorem 14.4. $\mathscr{L}(\Gamma_{CFG^{-\varepsilon}}, {}_j\Rightarrow) = \mathscr{L}(\Gamma_{CFG}, {}_j\Rightarrow)$.

Proof. It is straightforward to establish this theorem by analogy with the same statement reformulated in terms of ordinary CFGs, which works based on ${}_s\Rightarrow$ (see Theorem 5.1.3.2.4 on page 328 in [52]). ■

Lemma 14.2. $\mathbf{RE} \subseteq \mathscr{L}(\Gamma_{PSG}, {}_j\Rightarrow)$.

Proof. Construction. For every PSG $G = (\Sigma_G, \Delta, R_G, S_G)$, we construct another PSG $H = (\Sigma_H = \Sigma_G \cup \{S_H, \$, \#, \lfloor, \rfloor\}, \Delta, R_H, S_H)$ such that $L(G, {}_s\Rightarrow) = L(H, {}_j\Rightarrow)$. $S_H, \$, \#, \lfloor$, and $\rfloor$ are new nonterminal symbols in H. Set

$$R_H = \{S_H \to \#S_G, \# \to \lfloor\$, \lfloor\rfloor \to \#, \# \to \varepsilon\} \\ \cup \{\$\alpha \to \rfloor\beta \mid \alpha \to \beta \in R_G\}.$$

Basic Idea. Nonterminal # has at most one occurrence in the sentential form. # is generated by the initial rule $S_H \to \#S_G$. This symbol participates in the beginning and end of every simulation of the application of a rule from R_G. Each simulation consists of several jumping derivation steps:

(i) # is expanded to a string of two nonterminals—marker of a position ($\lfloor$), where the rule is applied in the sentential form, and auxiliary symbol ($) presented as a left context symbol in the left-hand side of every simulated rule from R_G.
(ii) For each $x \to y$ from R_G, $\$x \to \rfloor y$ is applied in H. To be able to finish the simulation properly, the right-hand side ($\rfloor y$) of applied rule has to be placed right next to the marker symbol $\lfloor$; otherwise, we cannot generate a sentence.
(iii) The end of the simulation (rule $\lfloor\rfloor \to \#$) checks that the jumping derivation was applied like in terms of ${}_s\Rightarrow$.
(iv) In the end, # is removed to finish the generation of a string of terminal symbols.

Claim 1. *Let y be a sentential form of H, that is, $S_H\,{}_j\Rightarrow^* y$. For every $X \in \{\#, \$, \lfloor, \rfloor, S_H\}$,* occur$(\{X\}, y) \leq 1$.

Proof. The claim follows from the rules in R_H (see the construction in the proof of Lemma 14.2). Note that occur$(\{\#, \$, \lfloor, \rfloor, S_H\}, y) \leq 2$ and in addition, if symbol # occurs in y, then occur$(\{\$, \lfloor, \rfloor, S_H\}, y) = 0$. □

Define the homomorphism $h\colon \Sigma_H^* \to \Sigma_G^*$ as $h(X) = X$ for all $X \in \Sigma_G$, $h(S_H) = S_G$, and $h(Y) = \varepsilon$ for all $Y \in \{\$, \#, \lfloor, \rfloor\}$.

Claim 2. *If $S_G\,{}_s\Rightarrow^m w$ in G, where $w \in \Delta^*$ and $m \geq 0$, then $S_H\,{}_j\Rightarrow^* w$ in H.*

Proof. First, we prove by induction on $m \geq 0$ that for every $S_G\,{}_s\Rightarrow^m x$ in G with $x \in \Sigma_G^*$, there is $S_H\,{}_j\Rightarrow^* x'$ in H such that $h(x') = x$.

Basis. For $S_G\,{}_s\Rightarrow^0 S_G$ in G, there is $S_H\,{}_j\Rightarrow \#S_G$ in H.

Induction Hypothesis. Suppose there exists $k \geq 0$ such that $S_G\,{}_s\Rightarrow^m x$ in G implies that $S_H\,{}_j\Rightarrow^* x'$ in H, where $h(x') = x$, for all $0 \leq m \leq k$.

Induction Step. Assume that $S_G\,{}_s\Rightarrow^k y\,{}_s\Rightarrow x$ in G. By the induction hypothesis, $S_H\,{}_j\Rightarrow^* y'$ in H with $h(y') = y$.

The derivation step $y\ _s\!\Rightarrow x$ in G is simulated by an application of three jumping rules from R_H in H to get $y'\ _j\!\Rightarrow^3 x'$ with $h(x') = x$ as follows:

$$\begin{aligned} y' = u'\#v'\ _j\!\Rightarrow u''\lfloor\$\alpha v'' \quad & [\# \to \lfloor\$] \\ _j\!\Rightarrow u''\lfloor\rfloor\beta v'' \quad & [\lfloor\rfloor \to \#] \\ _j\!\Rightarrow u'''\#v''' \quad & [\# \to \varepsilon] \quad = x', \end{aligned}$$

where $u'v' = u''\alpha v''$ and $u''\beta v'' = u'''v'''$.

In case $x \in \Delta^*$, there is one additional jumping derivation step during the simulation that erases the only occurrence of #-symbol (see Claim 1) by rule $\# \to \varepsilon$.

Note that $h(x)$ for $x \in \Delta^*$ is the identity. Therefore, in case $x \in \Delta^*$, the induction proves the claim. □

Claim 3. *If $S_H\ _j\!\Rightarrow^m w$ in H, for some $m \geq 0$, where $w \in \Delta^*$, then $S_G\ _s\!\Rightarrow^* w$ in G.*

Proof. To prove this claim, first, we prove by induction on $m \geq 0$ that for every $S_H\ _j\!\Rightarrow^m x$ in H with $x \in \Sigma_H^*$ such that there exists a jumping derivation $x\ _j\!\Rightarrow^* w$, where $w \in \Delta^*$, then $S_G\ _s\!\Rightarrow^* x'$ in G such that $h(x) = x'$.

Basis. For $m = 0$, when we have $S_H\ _j\!\Rightarrow^0 S_H\ _j\!\Rightarrow^* w$ in H, then there is $S_G\ _s\!\Rightarrow^0 S_G$ in G such that $h(S_H) = S_G$. Furthermore, for $m = 1$, we have $S_H\ _j\!\Rightarrow^1 \#S_G\ _j\!\Rightarrow^* w$ in H, then again there is $S_G\ _s\!\Rightarrow^0 S_G$ in G such that $h(\#S_G) = S_G$, so the basis holds.

Induction Hypothesis. Suppose there exists $k \geq 1$ such that $S_H\ _j\!\Rightarrow^m x\ _j\!\Rightarrow^* w$ in H implies that $S_G\ _s\!\Rightarrow^* x'$ in G, where $h(x) = x'$, for all $1 \leq m \leq k$.

Induction Step. Assume that $S_H\ _j\!\Rightarrow^k y\ _j\!\Rightarrow x\ _j\!\Rightarrow^* w$ in H with $w \in \Delta^*$. By the induction hypothesis, $S_G\ _s\!\Rightarrow^* y'$ in G such that $h(y) = y'$. Let $u, v \in \Sigma_G^*$ and $\bar{u}, \bar{v} \in \Sigma_H^*$. Let us examine the following possibilities of $y\ _j\!\Rightarrow x$ in H:

(i) $y = u\#v\ _j\!\Rightarrow \bar{u}\lfloor\$\bar{v} = x$ in H such that $uv = \bar{u}\bar{v}$: Simply, $y' = uv\ _s\!\Rightarrow^0 uv$ in G and by Claim 1 $h(\bar{u}\lfloor\$\bar{v}) = h(\bar{u}\bar{v}) = h(uv) = uv$.

(ii) $u\lfloor\$\alpha v\ _j\!\Rightarrow \bar{u}\rfloor\beta\bar{v}$ in H by rule $\$\alpha \to \rfloor\beta$ such that $uv = \bar{u}\bar{v}$: In fact, to be able to rewrite $\lfloor$, the symbol $\lfloor$ needs $\rfloor$ as its right neighbor, so $u = \bar{u}$ and $v = \bar{v}$ in this jumping derivation step; otherwise, the jumping derivation is prevented from generating a string of terminals. According to rule $\alpha \to \beta$, $u\alpha v\ _s\!\Rightarrow u\beta v$ in G and $h(\bar{u}\rfloor\beta\bar{v}) = u\beta v$.

(iii) $u\lfloor\rfloor v\ _j\!\Rightarrow \bar{u}\#\bar{v}$ in H such that $uv = \bar{u}\bar{v}$: In G, $uv\ _s\!\Rightarrow^0 uv$ and $h(\bar{u}\#\bar{v}) = h(\bar{u}\bar{v}) = h(uv) = uv$.

(iv) $u\#v\ _j\!\Rightarrow uv$ in H by $\# \to \varepsilon$: Trivially, $uv\ _s\!\Rightarrow^0 uv$ in G and $h(uv) = uv$.

If $x \in \Delta^*$, then the induction proves the claim. □

This closes the proof of Lemma 14.2. ■

Theorem 14.5. $\mathscr{L}(\Gamma_{PSG}, {}_j\!\Rightarrow) = \mathbf{RE}$.

Proof. By Turing–Church thesis, $\mathscr{L}(\Gamma_{PSG}, {}_j\!\Rightarrow) \subseteq \mathbf{RE}$. The opposite inclusion holds by Lemma 14.2 that is proved in details by Claims 2 and 3. ■

Properties of jumping derivations

We demonstrate that the order of nonterminals in a sentential form of jumping CFGs is irrelevant. Then, in this section, we study the semilinearity of language families generated by various jumping grammars.

As a generalization of the proof of Theorem 14.2, we give the following lemma demonstrating that the order in which nonterminals occur in sentential forms is irrelevant in jumping derivation mode based on context-free rules in terms of generative power.

Lemma 14.3. *Let η and τ be the homomorphisms from the proof of Theorem 14.2. For every $G \in \Gamma_X$ with $X \in \{RG, RLG, LG, CFG\}$ and $G = (\Sigma, \Delta, R, S)$ with $N = \Sigma - \Delta$, if $S\ {}_j\!\Rightarrow^* \gamma\ {}_j\!\Rightarrow^m w$ in G, $m \geq 0$, $\gamma \in \Sigma^*$, $w \in \Delta^*$, then for every $\delta \in \Sigma^*$ such that $\tau(\gamma) = \tau(\delta)$ and $\eta(\delta) \in \mathrm{perm}(\eta(\gamma))$, there is $\delta\ {}_j\!\Rightarrow^* w$ in G.*

Proof. We prove this lemma by induction on $m \geq 0$.

Basis. Let $m = 0$. That is, $S\ {}_j\!\Rightarrow^* \gamma\ {}_j\!\Rightarrow^0 w$ in G, so $\gamma = w$. By $\tau(\delta) = \tau(\gamma)$, we have $\gamma = w = \delta$, so $\delta\ {}_j\!\Rightarrow^0 w$ in G.

Induction Hypothesis. Assume that there exists $k \geq 0$ such that the lemma holds for all $0 \leq m \leq k$.

Induction Step. Assume that $S\ {}_j\!\Rightarrow^* \gamma\ {}_j\!\Rightarrow \gamma'\ [A \to x]\ {}_j\!\Rightarrow^k w$ in G with $k \geq 0$. Observe that $\tau(\delta) = \tau(\gamma)$ and $\eta(\delta) \in \mathrm{perm}(\eta(\gamma))$. By the abovementioned assumption, $|\eta(\gamma)| \geq 1$—that is $|\eta(\delta)| \geq 1$. Thus, the jumping derivation $\delta\ {}_j\!\Rightarrow^* w$ in G can be written as $\delta\ {}_j\!\Rightarrow \delta'\ [A \to x]\ {}_j\!\Rightarrow^* w$. Since all the rules in G are context-free, the position of A in δ and its context is irrelevant, and the occurrence of A in δ is guaranteed by the lemma precondition. During the application of $A \to x$, (1) an occurrence of A is found in δ, (2) removed, and (3) the right-hand side of the rule, x, is inserted anywhere in δ instead of A without preserving the position of the rewritten A. Assume x is inserted into δ' so that $\tau(\delta') = \tau(\gamma')$. We also preserve that $\eta(\delta') \in \mathrm{perm}(\eta(\gamma'))$; therefore, the lemma holds. ∎

Notice that even if there is no derivation $S\ {}_j\!\Rightarrow^* \delta$ in G, the lemma holds.

Note that based on the proof of Lemma 14.3, we can turn any jumping version of a CFG to an equivalent jumping CFG satisfying a modified Greibach normal form, in which each rule is of the form $A \to \alpha\beta$, where $\alpha \in \Delta^*$, $\beta \in N^*$. Observe that $\alpha \notin \Delta$. Consider, for instance, a context-free rule p with $\alpha = a_1 \cdots a_n$. By an application of p during a derivation of a string of terminals w, we arrange that a_1 appears somewhere in front of a_n in w. In other words, from Theorem 13 and Corollary 14 in [53] together with Theorem 14.55, it follows that for any language L, $L \in \mathscr{L}(\Gamma_{RG}, {}_j\!\Rightarrow)$ implies $L = \mathrm{perm}(L)$, which means that the order of all terminals in $w \in L$ is utterly irrelevant.

Corollary 14.2. *For every $G \in \Gamma_X$ with $X \in \{RG, RLG, LG, CFG\}$, $S\ {}_j\!\Rightarrow^* \gamma\ {}_j\!\Rightarrow^* w$ in G implies an existence of a derivation of the form*

$$S\ {}_j\!\Rightarrow^* \alpha\beta\ {}_j\!\Rightarrow^* w \text{ in } G$$

where $\alpha = \tau(\gamma)$*,* $\beta \in \mathrm{perm}(\eta(\gamma))$*, S is the start nonterminal, and w is a string of terminals.*

Definition 14.2. *([54]) Let* $w \in \Sigma^*$ *with* $\Sigma = \{a_1, \ldots, a_n\}$*. We define* Parikh vector *of w by* $\psi_\Sigma(w) = (\mathrm{occur}(a_1, w), \mathrm{occur}(a_2, w), \ldots, \mathrm{occur}(a_n, w))$*. A set of vectors is called* semilinear *if it can be represented as a union of a finite number of sets of the form* $\{v_0 + \sum_{i=1}^{m} \alpha_i v_i \mid \alpha_i \in \mathbb{N}, 1 \leq i \leq m\}$*, where* v_i *for* $0 \leq i \leq m$ *is an n-dimensional vector. A language* $L \subseteq \Sigma^*$ *is called* semilinear *if the set* $\psi_\Sigma(L) = \{\psi_\Sigma(w) \mid w \in L\}$ *is a semilinear set. A language family is* semilinear *if all its languages are semilinear.*

Lemma 14.4. *For X* $\in$ *{RG, RLG, LG, CFG},* $\mathscr{L}(\Gamma_X, {}_j\Rightarrow)$ *is semilinear.*

Proof. By Parikh's Theorem (see Theorem 6.9.2 on page 228 in [22]), for each context-free language $L \subseteq \Sigma^*$, $\psi_\Sigma(L)$ is semilinear. Let G be a CFG such that $L(G, {}_s\Rightarrow) = L$. From the definition of ${}_j\Rightarrow$ and CFG, it follows that $\psi(L(G, {}_s\Rightarrow)) = \psi(L(G, {}_j\Rightarrow))$, therefore $\psi(L(G, {}_j\Rightarrow))$ is semilinear as well. ∎

Recall that the family of context-sensitive languages is not semilinear (for instance, Example 2.3.1 and Theorem 2.3.1 in [12] implies that $\{a^{2^n} \mid n \geq 0\} \in \mathbf{CS}$, but is not semilinear language). By no means, this result rules out that $\mathscr{L}(\Gamma_{CSG}, {}_j\Rightarrow)$ or $\mathscr{L}(\Gamma_{MONG}, {}_j\Rightarrow)$ are semilinear. There is, however, other kind of results concerning multiset grammars (see [55]) saying that a context-sensitive multiset grammar generates a non-semilinear language. The multiset grammars work with Parikh vector of a sentential form, so the order of symbols in the sentential form is irrelevant. Then, all permutations of terminal strings generated by the grammar belong to the generated language.

Instead of the full definition of multiset grammars (see [55]), based on notions from the theory of macrosets, we introduce *multiset derivation mode* concerning the classical string formal language theory.

Definition 14.3. *Let* $G = (\Sigma, \Delta, R, S) \in \Gamma_{PSG}$ *be a grammar and* $u, v \in \Sigma^*$*; then,* $u \;{}_m\Rightarrow v\; [x \to y]$ *in G iff there exist* $x \to y \in R$ *and* $t, t', z, z' \in \Sigma^*$ *such that* $txt' \in \mathrm{perm}(u)$*,* $zyz' \in \mathrm{perm}(v)$*, and* $tt' \in \mathrm{perm}(zz')$*.*

Lemma 14.5. *Let* $G \in \Gamma_{PSG}$*; then,* $w \in L(G, {}_m\Rightarrow)$ *implies that* $\mathrm{perm}(w) \subseteq L(G, {}_m\Rightarrow)$*.*

Proof. Consider Definition 14.3 with v representing every permutation of v in every $u \;{}_m\Rightarrow v$ in G to see that this lemma holds true. ∎

Recall that $\mathscr{L}(\Gamma_{MONG}, {}_m\Rightarrow)$ is not semilinear (see [55]). As every context-sensitive multiset grammar can be transformed into a CSG that generates the same language under jumping derivation mode, we establish the following theorem:

Theorem 14.6. $\mathscr{L}(\Gamma_{CSG}, {}_j\Rightarrow)$ *is not semilinear. Neither is* $\mathscr{L}(\Gamma_{MONG}, {}_j\Rightarrow)$*.*

Proof. Recall that $\mathscr{L}(\Gamma_{MONG}, {}_m\Rightarrow)$ contains non-semilinear languages (see Theorem 1 in [55]). Thus, to prove Theorem 14.6, we only need to prove that $\mathscr{L}(\Gamma_{MONG}, {}_{m}\Rightarrow) \subseteq \mathscr{L}(\Gamma_{CSG}, {}_{j}\Rightarrow)$ because $\mathscr{L}(\Gamma_{CSG}, {}_{j}\Rightarrow) \subseteq \mathscr{L}(\Gamma_{MONG}, {}_{j}\Rightarrow)$ follows from Definition 14.1.

Construction. For every MONG $G = (\Sigma_G, \Delta, R_G, S)$, we next construct a CSG $H = (\Sigma_H, \Delta, R_H, S)$ such that $L(G, {}_{m}\Rightarrow) = L(H, {}_{j}\Rightarrow)$. Let $N_G = \Sigma_G - \Delta$ and h be the homomorphism $h\colon \Sigma_G^* \to \Sigma_H^*$ defined as $h(X) = X$ for all $X \in N_G$ and $h(a) = \langle a \rangle$ for all $a \in \Delta$. First, set $\Sigma_H = \Sigma_G \cup N_t \cup N_{cs}$, where $N_t = \{\langle a \rangle \mid a \in \Delta\}$ and $N_{cs} = \{{}_pX \mid X \in N_G \cup N_t, p \in R_G \text{ with } |\operatorname{lhs} p| > 1\}$. For every $p \in R_G$ with $|\operatorname{lhs} p| > 1$, let $g_p\colon (N_G \cup N_t)^* \to N_{cs}^*$ be the homomorphism defined as $g_p(X) = {}_pX$ for all $X \in N_G \cup N_t$. Set $R_t = \{\langle a \rangle \to a \mid a \in \Delta\}$, $R_{cf} = \{A \to h(x) \mid A \to x \in R_G, A \in \Sigma_G - \Delta \text{ and } x \in \Sigma_G^*\}$, and $R_{cs} = \emptyset$. For every rule $p\colon X_1X_2 \cdots X_n \to Y_1Y_2 \cdots Y_m \in R_G$ with $2 \le n \le m$, where $X_i, Y_{i'} \in \Sigma_G$, $1 \le i \le n$, and $1 \le i' \le m$, add these $2n$ new rules with labels $p_1, p_2, \ldots, p_{2n}$

$$
\begin{aligned}
p_1\colon &\quad h(X_1X_2\cdots X_n) \to g_p(h(X_1))h(X_2\cdots X_n),\\
p_2\colon &\quad g_p(h(X_1))h(X_2\cdots X_n) \to g_p(h(X_1X_2))h(X_3\cdots X_n),\\
&\quad\vdots\\
p_n\colon &\quad g_p(h(X_1X_2\cdots X_{n-1}))h(X_n) \to g_p(h(X_1X_2\cdots X_{n-1}X_n)),\\
p_{n+1}\colon &\quad g_p(h(X_1X_2\cdots X_n)) \to h(Y_1)g_p(h(X_2\cdots X_n)),\\
p_{n+2}\colon &\quad h(Y_1)g_p(h(X_2\cdots X_n)) \to h(Y_1Y_2)g_p(h(X_3\cdots X_n)),\\
&\quad\vdots\\
p_{2n}\colon &\quad h(Y_1Y_2\cdots Y_{n-1})g_p(h(X_n)) \to h(Y_1Y_2\cdots Y_{n-1}Y_nY_{n+1}\cdots Y_m)
\end{aligned}
$$

into R_{cs}. Set $R_c = \{A \to A \mid A \in \Sigma_H - \Delta\}$. Finally, set $R_H = R_{cf} \cup R_t \cup R_c \cup R_{cs}$.

Basic Idea. There are two essential differences between multiset derivation mode of a MONG and jumping derivation mode of a CSG.

(I) While a MONG rewrites a string at once in a single derivation step, a CSG rewrites only a single nonterminal that occurs within a given context during a single derivation step.

(II) In the multiset derivation mode, the mutual neighborhood of the rewritten symbols is completely irrelevant—that is, G applies any rule without any restriction placed upon the mutual adjacency of the rewritten symbols in the multiset derivation mode (see Definition 14.3). To put this in a different way, G rewrites any permutation of the required context in this way.

In the construction of the jumping CSG H, which simulates the multiset MONG G, we arrange (II) as follows:

(I.a) In H, the only rules generating terminals belong to R_t. By using homomorphism h, in every other rule, each terminal a is changed to the corresponding nonterminal $\langle a \rangle$.

(II.b) In R_c, there are rules that can rearrange the order of all nonterminals arbitrarily in any sentential form of H. Thus, considering (I.a), just like in G, no context restriction placed upon the mutual adjacency of rewritten symbols occurs in H. Indeed, H only requires the occurrence of the symbols from $h(\operatorname{lhs} p)$ during the simulation of an application of $p \in R_G$.

In order to arrange (I), an application of a monotonous context-sensitive rule $p\colon X_1X_2\cdots X_n \to Y_1Y_2\cdots Y_m \in R_G$, $2 \le n \le m$ in $u\ {}_m{\Rightarrow}\ v\ [p]$ in G is simulated in H by the following two phases:

(i) First, H verifies that a sentential form u contains all symbols from $h(\text{lhs}\,p)$ and marks them by subscript p for the consecutive rewriting. Therefore, to finish the simulation of the application of p, H has to use rules created based on p during the construction of R_{cs} since no other rules from R_H rewrite symbols ${}_pX$, $X \in N_G \cup N_t$.

$$\begin{array}{llll} u\ {}_j{\Rightarrow}^* & \alpha_0 X_1'X_2'\cdots X_n'\,\beta_0\ [\rho_0] & {}_j{\Rightarrow}\ u_1\ [p_1] \\ {}_j{\Rightarrow}^* & \alpha_{1p}X_1'X_2'\cdots X_n'\,\beta_1\ [\rho_1] & {}_j{\Rightarrow}\ u_2\ [p_2] \\ {}_j{\Rightarrow}^* & \alpha_{2p}X_{1p}'X_2'\cdots X_n'\,\beta_2\ [\rho_2] & {}_j{\Rightarrow}\ u_3\ [p_3] \\ \vdots & & \\ {}_j{\Rightarrow}^* & \multicolumn{2}{l}{\alpha_{n-1p}X_{1p}'X_2'\cdots {}_pX_{n-1}'X_n'\,\beta_{n-1}\ [\rho_{n-1}]\ {}_j{\Rightarrow}\ u_n\ [p_n],} \end{array}$$

where $\rho_i \in R_c^*$ for $0 \le i < n$ and $X_\ell' = h(X_\ell)$ for $1 \le \ell \le n$.

(ii) Then, by performing $u_n\ {}_j{\Rightarrow}^*\ v$, H simulates the application of p in G.

$$\begin{array}{llll} u_n\ {}_j{\Rightarrow}^* & \alpha_{np}X_{1p}'X_2'\cdots {}_pX_n'\,\beta_n\ [\rho_n] & {}_j{\Rightarrow}\ u_{n+1}\ [p_{n+1}] \\ {}_j{\Rightarrow}^* & \alpha_{n+1}Y_{1p}'X_2'\cdots {}_pX_n'\,\beta_{n+1}\ [\rho_{n+1}] & {}_j{\Rightarrow}\ u_{n+2}\ [p_{n+2}] \\ \vdots & & \\ {}_j{\Rightarrow}^* & \alpha_{2n-1}Y_1'Y_2'\cdots Y_{n-1p}'X_n'\,\beta_{2n-1}\ [\rho_{2n-1}] & {}_j{\Rightarrow}\ u_{2n}\ [p_{2n}] \\ = & \alpha_{2n}\,Y_1'Y_2'\cdots Y_m'\,\beta_{2n} & {}_j{\Rightarrow}^*\ v\ [\rho_{2n}], \end{array}$$

where $\rho_i \in R_c^*$ for $n \le i \le 2n$, $X_\ell' = h(X_\ell)$ for $1 \le \ell \le n$, and $Y_k' = h(Y_k)$ for $1 \le k \le m$.

The simulation of application of rules of R_G is repeated using rules from $R_c \cup R_{cf} \cup R_{cs}$ in H until a multiset derivation of a string of terminals in G is simulated. (In fact, we can simultaneously simulate more than one application of a rule from R_G if there is no interference in H.)

Then, in the final phase of the entire simulation, each nonterminal $\langle a\rangle$ is replaced with terminal a by using rules from R_t. To be precise, the rules of R_t can be applied even sooner, but symbols rewritten by these rules can be no longer rewritten by rules from $R_c \cup R_{cf} \cup R_{cs}$ in H.

To formally prove that $L(G,\ {}_m{\Rightarrow}) = L(H,\ {}_j{\Rightarrow})$, we establish the following claims:

Claim 1. *Every $w \in L(H,\ {}_j{\Rightarrow})$ can be generated by a derivation of the form*

$$S\ {}_j{\Rightarrow}^*\ w'\ {}_j{\Rightarrow}^*\ w \text{ in } H \text{ such that } w' = h(w) \text{ and } w \in \Delta^*.$$

Proof. In the construction given in the proof of Theorem 14.6, we introduce R_{cf} and R_{cs} such that for every $p \in R_H - R_t$, $\text{rhs}\,p \in (\Sigma_H - \Delta)^*$. In $S\ {}_j{\Rightarrow}^*\ w'$, we apply rules only from $R_H - R_t$ so $w' \in N_t^*$, and no terminal symbol occurs in any sentential form in $S\ {}_j{\Rightarrow}^*\ w'$. Then, by rules from R_t, we generate w such that $w = h(w')$. □

Claim 2. *If* $w \in L(H, {}_j\Rightarrow)$, *then* $\mathrm{perm}(w) \subseteq L(H, {}_j\Rightarrow)$.

Proof. Let $w \in \Delta^*$. Assume that w is generated in H as described in Claim 1—that is, $S\ {}_j\Rightarrow^* w'\ {}_j\Rightarrow^* w$ such that $w' = h(w)$. Since rules from R_t rewrite nonterminals in w' one by one in the jumping derivation mode, we have $w'\ {}_j\Rightarrow^* w''$ in H for every $w'' \in \mathrm{perm}(w)$. □

Claim 3. *If* $S\ {}_m\Rightarrow^\ell v$ *in* G *for some* $\ell \geq 0$, *then* $S\ {}_j\Rightarrow^* v'$ *in* H *such that* $v' \in \mathrm{perm}(h(v))$.

Proof. We prove this claim by induction on $\ell \geq 0$.

Basis. Let $\ell = 0$. That is, $S\ {}_m\Rightarrow^0 S$ in G, so $S\ {}_j\Rightarrow^0 S$ in G. By $h(S) = S$, $S \in \mathrm{perm}(h(S))$.

Induction Hypothesis. Assume that the claim holds for all $0 \leq \ell \leq k$, for some $k \geq 0$.

Induction Step. Take any $S\ {}_m\Rightarrow^{k+1} v$. Express $S\ {}_m\Rightarrow^{k+1} v$ as

$$S\ {}_m\Rightarrow^k u\ {}_m\Rightarrow v\ [p\colon x \rightarrow y]$$

in G. By the induction hypothesis, $S\ {}_j\Rightarrow^* u'$ in H such that $u' \in \mathrm{perm}(h(u))$. According to the form of monotonous rule $p\colon x \rightarrow y \in R_G$, there are the following two cases, (i) and (ii), concerning $u\ {}_m\Rightarrow v$ in G to examine.

(i) $|x| = 1$: Let $x = A$. By the induction hypothesis, $\mathrm{occur}(\{A\}, u) \geq 1$ implies $\mathrm{occur}(\{A\}, u') \geq 1$. By the construction according to p, we have $p'\colon A \rightarrow h(y) \in R_{cf}$. Assume $u = u_1 A u_2\ {}_m\Rightarrow v$ in G with $u_1 y u_2 \in \mathrm{perm}(v)$. Then, $u' = u_1' A u_2'\ {}_j\Rightarrow u_3' h(y) u_4'\ [p'] = v'$ in H, where $u_1' u_2' = u_3' u_4'$, so $v' \in \mathrm{perm}(h(v))$.

(ii) $|x| \geq 2$: Let $x = X_1 X_2 \cdots X_n$, $y = Y_1 Y_2 \cdots Y_m$, where $|x| = n \leq m = |y|$, $X_i \in \Sigma_G$, $1 \leq i \leq n$, but $x \notin \Delta^*$, $Y_{i'} \in \Sigma_G$, $1 \leq i' \leq m$. By construction of R_{cs}, we have $p_1, p_2, \ldots, p_{2n} \in R_H$. If p can be applied in G, then, by the induction hypothesis, $\mathrm{occur}(\{X_i\}, u) = \mathrm{occur}(\{h(X_i)\}, u')$ for $1 \leq i \leq n$. To simulate the application of p in H, first, apply rules from R_c to yield $u'\ {}_j\Rightarrow^* u_1' h(X_1 X_2 \cdots X_n) u_2'$. Next, consecutively apply $p_1, p_2, \ldots, p_{2n}$ so $u_1' h(X_1 X_2 \cdots X_n) u_2'\ {}_j\Rightarrow^* u_3' h(Y_1 Y_2 \cdots Y_m) u_4' = v'$ with $u_1' u_2' = u_3' u_4'$ and $v' \in \mathrm{perm}(h(v))$. □

By Claim 3 with $v = w$ and $w \in \Delta^*$, for every $S\ {}_m\Rightarrow^* w$ in G, there is a derivation $S\ {}_j\Rightarrow^* w''$ in H such that $w'' \in \mathrm{perm}(h(w))$. By Claim 1, there is a jumping derivation in H from w'' to w' such that $w' \in \Delta^*$ and $w' \in \mathrm{perm}(w)$. Therefore, by Lemma 14.5 and Claim 2, if $w \in L(G, {}_m\Rightarrow)$, then $\mathrm{perm}(w) \subseteq L(H, {}_j\Rightarrow)$, so $L(G, {}_m\Rightarrow) \subseteq L(H, {}_j\Rightarrow)$.

Claim 4. *If* $S\ {}_j\Rightarrow^\ell v\ {}_j\Rightarrow^* \bar{v}$ *in* H *for some* $\ell \geq 0$, *then* $S\ {}_m\Rightarrow^* v'$ *in* G *such that* $\bar{v} \in \mathrm{perm}(h(v'))$.

Proof. We prove this claim by induction on $\ell \geq 0$.

Basis. Let $\ell = 0$. Express $S\ {}_j\Rightarrow^0 S\ {}_j\Rightarrow^* S$ as $S\ {}_j\Rightarrow^0 S\ {}_j\Rightarrow^0 S$ in H, therefore $S\ {}_m\Rightarrow^0 S$ in G. By $h(S) = S$, $S \in \mathrm{perm}(h(S))$.

Induction Hypothesis. Assume that the claim holds for all $0 \leq \ell \leq k$, for some $k \geq 0$.

Induction Step. Take any $S\ _j\Rightarrow^{k+1} v\ _j\Rightarrow^* \bar{v}$. Express $S\ _j\Rightarrow^{k+1} v\ _j\Rightarrow^* \bar{v}$ as

$$S\ _j\Rightarrow^k u\ _j\Rightarrow v\ [q\colon x \to y]_j\Rightarrow^* \bar{v}$$

in H. Without any loss of generality, assume that $q \in R_H - R_t$ so $u, v \in (\Sigma_H - \Delta)^*$ (see Claim 1). If $q \in R_{cf} \cup R_{cs}$, then p denotes the rule from R_G that implied the addition of q into R_{cf} or R_{cs} during the construction in the proof of Theorem 14.6. Without any loss of generality and with respect to p from R_G, assume that there is no simulation of another context-sensitive rule from R_G in progress in H, so $\text{occur}(N_{cs}, u_1u_2) = \text{occur}(N_{cs}, v_1v_2) = 0$, where $u = u_1xu_2$ and $v = v_1yv_2$. By the induction hypothesis, $S\ _j\Rightarrow^* u\ _j\Rightarrow^* \bar{u}$ in H implies $S\ _m\Rightarrow^* u'$ in G such that $\bar{u} \in \text{perm}(h(u'))$. Now, we study several cases based on the form of q:

(i) $q \in R_c$ and $x = y = A$: Then, in a jumping derivation $u\ _j\Rightarrow v\ [q]_j\Rightarrow^0 \bar{v}$ in H, $u = u_1Au_2$ and $v = v_1Av_2$, where $u_1u_2 = v_1v_2$, so $v = \bar{v} \in \text{perm}(u)$. By the induction hypothesis, with $u\ _j\Rightarrow^0 \bar{u}$ in H so $u = \bar{u}$, there is a derivation $S\ _m\Rightarrow^* u'$ in G such that $u \in \text{perm}(h(u'))$. Together with $\bar{v} \in \text{perm}(u)$, there is also a derivation $S\ _m\Rightarrow^* u'\ _m\Rightarrow^0 v'$ in G with $\bar{v} \in \text{perm}(h(v'))$.

(ii) $q \in R_{cf}$ and $x = A$: Then, $u = u_1Au_2$ and $v = v_1yv_2$ with $u_1u_2 = v_1v_2$ and $v\ _j\Rightarrow^0 \bar{v}$ in H, so $v = \bar{v}$. By the induction hypothesis, with $u\ _j\Rightarrow^0 \bar{u}$ in H so $u = \bar{u}$, there is $S\ _m\Rightarrow^* u'$ in G with $u \in \text{perm}(h(u'))$, and we can write $u' = u_1'Au_2'$. By the construction, $p\colon A \to y \in R_G$, so together with the induction hypothesis, we have $S\ _m\Rightarrow^* u_1'Au_2'\ _m\Rightarrow v'\ [p]$ in G, where $v' \in \text{perm}(u_1'yu_2')$, so $\bar{v} \in \text{perm}(h(v'))$.

(iii) $q = p_i \in R_{cs}$, where $1 \le i \le 2n$ and $n = |\,\text{lhs}\,p|$: Express $S\ _j\Rightarrow^k u\ _j\Rightarrow v\ _j\Rightarrow^* \bar{v}$ in H as

$$S\ _j\Rightarrow^{k-i+1} \tilde{u}\ _j\Rightarrow^{i-1} u\ [\tilde{\rho}]_j\Rightarrow v\ [p_i]_j\Rightarrow^* \alpha_{2n}h(Y_1Y_2\cdots Y_m)\beta_{2n}\ [\bar{\rho}] = \bar{v}$$

in H. By the construction of R_{cs} according to p and by the induction hypothesis, $\tilde{\rho} = p_1 \cdots p_{i-1}$ and $\bar{\rho} = p_{i+1} \cdots p_{2n}$. By the induction hypothesis, $S\ _m\Rightarrow^* \tilde{u}'$ in G such that $\tilde{u} \in \text{perm}(h(\tilde{u}'))$. Then, by the application of $p \in R_G$, we have $S\ _m\Rightarrow^* \tilde{u}'\ _m\Rightarrow v'$ such that $\bar{v} \in \text{perm}(h(v'))$.

In (iii), there are three subcases of $u\ _j\Rightarrow v$ with $u_1u_2 = v_1v_2$ in H:

(iii.a) $1 \le i \le n$: Then, $u = u_1g_p(h(X_1 \cdots X_{i-1}))h(X_iX_{i+1} \cdots X_n)u_2$ and $v = v_1g_p(h(X_1 \cdots X_{i-1}X_i))h(X_{i+1} \cdots X_n)v_2$.

(iii.b) $n < i < 2n$ and $i' = i - n$: Then, $u = u_1h(Y_1 \cdots Y_{i'-1})g_p(h(X_{i'}X_{i'+1} \cdots X_n))u_2$ and $v = v_1h(Y_1 \cdots Y_{i'})g_p(h(X_{i'+1} \cdots X_n))v_2$.

(iii.c) $i = 2n$: Then, $u = u_1h(Y_1 \cdots Y_{n-1})g_p(h(X_n))u_2$ and $v = v_1h(Y_1 \cdots Y_{n-1}Y_n \cdots Y_m)v_2$.

Therefore, the claim holds for $k + 1$ as well. □

Assume $v \in N_t^*$ in Claim 4 so $v' \in \Delta^*$. Based on Claim 1, without any loss of generality, we can assume that all rules from R_t are applied in the end of a derivation of $w \in \Delta^*$ in H. Specifically, $S\ _j\Rightarrow^* v\ [\rho_v]_j\Rightarrow^* w\ [\rho_w]$ in H, where $\rho_v \in (R_H - R_t)^*$, $\rho_w \in R_t^*$, and $v = h(w)$. By Claim 4, we have $S\ _m\Rightarrow^* v'$ in G with $v \in \text{perm}(h(v'))$. Recall that $v \in N_t^*$ and $v' \in \Delta^*$. Therefore, $S\ _m\Rightarrow^* v'$ in G and $w \in \text{perm}(v')$.

Next, by Claim 2, $w \in L(H, {}_j\Rightarrow)$ implies perm(w) $\subseteq L(H, {}_j\Rightarrow)$. By the previous paragraph and Lemma 14.5, for w, we generate perm(w) in G included in $L(G, {}_m\Rightarrow)$, that is, $L(H, {}_j\Rightarrow) \subseteq L(G, {}_m\Rightarrow)$.

This closes the proof of Theorem 14.6. ■

Concerning the semilinearity of language families defined by jumping grammars under investigation, the following corollary sums up all important properties established in this section.

Corollary 14.3. *$\mathscr{L}(\Gamma_X, {}_j\Rightarrow)$ is semilinear for $X \in$ {RG, RLG, LG, CFG} and not semilinear for $X \in$ {CSG, MONG, PSG}.*

Proof. For $\mathscr{L}(\Gamma_{PSG}, {}_j\Rightarrow)$, the non-semilinearity follows from the well-known facts that **CS** is not semilinear (see Example 2.3.1 and Theorem 2.3.1 in [12]) and **CS** $\subset$ **RE** and from Theorem 14.5. The rest follows from Lemma 14.4 and Theorem 14.6. ■

Corollary 14.4. $\mathscr{L}(\Gamma_{CFG}, {}_j\Rightarrow) \subset \mathscr{L}(\Gamma_{CSG}, {}_j\Rightarrow)$.

Proof. Obviously, by Definition 14.1, $\mathscr{L}(\Gamma_{CFG}, {}_j\Rightarrow) \subseteq \mathscr{L}(\Gamma_{CSG}, {}_j\Rightarrow)$. By Corollary 14.3, $\mathscr{L}(\Gamma_{CSG}, {}_j\Rightarrow)$ contains a non-semilinear language that does not belong to $\mathscr{L}(\Gamma_{CFG}, {}_j\Rightarrow)$. ■

We close this section by proposing several future investigation areas concerning jumping grammars. Some of them relate to specific open questions pointed out earlier in the section; the present section, however, formulates them more generally and broadly.

I *Other Types of Grammars*. The present section has concentrated its attention to the language families resulting from classical grammars, such as the grammars classified by Chomsky (see [9]). Apart from them, however, the formal language theory has introduced many other types of grammars, ranging from regulated grammars through parallel grammars up to grammar systems. Reconsider the present study in their terms.

II *Left and Right Jumping Mode*. Considering the left and right jumps introduced in Definition 14.1, study them in terms of classical types of grammars. Later in Section 14.3.2.5, this book gives an introduction to discussion of left and right jumping derivation modes in terms of automata.

III *Closure Properties*. Several results and some open problems concerning closure properties follows from Section 14.3.2.7. Additionally, study closure properties of language families generated in a jumping way. Specifically, investigate these properties in terms of CFGs, CSGs, and MONGs.

IV *Alternative Definition of Jumping Mode with Context*. Assume context-sensitive rules (CSG) of the following form:

$$\alpha A \beta \rightarrow \alpha \gamma \beta, \text{ where } A \in N, \alpha, \beta, \gamma \in \Sigma^*, \gamma \neq \varepsilon.$$

There are three interesting ways of defining a jumping derivation step:

IV.a Using the previous definition (see Definition 14.1) of jumping derivation; that is, find $\alpha A \beta$ in the current sentential form $u\alpha A\beta v$, remove $\alpha A\beta$, and place $\alpha\gamma\beta$ anywhere in uv. For instance,
$aAbc \ {}_j\Rightarrow caxb \ [aAb \to axb]$.

IV.b Do not move the context of the rewritten nonterminal, that is, find A with left context α and right context β, remove this A from the current sentential form, and place γ in the new sentential form, such that string γ will be again in the context of both α and β (but it can be different occurrence of α and β). For instance,
$aAbab \ {}_{j'}\Rightarrow abaxb \ [aAb \to axb]$.

IV.c Similar to (b), in the third variant, we do not move the context of the rewritten nonterminal either and, in addition, γ has to be placed between the same occurrence of α and β. As a consequence, context-sensitive rules are applied sequentially even in this jumping derivation mode. For instance,
$aAbab \ {}_{j''}\Rightarrow axbab \ [aAb \to axb]$.
Notice that this derivation mode influences only the application of context-free rules (i.e., $\alpha = \beta = \varepsilon$).

Example 14.4. *Example 14.2 shows a CSG that generates* $\{a^n b^n \mid n \geq 1\}$ *when the alternative jumping derivation mode* ${}_{j'}\Rightarrow$ *for CSGs is used. In context of Lemma 14.1, the alternative jumping derivation mode (b) can increase the generative power of jumping CSGs (a). In fact, it is an open question whether* $\mathscr{L}(\Gamma_{CSG}, {}_{j'}\Rightarrow) \subseteq \mathscr{L}(\Gamma_{MONG}, {}_{j'}\Rightarrow)$.

V *Relationship with Formal Macroset Theory*. Recently, formal language theory has introduced various rewriting devices that generate different objects than classical formal languages. Specifically, in this way, Formal Macroset Theory has investigated the generation of macrosets—that is, sets of multisets over alphabets. Notice that some of its results resemble results achieved in the present study (cf., for instance, Theorem 1 in [55] and Theorems 14.2 and 14.3 above). Explain this resemblance mathematically.

14.2 Parallel jumping grammars

This section introduces and studies jumping versions of scattered context grammars (SCGs) (see Section 13.1). To give an insight into the key motivation and reason for this study, let us take a closer look at a more specific kind of information processing in a discontinuous way. Consider a process p that deals with information i. Typically, during a single computational step, p (1) reads n pieces of information, x_1–x_n, in i, (2) erases them, (3) generate n new pieces of information, y_1–y_n, and (4) inserts them into i possibly at different positions than the original occurrence of x_1–x_n, which was erased. To explore computation like this systematically and rigorously, the present section introduces and discusses jumping versions of SCGs (see [56]), which represent suitable grammatical models of computation like this.

To see this suitability, recall that the notion of an SCG G represents a language-generating rewriting system based upon an alphabet of symbols and a finite set of rules. The alphabet of symbols is divided into two disjoint subalphabets—the alphabet of terminal symbols and the alphabet of nonterminal symbols. In G, a rule r is of the form

$$(A_1, A_2, \ldots, A_n) \rightarrow (x_1, x_2, \ldots, x_n)$$

for some positive integer n. On the left-hand side of r, the As are nonterminals. On the right-hand side, the xs are strings. G can apply r to any string u of the form

$$u = u_0 A_1 u_1 \cdots u_{n-1} A_n u_n,$$

where us are any strings. Notice that A_1–A_n are scattered throughout u, but they occur in the order prescribed by the left-hand side of r. In essence, G applies r to u so

(1) it deletes $A_1, A_2, \ldots, A_n$ in u, after which
(2) it inserts $x_1, x_2, \ldots, x_n$ into the string resulting from the deletion (1).

By this application, G makes a derivation step from u to a string v of the form

$$v = v_0 x_1 v_1 \cdots v_{n-1} x_n v_n.$$

Notice that $x_1, x_2, \ldots, x_n$ are inserted in the order prescribed by the right-hand side of r. However, they are inserted in a scattered way—that is, in between the inserted xs, some substrings vs occur.

To formalize the above-described computation, consisting of phases (1)–(4), the present section introduces and studies the following nine jumping derivation modes of the standard application:

(1) Mode 1 requires that $u_i = v_i$ for all $i = 0, \ldots, n$ in the above-described derivation step.
(2) Mode 2 obtains v from u as follows:
    (2.a) $A_1, A_2, \ldots, A_n$ are deleted;
    (2.b) x_1–x_n are inserted in between u_0 and u_n.
(3) Mode 3 obtains v from u, so it changes u by performing (3.a)–(3.c), described next:
    (3.a) $A_1, A_2, \ldots, A_n$ are deleted.
    (3.b) x_1 and x_n are inserted into u_0 and u_n, respectively.
    (3.c) x_2 to x_{n-1} are inserted in between the newly inserted x_1 and x_n.
(4) In mode 4, the derivation from u to v is performed by the following steps:
    (4.a) $A_1, A_2, \ldots, A_n$ are deleted.
    (4.b) A central u_i is nondeterministically chosen, for some $0 \leq i \leq n$.
    (4.c) x_i and x_{i+1} are inserted into u_i.
    (4.d) x_j is inserted between u_j and u_{j+1}, for all $j < i$.
    (4.e) x_k is inserted between u_{k-2} and u_{k-1}, for all $k > i + 1$.
(5) In mode 5, v is obtained from u by (5.a)–(5.e), given as follows:
    (5.a) $A_1, A_2, \ldots, A_n$ are deleted.
    (5.b) A central u_i is nondeterministically chosen, for some $0 \leq i \leq n$.
    (5.c) x_1 and x_n are inserted into u_0 and u_n, respectively.

(5.d) x_j is inserted between u_{j-2} and u_{j-1}, for all $1 < j \leq i$.
(5.e) x_k is inserted between u_k and u_{k+1}, for all $i + 1 \leq k < n$.

(6) Mode 6 derives v from u applying the next steps:
(6.a) $A_1, A_2, \ldots, A_n$ are deleted.
(6.b) A central u_i is nondeterministically chosen, for some $0 \leq i \leq n$.
(6.c) x_j is inserted between u_j and u_{j+1}, for all $j < i$.
(6.d) x_k is inserted between u_{k-2} and u_{k-1}, for all $k > i + 1$.

(7) Mode 7 obtains v from u performing the steps stated as follows:
(7.a) $A_1, A_2, \ldots, A_n$ are deleted.
(7.b) A central u_i is nondeterministically chosen, for some $0 \leq i \leq n$.
(7.c) x_j is inserted between u_{j-2} and u_{j-1}, for all $1 < j \leq i$.
(7.d) x_k is inserted between u_k and u_{k+1}, for all $i + 1 \leq k < n$.

(8) In mode 8, v is produced from u by following the given steps:
(8.a) $A_1, A_2, \ldots, A_n$ are deleted.
(8.b) x_1 and x_n are inserted into u_1 and u_{n-1}, respectively.
(8.c) x_i is inserted into $u_{i-1}u_i$, for all $1 < i < n$, to the right of x_{i-1} and to the left of x_{i+1}.

(9) Mode 9 derives v from u by the next procedure:
(5.a) $A_1, A_2, \ldots, A_n$ are deleted.
(5.b) x_1 and x_n are inserted into u_0 and u_n, respectively.
(5.c) x_i is inserted into $u_{i-1}u_i$, for all $1 < i < n$, to the right of x_{i-1} and to the left of x_{i+1}.

As obvious, all these jumping derivation modes reflect and formalize the above-described four-phase computation performed in a discontinuous way more adequately than their standard counterpart. Consequently, applications of these grammars are expected in any scientific area involving this kind of computation, ranging from applied mathematics through computational linguistics and compiler writing up to data mining and bioinformatics.

This section is organized as follows. It formally introduces all the new jumping derivation modes in SCGs. After that, each of them is illustrated and investigated in a separate subsection. Most importantly, it is demonstrated that SCGs working under any of the newly introduced derivation modes are computationally complete—that is, they characterize the family of recursively enumerable languages. Finally, it suggests four open problem areas to be discussed in the future.

14.2.1 Definitions

Let us recall notation concerning SCGs (see Section 13.1). In this section, we formally define nine derivation modes (1)–(9), sketched in the previous introductory section.

Definition 14.4. *Let $G = (\Sigma, \Delta, R, S)$ be an SCG, and let ρ be a relation over Σ^*. Set*

$$\mathscr{L}(G, \rho) = \{x \mid x \in \Delta^*, S\ \rho^*\ x\}.$$

$\mathscr{L}(G, \rho)$ is said to be the language that G generates by ρ. *Set*

$$\mathbf{SC}(\rho) = \{\mathscr{L}(G, \rho) \mid G \textit{ is an SCG}\}.$$

SC(ρ) *is said to be* the language family that SCGs generate by ρ.

Definition 14.5. *Let* $G = (\Sigma, \Delta, R, S)$ *be an SCG. Next, we rigorously define the following direct derivation relations* ${}_1\Rightarrow$ *through* ${}_9\Rightarrow$ *over* Σ^*, *intuitively sketched in the previous introductory section.*

First, let $(A) \to (x) \in R$ *and* $u = w_1 A w_2 \in \Sigma^*$. *Then,*

$$w_1 A w_2 \ {}_i\Rightarrow w_1 x w_2, \ \text{for } i = 1, \ldots, 9.$$

Second, let

$$(A_1, A_2, \ldots, A_n) \to (x_1, x_2, \ldots, x_n) \in R,$$

$$u = u_0 A_1 u_1 \cdots A_n u_n,$$

and

$$u_0 u_1 \cdots u_n = v_0 v_1 \cdots v_n,$$

where $u_i, v_i \in \Sigma^*$, $0 \leq i \leq n$, *for some* $n \geq 2$. *Then,*

(1) $u_0 A_1 u_1 A_2 u_2 \cdots A_n u_n \ {}_1\Rightarrow u_0 x_1 u_1 x_2 v_2 \cdots x_n u_n$;

(2) $u_0 A_1 u_1 A_2 u_2 \cdots A_n u_n \ {}_2\Rightarrow v_0 x_1 v_1 x_2 v_2 \cdots x_n v_n$,
where $u_0 z_1 = v_0$, $z_2 u_n = v_n$;

(3) $u_0 A_1 u_1 A_2 u_2 \cdots A_n u_n \ {}_3\Rightarrow v_0 x_1 v_1 x_2 v_2 \cdots x_n v_n$,
where $u_0 = v_0 z_1$, $u_n = z_2 v_n$;

(4) $u_0 A_1 u_1 A_2 u_2 \cdots u_{i-1} A_i u_i A_{i+1} u_{i+1} \cdots u_{n-1} A_n u_n \ {}_4\Rightarrow$
$u_0 u_1 x_1 u_2 x_2 \cdots u_{i-1} x_{i-1} u_{i_1} x_i u_{i_2} x_{i+1} u_{i_3} x_{i+2} u_{i+1} \cdots x_n u_{n-1} u_n$,
where $u_i = u_{i_1} u_{i_2} u_{i_3}$;

(5) $u_0 A_1 u_1 A_2 \cdots u_{i-1} A_{i-1} u_i A_i u_{i+1} \cdots A_n u_n \ {}_5\Rightarrow$
$u_{0_1} x_1 u_{0_2} x_2 u_1 \cdots x_{i-1} u_{i-1} u_i u_{i+1} x_i \cdots u_{n_1} x_n u_{n_2}$,
where $u_0 = u_{0_1} u_{0_2}$, $u_n = u_{n_1} u_{n_2}$;

(6) $u_0 A_1 u_1 A_2 u_2 \cdots u_{i-1} A_i u_i A_{i+1} u_{i+1} \cdots u_{n-1} A_n u_n \ {}_6\Rightarrow$
$u_0 u_1 x_1 u_2 x_2 \cdots u_{i-1} x_{i-1} u_i x_{i+2} u_{i+1} \cdots x_n u_{n-1} u_n$;

(7) $u_0 A_1 u_1 A_2 \cdots u_{i-1} A_i u_i A_{i+1} u_{i+1} \cdots A_n u_n \ {}_7\Rightarrow$
$u_0 x_2 u_1 \cdots x_i u_{i-1} u_i u_{i+1} x_{i+1} \cdots u_n$;

(8) $u_0 A_1 u_1 A_2 u_2 \cdots A_n u_n \ {}_8\Rightarrow v_0 x_1 v_1 x_2 v_2 \cdots x_n v_n$,
where $u_0 z_1 = v_0$, $z_2 u_n = v_n$, $|u_0 u_1 \cdots u_{j-1}| \leq |v_0 v_1 \cdots v_j|$,
$|u_{j+1} \cdots u_n| \leq |v_j v_{j+1} \cdots v_n|$, $0 < j < n$;

(9) $u_0 A_1 u_1 A_2 u_2 \cdots A_n u_n \ {}_9\Rightarrow v_0 x_1 v_1 x_2 v_2 \cdots x_n v_n$,
where $u_0 = v_0 z_1$, $u_n = z_2 v_n$, $|u_0 u_1 \cdots u_{j-1}| \leq |v_0 v_1 \cdots v_j|$,
$|u_{j+1} \cdots u_n| \leq |v_j v_{j+1} \cdots v_n|$, $0 < j < n$.

We close this section by illustrating the above-introduced notation in Definition 14.4. Let $G = (\Sigma, \Delta, R, S)$ be an SCG, then, $\mathscr{L}(G, {}_5\Rightarrow) = \{x \mid x \in \Delta^*, S \ {}_5\Rightarrow^* x\}$ and **SC**$({}_5\Rightarrow) = \{\mathscr{L}(G, {}_5\Rightarrow) \mid G$ is an SCG$\}$. To give another example, **SC**$({}_1\Rightarrow)$ denotes the family of all scattered context languages.

14.2.2 Results

This section is divided into nine subsections, each of which is dedicated to the discussion of one of the nine jumping derivation modes introduced in the previous section. More specifically, the section (1) repeats the definition of the mode in question, (2) illustrates it by an example, and (3) determines the generative power of SCGs using this mode. Most importantly, the section demonstrates that SCGs working under any of these newly introduced derivation modes are computationally complete—that is, they characterize the family of recursively enumerable languages.

14.2.2.1 Jumping derivation mode 1

${}_1\Rightarrow$ represents, in fact, the ordinary scattered context-derivation mode.

Definition 14.6. *Let $G = (\Sigma, \Delta, R, S)$ be an SCG. Let $u_0A_1u_1 \cdots A_nu_n \in \Sigma^*$ and $(A_1, A_2, \ldots, A_n) \to (x_1, x_2, \ldots, x_n) \in R$, for $n \geq 1$. Then,*

$$u_0A_1u_1A_2u_2 \cdots A_nu_n \ {}_1\Rightarrow u_0x_1u_1x_2v_2 \cdots x_nu_n.$$

Example 14.5. *Let $G = (\Sigma, \Delta, R, S)$ be an SCG, where $\Sigma = \{S, S', S'', S''', A, B, C$ $A', B', C', a, b, c\}$, $\Delta = \{a, b, c\}$, and R contains the following rules:*

(i) $(S) \to (aSA)$,	*(vii)* $(S', C) \to (cS', C')$,
(ii) $(S) \to (bSB)$,	*(viii)* $(S', S'') \to (\varepsilon, S''')$,
(iii) $(S) \to (cSC)$,	*(ix)* $(S''', A') \to (S''', a)$,
(iv) $(S) \to (S'S'')$,	*(x)* $(S''', B') \to (S''', b)$,
(v) $(S', A) \to (aS', A')$,	*(xi)* $(S''', C') \to (S''', c)$,
(vi) $(S', B) \to (bS', B')$,	*(xii)* $(S''' \to \varepsilon)$.

Consider ${}_1\Rightarrow$. Then, the derivation of G is as follows:

First, G generates any string $w \in \Delta^*$ to the left of S and its reversal in capital letters to the right of S with linear rules. Then, it replaces S with $S'S''$. Next, while nondeterministically rewriting nonterminal symbols to the right of S'' to their prime versions, it generates the sequence of terminals in the same order to the left of S', which we denote w'. Since all the symbols to the right of S' must be rewritten, the sequence of symbols generated to the left of S' must have the same composition of symbols. Otherwise, no terminal string can be generated, so the derivation is blocked. Thereafter, S' is erased, and S'' is rewritten to S'''. Finally, the prime versions of symbols to the right of S''' are rewritten to the terminal string denoted w''. Consequently,

$$\mathscr{L}(G, {}_1\Rightarrow) = \{x \in \Delta^* \mid x = ww'w'', w = \text{reversal}\,(w''), w' \text{ is any permutation of } w\}.$$

For instance, the string abccabcba is generated by G in the following way:

$$\begin{aligned} S &\ {}_1\Rightarrow aSA \ {}_1\Rightarrow abSBA \ {}_1\Rightarrow abcSCBA \ {}_1\Rightarrow abcS'S''CBA \ {}_1\Rightarrow abccS'S''C'BA \\ &{}_1\Rightarrow abccaS'S''C'BA' \ {}_1\Rightarrow abccabS'S''C'B'A' \ {}_1\Rightarrow abccabS'''C'B'A' \\ &{}_1\Rightarrow abccabS'''cB'A' \ {}_1\Rightarrow abccabS'''cbA' \ {}_1\Rightarrow abccabS'''cba \ {}_1\Rightarrow abccabcba. \end{aligned}$$

Next, we prove that SCGs working under ${}_1\Rightarrow$ characterize **RE**.

Theorem 14.7. *[57]* $\mathbf{SC}({}_1\Rightarrow) = \mathbf{RE}$.

Proof. As obvious, any SCG G can be turned to a Turing machine M, so M accepts $\mathscr{L}(G, {}_1\Rightarrow)$. Thus, $\mathbf{SC}({}_1\Rightarrow) \subseteq \mathbf{RE}$. Therefore, we only need to prove $\mathbf{RE} \subseteq \mathbf{SC}({}_1\Rightarrow)$.

Let $L \in \mathbf{RE}$. Recall that there are context-free languages L_1 and L_2 and a homomorphism h such that

$$L = h(L_1 \cap L_2)$$

(see Theorem 10.3.1 in [22]). Since L_2 is context-free, so is reversal(L_2) (see page 419 in [32]). Thus, there are CFGs G_1 and G_2 that generate L_1 and reversal(L_2), respectively. More precisely, let $G_i = (\Sigma_i, \Delta, R_i, S_i)$ for $i = 1, 2$. Let $\Delta = \{a_1, \ldots, a_n\}$ and $0, 1, \$, S \notin \Sigma_1 \cup \Sigma_2$ be the new symbols. Without any loss of generality, assume that $\Sigma_1 \cap \Sigma_2 = \emptyset$. Define the new morphisms

(I) $c : a_i \mapsto 10^i1$;

(II) $C_1 : \Sigma_1 \cup \Delta \to \Sigma_1 \cup \Delta \cup \{0, 1\}^*$, $\begin{cases} A \mapsto A, & A \in \Sigma_1, \\ a \mapsto f(a), & a \in \Delta; \end{cases}$

(III) $C_2 : \Sigma_2 \cup \Delta \to \Sigma_2 \cup \{0, 1\}^*$, $\begin{cases} A \mapsto A, & A \in \Sigma_2, \\ a \mapsto c(a), & a \in \Delta; \end{cases}$

(IV) $f : a_i \mapsto h(a_i)c(a_i)$;

(V) $t : \Delta \cup \{0, 1, \$\} \to \Delta$, $\begin{cases} a \mapsto a, & a \in \Delta, \\ A \mapsto \varepsilon, & A \notin \Delta; \end{cases}$

(VI) $t' : \Delta \cup \{0, 1, \$\} \to \{0, 1\}$, $\begin{cases} a \mapsto a, & a \in \{0, 1\}, \\ A \mapsto \varepsilon, & A \notin \{0, 1\}. \end{cases}$

Finally, let $G = (\Sigma, \Delta, R, S)$ be SCG, with $\Sigma = \Sigma_1 \cup \Sigma_2 \cup \{S, 0, 1, \$\}$ and R containing the rules

(1) $(S) \to (\$S_1 1111 S_2\$)$;
(2) $(A) \to (C_i(w))$, for all $A \to w \in R_i$, where $i = 1, 2$;
(3) $(\$, a, a, \$) \to (\varepsilon, \$, \$, \varepsilon)$, for $a = 0, 1$;
(4) $(\$) \to (\varepsilon)$.

Claim 1. $\mathscr{L}(G, {}_1\Rightarrow) = L$.

Proof. Basic idea. First, the starting rule (1) is applied. The starting nonterminals S_1 and S_2 are inserted into the current sentential form. Then, by using rule (2) G simulates derivations of both G_1 and G_2 and generates the sentential form $w = \$w_1 1111 w_2\$$.

Suppose $S\ {}_1\Rightarrow^* w$, where symbols$(w) \cap (N_1 \cup N_2) = \emptyset$. Recall, N_1 and N_2 denote the nonterminal alphabets of G_1 and G_2, respectively. If $t'(w_1) =$ reversal(w_2), then $t(w_1) = h(v)$, where $v \in L_1 \cap L_2$ and $h(v) \in L$. In other words, w represents a successful derivation of both G_1 and G_2, where both grammars have generated the same sentence v; therefore, G must generate the sentence $h(v)$.

Rules (3) serve to check whether the simulated grammars have generated the identical words. Binary codings of the generated words are erased while checking the equality. Always the leftmost and the rightmost symbols are erased; otherwise, some symbol is skipped. If the codings do not match, some 0 or 1 cannot be erased, and no terminal string can be generated.

Finally, the symbols \$ are erased with rule (4). If G_1 and G_2 generated the same sentence and both codings were successfully erased, G has generated the terminal sentence $h(v) \in L$. □

Claim 1 implies $\mathbf{RE} \subseteq \mathbf{SC}({}_1\Rightarrow)$. Thus, Theorem 14.7 holds. ■

14.2.2.2 Jumping derivation mode 2

Definition 14.7. *Let $G = (\Sigma, \Delta, R, S)$ be an SCG. Let $u = u_0A_1u_1 \cdots A_nu_n \in \Sigma^*$ and $(A_1, A_2, \ldots, A_n) \to (x_1, x_2, \ldots, x_n) \in R$, for $n \geq 1$. Then,*

$$u_0A_1u_1A_2u_2 \cdots A_nu_n \;{}_2\Rightarrow v_0x_1v_1x_2v_2 \cdots x_nv_n,$$

where $u_0u_1 \cdots u_n = v_0v_1 \cdots v_n$, $u_0z_1 = v_0$ and $z_2u_n = v_n$, $z_1, z_2 \in \Sigma^*$.

Informally, by using $(A_1, A_2, \ldots, A_n) \to (x_1, x_2, \ldots, x_n) \in R$ G obtains

$$v = v_0x_1v_1x_2v_2 \cdots x_nv_n$$

from

$$u = u_0A_1u_1A_2u_2 \cdots A_nu_n$$

in ${}_2\Rightarrow$ as follows:

(1) $A_1, A_2, \ldots, A_n$ are deleted.
(2) x_1–x_n are inserted in between u_0 and u_n.

Notice, the mutual order of inserted right-hand-side strings must be always preserved.

Example 14.6. *Consider SCG defined in Example 14.5 and ${}_2\Rightarrow$. Context-free rules act in the same way as in ${}_1\Rightarrow$ unlike context-sensitive rules. Let us focus on the differences.*

First, G generates the sentential form $wS'S''\overline{w}$, where $w \in \Delta^*$ and $\overline{w}$ is the reversal of w in capital letters, with context-free derivations. Then, the nonterminals to the right of S' are rewritten to their prime versions and possibly randomly shifted closer to S', which may arbitrarily change their order. Additionally, the sequence of terminals in the same order is generated to the left of S', which we denote w'. S' may be also shifted; however, in such case, it appears to the right of S'' and future application of rule (viii) is excluded and no terminal string can be generated. Since all the symbols to the right of S' must be rewritten, the sequence generated to the left of S' must have the same composition of symbols. Next, S' is erased and S'' is rewritten to S''' at once, which ensures their mutual order is preserved. If any prime symbol occurs to the left of S''', it cannot be erased, and the derivation is blocked. Finally, the prime versions of symbols to the right of S''' are rewritten to the terminal string denoted w'', which also enables random disordering. Consequently,

$$\mathscr{L}(G, {}_2\Rightarrow) = \{x \in \Delta^* \mid x = ww'w'', w', w'' \text{ are any permutations of } w\}.$$

For example, the string abcacbbac is generated by G in the following way:

$$\begin{aligned} S &\;{}_2\Rightarrow aSA \;{}_2\Rightarrow abSBA \;{}_2\Rightarrow abcSCBA \;{}_2\Rightarrow abcS'S''CBA \;{}_2\Rightarrow abcaS'S''A'CB \\ &\;{}_2\Rightarrow abcacS'S''A'C'B \;{}_2\Rightarrow abcacbS'S''B'A'C' \;{}_2\Rightarrow abcacbS'''B'A'C' \\ &\;{}_2\Rightarrow abcacbS'''B'A'c \;{}_2\Rightarrow abcacbS'''bA'c \;{}_2\Rightarrow abcacbS'''bac \;{}_2\Rightarrow abcacbbac. \end{aligned}$$

Theorem 14.8. $\mathbf{SC}({}_2\Rightarrow) = \mathbf{RE}$.

Proof. Clearly $\mathbf{SC}({}_2\Rightarrow) \subseteq \mathbf{RE}$, so we only need to prove $\mathbf{RE} \subseteq \mathbf{SC}({}_2\Rightarrow)$.

Let $G = (\Sigma, \Delta, R, S)$ be the SCG constructed in the proof of Theorem 14.7. First, we modify G to a new SCG G' so $\mathscr{L}(G, {}_1\Rightarrow) = \mathscr{L}(G', {}_1\Rightarrow)$. Then, we prove $\mathscr{L}(G', {}_2\Rightarrow) = \mathscr{L}(G', {}_1\Rightarrow)$.

Construction. Set

$$N = \{\lceil, \rceil, \lfloor, \rfloor, |, X, \underline{X}, \overline{X}, \overline{\underline{X}}, Y, \underline{Y}, \overline{Y}, \overline{\underline{Y}}\},$$

where $\Sigma \cap N = \emptyset$. Define the new morphisms

(I) $\overline{C}_1 : \Sigma_1 \cup \Delta$,
$$\begin{cases} A \mapsto A, & A \in \Sigma_1, \\ a \mapsto \lceil f(a) \rceil\ |, & a \in \Delta; \end{cases}$$

(II) $\overline{C}_2 : \Sigma_2 \cup \Delta$,
$$\begin{cases} A \mapsto A & A \in \Sigma_2, \\ a \mapsto |\ \lceil c(a) \rceil, & a \in \Delta; \end{cases}$$

(III) $b : \Delta \cup \{0, 1, \$\} \cup N \to \{0, 1\}$,
$$\begin{cases} A \mapsto A, & A \in \{0, 1\}, \\ A \mapsto \varepsilon, & A \notin \{0, 1\}. \end{cases}$$

(IV) $\overline{t'} : \Delta \cup \{0, 1, \$\} \cup N \to \{0, 1, \$\} \cup N$,
$$\begin{cases} A \mapsto A, & A \in \{\$\} \cup N, \\ A \mapsto t'(A), & A \notin \{\$\} \cup N. \end{cases}$$

Let $G' = (\Sigma', \Delta, R', S)$ be SCG, with $\Sigma' = \Sigma \cup N$ and R' containing

(1) $(S) \to (\rceil X \$ S_1 \lceil 11 \,||\, 11 \rceil S_2 \$ Y \lceil)$;
(2) $(A) \to (\overline{C}_i(w))$ for $A \to w \in R_i$, where $i = 1, 2$;
(3) $(\rceil, X, \lceil) \to (\rfloor, \overline{\underline{X}}, \rfloor), (\rceil, Y, \lceil) \to (\lfloor, \overline{\underline{Y}}, \lfloor)$;
(4) $(\rfloor, \overline{\underline{X}}, \rfloor) \to (\rfloor, \overline{X}, \rfloor), (\lfloor, \overline{\underline{Y}}, \lfloor) \to (\lfloor, \overline{Y}, \lfloor)$;
(5) $(\$, 0, \overline{X}, \overline{Y}, 0, \$) \to (\varepsilon, \$, \overline{\underline{X}}, \overline{\underline{Y}}, \$, \varepsilon)$;
(6) $(\$, \overline{X}, \overline{Y}, \$) \to (\varepsilon, \overline{X}\$, \$\overline{Y}, \varepsilon)$;
(7) $(\rfloor, \overline{X}, \$, \rfloor, \lfloor, \$, \overline{Y}, \lfloor) \to (\varepsilon, \varepsilon, \varepsilon, \underline{X}\$, \$\underline{Y}, \varepsilon, \varepsilon, \varepsilon)$;
(8) $(\underline{X}, 1, 1, |, |, 1, 1, \underline{Y}) \to (\varepsilon, \varepsilon, \varepsilon, X, Y, \varepsilon, \varepsilon, \varepsilon)$;
(9) $(\$) \to (\varepsilon), (X) \to (\varepsilon), (Y) \to (\varepsilon)$.

Notice that X and Y hold the current state of computation and force the context-sensitive rules to be used in the following order:

(a) After applying rule (3), only rule (4) may be applied.
(b) After applying rule (4), only rule (5) or (6) may be applied.
(c) After applying rule (5), only rule (4) may be applied.
(d) After applying rule (6), only rule (7) may be applied.
(e) After applying rule (7), only rule (8) may be applied.
(f) After applying rule (8), only rule (3) may be applied.

Claim 1. $\mathscr{L}(G', {}_1\Rightarrow) = \mathscr{L}(G, {}_1\Rightarrow)$.

Proof. The context-free rules (1) and (2) of G' correspond one to one to rules (1) and (2) of G, only the codings of terminals contain additional symbols. Thus, for every derivation in G

$$S \;{}_1\Rightarrow^* \$v_1 1111 v_2\$ = v,$$

where v is generated by using rules (1) and (2) and $\text{symbols}\,(v) \cap (N_1 \cup N_2) = \emptyset$, there is

$$S \;{}_1\!\Rightarrow^* \rceil X\$ w_1 \lceil 11 \mid\mid 11 \rceil w_2 \$ Y \lceil = w$$

in G' generated by rules (1) and (2), where $b(w_1) = t'(v_1)$, $b(w_2) = v_2$. This also holds vice versa. Since such a sentential form represents a successful derivations of both G_1 and G_2, without any loss of generality, we can consider it in every successful derivation of either G, or G'. Additionally, in G

$$v \;{}_1\!\Rightarrow^* v', v' \in \Delta^*$$

if and only if $t'(v_1) = \text{reversal}\,(v_2)$. Note, $v' = t(v)$. Therefore, we have to prove

$$w \;{}_1\!\Rightarrow^* w', w' \in \Delta^*$$

if and only if $\overline{t'}(w_1) = \text{reversal}\,(w_2)$. Then, $v' = w'$.

Claim 2. *In G', for*

$$S \;{}_1\!\Rightarrow^* \rceil X\$ w_1 \lceil 11 \mid\mid 11 \rceil w_2 \$ Y \lceil = w, \text{symbols}\,(w) \cap (N_1 \cup N_2) = \emptyset,$$

where w is generated by using rules (1) and (2),

$$w \;{}_1\!\Rightarrow^* w',$$

where $w' \in \Delta^*$ if and only if $\overline{t'}(w_1) = \text{reversal}\,(w_2)$.

For the sake of readability, in the next proof, we omit all symbols from Δ in w_1—that is, we consider only nonterminal symbols, which are to be erased.

Proof. If. Suppose $w_1 = \text{reversal}\,(w_2)$, then $w \;{}_1\!\Rightarrow^* \varepsilon$. From the construction of G', $w_1 = (\lceil 10^{i_1} 1 \rceil \mid)(\lceil 10^{i_2} 1 \rceil \mid) \cdots (\lceil 10^{i_n} 1 \rceil \mid)$, where $i_j \in \{1, \ldots, |\Delta|\}$, $1 \le j \le n$, $n \ge 0$. Consider two cases—(I) $n = 0$ and (II) $n \ge 1$.

(I) If $n = 0$, $w = \rceil X\$\lceil 11 \mid\mid 11 \rceil \$ Y \lceil$. Then, by using rules (3) and (4), rules (7) and (8), and four times rule (9), we obtain

$$\begin{aligned}
&\rceil X\$\lceil 11 \mid\mid 11 \rceil \$ Y \lceil \;{}_1\!\Rightarrow \rfloor \bar{\underline{\underline{X}}}\$\rfloor 11 \mid\mid 11 \rceil \$ Y \lceil \;{}_1\!\Rightarrow \\
&\rfloor \bar{\underline{\underline{X}}}\$\rfloor 11 \mid\mid 11 \lfloor \$ \bar{\underline{\underline{Y}}} \lfloor \;{}_1\!\Rightarrow \rfloor \bar{\bar{X}}\$\rfloor 11 \mid\mid 11 \lfloor \$ \bar{\underline{Y}} \lfloor \;{}_1\!\Rightarrow \\
&\rfloor \bar{\bar{X}}\$\rfloor 11 \mid\mid 11 \lfloor \$ \bar{\bar{Y}} \lfloor \;{}_1\!\Rightarrow \underline{X}\$11 \mid\mid 11\$\underline{Y} \;{}_1\!\Rightarrow \\
&\$XY\$ \;{}_1\!\Rightarrow XY\$ \;{}_1\!\Rightarrow Y\$ \;{}_1\!\Rightarrow \$ \;{}_1\!\Rightarrow \varepsilon
\end{aligned}$$

and the claim holds.

(II) Let $n \ge 1$,

$$\begin{aligned}
w &= \rceil X\$\lceil 10^{i'} 1 \rceil \mid (\lceil 10^{i_m} 1 \rceil \mid)^k \lceil 11 \mid\mid 11 \rceil (\mid \lceil 10^{j_{m'}} 1 \rceil)^k \mid \lceil 10^{j'} 1 \rceil \$ Y \lceil \\
&= \rceil X\$\lceil 10^{i'} 1 \rceil \mid u \mid \lceil 10^{j'} 1 \rceil \$ Y \lceil,
\end{aligned}$$

where $k \ge 0$, $m, m' \in \{1, \ldots, k\}$, $i', i_m, j', j_{m'} \in \{1, \ldots, |\Delta|\}$. Sequentially using both rules (3) and (4) and rule (7), we obtain the derivation

$$
\begin{aligned}
&\rceil X\$\lceil 10^{i'}1\rceil \mid u \mid \lceil 10^{j'}1\rceil\$Y\lceil & {}_1\Rightarrow\ & \rfloor\overline{\underline{X}}\$\rfloor 10^{i'}1\rceil \mid u \mid \lceil 10^{j'}1\rceil\$Y\lceil\ {}_1\Rightarrow\\
&\rfloor\overline{\underline{X}}\$\rfloor 10^{i'}1\rceil \mid u \mid \lceil 10^{j'}1\lfloor\$\overline{\underline{Y}}\lfloor & {}_1\Rightarrow\ & \rfloor\overline{X}\$\rfloor 10^{i'}1\rceil \mid u \mid \lceil 10^{j'}1\lfloor\$\overline{\underline{Y}}\lfloor\ {}_1\Rightarrow\\
&\rfloor\overline{X}\$\rfloor 10^{i'}1\rceil \mid u \mid \lceil 10^{j'}1\lfloor\$\overline{Y}\lfloor & {}_1\Rightarrow\ & \underline{X}\$10^{i'}1\rceil \mid u \mid \lceil 10^{j'}1\$\underline{Y}.
\end{aligned}
$$

Next, we prove

$$w' = \underline{X}\$10^{i'}1\rceil \mid (\lceil 10^{i_m}1\rceil \mid)^k\lceil 11 \parallel 11\rceil(\mid \lceil 10^{j_{m'}}1\rceil)^k \mid \lceil 10^{j'}1\$\underline{Y}\ {}_1\Rightarrow^* \varepsilon$$

by induction on $k \geq 0$.

Basis. Let $k = 0$. Then,

$$w' = \underline{X}\$10^{i'}1\rceil \mid \lceil 11 \parallel 11\rceil \mid \lceil 10^{j'}1\$\underline{Y}.$$

By using a rule (8) and twice a rule (3) G' performs

$$
\begin{aligned}
&\underline{X}\$10^{i'}1\rceil \mid \lceil 11 \parallel 11\rceil \mid \lceil 10^{j'}1\$\underline{Y} & {}_1\Rightarrow\ & \$0^{i'}\rceil X\lceil 11 \parallel 11\rceil Y\lceil 0^{j'}\$\\
&{}_1\Rightarrow \$0^{i'}\rfloor\overline{\underline{X}}\rfloor 11 \parallel 11\rceil Y\lceil 0^{j'}\$ & {}_1\Rightarrow\ & \$0^{i'}\rfloor\overline{\underline{X}}\rfloor 11 \parallel 11\lfloor\overline{\underline{Y}}\lfloor 0^{j'}\$.
\end{aligned}
$$

Since $i' = j'$, both sequences of 0s are simultaneously erased by repeatedly using both rules (4) and rule (5). Observe that

$$\$0^{i'}\rfloor\overline{\underline{X}}\rfloor 11 \parallel 11\lfloor\overline{\underline{Y}}\lfloor 0^{j'}\$\ {}_1\Rightarrow^* \$\rfloor\overline{X}\rfloor 11 \parallel 11\lfloor\overline{Y}\lfloor\$.$$

Finally, by applying rules (4), (6), (7), (8), and (9), we finish the derivation as

$$
\begin{aligned}
&\$\rfloor\overline{X}\rfloor 11 \parallel 11\lfloor\overline{Y}\lfloor\$\ {}_1\Rightarrow \rfloor\overline{X}\$\rfloor 11 \parallel 11\lfloor\$\overline{Y}\lfloor\ {}_1\Rightarrow\\
&\underline{X}\$11 \parallel 11\$\underline{Y}\ {}_1\Rightarrow \$XY\$\ {}_1\Rightarrow^* \varepsilon
\end{aligned}
$$

and the basis holds.

Induction Hypothesis. Suppose there exists $k \geq 0$ such that

$$w' = \underline{X}\$10^{i'}1\rceil \mid (\lceil 10^{i_m}1\rceil \mid)^l\lceil 11 \parallel 11\rceil(\mid \lceil 10^{j_{m'}}1\rceil)^l \mid \lceil 10^{j'}1\$\underline{Y}\ {}_1\Rightarrow^* \varepsilon.$$

where $m, m' \in \{1, \ldots, l\}$, $i', i_m, j', j_{m'} \in \{1, \ldots, |\Delta|\}$, for all $0 \leq l \leq k$.

Induction Step. Consider any

$$w' = \underline{X}\$10^{i'}1\rceil \mid (\lceil 10^{i_m}1\rceil \mid)^{k+1}\lceil 11 \parallel 11\rceil(\mid \lceil 10^{j_{m'}}1\rceil)^{k+1} \mid \lceil 10^{j'}1\$\underline{Y},$$

where $m, m' \in \{1, \ldots, k+1\}$, $i', i_m, j', j_{m'} \in \{1, \ldots, |\Delta|\}$. Since $k + 1 \geq 1$

$$
\begin{aligned}
w' &= \underline{X}\$10^{i'}1\rceil \mid \lceil 10^{i''}1\rceil \mid u \mid \lceil 10^{j''}1\rceil \mid \lceil 10^{j'}1\$\underline{Y},\\
u &= (\lceil 10^{i_m}1\rceil \mid)^k\lceil 11 \parallel 11\rceil(\mid \lceil 10^{j_{m'}}1\rceil)^k.
\end{aligned}
$$

By using rule (8) and both rules (3) G' performs

$$
\begin{aligned}
&\underline{X}\$10^{i'}1\rceil \mid \lceil 10^{i''}1\rceil \mid u \mid \lceil 10^{j''}1\rceil \mid \lceil 10^{j'}1\$\underline{Y}\ {}_1\Rightarrow\\
&\$0^{i'}\rceil X\lceil 10^{i''}1\rceil \mid u \mid \lceil 10^{j''}1\rceil Y\lceil 0^{j'}\$ \quad {}_1\Rightarrow\\
&\$0^{i'}\rfloor\overline{\underline{X}}\rfloor 10^{i''}1\rceil \mid u \mid \lceil 10^{j''}1\rceil Y\lceil 0^{j'}\$ \quad {}_1\Rightarrow\\
&\$0^{i'}\rfloor\overline{\underline{X}}\rfloor 10^{i''}1\rceil \mid u \mid \lceil 10^{j''}1\lfloor\overline{\underline{Y}}\lfloor 0^{j'}\$.
\end{aligned}
$$

Since $i' = j'$, the prefix and the suffix of 0s are simultaneously erased by repeatedly using rules (4) and (5).

$$\$0^{i'}\rfloor\overline{\underline{X}}\rfloor 10^{i''}1\rceil \mid u \mid \lceil 10^{j''}1\lfloor\overline{\underline{Y}}\lfloor 0^{j'}\$\ {}_1\Rightarrow^* \$\rfloor\overline{X}\rfloor 10^{i''}1\rceil \mid u \mid \lceil 10^{j''}1\lfloor\overline{Y}\lfloor\$.$$

Finally, G' uses rules (6) and (7)

$\$\rfloor\overline{X}\rfloor 10^{i''}1\rceil \mid u \mid \lceil 10^{j''}1\lfloor\overline{Y}\lfloor\$ \ {}_1\!\Rightarrow\ \rfloor\overline{X}\$\rfloor 10^{i''}1\rceil \mid u \mid \lceil 10^{j''}1\lfloor\$\overline{Y}\lfloor\ {}_1\!\Rightarrow\ \underline{X}\$10^{i''}1\rceil \mid$
$u \mid \lceil 10^{j''}1\$\underline{Y} = w''$,

where

$$w'' = \underline{X}\$10^{i''}1\rceil \mid (\lceil 10^{i_m}1\rceil \mid)^k \lceil 11 \mid\mid 11\rceil(\mid \lceil 10^{j_{m'}}1\rceil)^k \mid \lceil 10^{j''}1\$\underline{Y}.$$

By the induction hypothesis, $w''\ {}_1\!\Rightarrow^* \varepsilon$, which completes the proof.

Only if. Suppose that $w_1 \neq \text{reversal}\,(w_2)$, then there is no w' satisfying $w\ {}_1\!\Rightarrow^* w'$ and $w' = \varepsilon$.

From the construction of G', there is no rule shifting the left \$ to the left and no rule shifting the right \$ to the right. Since rule (5) is the only one erasing 0s and these 0s must occur between two \$s, if there is any 0, which is not between the two \$s, it is unable to be erased. Moreover, an application of rule (5) moves the left \$ on the previous position of erased left 0; if it is not the leftmost, the derivation is blocked. It is symmetric on the right. A similar situation is regarding 1s, X, and Y. Thus, for the sentential form w, if 0 or 1 is the rightmost or the leftmost symbol of w, no terminal string can be generated.

Since $w_1 \neq \text{reversal}\,(w_2)$, the codings of terminal strings generated by G_1 and G_2 are different. Then, there is a and a', where $w_1 = vau$, $w_2 = u'a'v$, and $a \neq a'$. For always, the outermost 0 or 1 is erased, otherwise the derivation is blocked, suppose the derivation correctly erases both strings v, so a and a' are the outermost symbols. The derivation can continue in the following two ways:

(I) Suppose the outermost 0s are erased before the outermost 1s. Then, rule (5) is used, which requires $\overline{X}$ and $\overline{Y}$ between the previous positions of 0s. However, there is 1, a or a', which is not between X and Y.

(II) Suppose the outermost 1s are erased before the outermost 0s. Then, rule (8) is used, which requires $\underline{X}$ and $\underline{Y}$ in the current sentential form. The symbols $\underline{X}$ and $\underline{Y}$ are produced by rule (7), which requires X and \$ between two symbols $\rfloor$ and Y and \$ between two symbols $\lfloor$. Suppose w' is the current sentential form. Since w_1 or reversal (w_2) is of the form

$$\cdots\lceil 10^{i_0}1\rceil \mid \lceil 10^{i_1}1\rceil \mid \lceil 10^{i_2}1\rceil \mid \cdots,$$

where $i_0, i_1, i_2 \in \{1, \ldots, |\Delta|\}$, there is 0 as the leftmost or rightmost symbol of w' and $X\$$ and $\$Y$ occurs between $\rfloor$s and $\lfloor$s, respectively. However, this 0 is obviously not between the two \$ and remains permanently in the sentential form.

We showed that G' can generate the terminal string from the sentential form w if and only if $\overline{t'}(w_1) = \text{reversal}\,(w_2)$, so the claim holds. □

We proved that for any $w \in \Delta^*$, $S\ {}_1\!\Rightarrow^* w$ in G if and only if $S\ {}_1\!\Rightarrow^* w$ in G', and Claim 1 holds. □

Let us turn to ${}_2\!\Rightarrow$.

Claim 3. $\mathscr{L}(G', {}_2\Rightarrow) = \mathscr{L}(G', {}_1\Rightarrow)$.

Proof. In ${}_2\Rightarrow$, applications of context-free rules progress in the same way as in ${}_1\Rightarrow$. While using context-sensitive rules, inserted right-hand-side strings can be nondeterministically scattered between the previous positions of the leftmost and rightmost affected nonterminals, only their order is preserved. We show, we can control this by the construction of G'.

Recall the observations made at the beginning of the proof of Claim 1. Since the behavior of context-free rules remains unchanged in terms of ${}_2\Rightarrow$, these still hold true. It remains to prove that Claim 2 also holds in ${}_2\Rightarrow$.

In a special case, ${}_2\Rightarrow$ behave exactly as ${}_1\Rightarrow$, hence definitely $\mathscr{L}(G', {}_1\Rightarrow) \subseteq \mathscr{L}(G', {}_2\Rightarrow)$. We prove

$$w \notin \mathscr{L}(G', {}_1\Rightarrow) \Rightarrow w \notin \mathscr{L}(G', {}_2\Rightarrow).$$

Therefore, to complete the proof of Claim 3, we establish the following claim:

Claim 4. *In G', for*

$$S\ {}_1\Rightarrow^*\ \rceil X\$w_1\lceil 11 \mid\mid 11\rceil w_2\$Y\lceil = w, \text{symbols}\,(w) \cap (N_1 \cup N_2) = \emptyset,$$

where w is generated only by using rules (1) and (2), and $\overline{t'}(w_1) \neq \text{reversal}\,(w_2)$, *there is no w', where*

$$w\ {}_1\Rightarrow^*\ w', w' \in \Delta^*.$$

For the sake of readability, in the next proof, we omit all symbols from Δ in w_1—we consider only nonterminal symbols, which are to be erased.

Proof. Suppose any w, where

$$S\ {}_1\Rightarrow^*\ w = \rceil X\$w_1\lceil 11 \mid\mid 11\rceil w_2\$Y\lceil$$

in G' and w is generated by using rules (1) and (2), symbols $(w) \cap (N_1 \cup N_2) = \emptyset$, and $w_1 \neq \text{reversal}\,(w_2)$.

From the construction of G', there is no rule shifting the left \$ to the left and no rule shifting the right \$ to the right. Neither ${}_2\Rightarrow$ can do this. Since rule (5) is the only one erasing 0s and these 0s must be between two \$s, if there is any 0, which is not between the two \$s, it cannot be erased. A similar situation is regarding 1s, X, and Y. Thus, for the sentential form w, if 0 or 1 is the outermost symbol of w, no terminal string can be generated.

Consider two cases (I) $w_1 = \varepsilon$ or $w_2 = \varepsilon$ and (II) $w_1 \neq \varepsilon$ and $w_2 \neq \varepsilon$.

(I) Suppose the condition does not apply. Without any loss of generality, suppose $w_1 = \varepsilon$. Since $w_1 \neq \text{reversal}\,(w_2)$, $w_2 \neq \varepsilon$. Then,

$$w = \rceil X\$\lceil 11 \mid\mid 11\rceil(\mid \lceil 10^{i_m}1\rceil)^k \mid \lceil 10^{i'}1\rceil\$Y\lceil,$$

where $k \geq 0$, $m \in \{1, \ldots, k\}$, $i_m, i' \in \{1, \ldots, |\Delta|\}$.

First, rules (3) and (9) are the only applicable; however, application of rule (9) would block the derivation, so we do not consider it. While rewriting X, the leftmost $\rceil$ is rewritten. Unless the leftmost $\lceil$ is chosen, it becomes unpaired and, thus, cannot be erased. It is symmetric with Y. After the application of rule (3), rule (4) becomes applicable. The positions of the symbols \$ must be preserved for future usage of rule (7). Then, the only way of continuing a successful derivation is

$$
\begin{aligned}
&\rceil X\$\lceil 11 \mid\mid 11\rceil(\mid \lceil 10^{i_m}1\rceil)^k \mid \lceil 10^{i'}1\rceil\$Y\lceil\ {}_2\Rightarrow\\
&\rfloor\underline{\overline{X}}\$\rfloor 11 \mid\mid 11\rceil(\mid \lceil 10^{i_m}1\rceil)^k \mid \lceil 10^{i'}1\rceil\$Y\lceil\ {}_2\Rightarrow\\
&\rfloor\underline{\overline{X}}\$\rfloor 11 \mid\mid 11\rceil(\mid \lceil 10^{i_m}1\rceil)^k \mid \lceil 10^{i'}1\lfloor\$\underline{\overline{Y}}\lfloor\ {}_2\Rightarrow\\
&\rfloor\overline{X}\$\rfloor 11 \mid\mid 11\rceil(\mid \lceil 10^{i_m}1\rceil)^k \mid \lceil 10^{i'}1\lfloor\$\underline{\overline{Y}}\lfloor\ {}_2\Rightarrow\\
&\rfloor\overline{X}\$\rfloor 11 \mid\mid 11\rceil(\mid \lceil 10^{i_m}1\rceil)^k \mid \lceil 10^{i'}1\lfloor\$\overline{Y}\lfloor.
\end{aligned}
$$

Notice that if neighboring nonterminals are rewritten, ${}_2\Rightarrow$ do not shift any symbol.

Next, rule (7) is the only applicable possibly shifting $\underline{X}$, $\underline{Y}$, and \$s anywhere into the current sentential form. However, if any shift is performed, there is a symbol 1 as the outer most symbol, which is obviously unable to be erased. Thus,

$$
\begin{aligned}
&\rfloor\overline{X}\$\rfloor 11 \mid\mid 11\rceil(\mid \lceil 10^{i_m}1\rceil)^k \mid \lceil 10^{i'}1\lfloor\$\overline{Y}\lfloor_2\Rightarrow\\
&\underline{X}\$11 \mid\mid 11\rceil(\mid \lceil 10^{i_m}1\rceil)^k \mid \lceil 10^{i'}1\$\underline{Y} = w'.
\end{aligned}
$$

Next, consider two cases depending on k.

(I.i) Suppose $k = 0$. Then,

$$w' = \underline{X}\$11 \mid\mid 11\rceil \mid \lceil 10^{i'}1\$\underline{Y}.$$

Since $i' > 0$, rule (5) must be used. It requires presence of $\overline{X}$ and $\overline{Y}$ in the current sentential form. These can be obtained only by the application of rule (8) and both rules from (3) and (4). However, it must rewrite two pairs of $\rceil, \lceil$, but there is only one remaining. Therefore, there are i' symbols 0, which cannot be erased, and no terminal string can be generated.

(I.ii) Suppose $k > 0$. Then, w' is of the form

$$\underline{X}\$11 \mid\mid 11\rceil \mid \lceil u\rceil \mid \lceil 10^{i'}1\$\underline{Y}.$$

Rule (8) is the only applicable. It rewrites $\underline{X}$ to X, $\underline{Y}$ to Y and put them potentially anywhere into the current sentential form. However, rules (3), which are the only ones containing X and Y on the left-hand side, require X and Y situated between $\rceil$ and $\lceil$.

$$\underline{X}\$11 \mid\mid 11\rceil \mid \lceil u\rceil \mid \lceil 10^{i'}1\$\underline{Y}\ {}_2\Rightarrow\ \$11 \mid\mid 11\rceil X\lceil u\rceil Y\lceil 0^{i'}\$.$$

Without any loss of generality, we omit other possibilities of erasing the symbols | or 1, because the derivation would be blocked in the same way. Since there is no 0 to the left of X, the future application of rule (5) is excluded and the rightmost sequence of 0s is obviously skipped and cannot be erased any more.

(II) Suppose the condition applies. Then,

$$\begin{aligned} w &= \rceil X\$\lceil 10^{i}1\rceil \mid (\lceil 10^{j_m}1\rceil \mid)^{k}\lceil 11 \mid\mid 11\rceil(\mid \lceil 10^{j_{m'}}1\rceil)^{k'} \mid \lceil 10^{i'}1\rceil\$Y\lceil \\ &= \rceil X\$\lceil 10^{i}1\rceil \mid \lceil u\rceil \mid \lceil 10^{i'}1\rceil\$Y\lceil, \end{aligned}$$

where $k, k' \geq 0$, $m \in \{1, \ldots, k\}$, $m' \in \{1, \ldots, k'\}$, $i_m, i'_m, j, j' \in \{1, \ldots, |\Delta|\}$.

First, the situation is completely the same as in (I), the only possibly non-blocking derivation consists of application of both rules (3) and (4) followed by application of rule (7). No left-hand-side string may be shifted during the application of these rules or the derivation is blocked.

$$\begin{aligned} &\rceil X\$\lceil 10^{i}1\rceil \mid \lceil u\rceil \mid \lceil 10^{i'}1\rceil\$Y\lceil \;{}_2\!\Rightarrow\; \rfloor\underline{X}\$\rfloor 10^{i}1\rceil \mid \lceil u\rceil \mid \lceil 10^{i'}1\rceil\$Y\lceil \;{}_2\!\Rightarrow \\ &\rfloor\overline{\underline{X}}\$\rfloor 10^{i}1\rceil \mid \lceil u\rceil \mid \lceil 10^{i'}1\lfloor\$\overline{\underline{Y}}\lfloor \;{}_2\!\Rightarrow\; \rfloor\overline{X}\$\rfloor 10^{i}1\rceil \mid \lceil u\rceil \mid \lceil 10^{i'}1\lfloor\$\overline{\underline{Y}}\lfloor \;{}_2\!\Rightarrow \\ &\rfloor\overline{X}\$\rfloor 10^{i}1\rceil \mid \lceil u\rceil \mid \lceil 10^{i'}1\lfloor\$\overline{Y}\lfloor \;{}_2\!\Rightarrow\; \underline{X}\$10^{i}1\rceil \mid \lceil u\rceil \mid \lceil 10^{i'}1\$\underline{Y}. \end{aligned}$$

Next, rule (8) is the only applicable rule, which erases four symbols 1, two $|$, rewrites $\underline{X}$ to X and $\underline{Y}$ to Y and inserts them possibly anywhere into the current sentential form. However, X must be inserted between $\rceil$ and $\lceil$; otherwise rule (3) is not applicable and X remains permanently in the sentential form. Unless the leftmost pair of $\rceil$ and $\lceil$ is chosen, there are skipped symbols 1 remaining to the left of X. Rules (6) and (7) ensures the derivation is blocked, if X is shifted to the right. Additionally, the only way to erase 1s is rule (8), but these 1s must be to the right of X. Thus, the skipped symbols 1 cannot be erased. Therefore, the pair of $\rceil$ and $\lceil$ is the leftmost or the derivation is blocked. Moreover, the two erased 1s are also the leftmost or they cannot be erased in the future and the same holds for the left erased symbol $|$. A similar situation is regarding Y. Then,

$$\underline{X}\$10^{i}1\rceil \mid \lceil u\rceil \mid \lceil 10^{i'}1\$\underline{Y} \;{}_2\!\Rightarrow\; \$0^{i}\rceil X\lceil u\rceil Y\lceil 0^{i'}\$$$

and by using rule (3) and repeatedly rules (4) and (5), both outer most sequences of 0s can be erased, if $i = i'$. Additionally, rules (4) ensure that X and Y are never shifted. If there is any 0 skipped, it cannot be erased and the derivation is blocked.

$$\$0^{i}\rceil X\lceil u\rceil Y\lceil 0^{i'}\$ \;{}_2\!\Rightarrow^{*}\; \$0^{i}\rfloor\overline{\underline{X}}\rfloor u\lfloor\overline{\underline{Y}}\lfloor 0^{i'}\$ \;{}_2\!\Rightarrow^{*}\; \$\rfloor\overline{X}\rfloor u\lfloor\overline{Y}\lfloor\$.$$

Finally, by rules (6) and (7), both terminal codings can be completely erased and $\underline{X}$, $\underline{Y}$, and two \$ are the outermost symbols, if no symbol is skipped.

$$\$\rfloor\overline{X}\rfloor u\lfloor\overline{Y}\lfloor\$ \;{}_2\!\Rightarrow\; \rfloor\underline{X}\$\rfloor u\lfloor\$\underline{Y}\lfloor \;{}_2\!\Rightarrow\; \underline{X}\$u\$\underline{Y}.$$

Since $w_1 \neq w_2$, $w_1 = vau$ and $w_2 = u'a'v$, where $a \neq a'$ are the outermost non-identical terminal codings. Derivation can always erase vs, as it was described, or be blocked before. Without any loss of generality, we have to consider two cases.

(II.i) Suppose $au = \varepsilon$. Then, $u'a' \neq \varepsilon$ and the situation is the same as in (I), no terminal string can be generated and the derivation is blocked.

(II.ii) Suppose $au \neq \varepsilon, u'a' \neq \varepsilon$. If the derivation is not blocked before, it may generate the sentential form

$$\$0^{i}\rceil X \lceil u \rceil Y \lceil 0^{i'}\$,$$

where $10^{i}1 = a$, $10^{i'}1 = a'$. Then, $i \neq i'$, and while simultaneously erasing the sequences of 0s of both codings, one is erased before the second one. Rule (5) becomes inapplicable and there is no way not to skip the remaining part of the second sequence of 0s. The derivation is blocked.

We covered all possibilities and showed that there is no way to generate terminal string $w' \notin \mathscr{L}(G', {}_1\Rightarrow)$, and the claim holds. □

Since $S\ {}_1\Rightarrow^* w$, $w \in \Delta^*$ if and only if $S\ {}_2\Rightarrow^* w$, Claim 3 holds. □

We proved that $\mathscr{L}(G', {}_2\Rightarrow) = \mathscr{L}(G', {}_1\Rightarrow)$, $\mathscr{L}(G', {}_1\Rightarrow) = \mathscr{L}(G, {}_1\Rightarrow)$, and $\mathscr{L}(G, {}_1\Rightarrow) = L$, then $\mathscr{L}(G', {}_2\Rightarrow) = L$, so the proof of Theorem 14.8 is completed. ■

14.2.2.3 Jumping derivation mode 3

Definition 14.8. *Let $G = (\Sigma, \Delta, R, S)$ be an SCG. Let $u = u_0A_1u_1 \cdots A_nu_n \in \Sigma^*$ and $(A_1, A_2, \ldots, A_n) \rightarrow (x_1, x_2, \ldots, x_n) \in R$, for $n \geq 1$. Then,*

$$u_0A_1u_1A_2u_2 \cdots A_nu_n\ {}_3\Rightarrow v_0x_1v_1x_2v_2 \cdots x_nv_n,$$

where $u_0u_1 \cdots u_n = v_0v_1 \cdots v_n$, $u_0 = v_0z_1$ and $u_n = z_2v_n$, $z_1, z_2 \in \Sigma^*$.

Informally, G obtains $v = v_0x_1v_1x_2v_2 \cdots x_nv_n$ from $u = u_0A_1u_1A_2u_2 \cdots A_nu_n$ by $(A_1, A_2, \ldots, A_n) \rightarrow (x_1, x_2, \ldots, x_n) \in R$ in terms of ${}_3\Rightarrow$ as follows:

(1) $A_1, A_2, \ldots, A_n$ are deleted;
(2) x_1 and x_n are inserted into u_0 and u_n, respectively;
(3) x_2 through x_{n-1} are inserted in between the newly inserted x_1 and x_n.

Example 14.7. *Let $G = (\Sigma, \Delta, R, S)$, where $\Sigma = \{S, A, \$, a, b\}$, $\Delta = \{a, b\}$, be an SCG with R containing the following rules:*

(i)	$(S) \rightarrow (A\$)$,	*(iv)*	$(A) \rightarrow (\varepsilon)$,
(ii)	$(A) \rightarrow (aAb)$,	*(v)*	$(\$) \rightarrow (\varepsilon)$.
(iii)	$(A, \$) \rightarrow (A, \$)$,		

Consider G uses ${}_3\Rightarrow$. Notice that context-free rules are not influenced by ${}_3\Rightarrow$.

After applying starting rule (i), G generates a^nb^n, where $n \geq 0$, by using rule (ii) or finishes the derivation with rules (iv) and (v). However, at any time during the derivation, rule (iii) can be applied. It inserts or erases nothing, but it potentially *shifts A to the left. Notice, the symbol \$ is always the rightmost and, thus, cannot be shifted. Then,*

$$\mathscr{L}(G, {}_3\Rightarrow) = \{x \in \Delta^* \mid x = \varepsilon \text{ or } x = uvwb^n, uw = a^n, n \geq 0, \text{ and } v \text{ is defined recursively as } x\}.$$

For example, the string aaaababbabbb is generated by G in the following way:

$$S \;{}_3\Rightarrow A\$ \;{}_3\Rightarrow aAb\$ \;{}_3\Rightarrow aaAbb\$ \;{}_3\Rightarrow aaaAbbb\$ \;{}_3\Rightarrow aaAabbb\$ \;{}_3\Rightarrow aaaAbabbb\$ \;{}_3\Rightarrow aaaaAbbabbb\$ \;{}_3\Rightarrow aaaAabbabbb\$ \;{}_3\Rightarrow aaaaAbabbabbb\$ \;{}_3\Rightarrow aaaababbabbb\$ \;{}_3\Rightarrow aaaababbabbb.$$

Theorem 14.9. $\mathbf{SC}({}_3\Rightarrow) = \mathbf{RE}$.

Proof. Clearly $\mathbf{SC}({}_3\Rightarrow) \subseteq \mathbf{RE}$, so we only need to prove $\mathbf{RE} \subseteq \mathbf{SC}({}_3\Rightarrow)$.

Let $G = (\Sigma, \Delta, R, S)$ be the SCG constructed in the proof of Theorem 14.7. Next, we modify G to a new SCG G' satisfying $\mathscr{L}(G, {}_1\Rightarrow) = \mathscr{L}(G', {}_1\Rightarrow)$. Finally, we prove $\mathscr{L}(G', {}_3\Rightarrow) = \mathscr{L}(G', {}_1\Rightarrow)$.

Construction. Let $G' = (\Sigma, \Delta, R', S)$ be SCG with R' containing

(1) $(S) \to (S_1 11\$\$11 S_2)$;
(2) $(A) \to (C_i(w))$ for $A \to w \in R_i$, where $i = 1, 2$;
(3) $(a, \$, \$, a) \to (\$, \varepsilon, \varepsilon, \$)$, for $a = 0, 1$;
(4) $(\$) \to (\varepsilon)$.

We establish the proof of Theorem 14.9 by demonstrating the following two claims:

Claim 1. $\mathscr{L}(G', {}_1\Rightarrow) = \mathscr{L}(G, {}_1\Rightarrow)$.

Proof. G' is closely related to G, only rules (1) and (3) are slightly modified. As a result, the correspondence of the sentences generated by the simulated G_1, G_2, respectively, is not checked in the direction from the outermost to the central symbols but from the central to the outermost symbols. Again, if the current two symbols do not match, they cannot be erased both and the derivation blocks. □

Claim 2. $\mathscr{L}(G', {}_3\Rightarrow) = \mathscr{L}(G', {}_1\Rightarrow)$.

Proof. Without any loss of generality, we can suppose rules (1) and (2) are used only before the first usage of rule (3). The context-free rules work unchanged with ${}_3\Rightarrow$. Then, for every derivation,

$$S \;{}_1\Rightarrow^* w = w_1 11\$\$11 w_2$$

generated only by rules (1) and (2), where $\text{symbols}(w) \cap (N_1 \cup N_2) = \emptyset$, there is the identical derivation

$$S \;{}_3\Rightarrow^* w$$

and vice versa. Since

$$w\ {}_1\!\Rightarrow^* w', w' \in \Delta^*$$

if and only if $t'(w_1) = \text{reversal}\,(w_2)$, we can complete the proof of the previous claim by the following one.

Claim 3. *Let the sentential form w be generated only by rules (1) and (2). Without any loss of generality, suppose* $\text{symbols}\,(w) \cap (N_1 \cup N_2) = \emptyset$. *Consider*

$$S\ {}_3\!\Rightarrow^* w = w_1 11\$\$11 w_2.$$

Then, $w\ {}_3\!\Rightarrow^* w'$, *where* $w' \in \Delta^*$ *if and only if* $t'(w_1) = \text{reversal}\,(w_2)$.

For better readability, in the next proof, we omit all symbols of w_1 from Δ—we consider only nonterminal symbols, which are to be erased.

Basic idea. Both rules (3) are the only ones with 0s and 1s on their left-hand sides. These symbols are simultaneously erasing to the left and to the right of \$s checking the equality. While proceeding from the center to the edges, when there is any symbol skipped, which is remaining between \$s, there is no way, how to erase it, and no terminal string can be generated.

Consider ${}_3\!\Rightarrow$. Even when the symbols are erasing one after another from the center to the left and right, ${}_3\!\Rightarrow$ can potentially shift the left \$ to the left and the right \$ to the right skipping some symbols. Also in this case, the symbols between \$s cannot be erased anymore.

Proof. If. Recall

$$w = 10^{m_1}110^{m_2}1\cdots10^{m_l}111\$\$1110^{m_l}1\cdots10^{m_2}110^{m_1}1.$$

Suppose, the check works properly not skipping any symbol. Then,

$$w\ {}_3\!\Rightarrow^* w' = \$\$$$

and twice applying rule (4) the derivation finishes. □

Proof. Only if. If $w_1 \neq \text{reversal}\,(w_2)$, though the check works properly,

$$w\ {}_1\!\Rightarrow^* w' = w_1' x\$\$x' w_2'$$

and $x, x' \in \{0, 1\}$, $x \neq x'$. Continuing the check with application of rules (3) will definitely skip x or x'. Consequently, no terminal string can be generated.

We showed that G' can generate the terminal string from the sentential form w if and only if $t'(w_1) = \text{reversal}\,(w_2)$, and the claim holds. □

Since $S\ {}_1\!\Rightarrow^* w$, $w \in \Delta^*$ if and only if $S\ {}_3\!\Rightarrow^* w$, Claim 2 holds. □

We proved that $\mathscr{L}(G, {}_1\!\Rightarrow) = L$, $\mathscr{L}(G', {}_1\!\Rightarrow) = \mathscr{L}(G, {}_1\!\Rightarrow)$, $\mathscr{L}(G', {}_3\!\Rightarrow) = \mathscr{L}(G', {}_1\!\Rightarrow)$; therefore, $\mathscr{L}(G', {}_3\!\Rightarrow) = L$ holds. Thus, the proof of Theorem 14.9 is completed. ■

14.2.2.4 Jumping derivation mode 4

Definition 14.9. *Let $G = (\Sigma, \Delta, R, S)$ be an SCG. Let $uAv \in \Sigma^*$ and $(A) \to (x) \in R$. Then, $uAv \; {}_4\!\Rightarrow uxv$. Let $u = u_0A_1u_1 \cdots A_nu_n \in \Sigma^*$ and $(A_1, A_2, \ldots, A_n) \to (x_1, x_2, \ldots, x_n) \in R$, for $n \geq 2$. Then,*

$$u_0A_1u_1A_2u_2 \cdots u_{i-1}A_iu_iA_{i+1}u_{i+1} \cdots u_{n-1}A_nu_n \; {}_4\!\Rightarrow$$
$$u_0u_1x_1u_2x_2 \cdots u_{i-1}x_{i-1}u_{i_1}x_iu_{i_2}x_{i+1}u_{i_3}x_{i+2}u_{i+1} \cdots x_nu_{n-1}u_n,$$

where $u_i = u_{i_1}u_{i_2}u_{i_3}$.

Informally,

$$v = u_0u_1x_1u_2x_2 \cdots u_{i-1}x_{i-1}u_{i_1}x_iu_{i_2}x_{i+1}u_{i_3}x_{i+2}u_{i+1} \cdots x_nu_{n-1}u_n$$

is obtained from

$$u = u_0A_1u_1A_2u_2 \cdots u_{i-1}A_iu_iA_{i+1}u_{i+1} \cdots u_{n-1}A_nu_n$$

in G by $(A_1, A_2, \ldots, A_n) \to (x_1, x_2, \ldots, x_n) \in R$ in ${}_4\!\Rightarrow$ as follows:

(1) $A_1, A_2, \ldots, A_n$ are deleted.
(2) A central u_i is nondeterministically chosen, for some $i \in \{0, \ldots, n\}$.
(3) x_i and x_{i+1} are inserted into u_i.
(4) x_j is inserted between u_j and u_{j+1}, for all $j < i$.
(5) x_k is inserted between u_{k-2} and u_{k-1}, for all $k > i + 1$.

Example 14.8. *Let $G = (\Sigma, \Delta, R, S)$, where $\Sigma = \{S, A, B, C, \$, a, b, c, d\}$, $\Delta = \{a, b, c, d\}$, be an SCG with R containing the following rules:*

(i)	$(S) \to (AB\$\$BA)$,	*(iv)*	$(A, B, B, A) \to (A, C, C, A)$,
(ii)	$(A) \to (aAb)$,	*(v)*	$(\$, C, C, \$) \to (\varepsilon, \varepsilon, \varepsilon, \varepsilon)$,
(iii)	$(B) \to (cBd)$,	*(vi)*	$(A) \to (\varepsilon)$.

Consider G uses ${}_4\!\Rightarrow$. Then, every context-sensitive rule is applied in the following way. First, all affected nonterminals are erased. Next, some position of the current sentential form called center is nondeterministically chosen. Finally, the corresponding right-hand sides of the selected rule are inserted with each at the original place of the neighboring erased nonterminal closer to the center. The central right-hand-side strings are randomly put closer to the chosen central position. In this example, we show how to control the choice.

First rule (i) rewrites S to $AB\$\$BA$. Then, G uses rules (ii) and (iii) generating a sentential form

$$a^{n_1}Ab^{n_1}c^{n_2}Bd^{n_2}\$\$c^{n_3}Bd^{n_3}a^{n_4}Ab^{n_4},$$

where $n_i \geq 0$, for $i \in \{1, 2, 3, 4\}$. If rule (vi) is used, derivation is blocked. Next, G uses the context-sensitive rule (iv), which may act in several different ways. In any case, it inserts two Cs into the current sentential form and the only possibility to erase them is rule (v). However, thereby we force rule (iv) to choose the center for interchanging nonterminals between Bs and moreover to insert Cs between the *two symbols \$. Finally, G continues by using rule (ii) and eventually finishes twice rule (vi). Consequently,*

$$\mathcal{L}(G, {}_4\Rightarrow) = \{x \in \Delta^* \mid x = a^{n_1} b^{n_1} c^{n_2} a^{n_3} b^{n_3} d^{n_2} c^{n_4} a^{n_5} b^{n_5} d^{n_4} a^{n_6} b^{n_6}, n_i \geq 0, i \in \{1,2,3,4,5,6\}\}.$$

Then, the string aabbcabdccddab is generated by G in the following way:

$$\begin{aligned} S &{}_4\Rightarrow AB\$\$BA {}_4\Rightarrow aAbB\$\$BA {}_4\Rightarrow aaAbbB\$\$BA {}_4\Rightarrow aaAbbcBd\$\$BA \\ &{}_4\Rightarrow aaAbbcBd\$\$cBdA {}_4\Rightarrow aaAbbcBd\$\$ccBddA {}_4\Rightarrow aaAbbcBd\$\$ccBddaAb \\ &{}_4\Rightarrow aabbcAd\$CC\$ccAddab {}_4\Rightarrow aabbcAdccAddab {}_4\Rightarrow aabbcaAbdccAddab \\ &{}_4\Rightarrow aabbcabdccAddab {}_4\Rightarrow aabbcabdccddab. \end{aligned}$$

Theorem 14.10. $\mathbf{SC}({}_4\Rightarrow) = \mathbf{RE}$.

Proof. As is obvious, $\mathbf{SC}({}_4\Rightarrow) \subseteq \mathbf{RE}$, so we only prove $\mathbf{RE} \subseteq \mathbf{SC}({}_4\Rightarrow)$.

Let $G = (\Sigma, \Delta, R, S)$ be the SCG constructed in the proof of Theorem 14.7. Next, we modify G to a new SCG G' so $\mathcal{L}(G, {}_1\Rightarrow) = \mathcal{L}(G', {}_4\Rightarrow)$.

Construction. Introduce five new symbols—D, E, F, $|$, and $\top$. Set $N = \{D, E, F, |, \top\}$. Let $G' = (\Sigma', \Delta, R', S)$ be SCG, with $\Sigma' = \Sigma \cup N$ and R' containing the rules

(1) $(S) \rightarrow (F\$S_1 11|E|11S_2\$F)$;
(2) $(A) \rightarrow (C_i(w))$ for $A \rightarrow w \in R_i$, where $i = 1, 2$;
(3) $(F) \rightarrow (FF)$;
(4) $(\$, a, a, \$) \rightarrow (\varepsilon, D, D, \varepsilon)$, for $a = 0, 1$;
(5) $(F, D, |, |, D, F) \rightarrow (\$, \varepsilon, \top, \top, \varepsilon, \$)$;
(6) $(\top, E, \top) \rightarrow (\varepsilon, |E|, \varepsilon)$; and
(7) $(\$) \rightarrow (\varepsilon)$, $(E) \rightarrow (\varepsilon)$, $(|) \rightarrow (\varepsilon)$.

Claim 1. $\mathcal{L}(G, {}_1\Rightarrow) = \mathcal{L}(G', {}_4\Rightarrow)$.

Proof. The behavior of context-free rules remains unchanged under ${}_4\Rightarrow$. Since the rules of G' simulating the derivations of G_1 and G_2 are identical to the ones of G simulating both grammars, for every derivation of G

$$S {}_1\Rightarrow^* \$w_1 1111 w_2\$ = w,$$

where w is generated only by using rules (1) and (2) and symbols $(w) \cap (N_1 \cup N_2) = \emptyset$, there is

$$S {}_4\Rightarrow^* F\$w_1 11|E|11 w_2\$\#\#F = w'$$

in G', generated by the corresponding rules (1) and (2), and vice versa. Without any loss of generality, we can consider such a sentential form in every successful derivation. Additionally, in G

$$w {}_1\Rightarrow^* v, v \in \Delta^*$$

if and only if $t'(w_1) = \text{reversal}(w_2)$; then $v = t(w)$. Therefore, we have to prove

$$w' {}_4\Rightarrow^* v', v' \in \Delta^*$$

if and only if $t'(w_1) = \text{reversal}\,(w_2)$. Then, obviously $v' = v$, and we can complete the proof by the following claim:

Claim 2. *In G', for*

$$S\ {}_4\Rightarrow^* w = F^{i_1}\$w_1 11|E|11w_2\$\#\#F^{i_2},\ \text{symbols}\,(w) \cap (N_1 \cup N_2) = \emptyset,$$

where w is generated only by using rules (1) and (2),

$$w\ {}_4\Rightarrow^* w',$$

where $w' \in \Delta^*$ if and only if $t'(w_1) = \text{reversal}\,(w_2)$, for some $i_1, i_2 \geq 0$.

The new rule (3) potentially arbitrarily multiplies the number of Fs to the left and right. Then, Fs from both sequences are simultaneously erasing by using rule (5). Thus, without any loss of generality, suppose $i_1 = i_2$ equal the number of future usages of rule (5).

For the sake of readability, in the next proof, in w_1, we omit all symbols from Δ—we consider only nonterminal symbols, which are to be erased.

Proof. If. Suppose $w_1 = \text{reversal}\,(w_2)$, then $w\ {}_4\Rightarrow^* \varepsilon$. We prove this by the induction on the length of w_1,w_2, where $|w_1| = |w_2| = k$.

Basis. Let $k = 0$. Then, $w = FF\$11|E|11\$FF$. Except rules (7), rules (4) are the only ones applicable. The center for interchanging the right-hand-side strings must be chosen between the two rewritten 1s and additionally inserted Ds must remain on the different sides of the central string $|E|$. Moreover, if any 1 stays outside the two Ds, it cannot be erased, so

$$FF\$11|E|11\$FF\ {}_4\Rightarrow FFD1|E|1DFF.$$

Next, rule (5) rewrites Ds back to \$s, erases Fs, and changes |s to ⊤s. The center must be chosen between the two |s and inserted ⊤s may not be shifted; otherwise, they appear on the same side of E, and rule (6) is inapplicable. It secures the former usage of rule (4) was as expected, so

$$FFD1|E|1DFF\ {}_4\Rightarrow F\$1\top E\top 1\$F.$$

By rule (6), the symbols ⊤ may be rewritten back to |s. No left-hand-side string may be shifted during the application of the rule and the choice of the central position has no influence, because the neighboring symbols are rewritten. It secures the former usage of rule (5) was as expected; therefore,

$$F\$1\top E\top 1\$F\ {}_4\Rightarrow F\$1|E|1\$F.$$

Then, the same sequence of rules with the same restrictions can be used again to erase remaining 1s and the check is finished by rule (7) as

$$F\$1|E|1\$F\ {}_4\Rightarrow FD|E|DF\ {}_4\Rightarrow \$\top E\top\$\ {}_4\Rightarrow \$|E|\$\ {}_4\Rightarrow^* \varepsilon$$

and the basis holds.

Induction Hypothesis. Suppose there exists $k \geq 0$ such that the claim holds for all $0 \leq m \leq k$, where

$$w = F^{i_1}\$w_1 11|E|11w_2\$F^{i_2}, |w_1| = |w_2| = m.$$

Induction Step. Consider G' generating w with

$$w = F^{i_1}\$w_1 11|E|11w_2\$F^{i_2},$$

where $|w_1| = |w_2| = k + 1$, $w_1 = \text{reversal}(w_2) = aw_1'$, and $a \in \{0, 1\}$. Except rules (7), rules (4) are the only ones applicable. The center for interchanging of the right-hand-side strings must be chosen between the two rewritten 0s or 1s and additionally inserted Ds must remain on the different sides of the central string $|E|$. Moreover, the outermost 0s or 1s must be rewritten and Ds may not be shifted between the new outermost ones; otherwise, they cannot be erased.

$$F^{i_1}\$w_1 11|E|11w_2\$F^{i_2}\,{}_4\!\Rightarrow F^{i_1}Dw_1' 11|E|11w_2'DF^{i_2}.$$

Next, rule (5) rewrites Ds back to \$s, erases Fs, and changes |s to $\top$s. The center must be chosen between the two |s and inserted $\top$s may not be shifted; otherwise they appear on the same side of E and the rule (6) is inapplicable. It secures the former usage of rule (4) was as expected.

$$F^{i_1}Dw_1' 11|E|11w_2'DF^{i_2}\,{}_4\!\Rightarrow F^{i_1'}\$w_1' 11\top E\top 11w_2'\$F^{i_2'}.$$

By rule (6), the symbols $\top$ may be rewritten back to |s. No left-hand-side string may be shifted during the application of the rule, and the position of the chosen center has no influence, because the neighboring symbols are rewritten. It secures the former usage of rule (5) was as expected.

$$F^{i_1'}\$w_1' 11\top E\top 11w_2'\$F^{i_2'}\,{}_4\!\Rightarrow F^{i_1'}\$w_1' 11|E|11w_2'\$F^{i_2'} = w'.$$

By the induction hypothesis, $w'\,{}_4\!\Rightarrow^* \varepsilon$, which completes the proof.

Only if. Suppose $w_1 \neq \text{reversal}(w_2)$; there is no w', where $w\,{}_4\!\Rightarrow^* w'$ and $w' = \varepsilon$.

Since $w_1 \neq \text{reversal}(w_2)$, $w_1 = vau$, $w_2 = u'a'v$, and $a \neq a'$. Suppose both vs are correctly erased and no symbol is skipped producing the sentential form

$$F^{i_1}\$au11|E|11u'a'\$F^{i_2}.$$

Next, rule (4) can be applied to erase outermost 0s or 1s. However, then, there is 0 or 1 outside inserted Ds and, thus, unable to be erased, which completes the proof.

We showed that G' can generate the terminal string from the sentential form w if and only if $t'(w_1) = \text{reversal}(w_2)$, and the claim holds. □

We proved that for some $w \in \Delta^*$, $S\,{}_1\!\Rightarrow^* w$ in G if and only if $S\,{}_4\!\Rightarrow^* w$ in G', and the claim holds. □

Since $\mathscr{L}(G, {}_1\!\Rightarrow) = \mathscr{L}(G', {}_4\!\Rightarrow) = L$, the proof of Theorem 14.10 is completed. ■

14.2.2.5 Jumping derivation mode 5

Definition 14.10. *Let $G = (\Sigma,\ \Delta,\ R,\ S)$ be an SCG. Let $uAv \in \Sigma^*$ and $(A) \rightarrow (x) \in R$. Then, $uAv\ {}_5\!\Rightarrow uxv$. Let $u = u_0A_1u_1 \cdots A_nu_n \in \Sigma^*$ and $(A_1,A_2,\ldots,A_n) \rightarrow (x_1,x_2,\ldots,x_n) \in R$, for $n \geq 2$. Then,*

$$u_0A_1u_1A_2 \cdots u_{i-1}A_{i-1}u_iA_iu_{i+1} \cdots A_nu_n\ {}_5\!\Rightarrow$$
$$u_{0_1}x_1u_{0_2}x_2u_1 \cdots x_{i-1}u_{i-1}u_iu_{i+1}x_i \cdots u_{n_1}x_nu_{n_2},$$

where $u_0 = u_{0_1}u_{0_2}$, $u_n = u_{n_1}u_{n_2}$.

Informally, G obtains

$$u_{0_1}x_1u_{0_2}x_2u_1 \cdots x_{i-1}u_{i-1}u_iu_{i+1}x_i \cdots u_{n_1}x_nu_{n_2}$$

from

$$u_0A_1u_1A_2 \cdots u_{i-1}A_{i-1}u_iA_iu_{i+1} \cdots A_nu_n$$

by $(A_1, A_2, \ldots, A_n) \rightarrow (x_1, x_2, \ldots, x_n) \in R$ in ${}_5\!\Rightarrow$ as follows:

(1) $A_1, A_2, \ldots, A_n$ are deleted.
(2) A central u_i is nondeterministically chosen, for some $i \in \{0, \ldots, n\}$.
(3) x_1 and x_n are inserted into u_0 and u_n, respectively.
(4) x_j is inserted between u_{j-2} and u_{j-1}, for all $1 < j \leq i$.
(5) x_k is inserted between u_k and u_{k+1}, for all $i + 1 \leq k < n$.

Example 14.9. *Let $G = (\Sigma,\ \Delta,\ R,\ S)$, where $\Sigma = \{S,\ A,\ B,\ \$,\ a,\ b\}$, $\Delta = \{a,\ b\}$, be an SCG with R containing the following rules:*

(i)	$(S) \rightarrow (\$AA\$)$,	*(iv)*	$(B,\$,\$,B) \rightarrow (A,\varepsilon,\varepsilon,A)$,
(ii)	$(A) \rightarrow (aAb)$,	*(v)*	$(A) \rightarrow (\varepsilon)$.
(iii)	$(A,A) \rightarrow (B,B)$,		

Recall Example 14.8. ${}_4\!\Rightarrow$ interchanges the positions of nonterminals influenced by context-sensitive rules in the direction from the outer to the central ones. Opposed to ${}_4\!\Rightarrow$, ${}_5\!\Rightarrow$ interchanges nonterminals in the direction from a nondeterministically chosen center. In the present example, we show one possibility to control the choice.

Consider G uses ${}_5\!\Rightarrow$. First rule (i) rewrites S to \$AA\$. Then, G uses rule (ii) generating the sentential form

$$\$a^mAb^ma^nAb^n\$,$$

where $m,n \geq 0$. If rule (v) is used, derivation is blocked, because there is no way to erase the symbols \$. Next, G uses the context-sensitive rule (iii), which nondeterministically chooses a center and nondeterministically shifts Bs from the previous positions of As in the direction from this center. However, for the future application of rule (iv), the chosen center must lie between As, and moreover Bs must be inserted as the leftmost and the rightmost symbols of the current sentential form. The subsequent usage of rule (iv) preserves As as the leftmost and the rightmost symbols independently of the effect of ${}_5\!\Rightarrow$. Finally, G continues by using rule (ii) and eventually finishes *twice rule (v). If rule (iii) is used again, there is no possibility to erase inserted Bs. Consequently,*

$$\mathscr{L}(G, {}_5\Rightarrow) = \{x \in \Delta^* \mid x = a^k b^k a^l b^l a^m b^m a^n b^n, k, l, m, n \geq 0\}.$$

Then, the string aabbabaaabbb is generated by G in the following way:

$$S \;{}_5\Rightarrow \$AA\$ \;{}_5\Rightarrow \$aAbA\$ \;{}_5\Rightarrow \$aaAbbA\$ \;{}_5\Rightarrow \$aaAbbaAb\$$$
$${}_5\Rightarrow B\$aabbab\$B \;{}_5\Rightarrow AaabbabA \;{}_5\Rightarrow AaabbabaAb \;{}_5\Rightarrow AaabbabaaAbb$$
$${}_5\Rightarrow AaabbabaaaAbbb \;{}_5\Rightarrow aabbabaaaAbbb \;{}_5\Rightarrow aabbabaaabbb.$$

Theorem 14.11. $\mathbf{SC}({}_5\Rightarrow) = \mathbf{RE}$.

Proof. As obvious, $\mathbf{SC}({}_5\Rightarrow) \subseteq \mathbf{RE}$, so we only prove $\mathbf{RE} \subseteq \mathbf{SC}({}_5\Rightarrow)$.

Let $G = (\Sigma, \Delta, R, S)$ be the SCG constructed in the proof of Theorem 14.7. Next, we modify G to a new SCG G' so $\mathscr{L}(G, {}_1\Rightarrow) = \mathscr{L}(G', {}_5\Rightarrow)$.

Construction. Introduce four new symbols—D, E, F, and $\circ$. Set $N = \{D, E, F, \circ\}$. Let $G' = (\Sigma', \Delta, R', S)$ be SCG, with $\Sigma' = \Sigma \cup N$ and R' containing the rules

(1) $(S) \rightarrow (\$S_1 1111 S_2\$ \circ E \circ F)$,
(2) $(A) \rightarrow (C_i(w))$ for $A \rightarrow w \in R_i$, where $i = 1, 2$,
(3) $(F) \rightarrow (FF)$,
(4) $(\$, a, a, \$, E, F) \rightarrow (\varepsilon, \varepsilon, \$, \$, \varepsilon, D)$, for $a = 0, 1$,
(5) $(\circ, D, \circ) \rightarrow (\varepsilon, \circ E \circ, \varepsilon)$,
(6) $(\$) \rightarrow (\varepsilon)$, $(E) \rightarrow (\varepsilon)$, $(\circ) \rightarrow (\varepsilon)$.

Claim 3. $\mathscr{L}(G, {}_1\Rightarrow) = \mathscr{L}(G', {}_5\Rightarrow)$.

Proof. Context-free rules are not influenced by ${}_5\Rightarrow$. Rule (3) must generate precisely as many Fs as the number of applications of rule (4). Context-sensitive rules of G' correspond to context-sensitive rules of G, except the special rule (5). We show, the construction of G' forces context-sensitive rules to work exactly in the same way as the rules of G do.

Every application of rule (4) must be followed by the application of rule (5) to rewrite D back to E, which requires the symbol D between two $\circ$s. It ensures the previous usage of context-sensitive rule selected the center to the right of the rightmost affected nonterminal and all right-hand-side strings changed their positions with the more left ones. The leftmost right-hand-side string is then shifted randomly to the left, but it is always ε. ${}_5\Rightarrow$ has no influence on rule (5).

From the construction of G', it works exactly in the same way as G does. □

$\mathscr{L}(G, {}_1\Rightarrow) = \mathscr{L}(G', {}_5\Rightarrow)$ and $\mathscr{L}(G, {}_1\Rightarrow) = L$; therefore $\mathscr{L}(G', {}_5\Rightarrow) = L$. Thus, the proof of Theorem 14.11 is completed. ■

14.2.2.6 Jumping derivation mode 6

Definition 14.11. *Let $G = (\Sigma, \Delta, R, S)$ be an SCG. Let $uAv \in \Sigma^*$ and $(A) \rightarrow (x) \in R$. Then, $uAv \;_6\!\Rightarrow uxv$. Let $u = u_0A_1u_1 \cdots A_nu_n \in \Sigma^*$ and $(A_1,A_2,\ldots,A_n) \rightarrow (x_1,x_2,\ldots,x_n) \in R$, for $n \geq 2$. Then,*

$$u_0A_1u_1A_2u_2 \cdots u_{i-1}A_iu_iA_{i+1}u_{i+1} \cdots u_{n-1}A_nu_n \;_6\!\Rightarrow$$
$$u_0u_1x_1u_2x_2 \cdots u_{i-1}x_{i-1}u_ix_{i+2}u_{i+1} \cdots x_nu_{n-1}u_n.$$

Informally, G obtains

$$u_0u_1x_1u_2x_2 \cdots u_{i-1}x_{i-1}u_ix_{i+2}u_{i+1} \cdots x_nu_{n-1}u_n$$

from

$$u_0A_1u_1A_2u_2 \cdots u_{i-1}A_iu_iA_{i+1}u_{i+1} \cdots u_{n-1}A_nu_n$$

by using $(A_1, A_2, \ldots, A_n) \rightarrow (x_1, x_2, \ldots, x_n) \in R$ in $_6\!\Rightarrow$ as follows:

(1) $A_1, A_2, \ldots, A_n$ are deleted.
(2) A central u_i is nondeterministically chosen, for some $i \in \{0, \ldots, n\}$.
(3) x_j is inserted between u_j and u_{j+1}, for all $j < i$.
(4) x_k is inserted between u_{k-2} and u_{k-1}, for all $k > i + 1$.

Example 14.10. *Let $G = (\Sigma, \Delta, R, S)$, where $\Sigma = \{S, A, B, a, b\}$, $\Delta = \{a, b\}$, be an SCG with R containing the following rules:*

(i)	$(S) \rightarrow (ABBA)$,	*(iii)*	$(A, B, B, A) \rightarrow (AB, B, B, BA)$,
(ii)	$(A) \rightarrow (aAb)$,	*(iv)*	$(A, B, B, A) \rightarrow (\varepsilon, B, B, \varepsilon)$.

Consider G uses $_6\!\Rightarrow$. $_6\!\Rightarrow$ interchanges nonterminals similarly as $_4\!\Rightarrow$ does in Example 14.8; however, the central nonterminals are removed. This property can be used to eliminate nondeterminism of choosing of the center, which we demonstrate next.

Rules (i) and (ii) are context-free, not affected by $_6\!\Rightarrow$. First the starting rule (i) rewrites S to ABBA. Then, G uses rule (ii) generating the sentential form

$$a^mAb^mBBa^nAb^n,$$

where $m, n \geq 0$. Next, G uses the context-sensitive rule (iii) or (iv). Notice, there is no rule erasing Bs; thus in both cases, the center of interchanging of nonterminals must be chosen between the two Bs. Otherwise, in both cases, there is exactly one A remaining; thus, the only applicable rule is rule (ii), which is context-free and not erasing. Therefore, G uses rule (iii) generating the sentential form

$$a^mb^mABBAa^nb^n$$

and continues by using rule (ii) or it uses rule (iv) and finishes the derivation.

Subsequently, the language G generates is

$$\mathscr{L}(G, {}_6\!\Rightarrow) = \{x \in \Delta^* \mid x = a^{n_1}b^{n_1}a^{n_2}b^{n_2} \cdots a^{n_{2k}}b^{n_{2k}}, k, n_i \geq 0, 1 \leq i \leq 2k\}.$$

Then, the string aabbabaabbab is generated by G in the following way:

$$S\ {}_6\!\Rightarrow ABBA\ {}_6\!\Rightarrow aAbBBA\ {}_6\!\Rightarrow aaAbbBBA\ {}_6\!\Rightarrow aaAbbBBaAb$$
$${}_6\!\Rightarrow aabbABBAab\ {}_6\!\Rightarrow aabbaAbBBAab\ {}_6\!\Rightarrow aabbaAbBBaAbab$$
$${}_6\!\Rightarrow aabbaAbBBaaAbbab\ {}_6\!\Rightarrow aabbabaabbab.$$

Theorem 14.12. $\mathbf{SC}({}_6\!\Rightarrow) = \mathbf{RE}$.

Proof. Clearly, $\mathbf{SC}({}_6\!\Rightarrow) \subseteq \mathbf{RE}$. Next, we prove $\mathbf{RE} \subseteq \mathbf{SC}({}_6\!\Rightarrow)$.

Let $G = (\Sigma, \Delta, R, S)$ be the SCG constructed in the proof of Theorem 14.7. Next, we modify G to a new SCG G' so $\mathscr{L}(G, {}_1\!\Rightarrow) = \mathscr{L}(G', {}_6\!\Rightarrow)$.

Construction. Introduce two new symbols—E and F. Let $G' = (\Sigma', \Delta, R', S)$ be SCG, with $\Sigma' = \Sigma \cup \{E, F\}$ and R' containing the rules

(1) $(S) \rightarrow (F\$S_1 1111 S_2\$)$;
(2) $(A) \rightarrow (C_i(w))$ for $A \rightarrow w \in R_i$, where $i = 1, 2$;
(3) $(F) \rightarrow (FF)$;
(4) $(F, \$, a, a, \$) \rightarrow (E, E, \varepsilon, \$, \$)$, for $a = 0, 1$;
(5) $(\$) \rightarrow (\varepsilon)$.

Claim 1. $\mathscr{L}(G, {}_1\!\Rightarrow) = \mathscr{L}(G', {}_6\!\Rightarrow)$.

Proof. Context-free rules are not influenced by ${}_6\!\Rightarrow$. Context-sensitive rules of G' closely correspond to context-sensitive rules of G. The new symbols are used to force modified rules to act in the same way as sample ones do. The symbols F are first multiplied and then consumed by context-sensitive rules, so their number must equal the number of usages of these rules. The new symbols E are essential. E never appears on the left-hand side of any rule; thus, whenever it is inserted into the sentential form, no terminal string can be generated. Therefore, the center is always chosen between two Es, which are basically never inserted, and other right-hand-side strings are then inserted deterministically.

G' with ${}_6\!\Rightarrow$ works in the same way as G with ${}_1\!\Rightarrow$ does. □

$\mathscr{L}(G, {}_1\!\Rightarrow) = \mathscr{L}(G', {}_6\!\Rightarrow)$, hence $\mathscr{L}(G', {}_6\!\Rightarrow) = L$. Thus, the proof of Theorem 14.12 is completed. ■

14.2.2.7 Jumping derivation mode 7

Definition 14.12. *Let $G = (\Sigma, \Delta, R, S)$ be an SCG. Let $(A) \rightarrow (x) \in R$ and $uAv \in \Sigma^*$. Then, $uAv\ {}_7\!\Rightarrow uxv$. Let $u = u_0A_1u_1 \cdots A_nu_n \in \Sigma^*$ and $(A_1, A_2, \ldots, A_n) \rightarrow (x_1, x_2, \ldots, x_n) \in R$, for $n \geq 2$. Then,*

$$u_0A_1u_1A_2 \cdots u_{i-1}A_iu_iA_{i+1}u_{i+1} \cdots A_nu_n\ {}_7\!\Rightarrow$$
$$u_0x_2u_1 \cdots x_iu_{i-1}u_iu_{i+1}x_{i+1} \cdots u_n.$$

Informally, by using the rule $(A_1, A_2, \ldots, A_n) \rightarrow (x_1, x_2, \ldots, x_n) \in R$, G obtains

$$u_0x_2u_1 \cdots x_iu_{i-1}u_iu_{i+1}x_{i+1} \cdots u_n$$

from

$$u_0A_1u_1A_2 \cdots u_{i-1}A_iu_iA_{i+1}u_{i+1} \cdots A_nu_n$$

in ${}_7\Rightarrow$ as follows:

(1) $A_1, A_2, \ldots, A_n$ are deleted.
(2) A central u_i is nondeterministically chosen, for some $i \in \{0 \ldots, n\}$.
(3) x_j is inserted between u_{j-2} and u_{j-1}, for all $1 < j \leq i$.
(4) x_k is inserted between u_k and u_{k+1}, for all $i + 1 \leq k < n$.

Example 14.11. *Let $G = (\Sigma, \Delta, R, S)$, where $\Sigma = \{S, A, B, C, \$, a, b, c\}$, $\Delta = \{a, b, c\}$, be an SCG with R containing the following rules:*

(i)	$(S) \to (ABC\$)$,	*(v)*	$(A, B, C) \to (A, B, C)$,
(ii)	$(A) \to (aAa)$,	*(vi)*	$(A, B) \to (A, B)$,
(iii)	$(B) \to (bBb)$,	*(vii)*	$(A, \$) \to (\varepsilon, \varepsilon)$.
(iv)	$(C) \to (cCc)$,		

Consider G uses ${}_7\Rightarrow$. ${}_7\Rightarrow$ interchanges nonterminals in the direction from the nondeterministically chosen center and erases the outermost nonterminals. In this example, we show that we may force the center to lie outside the part of a sentential form between the affected nonterminals.

The derivation starts by using the starting rule (i) and continues by using rules (ii)–(iv) generating the sentential form

$$a^m A a^m b^n B b^n c^l C c^l \$,$$

where $m, n, l \geq 0$. Next, G uses the context-sensitive rule (v) choosing the center to the left of A erasing C. If a different central position is chosen, the symbol A is erased while B or C cannot be erased in the future and the derivation is blocked. There is the same situation, if one of rules (vi) or (vii) is used instead. Notice, no rule erases B or C. Then, the derivation continues by using rules (ii) and (iii) and eventually rule (vi) rewriting B to A and erasing B. Otherwise, A is erased and the symbol \$ cannot be erased any more. G continues by using rule (ii) and finally finishes the derivation with rule (vii). Subsequently,

$$\mathcal{L}(G, {}_7\Rightarrow) = \{x \in \Delta^* \mid x = a^{2m_1} b^{n_1} a^{2m_2} b^{n_1} c^l b^{n_2} a^{2m_3} b^{n_2} c^l, m_1, m_2, m_3, n_1, n_2, l \geq 0\}.$$

Then, the string aabaabccbaabcc is generated by G in the following way:

$$S \;{}_7\Rightarrow ABC\$ \;{}_7\Rightarrow aAaBC\$ \;{}_7\Rightarrow aAabBbC\$ \;{}_7\Rightarrow aAabBbcCc\$$$
$${}_7\Rightarrow aAabBbccCcc\$ \;{}_7\Rightarrow aabAbccBcc\$ \;{}_7\Rightarrow aabaAabccBcc\$ \;{}_7\Rightarrow aabaAabccbBbcc\$$$
$${}_7\Rightarrow aabaabccbAbcc\$ \;{}_7\Rightarrow aabaabccbaAabcc\$ \;{}_7\Rightarrow aabaabccbaabcc.$$

Theorem 14.13. $\mathbf{SC}({}_7\Rightarrow) = \mathbf{RE}$.

Proof. Clearly, $\mathbf{SC}({}_7\Rightarrow) \subseteq \mathbf{RE}$. We prove $\mathbf{RE} \subseteq \mathbf{SC}({}_7\Rightarrow)$.

Let $G = (\Sigma, \Delta, R, S)$ be the SCG constructed in the proof of Theorem 14.7. Next, we modify G to a new SCG G' so $\mathcal{L}(G, {}_1\Rightarrow) = \mathcal{L}(G', {}_7\Rightarrow)$.

Construction. Introduce four new symbols—E, F, H, and $|$. Set $N = \{E, F, H, |\}$. Let $G' = (\Sigma', \Delta, R', S)$ be SCG, with $\Sigma' = \Sigma \cup N$ and R' containing the rules

(1) $(S) \rightarrow (FHS_1 11\$|\$11S_2)$;
(2) $(A) \rightarrow (C_i(w))$ for $A \rightarrow w \in R_i$, where $i = 1, 2$;
(3) $(F) \rightarrow (FF)$;
(4) $(a, \$, \$, a) \rightarrow (\varepsilon, E, E, \varepsilon)$, for $a = 0, 1$;
(5) $(F, H, E, |, E) \rightarrow (H, \$, |, \$, \varepsilon)$;
(6) $(\$) \rightarrow (\varepsilon)$, $(H) \rightarrow (\varepsilon)$, $(|) \rightarrow (\varepsilon)$.

Claim 1. $\mathscr{L}(G, {}_1\Rightarrow) = \mathscr{L}(G', {}_7\Rightarrow)$.

Proof. The behavior of context-free rules remains unchanged under ${}_7\Rightarrow$. Since the rules of G' simulating the derivations of G_1, G_2, respectively, are identical to the ones of G simulating both grammars, for every derivation of G,

$$S \;{}_1\Rightarrow^* \$w_1 1111 w_2\$ = w,$$

where w is generated only by using rules (1) and (2) and $\text{symbols}(w) \cap (N_1 \cup N_2) = \emptyset$, there is

$$S \;{}_7\Rightarrow^* FHw_1 11\$|\$11w_2 = w'$$

in G', generated by the corresponding rules (1) and (2), and vice versa. Without any loss of generality, we can consider such a sentential form in every successful derivation. Additionally, in G

$$w \;{}_1\Rightarrow^* v, v \in \Delta^*$$

if and only if $t'(w_1) = \text{reversal}\,(w_2)$, then $v = t(w)$. Therefore, we have to prove

$$w' \;{}_4\Rightarrow^* v', v' \in \Delta^*$$

if and only if $t'(w_1) = \text{reversal}\,(w_2)$. Then, obviously $v' = v$ and we can complete the proof by the following claim.

Claim 2. *In G', for some $i \geq 1$,*

$$S \;{}_7\Rightarrow^* w = F^i Hw_1\$|\$w_2E$$

where w is generated only by using rules (1)–(3) and $\text{symbols}(w) \cap (N_1 \cup N_2) = \emptyset$. *Then,*

$$w \;{}_7\Rightarrow^* w',$$

where $w' \in \Delta^*$ if and only if $t'(w_1) = $ $\text{reversal}\,(w_2)$.

The new rule (3) may potentially arbitrarily multiply the number of Fs to the left. Then, Fs are erasing by using rule (5). Thus, without any loss of generality, suppose i equals the number of the future usages of rule (5).

For the sake of readability, in the next proof, we omit all symbols in w_1 from Δ—we consider only nonterminal symbols, which are to be erased.

Proof. If. Suppose $w_1 = \text{reversal}(w_2)$, then $w\ {}_7\!\Rightarrow^* \varepsilon$. We prove this by the induction on the length of w_1, w_2, where $|w_1| = |w_2| = k$. Then, obviously $i = k$. By the construction of G', the least k equals 2, but we prove the claim for all $k \geq 0$.

Basis. Let $k = 0$. Then,

$$w = H\$|\$.$$

By rules (6)

$$H\$|\$\ {}_7\!\Rightarrow^* \varepsilon$$

and the basis holds.

Induction Hypothesis. Suppose there exists $k \geq 0$ such that the claim holds for all m, where

$$w = F^m H w_1 \$|\$ w_2, |w_1| = |w_2| = m, 0 \leq m \leq k.$$

Induction Step. Consider G' generates w, where

$$w = F^{k+1} H w_1 \$|\$ w_2, |w_1| = |w_2| = k + 1.$$

Since $w_1 = \text{reversal}(w_2)$ and $|w_1| = |w_2| = k + 1$, $w_1 = w_1' a$, $w_2 = a w_2'$. The symbols a can be erased by application of rules (4) and (5) under several conditions. First, when rule (4) is applied, the center for interchanging right-hand-side strings must be chosen between the two \$s; otherwise, both Es appear on the same side of the symbol, | and rule (5) is not applicable. Next, no 0 or 1 may be skipped, while proceeding in the direction from the center to the edges. Finally, when rule (5) is applied, a center must be chosen to the left of F; otherwise, H is erased and the future application of this rule is excluded.

$$F^{k+1} H w_1' a \$|\$ a w_2'\ {}_7\!\Rightarrow F^{k+1} H w_1' D|D w_2'\ {}_7\!\Rightarrow F^k H w_1' \$|\$ w_2' = w'.$$

By the induction hypothesis, $w'\,{}_7\!\Rightarrow^* \varepsilon$, which completes the proof.

Only if. Suppose $w_1 \neq \text{reversal}(w_2)$, then, there is no w', where $w\ {}_7\!\Rightarrow^* w'$ and $w' = \varepsilon$.

Since $w_1 \neq \text{reversal}(w_2)$, $w_1 = uav$, $w_2 = va'u'$, and $a \neq a'$. Suppose both vs are correctly erased and no symbol is skipped producing the sentential form

$$F^i H u a \$|\$ a' u'.$$

Next rule (4) can be applied to erase the innermost 0s or 1s. However, since $a \neq a'$, even if the center is chosen properly between the two \$s, there is 0 or 1 between inserted Es and, thus, unable to be erased, which completes the proof.

We showed that G' can generate the terminal string from the sentential form w if and only if $t'(w_1) = \text{reversal}(w_2)$, and the claim holds. □

We proved $S\ {}_1\!\Rightarrow^* w$, $w \in \Delta^*$, in G if and only if $S\ {}_7\!\Rightarrow^* w$ in G'; hence, $\mathscr{L}(G, {}_1\!\Rightarrow) = \mathscr{L}(G', {}_7\!\Rightarrow)$ and the claim holds. □

Since $\mathscr{L}(G, {}_1\Rightarrow) = \mathscr{L}(G', {}_7\Rightarrow)$ and $\mathscr{L}(G, {}_1\Rightarrow) = L$, the proof of Theorem 14.13 is completed. ■

14.2.2.8 Jumping derivation mode 8

Definition 14.13. *Let $G = (\Sigma, \Delta, R, S)$ be an SCG. Let $u = u_0A_1u_1 \cdots A_nu_n \in \Sigma^*$ and $(A_1, A_2, \ldots, A_n) \to (x_1, x_2, \ldots, x_n) \in R$, for $n \geq 1$. Then,*

$$u_0A_1u_1A_2u_2 \cdots A_nu_n \ {}_8\Rightarrow v_0x_1v_1x_2v_2 \cdots x_nv_n,$$

where $u_0z_1 = v_0$, $z_2u_n = v_n$, $|u_0u_1 \cdots u_{j-1}| \leq |v_0v_1 \cdots v_j|$, $|u_{j+1} \cdots u_n| \leq |v_jv_{j+1} \cdots v_n|$, $0 < j < n$, and $z_1, z_2 \in \Sigma^*$.

Informally, G obtains

$$v_0x_1v_1x_2v_2 \cdots x_nv_n$$

from

$$u_0A_1u_1A_2u_2 \cdots A_nu_n$$

by using $(A_1, A_2, \ldots, A_n) \to (x_1, x_2, \ldots, x_n) \in R$ in ${}_8\Rightarrow$ as follows:

(1) $A_1, A_2, \ldots, A_n$ are deleted.
(2) x_1 and x_n are inserted into u_1 and u_{n-1}, respectively.
(3) x_i is inserted into $u_{i-1}u_i$, for all $1 < i < n$, to the right of x_{i-1} and to the left of x_{i+1}.

Example 14.12. *Let $G = (\Sigma, \Delta, R, S)$, where $\Sigma = \{S, \overline{S}, A, B, C, a, b, c\}$, $\Delta = \{a, b, c\}$, be an SCG with R containing the following rules:*

(i)	$(S) \to (AS)$,	*(iv)*	$(\overline{S}) \to (B)$,
(ii)	$(S) \to (\overline{S})$,	*(v)*	$(B) \to (BB)$,
(iii)	$(\overline{S}) \to (b\overline{S}cC)$,	*(vi)*	$(A, B, C) \to (a, \varepsilon, \varepsilon)$.

Consider G uses ${}_8\Rightarrow$. ${}_8\Rightarrow$ acts in a similar way as ${}_2\Rightarrow$ does. When a rule is to be applied, there is a nondeterministically chosen center in between the affected nonterminals and rule right-hand-side strings can be shifted in the direction to this center, but not farther than the neighboring affected nonterminal was.

Rules (i)–(v) are context-free. Without any loss of generality, we suppose these rules are used only before the first application of rule (vi) producing the string

$$A^m b^n B^l (cC)^n.$$

The derivation finishes with the sequence of applications of rule (vi). For As, Bs, and Cs are being rewritten together, $m = n = l$. Moreover, inserted a is always between the rewritten A and B. Subsequently,

$$\mathscr{L}(G, {}_8\Rightarrow) = \{x \in \Delta^* \mid x = wc^n, w \in \{a, b\}^*, \text{occur}(a, w) = \text{occur}(b, w) = n, n \geq 1\}.$$

For example, the string baabbaccc is generated by G in the following way:

$$S \ {}_8{\Rightarrow} AS \ {}_8{\Rightarrow} AAS \ {}_8{\Rightarrow} AAAS \ {}_8{\Rightarrow} AAA\overline{S} \ {}_8{\Rightarrow} AAAb\overline{S}cC \ {}_8{\Rightarrow} AAAbb\overline{S}cCcC$$
$${}_8{\Rightarrow} AAAbbb\overline{S}cCcCcC \ {}_8{\Rightarrow} AAAbbbBcCcCcC \ {}_8{\Rightarrow} AAAbbbBBcCcCcC$$
$${}_8{\Rightarrow} AAAbbbBBBcCcCcC \ {}_8{\Rightarrow} AAbbbaBBccCcC \ {}_8{\Rightarrow} AbabbaBcccC \ {}_8{\Rightarrow} baabbaccc.$$

Theorem 14.14. $\mathbf{SC}({}_8{\Rightarrow}) = \mathbf{RE}$.

Proof. Prove this theorem by analogy with the proof of Theorem 14.8. ∎

14.2.2.9 Jumping derivation mode 9

Definition 14.14. *Let $G = (\Sigma, \Delta, R, S)$ be an SCG. Let $u = u_0A_1u_1 \cdots A_nu_n \in \Sigma^*$ and $(A_1, A_2, \ldots, A_n) \rightarrow (x_1, x_2, \ldots, x_n) \in R$, for $n \geq 1$. Then,*

$$u_0A_1u_1A_2u_2 \cdots A_nu_n \ {}_9{\Rightarrow} \ v_0x_1v_1x_2v_2 \cdots x_nv_n,$$

where $u_0 = v_0z_1$, $u_n = z_2v_n$, $|u_0u_1 \cdots u_{j-1}| \leq |v_0v_1 \cdots v_j|$, $|u_{j+1} \cdots u_n| \leq |v_jv_{j+1} \cdots v_n|$, $0 < j < n$, and $z_1, z_2 \in \Sigma^*$.

Informally, G obtains

$$v_0x_1v_1x_2v_2 \cdots x_nv_n$$

from

$$u_0A_1u_1A_2u_2 \cdots A_nu_n$$

by using $(A_1, A_2, \ldots, A_n) \rightarrow (x_1, x_2, \ldots, x_n) \in R$ in ${}_9{\Rightarrow}$ as follows:

(1) $A_1, A_2, \ldots, A_n$ are deleted.
(2) x_1 and x_n are inserted into u_0 and u_n, respectively.
(3) x_i is inserted into $u_{i-1}u_i$, for all $1 < i < n$, to the right of x_{i-1} and to the left of x_{i+1}.

Example 14.13. *Let $G = (\Sigma, \Delta, R, S)$, where $\Sigma = \{S, \overline{S}, A, B, C, \$, a, b, c\}$, $\Delta = \{a, b, c\}$, be an SCG with R containing the following rules:*

(i) $(S) \rightarrow (aSa)$,
(ii) $(S) \rightarrow (A)$,
(iii) $(A) \rightarrow (\$A)$,
(iv) $(A) \rightarrow (C)$,
(v) $(C) \rightarrow (cBC\$)$,
(vi) $(C) \rightarrow (\varepsilon)$,
(vii) $(\$, B, \$) \rightarrow (\varepsilon, b, \varepsilon)$.

Consider G uses ${}_9{\Rightarrow}$. ${}_9{\Rightarrow}$ acts similarly to ${}_3{\Rightarrow}$ with respect to the direction of shift of the rule right-hand sides, but with limitation as in ${}_8{\Rightarrow}$. When a rule is to be applied, there is a nondeterministically chosen center in between the affected nonterminals and rule right-hand-side strings can be shifted in the direction from this center, but not farther than the neighboring affected nonterminal was.

Rules (i)–(vi) are context-free. Without any loss of generality, we can suppose these rules are used only before the first application of rule (vii), which produce the sentential form

$$a^m\$^n(cB)^l\$^la^m.$$

The derivation finishes with the sequence of applications of rule (vii). The symbols \$ and Bs are being rewritten together, thus $n = l$ must hold. Additionally, ${}_9\Rightarrow$ ensures, b is always inserted between the rewritten \$s. Subsequently,

$$\mathcal{L}(G, {}_9\Rightarrow) = \{x \in \Delta^* \mid x = a^m w a^m, w \in \{b, c\}^*, \text{occur}(b, w) = \text{occur}(c, w), m \geq 0\}.$$

For example, the string aabcbcaa is generated by G in the following way:

$$\begin{aligned} S &{}_9\Rightarrow aSa {}_9\Rightarrow aaSaa {}_9\Rightarrow aaAaa {}_9\Rightarrow aa\$Aaa {}_9\Rightarrow aa\$\$Aaa \\ &{}_9\Rightarrow aa\$\$Caa {}_9\Rightarrow aa\$\$cBC\$aa {}_9\Rightarrow aa\$\$cBcBC\$\$aa \\ &{}_9\Rightarrow aa\$\$cBcB\$\$aa {}_9\Rightarrow aa\$bccB\$aa {}_9\Rightarrow aabcbcaa. \end{aligned}$$

Theorem 14.15. $\mathbf{SC}({}_9\Rightarrow) = \mathbf{RE}$.

Proof. Prove this theorem by analogy with the proof of Theorem 14.9. ■

14.2.2.10 Open problem areas

Finally, let us suggest some open problem areas concerning the subject of this section.

Open Problem 14.2. *Return to derivation modes (1)–(9) in Section 14.2.2. Introduce and study further modes. For instance, in a more general way, discuss a jumping derivation mode, in which the only restriction is to preserve a mutual order of the inserted right-hand-side strings, which can be nondeterministically spread across the whole sentential form regardless of the positions of the rewritten nonterminals. In a more restrictive way, study a jumping derivation mode over words satisfying some prescribed requirements, such as a membership in a regular language.*

Open Problem 14.3. *Consider propagating versions of jumping SCGs. In other words, rule out erasing rules in them. Reconsider the investigation of the present section in its terms.*

Open Problem 14.4. *The present section has often demonstrated that some jumping derivation modes work just like ordinary derivation modes in SCGs. State general combinatorial properties that guarantee this behavior.*

Open Problem 14.5. *Establish normal forms of SCGs working in jumping ways.*

14.3 Jumping automata

Recall that jumping grammars represent language-generating models for discontinuous computation. The present section explores their automata-based counterparts, called jumping automata. As their name suggests, they jump across their input words discontinuously, and in this way, they also formalize computation performed in a discontinuous way.

To give an insight into the notion of a jumping automaton, reconsider the basic notion of a classical finite automaton M (see Chapter 5). Recall that M consists of an input tape, a read head, and a finite state control. The input tape is divided into cells. Each cell contains one symbol of an input string. The symbol under the read head, a, is the current input symbol. The finite control is represented by a finite set of states together with a control relation, which is usually specified as a set of computational rules. M computes by making a sequence of moves. Each move is made according to a computational rule that describes how the current state is changed and whether the current input symbol is read. If the symbol is read, the read head is shifted precisely one cell to the right. M has one state defined as the start state and some states designated as final states. If M can read w by making a sequence of moves from the start state to a final state, M accepts w; otherwise, M rejects w.

Unfortunately, the classical versions of finite automata work in a way that often fails to reflect the real needs of today's informatics. Perhaps most significantly, they fail to formalize discontinuous information processing, which is central to today's computation, while it was virtually unneeded and, therefore, unknown in the past. Indeed, in the previous century, most classical computer science methods were developed for continuous information processing. Accordingly, their formal models, including finite automata, work on strings, representing information, in a strictly continuous left-to-right symbol-by-symbol way. Modern information methods, however, frequently process information in a discontinuous way [58–63]. Within a particular running process, a typical computational step may be performed somewhere in the middle of information, while the very next computational step is executed far away from it; therefore, before the next step is carried out, the process has to jump over a large portion of the information to the desired position of execution. Of course, classical finite automata, which work on strings strictly continuously, inadequately, and inappropriately, reflect discontinuous information processing of this kind.

Formalizing discontinuous information processing adequately gives rise to the idea of adapting classical finite automata in a discontinuous way. In this way, the present chapter introduces and studies the notion of a jumping finite automaton (JFA), H. In essence, H works just like a classical finite automaton except it does not read the input string in a symbol-by-symbol left-to-right way. That is, after reading a symbol, H can jump over a portion of the tape in either direction and continue making moves from there. Once an occurrence of a symbol is read on the tape, it cannot be reread again later during computation of H. Otherwise, it coincides with the standard notion of a finite automaton, and as such, it is based upon a regulated mechanism consisting of its finite state control. Therefore, we study them in detail in this book.

More precisely, concerning JFAs, this section considers commonly studied areas of the formal language theory, such as decidability and closure properties, and establishes several results concerning JFAs regarding these areas. It concentrates its attentions on results that demonstrate differences between JFAs and their classical versions. As a whole, this chapter gives a systematic body of knowledge concerning

JFAs. At the same time, however, it points out several open questions regarding these automata, which may represent a new, attractive, significant investigation area of automata theory in the future.

This section is further divided into two subsections. The first subsection formalizes and illustrates JFAs. The second subsection demonstrates their fundamental properties, including a comparison of their power with the power of well-known language-defining formal devices, closure properties, decidability. In addition, it establishes an infinite hierarchy of language families resulting from these automata, one-directional jumps, and various start configurations.

14.3.1 Definitions and examples

In this subsection, we define a variety of JFAs discussed in this section and illustrate them by examples.

Definition 14.15. *A* general jumping finite automaton, *a GJFA for short, is a quintuple* $M = (Q, D, R, s, F)$, *where* D *is the input alphabet of* M, *and* Q, s, R *have the same meaning as in Definition 5.1, except that* $a \in D^*$ *for every* $qa \to p \in R$. *Furthermore, we define the binary* jumping relation, *symbolically denoted by* $\curvearrowright$, *over* D^*QD^*, *is defined as follows. Let* $x, z, x', z' \in D^*$ *such that* $xz = x'z'$ *and* $py \to q \in R$, *then,* M *makes a* jump *from* $xpyz$ *to* $x'qz'$, *symbolically written as* $xpyz \curvearrowright x'qz'$. *In the standard manner, we extend* $\curvearrowright$ *to* $\curvearrowright^m$, *where* $m \geq 0$, $\curvearrowright^+$, *and* $\curvearrowright^*$.

The language *accepted by* M *with* $\curvearrowright$ *denoted by* $L(M, \curvearrowright)$, *is defined as* $L(M, \curvearrowright) = \{uv \mid u, v \in D^*, usv \curvearrowright^* f, f \in F\}$. *Let* $w \in D^*$. *We say that* M accepts w *if and only if* $w \in L(M, \curvearrowright)$; M rejects w *otherwise. Two GJFAs* M *and* M' *are said to be* equivalent *if and only if* $L(M, \curvearrowright) = L(M', \curvearrowright)$.

Definition 14.16. *Let* $M = (Q, D, R, s, F)$ *be a GJFA.* M *is an* ε-free GJFA *if* $py \to q \in R$ *implies that* $|y| \geq 1$. M *is of* degree n, *where* $n \geq 0$, *if* $py \to q \in R$ *implies that* $|y| \leq n$. M *is a* JFA *if its degree is* 1.

Definition 14.17. *Let* $M = (Q, D, R, s, F)$ *be a JFA. Analogously to a GJFA,* M *is an* ε-free JFA *if* $py \to q \in R$ *implies that* $|y| = 1$. M *is a* deterministic JFA *(a DJFA for short) if (1) it is an* ε*-free JFA and (2) for each* $p \in Q$ *and each* $a \in D$, *there is no more than one* $q \in Q$ *such that* $pa \to q \in R$. M *is a* complete JFA *(a CJFA for short) if (1) it is a DJFA and (2) for each* $p \in Q$ *and each* $a \in D$, *there is precisely one* $q \in Q$ *such that* $pa \to q \in R$.

Definition 14.18. *Let* $M = (Q, D, R, s, F)$ *be a GJFA. The* transition graph *of* M, *denoted by* $\Delta(M)$, *is a multigraph, where nodes are states from* Q, *and there is an edge from* p *to* q *labeled with* y *if and only if* $py \to q \in R$. *A state* $q \in Q$ *is* reachable *if there is a walk from* s *to* q *in* $\Delta(M)$; q *is* terminating *if there is a walk from* q *to some* $f \in F$. *If there is a walk from* p *to* q, $p = q_1, q_2, \ldots, q_n = q$, *for some* $n \geq 2$, *where* $q_i y_i \to q_{i+1} \in R$ *for all* $i = 1, \ldots, n-1$, *then we write*

$$py_1y_2 \cdots y_n \rightsquigarrow q.$$

Next, we illustrate the previous definitions by two examples.

Example 14.14. *Consider the DJFA*

$$M = (\{s, r, t\}, D, R, s, \{s\}),$$

where $D = \{a, b, c\}$ *and*

$$R = \{sa \to r, rb \to t, tc \to s\}.$$

Starting from s, M has to read some a, some b, and some c, entering again the start (and also the final) state s. All these occurrences of a, b, and c can appear anywhere in the input string. Therefore, the accepted language is clearly

$$L(M, \curvearrowright) = \{w \in D^* \mid \text{occur}(a, w) = \text{occur}(b, w) = \text{occur}(c, w)\}.$$

Recall that $L(M, \curvearrowright)$ in Example 14.14 is a well-known non-context-free context-sensitive language.

Example 14.15. *Consider the GJFA*

$$M = (\{s, t, f\}, \{a, b\}, R, s, \{f\}),$$

where

$$R = \{sba \to f, fa \to f, fb \to f\}.$$

Starting from s, M has to read string ba, which can appear anywhere in the input string. Then, it can read an arbitrary number of symbols a and b, including no symbols. Therefore, the accepted language is $L(M, \curvearrowright) = \{a, b\}^*\{ba\}\{a, b\}^*$.

14.3.1.1 Denotation of language families

Throughout the rest of this chapter, **GJFA**, $\mathbf{GJFA}^{-\varepsilon}$, **JFA**, $\mathbf{JFA}^{-\varepsilon}$, and **DJFA**, denote the families of languages accepted by GJFAs, ε-free GJFAs, JFAs, ε-free JFAs, and DJFAs, respectively.

14.3.2 Properties

In this section, we discuss the generative power of GJFAs and JFAs and some other basic properties of these automata.

Theorem 14.16. *For every DJFA M, there is a CJFA M′ such that* $L(M, \curvearrowright) = L(M', \curvearrowright)$.

Proof. Let $M = (Q, D, R, s, F)$ be a DJFA. We next construct a CJFA M' such that $L(M, \curvearrowright) = L(M', \curvearrowright)$. Without any loss of generality, we assume that $\bot \notin Q$. Initially, set

$$M' = (Q \cup \{\bot\}, D, R', s, F),$$

where $R' = R$. Next, for each $a \in D$ and each $p \in Q$ such that $pa \to q \notin R$ for all $q \in Q$, add $pa \to \bot$ to R'. For each $a \in D$, add $\bot a \to \bot$ to R'. Clearly, M' is a CJFA and $L(M, \curvearrowright) = L(M', \curvearrowright)$. ∎

Lemma 14.6. *For every GJFA M of degree* $n \geq 0$, *there is an* ε*-free GJFA M′ of degree n such that* $L(M', \curvearrowright) = L(M, \curvearrowright)$.

Proof. This lemma can be demonstrated by using the standard conversion of finite automata to ε-free finite automata (see Algorithm 3.2.2.3 in [52]). ∎

Theorem 14.17. $\mathbf{GJFA} = \mathbf{GJFA}^{-\varepsilon}$.

Proof. $\mathbf{GJFA}^{-\varepsilon} \subseteq \mathbf{GJFA}$ follows from the definition of a GJFA. $\mathbf{GJFA} \subseteq \mathbf{GJFA}^{-\varepsilon}$ follows from Lemma 14.6. ∎

Theorem 14.18. $\mathbf{JFA} = \mathbf{JFA}^{-\varepsilon} = \mathbf{DJFA}$.

Proof. $\mathbf{JFA} = \mathbf{JFA}^{-\varepsilon}$ can be proved by analogy with the proof of Theorem 14.17, so we only prove that $\mathbf{JFA}^{-\varepsilon} = \mathbf{DJFA}$. $\mathbf{DJFA} \subseteq \mathbf{JFA}^{-\varepsilon}$ follows from the definition of a DJFA. The converse inclusion can be proved by using the standard technique of converting ε-free finite automata to deterministic finite automata (see Algorithm 3.2.3.1 in [52]). ∎

The next theorem shows a property of languages accepted by GJFAs with unary input alphabets.

Theorem 14.19. *Let* $M = (Q, D, R, s, F)$ *be a GJFA such that* card $(D) = 1$. *Then,* $L(M, \curvearrowright)$ *is regular.*

Proof. Let $M = (Q, D, R, s, F)$ be a GJFA such that card $(D) = 1$. Since card $(D) = 1$, without any loss of generality, we can assume that the acceptance process for $w \in D^*$ starts from the configuration sw, and M does not jump over any symbols. Therefore, we can treat M as an equivalent *general finite automaton* defined just like an ordinary finite automaton except that it can read a string, not just a symbol, during a single move (see Definition 3.4.1 in [23]). As general finite automata accept only regular languages (see Theorem 3.4.4 in [23]), $L(M, \curvearrowright)$ is regular. ∎

As a consequence of Theorem 14.19, we obtain the following corollary (recall that K below is not regular):

Corollary 14.5. *The language* $K = \{a^p \mid p \text{ is a prime number}\}$ *cannot be accepted by any GJFA.*

The following theorem gives a necessary condition for a language to be in **JFA**.

Theorem 14.20. *Let* K *be an arbitrary language. Then,* $K \in \mathbf{JFA}$ *only if* $K =$ perm(K).

Proof. Let $M = (Q, D, R, s, F)$ be a JFA. Without any loss of generality, we assume that M is a DJFA (recall that $\mathbf{JFA} = \mathbf{DJFA}$ by Theorem 14.18). Let $w \in L(M, \curvearrowright)$. We next prove that perm$(w) \subseteq L(M, \curvearrowright)$. If $w = \varepsilon$, then perm$(\varepsilon) = \varepsilon \in L(M, \curvearrowright)$, so we assume that $w \neq \varepsilon$. Then, $w = a_1 a_2 \cdots a_n$, where $a_i \in D$ for all $i = 1, \ldots, n$, for some $n \geq 1$. Since $w \in L(M, \curvearrowright)$, R contains

$$\begin{aligned} s a_{i_1} &\rightarrow s_{i_1}, \\ s_{i_1} a_{i_2} &\rightarrow s_{i_2}, \\ &\vdots \\ s_{i_{n-1}} a_{i_n} &\rightarrow s_{i_n}, \end{aligned}$$

where $s_j \in Q$ for all $j \in \{i_1, i_2, \ldots, i_n\}$, $(i_1, i_2, \ldots, i_n)$ is a permutation of $(1, 2, \ldots, n)$, and $s_{i_n} \in F$. However, this implies that $a_{k_1} a_{k_2} \cdots a_{k_n} \in L(M, \curvearrowright)$, where $(k_1, k_2, \ldots, k_n)$ is a permutation of $(1, 2, \ldots, n)$, so $\mathrm{perm}(w) \subseteq L(M, \curvearrowright)$. ■

From Theorem 14.20, we obtain the following two corollaries, which are used in subsequent proofs.

Corollary 14.6. *There is no JFA that accepts* $\{ab\}^*$.

Corollary 14.7. *There is no JFA that accepts* $\{a, b\}^*\{ba\}\{a, b\}^*$.

Consider the language of primes K from Corollary 14.5. Since $K = \mathrm{perm}(K)$, the condition from Theorem 14.20 is not sufficient for a language to be in **JFA**. This is stated in the following corollary:

Corollary 14.8. *There is a language K satisfying* $K = \mathrm{perm}(K)$ *that cannot be accepted by any JFA.*

The next theorem gives both a necessary and sufficient condition for a language to be accepted by a JFA.

Theorem 14.21. *Let L be an arbitrary language. $L \in$* **JFA** *if and only if* $L = \mathrm{perm}(K)$, *where K is a regular language.*

Proof. The proof is divided into the only-if part and the if part.

Only if. Let M be a JFA. Consider M as a finite automaton M'. Set $K = L(M')$. K is regular, and $L(M, \curvearrowright) = \mathrm{perm}(K)$. Hence, the only-if part holds.

If. Take $\mathrm{perm}(K)$, where K is any regular language. Let $K = L(M)$, where M is a finite automaton. Consider M as a JFA M'. Observe that $L(M', \curvearrowright) = \mathrm{perm}(K)$, which proves the if part of the proof. ■

Finally, we show that GJFAs are stronger than JFAs.

Theorem 14.22. JFA ⊂ GJFA.

Proof. **JFA** ⊆ **GJFA** follows from the definition of a JFA. From Corollary 14.7, **GJFA** − **JFA** $\neq \emptyset$, because $\{a, b\}^*\{ba\}\{a, b\}^*$ is accepted by the GJFA from Example 14.15. ■

Open Problem 14.6. *Is there a necessary and sufficient condition for a language to be in* **GJFA**?

14.3.2.1 Relations with well-known language families

In this section, we establish relations between **GJFA**, **JFA**, and some well-known language families, including **FIN**, **REG**, **CF**, and **CS**.

Theorem 14.23. **FIN** $\subset$ **GJFA**.

Proof. Let $K \in$ **FIN**. Since K is a finite, there exists $n \geq 0$ such that $\text{card}(K) = n$. Therefore, we can express K as $K = \{w_1, w_2, \ldots, w_n\}$. Define the GJFA

$$M = (\{s, f\}, D, R, s, \{f\}),$$

where $D = \text{symbols}(K)$ and $R = \{sw_1 \rightarrow f, sw_2 \rightarrow f, \ldots, sw_n \rightarrow f\}$. Clearly, $L(M, \curvearrowright) = K$. Therefore, **FIN** $\subseteq$ **GJFA**. From Example 14.14, **GJFA** $-$ **FIN** $\neq \emptyset$, which proves the theorem. ■

Lemma 14.7. *There is no GJFA that accepts* $\{a\}^*\{b\}^*$.

Proof. By contradiction. Let $K = \{a\}^*\{b\}^*$. Assume that there is a GJFA, $M = (Q, D, R, s, F)$, such that $L(M, \curvearrowright) = K$. Let $w = a^n b$, where n is the degree of M. Since $w \in K$, during an acceptance of w, a rule, $pa^i b \rightarrow q \in R$, where $p, q \in Q$ and $0 \leq i < n$, has to be used. However, then M also accepts from the configuration $a^i bsa^{n-i}$. Indeed, as $a^i b$ is read in a single step and all the other symbols in w are just as, $a^i ba^{n-i}$ may be accepted by using the same rules as during an acceptance of w. This implies that $a^i ba^{n-i} \in K$—a contradiction with the assumption that $L(M, \curvearrowright) = K$. Therefore, there is no GJFA that accepts $\{a\}^*\{b\}^*$. ■

Theorem 14.24. **REG** *and* **GJFA** *are incomparable.*

Proof. **GJFA** $\not\subseteq$ **REG** follows from Example 14.14. **REG** $\not\subseteq$ **GJFA** follows from Lemma 14.7. ■

Theorem 14.25. **CF** *and* **GJFA** *are incomparable.*

Proof. **GJFA** $\not\subseteq$ **CF** follows from Example 14.14, and **CF** $\not\subseteq$ **GJFA** follows from Lemma 14.7. ■

Theorem 14.26. **GJFA** $\subset$ **CS**.

Proof. Clearly, jumps of GJFAs can be simulated by CSGs, so **GJFA** $\subseteq$ **CS**. From Lemma 14.7, it follows that **CS** $-$ **GJFA** $\neq \emptyset$. ■

Theorem 14.27. **FIN** *and* **JFA** *are incomparable.*

Proof. **JFA** $\not\subseteq$ **FIN** follows from Example 14.14. Consider the finite language $K = \{ab\}$. By Theorem 14.20, $K \notin$ **JFA**, so **FIN** $\not\subseteq$ **JFA**. ■

14.3.2.2 Closure properties

In this section, we show the closure properties of the families **GJFA** and **JFA** under various operations.

Theorem 14.28. *Both* **GJFA** *and* **JFA** *are not closed under endmarking.*

Proof. Consider the language $K = \{a\}^*$. Clearly, $K \in$ **JFA**. A proof that no GJFA accepts $K\{\#\}$, where # is a symbol such that $\# \neq a$, can be made by analogy with the proof of Lemma 14.7. ■

Theorem 14.28 implies that both families are not closed under concatenation. Indeed, observe that the JFA

$$M = (\{s, f\}, \{\#\}, \{s\# \rightarrow f\}, s, \{f\})$$

accepts $\{\#\}$.

Corollary 14.9. *Both* **GJFA** *and* **JFA** *are not closed under concatenation.*

Theorem 14.29. **JFA** *is closed under shuffle.*

Proof. Let $M_1 = (Q_1, D_1, R_1, s_1, F_1)$ and $M_2 = (Q_2, D_2, R_2, s_2, F_2)$ be two JFAs. Without any loss of generality, we assume that $Q_1 \cap Q_2 = \emptyset$. Define the JFA

$$H = (Q_1 \cup Q_2, D_1 \cup D_2, R_1 \cup R_2 \cup \{f \rightarrow s_2 \mid f \in F_1\}, s_1, F_2).$$

To see that $L(H) = \text{shuffle}\,(L(M_1, \curvearrowright), L(M_2, \curvearrowright))$, observe how H works. On an input string, $w \in (D_1 \cup D_2)^*$, H first runs M_1 on w, and if it ends in a final state, it runs M_2 on the rest of the input. If M_2 ends in a final state, H accepts w. Otherwise, it rejects w. By Theorem 14.20, $L(M_i, \curvearrowright) = \text{perm}(L(M_i, \curvearrowright))$ for all $i \in \{1, 2\}$. Based on these observations, since H can jump anywhere after a symbol is read, we see that $L(H) = \text{shuffle}\,(L(M_1, \curvearrowright), L(M_2, \curvearrowright))$. ■

Notice that the construction used in the previous proof coincides with the standard construction of a concatenation of the two finite automata (see [52]).

Theorem 14.30. *Both* **GJFA** *and* **JFA** *are closed under union.*

Proof. Let $M_1 = (Q_1, D_1, R_1, s_1, F_1)$ and $M_2 = (Q_2, D_2, R_2, s_2, F_2)$ be two GJFAs. Without any loss of generality, we assume that $Q_1 \cap Q_2 = \emptyset$ and $s \notin (Q_1 \cup Q_2)$. Define the GJFA

$$H = (Q_1 \cup Q_2 \cup \{s\}, D_1 \cup D_2, R_1 \cup R_2 \cup \{s \rightarrow s_1, s \rightarrow s_2\}, s, F_1 \cup F_2).$$

Clearly, $L(H) = L(M_1, \curvearrowright) \cup L(M_2, \curvearrowright)$, and if both M_1 and M_2 are JFAs, then H is also a JFA. ■

Theorem 14.31. **GJFA** *is not closed under complement.*

Proof. Consider the GJFA M from Example 14.15. Observe that the complement of $L(M, \curvearrowright)$ (with respect to $\{a, b\}^*$) is $\{a\}^*\{b\}^*$, which cannot be accepted by any GJFA (see Lemma 14.7). ■

Theorem 14.32. **JFA** *is closed under complement.*

Proof. Let $M = (Q, D, R, s, F)$ be a JFA. Without any loss of generality, we assume that M is a CJFA (**JFA** = **DJFA** by Theorem 14.18, and every DJFA can be converted to an equivalent CJFA by Theorem 14.16). Then, the JFA

$$M' = (Q, D, R, s, Q - F)$$

accepts $\overline{L(M, \curvearrowright)}$. ∎

By using De Morgan's laws, we obtain the following two corollaries of Theorems 14.30, 14.31, and 14.32.

Corollary 14.10. **GJFA** *is not closed under intersection.*

Corollary 14.11. **JFA** *is closed under intersection.*

Theorem 14.33. *Both* **GJFA** *and* **JFA** *are not closed under intersection with regular languages.*

Proof. Consider the language $J = \{a, b\}^*$, which can be accepted by both GJFAs and JFAs. Consider the regular language $K = \{a\}^*\{b\}^*$. Since $J \cap K = K$, this theorem follows from Lemma 14.7. ∎

Theorem 14.34. **JFA** *is closed under reversal.*

Proof. Let $K \in$ **JFA**. Since $\text{perm}(w) \subseteq K$ by Theorem 14.20 for all $w \in K$, also $\text{reversal}\,(w) \in K$ for all $w \in K$, so the theorem holds. ∎

Theorem 14.35. **JFA** *is not closed under Kleene star or under Kleene plus.*

Proof. Consider the language $K = \{ab, ba\}$, which is accepted by the JFA

$$M = (\{s, r, f\}, \{a, b\}, \{sa \to r, rb \to f\}, s, \{f\}).$$

However, by Theorem 14.20, there is no JFA that accepts K^* or K^+ (notice that, for example, $abab \in K^+$, but $aabb \notin K^+$). ∎

Lemma 14.8. *There is no GJFA that accepts* $\{a\}^*\{b\}^* \cup \{b\}^*\{a\}^*$.

Proof. This lemma can be proved by analogy with the proof of Lemma 14.7. ∎

Theorem 14.36. *Both* **GJFA** *and* **JFA** *are not closed under substitution.*

Proof. Consider the language $K = \{ab, ba\}$, which is accepted by the JFA M from the proof of Theorem 14.35. Define the substitution σ from $\{a, b\}^*$ to $2^{\{a,b\}^*}$ as $\sigma(a) = \{a\}^*$ and $\sigma(b) = \{b\}^*$. Clearly, both $\sigma(a)$ and $\sigma(b)$ can be accepted by JFAs. However, $\sigma(K)$ cannot be accepted by any GJFA (see Lemma 14.8). ∎

Since the substitution σ in the proof of Theorem 14.36 is regular, we obtain the following corollary:

Corollary 14.12. *Both* **GJFA** *and* **JFA** *are not closed under regular substitution.*

Theorem 14.37. JFA *is not closed under* ε*-free homomorphism.*

Proof. Define the ε-free homomorphism ϕ from $\{a\}$ to $\{a,b\}^+$ as $\phi(a) = ab$ and consider the language $\{a\}^*$, which is accepted by the JFA

$$M = (\{s\}, \{a\}, \{sa \rightarrow s\}, \{s\}).$$

Notice that $\phi(L(M, \curvearrowright)) = \{ab\}^*$, which cannot be accepted by any JFA (see Corollary [64]. ■

The analogous result was recently proved for GJFAs in [64].

Theorem 14.38 (see Theorem 2 in [64]). GJFA *is not closed under* ε*-free homomorphism.*

Since ε-free homomorphism is a special case of homomorphism and since homomorphism is a special case of finite substitution, we obtain the following corollary of Theorems 14.37 and 14.38.

Corollary 14.13. GJFA *and* **JFA** *are not closed under homomorphism.*

Corollary 14.14. GJFA *and* **JFA** *are not closed under finite substitution.*

Theorem 14.39. JFA *is closed under inverse homomorphism.*

Proof. Let $M = (Q, \Gamma, R, s, F)$ be a JFA, D be an alphabet, and ϕ be a homomorphism from D^* to Γ^*. We next construct a JFA M' such that $L(M', \curvearrowright) = \phi^{-1}(L(M, \curvearrowright))$. Define

$$M' = (Q, D, R', s, F),$$

where

$$R' = \{pa \rightarrow q \mid a \in D, p\phi(a) \rightsquigarrow q \text{ in } \Delta(M)\}.$$

Observe that $w_1 s w_2 \curvearrowright^* q$ in M if and only if $w_1' s w_2' \curvearrowright^* q$ in M', where $w_1 w_2 = \phi(w_1' w_2')$ and $q \in Q$, so $L(M', \curvearrowright) = \phi^{-1}(L(M, \curvearrowright))$. A fully rigorous proof is left to the reader. ■

However, the same does not hold for GJFAs.

Theorem 14.40 (see Theorem 3 in [64]). GJFA *is not closed under inverse homomorphism.*

Moreover, in [64] it was shown that **GJFA** is not close under shuffle, Kleene star, and Kleene plus, while it is closed under reversal.

Theorem 14.41 (see Theorems 2 and 4 in [64]). GJFA *is not closed under shuffle, Kleene star, and Kleene plus.*

Theorem 14.42 (see Theorem 5 in [64]). GJFA *is closed under reversal.*

Table 14.1 Summary of closure properties

	GJFA	JFA
Endmarking	−	−
Concatenation	−	−
Shuffle	−	+
Union	+	+
Complement	−	+
Intersection	−	+
Int. with regular languages	−	−
Kleene star	−	−
Kleene plus	−	−
Mirror image	+	+
Substitution	−	−
Regular substitution	−	−
Finite substitution	−	−
Homomorphism	−	−
ε-Free homomorphism	−	−
Inverse homomorphism	−	+

The summary of closure properties of the families **GJFA** and **JFA** is given in Table 14.1, where + marks closure and − marks non-closure. It is worth noting that **REG**, characterized by finite automata, is closed under all of these operations.

14.3.2.3 Decidability

In this section, we prove the decidability of some decision problems with regard to **GJFA** and **JFA**.

Lemma 14.9. *Let $M = (Q, D, R, s, F)$ be a GJFA. Then, $L(M, \curvearrowright)$ is infinite if and only if $py \rightsquigarrow p$ in $\Delta(M)$, for some $y \in D^+$ and $p \in Q$ such that p is both reachable and terminating in $\Delta(M)$.*

Proof. If. Let $M = (Q, D, R, s, F)$ be a GJFA such that $py \rightsquigarrow p$ in $\Delta(M)$, for some $y \in D^+$ and $p \in Q$ such that p is both reachable and terminating in $\Delta(M)$. Then,

$$w_1 s w_2 \curvearrowright^* upv \curvearrowright^+ xpz \curvearrowright^* f,$$

where $w_1 w_2 \in L(M, \curvearrowright)$, $u, v, x, z \in D^*, p \in Q$, and $f \in F$. Consequently,

$$w_1 s w_2 \curvearrowright^* upvy' \curvearrowright^+ xpz \curvearrowright^* f,$$

where $y' = y^n$ for all $n \geq 0$. Therefore, $L(M, \curvearrowright)$ is infinite, so the if part holds.

Only if. Let $M = (Q, D, R, s, F)$ be a GJFA such that $L(M, \curvearrowright)$ is infinite. Without any loss of generality, we assume that M is ε-free (see Lemma 14.6). Then,

$$w_1 s w_2 \curvearrowright^* upv \curvearrowright^+ xpz \curvearrowright^* f$$

for some $w_1w_2 \in L(M, \curvearrowright)$, $u, v, x, z \in D^*$, $p \in Q$, and $f \in F$. This implies that p is both terminating and reachable in $\Delta(M)$. Let $y \in D^+$ be a string read by M during $upv \curvearrowright^+ xpz$. Then, $py \rightsquigarrow p$ in $\Delta(M)$, so the only-if part holds. ■

Theorem 14.43. *Both finiteness and infiniteness are decidable for* **GJFA**.

Proof. Let $M = (Q, D, R, s, F)$ be a GJFA. By Lemma 14.9, $L(M, \curvearrowright)$ is infinite if and only if $py \rightsquigarrow p$ in $\Delta(M)$, for some $y \in D^+$ and $p \in Q$ such that p is both reachable and terminating in $\Delta(M)$. This condition can be checked by any graph searching algorithm, such as breadth-first search (see page 73 in [65]). Therefore, the theorem holds. ■

Corollary 14.15. *Both finiteness and infiniteness are decidable for* **JFA**.

Observe that since there is no deterministic version of a GJFA, the following proof of Theorem 14.44 is not as straightforward as in terms of regular languages and classical deterministic finite automata.

Theorem 14.44. *The membership problem is decidable for* **GJFA**.

Proof. Let $M = (Q, D, R, s, F)$ be a GJFA, and let $x \in D^*$. Without any loss of generality, we assume that M is ε-free (see Theorem 14.17). If $x = \varepsilon$, then $x \in L(M, \curvearrowright)$ if and only if $s \in F$, so assume that $x \neq \varepsilon$. Set

$$\Gamma = \{(x_1, x_2, \ldots, x_n) \mid x_i \in D^+, 1 \leq i \leq n, x_1x_2 \cdots x_n = x, n \geq 1\}$$

and

$$\Gamma_p = \{(y_1, y_2, \ldots, y_n) \mid (x_1, x_2, \ldots, x_n) \in \Gamma, n \geq 1, (y_1, y_2, \ldots, y_n) \text{ is a permutation of } (x_1, x_2, \ldots, x_n)\}.$$

If there exist $(y_1, y_2, \ldots, y_n) \in \Gamma_p$ and $q_1, q_2, \ldots, q_{n+1} \in Q$, for some n, $1 \leq n \leq |x|$, such that $s = q_1$, $q_{n+1} \in F$, and $q_iy_i \rightarrow q_{i+1} \in R$ for all $i = 1, 2, \ldots, n$, then $x \in L(M, \curvearrowright)$; otherwise, $x \notin L(M, \curvearrowright)$. Since both Q and Γ_p are finite, this check can be performed in finite time. ■

Corollary 14.16. *The membership problem is decidable for* **JFA**.

Theorem 14.45. *The emptiness problem is decidable for* **GJFA**.

Proof. Let $M = (Q, D, R, s, F)$ be a GJFA. Then, $L(M, \curvearrowright)$ is empty if and only if no $f \in F$ is reachable in $\Delta(M)$. This check can be done by any graph searching algorithm, such as breadth-first search (see page 73 in [65]). ■

Corollary 14.17. *The emptiness problem is decidable for* **JFA**.

The summary of decidability properties of the families **GJFA** and **JFA** is given in Table 14.2, where + marks decidability.

Table 14.2 Summary of decidability properties

	GJFA	JFA
Membership	+	+
Emptiness	+	+
Finiteness	+	+
Infiniteness	+	+

14.3.2.4 An infinite hierarchy of language families

In this section, we establish an infinite hierarchy of language families resulting from GJFAs of degree n, where $n \geq 0$. Let $\mathbf{GJFA}_n$ and $\mathbf{GJFA}_n^{-\varepsilon}$ denote the families of languages accepted by GJFAs of degree n and by ε-free GJFAs of degree n, respectively. Observe that $\mathbf{GJFA}_n = \mathbf{GJFA}_n^{-\varepsilon}$ by the definition of a GJFA and by Lemma 14.6, for all $n \geq 0$.

Lemma 14.10. *Let D be an alphabet such that* card $(D) \geq 2$. *Then, for any $n \geq 1$, there is a GJFA of degree n, $M_n = (Q, D, R, s, F)$, such that $L(M_n)$ cannot be accepted by any GJFA of degree $n - 1$.*

Proof. Let D be an alphabet such that card $(D) \geq 2$, and let $a, b \in D$ such that $a \neq b$. The case when $n = 1$ follows immediately from the definition of a JFA, so we assume that $n \geq 2$. Define the GJFA of degree n

$$M_n = (\{s, f\}, D, \{sw \to f\}, s, \{f\}),$$

where $w = ab(a)^{n-2}$. Clearly, $L(M_n, \curvearrowright) = \{w\}$. We next prove that $L(M_n, \curvearrowright)$ cannot be accepted by any GJFA of degree $n - 1$.

Suppose, for the sake of contradiction, that there is a GJFA of degree $n - 1$, $H = (Q, D, R, s', F)$, such that $L(H) = L(M_n, \curvearrowright)$. Without any loss of generality, we assume that H is ε-free (see Lemma 14.6). Since $L(H) = L(M_n, \curvearrowright) = \{w\}$ and $|w| > n - 1$, there has to be

$$us'xv \curvearrowright^m f$$

in H, where $w = uxv$, $u, v \in D^*$, $x \in D^+$, $f \in F$, and $m \geq 2$. Thus,

$$s'xuv \curvearrowright^m f$$

and

$$uvs'x \curvearrowright^m f$$

in H, which contradicts the assumption that $L(H) = \{w\}$. Therefore, $L(M_n, \curvearrowright)$ cannot be accepted by any GJFA of degree $n - 1$. ■

Theorem 14.46. $\mathbf{GJFA}_n \subset \mathbf{GJFA}_{n+1}$ *for all* $n \geq 0$.

Proof. $\mathbf{GJFA}_n \subseteq \mathbf{GJFA}_{n+1}$ follows from the definition of a GJFA of degree n, for all $n \geq 0$. From Lemma 14.10, $\mathbf{GJFA}_{n+1} - \mathbf{GJFA}_n \neq \emptyset$, which proves the theorem. ∎

Taking Lemma 14.6 into account, we obtain the following corollary of Theorem 14.46.

Corollary 14.18. $\mathbf{GJFA}_n^{-\varepsilon} \subset \mathbf{GJFA}_{n+1}^{-\varepsilon}$ *for all* $n \geq 0$.

14.3.2.5 Left and right jumps

We define two special cases of the jumping relation.

Definition 14.19. *Let* $M = (Q, D, R, s, F)$ *be a GJFA. Let* $w, x, y, z \in D^*$, *and* $py \rightarrow q \in R$; *then, (1) M makes a* left jump *from* $wxpyz$ *to* $wqxz$, *symbolically written as*

$$wxpyz \; {}_{l}\!\curvearrowright wqxz$$

and (2) M makes a right jump *from* $wpyxz$ *to* $wxqz$, *written as*

$$wpyxz \; {}_{r}\!\curvearrowright wxqz.$$

Let $u, v \in D^*QD^*$; *then,* $u \curvearrowright v$ *if and only if* $u \; {}_{l}\!\curvearrowright v$ *or* $u \; {}_{r}\!\curvearrowright v$. *Extend* ${}_{l}\!\curvearrowright$ *and* ${}_{r}\!\curvearrowright$ *to* ${}_{l}\!\curvearrowright^m$, ${}_{l}\!\curvearrowright^*$, ${}_{l}\!\curvearrowright^+$, ${}_{r}\!\curvearrowright^m$, ${}_{r}\!\curvearrowright^*$, *and* ${}_{r}\!\curvearrowright^+$, *where* $m \geq 0$, *by analogy with extending* $\curvearrowright$. *Set*

$${}_{l}L(M, \curvearrowright) = \{uv \mid u, v \in D^*, usv \; {}_{l}\!\curvearrowright^* f \text{ with } f \in F\}$$

and

$${}_{r}L(M, \curvearrowright) = \{uv \mid u, v \in D^*, usv \; {}_{r}\!\curvearrowright^* f \text{ with } f \in F\}.$$

Let ${}_{l}\mathbf{GJFA}$, ${}_{l}\mathbf{JFA}$, ${}_{r}\mathbf{GJFA}$, and ${}_{r}\mathbf{JFA}$ denote the families of languages accepted by GJFAs using only left jumps, JFAs using only left jumps, GJFAs using only right jumps, and JFAs using only right jumps, respectively.

Theorem 14.47. ${}_{r}\mathbf{GJFA} = {}_{r}\mathbf{JFA} = \mathbf{REG}$.

Proof. We first prove that ${}_{r}\mathbf{JFA} = \mathbf{REG}$. Consider any JFA, $M = (Q, D, R, s, F)$. Observe that if M occurs in a configuration of the form xpy, where $x \in D^*, p \in Q$, and $y \in D^*$, then it cannot read the symbols in x anymore because M can make only right jumps. Also, observe that this covers the situation when M starts to accept $w \in D^*$ from a different configuration than sw. Therefore, to read the whole input, M has to start in configuration sw, and it cannot jump to skip some symbols. Consequently, M behaves like an ordinary finite automaton, reading the input from the left to the right, so $L(M, \curvearrowright)$ is regular and, therefore, ${}_{r}\mathbf{JFA} \subseteq \mathbf{REG}$. Conversely, any finite automaton can be viewed as a JFA that starts from configuration sw and does not jump to skip some symbols. Therefore, $\mathbf{REG} \subseteq {}_{r}\mathbf{JFA}$, which proves that ${}_{r}\mathbf{JFA} = \mathbf{REG}$. ${}_{r}\mathbf{GJFA} = \mathbf{REG}$ can be proved by the same reasoning using general finite automata instead of finite automata. ∎

Next, we show that JFAs using only left jumps accept some non-regular languages.

Theorem 14.48. ${}_l$**JFA** − **REG** $\neq \emptyset$.

Proof. Consider the JFA

$$M = (\{s, p, q\}, \{a, b\}, R, s, \{s\}),$$

where

$$R = \{sa \to p, pb \to s, sb \to q, qa \to s\}.$$

We argue that

$${}_lL(M, \curvearrowright) = \{w \mid \text{occur}(a, w) = \text{occur}(b, w)\}.$$

With $w \in \{a, b\}^*$ on its input, M starts over the last symbol. M reads this symbol by using $sa \to p$ or $sb \to q$, and jumps to the left in front of the rightmost occurrence of b or a, respectively. Then, it consumes it by using $pb \to s$ or $qa \to s$, respectively. If this read symbol was the rightmost one, it jumps one symbol to the left and repeats the process. Otherwise, it makes no jumps at all. Observe that in this way, every configuration is of the form urv, where $r \in \{s, p, q\}$, $u \in \{a, b\}^*$, and either $v \in \{a, \varepsilon\}\{b\}^*$ or $v \in \{b, \varepsilon\}\{a\}^*$.

Based on the previous observations, we see that

$${}_lL(M, \curvearrowright) = \{w \mid \text{occur}(a, w) = \text{occur}(b, w)\}.$$

Since $L(M, \curvearrowright)$ is not regular, ${}_l$**JFA** − **REG** $\neq \emptyset$, so the theorem holds. ∎

Open Problem 14.7. *Study the effect of left jumps to the acceptance power of JFAs and GJFAs.*

14.3.2.6 A variety of start configurations

In general, a GJFA can start its computation anywhere in the input string (see Definition 14.15). In this section, we consider the impact of various start configurations on the acceptance power of GJFAs and JFAs.

Definition 14.20. *Let $M = (Q, D, R, s, F)$ be a GJFA. Set*

$${}^bL(M, \curvearrowright) = \{w \in D^* \mid sw \curvearrowright^* f \text{ with } f \in F\},$$
$${}^aL(M, \curvearrowright) = \{uv \mid u, v \in D^*, usv \curvearrowright^* f \text{ with } f \in F\}, \text{ and}$$
$${}^eL(M, \curvearrowright) = \{w \in D^* \mid ws \curvearrowright^* f \text{ with } f \in F\}.$$

Intuitively, b, a, and e stand for *beginning*, *anywhere*, and *end*, respectively; in this way, we express where the acceptance process starts. Observe that we simplify ${}^aL(M, \curvearrowright)$ to $L(M, \curvearrowright)$ because we pay a principal attention to the languages accepted in this way in this chapter. Let ^{b}**GJFA**, ^{a}**GJFA**, ^{e}**GJFA**, ^{b}**JFA**, ^{a}**JFA**, and ^{e}**JFA** denote the families of languages accepted by GJFAs starting at the beginning, GJFAs starting anywhere, GJFAs starting at the end, JFAs starting at the beginning, JFAs starting anywhere, and JFAs starting at the end, respectively.

We show that

(1) starting at the beginning increases the acceptance power of GJFAs and JFAs and
(2) starting at the end does not increase the acceptance power of GJFAs and JFAs.

Theorem 14.49. ${}^{a}\mathbf{JFA} \subset {}^{b}\mathbf{JFA}$.

Proof. Let $M = (Q, D, R, s, F)$ be a JFA. The JFA

$$M' = (Q, D, R \cup \{s \to s\}, s, F)$$

clearly satisfies ${}^{a}L(M, \curvearrowright) = {}^{b}L(M', \curvearrowright)$, so ${}^{a}\mathbf{JFA} \subseteq {}^{b}\mathbf{JFA}$. We prove that this inclusion is, in fact, proper. Consider the language $K = \{a\}\{b\}^*$. The JFA

$$H = (\{s, f\}, \{a, b\}, \{sa \to f, fb \to f\}, s, \{f\})$$

satisfies ${}^{b}L(H) = K$. However, observe that ${}^{a}L(H) = \{b\}^*\{a\}\{b\}^*$, which differs from K. By Theorem 14.20, for every JFA N, it holds that ${}^{a}L(N) \neq K$. Hence, ${}^{a}\mathbf{JFA} \subset {}^{b}\mathbf{JFA}$. ■

Theorem 14.50. ${}^{a}\mathbf{GJFA} \subset {}^{b}\mathbf{GJFA}$.

Proof. This theorem can be proved by analogy with the proof of Theorem 14.49. ■

Lemma 14.11. *Let M be a GJFA of degree $n \geq 0$. Then, there is a GJFA M' of degree n such that ${}^{a}L(M, \curvearrowright) = {}^{e}L(M', \curvearrowright)$.*

Proof. Let $M = (Q, D, R, s, F)$ be a GJFA of degree n. Then, the GJFA

$$M' = (Q, D, R \cup \{s \to s\}, s, F)$$

is of degree n and satisfies ${}^{a}L(M, \curvearrowright) = {}^{e}L(M', \curvearrowright)$. ■

Lemma 14.12. *Let M be a GJFA of degree $n \geq 0$. Then, there is a GJFA $\hat{M}$ of degree n such that ${}^{e}L(M, \curvearrowright) = {}^{a}L(\hat{M})$.*

Proof. Let $M = (Q, D, R, s, F)$ be a GJFA of degree n. If ${}^{e}L(M, \curvearrowright) = \emptyset$, then the GJFA

$$M' = (\{s\}, D, \emptyset, s, \emptyset)$$

is of degree n and satisfies ${}^{a}L(M', \curvearrowright) = \emptyset$. If ${}^{e}L(M, \curvearrowright) = \{\varepsilon\}$, the GJFA

$$M'' = (\{s\}, D, \emptyset, s, \{s\})$$

is of degree n and satisfies ${}^{a}L(M'', \curvearrowright) = \{\varepsilon\}$. Therefore, assume that $w \in {}^{e}L(M, \curvearrowright)$, where $w \in D^+$. Then, $s \to p \in R$, for some $p \in Q$. Indeed, observe that either ${}^{e}L(M, \curvearrowright) = \emptyset$ or ${}^{e}L(M, \curvearrowright) = \{\varepsilon\}$, which follows from the observation that if M starts at the end of an input string, it first has to jump to the left to be able to read some symbols.

Define the GJFA $\hat{M} = (Q, D, \hat{R}, s, F)$, where

$$\hat{R} = R - \{su \to q \mid u \in D^+, q \in Q, \text{ and there is no } x \in D^+ \text{ such that } sx \rightsquigarrow s \text{ in } \Delta(M)\}.$$

The reason for excluding such $su \to q$ from $\hat{R}$ is that M first has to use a rule of the form $s \to p$, where $p \in Q$ (see the argumentation above). However, since $\hat{M}$ starts anywhere in the input string, we need to force it to use $s \to p$ as the first rule, thus changing the state from s to p, just like M does.

Clearly, $\hat{M}$ is of degree n and satisfies ${}^{e}L(M, \curvearrowright) = {}^{a}L(\hat{M})$, so the lemma holds. ■

Theorem 14.51. ${}^{e}\mathbf{GJFA} = {}^{a}\mathbf{GJFA}$ *and* ${}^{e}\mathbf{JFA} = {}^{a}\mathbf{JFA}$.

Proof. This theorem follows from Lemmas 14.11 and 14.12. ■

We also consider combinations of left jumps, right jumps, and various start configurations. For this purpose, by analogy with the previous denotations, we define ${}^{b}_{l}\mathbf{GJFA}$, ${}^{a}_{l}\mathbf{GJFA}$, ${}^{e}_{l}\mathbf{GJFA}$, ${}^{b}_{r}\mathbf{GJFA}$, ${}^{a}_{r}\mathbf{GJFA}$, ${}^{e}_{r}\mathbf{GJFA}$, ${}^{b}_{l}\mathbf{JFA}$, ${}^{a}_{l}\mathbf{JFA}$, ${}^{e}_{l}\mathbf{JFA}$, ${}^{b}_{r}\mathbf{JFA}$, ${}^{a}_{r}\mathbf{JFA}$, and ${}^{e}_{r}\mathbf{JFA}$. For example, ${}^{b}_{r}\mathbf{GJFA}$ denotes the family of languages accepted by GJFAs that perform only right jumps and starts at the beginning.

Theorem 14.52. ${}^{a}_{r}\mathbf{GJFA} = {}^{a}_{r}\mathbf{JFA} = {}^{b}_{r}\mathbf{GJFA} = {}^{b}_{r}\mathbf{JFA} = {}^{b}_{l}\mathbf{GJFA} = {}^{b}_{l}\mathbf{JFA} = \mathbf{REG}$.

Proof. Theorem 14.47, in fact, states that ${}^{a}_{r}\mathbf{GJFA} = {}^{a}_{r}\mathbf{JFA} = \mathbf{REG}$. Furthermore, ${}^{b}_{r}\mathbf{GJFA} = {}^{b}_{r}\mathbf{JFA} = \mathbf{REG}$ follows from the proof of Theorem 14.47 because M has to start the acceptance process of a string w from the configuration sw—that is, it starts at the beginning of w. ${}^{b}_{l}\mathbf{GJFA} = {}^{b}_{l}\mathbf{JFA} = \mathbf{REG}$ can be proved analogously. ■

Theorem 14.53. ${}^{e}_{r}\mathbf{GJFA} = {}^{e}_{r}\mathbf{JFA} = \{\emptyset, \{\varepsilon\}\}$.

Proof. Consider JFAs $M = (\{s\}, \{a\}, \emptyset, s, \emptyset)$ and $M' = (\{s\}, \{a\}, \emptyset, s, \{s\})$ to see that $\{\emptyset, \{\varepsilon\}\} \subseteq {}^{e}_{r}\mathbf{GJFA}$ and $\{\emptyset, \{\varepsilon\}\} \subseteq {}^{e}_{r}\mathbf{JFA}$. The converse inclusion also holds. Indeed, any GJFA that starts the acceptance process of a string w from ws and that can make only right jumps accepts either $\emptyset$ or $\{\varepsilon\}$. ■

Open Problem 14.8. *What are the properties of* ${}^{e}_{l}\mathbf{GJFA}$ *and* ${}^{e}_{l}\mathbf{JFA}$*?*

Notice that Open Problem 14.7, in fact, suggests an investigation of the properties of ${}^{a}_{l}\mathbf{GJFA}$ and ${}^{a}_{l}\mathbf{JFA}$.

14.3.2.7 Relations between jumping automata and jumping grammars

Next, we demonstrate that the generative power of regular and right-linear jumping grammars (see Section 14.1) is the same as the accepting power of JFAs and GJFAs, respectively. Consequently, the following equivalence and the previous results in this chapter imply several additional properties of languages that are generated by regular and right-linear jumping grammars such as closure properties and decidability.

Lemma 14.13. $\mathbf{GJFA} \subseteq \mathscr{L}(\Gamma_{RLG}, {}_{j}\Rightarrow)$.

Proof. Construction. For every GJFA $M = (Q, D, R, s, F)$, we construct an RLG $G = (Q \cup D \cup \{S\}, D, R', S)$, where S is a new nonterminal, $S \notin Q \cup D$, such that $L(M, \curvearrowright) = L(G, {}_{j}\Rightarrow)$. Set $R' = \{S \to f \mid f \in F\} \cup \{q \to xp \mid px \to q \in R\} \cup \{q \to x \mid sx \to q \in R\}$.

Basic Idea. The principle of the conversion is analogical to the conversion from classical lazy finite automata to equivalent RLGs with sequential derivation mode (see Section 2.6.2 in [32] and Theorem 4.1 in [11]).

The states of M are used as nonterminals in G. In addition, we introduce new start nonterminal S in G. The input symbols D are terminal symbols in G.

During the simulation of M in G, there is always exactly one nonterminal symbol in the sentential form until the last jumping derivation step that produces the string of terminal symbols. If there is a sequence of jumping moves $usv \curvearrowright^* ypxy' \curvearrowright zqz'z'' \curvearrowright^* f$ in M, then G simulates it by jumping derivation

$$S \ {}_j\!\Rightarrow f \ {}_j\!\Rightarrow^* zz'qz'' \ {}_j\!\Rightarrow yxpy' \ {}_j\!\Rightarrow^* w,$$

where $yy' = zz'z''$ and $w = uv$. First, S is nondeterministically rewritten to some f in G to simulate the entrance to the corresponding accepting final state of M. Then, for each rule $px \rightarrow q$ in M that processes substring x in the input string, there is x generated by the corresponding rule of the form $q \rightarrow xp$ in G. As the last jumping derivation step in G, we simulate the first jumping move of M from the start state s by rewriting the only nonterminal in the sentential form of G to a string of terminals and the simulation of M by G is completed. ∎

Lemma 14.14. $\mathscr{L}(\Gamma_{RLG}, {}_j\!\Rightarrow) \subseteq$ **GJFA**.

Proof. Construction. For every RLG $G = (\Sigma, \Delta, R', S)$, we construct a GJFA $M = (N \cup \{\sigma\}, \Delta, R, \sigma, \{S\})$, where σ is a new start state, $\sigma \notin \Sigma$ and $N = \Sigma - \Delta$, such that $L(G, {}_j\!\Rightarrow) = L(M, \curvearrowright)$. Set $R = \{Bx \rightarrow A \mid A \rightarrow xB \in R', A, B \in N, x \in \Delta^*\} \cup \{\sigma x \rightarrow A \mid A \rightarrow x \in R', x \in \Delta^*\}$.

Basic Idea. In the simulation of G in M we use nonterminals N as states, new state σ as the start state, and terminals Δ corresponds to input symbols of M. In addition, the start nonterminal of G corresponds to the only final state of M. Every application of a rule from R' in G is simulated by a move according to the corresponding rule from R constructed above. If there is a jumping derivation $S \ {}_j\!\Rightarrow^* yy'Ay'' \ {}_j\!\Rightarrow zxBz' \ {}_j\!\Rightarrow^* w$ in G, then M simulates it by jumping moves $u\sigma v \curvearrowright^* zBxz' \curvearrowright yAy'y'' \curvearrowright^* S$, where $yy'y'' = zz'$ and $w = uv$. ∎

Theorem 14.54. GJFA $= \mathscr{L}(\Gamma_{RLG}, {}_j\!\Rightarrow)$.

Proof. This theorem holds by Lemmas 14.13 and 14.14. ∎

In the following theorem, consider JFAs that processes only one input symbol in one move. We state their equivalence with jumping RGs.

Theorem 14.55. JFA $= \mathscr{L}(\Gamma_{RG}, {}_j\!\Rightarrow)$.

Proof. Prove this statement by analogy with the proof of Theorem 14.54. ∎

Figure 14.1 summarizes the achieved results on the descriptional complexity of jumping grammars and automata.

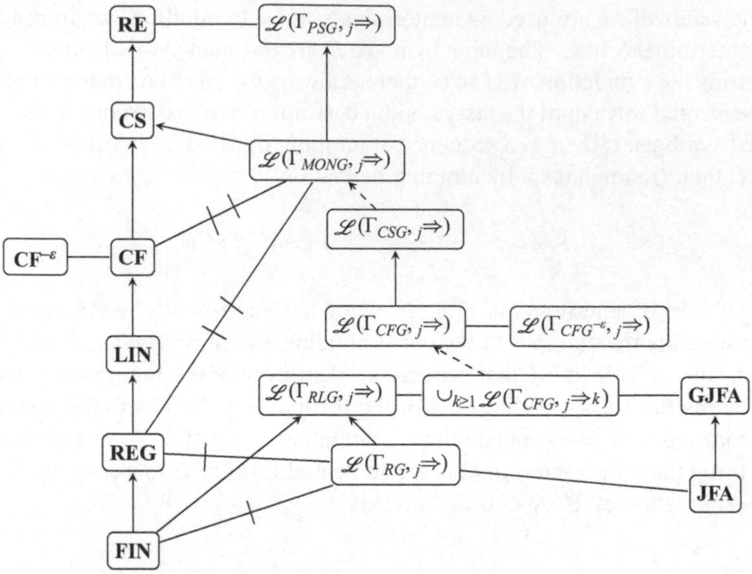

Figure 14.1 A hierarchy of language families closely related to the language families resulting from jumping grammars and automata is shown. If there is a line or an arrow from family X to family Y in the figure, then $X = Y$ or $X \subset Y$, respectively. If there is a dashed arrow from X to Y, then $X \subseteq Y$, but $X \subset Y$ represents an open problem. A crossed line represents the incomparability between connected families. (It is noteworthy that the figure describes only some of the language-family relations that are crucially important in terms of the present section; however, by no means, it gives an exhaustive description of these relations.)

14.3.2.8 A summary of open problems

Within the previous sections, we have already pointed out several specific open problems concerning them. We close the present chapter by pointing out some crucially important open-problem areas as suggested topics of future investigations:

(1) Concerning closure properties, study the closure of **GJFA** under shuffle, Kleene star, Kleene plus, and under reversal.
(2) Regarding decision problems, investigate other decision properties of **GJFA** and **JFA**, like equivalence, universality, inclusion, or regularity. Furthermore, study their computational complexity. Do there exist undecidable problems for **GJFA** or **JFA**?
(3) Section 14.3.2.5 has demonstrated that GJFAs and JFAs using only right jumps define the family of regular languages. How precisely do left jumps affect the acceptance power of JFAs and GJFAs?

(4) Broaden the results of Section 14.3.2.6 concerning various start configurations by investigating the properties of ${}_{l}^{e}$**GJFA** and ${}_{l}^{e}$**JFA**.
(5) Determinism represents a crucially important investigation area in terms of all types of automata. In essence, the nondeterministic versions of automata can make several different moves from the same configuration, while their deterministic counterparts cannot—that is, they make no more than one move from any configuration. More specifically, the deterministic version of classical finite automata require that for any state q and any input symbol a, there exists no more than one rule with qa on its left-hand side; in this way, they make no more than one move from any configuration. As a result, with any input string w, they make a unique sequence of moves. As should be obvious, in terms of JFAs, this requirement does not guarantee their determinism in the above sense. Modify the requirement so it guarantees the determinism.

Chapter 15
Deep pushdown automata

While the ordinary pushdown lists can be modified only on their tops, deep pushdown lists, as their name suggests, can be modified under them. Accordingly, while the ordinary versions of pushdown automata can expand only the topmost pushdown symbols, deep pushdown automata (DPDAs) can make expansions deeper in their pushdown lists; otherwise, they both work identically.

This chapter proves that the power of DPDAs is similar to the generative power of regulated context-free grammars without erasing rules. Indeed, just like these grammars, DPDAs are stronger than ordinary pushdown automata but less powerful than context-sensitive grammars. More precisely, they give rise to an infinite hierarchy of language families coinciding with the hierarchy resulting from n-limited state grammars (see Section 12.1).

The chapter is divided into two sections—Sections 15.1 and 15.2. The former introduces the basic versions of DPDAs. The latter places some natural restrictions on them.

15.1 Basic model

The concept of DPDAs is inspired by the well-known transformation of a context-free grammar to an equivalent pushdown automaton M, referred to as the general top-down parser for the grammar (see, page 176 in [39]). During every move, M either pops or expands its pushdown. More precisely, if an input symbol occurs on the pushdown top, M compares the pushdown top symbol with the current input symbol, and if they coincide, M pops the topmost symbol from the pushdown and proceeds to the next input symbol on the input tape. If a nonterminal occurs on the pushdown top, the parser expands its pushdown, so it replaces the top nonterminal with a string. M accepts an input string if it makes a sequence of moves, so it completely reads the string, empties its pushdown, and enters a final state.

Compared to M, a DPDA $_{deep}M$ works in a slightly generalized way. Indeed, $_{deep}M$ functions exactly as M except that it may make expansions of depth m so $_{deep}M$ replaces the mth topmost pushdown symbol with a string, for some $m \geq 1$. We demonstrate that the DPDAs that make expansions of depth m or less, where $m \geq 1$, are equivalent to m-limited state grammars, so these automata accept a proper language subfamily of the language family accepted by DPDAs that make expansions of depth

$m + 1$ or less. The resulting infinite hierarchy of language families obtained in this way occurs between the families of context-free and context-sensitive languages. For every positive integer n, however, there exist some context-sensitive languages that cannot be accepted by any DPDAs that make expansions of depth n or less.

15.1.1 Definitions and examples

Without further ado, we define the notion of a DPDA, after which we illustrate it by an example. Let $\mathbb{N}$ denote the set of all positive integers.

Definition 15.1. A *DPDA* is a septuple

$$M = (Q, D, \Gamma, R, s, S, F),$$

where

- Q is a finite set of *states*;
- D is an *input alphabet*;
- Γ is a *pushdown alphabet*, $\mathbb{N}$, Q, and Γ are pairwise disjoint, $D \subseteq \Gamma$, and $\Gamma - D$ contains a special *bottom symbol*, denoted by #;
- $R \subseteq (\mathbb{N} \times Q \times (\Gamma - (D \cup \{\#\})) \times Q \times (\Gamma - \{\#\})^+)$ $\cup (\mathbb{N} \times Q \times \{\#\} \times Q \times (\Gamma - \{\#\})^* \{\#\})$ is a finite relation;
- $s \in Q$ is the *start state*;
- $S \in \Gamma$ is the *start pushdown symbol*;
- $F \subseteq Q$ is the set of *final states*.

Instead of $(m, q, A, p, v) \in R$, we write $mqA \rightarrow pv \in R$ and call $mqA \rightarrow pv$ a *rule*; accordingly, R is referred to as the *set of rules* of M. A *configuration* of M is a triple in $Q \times \Delta^* \times (\Gamma - \{\#\})^* \{\#\}$. Let χ denote the set of all configurations of M. Let $x, y \in \chi$ be two configurations. M *pops* its pushdown from x to y, symbolically written as

$$x \;_p\!\vdash y,$$

if $x = (q, au, az), y = (q, u, z)$, where $a \in D, u \in D^*, z \in \Gamma^*$. M *expands* its pushdown from x to y, symbolically written as

$$x \;_e\!\vdash y,$$

if $x = (q, w, uAz)$, $y = (p, w, uvz)$, $mqA \rightarrow pv \in R$, where $q, p \in Q$, $w \in D^*$, $A \in \Gamma$, $u, v, z \in \Gamma^*$, and $\text{occur}(u, \Gamma - D) = m - 1$. To express that M makes $x \;_e\!\vdash y$ according to $mqA \rightarrow pv$, we write

$$x \;_e\!\vdash y \; [mqA \rightarrow pv].$$

We say that $mqA \rightarrow pv$ is a *rule of depth m*; accordingly, $x \;_e\!\vdash y \; [mqA \rightarrow pv]$ is an *expansion of depth m*. M makes a *move* from x to y, symbolically written as

$$x \vdash y,$$

if M makes either $x \;_e\!\vdash y$ or $x \;_p\!\vdash y$. If $n \in \mathbb{N}$ is the minimal positive integer such that each rule of M is of depth n or less, we say that M *is of depth n*, symbolically written as ${}_nM$. In the standard manner, we extend ${}_p\vdash$, ${}_e\vdash$, and $\vdash$ to ${}_p\vdash^m$, ${}_e\vdash^m$, and $\vdash^m$, respectively, for $m \geq 0$; then, based on ${}_p\vdash^m$, ${}_e\vdash^m$, and $\vdash^m$, we define ${}_p\vdash^+$, ${}_p\vdash^*$, ${}_e\vdash^+$, ${}_e\vdash^*$, $\vdash^+$, and $\vdash^*$.

Let M be of depth n, for some $n \in \mathbb{N}$. We define the *language accepted by* ${}_nM$, $L({}_nM)$, as

$$L({}_nM) = \{w \in D^* \mid (s, w, S\#) \vdash^* (f, \varepsilon, \#) \text{ in } {}_nM \text{ with } f \in F\}.$$

In addition, we define the *language that* ${}_nM$ *accepts by empty pushdown*, $E({}_nM)$, as

$$E({}_nM) = \{w \in D^* \mid (s, w, S\#) \vdash^* (q, \varepsilon, \#) \text{ in } {}_nM \text{ with } q \in Q\}.$$

For every $k \geq 1$, $\mathbf{DPDA}_k$ denotes the family of languages defined by deep pushdown automata of depth i, where $1 \leq i \leq k$. Analogously, $\mathbf{DEPDA}_k$ denotes the family of languages defined by deep pushdown automata of depth i by empty pushdown, where $1 \leq i \leq k$.

The following example gives a DPDA accepting a language from

$$\left(\mathbf{DPDA}_2 \cap \mathbf{DEPDA}_2 \cap \mathbf{CS}\right) - \mathbf{CF}.$$

Example 15.1. Consider the DPDA

$${}_2M = (\{s, q, p\}, \{a, b, c\}, \{A, S, \#\}, R, s, S, \{f\})$$

with R containing the following five rules:

$1sS \to qAA$	$1qA \to fab$	$1fA \to fc$
$1qA \to paAb$	$2pA \to qAc$	

On $aabbcc$, M makes

$$\begin{aligned}
(s, aabbcc, S\#) \;&{}_e\vdash (q, aabbcc, AA\#) & [1sS \to qAA] \\
&{}_e\vdash (p, aabbcc, aAbA\#) & [1qA \to paAb] \\
&{}_p\vdash (p, abbcc, AbA\#) & \\
&{}_e\vdash (q, abbcc, AbAc\#) & [2pA \to qAc] \\
&{}_e\vdash (q, abbcc, abbAc\#) & [1qA \to fab] \\
&{}_p\vdash (f, bcc, bAc\#) & \\
&{}_p\vdash (f, cc, Ac\#) & \\
&{}_e\vdash (f, cc, Ac\#) & [1fA \to fc] \\
&{}_p\vdash (f, cc, cc\#) & \\
&{}_p\vdash (f, c, c\#) & \\
&{}_p\vdash (f, \varepsilon, \#). &
\end{aligned}$$

In brief, $(s, aabbcc, S\#) \vdash^* (f, \varepsilon, \#)$. Observe that $L({}_2M) = E({}_2M) = \{a^n b^n c^n \mid n \geq 1\}$, which belongs to $\mathbf{CS} - \mathbf{CF}$.

15.1.2 Accepting power

In the present section, we establish the main results of this chapter. That is, we demonstrate that DPDAs that make expansions of depth m or less, where $m \geq 1$, are equivalent to m-limited state grammars, so these automata accept a proper subfamily of the language family accepted by DPDAs that make expansions of depth $m+1$ or less. Then, we point out that the resulting infinite hierarchy of language families obtained in this way occurs between the families of context-free and context-sensitive languages. However, we also show that there always exist some context-sensitive languages that cannot be accepted by any DPDAs that make expansions of depth n or less, for every positive integer n.

To rephrase these results briefly and formally, we prove that

$$\mathbf{DPDA}_1 = \mathbf{DEPDA}_1 = \mathbf{CF}$$

and for every $n \geq 1$,

$$\mathbf{DEPDA}_n = \mathbf{DPDA}_n \subset \mathbf{DEPDA}_{n+1} = \mathbf{DPDA}_{n+1} \subset \mathbf{CS}.$$

After proving all these results, we formulate several open-problem areas, including some suggestions concerning new deterministic and generalized versions of DPDAs.

Lemma 15.1. For every state grammar G and for every $n \geq 1$, there exists a DPDA of depth n, ${}_nM$, such that $L(G, n) = L({}_nM)$.

Proof. Let $G = (\Sigma, W, \Delta, R, S)$ be a state grammar and let $n \geq 1$. Set $N = \Sigma - \Delta$. Define the homomorphism f over $(\{\#\} \cup \Sigma)^*$ as $f(A) = A$, for every $A \in \{\#\} \cup N$, and $f(a) = \varepsilon$, for every $a \in \Delta$. Introduce the DPDA of depth n

$${}_nM = (Q, \Delta, \{\#\} \cup \Sigma, R, s, S, \{\$\}),$$

where

$$Q = \{S, \$\} \cup \{\langle p, u\rangle \mid p \in W, u \in N^*\{\#\}^n, |u| \leq n\},$$

and R is constructed by performing the following four steps:

(i) For each $(p, S) \to (q, x) \in R$, $p, q \in W$, $x \in \Sigma^+$, add
$1sS \to \langle p, S\rangle S$ to R;

(ii) If $(p, A) \to (q, x) \in R$, $\langle p, uAv\rangle \in Q$, $p, q \in W$, $A \in N$, $x \in \Sigma^+$, $u \in N^*$, $v \in N^*\{\#\}^*$, $|uAv| = n$, $p \notin {}_G states(u)$, add
$|uA|\langle p, uAv\rangle A \to \langle q, \text{prefix}(uf(x)v, n)\rangle x$ to R;

(iii) If $A \in N$, $p \in W$, $u \in N^*$, $v \in \{\#\}^*$, $|uv| \leq n-1$, $p \notin {}_G states(u)$, add
$|uA|\langle p, uv\rangle A \to \langle p, uAv\rangle A$ and
$|uA|\langle p, uv\rangle \# \to \langle p, uv\#\rangle \#$ to R;

(iv) For each $q \in W$, add
$1\langle q, \#^n\rangle \# \to \$\#$ to R.

${}_nM$ simulates n-limited derivations of G, so it always records the first n nonterminals occurring in the current sentential form in its state (if there appear fewer than n nonterminals in the sentential form, it completes them to n in the state by #s from behind). ${}_nM$ simulates a derivation step in the pushdown and, simultaneously, records the newly generated nonterminals in the state. When G successfully completes the generation of a terminal string, ${}_nM$ completes reading the string, empties its pushdown, and enters the final state \$.

To establish $L(G, n) = L({}_nM)$, we first prove two claims.

Claim 1. Let $(p, S)\ {}_n\!\Rightarrow^m (q, dy)$ in G, where $d \in \Delta^*, y \in (N\Delta^*)^*, p, q \in W, m \geq 0$. Then, $(\langle p, S\rangle, d, S\#) \vdash^* (\langle q, \text{prefix}(f(y\#^n), n)\rangle, \varepsilon, y\#)$ in ${}_nM$.

Proof. This claim is proved by induction on $m \geq 0$.

Basis. Let $i = 0$, so $(p, S)\ {}_n\!\Rightarrow^0 (p, S)$ in G, $d = \varepsilon$ and $y = S$. By using rules introduced in steps (i) and (iv),

$$(\langle p, S\rangle, \varepsilon, S\#) \vdash^* (\langle p, \text{prefix}(f(S\#^n), n)\rangle, \varepsilon, S\#) \text{ in } {}_nM$$

so the basis holds.

Induction Hypothesis. Assume that the claim holds for all m, $0 \leq m \leq k$, where k is a nonnegative integer.

Induction Step. Let $(p, S)\ {}_n\!\Rightarrow^{k+1} (q, dy)$ in G, where $d \in \Delta^*, y \in (N\Delta^*)^*, p, q \in W$. Since $k + 1 \geq 1$, express $(p, S)\ {}_n\!\Rightarrow^{k+1} (q, dy)$ as

$$(p, S)\ {}_n\!\Rightarrow^k (h, buAo)\ {}_n\!\Rightarrow (q, buxo)\ [(h, A) \to (q, x)],$$

where $b \in \Delta^*$, $u \in (N\Delta^*)^*$, $A \in N$, $h, q \in W$, $(h, A) \to (q, x) \in R$, max-suffix($buxo$, $(N\Delta^*)^*$) $= y$, and max-prefix($buxo$, Δ^*) $= d$. By the induction hypothesis,

$$(\langle p, S\rangle, w, S\#) \vdash^* (\langle h, \text{prefix}(f(uAo\#^n), n)\rangle, \varepsilon, uAo\#) \text{ in } M,$$

where $w =$ max-prefix($buAo$, Δ^*). As $(p, A) \to (q, x) \in R$, step (ii) of the construction introduces rule

$$|uA|\langle h, \text{prefix}(f(uAo\#^n), n)\rangle A \to \langle q, \text{prefix}(f(uxo\#^n), n)\rangle x \text{ to } R.$$

By using this rule, ${}_nM$ simulates $(buAo, h)\ {}_n\!\Rightarrow (buxo, q)$ by making

$$(\langle h, \text{prefix}(f(uAo\#^n), n)\rangle, \varepsilon, uAo\#) \vdash (\langle q, z\rangle, \varepsilon, uxo\#),$$

where $z =$ prefix($f(uxo\#^n)$, n) if $x \in \Sigma^+ - \Delta^+$ and $z =$ prefix($f(uxo\#^n)$, $n - 1$) $=$ prefix($f(uo\#^n)$, $n - 1$) if $x \in \Delta^+$. In the latter case, ($z =$ prefix($f(uo\#^n)$, $n - 1$), so $|z| = n - 1$), ${}_nM$ makes

$$(\langle q, \text{prefix}(f(uo\#^n), n - 1)\rangle, \varepsilon, uxo\#) \vdash (\langle q, \text{prefix}(f(uo\#^n), n)\rangle, \varepsilon, uxo\#)$$

by a rule introduced in (iii). If $uxo \in (N\Delta^*)^*$, $uxo = y$ and the induction step is completed. Therefore, assume that $uxo \neq y$, so $uxo = ty$ and $d = wt$, for some $t \in \Delta^+$. Observe that prefix($f(uxo\#^n)$, n) $=$ prefix($f(y\#^n)$, n) at this point. Then, ${}_nM$ removes t by making $|t|$ popping moves so that

$$(\langle q, \text{prefix}(f(uxo\#^n), n)\rangle, t, ty\#)\ {}_p\!\vdash^{|t|} (\langle q, \text{prefix}(f(y\#^n), n)\rangle, \varepsilon, y\#^n).$$

Thus, putting the previous sequences of moves together, we obtain

$$\begin{aligned}(p, wt, S\#^n) &\vdash^* (\langle q, \text{prefix}(f(uxo\#^n), n)\rangle, t, ty\#)\ [1sS \to qAA]\\ &{}_p\!\vdash^{|t|} (\langle q, \text{prefix}(f(y\#^n), n)\rangle, \varepsilon, y\#),\end{aligned}$$

which completes the induction step. □

By the previous claim for $y = \varepsilon$, if $(p, S)\ {}_n\!\Rightarrow^* (q, d)$ in G, where $d \in \Delta^*, p, q \in W$, then

$$(\langle p, S\rangle, d, S\#) \vdash^* (\langle q, \text{prefix}(f(\#^n), n)\rangle, \varepsilon, \#) \text{ in } {}_nM.$$

Observe that prefix$(f(\#^n), n) = \#$. As R contains rules introduced in (i) and (iv), we also have

$$\begin{aligned}(s, d, S\#) &\vdash (\langle p, S\rangle, d, S\#)\\ &\vdash^* (\langle q, \#^n, n)\rangle, \varepsilon, \#)\\ &\vdash^* (\$, \varepsilon, \#) \text{ in } {}_nM.\end{aligned}$$

Thus, $d \in L(G)$ implies that $d \in L({}_nM)$, so $L(G, n) \subseteq L({}_nM)$.

Claim 2. Let $(\langle p, S\#^{n-1}\rangle, c, S\#) \vdash^m (\langle q, \text{prefix}(f(y\#^n), n)\rangle, \varepsilon, by\#)$ in ${}_nM$ with $c, b \in \Delta^*, y \in (N\Delta^*)^*, p, q \in W$, and $m \geq 0$. Then, $(p, S)\ {}_n\!\Rightarrow^* (q, cby)$ in G.

Proof. This claim is proved by induction on $m \geq 0$.

Basis. Let $m = 0$. Then, $c = b = \varepsilon, y = S$, and

$$(\langle p, S\#^{n-1}\rangle, \varepsilon, S\#) \vdash^0 (\langle q, \text{prefix}(f(S\#^n), n)\rangle, \varepsilon, S\#) \text{ in } {}_nM.$$

As $(p, S)\ {}_n\!\Rightarrow^0 (p, S)$ in G, the basis holds.

Induction Hypothesis. Assume that the claim holds for all m, $0 \leq m \leq k$, where k is a nonnegative integer.

Induction Step. Let

$$(\langle p, S\#^{n-1}\rangle, c, S\#) \vdash^{k+1} (\langle q, \text{prefix}(f(y\#^n), n)\rangle, \varepsilon, by\#) \text{ in } {}_nM,$$

where $c, b \in \Delta^*, y \in (N\Delta^*)^*, p, q \in W$ in ${}_nM$. Since $k + 1 \geq 1$, we can express

$$(\langle p, S\#^{n-1}\rangle, c, S\#) \vdash^{k+1} (\langle q, \text{prefix}(f(y\#^n), n)\rangle, \varepsilon, by\#)$$

as

$$\begin{aligned}(\langle p, S\#^{n-1}\rangle, c, S\#) &\vdash^k \alpha\\ &\vdash (\langle q, \text{prefix}(f(y\#^n), n)\rangle, \varepsilon, by\#) \text{ in } {}_nM,\end{aligned}$$

where α is a configuration of ${}_nM$ whose form depend on whether the last move is (i) a popping move or (ii) an expansion, described as follows:

(i) Assume that $\alpha\ {}_p\!\vdash (\langle q, \text{prefix}(f(y\#^n), n)\rangle, \varepsilon, by\#)$ in ${}_nM$. In a greater detail, let $\alpha = (\langle q, \text{prefix}(f(y\#^n), n)\rangle, a, aby\#)$ with $a \in \Delta$ such that $c = \text{prefix}(c, |c| - 1)a$. Thus,

$$\begin{aligned}(\langle p, S\#^{n-1}\rangle, c, S\#) &\vdash^k (\langle q, \text{prefix}(f(y\#^n), n)\rangle, a, aby\#)\\ &{}_p\!\vdash (\langle q, \text{prefix}(f(y\#^n), n)\rangle, \varepsilon, by\#).\end{aligned}$$

Since $(\langle p, S\#^{n-1}\rangle, c, S\#) \vdash^k (\langle q, \text{prefix}(f(y\#^n), n)\rangle, a, aby\#)$, we have

$$(\langle p, S\#^{n-1}\rangle, \text{prefix}(c, |c| - 1), S\#) \vdash^k (\langle q, \text{prefix}(f(y\#^n), n)\rangle, \varepsilon, aby\#).$$

By the induction hypothesis, $(p, S)\ {}_n\!\Rightarrow^* (q, \text{prefix}(c, |c| - 1)aby)$ in G. As $c = \text{prefix}(c, |c| - 1)a$, $(p, S)\ {}_n\!\Rightarrow^* (q, cby)$ in G.

(ii) Assume that $\alpha\ {}_e\vdash (\langle q, \text{prefix}(f(y\#^n), n)\rangle, \varepsilon, by\#)$ in ${}_nM$. Observe that this expansion cannot be made by rules introduced in steps (i) or (iv). If this expansion is made by a rule introduced in (iii), which does not change the pushdown contents at all, the induction step follows from the induction hypothesis. Finally, suppose that this expansion is made by a rule introduced in step (ii). In a greater detail, suppose that

$$\alpha = (\langle o, \text{prefix}(f(uAv\#^n), n)\rangle, \varepsilon, uAv\#)$$

and ${}_nM$ makes

$$(\langle o, \text{prefix}(f(uAv\#^n), n)\rangle, \varepsilon, uAv\#)\ {}_e\vdash (\langle q, \text{prefix}(f(uxv\#^n), n)\rangle, \varepsilon, uxv\#)$$

by using

$$|f(uA)|\langle o, \text{prefix}(f(uAv\#^n), n)\rangle A \rightarrow \langle q, \text{prefix}(f(uxv\#^n), n)\rangle x \in R$$

introduced in step (ii) of the construction, where $A \in N$, $u \in (N\Delta^*)^*$, $v \in (N \cup \Delta)^*$, $o \in W$, $|f(uA)| \leq n$, $by\# = uxv\#$. By the induction hypothesis,

$$(\langle p, S\#^{n-1}\rangle, c, S\#) \vdash^k (\langle o, \text{prefix}(f(uAv\#^n), n)\rangle, \varepsilon, uAv\#) \text{ in } {}_nM$$

implies that $(p, S)\ {}_n\Rightarrow^* (o, cuAv)$ in G. From

$$|f(uA)|\langle o, \text{prefix}(f(uAv\#^n), n)\rangle A \rightarrow \langle q, \text{prefix}(f(uxv\#^n), n)\rangle x \in R,$$

it follows that $(o, A) \rightarrow (q, x) \in R$ and $A \notin {}_G\mathit{states}(f(u))$. Thus,

$$\begin{aligned}(p, S)\ &{}_n\Rightarrow^* (o, cuAv)\\ &{}_n\Rightarrow (q, cuxv) \text{ in } G.\end{aligned}$$

Therefore, $(p, S)\ {}_n\Rightarrow^* (q, cby)$ in G because $by\# = uxv\#$.

□

Consider the previous claim for $b = y = \varepsilon$ to see that

$$(\langle p, S\#^{n-1}\rangle, c, S\#) \vdash^* (\langle q, \text{prefix}(f(\#), n)\rangle, \varepsilon, \#^n) \text{ in } {}_nM$$

implies that $(p, S)\ {}_n\Rightarrow^* (q, c)$ in G. Let $c \in L({}_nM)$. Then,

$$(s, c, S\#) \vdash^* (\$, \varepsilon, \#) \text{ in } {}_nM.$$

Examine the construction of ${}_nM$ to see that $(s, c, S) \vdash^* (\$, \varepsilon, \#)$ starts by using a rule introduced in (i), so $(s, c, S) \vdash^* (\langle p, S\#^{n-1}\rangle, c, S\#)$. Furthermore, notice that this sequence of moves ends $(s, c, S) \vdash^* (\$, \varepsilon, \varepsilon)$ by using a rule introduced in step (iv). Thus, we can express

$$(s, c, \#) \vdash^* (\$, \varepsilon, \#)$$

as

$$\begin{aligned}(s, c, \#) &\vdash^* (\langle p, S\#^{n-1}\rangle, c, S\#)\\ &\vdash^* (\langle q, \text{prefix}(f(\#^n), n)\rangle, \varepsilon, \#)\\ &\vdash (\$, \varepsilon, \#) \text{ in } {}_nM.\end{aligned}$$

Therefore, $c \in L({}_nM)$ implies that $c \in L(G, n)$, so $L({}_nM) \subseteq L(G, n)$.

As $L({}_nM) \subseteq L(G, n)$ and $L(G, n) \subseteq L({}_nM)$, $L(G, n) = L({}_nM)$. Thus, Lemma 15.1 holds. ■

Lemma 15.2. For every $n \geq 1$ and every DPDA ${}_nM$, there exists a state grammar G such that $L(G, n) = L({}_nM)$.

Proof. Let $n \geq 1$ and ${}_nM = (Q, \Delta, \Sigma, R, s, S, F)$ be a DPDA. Let Z and \$ be two new symbols that occur in no component of ${}_nM$. Set $N = \Sigma - \Delta$. Introduce sets

$$C = \{\langle q, i, \rhd\rangle \mid q \in Q, 1 \leq i \leq n - 1\}$$

and

$$D = \{\langle q, i, \lhd\rangle \mid q \in Q, 0 \leq i \leq n - 1\}.$$

Moreover, introduce an alphabet W such that $\text{card}\,(\Sigma) = \text{card}\,(W)$, and for all i, $1 \leq i \leq n$, an alphabet U_i such that $\text{card}\,(U_i) = \text{card}\,(N)$. Without any loss of generality, assume that Σ, Q, and all these newly introduced sets and alphabets are pairwise disjoint. Set $U = \bigcup_{i=1}^{n} U_i$. For each i, $1 \leq i \leq n - 1$, set $C_i = \{\langle q, i, \rhd\rangle \mid q \in Q\}$ and for each i, $0 \leq i \leq n - 1$, set $D_i = \{\langle q, i, \lhd\rangle \mid q \in Q\}$. Introduce a bijection h from Σ to W. For each i, $1 \leq i \leq n$, introduce a bijection ${}_ig$ from N to U_i. Define the state grammar

$$G = (\Sigma \cup W \cup U \cup \{Z\}, Q \cup C \cup D \cup \{\$\}, \Delta, R, Z),$$

where R is constructed by performing the following steps:

(i) Add $(s, Z) \rightarrow (\langle s, 1, \rhd\rangle, h(S))$ to R.
(ii) For each $q \in Q$, $A \in N$, $1 \leq i \leq n - 1$, $x \in \Sigma^+$, add
  (a) $(\langle q, i, \rhd\rangle, A) \rightarrow (\langle q, i + 1, \rhd\rangle, {}_ig(A))$ and
  (b) $(\langle q, i, \lhd\rangle, {}_ig(A)) \rightarrow (\langle p, i - 1, \lhd\rangle, A)$ to R.
(iii) If $ipA \rightarrow qxY \in R$, for some $p, q \in Q$, $A \in N$, $x \in \Sigma^*$, $Y \in \Sigma$, $i = 1, \ldots, n$, add
  $(\langle p, i, \rhd\rangle, A) \rightarrow (\langle q, i - 1, \lhd\rangle, xY)$ and
  $(\langle p, i, \rhd\rangle, h(A)) \rightarrow (\langle q, i - 1, \lhd\rangle, xh(Y))$ to R.
(iv) For each $q \in Q$, $A \in N$, add
  $(\langle q, 0, \lhd\rangle, A) \rightarrow (\langle q, 1, \rhd\rangle, A)$ and
  $(\langle q, 0, \lhd\rangle, h(Y)) \rightarrow (\langle q, 1, \rhd\rangle, h(Y))$ to R.
(v) For each $q \in F$, $a \in \Delta$, add
  $(\langle q, 0, \lhd\rangle, h(a)) \rightarrow (\$, a)$ to R.

G simulates the application of $ipA \rightarrow qy \in R$, so it makes a left-to-right scan of the sentential form, counting the occurrences of nonterminals until it reaches the ith occurrence of a nonterminal. If this occurrence equals A, it replaces this A with y and returns to the beginning of the sentential form in order to analogously simulate a move from q. Throughout the simulation of moves of ${}_nM$ by G, the rightmost symbol of every sentential form is from W. G completes the simulation of an acceptance of a string x by ${}_nM$, so it uses a rule introduced in step (v) of the construction of R to change the rightmost symbol of x, $h(a)$, to a and, thereby, to generate x.

We next establish $L(G,n) = L({}_nM)$. To keep the rest of the proof as readable as possible, we omit some details in what follows. The reader can easily fill them in.

Claim 1. $L(G,n) \subseteq L({}_nM)$

Proof. Consider any $w \in L(G,n)$. Observe that G generates w as

$$\begin{aligned}(p,Z) \ {}_n\!\Rightarrow\ & (\langle s,1,\rhd\rangle, h(S))\ [(s,Z) \to (\langle s,1,\rhd\rangle, h(S))]\\ {}_n\!\Rightarrow^*\ & (f, yh(a))\\ {}_n\!\Rightarrow\ & (\$, w),\end{aligned}$$

where $f \in F$, $a \in \Delta$, $y \in \Delta^*$, $ya = w$, $(s,Z) \to (\langle s,1,\rhd\rangle, h(S))$ in step (i) of the construction of R, $(\langle q,0,\lhd\rangle, h(a)) \to (\$, a)$ in (v), every

$$u \in \text{strings}((\langle s,1,\rhd\rangle, h(S)) \ {}_n\!\vdash^* (q, yh(a)))$$

satisfies $u \in (\Sigma \cup U)^* W$, and every step in

$$(\langle s,1,\rhd\rangle, h(S)) \ {}_n\!\vdash^* (f, yh(S))$$

is made by a rule introduced in (ii)–(iv). Indeed, the rule constructed in (i) is always used in the first step and a rule constructed in (v) is always used in the very last step of any successful generation in G; during any other step, neither of them can be applied. Notice that the rule of (i) generates $h(S)$. Furthermore, examine the rules of (ii)–(iv) to see that by their use, G always produces a string that has exactly one occurrence of a symbol from W in any string, and this occurrence appears as the rightmost symbol of the string; formally,

$$u \in \text{strings}((\langle s,1,\rhd\rangle, h(S)) \ {}_n\!\Rightarrow^* (f, yh(a)))$$

implies that $u \in (\Sigma \cup U)^* W$. In a greater detail,

$$(\langle s,1,\rhd\rangle, h(S)) \ {}_n\!\Rightarrow^* (f, yh(a))$$

can be expressed as

$$\begin{array}{lllllllll}(q_0, z_0) & {}_n\!\Rightarrow^* & (c_0, y_0) & {}_n\!\Rightarrow & (d_0, u_0) & {}_n\!\Rightarrow^* & (p_0, v_0) & {}_n\!\Rightarrow \\ (q_1, z_1) & {}_n\!\Rightarrow^* & (c_1, y_1) & {}_n\!\Rightarrow & (d_1, u_1) & {}_n\!\Rightarrow^* & (p_1, v_1) & {}_n\!\Rightarrow \\ & \vdots & & \vdots & & \vdots & & \vdots \\ (q_m, z_m) & {}_n\!\Rightarrow^* & (c_m, y_m) & {}_n\!\Rightarrow & (d_m, u_m) & {}_n\!\Rightarrow^* & (p_m, v_m) & {}_n\!\Rightarrow \\ (q_{m+1}, z_{m+1}) & & & & & & & \end{array}$$

for some $m \geq 1$, where $z_0 = h(S)$, $z_{m+1} = yh(a)$, $f = q_{m+1}$, and for each j, $0 \leq j \leq m$, $q_j \in C_1$, $p_j \in D_0$, $z_j \in \Sigma^* W$, and there exists $i_j \in \{1, \ldots, n\}$ so $c_j \in C_{i_j}$, $y_j \in \Delta^* C_1 \Delta^* C_2 \cdots \Delta^* C_{i_j - 1} \Sigma^* W$, $d_j \in D_{i_j - 1}$, $u_j \in \Delta^* C_1 \Delta^* C_2 \cdots \Delta^* D_{i_j - 1} \Sigma^* W$, and

$$(q_j, z_j) \ {}_n\!\Rightarrow^* (c_j, y_j) \ {}_n\!\Rightarrow (d_j, u_j) \ {}_n\!\Rightarrow^* (p_j, v_j) \ {}_n\!\Rightarrow (q_{j+1}, z_{j+1})$$

satisfies (i)–(iv), given next.

For brevity, we first introduce the following notation. Let w be any string. For $i = 1, \ldots, |w|$, $\lfloor w, i, N \rfloor$ denotes the ith occurrence of a nonterminal from N in w, and if such a nonterminal does not exist, $\lfloor w, i, W \rfloor = 0$; for instance,

$$\lfloor ABABC, 2, \{A, C\} \rfloor$$

denotes the underlined $\underline{A}$ in $AB\underline{A}BC$.

(i) $(q_j, z_j)\ {}_n\!\Rightarrow^* (c_i, y_i)$ consists of $i_j - 1$ steps during which G changes $\lfloor z_j, 1, N \rfloor, \ldots, \lfloor z_j, i_j - 1, N \rfloor$ to ${}_1g(\langle \lfloor z_j, 1, N \rfloor, 2 \rangle), \ldots, {}_{i_j}g(\langle \lfloor z_j, i_j - 1, N \rfloor, i_j - 1 \rangle)$, respectively, by using rules of (ii)(a) in the construction of R.

(ii) If $i_j \leq \text{occur}(z_j, N)$, then $(c_j, y_j)\ {}_n\!\Rightarrow (d_j, u_j)$ have to consist of a step according to $(\langle q, i, \rhd \rangle, A_j) \to (\langle q, i-1, \lhd \rangle, x_j X_j)$, where $\lfloor z_j, i_j, N \rfloor$ is an occurrence of $A_j, x_j \in \Sigma^*, X_j \in \Sigma$, and if $i_j = \text{occur}(z_j, N \cup W)$, then $(c_j, y_j)\ {}_n\!\Rightarrow (d_j, u_j)$ consists of a step according to $(\langle p, i, \rhd \rangle, h(A_j)) \to (\langle q, i-1, \lhd \rangle, x_j h(X_j))$ constructed in (iii), where $\lfloor z_j, i_j, N \cup W \rfloor$ is an occurrence of $h(A_j), x_j \in \Sigma^*, X_j \in \Sigma$.

(iii) $(d_j, u_j)\ {}_n\!\Rightarrow^* (p_j, v_j)$ consists of $i_j - 1$ steps during which G changes ${}_{i_j}g(\langle \lfloor z_j, i_j - 1, N \rfloor, i_j - 1 \rangle), \ldots, {}_1g(\langle \lfloor z_j, 1, N \rfloor, 1 \rangle)$ back to $\lfloor z_j, i_j - 1, N \rfloor, \ldots, \lfloor z_j, 1, N \rfloor$, respectively, in a right-to-left way by using rules constructed in (ii)(b).

(iv) $(p_j, v_j)\ {}_n\!\Rightarrow (q_{j+1}, z_{j+1})$ is made by a rule constructed in (iv).

For every

$$\begin{aligned}(q_j, z_j)\ &{}_n\!\Rightarrow^* (c_j, y_j)\\ &{}_n\!\Rightarrow (d_j, u_j)\\ &{}_n\!\Rightarrow^* (p_j, v_j)\\ &{}_n\!\Rightarrow (q_{j+1}, z_{j+1}) \text{ in } G,\end{aligned}$$

where $0 \leq j \leq m$, ${}_nM$ makes

$$(q_j, o_j, \text{suffix}(z_j, t_j)) \vdash^* (q_{j+1}, o_{j+1}, \text{suffix}(z_{j+1}, t_{j+1}))$$

with $o_0 = w$, $z_0 = S\#$, $t_{j+1} = |\text{max-prefix}(z_{j+1}, \Delta^*)|$, $o_{j+1} = \text{suffix}(o_j, |o_j| + t_{j+1})$, where $o_0 = w$, $z_0 = S\#$, and $t_0 = |z_0|$. In this sequence of moves, the first move is an expansion made according to $i_j q_j A_j \to q_{j+1} x_j X_j$ (see steps (ii) and (iii) of the construction) followed by t_{j+1} popping moves (notice that $i_j \geq 2$ implies that $t_{j+1} = 0$). As $f \in F$ and $ya = w$, $w \in L({}_nM)$. Therefore, $L(G, n) \subseteq L({}_nM)$. □

Claim 2. $L({}_nM) \subseteq L(G, n)$

Proof. This proof is simple and left to the reader. □

As $L({}_nM) \subseteq L(G, n)$ and $L(G, n) \subseteq L({}_nM)$, we have $L(G, n) = L({}_nM)$, so this lemma holds true. ■

Theorem 15.1. For every $n \geq 1$ and for every language $L, L = L(G, n)$ for a state grammar G if and only if $L = L({}_nM)$ for a DPDA ${}_nM$.

Proof. This theorem follows from Lemmas 15.1 and 15.2. ■

By analogy with the demonstration of Theorem 15.1, we can establish the next theorem.

Theorem 15.2. For every $n \geq 1$ and for every language $L, L = L(G, n)$ for a state grammar G if and only if $L = E({}_nM)$ for a DPDA ${}_nM$.

The main result of this chapter follows next.

Corollary 15.1. *For every* $n \geq 1$,

$$\mathbf{DEPDA}_n = \mathbf{DPDA}_n \subset \mathbf{DPDA}_{n+1} = \mathbf{DEPDA}_{n+1}.$$

Proof. This corollary follows from Theorems 15.1 and 15.2 and from Theorem 12.1, which says that the m-limited state grammars generate a proper subfamily of the family generated by $(m + 1)$-limited state grammars, for every $m \geq 1$. ■

Finally, we state two results concerning **CF** and **CS**.

Corollary 15.2. $\mathbf{DPDA}_1 = \mathbf{DEPDA}_1 = \mathbf{CF}$.

Proof. This corollary follows from Lemmas 15.1 and 15.2 for $n = 1$, and from Theorem 12.1, which says that one-limited state grammars characterize **CF**. ■

Corollary 15.3. *For every* $n \geq 1$, $\mathbf{DPDA}_n = \mathbf{DEPDA}_n \subset \mathbf{CS}$.

Proof. This corollary follows from Lemmas 15.1 and 15.2, Theorems 15.1 and 15.2, and from Theorem 12.1, which says that $\mathbf{ST}_m$, for every $m \geq 1$, is properly included in **CS**. ■

15.1.3 Open problems

Finally, we suggest two open-problem areas concerning DPDAs.

Determinism

This chapter has discussed a general version of DPDAs, which work nondeterministically. Undoubtedly, the future investigation of these automata should pay a special attention to their deterministic versions, which fulfill a crucial role in practice. In fact, we can introduce a variety of deterministic versions, including the following two types. First, we consider the fundamental strict form of determinism.

Definition 15.2. Let $M = (Q, D, \Gamma, R, s, S, F)$ be a DPDA. We say that M is *deterministic* if for every $mqA \rightarrow pv \in R$,

$$\text{card}(\{mqA \rightarrow ow \mid mqA \rightarrow ow \in R, o \in Q, w \in \Gamma^+\} - \{mqA \rightarrow pv\}) = 0.$$

As a weaker form of determinism, we obtain the following definition:

Definition 15.3. Let $M = (Q, D, \Gamma, R, s, S, F)$ be a DPDA. We say that M is *deterministic with respect to the depth of its expansions* if for every $q \in Q$

$$\text{card}(\{m \mid mqA \rightarrow pv \in R, A \in \Gamma, p \in Q, v \in \Gamma^+\}) \leq 1,$$

because at this point from the same state, all expansions that M can make are of the same depth.

To illustrate, consider, for instance, the DPDA ${}_2M$ from Example 15.1. This automaton is deterministic with respect to the depth of its expansions; however, it does not satisfy the strict determinism. Notice that ${}_nM$ constructed in the proof of Lemma 15.1 is deterministic with respect to the depth of its expansions, so we obtain this corollary.

Corollary 15.4. *For every state grammar G and for every $n \geq 1$, there exists a DPDA ${}_nM$ such that $L(G, n) = L({}_nM)$ and ${}_nM$ is deterministic with respect to the depth of its expansions.*

Open Problem 1. Can an analogical statement to Corollary 15.4 be established in terms of the strict determinism?

15.1.3.1 Generalization

Let us note that throughout this chapter, we have considered only true pushdown expansions in the sense that the pushdown symbol is replaced with a nonempty string rather than with the empty string; at this point, no pushdown expansion can result in shortening the pushdown length. Nevertheless, the discussion of moves that allow DPDAs to replace a pushdown symbol with ε and, thereby, shorten its pushdown represents a natural generalization of DPDAs discussed in this chapter.

Open Problem 2. What is the language family defined by DPDAs generalized in this way?

15.2 Restricted versions

In essence, DPDAs represent language-accepting models based upon new stack-like structures, which can be modified deeper than on their top. As a result, these automata can make expansions deeper in their pushdown lists as opposed to ordinary pushdown automata, which can expand only the very pushdown top.

The section narrows its attention to n-expandable DPDAs, where n is a positive integer. In essence, during any computation, their pushdown lists contain #, which always appears as the pushdown bottom, and no more than $n - 1$ occurrences of other non-input symbols. This section demonstrates how to reduce the number of their non-input pushdown symbols different from # to one symbol, denoted by \$, without affecting the power of these automata. Based on the main result, we establish an infinite hierarchy of language families resulting from these reduced versions of n-expandable DPDAs. More precisely, consider n-expandable DPDAs with pushdown alphabets containing #, \$, and input symbols. This section shows that $(n + 1)$-expandable versions of these automata are stronger than their n-expandable versions, for every positive integer n. In addition, it points out that these automata with # as its only non-input symbol characterize the family of regular languages. In its conclusion, this section formulates several open-problem areas related to the subject for the future study.

15.2.1 Preliminaries and definitions

As usual, let $\mathbb{N}$ denote the set of all positive integers. For an alphabet Γ, Γ^* represents the free monoid generated by Γ under the operation of concatenation. The identity of Γ^* is denoted by ε. For $w \in \Gamma^*$, $|w|$ denotes the length of w.

Definition 15.4. Let M be a DPDA (see Definition 15.1) and $n \in \mathbb{N}$. If during any $\alpha \vdash^* \beta$ in M, $\alpha, \beta \in \Xi$, M has no more than n occurrences of symbols from $\Gamma - D$ in its pushdown, then M is an *n-expandable DPDA*.

Let $n, r \in \mathbb{N}$. $_n\mathbf{DPDA}$ denotes the language family accepted by n-expandable DPDAs. $_n\mathbf{DPDA}_r$ denotes the language family accepted by n-expandable DPDAs with # and no more than $(r-1)$ non-input pushdown symbols.

A *right-linear grammar* is a quadruple $G = (N, \Delta, R, S)$, where N is an alphabet of nonterminals, Δ is an alphabet of terminals such that $N \cap \Delta = \emptyset$, R is a finite subset of $N \times \Delta^*(N \cup \{\varepsilon\})$, and $S \in N$. R is called the *set of rules* in G; instead of $(A, x) \in R$, we write $A \to x$. Define the language of G, $L(G)$, as usual (see [52]).

REG denotes the regular language family. Recall that **REG** is characterized by right-linear grammars (see Theorem 7.2.2. in [52]).

15.2.2 Results

Next, we establish Lemma 15.3, which implies the main result of this section.

Lemma 15.3. Let $n \in \mathbb{N}$. For every n-expandable DPDA M, there exists an n-expendable DPDA M_R such that $L(M) = L(M_R)$ and M_R contains only two non-input pushdown symbols—\$ and #.

Proof. Construction. Let $n \in \mathbb{N}$. Let

$$M = (Q, D, \Gamma, R, s, S, F)$$

be an n-expandable DPDA. Recall that rules in R are of the form $mqA \to pv$, where $m \in \mathbb{N}$, $q, p \in Q$, either $A \in N$ and $v \in (\Gamma - \{\#\})^+$ or $A = \#$ and $v \in (\Gamma - \{\#\})^*\{\#\}$, where # denotes the pushdown bottom.

Let \$ be a new symbol, $\$ \notin Q \cup \Gamma$, and let homomorphisms f and g over Γ^* be defined as $f(A) = A$ and $g(A) = \$$, for every $A \in N$, and $f(a) = \varepsilon$ and $g(a) = a$, for every $a \in (D \cup \{\#\})$. Next, we construct an n-expandable DPDA

$$M_R = (Q_R, D, D \cup \{\$, \#\}, R_R, s_R, \$, F_R)$$

by performing (i)–(iv), given as follows:

(i) Add $m\langle q; uAz\rangle\$ \to \langle p; uf(v)z\rangle g(v)$ to R_R and add $\langle q; uAz\rangle$, $\langle p; uf(v)z\rangle$ to Q_R if $mqA \to pv \in R$, $u, z \in N^*$, $|u| = m - 1$, $|z| \leq n - m - 1$, $|uf(v)z| < n$, $m \in \mathbb{N}$, $q, p \in Q$, $A \in N$, and $v \in (\Gamma - \{\#\})^+$.

(ii) Add $m\langle q; u\rangle\# \rightarrow \langle p; uf(v)\rangle g(v)\#$ to R_R and add $\langle q; u\rangle$, $\langle p; uf(v)\rangle$ to Q_R if $mq\# \rightarrow pv\# \in R$, $u \in N^*$, $|u| = m - 1$, $|uf(v)| < n$, $m \in \mathbb{N}$, $q, p \in Q$, and $v \in (\Gamma - \{\#\})^*$.
(iii) Set $s_R = \langle s; S\rangle$.
(iv) Add all $\langle p; u\rangle$ to F_R, where $p \in F$, $u \in N^*$, $u < n$.

Later in this proof, we demonstrate that $L(M) = L(M_R)$.
Basic Idea. States in Q_R include not only the states corresponding to the states in Q but also strings of non-input symbols. Whenever M pushes a non-input symbol onto the pushdown, M_R records this information within its current state and pushes \$ onto the pushdown instead.

By Lemma 3.1. in [344], any n-expandable DPDA M can accept every $w \in L(M)$, so all expansions precede all pops during the accepting process. Without any loss of generality, we assume that M and M_R work in this way in what follows, too.

To establish $L(M) = L(M_R)$, we prove the following four claims:

Claim 1. Let $(s, w, S\#) \vdash^j (q, v, x\#)$ in M, where $s, q \in Q$, $w, v \in D^*$, and $x \in (\Gamma - \{\#\})^*$. Then, $(\langle s; S\rangle, w, \$\#) \vdash^* (\langle q; f(x)\rangle, v, g(x)\#)$ in M_R, where $\langle s; S\rangle$, $\langle q; f(x)\rangle \in Q_R$, and $g(x) \in (D \cup \{\$\})^*$.

Proof. This claim is proved by induction on $j \geq 0$.

Basis. Let $j = 0$, so $(s, w, S\#) \vdash^0 (s, w, S\#)$ in M, where $s \in Q$ and $S \in N$. Then, from (iii) in the construction, we obtain

$$(\langle s; S\rangle, w, \$\#) \vdash^0 (\langle s; S\rangle, w, \$\#)$$

in M_R, so the basis holds.

Induction Hypothesis. Assume there is $i \geq 0$ such that Claim 1 holds true for all $0 \leq j \leq i$.

Induction Step. Let $(s, w, S\#) \vdash^{i+1} (q, w, x\#)$ in M, where $x \in (\Gamma - \{\#\})^*$, $s, q \in Q$, $w \in D^*$, $k, \ell \geq 1$, $k + \ell < n$. Since $i + 1 \geq 1$, we can express $(s, w, S\#) \vdash^{i+1} (q, w, x\#)$ as

$$(s, w, S\#) \vdash^i (p, w, x_0A_1x_1 \cdots A_m \cdots A_kx_k\#)$$

$$\vdash (q, w, x_0A_1x_1 \cdots A_{m-1}x_{m-1}y_0B_1y_1 \cdots B_\ell y_\ell x_mA_{m+1} \cdots x_{k-1}A_kx_k\#)$$

$$[mpA_m \rightarrow qy_0B_1y_1 \cdots B_\ell y_\ell],$$

where $A_1, \ldots, A_k, B_1, \ldots, B_\ell \in N$ and $x_0x_1 \cdots x_k, y_0y_1 \cdots y_\ell \in D^*$. By the induction hypothesis, we have

$$(\langle s; S\rangle, w, \$\#) \vdash^* (\langle p; A_1 \cdots A_m \cdots A_k\rangle, w, x_0\$x_1\$ \cdots \$x_k\#),$$

Since $mpA_m \rightarrow qy_0B_1y_1 \cdots B_\ell y_\ell \in R$, we also have

$$m\langle p; A_1 \cdots A_m \cdots A_k\rangle\$ \rightarrow \langle q; A_1 \cdots A_{m-1}B_1 \cdots B_\ell A_{m+1} \cdots A_k\rangle y_0\$y_1\$ \cdots \$y_\ell \in R_R$$

(see (i) in the construction). Thus,

$$(\langle p; A_1 \cdots A_m \cdots A_k\rangle, w, x_0\$x_1\$ \cdots \$x_k\#) \vdash$$

$$(\langle q; A_1 \cdots A_{m-1} B_1 \cdots B_\ell A_{m+1} \cdots A_k \rangle, w, x_0\$x_1\$ \cdots \$x_{m-1}y_0\$y_1\$ \cdots \$y_\ell x_m\$ \cdots \$x_k\#)$$
$$[m\langle p; A_1 \cdots A_m \cdots A_k \rangle\$ \to \langle q; A_1 \cdots A_{m-1} B_1 \cdots B_\ell A_{m+1} \cdots A_k \rangle y_0\$y_1\$ \cdots \$y_\ell].$$

Analogically, we can prove the induction step for the case when # is rewritten (see (ii) in the construction). Therefore, Claim 1 holds true. □

Claim 2. $L(M) \subseteq L(M_R)$.

Proof. Consider Claim 1 for $v = \varepsilon$, $q \in F$, and $x = \varepsilon$. Under this consideration Claim 1 implies Claim 2. □

Claim 3. Let $(\langle s; S \rangle, w, \$\#) \vdash^j (\langle q; A_1 \cdots A_k \rangle, v, x\#)$ in M_R, where

$$s_R = \langle s; S \rangle,$$
$$\langle q; A_1 \cdots A_k \rangle \in Q_R,$$
$$w, v \in D^*,$$
$$A_1, \ldots, A_k \in N,$$
$$x = x_0\$x_1\$ \cdots \$x_k,$$

and

$$x_0 \cdots x_k \in D^*.$$

Then, $(s, w, S\#) \vdash^* (q, v, x_0 A_1 x_1 \cdots A_k x_k\#)$ in M, where $s, q \in Q$.

Proof. This claim is proved by induction on $j \geq 0$.

Basis. Let $j = 0$, so $(\langle s; S \rangle, w, \$\#) \vdash^0 (\langle s; S \rangle, w, \$\#)$ in M_R, where $s_R = \langle s; S \rangle$. From (iii) in the construction, we have

$$(s, w, S\#) \vdash^0 (s, w, S\#)$$

in M, so the basis holds.

Induction Hypothesis. Assume there is $i \geq 0$ such that Claim 3 holds true for $0 \leq j \leq i$.

Induction Step. Let $(\langle s; S \rangle, w, \$\#) \vdash^{i+1} (\langle q; A_1 \cdots A_k \rangle, w, x_0\$x_1\$ \cdots \$x_k\#)$ in M_R, where $\langle q; A_1 \cdots A_k \rangle \in Q_R$, $A_1, \ldots, A_k \in N$, $w \in D^*$, and $x_0 \cdots x_k \in D^*$, $k, \ell \geq 1$, $k + \ell < n$. Since $i + 1 \geq 1$, we can express

$$(\langle s; S \rangle, w, \$\#) \vdash^{i+1} (\langle q; A_1 \cdots A_k \rangle, w, x_0\$x_1\$ \cdots \$x_k\#)$$

as

$$(\langle s; S \rangle, w, \$\#) \vdash^i (\langle p; A_1 \cdots A_m \cdots A_k \rangle, w, x_0\$x_1\$ \cdots \$x_k\#)$$
$$\vdash (\langle q; A_1 \cdots A_{m-1} B_1 \cdots B_\ell A_{m+1} \cdots A_k \rangle, w, x_0\$x_1\$ \cdots \$x_{m-1}y_0\$y_1\$ \cdots \$y_\ell x_m\$ \cdots \$x_k\#)$$
$$[m\langle p; A_1 \cdots A_m \cdots A_k \rangle\$ \to \langle q; A_1 \cdots A_{m-1} B_1 \cdots B_\ell A_{m+1} \cdots A_k \rangle y_0\$y_1\$ \cdots \$y_\ell].$$

By the induction hypothesis, we obtain

$$(s, w, S\#) \vdash^i (p, w, x_0 A_1 x_1 \cdots A_m \cdots A_k x_k\#)$$

Since $m\langle p; A_1 \cdots A_m \cdots A_k \rangle\$ \to \langle q; A_1 \cdots A_{m-1} B_1 \cdots B_\ell A_{m+1} \cdots A_k \rangle y_0 \$ y_1 \$ \cdots \$ y_\ell \in R_R$, we also have $mpA_m \to qy_0 B_1 y_1 \cdots B_\ell y_\ell \in R$ as follows from (i) in the construction. We obtain

$$
\begin{aligned}
&(p, w, x_0 A_1 x_1 \cdots A_m \cdots A_k x_k \#) \\
&\vdash (q, w, x_0 A_1 x_1 \cdots A_{m-1} x_{m-1} y_0 B_1 y_1 \cdots B_\ell y_\ell x_m A_{m+1} \cdots x_{k-1} A_k x_k \#) \\
&[mpA_m \to qy_0 B_1 y_1 \cdots B_\ell y_\ell].
\end{aligned}
$$

Analogically, we can prove the case when # is expanded (see (ii) in the construction). Therefore, Claim 3 holds true. □

Claim 4. $L(M_R) \subseteq L(M)$.

Proof. Consider Claim 3 with $v = \varepsilon$, $\langle q; A_1 \cdots A_k \rangle \in F_R$, and $x = \varepsilon$. Under this consideration, Claim 3 implies Claim 4. □

As $L(M) \subseteq L(M_R)$ (see Claim 2) and $L(M_R) \subseteq L(M)$ (see Claim 4),

$$L(M_R) = L(M).$$

Thus, Lemma 15.3 holds. ■

The next example illustrates the construction described in the previous proof.

Example. Take this three-expandable DPDA

$$M = (\{s, q, p\}, \{a, b, c\}, \{a, b, c, A, S, \#\}, R, s, S, \{f\}),$$

with the set of rules defined as

$$
\begin{aligned}
R = \{&1sS \to qAA, \\
&1qA \to fab, \\
&1fA \to fc, \\
&1qA \to paAb, \\
&2pA \to qAc\}.
\end{aligned}
$$

By the construction given in the proof of Lemma 15.3, we construct $M_R = (Q_R, \{a, b, c\}, \{a, b, c, \$, \#\}, R_R, \langle s; S \rangle, \$, \{\langle f; A \rangle, \langle f; \varepsilon \rangle\})$, where $Q_R = \{\langle s; S \rangle, \langle q; AA \rangle, \langle f; A \rangle, \langle f; \varepsilon \rangle, \langle p; AA \rangle\}$ and

$$
\begin{aligned}
R_R = \{&1\langle s; S \rangle\$ \to \langle q; AA \rangle\$\$, \\
&1\langle q; AA \rangle\$ \to \langle f; A \rangle ab, \\
&1\langle f; A \rangle\$ \to \langle f; \varepsilon \rangle c, \\
&1\langle q; AA \rangle\$ \to \langle p; AA \rangle a\$b, \\
&2\langle p; AA \rangle\$ \to \langle q; AA \rangle\$c\}.
\end{aligned}
$$

For instance, M_R makes

$$
\begin{aligned}
(\langle s; S\rangle, aabbcc, \$\#) \;{}_e\vdash\; & (\langle q; AA\rangle, aabbcc, \$\$\#) && [1\langle s; S\rangle\$ \rightarrow \langle q; AA\rangle\$\$] \\
{}_e\vdash\; & (\langle p; AA\rangle, aabbcc, a\$b\$\#) && [1\langle q; AA\rangle\$ \rightarrow \langle p; AA\rangle a\$b] \\
{}_p\vdash\; & (\langle p; AA\rangle, abbcc, \$b\$\#) && \\
{}_e\vdash\; & (\langle q; AA\rangle, abbcc, \$b\$c\#) && [2\langle p; AA\rangle\$ \rightarrow \langle q; AA\rangle\$c] \\
{}_e\vdash\; & (\langle f; A\rangle, abbcc, abb\$c\#) && [1\langle q; AA\rangle\$ \rightarrow \langle f; A\rangle ab] \\
{}_p\vdash\; & (\langle f; A\rangle, cc, \$c\#) && \\
{}_e\vdash\; & (\langle f; \varepsilon\rangle, cc, cc\#) && [1\langle f; A\rangle\$ \rightarrow \langle f; \epsilon\rangle c] \\
{}_p\vdash\; & (\langle f; \varepsilon\rangle, \varepsilon, \#).
\end{aligned}
$$

Theorem 15.3. For all $n \geq 1$, ${}_n\mathbf{DPDA} = {}_n\mathbf{DPDA}_2$.

Proof. This theorem follows from Lemma 15.3. ■

Corollary 15.5. *For all* $n \geq 1$, ${}_n\mathbf{DPDA}_2 \subset {}_{n+1}\mathbf{DPDA}_2$.

Proof. This corollary follows from Theorem 15.3 in this section and Corollary 3.1. in [344]. ■

Can we reformulate Theorem 15.3 and Corollary 15.5 in terms of ${}_n\mathbf{DPDA}_1$? The answer is no as we show next.

Lemma 15.4. Let $M = (Q, D, \Gamma, R, s, S, F)$ be a DPDA with $\Gamma - D = \{\#\}$. Then, there is a right-linear grammar G such that $L(G) = L(M)$.

Proof. Let $M = (Q, D, \Gamma, R, s, S, F)$ with $\Gamma - D = \{\#\}$. Thus, every rule in R is of the form $1q\# \rightarrow px\#$, where $q, p \in Q$, $x \in D^*$. Next, we construct a right-linear grammar $G = (Q, D, R, s)$ so $L(M) = L(G)$. We construct R as follows.

(i) For every $1q\# \rightarrow px\# \in R$, where $p, q \in Q$, $x \in D^*$, add $q \rightarrow xp$ to R.
(ii) For every $f \in F$, add $f \rightarrow \varepsilon$ to R.

A rigorous proof that $L(M) = L(G)$ is left to the reader. ■

Theorem 15.4. $\mathbf{REG} =_1 \mathbf{DPDA}_1 =_n \mathbf{DPDA}_1$, for any $n \geq 1$.

Proof. Let $n \geq 1$. $\mathbf{REG} \subseteq {}_1\mathbf{DPDA}_1 =_n \mathbf{DPDA}_1$ is clear. Recall that right-linear grammars characterize **REG**, so ${}_n\mathbf{DPDA}_1 \subseteq \mathbf{REG}$ follows from Lemma 15.4. Thus, $\mathbf{REG} = {}_n\mathbf{DPDA}_1$. ■

Corollary 15.6. $\mathbf{REG} =_1 \mathbf{DPDA}_1 =_n \mathbf{DPDA}_1 \subset {}_n\mathbf{DPDA}_2$, *for all* $n \geq 2$.

Proof. Let $n \geq 1$. As obvious, ${}_1\mathbf{DPDA}_1 =_n \mathbf{DPDA}_1 \subseteq {}_n\mathbf{DPDA}_2$. Observe that

$$\{a^n b^n \mid n \geq 1\} \in {}_n\mathbf{DPDA}_2 - {}_n\mathbf{DPDA}_1.$$

Therefore, Corollary 15.6 holds. ■

15.2.3 Open problems

In the present section, we have reduced finitely expandable DPDAs with respect to the number of non-input pushdown symbols. Before closing this section, we suggest some open-problem areas related to this subject for the future investigation.

1. Can we reduce these automata with respect to the number of states?
2. Can we simultaneously reduce them with respect to the number of both states and non-input pushdown symbols?
3. Can we achieve the reductions described above in terms of general DPDAs, which are not finitely expandable? In fact, Lemma 15.4 holds for these automata, so it can be considered as a preliminary result related to this investigation area.

Part IV

Applications

This four-chapter part sketches computational applications of mathematical models studied earlier in the book. It also discusses their perspectives in computer science in the near future. Of course, many models can be applied to numerous application areas. Rather than looking all over them in an encyclopedic way, we focus our principal attention on two computer science application areas—syntax analysis and computational biology. Apart from this restriction, we narrow our attention only to applications based on four types of models covered earlier in this book, namely regulated grammars (see Chapter 12), scattered context grammars (see Section 11.2), grammar systems (see Section 13.3), and regulated pushdown automata (see Section 12.5).

Chapter 16 makes several utterly general remarks on applications in computational linguistics and biology. Then, more specifically, Chapters 17 and 18 describe applications in syntax analysis of programming and natural languages, respectively. Chapter 19 presents applications in computational biology.

Chapter 16
Applications in general

This chapter makes several general remarks about computational applications of modern language models covered earlier in this book. It also discusses their application perspectives in computer science in the near future.

As we know by now, however, all these models represent an enormously large variety of grammars and automata. Therefore, we narrow our attention only to some of them. Specifically, we choose regulated grammars (see Chapter 12), scattered context grammars (see Section 13.1), grammar systems (see Section 13.3), and regulated pushdown automata (see Chapter 12) for this purpose. Regarding the computer-science-application areas, we focus our principle attention on two areas—computational linguistics and computational biology.

16.1 Applications in computational linguistics: general comments

In terms of English syntax, grammatical regulation can specify a number of relations between individual syntax-related elements of sentences in natural languages. For instance, relative clauses are introduced by *who* or *which* depending on the subject of the main clause. If the subject in the main clause is a person, the relative clause is introduced by *who*; otherwise, it starts by *which*. We encourage the reader to design a regulated grammar that describes this dependency (consult [66]).

In other natural languages, there exist syntax relations that can be elegantly handled by regulated grammars, too. To illustrate, in Spanish, all adjectives inflect according to gender of the noun they characterize. Both the noun and the adjective may appear at different parts of a sentence, which makes their syntactical dependency difficult to capture by classical grammars; obviously, regulated grammars, discussed in Chapter 12, can describe this dependency in a more elegant and simple way. As a result, parsing is expected as their principle application field.

Ordinary parsers represent crucially important components of translators, and they are traditionally underlined by ordinary context-free grammars. As their name indicates, regulated parsers are based upon regulated context-free grammars. Considering their advantages, including properties (1)–(4) listed next, it comes as no surprise that they became increasingly popular in modern design of language translators.

1. Regulated parsers work in a faster way than classical parsers do. Indeed, ordinary parsers control their parsing process, so they consult their parsing tables during every single step. As opposed to this exhaustively busy approach, in regulated parsers, regulated grammatical mechanisms take control over the parsing process to a large extent; only during very few predetermined steps, they consult their parsing tables to decide how to continue the parsing process under the guidance of regulating mechanism. Such a reduction of communication with the parsing tables obviously results into a significant acceleration of the parsing process as a whole.
2. Regulated context-free grammars are much stronger than ordinary context-free grammars. Accordingly, parsers based upon regulated grammars are more powerful than their ordinary versions. As an important practical consequence, they can parse syntactical structures that cannot be parsed by ordinary parsers.
3. Regulated parsers make use of their regulation mechanisms to perform their parsing process in a deterministic way.
4. Compared to ordinary parsers, regulated parsers are often written more succinctly and, therefore, readably as follows from reduction-related results concerning the number of their components, such as nonterminals and rules, which were achieved earlier in this book (see Sections 11.4.2, 11.6.2, 13.1.4, 13.2.2, 13.2.3, and 13.2.4).

From a general point of view, some fundamental parts of translators, such as syntax-directed translators, run within the translation process under the parser-based regulation. Furthermore, through their symbol tables, parsers also regulate exchanging various pieces of information between their components, further divided into several subcomponents. Indeed, some parts of modern translators may be further divided into various subparts, which are run in a regulated way, and within these subparts, a similar regulation can be applied again, and so on. As a matter of fact, syntax-directed translation is frequently divided into two parts, which work concurrently. One part is guided by a precedence parser that works with expressions and conditions, while the other part is guided by a predictive parser that processes the general program flow. In addition, both parts are sometimes further divided into several subprocesses or threads. Of course, this two-parser design of syntax-directed translation requires an appropriate regulation of translation as a whole. Indeed, prior to this syntax-directed translation, a pre-parsing decomposition of the tokenized source program separates the syntax constructs for both parsers. On the other hand, after the syntax-directed translation based upon the two parsers is successfully completed, all the produced fragments of the intermediate code are carefully composed together, so the resulting intermediate code is functionally equivalent to the source program. Of course, handling translation like this requires a proper regulation of all these translation subphases.

To give one more example in terms of modern translator design, various optimization methods are frequently applied to the generation of the resulting target code to speed the code up as much as possible. This way of code generation may result from an explicit requirement in the source program. More often, however, modern translators themselves recognize that a generation like this is appropriate within the given computer framework, so they generate the effective target code to speed up its subsequent execution. Whatever they do, however, they always have to guarantee that the generated target code is functionally equivalent to the source program. Clearly, this design of translators necessitates an extremely careful control over all the optimization routines involved, and this complicated control has to be based upon a well-developed theory of computational regulation. Within formal language theory, which has always provided translation techniques with their formal models, this control can be accomplished by regulated grammars, which naturally and elegantly formalize computational regulation.

Apart from description, specification, and transformation of language syntax, regulated grammars can be applied to other linguistically oriented fields, such as *morphology* (see [67,68]).

16.2 Applications in computational biology: general comments

Mathematical models for languages and computation are applied in many fields of biology. Instead of covering them all, we restrict our attention only to microbiology, which also makes use of the systematically developed knowledge concerning these models significantly. Even more specifically, we narrow our attention to *molecular genetics* (see [69–71]).

A solidly developed control of information processing is central to this scientific field although it approaches this processing in a specific way. Indeed, genetically oriented studies usually investigate how to prescribe the modification of several symbols within strings that represent a molecular organism. To illustrate a modification like this, consider a typical molecular organism consisting of several groups of molecules; for instance, take any organism consisting of several parts that slightly differ in behavior of DNA molecules made by specific sets of enzymes. During their development, these groups of molecules communicate with each other, and this communication usually influences the future behavior of the whole organism. A simulation of such an organism might be formally based upon language models, which can control these changes at various places. Consequently, genetic dependencies of this kind represent another challenging application area of models for languages and computation in the future.

To sketch the applicability of these models in this scientific area in a greater detail, consider, for instance, forbidding grammars, studied earlier in Section 11.2. These grammars can formally and elegantly simulate processing information in molecular genetics, including information concerning macromolecules, such as DNA, RNA, and polypeptides. For instance, consider an organism consisting of DNA molecules made by enzymes. It is a common phenomenon that a molecule m made by a specific enzyme can be modified unless molecules made by some other enzymes occur either to the left or to the right of m in the organism. Consider a string w that formalizes this organism, so every molecule is represented by a symbol. As obvious, to simulate a change of the symbol a that represents m requires forbidding occurrences of some symbols that either precede or follow a in w. As obvious, forbidding grammars can provide a string-changing formalism that can capture this forbidding requirement in a very succinct and elegant way.

To put it more generally, mathematical models for languages and computation can simulate the behavior of molecular organisms in a rigorous and uniform way. Application-oriented topics like this obviously represent a future investigation area concerning these models. Indeed, to take advantage of highly effective parallel and mutually connected computers as much as possible, a modern software product simultaneously run several processes, each of which gather, analyze, and modify various elements occurring within information of an enormous size, largely spread and constantly growing across the virtually endless and limitless computer environment. During a single computational step, a particular running process selects a finite set of mutually related information elements, from which it produces new information as a whole and, thereby, completes the step. In many respects, the newly created information affects the way the process performs the next computational step, and from a more broad perspective, it may also significantly change the way by which the other processes work as well. Clearly, a product conceptualized in this modern way requires a very sophisticated regulation of its computation performed within a single process as well as across all the processes involved. Many mathematical models studied earlier in this book represent appropriate formal models for this modern computation, which is likely to fulfill a central role in computer science as a whole in the near future. As such, from a theoretical perspective, these models will allow us to express the theoretical fundamentals of this computation rigorously and systematically. From a more pragmatic perspective, based upon them, computer science can create a well-designed methodology concerning modern information processing. Simply put, as their main perspective in near future, these models allow us to create a systematized body of knowledge representing an in-depth theory of highly regulated computation as well as a sophisticated methodology concerning modern information processing, based upon this computation.

Chapter 17

Applications in syntax analysis: programming languages

Every solid operating system provides its users with a large variety of software components customarily referred to compilers. These components translate programs written in high-level programming languages, such as C#, to machine-language programs that perform the computation specified by the translated programs to make them computer executable. A crucially important part of every compiler represents a syntax analyzer or, more briefly, a parser. In this chapter, we describe how to design a parser based upon context-free grammars (CFGs) and pushdown automata (PDAs) (see Chapters 6 and 7).

CFGs are recognized as the most widely used specification tool for the syntactic structures of programming languages. Accordingly, PDAs, which represent the basic automaton-based counterpart to CFGs (see Theorem 7.6), usually underlie syntax analyzers, whose fundamental task is to decide whether the syntactic structures are correctly specified according to the grammatical rules. If they are not, the syntax analyzers detect and specify all the errors in them. If the structures are syntactically correct, the syntax analyzers produce parses—that is, the sequences of rules according to which the syntactic structures are generated because these parses are usually important to engineering techniques for language processing within which the syntax analyzer is applied. For instance, compilers make use of parses obtained in this way to direct the translation of programs written in high-level programming languages to functionally equivalent machine-language programs, which perform the computation specified by the input high-level programs.

The present chapter consists of four sections. Section 17.1 conceptualizes two fundamental approaches to syntax analysis—top-down parsing and bottom-up parsing. Then, Section 17.2 describes the former approach, while Section 17.3 explores the latter. Section 17.4 explains how to implement a syntax-directed translation, which is completely driven by a parser when producing target machine-language programs.

Note on notation. Throughout this chapter, we specify CFGs and PDAs as pairs just like in Chapters 6 and 7.

17.1 General parsers

The section gives the basics of syntax analysis in terms of CFGs and PDAs, introduced in Chapters 6 and 7. First, it gives a quite general insight into the syntax analysis of programming languages. Then, it explains how CFGs and PDAs conceptually underlie syntax analyzers.

The syntax of a programming language L is almost always specified by a CFG, $G = (\Sigma, R)$, satisfying $L = L(G)$. In essence, a syntax analyzer for G is a PDA M that decides whether a string $w \in L(G)$. M makes this decision by accepting w exactly when G generates w; consequently, $L(M) = L(G)$. In greater detail, to demonstrate that $w \in L(G)$, M simulates the construction of ${}_GS \Rightarrow^* w[\rho]$, where ρ represents a parse of w—that is, a sequence of rules from ${}_GR$ by which G derives w in G. If M successfully completes this construction, it usually produces the parse ρ as its output; hence, it is customarily referred to as a G-based parser. Typically, M is designed so it constructs ${}_GS \Rightarrow^* w$ either in a leftmost way or in a rightmost way. Accordingly, there exist two different approaches to parsing, customarily referred to as *top-down parsing* and *bottom-up parsing*, which produce *left parses* and *right parses*, respectively. Next, (1) and (2) describe both approaches together with the following two notions of parses:

1. M simulates ${}_GS \Rightarrow^*_{lm} w[\rho]$ so it starts from ${}_GS$ and proceeds toward w by simulating leftmost derivation steps according to rules from ${}_GR$. If and when it completes ${}_GS \Rightarrow^*_{lm} w[\rho]$, it usually also produces ρ as the *left parse of w corresponding to* ${}_GS \Rightarrow^*_{lm} w[\rho]$—the sequence of rules according to which G makes this leftmost derivation. In terms of the corresponding derivation tree $\perp({}_GS \Rightarrow^*_{lm} w[\rho])$, this approach can be naturally rephrased as the construction of $\perp({}_GS \Rightarrow^*_{lm} w[\rho])$, so it starts from the root and proceeds down toward the frontier; hence, a parser that works in this top-down way is called a *G-based top-down parser*.
2. If M simulates ${}_GS \Rightarrow^*_{rm} w[\rho]$, it makes this simulation in reverse. That is, it starts from w and proceeds toward ${}_GS$ by making rightmost derivation steps, each of which is performed in reverse by reducing the right-hand side of a rule to its left-hand side. If and when it completes this reverse construction of ${}_GS \Rightarrow^*_{rm} w[\rho]$, it produces reversal (ρ) as *the right parse of w corresponding to* ${}_GS \Rightarrow^*_{rm} w[\rho]$—the reverse sequence of rules according to which G makes this rightmost derivation. To express this construction in terms of $\perp({}_GS \Rightarrow^*_{rm} w[\rho])$, a parser like this constructs this tree, so it starts from its frontier w and proceeds up toward the root; hence, a parser that works in this way is referred to as a *G-based bottom-up parser.*

Whichever way a parser is designed, it is always based upon a PDA. Convention 17.1 simplifies the upcoming discussion of parsers by considering only one-state PDAs, which are equivalent with ordinary PDAs as follows from Algorithm 7.1, Theorem 7.1, and Theorem 7.6. In addition, some pragmatically motivated conventions concerning configurations are introduced too.

Convention 17.1. *Throughout this chapter, we assume that every PDA M has a single state denoted by $\Diamond$, so ${}_MQ = {}_MF = \{\Diamond\}$. Instead of a configuration of the form $x\Diamond y$*

from $_MX$ *(see Definition 7.1), we write* $\triangleright x\diamond y\triangleleft$*, where* $\triangleright$ *and* $\triangleleft$ *are two special symbols such that* $\{\triangleright, \triangleleft\} \cap {}_M\Sigma = \emptyset$*. By* pd*, we refer to the pushdown* $\triangleright x$*, whose rightmost symbol represents the* pd *top symbol and* $\triangleright$ *is called the* pd bottom*. We consider* pd *empty if* $x = \varepsilon$ *and, therefore,* $\triangleright$ *occurs on the pushdown top. By* ins*, we refer to the* input symbol *defined as the leftmost symbol of* $y\triangleleft$*. When ins* $= \triangleleft$*, referred to as the* input end*, all the input string has been read. As a result, M always accepts in a configuration of the form* $\triangleright\diamond\triangleleft$*.*

17.1.1 Syntax specified by context-free grammars

Of course, parsers can verify the syntax of a programming language only if it is precisely specified. Today, CFGs are almost exclusively used for this purpose. The following example illustrates how to specify the syntax of common syntactical structures, such as logical expressions, by using CFGs.

Example 17.1. We want to describe logical expression of the form

$$\iota_0 o_1 \iota_1 o_2 \iota_2 \cdots \iota_{n-1} o_n \iota_n,$$

where $o_j \in \{\vee, \wedge\}$, and ι_k is a logical variable, symbolically denoted by i (intuitively, i stands for an $i$dentifier) or another logical expression enclosed in parentheses, for all $1 \leq j \leq n$ and $0 \leq k \leq n$, for some $n \in {}_0\mathbb{N}$. For instance, $(i \vee i) \wedge i$ is an expression like this. A logical variable can be simply derived by this rule

$$S \rightarrow i.$$

We also introduce

$$S \rightarrow (S)$$

to derive a parenthesized expression—that is, any valid expression enclosed by parentheses. To derive logical operators $\vee$ and $\wedge$, we add these two rules

$$S \rightarrow S \vee S \text{ and } S \rightarrow S \wedge S.$$

As a result, we define the expressions by the four-rule CFG defined as

$$\begin{aligned}
1 &: S \rightarrow S \vee S,\\
2 &: S \rightarrow S \wedge S,\\
3 &: S \rightarrow (S),\\
4 &: S \rightarrow i.
\end{aligned}$$

This CFG is obviously ambiguous (see Definition 6.5); for instance, $S \Rightarrow^*_{lm} i \vee i \wedge i$ [14244] as well as $S \Rightarrow^*_{lm} i \vee i \wedge i$ [21444]. Observe, however, that the same language that the four-rule CFG generates is also generated by the unambiguous six-rule CFG defined as

$$\begin{aligned}
1 &: S \rightarrow S \vee A,\\
2 &: S \rightarrow A,\\
3 &: A \rightarrow A \wedge B,\\
4 &: A \rightarrow B,\\
5 &: B \rightarrow (S),\\
6 &: B \rightarrow i.
\end{aligned}$$

However, both of the previous CFGs are left-recursive (see Definition 6.14). Some important methods of syntax analysis work only with non-left-recursive CFGs; in fact, all the methods described in Section 17.2 are of this kind. Therefore, we give one more equivalent non-left-recursive unambiguous CFG, obtained from the previous CFG by Algorithm 6.8:

$$\begin{aligned}
1 &: S \rightarrow AC,\\
2 &: C \rightarrow \vee AC,\\
3 &: C \rightarrow \varepsilon,\\
4 &: A \rightarrow BD,\\
5 &: D \rightarrow \wedge BD,\\
6 &: D \rightarrow \varepsilon,\\
7 &: B \rightarrow (S),\\
8 &: B \rightarrow i.
\end{aligned}$$

Compare the three equivalent CFGs introduced in this example. Intuitively, we obviously see that in the syntax analysis, any grammatical ambiguity may represent an undesirable phenomenon, and if it does, we prefer the second CFG to the first CFG. On the other hand, the definition of the former is more succinct than the definition of the latter because the former contains a single nonterminal and four rules, while the latter has three nonterminals and six rules. As already noted, some methods of syntax analysis necessities using non-left-recursive CFGs, in which case we obviously use the third CFG, which has more nonterminals and rules than the other two CFGs in this example. Simply put, all three CFGs have their pros and cons.

Consequently, from a broader perspective, the previous example illustrates a typical process of designing an appropriate grammatical specification for a programming language in practice. Indeed, we often design several equivalent CFGs that generate the language, carefully consider their advantages and disadvantages, and based on this consideration, we choose the CFG that is optimal under given circumstances.

In what follows, we make use of the CFGs from the previous example so often that we introduce the next convention for the sake of brevity.

Convention 17.2. *Consider the CFGs that were defined in Example 17.1. Throughout the rest of this chapter, E, H, and J denotes its first, the second, and the third CFG, respectively. That is,* *(i)* *E denotes*

$$\begin{aligned}
1 &: S \rightarrow S \vee S,\\
2 &: S \rightarrow S \wedge S,\\
3 &: S \rightarrow (S),\\
4 &: S \rightarrow i,
\end{aligned}$$

(ii) *H denotes*

$$\begin{aligned}
1 &: S \rightarrow S \vee A,\\
2 &: S \rightarrow A,\\
3 &: A \rightarrow A \wedge B,\\
4 &: A \rightarrow B,\\
5 &: B \rightarrow (S),\\
6 &: B \rightarrow i,
\end{aligned}$$

(iii) *J denotes*

$$\begin{aligned}
1 &: S \rightarrow AC,\\
2 &: C \rightarrow \vee AC,\\
3 &: C \rightarrow \varepsilon,\\
4 &: A \rightarrow BD,\\
5 &: D \rightarrow \wedge BD,\\
6 &: D \rightarrow \varepsilon,\\
7 &: B \rightarrow (S),\\
8 &: B \rightarrow i.
\end{aligned}$$

17.1.2 Top-down parsing

Let I be a CFG. Given $w \in \Delta^*$, an I-based top-down parser works on w, so it simulates a leftmost derivation of w in I. If there is no leftmost derivation of w in I, the parser rejects w because $w \notin L(I)$. On the other hand, if the parser successfully completes the simulation of $S \Rightarrow_{lm}^{*} w[\rho]$ in I, which means that $w \in L(I)$, the parser accepts w to express that I generates w; in addition, it often produces the left parse ρ as output too.

Algorithm 17.1 transforms any CFG I to an equivalent PDA O that acts as an I-based top-down parser. In many respects, this transformation resembles Algorithm 7.1, reformulated in terms of Convention 17.1. Notice that O performs only the following two pushdown operations—*popping* and *expanding*.

1. If a terminal a occurs as the pushdown top symbol, O *pops* a off the pushdown by a rule of the form $a\Diamond a \rightarrow \Diamond$, by which O removes a from the pushdown top and, simultaneously, reads the input symbol a, so it actually verifies their identity.
2. If a nonterminal A occurs as the pushdown top symbol, O simulates a leftmost derivation step made by a rule $r: A \rightarrow X_1X_2 \cdots X_n \in {}_IR$, where each $X_i \in {}_I\Sigma$, $1 \leq i \leq n$, for some $n \in {}_0\mathbb{N}$ ($n = 0$ means $X_1X_2 \cdots X_n = \varepsilon$). O performs this simulation, so it *expands* its pushdown by using $A\Diamond \rightarrow \text{reversal}\,(X_1X_2 \cdots X_n)\Diamond$

Algorithm 17.1: Top-down parser

Input: A context-free grammar I.
Output: A pushdown automaton O such that O works as an I-based top-down parser.

begin
  set ${}_O\Sigma = {}_I\Sigma$ with ${}_O\Gamma = {}_IN \cup {}_I\Delta$, ${}_O\Delta = {}_I\Delta$, ${}_OS = {}_IS$
  set ${}_OR = \emptyset$
  for *each* $A \to x \in {}_IR$ **do**
    add $A\diamond \to \text{reversal}\,(x)\diamond$ to ${}_OR$ `// expansion rules`
  end
  for *each* $a \in {}_I\Delta$ **do**
    add $a\diamond a \to \diamond$ to ${}_OR$ `// popping rules`
  end
end

---

so it replaces the pushdown top A with $X_n \cdots X_1$. To describe an expansion like this more formally, consider ${}_IS \Rightarrow^*_{lm} w[\rho]$ in I, where $w \in {}_I\Delta^*$, expressed as

$$\begin{aligned} {}_IS &\Rightarrow^*_{lm} vAy \\ &\Rightarrow_{lm} vX_1X_2\cdots X_ny \\ &\Rightarrow^*_{lm} vu, \end{aligned}$$

where $w = vu$, so $v, u \in {}_I\Delta^*$. Suppose that I has just simulated the first portion of this derivation, $S \Rightarrow^*_{lm} vAy$; at this point, the pushdown of O contains Ay in reverse, and u is the remaining input to be read. In symbols, the PDA O occurs in the configuration $\triangleright\,\text{reversal}\,(y)A\diamond u\triangleleft$, from which it simulates $vAy \Rightarrow_{lm} vX_1X_2\cdots X_ny\ [r]$ by performing this expansion

$$\triangleright\,\text{reversal}\,(y)A\diamond y\triangleleft \Rightarrow \triangleright\,\text{reversal}\,(y)X_n\cdots X_1\diamond u\triangleleft$$

according to the rule $A\diamond \to X_n\cdots X_1\diamond$ from the set of rules in O; notice that $\text{reversal}\,(y)X_n\cdots X_1 = \text{reversal}\,(X_1\cdots X_ny)$.

Prove the next lemma as an exercise.

Lemma 17.1. *Algorithm 17.1 is correct.*

Left Parses. Consider the top-down parser O produced by Algorithm 17.1 from a CFG I. Observe that the expansion rules in O correspond to the grammatical rules in I according to this equivalence

$$A \to x \in {}_IR \text{ iff } A\diamond \to \text{reversal}\,(x)\diamond \in {}_OR.$$

Suppose that O simulates $S \Rightarrow^*_{lm} w[\rho]$ in I. To obtain ρ as the left parse of w corresponding to this derivation, record the grammatical rules corresponding to the

Table 17.1 Top-down parsing of $i \vee i \wedge i$

Derivation in I	**Left parse**	**Computation in O**
$\underline{S}$		$\triangleright S\Diamond i \vee i \wedge i \triangleleft$
$\Rightarrow_{lm} \underline{S} \vee S$	1	$\triangleright S \vee S\Diamond i \vee i \wedge i \triangleleft$
$\Rightarrow_{lm} i \vee \underline{S}$	4	$\triangleright S \vee i\Diamond i \vee i \wedge i \triangleleft$
		$\triangleright S \vee \Diamond \vee i \wedge i \triangleleft$
		$\triangleright S\Diamond i \wedge i \triangleleft$
$\Rightarrow_{lm} i \vee \underline{S} \wedge S$	2	$\triangleright S \wedge S\Diamond i \wedge i \triangleleft$
$\Rightarrow_{lm} i \vee i \wedge \underline{S}$	4	$\triangleright S \wedge i\Diamond i \wedge i \triangleleft$
		$\triangleright S \wedge \Diamond \wedge i \triangleleft$
		$\triangleright S\Diamond i \triangleleft$
$\Rightarrow_{lm} i \vee i \wedge i$	4	$\triangleright i\Diamond i \triangleleft$
		$\triangleright \Diamond \triangleleft$

expansion rules applied by O during this simulation. Specifically, if O makes an expansion by $A \rightarrow \text{reversal}(x)\Diamond$ to simulate the application of $r\colon A \rightarrow x \in {}_IR$ in I, write r. After the simulation of $S \Rightarrow^*_{lm} w$ is completed, the sequence of all rules recorded in this way is the left parse ρ. The next example describes O that produces left parses in this way.

Example 17.2. *Take the grammar E (see Convention 17.2), defined as*

$$1 : S \rightarrow S \vee S,$$
$$2 : S \rightarrow S \wedge S,$$
$$3 : S \rightarrow (S).$$
$$4 : S \rightarrow i$$

Consider E as the input grammar I of Algorithm 17.1. This algorithm turns I to a top-down parser for I, O, which has these expansion rules

$$S\Diamond \rightarrow S \vee S\Diamond,$$
$$S\Diamond \rightarrow S \wedge S\Diamond,$$
$$S\Diamond \rightarrow)S(\Diamond,$$
$$S\Diamond \rightarrow i\Diamond.$$

Apart from these rules, the second for loop of the algorithm introduces the popping rules $a\Diamond a \rightarrow \Diamond$, *for all* $a \in \{\vee, \wedge, (,), i\}$.

For instance, consider $S \Rightarrow^*_{lm} i \vee i \wedge i$ [14244] *in I. O parses* $i \vee i \wedge i$ *as described in Table 17.1, whose columns contain the following information:*

Column 1 $S \Rightarrow^*_{lm} i \vee i \wedge i$ [14244] *in I;*
Column 2 *the production of the left parse* 14244*;*
Column 3 $S \triangleright \Diamond i \vee i \wedge i \triangleleft \Rightarrow^* \triangleright \Diamond \triangleleft$ *in O.*

Algorithm 17.2: Bottom-up parser

Input: A context-free grammar I.
Output: A pushdown automaton O such that O works as an I-based bottom-up parser.

begin
  set ${}_O\Sigma = {}_I\Sigma \cup \{{}_OS\}$ with ${}_O\Delta = {}_I\Delta$ and ${}_O\Gamma = {}_IN \cup {}_I\Delta \cup \{{}_OS\}$, where ${}_OS \notin {}_I\Sigma$
  set ${}_OR = \{{}_OS{}_IS\diamond \rightarrow \diamond\}$
  for *each* $A \rightarrow x \in {}_IR$ **do**
    add $x\diamond \rightarrow A\diamond$ to ${}_OR$ `// reducing rules`
  end
  for *each* $a \in {}_I\Delta$ **do**
    add $\diamond a \rightarrow a\diamond$ to ${}_OR$ `// shifting rules`
  end
end

17.1.3 Bottom-up parsing

Let G be a CFG. Given $w \in \Delta^*$, a G-based bottom-up parser works on w, so it reversely simulates a rightmost derivation of w in G. If there is no rightmost derivation of w in G, the parser rejects w because $w \notin L(G)$. However, if the parser successfully completes the reverse simulation of $S \Rightarrow^*_{rm} w[\rho]$ in G, the parser accepts w to express that $w \in L(G)$, and in addition, it usually produces the right parse reversal (ρ) as output.

Next, we give Algorithm 17.2 that turns any CFG I to a PDA O, so O acts as an I-based bottom-up parser. To give an insight into this algorithm, consider any rightmost derivation ${}_IS \Rightarrow^*_{rm} w$ in I, where $w \in \Delta^*$. In essence, O simulates this derivation in reverse, proceeding from w toward ${}_IS$, and during all this simulation, it keeps its start symbol ${}_OS$ as the deepest symbol, occurring right behind $\triangleright$. When it reaches the configuration $\triangleright{}_OS{}_IS\diamond\triangleleft$, it moves to $\triangleright\diamond\triangleleft$ and, thereby, successfully completes the parsing of w. More specifically, express ${}_IS \Rightarrow^*_{rm} w$ in I as ${}_IS \Rightarrow^*_{rm} zv \Rightarrow^*_{rm} tv$, where $t, v \in \Delta^*$, $w = tv$, and $z \in \Sigma^*$. After reading t and making a sequence of moves corresponding to $zv \Rightarrow^*_{rm} tv$, O uses its pushdown to record z and contains v as the remaining input to read. In brief, it occurs in the configuration $\triangleright{}_OSz\diamond v\triangleleft$. To explain the next move of O that simulates the rightmost derivation step in I, express ${}_IS \Rightarrow^*_{rm} zv \Rightarrow^*_{rm} tv$ in greater detail as

$$\begin{aligned} {}_IS &\Rightarrow^*_{rm} yAv \\ &\Rightarrow_{rm} yxv \;\; [A \rightarrow x] \\ &\Rightarrow^*_{rm} tv, \end{aligned}$$

where $yx = z$ and $A \rightarrow x \in {}_IR$. From $\triangleright_O Syx\diamond v\triangleleft$, which equals $\triangleright_O Sz\diamond v\triangleleft$, M simulates $yAv \Rightarrow_{rm} yxv$ $[A \rightarrow x]$ in reverse as

$$\triangleright_O Syx\diamond v\triangleleft \Rightarrow \triangleright_O SyA\diamond v \triangleleft.$$

In addition, whenever needed, O can shift the first symbol of the remaining input onto the pushdown. In this way, step by step, O simulates ${}_IS \Rightarrow^*_{rm} zv \Rightarrow^*_{rm} tv$ in I until it reaches the configuration $\triangleright_O S_I S\diamond\triangleleft$. To reach $\triangleright\diamond\triangleleft$ and complete the acceptance of w, we add $\triangleright_O S_I S\diamond\triangleleft \rightarrow \triangleright\diamond\triangleleft$ to ${}_OR$.

Next we prove that $L(O) = L(I)$. In addition, in this proof, we demonstrate that O works as an I-based bottom-up parser in the sense that O simulates the construction of rightmost derivations in I in reverse.

Lemma 17.2. *Algorithm 17.2 is correct—that is,* $L(O) = L(I)$ *and* O *acts as an* I*-based bottom-up parser.*

Proof. To prove $L(I) = L(O)$, we first establish Claims A and B.

Claim A. Let

$$\begin{aligned} {}_IS &\Rightarrow^*_{rm} xv \\ &\Rightarrow^*_{rm} uv \ [\pi] \end{aligned}$$

in I, where $v, u \in {}_I\Delta^*$, $x \in {}_I\Sigma^*$, and $\pi \in {}_IR^*$. Then, O computes

$$\triangleright_O S\diamond uv\triangleleft \Rightarrow^* \triangleright_O Sx\diamond v \triangleleft.$$

Proof of Claim A by induction on $|\pi| \geq 0$.

Basis. Let $|\pi| = 0$. That is, $S \Rightarrow^*_{rm} xv \Rightarrow^0_{rm} uv$ in I, so $u = x$. Observe that O computes $\triangleright_O S\diamond uv\triangleleft \Rightarrow^{|u|} \triangleright_O Su\diamond v\triangleleft$ by shifting u onto the pushdown by $|u|$ consecutive applications of shifting rules of the form $\diamond a \rightarrow a\diamond$, where $a \in {}_I\Delta$ (see Algorithm 17.2). Thus, the basis holds true.

Induction hypothesis. Suppose that the claim holds for each $\pi \in {}_IR^*$ with $|\pi| \leq i$, for some $i \in {}_0\mathbb{N}$.

Induction step. Consider

$$\begin{aligned} {}_IS &\Rightarrow^*_{rm} xv \\ &\Rightarrow^*_{rm} uv \ [\pi] \end{aligned}$$

in I, where $\pi \in {}_IR^*$, $|\pi| = i$, and $p \in {}_IR$, so $|p\pi| = i + 1$. Express $xv \Rightarrow^*_{rm} uv\,[p\pi]$ as

$$\begin{aligned} xv &\Rightarrow_{rm} y\,\mathrm{rhs}(p)v \ [p] \\ &\Rightarrow^*_{rm} uv \qquad\quad [\pi], \end{aligned}$$

where $x = y\,\mathrm{lhs}(p)$ (see Definition 6.1 for lhs and rhs). By inspecting Algorithm 17.2, we see that $p \in {}_IR$ implies $\mathrm{rhs}(p)\diamond \rightarrow \mathrm{lhs}(p)\diamond \in {}_OR$. In the rest of this proof, we distinguish these two cases—(i) $y\,\mathrm{rhs}(p) \in {}_I\Delta^*$ and (ii) $y\,\mathrm{rhs}(p) \notin {}_I\Delta^*$.

(i) Let $y\,\mathrm{rhs}(p) \in {}_I\Delta^*$. Then, $y\,\mathrm{rhs}(p) = u$. Construct

$$\triangleright_O S\Diamond uv\triangleleft \Rightarrow^{|u|} \triangleright_O Sy\,\mathrm{rhs}(p)\Diamond v\triangleleft$$

in O by shifting u onto the pushdown, so

$$\begin{aligned}\triangleright_O S\Diamond uv\triangleleft &\Rightarrow^{|u|} \triangleright_O Sy\,\mathrm{rhs}(p)\Diamond v\triangleleft\\ &\Rightarrow \triangleright_O Sy\,\mathrm{lhs}(p)\Diamond v\triangleleft\ [\mathrm{rhs}(p)\Diamond \to \mathrm{lhs}(p)\Diamond].\end{aligned}$$

As $x = y\,\mathrm{lhs}(p)$, we have just proved $\triangleright_O S\Diamond uv\triangleleft \Rightarrow^* \triangleright_O Sx\Diamond v\triangleleft$ in O.

(ii) Let $y\,\mathrm{rhs}(p) \notin {}_I\Delta^*$. Express $y\,\mathrm{rhs}(p)$ as $y\,\mathrm{rhs}(p) = zBt$, where $t \in {}_I\Delta^*, z \in {}_I\Sigma^*$, and $B \in {}_IN$, so B is the rightmost nonterminal appearing in $y\,\mathrm{rhs}(p)$. Consider

$$\begin{aligned}{}_IS &\Rightarrow^*_{rm} xv\\ &\Rightarrow_{rm} zBtv\ [p]\\ &\Rightarrow^*_{rm} uv\quad [\pi].\end{aligned}$$

Since $|\pi| = i$, $\triangleright_O S\Diamond uv\triangleleft \Rightarrow^* \triangleright_O SzB\Diamond tv\triangleleft$ by the inductive hypothesis. By shifting t onto the pushdown, we obtain $\triangleright_O SzB\Diamond tv\triangleleft \Rightarrow^* \triangleright_O SzBt\Diamond v\triangleleft$. As $y\,\mathrm{rhs}(p) = zBt$, we have

$$\begin{aligned}\triangleright_O S\Diamond uv\triangleleft &\Rightarrow^{|t|} \triangleright_O Sy\,\mathrm{rhs}(p)\Diamond v\triangleleft\\ &\Rightarrow \triangleright_O Sy\,\mathrm{lhs}(p)\Diamond v\triangleleft\ [\mathrm{rhs}(p)\Diamond \to \mathrm{lhs}(p)\Diamond].\end{aligned}$$

Therefore, $\triangleright_O S\Diamond uv\triangleleft \Rightarrow^* \triangleright_O SzB\Diamond tv\triangleleft$ in O because $x = y\,\mathrm{lhs}(p)$, which completes (ii).

Consequently, Claim A holds true.

Claim B. Let $\triangleright_O S\Diamond uv\triangleleft \Rightarrow^* \triangleright_O Sx\Diamond v \triangleleft\ [\rho]$ in O, where $u, v \in {}_O\Delta^*$, $x \in {}_I\Sigma^*$, and $\rho \in ({}_OR - \{{}_OS_IS\Diamond \to \Diamond\})^*$. Then, $xv \Rightarrow^*_{rm} uv$ in I.
Proof of Claim B by induction on $|\rho| \geq 0$.

Basis. Let $|\rho| = 0$, so $u = x = \varepsilon$ and $\triangleright_O S\Diamond v\triangleleft \Rightarrow^0 \triangleright_O S\Diamond v\triangleleft$ in O. Clearly, $v \Rightarrow^0_{rm} v$ in I.

Induction hypothesis. Suppose that the claim holds for each $\rho \in ({}_OR - \{{}_OS_IS\Diamond \to \Diamond\})^*$ with $|\rho| \leq i$, for some $i \geq 0$.

Induction step. Consider any sequence of $i + 1$ moves of the form $\triangleright_O S\Diamond uv\triangleleft \Rightarrow^* \triangleright_O Sx\Diamond v \triangleleft\ [\rho r]$ in O, where $u, v \in {}_O\Delta^*$, $x \in {}_I\Sigma^*$, $\rho \in ({}_OR - \{{}_OS_IS\Diamond \to \Diamond\})^*$, $|\rho| = i$, and $r \in {}_OR$. Express $\triangleright_O S\Diamond uv\triangleleft \Rightarrow^* \triangleright_O Sx\Diamond v \triangleleft\ [\rho r]$ as

$$\begin{aligned}\triangleright_O S\Diamond uv\triangleleft &\Rightarrow^* \triangleright_O Sy\Diamond t\triangleleft\ [\rho]\\ &\Rightarrow \triangleright_O Sx\Diamond v\triangleleft\ [r],\end{aligned}$$

where $y \in {}_I\Sigma^*$ and $t \in {}_O\Delta^*$. As $r \neq {}_OS\Diamond \to \Diamond$, either $\mathrm{rhs}(r) = A\Diamond$ with $A \in {}_IN$ or $\mathrm{rhs}(r) = a\Diamond$ with $a \in {}_O\Delta^*$. Next, we distinguish these two cases—(i) $\mathrm{rhs}(r) = A\Diamond$ with $A \in {}_IN$ and (ii) $\mathrm{rhs}(r) = a\Diamond$ with $a \in {}_O\Delta^*$.

(i) Let rhs(r) $= A\diamond$ with $A \in {}_IN$, so $t = v$, r is of the form $z\diamond \to A\diamond$, $x = hA$, and $y = hz$, for some $A \to z \in {}_IR$ and $h \in {}_I\Sigma^*$. By using $A \to z \in {}_IR$, I makes $hAv \Rightarrow_{rm} hzv$. By the induction hypothesis, $yv \Rightarrow^*_{rm} uv$ in I. Thus, $xv \Rightarrow^*_{rm} uv$ in I.

(ii) Let rhs(r) $= a\diamond$ with $a \in {}_O\Delta^*$, so $t = av$, r is of the form $\diamond a \to a\diamond$, $x = ya$. Thus, $xv = yt$. Recall that $\triangleright_O S\diamond uv\triangleleft \Rightarrow^* \triangleright_O Sy\diamond t \triangleleft\ [\rho]$ with $|\rho| = i$. By the induction hypothesis, $yt \Rightarrow^*_{rm} uv$ in I. Since $xv = yt$, $xv \Rightarrow^*_{rm} uv$ in I.

Thus, Claim B holds true.

Consider Claim A for $v = \varepsilon$ and $x = {}_IS$. At this point, for all $u \in {}_I\Delta^*$, ${}_IS \Rightarrow^*_{rm} u$ in I implies $\triangleright_O S\diamond u\triangleleft \Rightarrow^* \triangleright_O S_I S\diamond\triangleleft$ in O. By using ${}_OS_IS\diamond \to \diamond$, O makes $\triangleright_O S_I S\diamond\triangleleft \Rightarrow \triangleright\diamond\triangleleft$ in O. Hence, $L(I) \subseteq L(O)$.

Consider Claim B for $v = \varepsilon$ and $x = {}_IS$. Under this consideration, if $\triangleright_O S\diamond u\triangleleft \Rightarrow^* \triangleright_O S_I S\diamond \triangleleft\ [\rho]$ in O, then ${}_IS \Rightarrow^*_{rm} u$ in I, for all $u \in {}_I\Delta^*$. During any acceptance of a string, $u \in {}_I\Delta^*$, O applies ${}_OS_IS\diamond \to \diamond$ precisely once, and this application occurs during the very last step in order to remove ${}_OS_IS$ and reach the configuration $\triangleright\diamond\triangleleft$. Indeed, observe that any earlier application of this rule implies that subsequently O can never completely read u and, simultaneously, empty the push-down; the details of this observation is left as an exercise. Thus, $\triangleright_O S\diamond u\triangleleft \Rightarrow^* \triangleright\diamond\triangleleft$ in O implies ${}_IS \Rightarrow^*_{rm} u$ in I, so $L(O) \subseteq L(I)$.

Consequently, $L(I) = L(O)$ because $L(I) \subseteq L(O)$ and $L(O) \subseteq L(I)$. As an exercise, examine the proof of Claims A to see that O works so it simulates rightmost derivations in I in reverse. Thus, O works as an I-based bottom-up parser, and Lemma 17.2 holds true. ■

Right Parses. Consider the I-based bottom-up parser O produced by Algorithm 17.2 from a CFG I. Observe that the reducing rules in O correspond to the grammatical rules in I according to this equivalence

$$A \to x \in {}_IR \text{ iff } x\diamond \to A\diamond \in {}_OR.$$

Suppose that O reversely simulates ${}_IS \Rightarrow^*_{rm} w[\rho]$ in I. To obtain reversal (ρ) as the right parse of w corresponding to ${}_IS \Rightarrow^*_{rm} w[\rho]$, record the reducing rules applied by O during this simulation. That is, if O makes a reduction by $x\diamond \to A\diamond$ to simulate the application of $A \to x \in {}_IR$ in I, write out r. When the simulation of ${}_IS \Rightarrow^*_{rm} w[\rho]$ is completed, the corresponding right parse is obtained in this way. The next example illustrates O extended in this way.

We have described O in terms of reverse simulation of rightmost derivations in I. As noted in the beginning of this section, instead of this description, the way O works can be also described in terms of derivation trees constructed in a bottom-up way, so this construction starts from their frontiers and proceeds up toward the roots. Leaving a general version of this alternative description as an exercise, we include such a bottom-up construction of a derivation tree within the next example.

Example 17.3. *Consider the CFG H (see Convention 17.2), defined as*

$$\begin{aligned} 1 &: S \rightarrow S \vee A, \\ 2 &: S \rightarrow A, \\ 3 &: A \rightarrow A \wedge B, \\ 4 &: A \rightarrow B, \\ 5 &: B \rightarrow (S), \\ 6 &: B \rightarrow i. \end{aligned}$$

Consider H as the input grammar I of Algorithm 17.2. This algorithm turns it to the H-based bottom-up parser O, which has these reducing rules

$$\begin{aligned} 1 &: S \vee A\diamond \rightarrow S\diamond, \\ 2 &: A\diamond \rightarrow S\diamond, \\ 3 &: A \wedge B\diamond \rightarrow A\diamond, \\ 4 &: B\diamond \rightarrow A\diamond, \\ 5 &: (S)\diamond \rightarrow B\diamond, \\ 6 &: i\diamond \rightarrow B\diamond. \end{aligned}$$

We have labeled these rules by the labels that denote the grammatical rules from which they are constructed; for instance, $1\colon S \vee A\diamond \rightarrow S\diamond$ *is constructed from* $1\colon S \rightarrow S \vee A$. *Apart from these six rules, the algorithm adds the shifting rules* $\diamond a \rightarrow a\diamond$, *for all* $a \in \{\vee, \wedge, (,), i\}$. *It also introduces* $ZS\diamond \rightarrow \diamond$, *where Z is declared as the start pushdown symbol of O.*

For instance, take $i \vee i \wedge i$ *as the input string. Consider Table 17.2. This table explains how O parses* $i \vee i \wedge i$ *by using its three columns, whose contents are described next.*

Table 17.2 Bottom-up parsing of $i \vee i \wedge i$

Derivation tree in *I*	**Right parse**	**Computation in *O***
$i \vee i \wedge i$		$\triangleright Z\diamond i \vee i \wedge i\triangleleft$
		$\Rightarrow \triangleright Zi\diamond \vee i \wedge i\triangleleft$
$B\langle i\rangle \vee i \wedge i$	6	$\Rightarrow \triangleright ZB\diamond \vee i \wedge i\triangleleft$
$A\langle B\langle i\rangle\rangle \vee i \wedge i$	4	$\Rightarrow \triangleright ZA\diamond \vee i \wedge i\triangleleft$
$S\langle A\langle B\langle i\rangle\rangle\rangle \vee i \wedge i$	2	$\Rightarrow \triangleright ZS\diamond \vee i \wedge i\triangleleft$
		$\Rightarrow \triangleright ZS \vee \diamond i \wedge i\triangleleft$
		$\Rightarrow \triangleright ZS \vee i\diamond \wedge i\triangleleft$
$S\langle A\langle B\langle i\rangle\rangle\rangle \vee B\langle i\rangle \wedge i$	6	$\Rightarrow \triangleright ZS \vee B\diamond \wedge i\triangleleft$
$S\langle A\langle B\langle i\rangle\rangle\rangle \vee A\langle B\langle i\rangle\rangle \wedge i$	4	$\Rightarrow \triangleright ZS \vee A\diamond \wedge i\triangleleft$
		$\Rightarrow \triangleright ZS \vee A \wedge \diamond i\triangleleft$
		$\Rightarrow \triangleright ZS \vee A \wedge i\diamond\triangleleft$
$S\langle A\langle B\langle i\rangle\rangle\rangle \vee A\langle B\langle i\rangle\rangle \wedge B\langle i\rangle$	6	$\Rightarrow \triangleright ZS \vee A \wedge B\diamond\triangleleft$
$S\langle A\langle B\langle i\rangle\rangle\rangle \vee A\langle A\langle B\langle i\rangle\rangle \wedge B\langle i\rangle\rangle$	3	$\Rightarrow \triangleright ZS \vee A\diamond\triangleleft$
$S\langle S\langle A\langle B\langle i\rangle\rangle\rangle \vee A\langle A\langle B\langle i\rangle\rangle \wedge B\langle i\rangle\rangle\rangle$	1	$\Rightarrow \triangleright ZS\diamond\triangleleft$
		$\Rightarrow \triangleright\diamond\triangleleft$

Column 1 *the bottom-up construction of* $\perp(S \Rightarrow^*_{rm} i \vee i \wedge i)$ *in I;*
Column 2 *the construction of* 64264631 *as the right parse;*
Column 3 $\triangleright Z\diamond i \vee i \wedge i\triangleleft \Rightarrow^* \triangleright\diamond\triangleleft$ *in O.*

Take the resulting right parse 64264631. *Reverse it to obtain* 13646246, *according to which I makes this rightmost derivation*

$$\begin{aligned} S &\Rightarrow_{rm} S \vee A & [1] \\ &\Rightarrow_{rm} S \vee A \wedge B & [3] \\ &\Rightarrow_{rm} S \vee A \wedge i & [6] \\ &\Rightarrow_{rm} S \vee B \wedge i & [4] \\ &\Rightarrow_{rm} S \vee i \wedge i & [6] \\ &\Rightarrow_{rm} A \vee i \wedge i & [2] \\ &\Rightarrow_{rm} B \vee i \wedge i & [4] \\ &\Rightarrow_{rm} i \vee i \wedge i & [6]. \end{aligned}$$

In brief, $S \Rightarrow^*_{rm} i \vee i \wedge i$ [13646246].

The algorithms and lemmas achieved earlier in this section have their important theoretical consequences. Let **CFG** and **PDA** denote the family of languages generated by CFGs and the family of languages accepted by PDA, respectively. In Section 7.2 we have left a proof that **CFG** $\subseteq$ **PDA** as an exercise (see Theorem 7.1). Observe that this inclusion follows from Algorithm 17.1 and Lemma 17.1. Alternatively, Algorithm 17.2 and Lemma 17.2 imply **CFG** $\subseteq$ **PDA** too.

Corollary 17.1. *For every CFG I there exists an equivalent PDA O, so* **CFG** $\subseteq$ **PDA**.

The parsers constructed in Algorithms 17.1 and 17.2 represent a framework of the most top-down and bottom-up parsers, respectively. In general, however, they work in a nondeterministic way, and, as such, they are difficult to implement and apply. Therefore, throughout the upcoming two application-oriented sections, we concentrate our attention solely on their deterministic versions, which are central to parsing in practice. Furthermore, up to now, this chapter has still maintained the mathematical terminology used in the previous chapter. The following convention relaxes this strict formalism in order to make the upcoming parsers easy to implement.

Convention 17.3. *Every parser discussed throughout the upcoming Sections 17.2 and 17.3 is deterministic. Rather than its strictly mathematical rule-based specification, we describe it as a* parsing algorithm *based upon its* parsing table. *Although every parsing table always depends on the parser in question, its general format represents a two-dimensional array with rows and columns denoted by top pushdown symbols and input symbols, respectively. If A occurs on the pushdown top and* ins *is the current input symbol, the entry corresponding to A and* ins *specifies the proper parsing action to be performed in this configuration.*

Consider the two special symbols, $\triangleright$ *and* $\triangleleft$, *which always denote the pushdown bottom and the input end, respectively (see Convention 17.1). The parser finds out that the pushdown is empty when* $\triangleright$ *appears on the pushdown top. Similarly, when* $\triangleleft$

occurs as the input symbol, all the input string has been read. Of course, $\rhd$ *or* $\lhd$ *can never be removed.*

17.2 Top-down parsers

Consider a CFG G and a G-based top-down parser working on an input string w (see Section 17.1). Recall that a top-down parser verifies that w is syntactically correct, so it simulates the construction of a derivation tree for w in a top-down way. That is, reading w from left to the right, the parser starts from the tree root and proceeds down toward the frontier denoted by w. To put it in derivation terms, it builds up the leftmost derivation of w so it starts from ${}_GS$ and proceeds toward w. If the parser works deterministically, the parser makes a completely deterministic selection of an applied rule during every single computational step.

The present section concentrates its attention on *predictive parsing*, which is the most frequently used deterministic top-down parsing method in practice. First, it defines and discusses *predictive sets* and *LL grammars*, where the first L stands for the *l*eft-to-right scan of the input string w, while the second L means that the parser simulates the *l*eftmost derivation of w. By using the predictive sets, the parser makes the simulation of leftmost derivations in a completely deterministic way. Then, this section describes two fundamental versions of predictive parsing. First, it explains *recursive descent parsing*, which frees us from explicitly implementing a pushdown list. Then, it uses the LL grammars and predictive sets to construct predictive tables used by *predictive table-driven parsing*, which explicitly implements a pushdown list. In this version of predictive parsing, any grammatical change only leads to a modification of the table, while its control procedure remains unchanged, which is obviously its great advantage. We also explain how predictive parsers handle the syntax errors to recover from them.

Throughout this section, we make frequent use of the terminology introduced in Section 1.3, such as *suffixes*, *prefixes*, and *symbol*. In the examples, we illustrate the material under discussion in terms of the CFG J from Convention 17.2.

17.2.1 Predictive sets and LL grammars

Consider a CFG G and an input string w. Let M be a G-based top-down parser constructed by Algorithm 17.1. Suppose that M has already found the beginning of the leftmost derivation for w, $S \Rightarrow_{lm}^{*} tAv$, where t is a prefix of w. More precisely, let $w = taz$, where a is the current input symbol, which follows t in w, and z is the suffix of w, which follows a. In tAv, A is the leftmost nonterminal to be rewritten in the next step. Suppose that there exist several different A-rules. Under the assumption that M works deterministically (see Convention 17.3), M has to select one of the A-rules to continue the parsing process, and it cannot revise this selection later on. If M represents a *predictive parser*, it selects the right rule by predicting whether its application gives rise to a leftmost derivation of a string starting with a. To make this prediction, every rule $r \in {}_GR$ is accompanied with its *predictive set* containing all terminals that can begin a string resulting from a derivation whose first step is made by r. If the A-rules have their predictive sets pairwise disjoint, M deterministically selects the rule whose predictive set contains a. To construct the predictive sets, we first need the *first* and *follow* sets, described next.

The predictive set corresponding to $r \in {}_GR$ obviously contains the terminals that occur as the first symbol in a string derived from rhs(r), and this observation gives rise to the next useful definition.

Definition 17.1. *Let $G = ({}_G\Sigma, {}_GR)$ be a CFG. For every string $x \in {}_G\Sigma^*$,*

$$\text{first}(x) = \{a \mid x \Rightarrow^* w, \textit{ where either } w \in {}_G\Delta^+ \textit{ with } a = \textit{symbol}(w, 1) \textit{ or } w = \varepsilon = a\},$$

where symbol$(w, 1)$ denotes the leftmost symbol of w (see Section 1.3).

In general, first is defined in terms of $\Rightarrow$, but we could rephrase this definition in terms of the leftmost derivations, which play a crucial role in top-down parsing, because for every $w \in {}_G\Delta^*$, $x \Rightarrow^* w$ iff $x \Rightarrow^*_{lm} w$ (see Theorem 6.1). That is,

$$\text{first}(x) = \{a \mid x \Rightarrow^*_{lm} w, \text{ where either } w \in {}_G\Delta^+ \text{ with } a = \textit{symbol}(w, 1) \text{ or } w = \varepsilon = a\}.$$

It is worth noticing that if $x \Rightarrow^* \varepsilon$, where $x \in \Sigma^*$, then ε is in first(x); as a special case, for $x = \varepsilon$, first$(\varepsilon) = \{\varepsilon\}$.

Next, we will construct the first sets for all strings contained in ${}_G\Delta \cup \{\text{lhs}(r) \mid r \in {}_GR\} \cup \{y \mid y \in \text{suffixes}(\text{rhs}(r)) \text{ with } r \in {}_GR\}$. We make use of some subsets of these first sets later in this section (see Algorithm 17.4 and Definition 17.3).

Basic Idea. To construct first(x) for every $x \in {}_G\Delta \cup \{\text{lhs}(r) \mid r \in {}_GR\} \cup \{y \mid y \in \text{suffixes}(\text{rhs}(r)) \text{ with } r \in {}_GR\}$, we initially set first(a) to $\{a\}$ for every $a \in {}_G\Delta \cup \{\varepsilon\}$ because $a \Rightarrow^0_{lm} a$ for these as. first$(w) = \textit{symbol}(w, 1)$ for every $w \in \{y \mid y \in \text{suffixes}(\text{rhs}(r) \text{ with } r \in {}_GR,\ y = au \text{ with } a \in {}_G\Delta,\ u \in {}_G\Sigma^*\}$ because $w \Rightarrow^0_{lm} w$ for these ws. If $A \to uw \in {}_GR$ with $u \Rightarrow^* \varepsilon$, then $A \Rightarrow^* w$, so we add the symbols of first(w) to first(A) (by Algorithm 6.4, we can determine whether u is a string consisting of ε-nonterminals, in which case $u \Rightarrow^*_{lm} \varepsilon$). Keep extending all the first sets in this way until no more symbols can be added to any of the first sets.

Implementation 17.1. To implement Algorithm 17.3, we define a new module `Parsing`. In this module, we define two special symbols which represent *pd* bottom and input end. In subsequent implementations throughout this chapter, we make frequent use of these symbols and furthermore assume that they are not present as terminals or nonterminals in any `ContextFreeGrammar` given as input.

```
public static class Parsing
{
    public static readonly Symbol PdBottom = "|>";
    public static readonly Symbol InputEnd = "<|";
}
```

We create two helper methods in `Parsing`: first, a method to add all symbols from one set to another.

Algorithm 17.3: first

Input: A context-free grammar, $G = ({}_G\Sigma, {}_GR)$.
Output: Sets first(u) for all
$u \in {}_G\Delta \cup \{\text{lhs}(r) \mid r \in {}_GR\} \cup \{y \mid y \in \text{suffixes}(\text{rhs}(r)) \text{ with } r \in {}_GR\}$.
begin
set first(a) = $\{a\}$ for every $a \in {}_G\Delta \cup \{\varepsilon\}$,
set first(w) = $\{symbol(w, 1)\}$ for every
$w \in \{y \mid y \in \text{suffixes}(\text{rhs}(r)) \text{ with } r \in {}_GR,\ y = au \text{ with } a \in {}_G\Delta,\ u \in {}_G\Sigma^*\}$
and
set all the other constructed first sets to $\emptyset$
repeat
if $r \in {}_GR$, $u \in \text{prefixes}(\text{rhs}(r))$, *and* $u \Rightarrow^*_{lm} \varepsilon$ **then**
extend first($suffix(\text{rhs}(r)|\text{rhs}(r)| - |u|)$) by
first($symbol(\text{rhs}(r), |u| + 1)$) and
extend first(lhs(r)) by first($suffix(\text{rhs}(r), |\text{rhs}(r)| - |u|)$)
end
until no change
end

```
private static bool ExtendSet<T>(FiniteSet<T> setToExtend,
                                 FiniteSet<T> extension)
{
    bool changed = false;

    foreach (T element in extension)
    {
        if (setToExtend.Add(element))
        {
            changed = true;
        }
    }

    return changed;
}
```

Second, we need to check if a prefix of a rule's right-hand side contains only erasable nonterminals (see Implementation 6.12). More generally, we implement a method which determines whether a given string contains only symbols from a given set.

```
private static bool HasOnlyGivenSymbols(HmmlcString s,
                                        FiniteSet<Symbol> symbols)
{
    foreach (Symbol a in s)
```

```
    {
        if (!symbols.Contains(a)) return false;
    }
    return true;
}
```

A straightforward implementation of Algorithm 17.3 follows. The result is represented as a standard generic `Dictionary` (from the .NET Framework), which maps strings to their respective first sets.

```
public static IDictionary<HmmlcString, FiniteSet<HmmlcString>>
    ComputeFirstSets(ContextFreeGrammar G)
{
    var first = new Dictionary<HmmlcString, FiniteSet<HmmlcString>>();

    foreach (Symbol a in G.Terminals)
    {
        var aAsString = new HmmlcString(a);
        first[aAsString] = new FiniteSet<HmmlcString> { aAsString };
    }
    first[HmmlcString.Empty] =
        new FiniteSet<HmmlcString> { HmmlcString.Empty };

    foreach (ContextFreeRule r in G.Rules)
    {
        var lhsAsString = new HmmlcString(r.LeftHandSide);
        if (!first.ContainsKey(lhsAsString))
        {
            first[lhsAsString] = new FiniteSet<HmmlcString>();
        }

        foreach (HmmlcString y in r.RightHandSide.GetAllSuffixes())
        {
            if (!first.ContainsKey(y))
            {
                if (y.Length > 1 && G.Terminals.Contains(y[0]))
                {
                    first[y] =
                        new FiniteSet<HmmlcString>
                        {
                            new HmmlcString(y[0])
                        };
                }
                else
                {
                    first[y] = new FiniteSet<HmmlcString>();
                }
            }
        }
    }

    FiniteSet<Symbol> erasableNonterminals =
        G.DetermineErasableNonterminals();
```

```
    bool change;
    do
    {
        change = false;

        foreach (ContextFreeRule r in G.Rules)
        {
            foreach (
                HmmlcString u in r.RightHandSide.GetAllPrefixes())
            {
                if (HasOnlyGivenSymbols(u, erasableNonterminals))
                {
                    FiniteSet<HmmlcString> f =
                        first[r.RightHandSide.GetSuffix(
                            r.RightHandSide.Length - u.Length)];

                    if (r.RightHandSide != HmmlcString.Empty)
                    {
                        if (ExtendSet(f,
                            first[new HmmlcString
                                r.RightHandSide[u.Length]])))
                        {
                            change = true;
                        }
                    }

                    if (ExtendSet(first[new HmmlcString(
                            r.LeftHandSide)], f))
                    {
                        change = true;
                    }
                }
            }
        }
    }
    while (change);

    return first;
}
```

The ε-rules deserve our special attention because they may give rise to derivations that erase substrings of sentential forms, and this possible erasure complicates the selection of the next applied rule. Indeed, consider a CFG, $G = ({}_G\Sigma, {}_GR)$, and suppose that $A \to x \in {}_GR$ with $x \Rightarrow^*_{lm} \varepsilon$. At this point, the parser needs to decide whether from A, it should make either $A \Rightarrow_{lm} x \Rightarrow^*_{lm} \varepsilon$ or a derivation that produces a non-empty string. To make this decision, we need to determine the set follow (A) containing all terminals that can follow A in any sentential form; if this set contains the current input symbol that is out of first(x), the parser simulates $A \Rightarrow_{lm} x \Rightarrow^*_{lm} \varepsilon$. In addition, to express that a sentential form ends with A, we include $\lhd$ into follow (A) (see Convention 17.1 for $\lhd$).

Definition 17.2. *Let $G = ({}_G\Sigma, {}_GR)$ be a CFG. For every $A \in {}_GN$,*

$$\text{follow}\,(A) = \{a \in {}_G\Delta \cup \{\lhd\} \mid Aa \in \text{substrings}\,(F(G)\{\lhd\})\},$$

where $F(G)$ denotes the set of sentential forms of G (see Definition 6.1).

Basic Idea. We next construct follow (A) for every $A \in N$. As S is a sentential form, we initialize follow (S) with $\{\lhd\}$. Consider any $B \to uAv \in {}_GR$. If a is a terminal in first(v), then $Aa \in$ substrings $(F(G))$, so we add a to follow (A). In addition, if ε is in first(v), then $v \Rightarrow^*_{lm} \varepsilon$ and, consequently, follow $(B) \subseteq$ follow (A), so we add all symbols from follow (B) to follow (A). Keep extending all the follow sets in this way until no symbol can be added to any of them.

Implementation 17.2. We now extend module `Parsing` introduced in Implementation 17.1 with an implementation of Algorithm 17.4.

At one point, we have to add symbols from a first set to a follow set. In our implementation of first, the result is a set of strings (`FiniteSet<HmmlcString>`) rather than a set of symbols (`FiniteSet<Symbol>`), to account for the empty string. We could use a `FiniteSet<HmmlcString>` for follow as well, but this makes little sense as it would only ever contain single-symbol strings. Instead, we convert first sets to sets of symbols (excluding ε) before performing the extension. This is possible because each member is either the empty string, which is skipped, or a string of length 1, in which case we take its first (and only) symbol.

Algorithm 17.4: follow

Input: A context-free grammar, $G = ({}_G\Sigma, {}_GR)$, and first(u) for every
$u \in {}_G\Delta \cup \{\text{lhs}(r) \mid r \in {}_GR\} \cup \{y \mid y \in \text{suffixes}(\text{rhs}(r)) \text{ with } r \in {}_GR\}$.
Output: Sets follow (u) for all $A \in {}_GN$.

begin
  set follow $(S) = \{\lhd\}$, and
  set all the other constructed follow sets to $\emptyset$
  repeat
    if $r \in {}_GR$ *and* $Au \in$ suffixes(rhs(r)), *where* $A \in {}_GN$, $u \in {}_G\Sigma^*$ **then**
      add the symbols in (first(u) $- \{\varepsilon\}$) to follow (A)
      if $\varepsilon \in$ first(u) **then**
        add the symbols in follow (lhs(r)) to follow (A)
      end
    end
  until no change
end

```
private static FiniteSet<Symbol> ExcludeEpsilon(
    FiniteSet<HmmlcString> A)
{
    var result = new FiniteSet<Symbol>();

    foreach (HmmlcString s in A)
    {
        if (s != HmmlcString.Empty)
        {
            result.Add(s[0]);
        }
    }

    return result;
}
```

Making use of the previous method, we now implement Algorithm 17.4. Recall that symbol `Parsing.InputEnd` and method `ExtendSet` were added in Implementation 17.1. Similar to the implementation of first, we represent the result as a generic .NET `Dictionary`.

```
public static IDictionary<Symbol, FiniteSet<Symbol>>
    ComputeFollowSets(ContextFreeGrammar G,
                      IDictionary<HmmlcString,
                      FiniteSet<HmmlcString>> first)
{
    var follow = new Dictionary<Symbol, FiniteSet<Symbol>>();

    foreach (Symbol A in G.Nonterminals)
    {
        follow[A] = new FiniteSet<Symbol>();
    }

    follow[G.StartSymbol]
        = new FiniteSet<Symbol>  Parsing.InputEnd ;

    bool change;
    do
    {
        change = false;

        foreach (ContextFreeRule r in G.Rules)
        {
            foreach (
                HmmlcString Au in r.RightHandSide.GetAllSuffixes())
            {
                if (Au != HmmlcString.Empty)
                {
                    Symbol A = Au[0];
                    if (G.Nonterminals.Contains(A))
                    {
                        HmmlcString u = Au.GetSuffix(Au.Length - 1);
```

```
                        if (ExtendSet(follow[A],
                                      ExcludeEpsilon(first[u])))
                        {
                            change = true;
                        }

                        if (first[u].Contains(HmmlcString.Empty))
                        {
                            if (ExtendSet(follow[A],
                                          follow[r.LeftHandSide]))
                            {
                                change = true;
                            }
                        }
                    }
                }
            }
        }
    }
    while (change);

    return follow;
}
```

Based on the first and follow sets, we define the predictive sets as follows:

Definition 17.3. *For each* $r \in {}_G R$*, its* predictive set *is denoted by* predictive-set (r) *and defined as follows:*

(i) *If* $\varepsilon \notin$ first(rhs(r)), predictive-set $(r) =$ first(rhs(r)).
(ii) *If* $\varepsilon \in$ first(rhs(r)), predictive-set $(r) =$ (first(rhs(r)) $- \{\varepsilon\}) \cup$ follow (lhs(r)).

17.2.2 LL grammars

Reconsider the discussion in the very beginning of this section. Recall that G, M, and w denote a CFG, a G-based top-down parser, and an input string w, respectively. Suppose that M has already simulated the beginning of the leftmost derivation $S \Rightarrow^*_{lm} tAv$ for an input string taz, where a is the current input symbol and $taz = w$, and it needs to select one of several different A-rules to rewrite A in tAv and, thereby, make another step. If for an A-rule r, $a \in$ predictive-set (r) and for any other A-rule p, $a \notin$ predictive-set (p), M deterministically selects r. This idea leads to the next definition of LL grammars.

Definition 17.4. *A CFG* $G = ({}_G\Sigma, {}_G R)$ *is an* LL grammar *if for each* $A \in N$*, any two different A-rules,* $p, q \in {}_G R$ *and* $p \neq q$*, satisfy* predictive-set $(p) \cap$ predictive-set $(q) = \emptyset$.

As already noted, in *LL grammars*, the first *L* stands for a *l*eft-to-right scan of symbols and the other *L* stands for a *l*eftmost derivation. Sometimes, in greater detail, the literature refers to the LL grammars as *LL(1) grammars* to point out that the top-down parsers based on these grammars always look at one input symbol during each step of the parsing process. Indeed, these grammars represent a special case of *LL(k) grammars*, where $k \geq 1$, which underlie parsers that make a k-symbol lookahead. In this introductory text, however, we discuss only LL(1) grammars and simply refer to them as LL grammars for brevity.

Example 17.4. *Consider the CFG J (see Convention 17.2) defined as*

$$\begin{aligned}
1 &: S \rightarrow AC, \\
2 &: C \rightarrow \vee AC, \\
3 &: C \rightarrow \varepsilon, \\
4 &: A \rightarrow BD, \\
5 &: D \rightarrow \wedge BD, \\
6 &: D \rightarrow \varepsilon, \\
7 &: B \rightarrow (S), \\
8 &: B \rightarrow i.
\end{aligned}$$

Algorithm 17.3 first. *For each rule in J, we construct* first(u) *for every* $u \in {}_J\Delta \cup \{\text{lhs}(r) \mid r \in {}_JR\} \cup \{y \mid y \in \text{suffixes}(\text{rhs}(r))$ *with* $r \in {}_JR\}$ *by Algorithm 17.3. First, we set* first(a) $= \{a\}$ *for every* $a \in \{i, (,), \vee, \wedge\} \cup \{\varepsilon\}$. *Consider* $B \rightarrow i$. *By the repeat loop of Algorithm 17.3, as* first(i) $= \{i\}$, *we include* i *into* first(B). *As* $i \in$ first(B) *and* $A \rightarrow BD \in {}_JR$, *we add* i *to* first(BD) *as well. Complete this construction as an exercise. However, to construct* predictive-set (r) *for each* $r \in {}_JR$, *we only need* $\{\text{first}(\text{rhs}(r)) \mid r \in {}_JR\}$, *which represents a subset of all the* first *sets constructed by Algorithm 17.3. The members of* $\{\text{first}(\text{rhs}(r)) \mid r \in {}_JR\}$ *are listed in the second column of Table 17.3.*

Algorithm 17.4 follow. *Consider* first(u) *for each* $u \in \{y \mid y \in$ *suffs*(rhs(r)) *with* $r \in {}_JR\}$. *We construct* follow (X), *for every* $X \in {}_JN$ *by Algorithm 17.4 as follows: we initially have* follow (S) $= \{\lhd\}$. *As* $B \rightarrow (S) \in {}_JR$ *and* $) \in$ first()), *we add*) *to* follow (S). *Since (1)* $S \rightarrow AC \in {}_JR$, *(2)* $\varepsilon \in$ first(C), *and (3)* follow (S) *contains*) *and* $\lhd$, *we add*) *and* $\lhd$ *to* follow (A). *As* $\vee \in$ first(C), *we add* $\vee$ *to* follow (A) *too. Complete this construction as an exercise. The third column of Table 17.3 contains* follow (lhs(r)) *for each* $r \in {}_JR$.

Table 17.3 Predictive sets for rules in ${}_JR$

Rule r	**first(rhs(**r**))**	**follow(lhs(**r**))**	**predictive-set(**r**)**
$S \rightarrow AC$	i, (	), $\lhd$	i, (
$C \rightarrow \vee AC$	$\vee$	), $\lhd$	$\vee$
$C \rightarrow \varepsilon$	ε	), $\lhd$	), $\lhd$
$A \rightarrow BD$	i, (	$\vee$,), $\lhd$	i, (
$D \rightarrow \wedge BD$	$\wedge$	$\vee$,), $\lhd$	$\wedge$
$D \rightarrow \varepsilon$	ε	$\vee$,), $\lhd$	$\vee$,), $\lhd$
$B \rightarrow (S)$	(	$\wedge$, $\vee$,), $\lhd$	(
$B \rightarrow i$	i	$\wedge$, $\vee$,), $\lhd$	i

Predictive sets *(Definition 17.3). The fourth column of Table 17.3 contains the set* predictive-set (r) *for each* $r \in {}_JR$. *Notice that* follow $(\mathrm{lhs}(r))$ *is needed to determine* predictive-set (r) *if* $\varepsilon \in \mathrm{first}(\mathrm{rhs}(r))$ *because at this point,* predictive-set $(r) = (\mathrm{first}(\mathrm{rhs}(r)) - \{\varepsilon\}) \cup \mathrm{follow}\,(\mathrm{lhs}(r))$; *if* $\varepsilon \notin \mathrm{first}(\mathrm{rhs}(r))$, *it is not needed because* predictive-set $(r) = \mathrm{first}(\mathrm{rhs}(r))$ *(see Definition 17.3). Take, for instance,* $S \to AC \in {}_JR$ *with* $\mathrm{first}(AC)) = \{i, (\}$. *As* $\varepsilon \notin \mathrm{first}(\mathrm{rhs}(S \to AC))$, predictive-set $(S \to AC) = \mathrm{first}(AC) = \{i, (\}$. *Consider* $C \to \varepsilon \in {}_JR$ *with* $\mathrm{first}(\varepsilon) = \{\varepsilon\}$ *and* follow $(C) = \{), \lhd\}$. *As* $\varepsilon \in \mathrm{first}(\mathrm{rhs}(C \to \varepsilon))$, predictive-set $(C \to \varepsilon) = (\mathrm{first}(\varepsilon) - \{\varepsilon\}) \cup \mathrm{follow}\,(C) = \emptyset \cup \{), \lhd\} = \{), \lhd\}$. *Complete this construction as an exercise.*

LL grammar. *Observe that* predictive-set $(C \to \vee AC) \cap$ predictive-set $(C \to \varepsilon) = \{\vee\} \cap \{), \lhd\} = \emptyset$. *Analogously,* predictive-set $(D \to \wedge BD) \cap$ predictive-set $(D \to \varepsilon) = \emptyset$ *and* predictive-set $(B \to (S)) \cap$ predictive-set $(B \to i) = \emptyset$. *Thus, J is an LL grammar.*

17.2.3 Predictive parsing

In this section, we first describe the recursive-descent parsing method. Then, we use the LL grammars and their predictive sets to create predictive tables and deterministic top-down parsers driven by these tables. Finally, we explain how to handle errors in predictive parsing.

17.2.4 Predictive recursive-descent parsing

Given an LL grammar, $G = ({}_G\Sigma, {}_GR)$, we next explain how to construct a *G-based predictive recursive-descent parser*, which makes use of programming routines SUCCESS and ERROR, described in the next convention.

Convention 17.4. *SUCCESS announces a successful completion of the parsing process, while ERROR announces a syntax error in the parsed program.*

It is worth noting that the following parser moves back to the symbol preceding the current input symbol. As demonstrated shortly, it performs this return when a rule selection is made by using a symbol from the follow set; at this point, this symbol is not actually used up, so the parser needs to move back to the symbol preceding *ins*.

Reconsider Algorithm 17.1, which turns a CFG G to a G-based top-down parser M as a PDA, which requires, strictly speaking, an implementation of a pushdown list. As a crucial advantage, *recursive descent*—that is, a top-down parsing method discussed next—frees us from this implementation. Indeed, the pushdown list is invisible in this method because it is actually realized by the pushdown used to support recursion in the programming language in which we write the recursive-descent parser. As this method does not require an explicit manipulation with the pushdown list, it comes as no surprise that it is popular in practice. Therefore, in its next description, we pay a special attention to its implementation.

Basic Idea. Consider a programming language defined by an LL grammar G. Let $w = t_1 \cdots t_j t_{j+1} \cdots t_m$ be an input string. Like any top-down parser, a G-based recursive-descent parser simulates the construction of a derivation tree with its frontier equal to w by using the grammatical rules, so it starts from the root and works down to the leaves, reading w in a left-to-right way. In terms of derivations, the parser looks for the leftmost derivation of w. To find it, for each nonterminal Y, the parser has a Boolean function, *rd-function* Y, which simulates rewriting the leftmost nonterminal Y. More specifically, with the right-hand side of a Y-rule, $Y \rightarrow X_1 \cdots X_i X_{i+1} \cdots X_n$, *rd-function* Y proceeds from X_1 to X_n. Assume that *rd-function* Y currently works with X_i and that t_j is the input symbol. At this point, depending on whether X_i is a terminal or a nonterminal, this function works as follows:

- If X_i is a terminal, *rd-function* Y matches X_i against t_j. If $X_i = t_j$, it reads t_j and proceeds to X_{i+1} and t_{j+1}. If $X_i \neq t_j$, a syntax error occurs, which the parser has to handle.
- If X_i is a nonterminal, the parser finds out whether there is an X_i-rule r satisfying $t_j \in$ predictive-set (r). If so, the parser calls *rd-function* X_i, which simulates rewriting X_i according to r. If not, a syntax error occurs, and the parser has to handle it.

The parser starts the parsing process from *rd-function* S, which corresponds to the start symbol of G, and ends when it eventually returns to this function after completely reading w. If during this entire process no syntax error occurs, G-based recursive-descent parser has found the leftmost derivation of w, which thus represents a syntactically well-formed program; otherwise, w is syntactically incorrect.

As this method does not require explicitly manipulating a pushdown list, it is very popular in practice; in particular, it is suitable for parsing declarations and general program flow as the next implementation illustrates. This implementation describes every *rd-function* Y as a C# function

```
bool Y()
{
    .
    .
    .
}
```

Implementation 17.3. First, we define a common interface for all parser implementations throughout this chapter. A parser takes as its input a string and returns either SUCCESS or ERROR.

```
public enum ParseResult
{
    Success,
    Error
}

public interface IParser
{
    ParseResult Parse(HmmlcString input);
}
```

Table 17.4 Rules in $_J R$ together with their predictive sets

Rule r	predictive-set (r)
$S \to AC$	i, (
$C \to \vee AC$	$\vee$
$C \to \varepsilon$	), $\lhd$
$A \to BD$	i, (
$D \to \wedge BD$	$\wedge$
$D \to \varepsilon$	$\vee$,), $\lhd$
$B \to (S)$	(
$B \to i$	i

A predictive recursive-descent parser which implements this interface might have the following structure. Note that we store the whole input and keep track of the current input position by index.

```
public class PredictiveRecursiveDescentParser : IParser
{
    private HmmlcString input;
    private int inputPosition;
    private void AdvanceInput() { inputPosition++; }
    private Symbol ins { get { return input[inputPosition]; } }

    public ParseResult Parse(HmmlcString input)
    {
        this.input = input;
        this.inputPosition = 0;

        // implementation for a specific context-free grammar
        // is to be placed here
        throw new NotImplementedException();
    }
}
```

Reconsider the LL grammar J (see Convention 17.2 and Example 17.4). Table 17.4 repeats its rules together with the corresponding predictive sets.

Next, we construct a J-based recursive-descent parser as a collection of Boolean *rd-functions* corresponding to nonterminals S, A, B, C, and D. By using the predictive sets, we make this construction, so the parser always selects the next applied rule deterministically.

Consider the start symbol S and the only S-rule $S \to AC$ with predictive-set $(S \to AC) = \{i, (\}$. As a result, *rd-function* S has this form

```
private bool S()
{
    if (ins == "i" || ins == "(")
```

```
    {
        if (A())
        {
            if (C())
            {
                return true;
            }
        }
    }

    return false;
}
```

Consider the two C-rules that include $C \to \vee AC$ with predictive-set $(C \to \vee AC) = \{\vee\}$ and $C \to \varepsilon$ with predictive-set $(C \to \varepsilon) = \{), \lhd\}$. Therefore, *rd-function* C selects $C \to \vee AC$ if the input symbol is $\vee$ and this function selects $C \to \varepsilon$ if this symbol is in $\{), \lhd\}$. If the input symbol differs from $\vee$,), or $\lhd$, the syntax error occurs. Thus, *rd-function* C has this form

```
private bool C()
{
    if (ins == "v")
    {
        // C -> vAC

        AdvanceInput();

        if (A())
        {
            if (C())
            {
                return true;
            }
        }
    }
    else if (ins == ")" || ins == Parsing.InputEnd)
    {
        // C -> eps
        // ) and <| are in follow(C)

        return true;
    }

    return false;
}
```

There exists a single A-rule of the form $A \to BD$ in J with predictive-set $(A \to BD) = \{i, (\}$. Its *rd-function* A, given next, is similar to *rd-function* S.

```
private bool A()
{
    if (ins == "i" || ins == "(")
    {
        if (B())
        {
            if (D())
            {
                return true;
            }
        }
    }

    return false;
}
```

Consider the two D-rules $D \to \wedge BD$ with *predict*$(D \to \wedge BD) = \{\wedge\}$ and $D \to \varepsilon$ with predictive-set $(D \to \varepsilon) = \{\wedge,), \lhd\}$. Therefore, *rd-function D* selects $D \to \wedge BD$ if the input symbol is $\wedge$, and it selects $D \to \varepsilon$ if this symbol is in $\{\wedge,), \lhd\}$. The *rd-function D* has thus this form

```
private bool D()
{
    if (ins == "^")
    {
        // B -> ^BD

        AdvanceInput();

        if (B())
        {
            if (D())
            {
                return true;
            }
        }
    }
    else if (ins == "v" || ins == ")" || ins == Parsing.InputEnd)
    {
        // D -> eps
        // v, ), <| are in follow(D)

        return true;
    }

    return false;
}
```

Finally, consider the *B*-rules $B \to (S)$ with predictive-set $(B \to (S)) = \{(\}$ and $B \to i$ with predictive-set $(B \to i) = \{i\}$. Therefore, *rd-function B* selects $B \to (S)$ if the input symbol is (, and this function selects $B \to i$ if the input symbol is *i*. If the input symbol differs from (or *i*, the syntax error occurs. Thus, *rd-function B* has this form

```
private bool B()
{
    if (ins == "(")
    {
        AdvanceInput();

        if (S())
        {
            // B -> S

            if (ins == ")")
            {
                AdvanceInput();
                return true;
            }
        }
    }
    else if (ins == "i")
    {
        AdvanceInput();
        return true;
    }

    return false;
}
```

Having all these functions in the parser, we can now implement the `Parse` method based on the following simple `if` statement, which decides whether the source program is syntactically correct by the final Boolean value of *rd-function S*:

```
public ParseResult Parse(HmmlcString input)
{
    this.input = input;
    this.inputPosition = 0;

    if (S())
    {
        return ParseResult.Success;
    }
    else
    {
        return ParseResult.Error;
    }
}
```

In the previous functions, we frequently make an advance within the string of input symbols.

17.2.5 Predictive table-driven parsing

In the predictive recursive-descent parsing, for every nonterminal A and the corresponding A-rules, there exists a specific Boolean function, so any grammatical change usually necessitates reprogramming several of these functions. Therefore, unless a change of this kind is ruled out, we often prefer an alternative *predictive table-driven parsing* based on a single general control procedure that is completely based upon a predictive table. At this point, a change of the grammar only implies an adequate modification of the table, while the control procedure remains unchanged. As opposed to the predictive recursive-descent parsing, however, this parsing method maintains a pushdown explicitly, not implicitly via recursive calls like in predictive recursive-descent parsing.

Consider an LL grammar G. Just like a general top-down parser (see Algorithm 17.1), a *G-based predictive table-driven parser* is underlain by a PDA, $M = ({}_M\Sigma, {}_MR)$ (see Definition 7.1). However, a strictly mathematical specification of M, including all its rules in ${}_MR$, would be somewhat tedious and lengthy from a practical point of view. Therefore, to make the parser easy to implement, we describe the parser in the way announced in Convention 17.3—that is, M is specified as an algorithm together with a *G-based predictive table*, denoted by ${}_GPT$, by which the parser determines a move from every configuration. The rows and columns of ${}_GPT$ are denoted by the members of ${}_GN$ and ${}_G\Sigma \cup \{\lhd\}$, respectively. Each of its entry contains a member of ${}_GR$, or it is blank. More precisely, for each $A \in {}_GN$ and each $t \in {}_G\Delta$, if there exists $r \in {}_GR$ such that lhs(r) $= A$ and $t \in$ predictive-set (r), ${}_GPT[A, t] = r$; otherwise, ${}_GPT[A, t]$ is blank, which signalizes a syntax error. Making use of ${}_GPT$, M works with the input string as described next. Before giving this description, we want to point out once again that G represents an LL grammar. Indeed, unless G is an LL grammar, we might place more than one rule into a single ${}_GPT$ entry and, thereby, make M nondeterministic.

Let X be the *pd* top symbol. Initially, set *pd* to $\rhd S$. Perform one of actions (1)–(5), given as follows:

1. If $X \in {}_G\Delta$ and $X = ins$, the *pd* top symbol is a terminal coinciding with *ins*, so M pops the pushdown by removing X from its top and, simultaneously, advances to the next input symbol.
2. If $X \in {}_G\Delta$ and $X \neq ins$, the pushdown top symbol is a terminal that differs from *ins*, so the parser announces an error by ERROR.
3. If $X \in {}_G\Delta$ and ${}_GPT[X, ins] = r$ with $r \in {}_GR$, where lhs(r) $= X$, M expands the pushdown by replacing X with reversal (rhs(r)).
4. If $X \in {}_G\Delta$ and ${}_GPT[X, ins]$ is blank, M announces an error by ERROR.
5. If $\rhd = X$ and $ins = \lhd$, the pushdown is empty and the input string is completely read, so M halts and announces a successful completion of parsing by SUCCESS.

Throughout the rest of this section, we also often make use of the operations EXPAND and POP. We next define them in terms of the general version of a top-down parser constructed by Algorithm 17.1.

Definition 17.5. *Let $G = ({}_G\Sigma, {}_GR)$ be a CFG. Let $M = ({}_M\Sigma, {}_MR)$ be a PDA that represents a G-based top-down parser produced by Algorithm 17.1.*

(i) *Let $r: A \rightarrow x \in {}_GR$.* EXPAND (r) *applies* $A\diamond \rightarrow$ reversal $(x)\diamond$ *in* M.
(ii) POP *applies* $a\diamond a \rightarrow \diamond$ *in* M.

Less formally, EXPAND $(A \rightarrow x)$ replaces the *pd* top with the reversal of x. If *ins* coincides with the *pd* top, POP removes the *pd* top and, simultaneously, advances to the next input symbol.

Implementation 17.4. Before we can implement a predictive table-driven parser, we need a representation of the predictive table. The following implementation makes use of standard generic `Dictionary` from the .NET Framework, in two layers. The first layer maps a symbol `A` to the corresponding table row, and the second selects the appropriate entry within that row for a symbol `t`. The entry is either a `ContextFreeRule`, or **`null`** which represents a blank entry.

```
public class PredictiveTable
{
    private Dictionary<Symbol, Dictionary<Symbol, ContextFreeRule>>
        table = new Dictionary<Symbol, Dictionary<Symbol,
                                              ContextFreeRule>>();

    public ContextFreeRule this[Symbol A, Symbol t]
    {
        get
        {
            Dictionary<Symbol, ContextFreeRule> row;
            if (table.TryGetValue(A, out row))
            {
                ContextFreeRule rule;
                if (row.TryGetValue(t, out rule))
                {
                    return rule;
                }
                else
                {
                    return null;
                }
            }
            else
            {
                return null;
            }
        }
        set
        {
            Dictionary<Symbol, ContextFreeRule> row;
            if (!table.TryGetValue(A, out row))
```

```
            {
                row = new Dictionary<Symbol, ContextFreeRule>();
                table[A] = row;
            }

            row[t] = value;
        }
    }
}
```

A predictive table-driven parser (see Algorithm 17.5) is based on a CFG and its predictive table.

```
public class PredictiveTableDrivenParser : IParser
{
    private ContextFreeGrammar G;
    private PredictiveTable PT;

    public PredictiveTableDrivenParser(ContextFreeGrammar G,
                                       PredictiveTable PT)
    {
        this.G = G;
        this.PT = PT;
    }
}
```

Following the interface `IParser` defined in Implementation 17.3, we can now implement Algorithm 17.5 as follows:

```
public ParseResult Parse(HmmlcString input)
{
    var pd = new Stack<Symbol>();

    pd.Push(Parsing.PdBottom);
    pd.Push(G.StartSymbol);

    int inputPosition = 0;

    while (true)
    {
        Symbol ins = input[inputPosition];
        Symbol X = pd.Peek();

        if (G.Terminals.Contains(X))
        {
            if (X == ins)
            {
                // pop
                pd.Pop();
                inputPosition++;
            }
            else
            {
```

Algorithm 17.5: Predictive table-driven parser

Input: An LL grammar G, its predictive table ${}_GPT$, and an input string, $w\lhd$, where $w \in {}_G\Sigma^*$.
Output: SUCCESS if $w \in L(G)$, and ERROR if $w \notin L(G)$.

```
begin
    set pd to ▷S
    repeat
        let X denote the current pd top symbol
        switch X do
            case in GΔ do
                if X = ins then
                    POP                                   // pop pd
                else
                    ERROR  // the pd top symbol differs from
                      ins
                end
            end
            case in GN do
                if GPT[X, ins] = r with r ∈ GR then
                    EXPAND (r)
                else
                    ERROR                  // the table entry is blank
                end
            end
            case ▷ do
                if ins = ◁ then
                    SUCCESS
                else
                    ERROR  // the pushdown is empty, but the
                      input string is not completely read
                end
            end
        end
    until SUCCESS or ERROR
end
```

```
            return ParseResult.Error;
        }
    }
    else if (G.Nonterminals.Contains(X))
    {
        ContextFreeRule r = PT[X, ins];
```

```
            if (r != null)
            {
                // expand(r)
                pd.Pop();
                foreach (Symbol a in r.RightHandSide.Reverse())
                {
                    pd.Push(a);
                }
            }
            else
            {
                // table entry is blank
                return ParseResult.Error;
            }
        }
        else if (X == Parsing.PdBottom)
        {
            if (ins == Parsing.InputEnd)
            {
                return ParseResult.Success;
            }
            else
            {
                // empty pushdown, but input is not completely read
                return ParseResult.Error;
            }
        }
        else
        {
            return ParseResult.Error;
        }
    }
}
```

Observe that, in contrast to Implementation 17.3, an explicit implementation of a pushdown is required; here we use a standard generic `Stack` provided by .NET Framework so that we do not need to reimplement it ourselves.

As explained in Section 17.1, apart from deciding whether $w \in L(G)$, a G-based top-down parser frequently produces the left parse of w—that is, the sequence of rules according to which the leftmost derivation of w is made in G provided that $w \in L(G)$. Consider the parser represented by Algorithm 17.5. To obtain left parses, extend this parser by writing out r whenever this algorithm performs EXPAND (r), where $r \in {}_{G}R$. In this way, we produce the left parse of an input string in the conclusion of the next example.

Example 17.5. *Reconsider the LL grammar J (see Example 17.4). Table 17.4 recalls its rules with the corresponding predictive sets.*

By using the predictive sets corresponding to these rules, we construct the predictive table ${}_{J}PT$ *(see Table 17.5).*

Table 17.5 $_J PT$

	$\vee$	$\wedge$	(	)	i	$\lhd$
S			1		1	
C	2			3		3
A			4		4	
D	6	5		6		6
B			7		8	
$\rhd$						☺

Table 17.6 Predictive table-driven parsing

Configuration	**Table entry and rule**	**Action**	**Sentential form**
			$\underline{S}$
$\rhd S\diamond i \wedge i \vee i \lhd$	$[S,i] = 1\colon S \to AC$	EXPAND (1)	$\Rightarrow_{lm} \underline{A}C$ [1]
$\rhd CA\diamond i \wedge i \vee i \lhd$	$[A,i] = 4\colon A \to BD$	EXPAND (4)	$\Rightarrow_{lm} \underline{B}DC$ [4]
$\rhd CDB\diamond i \wedge i \vee i \lhd$	$[B,i] = 8\colon B \to i$	EXPAND (8)	$\Rightarrow_{lm} i\underline{D}C$ [8]
$\rhd CDi\diamond i \wedge i \vee i \lhd$		POP	
$\rhd CD\diamond \wedge i \vee i \lhd$	$[D,\wedge] = 5\colon D \to \wedge BD$	EXPAND (5)	$\Rightarrow_{lm} i \wedge \underline{B}DC$ [5]
$\rhd CDB \wedge \diamond \wedge i \vee i \lhd$		POP	
$\rhd CDB\diamond i \vee i \lhd$	$[B,i] = 8\colon B \to i$	EXPAND (8)	$\Rightarrow_{lm} i \wedge i\underline{D}C$ [8]
$\rhd CDi\diamond i \vee i \lhd$		POP	
$\rhd CD\diamond \vee i \lhd$	$[D,\vee] = 6\colon D \to \varepsilon$	EXPAND (6)	$\Rightarrow_{lm} i \wedge i\underline{C}$ [6]
$\rhd C\diamond \vee i \lhd$	$[C,\vee] = 2\colon C \to \vee AC$	EXPAND (2)	$\Rightarrow_{lm} i \wedge i \vee \underline{A}C$ [2]
$\rhd CA \vee \diamond \vee i \lhd$		POP	
$\rhd CA\diamond i \lhd$	$[A,i] = 4\colon A \to BD$	EXPAND (4)	$\Rightarrow_{lm} i \wedge i \vee \underline{B}DC$ [4]
$\rhd CDB\diamond i \lhd$	$[B,i] = 8\colon B \to i$	EXPAND (8)	$\Rightarrow_{lm} i \wedge i \vee i\underline{D}C$ [8]
$\rhd CDi\diamond i \lhd$		POP	
$\rhd CD\diamond \lhd$	$[D,\lhd] = 6\colon D \to \varepsilon$	EXPAND (6)	$\Rightarrow_{lm} i \wedge i \vee i\underline{C}$ [6]
$\rhd C\diamond \lhd$	$[C,\lhd] = 3\colon C \to \varepsilon$	EXPAND (3)	$\Rightarrow_{lm} i \wedge i \vee i$ [3]
$\rhd\diamond\lhd$	$[\rhd,\lhd] =$ ☺	SUCCESS	

Take $i \wedge i \vee i$. Algorithm 17.5 parses this string as described in Table 17.6. The first column gives the configurations of the parser. The second column states the corresponding $_J PT$ entries together with the rules they contain. The third column gives the action made by the parser. The fourth column gives the sentential forms derived in the leftmost derivation.

Suppose that the parser should produce the left parse of $i \wedge i \vee i$—that is, the sequence of rules according to which the leftmost derivation of $i \wedge i \vee i$ is made in J (see (1) in the beginning of Section 17.1). The parser can easily obtain this parse by writing out the applied rules according to which the expansions are performed during the parsing process. Specifically, take the sequence of rules in the second column of Table 17.6 to obtain 14858624863 *as the left parse of $i \wedge i \vee i$ in J. Indeed,* $S \Rightarrow_{lm}^{*} i \wedge i \vee i$ [14858624863] *in J.*

Before closing this example, let us point out that from Algorithm 17.5 and $_J PT$, we could obtain a strictly mathematical specification of the parser as a PDA M. In essence, M has the form of the parser constructed in Algorithm 17.1 in Section 17.1. That is, M makes SUCCESS by $\triangleright\Diamond\triangleleft \rightarrow \Diamond$. If a pair of the pd *top X and the current input symbol b leads to ERROR, $_M R$ has no rule with $X\Diamond b$ on its left-hand side. It performs POP by rules of the form $a\Diamond a \rightarrow \Diamond$ for each $a \in {}_J\Delta$. Finally, if a pair of the* pd *top and the current input symbol leads to* EXPAND (r), *where r is a rule from $_J R$, M makes this expansion according to r by $A\Diamond \rightarrow$* reversal (x)$\Diamond$. *For instance, as $_J PT[S, i] = 1$ and $1: S \rightarrow AC \in {}_J R$, $_M R$ has $S\Diamond \rightarrow CA\Diamond$ to make an expansion according to* 1. *A completion of this mathematical specification of M is left as an exercise. However, not only is this completion a tedious task, but also the resulting parser M specified in this way is difficult to understand what it actually does with its incredibly many rules. That is why, as already pointed out (see Convention 17.3), we always prefer the description of a parser as an algorithm together with a parsing table throughout the rest of this book.*

17.2.6 Handling errors

Of course, a predictive parser struggles to handle each syntax error occurrence as best as it can. It carefully diagnoses the error and issues an appropriate error message. Then, it recovers from the error by slightly modifying *pd* or skipping some input symbols. After the recovery, the parser resumes its analysis of the syntactically erroneous program, possibly discovering further syntax errors. Most importantly, no matter what it does, the parser has to avoid any endless loop during the error recovery so that all the input symbols are read eventually. Throughout the rest of this section, we sketch two simple and popular error-recovery methods in terms of predictive table-driven parsing while leaving their straightforward adaptation for recursive descent parsing as an exercise.

Panic-mode error recovery. Let $G = ({}_G\Sigma, {}_G R)$ be an LL grammar, and let M be a predictive table-driven parser. For every nonterminal $A \in {}_G N$, we define a set of synchronizing input symbols as synchronizing-set (A) = first(A) ∪ follow (A). Suppose that M occurs in a configuration with X as the *pd* top and *ins* as the input symbol when a syntax error occurs. At this point, this error recovery method handles the error as follows:

- If $X \in {}_G N$ and $_G PT[X, ins]$ is blank, skip the input symbols until the first occurrence of t that belongs to synchronizing-set (X). If $t \in$ first(X), resume parsing according to the rule in $_G PT[X, t]$ without any further change. If $t \in$ follow (X), pop the *pd* top and resume parsing.
- If $X \in {}_G\Delta$ and $X \neq ins$, pop the *pd* top, X, and resume parsing.

As an exercise, we discuss further variants of this method, most of which are based on alternative definitions of the synchronizing sets.

Ad-hoc recovery. Let $G = ({}_G\Sigma, {}_G R)$ be an LL grammar, and let M be a predictive table-driven parser. In this method, we design a specific recovery routine, RECOVER [X, t], for every error-implying pair of a top *pd* symbol X and an input symbol t. That is, if X and t are the two different input symbols, we call RECOVER $[X, t]$. We also design RECOVER $[X, t]$ if $X \in {}_GN \cup \{\lhd\}$ and ${}_GPT[X, t]$ is blank. A call to RECOVER $[X, t]$ figures out the most probable mistake that leads to the given syntax error occurrence, issues an error message, and decides on a recovery procedure that takes a plausible action to resume parsing. Typically, RECOVER $[X, t]$ skips a tiny portion of the input string or modifies *pd* by changing, inserting, or deleting some symbols; whatever it does, however, the recovery procedure needs to guarantee that this modification surely avoids any infinite loop so that the parser eventually proceeds its normal process. Otherwise, the parser with this type of error recovery works just like Algorithm 17.5 except that if the error occurs in a configuration such that its *pd* top and the input symbol t represent an error-implying pair, it performs the RECOVER routine corresponding to this pair. In this way, the parser detects and recovers from the syntax error, after which it resumes the parsing process. Of course, once the parser detects a syntax error and recovers from it, it can never proclaim that the program is syntactically correct later during the resumed parsing process. That is, even if the parser eventually reaches ${}_GPT[\rhd, \lhd] = ☺$ after a recovery from a syntax error, it performs ERROR, not SUCCESS.

Example 17.6. *Return to the LL grammar J (see Example 17.4), defined as*

$$
\begin{aligned}
1 &: S \rightarrow AC \\
2 &: C \rightarrow \vee AC \\
3 &: C \rightarrow \varepsilon \\
4 &: A \rightarrow BD \\
5 &: D \rightarrow \wedge BD \\
6 &: D \rightarrow \varepsilon \\
7 &: B \rightarrow (S) \\
8 &: B \rightarrow i
\end{aligned}
$$

Consider the J-based predictive table-driven parser discussed in Example 17.5. Take input)i. As obvious,)i $\notin L(J)$. With)i, the parser immediately interrupts its parsing because ${}_JPT[S,)]$ is blank (see Table 17.5). Reconsidering this interruption in detail, we see that if S occurs as the pd *top and) is the input symbol, the following error-recovery routine is appropriate. Design the other error-recovery routines as an exercise.*

Name RECOVER $[S,)]$
Diagnostic) *equals* ins *or no expression occurs between parentheses*
Recovery *If*) *is* ins, *skip it. If no expression occurs between* (*and*), *remove* S) *from* pd *and skip*) *as* ins; *in this way,* pd *and* ins *are changed so that the missing expression problem can be ignored. Resume parsing.*

With)i, the parser works as described in Table 17.7, in which the error-recovery information is pointed up.

Table 17.7 Predictive table-driven parsing with error recovery

Configuration	Table entry
$\triangleright S\diamond)i\triangleleft$	$[S,)]$ is blank, so RECOVER $[S,)]$
$\triangleright S\diamond i\triangleleft$	$[S, i] = 1$: $S \rightarrow AC$
$\triangleright CA\diamond i\triangleleft$	$[A, i] = 4$: $A \rightarrow BD$
$\triangleright CDB\diamond i\triangleleft$	$[B, i] = 8$: $B \rightarrow i$
$\triangleright CDi\diamond i\triangleleft$	
$\triangleright CD\diamond\triangleleft$	$[D, \triangleleft] = 6$: $D \rightarrow \varepsilon$
$\triangleright C\diamond\triangleleft$	$[C, \triangleleft] = 3$: $C \rightarrow \varepsilon$
$\triangleright\diamond\triangleleft$	ERROR

17.2.7 Exclusion of left recursion

Deterministic top-down parsing places some nontrivial restrictions upon the CFGs it is based on. Perhaps most importantly, no deterministic top-down parser can be based upon a left-recursive CFG (see Section 6.7). Indeed, suppose that in order to simulate a leftmost derivation step, a deterministic top-down parser would select a directly left-recursive rule of the form $A \rightarrow Ax$, where A is a nonterminal and x is a string (see Definition 6.14). Since the right-hand side starts with A, the parser would necessarily simulate the next leftmost derivation step according to the same rule, and it would loop in this way endlessly. As an exercise, demonstrate that general left recursion would also lead to an infinite loop like this. Therefore, deterministic top-down parsing is always underlain by non-left-recursive CFGs.

As demonstrated in Example 17.1, however, left-recursive CFGs specify some common programming-language syntactical constructions, such as conditions and expressions, in a very elegant and succinct way, so we want deterministic parsers based upon them too. Fortunately, deterministic bottom-up parsers work with left-recursive CFGs perfectly well, which brings us to the topic of the next section—bottom-up parsers.

17.3 Bottom-up parsers

A standard bottom-up parser simulates the construction of a derivation tree with frontier w in a bottom-up way, where w is an input string. That is, reading w from left to right, the parser starts from frontier w and proceeds up toward the root. To put it in terms of derivations, it builds up the rightmost derivation of w in reverse, so it starts from w and proceeds toward the start symbol. Each action during this parsing process represents a *shift* or a *reduction*. The former consists of shifting the current input symbol onto the pushdown. During a reduction, the parser selects a *handle*—that is, an occurrence of the right-hand side of a rule in the current sentential form—and after this selection, it reduces the handle to the left-hand side of the rule so that this reduction, seen in reverse, represents a rightmost derivation step.

As already pointed out in Section 17.1, in practice, we are primarily interested in deterministic bottom-up parsing, which always precisely determines how to make every single step during the parsing process. That is why we narrow our attention to fundamental deterministic bottom-up parsing methods in this section. We describe two of them. First, we describe *precedence parsing*, which is a popular deterministic bottom-up parsing method for expressions whose operators and their priorities actually control the parsing process. Then, we describe *LR parsing*, where *L* stands for a *l*eft-to-right scan of the input string and *R* stands for a *r*ightmost derivation constructed by the parser. LR parsers are as powerful as deterministic PDAs, so they represent the strongest possible parsers that work in a deterministic way. That is probably why they are so often implemented in practice, and we discuss them in detail later in this section.

Both sections have a similar structure. First, they describe fundamental parsing algorithms together with parsing tables the algorithms are based on. Then, they explain how to construct these tables. Finally, they sketch how to handle syntax errors.

Throughout the section, we use the same notions and conventions as in Section 17.2, including SUCCESS and ERROR (see Convention 17.4).

17.3.1 Operator-precedence parsing

In practice, we almost always apply an operator-precedence parser to expressions, such as the logical expressions defined by the CFG *E* (see Convention 17.2), and we explain how to make this parser based upon this CFG rather than give a general explanation. First, we explain how an operator-precedence parser based upon *E* works, describe the construction of its parsing table, and sketch how to handle syntax errors. Then, we base this parser upon other expression-generating grammars. Finally, we outline advantages and disadvantages of operator-precedence parsing from a general viewpoint.

Recall that $E = ({}_E\Sigma, {}_ER)$ is defined as

$$\begin{aligned} &1: S \rightarrow S \vee S, \\ &2: S \rightarrow S \wedge S, \\ &3: S \rightarrow (S), \\ &4: S \rightarrow i, \end{aligned}$$

where ${}_E\Delta = \{\vee, \wedge, (,), i\}$ and ${}_EN = \{S\}$. The *operator-precedence parsing table of* E, ${}_EOP$, has a relatively simple format. Indeed, this table has its rows and columns denoted by the members of ${}_E\Delta \cup \{\triangleright\}$ and ${}_E\Delta \cup \{\triangleleft\}$, respectively. Each ${}_EOP$ entry is a member of $\{\lfloor, \rfloor, \square, ☺\}$, where $\square$ denotes a blank entry. Table 17.8 presents ${}_EOP$, whose construction is explained later in this section.

17.3.2 Operator-precedence parser

An *E*-based operator-precedence parser makes shifts and reductions by operations OP-REDUCE and OP-SHIFT, respectively. We define both operations next, making use of the *pd* and *ins* notation introduced in Convention 17.1.

Table 17.8 $_{E}OP$

	$\wedge$	$\vee$	i	(	)	$\lhd$
$\wedge$	$\rfloor$	$\rfloor$	$\lfloor$	$\lfloor$	$\rfloor$	$\rfloor$
$\vee$	$\lfloor$	$\rfloor$	$\lfloor$	$\lfloor$	$\rfloor$	$\rfloor$
i	$\rfloor$	$\rfloor$			$\rfloor$	$\rfloor$
(	$\lfloor$	$\lfloor$	$\lfloor$	$\lfloor$		
)	$\rfloor$	$\rfloor$			$\rfloor$	$\rfloor$
$\rhd$	$\lfloor$	$\lfloor$	$\lfloor$	$\lfloor$		☺

Definition 17.6. *Let $E = ({}_{E}\Sigma, {}_{E}R)$ and $_{E}OP$ have the same meaning as discussed previously. Operations* OP-REDUCE *and* OP-SHIFT *are defined in the following way:*

(i) OP-REDUCE *performs (a) through (c) given as follows:*
  - *(a)* *Let $pd = y$, where $y \in \{\rhd\}_{E}\Sigma^*$, and let a be the topmost* pd *symbol such that $a \in \{\rhd\} \cup {}_{E}\Delta$ and $y = xaubv$ with $_{E}OP[a, b] = \lfloor$, where $x \in \{\rhd\}_{E}\Sigma^* \cup \{\varepsilon\}$ ($a = \rhd$ iff $x = \varepsilon$). Then, the current* handle *is ubv.*
  - *(b)* *Select $r \in {}_{E}R$ with* $\text{rhs}(r) = ubv$.
  - *(c)* *Change ubv to* $\text{lhs}(r)$ *on the* pd *top.*

  To express, in a greater detail, that OP-REDUCE *is performed according to $r \in {}_{E}R$, write* OP-REDUCE (r).

(ii) OP-SHIFT *pushes* ins *onto the* pd *top and advances to the next input symbol.*

To illustrate OP-REDUCE, suppose that the current configuration of the parser is of the form $\rhd(S)\diamond\lhd$. In terms of (i) in Definition 17.6, $y = \rhd(S)$, and the topmost *pd* terminal a satisfying (i) is $\rhd$; to be quite precise, $x = \varepsilon$, $a = \rhd$, $u = \varepsilon$, $b =$ (, and $v = S$). Thus, (S) is the handle. In (ii), select $3: S \to (S)$. In (iii), reduce (S) to S and, thereby, change $\rhd(S)\diamond\lhd$ to $\rhd\diamond\lhd$; in symbols, perform OP-REDUCE (3). It is worth noting that the case when $a = \rhd$ is not ruled out as illustrated by this example as well. To give another example, in a briefer manner, apply OP-REDUCE to the configuration $\rhd(S \vee S\diamond) \wedge S\lhd$. This application actually performs OP-REDUCE (1) and changes $\rhd(S \vee S\diamond) \wedge S\lhd$ to $\rhd(S\diamond) \wedge S\lhd$. Observe that there are configurations to which OP-REDUCE is not applicable. Indeed, consider $\rhd()\diamond\lhd$. As E contains no rule with the right-hand side equal to (), OP-REDUCE is inapplicable to $\rhd()\diamond\lhd$.

To illustrate the other operation, OP-SHIFT, take, for instance, $\rhd S \vee \diamond i\lhd$. Notice that OP-SHIFT changes $\rhd S \vee \diamond i\lhd$ to $\rhd S \vee i\diamond\lhd$.

Basic Idea. Let X be the *pd* topmost terminal. The parser determines each parsing step based upon the entry $_{E}OP[X, ins]$. According to this entry, the parser performs one of the following actions:

(i) If $_{E}OP[X, ins]$ contains $\lfloor$, the parser performs OP-SHIFT.
(ii) If $_{E}OP[X, ins]$ is $\rfloor$, the parser performs OP-REDUCE.
(iii) Let $_{E}OP[X, ins] = \square$. If $X =$ (and $ins =$), the parser performs OP-SHIFT onto *pd* to prepare the performance of OP-REDUCE according to $3: S \to (S)$

right after this shift; otherwise, $X \neq ($ or $ins \neq)$, the blank entry signalizes a syntax error, so the parser performs ERROR.

(iv) If $_EOP[X, ins] = \smiley$, the parser performs SUCCESS and successfully completes the parsing process.

Implementation 17.5. In order to implement an operator-precedence parser, an implementation of the operator-precedence table is required. First, recall that each of its entry may be either blank, $\lfloor$, $\rfloor$, or SUCCESS. Below, `LeftLower` corresponds to $\lfloor$ (left operand has lower priority), and `LeftHigher` to $\rfloor$.

```
public enum OperatorPrecedenceTableEntry
{
    Blank,
    LeftLower,
    LeftHigher,
    Success
}
```

We implement the table itself with a two-layer dictionary structure, using the pattern introduced in the implementation of the predictive table (see Implementation 17.4).

```
public class OperatorPrecedenceTable
{
    private Dictionary<Symbol,
                       Dictionary<Symbol,
                                  OperatorPrecedenceTableEntry>>
        table = new Dictionary<Symbol,
                               Dictionary<Symbol,
                                          OperatorPrecedenceTableEntry
                                         >>();

    public OperatorPrecedenceTableEntry this[Symbol left,
                                             Symbol right]
    {
        get
        {
            Dictionary<Symbol, OperatorPrecedenceTableEntry> row;
            if (table.TryGetValue(left, out row))
            {
                OperatorPrecedenceTableEntry entry;
                if (row.TryGetValue(right, out entry))
                {
                    return entry;
                }
                else
                {
                    return OperatorPrecedenceTableEntry.Blank;
                }
            }
            else
```

```
            {
                return OperatorPrecedenceTableEntry.Blank;
            }
        }
        set
        {
            Dictionary<Symbol, OperatorPrecedenceTableEntry> row;
            if (!table.TryGetValue(left, out row))
            {
                row = new Dictionary<Symbol,
                                    OperatorPrecedenceTableEntry>();
                table[left] = row;
            }

            row[right] = value;
        }
    }
}
```

An operator-precedence parser based on a CFG and its respective operator-precedence table, which implements interface `IParser` defined in Implementation 17.3, may start out as follows:

```
public class OperatorPrecedenceParser : IParser
{
    private ContextFreeGrammar E;
    private OperatorPrecedenceTable OP;

    public OperatorPrecedenceParser(ContextFreeGrammar E,
                                    OperatorPrecedenceTable OP)
    {
        this.E = E;
        this.OP = OP;
    }

    public ParseResult Parse(HmmlcString input)
    {
        throw new NotImplementedException();
    }
}
```

One of the key parts of Algorithm 17.6 is OP-REDUCE. As its first step, we look for a handle to replace. The following implementation directly follows part (i) of OP-REDUCE in Definition 17.6, while storing symbols which potentially form the handle in a pushdown. If a handle is found, the method returns it; otherwise, it returns **null** and, thereby, indicates a parsing error.

```
private static HmmlcString FindHandle(Stack<Symbol> pd,
                                      ContextFreeGrammar E,
                                      OperatorPrecedenceTable OP)
{
```

Algorithm 17.6: Operator precedence parser

Input: E, ${}_EOP$, and $w\lhd$, where $w \in {}_E\Delta^*$, where E and ${}_EOP$ have the same meaning as above.

Output: If $w \in L(E)$, SUCCESS, and if $w \notin L(E)$, ERROR.

begin
  set pd to $\rhd$
  repeat
    switch ${}_EOP[X, ins]$ **do**
      case ⌊ **do**
        OP-SHIFT
      end
      case ⌋ **do**
        OP-REDUCE
      end
      case □ **do** `// □ denotes a blank`
        if $X =$ (*and* $ins =$) **then**
          OP-SHIFT
        else
          ERROR
        end
      end
      case ☺ **do**
        SUCCESS
      end
    end
  until *SUCCESS or ERROR*
end

```
Symbol a = null;
Symbol b = null;

var handleSymbols = new Stack<Symbol>();

foreach (Symbol x in pd) // iterates from top to bottom
{
    if (E.Terminals.Contains(x) || x == Parsing.PdBottom)
    {
        if (b == null)
        {
            b = x;
        }
        else
```

```
                {
                    if (OP[x, b] ==
                        OperatorPrecedenceTableEntry.LeftLower)
                    {
                        a = x;
                        break;
                    }
                    else
                    {
                        b = x;
                    }
                }
            }

            handleSymbols.Push(x);
        }

        if (a != null)
        {
            return new HmmlcString(handleSymbols.ToArray());
        }
        else
        {
            return null;
        }
    }
```

Part (ii) of OP-REDUCE (see Definition 17.6) consists of finding a rule with the handle as its right-hand side. Again, this method returns **`null`** if no such rule is found.

```
private static ContextFreeRule FindRule(ContextFreeGrammar E,
                                        HmmlcString rightHandSide)
{
    foreach (ContextFreeRule r in E.Rules)
    {
        if (r.RightHandSide == rightHandSide)
        {
            return r;
        }
    }

    return null;
}
```

With the methods `FindHandle` and `FindRule` already implemented, the implementation of OP-REDUCE is now straightforward. If we find a handle and a corresponding rule *r*, we replace the handle on the *pd* top with lhs(*r*); otherwise, the method communicates that it is impossible to perform OP-REDUCE by returning **false**.

```
private static bool Reduce(Stack<Symbol> pd,
                           ContextFreeGrammar E,
                           OperatorPrecedenceTable OP)
{
    HmmlcString handle = FindHandle(pd, E, OP);
    if (handle != null)
    {
        ContextFreeRule r = FindRule(E, handle);
        if (r != null)
        {
            for (int i = 0; i < handle.Length; i++)
            {
                pd.Pop();
            }
            pd.Push(r.LeftHandSide);

            return true;
        }
    }

    return false;
}
```

An implementation of Algorithm 17.6 follows next.

```
public ParseResult Parse(HmmlcString input)
{
    var pd = new Stack<Symbol>();

    pd.Push(Parsing.PdBottom);

    int inputPosition = 0;

    while (true)
    {
        Symbol ins = input[inputPosition];

        Symbol X = Parsing.PdBottom;
        foreach (Symbol a in pd) // iterates from top to bottom
        {
            if (E.Terminals.Contains(a))
            {
                X = a;
                break;
            }
        }
```

```
        switch (OP[X, ins])
        {
            case OperatorPrecedenceTableEntry.LeftLower:
                // OP-SHIFT
                pd.Push(ins);
                inputPosition++;
                break;
            case OperatorPrecedenceTableEntry.LeftHigher:
                // OP-REDUCE
                if (!Reduce(pd, E, OP))
                {
                    return ParseResult.Error;
                }
                break;
            case OperatorPrecedenceTableEntry.Blank:
                if (X == "(" && ins == ")")
                {
                    // OP-SHIFT
                    pd.Push(ins);
                    inputPosition++;
                }
                else
                {
                    return ParseResult.Error;
                }
                break;
            case OperatorPrecedenceTableEntry.Success:
                return ParseResult.Success;
        }
    }
}
```

As already explained in Section 17.1, apart from deciding whether $w \in L(E)$, we may want Algorithm 17.6 to produce the right parse of w, defined as the reverse sequence of rules according to which E makes this rightmost derivation (see (2) in the beginning of Section 17.1), if w belongs to $L(E)$. To obtain this parse, we extend the parser by writing out r whenever this algorithm performs OP-REDUCE (r), where $r \in {}_ER$. In this way, we produce the right parse of an input string in the conclusion of the next example.

Example 17.7. *Let us take, for instance, $w = i \wedge (i \vee i)$ in Algorithm 17.6, which represents the E-based operator-precedence parser, whose parsing table ${}_EOP$ is shown in Table 17.8. In Table 17.9, we describe the parse of $i \wedge (i \vee i)$ by Algorithm 17.6. In the first column, we give the ${}_EOP$ entries, and in the second, we present the actions taken by the parser according to these entries. In the third column, we give the parser configurations, which have the form $\rhd x\diamond y\lhd$, where $\rhd x$ is the current* pd, *and $y\lhd$ is the input suffix that remains to be parsed; the leftmost symbol of $y\lhd$ represents* ins. *We underline the topmost* pd *terminals in these configurations.*

Table 17.9 Operator-precedence parsing

Table entry	Action	Configuration
		$\underline{\triangleright}\diamond i \wedge (i \vee i)\triangleleft$
$[\triangleright, i] = \lfloor$	OP-SHIFT	$\triangleright\underline{i}\diamond \wedge (i \vee i)\triangleleft$
$[i, \wedge] = \rfloor$	OP-REDUCE (4)	$\underline{\triangleright}S\diamond \wedge (i \vee i)\triangleleft$
$[\triangleright, \wedge] = \lfloor$	OP-SHIFT	$\triangleright S\underline{\wedge}\diamond(i \vee i)\triangleleft$
$[\wedge, (] = \lfloor$	OP-SHIFT	$\triangleright S \wedge \underline{(}\diamond i \vee i)\triangleleft$
$[(, i] = \lfloor$	OP-SHIFT	$\triangleright S \wedge (\underline{i}\diamond \vee i)\triangleleft$
$[i, \vee] = \rfloor$	OP-REDUCE (4)	$\triangleright S \wedge \underline{(}S\diamond \vee i)\triangleleft$
$[(, \vee] = \lfloor$	OP-SHIFT	$\triangleright S \wedge (S\underline{\vee}\diamond i)\triangleleft$
$[\vee, i] = \lfloor$	OP-SHIFT	$\triangleright S \wedge (S \vee \underline{i}\diamond)\triangleleft$
$[i,)] = \rfloor$	OP-REDUCE (4)	$\triangleright S \wedge (S\underline{\vee}S\diamond)\triangleleft$
$[\vee,)] = \rfloor$	OP-REDUCE (1)	$\triangleright S \wedge \underline{(}S\diamond)\triangleleft$
$[(,)] = \Box$	OP-SHIFT	$\triangleright S \wedge (S\underline{)}\diamond\triangleleft$
$[), \triangleleft] = \rfloor$	OP-REDUCE (3)	$\triangleright S\underline{\wedge}S\diamond\triangleleft$
$[\wedge, \triangleleft] = \rfloor$	OP-REDUCE (2)	$\underline{\triangleright}S\diamond\triangleleft$
$[\triangleright, \triangleleft] =$ ☺	SUCCESS	

Suppose that the parser should produce the right parse of $i \wedge (i \vee i)$. *The parser can easily obtain this parse by writing out the applied rules according to which the reductions are performed during the parsing process. Specifically, take the sequence of rules in the second column of Table 17.9 to obtain* 444132 *as the right parse of* $i \wedge (i \vee i)$ *in E.*

17.3.3 Construction of operator-precedence parsing table

The parsing table ${}_EOP$ (see Table 17.8) can be easily constructed by using common sense and elementary mathematical rules concerning precedence and associativity of operators occurring in the expressions generated by E. This construction thus assumes that for every pair of two operators, their mutual precedence is stated, and in addition, for every operator, it is specified whether it is left-associative or right-associative.

Basic Idea. Mathematically, $\lfloor$ and $\rfloor$ can be viewed as two binary relations over Δ, defined as follows. For any pair of operators a and b, $a\lfloor b$ means that a has a lower precedence than b, so a handle containing a is reduced after a handle containing b. Regarding the other relation, $a\rfloor b$ says that a has a precedence before b, meaning that a handle containing a is reduced before a handle containing b. To obtain the complete definition of $\lfloor$ and $\rfloor$, perform (1)–(4), in which $a \in {}_E\Delta \cup \{\triangleright\}$ and $b \in {}_E\Delta \cup \{\triangleleft\}$.

1. If a and b are operators such that a has a higher mathematical precedence than b, then $a\rfloor b$ and $b\lfloor a$.
2. If a and b are left-associative operators of the same precedence, then $a\rfloor b$ and $b\rfloor a$. If a and b are right-associative operators of the same precedence, then $a\lfloor b$ and $b\lfloor a$.

3. In ${}_E\Delta$, consider i, which represents an identifier and occurs on the right-hand side of rule 4: $S \to i$ in ${}_ER$. If a is a terminal that can legally precede operand i, then $a\lfloor i$, and if a can legally follow i, then $i\rfloor a$.
4. If a is a terminal that can legally precede (, then $a\lfloor($. If a can legally follow (, then $(\lfloor a$. Similarly, if a can legally precede), then $a\rfloor)$, and if a can legally follow), then $)\rfloor a$.

Following (1)–(4), we now construct ${}_EOP$ by using these two equivalences

$$ {}_EOP[a,b] = \lfloor \text{ iff } a\lfloor b, \text{ and } {}_EOP[a,b] = \rfloor \text{ iff } a\rfloor b $$

for all $a \in {}_E\Delta \cup \{\rhd\}$ and $b \in {}_E\Delta \cup \{\lhd\}$. The other entries are blank. All these blank entries signalize syntax errors except ${}_EOP[(,)]$; if the parser occurs in ${}_EOP[(,)]$, it shifts) onto pd in order to perform OP-REDUCE according to $3: S \to (S)$ right after this shift.

Example 17.8. *In E, suppose that* $\vee$ *and* $\wedge$ *satisfy the standard mathematical precedence and associative rules. That is,* $\wedge$ *has a precedence before* $\vee$*, and both operators are left-associative. From (1) stated previously, as* $\wedge$ *has a precedence before* $\vee$, $\wedge\rfloor\vee$ *and* $\vee\lfloor\wedge$*. From (2), since* $\wedge$ *is left-associative, define* $\wedge\rfloor\wedge$*. Regarding i, as* $\vee$ *can legally precede i, define* $\vee\lfloor i$ *according to (3). Considering the parentheses, (4) implies* $\wedge\lfloor($*. Complete the definitions of* $\lfloor$ *and* $\rfloor$ *and use them to construct* ${}_EOP$ *(see Table 17.8).*

17.3.4 Handling errors

In practice, after detecting the first error, a well-written bottom-up parser does not stop. Instead, it somehow deals with that error, so it eventually resumes the parsing process and allows further possible errors to be detected. Next, we sketch how to handle errors in this pragmatically sophisticated way in terms of operator-precedence parsing, in which we distinguish two basic kinds of errors:

1. table-detected errors,
2. reduction errors.

Let X be the pd topmost terminal.

Table-detected errors. If ${}_EOP[X, ins]$ is blank, an error is detected by the table (an exception represents ${}_EOP[(,)]$ as already explained previously). To handle it, the parser modifies its pushdown or the input by changing, inserting, or deleting some symbols. Whatever the parser does, it has to guarantee a recovery from the error. After the recovery, it resumes the parsing process so that all the input string is eventually processed. The precise modification depends on the type of an error that the table detects, and the exact recovery action chosen always requires some ingeniousness from the compiler author to select the best possible action. When the parser reaches a blank entry, the error-recovery routine corresponding to this entry is performed.

Reduction errors. If ${}_EOP[X, ins] = \rfloor$, the parser should perform a reduction. If there is no rule by which the parser can make this reduction, a reduction error occurs.

More precisely, this error occurs when no grammatical rule has the right-hand side equal to the string y delimited by $\lfloor$ and $\rfloor$ on the *pd* top. After issuing a diagnostic of this error, the parser selects a *recovery rule* $A \to x$ such that x can be obtained from y by a slight modification, such as the deletion of a single symbol. To recover, it changes y to A on the *pd* top, then it resumes the parsing process.

In practice, operator-precedence parsers frequently handle errors more sophisticatedly and effectively. Indeed, they detect most errors described above earlier during the parsing process by some additional checks. They usually make the *length-of-handle check* to verify that a handle always occurs within the pushdown top consisting of no more than j symbols, where j is the length of the longest right-hand side of a rule in G. At this point, they can narrow its attention to finitely many illegal strings of length j or less and associate a recovery rule with each of them in advance. Furthermore, a reduction error can be frequently detected earlier by a *valid handle-prefix check*, which verifies that there is a rule r whose prefix occurs on the pushdown top; if there is none, a reduction error is inescapable.

When a recovery action leads to skipping some input symbols, it represents a rather straightforward task. Consider, for instance, ${}_EOP[\rhd,)] = \Box$, which detects an error. To recover, the parser skips) by advancing to the input symbol behind this), issues an error diagnostic stating that an unbalanced right parenthesis has occurred, and continues with the parsing process. A recovery action that modifies *pd* is usually more difficult. Consider ${}_EOP[i, (] = \Box$. To recover, the parser first changes the *pd* top symbol, $X = i$, to S, then pushes $\wedge$ onto the pushdown top. As a result, after this modification of the pushdown, $\wedge$ is the topmost pushdown symbol under which S occurs. To complete this recovery, the parser issues an error diagnostic that an operator is missing and resumes the parsing process. Unfortunately, we can hardly determine whether the source program's author left out $\wedge$ or $\vee$ in front of (. We can only speculate that the input left parenthesis might indicate that the author left out $\wedge$ because the parentheses are normally used to change the common priorities of operators in the expressions; for instance, the parentheses are necessary in $i \wedge (i \vee i)$, but they are superfluous in $i \vee (i \wedge i)$. Therefore, we have chosen $\wedge$ as the operator inserted onto the pushdown in this recovery action although we can never be absolutely sure that this is what the source program's author improperly left out. In Table 17.10, we give

Table 17.10 ${}_E$*OP with error-recovery routines*

	$\wedge$	$\vee$	i	(	)	$\lhd$
$\wedge$	$\rfloor$	$\rfloor$	$\lfloor$	$\lfloor$	$\rfloor$	$\rfloor$
$\vee$	$\lfloor$	$\rfloor$	$\lfloor$	$\lfloor$	$\rfloor$	$\rfloor$
i	$\rfloor$	$\rfloor$	$\boxed{1}$	$\boxed{2}$	$\rfloor$	$\rfloor$
(	$\lfloor$	$\lfloor$	$\lfloor$	$\lfloor$		$\boxed{3}$
)	$\rfloor$	$\rfloor$	$\boxed{4}$	$\boxed{5}$	$\rfloor$	$\rfloor$
$\rhd$	$\lfloor$	$\lfloor$	$\lfloor$	$\lfloor$	$\boxed{6}$	☺

$_EOP$ with the error entries filled with the names of the error-recovery routines, [1]–[6], schematically described next.

[1] $_EOP$ **entry** $[i, i]$
Diagnostic missing operator between two *i*s
Recovery X equals i; replace it with $S\wedge$

[2] $_EOP$ **entry** $[i, (]$
Diagnostic missing operator between i and (
Recovery X equals i; replace it with $S\wedge$

[3] $_EOP$ **entry** $[(, \lhd]$
Diagnostic missing right parenthesis
Recovery *ins* equals $\lhd$; insert) in front of it, and after this insertion, set *ins* to the newly inserted)

[4] $_EOP$ **entry** $[), i]$
Diagnostic missing operator between) and i
Recovery *ins* equals i; insert $\wedge$ in front of it, and after this insertion, set *ins* to the newly inserted $\wedge$

[5] $_EOP$ **entry** $[), (]$
Diagnostic missing operator between) and (
Recovery *ins* equals (; insert $\wedge$ in front of it, and after this insertion, set *ins* to the newly inserted $\wedge$

[6] $_EOP$ **entry** $[\rhd,)]$
Diagnostic unbalanced)
Recovery ignore *ins* and advance to the next input symbol

To illustrate the reduction errors, consider $()\lhd$. By $_EOP$, the parser detects no table-detected error in this obviously incorrect expression. However, when () occurs as the two-symbol pushdown top, a reduction error is reported because () does not coincide with the right-hand side of any rule. To recover, the parser replaces () with (S) on the pushdown top and resumes the parsing process as usual. Observe that this reduction error is detectable earlier provided that the parser makes a valid handle-prefix check. Indeed, when (is on the pushdown top and the parser is about to shift) onto the pushdown, it checks whether there is a rule whose right-hand side begins with (). As there is none, the parser detects and reports a reduction error even before shifting) onto the pushdown. To recover, it pushes S onto the pushdown and then resumes the parsing process. Next, we describe three kinds of reduction errors, ①–③, from each of which the parser recovers by pushing S onto the pushdown top before it makes a shift.

① **Configuration** $X =$ (and $ins =$)
Diagnostic no expression between parenthesis
Recovery push S onto the *pd* top

② **Configuration** $X \in \{\wedge, \vee\}$ and $ins \notin \{i, (\}$
Diagnostic missing right operand
Recovery push S onto the *pd* top

③ **Configuration** S is the *pd* top symbol and *ins* $\in \{\wedge, \vee\}$
Diagnostic missing left operand
Recovery push S onto the *pd* top

Example 17.9. *Consider $i(i\vee)\lhd$. As obvious, this expression is ill-formed. Working on $i(i\vee)\lhd$, Algorithm 17.6 interrupts its parsing process after making only the first two steps described in Table 17.11 because it reaches a blank entry in ${}_EOP$, which means a syntax error.*

The parser that handles syntax errors by the routines described above works with this expression as described in Table 17.12, which points up information related to handling errors. In the third column, apart from giving the parser configurations presented in the same way previously, we point out the parts related to error recovery. Observe that the parser recovers from both errors occurring in the expressions. As a result, the parser completes the parsing of this expression. The parsing process obviously ends by ERROR for the previously detected errors.

Table 17.11 Operator-precedence parser working on $\rhd\diamond i(i\vee)\lhd$

Table entry	Action	Configuration
		$\rhd\diamond i(i\vee)\lhd$
$[\rhd, i] = \lfloor$	OP-SHIFT	$\rhd\underline{i}\diamond(i\vee)\lhd$
$[i, (]$ is blank	ERROR	

Table 17.12 Operator-precedence parser that recovers from errors in $\rhd\diamond i(i\vee)\lhd$

Table entry	Action	Configuration
		$\rhd\diamond i(i\vee)\lhd$
$[\rhd, i] = \lfloor$	OP-SHIFT	$\rhd\underline{i}\diamond(i\vee)\lhd$
$[i, (] = \boxed{2}$	recovery $\boxed{2}$	$\rhd S\underline{\wedge}\diamond(i\vee)\lhd$
$[\wedge, (] = \lfloor$	OP-SHIFT	$\rhd S\wedge\underline{(}\diamond i\vee)\lhd$
$[(, i] = \lfloor$	OP-SHIFT	$\rhd S\wedge(\underline{i}\diamond\vee)\lhd$
$[i, \vee] = \rfloor$	OP-REDUCE (4)	$\rhd S\wedge\underline{(}S\diamond\vee)\lhd$
$[(, \vee] = \rfloor$	recovery ②	$\rhd S\wedge(S\underline{\vee}S\diamond)\lhd$
$[\vee,)] = \rfloor$	OP-REDUCE (1)	$\rhd S\wedge\underline{(}S\diamond)\lhd$
$[(,)] = \square$	OP-SHIFT	$\rhd S\wedge(S\underline{)}\diamond\lhd$
$[), \lhd] = \rfloor$	OP-REDUCE (3)	$\rhd S\underline{\wedge}S\diamond\lhd$
$[\wedge, \lhd] = \rfloor$	OP-REDUCE (2)	$\underline{\rhd}S\diamond\lhd$
$[\rhd, \lhd]$	ERROR	

In the second step, the parser detects that an operator is missing between i and (, and recovery routine 2 *handles this error by replacing i with S and, then, pushing* $\wedge$ *on the* pd *top. In the seventh step, the parser detects a reduction error because* $\vee$ *occurs on the* pd *top and the next input symbol equals*). *Indeed, at this point,* $S\vee$ *forms the handle but there is no rule with the right-hand side equal to* $S\vee$. *To recover, recovery routine* ② *pushes S onto the* pd *top. As a result, the parser completes the parsing of* $i(i\vee)$ *rather than getting stuck inside of this expression like in Table 17.11.*

17.3.5 Operator-precedence parsers for other expressions

Up until now, we have based the explanation of operator-precedence parsing strictly upon E. Of course, apart from the logical expressions generated by E, this parsing method elegantly handles other expressions. Next, we explain how this method handles unary operators. Then, we sketch how to adapt it for arithmetic expressions. Finally, we point out that it works well with both ambiguous and unambiguous grammars.

Unary operators. Consider $\neg$ as a unary operator that denotes a logical negation. To incorporate this operator, we extend the CFG E by adding a rule of the form $S \rightarrow \neg S$ to obtain the CFG defined as

$$S \rightarrow \neg S,$$
$$S \rightarrow S \vee S,$$
$$S \rightarrow S \wedge S,$$
$$S \rightarrow (S),$$
$$S \rightarrow i.$$

Assume that $\neg$ satisfies the standard precedence and associative rules used in logic. That is, $\neg$ is a right-associative operator having a higher precedence than $\wedge$ and $\vee$. Return to rules (1)–(4), preceding Example 17.8 in this section. By using these rules, we easily obtain the table that includes this unary operator (see Table 17.13).

Table 17.13 Operator-precedence parsing with unary operator $\neg$

	$\neg$	$\wedge$	$\vee$	i	(	)	$\lhd$
$\neg$	$\lfloor$	$\rfloor$	$\rfloor$	$\lfloor$	$\lfloor$	$\rfloor$	$\rfloor$
$\wedge$	$\lfloor$	$\rfloor$	$\rfloor$	$\lfloor$	$\lfloor$	$\rfloor$	$\rfloor$
$\vee$	$\lfloor$	$\lfloor$	$\rfloor$	$\lfloor$	$\lfloor$	$\rfloor$	$\rfloor$
i	$\rfloor$	$\rfloor$	$\rfloor$			$\rfloor$	$\rfloor$
(	$\lfloor$	$\lfloor$	$\lfloor$	$\lfloor$	$\lfloor$		
)		$\rfloor$	$\rfloor$			$\rfloor$	$\rfloor$
$\rhd$	$\lfloor$	$\lfloor$	$\lfloor$	$\lfloor$	$\lfloor$		☺

Table 17.14 Arithmetic-operator precedence table

	$\uparrow$	$\times$	$\div$	$+$	$-$	i	(	)	$\lhd$
$\uparrow$	⌊	⌋	⌋	⌋	⌋	⌊	⌊	⌋	⌋
$\times$	⌊	⌋	⌋	⌋	⌋	⌊	⌊	⌋	⌋
$\div$	⌊	⌋	⌋	⌋	⌋	⌊	⌊	⌋	⌋
$+$	⌊	⌊	⌊	⌋	⌋	⌊	⌊	⌋	⌋
$-$	⌊	⌊	⌊	⌋	⌋	⌊	⌊	⌋	⌋
i	⌋	⌋	⌋	⌋	⌋			⌋	⌋
(	⌊	⌊	⌊	⌊	⌊	⌊	⌊		
)	⌋	⌋	⌋	⌋	⌋			⌋	⌋
$\rhd$	⌊	⌊	⌊	⌊	⌊	⌊	⌊		☺

Arithmetic expressions with right-associative operators. Consider this CFG

$$
\begin{aligned}
S &\rightarrow S + S,\\
S &\rightarrow S - S,\\
S &\rightarrow S \times S,\\
S &\rightarrow S \div S,\\
S &\rightarrow S \uparrow S,\\
S &\rightarrow (S),\\
S &\rightarrow i,
\end{aligned}
$$

in which the operators have the standard meaning and satisfy the common arithmetic precedence and associative rules ($\uparrow$ denotes the operator of exponentiation). That is, $\uparrow$ has a precedence before $\times$ and $\div$, which have a precedence before $+$ and $-$. The exponentiation operator $\uparrow$ is right-associative, while the others are left-associative. The precedence table for this grammar is straightforwardly made by construction rules (1)–(4) (see Table 17.14).

Expressions involving relational operators are handled analogously, so we leave their discussion as an exercise.

Ambiguity. As opposed to the most top-down parsers, such as the predictive parsers (see Section 17.2), the precedence parsers work with ambiguous grammars without any problems. In fact, all the previous precedence parsers discussed in this section are based on ambiguous grammars, such as E. As obvious, these parsers can be based upon unambiguous grammars too. To illustrate, consider the unambiguous grammar H (see Convention 17.2), defined as

$$
\begin{aligned}
1 &: S \rightarrow S \vee A,\\
2 &: S \rightarrow A,\\
3 &: A \rightarrow A \wedge B,\\
4 &: A \rightarrow B,\\
5 &: B \rightarrow (S),\\
6 &: B \rightarrow i.
\end{aligned}
$$

Suppose that all the operators satisfy the same precedence and associative rules as in the equivalent ambiguous grammar above. As an exercise, by rules (1)–(4), construct $_{H}OP$ and observe that this table coincides with Table 17.8.

On the one hand, as demonstrated earlier in this section, operator-precedence parsers work nicely for the CFGs that generate expressions even if these grammars are ambiguous. On the other hand, they place several strict restrictions on the CFGs they are based on; perhaps, most significantly, they exclude any involvement of ε-rules or rules having the same right-hand side but different left-hand sides. As a result, in practice, these parsers are frequently used in a combination with predictive parsers discussed in Section 17.2. Combined in this way, the precedence parsers handle the syntax of expressions, while the other parsers handle the rest. Alternatively, bottom-up parsers are designed as LR parsers, discussed next.

17.3.6 LR parsing

This section discusses the *LR parsers* (*L* stands for the *l*eft-to-right scan of symbols, and *R* is for the *r*ightmost derivation, which the bottom-up parsers construct in reverse as already explained in Section 17.1). LR parsers are based on *LR tables* constructed from *LR CFGs*—that is, the CFGs for which LR tables can be constructed; let us point out that there are *non-LR CFGs* for which these tables cannot be built up.

In practice, LR parsers belong to the most popular parsers for their several indisputable advantages. First, they work fast. Furthermore, they easily and elegantly handle syntax errors because they never shift an erroneous input symbol onto the pushdown, and this property obviously simplifies the error-recovery process. Most importantly, out of all deterministic parsers, they are ultimately powerful because LR CFGs generate the language family coinciding with the language family accepted by deterministic PDAs by final state (see Section 10.7 in [84]).

In this section, we first describe the fundamental LR parsing algorithm. Then, we explain how to construct the LR tables, which the algorithm makes use of. Finally, we discuss how this parsing method handles errors.

17.3.7 LR parsing algorithm

Consider an LR grammar, $G = ({}_{G}\Sigma, {}_{G}R)$. Its *G-based LR table* consists of the *G-based action part* and the *G-based goto part*, denoted by $_{G}action$ and $_{G}goto$, respectively. Both parts have their rows denoted by members of the set $_{G}\Theta = \{\theta_1, \ldots, \theta_m\}$, whose construction is described later in this section. The columns of $_{G}action$ and $_{G}goto$ are denoted by the symbols of $_{G}\Delta$ and $_{G}N$, respectively; recall that $_{G}\Delta$ and $_{G}N$ denote G's alphabets of terminals and nonterminals, respectively. For each $\theta_j \in {}_{G}\Theta$ and $t_i \in {}_{G}\Delta \cup \{\lhd\}$, $_{G}action[\theta_j, t_i]$ entry is either a member of $_{G}\Theta \cup {}_{G}R \cup \{☺\}$ or a blank entry (see Table 17.15). Frequently, the rules of $_{G}R$ are labeled throughout this section, and instead of the rules themselves, only their labels are written in $_{G}action$ for brevity. For each $\theta_j \in {}_{G}\Theta$ and $A_i \in {}_{G}N$, $_{G}goto[\theta_j, A_i]$ is either a member of $_{G}\Theta$ or a blank entry (see Table 17.16).

Table 17.15 action

	t_1	$\ldots$	t_i	$\ldots$	t_n
θ_1					
$\vdots$					
θ_j			$action[\theta_j, t_i]$		
$\vdots$					
θ_m					

Table 17.16 goto

	A_1	$\ldots$	A_i	$\ldots$	A_k
θ_1					
$\vdots$					
θ_j			$goto[\theta_j, t_i]$		
$\vdots$					
θ_m					

Convention 17.5. *As usual, whenever there is no danger of confusion, we omit G in the denotation above, so we simplify* $_G\Theta$ $_G$*action,* $_G$*goto,* $_G\Delta$*, and* $_GN$ *to* Θ*, action, goto,* Δ*, and N, respectively.*

Basic Idea. Like an operator-precedence parser (see Algorithm 17.6), an LR parser scans w from left to right, and during this scan, it makes shifts and reductions. If $w \in L(G)$, it accepts w; otherwise, it rejects w. During the parsing process, every configuration of the parser is of the form $\triangleright q_0 Y_1 q_1 \cdots Y_{m-1} q_{m-1} Y_m q_m \diamond v \triangleleft$, where the qs and the Ys are in $_G\Theta$ and $_G\Sigma$, respectively, and $v \in$ suffixes(w). Recall that according to Definition 7.1, the pushdown is written in the right-to-left way, so q_m is the topmost *pd* symbol, Y_m occurs as the second *pd* symbol, and so on up to the *pd* bottom, $\triangleright$. As a result, a member of $_G\Theta$ always appears as the topmost *pd* symbol. The LR parser makes shifts and reductions in a specific LR way, though. Next, we describe operations LR-REDUCE and LR-SHIFT that denote the actions by which the LR parser makes its reductions and shifts, respectively (as usual, in the definition of LR-REDUCE and LR-SHIFT, we make use of the *pd* and *ins* notation introduced in Convention 17.1).

Definition 17.7. (Operations LR-REDUCE and LR-SHIFT). *Let* $G = ({_G\Sigma}, {_GR})$*,* $_G\Theta$*,* $_G$*action, and* $_G$*goto have the same meaning as above. In a G-based LR parser, we use operations* LR-REDUCE *and* LR-SHIFT *defined as follows:*

LR-REDUCE *If* $p\colon A \to X_1X_2\cdots X_n \in {_GR}$, $X_j \in {_G\Sigma}$, $1 \le j \le n$, *for some* $n \geq 0$ *(*$n = 0$ *means* $X_1X_2\cdots X_n = \varepsilon$*),* $o_0X_1o_1X_2o_2\cdots o_{n-1}X_no_n$ *occurs as the*

$(2n+1)$-symbol pd *top—that is, the current configuration of the parser is of the form* $\triangleright \cdots o_0 X_1 o_1 X_2 o_2 \cdots o_{n-1} X_n o_n \diamond \cdots \triangleleft$ *with* o_n *as the topmost* pd *symbol, where* $o_k \in {}_G\Theta$, $0 \leq k \leq n$, *then* LR-REDUCE(p) *replaces* $X_1 o_1 X_2 o_2 \cdots o_{n-1} X_n o_n$ *with* Ah *on the pushdown top, where* $h \in {}_G\Theta$ *is defined as* $h = {}_G goto[o_0, A]$*; otherwise, ERROR.*

LR-SHIFT *Let t and q denote* ins *and the* pd *top symbol, respectively. Furthermore, let* $action[q, t] = o$, *where* $o \in {}_G\Theta$. *At this point,* LR-SHIFT *extends* pd *by to, so o is the topmost pushdown symbol after this extension. In addition, it sets* ins *to the input symbol that follows t and, thereby, advances to the next input symbol.*

Notice that the following LR parser has always its *pd* top symbol from ${}_G\Theta$ as follows from Definition 17.7.

Implementation 17.6. Here we present a C# implementation of an LR parser. First, we implement the two parts of the LR table: *goto* and *action*. For both parts, we once again follow the pattern from Implementation 17.3. We present *goto* part first because it is simpler—each entry is either a symbol (`Symbol`) or is blank (**`null`**).

```
public class GotoTable
{
    private Dictionary<Symbol, Dictionary<Symbol, Symbol>> table =
        new Dictionary<Symbol, Dictionary<Symbol, Symbol>>();

    public Symbol this[Symbol r, Symbol c]
    {
        get
        {
            Dictionary<Symbol, Symbol> row;
            if (table.TryGetValue(r, out row))
            {
                Symbol theta;
                if (row.TryGetValue(c, out theta))
                {
                    return theta;
                }
                else
                {
                    return null;
                }
            }
            else
            {
                return null;
            }
        }
        set
        {
            Dictionary<Symbol, Symbol> row;
```

```
                if (!table.TryGetValue(r, out row))
                {
                    row = new Dictionary<Symbol, Symbol>();
                    table[r] = row;
                }

                row[c] = value;
            }
        }
    }
```

For the *action* part, there are three types of (non-blank) entries.

```
public enum ActionTableEntryType
{
    Theta,
    Rule,
    Success
}

public class ActionTableEntry
{
    public ActionTableEntryType Type { get; private set; }
    public Symbol Theta { get; private set; }
    public ContextFreeRule Rule { get; private set; }

    private ActionTableEntry()
    {
    }

    public static readonly ActionTableEntry Success =
        new ActionTableEntry { Type = ActionTableEntryType.Success };

    public static ActionTableEntry ForTheta(Symbol theta)
    {
        return new ActionTableEntry
        {
            Type = ActionTableEntryType.Theta,
            Theta = theta
        };
    }

    public static ActionTableEntry ForRule(ContextFreeRule r)
    {
        return new ActionTableEntry
        {
            Type = ActionTableEntryType.Rule,
            Rule = r
        };
    }
}
```

Using the class to represent *action* table entries, we next implement the *action* part by analogy with the *goto* part.

```
public class ActionTable
{
    private Dictionary<Symbol,
                       Dictionary<Symbol, ActionTableEntry>>
        table =
            new Dictionary<Symbol,
                           Dictionary<Symbol, ActionTableEntry>>();

    public ActionTableEntry this[Symbol r, Symbol c]
    {
        get
        {
            Dictionary<Symbol, ActionTableEntry> row;
            if (table.TryGetValue(r, out row))
            {
                ActionTableEntry entry;
                if (row.TryGetValue(c, out entry))
                {
                    return entry;
                }
                else
                {
                    return null;
                }
            }
            else
            {
                return null;
            }
        }
        set
        {
            Dictionary<Symbol, ActionTableEntry> row;
            if (!table.TryGetValue(r, out row))
            {
                row = new Dictionary<Symbol, ActionTableEntry>();
                table[r] = row;
            }

            row[c] = value;
        }
    }
}
```

The LR table implementation simply combines the *action* and the *goto* part.

```
public class LRTable
{
    public ActionTable Action { get; private set; }
    public GotoTable Goto { get; private set; }

    public LRTable()
```

```
    {
        this.Action = new ActionTable();
        this.Goto = new GotoTable();
    }
}
```

The basic structure of an LR parser conforming to our `IParser` interface (see Implementation 17.3) as follows:

```
public class LRParser : IParser
{
    private LRTable table;

    public LRParser(LRTable table)
    {
        this.table = table;
    }

    public ParseResult Parse(HmmlcString input)
    {
        throw new NotImplementedException();
    }
}
```

Finally, we can implement the parsing algorithm itself. We first create a helper method which finds the o_0 symbol on pushdown according to the right-hand side of a rule (see Definition 17.7), so that we can perform LR-REDUCE.

```
private static Symbol CheckPdTop(Stack<Symbol> pd, HmmlcString s)
{
    int index = s.Length - 1;

    bool isTheta = true; // pd top is theta

    foreach (Symbol a in pd) // iterates from top to bottom
    {
        if (a == Parsing.PdBottom) return null;
            // not enough symbols on pd

        if (isTheta)
        {
            if (index < 0) // whole string checked
            {
                return a; // o0 found
            }
        }
        else
        {
            if (s[index] != a) return null;
            index--;
        }
```

```
        isTheta = !isTheta;
    }

    return null;
}
```

By making use of this method, we implement LR-REDUCE as follows:

```
private static bool Reduce(Stack<Symbol> pd,
                           ContextFreeRule r,
                           GotoTable gotoTable)
{
    Symbol o0 = CheckPdTop(pd, r.RightHandSide);
    if (o0 == null) return false;

    int pdTopLength = 2 * r.RightHandSide.Length + 1;
    for (int i = 0; i < pdTopLength - 1; i++)  pd.Pop();

    Symbol A = r.LeftHandSide;
    Symbol h = gotoTable[o0, A];
    pd.Push(A);
    pd.Push(h);

    return true;
}
```

The main parsing method implementation now mirrors Algorithm 17.7.

```
public ParseResult Parse(HmmlcString input)
{
    var pd = new Stack<Symbol>();
    pd.Push(Parsing.PdBottom);
    pd.Push("theta1");

    int inputPosition = 0;

    while (true)
    {
        Symbol ins = input[inputPosition];
        Symbol q = pd.Peek();

        var actionEntry = table.Action[q, ins];

        if (actionEntry == null) // blank
        {
            return ParseResult.Error;
        }

        switch (actionEntry.Type)
        {
            case ActionTableEntryType.Theta:
```

Algorithm 17.7: LR parser

Input: An LR grammar $G = ({}_G\Sigma, {}_GR)$, an input string, w, with $w \in {}_G\Delta^*$, and G-based LR table consisting of *action* and *goto*.
Output: SUCCESS if $w \in L(G)$, or ERROR if $w \notin L(G)$.

begin
  set $pd = \triangleright\theta_1$ // θ_1 denotes the first row of *action* and *goto*
  repeat
    let q denote the pd topmost symbol
    switch *action*$[q, ins]$ **do**
      case *in* ${}_G\Theta$ **do**
        LR-SHIFT
      end
      case *in* ${}_GR$ **do**
        LR-REDUCE (r) with $r = action[q, ins]$
      end
      case □ **do**
        ERROR   // □ denotes a blank
      end
      case ☺ **do**
        SUCCESS
      end
    end
  until *SUCCESS or ERROR*
end

```
                // LR-SHIFT
                pd.Push(ins);
                pd.Push(actionEntry.Theta);
                inputPosition++;
                break;
            case ActionTableEntryType.Rule:
                // LR-REDUCE
                if (!Reduce(pd, actionEntry.Rule, table.Goto))
                {
                    return ParseResult.Error;
                }
                break;
            case ActionTableEntryType.Success:
                return ParseResult.Success;
        }
    }
}
```

To obtain the right parse of w, extend Algorithm 17.7 by writing out r whenever LR-REDUCE (r) occurs, where $r \in {}_G R$. This straightforward extension is left as an exercise.

Example 17.10. *Consider the CFG H (see Convention 17.2), whose rules are*

$$1 : S \to S \vee A$$
$$2 : S \to A$$
$$3 : A \to A \wedge B$$
$$4 : A \to B$$
$$5 : B \to (S)$$
$$6 : B \to i$$

where S is the start symbol. This grammar has its two-part LR table, consisting of action and goto, depicted in Tables 17.17 and 17.18, respectively. Both action and goto have their rows denoted by the members of ${}_H\Theta = \{\theta_1, \theta_2, \ldots, \theta_{12}\}$. *The columns*

Table 17.17 ${}_H$*action*

	$\wedge$	$\vee$	i	(	)	$\triangleleft$
θ_1			θ_6	θ_5		
θ_2		θ_7				☺
θ_3	θ_8	2			2	2
θ_4	4	4			4	4
θ_5			θ_6	θ_5		
θ_6	6	6			6	6
θ_7			θ_6	θ_5		
θ_8			θ_6	θ_5		
θ_9		θ_7			θ_{12}	
θ_{10}	θ_8	1			1	1
θ_{11}	3	3			3	3
θ_{12}	5	5			5	5

Table 17.18 ${}_H$*goto*

	S	A	B
θ_1	θ_2	θ_3	θ_4
θ_2			
θ_3			
θ_4			
θ_5	θ_9	θ_3	θ_4
θ_6			
θ_7		θ_{10}	θ_4
θ_8			θ_{11}
θ_9			
θ_{10}			
θ_{11}			
θ_{12}			

Table 17.19 LR parsing

Configuration	Table entry	Parsing action
$\triangleright\theta_1\diamond i \wedge i \vee i\triangleleft$	$action[\theta_1, i] = \theta_6$	LR-SHIFT (i)
$\triangleright\theta_1 i\theta_6\diamond \wedge i \vee i\triangleleft$	$action[\theta_6, \wedge] = 6$, $goto[\theta_1, B] = \theta_4$	LR-REDUCE (6)
$\triangleright\theta_1 B\theta_4\diamond \wedge i \vee i\triangleleft$	$action[\theta_4, \wedge] = 4$, $goto[\theta_1, A] = \theta_3$	LR-REDUCE (4)
$\triangleright\theta_1 A\theta_3\diamond \wedge i \vee i\triangleleft$	$action[\theta_3, \wedge] = \theta_8$	LR-SHIFT ($\wedge$)
$\triangleright\theta_1 A\theta_3 \wedge \theta_8\diamond i \vee i\triangleleft$	$action[\theta_8, i] = \theta_6$	LR-SHIFT (i)
$\triangleright\theta_1 A\theta_3 \wedge \theta_8 i\theta_6\diamond \vee i\triangleleft$	$action[\theta_6, \vee] = 6$, $goto[\theta_8, B] = \theta_{11}$	LR-REDUCE (6)
$\triangleright\theta_1 A\theta_3 \wedge \theta_8 B\theta_{11}\diamond \vee i\triangleleft$	$action[\theta_{11}, \vee] = 3$, $goto[\theta_1, A] = \theta_3$	LR-REDUCE (3)
$\triangleright\theta_1 A\theta_3\diamond \vee i\triangleleft$	$action[\theta_3, \vee] = 2$, $goto[\theta_1, S] = \theta_2$	LR-REDUCE (2)
$\triangleright\theta_1 S\theta_2\diamond \vee i\triangleleft$	$action[\theta_2, \vee] = \theta_7$	LR-SHIFT ($\vee$)
$\triangleright\theta_1 S\theta_2 \vee \theta_7\diamond i\triangleleft$	$action[\theta_7, i] = \theta_6$	LR-SHIFT (i)
$\triangleright\theta_1 S\theta_2 \vee \theta_7 i\theta_6\diamond\triangleleft$	$action[\theta_6, \triangleleft] = 6$, $goto[\theta_7, B] = \theta_4$	LR-REDUCE (6)
$\triangleright\theta_1 S\theta_2 \vee \theta_7 B\theta_4\diamond\triangleleft$	$action[\theta_4, \triangleleft] = 4$, $goto[\theta_7, A] = \theta_{10}$	LR-REDUCE (4)
$\triangleright\theta_1 S\theta_2 \vee \theta_7 A\theta_{10}\diamond\triangleleft$	$action[\theta_{10}, \triangleleft] = 1$, $goto[\theta_1, S] = \theta_2$	LR-REDUCE (1)
$\triangleright\theta_1 S\theta_2\diamond\triangleleft$	$action[\theta_2, \triangleleft] = ☺$	SUCCESS

of action are denoted by terminals $\wedge$, $\vee$, (,), i, *and* $\triangleleft$. *The columns of goto are denoted by nonterminals S, A, and B.*

With $i \wedge i \vee i \in L(H)$ *as the expression, Algorithm 17.7 works as described in Table 17.19. The algorithm makes the successful parsing of* $i \wedge i \vee i$ *by the sequence of configurations given in the first column of this figure. The second column gives the relevant entries of action and goto, and the third column specifies the actions made by the algorithm. Notice that goto is relevant only when a reduction is performed; regarding a shift, it is not needed at all.*

By writing out the rules according to which the LR parser makes each reduction, we obtain 64632641 *as the right parse of* $i \wedge i \vee i$ *in* H.

17.3.8 Construction of the LR table

The parsing theory has developed many sophisticated methods of constructing the LR tables. Most of them are too complicated to include them into this introductory text, however. Therefore, we just restrict our explanation of this construction to the fundamental ideas underlying a *simple LR table construction*. As its name indicates, it is simpler than the other constructions of LR tables, and this aspect represents its principal advantage. On the other hand, there exist LR CFGs for which this construction does not work. In other words, the LR parsers based upon tables constructed in this way are slightly less powerful than LR parsers based upon tables produced by more complicated methods, which are equivalent with LR CFGs and, therefore, characterize the family of languages accepted by deterministic PDAs, as already pointed out in the beginning of Section 17.3.6. However, these complicated LR-table constructions are too complex to be included into this introductory text.

As a matter of fact, even if we restrict our attention to the simple LR-table construction, this construction still belongs to the most complicated topics of this introductory book. Therefore, we only give its gist while reducing the formalism concerning this construction as much as possible.

Items. Let G be an LR CFG. In every configuration, the *pd* top contains a handle prefix, which the G-based LR parser tries to extend so a complete handle occurs on the *pd* top. As soon as the *pd* top contains a complete handle, the parser can make a reduction according to a rule $r \in {}_MR$ with rhs(r) equal to the handle. To express that a handle prefix appears as the *pd* top, we introduce an *item* of the form

$$A \to x \bullet y$$

for each rule $A \to z \in {}_GR$ and any two strings x and y such that $z = xy$. Intuitively, $A \to x \bullet y$ means that if x occurs as the *pd* top and the parser makes a sequence of moves resulting into producing y right behind x on the *pd* top, the parser gets z as the handle on the *pd* top, which can be reduced to A according to $A \to z$. An item of the form $A \to \bullet z$ is called a *start item*, while an item of the form $A \to z\bullet$ is called an *end item*.

Example 17.11. *Recall the six-rule CFG H from Convention 17.2, defined as*

$$\begin{aligned}
1 &: S \to S \vee A \\
2 &: S \to A \\
3 &: A \to A \wedge B \\
4 &: A \to B \\
5 &: B \to (S) \\
6 &: B \to i
\end{aligned}$$

From $S \to S \vee A$, *we obtain these four items*

$$\begin{aligned}
&S \to \bullet S \vee A \\
&S \to S \bullet \vee A \\
&S \to S \vee \bullet A \\
&S \to S \vee A\bullet
\end{aligned}$$

in which $S \to \bullet S \vee A$ *and* $S \to S \vee A\bullet$ *represent a start item and an end item, respectively. Consider* $S \to S \bullet \vee A$. *In essence, this item says that if S currently appears as the* pd *top and a prefix of the input is reduced to* $\vee A$, *the parser obtains* $S \vee A$ *as the handle, which can be reduced to S by using* $S \to S \vee A$.

Before going any further, notice that several different items may be relevant to the same pd *top string. To illustrate, take* $S \to S \vee A\bullet$ *and* $A \to A \bullet \wedge B$. *Notice that both items have to be taken into account whenever the LR parser occurs in a configuration with the three-symbol string* $S \vee A$ *as the* pd *top. Consider, for instance,* $\triangleright S \vee A \diamond \triangleleft$ *and* $\triangleright S \vee A \diamond \wedge i \triangleleft$. *From* $\triangleright S \vee A \diamond \triangleleft$, *the H-based LR parser makes a reduction* *according to $S \to S \vee A$ and, thereby, successfully completes the parsing process. More formally, the parser performs*

$$\triangleright S \vee A \diamond \triangleleft \Rightarrow \triangleright S \diamond \triangleleft.$$

In $\triangleright S \vee A \diamond \wedge i \triangleleft$, the parser has actually A as a prefix of the handle $A \wedge B$ on the pushdown. As a result, from $\triangleright S \vee A \diamond \wedge i \triangleleft$, it first makes several shifts and reductions before it obtains $A \wedge B$ as the handle on the pushdown top. Then, it reduces $A \wedge B$ to A according to $A \to A \wedge B$, after which it obtains $S \vee A$ as the handle, makes a reduction according to $S \to S \vee A$, and, thereby, completes the parsing process. To summarize this part of parsing process formally, from $\triangleright S \vee A \diamond \wedge i \triangleleft$, the H-based LR parser computes

$$\begin{aligned}\triangleright S \vee A \diamond \wedge i \triangleleft &\Rightarrow \triangleright S \vee A \wedge \diamond i \triangleleft \\ &\Rightarrow \triangleright S \vee A \wedge i \diamond \triangleleft \\ &\Rightarrow \triangleright S \vee A \wedge B \diamond \triangleleft \\ &\Rightarrow \triangleright S \vee A \diamond \triangleleft \\ &\Rightarrow \triangleright S \diamond \triangleleft.\end{aligned}$$

Convention 17.6. *Throughout the rest of this chapter, for an LR CFG G, ${}_GI$, ${}_GI_{start}$, and ${}_GI_{end}$ denote the set of all its items, the set of start items, and the set of end items, respectively, so ${}_GI_{start} \subseteq {}_GI$ as well as ${}_GI_{end} \subseteq {}_GI$. Furthermore, ${}_G\Omega = \text{power}({}_GI)$—that is, ${}_G\Omega$ denotes the power set of ${}_GI$, defined as the set of all subsets of ${}_GI$ (see Section 1.1). As usual, we omit the subscript G in this notation if no confusion exists; for instance, we often write I instead of ${}_GI$ if G is understood.*

As sketched in the conclusion of the previous example, several items are usually related to a single prefix of the right-hand side of some rules when the prefix occurs on the *pd* top in order to determine the next LR parsing step. Next, we construct the item sets corresponding to all prefixes of the right-hand sides of rules in ${}_GR$, and these sets are then used as members of ${}_G\Theta$, so ${}_G\Theta \subseteq {}_G\Omega$. By using the members of ${}_G\Theta$, we then construct the G-based LR table.

Construction of ${}_G\Theta$. Initially, we change the start symbol S to a new start symbol Z in G and add a dummy rule of the form $Z \to S$. As a result, we can be sure that in G, every derivation that generates a sentence in $L(G)$ starts by applying $Z \to S$. Apart from ${}_G\Theta$, we introduce an auxiliary item set ${}_GW$. Initially, we set ${}_G\Theta$ and ${}_GW$ to $\emptyset$ and $\{Z \to \bullet S\}$, respectively. We repeat extensions (i) and (ii), described next, until no new item set can be included into ${}_GW$ in order to obtain all item sets in ${}_G\Theta$. Let us note that during the computation of (i) and (ii), ${}_G\Theta$ and ${}_GW$ always represent subsets of ${}_G\Omega$.

(i) Let $I \in {}_GW$. Suppose that u appears on the *pd* top, and let $A \to uBv \in {}_GR$, where $A, B \in {}_GN$, and $u, v \in {}_G\Sigma^*$. Observe that if $A \to u \bullet Bv \in I$ and $B \to \bullet y \in {}_GI_{start}$, then by using $B \to y$, the G-based LR parser can reduce y to B, and this reduction does not affect u appearing on the *pd* top at all because $B \to \bullet y$ is a start item. Thus, extend I by adding $B \to \bullet y$ into it. Repeat this extension until I can no longer be extended in this way. Take the resulting I and add it to ${}_G\Theta$ (if I was already there, ${}_G\Theta$ remains unchanged). To summarize this extension as a

Pascal-like procedure, for $I \in {}_GW$, perform

repeat
  if $A \to u \bullet Bv \in I$ and $B \to z \in {}_GR$ **then**
    include $B \to \bullet z$ into I
  end
until no change
include I into ${}_G\Theta$

(ii) This extension is based upon a relation ${}_G\circlearrowright$ from ${}_G\Omega \times {}_G\Sigma$ to ${}_G\Omega$, defined next. Intuitively, for $I \in {}_G\Omega$ and $X \in {}_G\Sigma$, ${}_G\circlearrowright(I, X)$ specifies the set of items related to the configuration that M enters from I by pushing X on the *pd* top. Formally, for all $I \in {}_G\Omega$ and all $X \in {}_G\Sigma$,

$$ {}_G\circlearrowright(I,X) = \{A \to uX \bullet v \mid A \to u \bullet Xv \in I,\ A \in {}_GN,\ u, v \in {}_G\Sigma^*\}. $$

Let $I \in {}_GW$ and $A \to uX \bullet v \in I$, where $A \in {}_GN, u, v \in {}_G\Sigma^*$, and $X \in {}_G\Sigma$. Consider a part of a rightmost derivation in G in reverse during which a portion of the input string is reduced to X. Simulating this derivation part, the G-based LR parser actually obtains X on the *pd*. As a result, for every $I \in {}_GW$ and $X \in {}_G\Sigma$, the following for loop extends ${}_GW$ by ${}_G\circlearrowright(I, X)$ unless ${}_G\circlearrowright(I, X)$ is empty.

for each $X \in {}_G\Sigma$ with ${}_G\circlearrowright(I, X) \neq \emptyset$
  include ${}_G\circlearrowright(I, X)$ into ${}_GW$
end

Based upon (i) and (ii), we next construct ${}_G\Theta$.

Implementation 17.7. Here we implement Algorithm 17.8 in C#. First, we create a class to represent an item.

```
public class LRItem : IEquatable<LRItem>
{
    public ContextFreeRule Rule { get; private set; }
    public int SeparatorPosition { get; private set; }

    public LRItem(ContextFreeRule rule, int separatorPosition)
    {
        this.Rule = rule;
        this.SeparatorPosition = separatorPosition;
    }

    public static bool Equals(LRItem item1, LRItem item2)
    {
        if (ReferenceEquals(item1, item2)) return true;
        else if (ReferenceEquals(item1, null) ||
                 ReferenceEquals(item2, null))
        {
            return false;
        }
        else
        {
```

Algorithm 17.8: Construction of ${}_G\Theta$

Input: An LR grammar, $G = ({}_G\Sigma, {}_GR)$, extended by the dummy rule $Z \to S$, where Z is the new start symbol.
Output: ${}_G\Theta$.
Note: Apart from ${}_G\Theta$, an auxiliary set ${}_GW \subseteq {}_G\Omega$ is used.

begin
  set ${}_GW = \{\{Z \to \bullet S\}\}$
  set ${}_G\Theta = \emptyset$
  repeat
    for *each* $I \in {}_GW$ **do**
                        `// start of extension (i)`
      repeat
        if $A \to u \bullet Bv \in I$ *and* $B \to z \in {}_GR$ **then**
          include $B \to \bullet z$ into I
        end
      until no change
      include I into ${}_G\Theta$ `// end of extension (i)`
                        `// start of extension (ii)`
      for *each* $X \in {}_G\Sigma$ *with* ${}_G\circlearrowright(I, X) \neq \emptyset$ **do**
        include ${}_G\circlearrowright(I, X)$ into ${}_GW$
      end
                        `// end of extension (ii)`
    end
  until no change
end

```
            return item1.Rule == item2.Rule &&
                item1.SeparatorPosition == item2.SeparatorPosition;
        }
    }
    public override bool Equals(object obj)
    {
        return LRItem.Equals(this, obj as LRItem);
    }
    public bool Equals(LRItem other)
    {
        return LRItem.Equals(this, other);
    }
    public static bool operator ==(LRItem item1, LRItem item2)
    {
        return LRItem.Equals(item1, item2);
    }
    public static bool operator !=(LRItem item1, LRItem item2)
```

```
    {
        return !LRItem.Equals(item1, item2);
    }
    public override int GetHashCode()
    {
        int hash = 17;
        hash = hash * 23 + this.Rule.LeftHandSide.GetHashCode();
        hash = hash * 23 + this.Rule.RightHandSide.GetHashCode();
        hash = hash * 23 + this.SeparatorPosition.GetHashCode();
        return hash;
    }

    public override string ToString()
    {
        if (this.SeparatorPosition == 0)
        {
            return this.Rule.LeftHandSide + " -> |"
                    + this.Rule.RightHandSide;
        }
        else if (this.SeparatorPosition ==
                this.Rule.RightHandSide.Length)
        {
            return this.Rule.LeftHandSide + " -> "
                    + this.Rule.RightHandSide + "|";
        }
        else
        {
            return this.Rule.LeftHandSide + " -> "
                    + this.Rule.RightHandSide.GetPrefix(
                        this.SeparatorPosition)
                    + "|" + this.Rule.RightHandSide.GetSuffix(
                        this.Rule.RightHandSide.Length
                        - this.SeparatorPosition);
        }
    }
}
```

Next we add two properties which tell us if an item is a start item, an end item, or neither.

```
public bool IsStartItem
{
    get { return this.SeparatorPosition == 0; }
}
public bool IsEndItem
{
    get
    {
        return this.SeparatorPosition ==
```

```
                this.Rule.RightHandSide.Length;
    }
}
```

We also add a property which returns the first symbol after the separator, if applicable.

```
public Symbol FirstSuffixSymbol
{
    get
    {
        if (this.SeparatorPosition < this.Rule.RightHandSide.Length)
        {
            return this.Rule.RightHandSide[this.SeparatorPosition];
        }
        else
        {
            return null;
        }
    }
}
```

Recall that extension (ii) is based on relation $_G\circlearrowright$. The following method, added to `LRParser` class (see Implementation 17.6), implements this relation.

```
private static FiniteSet<LRItem> NextItems(FiniteSet<LRItem> I,
                                           Symbol X)
{
    var result = new FiniteSet<LRItem>();

    foreach (LRItem i in I)
    {
        if (i.FirstSuffixSymbol == X)
        {
            result.Add(new LRItem(i.Rule, i.SeparatorPosition + 1));
        }
    }

    return result;
}
```

We will also need a helper method which adds a given set to a given family.

```
private static bool AddSet<T>(FiniteSet<FiniteSet<T>> family,
                              FiniteSet<T> setToAdd)
{
    foreach (var existingSet in family)
    {
        if (setToAdd.SetEquals(existingSet))
        {
            return false;
        }
    }
```

```
    family.Add(setToAdd);

    return true;
}
```

Now we are ready to implement Algorithm 17.8 in `LRParser` class by adding a method as follows:

```
public static FiniteSet<FiniteSet<LRItem>> ConstructTheta(
    ContextFreeGrammar G)
{
    var W = new FiniteSet<FiniteSet<LRItem>>
    {
        new FiniteSet<LRItem>
        {
            new LRItem(new ContextFreeRule("Z",
                                            new HmmlcString("S")), 0)
        }
    };
    var Theta = new FiniteSet<FiniteSet<LRItem>>();

    bool change;
    do
    {
        change = false;

        var currentW = new FiniteSet<FiniteSet<LRItem>>(W);

        foreach (FiniteSet<LRItem> I in currentW)
        {
            var newI = new FiniteSet<LRItem>(I);

            // start of extension I
            bool extension1change;
            do
            {
                extension1change = false;
                var currentI = new FiniteSet<LRItem>(newI);
                foreach (LRItem i in currentI)
                {
                    foreach (ContextFreeRule r in G.Rules)
                    {
                        if (i.FirstSuffixSymbol == r.LeftHandSide)
                        {
                            if (newI.Add(new LRItem(r, 0)))
                            {
                                extension1change = true;
                            }
                        }
                    }
                }
            }
            while (extension1change);
```

```
            if (AddSet(Theta, newI))
            {
                change = true;
            }
            // end of extension I

            // start of extension II
            foreach (Symbol X in G.Nonterminals)
            {
                var nextItems = NextItems(newI, X);
                if (!nextItems.IsEmpty)
                {
                    if (AddSet(W, nextItems))
                    {
                        change = true;
                    }
                }
            }
            foreach (Symbol X in G.Terminals)
            {
                var nextItems = NextItems(newI, X);
                if (!nextItems.IsEmpty)
                {
                    if (AddSet(W, nextItems))
                    {
                        change = true;
                    }
                }
            }
            // end of extension II
        }
    }
    while (change);

    return Theta;
}
```

Example 17.12. *Consider again H (see Convention 17.2). Add a dummy rule of the form $Z \to S$ to its rules and define Z as the start symbol. The resulting LR CFG is defined as*

$$
\begin{aligned}
0 &: Z \to S \\
1 &: S \to S \vee A \\
2 &: S \to A \\
3 &: A \to A \wedge B \\
4 &: A \to B \\
5 &: B \to (S) \\
6 &: B \to i
\end{aligned}
$$

Table 17.20 $_H\Theta$

$_H\Theta$	**Item sets**
θ_1	$\{Z \rightarrow \bullet S, S \rightarrow \bullet S \vee A, S \rightarrow \bullet A, A \rightarrow \bullet A \wedge B, A \rightarrow \bullet B, B \rightarrow \bullet(S), B \rightarrow \bullet i\}$
θ_2	$\{Z \rightarrow S\bullet, S \rightarrow S \bullet \vee A\}$
θ_3	$\{S \rightarrow A\bullet, A \rightarrow A \bullet \wedge B\}$
θ_4	$\{A \rightarrow B\bullet\}$
θ_5	$\{B \rightarrow (\bullet S), S \rightarrow \bullet S \vee A, S \rightarrow \bullet A, A \rightarrow \bullet A \wedge B, A \rightarrow \bullet B, B \rightarrow \bullet(S), B \rightarrow \bullet i\}$
θ_6	$\{B \rightarrow i\bullet\}$
θ_7	$\{S \rightarrow S \vee \bullet A, A \rightarrow \bullet A \wedge B, A \rightarrow \bullet B, B \rightarrow \bullet(S), B \rightarrow \bullet i\}$
θ_8	$\{A \rightarrow A \wedge \bullet B, B \rightarrow \bullet(S), B \rightarrow \bullet i\}$
θ_9	$\{B \rightarrow (\bullet S), S \rightarrow S \bullet \vee A\}$
θ_{10}	$\{S \rightarrow S \vee A\bullet, A \rightarrow A \bullet \wedge B\}$
θ_{11}	$\{A \rightarrow A \wedge B\bullet\}$
θ_{12}	$\{B \rightarrow (S)\bullet\}$

Next, apply Algorithm 17.8 with H as its input. At the beginning, set $_H\Theta = \emptyset$ *and* $W = \{\{Z \rightarrow \bullet S\}\}$. *By extension (i), the algorithm extends* $\{Z \rightarrow \bullet S\} \in {_H}W$ *to*

$$
\begin{aligned}
\{\, Z &\rightarrow \bullet S,\\
S &\rightarrow \bullet S \vee A,\\
S &\rightarrow \bullet A,\\
A &\rightarrow \bullet A \wedge B,\\
A &\rightarrow \bullet B,\\
B &\rightarrow \bullet(S),\\
B &\rightarrow \bullet i \quad \}.
\end{aligned}
$$

Include this item set into $_H\Theta$. *Notice that this new item set I contains* $Z \rightarrow \bullet S$, $S \rightarrow \bullet S \vee A$, *and for* $I = \{Z \rightarrow \bullet S, S \rightarrow \bullet S \vee A\}$, *we have* $_H\circlearrowleft(I, S) = \{Z \rightarrow S\bullet, S \rightarrow S \bullet \vee A\}$. *Thus, by performing extension (ii), the algorithm includes* $\{Z \rightarrow S\bullet, S \rightarrow S \bullet \vee A\}$ *into* $_HW$, *after which it performs the second iteration of (i) and (ii), and so on. Continuing in this way, this algorithm eventually produces the 12 item sets listed in the second column of Table 17.20. For brevity, these 12 item sets are referred to as* θ_1 *to* θ_{12} *according to the first column of this table.*

Construction of LR table. Making use of $_G\Theta$, we construct the *action* and *goto* parts of LR table by performing (i)–(iii), given next, in which we automatically suppose that θ_i and θ_j belong to $_G\Theta$. Concerning (i) and (ii), given next, it is important to realize that for all $\theta_i \in {_G}\Omega$ and all $X \in {_G}\Sigma$, $_G\circlearrowleft(\theta_i, X)$ and $_GI_{start}$ (see Convention 17.6) are necessarily disjoint.

(i) To explain the construction of *goto*, consider item $A \rightarrow u \bullet Bv \in I$, where $I \in {_G}\Theta$, $A, B \in {_G}N$ and $u, v \in {_G}\Sigma^*$. At this point, after reducing a portion of the input string to B, M actually extends the prefix u of the handle by B, so uB occurs on the *pd* top, which leads to this extension:

if ${}_G\circlearrowleft(\theta_i, B) = \theta_j - {}_GI_{start}$, where $B \in {}_GN$ **then**
  $goto[\theta_i, B] = \theta_j$
end

(ii) By analogy with the construction of the *goto* entries in (i), we obtain the *action* shift entries in this way

if ${}_G\circlearrowleft(\theta_i, b) = \theta_j - {}_GI_{start}$, where $b \in {}_G\Delta$ **then**
  $action[\theta_i, b] = \theta_j$
end

(iii) To explain the construction of the reduction entries in *action*, consider a rule $r: A \to u \in {}_GR$ and $A \to u\bullet \in {}_GI_{end}$ (see Convention 17.6), which means that a complete handle u occurs on the pushdown top. At this point, the parser reduces u to A according to this rule provided that after this reduction, A is followed by a terminal a that may legally occur after A in a sentential form. As a result, we obtain

if $A \to u\bullet \in \theta_i$, $a \in$ follow (A), $r: A \to u \in {}_GR$ **then**
  $action[\theta_i, b] = r$
end

(see Definition 17.2 and Algorithm 17.4 for the definition and construction of follow, respectively).

Recall that G starts every derivation by applying $0: Z \to S$, and the LR parser works, so it simulates rightmost derivations in G in reverse. Furthermore, notice that when the input symbol equals $\lhd$, all the input has been read by the parser. Consequently, if $Z \to S\bullet \in \theta_i$, we set $action[\theta_i, \lhd] = ☺$ to signalize that the parsing process has been successfully completed. Therefore,

if $Z \to s\bullet \in \theta_i$ **then**
  $action[\theta_i, \lhd] = ☺$
end

Implementation 17.8. The following C# implementation of LR table construction directly follows Algorithm 17.9.

```
public static LRTable ConstructLRTable(
    ContextFreeGrammar G,
    FiniteSet<FiniteSet<LRItem>> Theta,
    IDictionary<Symbol, FiniteSet<Symbol>> follow)
{
    var table = new LRTable();

    var endItemZtoS = new LRItem(
        new ContextFreeRule("Z", new HmmlcString("S")),
        1);

    int iNumber = 0;

    foreach (FiniteSet<LRItem> i in Theta)
    {
```

Algorithm 17.9: LR table

Input: An LR grammar, $G = ({}_G\Sigma, {}_GR)$, in which Z and $0\colon Z \to S$ have the same meaning as in Algorithm 17.8, and ${}_G\Theta$, which is constructed by Algorithm 17.8.
Output: A G-based LR table, consisting of the *action* and *goto* parts.
Note: We suppose that $A, B \in {}_GN$, $b \in {}_G\Delta$, and $u, v \in {}_G\Sigma^*$ in this algorithm.

begin
  denote the rows of *action* and *goto* with the members of ${}_G\Theta$
  denote the columns of *action* and *goto* with the members of ${}_G\Delta$ and ${}_GN$, respectively
  repeat
    for *all* $\theta_i, \theta_j \in {}_G\Theta$ **do**
      if $\theta_j - {}_GI_{start} \neq \emptyset$ **then**
        if ${}_G\circlearrowleft(\theta_i, B) = \theta_j - {}_GI_{start}$, *where* $B \in {}_GN$ **then**
          $goto[\theta_i, B] = \theta_j$ `//` *goto* `entries; see (i)`
        end
        if ${}_G\circlearrowleft(\theta_i, b) = \theta_j - {}_GI_{start}$, *where* $b \in {}_G\Delta$ **then**
          $action[\theta_i, b] = \theta_j$ `//` *action* `shift entries; see (ii)`
        end
      end
      if $A \to u\bullet \in \theta_i \cap {}_GI_{end}$, $a \in$ follow (A), $r\colon A \to u \in {}_GR$ **then**
        $action[\theta_i, a] = r$ `//` *action* `reduction entries; see (iii)`
      end
    end
  until no change
  if $Z \to S\bullet \in \theta_i$ **then**
    $action[\theta_i, \lhd] = ☺$ `// success`
  end
    `// all the other entries remain blank and, thereby, signalize a syntax error`
end

```
iNumber++;
Symbol iTheta = "theta" + iNumber;

int jNumber = 0;

foreach (FiniteSet<LRItem> j in Theta)
{
    jNumber++;
```

```
            Symbol jTheta = "theta" + jNumber;

            var jWithoutStartItems = new FiniteSet<LRItem>();
            foreach (LRItem item in j)
            {
                if (!item.IsStartItem)
                {
                    jWithoutStartItems.Add(item);
                }
            }

            if (!jWithoutStartItems.IsEmpty)
            {
                foreach (Symbol B in G.Nonterminals)
                {
                    if (NextItems(i, B).SetEquals(jWithoutStartItems))
                    {
                        table.Goto[iTheta, B] = jTheta;
                    }
                }

                foreach (Symbol b in G.Terminals)
                {
                    if (NextItems(i, b).SetEquals(jWithoutStartItems))
                    {
                        table.Action[iTheta, b] =
                            ActionTableEntry.ForTheta(jTheta);
                    }
                }
            }
        }

        foreach (LRItem item in i)
        {
            if (item.IsEndItem)
            {
                ContextFreeRule r = item.Rule;
                Symbol A = r.LeftHandSide;
                foreach (Symbol a in follow[A])
                {
                    table.Action[iTheta, a] =
                        ActionTableEntry.ForRule(r);
                }
            }
        }

        if (i.Contains(endItemZtoS))
        {
            table.Action[iTheta, Parsing.InputEnd] =
                ActionTableEntry.Success;
        }
    }

    return table;
}
```

Example 17.13. *Consider the same grammar as in Example 17.12, defined as*

$$\begin{aligned}
0 &: Z \rightarrow S,\\
1 &: S \rightarrow S \vee A,\\
2 &: S \rightarrow A,\\
3 &: A \rightarrow A \wedge B,\\
4 &: A \rightarrow B,\\
5 &: B \rightarrow (S),\\
6 &: B \rightarrow i.
\end{aligned}$$

Consider $_H\Theta = \{\theta_1, \theta_2, \ldots, \theta_{12}\}$, *obtained in Example 17.12 (see Table 17.20). Denote the rows of action and goto with the members of* $_H\Theta$. *Denote the columns of action and goto with the members of* $\{\vee, \wedge, (,), i, \lhd\}$ *and* $\{S, A, B\}$, *respectively.*

According to the first if statement in Algorithm 17.9, goto$[\theta_1, S] = \theta_2$ *because* $S \rightarrow \bullet S \vee A \in \theta_1$ *and* $S \rightarrow S \bullet \vee A \in \theta_2$. *By the second if statement, action*$[\theta_2, \vee] = theta_7$ *because* $S \rightarrow S \bullet \vee A \in \theta_2$ *and* $S \rightarrow S \vee \bullet A \in \theta_7$. *By the third if statement, action*$[\theta_3, \vee] = 2$ *because* $2: S \rightarrow A\bullet \in \theta_3$ *and* $\vee \in$ follow (A). *As an exercise, perform a complete execution of the repeat loop, containing the three if statements. After this, according to the conclusion of Algorithm 17.9, set action*$[\theta_2, \lhd] =$ ☺ *because* θ_2 *contains* $Z \rightarrow S\bullet$. *The resulting table produced by this algorithm is given in Tables 17.17 and 17.18.*

Out of the existing constructions of LR tables, the construction described in this section belongs to the simplest methods of obtaining LR tables. Unfortunately, there exist LR grammars for which this construction does not work. In fact, it breaks down even when some quite common grammatical phenomenon occurs. Specifically, it cannot handle *reduction-shift conflict*, whose decision requires to figure out whether the parser should perform a shift or a reduction when both actions are possible. Furthermore, if two or more different reductions can be made in the given configuration, it cannot decide which of them it should select. To give an insight into this latter *reduction-reduction conflict*, suppose that the same set in $_H\Theta$ contains two end items, $A \rightarrow u\bullet$ and $B \rightarrow v\bullet$, but follow $(A) \cap$ follow $(B) \neq \emptyset$. At this point, Algorithm 17.9 would illegally place both rules, $A \rightarrow u$ and $B \rightarrow v$, into the same entry in the action part of the LR table. There exists a number of complicated constructions that resolve these conflicts. However, these constructions are too complex to be included into this introductory text as already pointed out.

17.3.9 Handling errors in LR parsing

Compared to handling errors in precedence parsing, LR parsing handles syntax errors more exactly and elegantly. Indeed, LR parsing detects an error as soon as there is no valid continuation for the portion of the input thus far scanned. As a result, it detects all possible errors by using only the *action* part of the table; as a side effect, this property allows us to significantly reduce the size of the *goto* part by removing its unneeded blank entries. Next, we sketch two frequently used methods of LR error recovery. As before, we suppose that $G = ({}_G\Sigma, {}_GR)$ is an LR grammar, and M is a G-based LR parser, which uses LR-table, consisting of *action* and *goto*.

A *panic-mode error recovery* represents a method that tries to isolate the shortest possible erroneous substring derivable from a selected nonterminal, skips this substring, and resumes the parsing process. This method has a selected set of nonterminals, ${}_GO$, which usually represents major program pieces, such as expressions or statements. In principle, this method finds the shortest string uv such that $u \in {}_G\Sigma^*$ is a string obtained from a current pushdown top $x \in ({}_G\Sigma\, {}_G\Theta)^*$ by deleting all symbols from ${}_G\Theta$, and v is the shortest input prefix followed by an input symbol a from follow (A), where $A \in O$ and $A \Rightarrow^*_{rm} uv$. Let x be preceded by $o \in {}_G\Theta$ and $goto[o, A] = \theta$. To recover, this method replaces x with $A\theta$ on the *pd* top and skips the input prefix v. In this way, it pretends that the parser has reduced a portion of the input string that ends with v to A. After this, it resumes the parsing process from $action[\theta, a]$. As an exercise, we discuss this method in detail as well as its more sophisticated variants.

Ad-hoc recovery. This method resembles the way the precedence parser handles the table-detected errors. That is, this method considers each blank *action* entry, which only signalizes an error without any diagnostic specification. Based on a typical language usage, it decides the most probable mistake that led to the particular error in question, and according to this decision, it designs an ingenious recovery procedure that takes an appropriate recovery action. This design always requires some ingeniousness from the compiler's author, who is encouraged to consult some other computer-science areas, ranging from computational psychology through artificial intelligence to the formal language theory, in order to design the best possible error-recovery routine. Typically, this routine handles an error of this kind so that it modifies the pushdown or the input by changing, inserting, or deleting some symbols; whatever modification it performs, however, it has to guarantee that this modification surely avoids any infinite loop so that the parser eventually proceeds its normal process. Finally, each blank entry is filled with the reference to the corresponding recovery routine. In practice, this method is very popular, and we illustrate its application in the next example.

Example 17.14. *To demonstrate how LR parsing handles syntax errors by using the ad-hoc recovery method, consider the grammar H (see Convention 17.2), defined as*

$$
\begin{aligned}
1 &: S \rightarrow S \vee A,\\
2 &: S \rightarrow A,\\
3 &: A \rightarrow A \wedge B,\\
4 &: A \rightarrow B,\\
5 &: B \rightarrow (S),\\
6 &: B \rightarrow i,
\end{aligned}
$$

and its LR table consisting of action and goto given in Tables 17.17 and 17.18, respectively. Consider the ill-formed expression $i\vee)$*. With* $i\vee)$*, the* H*-based LR parser interrupts its parsing process after making the six steps described in Table 17.21 because it reaches a blank entry in action, so the error recovery is in order.*

Next, we schematically describe four diagnoses together with the corresponding recovery procedures—$\boxed{1}$*–*$\boxed{4}$*, whose straightforward incorporation into Algorithm 7.25*

Table 17.21 H-based LR parser working on i∨) without error recovery

Configuration	**Table entry**	**Parsing action**
$\triangleright\theta_1\diamond i\vee)\triangleleft$	$action[\theta_1, i] = \theta_6$	LR-SHIFT (i)
$\triangleright\theta_1 i\theta_6\diamond\vee)\triangleleft$	$action[\theta_6, \vee] = 6, goto[\theta_1, B] = \theta_4$	LR-REDUCE (6)
$\triangleright\theta_1 B\theta_4\diamond\vee)\triangleleft$	$action[\theta_4, \vee] = 4, goto[\theta_1, A] = \theta_3$	LR-REDUCE (4)
$\triangleright\theta_1 A\theta_3\diamond\vee)\triangleleft$	$action[\theta_3, \vee] = 2, goto[\theta_1, S] = \theta_2$	LR-REDUCE (2)
$\triangleright\theta_1 S\theta_2\diamond\vee)\triangleleft$	$action[\theta_2, \vee] = \theta_7$	LR-SHIFT ($\vee$)
$\triangleright\theta_1 S\theta_2 \vee \theta_7\diamond)\triangleleft$	$action[\theta_7,)] = \square$	ERROR

Table 17.22 $_H$action with error-recovery routines

	$\wedge$	$\vee$	i	(	)	$\triangleleft$
θ_1	$\boxed{1}$	$\boxed{1}$	θ_6	θ_5	$\boxed{2}$	$\boxed{1}$
θ_2		θ_7			$\boxed{1}$	☺
θ_3	θ_8	2			2	2
θ_4	4	4			4	4
θ_5	$\boxed{1}$	$\boxed{1}$	θ_6	θ_5	$\boxed{2}$	$\boxed{1}$
θ_6	6	6	$\boxed{3}$	$\boxed{3}$	6	6
θ_7	$\boxed{1}$	$\boxed{1}$	θ_6	θ_5	$\boxed{2}$	$\boxed{1}$
θ_8	$\boxed{1}$	$\boxed{1}$	θ_6	θ_5	$\boxed{2}$	$\boxed{1}$
θ_9		θ_7			θ_{12}	$\boxed{4}$
θ_{10}	θ_8	1			1	1
θ_{11}	3	3			3	3
θ_{12}	5	5	$\boxed{3}$	$\boxed{3}$	5	5

is left as an exercise. Table 17.22 presents a new version of action with the appropriate error-recovery routine placed into each blank entry. With i∨) as its input, the H-based LR parser makes the error recovery described in Table 17.24. As an exercise, prove that the parser can never detect an error in the blank entries of the table. Indeed, the parser cannot detect an error in any entry of the goto part, which thus contains no recovery routines, as shown in Table 17.23. However, for the same reason, the action part contains some blank entries too.

$\boxed{1}$ **Diagnostic** *missing i or (*
Recovery *insert $i\theta_6$ onto the pushdown*

$\boxed{2}$ **Diagnostic** *unbalanced)*
Recovery *delete the input symbol) and, thereby, advance to the next input symbol*

$\boxed{3}$ **Diagnostic** *missing operator*
Recovery *insert ∨ in front of the current input symbol* ins, *and after this insertion, set* ins *to the newly inserted ∨*

$\boxed{4}$ **Diagnostic** *missing)*
Recovery *insert $)\theta_{12}$ onto the pushdown*

Table 17.23 $_H goto$

	S	A	B
θ_1	θ_2	θ_3	θ_4
θ_2			
θ_3			
θ_4			
θ_5	θ_9	θ_3	θ_4
θ_6			
θ_7		θ_{10}	θ_4
θ_8			θ_{11}
θ_9			
θ_{10}			
θ_{11}			
θ_{12}			

Table 17.24 H-based LR parser working on i∨) with ad-hoc error recovery

Configuration	**Table entry**	**Parsing action**
$\triangleright\theta_1\diamond i\vee)\triangleleft$	$action[\theta_1, i] = \theta_6$	LR-SHIFT (i)
$\triangleright\theta_1 i\theta_6\diamond\vee)\triangleleft$	$action[\theta_6, \vee] = 6$, $goto[\theta_1, B] = \theta_4$	LR-REDUCE (6)
$\triangleright\theta_1 B\theta_4\diamond\vee)\triangleleft$	$action[\theta_4, \vee] = 4$, $goto[\theta_1, A] = \theta_3$	LR-REDUCE (4)
$\triangleright\theta_1 A\theta_3\diamond\vee)\triangleleft$	$action[\theta_3, \vee] = 2$, $goto[\theta_1, S] = \theta_2$	LR-REDUCE (2)
$\triangleright\theta_1 S\theta_2\diamond\vee)\triangleleft$	$action[\theta_2, \vee] = \theta_7$	LR-SHIFT ($\vee$)
$\triangleright\theta_1 S\theta_2 \vee \theta_7\diamond)\triangleleft$	$action[\theta_7,)] = \boxed{2}$	$\boxed{2}$—skip)
$\triangleright\theta_1 S\theta_2 \vee \theta_7\diamond\triangleleft$	$action[\theta_7, \triangleleft] = \boxed{1}$	$\boxed{1}$—push $i\theta_6$ onto *pd*
$\triangleright\theta_1 S\theta_2 \vee \theta_7 i\theta_6\diamond\triangleleft$	$action[\theta_6, \triangleleft] = 6$, $goto[\theta_7, B] = \theta_4$	LR-REDUCE (6)
$\triangleright\theta_1 S\theta_2 \vee \theta_7 B\theta_4\diamond\triangleleft$	$action[\theta_4, \triangleleft] = 4$, $goto[\theta_7, A] = \theta_{10}$	LR-REDUCE (4)
$\triangleright\theta_1 S\theta_2 \vee \theta_7 A\theta_{10}\diamond\triangleleft$	$action[\theta_{10}, \triangleleft] = 1$, $goto[\theta_1, S] = \theta_2$	LR-REDUCE (1)
$\triangleright\theta_1 S\theta_2\diamond\triangleleft$	$action[\theta_2, \triangleleft] = ☺$	ERROR

17.4 Syntax-directed translation: an implementation

Parsers often represent important components of other software tools, such as compilers, which not only analyze but also translate input programs written in a programming language. That is, if the programs are correct, they are translated into functionally equivalent programs written in output codes, such as machine-independent codes or the machine code of a particular computer. This translation is usually directed by the parsers during their syntax analysis of the input programs, hence its name—*syntax-directed translation*. Recall that the parsers produce parses as the sequences of grammatical rules according to which the input programs are generated, so the translation could take advantage of these parses once the syntax analysis is over to produce the equivalent output code. In practice, however, most parsers perform their analysis simultaneously with the translation to speed up the translation process. That is, during a parsing step according to a rule, this translation performs an action with *attributes* attached to the pushdown symbols the parsing step is performed with. Regarding the code generation, these attributes usually address fragments of the code produced so far from which the attached action creates a larger piece of the generated code by composing these fragments together. In this way, the action generates the code that determines how to interpret the rule it is attached to. From a broader perspective, these actions bridge the gap between the syntax analysis of the input programs and their interpretation in terms of the output code. In other words, they actually define the *meaning* of the rules they are attached to, and that is why these actions are often called *semantic actions*.

In this section, we sketch a precedence parser (see Section 17.3) so the parser guides the syntax-directed translation of infix logical expressions to their postfix equivalents. The syntax-directed translation is defined by the grammar extended by semantic actions with attributes, which are placed into braces behind the grammatical rules as follows next. When a parser applies a rule, its action is performed too.

$$
\begin{array}{ll}
C \to \neg C & \{\text{POSTFIX}\,(!)\} \\
C \to C \vee C & \{\text{POSTFIX}\,(|)\} \\
C \to C \wedge C & \{\text{POSTFIX}\,(\&)\} \\
C \to (C) & \{\} \\
C \to i\ \{var\} & \{\text{POSTFIX}\,(var)\} \\
C \to \#\ \{int\} & \{\text{POSTFIX}\,(int)\}
\end{array}
$$

In a greater detail, as their operands, the infix expressions may contain the identifiers, denoted by i, and integers, denoted by # (every positive integer represents the logical value *true* while the zero means *false*). Logical operators *and*, *or*, and *not* are denoted by &, |, and !, respectively. Suppose that the syntax-directed translation applies $C \to i$ {POSTFIX (var)}. Apart from the usual reduction as a parsing action (see the beginning of Section 17.3), the translation emits the specific variable acting as an attribute attached to the identifier. Similarly, by $C \to \#$ {POSTFIX (int)}, the translation emits the integer attribute attached to #. During the application of $C \to C \vee C$ {POSTFIX (|)}, the translation has generated the operands corresponding to the two Cs on the right-hand side, so it is the right moment to generate | behind them. In a similar way, the translation uses $C \to \neg C$ {POSTFIX (!)} and $C \to C \wedge C$ {POSTFIX (&)}. As postfix notation uses no parentheses, a reduction according to $C \to (C)$ makes no semantic action. Leaving a more detailed discussion of this postfix-notation-generating syntax-directed translation in general as an exercise, we now consider the expression $i\{x\} \wedge (i\{y\} \vee \{z\})$, so in this expression, variables x, y, and z represent attributes attached to the first i, the second i, and the third i, respectively. In Table 17.25, we describe how the syntax-directed translation based

Table 17.25 Syntax-directed generation of postfix notation

Configuration	Parsing action	Semantic action	Postfix notation
$\triangleright\diamond i\{x\} \wedge (i\{y\} \vee i\{z\})\triangleleft$	SHIFT		
$\triangleright\underline{i\{x\}}\diamond \wedge (i\{y\} \vee i\{z\})\triangleleft$	REDUCE ($C \rightarrow i$)	POSTFIX (x)	x
$\triangleright C\diamond \wedge (i\{y\} \vee i\{z\})\triangleleft$	SHIFT		
$\triangleright C \wedge \diamond(i\{y\} \vee i\{z\})\triangleleft$	SHIFT		
$\triangleright C \wedge (\diamond i\{y\} \vee i\{z\})\triangleleft$	SHIFT		
$\triangleright C \wedge (\underline{i\{y\}}\diamond \vee i\{z\})\triangleleft$	REDUCE ($C \rightarrow i$)	POSTFIX (y)	xy
$\triangleright C \wedge (C\diamond \vee i\{z\})\triangleleft$	SHIFT		
$\triangleright C \wedge (C \vee \diamond i\{z\})\triangleleft$	SHIFT		
$\triangleright C \wedge (C \vee \underline{i\{z\}}C\diamond)\triangleleft$	REDUCE ($C \rightarrow i$)	POSTFIX (z)	xyz
$\triangleright C \wedge (\underline{C \vee C}\diamond)\triangleleft$	REDUCE ($C \rightarrow C \vee C$)	POSTFIX ($\vert$)	$xyz\vert$
$\triangleright C \wedge (C\diamond)\triangleleft$	SHIFT		
$\triangleright C \wedge \underline{(C)}\diamond\triangleleft$	REDUCE ($C \rightarrow (C)$)	no action	
$\triangleright\underline{C \wedge C}\diamond\triangleleft$	REDUCE ($C \rightarrow C \wedge C$)	POSTFIX (&)	$xyz\vert\&$
$\triangleright C\diamond\triangleleft$	*ACCEPT*		

upon the above attribute grammar and guided by an operator-precedence parser turns this expression to the postfix notation $xyz|\&$.

Implementation 17.9. Recall that we have already provided an example implementation of an operator-precedence parser (see Implementation 17.5). Although the implementation presented here shares many similarities, it is more practically oriented and, as a result, follows Algorithm 17.6 less closely. For instance, it makes use of a special symbol stored on the pushdown to mark the beginning of handle, which obviously makes the delimitation of a handle simpler and faster. Moreover, instead of our specific `HmmlcString` and `Symbol` classes, we obtain the input in a standard way and use a lexical analyzer to recognize lexemes and produce the corresponding tokens. As the parser makes the syntax analysis of the tokenized infix expression, it additionally performs semantic actions to produce the postfix equivalent to the infix expression.

First, we define the types of symbol which can occur in the input or on the pushdown.

```
public enum SymbolType
{
    Token_Identifier = 0,        // i
    Token_Integer = 1,           // #
    Token_And = 2,               // &
    Token_Or = 3,                // |
    Token_Neg = 4,               // !
    Token_LeftParen = 5,         // (
```

```
    Token_RightParen = 6,          // )
    EndMarker = 7,                 // $
    Nonterminal_Condition = 8, // C
    HandleMarker = 9
}
```

The only nonterminal *C* is represented by `Nonterminal_Condition`. The symbol `EndMarker` marks the input end as well as the pushdown bottom. The symbol `HandleMarker` is a special type of pushdown symbol introduced to delimit a handle. The other symbols correspond to the input tokens.

The lexical analyzer, as defined by `ILex` interface, recognizes the next lexeme and produces its token that specifies the lexeme. Moreover, for an identifier, the token has an attribute which specifies its name, and for an integer, an attribute with its value.

```
public class Token
{
    public SymbolType Type { get; private set; }
    public string Name { get; private set; }
    public int Value { get; private set; }

    public Token(SymbolType type, string name, int value)
    {
        this.Type = type;
        this.Name = name;
        this.Value = value;
    }
}

public interface ILex
{
    Token GetNextToken();
}
```

The following class represents a context-free rule extended with a semantic action. In this example, the action is either a string to be appended to the postfix notation or **`null`** if no action is to be performed.

```
public class ExtendedRule
{
    public SymbolType LeftHandSide { get; set; }
    public IList<SymbolType> RightHandSide { get; private set; }
    public string Action { get; set; }

    public ExtendedRule()
    {
        this.RightHandSide = new List<SymbolType>();
    }
}
```

We now implement an operator-precedence parser which uses a provided lexical analyzer.

```
public class PrecedenceParser
{
    private ILex lex;

    public PrecedenceParser(ILex lex)
    {
        this.lex = lex;
    }
}
```

In this example, we specify both the precedence table and the rules directly inside `PrecedenceParser` class. In the precedence table, `'<'`, `'>'`, and `'='` represent $\lfloor$, $\rfloor$, and $|$, respectively. Symbol `'_'` denotes a blank entry and `'+'` means that parsing is successfully completed.

```
private static readonly char[,] precedenceTable = new char[,]
{
    /*         i    #    &    |    !    (    )    $ */
    /* i */ { '_', '_', '>', '>', '_', '_', '>', '>' },
    /* # */ { '_', '_', '>', '>', '_', '_', '>', '>' },
    /* & */ { '<', '<', '>', '>', '<', '<', '>', '>' },
    /* | */ { '<', '<', '<', '>', '<', '<', '>', '>' },
    /* ! */ { '<', '<', '>', '>', '<', '<', '>', '>' },
    /* ( */ { '<', '<', '<', '<', '<', '<', '=', '_' },
    /* ) */ { '_', '_', '>', '>', '_', '_', '>', '>' },
    /* $ */ { '<', '<', '<', '<', '<', '<', '_', '+' }
};

private static readonly List<ExtendedRule> rules =
    new List<ExtendedRule>
{
    new ExtendedRule
    {
        LeftHandSide = SymbolType.Nonterminal_Condition,
        RightHandSide = { SymbolType.Token_Neg,
                          SymbolType.Nonterminal_Condition },
        Action = "!"
    },
    new ExtendedRule
    {
        LeftHandSide = SymbolType.Nonterminal_Condition,
        RightHandSide = { SymbolType.Nonterminal_Condition,
                          SymbolType.Token_Or,
                          SymbolType.Nonterminal_Condition },
        Action = "|"
    },
    new ExtendedRule
```

```
    {
        LeftHandSide = SymbolType.Nonterminal_Condition,
        RightHandSide = { SymbolType.Nonterminal_Condition,
                          SymbolType.Token_And,
                          SymbolType.Nonterminal_Condition },
        Action = "&"
    },
    new ExtendedRule
    {
        LeftHandSide = SymbolType.Nonterminal_Condition,
        RightHandSide = { SymbolType.Token_LeftParen,
                          SymbolType.Nonterminal_Condition,
                          SymbolType.Token_RightParen },
        Action = null // no postfix action defined for parenthesis
    },
    new ExtendedRule
    {
        LeftHandSide = SymbolType.Nonterminal_Condition,
        RightHandSide = { SymbolType.Token_Identifier },
        Action = "i"
    },
    new ExtendedRule
    {
        LeftHandSide = SymbolType.Nonterminal_Condition,
        RightHandSide = { SymbolType.Token_Integer },
        Action = "#"
    }
};
```

First, we implement the pushdown. For each symbol, it stores its type and the corresponding token if there is one (**null** otherwise).

```
public class PdSymbol
{
    public SymbolType Type { get; private set; }
    public Token Token { get; private set; }

    public PdSymbol(Token token)
    {
        this.Type = token.Type;
        this.Token = token;
    }

    public PdSymbol(SymbolType type)
    {
        this.Type = type;
        this.Token = null;
    }
}
```

Making use of the standard generic `Stack` class from .NET Framework, the pushdown is implemented simply as `Stack<PdSymbol>`. We now add several helper methods to `PrecedenceParser` class which operate on it. The first one finds the topmost terminal, which determines the parsing action.

```
private static PdSymbol GetTopmostTerminal(Stack<PdSymbol> pd)
{
    foreach (var symbol in pd)
    {
        if (symbol.Type <= SymbolType.EndMarker)
        {
            return symbol;
        }
    }

    return null;
}
```

The next method inserts the handle delimiter symbol directly after the topmost occurrence of the given symbol on the pushdown.

```
private static void InsertHandleMarkerAfter(Stack<PdSymbol> pd,
                                            PdSymbol symbol)
{
    var pdTop = new Stack<PdSymbol>();

    while (pd.Peek() != symbol)
    {
        pdTop.Push(pd.Pop());
    }

    pd.Push(new PdSymbol(SymbolType.HandleMarker));

    while (pdTop.Count > 0)
    {
        pd.Push(pdTop.Pop());
    }
}
```

Making use of the special handle delimiter symbol, the following method retrieves the handle on the pushdown top.

```
private static List<PdSymbol> FindHandle(Stack<PdSymbol> pd)
{
    var handle = new List<PdSymbol>();

    foreach (var symbol in pd)
    {
        if (symbol.Type == SymbolType.HandleMarker)
        {
            break;
```

```
        }

        handle.Add(symbol);
    }

    handle.Reverse();

    return handle;
}
```

Once we have a handle, we need to find a rule whose right-hand side equals it.

```
private ExtendedRule FindRule(List<PdSymbol> handle)
{
    foreach (var rule in rules)
    {
        if (rule.RightHandSide.Count == handle.Count)
        {
            bool match = true;

            for (int i = 0; i < handle.Count; i++)
            {
                if (handle[i].Type != rule.RightHandSide[i])
                {
                    match = false;
                    break;
                }
            }

            if (match)
            {
                return rule;
            }
        }
    }

    return null;
}
```

If a handle and a matching rule is determined successfully, we replace the handle on the pushdown top by the left-hand side of the rule.

```
private static void Reduce(Stack<PdSymbol> pd, ExtendedRule rule)
{
    for (int i = 0; i <= rule.RightHandSide.Count; i++)
    {
        pd.Pop();
    }

    pd.Push(new PdSymbol(rule.LeftHandSide));
}
```

Finally, the rule may have a postfix action specified. The following method performs the action.

```
private static void PerformPostfixAction(string action,
                                         List<PdSymbol> handle)
{
    switch (action)
    {
        case null: // no action prescribed
            break;
        case "i": // identifier
            Console.Write(handle[handle.Count - 1].Token.Name);
            Console.Write(' ');
            break;
        case "#": // integer value
            Console.Write(handle[handle.Count - 1].Token.Value);
            Console.Write(' ');
            break;
        default: // other action (operator)
            Console.Write(action);
            Console.Write(' ');
            break;
    }
}
```

We are now ready to implement the main parsing method. It reads tokens from the provided lexical analyzer and writes out the postfix notation to the standard output as semantic actions during syntax analysis. If a parsing error occurs, it is reported to the standard error output, and the method returns **false**; otherwise, **true** is returned.

```
public bool RunParsing()
{
    var pd = new Stack<PdSymbol>();
    pd.Push(new PdSymbol(SymbolType.EndMarker));

    Token token = lex.GetNextToken();

    while (true)
    {
        if (token == null) return false;

        PdSymbol topmostTerminal = GetTopmostTerminal(pd);

        switch (precedenceTable[(int)topmostTerminal.Type,
                                (int)token.Type])
        {
            case '+': // success
                return true;
            case '=':
                pd.Push(new PdSymbol(token));
```

```
                    token = lex.GetNextToken();
                    break;
                case '<':
                    InsertHandleMarkerAfter(pd, topmostTerminal);
                    pd.Push(new PdSymbol(token));
                    token = lex.GetNextToken();
                    break;
                case '>':
                    List<PdSymbol> handle = FindHandle(pd);
                    if (handle.Count > 0)
                    {
                        ExtendedRule rule = FindRule(handle);
                        if (rule != null)
                        {
                            Reduce(pd, rule);
                            PerformPostfixAction(rule.Action, handle);
                        }
                        else
                        {
                            Console.Error.WriteLine("Syntax error: "
                                + "no rule has the current handle as "
                                + "its right-hand side.");
                            return false;
                        }
                    }
                    else
                    {
                        Console.Error.WriteLine("Syntax error: "
                            + "no symbol < occurs in the pushdown, "
                            + "so no handle is delimited.");
                        return false;
                    }
                    break;
                default:
                    Console.Error.WriteLine("Syntax error: "
                        + "table-detected error by a blank entry.");
                    return false;
            }
        }
    }
```

Next, we present a concrete implementation of a lexical analyzer, and an example of its usage along with the operator-precedence parser.

Implementation 17.10. We implement `ILex` interface specified in the previous Implementation 17.9 using a finite automaton to recognize a lexeme.

```
public class Lex : ILex
{
    private enum State
```

```
    {
        Start,
        Identifier,
        Integer
    }

    private int lineNumber;
    private int position;
    private bool advanceInput = true;
    private bool endOfFile = false;
    private char c = ' ';

    public Lex()
    {
        this.lineNumber = 1;
        this.position = 0;
    }

    public Token GetNextToken()
    {
        var state = State.Start;

        var lexeme = new StringBuilder();

        while (true)
        {
            if (advanceInput)
            {
                int nextCharacterOrEndOfFile = Console.Read();

                endOfFile = nextCharacterOrEndOfFile < 0;

                if (!endOfFile)
                {
                    c = (char)nextCharacterOrEndOfFile;

                    if (c == '/ n')
                    {
                        lineNumber++;
                        position = 0;
                    }

                    position++;
                }
            }

            advanceInput = true;

            switch (state)
            {
                case State.Start:
                    if (endOfFile)
                    {
```

```
            return new Token(SymbolType.EndMarker,
                             string.Empty, 0);
        }
        else if (char.IsWhiteSpace(c))
        {
            continue;
        }
        else if (char.IsLetter(c))
        {
            lexeme.Append(c);
            state = State.Identifier;
        }
        else if (char.IsDigit(c))
        {
            lexeme.Append(c);
            state = State.Integer;
        }
        else
        {
            switch (c)
            {
                case '&':
                    return new Token(
                        SymbolType.Token_And, "&", 0);
                case '|':
                    return new Token
                        SymbolType.Token_Or, "|", 0);
                case '!':
                    return new Token(
                        SymbolType.Token_Neg, "!", 0);
                case '(':
                    return new Token(
                        SymbolType.Token_LeftParen,
                        "(", 0);
                case ')':
                    return new Token(
                        SymbolType.Token_RightParen,
                        ")", 0);
                default:
                    Console.Error.WriteLine("Undefined "
                        + "symbol at line: 0 "
                        + "position: 1",
                        lineNumber, position);
                    return null;
            }
        }
        break;
    case State.Identifier:
        if (endOfFile || char.IsWhiteSpace(c))
        {
            state = State.Start;
            advanceInput = false;
```

```
                        return new Token(SymbolType.Token_Identifier,
                                         lexeme.ToString(), 0);
                    }
                    else if (char.IsLetterOrDigit(c))
                    {
                        lexeme.Append(c);
                    }
                    else
                    {
                        switch (c)
                        {
                            case '&':
                            case '|':
                            case '!':
                            case '(':
                            case ')':
                                state = State.Start;
                                advanceInput = false;
                                return new Token(
                                    SymbolType.Token_Identifier,
                                    lexeme.ToString(), 0);
                            default:
                                Console.Error.WriteLine("Illegal "
                                    + "symbol at line: 0 "
                                    + "position: 1",
                                    lineNumber, position);
                                return null;
                        }
                    }
                    break;
                case State.Integer:
                    if (endOfFile || char.IsWhiteSpace(c))
                    {
                        state = State.Start;
                        advanceInput = false;

                        // we define 0 for zero input,
                        // and 1 for nonzero input
                        int value = int.Parse(lexeme.ToString()) == 0
                            ? 0
                            : 1;
                        return new Token(SymbolType.Token_Integer,
                                         string.Empty, value);
                    }
                    else if (char.IsDigit(c))
                    {
                        lexeme.Append(c);
                    }
                    else
                    {
                        switch (c)
                        {
                            case '&':
```

```
                        case '|':
                        case '!':
                        case '(':
                        case ')':
                            state = State.Start;
                            advanceInput = false;

                            // we define 0 for zero input,
                            // and 1 for nonzero input
                            int value =
                                int.Parse(lexeme.ToString()) == 0
                                ? 0
                                : 1;
                            return new Token(
                                SymbolType.Token_Integer,
                                string.Empty, value);
                        default:
                            Console.Error.WriteLine("Lexical "
                                + "error at line: 0 "
                                + "position: 1",
                                lineNumber, position);
                            return null;
                    }
                }
                break;
            }
        }
    }
}
```

The following code reads an infix expression from the standard input and produces the corresponding postfix notation using the standard output.

```
var lex = new Lex();
var precedenceParser = new PrecedenceParser(lex);

precedenceParser.RunParsing();
```

As stated in the preface, this book is supported by a web page, which includes several other substantial portions of various syntax-directed translations.

Chapter 18

Applications in syntax analysis: natural languages

In Chapter 17, we describe the syntax analysis of programming languages by using classical language models—context-free grammars and pushdown automata. In the present chapter, however, we sketch the syntax analysis of natural languages based upon alternative grammatical models—namely, scattered context grammars, introduced in Section 13.1.

While in Section 13.1, we discuss these grammars in a strictly theoretical way, we next informally sketch how to apply them to the English syntax, which consists of the rules concerning how words relate to each other in order to form well-formed grammatical English sentences. We have selected the syntax of this language because the reader is surely familiar with English very well. Nevertheless, analogical ideas can be applied to members of other language families, including Indo-European, Sino-Tibetan, Niger–Congo, Afro-Asiatic, Altaic, and Japonic families of languages. We explore several common linguistic phenomena involving scattered context in English syntax and explain how to express these phenomena by scattered context grammars. By no means is this chapter intended to be exhaustive in any way. Rather, we consider only selected topics concerning English syntax and demonstrate how scattered context grammars allow us to explore them clearly, elegantly, and precisely.

18.1 Syntax and related linguistic terminology

In this section, we discuss and describe the principles and rules according to which we correctly construct and transform grammatical English sentences. To give an insight into the discussion of English syntax, we open this section by some simple examples that illustrate how we connect the theoretically oriented discussion of scattered context grammars in Section 13.1 with the application-oriented discussion of English syntax in the present chapter.

18.1.1 Introduction by way of examples

Observe that many common English sentences contain expressions and words that mutually depend on each other although they are not adjacent to each other in the sentences. For example, consider this sentence:

He usually goes to work early.

The subject (*he*) and the predicator (*goes*) are related; sentences

**He usually go to work early.*

and

**I usually goes to work early.*

are ungrammatical because the form of the predicator depends on the form of the subject, according to which the combinations **he...go* and **I...goes* are illegal (throughout this chapter, * denotes ungrammatical sentences or their parts). Clearly, any change of the subject implies the corresponding change of the predicator as well. Linguistic dependencies of this kind can be easily and elegantly captured by scattered context grammars. Let us construct a scattered context grammar that contains this production:

(He, goes) $\rightarrow$ (We, go).

This production checks whether the subject is the pronoun *he* and whether the verb *go* is in third person singular. If the sentence satisfies this property, it can be transformed to the grammatically correct sentence

We usually go to work early.

Observe that the related words may occur far away from each other in the sentence in question. In the above example, the word *usually* occurs between the subject and the predicator. While it is fairly easy to use context-sensitive grammars to model context dependencies where only one word occurs between the related words, note that the number of the words appearing between the subject and the predicator can be virtually unlimited. We can say

He almost regularly goes to work early.

but also

He usually, but not always, goes to work early.

and many more grammatical sentences like this. To model these context dependencies by ordinary context-sensitive grammars, many auxiliary productions have to be introduced to send the information concerning the form of a word to another word, which may occur at the opposite end of the sentence. As opposed to this awkward and tedious description, the single scattered context production above is needed to perform the same job regardless of the number of the words appearing between the subject and the predicator.

We next give another example that illustrates the advantage of scattered context grammars over classical context-sensitive grammars under some circumstances. Consider these two sentences:

John recommended it.

and

Did John recommend it?

There exists a relation between the basic clause and its interrogative counterpart. Indeed, we obtain the second, interrogative clause by adding *did* in front of *John* and by changing *recommended* to *recommend* while keeping the rest of the sentence unchanged. In terms of scattered context grammars, this transformation can be described by the scattered context production

$$(\text{John, recommended}) \rightarrow (\text{Did John, recommend});$$

clearly, when applied to the first sentence, this production performs exactly the same transformation as we have just described. Although this transformation is possible by using an ordinary context production, the inverse transformation is much more difficult to achieve. The inverse transformation can be performed by a scattered context production

$$(\text{Did, recommend}) \rightarrow (\varepsilon, \text{recommended});$$

obviously, by erasing *did* and changing *recommend* to *recommended*, we obtain the first sentence from the second one. Again, instead of *John*, the subject may consist of a noun phrase containing several words, which makes it difficult to capture this context dependency by ordinary context-sensitive grammars.

Considering the examples above, the advantage of scattered context grammars is more than obvious: scattered context grammars allow us to change only some words during the transformation while keeping the others unchanged. On the other hand, context-sensitive grammars are inconvenient to perform transformations of this kind. A typical context-sensitive grammar that performs this job usually needs many more context-sensitive productions by which it repeatedly traverses the transformed sentence in question just to change very few context-dependent words broadly spread across the sentence.

18.1.2 Terminology

Taking into account the intuitive insight given above, we see that there are structural rules and regularities underlying syntactically well-formed English sentences and their transformations. Although we have already used some common linguistic notions, such as subject or predicator, we now introduce this elementary linguistic terminology more systematically so we can express these English sentences in terms of their syntactic structure in a more exact and general way. However, we restrict this introduction only to the very basic linguistic notions, most of which are taken from [66,72]. In the next chapter, which concludes this book, we recommend several further excellent linguistic treatments closely related to the discussion of this chapter.

Throughout the rest of this section, we narrow our discussion primarily to verbs and personal pronouns, whose proper use depends on the context in which they occur. For instance, *is*, *are*, *was*, and *been* are different forms of the same verb *be*, and their proper use depends on the context in which they appear. We say that words in these categories *inflect* and call this property *inflection*. Verbs and personal pronouns often represent the key elements of a clause—the *subject* and the *predicate*. In simple clauses like

She loves him.

we can understand the notion of the subject and the predicate so that some information is "predicated of" the subject (*she*) by the predicate (*loves him*). In more complicated clauses, the best way to determine the subject and the predicate is the examination of their syntactic properties (see [72] for more details). The predicate is formed by a *verb phrase*—the most important word of this phrase is the verb, also known as the *predicator*. In some verb phrases, there occur several verbs. For example, in the sentence

He has been working for hours.

the verb phrase contains three verbs—*has*, *been*, and *working*. The predicator is, however, always the first verb of a verb phrase (*has* in the above example). In this study, we focus on the most elementary clauses—*canonical clauses*. In these clauses, the subject always precedes the predicate, and these clauses are positive, declarative, and without subordinate or coordinate clauses.

Next, we describe the basic categorization of verbs and personal pronouns and further characterize their inflectional forms in greater detail.

18.1.3 Verbs

We distinguish several kinds of verbs based upon their grammatical properties. The set of all verbs is divided into two subsets—the set of *auxiliary verbs*, and the set of *lexical verbs*. Further, the set of auxiliary verbs consists of *modal verbs* and *non-modal verbs*. The set of modal verbs includes the following verbs—*can*, *may*, *must*, *will*, *shall*, *ought*, *need*, *dare*; the verbs *be*, *have*, and *do* are non-modal. All the remaining verbs are lexical. In reality, the above-defined classes overlap in certain situations; for example, there are sentences, where *do* appears as an auxiliary verb, and in different situations, *do* behaves as a lexical verb. For simplicity, we do not take into account these special cases in what follows.

Inflectional forms of verbs are called *paradigms*. In English, every verb, except for the verb *be*, may appear in each of the six paradigms described in Table 18.1 (see [72]). Verbs in *primary form* may occur as the only verb in a clause and form the head of its verb phrase (predicator); on the other hand, verbs in *secondary form* have to be accompanied by a verb in primary form.

The verb *be* has nine paradigms in its neutral form. All primary forms have, in addition, their negative contracted counterparts. Compared to other verbs, there is one more verb paradigm called *irrealis*. The irrealis form *were* (and *weren't*) is used in sentences of an unrealistic nature, such as

I wish I were rich.

All these paradigms are presented in Table 18.2.

18.1.4 Personal pronouns

Personal pronouns exhibit a great amount of inflectional variation as well. Table 18.3 summarizes all their inflectional forms. The most important for us is the class of pronouns in *nominative* because these pronouns often appear as the subject of a clause.

Table 18.1 Paradigms of English verbs

Form	Paradigm	Person	Example
Primary	Present	Third sg	*She* walks *home.*
		Other	*They* walk *home.*
	Preterite		*She* walked *home.*
Secondary	Plain form		*They should* walk *home.*
	Gerund-participle		*She is* walking *home.*
	Past participle		*She has* walked *home.*

Table 18.2 Paradigms of the verb be

Form	Paradigm	Person	Neutral	Negative
Primary	Present	First sg	*Am*	*Aren't*
		Third sg	*Is*	*Isn't*
		Other	*Are*	*Aren't*
	Preterite	First sg, third sg	*Was*	*Wasn't*
		Other	*Were*	*Weren't*
	Irrealis	First sg, third sg	*Were*	*Weren't*
Secondary	Plain form		*Be*	—
	Gerund-participle		*Being*	—
	Past participle		*Been*	—

Table 18.3 Personal pronouns

Nonreflexive				Reflexive
Nominative	**Accusative**	**Genitive**		
Plain		**Dependent**	**Independent**	
I	*Me*	*My*	*Mine*	*Myself*
You	*You*	*Your*	*Yours*	*Yourself*
He	*Him*	*His*	*His*	*Himself*
She	*Her*	*Her*	*Hers*	*Herself*
It	*It*	*Its*	*Its*	*Itself*
We	*Us*	*Our*	*Ours*	*Ourselves*
You	*You*	*Your*	*Yours*	*Yourselves*
They	*Them*	*Their*	*Theirs*	*Themselves*

18.2 Transformational scattered context grammars

As we have already mentioned, in this chapter, we primarily apply scattered context grammars to transform grammatical English sentences to other grammatical English sentences. To do so, we next slightly modify scattered context grammars, so they start their derivations from a language rather than a single start symbol. Even more importantly, these grammars define transformations of languages, not just their generation.

Definition 18.1. A *transformational scattered context grammar* is a quadruple

$$G = (\Sigma, \Delta, R, I),$$

where

- Σ is the *total vocabulary*,
- $\Delta \subset \Sigma$ is the set of terminals (or the *output vocabulary*),
- R is a finite set of scattered context productions, and
- $I \subset \Sigma$ is the *input vocabulary*.

The derivation step is defined as in scattered context grammars (see Definition 13.1). The *transformation T that G defines from $K \subseteq I^*$* is denoted by $T(G,K)$ and defined as

$$T(G,K) = \{(x,y) \mid x \Rightarrow_G^* y, x \in K, y \in \Delta^*\}.$$

If $(x,y) \in T(G,K)$, we say that *x is transformed to y* by G; x and y are called the *input* and the *output sentence*, respectively.

As already pointed out, while scattered context grammars generate strings, transformational scattered context grammars translate them. In a sense, however, the language generated by any scattered context grammar $G = (\Sigma, \Delta, R, S)$ can be expressed by using a transformational scattered context grammar $H = (\Sigma, \Delta, R, \{S\})$ as well. Observe that

$$L(G) = \{y \mid (S,y) \in T(H, \{S\})\}.$$

Before we make use of transformational scattered context grammars in terms of English syntax in the next section, we give two examples to demonstrate a close relation of these grammars to the theoretically oriented studies given previously in this book. To link the theoretical discussions given in the previous chapters of this book to the present chapter, the first example presents a transformational scattered context grammar that works with purely abstract languages. In the second example, we discuss a transformational scattered context grammar that is somewhat more linguistically oriented.

Example 18.1. Define the transformational scattered context grammar

$$G = (\Sigma, \Delta, R, I),$$

where $\Sigma = \{A, B, C, a, b, c\}$, $\Delta = \{a, b, c\}$, $I = \{A, B, C\}$, and

$$R = \{(A, B, C) \rightarrow (a, bb, c)\}.$$

For example, for the input sentence $AABBCC$,

$$AABBCC \Rightarrow_G aABbbcC \Rightarrow_G aabbbbcc.$$

Therefore, the input sentence $AABBCC \in I^*$ is transformed to the output sentence $aabbbbcc \in \Delta^*$, and

$$(AABBCC, aabbbbcc) \in T(G, I^*).$$

If we restrict the input sentences to the language $L = \{A^nB^nC^n \mid n \geq 1\}$, we get

$$T(G, L) = \{(A^nB^nC^n, a^nb^{2n}c^n) \mid n \geq 1\},$$

so every $A^nB^nC^n$, where $n \geq 1$, is transformed to $a^nb^{2n}c^n$.

In the following example, we modify strings consisting of English letters by a transformational scattered context grammar, and in this way, we relate these grammars to lexically oriented linguistics—that is, the area of linguistics that concentrates its study on vocabulary analysis and dictionary design.

Example 18.2. We demonstrate how to lexicographically order alphabetic strings and, simultaneously, convert them from their uppercase versions to lowercase versions. More specifically, we describe a transformational scattered context grammar G that takes any alphabetic strings that consist of English uppercase letters enclosed in angle brackets, lexicographically orders the letters, and converts them to the corresponding lowercases. For instance, G transforms $\langle XXUY \rangle$ to $uxxy$.

More precisely, let J and Δ be alphabets of English uppercases and English lowercases, respectively. Let $\prec$ denote *lexical order* over J; that is, $A \prec B \prec \cdots \prec Z$. Furthermore, let h be the function that maps the uppercases to the corresponding lowercases; that is, $h(A) = a$, $h(B) = b$, …, $h(Z) = z$. Let i denote the inverse of h, so $i(a) = A$, $i(b) = B$, …, $i(z) = Z$. Let $N = \{\hat{a} \mid a \in \Delta\}$. We define the transformational scattered context grammar $G = (\Sigma, \Delta, R, I)$, where Δ is defined as above, $I = J \cup \{\langle, \rangle\}$, $\Sigma = I \cup N \cup \Delta$, and R is constructed as follows:

(1) For each $A, B \in I$, where $A \prec B$, add
$(B, A) \rightarrow (A, B)$ to R.
(2) For each $a \in \Delta$, add
$(\langle) \rightarrow (\hat{a})$ to R.
(3) For each $a \in \Delta$ and $A \in J$, where $i(a) = A$, add
$(\hat{a}, A) \rightarrow (a, \hat{a})$ to R.
(4) For each $a, b \in \Delta$, where $i(a) \prec i(b)$, add
$(\hat{a}) \rightarrow (\hat{b})$ to R.
(5) For each $a \in \Delta$, add
$(\hat{a}, \rangle) \rightarrow (\varepsilon, \varepsilon)$ to R.

Set $K = \{\langle\} J^* \{\rangle\}$. For instance, G transforms $\langle ORDER \rangle \in K$ to $deorr \in \Delta^*$ as

$$\begin{aligned}\langle ORDER \rangle &\Rightarrow_G \langle OEDRR \rangle \Rightarrow_G \langle DEORR \rangle \\ &\Rightarrow_G \hat{d}DEORR\rangle \Rightarrow_G d\hat{d}EORR\rangle \Rightarrow_G d\hat{e}EORR\rangle \Rightarrow_G de\hat{e}ORR\rangle \\ &\Rightarrow_G de\hat{o}ORR\rangle \Rightarrow_G deo\hat{o}RR\rangle \Rightarrow_G deo\hat{r}RR\rangle \Rightarrow_G deor\hat{r}R\rangle \\ &\Rightarrow_G deorr\hat{r}\rangle \Rightarrow_G deorr,\end{aligned}$$

so $(\langle ORDER\rangle, deorr) \in T(G,K)$. Clearly, G can make the same transformation in many more ways; on the other hand, notice that the set of all transformations of $\langle ORDER\rangle$ to *deorr* is finite.

More formally, we claim that G transforms every $\langle A_1 \cdots A_n\rangle \in K$ to $b_1 \cdots b_n \in \Delta^*$, for some $n \geq 0$, so that $i(b_1) \cdots i(b_n)$ represents a permutation of $A_1 \cdots A_n$, and for all $1 \leq j \leq n-1$, $i(b_j) \prec i(b_{j+1})$ (the case when $n = 0$ means that $A_1 \cdots A_n = b_1 \cdots b_n = \varepsilon$). To see why this claim holds, notice that $\Delta \cap I = \emptyset$, so every successful transformation of a string from K to a string from Δ^* is performed so that all symbols are rewritten during the computation. By productions introduced in (1), G lexicographically orders the input uppercases. By a production of the form $(\langle) \rightarrow (\hat{a})$ introduced in (2), G changes the leftmost symbol $\langle$ to $\hat{a}$. By productions introduced in (3) and (4), G verifies that the alphabetic string is properly ordered and, simultaneously, converts its uppercase symbols into the corresponding lowercases in a strictly left-to-right one-by-one way. Observe that a production introduced in (2) is applied precisely once during every successful transformation because the left-to-right conversion necessities its application, and on the other hand, no production can produce $\langle$. By a production from (5), G completes the transformation; notice that if this completion is performed prematurely with some uppercases left, the transformation is necessary unsuccessful because the uppercases cannot be turned to the corresponding lowercases. Based upon these observations, it should be obvious that G performs the desired transformation.

Having illustrated the lexically oriented application, we devote the next section solely to the applications of transformational scattered context grammars in English syntax.

18.3 Scattered context in English syntax

In this section, we apply transformational scattered context grammars to English syntax. Before opening this topic, let us make an assumption regarding the set of all English words. We assume that this set, denoted by Δ, is finite and fixed. From a practical point of view, this is obviously a reasonable assumption because we all commonly use a finite and fixed vocabulary of words in everyday English (purely hypothetically, however, this may not be the case as illustrated by the study that closes this section). Next, we subdivide this set into subsets with respect to the classification of verbs and pronouns described in Section 18.1:

- Δ is the set of all words including all their inflectional forms.
- $\Delta_V \subset \Delta$ is the set of all verbs including all their inflectional forms.
- $\Delta_{VA} \subset \Delta_V$ is the set of all auxiliary verbs including all their inflectional forms.
- $\Delta_{Vpl} \subset \Delta_V$ is the set of all verbs in plain form.
- $\Delta_{PPn} \subset \Delta$ is the set of all personal pronouns in nominative.

To describe all possible paradigms of a verb $v \in \Delta_{Vpl}$, we use the following notation:

- $\pi_{3rd}(v)$ is the verb v in third person singular present.

- $\pi_{pres}(v)$ is the verb v in present (other than third person singular).
- $\pi_{pret}(v)$ is the verb v in preterite.

There are several conventions we use throughout this section in order to simplify the presented case studies:

- We do not take into account capitalization and punctuation. Therefore, according to this convention,

  He is your best friend.

  and

  he is your best friend

  are equivalent.
- To make the following studies as simple and readable as possible, we expect every input sentence to be a canonical clause. In some examples, however, we make slight exceptions to this rule; for instance, sometimes we permit the input sentence to be negative. The first example and the last example also demonstrate a simple type of coordinated canonical clauses.
- The input vocabulary is the set $I = \{\langle x \rangle \mid x \in \Delta\}$, where Δ is the set of all English words as stated above. As a result, every transformational scattered context grammar in this section takes an input sentence over I and transforms it to an output sentence over Δ. For instance, in the case of the declarative-to-interrogative transformation,

  $\langle\text{he}\rangle\langle\text{is}\rangle\langle\text{your}\rangle\langle\text{best}\rangle\langle\text{friend}\rangle$

  is transformed to

  is he your best friend

  As we have already mentioned, we omit punctuation and capitalization, so the above sentence corresponds to

  Is he your best friend?

Next, we give several studies that describe how to transform various kinds of grammatical sentences to other grammatical sentences by using transformational scattered context grammars.

18.3.1 Clauses with neither *and* nor

The first example shows how to use transformational scattered context grammars to negate clauses that contain the pair of the words *neither* and *nor*, such as

Neither Thomas nor his wife went to the party.

Clearly, the words *neither* and *nor* are related, but there is no explicit limit of the number of the words appearing between them. The following transformational scattered context grammar G converts the above sentence to

Both Thomas and his wife went to the party.

In fact, the constructed grammar G is general enough to negate every grammatical clause that contains the pair of the words *neither* and *nor*.

Set $G = (\Sigma, \Delta, R, I)$, where $\Sigma = \Delta \cup I$, and R is defined as follows:

$$R = \{(\langle\text{neither}\rangle, \langle\text{nor}\rangle) \to (\text{both}, \text{and})\} \\ \cup \{(\langle x\rangle) \to (x) \mid x \in \Delta - \{\text{neither}, \text{nor}\}\}.$$

For example, for the above sentence, the transformation can proceed in this way:

$$\begin{aligned} &\langle\text{neither}\rangle\langle\text{thomas}\rangle\langle\text{nor}\rangle\langle\text{his}\rangle\langle\text{wife}\rangle\langle\text{went}\rangle\langle\text{to}\rangle\langle\text{the}\rangle\langle\text{party}\rangle \\ &\quad\Rightarrow_G \text{both } \langle\text{thomas}\rangle \text{ and } \langle\text{his}\rangle\langle\text{wife}\rangle\langle\text{went}\rangle\langle\text{to}\rangle\langle\text{the}\rangle\langle\text{party}\rangle \\ &\quad\Rightarrow_G \text{both thomas and } \langle\text{his}\rangle\langle\text{wife}\rangle\langle\text{went}\rangle\langle\text{to}\rangle\langle\text{the}\rangle\langle\text{party}\rangle \\ &\quad\Rightarrow_G \text{both thomas and his } \langle\text{wife}\rangle\langle\text{went}\rangle\langle\text{to}\rangle\langle\text{the}\rangle\langle\text{party}\rangle \\ &\quad\Rightarrow_G^5 \text{both thomas and his wife went to the party.} \end{aligned}$$

The production

$$(\langle\text{neither}\rangle, \langle\text{nor}\rangle) \to (\text{both}, \text{and})$$

replaces *neither* and *nor* with *both* and *and*, respectively. Every other word $\langle w\rangle \in I$ is changed to $w \in \Delta$. Therefore, if we denote all possible input sentences, described in the introduction of this example, by K, $T(G, K)$ represents the set of all negated sentences from K, and

$$(\langle\text{neither}\rangle\langle\text{thomas}\rangle\langle\text{nor}\rangle\langle\text{his}\rangle\langle\text{wife}\rangle\langle\text{went}\rangle\langle\text{to}\rangle\langle\text{the}\rangle\langle\text{party}\rangle, \\ \text{both thomas and his wife went to the party}) \in T(G, K).$$

18.3.2 Existential clauses

In English, clauses that indicate an existence are called *existential*. These clauses are usually formed by the dummy subject *there*; for example,

There was a nurse present.

However, this dummy subject is not mandatory in all situations. For instance, the above example can be rephrased as

A nurse was present.

We construct a transformational scattered context grammar G that converts any canonical existential clause without the dummy subject *there* to an equivalent existential clause with *there*.

Set $G = (\Sigma, \Delta, R, I)$, where $\Sigma = \Delta \cup I \cup \{X\}$ (X is a new symbol such that $X \notin \Delta \cup I$), and R is defined as follows:

$$\begin{aligned} R = \big\{&(\langle x\rangle, \langle\text{is}\rangle) \to (\text{there is } xX, \varepsilon), \\ &(\langle x\rangle, \langle\text{are}\rangle) \to (\text{there are } xX, \varepsilon), \\ &(\langle x\rangle, \langle\text{was}\rangle) \to (\text{there was } xX, \varepsilon), \\ &(\langle x\rangle, \langle\text{were}\rangle) \to (\text{there were } xX, \varepsilon) \mid x \in \Delta\big\} \\ \cup \big\{&(X, \langle x\rangle) \to (X, x) \mid x \in \Delta\big\} \\ \cup \{&(X) \to (\varepsilon)\}. \end{aligned}$$

For the above sample sentence, we get the following derivation:

$$\begin{aligned}&\langle\text{a}\rangle\langle\text{nurse}\rangle\langle\text{was}\rangle\langle\text{present}\rangle\\&\quad\Rightarrow_G \text{there was a } X\langle\text{nurse}\rangle\langle\text{present}\rangle\\&\quad\Rightarrow_G \text{there was a } X \text{ nurse } \langle\text{present}\rangle\\&\quad\Rightarrow_G \text{there was a } X \text{ nurse present}\\&\quad\Rightarrow_G \text{there was a nurse present.}\end{aligned}$$

A production from the first set has to be applied first because initially there is no symbol X in the sentential form and all other productions require X to be present in the sentential form. In our case, the production

$$(\langle\text{a}\rangle, \langle\text{was}\rangle) \rightarrow (\text{there was a } X, \varepsilon)$$

is applied; the use of other productions from this set depends on what tense is used in the input sentence and whether the subject is singular or plural. The production nondeterministically selects the first word of the sentence, puts *there was* in front of it, and the symbol X behind it; in addition, it erases *was* in the middle of the sentence. Next, all words $\langle w\rangle \in I$ are replaced with $w \in \Delta$ by productions from the second set. These productions also verify that the previous nondeterministic selection was made at the beginning of the sentence; if not, there remains a word $\langle w\rangle \in I$ in front of X that cannot be rewritten. Finally, the derivation ends by erasing X from the sentential form.

This form of the derivation implies that if we denote the input existential clauses described in the introduction of this example by K, $T(G,K)$ represents the set of these clauses with the dummy subject *there*. As a result,

$$(\langle\text{a}\rangle\langle\text{nurse}\rangle\langle\text{was}\rangle\langle\text{present}\rangle, \text{there was a nurse present}) \in T(G,K).$$

18.3.3 Interrogative clauses

In English, there are two ways of transforming declarative clauses into interrogative clauses depending on the predicator. If the predicator is an auxiliary verb, the interrogative clause is formed simply by swapping the subject and the predicator. For example, we get the interrogative clause

Is he mowing the lawn?

by swapping *he*, which is the subject, and *is*, which is the predicator, in

He is mowing the lawn.

On the other hand, if the predicator is a lexical verb, the interrogative clause is formed by adding the dummy *do* to the beginning of the declarative clause. The dummy *do* has to be of the same paradigm as the predicator in the declarative clause and the predicator itself is converted to its plain form. For instance,

She usually gets up early.

is a declarative clause with the predicator *gets*, which is in third person singular, and the subject *she*. By inserting *do* in third person singular to the beginning of the sentence and converting *gets* to its plain form, we obtain

Does she usually get up early?

To simplify the following transformational scattered context grammar G, which performs this conversion, we assume that the subject is a personal pronoun in nominative.

Set $G = (\Sigma, \Delta, R, I)$, where $\Sigma = \Delta \cup I \cup \{X\}$ (X is a new symbol such that $X \notin \Delta \cup I$), and R is defined as follows:

$$\begin{aligned}
R = &\left\{(\langle p\rangle, \langle v\rangle) \to (vp, X) \mid v \in \Delta_{VA}, p \in \Delta_{PPn}\right\} \\
\cup &\left\{(\langle p\rangle, \langle \pi_{pret}(v)\rangle) \to (\text{did}\, p, vX),\right. \\
&(\langle p\rangle, \langle \pi_{3rd}(v)\rangle) \to (\text{does}\, p, vX), \\
&\left.(\langle p\rangle, \langle \pi_{pres}(v)\rangle) \to (\text{do}\, p, vX) \mid v \in \Delta_{Vpl} - \Delta_{VA}, p \in \Delta_{PPn}\right\} \\
\cup &\left\{(\langle x\rangle, X) \to (x, X),\right. \\
&\left.(X, \langle y\rangle) \to (X, y) \mid x \in \Delta - \Delta_{V}, y \in \Delta\right\} \\
\cup &\{(X) \to (\varepsilon)\}.
\end{aligned}$$

For sentences whose predicator is an auxiliary verb, the transformation made by G proceeds as follows:

$$\begin{aligned}
&\langle\text{he}\rangle\langle\text{is}\rangle\langle\text{mowing}\rangle\langle\text{the}\rangle\langle\text{lawn}\rangle \\
&\quad\Rightarrow_G \text{is he } X\langle\text{mowing}\rangle\langle\text{the}\rangle\langle\text{lawn}\rangle \\
&\quad\Rightarrow_G \text{is he } X \text{ mowing } \langle\text{the}\rangle\langle\text{lawn}\rangle \\
&\quad\Rightarrow_G \text{is he } X \text{ mowing the } \langle\text{lawn}\rangle \\
&\quad\Rightarrow_G \text{is he } X \text{ mowing the lawn} \\
&\quad\Rightarrow_G \text{is he mowing the lawn.}
\end{aligned}$$

The derivation starts by the application of a production from the first set, which swaps the subject and the predicator, and puts X behind them. Next, productions from the third set rewrite every word $\langle w\rangle \in I$ to $w \in \Delta$. Finally, X is removed from the sentential form.

The transformation of the sentences in which the predicator is a lexical verb is more complicated:

$$\begin{aligned}
&\langle\text{she}\rangle\langle\text{usually}\rangle\langle\text{gets}\rangle\langle\text{up}\rangle\langle\text{early}\rangle \\
&\quad\Rightarrow_G \text{does she } \langle\text{usually}\rangle \text{ get } X\langle\text{up}\rangle\langle\text{early}\rangle \\
&\quad\Rightarrow_G \text{does she usually get } X\langle\text{up}\rangle\langle\text{early}\rangle \\
&\quad\Rightarrow_G \text{does she usually get } X \text{ up } \langle\text{early}\rangle \\
&\quad\Rightarrow_G \text{does she usually get } X \text{ up early} \\
&\quad\Rightarrow_G \text{does she usually get up early.}
\end{aligned}$$

As the predicator is in third person singular, a production from

$$\left\{(\langle p\rangle, \langle \pi_{3rd}(v)\rangle) \to (\text{does}\, p, vX) \mid v \in \Delta_{Vpl} - \Delta_{VA}, p \in \Delta_{PPn}\right\}$$

is applied at the beginning of the derivation. It inserts *does* to the beginning of the sentence, converts the predicator *gets* to its plain form *get*, and puts X behind it. Next, productions from

$$\{(\langle x\rangle, X) \rightarrow (x, X) \mid x \in \Delta - \Delta_V\}$$

rewrite every word $\langle w\rangle \in I$ appearing in front of the predicator to $w \in \Delta$. Notice that they do not rewrite verbs—in this way, the grammar verifies that the first verb in the sentence was previously selected as the predicator. For instance, in the sentence

He has been working for hours.

has must be selected as the predicator; otherwise, the derivation is unsuccessful. Finally, the grammar rewrites all words behind X, and erases X in the last step as in the previous case.

Based on this intuitive explanation, we can see that the set of all input sentences K described in the introduction of this example is transformed by G to $T(G, K)$, which is the set of all interrogative sentences constructed from K. Therefore,

$$(\langle\text{he}\rangle\langle\text{is}\rangle\langle\text{mowing}\rangle\langle\text{the}\rangle\langle\text{lawn}\rangle, \text{is he mowing the lawn}) \in T(G, K),$$
$$(\langle\text{she}\rangle\langle\text{usually}\rangle\langle\text{gets}\rangle\langle\text{up}\rangle\langle\text{early}\rangle, \text{does she usually get up early}) \in T(G, K).$$

18.3.4 Question tags

Question tags are special constructs that are primarily used in spoken language. They are used at the end of declarative clauses, and we customarily use them to ask for agreement or confirmation. For instance, in

Your sister is married, isn't she?

isn't she is a question tag, and we expect an answer stating that she is married. The polarity of question tags is always opposite to the polarity of the main clause—if the main clause is positive, the question tag is negative, and vice versa. If the predicator is an auxiliary verb, the question tag is formed by the same auxiliary verb. For lexical verbs, the question tag is made by using *do* as

He plays the violin, doesn't he?

There are some special cases that have to be taken into account. First, the verb *be* has to be treated separately because it has more paradigms than other verbs and the question tag for first person singular is irregular:

I am always right, aren't I?

Second, for the verb *have*, the question tag depends on whether it is used as an auxiliary verb or a lexical verb. In the first case, *have* is used in the question tag as

He has been working hard, hasn't he?

and in the latter case, the auxiliary *do* is used as

They have a dog, don't they?

To explain the basic concepts as simply as possible, we omit the special cases of the verb *have* in the following transformational scattered context grammar G, which supplements a canonical clause with a question tag. For the same reason, we only sketch its construction and do not mention all the created productions explicitly. In addition, we suppose that the subject is represented by a personal pronoun.

Set $G = (\Sigma, \Delta, R, I)$, where $\Sigma = \Delta \cup I \cup \{X, Y\}$ (X, Y are new symbols such that $X, Y \notin \Delta \cup I$), and R is defined as follows:

$$\begin{aligned}
R = \big\{ & (\langle p\rangle, \langle \text{will}\rangle, \langle x\rangle) \rightarrow (p, \text{will}\, X, Yx \text{ won't}\, p),\\
& (\langle p\rangle, \langle \text{won't}\rangle, \langle x\rangle) \rightarrow (p, \text{won't}\, X, Yx \text{ will}\, p),\\
& \ldots \mid p \in \Delta_{PPn}, x \in \Delta \big\}\\
\cup \big\{ & (\langle \text{I}\rangle, \langle \text{am}\rangle, \langle x\rangle) \rightarrow (\text{I}, \text{am}\, X, Yx \text{ aren't I}),\\
& (\langle \text{you}\rangle, \langle \text{are}\rangle, \langle x\rangle) \rightarrow (\text{you}, \text{are}\, X, Yx \text{ aren't you}),\\
& \ldots \mid x \in \Delta \big\}\\
\cup \big\{ & (\langle p\rangle, \langle v\rangle, \langle x\rangle) \rightarrow (p, vX, Yx \text{ doesn't}\, p),\\
& (\langle q\rangle, \langle v\rangle, \langle x\rangle) \rightarrow (q, vX, Yx \text{ don't}\, q) \mid\\
& p \in \{\text{he, she, it}\}, q \in \Delta_{PPn} - \{\text{he, she, it}\}, v \in \Delta_V - \Delta_{VA}, x \in \Delta \big\}\\
& \vdots\\
\cup \big\{ & (\langle x\rangle, X) \rightarrow (x, X),\\
& (X, \langle y\rangle, Y) \rightarrow (X, y, Y) \mid x \in \Delta - \Delta_V, y \in \Delta \big\}\\
\cup \{ & (X, Y) \rightarrow (\varepsilon, \varepsilon)\}.
\end{aligned}$$

First, we describe the generation of question tags for clauses whose predicator is an auxiliary verb:

$$\begin{aligned}
& \langle \text{I}\rangle \langle \text{am}\rangle \langle \text{always}\rangle \langle \text{right}\rangle\\
& \quad \Rightarrow_G \text{I am}\, X \langle \text{always}\rangle Y \text{ right aren't I}\\
& \quad \Rightarrow_G \text{I am}\, X \text{ always } Y \text{ right aren't I}\\
& \quad \Rightarrow_G \text{I am always right aren't I.}
\end{aligned}$$

Here, the production

$$(\langle \text{I}\rangle, \langle \text{am}\rangle, \langle \text{right}\rangle) \rightarrow (\text{I}, \text{am}\, X, Y \text{ right aren't I})$$

initiates the derivation. When it finds *I am* at the beginning of the sentence, it generates the question tag *aren't I* at its end. In addition, it adds X behind *I am* and Y in front of *right aren't I*. Next, it rewrites all words from $\langle w\rangle \in I$ to $w \in \Delta$. It makes sure that the predicator was chosen properly by productions from

$$\big\{ (\langle x\rangle, X) \rightarrow (x, X) \mid x \in \Delta - \Delta_V \big\}$$

similarly to the previous example. In addition, productions from

$$\big\{ (X, \langle y\rangle, Y) \rightarrow (X, y, Y) \mid x \in \Delta - \Delta_V, y \in \Delta \big\}$$

check whether the question tag was placed at the very end of the sentence. If not, there remains some symbol from the input vocabulary behind Y that cannot be rewritten. Finally, the last production removes X and Y from the sentential form.

When the predicator is a lexical verb in present, the question tag is formed by *does* or *do* depending on person in which the predicator occurs:

$$\begin{aligned}&\langle\text{he}\rangle\langle\text{plays}\rangle\langle\text{the}\rangle\langle\text{violin}\rangle\\ &\quad\Rightarrow_G \text{he plays } X\langle\text{the}\rangle Y \text{ violin doesn't he}\\ &\quad\Rightarrow_G \text{he plays } X \text{ the violin } Y \text{ doesn't he}\\ &\quad\Rightarrow_G \text{he plays the violin doesn't he.}\end{aligned}$$

The rest of the derivation is analogous to the first case.

Based on these derivations, we can see that the set of all input sentences K described in the introduction of this example is transformed by G to $T(G,K)$, which is the set of all sentences constructed from K that are supplemented with question tags. Therefore,

$$(\langle\text{I}\rangle\langle\text{am}\rangle\langle\text{always}\rangle\langle\text{right}\rangle, \text{I am always right aren't I}) \in T(G,K),$$
$$(\langle\text{he}\rangle\langle\text{plays}\rangle\langle\text{the}\rangle\langle\text{violin}\rangle, \text{he plays the violin doesn't he}) \in T(G,K).$$

18.3.5 Generation of grammatical sentences

The purpose of the next discussion, which closes this section, is 6-fold—(1)–(6), stated as follows:

1. We want to demonstrate that ordinary scattered context grammars, discussed in the previous chapters of this book, can be seen as a special case of transformational scattered context grammars, whose applications are discussed in the present section.
2. As pointed out in the notes following the general definition of a transformational scattered context grammar (see Definition 18.1), there exists a close relation between ordinary scattered context grammars and transformational scattered context grammars. That is, for every scattered context grammar $G = (\Sigma, \Delta, R, S)$, there is a transformational scattered context grammar $H = (\Sigma, \Delta, R, \{S\})$ satisfying

   $$L(G) = \{y \mid (S, y) \in T(H, \{S\})\},$$

   and in this way, $L(G)$ is defined by H. Next, we illustrate this relation by a specific example.
3. From a syntactical point of view, we want to show that scattered context grammars can generate an infinite non-context-free grammatical subset of English language in a very succinct way.
4. In terms of *morphology*—that is, the area of linguistics that studies the structure of words and their generation—we demonstrate how to use transformational scattered context grammars to create complicated English words within English sentences so that the resulting words and sentences are grammatically correct.
5. As stated in the beginning of the present section, so far we have assumed that the set of common English words is finite. Next, we want to demonstrate that from a strictly theoretical point of view, the set of all possible well-formed English words, including extremely rare words in everyday English, is infinite. Indeed, L, given next, includes infinitely many words of the form $(great\text{-})^i grandparents$,

(great-)^{i}grandfathers, and *(great-)^{i}grandmothers*, for all $i \geq 0$, and purely theoretically speaking, they all represent well-formed English words. Of course, most of them, such as

great-great-great-great-great-great-great-great-great-grandfathers

cannot be considered as common English words because most people never use them during their lifetime.

6. We illustrate that the language generation based upon scattered context grammars may have significant advantages over the generation based upon classical grammars, such as context-sensitive grammars.

Without further ado, consider the language L consisting of these grammatical English sentences:

Your grandparents are all your grandfathers and all your grandmothers.

Your great-grandparents are all your great-grandfathers and all your great-grandmothers.

Your great-great-grandparents are all your great-great-grandfathers and all your great-great-grandmothers.

⋮

In brief,

$$L = \{\text{your } \{\text{great-}\}^i\text{grandparents arc all your } \{\text{great-}\}^i\text{grandfathers and all your } \{\text{great-}\}^i\text{grandmothers} \mid i \geq 0\}.$$

Introduce the scattered context grammar $G = (\Sigma, \Delta, R, S)$, where

$$\Delta = \{\text{all, and, are, grandfathers, grandmothers, grandparents, great-, your}\},$$

$\Sigma = \Delta \cup \{S, \#\}$, and R consists of these three productions:

$$\begin{aligned}(S) &\to (\text{your \#grandparents are all your \#grandfathers} \\ &\qquad \text{and all your \#grandmothers}), \\ (\#, \#, \#) &\to (\text{\#great-, \#great-, \#great-}), \\ (\#, \#, \#) &\to (\varepsilon, \varepsilon, \varepsilon).\end{aligned}$$

Obviously, this scattered context grammar generates L; formally, $L = L(G)$. Consider the transformational scattered context grammar $H = (\Sigma, \Delta, R, \{S\})$. Notice that

$$L(G) = \{y \mid (S, y) \in T(H, \{S\})\}.$$

Clearly, L is not context-free, so its generation is beyond the power of context-free grammars. It would be possible to construct a context-sensitive grammar that generates L. However, a context-sensitive grammar like this would have to keep traversing across its sentential forms to guarantee the same number of occurrences of *great-* in the generated sentences. Compared to this awkward way of generating L, the scattered context grammar G generates L in a more elegant, economical, and effective way.

In this chapter, we have illustrated how to transform and generate grammatical sentences in English by using transformational scattered context grammars, which represent a very natural linguistic apparatus straightforwardly based on scattered context grammars. However, from a more general perspective, we can apply these grammars basically in any area of science that formalizes its results by strings containing some scattered context dependencies.

Chapter 19
Applications in biology

In this two-section chapter, we sketch applications of totally parallel grammars with context conditions (see Section 13.2). That is, we apply their special versions to microbiological organisms. We give three case studies that make use of these grammars. Section 19.1 presents two case studies of biological organisms whose development is affected by some abnormal conditions, such as a virus infection. From an even more practical point of view, by using these grammars, Section 19.2 makes a powerful and elegant implementation tool in the area of biological simulation and modeling. Specifically, it implements models of growing plants.

19.1 Applications

Consider simple context-conditional ET0L grammar (see Definition 13.9). By *simple semi-conditional 0L grammars*, we refer to these grammars that contain only terminals. We make use of them in the following application.

Case Study 1. Consider a cellular organism in which every cell divides itself into two cells during every single step of healthy development. However, when a virus infects some cells, all of the organism stagnates until it is cured again. During the stagnation period, all of the cells just reproduce themselves without producing any new cells. To formalize this development by a suitable simple semi-conditional L grammar (see Section 13.2), we denote a healthy cell and a virus-infected cell by A and B, respectively, and introduce the simple semi-conditional 0L grammar, $G = (\{A, B\}, R, A)$, where R contains the following productions:

$$
\begin{array}{ll}
(A \rightarrow AA, 0, B), & (B \rightarrow B, 0, 0), \\
(A \rightarrow A, B, 0), & (B \rightarrow A, 0, 0), \\
(A \rightarrow B, 0, 0). &
\end{array}
$$

Figure 19.1 describes G simulating a healthy development while Figure 19.2 gives a development with a stagnation period caused by the virus. □

In the next case study, we discuss an 0L grammar that simulates the developmental stages of a red alga (see [11,41]). Using context conditions, we can modify this grammar so that it describes some unhealthy development of this alga that leads to its partial death or degeneration.

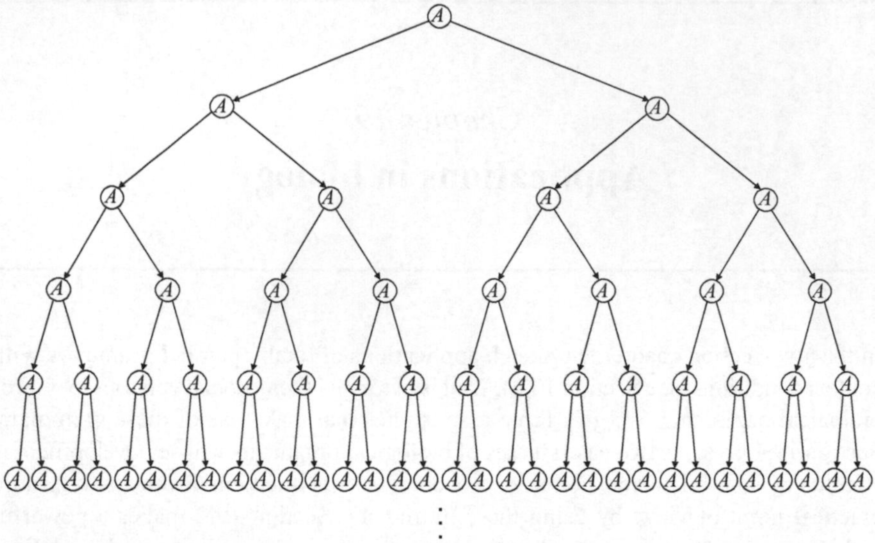

Figure 19.1 Healthy development

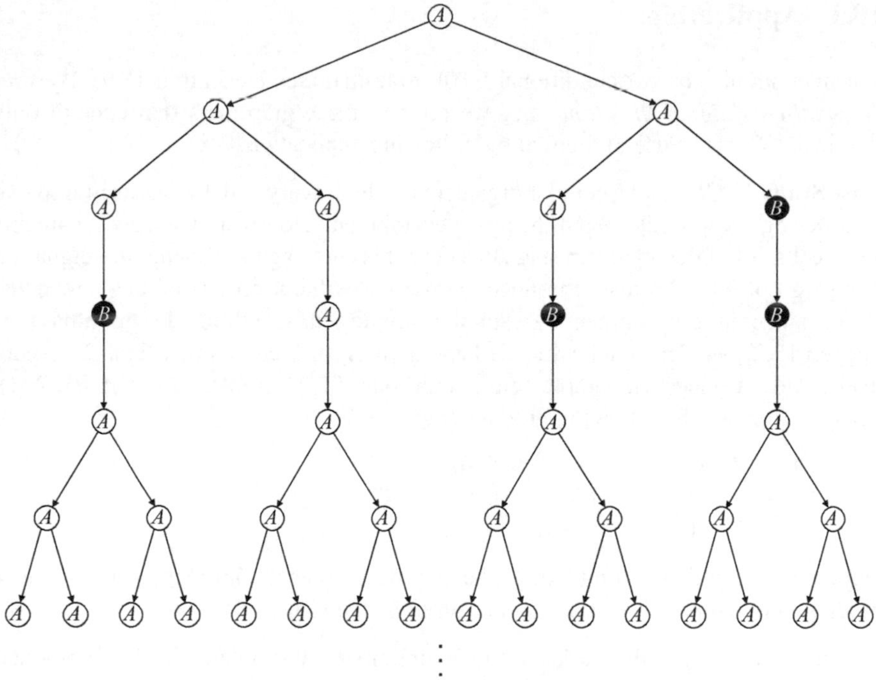

Figure 19.2 Development with a stagnating period

Case Study 2. Consider an 0L grammar

$$G = (\Sigma, R, 1),$$

where

$$\Sigma = \{1, 2, 3, 4, 5, 6, 7, 8, [,]\}$$

and the set of productions R contains

$$\begin{array}{lllll} 1 \to 23, & 2 \to 2, & 3 \to 24, & 4 \to 54, & [\to [, \\ 5 \to 6, & 6 \to 7, & 7 \to 8[1], & 8 \to 8, &] \to]. \end{array}$$

From a *biological viewpoint*, expressions in fences represent branches whose position is indicated by 8s. These branches are shown as attached at alternate sides of the branch on which they are born. Figure 19.3 gives a biological interpretation of

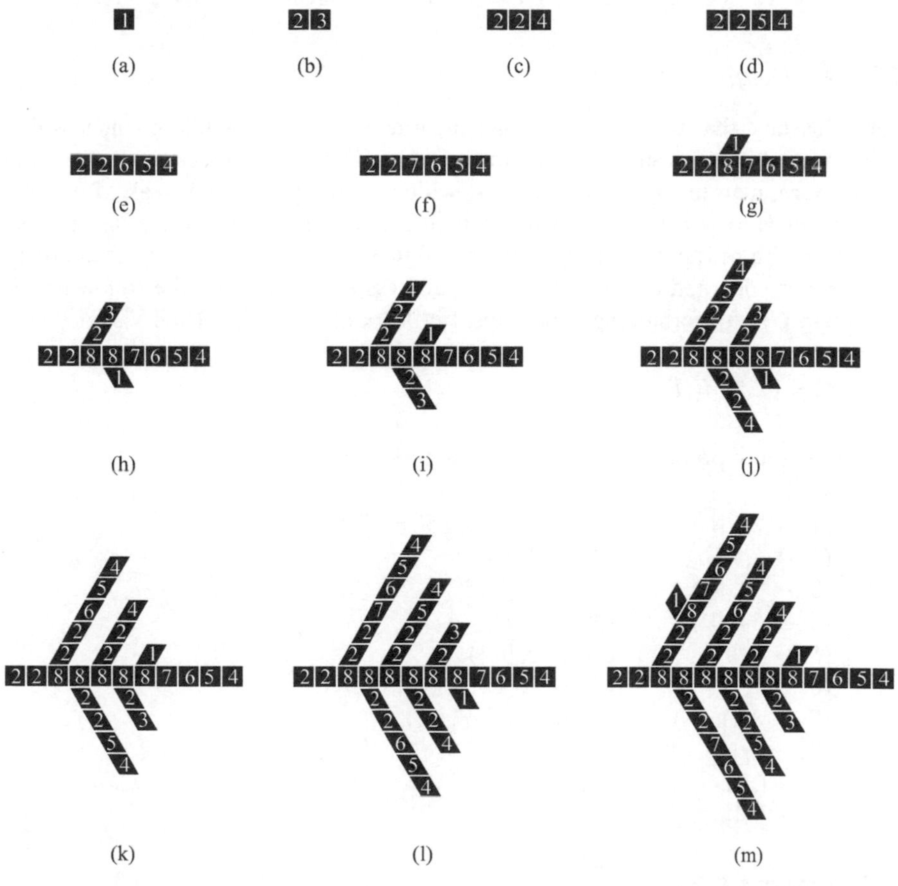

Figure 19.3 Healthy development

the developmental stages formally specified by the next derivation, which contain 13 strings corresponding to stages (a)–(m) in the figure.

$$
\begin{aligned}
1 &\Rightarrow_G 23\\
&\Rightarrow_G 224\\
&\Rightarrow_G 2254\\
&\Rightarrow_G 22654\\
&\Rightarrow_G 227654\\
&\Rightarrow_G 228[1]7654\\
&\Rightarrow_G 228[23]8[1]7654\\
&\Rightarrow_G 228[224]8[23]8[1]7654\\
&\Rightarrow_G 228[2254]8[224]8[23]8[1]7654\\
&\Rightarrow_G 228[22654]8[2254]8[224]8[23]8[1]7654\\
&\Rightarrow_G 228[227654]8[22654]8[2254]8[224]8[23]8[1]7654\\
&\Rightarrow_G 228[228[1]7654]8[227654]8[22654]8[2254]8[224]8[23]8[1]7654.
\end{aligned}
$$

19.1.1 Death

Let us assume that the red alga occurs in some unhealthy conditions under which only some of its parts survive while the rest dies. This dying process starts from the newly born, marginal parts of branches, which are too young and weak to survive, and proceeds toward the older parts, which are strong enough to live under these conditions. To be quite specific, all the red alga parts become gradually dead except for the parts denoted by 2s and 8s. This process is specified by the following 0L grammar, G, with forbidding conditions. Let $W = \{a' : a \in \Sigma\}$. Then,

$$G = (\Sigma \cup W, R, 1),$$

where the set of productions R contains the following:

$$
\begin{array}{ll}
(1 \rightarrow 23, W), & (1' \rightarrow 2', \{3', 4', 5', 6', 7'\}),\\
(2 \rightarrow 2, W), & (2' \rightarrow 2', \emptyset),\\
(3 \rightarrow 24, W), & (3' \rightarrow \varepsilon, \{4', 5', 6', 7'\}),\\
(4 \rightarrow 54, W), & (4' \rightarrow \varepsilon, \emptyset),\\
(5 \rightarrow 6, W), & (5' \rightarrow \varepsilon, \{4'\}),\\
(6 \rightarrow 7, W), & (6' \rightarrow \varepsilon, \{4', 5'\}),\\
(7 \rightarrow 8[1], W), & (7' \rightarrow \varepsilon, \{4', 5', 6'\}),\\
(8 \rightarrow 8, W), & \\
([\rightarrow [, \emptyset), & \\
(] \rightarrow], \emptyset), &
\end{array}
$$

and for every $a \in \Sigma$,

$$(a \rightarrow a', \emptyset), \qquad (a' \rightarrow a', \emptyset).$$

Figure 19.4 pictures the dying process corresponding to the next derivation, whose last eight strings correspond to stages (a)–(h) in the figure.

$$
\begin{aligned}
1 &\Rightarrow_G^* 228[228[1]7654]8[227654]8[22654]8[2254]8[224]8[23]8[1]7654\\
&\Rightarrow_G 2'2'8'[2'2'8'[1']7'6'5'4']8'[2'2'7'6'5'4']8'[2'2'6'5'4']8'[2'2'5'4']8'[2'2'4']\\
&\quad 8'[2'3']8'[1']7'6'5'4'\\
&\Rightarrow_G 2'2'8'[2'2'8'[1']7'6'5']8'[2'2'7'6'5']8'[2'2'6'5']8'[2'2'5']8'[2'2']8'[2'3']\\
&\quad 8'[1']7'6'5'\\
&\Rightarrow_G 2'2'8'[2'2'8'[1']7'6']8'[2'2'7'6']8'[2'2'6']8'[2'2']8'[2'2']8'[2'3']8'[1']7'6'\\
&\Rightarrow_G 2'2'8'[2'2'8'[1']7']8'[2'2'7']8'[2'2']8'[2'2']8'[2'2']8'[2'3']8'[1']7'\\
&\Rightarrow_G 2'2'8'[2'2'8'[1']]8'[2'2']8'[2'2']8'[2'2']8'[2'2']8'[2'3']8'[1']\\
&\Rightarrow_G 2'2'8'[2'2'8'[1']]8'[2'2']8'[2'2']8'[2'2']8'[2'2']8'[2']8'[1']\\
&\Rightarrow_G 2'2'8'[2'2'8'[2']]8'[2'2']8'[2'2']8'[2'2']8'[2'2']8'[2']8'[2'].
\end{aligned}
$$

19.1.2 Degeneration

Imagine a situation where the red alga has degenerated. During this degeneration, only the main stem was able to give a birth to new branches while all the other branches lengthened themselves without any branching out. This degeneration is specified by the forbidding 0L grammar $G = (\Sigma \cup \{D, E\}, R, 1)$, with R containing

$$
\begin{array}{llll}
(1 \to 23, \emptyset), & (2 \to 2, \emptyset), & (3 \to 24, \emptyset), & (4 \to 54, \emptyset),\\
(5 \to 6, \emptyset), & (6 \to 7, \emptyset), & (7 \to 8[1], \{D\}), & (8 \to 8, \emptyset),\\
([\to [, \emptyset), & (] \to], \emptyset), & (7 \to 8[D], \emptyset), & \\
(D \to ED, \emptyset), & (E \to E, \emptyset). & &
\end{array}
$$

Figure 19.5 pictures the degeneration specified by the following derivation, in which the last ten strings correspond to stages (a)–(j) in the figure.

$$
\begin{aligned}
1 &\Rightarrow_G^* 227654\\
&\Rightarrow_G 228[D]7654\\
&\Rightarrow_G 228[ED]8[D]7654\\
&\Rightarrow_G 228[E^2D]8[ED]8[D]7654\\
&\Rightarrow_G 228[E^3D]8[E^2D]8[ED]8[D]7654\\
&\Rightarrow_G 228[E^4D]8[E^3D]8[E^2D]8[ED]8[D]7654\\
&\Rightarrow_G 228[E^5D]8[E^4D]8[E^3D]8[E^2D]8[ED]8[D]7654\\
&\Rightarrow_G 228[E^6D]8[E^5D]8[E^4D]8[E^3D]8[E^2D]8[ED]8[D]7654\\
&\Rightarrow_G 228[E^7D]8[E^6D]8[E^5D]8[E^4D]8[E^3D]8[E^2D]8[ED]8[D]7654\\
&\Rightarrow_G 228[E^8D]8[E^7D]8[E^6D]8[E^5D]8[E^4D]8[E^3D]8[E^2D]8[ED]8[D]7654.
\end{aligned}
$$

□

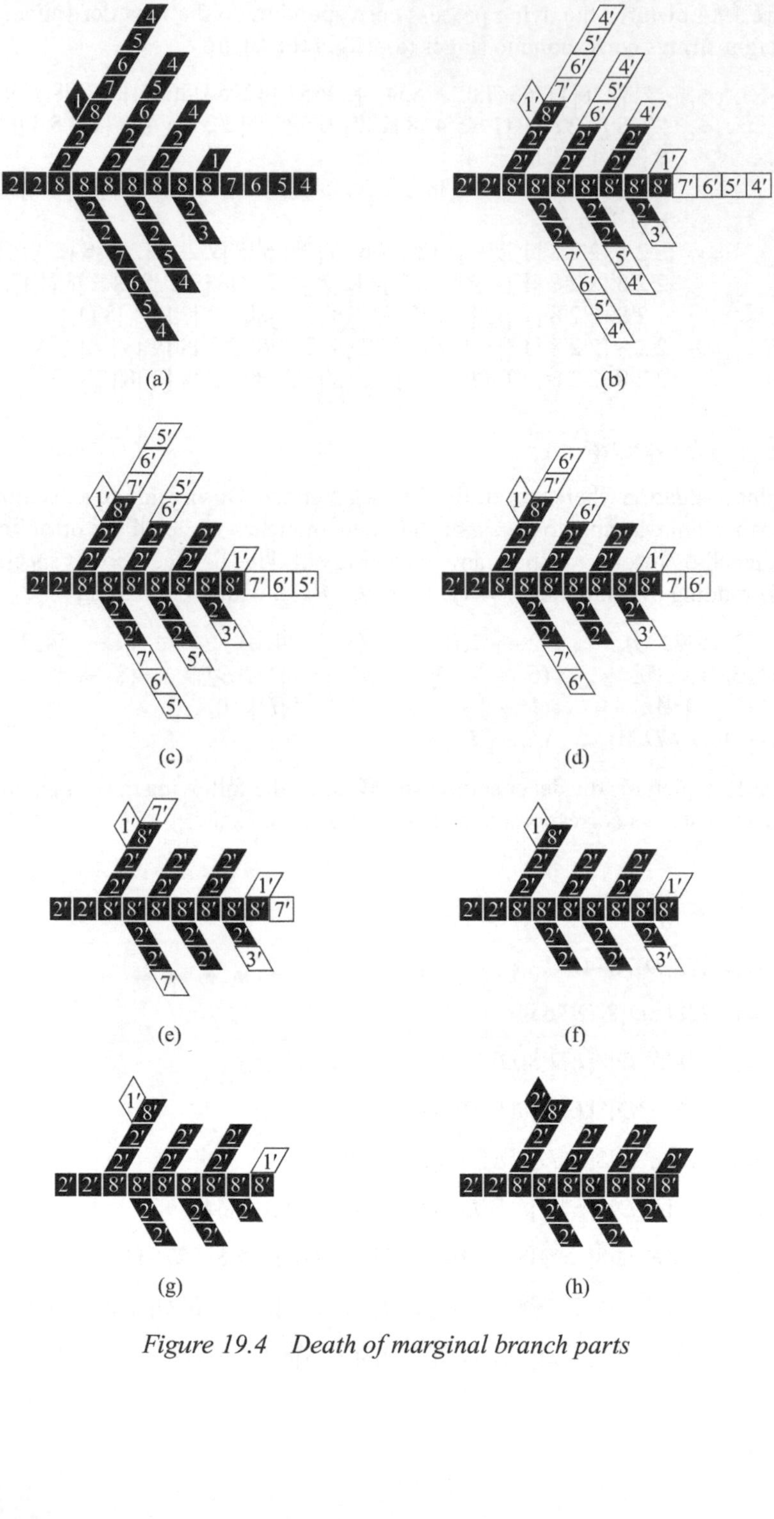

Figure 19.4 Death of marginal branch parts

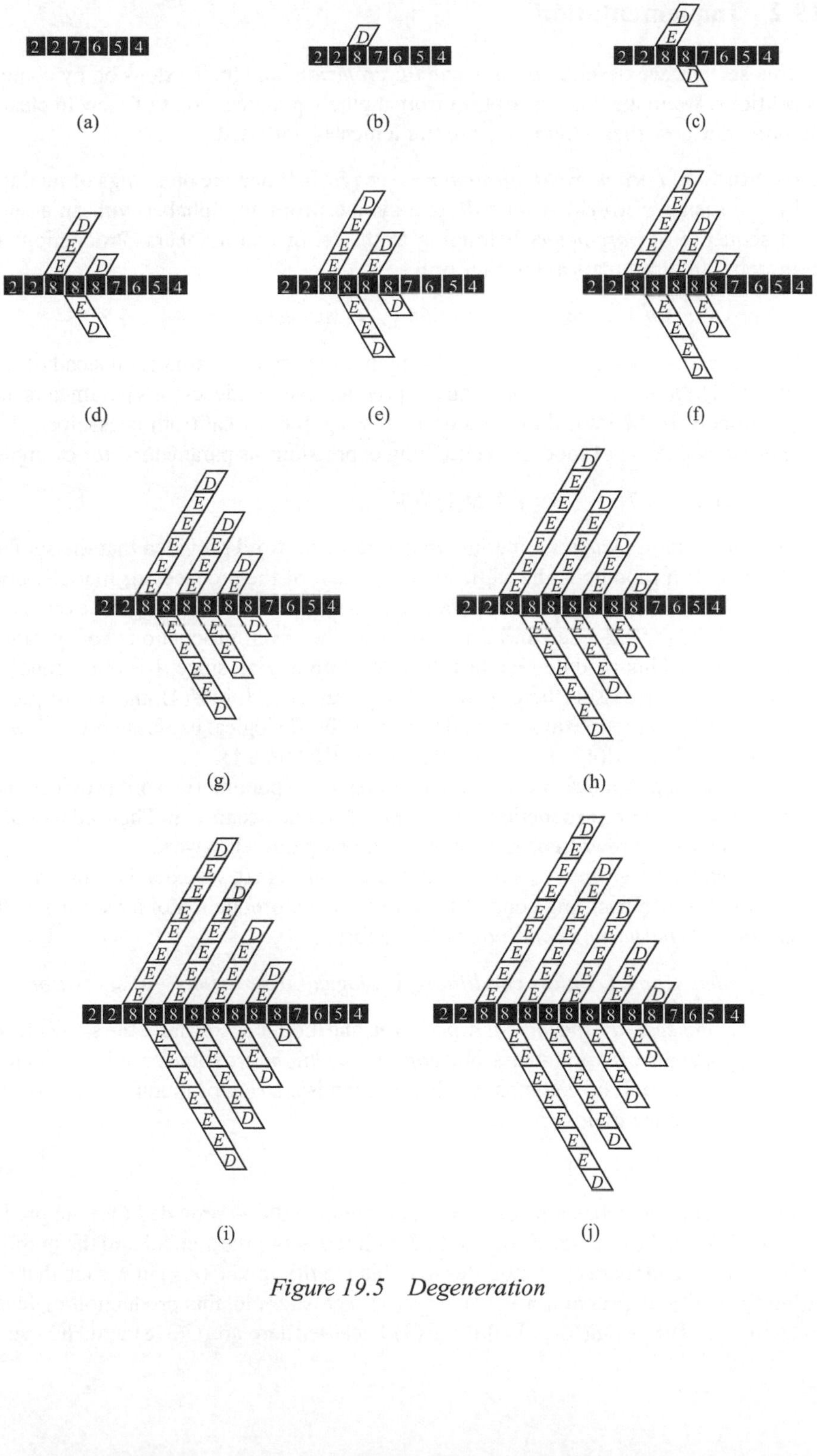

Figure 19.5 Degeneration

19.2 Implementation

In this section, we describe *parametric 0L grammars* and their extension by context conditions. We make this description from a purely practical point of view to clearly demonstrate how these grammars are implemented and used.

Case Study 3. *Parametric 0L grammars* (see [73,74]) operate on strings of modules called *parametric words*. A *module* is a symbol from an alphabet with an associated sequence of *parameters* belonging to the set of real numbers. Productions of parametric 0L grammars are of the form

$$predecessor\ [\ :\ logical\ expression\ ]\ \rightarrow\ successor.$$

The *predecessor* is a module having a sequence of formal parameters instead of real numbers. The *logical expression* is any expression over predecessor's parameters and real numbers. If the logical expression is missing, the logical truth is assumed. The *successor* is a string of modules containing expressions as parameters; for example,

$$A(x)\ :\ x < 7\ \rightarrow\ A(x+1)D(1)B(3-x).$$

Such a production *matches* a module in a parametric word provided that the symbol of the rewritten module is the same as the symbol of the predecessor module, both modules have the same number of parameters, and the value for the logical expression is true. Then, the module can be rewritten by the given production. For instance, consider $A(4)$. This module matches the above production since A is the symbol of production's predecessor, there is one actual parameter, 4, in $A(4)$, that corresponds to the formal parameter x in $A(x)$, and the value for the logical expression $x < 7$ with $x = 4$ is true. Thus, $A(4)$ can be rewritten to $A(5)D(1)B(-1)$.

As usual, a parametric 0L grammar can rewrite a parametric word provided that there exists a matching production for every module that occurs in it. Then, all modules are simultaneously rewritten, and we obtain a new parametric word.

Parametric 0L grammars with context conditions. Next, we extend the parametric 0L grammars by permitting context conditions. Each production of a *parametric 0L grammar with permitting conditions* has the form

$$predecessor\ [\ ?\ context\ conditions]\ [\ :\ logical\ expression]\ \rightarrow\ successor,$$

where the *predecessor*, the *logical expression*, and the *successor* have the same meaning as in parametric 0L grammars, and *context conditions* are some permitting context conditions separated by commas. Each condition is a string of modules with formal parameters. For example, consider

$$A(x)\ ?\ B(y),\ C(r,z)\ :\ x < y + r\ \rightarrow\ D(x)E(y+r).$$

This production matches a module in a parametric word w provided that the predecessor $A(x)$ matches the rewritten module with respect to the symbol and the number of parameters and there exist modules matching to $B(y)$ and $C(r, z)$ in w such that the value for logical expression $x < y + r$ is true. For example, this production matches $A(1)$ in $C(3, 8)D(-1)B(5)H(0, 0)A(1)F(3)$ because there are $C(3, 8)$ and $B(5)$ such that $1 < 5 + 3$ is true. If there are more substrings matching the context condition, any of them can be used.

Having described the parametric 0L grammars with permitting conditions, we next show how to use them to simulate the development of some plants.

In nature, developmental processes of multicellular structures are controlled by the quantity of substances exchanged between modules. In the case of plants, growth depends on the amount of water and minerals absorbed by the roots and carried upward to the branches. The model of branching structures making use of the resource flow was proposed by Borchert and Honda in [75]. The model is controlled by a *flux* of resources that starts at the base of the plant and propagates the substances toward the apexes. An apex accepts the substances, and when the quantity of accumulated resources exceeds a predefined threshold value, the apex bifurcates and initiates a new lateral branch. The distribution of the flux depends on the number of apexes that the given branch supports and on the type of the branch—plants usually carry a greater amount of resources to straight branches than to lateral branches (see [74,75]).

The following two examples illustrate the idea of plants simulated by parametric 0L grammars with permitting conditions:

1. Consider the model

$$\begin{array}{ll} axiom: & I(1,1,e_{root})A(1) \\ p_1: & A(id)\;?\;I(id_p,c,e)\;:\;id == id_p\;\wedge\;e \geq e_{th} \\ & \rightarrow\;[+(\alpha)I(2*id+1,\gamma,0)A(2*id+1)] \\ & \quad /(\pi)I(2*id,1-\gamma,0)A(2*id) \\ p_2: & I(id,c,e)\;?\;I(id_p,c_p,e_p)\;:\;id_p == \lfloor id/2 \rfloor \\ & \rightarrow\;I(id,c,c*e_p) \end{array}$$

This L grammar describes a simple plant with a constant resource flow from its roots and with a fixed distribution of the stream between lateral and straight branches. It operates on the following types of modules:

i. $I(id,c,e)$ represents an internode with a unique identification number id, a distribution coefficient c, and a flux value e.
ii. $A(id)$ is an apex growing from the internode with identification number equal to id.
iii. $+(\phi)$ and $/(\phi)$ rotate the segment orientation by angle ϕ (for more information, consult [74]).
iv. [and] enclose the sequence of modules describing a lateral branch.

We standardly assume that if no production matches a given module $X(x_1,\ldots,x_n)$, the module is rewritten by an implicit production of the form

$$X(x_1,\ldots,x_n) \rightarrow X(x_1,\ldots,x_n);$$

that is, it remains unchanged.

At the beginning, the plant consists of one internode $I(1,1,e_{root})$ with apex $A(1)$, where e_{root} is a constant flux value provided by the root. The first production, p_1, simulates the bifurcation of an apex. If an internode preceding the apex $A(id)$ reaches a sufficient flux $e \geq e_{th}$, the apex creates two new internodes I terminated by apexes A. The lateral internode is of the form $I(2 * id + 1, \gamma, 0)$ and the straight internode is of the form $I(2 * id, 1 - \gamma, 0)$. Clearly, the identification numbers of these internodes are unique. Moreover, every child internode can easily calculate the identification number of its parent internode; the parent internode has $id_p = \lfloor id/2 \rfloor$. The coefficient γ is a fraction of the parent flux to be directed to the lateral internode. The second production, p_2, controls the resource flow of a given internode. Observe that the permitting condition $I(id_p, c_p, e_p)$ with $id_p = \lfloor id/2 \rfloor$ matches only the parent internode. Thus, p_2 changes the flux value e of $I(id, c, e)$ to $c * e_p$, where e_p is the flux of the parent internode, and c is either γ for lateral internodes or $1 - \gamma$ for straight internodes. Therefore, p_2 simulates the transfer of a given amount of parent's flux into the internode. Figure 19.6 pictures 12 developmental stages of this plant, with e_{root}, e_{th}, and γ set to 12, 0.9, and 0.4, respectively. The numbers indicate the flow values of internodes.

It is easy to see that this model is unrealistically simple. Since the model ignores the number of apexes, its flow distribution does not depend on the size of branches, and the basal flow is set to a constant value. However, it sufficiently illustrates the technique of communication between adjacent internodes. Thus, it can serve as a template for more sophisticated models of plants, such as the following model.

2. We discuss a plant development with a resource flow controlled by the number of apexes. This example is based on Example 17 in [74].

$$
\begin{array}{ll}
axiom: & N(1)I(1, straight, 0, 1)A(1) \\
p_1: & N(k) \rightarrow N(k+1) \\
p_2: & I(id, t, e, c) \; ? \; N(k),\ A(id) \\
 & : id == 1 \\
 & \rightarrow I(id, t, \sigma_0 2^{(k-1)\eta^k}, 1) \\
p_3: & I(id, t, e, c) \; ? \; N(k),\ I(id_s, t_s, e_s, c_s),\ I(id_l, t_l, e_l, c_l) \\
 & : id == 1 \wedge id_s == 2 * id \wedge id_l == 2 * id + 1 \\
 & \rightarrow I(id, t, \sigma_0 2^{(k-1)\eta^k}, c_s + c_l) \\
p_4: & I(id, t, e, c) \; ? \; I(id_p, t_p, e_p, c_p),\ I(id_s, t_s, e_s, c_s),\ I(id_l, t_l, e_l, c_l) \\
 & : id_p == \lfloor id/2 \rfloor \wedge id_s == 2 * id \wedge id_l == 2 * id + 1 \\
 & \rightarrow I(id, t, \delta(t, e_p, c_p, c), c_s + c_l) \\
p_5: & Id(id, t, e, c) \; ? \; I(id_p, t_p, e_p, c_p),\ A(id_a) \\
 & : id_p == \lfloor id/2 \rfloor \wedge id_a == id \\
 & \rightarrow I(id, t, \delta(t, e_p, c_p, c), 1) \\
p_6: & A(id) \; ? \; I(id_p, t_p, e_p, c_p) \\
 & : id == id_p \wedge e_p \geq e_{th} \\
 & \rightarrow [+(\alpha)I(2 * id + 1, lateral, e_p * (1 - \lambda), 1)A(2 * id + 1)] \\
 & \quad /(\pi)I(2 * id, straight, e_p * \lambda, 1)A(2 * id)
\end{array}
$$

This L grammar uses the following types of modules:

i. $I(id, t, e, c)$ is an internode with a unique identification number id, where t is a type of this internode, $t \in \{straight, lateral\}$, e is a flux value, and c is a number of apexes the internode supports.

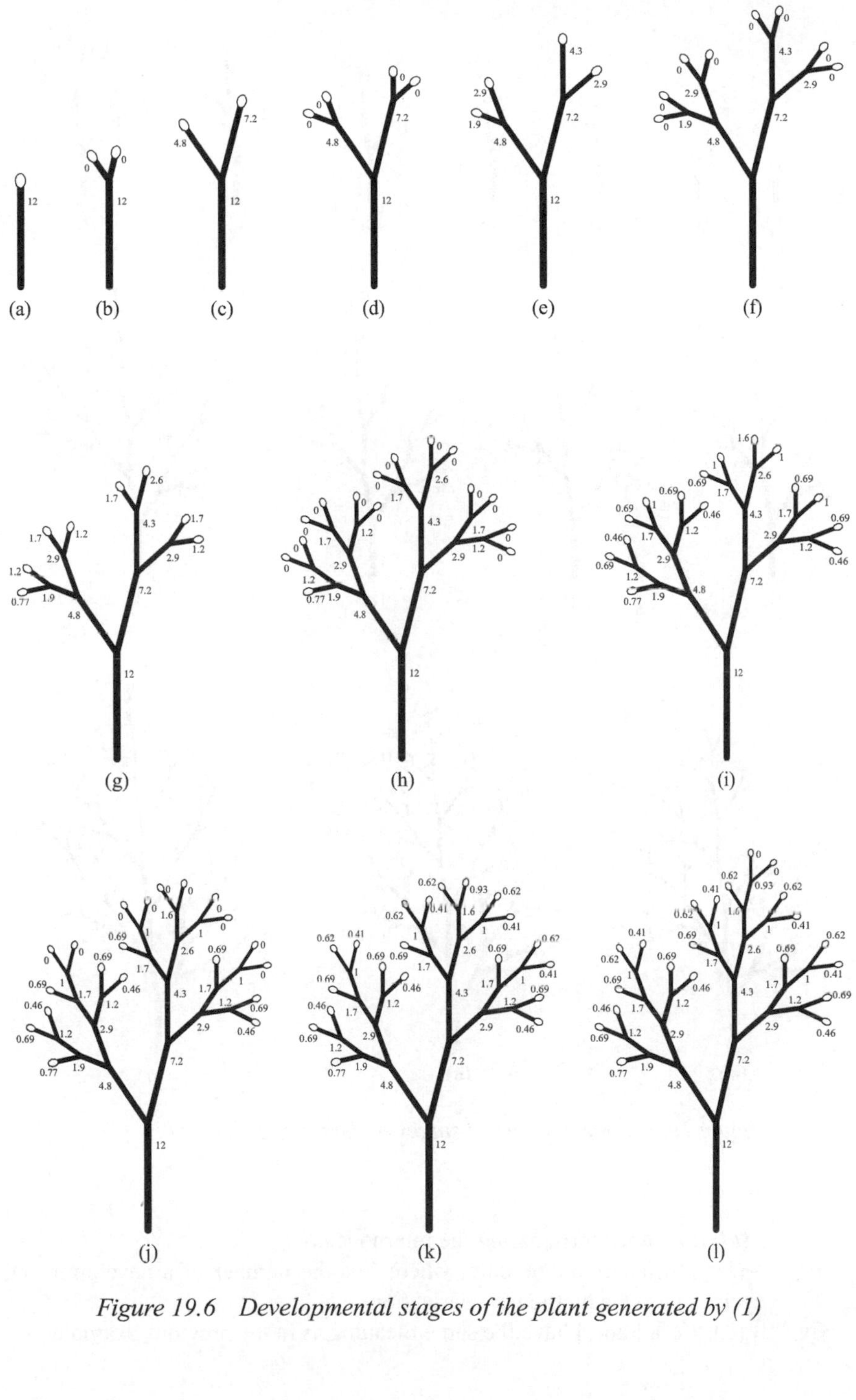

Figure 19.6 Developmental stages of the plant generated by (1)

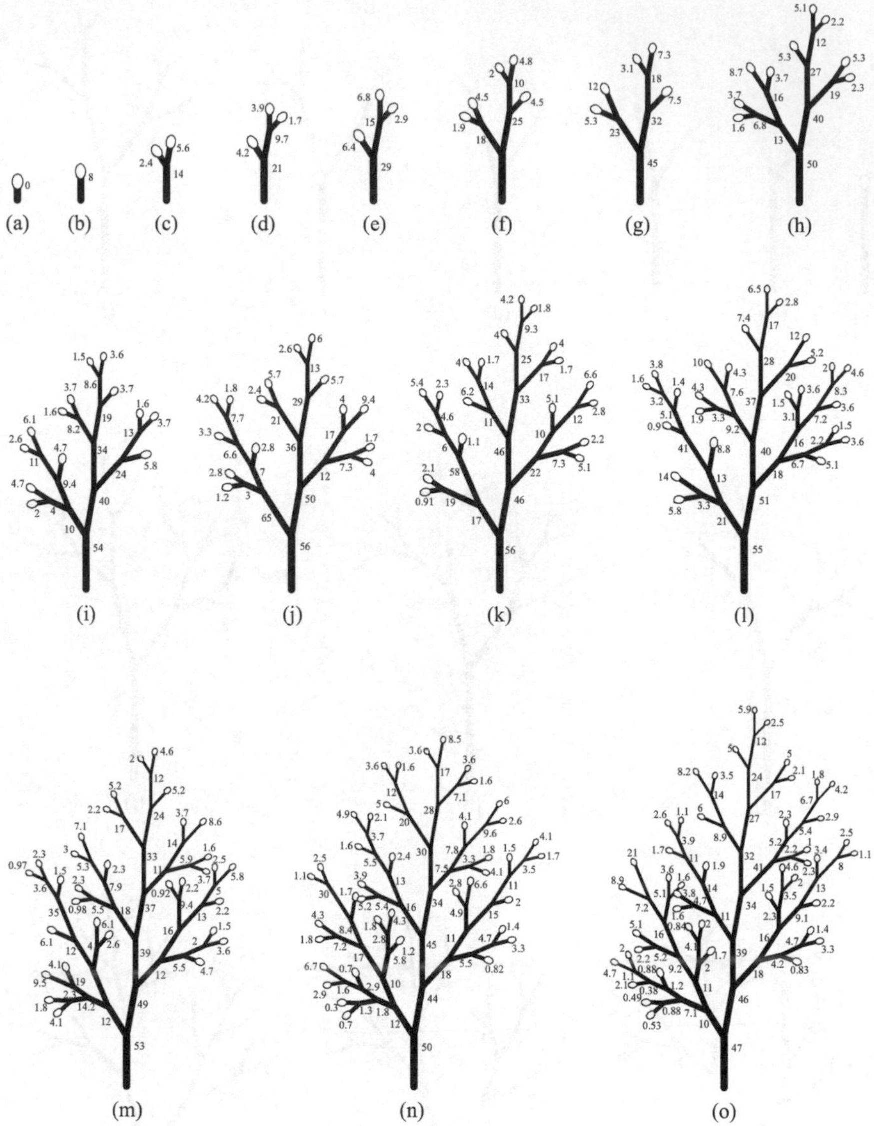

Figure 19.7 Developmental stages of the plant generated by (2)

ii. $A(id)$ is an apex terminating the internode *id*.
iii. $N(k)$ is an auxiliary module, where k is the number of a developmental cycle to be done by the next derivation.
iv. $+(\phi)$, $/(\phi)$, [and] have the same meaning as in the previous example.

The flux distribution function, δ, is defined as

$$\delta(t, e_p, c_p, c) = \begin{cases} e_p - e_p(1-\lambda)((c_p - c)/c) & \text{if } t = \textit{straight}, \\ e_p(1-\lambda)(c/(c_p - c)) & \text{if } t = \textit{lateral}. \end{cases}$$

The development starts from the axiom $N(1)I(1, \textit{straight}, 0, 1)A(1)$ containing one straight internode with one apex. In each derivation step, by application of p_4, every inner internode $I(id, t, e, c)$ gets the number of apexes of its straight $(I(id_s, t_s, e_s, c_s))$ and lateral $(I(id_l, t_l, e_l, c_l))$ descendant. Then, this number is stored in c. Simultaneously, it accepts a given part of the flux e_p provided by its parent internode $I(id_p, t_p, e_p, c_p)$. The distribution function δ depends on the number of apexes in the given branch and in the sibling branch, and on the type of this branch (straight or lateral). The distribution factor λ determines the amount of the flux that reaches the straight branch in case that both branches support the same number of apexes. Otherwise, the fraction is also affected by the ratio of apex counts. Productions p_2 and p_3 rewrite the basal internode, calculating its input flux value. The expression used for this purpose, $\sigma_0 2^{(k-1)\eta^k}$, was introduced by Borchert and Honda to simulate a sigmoid increase of the input flux; σ_0 is an initial flux, k is a developmental cycle, and η is a constant value scaling the flux change. Production p_5 rewrites internodes terminated by apexes. It keeps the number of apexes set to 1, and by analogy with p_4, it loads a fraction of parent's flux by using the δ function. The last production, p_6, controls the addition of new segments. By analogy with p_1 in the previous example, it erases the apex and generates two new internodes terminated by apexes. Figure 19.7 shows 15 developmental stages of a plant simulation based on this model.

Obviously, there are two concurrent streams of information in this model. The bottom-up (acropetal) stream carries and distributes the substances required for the growth. The top-down (basipetal) flow propagates the number of apexes that is used for the flux distribution. A remarkable feature of this model is the response of a plant to a pruning. Indeed, after a branch removal, the model redirects the flux to the remaining branches and accelerates their growth.

Let us note that this model is a simplified version of the model described in [74], which is very complex. Under this simplification, however, $c_p - c$ may be equal to zero as the denominator in the distribution function δ. If this happens, we change this zero value to the proper nonzero value so that the number of apexes supported by the parent internode corresponds to the number of apexes on the straight and lateral branches growing from the parent internode. Consult [74] for a more appropriate, but also complicated solution of this problem.

From the presented examples, we see that with permitting conditions, parametric 0L grammars can describe sophisticated models of plants in a very natural way. Particularly, compared to the context-sensitive L grammars, they allow one to refer to modules that are not adjacent to the rewritten module, and this property makes them more adequate, succinct, and elegant. □

Part V

Conclusion

We close the entire book by adding several important remarks concerning its coverage in the present concluding part. First, we sum up all the coverage contained in the text. Then, we sketch important current investigation trends. In addition, we make several bibliographical remarks. The whole part consists of a single chapter.

Chapter 20
Concluding remarks

First, Section 20.1 summarizes all the material covered in the text. Then, Section 20.2 points out modern investigation trends, including open-problem areas, and makes many bibliographical comments.

20.1 Summary of the book

This book gives a survey of crucially important mathematical models for languages and computation. Most of these models were introduced and studied within the framework of formal language theory. In essence, this theory represents a mathematically systematized body of knowledge concerning languages and their models, which allow us to formalize and investigate computation strictly scientifically. The book defines languages as sets of finite sequences consisting of symbols. As a result, this general definition encompasses almost all languages, including natural as well as artificial languages, such as programming languages. The strictly mathematical approach to languages necessitates an introduction of mathematical models that define them.

Traditionally, these language models are based upon finitely many rules by which they sequentially rewrite strings. They are classified into two basic categories—grammars and automata. Grammars define strings of their languages by generating them from special start symbols. Automata define strings of their languages by a rewriting process that starts from these strings and ends in a special set of strings, usually called final configurations. However, apart from these traditional versions of grammars and automata, language theory has also developed several language models that rewrite words in an alternative way.

These alternative language models are covered in this book, too. Many of them have their great advantages over their traditional counterparts. From a practical viewpoint, an important advantage of these models consists of controlling their language-defining process and, therefore, operating in a more deterministic way than classical language models, which perform their derivations in a quite traditional way. Indeed, in an everchanging environment in which real language processors work, the modern language models adequately reflect and simulate real communication technologies applied in such real-world areas as various engineering techniques for language analysis. Most importantly, the modern versions of language models are stronger than their traditional counterparts. Considering these significant advantages and properties, the alternative language models fulfill a highly beneficial role in many fields of science, ranging from mathematics through computer science up to linguistics and biology.

Discussing both traditional and alternative models for languages and computation, this book restricts its principal attention to these three crucially important investigation areas—their properties, transformations, and applications.

1. Concerning properties, the power of the models under consideration represents perhaps the most important property concerning them, so we always determined the language family defined by these models. Special attention was also paid to algorithms that modify modern language models so that they satisfy some prescribed properties without changing the generated language. Algorithms of this kind fulfill an important role in practice because many language processors strictly require that the prescribed properties be satisfied. From a theoretical viewpoint, these properties frequently simplified proofs demonstrating results about the models.
2. Transformations of language models were important to this book, too. Specifically, transformations that reduce the models represent one of its important investigation areas because reduced versions of these models define languages in a succinct and easy-to-follow way. As obvious, this reduction simplifies the development of language-processing technologies, which then work economically and effectively. Of course, the same languages can be defined by different language models. We obviously tend to define them by the most appropriate models under given circumstances. Therefore, whenever discussing different types of equally powerful language models, we also presented transformations that converted them to each other. More specifically, given a language model of one type, we explained how to convert it to a language model of another equally powerful type, so both the original model and the model produced by this conversion define the same language.
3. Finally, the book demonstrated applications of language models. It narrowed its attention to grammars rather than automata. First, it described these applications and their perspectives from a general viewpoint. Then, it gave many case studies to show quite specific real-world applications concerning computational linguistics and biology.

Part I, consisting of Chapters 1–3, reviews the most basic concepts concerning sets and sequences. Chapter 1 reviews basic concepts from set theory. Special attention is paid to languages defined as sets whose elements are finite sequences of symbols because languages play an important role later in this book. Chapter 2 gives the essentials concerning relations and their crucially important special cases, namely, functions. Chapter 3 reviews fundamental concepts from graph theory.

Part II, consisting of Chapters 4–10, covers classical models for languages and computation. Chapter 4 introduces the basic versions of rewriting systems while paying special attention to using them as language defining devices. Chapter 5 presents finite automata as the simplest versions of automata covered in this book. Chapter 6 discusses generative models called context-free grammars, while Chapter 7 discusses their accepting counterparts—pushdown automata; indeed, both are equally powerful. Chapters 8–10 are crucially important to Part II and, in fact, the book in its entirety. These chapters deal with Turing machines as basic language-defining models for computation. Indeed, based on them, Part II explores the very heart of the foundations of computation. More precisely, Chapter 8 introduces the mathematical notion of a Turing machine, which has become a universally accepted formalization of the intuitive notion of a procedure. Based upon this strictly mathematical notion, Chapters 9 and 10 study the general limits of computation in terms of computability and decidability. Regarding computability, Chapter 9 considers Turing machines as computers of functions over nonnegative integers and demonstrates the existence of functions whose computation cannot be specified by any procedure. As far as decidability is concerned, Chapter 10 formalizes problem-deciding algorithms by Turing machines that halt on every input. It formulates several important problems concerning the language models discussed in this book and constructs algorithms that decide them. On the other hand, Chapter 10 describes several problems that are not decidable by any algorithm. Apart from giving several specific undecidable problems, this book builds up a general theory of undecidability. Finally, the text approaches decidability in a much finer and realistic way. Indeed, it reconsiders problem-deciding algorithms in terms of their computational complexity measured according to time and space requirements. Perhaps most importantly, it shows that although some problems are decidable in principle, they are intractable for absurdly high-computational requirements of the algorithms that decide them.

Part III, consisting of Chapters 11–15, deals with the most important alternative versions of mathematical models. Chapter 11 gives the fundamentals of grammars based upon context conditions. Chapter 12 covers grammars that regulate their generation process by additional mechanisms, based upon simple mathematical concepts, such as finite sets of symbols. Chapter 13 studies grammars that generate their languages in parallel and, thereby, accelerate this generation significantly. Chapter 14 explores automata and grammars that work on their words in a discontinuous way. Finally, Chapter 15 studies deep pushdown automata that can expand their pushdown lists deeper in their pushdown lists; otherwise, they function just like classical pushdown automata (see Chapter 7).

Part IV, consisting of Chapters 16–19, sketches applications of mathematical models studied earlier in the book. First, Chapter 16 covers these applications and their perspectives, in general. Then, more specifically, Chapters 17 and 18 describe the syntax analysis of programming and natural languages, respectively. Chapters 19 gives some applications in microbiology.

Part V, consisting of the present chapter, closes the entire book by adding several remarks concerning its coverage. It summarizes all the material covered in the text. Furthermore, it sketches many brand new investigation trends and long-time open problems. It also makes several bibliographical remarks.

20.2 Latest trends and open problems

In this section, we point out several new directions in the investigation of mathematical models for languages and computation. We also point out many open problems.

Algebraically speaking, various kinds of modern language models can be viewed as restrictions placed upon relations by which the language models define their languages. Indeed, several modern versions of grammars are based on restrictions placed upon derivations, while modern versions of automata restrict the way they make moves. From this point of view, the investigation of modern grammars is closely related to many algebraically oriented studies in formal language theory. Areas of future research include the following investigation fields. Investigate how to replace some of the previous regulating mechanisms by suitable relation-domain restrictions and vice versa. Furthermore, study how some well-known special cases of these relations affect the resulting language-defining power. Specifically, perform this study under the assumptions that these relations represent functions, injections, or surjections. The algebraic theory of formal languages and their automata is discussed in a large number of articles and books (see [31,52,76–98]).

In formal language theory, the overwhelming majority of language models represent either grammars or automata. Although it is obviously quite natural to design language models based on a combination of both and, thereby, make the scale of language-defining models much richer and broader, only a tiny minority of these models is designed in this combined way. For instance, state grammars represent language models that have features of both grammars and automata (see Section 12.1), and some others were briefly investigated in [40,83,84,99–105]. It is thus highly expectable that formal language theory will introduce and investigate many more language models based upon a combination of grammars and automata.

Grammars and automata discussed in this book define languages. As obvious, they can be modified to translation-defining models. Most probably, formal language theory will reopen their investigation of translation-defining models by studying their properties from a theoretical point of view by analogy with other well-known studies of formal translation, including [106–116]. Simultaneously, however, we can expect a struggle to apply them to the translation of programming as well as natural languages. As a matter of fact, to some extent, [36,100,117,118] have already sketched applications concerning the specification and translation of natural languages in this way.

Throughout this book, we have already formulated many open problems. We close the present section by selecting and repeating the most important questions, which deserve our special attention. To see their significance completely, however, we suggest that the reader returns to the referenced parts of the book in order to view these questions in the full context of their formulation and discussion in detail.

Erasing. Over the last four decades, formal language theory has struggled to determine the precise impact of erasing rules to the power of alternative versions of grammars. Indeed, it is still an open question whether regular-controlled, matrix, programmed, and forbidding grammars are equivalent to their propagating versions (see Chapter 12). Furthermore, several transformation-related results are achieved for grammars with erasing rules. In the proof techniques by which we have demonstrated the results, these rules fulfill a crucial role. In other words, these techniques cannot be straightforwardly adapted for grammars without erasing rules. Can we achieve some uniform rewriting for grammars without erasing rules in a different way?

For some results regarding the role of erasing rules, see [12,14,18,19,23,35,40, 45,103–105,119–131].

Scattered context. Scattered context grammars were discussed in [34,36–38,56, 57,114,115,122,132–165]. It is a long-standing open problem whether propagating scattered context grammars and context-sensitive grammars are equivalent. Consider the results in Section 13.1 concerning the reduction of scattered context grammars. While one-nonterminal versions of scattered context grammars do not generate the entire family of recursively enumerable languages (see Theorem 13.5), their two-nonterminal versions do (see Theorem 13.8). Therefore, regarding the number of nonterminals, this open-problem area has been completely solved. By Theorem 13.9, the two-context-sensitive rule versions of scattered context grammars characterize the family of recursively enumerable languages. On the other hand, the generative power of their one-context-sensitive-rule versions has not been determined yet.

Determinism. In Section 12.5, we have proved that state-controlled and transition-controlled finite automata regulated by languages generated by propagating programmed grammars with appearance checking characterize the family of recursively enumerable languages (see Theorem 12.42 and Corollary 12.43). Let us point out, however, that these automata are, in a general case, nondeterministic. Does this characterization hold in terms of their deterministic versions, too? Furthermore, try to achieve an analogical characterization of the family of context-sensitive languages. In addition, reconsider deep pushdown automata, discussed in Chapter 15. In its conclusion, this section discusses special types of these automata—deterministic deep pushdown automata. Determine the language family defined by these two variants. Study [166–169] when investigating deterministic versions of mathematical models.

Multigeneration. The basics of multigenerative grammar systems are given in Chapter 13 and [170–173]. Recall that they are based upon a simultaneous generation of several strings, which are composed together by some basic operation, such as concatenation, after their generation is completed. Consider other operations, like intersection, and study languages generated in this way by multigenerative grammar systems. Furthermore, study multigenerative grammar systems based on special cases of context-free grammars. Specifically, what is the generative power of multigenerative grammar systems based upon regular or linear grammars?

Jumping. Consider jumping finite automata and their general versions, discussed in Chapter 14. Theorem 14.35 gives a necessary and sufficient condition for a language to belong to the family defined by jumping finite automata. Does there exist a similar necessary and sufficient condition for general jumping finite automata as well? Furthermore, how precisely do left jumps affect the power of these automata? Are there any undecidable problems concerning the family of languages accepted by these automata? Study [51,53,64,174] when investigating jumping versions of mathematical models.

20.3 Bibliographical remarks

In what follows, we give an overview of the crucially important studies published on the subject of this book.

Although the present book concerning mathematical models is self-contained, some background in formal language theory is definitely helpful to grasp them easily (see [11,22,31,52,54,78,80,88,91,95–98,175–179]). Early works about models for languages and computation are [1,6,7,9–11,15,16,25,29–31,40,56,76,78,84,88,92, 94,98,99,145,162,165,168,176,178,180–206]. Furthermore, [13,21,22,39,207–209] give an overview of results concerning grammars. In [52,81,83,84,87,88,92,94,95, 97,98,176,177,179], there are many algorithms that transform automata, grammars, and related mathematical models into equivalent models that in addition, satisfy some prescribed properties. Furthermore, [1,4,9,24–30,32,33,55,58–63,65–73,75,181,182, 184,186,193,194,197,201,202,210–263,309] are closely related to the subject of this book as well.

20.3.1 Grammars

Contextness. Most context-related normal forms of grammars were established in [6,8,10,192,264–267]. Grammars based on context conditions are discussed in [7, 14,16–19,34,36–38,40,45,47,56,57,99,114,115,122,123,130,132–135,138–154,156–158,160,161,163–165,183,187,189,191,198–200,203–206,265,268–291]. Specifically, random context grammars were introduced in [183]. Strictly speaking, in [183], their definition coincides with the definition of permitting grammars in this book. Forbidding grammars, also known as N-grammars (see [15]), together with other variants of random context grammars were originally studied in [189,191,200]. After these studies, many more works discussed these grammars, including [14,275,285,291,292]. In [293–295], simplified versions of random-context grammars, called restricted context-free grammars, were studied. Moreover, [296–299] studied grammar systems with their components represented by random context grammars. Generalized forbidding grammars were introduced in [300] and further investigated in [285,301]. Semi-conditional and simple semi-conditional grammars were introduced and investigated in [16] and [283], respectively. Their descriptional complexity was studied in [17–19,274,278,285,287].

Originally, scattered context grammars were defined in [56]. Their original version disallowed erasing rules, however. Four years later, [145] generalized them to scattered context grammars with erasing rules (see also [302]). The following studies represent the most important studies that have discussed these grammars: [19,34,37,38,56,57,122,132,133,135–141,143–146,148–152,155, 158,159,161–165,180,190,192,285,302,303]. Uniform generation of languages by scattered context grammars was investigated in [132]. For an in-depth overview of scattered context grammars and their applications, consult [36] and the references given therein.

Sequential rewriting over word monoids has been studied in [304,305]. Moreover, [306–308] investigate sequential rewriting over free groups.

Regulation. Grammars regulated by regular control languages over the set of rules were introduced in [195]. Their workspace conditions were established in [309] and [310]. Generation of sentences with their parses by these grammars was investigated in [123]. Matrix grammars were first defined and studied in [311]. For more results regarding the elimination of erasing rules from these grammars, see [14,119–121]. Programmed grammars were introduced in [185]. Their non-determinism has been investigated in [167,266,267,312,313]. Some other recent papers include [314–316]. State grammars were defined by Kasai in [20]. A generalized version of these grammars with erasing rules was originally studied in [188]. Consult [12,18,19,23,35,45,125,127–131,139,317–320] for more results about regulated grammars.

Parallelism. ET0L grammars have been studied in [5,12,15,40–42,48,50,74,128, 135,277,282,285,302,308,317–326]. Context-conditional ET0L grammars were studied in [285]. Forbidding ET0L grammars were introduced and investigated in [321]. Simple semi-conditional ET0L grammars were introduced in [277] and further studied in [276]. Left versions of ET0L grammars were introduced and studied in [326]. Their nonterminal complexity was investigated in [282]. Parallel rewriting over word monoids was studied in [135,324]. For modern versions of ET0L grammars, consult [128,196,317–320,323,325] and Chapter 8 in [12].

Multigeneration. Multigenerative grammar systems based upon leftmost derivations (see Section 13.3) were introduced in [171]. Their general versions were studied in [170]. Controlled pure grammar systems were introduced and investigated in [280]. Moreover, [327] gives a preliminary solution to four open problems raised in [280]. For more results about grammar systems, consult [2,42–49,170–173,264,296–299, 327–333].

20.3.2 Automata

Essentials. The theory of automata is covered in many books, including [13,39,52, 83,95,179,208,209].

Regulation. Self-regulated finite automata and self-regulated pushdown automata were introduced in [334]. Finite automata regulated by control languages were introduced in [23]. For a study of finite automata controlled by Petri nets, see [335]. Regulated pushdown automata were introduced in [3]. Their special versions, referred to as one-turn linear-regulated pushdown automata, were studied in [336–338]. Black-hole pushdown automata, which are closely related to regulated pushdown automata, were introduced and investigated in [339,340].

Deepness. Deep pushdown automata were defined and studied in [341]. For more results related to these automata, consult [342–346].

Algebra. The algebraic theory of automata is covered in [77–80,84,88,92,97,98]. Finite automata over free groups were studied in [89,90]. Pushdown automata with pushdowns defined over free groups were introduced and studied in [347]. Finally, #-rewriting systems were recently introduced and studied in [101–105].

Jumping computation. Jumping finite automata were introduced in [53]. Several open problems stated there were solved in [51,64]. Other related models involving discontinuity include nested word automata [348], bag automata [349], and input-revolving finite automata [169].

By no means does this handbook cover mathematical models for languages and computation in an exhaustive way. Further models of this kind are to be found in [350,351].

References

[1] Kleijn HCM, Rozenberg G. On the Generative Power of Regular Pattern Grammars. Acta Informatica. 1983;20:391–411.

[2] Meduna A. Two-Way Metalinear PC Grammar Systems and Their Descriptional Complexity. Acta Cybernetica. 2004;2004(16):385–397.

[3] Kolář D, Meduna A. Regulated Pushdown Automata. Acta Cybernetica. 2000;2000(4):653–664.

[4] Meduna A. Simultaneously One-Turn Two-Pushdown Automata. International Journal of Computer Mathematics. 2003;2003(80):679–687.

[5] Rozenberg G, Salomaa A. Mathematical Theory of L Systems. Academic Press, Orlando, FL; 1980.

[6] Kuroda SY. Classes of Languages and Linear-Bounded Automata. Information and Control. 1964;7(2):207–223.

[7] Penttonen M. One-Sided and Two-Sided Context in Formal Grammars. Information and Control. 1974;25(4):371–392.

[8] Geffert V. Normal Forms for Phrase-Structure Grammars. Theoretical Informatics and Applications. 1991;25(5):473–496.

[9] Chomsky N. On Certain Formal Properties of Grammars. Information and Control. 1959;2:137–167.

[10] Greibach SA. A New Normal-Form Theorem for Context-Free Phrase Structure Grammars. Journal of the ACM. 1965;12(1):42–52.

[11] Salomaa A. Formal Languages. Academic Press, London; 1973.

[12] Dassow J, Păun G. Regulated Rewriting in Formal Language Theory. Springer, New York, NY; 1989.

[13] Rozenberg G, Salomaa A, editors. Handbook of Formal Languages, vol. 2: Linear Modeling: Background and Application. Springer, New York, NY; 1997.

[14] Zetzsche G. On Erasing Productions in Random Context Grammars. In: ICALP'10: Proceedings of the 37th International Colloquium on Automata, Languages and Programming. Springer; 2010. p. 175–186.

[15] Penttonen M. ET0L-Grammars and N-Grammars. Information Processing Letters. 1975;4(1):11–13.

[16] Păun G. A Variant of Random Context Grammars: Semi-conditional Grammars. Theoretical Computer Science. 1985;41(1):1–17.

[17] Okubo F. A Note on the Descriptional Complexity of Semi-conditional Grammars. Information Processing Letters. 2009;110(1):36–40.

[18] Masopust T. An Improvement of the Descriptional Complexity of Grammars Regulated by Context Conditions. In: 2nd Doctoral Workshop on Mathematical and Engineering Methods in Computer Science. Faculty of Information Technology; 2006. p. 105–112.

[19] Vaszil G. On the Descriptional Complexity of some Rewriting Mechanisms Regulated by Context Conditions. Theoretical Computer Science. 2005;330(2):361–373.

[20] Kasai T. An Hierarchy Between Context-Free and Context-Sensitive Languages. Journal of Computer and System Sciences. 1970;4:492–508.

[21] Martín-Vide C, Mitrana V, Păun G, editors. Formal Languages and Applications. Springer, Berlin; 2004. p. 249–274.

[22] Harrison M. Introduction to Formal Language Theory. Addison-Wesley, Boston, MA; 1978.

[23] Meduna A, Zemek P. Regulated Grammars and Automata. New York, NY: Springer US; 2014.

[24] Rosebrugh RD, Wood D. A Characterization Theorem for n-Parallel Right Linear Languages. Journal of Computer and System Sciences. 1973;7:579–582.

[25] Rosebrugh RD, Wood D. Restricted Parallelism and Right Linear Grammars. Utilitas Mathematica. 1975;7:151–186.

[26] Wood D. Properties of n-Parallel Finite State Languages. McMaster University; 1973.

[27] Wood D. m-Parallel n-Right Linear Simple Matrix Languages. Utilitas Mathematica. 1975;8:3–28.

[28] Ibarra OH. Simple Matrix Languages. Information and Control. 1970;17: 359–394.

[29] Fischer PC, Rosenberg AL. Multitape One-Way Nonwriting Automata. Journal of Computer and System Sciences. 1968;2:38–101.

[30] Siromoney R. Finite-Turn Checking Automata. Journal of Computer and System Sciences. 1971;5:549–559.

[31] Siromoney R. Studies in the Mathematical Theory of Grammars and Its Applications. University of Madras, Madras, India; 1969.

[32] Wood D. Theory of Computation: A Primer. Addison-Wesley, Boston, MA; 1987.

[33] Autebert J, Berstel J, Boasson L, editors. Context-Free Languages and Pushdown Automata. In: Handbook of Formal Languages. Springer, Berlin; 1997. p. 111–174.

[34] Masopust T. Scattered Context Grammars Can Generate the Powers of 2. In: Proceedings of the 13th Conference and Competition EEICT 2007. vol. 4. Faculty of Electrical Engineering and Communication, Brno University of Technology; 2007. p. 401–404.

[35] Masopust T. Formal Models: Regulation and Reduction. Faculty of Information Technology, Brno University of Technology; 2007.

[36] Meduna A, Techet J. Scattered Context Grammars and Their Applications. WIT Press, Southampton; 2010.

[37] Meduna A. Terminating Left-Hand Sides of Scattered Context Grammars. Theoretical Computer Science. 2000;2000(237):424–427.
[38] Csuhaj-Varjú E, Vaszil G. Scattered Context Grammars Generate Any Recursively Enumerable Language With Two Nonterminals. Information Processing Letters. 2010;110:902–907.
[39] Rozenberg G, Salomaa A, editors. Handbook of Formal Languages, vol. 1: Word, Language, Grammar. Springer, New York, NY; 1997.
[40] Rozenberg G, Solms SH. Priorities on Context Conditions in Rewriting Systems. Information Sciences. 1978;14(1):15–50.
[41] Solms SH. Some Notes on ET0L Languages. International Journal of Computer Mathematics. 1976;5:285–296.
[42] Beek M, Csuhaj-Varjú E, Holzer M, *et al.* On Competence in CD Grammar Systems. In: Developments in Language Theory. vol. 3340 of Lecture Notes in Computer Science. Springer, Berlin, Heidelberg; 2005. p. 3–14.
[43] Beek M, Csuhaj-Varjú E, Holzer M, *et al.* On Competence in CD Grammar Systems With Parallel Rewriting. International Journal of Foundations of Computer Science. 2007;18(6):1425–1439.
[44] Bordihn H, Holzer M. Grammar Systems With Negated Conditions in their Cooperation Protocols. Journal of Universal Computer Science. 2000;6(12):1165–1184.
[45] Bordihn H, Holzer M. Random Context in Regulated Rewriting Versus Cooperating Distributed Grammar Systems. In: LATA'08: Proceedings of the 2nd International Conference on Language and Automata Theory and Applications. Springer; 2008. p. 125–136.
[46] Csuhaj-Varjú E, Dassow J, Vaszil G. Some New Modes of Competence-Based Derivations in CD Grammar Systems. In: Developments in Language Theory. vol. 5257 of Lecture Notes in Computer Science. Springer, Berlin, Heidelberg; 2008. p. 228–239.
[47] Csuhaj-Varjú E, Păun G, Salomaa A. Conditional Tabled Eco-Grammar Systems. Journal of Universal Computer Science. 1995;1(5):252–268.
[48] Dassow J. On Cooperating Distributed Grammar Systems With Competence Based Start and Stop Conditions. Fundamenta Informaticae. 2007;76: 293–304.
[49] Fernau H, Holzer M, Freund R. Hybrid Modes in Cooperating Distributed Grammar Systems: Internal Versus External Hybridization. Theoretical Computer Science. 2001;259(1–2):405–426.
[50] Sosík P. The Power of Catalysts and Priorities in Membrane Systems. Grammars. 2003;6(1):13–24.
[51] Madejski G. Jumping and Pumping Lemmas and Their Applications. In: Proceedings of NCMA 2016 – 8th Workshop on Non-Classical Models of Automata and Applications; 2016. p. 25–34.
[52] Meduna A. Automata and Languages: Theory and Applications. Springer, London; 2000.
[53] Meduna A, Zemek P. Jumping Finite Automata. International Journal of Foundations of Computer Science. 2012;23(7):1555–1578.

[54] Ginsburg S. The Mathematical Theory of Context-free Languages. McGraw Hill, New York, NY; 1966.
[55] Kudlek M, Martín-Vide C, Păun G. Toward FMT (Formal Macroset Theory). In: Pre-proceedings of the Workshop on Multiset Processing. Curtea de Arges; 2000. p. 149–158.
[56] Greibach SA, Hopcroft JE. Scattered Context Grammars. Journal of Computer and System Sciences. 1969;3(3):233–247.
[57] Fernau H, Meduna A. A Simultaneous Reduction of Several Measures of Descriptional Complexity in Scattered Context Grammars. Information Processing Letters. 2003;86(5):235–240.
[58] Grossman DA, Frieder O. Information Retrieval: Algorithms and Heuristics. 2nd ed. Springer, Berlin; 2004.
[59] Bouchon-Meunier B, Coletti G, Yager RR, editors. Modern Information Processing: From Theory to Applications. Elsevier Science, New York, NY; 2006.
[60] Buettcher S, Clarke CLA, Cormack GV. Information Retrieval: Implementing and Evaluating Search Engines. The MIT Press, Cambridge, MA; 2010.
[61] Manning CD, Raghavan P, Schütze H. Introduction to Information Retrieval. Cambridge University Press, New York, NY; 2008.
[62] Baeza-Yates R, Ribeiro-Neto B. Modern Information Retrieval: The Concepts and Technology behind Search. 2nd ed. Addison-Wesley Professional, Boston, MA; 2011.
[63] Nisan N, Schocken S. The Elements of Computing Systems: Building a Modern Computer from First Principles. The MIT Press, Cambridge, MA; 2005.
[64] Vorel V. On Basic Properties of Jumping Finite Automata. International Journal of Foundations of Computer Science. 2018;29(1):1–15.
[65] Russell S, Norvig P. Artificial Intelligence: A Modern Approach. 2nd ed. Upper Saddle River, NJ: Prentice-Hall, 2002.
[66] Huddleston R, Pullum G. A Student's Introduction to English Grammar. Cambridge University Press, New York, NY; 2005.
[67] Bauer L. Introducing Linguistic Morphology. 2nd ed. Georgetown University Press, Washington, DC; 2003.
[68] Aronoff M, Fudeman K. What is Morphology (Fundamentals of Linguistics). Hoboken, NJ: Wiley-Blackwell; 2004.
[69] Strachan T, Read A. Human Molecular Genetics. 4th ed. Garland Science, New York, NY; 2010.
[70] Watson JD, Baker TA, Bell SP, *et al.* Molecular Biology of the Gene. 6th ed. Benjamin Cummings Publishing, San Francisco, CA; 2007.
[71] Russel PJ. iGenetics: A Molecular Approach. 3rd ed. Benjamin Cummings Publishing, San Francisco, CA; 2009.
[72] Huddleston R, Pullum G. The Cambridge Grammar of the English Language. Cambridge University Press, New York, NY; 2002.
[73] Prusinkiewicz P, Lindenmayer A. The Algorithmic Beauty of Plants. Springer-Verlag New York Inc., New York, NY; 1990.

[74] Prusinkiewicz P, Hammel M, Hanan J, *et al.* L-Systems: From the Theory to Visual Models of Plants. In: Proceedings of the 2nd CSIRO Symposium on Computational Challenges in Life Sciences. Collingwood, Victoria, Australia: CSIRO Publishing; 1996.

[75] Borchert R, Honda H. Control of Development in the Bifurcating Branch System of Tabebuia Rosa: A Computer Simulation. Botanical Gazette. 1984;145: 184–195.

[76] Chomsky N. Three Models for the Description of Language. IRE Transactions on Information Theory. 1956;2(3):113–124.

[77] Carroll J, Long D. Theory of Finite Automata With an Introduction to Formal Languages. Upper Saddle River, NJ: Prentice-Hall; 1989.

[78] Kuich W, Salomaa A. Semirings, Automata, Languages. Springer, London; 1985.

[79] von zur Gathen J, Gerhard J. Modern Computer Algebra. 2nd ed. Cambridge University Press, New York, NY; 2003.

[80] Gilbert WJ, Gilbert WJ. Modern Algebra With Applications (Pure and Applied Mathematics: A Wiley Series of Texts, Monographs and Tracts). 2nd ed. Hoboken, NJ: Wiley-Blackwell; 2003.

[81] Sudkamp TA. Languages and Machines: An Introduction to the Theory of Computer Science. Addison-Wesley, Boston, MA; 2006.

[82] Sudkamp TA. Languages and Machines. Addison-Wesley, Boston, MA; 1988.

[83] Hopcroft JE, Motwani R, Ullman JD. Introduction to Automata Theory, Languages, and Computation. 3rd ed. Addison-Wesley, Boston, MA; 2006.

[84] Hopcroft JE, Ullman JD. Introduction to Automata Theory, Languages, and Computation. Addison-Wesley, Boston, MA; 1979.

[85] Gross JL, Yellen J. Graph Theory and Its Applications (Discrete Mathematics and Its Applications). 2nd ed. Chapman & Hall/CRC, London; 2005.

[86] Diestel R. Graph Theory. 3rd ed. Springer, New York, NY; 2005.

[87] Mordeson JN, Malik DS. Fuzzy Automata and Languages: Theory and Applications. Chapman & Hall/CRC, London; 2002.

[88] Hopcroft JE, Ullman JD. Formal Languages and Their Relation to Automata. Addison-Wesley, Boston, MA; 1969.

[89] Dassow J, Mitrana V. Finite Automata over Free Groups. International Journal of Algebra and Computation. 2000;10(6):725.

[90] Mitrana V, Stiebe R. Extended Finite Automata Over Groups. Discrete Applied Mathematics. 2001;108(3):287–300.

[91] Truss J. Discrete Mathematics for Computer Scientists (International Computer Science Series). 2nd ed. Addison-Wesley, Boston, MA; 1998.

[92] Salomaa A. Computation and Automata. Cambridge University Press, New York, NY; 1985.

[93] Jacobson N. Basic Algebra. 2nd ed. W.H. Freeman, New York, NY; 1989.

[94] Eilenberg S. Automata, Languages, and Machines. Academic Press, Orlando, FL; 1974.

[95] Kelley D. Automata and Formal Languages. Upper Saddle River, NJ: Prentice-Hall; 1995.

[96] McHugh JA. Algorithmic Graph Theory. Upper Saddle River, NJ: Prentice-Hall; 1990.
[97] Ito M. Algebraic Theory of Automata and Languages. 2nd ed. World Scientific Publishing Company, Singapore; 2003.
[98] Ginsburg S. Algebraic and Automata-Theoretic Properties of Formal Languages. Elsevier Science, New York, NY; 1975.
[99] Rozenberg G. Selective Substitution Grammars (Towards a Framework for Rewriting Systems). Part 1: Definitions and Examples. Elektronische Informationsverarbeitung und Kybernetik. 1977;13(9):455–463.
[100] Čermák M, Horáček P, Meduna A. Rule-Restricted Automaton-Grammar Transducers: Power and Linguistic Applications. Mathematics for Applications. 2012;1(1):13–35.
[101] Křivka Z. Rewriting Systems With Restricted Configurations. Faculty of Information Technology, Brno University of Technology; 2007.
[102] Křivka Z. Rewriting Systems With Restricted Configurations. Faculty of Information Technology BUT; 2008.
[103] Křivka Z, Meduna A, Smrček J. *n*-Right-Linear #-Rewriting Systems. In: Third Doctoral Workshop on Mathematical and Engineering Methods in Computer Science (MEMICS 2007). Znojmo, Czech Republic; 2007. p. 105–112.
[104] Křivka Z, Meduna A, Schönecker R. Generation of Languages by Rewriting Systems that Resemble Automata. International Journal of Foundations of Computer Science. 2006;17(5):1223–1229.
[105] Křivka Z, Meduna A. Generalized #-Rewriting Systems of Finite Index. In: Information Systems and Formal Models (Proceedings of 2nd International Workshop on Formal Models (WFM'07)). Opava, Czech Republic: Silesian University; 2007. p. 197–204.
[106] Aho AV, Ullman JD. The Theory of Parsing, Translation and Compiling, Volume I: Parsing. Upper Saddle River, NJ: Prentice-Hall; 1972.
[107] Aho AV, Lam MS, Sethi R, *et al.* Compilers: Principles, Techniques, and Tools. 2nd ed. Addison-Wesley, Boston, MA; 2006.
[108] Brookshear JG. Theory of Computation. Benjamin Cummings Publishing, San Francisco, CA; 1989.
[109] Chomsky N. Syntactic Structures. Mouton, New York, NY; 2002.
[110] Gries D. Compiler Construction for Digital Computers. John Wiley & Sons, New York, NY; 1971.
[111] Lewis PM, Rosenkrantz DJ, Stearns RE. Compiler Design Theory. Addison-Wesley, Boston, MA; 1976.
[112] Pagen FG. Formal Specifications of Programming Language: A Panoramic Primer. Upper Saddle River, NJ: Prentice-Hall; 1981.
[113] Sippu S, Soisalon-Soininen E. Parsing Theory. Springer, New York, NY; 1987.
[114] Jirák O. Table-Driven Parsing of Scattered Context Grammar. In: Proceedings of the 16th Conference and Competition EEICT 2010. Faculty of Information Technology, Brno University of Technology; 2010. p. 171–175.

[115] Kolář D. Scattered Context Grammars Parsers. In: Proceedings of the 14th International Congress of Cybernetics and Systems of WOCS. Wroclaw University of Technology; 2008. p. 491–500.

[116] Rußmann A. Dynamic LL(k) Parsing. Acta Informatica. 1997;34(4): 267–289.

[117] Horáček P, Meduna A. Synchronous Versions of Regulated Grammars: Generative Power and Linguistic Applications. Theoretical and Applied Informatics. 2012;24(3):175–190.

[118] Horáček P, Meduna A. Regulated Rewriting in Natural Language Translation. In: 7th Doctoral Workshop on Mathematical and Engineering Methods in Computer Science. Brno University of Technology, Brno, Czech Republic; 2011. p. 35–42.

[119] Zetzsche G. Erasing in Petri Net Languages and Matrix Grammars. In: DLT '09: Proceedings of the 13th International Conference on Developments in Language Theory. Springer; 2009. p. 490–501.

[120] Zetzsche G. Toward Understanding the Generative Capacity of Erasing Rules in Matrix Grammars. International Journal of Computer Mathematics. 2011;22(2):411–426.

[121] Zetzsche G. A Sufficient Condition for Erasing Productions to Be Avoidable. In: DLT'11: Developments in Language Theory. vol. 6795 of Lecture Notes in Computer Science. Springer, Berlin, Heidelberg; 2011. p. 452–463.

[122] Meduna A, Techet J. Scattered Context Grammars that Erase Nonterminals in a Generalized k-Limited Way. Acta Informatica. 2008;45(7): 593–608.

[123] Meduna A, Zemek P. On the Generation of Sentences With Their Parses by Propagating Regular-Controlled Grammars. Theoretical Computer Science. 2013;477(1):67–75.

[124] Kari L. On Insertion and Deletion in Formal Languages. University of Turku, Finland; 1997.

[125] Zemek P. On Erasing Rules in Regulated Grammars. Faculty of Information Technology, Brno University of Technology; 2010.

[126] Zemek P. k-Limited Erasing Performed by Regular-Controlled Context-Free Grammars. In: Proceedings of the 16th Conference and Competition EEICT 2010. Faculty of Information Technology, Brno University of Technology; 2010. p. 42–44.

[127] Fernau H. Unconditional Transfer in Regulated Rewriting. Acta Informatica. 1997;34(11):837–857.

[128] Fernau H, Wätjen D. Remarks on Regulated Limited ET0L Systems and Regulated Context-Free Grammars. Theoretical Computer Science. 1998; 194(1–2):35–55.

[129] Meduna A, Zemek P. Regulated Grammars and Their Transformations. Faculty of Information Technology, Brno, Czech Republic, Brno University of Technology; 2010.

[130] Masopust T, Meduna A. Descriptional Complexity of Grammars Regulated by Context Conditions. In: LATA '07 Pre-proceedings. Reports of the Research

Group on Mathematical Linguistics 35/07, Universitat Rovira i Virgili; 2007. p. 403–411.

[131] Bordihn H, Fernau H. Accepting Grammars With Regulation. International Journal of Computer Mathematics. 1994;53(1):1–18.

[132] Meduna A. Uniform Generation of Languages by Scattered Context Grammars. Fundamenta Informaticae. 2001;44:231–235.

[133] Masopust T, Meduna A, Šimáček J. Two Power-Decreasing Derivation Restrictions in Generalized Scattered Context Grammars. Acta Cybernetica. 2008;18(4):783–793.

[134] Meduna A. Syntactic Complexity of Scattered Context Grammars. Acta Informatica. 1995;1995(32):285–298.

[135] Kopeček T, Meduna A, Švec M. Simulation of Scattered Context Grammars and Phrase-Structured Grammars by Symbiotic E0L Grammars. In: Proceeding of 8th International Conference on Information Systems, Implementation and Modelling (ISIM'05). Brno, Czech Republic; 2005. p. 59–66.

[136] Gonczarowski J, Warmuth MK. Scattered Versus Context-Sensitive Rewriting. Acta Informatica. 1989;27:81–95.

[137] Meduna A. Scattered Rewriting in the Formal Language Theory. In: Missourian Annual Conference on Computing. Columbia, US; 1991. p. 26–36.

[138] Techet J. Scattered Context in Formal Languages. Faculty of Information Technology, Brno University of Technology; 2008.

[139] Fernau H. Scattered Context Grammars With Regulation. Annals of Bucharest University, Mathematics-Informatics Series. 1996;45(1):41–49.

[140] Meduna A, Židek S. Scattered Context Grammars Generating Sentences Followed by Derivation Trees. Theoretical and Applied Informatics. 2011;2011(2): 97–106.

[141] Meduna A, Techet J. Reduction of Scattered Context Generators of Sentences Preceded by Their Leftmost Parses. In: DCFS 2007 Proceedings. High Tatras, Slovakia; 2007. p. 178–185.

[142] Masopust T. On the Descriptional Complexity of Scattered Context Grammars. Theoretical Computer Science. 2009;410(1):108–112.

[143] Fernau H, Meduna A. On the Degree of Scattered Context-Sensitivity. Theoretical Computer Science. 2003;290(3):2121–2124.

[144] Păun G. On Simple Matrix Languages Versus Scattered Context Languages. Informatique Théorique et Applications. 1982;16(3):245–253.

[145] Virkkunen V. On Scattered Context Grammars. Acta Universitatis Ouluensis. 1973;20(6):75–82.

[146] Meduna A, Techet J. Maximal and Minimal Scattered Context Rewriting. In: FCT 2007 Proceedings. Budapest; 2007. p. 412–423.

[147] Meduna A, Vrábel L, Zemek P. LL Leftmost k-Linear Scattered Context Grammars. In: AIP Conference Proceedings. vol. 1389. Kassandra, Halkidiki, Greece: American Institute of Physics; 2011. p. 833–836.

[148] Masopust T, Techet J. Leftmost Derivations of Propagating Scattered Context Grammars: A New Proof. Discrete Mathematics and Theoretical Computer Science. 2008;10(2):39–46.

[149] Meduna A. Generative Power of Three-Nonterminal Scattered Context Grammars. Theoretical Computer Science. 2000;2000(246):279–284.
[150] Meduna A, Techet J. Generation of Sentences With Their Parses: the Case of Propagating Scattered Context Grammars. Acta Cybernetica. 2005;17:11–20.
[151] Meduna A. Four-Nonterminal Scattered Context Grammars Characterize the Family of Recursively Enumerable Languages. International Journal of Computer Mathematics. 1997;63:67–83.
[152] Meduna A. Erratum: Coincidental Extension of Scattered Context Languages. Acta Informatica. 2003;39(9):699.
[153] Meduna A. Economical Transformations of Phrase-Structure Grammars to Scattered Context Grammars. Acta Cybernetica. 1998;13:225–242.
[154] Masopust T, Meduna A. Descriptional Complexity of Three-Nonterminal Scattered Context Grammars: An Improvement. In: Proceedings of 11th International Workshop on Descriptional Complexity of Formal Systems. Otto-von-Guericke-Universität Magdeburg; 2009. p. 235–245.
[155] Meduna A. Descriptional Complexity of Scattered Rewriting and Multi-rewriting: An Overview. Journal of Automata, Languages and Combinatorics. 2002;2002(7):571–577.
[156] Jirák O, Kolář D. Derivation in Scattered Context Grammar via Lazy Function Evaluation. In: 5th Doctoral Workshop on Mathematical and Engineering Methods in Computer Science. Masaryk University; 2009. p. 118–125.
[157] Jirák O. Delayed Execution of Scattered Context Grammar Rules. In: Proceedings of the 15th Conference and Competition EEICT 2009. Faculty of Information Technology, Brno University of Technology; 2009. p. 405–409.
[158] Meduna A. Coincidental Extension of Scattered Context Languages. Acta Informatica. 2003;39(5):307–314.
[159] Meduna A. Canonical Scattered Rewriting. International Journal of Computer Mathematics. 1993;51:122–129.
[160] Meduna A, Techet J. Canonical Scattered Context Generators of Sentences With Their Parses. Theoretical Computer Science. 2007;2007(389):73–81.
[161] Masopust T. Bounded Number of Parallel Productions in Scattered Context Grammars With Three Nonterminals. Fundamenta Informaticae. 2010;99(4): 473–480.
[162] Ehrenfeucht A, Rozenberg G. An Observation on Scattered Grammars. Information Processing Letters. 1979;9(2):84–85.
[163] Meduna A, Techet J. An Infinite Hierarchy of Language Families Generated by Scattered Context Grammars With *n*-Limited Derivations. Theoretical Computer Science. 2009;410(21):1961–1969.
[164] Techet J. A Note on Scattered Context Grammars With Non-Context-Free Components. In: 3rd Doctoral Workshop on Mathematical and Engineering Methods in Computer Science. Brno University of Technology, Brno, Czech Republic; 2007. p. 225–232.
[165] Milgram D, Rosenfeld A. A Note on Scattered Context Grammars. Information Processing Letters. 1971;1:47–50.
[166] Valiant L. The Equivalence Problem for Deterministic Finite Turn Pushdown Automata. Information and Control. 1989;81:265–279.

[167] Meduna A, Vrábel L, Zemek P. On Nondeterminism in Programmed Grammars. In: 13th International Conference on Automata and Formal Languages. Debrecen, Hungary: Computer and Automation Research Institute, Hungarian Academy of Sciences; 2011. p. 316–328.

[168] Courcelle B. On Jump Deterministic Pushdown Automata. Mathematical Systems Theory. 1977;11:87–109.

[169] Bensch S, Bordihn H, Holzer M, *et al.* On Input-Revolving Deterministic and Nondeterministic Finite Automata. Information and Computation. 2009;207(11):1140–1155.

[170] Lukáš R, Meduna A. Multigenerative Grammar Systems and Matrix Grammars. Kybernetika. 2010;46(1):68–82.

[171] Lukáš R, Meduna A. Multigenerative Grammar Systems. Schedae Informaticae. 2006;2006(15):175–188.

[172] Lukáš R, Meduna A. Multigenerative Grammar Systems. In: Proceedings of 1st International Workshop – WFM; 2006. p. 19–26.

[173] Lukáš R, Meduna A. General Multigenerative Grammar Systems. In: WFM'07: Information Systems and Formal Models ISIM. Silesian University, Opava; 2007. p. 205–212.

[174] Křivka Z, Meduna A. Jumping Grammars. International Journal of Foundations of Computer Science. 2015;26(6):709–731.

[175] Floyd RW, Beigel R. The Language of Machines: An Introduction to Computability and Formal Languages. Computer Science Press, New York, NY; 1994.

[176] Lewis HR, Papadimitriou CH. Elements of the Theory of Computation. Upper Saddle River, NJ: Prentice-Hall; 1981.

[177] Martin JC. Introduction to Languages and the Theory of Computation. 3rd ed. McGraw-Hill, New York, NY; 2002.

[178] Moll RN, Arbib MA, Kfoury AJ. An Introduction to Formal Language Theory. Springer, New York, NY; 1988.

[179] Sipser M. Introduction to the Theory of Computation. 2nd ed. PWS Publishing Company, Boston, MA; 2006.

[180] Mayer O. Some Restrictive Devices for Context-Free Grammars. Information and Control. 1972;20:69–92.

[181] Moriya E. Some Remarks on State Grammars and Matrix Grammars. Information and Control. 1973;23:48–57.

[182] Kleijn HCM. Selective Substitution Grammars Based on Context-Free Productions. Leiden University, The Netherlands; 1983.

[183] van der Walt APJ. Random Context Grammars. In: Proceedings of Symposium on Formal Languages; 1970. p. 163–165.

[184] Sakarovitch J. Pushdown Automata With Terminating Languages. In: Languages and Automata Symposium, RIMS 421, Kyoto University; 1981. p. 15–29.

[185] Rosenkrantz DJ. Programmed Grammars and Classes of Formal Languages. Journal of the ACM. 1969;16(1):107–131.

[186] Ginsburg S, Greibach SA, Harrison M. One-Way Stack Automata. Journal of the ACM. 1967;14(2):389–418.

[187] Păun G. On the Generative Capacity of Conditional Grammars. Information and Control. 1979;43:178–186.

[188] Horváth G, Meduna A. On State Grammars. Acta Cybernetica. 1988;1988(8): 237–245.

[189] Lomkovskaya MV. On Some Properties of *c*-Conditional Grammars (in Russian). Nauchno-Tekhnicheskaya Informatsiya. 1972;2(1):16–21.

[190] Král J. On Multiple Grammars. Kybernetika. 1969;1:60–85.

[191] Lomkovskaya MV. On *c*-Conditional and Other Commutative Grammars (in Russian). Nauchno-Tekhnicheskaya Informatsiya. 1972;2(2):28–31.

[192] Cremers AB. Normal Forms for Context-Sensitive Grammars. Acta Informatica. 1973;3:59–73.

[193] Fris I. Grammars With Partial Ordering of the Rules. Information and Control. 1968;12:415–425.

[194] Wood D. Grammars and L Forms: An Introduction. Springer, New York, NY; 1980.

[195] Ginsburg S, Spanier E. Finite-turn Pushdown Automata. SIAM Journal on Control. 1968;4:429–453.

[196] Asveld PRJ. Controlled Iteration Grammars and Full Hyper-AFL's. Information and Control. 1977;34(3):248–269.

[197] Ginsburg S, Spanier EH. Control Sets on Grammars. Theory of Computing Systems. 1968;2(2):159–177.

[198] Navrátil E. Context-Free Grammars With Regular Conditions. Kybernetika. 1970;6(2):118–125.

[199] Kelemen J. Conditional Grammars: Motivations, Definition, and Some Properties. In: Proceedings on Automata, Languages and Mathematical Systems. K. Marx University of Economics, Budapest; 1984. p. 110–123.

[200] Lomkovskaya MV. Conditional Grammars and Intermediate Classes of Languages (in Russian). Soviet Mathematics – Doklady. 1972;207:781–784.

[201] Arbib MA, Moll RN, Kfoury AJ. Basis for Theoretical Computer Science. Springer, New York, NY; 1984.

[202] Kleijn HCM. Basic Ideas of Selective Substitution Grammars. In: Trends, Techniques, and Problems in Theoretical Computer Science. vol. 281 of Lecture Notes in Computer Science. Berlin, Heidelberg: Springer; 1987. p. 75–95.

[203] Ehrenfeucht A, Kleijn HCM, Rozenberg G. Adding Global Forbidding Context to Context-Free Grammars. Theoretical Computer Science. 1985;37:337–360.

[204] Cremers AB, Maurer HA, Mayer O. A Note on Leftmost Restricted Random Context Grammars. Information Processing Letters. 1973;2(2):31–33.

[205] Král J. A Note on Grammars With Regular Restrictions. Kybernetika. 1973;9(3):159–161.

[206] Urbanek FJ. A Note on Conditional Grammars. Revue Roumaine de Mathématiques Pures at Appliquées. 1983;28:341–342.

[207] Revesz GE. Introduction to Formal Language Theory. McGraw-Hill, New York, NY; 1983.

[208] Rozenberg G, Salomaa A, editors. Handbook of Formal Languages, vol. 3: Beyond Words. Springer, New York, NY; 1997.

[209] Meduna A. Formal Languages and Computation: Models and Their Applications. Taylor & Francis, New York, NY; 2014.

[210] Alur R, Madhusudan P. Visibly Pushdown Languages. In: Annual ACM Symposium on Theory of Computing. Chicago, IL, USA; 2004.

[211] Meduna A. Uniform Rewriting Based on Permutations. International Journal of Computer Mathematics. 1998;69(1–2):57–74.

[212] Kuich W, Maurer HA. Tuple Languages. In: International Computing Symposium, Bonn; 1970. p. 881–891.

[213] Rogers H. Theory of Recursive Functions and Effective Computability. The MIT Press, Cambridge, MA; 1987.

[214] Markov AA. The Theory of Algorithms. American Mathematical Society Translations. 1960;2(15):1–14.

[215] Kuich W, Maurer HA. The Structure Generating Function and Entropy of Tuple Languages. Information and Control. 1971;19(3):194–203.

[216] Srikant YN, Shankar P. The Compiler Design Handbook. CRC Press, London; 2002.

[217] Rytter W, Crochemore M. Text Algorithms. Oxford University Press, New York, NY; 1994.

[218] ter Beek MH, Csuhaj-Varjú E, Mitrana V. Teams of Pushdown Automata. International Journal of Computer Mathematics. 2004;81(2):141–156.

[219] Maurer HA. Simple Matrix Languages With a Leftmost Restriction. Information and Control. 1973;23:128–139.

[220] Jancar P, Mráz F, Plátek M, *et al.* Restarting Automata. In: Reichel H, editor. Fundamentals of Computation Theory. Berlin, Heidelberg: Springer-Verlag; 1995. p. 283–292.

[221] Moore C, Crutchfield J. Quantum Automata and Quantum Grammars. Theoretical Computer Science. 2000;237(1–2):275–306.

[222] Sarkar P. Pushdown Automaton With the Ability to Flip Its Stack. In: TR01-081, Electronic Colloquium on Computational Complexity (ECCC); 2001.

[223] Kari L. Power of Controlled Insertion and Deletion. In: Results and Trends in Theoretical Computer Science. vol. 812 of Lecture Notes in Computer Science. Berlin, Heidelberg: Springer; 1994. p. 197–212.

[224] Martí-Vide C, Mitrana V. Parallel Communicating Automata Systems – A Survey. Journal of Applied Mathematics and Computing. 2000;7(2): 237–257.

[225] Kennedy K, Allen JR. Optimizing Compilers for Modern Architectures: A Dependence-Based Approach. Morgan Kaufmann Publishers, San Francisco, CA; 2002.

[226] Kondacs A, Watrous J. On the Power of Quantum Finite State Automata. In: Proceedings of the 38th Annual Symposium on Foundations of Computer Science; 1997. p. 66–75.

[227] Freund R, Păun G. On the Number of Non-Terminal Symbols in Graph-Controlled, Programmed and Matrix Grammars. In: Machines,

Computations, and Universality. vol. 2055 of Lecture Notes in Computer Science. Springer; 2001. p. 214–225.

[228] Kuich W, Maurer HA. On the Inherent Ambiguity of Simple Tuple Languages. Computing. 1971;7:194–203.

[229] Moriya E, Hofbauer D, Huber M, *et al.* On State-Alternating Context-Free Grammars. Theoretical Computer Science. 2005;337:183–216.

[230] Vaszil G. On Simulating Non-returning PC Grammar Systems With Returning Systems. Theoretical Computer Science. 1998;209(1–2):319–329.

[231] Masopust T, Meduna A. On Pure Multi-Pushdown Automata that Perform Complete Pushdown Pops. Acta Cybernetica. 2009;19(2):537–552.

[232] Horáček P. On Generative Power of Synchronous Grammars With Linked Rules. In: Proceedings of the 18th Conference STUDENT EEICT 2012 Volume 3. Brno University of Technology, Brno, Czech Republic; 2012. p. 376–380.

[233] Sebesta RW. On Context-Free Programmed Grammars. Computer Languages. 1989;14(2):99–108.

[234] Turing AM. On Computable Numbers, With an Application to the Entscheidungsproblem. Proceedings of the London Mathematical Society. 1936;42(2):230–265.

[235] Čermák M, Meduna A. *n*-Accepting Restricted Pushdown Automata Systems. In: 13th International Conference on Automata and Formal Languages. Computer and Automation Research Institute, Hungarian Academy of Sciences; 2011. p. 168–183.

[236] Cherubini A, Breveglieri L, Citrini C, *et al.* Multipushdown languages and grammars. International Journal of Foundations of Computer Science. 1996;7(3):253–292.

[237] Gutiérrez-Naranjo MA, Pérez-Jiménez MJ, Riscos-Núñez A. Multidimensional Sevilla Carpets Associated With P Systems. In: Proceedings of the ESF Exploratory Workshop on Cellular Computing (Complexity Aspects); 2005. p. 225–236.

[238] Jancar P, Mráz F, Plátek M, *et al.* Monotonicity of Restarting Automata. Journal of Automata, Languages and Combinatorics. 2007;12(3): 355–371.

[239] Bal H, Grune D, Jacobs C, *et al.* Modern Compiler Design. John Wiley & Sons, Hoboken, NJ; 2000.

[240] Limaye N, Mahajan M. Membership Testing: Removing Extra Stacks from Multi-stack Pushdown Automata. In: 3rd International Conference on Language and Automata Theory and Applications. Tarragona, Spain; 2009. p. 493–504.

[241] Parsons TW. Introduction to Compiler Construction. Computer Science Press, New York, NY; 1992.

[242] Cormen TH, Leiserson CE, Rivest RL. Introduction to Algorithms. The MIT Press, Cambridge, MA; 1990.

[243] Cormen TH, Leiserson CE, Rivest RL, *et al.* Introduction to Algorithms. The MIT Press, Cambridge, MA; 2009.

[244] Meduna A, Kolář D. Homogenous Grammars With a Reduced Number of Non-Context-Free Productions. Information Processing Letters. 2002;81:253–257.

[245] Meduna A, Zemek P. Generalized One-Sided Forbidding Grammars. International Journal of Computer Mathematics. 2013;90(2):127–182.

[246] Post E. Formal Reductions of the General Combinatorial Decision Problem. American Journal of Mathematics. 1943;65(2):197–215.

[247] Baker CL. English Syntax. 2nd ed. The MIT Press, Cambridge, MA; 1995.

[248] Cooper KD, Torczon L. Engineering a Compiler. Morgan Kaufmann Publishers, San Francisco, CA; 2004.

[249] Meduna A. Elements of Compiler Design. Auerbach Publications, Boston, MA; 2007.

[250] Amos M. DNA Computation. University of Warwick, England; 1997.

[251] Seberry J, Pieprzyk J. Cryptography: An Introduction to Computer Security. Upper Saddle River, NJ: Prentice-Hall; 1989.

[252] Cytron R, Fischer C, LeBlanc R. Crafting a Compiler. Addison-Wesley, Boston, MA; 2009.

[253] Meduna A. Context-Free Multirewriting With a Reduced Number of Nonterminals. Faculty of Information Technology, Brno University of Technology; 2000.

[254] Cojocaru L, Mäkinen E, Tiplea FL. Classes of Szilard Languages in NC^1. In: Symbolic and Numeric Algorithms for Scientific Computing (SYNASC), 11th International Symposium; 2009. p. 299–306.

[255] Greibach SA. Checking Automata and One-Way Stack Languages. Journal of Computer and System Sciences. 1969;3:196–217.

[256] Bravo C, Neto JJ. Building Context-Sensitive Parsers from CF Grammars With Regular Control Language. In: Implementation and Application of Automata 8th International Conference. Springer; 2003. p. 306–308.

[257] Church A. An Unsolvable Problem of Elementary Number Theory. American Journal of Mathematics. 1936;58(2):345–363.

[258] Muchnick SS. Advanced Compiler Design and Implementation. Morgan Kaufmann Publishers, San Francisco, CA; 1997.

[259] Alur R, Madhusudan P. Adding Nesting Structure to Words. In: Developments in Language Theory. Santa Barbara, CA; 2006.

[260] Bordihn H, Fernau H. Accepting Grammars and Systems: An Overview. In: Proc. of Development in Language Theory Conf. Magdeburg; 1995. p. 199–208.

[261] Ginsburg S, Greibach S. Abstract Families of Languages. In: Studies in Abstract Families of Languages, Memoirs of the American Mathematical Society; 1969. p. 1–32.

[262] Church A. A Note on the Entscheidungsproblem. The Journal of Symbolic Logic. 1936;1(1):40–41.

[263] Mäkinen E. A Bibliography on Szilard Languages. Department of Computer Sciences, University of Tampere; 1998 Available on http://www.cs.uta.fi/reports/pdf/Szilard.pdf.

[264] Csuhaj-Varju E, Vaszil G. On Context-free Parallel Communicating Grammar Systems: Synchronization, Communication, and Normal Forms. Theoretical Computer Science. 2001;255:511–523.
[265] Zemek P. Normal Forms of One-Sided Random Context Grammars. In: Proceedings of the 18th Conference STUDENT EEICT 2012. vol. 3. Brno University of Technology, Brno, Czech Republic; 2012. p. 430–434.
[266] Vrábel L. A New Normal Form for Programmed Grammars With Appearance Checking. In: Proceedings of the 18th Conference STUDENT EEICT 2012. Brno University of Technology, Brno, Czech Republic; 2012. p. 420–425.
[267] Vrábel L. A New Normal Form for Programmed Grammars. In: Proceedings of the 17th Conference STUDENT EEICT 2011. Brno University of Technology, Brno, Czech Republic; 2011.
[268] Csuhaj-Varjú E. On Grammars With Local and Global Context Conditions. International Journal of Computer Mathematics. 1992;47:17–27.
[269] Dassow J, Păun G, Salomaa A. Grammars Based on Patterns. International Journal of Foundations of Computer Science. 1993;4(1):1–14.
[270] Ehrenfeucht A, Pasten P, Rozenberg G. Context-Free Text Grammars. Acta Informatica. 1994;31:161–206.
[271] Meduna A. Global Context Conditional Grammars. Journal of Automata, Languages and Combinatorics. 1991;1991(27):159–165.
[272] Kelemen J. Measuring Cognitive Resources Use (a Grammatical Approach). Computers and Artificial Intelligence. 1989;8(1):29–42.
[273] Kleijn HCM, Rozenberg G. Context-Free-Like Restrictions on Selective Rewriting. Theoretical Computer Science. 1981;16:237–239.
[274] Vaszil G. On the Number of Conditional Rules in Simple Semi-conditional Grammars. In: Descriptional Complexity of Formal Systems. MTA SZTAKI, Budapest, Hungary; 2003. p. 210–220.
[275] Ewert S, Walt A. The Power and Limitations of Random Context. In: Grammars and Automata for String Processing: From Mathematics and Computer Science to Biology. London: Taylor and Francis; 2003. p. 33–43.
[276] Kopeček T, Meduna A. Simple-Semi-Conditional Versions of Matrix Grammars With a Reduced Regulating Mechanism. Computing and Informatics. 2004;2004(23):287–302.
[277] Švec M. Simple Semi-Conditional ET0L Grammars. In: Proceedings of the International Conference and Competition Student EEICT 2003. Brno University of Technology, Brno, Czech Republic; 2003. p. 283–287.
[278] Meduna A, Švec M. Reduction of Simple Semi-conditional Grammars With Respect to the Number of Conditional Productions. Acta Cybernetica. 2002;15:353–360.
[279] Zemek P. One-Sided Random Context Grammars: Established Results and Open Problems. In: Proceedings of the 19th Conference STUDENT EEICT 2013. vol. 3. Brno University of Technology, Brno, Czech Republic; 2013. p. 222–226.
[280] Meduna A, Zemek P. One-Sided Random Context Grammars With Leftmost Derivations. In: LNCS Festschrift Series: Languages Alive. vol. 7300. Springer Verlag; 2012. p. 160–173.

[281] Meduna A, Zemek P. One-Sided Random Context Grammars. Acta Informatica. 2011;48:149–163.
[282] Zemek P. On the Nonterminal Complexity of Left Random Context E0L Grammars. In: Proceedings of the 17th Conference STUDENT EEICT 2011. vol. 3. Brno University of Technology, Brno, Czech Republic; 2011. p. 510–514.
[283] Meduna A, Gopalaratnam A. On Semi-conditional Grammars With Productions Having Either Forbidding or Permitting Conditions. Acta Cybernetica. 1994;11:307–323.
[284] Meduna A, Zemek P. Nonterminal Complexity of One-Sided Random Context Grammars. Acta Informatica. 2012;49(2):55–68.
[285] Meduna A, Švec M. Grammars With Context Conditions and Their Applications. Hoboken, NJ: Wiley; 2005.
[286] Meduna A, Csuhaj-Varjú E. Grammars With Context Conditions. EATCS Bulletin. 1993;32:112–124.
[287] Masopust T, Meduna A. Descriptional Complexity of Semi-Conditional Grammars. Information Processing Letters. 2007;104(1):29–31.
[288] Meduna A, Kopeček T. Conditional Grammars and Their Reduction. Faculty of Information Technology, Brno University of Technology; 2008.
[289] van der Walt APJ, Ewert S. A Shrinking Lemma for Random Forbidding Context Languages. Theoretical Computer Science. 2000;237(1–2): 149–158.
[290] van der Walt APJ, Ewert S. A Pumping Lemma for Random Permitting Context Languages. Theoretical Computer Science. 2002;270(1–2):959–967.
[291] Atcheson B, Ewert S, Shell D. A Note on the Generative Capacity of Random Context. South African Computer Journal. 2006;36:95–98.
[292] Ewert S, Walt A. Necessary Conditions for Subclasses of Random Context Languages. Theoretical Computer Science. 2013;475:66–72.
[293] Dassow J, Masopust T. On Restricted Context-Free Grammars. Journal of Computer and System Sciences. 2012;78(1):293–304.
[294] Masopust T, Meduna A. On Context-Free Rewriting With a Simple Restriction and Its Computational Completeness. RAIRO – Theoretical Informatics and Applications – Informatique Théorique et Applications. 2009;43(2):365–378.
[295] Masopust T. Simple Restriction in Context-Free Rewriting. Journal of Computer and System Sciences. 2010;76(8):837–846.
[296] Goldefus F, Masopust T, Meduna A. Left-Forbidding Cooperating Distributed Grammar Systems. Theoretical Computer Science. 2010;20(3):1–11.
[297] Csuhaj-Varjú E, Masopust T, Vaszil G. Cooperating Distributed Grammar Systems With Permitting Grammars as Components. Romanian Journal of Information Science and Technology. 2009;12(2):175–189.
[298] Masopust T. On the Terminating Derivation Mode in Cooperating Distributed Grammar Systems With Forbidding Components. International Journal of Foundations of Computer Science. 2009;20(2):331–340.
[299] Křivka Z, Masopust T. Cooperating Distributed Grammar Systems With Random Context Grammars as Components. Acta Cybernetica. 2011;20(2):269–283.

[300] Meduna A. Generalized Forbidding Grammars. International Journal of Computer Mathematics. 1990;36(1–2):31–38.

[301] Meduna A, Švec M. Descriptional Complexity of Generalized Forbidding Grammars. International Journal of Computer Mathematics. 2003;80(1):11–17.

[302] Meduna A. Symbiotic E0L Systems. Artificial Life: Gramatical Models. Bucharest, Black Sea University Press; 1995. p. 122–129.

[303] Masopust T, Meduna A. On Descriptional Complexity of Partially Parallel Grammars. Fundamenta Informaticae. 2008;87(3):407–415.

[304] Meduna A. Context Free Derivations on Word Monoids. Acta Informatica. 1990;27:781–786.

[305] Meduna A. Syntactic Complexity of Context-Free Grammars Over Word Monoids. Acta Informatica. 1996;1996(33):457–462.

[306] Bidlo R, Blatný P, Meduna A. Automata With Two-Sided Pushdowns Defined over Free Groups Generated by Reduced Alphabets. Kybernetika. 2007;2007(1):21–35.

[307] Bidlo R, Blatný P, Meduna A. Formal Models over Free Groups. In: 1st Doctoral Workshop on Mathematical and Engineering Methods in Computer Science. Faculty of Information Technology, Brno University of Technology, Brno, Czech Republi; 2005. p. 193–199.

[308] Bidlo R, Blatný P, Meduna A. Context-Free and E0L Derivations over Free Groups. Schedae Informaticae. 2007;2007(16):14–24.

[309] Meduna A, Zemek P. Workspace Theorems for Regular-Controlled Grammars. Theoretical Computer Science. 2011;412(35):4604–4612.

[310] Zemek P. k-Limited Erasing Performed by Regular-Controlled Context-Free Grammars. In: Proceedings of the 16th Conference STUDENT EEICT 2011. vol. 3. Brno University of Technology, Brno, Czech Republic; 2010. p. 42–44.

[311] Abraham S. Some Questions of Language Theory. In: Proceedings of the 1965 Conference on Computational Linguistics. Association for Computational Linguistics; 1965. p. 1–11.

[312] Barbaiani M, Bibire C, Dassow J, *et al.* The Power of Programmed Grammars With Graphs From Various Classes. Journal of Applied Mathematics & Computing. 2006;22(1–2):21–38.

[313] Bordihn H, Holzer M. Programmed Grammars and Their Relation to the LBA Problem. Acta Informatica. 2006;43(4):223–242.

[314] Fernau H, Stephan F. How Powerful is Unconditional Transfer? – When UT Meets AC. In: Developments in Language Theory, Aristotle University of Thessaloniki, Greece; 1997. p. 249–260.

[315] Fernau H. Nonterminal Complexity of Programmed Grammars. Theoretical Computer Science. 2003;296(2):225–251.

[316] Fernau H, Freund R, Oswald M, *et al.* Refining the Nonterminal Complexity of Graph-Controlled, Programmed, and Matrix Grammars. Journal of Automata, Languages and Combinatorics. 2007;12(1–2):117–138.

[317] Wätjen D. Regulations of Uniformly k-Limited ET0L Systems and Their Relations to Controlled Context-Free Grammars. Journal of Automata, Languages and Combinatorics. 1996;1(1):55–74.

[318] Wätjen D. Regulation of Uniformly k-Limited T0L Systems. Journal of Information Processing and Cybernetics. 1994;30(3):169–187.

[319] Wätjen D. Regulation of k-Limited ET0L Systems. International Journal of Computer Mathematics. 1993;47:29–41.

[320] Dassow J, Fest U. On Regulated L Systems. Rostocker Mathematisches Kolloquium. 1984;25:99–118.

[321] Meduna A, Švec M. Forbidding ET0L Grammars. Theoretical Computer Science. 2003;2003(306):449–469.

[322] Rozenberg G, Salomaa A. The Book of L. Springer-Verlag, New York, NY; 1986.

[323] Ginsburg S, Rozenberg G. T0L Schemes and Control Sets. Information and Control. 1974;27:109–125.

[324] Meduna A. Symbiotic E0L Systems. Acta Cybernetica. 1992;10:165–172.

[325] Wätjen D. On Regularly Controlled k-Limited T0L Systems. International Journal of Computer Mathematics. 1995;55(1–2):57–66.

[326] Meduna A, Zemek P. Left Random Context ET0L Grammars. Fundamenta Informaticae. 2013;123(3):289–304.

[327] Meduna A, Vrábel L, Zemek P. Solutions To Four Open Problems Concerning Controlled Pure Grammar Systems. International Journal of Computer Mathematics. 2014;91(6):1156–1169.

[328] Gaso J, Nehez M. Stochastic Cooperative Distributed Grammar Systems and Random Graphs. Acta Informatica. 2003;39:119–140.

[329] Fernau H. Parallel Communicating Grammar Systems With Terminal transmission. Acta Informatica. 2001;37:511–540.

[330] Csuhaj-Varju E, Vaszil G. Parallel Communicating Grammar Systems With Incomplete Information Communication. In: Developments in Language Theory. Berlin, Heidelberg; 2001. p. 381–392.

[331] Păun G, Salomaa A, Vicolov S. On the Generative Capacity of Parallel Communicating Grammar Systems. International Journal of Computer Mathematics. 1992;45:45–59.

[332] Fernau H, Holzer M. Graph-controlled Cooperating Distributed Grammar Systems With Singleton Components. In: Proceedings of the Third International Workshop on Descriptional Complexity of Automata, Grammars, and Related Structures; 2001. p. 79–90.

[333] Csuhaj-Varju E, Dassow J, Kelemen J, *et al.* Grammar Systems: A Grammatical Approach to Distribution and Cooperation. Gordon and Breach, Yverdon; 1994.

[334] Masopust T, Meduna A. Self-Regulating Finite Automata. Acta Cybernetica. 2007;18(1):135–153.

[335] Jantzen M, Kudlek M, Zetzsche G. Finite Automata Controlled by Petri Nets. In: Philippi S, Pini A, editors. Proceedings of the 14th Workshop; Algorithmen und Werkzeuge für Petrinetze. Technical Report Nr. 25/2007. University of Koblenz-Landau; 2007. p. 57–62.

[336] Kolář D, Meduna A. One-Turn Regulated Pushdown Automata and Their Reduction. Fundamenta Informaticae. 2001;2001(21):1001–1007.

[337] Kolář D, Meduna A. Regulated Automata: From Theory Towards Applications. In: Proceeding of 8th International Conference on Information Systems Implementation and Modelling (ISIM'05); 2005. p. 33–48.
[338] Rychnovský L. Regulated Pushdown Automata Revisited. In: Proceedings of the 15th Conference STUDENT EEICT 2009. Brno University of Technology, Brno, Czech Republic; 2009. p. 440–444.
[339] Csuhaj-Varjú E, Vaszil G, Masopust T. Blackhole State-Controlled Regulated Pushdown Automata. In: Second Workshop on Non-Classical Models for Automata and Applications; 2010. p. 45–56.
[340] Csuhaj-Varjú E, Masopust T, Vaszil G. Blackhole Pushdown Automata. Fundamenta Informaticae. 2011;112(2–3):137–156.
[341] Meduna A. Deep Pushdown Automata. Acta Informatica. 2006;2006(98): 114–124.
[342] Křivka Z, Meduna A, Schönecker R. Reducing Deep Pushdown Automata and Infinite Hierarchy. In: 2nd Doctoral Workshop on Mathematical and Engineering Methods in Computer Science. Brno University of Technology, Brno, Czech Republic; 2006. p. 214–221.
[343] Křivka Z, Meduna A, Schönecker R. General Top-Down Parsers Based On Deep Pushdown Expansions. In: Proceedings of 1st International Workshop on Formal Models (WFM'06). Ostrava, Czech Republic; 2006. p. 11–18.
[344] Leupold P, Meduna A. Finitely Expandable Deep PDAs. In: Automata, Formal Languages and Algebraic Systems: Proceedings of AFLAS 2008. Hong Kong University of Science and Technology; 2010. p. 113–123.
[345] Solár P. Parallel Deep Pushdown Automata. In: Proceedings of the 18th Conference STUDENT EEICT 2012. vol. 3. Brno University of Technology, Brno, Czech Republic; 2012. p. 410–414.
[346] Quesada AA, Stewart IA. On the Power of Deep Pushdown Stacks. Acta Informatica. 2009;46(7):509–531.
[347] Bidlo R, Blatný P. Two-Sided Pushdown Automata over Free Groups. In: Proceedings of the 12th Conference Student EEICT 2006 Volume 4. Faculty of Electrical Engineering and Communication BUT; 2006. p. 352–355.
[348] Alur R, Madhusudan P. Adding Nesting Structure to Words. Journal of the ACM. 2009;56(3):16:1–16:43.
[349] Daley M, Eramian M, McQuillan I. Bag Automata and Stochastic Retrieval of Biomolecules in Solution. In: Ibarra OH, Dang Z, editors. Implementation and Application of Automata, Eighth International Conference CIAA 2003, Santa Barbara, CA, July 16–18, 2003. No. 2759 in Lecture Notes in Computer Science. Springer-Verlag; 2003. p. 239–250.
[350] Meduna A. Syntactic Complexity of Scattered Context Grammars. Acta Informatica. 1995;32:285–298.
[351] Meduna A, Zemek P. One-Sided Random Context Grammars. Acta Informatica. 2011;48(3):149–163.

Index